P L A N E T

G E O G R A P H Y

Other books by Stephen Codrington

Appreciating Australia
    1994 (with Ken Scott)

Australia and its Neighbours: A Student Source Book
 1985

Australia's Pacific Neighbours
    1989 (with Michael Brooks)

Changing Communities
    1996 (with Ken Scott)

Foundations: The Principles and Characteristics of Education at St Paul's Grammar School, Penrith
 1991

Gold From Gold: The History of Dairying in the Bega Valley
    1979 1st edition
    1981 2nd edition

Investigating Our World
    1996 (with Ken Scott)

People's China
 1982

Senior Geography Case Studies
    1981 (editor)

Skills in Geography
    1985 (with Chris Chittenden)

The First of Many Decades: Recollections of St Paul's Grammar School, Penrith, 1983-1993
    1993 (editor)

The Geography Skills Book
    1989 (with Chris Chittenden)

Themes in Geographic Development
    1987 (with Brian Knapp)

Understanding Environments
    1995 (with Ken Scott)

Understanding Our Earth
    1985 (with David Chapman)

World of Contrasts
    1982 1st edition (with Dianne Codrington)
    1985 2nd edition (with Dianne Codrington)
    1991 3rd edition (with Dianne Codrington)
    1994 4th edition (with Dianne Codrington)

PLANET

GEOGRAPHY

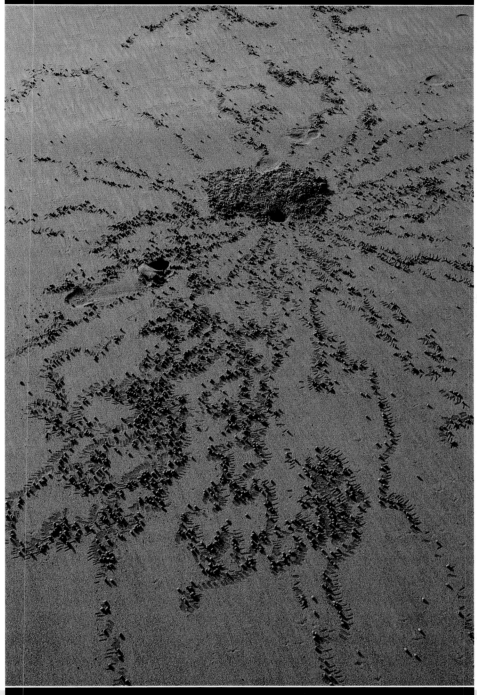

STEPHEN

CODRINGTON

SOLID STAR
PRESS

SYDNEY

http://www.stephencodrington.com
http://www.planetgeography5.com

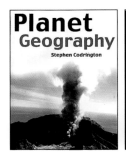

1st Edition
2002

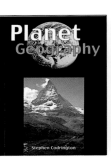

2nd Edition
2003

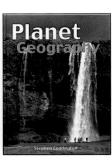

3rd Edition
2005

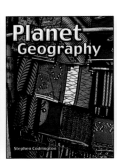

4th Edition
2007

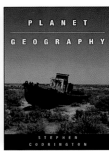

5th Edition
2009

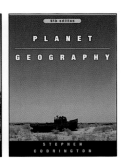

6th Edition
2011

ISBN 978 0 9803436 5 6

Proceeds from the sale of this book will be used to support the establishment of medical clinics and improved health care in poor rural areas of China's Guizhou province, as described in Chapter 10.

The author and publisher are grateful for permission to reproduce copyright material. Where copyright material has been reproduced, this is acknowledged beside the illustration. Every effort has been made to trace all holders of copyrights, but where this has not been possible the publisher will be pleased to make any necessary arrangements at the first opportunity.

All photographs, except where stated otherwise in the caption, were taken by the author.

Contents

Preface

Geography provides the ideal, integrated framework to understand contemporary world issues, and more importantly, it provides an effective framework of problem solving skills. If we understand the causes of problems, we are well on the way to finding an effective solution. And the reality is that we live in a world today that desperately needs young people equipped with the skills and insights to make our world a better place!

We know that our world is becoming more and more integrated. This trend shows itself in many ways, and to reflect this trend, cultural homogenisation is the topic of study in one of the chapters of this book. Global integration has now reached the point where a single senior secondary school Geography course is now taught in over 100 countries – that program is, of course, the International Baccalaureate Diploma for which this book was written.

This book is not designed to be a textbook in the traditional sense of one reference that covers everything for a course. In today's world of the internet, the traditional textbook no longer occupies the prime role that it once enjoyed. *Planet Geography* is intended to serve as a resource for IB Geography, but just one of many resources, including the book's own support website – www.planetgeography5.com. *Planet Geography* is deliberately richly illustrated with photographs, maps and diagrams. This is important because we know now that people absorb data from many sources, and many students gain information more easily from pictures and diagrams than the written word. Colour photographs have been used extensively to illustrate the material, with almost every photograph in the book being taken by the author. Photographs, maps and diagrams have been integrated carefully with text for clarity and relevance. Case studies are an integral part of the book, and serve not as 'add-ons', but as a means of developing concepts in a way that relates effectively to the real world.

The development of thinking skills and Theory of Knowledge perspectives are also encouraged by the types of exercises presented in the book, so that students are helped to develop skills and understanding, not just a mastery of content. This is supported by at least one dedicated 'ToK Box' in every chapter of the book. Through these approaches, it is hoped that young people using this book will acquire the wisdom that is necessary for the stewardship and survival of our planet.

It would be impossible to quantify the writing (and photographing!) period taken to prepare this book, as the field research alone spans most of my career as a teacher. The subject of Geography has given me enormous pleasure over the years, and this book is my attempt to share some of the insights of this great subject with another generation of learners. This book, like the earlier editions, is my way of saying 'thank you' to the thousands of people with whom I have worked over the years in the field of Geography.

More than anyone else I must thank and pay tribute to my family, and especially my children who have grown up with the notion that any family holiday is really a geography field study in disguise! My wife, Di, and my now-adult children – Liesl, Phillip, Tim and Andrew – have sacrificed having their husband and father with them on countless weekends and evenings while this book was written. This is not a small book, and the time they have sacrificed has been considerable.

About the author

An Australian by birth, Dr Stephen Codrington is the Principal of Li Po Chun United World College in Hong Kong. This is his fourth headship, having previously served as Principal at St Paul's Grammar School in Penrith (Sydney, Australia) between 1989 and 1997, Kristin School in Auckland, New Zealand from 1997 to 1999, followed by Prince Alfred College in Adelaide (Australia) from 2000 to 2004. Prior to that he taught at schools in both Australia and England including St Ignatius College, Riverview (Sydney, Australia) and Stonyhurst College (Lancashire, UK).

He is a former President of both the Geographical Society of New South Wales and the Geography Teachers' Association of New South Wales (twice). He has led several successful geographical study tours to such diverse destinations as China, Cambodia, Russia, Myanmar, Estonia, Uzbekistan, Papua New Guinea, Indonesia (Irian Jaya) and Thailand. In 2005, he led a group of the first foreign students ever to visit North Korea – the first of six trips he has now undertaken to that unknown and often misunderstood country. Stephen's work has taken him to more than 90 countries.

He has been honoured with election as a Fellow of the Australian College of Education, the Royal Geographical Society (UK), the International Biographical Association, and the Geographical Society of NSW, as well as being elected a Member of the Order of International Fellowship. He is a former Chairman of HICES (Heads of Independent Co-educational Schools). He was named International Man of the Year (Education) by the International Biographical Centre in Cambridge (England) in 1995-96. He has been listed in Who's Who in Australia every year since 2003.

He edited Geography Bulletin, the journal of the Geography Teachers' Association of New South Wales from 1980 to 1986. He continues to teach in the classroom, to the delight of his students.

Stephen has worked intensively in the area of change management of schools and in 2000 he was presented with an Outstanding Public Speaker award by IBC in England.

From 1996 to 2001 he served as Deputy Chief Examiner in Geography for the International Baccalaureate (I.B.), setting examination papers for the I.B. and assisting with curriculum development. During his terms as Deputy Chief Examiner, he led many teachers' workshops in places such as Melbourne, Guangzhou, Singapore, Brisbane, Auckland, Adelaide, Hong Kong and Mumbai. He maintains a personal website at www.stephencodrington.com.

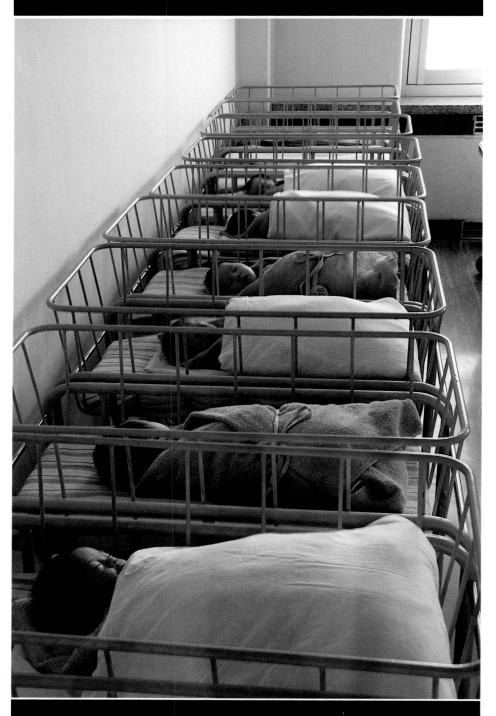

Populations in Transition

The changes in population today are unprecedented in the history of the planet.

Outline

ToK BoX – Page 35
Theory of Knowledge

Population Change

World Population Growth

At first sight, the statistics on world population seem frightening. Global population is now almost 6.5 billion. Last year, the world's population grew by almost 80 million people. Three billion young people are entering their reproductive years, a figure that is equal to the entire population of the world in 1960. There are currently about 50 million abortions, both legal and illegal, in the world every year. A quarter of all pregnancies in developing countries end in abortion.

However, it is important not to be alarmist. Even using common but emotive terms like 'population explosion' can pre-judge the population issue. In the late 1960s, a US Biology Professor, Paul Ehrlich, wrote a book called 'The Population Bomb' that opened with these words:

"Population control – or race to oblivion? Overpopulation is now the dominant problem in all our personal, national, and international planning. No one can do rational planning, nor can public policy be resolved in any area unless one first takes into account the population bomb... The battle to feed all of humanity is over. In the 1970s and 1980s hundreds of millions of people will starve to death in spite of any crash programmes embarked upon now... Population control is the conscious regulation of the numbers of human beings to meet the needs not just of individual families, but of society as a whole."

Although there were famines and wars during the 1970s and 1980s, Ehrlich's more catastrophic predictions did not come to pass. In some respects, Paul Ehrlich was echoing the predictions made by the English demographer Thomas Malthus in 1798. Malthus argued that the earth could only support a finite population size because food supplies are limited. He said that while the human population increases in a geometric progression (1→2→4→8→

>> Some Useful Definitions

Contemporary — an event that has taken place in your lifetime.

Geographic — all the demographic, environmental, social, cultural, economic, political and geopolitical factors that could influence or be influenced by the geography of an area.

Migration — the movement of people, involving a change of residence. It can be internal or external (international) and voluntary or forced. It does not include temporary circulation such as commuting or tourism.

Pattern — the arrangement of spatial elements.

Recent — refers to an event that has taken place since the year 2000.

Socio-economic — the combination of social factors (including demographic, cultural and political) and economic factors.

Trend — changes over time.

16→32 etc), food production only increases in an arithmetic progression (1→2→3→4→5→6 etc). Malthus believed this was the case because the amount of land is finite, and so food production could not continue increasing to keep pace with population growth (figure 1.1).

1.1 *Crowded scenes like this market in Djenné (Mali) might at first seem to confirm Malthusian views of population growth. However, standards of living, average life expectancies and availability of food in most countries in the world are now better than they have ever been.*

Malthus argued that when population growth outstripped food supply, as he felt was inevitable, then a correction could happen in one of two ways. On one hand, preventative checks would lower the fertility rate. This could happen, for example, if prices of food rose as it became scarcer, causing couples to delay marriage or reduce the number of children they had. On the other hand, Malthus argued that if preventative checks were insufficient, then positive checks would reduce the population size by catastrophic means such as famine, disease or war.

At the time Malthus wrote, he believed that Britain's population could not possibly grow beyond 10 million people. Today Britain's population is just over 58 million and the standards of living are much higher than Malthus could ever have imagined. Malthus' predictions were wrong because he underestimated the extent to which technology would improve farming yields. In the past 200 years since Malthus wrote, food production has increased more than population, and the vast food surpluses in many developed countries show that there is still room for food production to increase. Indeed, the world currently produces enough food for every man, woman and child to be obese. The fact that many millions of people

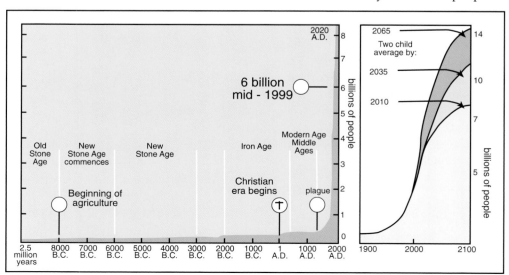

1.2 *The growth of world population through history.*

are still malnourished is a problem of distribution and capacity to pay, not a problem of production.

Since Malthus first raised the issue of the carrying capacity of the earth, many demographers (people who study population) have looked at the question of how many people the earth can support. In 1891, a scholarly study by Ravenstein suggested that the earth could support no more than 6 billion people, about the current population. In 1925, Penck suggested that the maximum should be raised to between 7.7 to 9.5 billion people, but in 1945 Pearson and Harper suggested lowering the figure to 0.9 to 2.8 billion, many fewer people than the world currently supports. Other estimates have varied widely, from only 7.5 million (Gilland, 1983), to 2 billion (Westing, 1981), under 5.5 billion (Ehrlich, 1993), 41 billion (Revelle, 1967), and 1 trillion (Marchetti, 1978). In 1981, the American economist Julian Simon argued there is no meaningful limit to the earth's population. He suggested each extra person is a resource that adds to our productive capacity, and should not be seen as a draining consumer of resources. Clearly, there is no consensus on the maximum number of people the earth can support.

Figure 1.2 shows the growth in world population over time, together with projections to the year 2050 based on various assumptions of family sizes in the future. This graph shows clearly the accelerating way in which population numbers are increasing, although not necessarily an accelerating rate of population increase. It took over one million years of human history for the world's population to grow to 1 billion; this figure was reached in 1830.

Table 1.2
Life Expectancy and Infant Mortality, Males and Females Combined, Year 33 to 1875

Country and Period	Life Expectancy at Birth (years)	Death Rate per 1000 people in 1st year of life
Roman Egypt, 33 - 258	24.0	329
England, 1301 - 1425	24.3	218
England, 1541 - 1526	33.7	-
England, 1620 - 1626	37.7	171
England, 1726 - 1751	34.6	195
England, 1801 - 1826	40.8	144
France, 1740 - 1749	24.8	296
France, 1820 - 1829	38.8	181
Sweden, 1751 - 1755	37.8	203
Japan, 1776 - 1875	32.2	277
Japan, 1800 - 1850	33.7	295
Japan, 1751 - 1869	37.4	216

Source: Maddison, A (2001) *The World Economy* p.29

Table 1.1
Level and rate of Growth of Population

Year	0	1000	1820	2000	0-1000	1000-1820	1820-2000
	millions of people				average annual growth rate (%)		
Western Europe	24.7	25.4	132.9	338	0	0.2	0.6
Societies established by European countries, such as colonies	1.2	2	11.2	323	0.05	0.21	1.91
Japan	3	7.5	31	126	0.09	0.17	0.7
Total of Group A (above)	28.9	34.9	175.1	838	0.02	0.2	0.88
Latin America	5.6	11.4	21.2	508	0.07	0.08	1.8
Eastern Europe and Former USSR	8.7	13.6	91.2	412	0.05	0.23	0.05
Asia (except Japan)	171.2	175.4	679.4	3390	0	0.17	0.91
Africa	16.5	33	74.2	760	0.07	0.1	1.32
Total of Group B (above)	202	233.4	866	5059	0.01	0.16	1
WORLD	230.8	268.3	1041.1	5908	0.02	0.17	0.98

Source: Maddison, A (2001) *The World Economy* p.28

Table 1.3
Birth rates and Life Expectancy, 1820 - 2000

	Births per 1000 population				Average life expectancy at birth (years)			
	1820	1900	1950	2000	1820	1900	1950	2000
France	3.19	2.19	2.05	1.26	37	47	65	78
Germany	3.99	3.60	1.65	0.96	41	47	67	77
Italy	3.90	3.30	1.94	0.93	30	43	66	78
Netherlands	3.50	3.16	2.27	1.27	32	52	72	78
Spain	4.00	3.39	2.00	0.92	28	35	62	78
Sweden	3.40	2.69	1.64	1.01	39	56	70	79
United Kingdom	4.02	2.93	1.62	1.30	40	50	69	77
Western Europe average	3.74	3.08	1.83	1.00	36	46	67	78
United States of America	5.52	3.23	2.40	1.44	39	47	68	77
Japan	2.62	3.24	2.81	0.95	34	44	61	81
Russia	4.13	4.80	2.65	0.88	28	32	65	67
Brazil	5.43	4.60	4.44	2.10	27	36	45	67
Mexico		4.69	4.56	2.70		33	50	72
Latin America average			4.19	2.51	27	35	51	69
China		4.12	3.70	1.60		24	41	71
India		4.58	4.50	2.80	21	24	32	60
Asia average			4.28	2.30	23	24	40	66
Africa average			4.92	3.90	23	24	38	52
World			3.74	2.30	**26**	**31**	**49**	**66**

Source: Maddison, A (2001) *The World Economy* p.30

It then took 100 years to add the second billion (1830 to 1930), 30 years to add the third billion (1930 to 1960), 15 years to add the fourth billion (1960 to 1975) and 12 years to add the fifth billion (1975 to 1987). However, the sixth billion also took 12 years to add (1987 to 1999), indicating that the rate of population increase has begun to slow.

It is important to understand that this growth in world population has not been evenly distributed across the world (see table 1.1).

The growth in world population has been caused by a combination of death rates being lowered and life expectancies increasing. The **death rate** is the proportion of the population that dies in a particular year. When we examine the death rate of young children, such as in the first year of life, or first five years of life, we refer to this as the **infant mortality rate**. The **average life expectancy** is the number of years that a child born in a particular country in a certain year can expect to live. Between the years 1 and 1820, a slow lowering of average death rates was the main cause of increasing population (table 1.2).

Table 1.4
Average Life Expectancy for Group A and Group B
Countries 1000 - 2000 (years at birth)

	1000	1820	1900	1950	2000
Group A	24	36	46	66	78
Group B	24	24	26	44	64
World	24	26	31	49	66

Group A and Group B countries defined in table 1.1.
Source: Maddison, A (2001) *The World Economy* p.31

Since 1820, the decrease in death rates has been much sharper, and it has been the main cause of population growth, offsetting the lowering of birth rates in the same period (table 1.3). As a consequence of the lowering of death rates, life expectancies have increased greatly – perhaps the greatest improvement in human welfare that is possible (tables 1.2 and 1.3). Between the year 1 and 1000, average life expectancy throughout the world was about 24 years. Life expectancy had risen to an average of only 26 years by 1820, although this figure was 36 years in the Group A countries shown in table 1.1, compared with 24 years in the group B countries. The changes since that time are shown in table 1.4.

Just as population growth has been unevenly distributed in the past, growth is likely to be unevenly distributed in the decades ahead. As figure 1.3 shows, 90% of future population increase will be in developing countries, the areas least able to cope with the resource demands of additional numbers. The increase in population numbers has been (and will be) greatest in Asia. In contrast, population growth in Europe seems to have stopped and population numbers have actually started to decline in Europe. About 80% of the world population today lives in less developed countries. People in the industrialised countries comprise only 20% of world population, and this proportion seems certain to come down to 16% in 2020, even though there will be more industrialised countries then. However, it is worth remembering that each baby born in the USA today will consume 80 times more resources in their lifetime than a baby born today in India.

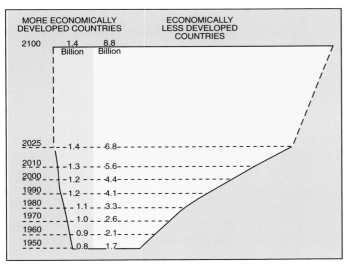

1.3 *Growth of world population, 1950 to 2100.*

Seventy-four countries, all from the less developed world, and including Nigeria, Iran, Ethiopia, Iraq, El Salvador, Pakistan, Guatemala, Syria, Honduras and Nicaragua, seem certain to double their populations in 30 years or less. Even though a number of countries in Asia and Latin America have registered significant falls in their total fertility rates, the annual number of births worldwide will remain over 132 million for several years to come.

The reason is that most of these countries already have a large population base, and a large number of women there are entering their reproductive years. Three billion people will enter their childbearing years within the next generation, while only about 1.8 billion people will leave that phase of life. This will leave a net gain of 600 million couples who could produce 1.8 billion children in the next generation at the current fertility rate of about three children per woman.

To take one example, India's total fertility rate, fell from 4.3 children per woman in 1985 to 3.2 in 1997. However, due to its already large population size of 920 million, almost 25 million babies were born there in 1997. India's fertility rate is still much higher than China's rate of 1.8 children per woman and the replacement level of 2.1 children per woman. India is likely to overtake China as the world's most populous country somewhere around 2050.

QUESTION BLOCK 1A

1. *Comment on Paul Ehrlich's statement from* The Population Bomb *(1969). Do you agree that 'overpopulation is now the dominant problem in all our personal, national, and international planning'? Give reasons for your answer.*

2. *Outline Thomas Malthus' argument, and explain why it did not happen as he predicted.*

3. *Examine figure 1.2. Describe the trend in world population shown in the graph.*

4. *Suggest the rationale for dividing countries into Group A and Group B in table 1.1.*

5. *Draw a line graph with seven lines, one each to show the growth in world population from 0 to 1998 in the seven regions listed in table 1.1. Do not include lines for the cumulative totals of Group A, Group B and the world.*

6. *Describe the changes shown in the average annual growth rates displayed in the right-hand three columns of table 1.1.*

7. *Using table 1.3, draw a line graph showing the changes in birth rates from 1820 to 2000 for each country shown. Describe the trend you have drawn, and discuss any significant differences between countries. Where data is missing, leave a blank section in that part of the line graph.*

8. *Using table 1.3, draw a series of column graphs showing the changes in average life expectancy from 1820 to 2000 for each country shown. Describe the trend you have drawn, and discuss any significant differences between countries.*

9. *Describe the pattern shown in table 1.4.*

10. *In the light of what you have read here, how would you define 'overpopulation'?*

Population Structure

The **structure** of a population refers to the age and sex distribution of the population. This is often shown as a graph with the number or proportion of each age group shown as horizontal bars from a central vertical column that represents age groups, as in figure 1.4. In general these graphs show males on the left hand side of the diagram and females to the right. These graphs are known as **population pyramids**, or **age-sex diagrams**. The graphs can show varying degrees of detail with the horizontal bands commonly representing age bands of one year, five years (as in figure 1.4), or ten years.

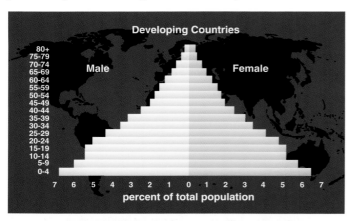

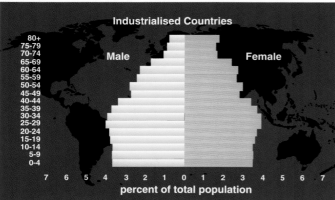

1.4 *Population structures for developing countries (top) and industrialised countries (bottom).*

Population pyramids reflect past and present demographic trends in the population being described. A population pyramid with a wide base that narrows quickly upwards represents a population with a high birth rate, a high proportion of young people and a rapidly growing population. A population pyramid with steep vertical sides represents an ageing population with a low birth rate. Such population pyramids typically have an excess of elderly females over males because females tend to have longer life expectancies than males.

As a result of the difference in population growth rates in developed and developing countries, a contrasting set of population structures has emerged (figure 1.4). Developing countries (Less Economically Developed Countries, or **LEDCs**) tend to have population structures with a wide base, indicating that a large proportion of the population is below 15 years of age. This has important implications for future population growth in these nations as the young people reach adulthood and begin to have children of their own, and it is evidence that the population size is growing rapidly. On the other hand, developed countries (More Economically Developed Countries, or **MEDCs**) have a population pyramid that has a narrower base. Because there are fewer young people entering their reproductive years, the size of the population can remain stable over time. Population pyramids with a narrower base are evidence of an ageing population and a slower rate of population increase, or even a declining population size.

Another way of looking at population growth trends is to consider **fertility rates**, or the average number of births per woman. As figure 1.5 shows, fertility rates are very high in developing regions such as Africa and the Middle East and low in most industrialised regions, especially Europe, where some countries have fertility rates below the replacement level. Indeed, almost all the countries in Europe, except Iceland and Albania, have below-replacement fertility rates. Spain (1.2 births per woman), Italy (1.2), Germany (1.3), Estonia (1.3) and Slovenia (1.3) have some of the world's lowest fertility rates. In Asia, China (1.8), Japan (1.5), Singapore (1.8) and South Korea (1.7), all have below-replacement fertility rates.

Sub-Saharan Africa and south central Asia continue to be the areas with the fastest population growth. Even in these regions, fertility fell between 1980 and 2000 in a number of countries. In Bangladesh, it dropped from 6.7 children per woman to 3.1; in Turkey from 4.3 to 1.7; in Myanmar from 5.3 to 3.3; and in Kenya from 8.1 to 4.9. The fertility level for Africa as a whole, however, is 5.3 births per woman, and in south central Asia 3.8. The current global average is 2.8 children per woman, well above the replacement level. It seems certain that Africa will double its population in 25 years.

The number of countries with a below-replacement fertility rate increased from 19 in 1970 to more than 50 today. Indeed, some demographers are claiming that the "population explosion is over", and there are even concerns about a "population implosion" as more and more countries fall below replacement level. Some estimates suggest that between 2040 and 2050 world population will decline by a total of 85 million.

QUESTION BLOCK 1B

1. *Contrast the population structures of LEDCs and MEDCs, and account for the differences.*

2. *What is the relationship between fertility rates and rates of population growth?*

3. *Describe the broad world pattern of fertility.*

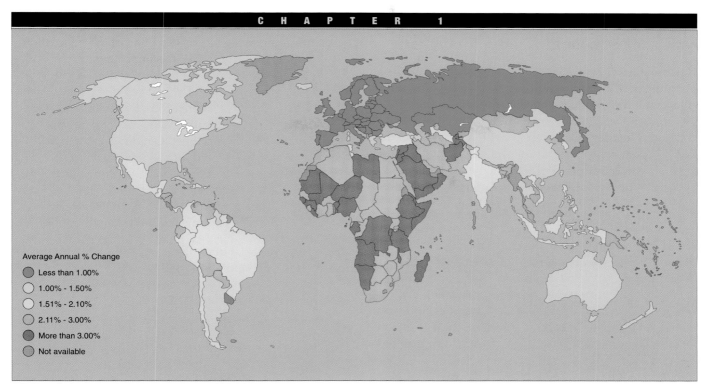

1.5 *Population growth rates per annum, 2000-2008.*

Demographic Transition Model

The rate of population increase in any area can be calculated by adding the rate of natural increase and the rate of net migration. The natural increase in turn is the difference between the birth rate and the death rate. The birth rate is the number of live births per 1000 people per year, while the death rate is number of deaths per 1000 people per year. If the birth rate exceeds the death rate, then the total population size will increase as long as this natural increase is not offset by losses due to migration.

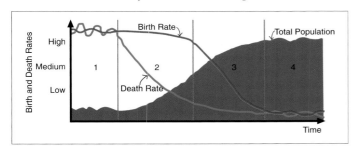

1.6 *The demographic transition model.*

These changes are often analysed with reference to the **demographic transition model** (figure 1.6). In this model, a society passes through four stages. In stage 1, both birth rates and death rates are high, so there is a small (if any) increase in population size. Stage 1 societies are those that are very traditional, such as might be found in isolated regions of the Himalayas, Irian Jaya, central Africa and the interior of South America. Birth rates are high for several sound, logical reasons. One important factor is that the infant mortality rate is high and many children die at a young age, so families often have additional children to compensate. Children are seen as economic assets as they do useful work for the family from the age of six

1.7 *In many countries, children are seen as an investment in the family's future. In countries where governments do not provide old age pensions, children provide security for parents in their old age. These children are with their father outside the family yurt in Mongolia.*

or seven. By the time children reach the age of 10 or 12 they are often producing more for the family than they consume. Moreover, children provide security for their parents in old age, an important consideration in countries that have no old age pension schemes (figure 1.7). The religious beliefs of people in traditional societies also encourage large families, and even where this is not the case, children may be seen as a sign of virility. Death rates are high because medical care is often inadequate and because poor sanitation allows the spread of disease.

Stage 2 occurs when death rates fall as a result of advances in medical care and sanitation. However, birth rates remain high because the cultural factors that lead to high birth rates are unaltered. Because there is a large gap between birth rates and death rates, population grows very rapidly. For example, in a society where the birth rate was 35 per 1000 people (i.e. 3.5%), and death rates had fallen to 20 per 1000 (i.e. 2.0%), then the rate of population increase would be 1.5% per annum. Countries at this stage of the demographic transition include Kenya, Paraguay, Afghanistan, Nepal and Ethiopia.

1.8 *A major factor in reducing birth rates in stage 3 countries such as Malaysia is the availability of family planning facilities, like this one in Kuala Trengganu.*

After a while, birth rates begin to fall, and this marks the beginning of stage 3. A fall in birth rates often follows a fall in death rates, as farmers and others realise that large families are no longer necessary to compensate for a high death rate. The birth rate may also be lowered as family planning facilities become available, as parents come to favour more material possessions rather than large families, and as women become more involved in the workforce (figure 1.8). As the birth rate lowers, the death rate continues to be reduced, although the decrease in the death rate is less than the fall of the birth rate in stage 3. Because the gap between the birth rate and the death rate is closing in stage 3, the rate of population increase slows down from stage 2, but as birth rates are still higher than death rates, the population continues to grow in size. Countries at stage 3 of the demographic transition include Malaysia, Israel, China and Chile.

1.9 *In countries at stage 4 of the demographic transition, even places normally associated with children, such as beaches, are dominated by the presence of adults. Only two children can be seen among hundreds of adults in this view of Scheveningen Beach, Netherlands.*

Stage 4 is reached when both birth rates and death rates are low. Like stage 1, the small gap between birth rates and death rates in stage 4 gives a slowly growing or declining population. This stage has been reached in several countries, especially in Europe, including Bulgaria, Latvia, Russia, Netherlands and the United Kingdom (figure 1.9). Today, Europe has a larger percentage of older people than any other continent (15% of the population over 65 years), and for this reason has a higher average death rate (12 deaths per 1000 people) than any continent other than Africa. The economies of Eastern Europe that are emerging from communism into capitalism, such as Russia, Ukraine and Latvia, are experiencing a gradual increase in death rates, largely due to the growing pressures of economic transition which have increased the rates of suicides and deaths caused by excessive alcoholism.

The demographic transition model is based on Europe's experience through its pre-industrial phase before the late 1700s (stage 1), through the Industrial Revolution in the early 1800s (stage 2), the expansion of manufacturing through to the 1960s (stage 3) and post-industrialisation (stage 4). The demographic transition leads to changes in a country's population structure as can be seen in the case of the Netherlands (figure 1.10).

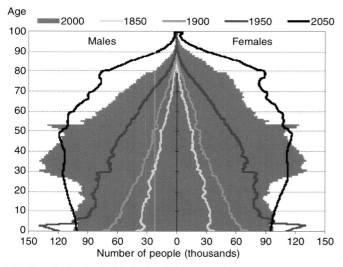

1.10 *Population in the Netherlands by age and sex, 1850 to 2050.*

Countries in other parts of the world such as Asia and South America seem to be passing through the stages of the demographic transition much more quickly than Europe. The demographic transition gives great hope to those people who are concerned about the rapid population growth in poorer countries, as it seems to suggest that as people become more affluent they will voluntarily reduce their family sizes.

Although the demographic transition has described the experience of many places in addition to Europe, it is possible that other countries in the future will not follow the pattern predicted. For example, most parts of Africa are

at stage 2 of the demographic transition at present, and in the years ahead we would expect their birth rates to drop dramatically as the death rates continue falling slowly as they move into stage 3. However, Rwanda, Liberia and Burundi in Africa and Iraq in western Asia have seen their death rates increase due to war. Furthermore, the spread of AIDS is increasing death rates quite dramatically in Africa. It is estimated that without the deaths caused by AIDS, the population of Africa would have been about 25% more than it is today. AIDS has also sharply reduced the life expectancy of people in Africa, and life expectancy in Eastern Africa is now estimated at 46.7 years, nearly four years lower than an earlier UN projection a few years ago (figure 1.11).

1.11 *This sign in central Dar-es-Salaam, Tanzania's largest city, reflects the huge concern about AIDS in Africa and the impact it is having on East Africa's death rates.*

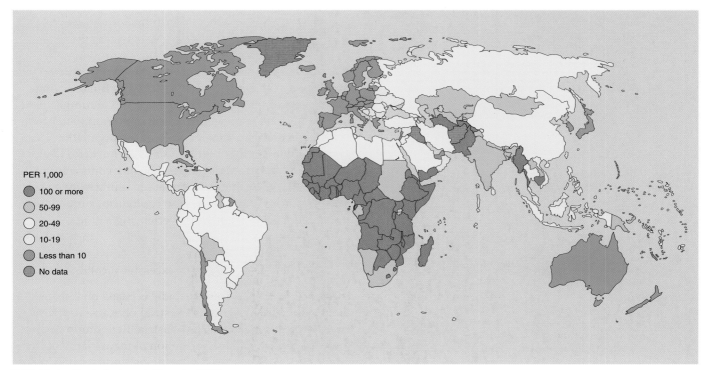

1.12 *Under-five infant mortality rate, 2008.*

The impact of AIDS has been most severe in sub-Saharan Africa where about 4.5 million people were killed by the disease between 1985 and 1997. Botswana, Malawi, Uganda, Zambia and Zimbabwe have been hit the hardest by the AIDS epidemic, and currently more than 10% of the adult population in these countries are infected with HIV. Sierra Leone in western Africa now has the world's highest death rate with 25.7 deaths per 1000 people, followed by 22.4 in Malawi and 21.0 in Uganda.

The contrast between countries at stages 2 and 4 of the demographic transition today – the rich and poor countries – can be seen by comparing their infant mortality rates (figure 1.12).

Infant mortality provides an even stronger measure of the contrasts. **Infant mortality** is defined as the proportion of children who die before they reach the age of one year. In Africa, the average number of infant deaths per 1000 live births is 86, reaching a peak at 283 in Sierra Leone and 235 in Liberia. The average infant mortality rate for South America is 36 and for Asia 56. On the other hand, in Western Europe, North America, Japan and Australia, infant mortality is 10 or less per 1000 live births.

QUESTION BLOCK 1C

1. Outline the main characteristics of each stage of the demographic transition model.

2. The birth rates and death rates for selected countries are given in table below for the year 2008. For each country, calculate the rate of population increase.

Country	Birth Rate (births per 1000 people)	Death Rate (deaths per 1000 people)
Australia	14	7
China	12	7
Czech Republic	11	10
Italy	9	10
Malawi	48	16
Malaysia	21	5
Myanmar	19	10
Nepal	29	9
Papua New Guinea	31	10
Swaziland	31	31
Uganda	48	16
United Kingdom	13	9

3. Give three examples of countries (or regions) at each stage of the demographic transition.

4. Draw a sketch of the shape of the population pyramid you think would apply at each stage of the demographic transition.

5. What causes the change between each stage of the demographic transition?

6. Why do developed nations such as the United Kingdom and Italy have higher death rates than developing countries such as China and Malaysia?

7. Three LEDCs listed in question 5 are Papua New Guinea, Swaziland and Uganda. Suggest reasons for the different rates of population growth in those three countries.

8. How reliable do you think the demographic transition is in predicting future changes in population in developing countries?

9. Describe the pattern shown in figure 1.12.

10. Compare the patterns shown in figures 1.12 and 10.2 (in chapter 10), and suggest reasons for any similarities you can identify.

Population Momentum and World Population Growth

As shown in the sections above, total fertility is declining in most countries of the world. Even when this occurs, however, there is a lag period before the rate of natural increase declines. This is because children and youths who have already been born but who have not yet reached childbearing age give the population momentum to continue growing. **Population momentum** is the tendency for a population to continue growing even after the time that a replacement level of fertility has been achieved. It occurs when a population contains quite high proportion of people at or before their childbearing years.

The population momentum factor (PMF) is calculated by multiplying the crude birth rate (CBR) with the average life expectancy at birth (LEB). A PMF of 1 indicates that natural increase is not contributing to population growth. A PMF greater than 1 means there is positive momentum in the population that will lead to future growth, while a PMF of less than 1 means there is negative momentum, or a high probability that the population will decline in size. The higher the PMF, the greater will be the population momentum for that country.

The population momentum for a selection of countries is shown in table 1.5. The figures are calculated using the formula PMF = CBR x LEB. Thus, the PMF for Nigeria is 0.043 x 47, or 2.021. This is a fairly typical situation for many countries in Africa where the population experiences short life expectancies but which are continuing to increase because of high fertility rates.

Table 1.5
Demographic Characteristics and Population Momentum for Selected Countries, 2008

	Population 2008	Estimated Population 2025	Estimated Population 2050	Projected Population Change 2008-50 (%)	Crude Birth Rate (CBR) in births per 1000 population	Life Expectancy at Birth (LEB) in years	Population Momentum Factor (PMF)
HIGH HUMAN DEVELOPMENT							
Norway	4.8	5.6	6.6	38	12	80	0.960
Australia	21.3	24.7	28.1	32	14	81	1.134
Sweden	9.2	9.9	10.4	13	12	81	0.972
Japan	127.7	119.3	95.2	-25	9	82	0.738
USA	304.5	355.7	438.2	44	14	78	1.092
United Kingdom	61.3	68.8	76.9	26	13	79	1.027
South Korea	48.6	49.1	42.3	-13	10	79	0.790
United Arab Emirates	4.5	6.2	7.8	75	15	78	1.170
Mexico	107.7	123.8	131.6	22	20	75	1.500
Malaysia	27.7	34.6	40.4	46	21	74	1.554
MEDIUM HUMAN DEVELOPMENT							
China	1,324.7	1,476.0	1,437.0	8	12	73	1.533
Iran	72.2	88.0	100.2	39	20	71	1.420
Vietnam	86.2	100.1	112.8	31	17	73	1.241
Indonesia	239.9	291.9	343.1	43	21	70	1.470
Bolivia	10.0	13.3	16.7	67	29	65	1.885
India	1,149.3	1,407.7	1,755.2	53	24	65	1.560
Myanmar	49.2	55.4	58.7	19	19	61	1.169
Nepal	27.0	36.5	48.7	81	29	64	1.856
Papua New Guinea	6.5	8.6	11.2	73	29	57	1.653
Kenya	38.0	51.3	65.2	72	40	53	2.120
LOW HUMAN DEVELOPMENT							
Eritrea	5.0	7.7	11.5	129	40	57	2.280
Nigeria	148.1	205.4	282.2	91	43	47	2.021
Tanzania	40.2	58.2	82.5	105	38	51	1.938
Rwanda	9.6	14.6	21.7	126	43	47	2.021
Malawi	13.6	20.4	30.5	124	48	46	2.208
Zambia	12.2	15.5	19.3	58	43	38	1.634
Ethiopia	79.1	110.5	147.6	87	40	49	1.960
Mali	12.7	20.6	34.2	169	48	56	2.688
Niger	14.7	26.3	53.2	261	46	57	2.622
Sierra Leone	5.5	7.6	10.9	99	48	48	2.304

Source: Derived from the Population Reference Bureau 2008 World Population Data Sheet, *Countries arranged by descending HDI (see chapter 2)*

Vietnam, also shown in table 1.5, is experiencing a different situation. Vietnam has experienced very rapid economic development since the early 1990s, and as we would expect from the typical trends of the demographic transition, it has seen a large decline in population fertility. However, Vietnam's population continues to grow because of the increase in life expectancy which has accompanied the improving living standards.

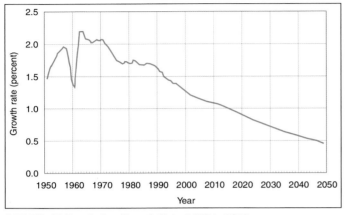

1.13 *World Population Growth Rate, 1950 to 2050.*

Japan has a momentum factor of 0.738, which is well below 1, suggesting that Japan is confronting the challenges of a declining population. Like many more economically developed countries (MEDCs) that experience both declining birth rates and increasing life expectancies, Japan has a large elderly population that is supported by welfare programs that must be funded through income taxes. As the number of people in the working population declines, Japan will struggle increasingly to maintain its economic growth as well as providing for the needs of the elderly.

As a result of all the factors described so far in this chapter, the world population growth rate has been slowing in recent decades, and this trend is expected to continue (figure 1.13). This does not mean that world population size will decline, merely that it will grow at a slowing rate of increase.

Figure 1.14 shows the density of the world's population. However, it is important to remember the limitations of a map such as this. The shadings shown are national averages, and population is seldom distributed evenly throughout an entire country. In Australia, for example, population is concentrated along the south-east coastline, in China in the eastern half of the country, and in Egypt along the Nile River valley.

In order to understand the density of world population, it is necessary to know something about the nature of individual countries. For example, many countries have topographic and climatic barriers to settlement over much of their land areas, resulting in uneven distributions of people. For example, China has high mountainous areas in the south-west, deserts in the north-west and very cold areas in the north-east, all of which combine to concentrate population in the east and south-east. Egypt has a narrow strip of well-watered land along the Nile River, and most of the country's population is concentrated along that strip. Most countries of the world have an uneven distribution of population within their borders (figures 1.15 and 1.16). On the other hand, some countries such as the Netherlands have almost nowhere that is unsettled.

In some parts of the world, humans have enhanced the natural environment to improve its capacity to house

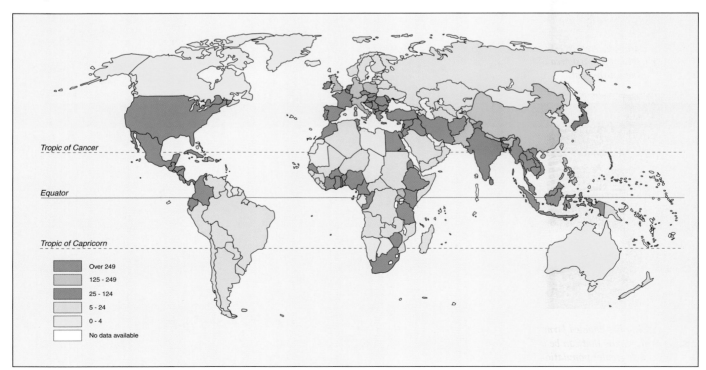

1.14 *Density of world population, measured in persons per square kilometre.*

people. In other words, the productivity of the resource base of the land has been increased, and this has allowed an increase in population density. A good example of this process is found in several countries in Asia (such as Philippines, Indonesia, Nepal and China) where hillsides have been terraced to allow irrigation of rice fields (figure 1.17).

1.15 *Although Germany is one of the world's most densely populated countries, there are variations in population density, as seen in this view of Berlin, compared with the view in the next photo.*

1.16 *A sparsely populated area of Germany; the Black Forest, near Freiburg in the south-west.*

1.17 *Terracing has enabled farmers in Nepal to transform steep hillsides into rice padis that can be irrigated and flooded, enabling the land to feed a much greater population density.*

Canada and Australia are also examples of countries where the impact of difficult topography and climate has affected the population distribution. In these two countries, the indigenous people did not develop an agricultural culture before European settlement. This limited the capacity of these populations to grow prior to European intrusion a little over two centuries ago. Both Australia and Canada occupy a large land area, and yet each has a very low total population and low population density.

China is perhaps an even more extreme example of these factors. China's population density can be described as following an 80-20 distribution, where 80% of the population occupies the eastern 20% of the land where the land is most fertile. On the other hand, only 20% of the population is found in the western 80% of the country where high mountains and arid deserts dominate the landscape.

QUESTION BLOCK 1D

1. *Examine figure 1.14, which shows the density of world population. Explain how a map such as this that shows national averages may be misleading when trying to locate concentrations of population.*

2. *Using the information in the table below, classify each of the countries shown into either (a) sparsely populated or (b) densely populated. Then comment on the relationship between population density and economic development.*

Country and its population	Population in millions 2008	Area of the country (sq. km)	GNI per capita 2007 ($US)
Australia	21.3	7,741,220	35,960
Bangladesh	147.3	144,000	470
Botswana	1.8	581,730	5,840
Canada	33.3	9,984,670	39,420
Germany	82.2	357,050	38,860
India	1,149.3	3,287,260	950
Japan	127.7	377,910	37,670
Mauritania	3.2	1,030,700	840
Mongolia	2.7	1,566,500	880
Netherlands	16.4	41,530	45,820
Singapore	4.8	699	32,470

3. *With reference to your answers to the last two questions, how would you define 'overpopulation'?*

4. *Using the statistics on the next page, calculate the population momentum factor for each country listed:*

Country	Crude Birth Rate (Births per 1000 people)	Life Expectancy at Birth (years)
Afghanistan	47	43
Bangladesh	24	63
Bulgaria	10	73
Canada	11	80
Germany	8	79
Israel	21	80
Liberia	50	46
Russia	12	67
Singapore	11	81
Swaziland	31	33
Uganda	48	48

Table 1.6
Population Growth in Papua New Guinea, 1950 to 2050

Year	Total Population
1950	1,412,000
1960	1,747,000.00
1970	2,288,000.00
1980	2,991,000.00
1990	3,825,000.00
2000	4,927,000.00
2010 (estimate)	6,771,000.00
2020 (estimate)	7,400,000.00
2030 (estimate)	8,592,000.00
2040 (estimate)	9,707,000.00
2050 (estimate)	10,670,000.00

Source: US Census Bureau

5. With reference to the statistics you calculated in the previous question, comment on the likely future trends of population growth in each of the countries listed.

6. Describe the pattern of population density shown in figure 1.14, and suggest reasons why particular areas of the world are more densely populated than others. In suggesting reasons for particular areas, you may find it helpful to use these sub-headings: climate, availability of water, topography, soils, resources, and history.

7. Outline the factors that can cause population within a country to be unevenly distributed.

Case Study – Papua New Guinea

One of the features that identifies Papua New Guinea as a developing country is its population growth pattern. The growth in Papua New Guinea's total population over the past few decades is shown in table 1.6.

Of Papua New Guinea's total population in 2000, 40% were under 15 years of age (the equivalent figure for Australia was 21%). This shows that Papua New Guinea's population will continue to grow rapidly for some time to come. However, the proportion of people under 15 years of age in Papua New Guinea is becoming smaller – in 1980 the figure was 43%. This shows that the birth rate of Papua New Guinea's population is also slowing a little, from 41 births per 1000 people in 1970-75 to 32 births per 1000 people in 1995-2000. Nonetheless, any village in Papua New Guinea will be noteworthy for the large number of children present (figures 1.18 and 1.19).

An important point to realise regarding Papua New Guinea's population is that it is spread very unevenly across the country (figure 1.20). In fact, the pattern of

1.18 Children are evident in most Papua New Guinean villages because 40% of the country's population are aged 15 years of age of less.

population distribution is quite different to that expected in most countries. Whereas most countries have the highest population densities in coastal areas, Papua New Guinea's Guinea's population density is greatest in the mountain valleys of the Highlands, with altitudes of between 1500 and 2000 metres. In this respect, as was the case in medieval Europe, the population is concentrated in the highest areas for safety, and are thus remote from roads and communications (figures 1.20 and 1.21).

This was a great surprise to the early European explorers who had presumed that the inland areas were uninhabited. A high mountain chain ran along the island of New Guinea like a spine from west to east. When viewed from the coastal areas on either side of the Highlands, the mountains appear to be an inhospitable, solid mass. However, when an Australian group ventured into the mountains for the first time in 1930 looking for gold, they discovered that a series of rugged valleys ran through the

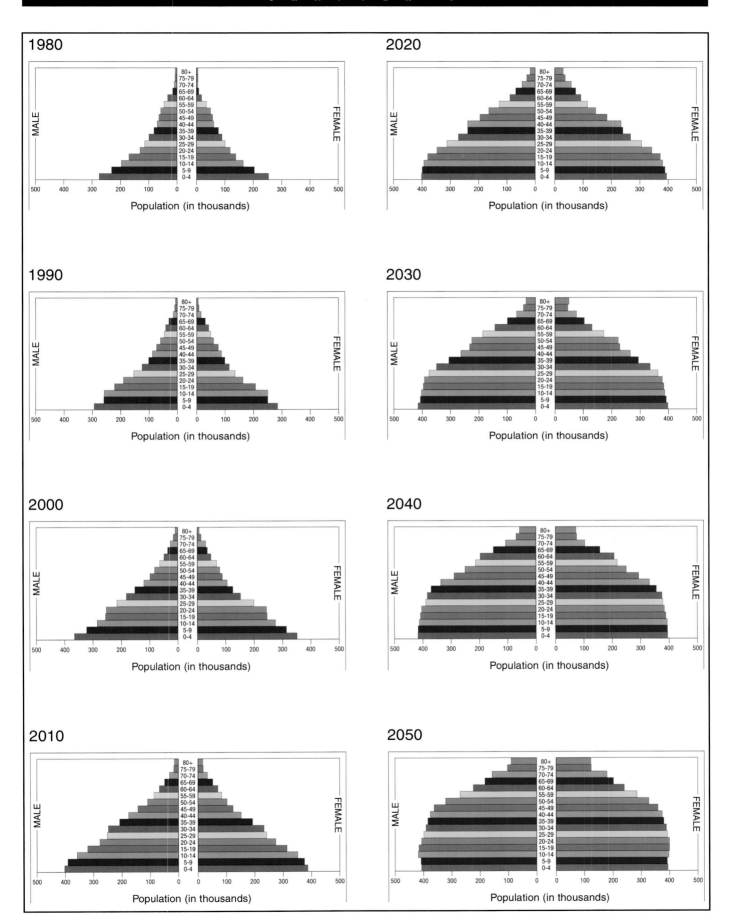

1.19 *Population pyramids for Papua New Guinea, 1980 to 2050.*

Populations in Transition

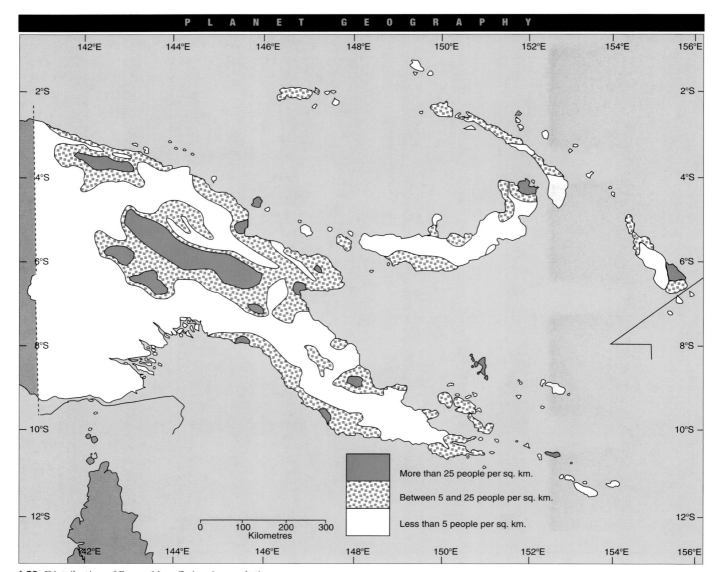

1.20 *Distribution of Papua New Guinea's population.*

elevated parts of the Highlands. These valleys contained almost one million people whose existence the rest of the world had not suspected.

There are good reasons for the high population density of the Highlands. These areas have rich volcanic soils that are well drained, a reliable and abundant rainfall, and unlike the low lying swampy coastal areas, they are free from malaria. Other areas with high population densities include the northern end of New Britain island, where the rich volcanic soils have encouraged plantations to be established, and the copper mining areas of Panguna, Arawa and Kieta in the outlying North Solomon Islands. In total, the Highlands comprise 37% of Papua New Guinea's population, with 28% from the rest of New Guinea, 20% from Papua and 15% from the islands.

The average population density of Papua New Guinea as a whole is 10 people per square kilometre. This is quite a low population density, and so in contrast with many developing countries, Papua New Guinea is generally regarded as being underpopulated. This means that the country has insufficient people to develop its resources

Table 1.7

Average Population Density of Selected Countries, 2006

Country	People per square kilometre
Australia	3
Bangladesh	1,178
China	140
Indonesia	122
Namibia	2
Netherlands	482
Papua New Guinea	13
Singapore	6,302
United Kingdom	249
United States	32
Zimbabwe	34

Source: World Bank

1.21 *In spite of its appearance, this is one of the most densely populated parts of Papua New Guinea. All the land in this view of Chimbu Gorge, in the rugged Highlands, is being used productively for cultivation, hunting or gathering.*

adequately. To place this figure in perspective, the average population densities of some other countries are shown in table 1.7.

Underpopulation can lead to a number of problems. Examples of significant problems include too little tax revenue to provide basic services such as schools and health clinics, too few roads to service an area, and low prices for cash crops due to the high cost of transport and lack of competition.

However, not all parts of Papua New Guinea are underpopulated. Some areas are overpopulated, which means that there are too many people for the amount of land and the resources available. Overpopulation can lead to:
- food shortages when too many people compete for too little food;
- over-exploitation of the land (which can lead in turn to soil erosion and land degradation), and
- land disputes as people fight over scarce resources.

Because of the unequal distribution of Papua New Guinea's population, people tend to move (or migrate) from areas of high population density into areas of lower population density. When people move from rural areas into urban areas, the movement is called rural-urban migration. Rural-urban migration is one of the main causes of urbanisation in Papua New Guinea.

QUESTION BLOCK 1E

1. *Draw a line graph showing the change in Papua New Guinea's population over the period 1950 to 2050.*

2. *On the basis of the information in this section, describe the changing shape of Papua New Guinea's population pyramid from 1980 to 2050.*

3. *Using figure 1.20, describe and account for the distribution of Papua New Guinea's population.*

4. *List the problems of (a) underpopulation and (b) overpopulation.*

5. *What is 'rural-urban migration'?*

1.22 *This Dani family is unusual because there are three children, two of whom are twins. The mother has followed the traditional custom and induced early menopause as a means of population control by Dani society, even though she is in her early twenties.*

Responses to high and low fertility

Dependency and Ageing Ratios

When a country has a declining population, as many in Europe now experience, it places great strains on social security and pension funds. This is because an increasing proportion of the population become dependent on the wealth produced by a declining workforce. The **dependency ratio** attempts to measure this phenomenon. For the purposes of international comparisons, the economically active, or working, population is usually defined as those between the ages of 15 and 65 years of age. The dependent population is defined as those under 15 or over 65 years of age. The dependency ratio can therefore be calculated using the formula:

$$\frac{\text{Number of dependent people} \times 100}{\text{Number of people of working age}}$$

In Australia, the calculation using 2008 figures would be as follows:

Total population size = 21 300 000 people
Percentage of people under 15 years = 19%
Percentage of people 15 to 65 years = 68%
Percentage of people over 65 years   = 13%

Therefore the number of people of dependent ages was (19 + 13)% of 21.3 million, or 6,816,000 people (rounded off to 6.8 million).

The number of working age people was 68% of 21.3 million, or 14,484,000 people (rounded off to 14.5 million).

Therefore, Australia's dependency ratio was:

$$\frac{6.8 \times 100}{14.5}$$

or 46.9%. This means that for every 100 people of working age, there were 46.9 people dependent on them. Back in 1975, Australia's dependency ratio had been 57%, so although the proportion of elderly people has increased since 1975, it has been more than offset by a decline in the proportion of school age children.

QUESTION BLOCK 1F

1. *Use the data in the table below to calculate the dependency ratio for each country shown (except Australia which is shown in the text as an example):*

Country and its population	Size in millions 2008	% under 15	% 15 - 65	% over 65
Australia	21.3	19	68	13
China	1,324.7	19	73	8
Iran	72.2	26	69	5
Japan	127.7	13	65	22
Papua New Guinea	6.5	40	58	2
Singapore	4.8	19	72	9
Uganda	29.2	49	48	3
United Kingdom	61.3	18	66	16

2   *Select three countries with contrasting dependency ratios from the previous question, and discuss the implications of the dependency ratios on the provision of services such as schools, hospitals and transport in the countries selected.*

Population Policies

Although traditional societies often have high birth rates and high death rates characteristic of stage 1 of the demographic transition, it would be wrong to think that people in such societies have no control over their population growth. For example, the Dani people of the Baliem Valley in the Highlands of Irian Jaya, Indonesia (discussed in more detail in chapter 16) represent a society which continues to function largely according to traditional customs. Even today, some polygamy is practised, as is common in many traditional societies where warfare is common and so the ratio of women to men might be artificially high. Among the Dani people, few men have more than two wives, and only very wealthy men would have as many as three or four wives. Indeed, just over half of Dani men today have only one wife, largely because of the impact of Christian missionaries.

As the average life expectancy of Dani people is only 38 years, men usually marry at the age of 20, but girls often marry earlier, usually at around the age of 12. It has always been very uncommon for Dani women to have more than two children as the Dani have known the need to live within the resource limits of their difficult mountain environment. After a Dani woman has given birth to her second child, usually at around the age of 18 to 20, she eats the sap of a particular species of tree that induces early menopause (figure 1.22). This causes her to stop menstruating and she becomes incapable of having any more children. In this way, the Dani population has remained stable for a long period of time.

However, many people are concerned at the effects of rapid population growth in countries at stages 2 and 3 of the demographic transition. Governments often feel the need to introduce policies to control the growth of their populations. Most of these policies are **anti-natalist**, which means they discourage births and try to slow population growth. A few countries with slow rates of population increase have introduced **pro-natalist** population polices which are designed to encourage more births. There are three approaches to anti-natalist population polices. The first is the **regulatory** approach, where governments impose regulations and restrictions that control the number of births. A second approach is to offer **incentives**, such as prizes or money to families that limit the number of children they have. The third anti-natalist approach is to argue that according to the demographic transition, fertility will decline as people become more affluent. Therefore, policies are implemented to **raise people's standards of living** in the hope that this will result in reduced population growth.

In reality, governments often use a mixture of these policy types, and this can be illustrated by examining the population policies of several countries.

China's Population Policy

China has the world's largest population, and its cities are among the most densely populated places in the world, as shown in figure 1.1 at the beginning of this chapter). China's anti-natalist population control policy is perhaps the best known such policy in the world. China's policy is certainly one of the most rigid of any country, and because it insists that each family limit itself to having only one child, it is commonly known as the 'One Child Policy'.

Before 1949 when the Communist Party came to power in a revolution, China was at stage 1 of the demographic transition. Birth rates were high, with the typical number of children per family being between five and eight. However, death rates were also high and life expectancies were short – in 1930 these were 23.7 years for females and 24.6 years for males. Infant mortality rates were high (about 300 deaths per 1000 live births), and so with both death rates and birth rates being very high, population growth was slow.

By 1949, China's population had reached 538 million people. In the early years of Communist rule, China followed a pro-natalist population policy in which large families were encouraged. This reflected traditional attitudes that had existed in China for many centuries, but it was supported by the leadership of the time. The new Communist government saw a large population as making China's position in the world stronger. When Mao Zedong announced the beginning of the People's Republic in 1949, he said "The Chinese people have stood up". Mao saw a large and healthy population as being necessary for China to take its proper place in the world as a nation-state of significance.

1.23 *Information outside a birth control office in Shanghai drawing attention to China's growing population — from 540 million in 1949 to 1.008 billion in 1982 and 1.133 billion in 1990.*

In the 1950s, however, a census revealed that China had 100 million people more than previously thought. This information came to light at the same time as many people were experiencing hardship and malnutrition as a re-

sult of the Great Leap Forward, a political campaign designed to catapult China into modern industrialisation that went terribly wrong. Indeed, many people died during the Great Leap Forward when abnormal floods and droughts reduced food production. Against this background, China entered stage 2 of the demographic transition in the early 1960s as a result of improvements made to medical services.

However, with Mao's death in 1976, the Chinese government began to advocate voluntary population control to reduce the birth rate and accelerate the beginning of stage 3 of the demographic transition. The argument put to the Chinese people was based on Malthusian logic – China was modernising, but there was only a certain fixed amount of wealth to divide among the population. If people would limit their family sizes, then 'a larger slice of cake' would be available for each person. From the 1970s, birth control offices were established throughout China to give advice about limiting family sizes and to distribute information about the need to control population growth (figure 1.23).

Table 1.8
Marital Status by Age Group in China, 1982
(all figures are percentages)

Age	Unmarried	Married	Widowed	Divorced
15 - 19	97.38	2.59	0.0004	0.02
20	84.12	15.76	0.02	0.10
21	74.79	25.06	0.03	0.12
22	62.73	37.07	0.04	0.16
23	48.88	50.87	0.06	0.19
24	36.60	63.09	0.09	0.22
25	25.70	73.91	0.12	0.27
26	18.09	81.45	0.15	0.31
27	12.69	86.76	0.20	0.35
28	9.42	89.91	0.26	0.41
29	7.32	91.91	0.32	0.45
30 - 34	4.93	93.49	0.55	0.58
35 - 39	3.70	94.33	1.23	0.74
40 - 44	3.13	93.39	2.54	0.94
45 - 49	2.39	91.45	5.00	1.16
50 - 59	1.66	84.48	12.58	1.28
60 - 79	1.37	56.70	40.98	0.95
80+	1.11	17.72	80.80	0.37

Source: Li Chengrui (1992) p.173

At the same time, the minimum legal age for marriage was raised to 20 for females and 22 for males so that couples would have fewer childbearing years available to them (figure 1.24). Moreover, the Marriage Law adopted in 1980 requires that 'husband and wife are duty bound to practice family planning'. At about the time the new Marriage Law was passed, half of Chinese people were married by the age of 23 (see table 1.8). The table also shows that China has a high marriage rate, low divorce rate and that marriages in China tend to be very stable. The marriages that occurred before the legal minimum marriage age were usually in remote areas among minority ethnic groups.

1.24 *A Chinese couple in Harbin on their wedding day. It is a condition of marriage in China that couples practice family planning.*

1.25 *A special music school for single children in Tangshan, China.*

In 1980, the One Child Policy was introduced, providing rewards and benefits for couples that agreed to have only one child. Additional health care subsidies were granted to one-child families, together with priority health care, priority in housing allocation, priority in educational provision, extra land for private farming and extra food rations (figure 1.25). Furthermore, every member of a work unit that meets its standard target of 100% one-child families receives a financial bonus, and this encourages fellow-workers to put pressure on their colleagues to have only one child. If parents change their minds and have a sec-

ond child, all the privileges that have been given are taken away.

Although the one-child policy is officially policed by the promise of incentives and rewards, in reality there are also punishments for violating family planning regulations. Punishments may arise for refusal to abort unapproved pregnancies, an unapproved birth for couples under the legal marriage age, or having an approved second child too soon. Family planning staff who violate regulations by accepting bribes, making false reports, or issuing false birth certificates are also open to be punished. Penalties generally include fines, losing government benefits, demotion or dismissal from employment or from Communist Party membership.

The punishments for violating family planning policies vary for urban and rural couples. Penalties for rural couples include loss of government land grants, food, loans, and farming supplies. For example, a rural couple with an unauthorised child may be disqualified from receiving plots of land for growing grain for the next seven years or, if they have another unapproved birth, for 14 years. For workers in urban areas who violate birth control policy, fines are imposed on a percentage of their income, usually between 20% to 50% of annual salary.

There are only a few exceptions to the one-child policy. The first applies to families in some backward rural areas who may have two children because children are a vital part of the farming work force. The second exception has applied since 1995 to couples where both husband and wife are themselves single children – they may have a second child. Other exceptions include families whose first child is disabled and unable to work, pregnancies occurring after a childless couple has adopted a child, couples facing difficulties in continuing the family line, and Chinese people returning to China after living abroad. In rural areas, couples with 'real difficulties' and certain peasants may be allowed a second child; the phrase 'real difficulties' is generally understood to include situations in which a couple has a single female child. In China, it is still common to say 'a little happiness has arrived' when describing the birth of a girl, but 'a great happiness has arrived' when a boy is born.

In the early 1990s, the guidelines were tightened further. The 'Decision on Strengthening the Family Planning Programme to Strictly Control Population Growth of 1991' (known as the '1991 Decision') contains provisions suggesting the use of IUDs and sterilisation, and allowing forced pregnancy termination (abortions) in certain circumstances. However, the official policy is that coercive action should not be used as part of the country's population policies.

The one-child policy is implemented in a manner that would be described as heavy handed outside China. Women's menstrual cycles are monitored publicly by the work unit, and compulsory pelvic examinations are performed on all those suspected of being pregnant. Insertion of IUDs in women with one child is usually mandatory, and these are checked by x-ray from time to time to ensure they have not been removed. Unauthorised pregnancies are usually terminated by abortion when detected, often regardless of stage of pregnancy.

1.26 *A typical 'One Child' propaganda poster in Beijing.*

There have been many reports of infanticide by drowning of girl babies in rural areas when couples have desperately wanted a son as their single child. According to Chinese tradition, daughters join the families of their husbands when they marry. Therefore, girls are seldom able to support or care for their parents in old age. By the 1990s, thousands of ultrasound machines were being imported to China so that couples could check the sex of their unborn baby. Domestic factories in China began manufacturing ultrasound machines at the rate of 10 000 a year. However, in 1993 authorities banned the use of ultrasound for the purpose of sex selection, but this ban cannot be enforced. Some parts of China report sex ratios at birth for of 300 males to 100 females, and reports predict that early next century China will have an excess of 70 million bachelors because of the abortion of girl babies.

1.27 *A 'One Child' painted ceramic tile street display in Guangzhou.*

This policy was supported in China's laws. Although China does not have a formal national family planning law, the idea of family planning is firmly embedded in national and provincial laws and regulations. Article 25 of China's Constitution affirms the importance of family planning to curb population growth, calling family planning a necessary part of development. Article 49, which grants government protection to marriage and the family, confirms the 'duty' of both wife and husband to 'practice family planning'. Under a 1982 regulation, couples with two or more children may be compulsorily sterilised, although the Women's Protection Law expresses this as 'women enjoy the freedom of choosing not to bear children'.

Since 1980, large propaganda posters encouraging families to have only one child have been a prominent feature of the Chinese landscape (figures 1.26 and 1.27). These posters almost always show two modern, well-dressed, smiling parents and their single daughter. Showing a girl counters the traditional Chinese preference for boys, as it is boys who carry on the family name. The posters carry slogans such as 'One child is best for you and best for the country' and 'Limit the numbers but raise the quality'.

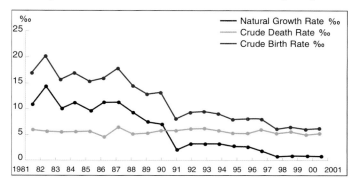

1.28 *Changes in Beijing's population growth rates, 1981 to 2001.*

In introducing the one-child policy, the Chinese government's stated target was to limit its population to 1.3 billion people by 2000 and to lower the natural population growth rate to less than 10 per thousand (i.e. 1%) by the year 2000. The introduction of the one-child policy certainly had an immediate effect on population growth in China (figure 1.28). In 1960, China's birth rate was 37 births per 1000 people. By 1988 this had fallen to 21 per 1000, and by 1998 to 16.2 births per 1000 people. In 1960, China's population was growing at an overall rate of 2% per annum. By 1978, shortly before the One Child Policy was introduced, the rate had fallen to 1.4%. In 1980 when the new policy was introduced, the growth rate fell to 1.2%. Further drops since then have continued slowly, and in 1998, the growth rate was 1.042%, still short of the target figure of 1.00%.

By 2008, China's population (including 7.6 million in Hong Kong and Macau) was 1.332.3 billion. As a result of the One Child Policy, it is now predicted by the Chinese authorities that the country's total population will peak at 1.519 billion by 2033. The proportion of women of child-bearing age decreased to 26.7% in 2000, and predicted

1990

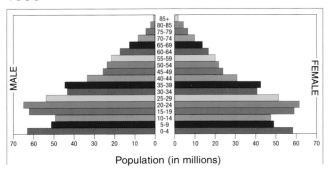

2030

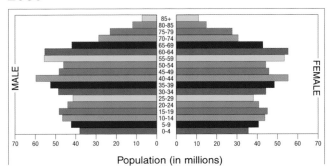

2000

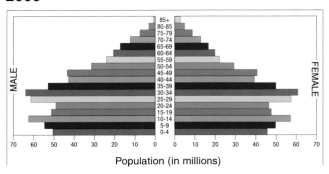

2040

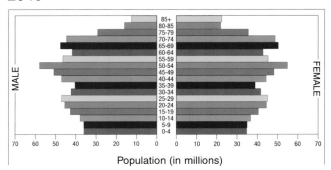

2010

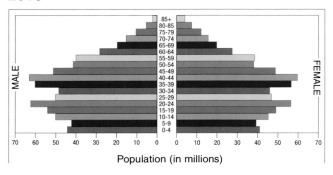

2050

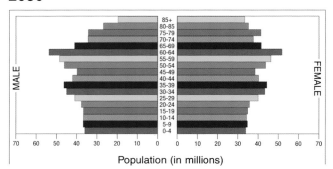

2020

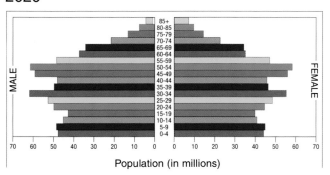

1.29 *China's changing population structure, 1990 to 2050.*

decreases will lower the figure to 24.5% by 2020 and 21.9% by 2040. Meanwhile the percentage of aged people increased from 7.63% in 1982 to 9.84% in 2000, and it is expected to increase to 21.9% by 2030. By 2050, the proportion of China's population that is aged will be 27.43%, and this will pose significant challenges for the provision of services for the elderly (figure 1.29).

1.30 *Many single children in China are dressed as 'little emperors' on special occasions. There is concern that China's single children are growing up to be very self-centred, an unforeseen consequence of the one-child policy.*

However, there have been consequences of this population control. In 1983 (the peak year), family planning work teams carried out 21 million sterilisations (79% on women), 18 million IUD insertions, and 14 million abortions. There is also concern that those children who are born and grow up without brothers or sisters are becoming very spoilt and selfish. Single children in China tend to have every desire fulfilled by doting parents and other adults, and they are commonly known in China as 'little emperors' (figure 1.30). In another generation, the concepts of 'aunt', 'uncle' and 'cousin' will have disappeared along with 'sister' and 'brother'.

1.31 *A family with TWO children rides on a motorbike Pingyao, China.*

In recent years, China's 'One Child' Policy has come to be treated less seriously in some parts of the country than others. In Guangdong province in China's south-east, for example, families with two children were becoming quite common by the early 2000s, and by 2010 it was almost the norm in many coastal areas and elsewhere (figure 1.31). This was because the province was quite wealthy and many people felt they could afford more than one child –

the opposite of what the Demographic Transition Model might predict! People who were self-employed felt free to have more children because, unlike government employees, they did not need official permission to have a child.

US Population Policy

In strong contrast with China, the United States does not have any formal population policy apart from its laws governing immigration. Where the US government has legislated in the area of population, it has intended to enhance individual people's right to choose their own family planning. This is the opposite of the Chinese approach, which is to make the overall goals paramount over individual people's rights.

Thus, the US government has enacted laws providing funding or refunds for family planning services. In this way, women with low-incomes have access to birth control. In most US states, a woman must have had a child or be pregnant, be single, and have an income that is less than 50% of the poverty level to be eligible for refunds for family planning.

In 1970, the US government established a national family planning programme. This programme now provides financial support to 76% of all family planning agencies in the US Each year, four million Americans use government funded family planning programmes to obtain abortions or sterilisations. As a condition of government funding, family planning agencies must provide services for adolescents including contraceptive information and devices, gynaecological examinations, pregnancy tests, and screening tests for STDs, HIV, and cancer.

Nigeria's Population Policy

Nigeria has one of the fastest growing populations in the world. In 1975, its birth rate was 46.3 per 1000 people and its death rate was 20.2 per 1000. Thus, Nigeria's annual population growth rate at that time was 2.61%, one of the highest in the world. In 2008, birth rates remained high at 43 per 1000 people, while death rates had fallen to 18 per 1000. Therefore, the population growth rate remained almost the same at 2.5%. In 1950, Nigeria's population was 32.9 million people. By 1990 this figure had climbed to 96.2 million, and by 2008 to 148.1 million. Current projections are that Nigeria will have a population of 205.4 million by 2025 and 282.2 million by 2050.

In 1981-82, Nigeria's fertility rate was 5.94 children per woman. In 1990, this had climbed to 6.01 and it is currently estimated to be 5.9. One reason for Nigeria's high level of fertility is the very low level of contraceptive use. Only about 6% of married women currently use a method of contraception. Knowledge of contraception is very low, with fewer than half of all women aged 15 to 49 knowing of any method.

At present, the average ideal family size desired by women in Nigeria is essentially the same as the total fertility rate: six children per woman. According to a government survey, half of women with five children say they want to have another child.

Another factor leading to high fertility is the early age of marriage and childbearing in Nigeria. Half of all women are married by age 17, and 50% of all women become mothers by age 20. More than a quarter of Nigerian women aged 15 to 19 are either pregnant or already have children.

The Nigerian government became concerned about the consequences of such rapid increases in population, and in 1988 it adopted the National Policy on Population for Development, Unity, Progress and Self-Reliance. This policy was designed to slow the rate of population growth and improve the standards of living for the people. The policy worked on a voluntary basis, assuming that couples wish to determine the number and the spacing of their children.

The National Policy on Population identifies several objectives that include:

- promoting an awareness of population problems and the effects of rapid population growth;

- providing information on the benefits of small family size; and

- making family planning services easily accessible to all couples at an affordable cost.

The specific targets of the policy included:

- reducing the proportion of women who marry before the age of 18 by 80% by the year 2000;

- reducing the number of children a woman bears over her lifetime from the average of more than six children to an average of four;

- reducing the percentage of women having more than four children by 80% by the year 2000;

- reducing the rate of population growth from 3% per year to 2% by 2000;

- extending family planning coverage to 80% of women of child bearing age by 2000;

- reducing the infant mortality rate from the 1975 level of 111 per 1000 live births to 30 per 1000 live births by 2000; and

- providing 75% of rural communities with basic social amenities by 2000 to stimulate and sustain self-reliant development.

The main way of implementing this policy has been through an aggressive campaign, organised by the government to educate people about the importance of small family sizes, both for their own good and for the benefit of the nation. The policy has particularly tried to promote the use of family planning methods, a difficult task in a nation that is mainly Muslim. Contraception has been promoted through day care centres that have been established for employed women to leave their children while they are working. In order to encourage women to use these centres and obtain the information, legislation has been introduced to eliminate discrimination against women in education and employment and the minimum age of marriage has been increased to 18 years.

1.32 *This young Nigerian mother near the northern town of Jos has two young children and is pregnant with a third. Any anti-natalist population policy in Nigeria must change the attitudes of women such as her.*

So far, the Nigerian policy has not achieved the ambitious targets set. However, some gains have been made even though aspects of the policy violate the religious beliefs of many Nigerians. Any policy in Nigeria can only be successful if it is communicated to people in the countryside where most people live, and if it works within rather than against people's cultural sensitivities (figure 1.32). However, while most families retain a preference for having large numbers of children, the government's policy to limit population growth is unlikely to succeed.

Singapore's Population Policy

Unlike many other countries in the world, Singapore has a pro-natalist population policy. The words of a Singaporean Government publication summarise the rationale for the policy:

"People are, and always will be, our most precious resource. More than anything else, it is the effort of Singaporeans, with their drive and talent, that has made the country what it is today. Overcoming great odds as a newly-independent nation without natural resources, we have turned our city-state into a thriving and modern economy.., In the next lap, the size of our population and the quality of our people will determine how successfully we fare. (But) the population is not growing fast enough to replace itself in the long term; many Singaporeans remain unmarried; and those who do marry tend to have fewer children... Too small a population will hinder our development."

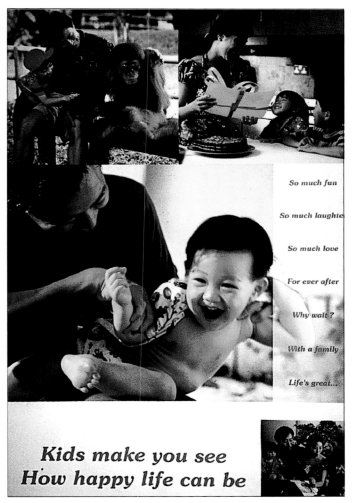

Kids make you see
How happy life can be

So much fun
So much laughter
So much love
For ever after
Why wait?
With a family
Life's great...

1.33 *A pro-natalist population poster in a subway in Singapore.*

At first, the claim that Singapore is underpopulated might seem surprising for a country with 4.8 million people in an area of only 685 square kilometres; its population density of 7,742 people per square kilometre is among the highest in the world. Furthermore, Singapore's birth rate of 11 births per 1000 people easily exceeds its death rate of 5 deaths per 1000 people. However, Singapore's population is ageing, and if current trends continue population numbers will peak in 2030 and then start to decline.

During the 1960s, when Singapore became an independent nation, it was rapidly rising population numbers that were causing concern. Large numbers of people had migrated to Singapore from China, Malaysia and India, and it was feared that the large numbers might cause strain in the new independent nation. At the time, an anti-natalist government policy of 'stop-at-two' was introduced. The policy was so successful that Singapore's population growth is now falling below replacement level.

In response to this situation, a new pro-natalist policy known as the New Population Policy was introduced in 1987. The target of the policy was young couples who were choosing to put their careers, leisure and personal interests above marriage and parenthood. Posters were placed on buses and trains with slogans such as 'Children – Life would be empty without them' and 'Now that you've married, take the next step' (figure 1.33).

The aim of the New Population Policy was to increase Singapore's fertility rate to 2.1, which is replacement rate. In 1986, the year before the policy was introduced, fertility in Singapore fell to a record low of 1.4. In 1988, the first full year of the pro-natalist policy, fertility rose to 2.0, a significant increase but still less than replacement level. If the New Population Policy is unsuccessful and fertility remains in the 1.8 to 2.1 range, Singapore's population will peak in the year 2030 at 5.3 to 5.4 million, and then decline. Furthermore, the proportion of elderly people in the population will rise as the post-war baby boomers reach old age; in the year 2030 25% of Singapore's population will be aged 60 or older compared with 9% today. The Singapore Government believes that the country can comfortably accommodate over 5 million people with substantial gains in the quality of life.

The New Population Policy particularly targets intellectually talented people. Whereas the policy in general encourages each married couple to have two children, couples that are university graduates are encouraged to have four children. In an effort to raise the talent level of the population further, Singapore is encouraging the immigration of well-educated people from other parts of Asia and actively discouraging the emigration of university graduates.

India's Population Policy

The Indian government was one of the first in the world to introduce an anti-natalist population policy. In 1952, a well-publicised programme was launched which offered incentives such as transistor radios to men who volunteered to be sterilised by having a vasectomy. The campaign was only partly successful, largely because many men became disillusioned when they realised that sterilisation was permanent whereas the batteries of transistor radios are not.

The campaign to encourage male sterilisations was strengthened during the 1970s when many men were forced to be sterilised against their wishes. This lowered birth rates, but gave population policies in India a bad reputation. One of the problems faced by population workers in India is that, like China, boy babies are traditionally favoured over girls. Although there are many reasons why this is so (see extract 1.1), the pressure remains on families with many daughters to continue trying to have a son.

Today, India's population policy aims to reduce fertility rates, largely by encouraging the use of contraceptives. The current Five Year Plan for India's economy identifies controlling population growth as the sixth most important objective of national government policy. The government established the specific target of reducing the birth rate from 29.9 per 1000 in 1990 to 26 per 1000 by 1997 and achieving an average of 2.1 children per family by 2000. The policy also set targets for the numbers of users of specific types of contraception, particularly sterilisation, abortions and IUDs.

The Indian government tries to use incentives to encourage people to achieve the targets set. Among the incentives offered are new schools, provision of drinking water facilities and new road links for areas that reduce their population growth. There are also cash incentives for people willing to be sterilised or have an IUD inserted, as well as commissions for health workers who successfully motivate individuals or couples to become sterilised. In an effort to promote population control, the central government proposed an amendment to the Constitution in the mid-1990s to disqualify from election to national Parliament or state legislatures any candidate with more than two children. This bill has not yet been passed, but the proposal remains pending.

To support its population policy, the Indian government provides large-scale family planning services. The network of population control centres is placed within government hospitals, clinics, and workplace sites. All services in these centres are provided free of charge to the user. The policy also aims to increase public awareness of family planning and to train medical personnel. The government organises mass public information campaigns, primary and adult education programmes, and the training of community workers to promote family planning in rural areas. Many of the government programmes feature motivators who talk with couples and maintain a register of their reproductive activities.

Despite the great efforts put into population control in India, the successes have been modest. In 1975, India's birth rate was 38.2 per 1000 people, and by 1995 this had declined to 29.1 births per 1000, falling further to 25.2

births per 1000 by 2000 and 24 per 1000 in 2008. However, there are significant differences between different regions of India which provide some useful insights – in the state of Uttah Pradesh the birth rate is 40 per 1000, but in the southern state of Kerala the birth rate is only 18 per 1000. The reasons that Kerala has been so successful in controlling births are examined in the section that follows.

The Kerala Approach to Population Control

Kerala is a state in southern India with an area of 38,864 square kilometres and a population of 30 million people (figure 1.34). It is largely an agricultural state with coconut plantations and rice farms, and its other crops include black pepper, rubber, tapioca, oilseeds, sugar cane, tea, coffee and teak timber. The capital city is Trivandrum with a population of 600,000, although the town of Cochin is larger (with over 700,000 people) and is one of India's largest ports.

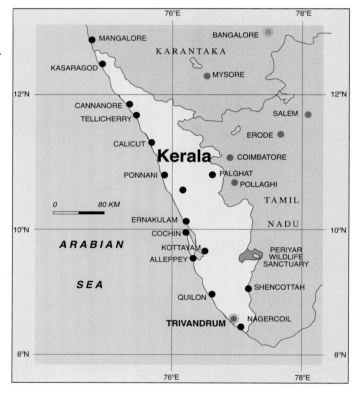

1.34 *Map of Kerala.*

Kerala has had spectacular success in lowering its birth rate without any strong regulations like China or even any financial incentives like other parts of India. Kerala is also attracting international attention for its success in controlling deaths, and especially for lowering its infant mortality rates. According to the demographic transition model, lowering birth rates occurs only when substantial economic changes such as industrialisation and urbanisation occur. However, Kerala's fall in fertility occurred at a time when Kerala had a dismal record in industrial and agricultural production and when there was high unemployment.

ToK BoX

Link to Theory of Knowledge.

In the IB Diploma Geography course, it is important to remember that Geography is just one subject within the wider context of all knowledge. The study of the 'Theory of Knowledge' is also called **epistemology**, and it is one of the most important branches of philosophy. It is the 'umbrella' that spans the entire scope of knowledge and understanding. The diagram in this ToK BoX shows one way to represent the Theory of Knowledge framework. The starting point is the centre of the circle, which is you — the knower. On the outside of the circle there are six broad areas of knowledge.

Most subjects fit into one of these six broad areas, but geography is somewhat different. Geography spans both the natural sciences (in physical geography) and the human sciences (in human geography). Indeed, one of the great distinctive features of geography is the way it links (or integrates) the physical and human facets of our world. Geography is therefore a good example of why the classification of knowledge into these six broad areas is somewhat imperfect.

The knower (you!) accesses the six broad areas of knowledge through four 'Ways of Knowing" — reasoning, the emotions, sense-perception and language.

In each chapter of this book, there will be a "ToK BoX" which is designed to help you place the understandings you acquire in Geography within the wider context of the areas of knowledge and the ways of knowing.

The next ToK BoX is on page 61.

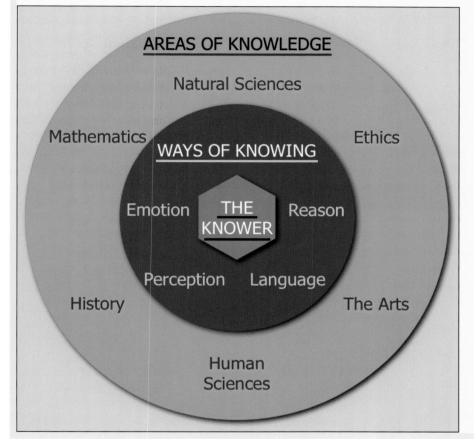

Kerala has always been one of the most densely populated parts of India. As long ago as 1901, Kerala's population density was double that of India as a whole. In the most recent census (1981), Kerala's population density of 654 people per square kilometre was three times India's national average. Kerala is also unusual in that unlike the rest of India (and most of the world), Kerala gives birth to more girls than boys, and the female to male ratio has been increasing over the years. In 1901, Kerala had 99.6 males for every 100 females; this figure fell to 98.9 in 1921, 97.3 in 1951 and 96.7 in 1981.

Traditionally, Kerala has had the highest fertility rates and one of the lowest death rates in India. Therefore, its population growth rate was among the fastest in India. In the mid-1960s, Kerala's birth rate was about 42 per 1000 people, but with the impact of the Indian government's population policies this fell to 35 per 1000 in 1970. By 1980, the birth rate had fallen to 30 per 1000 and by 1990 to 20 per 1000. The decline has continued since then, reaching 17 per 1000 in 1993 and 15 per 1000 in 1997. With a fertility rate of 1.7, Kerala's population growth has slowed to less than replacement level, a remarkable decline in fertility in the space of just over 30 years.

In the period 1991 to 1996, the average number of births in Kerala was 466 000 per year, but by 2021 to 2026, this figure will fall to 205 000. Today, many schools are already empty and industries catering to children's needs are likely to have a bleak future. On the other hand, the proportion of aged people in Kerala will grow in the years ahead. The proportion of people in Kerala aged 60 and over in 1961 was 5.8%. By 1981, this figure had risen to 7.5% and it is expected to rise further to 10.2% in 2001 and 18.4% in 2026.

The decline in birth rates has been matched by large falls in the death rates also. Although Kerala has traditionally lower death rates than the rest of India, it reached 13 per 1000 people in 1993 and has stayed at that level since that time. Between 1991 and 2031, the number of elderly people in Kerala will increase by 289% – from 2.6 million to about 9.6 million. In 1991, there were only 16 elderly people for every 100 people in the working ages of 20-59 years; by 2031 this figure will have risen to 60.

It is important to understand that even within Kerala, there are substantial differences in mortality rates depending on educational level, religion and occupation of the people concerned. This can be seen with reference to infant mortality rates, as shown in table 1.9.

Such major changes in birth rates and death rates in a relatively short period of time have significant implications. In the past, many resources have had to be allocated to the needs of children, such as in education, children's health, clothing and toys. In the future, these resources will need to be diverted to care of the needs of the elderly – housing, food, medical care, and so on.

Table 1.9
Infant and Child Mortality rates in Rural Areas of India and Kerala

Mother's Characteristic	Infant Mortality Rate		Under 5 Mortality Rate	
	Kerala	India	Kerala	India
Educational level				
Illiterate	55	145	100	176
Below Primary	44	101		
Primary			67	123
Middle			46	88
Matriculation	29	71	33	66
Graduate			25	46
Religion / Caste				
Hindu	45	138	74	168
Muslim	43	126	82	148
Christian	27		56	108
Lower caste	85	152	113	203
Tribal		120	157	193
Occupation				
Main Worker	74	142	96	177
- Cultivator			89	164
- Farm Labourer			111	190
- Non-manual			41	111
- Manual			103	171
Marginal Worker			87	188
Non Worker	34	134	64	154
All Women	**42**	**136**	**72**	**164**

Source: Zachariah & Rajan (1992) p.44

Why have such significant demographic changes occurred in Kerala? At first the changes seem puzzling, especially as Kerala lags behind the rest of India according to most economic measures. Kerala's elected state government has had long periods of Communist control. The Communists have believed that as most of Kerala's people live in the rural areas, then improving the quality of life of rural people is the key to economic development. Therefore, most government expenditure has gone into education and health care in rural areas – village schools and rural health clinics. The Kerala officials have not spent any more money on health and education than other Indian states, but they have ensured that money is spent on low cost rural facilities where the people live rather than on large prestigious projects in the cities. In 1988, there were 259 hospital beds per 100 000 people in Kerala compared with an average of only 77 for India as a whole. Of these beds, 56% were in rural areas, whereas for India in general, only 18% of hospital beds are in rural areas. In Kerala, 47% of villages have a health clinic within two kilometres, but for India in general the figure is only 12%.

Particular attention was placed on raising female literacy. Traditionally in India, girls were often denied an education, but in Kerala girls were treated equally with boys. At the last census for which data has been released (1981), 71% of all women in Kerala aged 15 and above were literate, compared with 26% for all of India. In Kerala, 13% of women had been educated to the end of senior high school or beyond, compared with 6% for all of India. As table 1.9 showed, the inverse relationship between a mother's education and early deaths of children is extremely clear. It is believed that more education makes mothers less fatalistic about illness, bolder to question their mother-in-law's authority, more demanding of better health care and better food for their children, and raises incomes and therefore standards of living.

With the exception of the rise in female literacy, there has been no substantial change in Kerala's economy that might have accelerated the demographic transition in the way that seems to have happened. However, there has been a fundamental shift in the attitudes of people of Kerala to want fewer children but to give each child a better quality of life. The decline in Kerala's fertility is a good example of diffusion. i.e. that an idea begins at one point and spreads from there. The evidence that the fertility decline is an example of diffusion is as follows:

• The increase in the minimum age for females to marry was not an important factor in Kerala's fertility decline; it accounted for only 15% of the decline between 1961 and 1981.

• Fertility declined at the same time as knowledge about contraception was becoming more widespread.

- The decline in fertility happened very quickly; over a period of 30 years fertility went from a typical developing country situation to below replacement level.

- The decline in fertility and the rise in female literacy seem very closely linked.

- Fertility declined more among non-Muslims than Muslims, suggesting that contraception is more likely to be adopted where it does not violate religious and social norms.

Does Kerala's experience have applicability to other areas of India and the world? For Kerala, the key to lowering fertility seems to have been raising the level of female literacy. Kerala has been successful in raising female literacy for three reasons. First, mass education has been a central policy of governments in Kerala for many decades. Second, Kerala has a high proportion of Christians in the population, and this group is more open to the education of females than most other religious groups in Kerala. Finally, the high population density in Kerala increases people's accessibility to schools, raising the participation rate in education. The rest of India lags some 40 years behind Kerala in the level of female literacy, and it is even possible that the rest of India will never bridge this gap because of the traditional barriers to educating females among many groups in India.

QUESTION BLOCK 1G

1. Explain how a traditional, isolated society might limit their population growth.

2. Draw a diagram to show a classification of the different types of population policies which are possible. Under each type of policy, list an example of a country which implements this type of policy.

3. Why did China have a pro-natalist population policy in the 1950s?

4. In what way does raising the minimum age for marriage control population growth?

5. Show the information in table 1.8 on a line graph. Draw the horizontal axis to show 'age' and the vertical axis to show 'percentage of population'. Remember to make the intervals on the horizontal axis proportionately spaced to reflect the gap in ages accurately.

6. What are the main findings you can draw from the information in table 1.8?

7. Outline the aims of China's 'One Child' Policy, and describe the ways in which the policy is implemented.

8. What exceptions are made under the 'One Child' Policy?

9. How successful has the 'One Child' Policy been in China?

10. What problems have been encountered with the 'One Child' Policy?

11. Contrast the aims of the U.S. and the Chinese population policies.

12. Comment on the rate of population increase in Nigeria. Use figures to quantify your answer.

13. Why is the rate of population growth in Nigeria increasing?

14. How successful is Nigeria's population policy? Give reasons why this is so.

15. In what way is the aim of Singapore's population policy different to population policies in China and Nigeria?

16. In what way has the aim of Singapore's population policy changed over the past decades?

17. Why is Singapore's population policy particularly targeting university graduates?

18. How successful has Singapore's population policy been?

19. What are the aims of India's population policy?

20. How does the Indian Government encourage people to conform to its population policy?

21. How successful has India's population policy been?

22. Describe the location of the Indian state of Kerala.

23. Write about half a page to describe the demographic change which has occurred in Kerala.

24. With reference to table 1.9, describe the relationship between infants' and children's mortality rates and the educational level of women.

25. What will be the impact of Kerala's demographic changes in the years ahead?

26. List and then briefly describe the factors that have caused Kerala's large demographic changes.

27. What is meant by the claim that 'the fertility decline (in Kerala) is an example of diffusion'?

28. To what extent could Kerala's approach in controlling population growth be applied to other parts of the world such as China and Nigeria?

Movement responses – migration

Migration

It was stated earlier in this chapter that total population is a function of natural increase plus net migration. **Migration** is the movement of people. It can be permanent or temporary, and if temporary it can be long-term (more than a year) or short-term. If a migrant returns home periodically, as is common with seasonal farm workers or rural-urban migrants in developing nations, it is known as circular migration. Although commuting each day to and from work is a movement of people, it is not usually classified as 'migration'. Migration can be within a country (internal migration, involving out-migration from one place and in-migration to another) or between countries (international migration, involving emigration from one country and immigration into another). Migration can be **voluntary**, such as for finding employment or moving to obtain an education, or **involuntary**, as with refugees or rural workers who have been evicted from their farms.

In 1885, the British Geographer E.G. Ravenstein proposed seven principles of migration. Although these principles were based on his research in the United Kingdom, they are often regarded as applying more widely. The seven rules were:

1. Most migrants move only a short distance;

2. Migration occurs as a step-by-step process, and as one group of migrants moves on to the next step, the people will be replaced by a new group from elsewhere;

3. Emigration is the opposite of immigration;

4. Each wave of migration encourages a counter-current in the opposite direction, and net migration is the balance between the two movements;

5. Migrants who travel long distances are more likely to finish up at a major centre of industry or commerce;

6. People in rural areas are more likely to migrate than urban dwellers;

7. Females are more likely than males to migrate within their own country, but males are more likely than females to migrate to another country.

Other geographers have added to Ravenstein's work, and proposed several additional 'rules' such as the following:

1. Large towns and cities grow more by migration than by natural increase;

2. People migrate mainly for economic reasons;

3. Most migrants are single and in the 20-35 age bracket;

4. Migration increases as towns, industries and transport links develop;

5. Many migrants are unable to find work when they arrive and eventually return to their place of origin.

The decision of whether or not to migrate is not taken lightly by any migrant. Often the decision is related to difference in wealth or development between a migrant's home and the intended destination. Factors that might force a person to leave their place of residence are called **push factors**, and these can be broadly divided into 'hard push factors' and 'soft push factors'. Hard push factors

include war, starvation and environmental catastrophes, while soft push factors include persecution, poverty and social loneliness.

Table 1.10

Factors Influencing a Rural-Urban Migration Decision

Push Factors	Pull Factors	Restraining Factors
Not enough land for farming due to rising population	A perception that many jobs are available in the city	Desire to stay with the family in the rural area
Boredom with rural farming life	A wish to get a better education	Security of being supported by the family at home
Forced off the land by a landlord	Easy access to the city along roads or railways	The cost of moving to the city
Low standard of living in a rural village	Better health facilities in the cities	People in the city may speak a different language
Risk of famine if the crop fails	Better entertainment in the city	Cost of living is higher in the cities
Work on the farm is too hard		Diseases spread more easily in the cities

The decision whether to migrate or not will often be based on a perception of the destination that may be quite different from the reality. Other factors that might be considered include where other members of the family live, whether or not employment is likely, the ease of transport and social factors. For migrants considering moving from the countryside to a city (**rural-urban migrants**), the decision on whether to migrate or not depends on a series of push factors, pull factors and restraining factors. As already described, **push factors** are forces that repel a person from their place of residence. **Pull factors** are forces that attract a person to a new area. **Restraining factors** are forces that encourage a person not to move but to remain in their present area of residence. Some of these factors are listed in table 1.10.

For many rural-urban migrants, the move to the city results in disappointment. Many migrants are unable to find employment and therefore they are unable to afford housing, living in shanty settlements instead (figures 1.35 and 1.36). **Shanty settlements** comprise self-help housing made from scrounged materials such as packing cases, corrugated iron and disused plastic sheeting. Rural-urban migrants who are even unable to obtain shanty housing become street-dwellers (figure 1.37).

The process of rural-urban migration has been responsible for more than half the massive growth in cities in the developing world over the past few decades. For example,

61% of Port Moresby's population were born elsewhere, while in Bangladesh's capital city, Dhaka, 80% of the city's growth is coming from rural-urban migration. In cities throughout the developing nations, rural-urban migration has given rise to massive urban sprawl and the establishment of sub-standard housing (figure 1.38).

1.35 *An area of shanty housing in Addis Ababa, capital city of Ethiopia.*

1.36 *Shanty housing on the outskirts of Djibouti City, Djibouti.*

1.37 *Street dwellers have taken over the entire pavement of this street in Addis Ababa, Ethiopia.*

Although most migrants make their own decisions whether or not to migrate, this is not always the case. In Indonesia, a planned programme of forced migration has moved almost 2 million people from the densely populated islands of Java and Sumatra to more sparsely settled islands such as Sulawesi and Irian Jaya (the western half of the island of New Guinea). The motive for this migration is partly political. The Indonesian Government asserts sovereignty over Irian Jaya even though the people living there are Melanesian and have no ethnic connection with the other peoples of Indonesia. By moving large numbers of migrants into Irian Jaya, the Indonesian government can claim that a large proportion of the residents of Irian Jaya are Javanese or Sumatran, legitimising the government's claim to the area.

1.38 *La Paz, the capital of Bolivia, is a city of over one million people. Most of the people are rural-urban migrants who live in sprawling housing areas like this on the escarpment overlooking the central part of the city.*

Refugees are migrants who are forced to move because of political unrest or persecution. Over recent decades, there have been refugees from conflicts in many parts of the world. Wars have forced refugees to move from Tibet to Nepal, from Vietnam to Canada and Australia, from Congo (formerly Zaire) to Tanzania, from Cambodia to Thailand, and from Kosovo to Albania to mention just a few examples (figure 1.39).

1.39 *Refugees in Bhodnath, Nepal. The Tibetan Buddhists felt constrained in practising their religious beliefs and therefore migrated to Nepal.*

Populations in Transition

On the other hand, economic circumstances have encouraged migration from Mexico and Puerto Rico to the USA, from Bolivia to Argentina, from Turkey to Germany, and from India to various Arab states in the Middle East among other examples (figure 1.40). In this respect, migration may be seen as a means of equalising economic inequalities between regions. If people migrate from areas where there is an excess of labour to an area where there is a shortage (and therefore higher wages), then pressure can be relieved both where are too many workers (as some leave) and where there is a labour shortage (because more workers arrive).

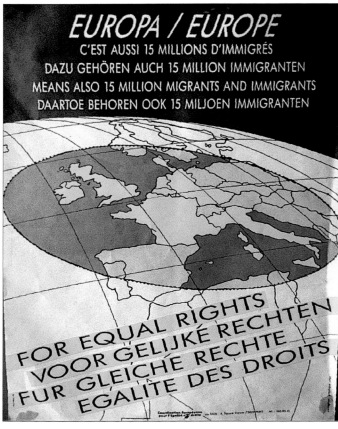

1.40 *The movement of migrant workers from Turkey into the European Community has caused ethnic tensions. This poster in Paris appeals for equal rights for migrants.*

QUESTION BLOCK 1H

1. Draw a diagram or a table to classify the different types of migration.

2. How accurate are Ravenstein's seven laws of migration today?

3. If you were to add three extra 'laws' of migration to the list of 12 presented in this section of the text, what would they be?

4. What is the difference between push factors, pull factors and restraining factors? Give two examples of each.

5. Why do many rural-urban migrants have trouble finding employment in the cities?

6. Give an example of each of the following types of migration:
a. international refugee
b. international voluntary
c. rural-urban
d. intra-urban
e. inter-urban
f. circular
g. internal forced

Case Study of Internal (National) Migration – Papua New Guinea

Any movement of people is called migration. When people leave a country, it is called **emigration**, but when people enter a country from overseas it is termed **immigration**. The movement of people within a country is called internal migration. When people move away from a particular district or town, it is called out-migration. On the other hand, in-migration is the movement of people into a particular town or district.

Table 1.11
Urbanisation in Papua New Guinea, 1960 - 2015

Year	Urban Population in PNG	
	in thousands of people	as a % of total population
1960	58	3
1970	240	10
1975	326	12
1980	403	13
1985	476	14
1990	582	13
1995	690	13
2000	766	13
2005	824	13
2015 (estimate)	1,095	15

Sources: Various

Table 1.11 shows that Papua New Guinea has experienced a spectacular increase in the number of people living in urban areas since 1960. This came about due to three factors:

a. about 20% of the growth was due to biological increase (the number of births exceeding the number of deaths) in the towns;

b. about 7% of the growth was due to urban boundaries being expanded to take in surrounding villages (i.e. a reclassification of existing settlements); and

c. the remainder of the growth (and thus the over-whelming majority) was due to rural-urban migration.

Rural-urban migration has been so important that today, well over half of Papua New Guinea's urban population are people who were born in rural areas. Papua New Guinea's two largest towns, Port Moresby and Lae, have 61% and 62% respectively of their populations born outside their areas (figure 1.41). In mining towns on Bougainville Island, the figure is 84%, with some towns (Arawa, Kieta and Panguna) having over 90% of their people having been born elsewhere.

1.41 *Due to rural-urban migration, over half the population of Port Moresby were born elsewhere.*

QUESTION BLOCK 1I

1. Use the information in table 1.11 to construct (a) a column graph of Papua New Guinea's urban population numbers from 1960 to 2015, and (b) a line graph to show this data as a percentage of total population.

2. What evidence is there that rural-urban migration has been important in Papua New Guinea?

Before World War II, there was some migration of Papua New Guineans under contract to coastal plantations. Most of these labourers came from coastal provinces such as Sepik, Gulf, Morobe and Milne Bay. Few migrants left the Highlands before World War II, as the area was still very isolated from the rest of the nation – Europeans only discovered that people lived in the Highlands in the early 1930s. However, after World War II, the Highlands became the main source for contract labour in the coastal provinces and islands. The movement of people under contract to work on plantations was circular migration, which meant that the workers returned home after a certain 'contract' period. Contract labourers who returned to their villages often spread wondrous, fanciful tales of city life, and this encouraged others to join the scheme. Thus, in recent years, there has been a shift towards chain migration. **Chain migration** is a 'one-way' movement of people in steps, first from villages to small towns, then to larger towns, and finally to cities.

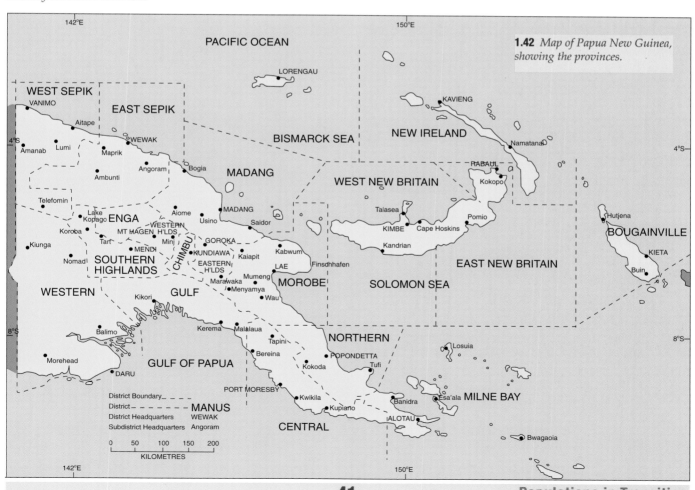

1.42 *Map of Papua New Guinea, showing the provinces.*

Table 1.12
Migration in Papua New Guinea

Province	Out-Migrants		In-Migrants	
	Number	% of people born in the province	Number	% of people living in the province
HIGHLANDS				
Chimbu	30,000	15	2,500	2
Eastern Highlands	20,000	7	12,500	5
Enga	12,500	7	2,500	1
Southern Highlands	20,000	9	2,500	1
Western Highlands	7,500	3	35,000	13
REST OF NEW GUINEA				
East Sepik	25,000	11	7,500	4
Madang	15,000	7	12,500	6
Morobe	25,000	8	32,500	11
West Sepik	7,500	6	2,500	3
PAPUA				
Central	20,000	17	10,000	9
Gulf	15,000	20	2,500	4
Milne Bay	10,000	7	2,500	2
Port Moresby	10,000	18	65,000	61
Northern	7,500	9	5,000	8
Western	5,000	7	2,500	2
ISLANDS				
East New Britain	15,000	13	20,000	16
Manus	5,000	19	2,500	8
New Ireland	5,000	9	7,500	12
Bougainville	2,500	3	17,500	13
West New Britain	5,000	7	20,000	23

Source: Based on tables in Ranck and Jackson (1986)

The movement of people in Papua New Guinea has certainly not been uniform, however. The pattern of movement can be described with reference to table 1.12 and figure 1.42.

QUESTION BLOCK 1J

1. *What type of provinces have experienced large scale out-migration?*

2. *What type of provinces have experienced large scale in-migration?*

3. *Suggest the effect of each of the following on migration in Papua New Guinea:*
   a. *The Highlands have the highest population densities in Papua New Guinea.*
   b. *The copper mines on Bougainville Island (Panguna, Arawa, etc) are in North Solomons Province.*

c. *The range of goods and services available in Port Moresby is much greater than anywhere else in Papua New Guinea.*

d. *There are many oil palm re-settlement schemes in West New Britain.*

e. *The world's largest single deposit of copper is located at Ok Tedi in Western Province. However, the mine is still being developed and is not yet fully operational.*

4. *Calculate Spearman's Rank Correlation Coefficient using the percentage figures in table 1.12. To do this:*

   a. *Draw up a table with five columns. In the first column, list the names of the twenty provinces.*

   b. *For each province listed, calculate its 'out-migrants' rank with '1' being the highest figure and 20 being the lowest. Where two figures are the same, split that ranking (i.e. two equal figures which would have been in 2nd and 3rd places receive a value of 2.5 each). Write the figures for each province in the second column.*

   c. *For each province listed, calculate its 'in-migrants' rank with '1' being the highest figure and 20 being the lowest. Where two figures are the same, split that ranking. Write the figures for each province in the third column.*

   d. *For each province, calculate the difference between the two rankings (i.e. for each province, subtract the column 3 figure from the column 2 figure). Write the answers in column 4 for each province.*

   e. *In column 5, calculate the square of each of the figures in column 4. At the foot of column 5, calculate the sum of the squared differences (i.e. calculate $\sum d^2$).*

   f. *Calculate Spearman's Rank Correlation Coefficient by applying the formula:*

   $$Rs = 1 - \frac{6 \times \sum d^2}{n(n^2 - 1)}$$

   where,

   Rs = Spearman's Rank Correlation Coefficient,

   $\sum d^2$ = the sum of column 5 (the sum of differences squared), and

   n = the number of cases (in this case, the number of provinces).

5. *Use the following diagram to interpret the result you calculated in question 2.14 and draw conclusions:*

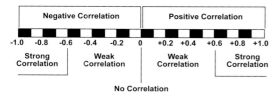

Overall, there has been a movement from densely populated interior regions (the Highlands) to the New Guinea Islands (plantations, Rabaul and mining towns on Bougainville) and to the coastal towns of Port Moresby, Lae, Madang and Wewak. The largest rates of out-migration are from Gulf, Manus and Chimbu Provinces. Between 13% and 20% of the people from these provinces now live outside them.

Because Chimbu Province is the most densely settled part of Papua New Guinea, migrants from that area tend to become very significant minorities in the coastal towns. This has led to some tension between Chimbu and people from other areas in the towns. Like most groups of rural-urban migrants, the Chimbu people tend to cluster together in certain parts of the towns, and this can attract hostility at times from other ethnic groups. The large community of poor rural-urban migrants living in shanties at the Six-Mile Rubbish Tip in Port Moresby, for example, often draws criticism from less poor people who have migrated from other parts of the country (figure 1.43).

1.43 *Squatters from the Highlands living at Six-Mile Rubbish Tip in Port Moresby.*

Circularity (returning home) is very common among rural-urban migrants in Papua New Guinea. Indeed, over 50% of rural-urban migrants return home within five years of their move. However, the situation is somewhat complex because many of these people return to the towns at a later time. Because work is easier to find for males, the typical rural-urban migrant in Papua New Guinea is a young, single, somewhat adventurous male.

The decision of whether or not to migrate is a complex one and it is not made lightly. Figure 1.44 describes the decision making process involved. The migration decision is influenced by a number of push factors and pull factors. **Push factors** are forces that repel a person away from an area. **Pull factors** are forces that attract a person into a particular area. In the specific case of Papua New Guinea, important push and pull factors include:

a. Push factors

• Pressure on the land due to rising population (especially in the Highlands)

• The need to raise fast cash (for tax, consumer goods or a bride price)

• A desire to avoid traditional obligations and authority

• An extended adolescence, due to abolition of initiation ceremonies

• Personal factors (such as arguments or family problems)

1.44 *The decision making process of a potential rural-urban migrant.*

influence the decision whether or not to migrate. Another term for this is **psychological motives**.

Although most Papua New Guineans have adequate amounts of land for subsistence farming, land pressure is growing with rising population and increased cash cropping. In areas where subsistence cultivation is hardest and where cash cropping does not occur (such as in Sepik, Gulf and Western Provinces), high rates of out-migration and low rates of circularity occur. Migration from the Chimbu area of the Highlands is also mostly due to shortages of land, although no-one is ever forced to move to avoid starvation.

• Boredom with village life (particularly among the young)

b. Pull factors
• A wish to acquire skills or education
• Easy access to towns (roads, air, shipping)
• Desire to join urban resident kin
• Belief that many more services are found in the towns
• Perception of migration as a rite of passage into manhood.

1.46 *This settlement for rural-urban migrants from Sepik Province is typical of the housing occupied by many people who have migrated to Port Moresby.*

1.45 *The downtown centre of Port Moresby is the image that many people in Papua New Guinea's villages have of urban life.*

Often, **opinions** may be more important than reality. Many people in Papua New Guinean villages think of the tall buildings and bright lights of the centre of Port Moresby when they consider migrating (figure 1.45). However, for most of them, migration to Port Moresby brings unemployment, poverty, poor accommodation and misery (figure 1.46). Nonetheless, it is people's opinions that

1.47 *Where community schools have been established, such as here at Maramba, rates of our-migration are reduced.*

In areas where plantations have been established, out-migration is much lower. This is because the plantations offer local work, and often lead to the establishment of local schools, shops, and so on (figure 1.47). Of course, since most subsistence cultivation in Papua New Guinea is done by women, men are relatively free to migrate *and* to increase their cash-cropping activities if they leave their wives at home to do the weeding and harvesting. Different towns have different attractions for migrants. For example, people from the Mount Hagen in the Western Highlands do not like to migrate to Lae because it is reached too easily by their relatives who might follow them! Therefore, people from Mount Hagen usually prefer to migrate to Port Moresby, even though that means an expensive flight.

QUESTION BLOCK 1K

1. *Would you say that rural-urban migrants consider carefully whether or not they will migrate? Give reasons for your answer.*

2. *Do you think push factors or pull factors are more important in influencing rural-urban migration in Papua New Guinea?*

Villages that have lost rural-urban migrants tend to have unbalanced population structures, with an excess of children, old people and women (figure 1.48). However, this does not usually affect food production as it is traditionally the women's role to tend the gardens. The traditional role of men was to fight, and as there is little calling for fighting nowadays, the men tend to spend their time sitting, talking and making money. In general, the loss of even the village's most able-bodied men is seldom a major economic problem.

1.48 *A typical scene in a village that has lost many of its young men to the towns as rural-urban migrants. The population structure of such villages is quite unbalanced.*

Migration is seen by Papua New Guineans as part of the process of 'modernisation'. So far, rural-urban migration

has not led to great differences in attitudes between urban dwellers and rural dwellers, as has occurred in parts of Asia. Most townspeople are first generation migrants who have maintained strong contacts with their villages, and rural-urban circulation is high. However, the absence of young men from the villages means that many traditional ceremonies are beginning to die away. For example, the *turnim het karim leg* ceremony has traditionally been an important part of courtship in the Highlands (figure 1.49). However, with the young women outnumbering the young men in many villages, the ceremony is declining in importance. Young people are now tending to choose their partners in what they see as the more modern fashion.

1.49 *In the 'turnim het karim leg' ceremony, young men and women get dressed up and go through a ceremony where they chant courtship songs. As they sing, they shake their heads and cross legs with each other. After several hours they pair off and go into the gardens to have sex.*

Naturally, there is some economic dislocation in the rural areas that the young male migrants have left behind. This dislocation is greatest in areas where migration has been greatest and where circulation least frequent. Migration to Port Moresby has so depopulated some Gulf Province areas that gardening has stopped in some places. Indeed, in some cases, settlements have broken up as people scatter to collect wild sago.

In most areas, however, the effects have not been as severe. The Orokaiva people from Northern Province always send money home to the villages to help those remaining behind, and their district does not seem adversely affected by its 30% absentee rate. The young people who leave the Mount Hagen district of the Western Highlands have no real productive role in their villages. Even when older Highlanders leave, there is little effect because their wives continue to care for the crops and they either send money home or visit periodically. The large number of Sio (an Islander group) working away from home also send money back and return when middle-aged to responsible positions in the community. In such circumstances, rural-urban migration is not disastrous for the village.

QUESTION BLOCK 1L

1. What are the good and bad effects of rural-urban migration on the rural villages which the migrants leave behind?

In traditional Papua New Guinean society, there were no towns. People lived in small, self-reliant villages. The way of life of the people was based on farming which avoided complex technology, and there was only limited trade between most villages (figure 1.50).

1.50 *A typical, traditional self-reliant Papua New Guinean village, west of Vanimo. Even in this village, the corrugated iron roofs provide evidence of contact with the outside world.*

The first towns in Papua New Guinea were built after the arrival of Europeans in 1884. Being built by European traders, missionaries and government officials, the towns were centres of trade, religion and administration. At first, local Papua New Guineans were not permitted to live in the towns. However, following World War II, this regulation became difficult to enforce, and local people began moving into urban centres. It was during this period that large scale rural-urban migration began in Papua New Guinea. Today, the rapidly growing size of Papua New Guinea's urban population reflects the importance of rural-urban migration.

In 1966, there were two males living in Papua New Guinea towns to every female. Since that time, more women have begun migrating to the towns (often to join their husbands), and today the ratio is 1.38 males to each female. Most towns have an abundance of young people of working age. One quarter of Papua New Guinea's males between 15 and 44 years old live in towns where they make up 50% of the urban population. This is particularly strong in the mining towns on Bougainville, which are almost entirely populated with single males from all parts of Papua New Guinea. In Port Moresby, the ratio of males to females is 3:2. However, for Highlanders in Port Moresby, there are almost six males for every female.

Over 95% of the migrants who come into the towns have had no formal job training. In Port Moresby, 46% of in-migrants have not even completed one year of schooling and only 1% received a leaving certificate. This means that employment in skilled and semi-skilled fields often eludes in-migrants, who wind up either working as houseboys or cleaners, or remaining unemployed. Port Moresby's crime rate is very high by any standards, and much of this crime is by 'raskals', unemployed young male in-migrants. Street bashings are unfortunately extremely common. Many residences in the towns are surrounded by two-metre-high barbed wire fences, often featuring security devices (figure 1.51). Unlike the situation in Africa or Asia, very few unemployed in-migrants turn to prostitution.

Unemployment is a problem in the towns. Between 15% and 25% of working age males and 80 to 90% of working age females are currently unemployed in Papua New Guinea's seven largest towns. These figures are a little misleading, however, as a substantial number of these people are not, in fact, looking for work. In Goroka, for example, about 20% of the unemployed are voluntarily outside the formal economy. In other words, they are engaged in subsistence activities or just visiting relatives, occasionally selling produce, and so on. Thus, the true unemployment rate is estimated as being between 5% and 12%.

1.51 *Typical security measures in Boroko, a suburb of Port Moresby.*

1.52 *Unemployed rural-urban migrants scavenging at Port Moresby's Six-Mile rubbish dump.*

Few of these unemployed people are really trapped in the towns. People who do not have work and would like to go home, but cannot, number only about 1% of males and 3% of females. An important exception to this, however, is the many Chimbu people who live in Port Moresby's Six-Mile rubbish dump (figure 1.52). They have a 27% unemployment rate as travel back to the Chimbu can only be undertaken by air, making the trip quite expensive.

Papua New Guinea is divided into four broad regions: Papua, the Highlands, the New Guinea coast and the New Guinea Islands. These divisions sometimes become the basis of ethnic conflict in the towns. In most towns, New Guinea Islanders and Papuans are the most educated and qualified for skilled positions, with Highlanders being easily the least qualified. In Mount Hagen, for example (which is in the Highlands), 18.5% of the Islanders, 7.4% of the Papuans, 3.0% of the New Guinea Coastals and only 0.7% of the Highlanders have formal job certification. Highlanders are the most recent group to begin living in towns, even in Highland towns.

Being the least educated and qualified, the Highlanders are concentrated in the lowest paying jobs, positions that are the least secure and hold the fewest opportunities for advancement. They are the least likely to have their wives and children in town, and tend not to reside in one urban centre continuously.

The shortage of housing in Papua New Guinean towns is very severe. Every night, thousands of rural-urban migrants sleep under shop awnings and petrol station fronts. In Papua New Guinea, nearly half the urban population live in **squatter settlements**. These consist of areas of land which are not zoned for a specific purpose which are then settled by people who do not own the land who construct shanty housing using scrounged materials (figure 1.53). Unlike many cities in Asia and South America, squatter settlements in Papua New Guinea do not generally have services such as electricity, street lighting, sewerage, rubbish collection or running water, as the authorities do not wish to encourage rural-urban migration.

Most squatter settlements are located on land not wanted by any other users, and close to possible places of work. These squatter settlements tend to be settled by people from the same ethnic background, and become, in effect, like a rural village moved into a town. The residents in squatter settlements cannot afford to buy, or even rent, the cheapest type of house, and have to make do with what they can build themselves. If possible, they will use the traditional village construction materials of sago leaves, bamboo or black palm, but generally all that will be available will be pieces of corrugated iron or packing cases. They are built in no apparent pattern, and certainly not in the neat ordered rows that the Europeans seem to prefer.

1.54 *In southern coastal areas of Papua New Guinea, the shortage of land encourages people to build houses over the water. Traditionally, this was also useful for defence. This view shows houses built over the water in the Port Moresby suburb of Koki.*

Overcrowding is a problem in the squatter settlements. Housing is scarce in most urban areas of Papua New Guinea. In part, this is because the colonial administration deliberately built few houses in order to discourage rural-urban migration. However, another reason is that there is so little flat land available in Papua New Guinean urban areas (figure 1.54). In nearly every major town, most of the land suitable for future urban expansion is under customary tenure, which means it is owned by the local native population who do not want to part with it. The average household in a squatter settlement has seven residents, compared with five residents for Papua New Guinean urban areas as a whole.

1.53 *Two views of a well-established area of poor housing at Hanuabada, a coastal suburb of Port Moresby.*

Populations in Transition

Traditional social systems tend to break down in the urban towns. In the villages, there is usually a 'big man' who has the charisma and oratory to influence people and settle disputes. However, no 'big man' would ever migrate from the Highlands to Port Moresby. The lack of 'big men' has led to problems of social control among Highlanders, since there is no-one with the ability to manage people and the social prestige necessary to settle disputes effectively.

QUESTION BLOCK 1M

1. *Make a point form list of the effects of rural-urban migration on the towns of Papua New Guinea.*

Gender and Change

The Role and Status of Women

The role and status of women varies from country to country. It varies from culture to culture even within one country, and is changing at different rates in different places. It is very difficult to generalise, but some statistics are so significant that they cannot be ignored. Particularly in LEDCs, the situation faced by women is generally inferior to that of men. In the words of a brochure produced by the NGO Community Aid Abroad, "(Women) often work twice as many hours as men, earn only one tenth of the income of men, consume less of the food than men and own only one hundredth the property of men."

In most LEDCs, women have much less scope than men to earn an income. In many cases where women cannot be supported by income earning men they must resort to begging to survive (figure 1.55).

1.55 Buddhist nuns begging for alms near Mandalay, Myanmar.

Since its formation in 1945, the United Nations has mirrored the practices in most of the world in having a high proportion of men as its national representatives, and also in its staff, where women have comprised less than 10% of the employees for most of its history. Nevertheless, the United Nations has been aware of the great inequalities faced by women and as long ago as 1975, it produced guidelines for release at the end of the first International Women's Year.

Among the points in the document were the following:

- The achievement of equality between men and women implies that they should have equal rights, opportunities and responsibilities to enable them to develop their talents and capabilities for their own personal fulfilment and the benefit of society.

- Governments should strive to ameliorate the hard working conditions and unreasonably heavy work loads that fall upon large groups of women in many countries, particularly among underprivileged social groups.

In many MEDCs, women have battled for many years to be able to enter forms of employment that have traditionally been regarded exclusively, or almost exclusively, as men's work. In spite of the widespread understanding that women and men are equally capable of performing most jobs, very low numbers of women continue enter many occupations that are still regarded in some societies as "men's work", especially those which have a component of great physical effort.

1.56 Women carrying heavy goods by hand, Djibouti.

It is worth noting that the United Nations' concern is somewhat different. In many countries, women continue to perform do the heavy – even unreasonably heavy – labour (figures 1.56 and 1.57). In some LEDCs, it is not uncommon to see men filling head baskets with rocks at a road construction site and then lifting them onto women's heads to be transported some hundreds of metres, or to see women engaged in heavy manual labour at road or building construction sites (figure 1.58).

Such expectations of women to be beasts of burden is seen as the norm in many nations. In some cases it is so blatant that a man may be seen walking along a road or track carrying nothing, while his wife is a short distance behind loaded with firewood and even a child as well. The practice begins at an early age where even young girls are often seen carrying heavy loads (figure 1.59).

1.57 *A woman carrying a heavy load of fuelwood, Addis Ababa, Ethiopia.*

1.58 *Women doing road work, near Kinka, Ethiopia.*

In many MEDCs, the exclusion of women from some work might once have been excused on the grounds of different physical strength. However, this could hardly explain the small numbers of women in fields such as law, academia or engineering. Perhaps it was once a valid argument in more strenuous occupations such as building and construction, factory employment, or driving heavy

vehicles, but during the male labour shortage during World War II, thousands of women proved they could handle such jobs. With improved technology, the heavy lifting component of most jobs has now disappeared.

Another reason that was once given for women to be denied a full education or access to top positions was that any investment made in their professional development would have less return than the equivalent investment in a man. The argument was that men tend to work fairly constantly from the age of 20 to about 60 or 65, while many women spend a number of these years outside the workforce having children or raising families. Whatever the truth of this argument, it is regarded as an unacceptable reason to deny women educational or employment opportunities in most MEDCs today. As seen in the adult literacy rates shown in table 1.13 a little later in the chapter, the same cannot usually be said for LEDCs.

1.59 *Girls carrying heavy loads in southern Ethiopia.*

Any bias in favour of men in MEDCs now seems to be a clear, if not always admitted, attempt to give men the first opportunity at key positions. Even with equal opportunity policies in place and positive discrimination in favour of women in many cases (i.e. deliberately giving women more than 50% of new promotion positions), many women feel that they hit a 'glass ceiling', an invisible but nonetheless real barrier to further promotions.

The male literacy rate is low in a number of the countries shown above, but in every case it is higher than that for women. Since education is crucial in gaining employment, the graph shows why the United Nations' action plan is really needed nearly 20 years after its implementation.

QUESTION BLOCK 1N

1. It is obvious that males and females are physically different. In our society there are many people, both men and women, who insist that the differences between the sexes are very important and that they result in quite different attitudes, thoughts, talents, speech patterns, behaviour, occupations and so on. They feel that men and women are totally different in almost all aspects of their lives. On the other hand, many others – again both men and women – support the view that although there are obvious physical differences, people should be treated the same. They maintain that a person's gender should make no difference if they are being considered as a pupil in school, a parent, a worker, a professional or whatever. In this context, what is your opinion of the accuracy of the assertion "men and women are different, but that does not mean they are not equal". Give reasons to explain your viewpoint.

Women in China

China is one of the best examples of how long-term attitudes of gender inequalities that suppressed the place in women could be largely overcome within a generation or two.

For thousands of years Chinese women lived under prolonged oppression, degradation and abasement in a very hierarchical, patriarchal (male-dominated) society. Women were considered inferior to men and this was shown in many ways:
- women had no political rights
- women were excluded from political and social life
- women were economically dependent on men
- women had no property or inheritance rights
- women were denied all sources of personal income
- women had no social status (they were kept at the 'bottom of society'
- women were forced to obey fathers and then husbands (or sons, if widowed)
- women were forced to marry men chosen by their parents and matchmakers
- women were not allowed to remarry if widowed
- women had almost no personal dignity
- women were denied formal education
- women were harassed by systems of polygamy and prostitution
- many women were forced to have their feet bound from childhood

When the Communists came to power in 1949, they promised to change this situation. From that date, a popular phrase became "Women hold up half the sky", and great steps were made to accept Chinese women as the full equals of men. Since 1949, Chinese women have certainly made extremely important contributions to such projects as industrial and agricultural production, science, culture, politics, education and health care.

The first meeting of the Chinese People's Consultative Conference (the forerunner to the National People's Congress) in 1949 was attended by 69 women, or more than 10% of the delegates. Although this figure may sound like a small percentage, in the context of traditional China it represented an earth-shattering change from previous practice.

In the years following the Communist Revolution (called Liberation in China), women were given the vote, given the right to own land, given the right to move out of the home to work or socialise, and prostitution (a form of slavery in pre-revolutionary China) was banned. A campaign to eradicate illiteracy was started, and the female illiteracy figure declined from over 90% in 1949 to 38% in 1992 and just 13% by 2005. New marriage laws were introduced making forced marriages illegal from 1950, prohibiting polygamy, and guaranteeing the rights of women and children. As a result of the changes, there was a reduction in wife bashing and arranged marriages.

Today, China's women are more liberated than many other parts of the world, and certainly much more than they were in the past. Chinese women occupy significant senior positions in industry, education, commerce, and politics. They are educated to very high levels and they often travel overseas to further their education. Chinese women today can be seen working in almost every job on an equal basis with men, including labouring and technological jobs (figure 1.60).

1.60 *A female doctor dispenses medicine at a medical clinic from a new medical clinic in Gonghe village, a poor rural area of China's Guizhou province.*

This is not to say that the situation is perfect. In rural areas, some families still feel that having a boy baby is preferable to having a girl baby. Often, the reason behind this attitude is that when they marry, girls leave their parents and become part of the husband's extended family, helping with the work to support that family rather than her own parents. Furthermore, boys carry the family name into the next generation, and in many isolated farming communities, reverence for ancestors is still an important part of the culture.

QUESTION BLOCK 1O

1. *Write your opinion of the rules and restrictions which governed the lives of Chinese women before 1949. Would you like your lives and your bodies to be controlled in such ways?*

2. *Research the topic of "foot binding" in China. Find out just how cruel this treatment was and imagine how Chinese girls suffered.*

3. *Summarise the impact of gender reforms in China upon women, children, and men, and on the social, political and family aspects of life in China.*

Women in Muslim (Islamic) Countries

1.61 *Women leaving a mosque at Jamal ad-Din, Turkmenistan.*

Few issues have greater potential to cause misunderstanding between the Islamic world and the West than the role and place of women in Muslim societies. To some extent, it is very difficult to make generalisations about this subject because of the extreme diversity across the Muslim world, a vast area that extends from Morocco in the west to Indonesia in the east, spanning many different countries, ethnic groups, communities, races and cultures. The one common factor is the Muslim religion, known as Islam, although there are variations within the beliefs and practices of Islam that influence the role of women in different Muslim countries. As the noted Muslim Pakistani development activist and writer on gender issues, Ms Khawar Mumtaz, commented: "The situation of Muslim women is differentiated by country and also, within each society, by class, ethnicity, rural or urban location, and level of development." Despite these different backgrounds, there are some aspects of Muslim women's lives which appear common to most of them. Again quoting Ms Khawar Mumtaz, "The desire to control women seems to pervade all Muslim societies."

According to the Qur'an (the Holy Book of Islam), men and women are equal before God (Allah). The Qur'an regards men and women as two units of a pair, complementing each other each other in various physical and psychological ways. Islam does not assign a lower status to the women, but it does assign different responsibilities to men and women. For example, in the family structure that the Qur'an prescribes, women are responsible for raising the children and domestic duties while men are responsible for providing security and livelihood for the family. When the practices of different countries are compared, there is less uniformity than the Qur'an might seem to suggest, and different Muslim countries assign women varying degrees of rights with regards to marriage, divorce, civil rights, legal status, dress code, and

education. This is especially so for countries that have had greater exposure to international linkages, and in such countries, many people have found themselves caught between tradition and change. In such situations, women may be used as symbols of both tradition *and* change, with some women being given equality with men and social position, while others were kept hidden behind the veil and in submission.

1.62 *Malaysian schoolgirls riding home on bicycles.*

1.63 *Women in Yemen dress more conservatively than in many other Muslim countries. This woman is in Sana'a, the capital city.*

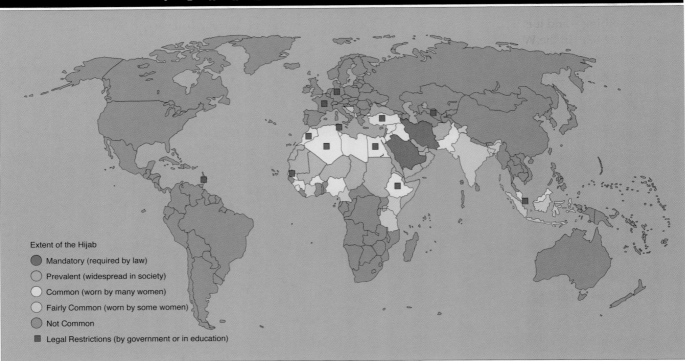

1.64 *Prevalence of Hijab clothing, and countries where there are restrictions on its display.*

Extent of the Hijab
- Mandatory (required by law)
- Prevalent (widespread in society)
- Common (worn by many women)
- Fairly Common (worn by some women)
- Not Common
- Legal Restrictions (by government or in education)

1.65 *Women in the central market of Sana'a, Yemen.*

In countries such as Tunisia, Malaysia, Egypt and Turkey the emancipation of women has progressed further than

in more isolated societies such as Saudi Arabia, Yemen and Afghanistan (figures 1.61 to 1.63). Perhaps the most visible symbol of this difference is clothing and dress. The Qur'an instructs all Muslims (men and women) to dress in a modest way. When this is applied to women, it is often referred to as *hijab,* which comes from the Arabic word meaning 'cover' but which in the context of clothing is used more broadly to mean 'modest dress for women' (figure 1.64). In most Islamic countries, *hijab* implies using loose clothing to cover all parts of the body except for the face, feet and hands when in public. Tight fitting clothing conflicts with the standards of modesty implied by *hijab,* so loose clothing that hides the shape of the body is the norm for Muslim women, and in some stricter societies, even the face must be covered (figure 1.65). In recent years, *hijab* has become a symbol of Muslim identity and morality that stand in defiance of Western values such as materialism, commercialism, and values. *Hijab* is a source of pride and distinctiveness for many Muslims, while for many Westerners it is a symbol of gender oppression.

Since the Islamic Revolution of 1979 in Iran, wearing the *chador* has been the usual way for women to comply with *hijab* when outside the house. The *chador* is a piece of (usually) black full-length fabric that is thrown over the head and held closed at the front (figure 1.66). Wearing the *chador* is not compulsory for Iranian women (although modesty in dress is enforced). Almost all Iranian women do choose to wear the *chador,* however, claiming simply that it is a respectable and pious way to dress. A smaller number of women claim to wear the *chador* as a sign of support for the country's Islamic rulers. Most Iranian women claim that they find the chador to be a very comfortable and liberating way to dress, as they can wear whatever they like underneath – including blue jeans and western clothing – and it is said to be extremely comfortable (figure 1.67). In the West, on the other hand, the *chador* is seen as a symbol of suppression of women's rights to express themselves as individuals in Iran.

1.66 *An Iranian woman wearing the chador.*

Perhaps the strictest expression of *hijab* for women in recent years occurred in Afghanistan during the period from 1996 to 2001 when the Taliban controlled Afghanistan. The Taliban adopted an extremely strict, fundamentalist ideology that opposed outside (especially Western) influences and took a very narrow interpretation of the Qur'an on moral and legal issues, imposing a code of Islamic law (called *sharia*) that included punishments that many outsiders saw as extremely harsh. One expression of Taliban rule was the requirement that all women wear the *burqa*, a traditional Afghan cloak that covered women completely, including the eyes. The perception outside Afghanistan (especially among women's groups in North America and Western Europe) that enforcing *burqa* wearing was a violation of women's rights became a significant issue in 2001 as the US Government was seeking support for an invasion to overthrow the Taliban. To many people in Afghanistan, enforcing the *burqa* was seen as more legitimate than many other Taliban actions that did not seem to stem from the Qur'an or sharia law, such as bans on clapping at sports events, bans on flying kites, bans on trimming beards and bans on sports for women.

Ironically, several of the European nations that protested about enforcing wearing the *burqa* on the grounds that it restricted women's right to choose are now debating whether to ban *burqas*, head scarves and other items of clothing associated with Islam such as the *niqāb*, which is the face veil shown in figures 1.63 and 1.65. France and several states in Germany have banned the wearing of head scarves in schools, the Netherlands announced in late 2006 that it would ban the *niqāb*, and in 2006 the British Foreign Secretary, Jack Straw, called on British Muslim women to abandon the full veil, a view that was subsequently endorsed by the then-Prime Minister Tony Blair (figure 1.68).

1.67 *Two women in a mosque in Esfahan, Iran, show how the chador is often combined with blue jeans.*

Some countries with large Muslim populations adopt very different approaches to the wearing of *hijab*. For example, 99% of Turkey's population are Muslims, and over 60% of women wear the *hijab*. However, Turkey has a strong tradition of secularism which separates government from any spiritual or religious basis. As a consequence, wearing headscarves is banned in private and state universities and schools, and it is not permitted in public offices, including all government buildings. Understandably, this policy is somewhat controversial, and many Muslim women claim that the bans represent discrimination against them.

Of course, the issue of gender equality in Muslim countries affects many more areas than clothing. Like clothing, however, the issues confronting women vary from country to country. One of the stricter Muslim societies is Saudi Arabia, where women are not allowed to leave their houses without a male relative such as their father, brother or husband. Women can only be educated in segregated (single-sex) schools, and when women demonstrated to be allowed to drive cars, their movement was crushed because they wanted something which was labelled as 'un-Islamic'. Under Saudi law, a male relative is permitted kill his female relative for offences such as premarital or extramarital sex, refusing an arranged marriage, attempting to obtain a divorce, or simply talking with a man without permission.

1.68 *A Muslim family in Blackburn, Lancashire, a city where Islam is the dominant religion.*

During law cases in Pakistan, the testimony of one man is equal to that of two women. For a woman to prove she has been raped, four adult males of 'impeccable character' must testify that they have witnessed the penetration. Understandably, as a result of this requirement, very few men are charged with rape in Pakistan. According to western media reports, 60% of Pakistani women finish up being charged with adultery if they are raped, for which the punishment is either imprisonment for the woman or an enforced marriage to their rapist.

In spite of these somewhat extreme examples, it would be wrong to label Muslim societies as looking down upon women. Such a view would be judging a culture by standards that are not its own. Indeed, many people in Muslim societies argue that their treatment of females elevates women to a much higher place than is common in Western societies. Most people in Muslim societies would argue that their women are protected from the kinds of exploitation that are often common in Western societies – one would never see a semi-nude woman draped over the bonnet of a motor car for advertising purposes in a Muslim society, for example.

It would also be wrong to claim that women can never rise to positions of power in Muslim societies. Among the Muslim women who have become heads of state in substantially Islamic countries are Benazir Bhutto of Pakistan, Mame Madior Boye of Senegal, Tansu Çiller of Turkey, Kaqusha Jashari of Kosovo, and Megawati Sukarnoputri of Indonesia. Furthermore, Bangladesh was the first country in the world to have two successive female heads of state as Khaleda Zia and Sheikh Hasina replaced each other as Prime Minister in 1996 and 2001.

The status of women in Muslim (Islamic) countries will probably continue to be a subject of debate between Muslims and non-Muslims. Women may be treated differently from men in Islamic societies, but it depends on one's point of view whether these differences also necessarily mean inferiority.

QUESTION BLOCK 1P

1. *With reference to figure 1.64, describe the distribution of the different ways in which* hijab *is practised.*

2. *Compare the dress and the relative numbers of men and women in the photos in this section. Do the differences imply any differences in the place of men vs women in these societies?*

3. *Giving reasons, explain why you think the differences between laws and expectations of men and women in Muslim societies imply (or do not imply) inferiority.*

Gender-related Equity Issues

When the issue of gender inequality is examined on a global scale, we find that on many measures females appear to be disadvantaged compared with males. Several measures of gender equality are shown in table 1.13.

One approach when examining gender equality is to try and develop a composite measure that quantifies the extent of the disadvantage faced by females. The United Nations Development Program has developed two such indices, the Gender-related Development Index (GDI) and the Gender Empowerment Index (GEM).

The **Gender-related Development index** (GDI) is calculated by averaging three measures:

a. **longevity**, as measured by the female and male life expectancy at birth;

b. **knowledge**, as measured by (1) female and male literacy rates, and (2) female and male combined school enrolment ratios; and

c. **income** per capita, in Purchasing Power Parity US dollars, based on female and male earned income shares.

The GDI figures for a number of countries is shown on the left side of table 1.13, together with some of the measures that have been used in its calculation.

It is often useful to compare a country's GDI to other composite measures of development, as discussed in detail in chapter 2, such as the Human Development Index (HDI) which is an overall measure of a country's development. In general, the closer a country's HDI and GDI rankings are, the greater gender equity that exists in that country. Where the GDI ranking is lower than the HDI ranking, there is a degree of gender inequity against females.

According to the United Nations Development Programme, the GDI rank is below the HDI rank in 43 of the 143 countries for which calculations have been completed. In these countries, gains in economic development have not brought as many benefits to women as they have to men (figure 1.69). The greatest negative differences between GDI and HDI occur in Arab territories such as Palestine (-15), Libya (-9), Saudi Arabia (-9), Oman (-8) and Yemen (-6).

1.69 *In many LEDCs, women must continue to raise children as well as earn an income, often by heavy physical work. This Malian woman carries her child on her back as she carries a heavy load of freight on her head.*

On the other hand, there are 60 countries for which the GDI rank is greater than the HDI rank. In these countries, economic development has served to advance the interests of women and reduce the inequities in quality of life between men and women. The countries where this has happened are very diverse, and include MEDCs such as Australia and Sweden, medium human development countries such as Russia and Brazil, and LEDCs such as Tanzania and Gambia. This suggests that it is possible to address gender equity issues in different countries regardless of levels of their economic development or culture.

The **Gender Empowerment Measure (GEM)** is a measure of the extent to which females as well as males participate in the decision making processes of a country. The GEM includes three components:

a. **political participation**, as measured by the percentage of seats held by women in national parliaments;

b. **economic participation**, as measured by as measured by the percentage of women among legislators, senior officials and managers, as well as in professional and technical fields; and

c. **power over economic resources**, as measured by the income earned by females compared with men's incomes.

GEM statistics are shown for a selection of countries in table 1.13. Unfortunately, many LEDCs do not collect the data required to calculate their GEM, which explains the large number of 'n.a.' (not available) entries in the table. Of course, the fact that a country does not even collect data on gender empowerment is itself a measure of the low importance placed on this issue by government decision-makers!

The right hand side of table 1.13 shows several measures of gender inequality, some of which are included in the calculation of either the GDI or GEM, while others are not. It can be seen from the data that males are the disadvantaged group in some areas, such as life expectancy (which is shorter for men in almost every country of the world), and in the proportion of prisoners who are male, which exceeds 90% in all the countries listed except two.

When issues of gender equality are discussed, it is usually matters of wealth, power or influence that are discussed. In these areas, females are almost universally disadvantaged compared with males, as the statistics in table 1.13 show. Compared with males, females tend to have fewer educational opportunities, they are less likely to assume positions of power in government or business, and they tend to earn lower wages for equivalent work. Although these generalisations are true globally, the extent to which they apply to individuals varies from country to country, and females tend to be less disadvantaged in more economically more developed countries.

Table 1.13
Gender-Related Development Index (GDI), 2008, for the same countries listed in table 2.1
(order of countries shown follows that in table 2.1)

	Measure of Gender Equality		Life Expectancy at Birth (years)		Adult Literacy Rate (%)		GDI as % of HDI
	GDI	GEM	Female	Male	Female	Male	
HIGH HUMAN DEVELOPMENT							
Norway	0.957	0.915	83	78	100	100	98.8%
Australia	0.960	0.866	84	79	100	100	99.8%
Sweden	0.955	0.925	83	79	100	100	99.9%
Japan	0.942	0.575	86	79	100	100	98.8%
USA	0.937	0.769	81	75	100	100	98.5%
United Kingdom	0.944	0.786	81	77	100	100	99.8%
South Korea	0.910	0.540	82	76	100	100	98.8%
United Arab Emirates	0.855	0.698	81	77	88	89	98.5%
Mexico	0.820	0.603	78	73	90	93	98.9%
Malaysia	0.802	0.538	76	72	85	92	98.8%
MEDIUM HUMAN DEVELOPMENT							
China	0.776	0.526	75	71	87	95	99.8%
Iran	0.750	0.345	72	69	77	88	98.8%
Vietnam	0.732	0.555	75	71	100	100	99.8%
Indonesia	0.721	0.441	72	69	87	94	99.1%
Bolivia	0.691	0.509	67	63	81	93	99.5%
India	0.600	n.a.	66	65	48	73	97.0%
Myanmar	0.575	n.a.	54	58	86	94	98.6%
Nepal	0.520	0.485	64	63	35	63	97.4%
Papua New Guinea	0.529	n.a.	60	54	51	63	99.7%
Kenya	0.521	n.a.	53	53	70	78	99.9%
LOW HUMAN DEVELOPMENT							
Eritrea	0.469	n.a.	59	54	21	43	97.0%
Nigeria	0.456	n.a.	47	46	60	78	96.9%
Tanzania	0.464	0.600	52	50	62	78	99.4%
Rwanda	0.450	n.a.	48	47	60	71	99.6%
Malawi	0.432	n.a.	47	45	58	77	98.9%
Zambia	0.425	0.425	37	38	72	79	97.9%
Ethiopia	0.393	0.474	51	48	23	50	96.8%
Mali	0.371	n.a.	59	54	16	33	97.6%
Niger	0.355	n.a.	56	58	15	43	94.9%
Sierra Leone	0.320	n.a.	49	48	24	47	95.2%

Source: Derived from data supplied by the UNDP, Population Reference Bureau, International Centre for Prison Studies

Ratio of girls to boys in primary & secondary schools	Ratio of female to male earned income	% males aged 15+ in the labour force	% females aged 15+ in the labour force	% of males who live to age 65	% of females who live to age 65	Women in Parliament % of total seats	% of prisoners who are female	
							HIGH HUMAN DEVELOPMENT	
101	0.79	73	64	86	92	38	5.2	Norway
97	0.73	70	56	87	93	25	6.8	Australia
100	0.84	67	59	88	93	47	5.2	Sweden
100	0.46	73	48	87	94	9	5.9	Japan
100	0.64	73	60	81	88	16	8.6	USA
101	0.70	69	55	85	90	20	5.7	United Kingdom
96	0.52	74	50	81	92	13	5.3	South Korea
101	0.25	93	41	86	91	23	n.a.	United Arab Emirates
99	0.42	80	40	78	86	23	5.0	Mexico
105	0.44	81	47	32	37	9	6.5	Malaysia
							MEDIUM HUMAN DEVELOPMENT	
100	0.65	82	69	75	82	20	4.6	China
105	0.41	74	40	73	81	4	3.5	Iran
97	0.71	78	72	78	84	26	12.4	Vietnam
97	0.46	85	51	71	79	11	4.7	Indonesia
98	0.58	84	63	63	71	17	7.0	Bolivia
91	0.32	82	34	59	69	8	4.0	India
101	0.61	86	68	54	66	n.a.	17.8	Myanmar
93	0.50	78	50	61	65	17	8.3	Nepal
80	0.70	75	72	41	55	1	5.0	Papua New Guinea
96	0.82	90	70	42	47	7	3.6	Kenya
							LOW HUMAN DEVELOPMENT	
72	0.50	90	58	41	54	22	n.a.	Eritrea
83	0.40	85	46	37	40	7	1.9	Nigeria
97	0.72	90	86	40	45	30	3.3	Tanzania
102	0.73	84	80	33	39	49	2.6	Rwanda
100	0.74	90	86	32	37	14	1.2	Malawi
96	0.54	91	66	23	26	15	2.6	Zambia
81	0.61	89	71	44	49	22	n.a.	Ethiopia
74	0.66	82	72	48	58	10	2.0	Mali
70	0.56	95	71	59	57	12	n.a.	Niger
86	0.45	94	56	33	39	13	n.a.	Sierra Leone

In many people's minds, the status of women and their perceived importance in society are indicated by the work they are allowed to do. The pictures in figures 1.70 to 1.73 show women from several nations working in occupations which are typical of countries at different levels of economic development.

1.70 *Most teachers in Russia are women.*

1.71 *A Dani woman using a digging stick for cultivating sweet potatoes in Irian Jaya.*

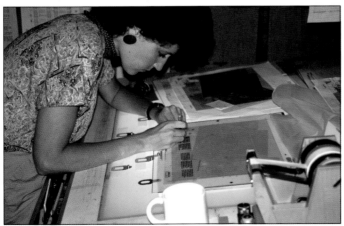

1.72 *A cartographer using computing equipment at the National Geographic Society in Washington DC (USA).*

1.73 *Women selling jewellery in the main market of Ashgabat, Turkmenistan.*

Women have been seen as 'beasts of burden', as sex objects, as inferior persons, or as not worthy of having a vote. Such perceptions can diminish the status of women and reduce their self esteem. It is in everyone's interests, men and women alike, to release the female half of the world's population from ideas and practices which may keep women in bondage, suffering and slavery.

QUESTION BLOCK 1Q

1. *Look at the female and male literacy rates shown in table 1.13. Draw column graphs for each country shown to compare the male and female literacy rates.*

2. *Describe the different patterns of female and male literacy rates in developed and developing nations.*

3. *Explain how the GDI can be used to indicate how effectively gender equity is being achieved in a country.*

4. *Which types of countries are (a) most effective, and (b) least effective in achieving gender equality?*

5. *For each of the variables shown on the right hand page of table 1.13, name the country that appears to be (a) most advantaged, and (b) most disadvantaged. What generalisations can you draw from these results?*

6. *In the text, it is stated that ' females tend to be less disadvantaged in more economically more developed countries'. Do you think some countries are more wealthy because their females are more empowered, or do you think the females in those countries are more empowered because the countries are more wealthy? In other words, is there a cause-and-effect between female empowerment and national wealth, and if so, in which direction does it operate? Give reasons to support your answer.*

Disparities in wealth and development

2

Differences in economic development in various parts of the world

Measurements of Global and Regional Disparities

**ToK BoX – Page 61
Emotion and Intuition**

include political, social, economic and cultural freedom, a sense of community, opportunities for being creative and productive, and self-respect and human rights. Yet human development is more than just achieving these capabilities; it is also the process of pursuing them in a way that is equitable, participatory, productive and sustainable".

Geographic Development

In introducing the United Nations Development Program's *Human Development Report*, Paul Streeten wrote these words:

"Human development is the process of enlarging people's choices – not just choices among different detergents, television channels or car models, but the choices that are created by expanding human capabilities and functionings – what people do and can do in their lives. At all levels of development a few capabilities are essential for human development, without which many choices in life would not be available. These capabilities are to lead long and healthy lives, to be knowledgeable and to have access to the resources needed for a decent standard of living… But many additional choices are valued by people. These

Paul Streeten's words are important, because they emphasise that development is a real issue that affects people very powerfully. The level of development in a country where a person happens to have been born affects their quality of life, and in many cases, even the number of years that life is likely to last. It is not surprising that developing the economy is a prime aim of many countries in the world (figure 2.1).

One of the problems faced by people who try to come to grips with the issue of development is that different books and internet resources use different terminology when describing it. It is important to clarify and understand the different terms that are used so ambiguity is avoided.

>> Some Useful Definitions

Core and periphery — the concept of a developed core surrounded by an undeveloped periphery. The concept can be applied at various scales.

GNI — Gross national Income (now often used in preference to GNP, or Gross National product): the total value of goods and services produced within a country together with the balance of income and payments from or to other countries.

Remittances — transfers of money and/or goods by foreign workers to their home countries.

Strategies — any (usually 'big picture') management policies, initiatives and/or plans.

In the 1950s and 1960s, when the issue of development first began to be studied seriously, the poorer countries of the world were labelled **backward** or **undeveloped**. These labels were inaccurate and gave a false impression, however. All peoples of the world have developed in some way, and therefore they cannot accurately be labelled 'undeveloped'. Some nations have chosen to emphasise cultural development rather than economic development, and indeed many of these countries would claim to be more 'culturally developed' than many of the world's richer nations (figure 2.2).

To overcome this inaccuracy, the label 'undeveloped' was replaced by **underdeveloped**. This term implied that at least some development had occurred, even if this was not as much as had occurred in some richer nations. However, this term caused offence to many people in the poorer countries, because it was felt the term implied they were inferior in some way. Therefore, this term came to be replaced by a new term – **less developed countries**. This term was meant to convey the idea that these countries had certainly developed, although not so much as the 'more developed countries'.

2.2 *Although Myanmar is economically a very poor country, it is remarkably rich culturally, and could not accurately be labelled 'undeveloped'. This view shows part of the Buddhist Shwedagon Pagoda complex in Yangon.*

Many people in these countries still felt that this term failed to address their concerns, so they came to be known as the **developing** countries. The thinking behind this label was that although they were poorer than other countries, they were in an active process of 'developing' their countries economically. The term still proved unsatisfactory for many people, however, as it seemed to imply that if the poorer countries worked hard enough, then one day they might be able to emerge just like one of the 'developed' countries. In other words, the term implied that there was only one pathway to development, and that these countries were further back along that pathway.

Other labels have also been proposed and tried to overcome these concerns. In the 1960s and 1970s it was common to use the term the **Third World**. The term arose during the Cold War period of tensions and rivalry between the capitalist United States and the communist Soviet Union. The idea behind the label was that the rich, capitalist countries are the 'First World', the developed socialist nations are the 'Second World', while the remaining poor countries of the world are the 'Third World', whether they are capitalist or communist. Once again, people in the poorer countries objected to this label, claiming that it implied there was a race to develop and

2.1 *'Development is the absolute need' is the message of this huge float on display in Beijing's Tian An Men Square.*

that they were being given last place in the race. A variation of this theme was the label the **Two-Thirds World**, which was inspired by the fact that the poorer countries contain about two-thirds of the world's population. However, this label never became widely used.

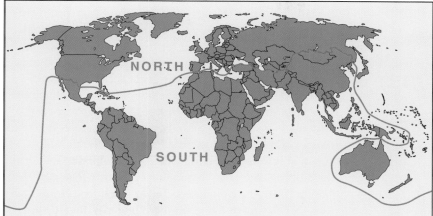

2.3 *'The North' and 'the South', as commonly defined by the Brandt Line.*

Other labels have also been suggested. One attempt to express the characteristics of the poorer countries more positively was to call them the **Human Resource Rich Countries**. This label emphasised that poorer countries have a great asset in their human resources (large populations), even if they have little machinery. Although this label had a positive intent and was not insulting or demeaning, it was too long to become widely used.

Another 'neutral' label that became popular during the 1980s was **the South** to refer to the poorer, less developed countries, and **the North** to refer to the richer, more developed countries. The idea behind these labels was that generally, the northern hemisphere is a world of wealth, industrialisation, consumption and comfort, while the southern hemisphere is a world of poverty, poor nutrition and disadvantage. The labels tried to point out that all countries, rich and poor, share the same world, and are just in different facets (north and south) of that one world.

Geographers were quick to point out the problems with these labels, however. Not all the richer countries are situated in the northern hemisphere, and despite their location, Australia and New Zealand were classified as 'the North'. Similarly, poorer nations spread far to the north. For example, Turkey extends as far north of the equator as Tasmania is to the south of it, while China and Mongolia extend beyond 50°N, well further north than the southern tip of New Zealand is south (figure 2.3).

ToK BoX

Emotion and Intuition.

The issue of disparities in wealth and development often evokes strong emotional responses from many people. Aid agencies provide heart-breaking photos of suffering children that are designed to move people in MEDCs to open their wallets and make donations to overcome whatever emotion has been triggered — guilt, sorrow, heartache, despair, shame, or whatever.

Emotion is certainly a very powerful driver of human behaviour, and it may be just as important as reason in helping us to make appropriate decisions. Making decisions according to an emotional response or instinct, without conscious reasoning, is often called intuition.

An experienced teacher once said that students are very attracted to intuition because it seems like being able to get knowledge and power for free — being able to express opinions without the demands of researching the facts. Intuition is sometimes called 'gut feelings'. Most people think they are very good at summing up other people and situations using intuition — they are rarely correct in that assumption.

The psychologist Edward de Bono developed a method of problem solving

called the 'Six Thinking Hats' that attempted to give emotion and intuition their rightful place in the array of thinking skills that people use to solve problems.

De Bono believes that true understanding comes from the ability to examine a problem or situation from a variety of viewpoints. He argues that if people work in parallel using different viewpoints in turn, collaboration will be fostered and ego will be removed from decision-making, thus making the process more productive

De Bono suggests that each approach to problem solving can be signified by a different coloured hat. One possible sequence for addressing a problem could be:

1. The Red Hat looks at problems using intuition, gut reaction, and emotion, also trying to think how other people might react emotionally.

2. The White Hat focuses on the data available, looking at the information and seeing what can be learnt from it.

3. The Yellow Hat is the optimistic viewpoint that helps the decision-

maker to see all the benefits of the decision and the positive value in it.

4. The Black Hat highlights the weak points, or negative aspects, of a plan, thus allowing contingency plans to be developed to counter these weaknesses.

5. The Green Hat focuses on creative solutions to a problem, looking at new possibilities through a freewheeling 'brain-storming' in which there should be no criticism of ideas.

6. The Blue Hat provides the overview, or 'big picture'. The Blue Hat is used by people chairing meetings so that when difficulties are encountered, activity may be re-directed into other types of thinking such as Green Hat or Black Hat.

By including emotion and intuition in the Six Thinking Hats, de Bono recognises that these 'ways of knowing' have a place in the decision-making process, though not at the expense of other 'ways of knowing' that should also be recognised and used.

The next ToK BoX is on page 114.

2.4 *The main railway station in Bamako, capital city of Mali, shows its French colonial origins. Mali is one of the world's poorest countries, perhaps partly because so much natural wealth was exported to France during colonial times. Today, the poverty is illustrated by the clock on the front of the railway station – the original one has gone and has been replaced by one that looks as though it may have come from someone's kitchen.*

Ironically, some scholars in the poorer countries are once again advocating the use of the term **undeveloped** countries. Their argument is that during the 1800s European colonial powers exploited the resources of their colonies, developing themselves and 'undeveloping' their colonies (figure 2.4). However, this label has not become widely accepted because many scholars in the richer nations are uncomfortable that they may once again be interpreted as insulting people in poorer countries by labelling them in this way.

In the United Kingdom, the terms **ELDC** (Economically Less Developed Countries) and **EMDC** (Economically More Developed Countries) became very popular during the 1990s. Although these are largely British terms, they have found their way into books produced and used in other countries also. Sometimes, the labels are used slightly differently, as in **LEDC** (Less Economically Developed Country) and **MEDC** (More Economically Developed Country). These labels emphasise that it is only the economic aspect of development that is being consid-

ered, not cultural, human or social development. However, the labels are also criticised for implying that the categories are fixed, and that once a country is an LEDC, it will always remain so.

Students should recognise that all these terms mean essentially the same thing; they are trying to separate and categorise economically poor countries from those that are wealthier. The different terms do, however, carry different implications for different users, and a term that is offensive to one person will be quite acceptable to another. Trends change with labels separating poorer from richer countries, and for this reason it is necessary for students to be familiar with them all. Therefore, this book (like most others) will use the terms somewhat interchangeably, often referring to LEDCs, but using the term 'developing countries' when the dynamic process of change is being emphasised. Importantly, the United Nations Development Program uses the term **developing countries**, referring also to some 42 of the world's poorest countries as the **least developed countries**.

The Development Countries Assistance Committee of the OECD also uses the term **developing countries**, defining these as including all countries and territories in Africa except South Africa, in Asia except Japan, in Oceania except Australia and New Zealand, in the Americas except Canada and the USA and the following countries in Europe: Albania, Cyprus, Gibraltar, Greece, Malta, Portugal, Turkey and the countries of the former Yugoslavia.

Having said all this, it is important to remember that the countries of the world cannot really be cleanly separated into two groups on the basis of their wealth. Development is a relative term. Therefore, while it may be accurate to say that one country is more economically developed than another, it is rarely accurate to claim a country is either developed or underdeveloped in absolute terms, as there will almost always be other countries that are both more and less developed than it is.

So, what do we really mean by the term **development**? The word 'development' is generally used in two ways. First, it is used to describe a process – the process of development. In this case, economic development refers to the changes occurring in a country that are enabling it to advance. In general, we can say a country is advancing, or developing, if the quality of the inhabitants' lives is improving.

The second use of the word 'development' describes a potential state of being. In other words, a country achieves a state of development when its people have achieved the full quality of life that they desire. It should be clear that this 'developed state' is something countries strive towards, but have never yet achieved.

It is important to distinguish between **economic development**, which advances the quality of life for people, and **economic growth**, which is simply an expansion in the size of a country's economy. Although economic growth often provides the wealth to drive economic development, economic growth can (and does) occur without economic development necessarily also occurring.

QUESTION BLOCK 2A

1. *Read Paul Streeten's comments about development. Do you agree, disagree or partially agree with his comments? Give reasons to support your answer.*

2. *What is the difference between economic growth and economic development?*

Characteristics of LEDCs

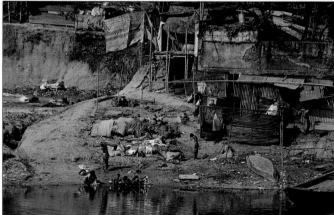

2.5 *Two views of Dhaka, the capital city of Bangladesh. The top view shows an area near the city centre, while the lower photo shows an area of poor housing in the northern suburbs.*

People who have never had the opportunity to live in an LEDC, or even visit such a country, can easily develop misunderstandings about what they are really like. The two photos of Dhaka in figure 2.5 show common notions of developing countries – crowded cities with large numbers of people who are poorer than people in MEDCs but who are nonetheless very hardworking. Certainly, some cities in LEDCs have high population densities, but many MEDCs also have high population densities – the Netherlands being an example of an MEDC with a high population density and a very high standard of living.

Although figure 2.6 is one image of an LEDC, figures 2.7 and 2.8 are also common scenes in many LEDCs, and show that there is no such thing as a single 'typical' image of an LEDC. There is more diversity in the characteristics of developing countries than among MEDCs. Some countries are developing rapidly, others are economically stagnant, while every country has its own distinctive national and cultural characteristics which make it unique.

2.6 *Arab nations tend to have had less success in improving the quality of life of women as measured by the GDI.*

2.7 *Daily village life in southern Ghana. A young boy leads his blind older sister by allowing her to place her hand on his head.*

2.8 *Bangkok, capital city of Thailand.*

Nonetheless, LEDCs do share some common characteristics, which may include some or all of the points listed below. When reading this list, however, it is important to remember that for every point shown, there are exceptions. There is no such thing as an LEDC that shows *all* these characteristics, which are by necessity, generalisations. Having said this, some common characteristics of LEDCs are:

- A very high proportion of the population is involved in **agriculture**, usually about 70% to 90% (figure 2.9). This implies that many farmers are subsistence producers and that commercial surpluses are very small.

- People are often **underemployed**. In other words, it would be possible to reduce the number of workers and still obtain the same total output.

- There is little **income per person**, and so many people exist near the subsistence level. The major proportion of people's expenditure, therefore, is on food and other necessities. Low incomes mean that most people have no savings. As savings are low, investment in new equipment and infrastructure is also low (figure 2.10).

In severe cases, malnutrition may result at a personal level.

- Most **exports** comprise a narrow range of primary products (agriculture and mining products, obtained directly from the ground), such as foodstuffs and minerals. Examples include sugar, cocoa, timber, rubber and tin. This causes long-term problems as the prices of primary products have tended to fall when measured against imports of secondary (manufactured) and tertiary (services) products. Over-dependence on one or two primary product exports makes LEDCs vulnerable to shifts in the global economy.

- **Housing** and other services, such as education, sanitation and transport are inadequate (figure 2.11).

- Levels of **technology** are low, tools and equipment are limited, simple and expensive (unless hand-made using traditional technology and local materials). There is an emphasis on animate energy – animals and people – rather than inanimate energy, based on energy sources such as oil or electricity (figures 2.12 and 2.13).

2.9 *Women work to winnow millet seeds, separating the husk from the grain by allowing the wind to blow away the chaff. This labour-intensive work is being done near San, Mali.*

2.11 *Very basic housing near Massawa in Eritrea. These houses have no electricity or running water, and are designed to be dismantled and moved quickly when food or water in the area becomes scarce.*

2.10 *Lack of funds to invest in new machinery often results in old buses and trucks being used for many years in many LEDCs, often in a very overcrowded state. This bus in Bamako (Mali) is being shared by a small farmyard of sheep and goats on the roof; the animals are being taken home to be sacrificed in the Muslim festival of Tabaski.*

2.12 *Animals of the Erebora tribe in southern Ethiopia gather in the shade of a tree in the village compound. The Erebora people are pastoralists who live by raising animals and moving from place to place in the semi-arid environment to find reliable water supplies.*

Disparities in wealth and development

2.13 *In sharp contrast to large petrol stations operated by transnational oil companies in MEDCs, this petrol station in Segou (Mali) stores petrol in used glass bottles and uses a hand pump to fill vehicles. The faded sign in French means 'Petrol sold here'.*

2.14 *Women and young girls pound millet to make flour. This is traditional women's work in many LEDCs, especially in Africa. None of the girls in this photo attends school; their labour is regarded as too valuable to be sacrificed.*

- Many **farms are very small** in area and dispersed, as holdings are continually sub-divided as population increases. This makes the use of machinery almost impossible.

- Depending on the stage of the demographic transition model reached, **birth rates** tend to be high, and if death rates have fallen with medical advances, **population growth rates** may be high also.

- There is **overcrowding** in many rural areas.

- There is high **illiteracy** and use of child labour (figure 2.14).

- **Governments** are often unstable, coups are relatively common, especially in South America and to some extent Africa, and quite a number of LEDCs are controlled by authoritarian regimes, and maybe even totalitarian military juntas.

- People are very **dependent on their natural environment**. People tend to live within the confines of their environment as they have limited means to change their surroundings.

Indicators of Development

In the Human Development Report that was mentioned at the beginning of this chapter, Paul Streeten makes another important observation:

"In investigating the priorities of poor people, one discovers that what matters most to them often differs from what outsiders assume. More income is only one of the things poor people desire. Adequate nutrition, safe water at hand, better medical services, more and better schooling for their children, cheap transport, adequate shelter, continuing employment and secure livelihoods and productive, remunerating, satisfying jobs do not show up in higher income per head, at least not for some time.

There are other non-material benefits that are often more highly valued by poor people than material improvements... Among these are good and safe working conditions, freedom to choose jobs and livelihoods, freedom of movement and speech, liberation from oppression, violence and exploitation, security from persecution and arbitrary arrest, a satisfying family life, the assertion of cultural and religious values, adequate leisure time and satisfying forms of its use, a sense of purpose in life and work, the opportunity to join and actively participate in the activities of civil society and a sense of belonging to a community".

This description gives a clear insight into the aspirations of people in LEDCs. It seems sensible, therefore, that the way we measure development should reflect these aspirations. In this way, we can be confident that we are measuring those characteristics of a country that will lead to real improvements in people's quality of life. Unfortunately, the indicators commonly used to measure development sometimes fall short of this ideal.

There are three main groups of indicators used to try and measure development. The three groups, which shall be considered in turn in the following paragraphs, are:
- Quantitative indicators of development;
- Qualitative indicators of development; and
- Composite indicators of development.

Quantitative indicators

Perhaps the most commonly used indicators are **quantitative** indicators of development, which use statistics to try and measure certain aspects of a country. Quantitative measures of development in turn usually fall into three groups – economic, social and demographic. Examples of economic indicators of development include percentage of the labour force in agriculture, energy consumption per capita, Gross Domestic Product (GDP) per capita and Gross National Income (GNI) per capita. Examples of social indicators include literacy rates and population per

Table 2.1
Some Indicators of Development for 30 Selected Countries

	Life Expectancy at Birth, in years, 2008	Access to Clean Water, % of population, 2006	Adult Literacy Rate, % of population, 2005	GNI per capita, US$, 2007	PPP GNI per capita, US$, 2007	Human Development Index (HDI), 2007	Agriculture as % of GDP, 2007
HIGH HUMAN DEVELOPMENT							
Norway	80	100	100	76,450	53,690	0.968	2
Australia	81	100	100	35,960	33,340	0.962	3
Sweden	81	100	100	46,060	35,840	0.956	1
Japan	82	100	100	37,670	34,600	0.953	2
USA	78	100	100	46,040	45,850	0.951	1
United Kingdom	79	100	100	42,740	34,370	0.946	1
South Korea	79	92	100	19,690	24,750	0.921	3
United Arab Emirates	78	100	89	23,950	23,990	0.868	2
Mexico	75	95	92	8,340	12,580	0.829	4
Malaysia	74	99	89	6,540	13,570	0.811	9
MEDIUM HUMAN DEVELOPMENT							
China	73	88	91	2,360	5,370	0.777	12
Iran	71	94	82	3,470	10,800	0.759	9
Vietnam	73	92	100	790	2,550	0.733	20
Indonesia	70	80	90	1,650	3,580	0.728	14
Bolivia	65	86	87	1,260	4,140	0.695	14
India	65	89	61	950	2,740	0.619	18
Myanmar	61	80	90	910	1,070	0.583	42
Nepal	64	89	49	340	1,040	0.534	35
Papua New Guinea	57	40	57	850	1,870	0.530	36
Kenya	53	57	74	680	1,540	0.521	23
LOW HUMAN DEVELOPMENT							
Eritrea	57	60	32	230	520	0.483	18
Nigeria	47	47	69	930	1,770	0.470	33
Tanzania	51	55	69	400	1,200	0.467	45
Rwanda	47	65	65	320	860	0.452	36
Malawi	46	76	61	250	750	0.437	34
Zambia	38	58	79	800	1,220	0.434	22
Ethiopia	49	42	36	220	780	0.406	46
Mali	56	60	24	500	1,040	0.380	37
Niger	57	42	29	280	630	0.374	39
Sierra Leone	48	53	36	260	660	0.336	44

Source: Derived from data supplied by the UNDP, World Bank, Population Reference Bureau

% of Population aged 0-14, 2008	Electricity Consumpt-ion per capita, kWh, 2006	CO$_2$ Emissions per capita, tonnes, 2006	% of Under-nourished people, 2005	Mobile Phone Subscribers per 100 people, 2007	Foreign Aid Received per capita, US$, 2007	Internet Users per 1000 people, 2007	
							HIGH HUMAN DEVELOPMENT
19	24,296	11.4	<2.5%	110	0	848	Norway
19	11,332	18.1	<2.5%	101	0	681	Australia
17	15,231	5.4	<2.5%	113	0	797	Sweden
13	8,220	9.6	<2.5%	84	0	690	Japan
20	13,564	19.5	<2.5%	85	0	735	USA
18	6,185	9.1	<2.5%	118	0	717	United Kingdom
18	8,063	9.4	<2.5%	90	0	759	South Korea
19	14,567	30.1	3%	177	0	518	United Arab Emirates
32	2,003	4.1	5%	63	1	227	Mexico
32	3,388	9.3	3%	88	8	557	Malaysia
							MEDIUM HUMAN DEVELOPMENT
19	2,041	4.3	12%	42	1	161	China
26	2,290	6.5	4%	42	1	324	Iran
26	598	1.2	16%	28	29	210	Vietnam
29	530	1.9	6%	36	4	58	Indonesia
38	485	1.0	23%	34	50	105	Bolivia
32	503	1.3	20%	21	1	72	India
27	93	0.2	5%	0	4	1	Myanmar
37	80	0.1	17%	12	21	14	Nepal
40	427	0.7	21%	5	50	18	Papua New Guinea
42	145	0.3	31%	30	34	80	Kenya
							LOW HUMAN DEVELOPMENT
43	49	0.2	75%	2	32	25	Eritrea
45	116	0.8	9%	27	14	68	Nigeria
44	59	0.1	44%	21	70	10	Tanzania
44	38	0.1	33%	7	73	11	Rwanda
46	94	0.1	35%	8	53	10	Malawi
46	730	0.2	46%	22	88	42	Zambia
43	38	0.1	46%	2	31	4	Ethiopia
48	16	0.0	29%	21	82	8	Mali
49	44	0.1	32%	6	38	3	Niger
42	59	0.2	51%	13	92	2	Sierra Leone

doctor, while examples of demographic indicators would be average life expectancy, percentage of the population undernourished and infant mortality rates. A selection of these single-factor indices are shown in table 2.1.

Of these indicators of development, the most commonly used are three very similar measurements – Gross Domestic Product (GDP) per capita, Gross National Product (GNP) per capita and Gross National Income (GNI) per capita. Unlike most quantitative indicators that measure a single aspect of a country's development, GDP is a broad measure of an economy's performance. It measures all the economic output in a country in a given year, quantifying the total value of all goods and services produced in the country. When the GDP is divided by the population of that country, then the **GDP per capita** is calculated. The GNP differs from the GDP by trying to isolate the economic activity of foreign-owned firms. **GNI**, which is increasingly preferred to GNP and GDP, measures the total value of goods and services produced within a country together with the balance of income and payments from or to other countries.

For most countries, the GNP, GDP and GNI are fairly similar figures.

The reason that GNP per capita, GDP per capita and GNI per capita are popular and widely used indicators of development is that they include every aspect of a country's economy that has a monetary value. On the other hand, most other quantitative indicators of development simply focus on a single aspect of the country, such as energy use or food consumption. However, all three measures have some significant shortcomings:

- Although these measures embrace all aspects of a country's economy, they do not give any information about the **distribution of wealth** within the country. For example, in 2006, the United Arab Emirates (UAE) had a GDP per capita of $US49,116, which is greater than many European countries, and almost double the figure for New Zealand. However, much of the wealth of the UAE comes from oil production,

and does not necessarily flow to the bulk of the population (figure 2.15). With the UAE, and most countries to a similar or lesser extent, there are great gaps between the rich and poor that a single figure for GNI per capita or GDP per capita masks.

- Only transactions in the formal (monetary) sector are included in calculations of GNP per capita, GDP per capita and GNI per capita. This means that work done on a **non-monetary** basis, such as subsistence agriculture (the main source of food in many LEDCs), or work which is not officially recorded such as undeclared 'cash-in-hand' work, smuggling, the black market and the drug trade are not included (figure 2.16). In some countries, these are major facets of the operation of the economy. Ignoring these aspects of the economy can significantly deflate a country's GNP per capita and GDP per capita.

2.16 *Subsistence farming accounts for about 80% of the workforce in many LEDCs, and is the basic pillar of the economy. However, it is only any small commercial component that is counted in calculations of GNP per capita and GDP per capita.*

- The statistics for GNP per capita, GDP per capita and GNI per capita are collected by the national government in each country. In many LEDCs, the **statistics may be unreliable** because the resources are not available to ensure accuracy. For example, in China during the Cultural Revolution (1966-1976) govern-

2.15 *Although the United Arab Emirates has a high GNI per capita, there are large gaps in wealth within the country, as these views of a bank in Abu Dhabi (left) and a residential area in Hatta (right)) illustrate.*

ment planners required each township to submit planned production statistics. One rural township with 20,000 inhabitants submitted a three-year plan which called for the construction of a farm for 10,000 pigs, another farm for 10,000 chickens, a third for 10,000 ducks, yet another for 10,000 head of cattle, the opening of 10,000 *mou* of orchards, 10,000 *mou* of fish ponds, a bee farm of 10,000 hives and new villages for 10,000 people. (A *mou* is equal to one-sixth of a hectare). In colloquial or slang Chinese, 10,000 commonly means 'lots of' or 'a very great number', and so this plan had no statistical accuracy whatsoever. Statistics collected in many countries today may well have little greater accuracy. Problems also occur when the countries that collect the data improve or change the bases of their data collection. This can make comparisons of figures over time unreliable. Furthermore, different countries often disagree about definitions and assumptions of the statistics they collect, making comparisons between countries unreliable. Finally, data quality can vary from country to country. For example, LEDCs tend to have reliable data on literacy rates whereas MEDCs do not, while data for other indicators may be more reliable in MEDCs than LEDCs.

- The measures of GNP per capita, GDP per capita and GNI per capita are almost always reported in US dollars. Therefore, international comparisons between different countries are affected by **changing currency exchange rates**. To take an example, in 2006 Australia's GDP per capita was $US33,035. If changes to international exchange rates had resulted in Australia's dollar declining by 5% against the US dollar, then this figure would have been about $US1,650 less, or about $US31,380, even though Australia was no less economically developed than previously.

- The measures of GNP per capita, GDP per capita and GNI per capita do not give any indication of the **happiness**, **satisfaction** or **welfare** of the population in a country. Happiness does not necessarily follow from being richer, and many studies actually show there is an inverse relationship between wealth and happiness.

- The measures of GNP per capita, GDP per capita and GNI per capita do not necessarily reflect the **purchasing power** of money in different countries. For example, the GDP per capita of Australia and Belgium are similar ($U33,035 and $US33,243 in 2006), but a litre of petrol that costs $1 in Australia may cost $2.40 in Belgium. Therefore, the purchasing power of money is very different in the two countries.

To overcome this last concern, GNP per capita is sometimes expressed at **purchasing power parity** (PPP) rates. PPP is defined as the number of units of a country's currency needed to buy the same amounts of goods and services in a country as $US1 would buy in the United States. PPP examines a wide range of goods and services, including food, transport, clothing and housing. It provides a measure of what people can actually afford, regardless of the local value and exchange rate of their currency.

Qualitative indicators

Qualitative indicators of development attempt to describe a country's development in terms of those factors that influence people's quality of life. Rather than trying to *measure* development, qualitative indicators attempt to *describe* development (figure 2.17). Qualitative indicators usually try to describe those facets of a country that directly affect the quality of life of the people in the country. Therefore, qualitative indicators of development would include analyses of things such as freedom from want, survival, welfare and security.

2.17 *Qualitative indicators of development attempt to describe aspects of the quality of life of people. A description of development for these people in Nepal would include their welfare, security, survival and freedom from want.*

Because they describe rather than measure a country's development, qualitative indicators of development are not very useful for the (perhaps questionable) task of ranking countries according to their level of development. However, they are useful for giving a fuller picture of the situation in a country than a simple statistic (a quantitative measure) is likely to convey.

Composite indicators

Composite indicators of development combine several other measures of development into a single figure. The aim is to present a measure which focuses on the quality of life of people like the qualitative indicators, but which is more precise like the quantitative measures. By combining several measures of development to create a composite indicator, it is hoped that an even broader and more useful indicator than GNP per capita can be developed.

The first attempt at generating a composite indicator of development occurred in the 1980s when the Overseas

Development Council (ODC) developed the **Physical Quality of Life Index** (PQLI). The PQLI was calculated by obtaining the average of three indicators of quality of life that were thought to be particularly important – literacy, life expectancy and infant mortality.

Literacy was included because it gave a crude indication of access to education, which was seen as necessary if people are to play a productive and rewarding role in society. Literacy was seen as the first step towards a sound education. As it was developed in primary school, it was accessible by many people in LEDCs where secondary schooling may be too expensive to pursue.

Life expectancy was seen as important on the assumption that having life is perhaps the most important indicator of quality of life; it is certainly a necessary prerequisite! Furthermore, it was suggested that a long life is preferable to a short life, and therefore average life expectancy at birth was seen as an important indicator. Life expectancy is also a reflection of other aspects of quality of life, such as access to medical care and adequate nutrition. Similar thinking lay behind the inclusion of infant mortality, or the proportion of infants who survive to their fifth birthday.

For each of the three indicators, countries were ranked and given a score, with the 'best' country being given a score of 100, and the 'worst' performing country being given a score of 0. Therefore, for example, when allocating scores for life expectancy, Japan would score 100 as its life expectancy of 82 years is the longest in the world. On the same basis, Zambia would score 0, as its average life

expectancy of 38 years was the shortest in the world. A similar approach was taken for the remaining two indicators. An average of the three scores was then obtained to calculate the PQLI.

During the 1990s, the PQLI tended to be replaced by a slightly different measure, the **Human Development Index** (HDI), which was developed in 1990 by the United Nations Development Program (UNDP). Like the PQLI, the HDI also uses three measures to generate an index, and two of the three measures are the same – literacy and life expectancy. However, rather than using infant mortality, the HDI uses GDP per capita on a PPP basis. This was done to balance the social measures of development with an economic measure, as control of personal resources and wealth was seen as an important aspect of people's quality of life.

Like the PQLI, calculation of the HDI involves ranking countries on a scale from 100 down to 0, and taking an average of the three rankings. However, the HDI is expressed on a scale from 0 to 1, usually to three decimal places. Countries are then classified into three groups – high human development with HDIs of 0.800 and above, medium human development with HDIs of 0.500 to 0.799 and low human development with HDIs of below 0.500.

Although HDI is the most commonly used composite indicator of development, other composite measures also exist, usually being calculated using similar methodology. Examples of other composite indicators are the **Gender-related Development Index** (GDI, developed in 1995) and the **Gender Empowerment Measure** (GEM, also

Table 2.2

Comparison of Composite Indicators of Development

Indicator	Index is calculated by averaging these three measures...		
	Longevity	Knowledge	Decent Standard of Living
HDI	Life expectancy at birth	1. Adult literacy rate 2. Combined school enrolment ratio	Adjusted per capita income in PPP $
GDI	Female and male life expectancy at birth	1. Female and male literacy rates 2. Female and male combined school enrolment ratios	Adjusted per capita in come in PPP $, based on female and male earned income shares
HPI-1 (for developing countries)	Percentage of people not expected to survive to age 40	Adult literacy rate	1. Percentage of people without access to safe water 2. Percentage of people without access to health services 3. Percentage of underweight children under five
HPI-2 (for industrialised countries)	Percentage of people not expected to survive to age 60	Adult functional illiteracy rate	Percentage of people living below the income poverty line (50% of median personal disposable income)

Source: UNDP

1995) that were discussed in chapter 1. Another composite indicator is the **Human Poverty Index** (HPI, developed in 1997). Two versions of the HPI exist, HPI-1 for developing countries and HPI-2 for industrialised countries, with different variables designed to reflect the characteristics of each group of countries. The difference between these measures, together with a comparison of the other composite indicators of development is given in table 2.2.

QUESTION BLOCK 2B

1. *What is the difference between (a) quantitative, (b) qualitative, and (c) composite indicators of development? Give three examples of each.*

2. *Why is GNI per capita so popular as an indicator of development?*

3. *List the shortcomings of GNI per capita as an indicator of development.*

4. *Explain the concepts underlying PPP.*

5. *Explain why the three variables used to calculate the PQLI were chosen.*

6. *How does the HDI differ from the PQLI?*

Origin of Disparities

Equity Issues

The indicators of economic development highlight the global inequities between countries very effectively. However, a shortcoming of these statistics is that they tend to mask inequities within countries. Even within a wealthy country such as Australia, Canada or Germany, very few people are of the 'average' wealth that the statistics state. In LEDCs, the gap between rich and poor is much greater than in industrialised countries.

The **internet** is a good indicator of the lack of equity that exists within many countries. Moreover, it is an important indicator because access to education and information is necessary if people are to make wise choices and advance economically. Within South Africa, to take one example, the average internet user earned seven times the national average income, while 90% of internet users in Latin America are in the upper income group. Furthermore, internet users tend to be those with higher education. Globally, 30% of internet users have at least one university degree, while in some countries the figure is even higher – 50% in the United Kingdom, almost 60% in China and almost 70% in Ireland (figure 2.18).

Internet users tend to be young males. Although women are about 38% of internet users in the United States, the proportion of women is much less in most other countries: 17% in Brazil, 16% in Russia, 7% in China and 4% in the Arab states. The average age of internet users in the United States is only 30 years, and it is below 30 years in China and the United Kingdom. Although less than 10% of the world's population speaks English, 80% of all websites are written in English.

2.18 *A very basic internet café in Asmara, the capital city of Eritrea.*

The differences in development within countries are usually based on income differences that arise because of ethnic, gender or locational differences. Because of this, the differences between **regions and districts** within a country can usually be quantified, either by using quantitative or composite indicators of development such as the HPI-1. Using the HPI-1, the UNDP found that human deprivation is much higher in Bihar (a state in north-eastern India where the HPI-1 is 54%) than in Kerala, a state in south India where the HPI-1 is only 23%. Similarly, two regions in Kazakhstan that have similar school enrolments and life expectancies have very different HDI values which reflect the different levels of income in the two areas. The statistics for these two regions are an HDI of 0.835 and a GDP per capita ($US PPP) of $8,285 in Mangistau, and an HDI of 0.594 and a GDP per capita ($US PPP) of $1,650 in Zhambyl.

In many LEDCs, significant differences arise between urban and rural areas. Few countries are equally developed in all geographical areas. For example, as China has developed economically since the 1980s, the cities have advanced greatly while development in rural areas has been much slower. Therefore, the process of economic development in China has widened the gap between rich and poor to levels greater than ever before (figure 2.19).

2.19 *As China has developed economically, the cities have modernised greatly but there has been much less progress in the rural areas where 80% of the population live. These views contrast the city of Beijing (top) with Xijiang, a typical rural village in Guizhou province (bottom).*

The gaps between rural and urban areas grow in many LEDCs as the process of economic development occurs, largely because the cities are the first areas to receive additional investment and improvements. In many ways this is a pity, because the bulk of the population in most LEDCs live in rural villages and farming areas.

Significant differences can arise between different **ethnic groups** living in the same country. In Nepal, the average life expectancy for upper-caste Hindus is 61 years, compared with 49 years for Muslims. Similarly, the adult literacy rates for upper-caste Hindus in Nepal is 58%, compared with only 22% for Muslims (figure 2.20).

Even in an MEDC such as Australia, there are significant differences in the incomes, life expectancy, access to edu-

2.20 *Although the quality of life of this Hindu family in Nepal (top) is not luxurious by the standards of most MEDCs, it is far better than the conditions experienced by this Muslim community living beside the river (bottom).*

cation, standards of health and literacy between Aboriginal people and the statistical average for Australia as a whole.

Statistics for 2008 showed that the average annual population growth rate of 2.0% for Indigenous population of Australia was nearly twice the rate for the total population (0.8%). Furthermore, the Aboriginal and Torres Strait Islander population, with a median age of 20 years, is younger than the total population by 14 years. Average life expectancy for Aboriginal and Torres Strait Islander people is 59 years for males and 66 years for females, nearly 20 years less than the averages for the total population.

In general, the **disparities within countries** tend to be greater in LEDCs than in MEDCs, with the disparities greatest in Africa and Latin America (figure 2.21). Brazil has one of the world's largest gaps between rich and poor. The disparity is so wide that the richest 20% of people in Brazil share an income and lifestyle that is equivalent to the most affluent countries in Europe. On the other hand, the poorest 20% have an HDI which is approximately equal to that of India. Expressed another way, the richest 20% of Brazil's population retains 65% of the total income

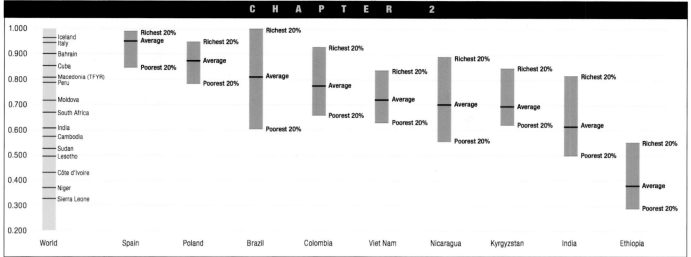

2.21 *Disparities in wealth, selected countries.*

while the poorest 50% earns just 12% of the country's income. The disparities in Brazil are spread unevenly through the country, with 5% of the poor being in the North (where 43% of the population in the area), 45% in the Northeast (46% of the area's population), 34% in the Southeast (23% of the population), 10% in the South (20% of the population), and 6% in the Centre-West (25% of that area's population). The reasons for the large disparities are complex, but some commentators blame government 'trickle-down' economic policies that have provided tax cuts and other benefits to businesses and rich individuals in the belief that this will indirectly benefit (trickle down to) the broad population.

India also has significant inequalities in human development achievements across income groups as measured by HDI. The richest 20% of India's population has an HDI that ranks within the range of some European countries such as Macedonia, whereas the poorest 20% of the population has an HDI that ranks below some poorer African countries such as Sudan. The reasons for the wide disparities in India are even more complex than those in Brazil, and may include a mix of government corruption, the inflexibility of the caste system, a breakdown of traditional forms of land ownership, and government policies to encourage privatisation.

QUESTION BLOCK 2C

1. There is a close positive relationship between economic development and internet access. In which direction is the 'cause-and-effect', in your opinion?

2. Explain how the internet both helps and hinders economic development.

3. Describe the pattern shown in figure 2.21.

4. Identify the types of countries with relatively small disparities and inequities as shown in figure 2.21. Suggest reasons why these countries may have smaller disparities than countries like Brazil and India.

Why do Disparities Arise?

Disparities in access to food

There are millions of people in the world who are malnourished, and whose main priority is securing an adequate food supply. Although most of these people live in LEDCs, it would be wrong to think that the typical person in developing countries is malnourished. Certainly average daily food intake in LEDCs is less than that of people in MEDCs, and statistics which support this were given in table 2.1.

The world has never produced so much food. We now have a situation in the world where enough grain (mainly wheat and rice) is produced to feed every man, woman and child in the world more than 3000 calories every day. This is **more than enough food** to feed everyone adequately – indeed more than adequately – even without allowing for any other food production such as vegetables, fruit, fish and meat.

In MEDCs in Europe and North America, there are huge surplus stocks of wheat, butter, wine and other foods that simply cannot be sold for a price that would cover the cost of production. Farmers would often prefer to **dump** food into the ground or into the ocean than sell it for a price that is too low. And yet in spite of this glut of food on world markets, there have never been so many people suffering from **starvation** or **malnutrition** than now. It has been estimated that between 18 and 20 million people are dying of starvation or starvation related disease each year.

The problem is not that the world is producing insufficient food, but that it not being distributed effectively. One reason for this is that commercial farmers (perhaps reasonably) will usually sell their produce to the person (or company) that will **pay the highest price**. Unfortunately, for many poor people in LEDCs, they are usually the ones who cannot afford to pay the top prices. To take one example, wheat is an important staple food for much of the world's population. However, wheat is also in demand by beef farmers in MEDCs who feed it to their cattle to produce high quality, lean meat. A beef farmer in an MEDC will almost always be able to afford to pay a higher price for wheat than a hungry peasant in an LEDC, which means that the peasant will usually miss out. This issue of the production and global distribution of food was developed in more detail in chapter 10.

One of the solutions often proposed is sending **food aid** to LEDCs from MEDCs. It is argued that if people in LEDCs are short of food when farmers in MEDCs have surplus stocks, the obvious solution must be to send food aid. Perhaps surprisingly, such food aid from MEDCs can actually make the situation even worse. When farmers in LEDCs are trying to establish a commercial food growing industry in their country, there could be no greater blow than to have to compete with free or subsidised grain or other food from an MEDC. Food aid is important on humanitarian grounds when there is a natural disaster, but it really hurts farmers in LEDCs when it continues for a long period of time. This issue must be considered carefully before food aid is sent to LEDCs, as the motive for such aid is sometimes to assist farmers in MEDCs rather than the needy in LEDCs.

2.22 *Traditional farming methods — using animal power and a wooden plough.*

2.23 *To overcome the shortage of farming land in LEDCs with a high population density, terracing of the hillsides is often practised.*

Although food production per capita is increasing in most parts of the world, it is declining in Africa. This is partly because Africa's rapidly growing population is outstripping the capacity of farmers to increase production, but it is also because of the characteristics of farming in Africa, and in other areas where the impact of agricultural reforms have not yet been felt. In general, farmers in LEDCs produce less food per capita than farmers in MEDCs. There are many reasons for the difference, including the following:

- In most LEDCs, and especially the low human development countries, the majority of farming is done on a **subsistence** basis. This means that most of the food that is produced is consumed by the farmer's immediate family, leaving only a small surplus for commercial sale. Subsistence farmers have neither the incentive nor the means to increase production in order to produce a surplus.

- **Traditional farming methods** that do not optimise productivity are still used by many farmers. Examples of such methods would include broadcasting seeds rather than sowing them in rows and using traditional implements such as wooden ploughs and animal power (figure 2.22).

- Because of poor storage facilities, there is a large loss of production due to **insect pests**. It is estimated that about 30% of the world's food production is destroyed by rats, grasshoppers and other pests.

- When plots of farming land are divided among the children of a farmer who has died, **small divided landholdings** often result. This is to ensure that each of the children has an equal share of land with different qualities, but it makes the use of machinery impractical and means that valuable time must be spent walking from one small plot to another. On the other hand, the practice does often provide some protection from natural disaster by providing each family with some land in the valley floor as well as on the slopes and ridges (figure 2.23).

- In many LEDCs, **absentee landlords** control much of the farming land. These landlords often charge excessive rental to the farmers, such as a large percentage of the crop grown. The farmers are therefore forced to continue working to pay off their debts to the landlord. This provides little incentive to the farmers to boost production more than is necessary.

- Farmers in LEDCs often **do not specialise** in one specific crop, but cultivate many crops. This is sensible for a subsistence farmer whose diet depends on what is grown, but it means that farmers seldom become experts in growing one particular crop.

- **Agribusiness** companies often convince farmers to abandon growing food, and switch instead to growing commercial crops such as cotton, rubber, tobacco or tea for export. Because the prices of such crops have fallen in real terms over recent decades, farmers who accepted this option may now find themselves not earning enough money to buy the food they once grew themselves.

Food security for people in LEDCs has improved greatly in recent decades. This has occurred for five main reasons. First, many farmers adopted new **high yielding varieties** of crops, especially rice and wheat. These were crops that were genetically engineered to shorten the growing cycle, enabling double cropping and even triple cropping of farmland. Many of these high yielding varieties (HYVs) were also more resistant to diseases that affected traditional species of crops. Second, **irrigation systems** became more widespread in many areas of the world. Third, there was a big increase in the use of **chemical pesticides and fertilisers** on farms. Although there can be undesirable side effects on the biophysical environment from the widespread use of chemicals, they also increase farm productivity, at least in the short-term. The increases in production that resulted from these three innovations were so great that their introduction has become known as the **Green Revolution**. Fourth, **mechanical technology** has become much more wide-spread on the world's farms, enabling a small number of people to achieve tasks that used to require a huge work force (figure 2.24). Finally, the changing nature of the **agricultural work force** has also affected productivity. The number of people engaged in agriculture around the world is declining. This decline is found in every part of the world, and is expected to continue into the future.

2.24 *A Chinese walking tractor. Originally developed from mechanised ploughs, these low cost, simple tractors have transformed Chinese farming.*

Disparities in access to shelter

A shortage of accommodation is one of the most common characteristics of cities in LEDCs. This situation arises because of a combination of circumstances. Governments in LEDCs usually collect less taxation per head than governments in MEDCs, and therefore have less money available for providing services such as providing hous-

ing. Furthermore, people in LEDCs spend a larger proportion of their incomes on food than people in MEDCs, and therefore have less disposable income available for housing and other needs. For this reason, there are few large profits available for private developers to provide large-scale low-cost housing, and so the situation tends to be neglected.

The situation is acute in many cities in LEDCs because of the influx of people who have moved there from rural areas of the country. This movement of people, known as **rural-urban migration**, is swelling the populations of cities in LEDCs to sometimes huge numbers today. In the cities of some LEDCs, well over half the population may not have been born in the city, having moved there from rural areas.

2.25 *Breakfast time for a homeless family in Mandalay, Myanmar. This family has spent the night sleeping on the footpath in the sacks or under the sheets of cardboard. The green and blue-striped sacks on the right still contained sleeping people when this photo was taken.*

Many of the rural-urban migrants find that employment is more difficult to find than they had expected. Lacking skills needed in cities, many find themselves unemployed and homeless, sometimes having to sleep on the streets (figure 2.25). Many of these people turn to begging, work in prostitution, or turn to crime.

Those people who are more fortunate than the street-dwellers live in **shanty** housing. This is self-help housing made from scrounged materials such as corrugated iron, packing cases, cloth and disused plastic sheeting (figure 2.26). It is estimated that between 70% and 95% of all new housing in LEDCs consists of shanty settlements. About 60% of the urban population in Africa live in shanty settlements. In Asia, the equivalent figure is 20% and in South America 30%.

Many governments are embarrassed to have shanty settlements and use the police or the army to demolish them from time to time. However, other governments realise that shanty housing is really a form of self-help housing, and provide support by connecting basic services such as electricity. Even where people live in more permanent

2.26 *Part of a large area of shanty housing in Soweto, South Africa.*

2.27 *Recently built housing in Phnom Penh, capital city of Cambodia (top) and an oblique aerial view of housing in Djibouti (bottom).*

housing than shanties, however, the quality of typical housing would often fall short of basic expectations in MEDCs (figure 2.27). Basic services such as water are often lacking, and houses accommodating a family often comprise just a single room (figure 2.28).

Some governments in LEDCs which are developing rapidly have the resources to build high-rise public housing to re-house the shanty dwellers. However, the replacement of shanty housing remains a major issue in many LEDCs. Where governments lack the money to provide housing, they can provide materials for people to build better quality self-help housing, provide people with loans or grants to improve their shanties or pay to improve the quality of shanty areas. Even these measures cost money, which is always in short supply in LEDCs. These issues of access to shelter are explored in more detail in chapter 16.

2.28 *Housing in LEDCs often lack basic services. In this view, people use public taps in the streets of Dhaka (Bangladesh) for washing themselves.*

Disparities in access to health and education

Perhaps the most important services needed by people in LEDCs are health and education. Health services are needed to cure even basic illnesses which, if left untreated, can lead to serious sickness and even death. Education is an important investment in a country's future, providing young people to contribute to and change their society for the better (figure 2.29). However, like all services in LEDCs, health and education can be seen as very expensive in countries where money is scarce. Table 2.3 highlights the differences in provision of health and education for the selection of 30 countries listed previously in tables 2.1 and 1.13.

Recent changes in both LEDCs and in the process of globalisation seem to have increased the health risks to people everywhere, but especially within LEDCs where medical services are less adequate. Viruses and bacteria constantly mutate, posing new risks for humans who may lack the resistance necessary to defend themselves against attack by new diseases. This is especially so in LEDCs where many people lack sufficient nutrition and body condition to have complete immunity anyway.

Improvements in global travel mean that viruses and bacteria can now travel around the world (with their human hosts) in just a few hours. Indeed, even greater travel opportunities within LEDCs encourages the spread of diseases. Traditionally, a villager in Africa who con-

Table 2.3
Selected Health and Education Indicators (for countries listed in tables 1.13 and 2.1)

	HEALTH INDICATORS					EDUCATION INDICATORS		
	Under 5 Mortality Rate per 1000 births, 1990	Under 5 Mortality Rate per 1000 births, 2007	Health Expenditure per capita, US$, 2006	Measles Immunis-ation Rate, % of 2 year olds, 2007	% of Births Attended by Skilled Health Staff, 2007	Primary School Completion Rate, %, 2007	% of Relevant Age Group in High School, 2007	Primary School Pupils per Teacher, 2007
HIGH HUMAN DEVELOPMENT								
Norway	9	4	6,267	92	100	96	100	11
Australia	10	6	3,302	94	100	100	100	14
Sweden	7	3	3,973	96	100	100	100	10
Japan	6	4	2,759	98	100	100	100	19
USA	11	8	6,719	93	99	95	94	14
United Kingdom	10	6	3,332	86	100	100	100	18
South Korea	9	5	1,168	92	100	100	96	28
United Arab Emirates	55	8	1,018	92	100	100	90	17
Mexico	46	35	527	96	93	100	85	28
Malaysia	22	11	259	90	98	98	72	17
MEDIUM HUMAN DEVELOPMENT								
China	49	22	94	94	98	98	76	18
Iran	72	33	215	97	72	100	81	19
Vietnam	53	15	46	83	88	94	76	21
Indonesia	91	31	39	80	72	99	62	20
Bolivia	125	57	79	81	67	100	82	24
India	123	72	29	67	47	86	54	40
Myanmar	168	103	5	81	68	58	49	29
Nepal	145	55	17	81	19	78	43	38
Papua New Guinea	94	65	29	58	42	54	22	36
Kenya	97	121	29	80	42	93	48	40
LOW HUMAN DEVELOPMENT								
Eritrea	147	70	8	95	28	46	31	48
Nigeria	230	189	33	62	35	72	32	40
Tanzania	161	116	23	90	43	72	28	53
Rwanda	173	181	33	99	39	35	13	69
Malawi	221	111	21	83	54	55	29	49
Zambia	180	170	58	85	43	88	36	49
Ethiopia	204	119	7	65	6	46	27	59
Mali	250	196	31	68	45	49	28	52
Niger	320	176	16	47	33	40	11	40
Sierra Leone	302	262	12	67	43	81	32	44

Disparities in wealth and development

tracted a newly mutated disease may well have died, and apart from a few relatives who may also have been infected, the virus would simply die out. Nowadays, an infected person is more likely to travel to neighbouring villages and even to the megacities where an epidemic is possible.

2.29 *Education at its most basic level – teaching basic literacy to children without a classroom in a village in Ghana.*

2.30 *Lack of clean running water is a major health risk for many people in LEDCs. In this view, people clamour to get water from an open well beside the road in Djibouti.*

Overcrowding and poverty provide ideal conditions for the spread of infection. To take one example, dengue is now the most important and fastest-growing insect-borne viral infection in the world. It is carried by the *aedes aegypti* mosquito which lives and breeds in the rubbish commonly found in overcrowded cities in the tropics, especially in the small pools of water which collect in abandoned car tyres.

Many diseases arise from **poor water quality** in LEDCs (figure 2.30). This is often because water is used for many different purposes which are not really compatible. For example, it is common to see people washing their clothes in the river even though the river bed might also be used to graze cattle and the water might be used as a toilet and garbage dump.

One of the main pollutants of water in LEDCs is human sewage. In many areas, a toilet is simply a hole in the ground or above a river. Even more often, there is not even a hole in the ground, and people must defecate on a river bank, in the bush or on a special area set aside for use as a toilet (figure 2.31). In such places, diseases can spread easily as flies and other vermin carry germs from the exposed excrement to people's food. It is difficult for people to maintain personal hygiene under such conditions, and diseases such as diarrhoea can spread easily.

2.31 *Signs on this wall in Kumasi (Ghana) implore residents not to urinate against the wall.*

Malaria kills thousands of people each year in tropical areas of the world, and it is one of the main health risks in LEDCs. Malaria is a parasite which is carried by one particular type of mosquito, the anopheles. The mosquitoes breed in stagnant water where the summer temperature is over 21°C. When an anopheles mosquito bites a person, the malaria parasite may be injected into the person's blood stream. Once in the blood, the parasite multiplies and can cause the person to experience fever and fits of shivering. It may kill a person directly, or else it can weaken a person so that they are unable to work properly. Sometimes, it weakens the immune system so that other diseases can infect and perhaps kill the sufferer. Malaria is largely found in tropical areas of LEDCs. In previous centuries it was found in other areas also, including parts of Europe. In cooler areas, malaria was eradicated by draining swamps and marshes, but this task is so great as to be impossible in the tropics.

Other water borne parasites also cause serious diseases in tropical areas of LEDCs. **Bilharzia** snails live in warm, still waters of tropical areas and cause about 20 million deaths each year. When people walk bare footed in the water, the snails enter the body through the soles of the feet or through a body orifice. Once in the human body, the snails reproduce in the kidney or the bladder. The person becomes weak and suffers from anaemia and failure of the bladder or kidney. When infected people urinate or defecate in a lake or river, the eggs of the bilharzia snail are released, starting the life cycle over once again.

It is extremely difficult to eliminate the causes of these and other water-borne diseases. It is almost impossible to drain all the stagnant water in tropical areas – after all, the staple food of much of the world (rice) is grown in flooded padi fields. Therefore, eliminating the parasites would probably involve the use of pesticides. However, the sprays involved are expensive for poor nations and they may cause damage to the environment. Perhaps the most effective way of reducing the impact of these diseases is to educate the local population in how to minimise the risks of catching them.

QUESTION BLOCK 2D

1. *If world food production per capita has never been higher, why are so many people in the world malnourished?*

2. *Explain how non-emergency food aid to LEDCs can hurt local farmers in those countries.*

3. *Why is food production per capita usually less in LEDCs than in MEDCs?*

4. *Outline the five major innovations which have increased crop yields in LEDCs.*

5. *Why is shortage of housing a problem in many LEDCs?*

6. *Why do the cities in many LEDCs have shanty housing? Are shanties a good or a bad thing?*

7. *Using table 2.3, describe the improvements in under-five mortality rates which occurred between 1990 and 2007. Were these gains evenly distributed? Explain your answer.*

8. *Rank the countries listed in table 2.3 from best to worst according to (a) health expenditure per capita, and (b) the most recent under 5 mortality rate. What conclusions can you draw from this?*

9. *Using table 2.3, describe the varying access to education for children in the countries listed.*

10. *Explain why globalisation increases the vulnerability of people to new diseases, especially those who live in LEDCs.*

Case Study of Disparities and Inequities within one country – Papua New Guinea

Papua New Guinea occupies the eastern half of the island of New Guinea, which is situated to the immediate north of Australia, plus many smaller islands to the east of New Guinea.

Before European contact, most production in Papua New Guinea came from small scale subsistence producers. Papua New Guinea consisted of many diverse cultural groupings who were largely independent from each other. Nonetheless, extensive trading networks existed with products often being bartered in exchange for customary gifts or compensations. While many of the characteristics of the traditional subsistence economy are still significant, they are not at the core of the economy today.

In the early 1800s, Europeans and Australians began trading with the more accessible coastal Papua New Guineans for products such as *bêche-de-mer* (an edible sea cucumber), turtle shell and pearl shell. Coconut oil produced in villages was traded to meet the increased European demand for vegetable oils which had begun to supplant the use of animal tallow. Despite the often unequal exchange involved with this trade, the indigenous people benefited from the introduction of steel tools and other new technologies, while maintaining the traditional structure of their economy.

However, when machinery was developed in 1850s for large scale extraction of oil from copra, the basis of the trading relationship changed. The indigenous technology for producing the oil was made redundant, and with it the value added in the processing of coconuts was lost. Eventually, it led to village producers moving to work for wages on plantations established by the Europeans (figure 2.32).

The early economic development of the German colonised part of New Guinea and the Australian/British colonised Papua were based on the plantation system. The main product produced on plantations was copra, although rubber, coffee and tobacco were also important. In New Guinea, the cultivated plantation area rose from 2,400 hectares in 1899 to 110,000 hectares in 1940.

2.32 *Tapping rubber on a plantation at Sogeri, in the hills to the east of Port Moresby.*

The plantation sector in Papua was much smaller. However, copra and rubber were the mainstays of the Papuan economy for the period up to 1940, except for short-lived copper and gold booms. Australian companies were the prime forces in the plantation economy. Although powerful within the Pacific area, these companies were no match for large transnational competitors such as Firestone, Brook-Bond, Unilever and Tate & Lyle, however.

Following the end of World War II in 1945, economic development became dependent on the expansion of agricultural production and the inflow of Australian government aid. Although exports of agricultural and fisheries products rose in value, the production of food for domestic consumption virtually stagnated in the period up to independence in 1975 while food imports grew markedly during the same 20-year period.

Australian aid led to the growth of an extremely large government sector of employment, stimulating a rapid increase in the rate of urbanisation (see chapter 11). Manufacturing industries expanded, although they remained a small sector in Papua New Guinea's economy. Most of the manufacturing establishments were foreign owned and concentrated on the processing of primary products (figure 2.33).

2.33 *Most manufacturing in Papua New Guinea involves the initial processing of primary products.*

During the decades leading up to independence in 1975, as well as during the post-independence years, the mining sector grew in importance. Large-scale projects for natural resource exploitation by transnational corporations, symbolised by the giant Bougainville Copper Company, resulted in copper taking over the role of agriculture as the country's chief export.

Even today, Papua New Guinea has an economy largely owned and managed by foreigners, with a heavy dependence on mineral and agricultural commodities, and a reliance on Australian government aid. However, given the almost non-existent capacity for local people to invest in capital projects, this may not have been entirely negative. Indeed, foreign companies operating in Papua New Guinea argue that the wealth generated by their contin-

ued activities flow on (or 'trickle down') throughout the Papua New Guinean economy, providing employment, technology, training and management expertise.

Measures of economic development in Papua New Guinea are difficult to obtain. In 2009, Papua New Guinea's GNP per capita was equivalent to $US1081, a significant decline from the figure about 15 years earlier (table 2.4). On a PPP (purchasing power parity) basis, the 2009 figure was $US2166. When adjusted for the effects of changes in prices, the GNP in Papua New Guinea has probably not increased greatly since independence.

Of course, GNP per capita is not the only way to measure economic development – improvements in living standards also provide important measures of development. During the period 1975 to 2008, life expectancy at birth increased from 48 years to 57 years. During the same period, infant mortality decreased from 90 per thousand live births to 62 per thousand live births. In education, only 1% of secondary school age children attended high school in 1960, compared with 14% by 1984; by 2006 the figure was still only 22%, comprising 26% of males and 18% of females attending high schools. Between 1970 and 2008, adult literacy increased from 33% to 51% for females and from 60% to 63% for males.

Agriculture still provides a subsistence livelihood for 85% of the population. Papua New Guinea's reliance on primary products, like many other LEDCs, has exposed it to economic fluctuations arising from changes in the global economy. The factors impacting on Papua New Guinea in recent years have included falling mineral prices, low commodity prices for most of the country's exports, currency inflation, and depreciating exchange rates. Two of the country's largest mining operations were particularly affected in the early 2000s. An El Niño induced drought reduced power supplies and stopped shipment of exports from the huge Ok Tedi copper mine in 2002, drastically reducing Papua New Guinea's export earnings. Local landowner unrest led to power pylons supplying the Porgera gold mine being destroyed shortly afterwards. This resulted in the closure of the mine and a loss of 1000 jobs. Furthermore, a series of natural disasters in the period 2000 to 2002, including a volcanic eruption in East New Britain and an earthquake in East Sepik province, have also made economic development difficult.

QUESTION BLOCK 2E

1. *In your opinion, did Papua New Guinea's colonial development help or hinder its current economic development? Give reasons to support your answer.*

2. *From your knowledge of other LEDCs, to what extent is Papua New Guinea's experience of economic development typical of other countries?*

Table 2.4
Papua New Guinea's GNP, 1976 to 2009

Year	Total GNP (millions of $US)	GNP per Capita ($US)	PPP per Capita ($US)
1976	1,068	473	
1977	1,251		
1978	1,299	560	
1979	1,413		
1980	1,633	816	
1981	1,708		
1982	1,697		
1983	1,765		
1984	1,967	760	
1985	2,239	663	
1986	2,470	690	
1987	2,706	730	
1988	3,030	700	
1989	3,444	890	
1990	3,464	871	
1991	3,693	932	1,830
1992	4,005	950	1,972
1993	4,644	1,130	
1994	4,978	1,314	
1995	4,990	1,134	2,420
1996	5,049	1,150	2,650
1997	4,185	930	
1998	4,104	876	2,205
1999	3,834	810	2,260
2000	3,607	700	2,180
2001	2,959	586	
2002	2,793	515	
2003	3,395	641	1,682
2004	3,909	695	1,731
2005	3,870	851	2,563
2006	5,654	943	2,410
2007	5,925	991	2,100
2008	6,091	1,027	2,085
2009	6,432	1,081	2,166

Disparities in Papua New Guinea today

Overall, the benefits of economic development in Papua New Guinea have not been spread evenly. To some extent, this is because the country's rugged terrain makes the cost of developing infrastructure such as roads very high (figures 2.34 and 2.35). The country has no railways whatsoever, and rivers provide the major transport network (figure 2.36).

2.34 *Freight transport in many parts of Papua New Guinea is confined to walking tracks because of the rugged terrain and lack of continuous road networks.*

2.35 *Even where roads exist in Papua New Guinea, access can be slow, difficult and dangerous. This view shows a PMV (Public Motor Vehicle, or small bus) negotiating a section of road in the swamps of the Sepik River floodplain.*

Immediately before independence (in the 1960s and early 1970s), the proportion of GNP going to Papua New Guineans declined as the earnings of expatriates (foreign managers and workers) grew faster than those of nationals (local people). After independence in 1975, the emergence of a government administration comprising local people reversed this inequality. In 1976, 86.5% of Papua New Guinea's public service comprised local people, but

2.36 *Rivers are an important means of transport in Papua New Guinea, but this is mainly transport of people rather than freight.*

2.37 *As economic development occurs, markets develop. In this view, local growers sell surplus food at the central markets in the northern coastal town of Wewak. In the left background, several crude buses (known locally PMVs public motor vehicles) provide evidence of emerging transport networks.*

this figure had risen to 94.3% by 1985 and it is about 98% today.

In this context, the concerns of local Papua New Guineans centre on the profits of foreign corporations and investors. As long ago as 1986, John Momis, a member of Papua New Guinea's Parliament, expressed local people's concern that the benefits of development were being concentrated in the hands of just a few people:

"A small political elite is rapidly growing rich, very much at the expense of the majority.

Here I am not talking about the growing number of Papua New Guineans who are struggling to penetrate the presently foreign dominated economy of our country. Indeed, it is much to my sorrow that there is no middle class as such.

The small elite I am talking about comprises politicians, senior bureaucrats and some businessmen, including some large rural coffee and cocoa producers. But apart from the few big rural businessmen, most of the elite are rich through activities that would cause some political analysts to call them compradors-they spin off benefits of foreign investment and urban real estate markets, where land is kept artificially scarce by the very rich people reaping the benefits.

What is worse, many grow rich through the corruption which is becoming ever more prevalent amongst politicians and bureaucrats."

Mining projects in Papua New Guinea have provided high incomes for people working in these areas. However, because mining is so capital intensive, the direct benefits are limited to a small number of people. In any case, most of Papua New Guinea's population are engaged in subsistence food production, and have very little contact with the cash economy (figure 2.37). The main crops grown are sweet potato, taro, yams, bananas and sago.

2.38 *Small-scale processing of coffee beans beside the road in Chimbu Gorge, a densely populated valley in the Highlands.*

The manufacturing sector accounts for about 10% of Papua New Guinea's GNP. Most manufacturing focuses on small-scale initial processing of mining or agricultural products (figure 2.38). Papua New Guinea faces several problems in developing a viable manufacturing sector, including:

- the domestic market is small and fragmented;

- transport networks, and other infrastructure such as water and electricity, are poorly developed;

- there is a shortage of entrepreneurial, management and labour skills and experience;

- law and order are problems, especially in urban areas where theft, muggings and violent crime cause widespread fear;

- high absenteeism due to poor medical facilities that cannot cope with the large number and types of tropical diseases and widespread malnutrition;

- high dropout rates from schools (especially among girls) means the population is largely unskilled;

- land ownership problems (because 97% of the land is under tribal laws, industrialists often find it extremely difficult and costly to obtain suitable land); and

- high wages and low productivity of workers compared with nearby countries in Asia.

Like most LEDCs, Papua New Guinea wishes to replace imported manufactured goods with local products, wherever possible, to save foreign currency. However, these problems made the development of manufacturing a major challenge.

The question of whether or not development in Papua New Guinea has been evenly distributed depends on the indicator of development used. In the sections that follow, a number of indicators will be examined: income distribution, health care, education and government services.

Income distribution

Papua New Guinea's GDP per capita was $US1950 in 2006. At that time, Papua New Guinea ranked 136th among the 178 nations surveyed annually in terms of GDP per capita, and 149th in terms of HDI. However, within the country there are major differences between at least four groups:

1. A small number of expatriates (Europeans) and an elite group of nationals in senior jobs. There are about 15,000 such people, and their average annual incomes are about 20 times higher than citizens in the rest of the workforce (figure 2.39).

2. About 43,000 nationals are employed by the government, earning on average double or triple the national average income.

3. Smallholders on oil palm estates in West New Britain, probably the most affluent rural producers, earn about double the average annual income, but all other rural producers would earn much less.

4. It is very difficult to impute an income value on the output of subsistence producers, but it has been estimated to be about $US 400 per annum (figure 2.40).

As time goes on, the gaps between these groups should narrow for several reasons. First, as nationals take over expatriates jobs, middle and higher incomes will become available to more and more local people. Second, more and more people are taking up cash cropping to supplement their subsistence production, giving them access to increased incomes.

Income differences do not have an even geographical distribution. Because most expatriates and government employees live in the towns or on resource projects, the provinces with the larger towns also have the larger average incomes. Moreover, because the major areas of cash cropping tend to be near towns, the effect is heightened. Thus, the areas of higher incomes tend to be urban and coastal.

2.39 *An area of high incomes — the Port Moresby suburb of Boroko.*

2.40 *An area of low incomes — the Sepik River village of Maramba.*

Health status and health care services

It is very difficult to collect accurate health statistics in a developing nation such as Papua New Guinea. Although most births now occur in hospitals or clinics, most deaths due to pneumonia, gastroenteritis or malaria occur away from hospitals in remote villages and at home. It is known that malnutrition is common in some isolated parts of the country. Indicators of health status and health services for each province are given in figure 2.41.

In this figure, two measures of health care are used. Health status is based on estimates of rural life expectancy and two measures of child health. Health service is based on the number of health extension officers and aid posts per unit of population and travelling time to aid posts.

Health status is lowest in the Highlands (possibly due to malnutrition) and in some of the malarial, swampy, lowland provinces (e.g. Sepik, Gulf), and highest in the island provinces where there is less malaria, where food sources

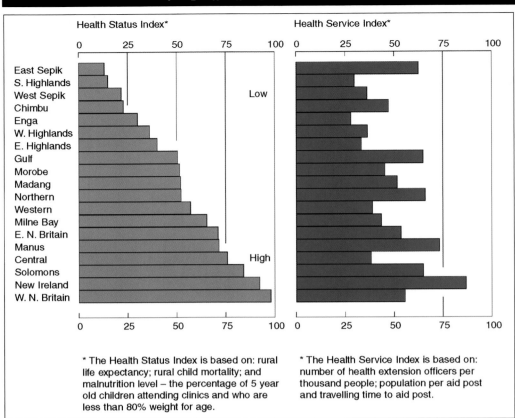

2.41 *Health status and health service indicators. The location of the provinces listed can be seen in figure 1.42.*

* The Health Status Index is based on: rural life expectancy; rural child mortality; and malnutrition level – the percentage of 5 year old children attending clinics and who are less than 80% weight for age.

* The Health Service Index is based on: number of health extension officers per thousand people; population per aid post and travelling time to aid post.

is based on both adult literacy and beginning enrolments in primary and secondary schools. It shows that educational services are distributed very unevenly among the provinces. The Highlands are disadvantaged by a double handicap – the lateness of the region's first contact with the outside world (which happened only in the 1930s), and the high density of the population. On the other hand, the coastal ports and their hinterlands have retained the advantage they gained from earlier contact with the outside world.

are more varied, and where smallholder farmers are richer. However, there are some strong contrasts between health services and health status. Health services are equally well provided in East Sepik and Gulf as in the islands, but these provinces still have a low health status.

It is important to remember that as an LEDC, even those schools which are better equipped may seem quite poor compared with schools in MEDCs.

Educational status

Education is seen in Papua New Guinea as a major key to personal advancement. It is highly prized by local people, and governments have always emphasised it strongly. In Papua New Guinea, the Education Department receives the largest allocation of government funds of all departments. However, school enrolments decline sharply as the level of education increases, and girls are especially poorly represented at higher levels. Educational status is shown in figure 2.42. This education index

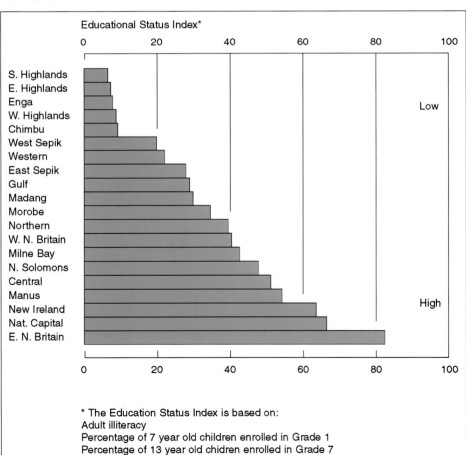

2.42 *Education status indicator. The location of the provinces listed can be seen in figure 1.42.*

* The Education Status Index is based on:
Adult illiteracy
Percentage of 7 year old children enrolled in Grade 1
Percentage of 13 year old chidren enrolled in Grade 7

2.43 *Inside the community school that is shown in figure 1.47. In this classroom there are no seats, and children sit cross-legged on the floor, resting a board across their laps to use as a desk.*

2.44 *Inside the library of Passam National High School, a well-equipped selective school south of Wewak.*

Figures 2.43 and 2.44 give an insight into the range of schools that are found in just one province (East Sepik) of Papua New Guinea.

Government services

Government services can be analysed by looking at the number of government officers per 1000 people in an

area. Once again, this measure shows a large gap between the Highlands on one hand (disadvantaged) and the islands (advantaged) on the other. However, the contrast is not as great as with the indicators for health or education (figure 2.45).

QUESTION BLOCK 2F

1. *In what ways has economic development affected Papua New Guinea unevenly? Give specific examples of provinces/areas in your answer.*

2. *What factors have led to inequalities in Papua New Guinea's economic development? Give specific examples of provinces/areas in your answer.*

3. *Make four copies of the map showing Papua New Guinea's provinces (figure 1.42). On each copy, colour the four provinces with the highest standards green, and the four provinces with the poorest standards red, using one copied map to show the information in figure 2.42, another copied map for figure 2.45 and two copies to show the two sets of data in figure 2.41).*

4. *Whenever economic development occurs, some people gain while others suffer. Has this been true for Papua New Guinea? Illustrate your argument with specific examples, facts and figures.*

Disparities and Change

Global Variations in Development

The links and interactions between the world's nations have never been stronger than they are today. **Globalisation**, which is the spread and acceptance of economic, social and cultural ideas across the world, is building linkages across national borders in the areas of economics, technology, culture and communications. The impact of globalisation is explained in greater detail in chapters 12 to 18.

The overall gains in economic development that have occurred are sometimes spectacular. Average world death rates of children fell by 55% between 1965 and 2008, and a child born today can expect to live 12 years longer than a child born in 1965. In LEDCs, the proportion of children enrolled in primary school has increased from less than half to about three-quarters. Furthermore, adult literacy rates have improved from 48% in 1970 to 82% in 2005. Global wealth also increased in material terms, and during the period 1947 to 2007, average per capita incomes more than tripled as global GDP increased 18-fold (from \$US3 trillion to \$US54 trillion).

Although these improvements are impressive, they mask huge differences from person to person, and between different countries. For example:

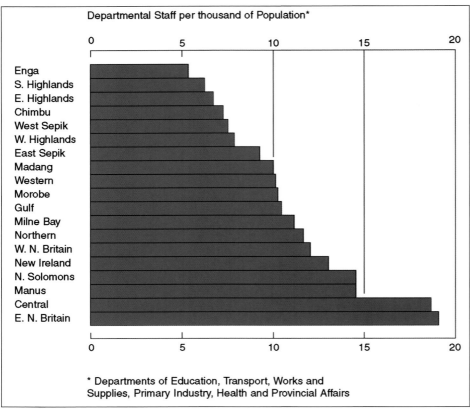

2.45 *Government officers staffing indicator. The location of the provinces listed can be seen in figure 1.42. (after Wilson & Woods)*

These points highlight the vast differences that exist, but they do little to help us get an overall picture or gain a total perspective. Table 2.1 attempts to provide a suitable framework to analyse the global variations in development that exist. The table lists a selection of countries and gives a variety of indicators of development, both quantitative and composite.

The data in table 2.1 suggest that high HDI countries tend to be in North America, Europe and Australasia, while low HDI countries tend to be in parts of Asia and Africa. However, as table 2.1 includes data for only 30 countries, we need to explore data for all countries before making any conclusions about the pattern of global variations in development. Table 2.5 ranks the top 5 and bottom 5 countries using the composite indicators of development discussed in the previous section.

- The three richest people in the world, Warren Buffett, Carlos Slim and Bill Gates, had total assets of $US180 billion (in 2008), which was greater than the GDP of the world's 57 least developed countries;

- Over 25% of the 5.5 billion people in LEDCs still have life expectancies below 40 years;

- More than 80 countries had a lower annual per capita income in 2008 than they did in 1995;

- Average income in the world's five richest countries is about 80 times the level of the poorest five, the widest the inequality gap has ever been;

- About 2.6 billion people have no access to clean water;

- About 115 million primary school aged children do not attend school, two-thirds of whom are girls;

- A Bangladeshi would need to save all of his or her wages for eight years to buy a computer; an American needs only one month's salary;

- The number of telephones per 100 people in Afghanistan is one; in Monaco it is 99;

- 20% of the world's people live in South Asia, but it has less than 1% of the world's internet users;

- About 2.7 billion people survive on incomes of less than two dollars (US) per day.

Table 2.5

Top and Bottom 5 Countries according to Composite Indicators of Development, 2008

Index	Top 5 Countries	Lowest 5 Countries
HDI	1. Iceland 2. Norway 3. Australia 4. Canada 5. Ireland	5th last. Mali 4th last. Niger 3rd last. Guinea-Bissau 2nd last. Burkina Faso Lowest. Sierra Leone
GDI	1. Iceland 2. Australia 3. Norway 4. Canada 5. Sweden	5th last. Central African Republic 4th last. Burkina Faso 3rd last. Niger 2nd last. Guinea-Bissau Lowest. Sierra Leone
GEM	1. Norway 2. Sweden 3. Finland 4. Denmark 5. Iceland	5th last. Kyrgyzstan 4th last. Turkey 3rd last. Egypt 2nd last. Saudi Arabia Lowest. Yemen
HPI-1	1. Barbados 2. Uruguay 3. Chile 4. Argentina 5. Costa Rica	5th last. Niger 4th last. Ethiopia 3rd last. Burkina Faso 2nd last. Mali Lowest. Chad
HPI-2	1. Sweden 2. Norway 3. Netherlands 4. Finland 5. Denmark	5th last. Spain 4th last. United Kingdom 3rd last. United States 2nd last. Ireland Lowest. Italy

Source: UNDP

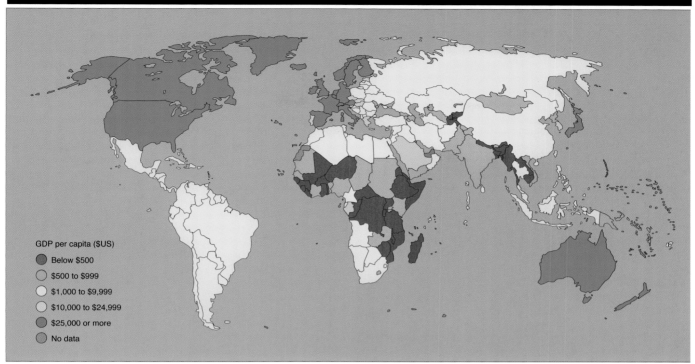

2.46 *World distribution of GNP per capita, 2007*

The data in tables 2.1 and 2.5, and in figures 2.46 to 2.48 all indicate that the LEDCs are concentrated in certain parts of the world. In general, the poorer countries are found in the tropical parts of Africa and in some scattered parts of south and south-east Asia. Similarly, the most highly developed economies tend to be found in North America and western Europe, with Japan and Australia being isolated exceptions to this generalisation.

Having said this, there are significant differences in many countries' rankings of development according to the measure used. This was seen clearly in tables 2.1 and 2.5. Although quantitative measures such as GNP per capita and composite measures such as HDI give broadly similar findings on which countries are most developed and which are least developed, there are some important differences. Table 2.6 lists a selection of countries with similar HDIs but quite different levels of income, while figure 2.49 shows an example of two countries with similar incomes but very different HDIs.

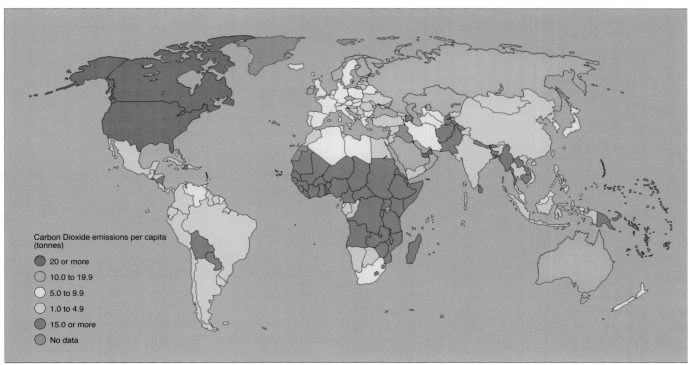

2.47 *World distribution of carbon dioxide emissions per capita, 2005.*

Disparities in wealth and development

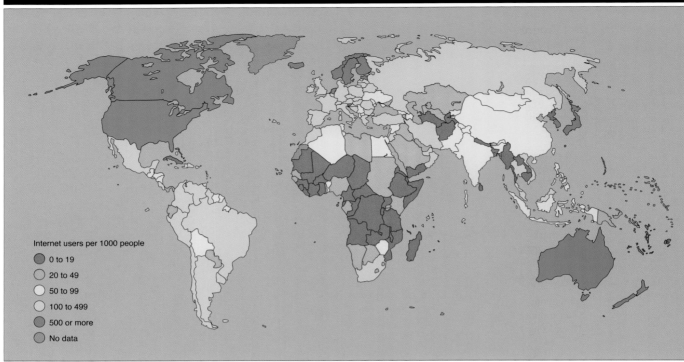

2.48 *World distribution of telephone fixed lines and mobile phone subscribers, 2006.*

Table 2.6

Three pairs of countries with similar HDI but differing incomes

| Country | HDI Value (2005) | The three factors contributing to HDI | | |
		Life expect-ancy at birth (years) 2006	Adult literacy rate (%) 2005	Real PPP GNI per capita ($US) 2007
Greece	0.926	79	96	32,520
Singapore	0.922	80	93	48,520
Turkey	0.775	71	87	12,090
Suriname	0.774	70	90	7,640
Botswana	0.654	50	81	12,420
Morocco	0.646	71	52	3,990

Source: UNDP

Changing Rates of Development

It is important to understand that economic development is not a static state for a country, but a dynamic process of change. The rate of change in GDP per capita between 1990 and 2005 is shown in figure 2.50. This figure presents quite a different distribution to the general patterns of world development that have been described above. In general, the most rapidly developing economies during the 15-year period were in southern and western South America, and in South, South-East and East Asia. These countries are often referred to as the **tiger economies** because of their rapid economic growth. Countries with particularly rapid and sustained growth between 190 and 2005 included China (8.8% p.a.), South Korea (4.5% p.a.), and Vietnam (5.9% p.a.).

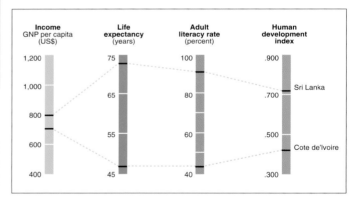

2.49 *Two countries with similar income but different human development – the case of Sri Lanka and Côte d'Ivoire.*

On the other hand, figure 2.50 also shows many countries where GDP per capita actually declined during the period 1990 to 2005. These countries fell into three main groups. The first group comprised many of the countries that were parts of the former Soviet Union until it dissolved in 1991, or were former communist countries in Eastern Europe. The process of adjusting to a market economy has forced many inefficient factories and companies to close, and this has affected economic growth and development, causing severe hardship to many people. Examples of countries where real GDP per capita fell markedly between 1990 and 2005 include Russia, Ukraine, Turkmenistan, Tajikistan and Kyrgyzstan.

Table 2.7
Fastest and Slowest Progress in Human Development, 1975 - 2005

	Country	1975 HDI	2005 HDI
Countries starting from high human development (0.800 to 1.000)			
Fastest Progress	Australia	0.844	0.962
	Norway	0.859	0.968
	Canada	0.868	0.961
Slowest Progress	Austria	0.840	0.948
	New Zealand	0.849	0.943
	Denmark	0.868	0.949
Countries starting from medium human development (0.500 to 0.799)			
Fastest Progress	Singapore	0.722	0.922
	South Korea	0.691	0.921
	Hong Kong	0.756	0.937
Slowest Progress	South Africa	0.649	0.674
	Romania	0.755	0.813
	Zimbabwe	0.547	0.513
Countries starting from low human development (0 to 0.499)			
Fastest Progress	Indonesia	0.469	0.728
	Egypt	0.435	0.708
	Swaziland	0.412	0.547
Slowest Progress	Burundi	0.280	0.413
	C.A.R	0.333	0.384
	Zambia	0.449	0.434

Source: UNDP

The second group of countries whose GDP per capita has declined are found in central areas of Africa. Many of these countries have been affected by AIDS/HIV, reducing average life expectancies and leading to reduced productivity in the workforce. In some cases, political instability has aggravated the economic decline. Examples of African countries affected in these ways include Congo, Sierra Leone and Zimbabwe.

The third group of countries with declining GDP per capita were the Arab oil producing states of the Arabian Peninsula. These countries are heavily dependent on oil exports for their income, and falling oil prices during the 1990s and early 2000s reduced incomes. Examples of countries affected in this way included Qatar, the United Arab Emirates and Saudi Arabia.

When composite indicators of development are examined, the changing pattern of economic development becomes more complex. Table 2.7 lists the fastest and slowest progress in human development (using the HDI) over the period 1975 to 2005 for the 179 countries for which data was collected.

Table 2.7 shows that almost no countries are experiencing a declining HDI – Zimbabwe and Zambia were the sole exceptions. However, it can also be seen that in general, the medium and high human development countries are improving at a faster rate than the low human development countries. In other words, although the level of development is rising (almost) everywhere, the gap between the rich and poor countries is widening.

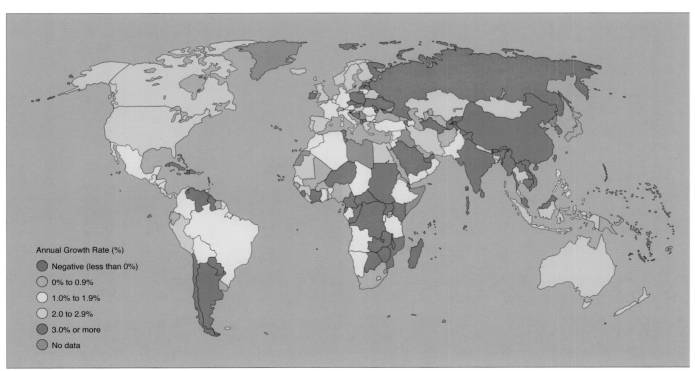

Annual Growth Rate (%)
- Negative (less than 0%)
- 0% to 0.9%
- 1.0% to 1.9%
- 2.0 to 2.9%
- 3.0% or more
- No data

2.50 *Rates of growth in GNP per capita, 1990-2005.*

QUESTION BLOCK 2G

1. *Provide evidence that shows substantial gains have occurred in world economic development.*

2. *Provide evidence that shows some substantial setbacks have occurred in world economic development.*

3. *What is the basis for the rank order of the countries in table 2.1?*

4. *For each indicator of development shown in table 2.1, list the 'most developed' and the 'least developed' country.*

5. *For each indicator in table 2.1, describe briefly how it relates to economic development.*

6. *From your answer to the previous question, write about two pages to describe and suggest reasons for the global pattern of disparities in life expectancy, education and income.*

7. *Choose three countries in table 2.1, one from each of the three development bands, and write about 12 lines to contrast their economic development.*

8. *Which of the indicators in table 2.1 do you think is least effective in describing development? Explain why you chose this indicator.*

9. *Use figure 2.50 to write about 12 lines describing the distribution of (a) rapidly growing economies, and (b) slow growing and stagnant economies.*

10. *Suggest reasons for the pattern you have described in your answer to the last question.*

Forces Affecting Different Rates of Economic Development

The reasons that a country's economy develops quickly or slowly are complex, and in many ways unique for each country. The factors affecting the rate of economic development may be political, social, physical or historical.

Another way to look at the forces affecting economic development is to consider **external forces**, which are forces affecting the country from elsewhere, and **internal forces**, which are factors operating from within the country. Examples of external forces include culture contact, trade, financial flows and investment, technological change, transnational corporations, and bilateral and multilateral agreements. Examples of internal forces include transport and other infrastructure, political systems and planning, population change, availability of natural resources, and internal capital formation. We will now consider each of these forces.

External forces

Historically, **culture contact** played a significant role in economic development. For countries that were colo-

nised by European powers, colonisation brought mixed blessings. On one hand, many resources were exported at very low prices with few direct benefits for the colony. On the other hand, transport and other **infrastructure** were often built, some of which still operates today. Of course, the infrastructure was designed to help the colonial power rather than the local population, and so railways (to take one example) were often built to the sites of mines or other resources rather than to centres of population. Notwithstanding these problems, culture contact inevitably brings new ideas to a country, some of which may be beneficial in speeding economic development.

2.51 *Trade enables countries to gain access to resources they lack. For many centuries, these large traditional sailing vessels have been bringing scarce timber from coastal regions of West Africa to inland areas of the Sahel Desert along the Niger River.*

Trade between countries allows countries to exchange resources and products it has in abundance for other goods that it lacks. In this way, trade helps most countries to advance, presuming the terms of trade are negotiated fairly for all parties (figure 2.51). Japan lacks most natural resources, but through trade it has overcome these shortcomings and has developed economically to a very high level.

2.52 *This water well has been donated as a gift by a British Islamic organisation to a small village near Kouroukou in central Mali. Providing a clean water supply brings great benefits for people's health as well as economic development.*

Financial flows into a country can help economic development by providing funds for investment that the country itself lacks. These funds allow factories to be built and resources to be developed, providing employment and taxation revenue for the government that can be used to provide services and build infrastructure elsewhere in the country. Of course, unless the financial flow is a gift in the form of aid, overseas investors always demand a profit on their investments, so the other side of financial flows is the outflow of profits and interest payments (figure 2.52). Today, the need to repay debt on borrowings and the profits on investments means that the net flow of money in the world is from LEDCs to MEDCs.

When foreign investment occurs in a country, it is often accompanied by an inflow of new technology, leading to **technological change**, new techniques and ways of doing things. Provided that the technology is appropriate for the country, this usually helps to encourage economic development. LEDCs usually have little capital (money) but large numbers of people, making wages cheap but machinery expensive. This '**resource endowment**' is the opposite of most MEDCs, which have shortages of labour (and thus high wages) but abundant money to invest in machinery (which is therefore relatively cheap). It follows from this that the technology which is suitable for an MEDC, such as a labour saving machine, will not be appropriate for an LEDC, which would have to find scarce money to buy a machine to replace labour, which is abundant. Appropriate technology for an LEDC will therefore be cheap, and will allow production processes to remain fairly labour intensive.

2.53 *Investment by transnational corporations brings cultural changes as well as economic expansion, as seen here where Coca-Cola is being distributed on the back of a donkey in Fez. Morocco.*

Transnational corporations can play an important role in LEDCs these days. Like colonisation, they can be a mixed blessing for LEDCs, and indeed some people believe that transnational corporations are a new form of colonialism in which corporations rather than countries oppress less powerful groups of people, but do so economically rather than politically (figure 2.53). Benefits that transnational corporations can bring to LEDCs include the investment

funds and the new technology they bring, but there are often large social costs as inappropriate capital intensive technology is sometimes imported from the home country such as USA, Japan, UK or France. Another difficulty is that transnational corporations have the flexibility to adjust the buying and selling prices of raw materials and components within the corporation to shift their profits to countries with low rates of taxation, and their losses to countries with higher rates of taxation. This flexibility is a strong incentive for LEDCs to minimise the rates of taxation they charge transnational corporations, reducing the financial benefits that may have otherwise arisen.

Bilateral (between two countries) and **multilateral** (between several countries) trade agreements can assist the economic development of countries within the agreement, but may slow the economic development for countries outside the agreement.

Internal forces

2.54 *Modern electric trams provide low pollution transport in Athens, Greece. Compare the transport infrastructure shown here with that in the next photo.*

2.55 *This river ferry near Djenné in Mali (an LEDC) uses a combination of human and diesel power to move vehicles across the river. In an MEDC, such a frequently used narrow river crossing would normally be served by a bridge.*

Turning to internal forces affecting the rate of economic development, **transport** and other infrastructure are very significant (figures 2.54 and 2.55). **Infrastructure** refers to the services and facilities needed to support productive activities, and as well as transport, examples include telecommunications, electricity, water, port facilities and other public services (figures 2.56 and 2.57). It is a general principle that countries with a high level of infrastructure will develop more rapidly than countries that do not have these facilities, everything else (such as political systems and levels of corruption) being equal.

2.56 *With a population of 1.3 million people, Dallas (Texas, USA) has several important industries, including banking, commerce, telecommunications, computer technology, energy, and transportation. Its well-developed infrastructure is essential to support hi-tech industry.*

2.57 *In comparison with the previous photo, the main street of Timbuktu in Mali shows little evidence of infrastructure, except perhaps the electricity lines beside the street.*

The **political systems** and **planning mechanisms** in a country also influence the rate of economic development. As a generalisation, economies with open policies towards trade and investment (such as Hong Kong, South Korea, Canada and Australia) have faster and more stable economic growth than economies with closed or less transparent political systems (such as North Korea, Russia and Saudi Arabia). In some countries, the nature of the political system influences the type of economic development that occurs. For example, the government in

Myanmar supports central planning and discourages foreign trade, and so a large proportion of the country's trade and economic growth comes from smuggling operations across the border with Thailand and, according to some sources, drug production in the hill areas near the Thai, Lao and Chinese borders where government control is weak.

Rapid population growth is considered by some people to slow down economic development, although opinions differ on this point. Malthusians argue that each extra person is a consumer, taking a share from a fixed pool of resources. Followers of writers such as Julian Simon and Bjørn Lomborg, on the other hand, argue that each extra person is a productive resource that produces more than it consumes, and providing creativity that solves problems and thus improves productivity. As we saw in chapter 1, there is no clear correlation between the rate of population growth and the rate of economic development.

At first sight, we would expect that **availability of natural resources** would significantly affect the rate of economic development. We would expect that the more natural resources a country possesses, the faster would be its rate of economic growth. In fact, there are examples of wealthy economies with very few natural resources (such as Japan, Hong Kong and the Netherlands) as well as wealthy countries with abundant resources (such as USA, Germany, Canada and Australia). Similarly, there are poor countries with abundant natural resources, such as Papua New Guinea, Myanmar, Venezuela and Nigeria – such countries either do not have the population or the finance to develop the resources, or the bureaucracy or corruption is so great that the rate of economic development is impeded.

Internal capital formation means the ability of a country to find its own funds to invest in development projects. People in LEDCs typically earn low incomes, forcing them to spend a large proportion of their income on basic necessities such as food, clothing and shelter. This leaves very little surplus for savings, and therefore banks have very little funds available for investment. This creates a cycle of impoverishment, known as the **Vicious Cycle of Poverty** (figure 2.58). In summary, low incomes lead to low investment, which lead to low levels of savings, which lead to low levels of productivity, which perpetuate low incomes. Unless some way can be found to break the vicious cycle of poverty, it becomes self-perpetuating.

In cases where the vicious cycle of poverty is broken successfully, the foundation of sustainable economic development is usually agriculture (figure 2.59). In LEDCs, a large proportion of the population are farmers. Therefore, if development is to have an impact on most of the population, it must have an impact on the agricultural sector of the economy. A sound farming sector is needed:
- to provide a food surplus to feed city dwellers;

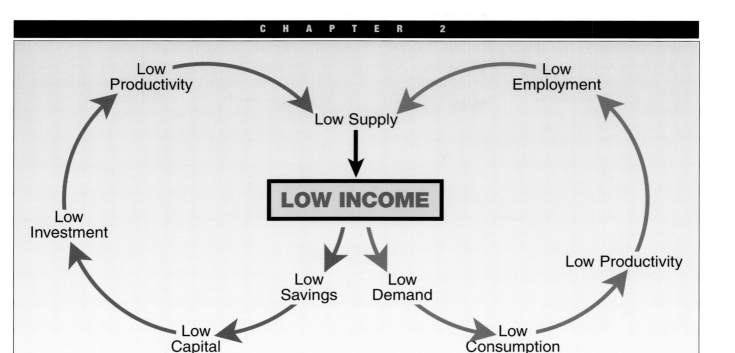

2.58 *The Vicious Cycle of Poverty.*

- to provide surplus labour for growing manufacturing and service sectors of the economy;
- to enlarge exports;
- to provide a market for manufactured goods; and
- to show the bulk of the population that development is actually occurring.

2.59 *Traditional labour-intensive farming methods are still very common in many parts of the world. This yak-drawn wooden plough is being used in a remote area near Bendiwan village in Tiger Leaping Gorge, south-west China.*

A more complete analysis of the importance of agriculture in providing a basis for sound economic development is shown in figure 2.62.

Millennium Development Goals (MDGs)

Widespread growing concern about the disastrous effects of the widening disparities between rich and poor in the world led the United Nations to adopt a set of eight goals to be achieved through international co-operation by

2015. These eight goals, which contain 21 specific targets, have become known as the **Millennium Development Goals** (MDGs). The MDGs, which were supported by the 189 member countries of the United Nations in 2000, are as follows:

1. **Eradicate extreme poverty and hunger:**
   - Halve, between 1990 and 2015, the proportion of people whose income is less than $1 a day.
   - Achieve full and productive employment and decent work for all, including women and young people.
   - Halve, between 1990 and 2015, the proportion of people who suffer from hunger.

2. **Achieve universal primary education:**
   - Ensure that, by 2015, children everywhere, boys and girls alike, will be able to complete a full course of primary schooling (figure 2.60).

2.60 *A primary school class at Chinsapo, an outer suburb if Lilongwe, capital city of Malawi.*

3. **Promote gender equality and empower women:**
   - Eliminate gender disparity in primary and secondary education, preferably by 2005, and in all levels of education no later than 2015.

4. **Reduce child mortality:**
   - Reduce by two-thirds, between 1990 and 2015, the under-five mortality rate.

5. **Improve maternal health:**
   - Reduce by three quarters, between 1990 and 2015, the maternal mortality ratio.
   - Achieve, by 2015, universal access to reproductive health.

6. **Combat HIV/AIDS, malaria, and other diseases:**
   - Have halted by 2015 and begun to reverse the spread of HIV/AIDS (figure 2.61).
   - Have halted by 2015 and begun to reverse the incidence of malaria and other major diseases.

7. **Ensure environmental sustainability:**
   - Integrate the principles of sustainable development into country policies and programmes and reverse loss of environmental resources.
   - Reduce biodiversity loss, achieving, by 2010, a significant reduction in the rate of loss.
   - Halve, by 2015, the proportion of people without sustainable access to safe drinking water and basic sanitation.
   - By 2020, to have achieved a significant improvement in the lives of at least 100 million slum dwellers.

8. **Develop a global partnership for development:**
   - Address the special needs of the least developed countries, landlocked countries and small island developing states.
   - Develop further an open, rule-based, predictable, non-discriminatory trading and financial system.
   - Deal comprehensively with developing countries' debt.
   - In co-operation with pharmaceutical companies, provide access to affordable essential drugs in developing countries.
   - In co-operation with the private sector, make available the benefits of new technologies, especially information and communications.

At the time this book was written, more than half the MDG period (2000 to 2015) had passed, and while many important and significant gains had been made in several areas, it seemed unlikely that all the targets would be met.

2.61 *A poster promoting VCT (voluntary counselling and testing) for AIDS in a medical clinic in Bai Shui, a remote rural village in Guizhou province, China.*

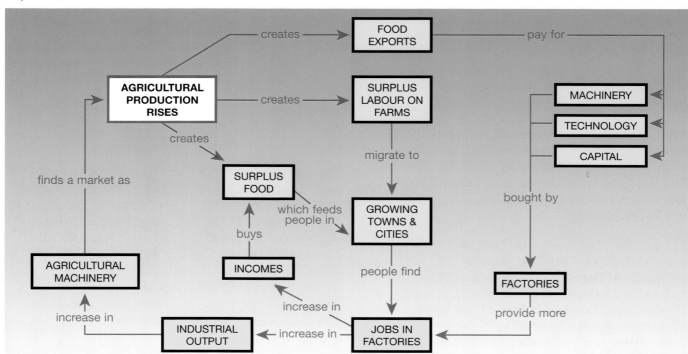

2.62 *The role of agriculture in economic development.*

1. *The United Nations maintains two websites with up-to-date reports on the progress of the Millennium Development Goals. The URLs of the sites are http://www.undp.org/mdg/ and http://www.un.org/millenniumgoals/. Visit these sites and analyse the progress made in the areas of poverty reduction, education and health.*

2. *The primary school class shown in figure 2.60 is a co-educational group in Chinsapo, an outer district of Lilongwe, the capital city of Malawi. Estimate the approximate proportion of girls in the class.*

Reducing Disparities

The Millennium Development Goals represent one of the most ambitious attempts the world has ever seen to harness international co-operation in order to reduce global disparities. Nonetheless, there are other important strategies that have also been shown to help reduce the gaps between rich and poor in the world.

Reducing Disparities through Industrialisation, Trade and Market Access

The first country to develop economically at a rapid rate was Britain, where industrialisation began with the construction of textile mills in the late 1700s. This pathway to development, known as the Industrial Revolution, was successfully copied by other countries in Europe and North America, and by Japan. Therefore, many LEDCs see industrialisation as the key to economic development.

Traditional manufacturing in LEDCs tends to be small in scale and labour intensive (figures 2.63 and 2.64). This is not as inefficient as it might first appear to outsiders. LEDCs tend to have an abundance of labour and a shortage of capital. Therefore, labour tends to be cheap while machinery tends to be expensive, and so it makes good economic sense to use people rather than machinery. MEDCs tend to have the opposite **endowment of resources**, and labour is scarce (and therefore expensive) while capital is plentiful (and therefore relatively cheap). This is why the common practice of replacing people with machines that is practised in MEDCs is inappropriate when applied in LEDCs.

The main advantage of industrialisation to LEDCs is that it allows **import substitution**. This means that it becomes possible to replace imported goods with products manufactured in the country itself, therefore saving scarce foreign currency. However, before industrialisation can occur, agriculture must be developed and commercialised to the point where it is producing enough surplus food to feed the industrial workers. Furthermore, it is important that the manufacturing industries which are developed

should produce goods which can find a market. In LEDCs where most of the population are farmers, this suggests that low-cost goods which can improve the productivity of farmers should be the priority.

2.63 *Manufacturing in LEDCs often involves the processing of raw materials produced by primary industries. This example shows the tanning of animal hides to produce leather in Marrakesh, Morocco.*

2.64 *In this example of labour intensive manufacturing, a woman provides the power to spin a pottery wheel with her foot while a man fashions a clay pot. It will be fired in a kiln fuelled by burning timber branches.*

One technique that several LEDCs have found effective in promoting manufacturing activity is developing **export processing zones** (EPZs). These zones are specially set aside areas with special regulations designed to encourage foreign investment in industries that will manufacture goods for export. Among the incentives offered to foreign firms are tax holidays, low interest loans, cheap labour, exemption from normal import taxes and duties, and assistance with setting up companies, offices and factories.

EPZs were first introduced in India and Puerto Rico during the 1960s, but the most successful examples are the

Special Economic Zones (SEZs) of China, where zones of capitalism are permitted in what is officially a socialist economy. The first large SEZ in China was in Shenzhen, which is situated against the Chinese side of the border with Hong Kong (figure 2.65). This SEZ was established in the early 1980s, and growth has been both rapid and successful. Since the return of Hong Kong to China in June 1997, manufacturing in Shenzhen and Hong Kong has become increasingly integrated. Several other SEZs have also been established in China. One of the most successful new SEZs is Pudong, an SEZ the size of Singapore on the east bank of the Huangpu River across from Shanghai (figure 2.66).

2.65 *Rapid change is seen throughout the Pearl River Delta, and Shenzhen is a spectacular example. In 1980 the area shown here was vacant land on the edge of a small fishing village. By 2005, Shenzhen had a population of over 8.5 million people, of whom 7 million were migrants from other parts of China. Shenzhen's population has an average age below 26 years. By 2008, Shenzhen had become a megacity with a population of almost 12 million people.*

2.66 *A section of Riverside Park, a large area of open space beside the Huangpu River in Pudong's Lujiazui Finance and Trade Zone. Scenes such as this are the dream of planners for Shanghai's future as a megacity.*

Reducing Disparities through Debt Relief

One of the most significant problems facing many LEDCs is paying the interest costs and repaying the borrowings on long-term debts. Some LEDCs are in serious trouble because their total debt exceeds their annual income, which means that these countries are technically bankrupt.

The current situation regarding global debt has grown over several decades. Most LEDCs are producers of primary products. These countries must earn income from the export of these commodities if they are to have the money to pay for imports of manufactured goods produced in MEDCs. However, the long-term trend of the past 50 years has been for the prices of primary product exports from LEDCs to have risen much less than the prices of the goods they wished to import. This has meant that the LEDCs have had to produce more and more of their exports simply to keep pace with the cost of imports. We say that the **terms of trade** have turned against the LEDCs because their imports have become relatively more expensive over time. As the situation is sometimes expressed, the LEDCs 'have to run just to stand still'. It is to overcome this problem that many LEDCs have tried to develop their manufacturing and tourism industries, as discussed in chapter 9.

Another strategy followed by many LEDCs was to borrow money from banks in MEDCs, and use these funds to invest in economic development projects such as factories, dams, railways and buildings. Many LEDCs found that the profits from these projects were less than anticipated, and so additional borrowing was needed to sustain the projects. This situation became an ongoing **debt trap** for many LEDCs. Today, the debt situation is so severe that many LEDCs are paying far more in debt repayments than they are receiving in aid payments from the same countries.

The problem of LEDC debt is a major one. The banks which lent the money are unwilling simply to wipe billions of dollars which are owed to them. However, for many LEDCs the debt has grown so large that it is quite impossible for it all to be repaid.

Reducing Disparities through Ecologically Sustainable Development

Development, and the gaps which exist between rich and poor in the world, have only been studied seriously since World War II ended in 1945. Since that time, there have been several phases of study with different emphases. The stages in thinking about development issues are shown in table 2.8.

During the **structural change** phase of the 1940s to the 1960s, it was argued that all countries would pass through a set of stages of economic development if given enough time. The pathway to development was seen as the route followed by Western Europe and North America during the Industrial Revolution. Following a model

Table 2.8

A brief history of ideas and strategies in development

School of Thought	Time Period	Main Ideas	Real World Strategies
Structural Change	1940s to 1960s	• Progressive stages of economic growth • Economic structural change • Trickle-down economics	• Investment • Technology transfer • Large-scale industrialisation projects
Dependency	1970s	• Emphasis on human welfare • Core-periphery model • Circular and cumulative causation • Neo-colonialism • Bottom-up economics	• Small scale and rural enterprises • Import substitution • Appropriate technology •Nationalisation
Neo-Liberal Counter-revolution	1980s	• Free market economics	• Privatisation • Foreign direct investment • Reduced role of government • Free global trade • Currency devaluation
Sustainable Development	1990s to 2000s	• Global environmental change • Environmental (green) economics	• Partnerships between LEDCS and MEDCs • Market mechanisms for environmental regulation • Resource conservation • Renewable resources

Source: Based on Kuby, M., Harner, J. & Gober, P. (1998), p.8-4

proposed by the US economist W.W. Rostow, it was argued that countries would progress through five stages – from a traditional society, through economic 'take-off' and on through maturity to a stage of high mass consumption. This thinking led to investment in large-scale projects that would 'kick-start' LEDCs into a process of 'development catch-up'.

During the 1970s it was acknowledged that many LEDCs were not following this fixed pathway to development. Countries such as China, Vietnam, Tanzania and Cuba were deliberately following strategies which encouraged small-scale self-sufficient rural technology. These countries were seeking to initiate development from the countryside where most people lived rather than through large-scale manufacturing. This approach impressed many observers, and so the **dependency** approach to development gained favour.

The dependency approach was based on the **core-periphery** model of development. This model tries to explain the distribution of human activity by unequal distribution of power in politics, societies and economies. The model suggests that **growth poles** have developed where economic and political power is concentrated. These areas, concentrated in Western Europe and North

America, have become the **core** which dominates world economic activity. The core is the area where wealth is greatest, and intensity of economic activity declines as one moves away from the core. In contrast to the core, the **periphery** (edge) is much poorer and lacks the decision-making power of the core.

In general, the periphery produces raw materials at relatively low cost for the industrial core. The core, in turn, processes these raw materials and re-exports them to the periphery at a profit in the form of manufactured goods. Between the core and the periphery is an area which exerts more power than the periphery but less than the core. This is known as the **semi-periphery**, and Australia would fit into this zone.

The core-periphery model attempts to explain global patterns of development. However, it is also useful for describing the process of change that occurs within a country as economic development occurs (figure 2.67). Followers of the dependency approach use the core-periphery model, arguing that continuing lack of development in the LEDCs is due to the lack of power they have in their positions on the periphery of global decision-making. It is claimed that this situation of dependence began when many of the LEDCs were colo-

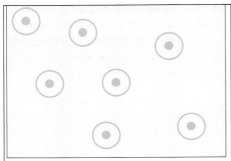

a. The preindustrial structure of independent local centres with small market areas and little interaction.

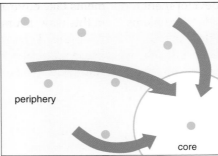

b. Early industrialisation brings concentration of investment, wealth, and power into a single, strong core. The periphery provides raw materials and labour to the core, while the core provides manufactured goods to the periphery. The net result is a draining of wealth from the periphery to the core.

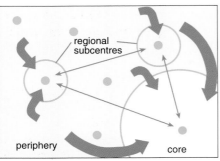

c. As industry develops, the core remains the dominant centre, but regional subcentres begin to emerge. The core and regional subcentres exchange manufactured goods and services while continuing to receive raw materials and labour from the periphery.

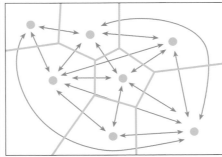

d. Ultimately a mature and functionally-interconnected space economy emerges in which the periphery has been absorbed into nearby metropolitan economies.

2.67 *The processes of industrialisation and economic development as described by the core-periphery model. Many countries remain in stages two or three, seemingly stalled in the global periphery and lacking a strong internal economy. This model could apply internationally or within a country.*

The definition of sustainable development presented in that report was 'development which meets the needs of the present without compromising the ability of future generations to meet their own needs'.

This definition was based on the principle of equity between generations, present and future. Using this definition, supporters of sustainable development argue that development must be done in such a way that the environment remains intact for future generations. Therefore, development that increases pollution, reduces the resource base, reduces biodiversity or changes the global environment is unacceptable because it cannot be sustained in the long-term.

In this context, sustainable development can be thought of as trying to achieve a balance between three types of sustainability — environmental sustainability, social sustainability and economic sustainability (figure 2.68).

nised, and continues today because the MEDCs (through transnational corporations) force them to produce unprofitable primary products. Certainly, many LEDCs are heavily dependent on single-product primary exports. Examples of this include Cuba (74% of whose exports are sugar), Cambodia (83% rubber), Zambia (85% copper) and Iraq (98% oil).

There was a reaction against the dependency model in the 1980s as free market economics dominated thinking in the US and UK. This led to a re-examination of development strategies, and the **neo-liberal counter-revolution** resulted. Followers of this approach argued that policies of encouraging and protecting small and inefficient industries in LEDCs was perpetuating dependency rather than curing it. It was argued that if LEDCs are to advance, they must do so with industries that are competitive with the rest of the world. In order to achieve this, protection should be removed, and the industries should either compete effectively or close down. Consequently, many LEDCs competed to attract foreign investment to introduce modern technology to upgrade inefficient industries.

In the 1990s, the concept of **sustainable development** came to dominate thinking. The concept of sustainable development first appeared in 1987 when the report of the World Commission on Environment and Development, known as the Brundtland Report, was published.

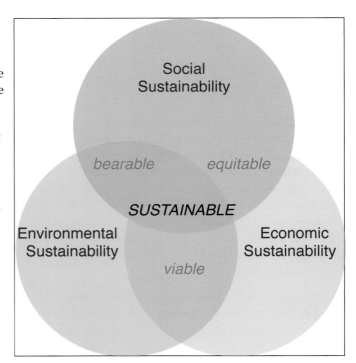

2.68 *A Model of Sustainable Development*
Source: World Conservation Union

There are several barriers to sustainable development. First, the heavy reliance on fossil fuels leads to problems such as acid rain, global warming, deforestation and health problems. Furthermore, reliance on fossil fuels perpetuates international inequalities by protecting the powerful positions of transnational oil and motor companies, which are among the largest TNCs. Transnational corporations can be defined as large business enterprises with a number of branches operating in several countries, but with usually a central head office in a developed country. The powers of TNCs transcend national boundaries, which is why they compete with the power of the nation-state, weakening the role of the nation-state in today's world.

2.69 *Sustainable development means meeting present needs while protecting the environment for future generations. Overgrazing here makes it unlikely that this man's children will be herding cattle in the same area.*

A second barrier to sustainable development is population growth. This was examined in detail in chapter 1. Brundtland argued that sustainable development is only possible if population grows in a way that is in harmony with the changing productive capacity of the world's ecosystems.

The third barrier to sustainable development is also the largest, according to the Brundtland Report. This barrier is the lack of a strong institutional framework to oversee the process of development. For sustainable development to occur, Brundtland argued that economic decisions must be fully integrated with ecological and environmental decision-making. In practice, few govern-

ments take environmental considerations into account in this way. Brundtland argued that unless there were widespread changes in people's attitudes and values and in the political will to implement changes, then sustainable development is unlikely to become a reality.

This last concern is very real. Most governments in LEDCs argue that while they would like to protect the environment, it is a luxury they cannot afford until their wealth increases. Such governments sometimes argue that concern for the environment is a luxury enjoyed by those who are already wealthy. 'Development is the absolute need' is the common argument (figures 2.1 and 2.69).

Perhaps the current challenge in studying development is to find a way in which sustainable development can become appealing, not only to people in LEDCs but everywhere. Economic development and preservation of the environment are not necessarily in conflict. In the words of Kuby, Harner and Gober:

"efficient energy and water use, renewable resources, pollution reduction, and protection of forests and wetlands actually make long-term economic sense. The sustainable development movement aims to help LEDCs skip the inefficient dependency on fossil-fuels that MEDCs experienced, and vault right to efficient, renewable technologies".

QUESTION BLOCK 2I

1. *Describe the different resource endowments of LEDCs and MEDCs, and explain why this makes the manufacturing shown in figures 2.63 and 2.64 quite efficient.*

2. *What is 'import substitution'? Why do many LEDCs seek to achieve import substitution?*

3. *What is an export processing zone?*

4. *How did debt among LEDCs grow into such a large problem?*

5. *Explain briefly how the idea of 'sustainable development' came about.*

6. *Describe the core-periphery model.*

7. *How realistic is it to think that Brundtland's three barriers to sustainable development can be overcome? Explain your answer.*

3 Patterns in environmental quality and sustainability

Changes in atmosphere, soils, water, biodiversity and sustainability

Outline

Atmosphere and change Page 100
The causes and environmental consequences of global climate change.

Soil and change Page 116
Causes of soil degradation, the environmental and socio-economic consequences of this process, together with management strategies.

Water and change Page 120
Ways water is used at the regional scale, environmental and human factors affecting patterns and trends in water scarcity, and factors affecting access to safe drinking water.

Biodiversity and change Page 129
The concept and importance of biodiversity in tropical rainforests, and the causes and consequences of reduced biodiversity in this biome.

Sustainability and the environment Page 136
The concept of environmental sustainability, and a management strategy designed to achieve environmental sustainability.

**ToK BoX — Page 114
Truth and Global Warming**

Atmosphere and Change

The Atmosphere

The atmosphere is like a thin film surrounding the earth. If the earth were the size of a soccer ball on a wet field, the atmosphere would be like the wet layer around it. In fact, the atmosphere is about 500 kilometres thick, although half the mass of the atmosphere is found in the lowest six kilometres and 99% of the atmosphere is contained in the lowest 40 kilometres.

Within the atmosphere there are four distinct layers, defined by whether the temperatures are rising or falling with altitude (figure 3.1). The layers are:

• **Thermosphere.** The thermosphere is the highest layer of the atmosphere, extending from about 80 kilometres above sea level out to the farthest limits of the atmosphere. The gases in this layer of the atmosphere are very thin, and the thermosphere makes up only 0.001% of the mass of the atmosphere. In fact, there is little difference between the thermosphere and a vacuum. The gases in this layer are oxygen, hydrogen and nitrogen, and these absorb ultra-violet radiation from the sun, heating up to very high temperatures exceeding 200°C and sometimes exceeding 1000°C.

• **Mesosphere.** The mesosphere is the second highest layer of the atmosphere, extending between about 50 and 80 kilometres above sea level. This is the coldest part of the atmosphere because there is very little cloud, dust, ozone or water vapour to absorb heat from the sun. The **mesopause**, which separates the mesosphere from the thermosphere above it, is always a constant -90°C. The mesosphere also has the strongest winds in the atmosphere, approaching 3,000 kilometres per hour in places.

• **Stratosphere.** The stratosphere is found below the mesosphere in a band from about 20 kilometres to 50

>> Some Useful Definitions

Global climate change — the changes in global patterns of rainfall and temperature, sea level, habitats and the incidences of droughts, floods and storms, resulting from changes in the Earth's atmosphere, believed to be mainly caused by the enhanced greenhouse effect.

Global scale — the world as a whole.

Local scale — areas of limited extent.

National scale — the area of a country.

Regional scale — an area that encompasses several countries sharing some common element (economic, political, locational).

Soil degradation — a severe reduction in the quality of soils. The term includes soil erosion, salinisation and soil exhaustion (loss of fertility).

Water scarcity — occurs in two forms: **physical water scarcity**, where water resource development is approaching or has exceeded unsustainable levels (this relates water availability to water demand and implies that arid areas are not necessarily water scarce); and **economic water scarcity**, where water is available locally but is not accessible for human, institutional or financial capital reasons.

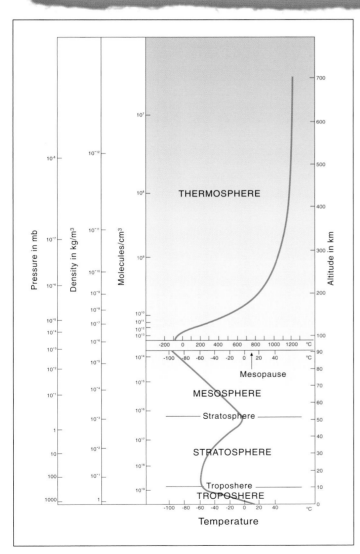

3.1 *A cross-section of the atmosphere showing the four layers and the temperatures at each level.*

- kilometres above sea level. There is a concentration of ozone in the stratosphere, and as ozone absorbs ultra-violet radiation very well, temperatures rise with increasing altitude in the stratosphere. In the lower parts of the stratosphere, most of the ultra-violet radiation has already been absorbed, so temperatures are cooler. The temperature at the top of the stratosphere is a fairly constant 0°C, but at its lower limit (the **tropopause**) the temperature is typically about -50°C.

- **Troposphere.** The troposphere is the lowest layer of the atmosphere, and it contains most of the mass of the atmosphere, as well as most of the dust, water vapour and pollution. It is the layer in which the weather occurs, and it behaves quite differently to the other three layers. Whereas the three upper layers obtain their heat directly from solar radiation, the troposphere is warmed indirectly by reflected heat from the earth's surface and clouds. Temperatures in the troposphere fall by about 6.5°C for every 1000 metres rise in altitude, although this figure varies from place to place. The troposphere comprises a mixture of gases, but the most important ones are nitrogen (78%), oxygen (21%), argon (almost 1%), and carbon dioxide (0.003%). Other gases such as hydrogen, helium, krypton, methane, neon, ozone and xenon together make up only 0.001% of the atmosphere. The troposphere also contains water vapour (the gaseous form of water), but the proportion of water vapour varies enormously from place to place and from day to day.

QUESTION BLOCK 3A

1. *Draw up a table to contrast the characteristics of the four layers of the earth's atmosphere.*

The Global Heat Budget and Atmospheric Circulation

All the processes of the atmosphere (and indeed all life on earth) depend on energy from the sun. The sun's energy is enormous. The surface area of the sun is 65 million billion square metres, and the energy sent from each square metre is enough to power one million light globes. A small part of the energy produced by the sun reaches the earth. The incoming solar radiation, known is **insolation**, arrives in the form of short-wave radiation. **Short-wave radiation** from the sun is mainly visible light towards the purple end of the spectrum with a wavelength of 0.39 to 0.76 µm (micrometres, or microns). The reason that the sun's energy is short-wave radiation is that the sun is so hot – 5300°C. Cooler bodies such as the moon and the earth, emit **long-wave radiation**, which is mainly infra-red heat with a wavelength of about 4 to 30 µm.

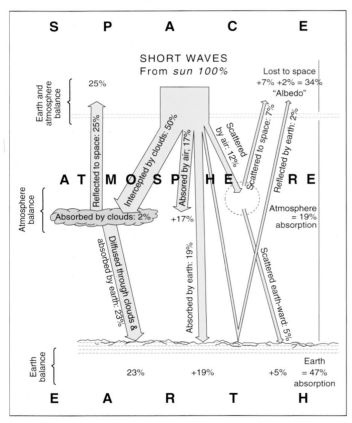

3.2 *The ways insolation is dispersed in the earth's atmosphere.*

When the sun's energy reaches the atmosphere, it is dispersed in different ways (figure 3.2). Although clouds cover about half of the earth at any time, they are poor absorbers of the sun's energy. Much more solar energy is absorbed by dust and gases in the atmosphere, especially water vapour. Altogether, 19% of incoming solar radiation is absorbed in the atmosphere.

The earth's surface absorbs 47% of the insolation, some directly and some after being reflected or scattered by the atmosphere. A small amount of radiation is reflected by

the earth's surface back into space. The amount of energy reflected from a particular place depends on the kind of surface on the earth at that point. Light, shiny surfaces, such as snow and ice, have much higher reflectivity (or **albedo**) than darker, duller surfaces, such as dark soil or a green forest (figure 3.3).

3.3 *Water has a high albedo (over 90%) if the sun's angle is low, but this falls to less than 5% under a noon sun or if the water is choppy. This early morning oblique aerial view of Myanmar's Irrawaddy Delta shows a high albedo from the sea and the rice padis, but high absorption in the clouds.*

The amount of heat received at the earth's surface varies according to latitude (figure 3.4). Less solar energy is absorbed by the ground in polar areas than equatorial areas for three reasons. First, the sun's rays strike the earth's surface at a lower angle near the poles. Therefore an equivalent amount of solar energy approaching the equator and the poles must be spread over a larger area in polar areas, meaning that there is less heat per square metre on the surface.

The second reason that the poles receive less solar radiation is that the sun's rays must penetrate a greater thickness of atmosphere near the poles than near the equator. This is because the rays penetrate the atmosphere at an oblique angle. As a result of this, the dust and gases of the atmosphere absorb more heat and light, and less reaches the earth's surface.

The third reason that the earth's surface at the poles absorbs less solar radiation is that more of the light that does reach the surface is reflected back into space. The shiny white ice and snow of the poles has a much higher albedo than the water and vegetation of the equatorial zones. In fact, snow and ice reflect about 80% of the solar energy whereas grass and trees will absorb between 65% and 85% of solar energy. Furthermore, any surface becomes shinier when light hits it at a low angle — even a black bitumen road seems shiny when viewed at a low angle. The light that reaches the polar surfaces does so at a very low angle, and therefore much of it is reflected rather than absorbed.

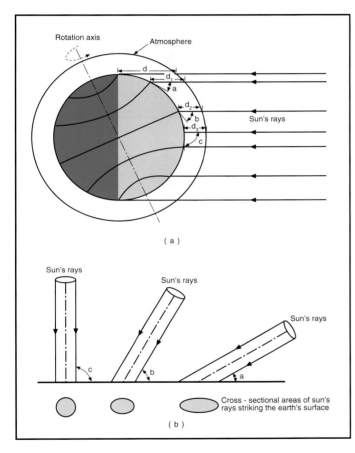

(a)

(b)

3.4 *The intensity of solar radiation depends on the angle which the sun's rays meet the earth's surface. The angle of the sun's rays (a, b and c) and the thickness of atmosphere through which they must pass (d1, d2 and d3) depends on the latitude. At high latitudes, the same amount of insolation is spread out over a larger area, making the heat less intense.*

When radiation is reflected from the earth's surface, the wavelength becomes longer, which means that the radiation shifts towards the red and infra-red end of the spectrum. In other words, less of the radiation is in the form of light, and more of it is in the form of heat. This is significant because the gases of the atmosphere are relatively good absorbers of long-wave radiation and thus absorb the energy emitted by the Earth's surface to a greater extent than they absorb the short-wave radiation coming from the sun.

If we examine the amount of energy received and lost at different latitudes over an entire year, the pattern shown in figure 3.5 emerges. The graph shows the average annual insolation at each latitude (curve I) and the average annual loss of long-wave energy (curve II). Although the total incoming energy (curve I) equals the total outgoing energy (curve II), there is a net surplus of energy between the equator and latitudes 38° North and South, while latitudes between 38° North and South and the poles have a net deficit.

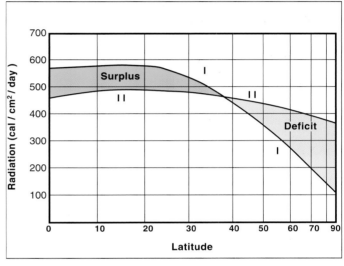

3.5 *The earth's heat budget. Average annual insolation at each latitude is shown by curve I, while average annual loss of long-wave energy is shown by curve II. Latitudes between the equator and 38° N and S have a net surplus of energy, while latitudes between 38° N and S and the poles have a net deficit. Note that the horizontal axis has been scaled in proportion to area.*

We know that over the history of the planet, the equatorial regions have not continued to heat up while the polar areas have not kept getting colder. The reason for this is that a complex mechanism of atmospheric circulation redistributes heat from the equatorial regions (low latitudes) to the polar regions (high latitudes). It is this redistribution of heat energy that creates the world's pressure systems and winds.

Of all the solar energy received by the earth, 34% is reflected back into space, either from the earth's surface (2%), from the atmosphere itself (7%) or from clouds (25%). However, before the energy is reflected back into space, some of it is retained in the atmosphere for a while, and this is the heat that provides the warmth that makes the earth habitable by humans. This process where the input of heat into the atmosphere equals the output while an amount is retained for a while is known as the **greenhouse effect**, because it is the same principle by which a greenhouse provides a warm environment for crops to grow (figure 3.6). Without the greenhouse effect, the earth would be 33C° cooler than it is now. (Note that when we refer to actual temperatures, we use the format 33°C, but when we discuss differences between two temperatures we use the format 33C°).

3.6 *Farmers use greenhouses to build up heat for the cultivation of vegetables in cool climates. This farmer near Wuhan in China has removed the plastic covering with the arrival of spring to show the cabbages that grew in the greenhouse while it was snowing outside. Heat builds up in the earth's atmosphere like a greenhouse.*

QUESTION BLOCK 3B

1. *With reference to figure 3.2, state the proportion of insolation which (a) is absorbed by the earth's surface, (b) is absorbed by the atmosphere, and (c) is lost to space.*

2. *Explain the significance of the shift in wavelength of the sun's radiation when it is reflected from the earth's surface.*

3. *Why does the equator receive more energy from the sun than the poles?*

4. *What is the greenhouse effect?*

Evidence for and Impact of Global Climate Change

There is overwhelming evidence that the earth's climate has changed often over the centuries. Figure 3.7 shows the changes in Greenland's climate over the past 75,000 years. We can see from

3.7 *Temperature changes in Greenland over the past 75,000 years. In (a) we see that the last great ice age ended about 11,000 years ago. In (b) we see that average temperatures for the past 1000 years were lower than in this century, with the period 1930 to 1970 being particularly mild. In (c) we note that large temperature changes can occur quite suddenly, and that both 'cooler' and 'warmer' periods can have warm or cold years.*

figure 3.7 that the climate has only been warmer than present levels for about 15% of the past 75,000 years. We can also see that temperatures have varied even within short periods of time, and in some cases this has had major effects on human activities such as fishing and farming.

Obviously, the changes shown in figure 3.7 are due to natural causes, as the number of humans for most of the past 75,000 years was far too small to have any significant impact on the environment at a global scale. The natural

3.8 *A small glacier in the Altay Mountains (Mongolia). A few decades ago, the ice of the glacier covered the entire valley area in the foreground where moraine has now been deposited.*

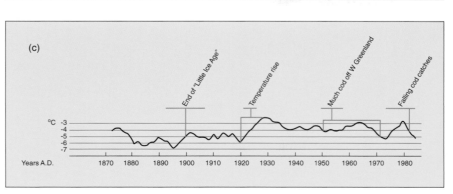

causes for climate change might include changes in levels of solar activity, the impact of volcanic activity (extra dust in the atmosphere can lead to cooling), variations in the earth's orbit (perhaps with changing distances from the sun) and changes in the humidity and cloud cover.

However, there is evidence of a different trend in global temperatures in recent decades, including the following:

• Arctic sea ice is melting at a rapid rate; it is 40% thinner now than it was forty years ago.

• All major non-polar glacial systems are in rapid retreat (figure 3.8); the 'permanent' snows on Mount Kilimanjaro in Africa may disappear within a decade or two.

• Throughout the northern hemisphere, ice forms on lakes about a week later than it did a century ago, and it melts about a week earlier.

• The timing of egg-laying for animals and the flowering of plants has changed as climates have warmed, and the distributions of plants and animals have also shifted as habitats have changed.

• Precipitation has increased across the northern hemisphere, especially destructive rain storms.

• El Niño events, which are huge and sometimes destructive effects caused by ocean warming in the tropical Pacific Ocean, have become more frequent, persistent and intense since the mid-1970s.

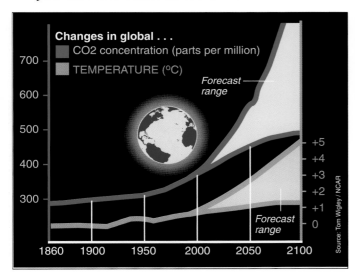

3.9 *Changes in carbon dioxide concentration and global temperatures from 1860 to the present (actual) and from the present to 2100 (projected).*

The scale of the changes in global temperatures since about 1980 are unprecedented, and this leads many researchers to hypothesise that human activity may be a significant part of the cause. There seems little doubt that global warming is occurring, although some researchers continue to question whether it is due to natural processes or human activities such as the consumption of fossil fuels. If global warming is mainly caused by human actions, then it could well be the most significant environmental issue faced by humanity because the implications are so great (figure 3.9).

It is expected that temperature increases will **reduce crop yields** in most tropical and sub-tropical regions of the world, where food is most scarce. On the other hand, increases in summer rainfall may benefit crop production and commercial forestry in some areas, particularly in South Asia.

Warming temperatures would also mean less **availability of water** in arid regions as well as a higher risk of flooding from heavier rainfall in temperate regions. This paradox arises because warm air holds more water vapour than cold, and so both evaporation in dry areas and downpours in wet areas increase. Some forecasters suggest that areas currently experiencing frequent water crises, such as north-east China and the flood-prone river deltas of Bangladesh and Vietnam, may experience large-scale **land degradation** and loss of soil in a changing climate. For the world's least developed countries, agricultural impacts such as these may threaten not only food security, but also national economic productivity.

3.10 *Global warming could melt polar ice caps and icebergs, causing a rise in the world's sea levels, flooding many low lying coastal areas and islands. The lake where these icebergs are floating at Jökulsárlón (Iceland) used to be filled with a glacier of solid ice. Will icebergs exist here in 50 years, or will this scene just be a coastal lagoon?*

It is also suggested that **rising sea levels** could flood many low-lying areas and even submerge some island and delta countries (figure 3.10). It is important to note that a rise in sea level does not happen simply because the polar ice caps begin melting, for the same reason that melting an ice cube in a drink does not raise the level of liquid in a glass. The rise in sea level of about 30 centimetres would result mostly from the thermal expansion of hotter water. If this occurs, other impacts will include aggravated erosion from the rising sea levels, the displacement of people in coastal communities, and increased costs to manage coastal defences (figures 3.11 and

3.12). The impacts of sea level changes are likely to affect the world's poorest most as they cannot afford the expensive engineering solutions required to give protection against rising sea levels.

3.11 *One of many houses built in very vulnerable locations on the beach front in North Carolina.*

3.12 *These dunes on the North Carolina coastline have been strengthened by planting salt-tolerant grasses to guard against erosion by wave attack.*

The evidence to support rising sea levels is mixed. According to satellite measurements, a global rise in sea levels is occurring, but it is only about 2 millimetres per year. However, there are wide local variations in the rise and fall of sea levels in various parts of the world, and these variations have a wide range of about 100 millimetres per year, with most parts of the world showing downward trends. Historical records show no acceleration in sea level rise during the 20th century. The situation continues to be monitored, especially in the places that would be most affected such as the low-lying river deltas of countries such as Bangladesh, India, Philippines, Vietnam, and China, as well as the small island states of the Pacific Ocean (figure 3.13).

Other predictions are that a warmer and wetter world will favour mosquitoes, and so more people will be exposed to **diseases** such as malaria and dengue fever. As many of the diseases that will spread are tropical, they are likely to

affect those who can least afford to pay for treatment and are thus the most vulnerable. On the other hand, many indigenous peoples who practise traditional lifestyles and live in harmony with their environments are so in-tune with the land and have such adaptable lifestyles that they may be able to withstand these impacts. Nonetheless, some forecasts suggest rising temperatures will expose millions of additional individuals to infectious diseases and heat-related deaths by 2100, although higher temperatures may also reduce the risk of cold-weather related deaths in other areas.

3.13 *These stilt houses, built over the shoreline near Manila (Philippines) are especially vulnerable to damage, especially during typhoons.*

3.14 *On the elevated Tibetan plateau in China, growth of vegetation is limited by the cold, dry climate.*

More and more people now believe that humans are reducing the earth's capacity to absorb greenhouse gases by reducing **biodiversity** and cutting down large areas of forest (**deforestation**). Through the process of deforestation, humans have increased the concentration of greenhouse gases in the atmosphere by releasing large quantities of stored carbon dioxide. These gases absorb infrared radiation, and therefore they retain energy that would have otherwise escaped back into space. The impact of climate change on ecosystems and biodiversity will vary in different environments. For example, coral reefs are likely to be damaged by increases in the frequency of bleaching events, while estimates suggest that the Asia-Pacific region may lose up to 13% of its mangrove wetlands. Changes in high altitude environments such as the Tibetan Plateau may see desert and steppe systems give way to forests and grasslands (figure 3.14). Meanwhile, the grasslands of central Asia are projected to decline, while wildfires and dieback diseases may affect some tropical forests.

ruption of utility services, such as electricity, sewers and communications, are also common occurrences during tropical cyclones.

The argument that global warming might cause tropical cyclones to become more severe is based on the assumption that sea surface temperatures will increase as the climate becomes warmer – warm oceans provide most of

Yet another concern is that global warming might cause tropical cyclones and hurricanes to become more frequent or more intense. **Tropical cyclones**, which are also known as **typhoons** and **hurricanes**, are highly intense low pressure cells, with winds generally exceeding 120 kilometres per hour. They spend most of their 'lives' over the warm oceans from which they draw their energy and moisture (figure 3.15). When tropical cyclones move over land or over cooler water, they tend to lose strength. When they move into populated areas, they create a significant hazard as buildings are destroyed, and debris is blown about (figure 3.16). The winds in tropical cyclones can tear roofs away from buildings, uproot trees, and damage power lines and communications. Additional hazards that can arise from tropical cyclones include coastal flooding and **storm surges**, which are rises in ocean levels produced by high winds and low atmospheric pressure. Besides causing flooding, storm surges can also increase coastal erosion, potentially causing slope failures. Tropical cyclones can even start fires by damaging power lines. Contamination of drinking water and dis-

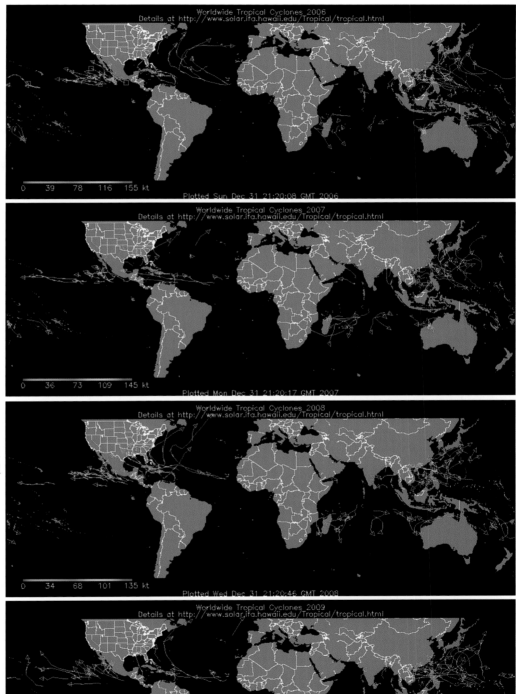

3.15 *The world distribution of tropical cyclones, 2006 (top) to 2009 (bottom).*

the energy supply for tropical cyclones. Once again, the evidence for this argument is ambiguous. According to Landsea (1996), there has been a general decrease in the number of intense tropical cyclones in the North Atlantic hurricanes since the mid-1970s, although the mid-1990s saw a more active tropical cyclone trend in the Atlantic. Many climatologists conclude that although global warming has some effects on the frequency and intensity of tropical cyclones, most of the variations are due to natural factors such as ocean temperatures and the movements of ocean currents..

3.16 *Typhoon damage in Manila, the capital city of the Philippines.*

It is possible that some other hazards may become more severe or frequent if global warming occurs. If climates become warmer, it seems likely that the number of **thunderstorms** with extreme rainfall, tornadoes and hail, heat waves, floods and drought will increase in specific areas; while the frequency of cold waves will become rarer. The relationship between the frequency and intensity of tropical cyclones and global warming is inconclusive. Some parts of the world will probably benefit if global warming occurs, because increased rainfall and warmer temperatures will enhance conditions for growing crops, and yields of food should increase.

Nonetheless, global warming is likely to carry serious **financial costs** in addition to the social costs mentioned above. Estimates of these financial costs vary depending on the impacts that are forecast, but estimates of about $US 5 trillion over the next century are common. These costs may be needed in areas such as agriculture, forestry, fisheries, water supply, energy, infrastructure, cyclone damage, drought damage, coastal protection, loss of land due to rising seas, loss of wetlands, loss of forests, loss of species, loss of human life, pollution and migration. Most of these costs will be felt in LEDCs because they are poorer and therefore have less capacity to cope with problems. It is said that the MEDCs in temperate areas may even benefit if global warming occurs, provided the extent of warming is only 2C° to 3C°, because of the improved crop yields mentioned earlier.

Another aspect of the financial costs are the **psychological costs**. In 2008, the first case of 'climate change delusion' was reported when an anxious and depressed 17-year-old boy was admitted to the psychiatric unit at the Royal Children's Hospital in Melbourne. He was refusing to drink water because he was so concerned that a drought at the time was related to climate change. The young man was convinced that if he drank water, millions of people would die as a consequence. There is evidence that extreme weather events, such as droughts, typhoons, floods, and cyclones, can cause emotional distress which in turn can trigger conditions such as as depression or post-traumatic stress disorder where the body's fear and arousal systems become heightened. If 'climate change delusion' becomes more common, the demands on the mental health industry could become significant.

On balance, researchers believe that the net effects of global warming are most likely to be negative for a majority of the world's economies. This will be the result of different factors in different countries. In those countries where long-term, sustainable economic development can be achieved, these economic impacts may simply serve to slow the rate of economic growth. In other countries, especially the poorer countries that are more dependent on the natural environment, then the impact of climate change on the economy could be extremely damaging, and in the case of some specific industries such as fishing and cropping, the impact could be ruinous.

QUESTION BLOCK 3C

1. *Most geographers agree that climate change is caused by a mix of natural and human factors. There is no consensus on how important each of these factors is in the global warming currently being experienced. Why do you think it has been so difficult to reach a consensus on the relative importance of natural and human factors?*

2. *Make a point form list of the impacts of global warming covered in this section in descending order of importance.*

3. *Give reasons to explain why you placed your first ranked and your last ranked points in the positions you chose when you answered the previous question.*

4. *How do the likely and possible effects of global warming impact people in LEDCs and MEDCs differently?*

5. *Does global warming cause more intense tropical cyclone activity? Give reasons to support your answer.*

Atmospheric Carbon Dioxide

Some gases retain heat especially well, and one of these is carbon dioxide (CO_2). Carbon dioxide is an important by-product of many manufacturing processes (figure 3.17). Since the beginning of the industrial revolution, the concentration of carbon dioxide has increased by 36%, while two other **greenhouse gases** (gases that retain heat), nitrous oxide and methane, have increased by 17% and 151% respectively. Although not all researchers agree, a majority claim that as a result of this build-up of greenhouse gases, average global temperatures rose by 0.8C° since 1880, and the trend seems to be accelerating.

Measurements of **atmospheric carbon dioxide** (CO_2) concentrations have been taken at Mauna Loa in Hawaii for a longer time than anywhere else in the world. Mauna Loa is considered one of the best locations for measuring undisturbed air because local influences on atmospheric CO_2 concentrations are minimal, and any influences from nearby volcanoes can easily be excluded from the records. The methods and equipment used to obtain measurements have remained unchanged since the monitoring program began in 1959.

The Mauna Loa record shows a mean annual increase of 17.4% in the average annual concentration of CO_2, rising from 315.98 parts per million by volume (ppmv) of dry air in 1959 to 383.57 ppmv in 2007. This is the highest level of CO_2 concentration at any time during the past 160,000 years. It represents an average annual growth rate of 1.43 ppmv per year, although in 1997-98 an abnormally large increase of 2.87 ppmv occurred. At the time the industrial revolution began, the concentration was about 280 ppmv, and this figure had remained fairly constant since the end of the last ice age 14,000 years ago, when the concentration increased from about 190 ppmv.

Scientists disagree over whether or not increasing the CO_2 concentration leads to global warming. Some argue that during the period 1940 to 1980, when carbon dioxide emissions were rising most rapidly, global temperatures actually fell, which is why there were widespread predictions of an imminent ice age during the 1970s. However, during the period with the most reliable data (since 1960), global average surface temperature has increased by between 0.2C° and 0.3C°.

Still other researchers dispute the cause-and-effect relationship between carbon dioxide and global warming. As outlined in the 'ToK Box' in this chapter, some researchers agree that there is a positive correlation between levels of atmospheric carbon dioxide and global warming, but claim it is rising temperatures that cause the increase in carbon dioxide levels, not vice versa.

If we take a long time frame, global mean surface air temperatures have increased by between about 0.3C° and 0.6C° since the 1890s. This trend has not been uniform across the world, however. Some areas, such as the continental areas between 40°N and 70°N, have warmed more than the average, while other parts of the world, such as the North Atlantic Ocean, have cooled slightly during the past century. Clearly, the physics behind the greenhouse

effect, and the atmosphere's capacity to regulate itself, are very complex and still not well understood.

3.17 *Greenhouse gas and particulate emissions from a coal-fired power station in Pyongyang, North Korea.*

The Kyoto Protocol and the IPCC

In December 1997, world leaders met in **Kyoto**, Japan, to consider a world treaty that would restrict emissions of greenhouse gases, especially carbon dioxide. It was agreed that carbon dioxide levels had increased substantially since the time of the industrial revolution, and that this trend was expected to continue. It was also agreed that humans had been responsible for much of this increase. However, there was disagreement over how much of the increase in temperatures had been due to the increase in carbon dioxide concentrations. Some argued that more greenhouse gases in the future would raise the earth's temperatures, causing the polar ice caps to melt partially, raising sea levels and flooding low-lying coastal areas and islands. On the other hand, others argued that greenhouse gases support plant life, and thus the animal life that depends upon it would thrive with an increase in carbon dioxide levels. These commentators argued that what humanity is doing is simply liberating carbon from beneath the earth's surface and putting it into the atmosphere, where it is available for conversion into living organisms.

It is agreed by people from all points of view that the greenhouse effect is certainly real. Greenhouse gases such as H_2O (water vapour) and CO_2 in the atmosphere reduce the escape of long-wave infrared radiation (heat) from the earth into space. Therefore, when we increase the concentration of carbon dioxide, we effectively increase the energy input to the earth. However, as shown in figure 3.2 earlier in this chapter, what happens to this heat energy is complex. The energy is redistributed vertically and horizontally by various physical processes, including advection, convection, and diffusion in the atmosphere and ocean.

At the end of the Kyoto meeting, 38 industrialised countries agreed to cut their emissions of six greenhouse gases that were linked to global warming. An agreement was signed, which has become known as the **Kyoto Protocol**. Then, in July 2001, a further meeting of delegates from 180 countries was held in Bonn (Germany) to work out details of implementing the Kyoto Protocol. It was agreed in Bonn that the Kyoto Protocol would not take effect until it is ratified by 55% of the nations responsible for at least 55% of the greenhouse gas emissions. The countries (mainly MEDCs) that agree to ratify the Protocol are obliged to reduce emissions of carbon dioxide to an average of 5.2% below 1990 levels during the five-year period 2008 to 2012. Compared with not doing anything, this initiative represents a reduction of almost 30% in greenhouse gas emissions. The emissions of LEDCs will be controlled by subsequent negotiations under the climate treaty.

Opinions differ as to how effective the Kyoto Protocol will be. It has been calculated that an expected increase in global temperatures of 2.1C° by 2100 will only be reduced to an increase of 1.9C° under the Kyoto Protocol. Expressed another way, the temperature that would have

been experienced in 2094 would merely be postponed by six years until 2100 under the Kyoto Protocol. For this reason, some critics of the Protocol say it is far too weak, while others argue that its financial cost ($US 150 billion to $US 350 billion annually) is not justified for the tokenistic gains that are achieved. As Lomborg (2001) comments:

"Because global warming will primarily hurt Third World countries, we have to ask if Kyoto is the best way to help them. The answer is no. For the cost of Kyoto in just 2010, we could once and for all solve the single biggest problem on earth: We could give clean drinking water and sanitation to every single human being on the planet. This would save two million lives and avoid half a billion severe illnesses every year. And for every following year we could then do something equally good."

In February 2005, the BBC conducted a survey of almost 2000 world-wide on the issue of climate change. Some of the key results are shown in figure 3.18.

Significant work on the issue of climate change has been undertaken by a group known as the **Intergovernmental Panel on Climate Change** (IPCC), established jointly by two United nations bodies, the UNEP and the WMO. The IPCC comprises several hundred of the world's leading

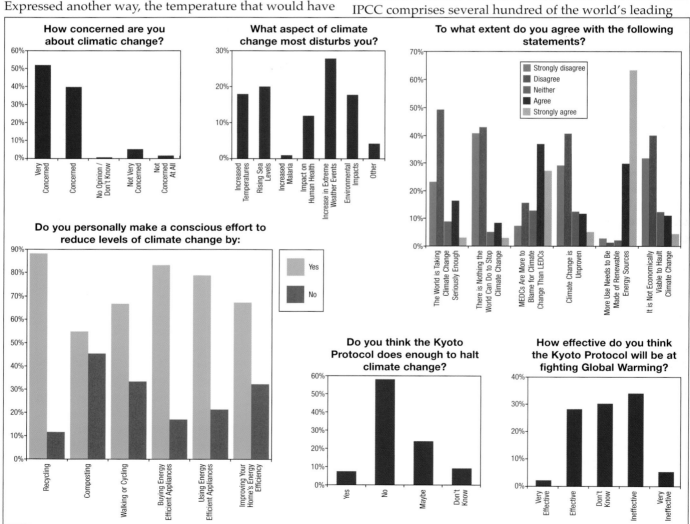

3.18 *Results from a world-wide survey on attitudes to climate change conducted by the BBC in February 2005 (Source: extracted from www.bbcworldpanel.com/reports.php?&aid=793523597). It would be interesting to compare these results to the attitudes of the members of your class.*

scientists and researchers. Several reports have been published by the IPCC that contrast strongly with views of some governments and critics such as Bjørn Lomborg.

The report of the IPCC consists of four large volumes that were finalised at conferences held in Shanghai, Geneva and Accra in late 2000 and early 2001. The report suggests that humanity stands 'on the edge of cataclysm' as a consequence of global warming. Extensive measurements have been undertaken in the upper atmosphere, under the sea, on tundra and desert, permafrost and ice caps, in tree rings and glacial ice cores, in pollen sediments and bird nesting records, with satellites and weather balloons. Computer models were developed to a high degree of accuracy, with the models being tested by looking at past climates, and tracking chemicals released in the 1991 eruption of Mount Pinatubo in the Philippines. The research has been analysed by an international team of researchers who were charged with reaching a consensus on global warming.

The preliminary finding in 1995 concluded that 'the balance of evidence suggests a discernible human influence on global climate'. The conclusion reached in 2001 was considerably more alarming. Using six different projections about how economies would grow and how they would make the transition to non-carbon forms of energy, it was concluded that the global average temperature would rise by 1.7C° to 6.1C° before 2100. This was a more pessimistic projection that the 1996 conclusion, which forecast a rise in temperatures before 2100 of between 1.1C° and 4.0C°.

If this forecast comes true, the earth will be transformed into a planet unlike anything that humans have ever experienced. The current global average temperature is 15°C, but this could rise to as much as 21°C. This temperature would mean a huge rise in the amount of energy trapped in the lower atmosphere, increasing the rate of almost every natural process except the volcanic and the tectonic.

The IPCC argues that there is now no doubt that the earth's climate is warming. Among the evidence of this, the IPCC says that average global surface temperatures increased by about 0.6C° between 1900 and 2000, snow cover and ice extent have decreased, hurricane activity has increased ,and average sea levels have increased. The IPCC notes that the biggest increases in temperatures have been in the lowest 8 kilometres of the atmosphere, which is where human impacts are greatest. The IPCC is extremely critical of the emissions of greenhouse gases and aerosols because of the impact they cause (figure 3.19). This is why the Kyoto Protocol calls for immediate reductions of greenhouse gas emissions by MEDCs.

The trend of global warming has been likened to the shape of hockey stick, as there is a sharp rise beginning at the start of the Industrial Revolution. The IPCC predicts that this trend will continue unless significant actions are taken to reverse the production of greenhouse gases and strengthen the directions of the Kyoto Protocol.

The IPCC's predictions have been challenged, however. The IPCC used market-based exchange rates as the financial basis of its predictions, whereas critics argue it should have used the more realistic Purchasing Power Parity (PPP) method, as described in chapter 2 of this book. The PPP method adjusts wealth according to the spending power of different countries rather than an often artificial exchange rate. Critics of the IPCC claim that in using market-based exchange rates, the IPCC has over-predicted future economic growth, and therefore emissions growth.

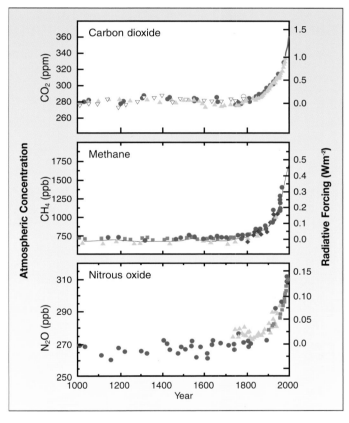

3.19 *Global atmospheric concentrations of three greenhouse gases. The left axes show concentrations in parts per billion (ppb). The right axes show the estimated radiative forcing, which is the change in the balance between radiation entering the atmosphere and radiation leaving. It is thus a measure of the temperature rise that results from the change in gas concentration. Because these three gases have atmospheric lifetimes of over a decade, they are well mixed and the concentrations reflect figures throughout the globe. All three gases show sharp rises as a result of human activity during the industrial era. The shapes of the curves are sometimes known as 'the hockey stick' effect. (Source: IPCC, 'Third Assessment Report)*

The IPCC's predictions are certainly serious, and if true, represent a very significant global challenge for humanity. According to the organisation, average global temperatures will rise between 1.4C° and 5.8C°, which is a more rapid rate than 1900 to 1990, and probably the most rapid

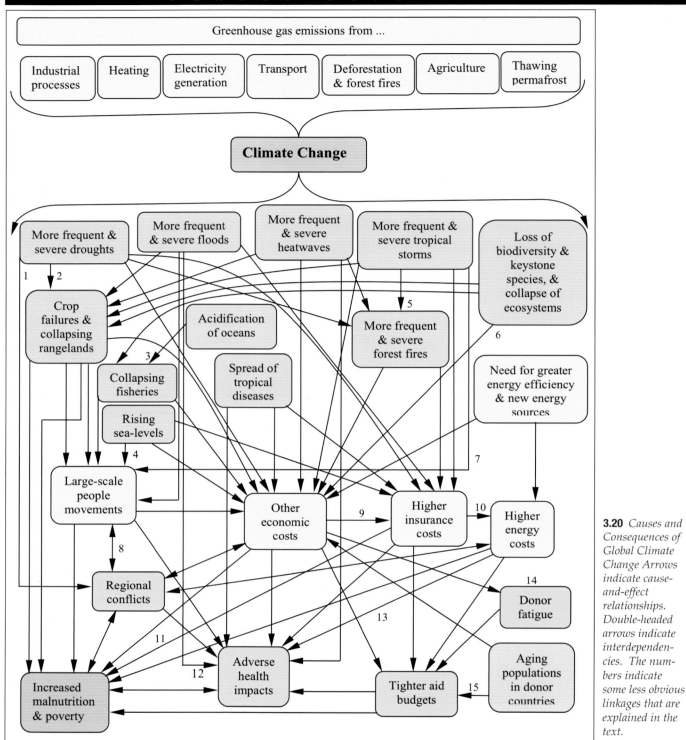

3.20 *Causes and Consequences of Global Climate Change Arrows indicate cause-and-effect relationships. Double-headed arrows indicate interdependencies. The numbers indicate some less obvious linkages that are explained in the text.*

rise for at least 10,000 years. This will result in higher maximum and minimum temperatures, more hot days, fewer cold days, reduced diurnal ranges of temperatures, shrinking ice and snow cover, retreat of glaciers, more frequent droughts and more intense tropical cyclones. The IPCC also predicts that the tropical Pacific Ocean will become more El Niño-like, with the eastern Pacific warming more than the western Pacific, and therefore a shift in precipitation in the same direction. Among the other predictions made by the IPCC are that average global precipitation will increase, although variations in

precipitation from year to year will also increase, while global sea levels will increase by between 0.09 and 0.88 metres between 1990 and 2100.

If the predictions are correct, the consequences of global warming are likely to be felt globally in a multitude of ways. Figure 3.20 looks complex, but it is an attempt to simplify the intricate and convoluted consequences of global climate change. Some of the consequences have already been examined, but 15 of the links that are identified by number in figure 3.20 require a little more explanation:

1. More frequent and severe droughts could lead directly to conflict because of tensions over water resources, especially between upstream and downstream areas of the same catchment, or between different countries that share the same underground aquifer, especially if one side accuses the other of stealing water. The IPCC projects that by 2050, more than one billion people in Asia could be adversely affected by decreased water availability.

2. More frequent and severe droughts can ruin harvests, leading to malnutrition and migrations in search of water and pasture. The IPCC forecasts that in Africa "By 2020, between 75 and 250 million people are projected to be exposed to an increase of water stress due to climate change."

3. Acidification of the oceans due to increased absorption of CO_2 can hinder the formation of shells and skeletons of marine organisms, adversely affecting marine ecosystems. This is discussed in greater detail in chapter 6.

4. Rising sea levels are expected to cause large-scale migrations of people, escaping not only the permanently higher sea levels, but also the increased frequency of flooding in more elevated areas due to storm surges that cover farmlands with salt water, as well as contaminating fresh water wells and aquifers. A World Bank study in 2007 calculated that a 1 metre rise in sea levels would affect at least 56 million people globally.

5. More frequent tropical storms increase the number of fires started by lightning strikes.

6. Loss of biodiversity occurs when climate changes faster than organisms can migrate or adapt. When critically important species in a food web are lost, the ecosystem can collapse. This may have devastating consequences for the species directly involved, but it also has severe consequences on economic systems because of its impact on agriculture and tourism, as well as through the loss of irreplaceable natural chemical compounds for pharmaceutical and bioscience research.

7. More frequent and severe tropical storms can lead directly to migrations of people from low-lying areas trying to escape the devastation and the loss of farmland and clean water due to saltwater contamination by storm surges.

8. Large-scale population movements are very likely to lead to conflicts as people try to cross borders and settle on land that is already claimed by others.

9. All of the economic costs of global warming will indirectly affect the insurance industry, which will result in higher premiums.

10. Higher insurance costs will affect companies that generate energy, and these higher energy costs will be passed on to consumers.

11. Higher insurance costs directly impoverish people by making insurance unaffordable to some folk who previously would have been able to afford it.

12. More frequent and severe floods contaminate water supplies leading directly to outbreaks of cholera, diarrhoea and other water-borne diseases.

13. Higher energy costs lead directly to worse health care since they increase transport, heating and electricity costs for the health sector.

14. Donor fatigue is likely to become a significant problem with the increased frequency and severity of droughts, floods, tropical storms, heat waves and forest fires, the spread of tropical diseases, a likely increase in conflicts and the increased costs of energy and other economic costs facing donor countries.

15. The ageing of donor countries' populations will increase donors' health care costs at the same time as it shrinks their tax bases. This is likely to be one of the main sources of pressure on donors' aid budgets – not because older people are any less generous than younger people, but because the higher health care costs will erode public finances as people live longer and there are fewer workers per retiree.

Not all climate change forecasts predict catastrophe. Perhaps Russia has the potential to gain the most from climate warming. Russia has huge untapped reserves of natural gas and oil in Siberia and also offshore in the Arctic Sea, and warmer temperatures would make these energy reserves much more accessible. Presuming (maybe wrongly) that oil and natural gas continue be used in large quantities as global warming continues, then this would mean a big boost for the Russian economy given that 80% of its exports and 32% of its government revenues presently come from the production of energy and raw materials. Furthermore, the opening of an Arctic waterway for shipping could provide economic and commercial advantages for Russia's foreign trade.

Canada is another country that might benefit from global warming as it would escape several climate-related developments such as intense hurricanes and heat waves. Furthermore, global warming could open up vast areas of land that is currently covered by snow for most of the year to development. If temperatures rose, access for shipping to Hudson Bay would be improved, and it is possible that new polar shipping routes could be opened. Furthermore, the length of the growing seasons for agriculture would increase, the energy demand for heating and cooling will probably fall, and productive forests would be expected to expand into the tundra.

ToK BoX

Truth and Global Warming.

In 2006, Al Gore released a movie about climate change called 'An Inconvenient Truth'. The movie's release was widely regarded as one of the most important actions in making the general public aware of climate change as an issue. Al Gore was awarded the Nobel Peace Prize, largely in recognition of the movie's effectiveness in alerting people to the issue of climate change.

By using the title 'An Inconvenient Truth', Al Gore was stating that the claims made in the movie are 'truth'. Every geographer would acknowledge that global temperatures change over time — how else could we have had ice ages? However, the central claim of 'An Inconvenient Truth' is that the warming of the world's temperatures today is unprecedented in human history, and these changes are primarily caused by human actions. This claim is not accepted by all geographers.

2. Climate change is mainly attributable to human-generated emissions of carbon dioxide, methane and nitrous oxide (greenhouse gases);

3. Climate change will, if unchecked, have significant adverse effects on the world and its populations; and

4. There are measures which individuals and governments can take which will help to reduce climate change or mitigate its effects.

The central piece of evidence used in the film was an analysis of the trend of annual temperatures and carbon dioxide (CO_2) levels for the past 650,000 years in Antarctic ice core samples. In the movie, Al Gore discusses the possibility of the collapse of a major ice sheet in Greenland or in West Antarctica, either of which could raise global sea levels, flooding coastal areas and producing millions of refugees. Melt water from

energy industry, while still others were from dissenting scientists and geographers who disputed Gore's interpretation of the evidence he had selected to present.

In 2007, as a response to 'An Inconvenient Truth', a documentary called 'The Great Global Warming Swindle' was shown by Britain's Channel 4. This documentary quoted an impressive array of scientists and geographers from around the world and provided evidence to support 14 claims against the thesis of man-made (anthropogenic, or human-induced) global warming:

1. Evidence from many sources, including Antarctic ice cores and the lag effects shown in contemporary measurements, shows that although there is a relationship between atmospheric carbon dioxide and global temperatures, it is rising temperatures that cause the rise in CO_2, not vice versa as is often claimed.

2. From the 1940s to the early 1980s, the earth experienced a significant period of cooling, even though this was the period during which industrial production and carbon dioxide production rose most sharply. That explains the widespread concerns about the onset of an imminent ice age during the 1970s.

3. Water vapour and methane are far more significant greenhouse gases than carbon dioxide, both in terms of volume and impact. To ignore them and focus on carbon dioxide is to miss the real causes of climate change. Statistically, fluctuations in all three gases are overwhelmingly dominated by natural rather than human causes.

4. Sun spot activity and levels of solar radiation parallel temperature changes much more closely than carbon dioxide levels, and these natural causes have a direct bearing on atmospheric water vapour and (to a lesser extent) methane levels.

5. If rising carbon dioxide levels were the main cause of anthropogenic (human-induced) global warming, then the troposphere (the layer of the earth's atmosphere about 10 to 15 kilometres above the surface) should heat up faster than the earth's surface. However, data collected from satellites and weather balloons show that this is not so, and in fact there is a slight opposite trend.

6. The proportion of carbon dioxide in the atmosphere produced by humans is extremely small (about 3%) compared

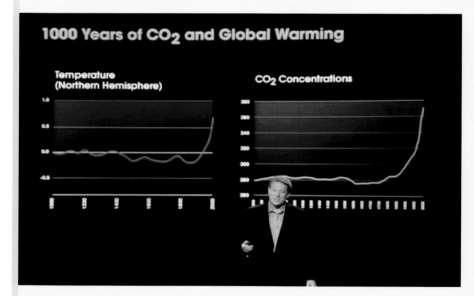

The central theses of 'An Inconvenient Truth' are that global warming is real, that anthropogenic forcing (human actions) is the primary cause, that global warming will result in a catastrophic loss of both human and animal life, that global warming is causing increased storm intensity, and that we have passed the tipping point so that global warming will continue to accelerate out of control.

The four main scientific points made in 'An Inconvenient Truth' were:

1. Global average temperatures have been rising significantly over the past half century and are likely to continue to rise (climate change);

Greenland, because of its lower salinity, could halt the currents that keep northern Europe warm and quickly trigger dramatic local cooling there.

Gore quoted US Geological Survey predictions that that by 2030, Glacier National Park will have no glaciers left. He also quoted figures, such as in the last 30 years, over one million square kilometres of Arctic sea ice have melted, and thus polar bears today drown when they cannot find an ice floe on which to rest.

Almost as soon as it was released, 'An Inconvenient Truth' provoked controversy. Some of the attacks were from political lobby groups, others from the

with the amounts produced naturally by animals, bacteria, decaying vegetation, the ocean and volcanoes; the human "carbon footprint" is vastly outweighed by these other factors.

7. In the 1970s, scientific concerns focused on the imminent onset of a new ice age. The more recent concern about global warming since the 1980s was politically motivated, the origins being the British Prime Minister, Margaret Thatcher's wish to promote nuclear energy by denigrating coal-based electricity generation.

8. There is a vested interest among researchers today to highlight and exaggerate the potential catastrophe of global warming because so much funding is available for this purpose, and a very powerful anti-global warming industry has grown up. There is evidence of research being falsified to sensationalise the potential dangers of global warming.

9. Rising sea levels due to melting ice caps are extremely unlikely because sea levels are less dependent on the volume of ocean water than thermal expansion and contraction. The video clips we often see of collapsing ice sheets are simply the annual spring thawing.

10. Historical evidence of past warm interglacial periods shows that although farmers in some areas may suffer, many more farmers are likely to prosper if global warming continues due to increased rainfall that is more reliable than at present.

11. Global warming activists claim that natural disasters such as hurricanes and typhoons are likely to increase in frequency and severity with global warming. However, between the equator and the poles the opposite is more likely because the severity of extreme atmospheric events is determined by the differential conditions, but with global warming these differences are reduced, not increased.

12. Global warming activists argue that LEDCs (less economically developed countries) need to adopt pathways to development that produce less carbon (such as wind, tidal and solar power), even though these strategies are usually too expensive even for MEDCs (More Economically Developed Countries) to adopt. This is a concern because it is seen by people in LEDCs to be an attempt to perpetuate and even widen the gap between rich and poor.

13. Global warming is being used as a weapon by some governments to impose taxes, reduce personal freedoms,

change labour regulations etc for purposes that are not connected with global warming. Carbon futures trading is an especially insidious form of the rich profiteering at the expense of the poor.

14. At the time that the UN report by the Intergovernmental Panel on Climate Change (IPCC) was published, it was said to have been supported unanimously by more than 2,000 of the world's leading scientists. However, several scientists now claim it was a 'sham' given that this list included the names of scientists who disagreed with its findings. Professor Reiter, of the Pasteur Institute in Paris, for example, said his name was removed from an assessment only when he threatened legal action against the panel. Other scientists claim their names were included in the report against their wishes.

15. NASA data suggests that all the planets of our solar system may be warming at about the same percentage rate as Earth — with no help from humans.

How can we judge 'truth claims' such as those made in 'An Inconvenient Truth' and 'The Great Global Warming Swindle'? Many — maybe most — people today would probably agree with the

claim that humans are the main cause of global warming, but that would be a very weak basis to say the statement is true.

It may be helpful to understand that there are three different theories of truth against which we can test this (and any other) truth claim!

One theory is the Correspondence Theory of Truth. Under this theory, a statement is true if and only if it corresponds to a fact. The fact should be independent of language, society and culture. "Grass is green" is true if and only if the grass the green. People who hold the

correspondence theory of truth are called realists.

Another theory is the Coherence Theory of Truth. Under this theory, a statement is true if it is consistent with other true statements within a belief system. People who hold the coherence theory of truth are called anti-realists. Whereas realists go out and look for evidence, anti-realists sit and think about consistency. For an anti-realist, the statement 'the world is flat' was once true because it conformed to the broad consensus of how people viewed the world, but it is no longer true.

The third theory is the Pragmatic Theory of Truth. Under this theory, a statement is true if it is useful or works in practice. People who hold the pragmatic theory of truth are called pragmatists. Pragmatism does not concern itself with facts or coherence. This theory could be summarised as 'If it works, it must be true'.

So, to return to the question of global warming, consider the claim 'global warming is caused by human actions'. For a realist, this would be true if and only if the factual data supports the statement.

For an anti-realist, the statement would be true if it reflects the broad consensus of opinion.

For a pragmatist, it would be true if it is useful, for example, if you can make money from the belief, or if it makes you feel better, or more passionate about a cause, or if it serves you politically, and so on.

Being aware of the various theories of truth, how would YOU go about evaluating the claim that 'global warming is caused by human actions'?

The next ToK BoX is on page 150.

Further information on climate change, especially its effects on extreme environments, is provided towards the end of chapter 7. Further information on the interrelationship between climate change and the oceans is given in chapter 6.

QUESTION BLOCK 3D

1. *Describe and account for the rising level of carbon dioxide in the atmosphere over the last century or so.*

2. *Is the growing concentration of CO₂ in the atmosphere causing global warming? Give reasons to support your answer.*

3. *What is the Kyoto Protocol?*

4. *How effective do you think the Kyoto Protocol has been in addressing the challenges of climate change?*

5. *What is the IPCC?*

6. *How effective do you think the IPCC has been in addressing the challenges of climate change?*

7. *Study figure 3.20. Identify the three consequences of climate change that you think are most significant, and justify your choice.*

7. *If countries such as Canada and Russia are expected to benefit from global warming, does that mean they have no interest in working to slow down climate change?*

Soil and Change

Soil Formation and Erosion

When rocks are broken down by the processes of weathering, small particles become available to be mixed with organic matter such as humus (decaying plant matter) and animal faeces. Over time, this process results in the formation of a thin layer of soil. As the soil forms, it can support the growth of small plants, which add additional organic matter when they die. Over time, the soil thus develops more fully and becomes thicker. Eventually, a mature soil may form with layers (called **horizons**) of different colours that are roughly parallel to the ground surface. The collection of horizons at one point is called a **soil profile**, and it reflects the movement of water and minerals upwards and downwards.

However, the process of soil formation can be arrested and reversed as soils are degraded. **Soil erosion** is the removal and transfer of soil particles from one place to another, usually by wind or running water. It occurs in varying degrees on all soils and while it may be a natural process, it is often aggravated by the actions of people.

When erosion proceeds slowly, soils adjust to the surface changes and the profile will not change noticeably in the short-term. Rapid additions of sediment from flooding or erosion of soils from upslope can bury a soil profile, and the soil-forming processes will then begin acting on the newly deposited surface. The previous profile is often preserved if the burial is deep.

Erosion that has taken place over a very long period (which we can refer to as geological time), it is termed **normal erosion**. Its rate is affected by factors such as:

- *rainfall* (its intensity, duration, amount, seasonality);

- the nature and intensity of the *vegetation* cover;

- the length and angle of the *slopes*; and

- the *likelihood* of soils to erode. This is mainly a result of characteristics like texture, structure and dispersibility. These properties influence infiltration rates and ease of particle detachment from the soil surface.

Human activities have often caused an increase in normal erosion rates, and this is termed **accelerated erosion** (figure 3.21). In both urban and rural areas, tree vegetation has often been removed. This alters the surface cover in a way which exposes soils to additional risks of erosion by wind or water.

3.21 *This large sign in China reminds people of the importance of soil conservation. An example of the consequences of ignoring such messages can be seen in the right-hand lead photo of this chapter (on page 100), which shows severe soil erosion near Konso, Ethiopia.*

The scale of the global problem of soil degradation is causing increasing concern. According to a study done at Cornell University, soil is being eroded at a rate ten to forty times faster than it is being replenished on an average world-wide basis. As the vast majority of human food comes directly or indirectly from croplands, which are shrinking by more than ten million hectares per annum due to soil erosion, the potential impact on the human food supply is obvious. The pressure on soils to produce food is increasing also as the demand increases to grow vegetable-based biofuels and and industrial crops such as cotton, both of which require vast areas of farmland and cleared rainforests.

Wind Erosion

Wind erosion occurs in areas where the soil particles are loosely bound together. In many farming areas, the land is cultivated to eliminate weeds which compete with the crops for the limited supplies of moisture and nutrients in the soil. Soil structures are broken up by cultivation and this makes the soil particles more vulnerable to being blown by the wind when they are dry (figure 3.22). Finer particles such as clay can be transported over great distances, while sand can drift across fences, railway lines, crops and roads (figure 3.23).

3.22 *Wind erosion of topsoil at Merv, Turkmenistan.*

3.23 *A sand drift almost blocks the highway near Konye-Urgench in northern Turkmenistan.*

Wheat cultivation in countries like Australia is a marginal activity where rainfall is relatively low and unreliable. Cultivation of light textured soils in marginal wheat lands has led to **desertification**, which is the extension or intensification of desert conditions. Desertification leads to reductions in plant productivity, accelerated decline in soil quality and increasing hazards for human occupancy. Large areas of the world are being threatened by desertifi-

cation including west and central Africa as well as parts of Australia. Over-grazing in areas south of the Sahara Desert has contributed to an expansion of the desert, with the edge of the Sahara advancing southwards by about 25 kilometres per year, on average, according to some commentators (figure 3.24).

3.24 *Cattle owned by nomadic pastoralists graze on the outskirts of Timbuktu. Mali.*

Water Erosion

Human disturbance of the vegetation cover has sped up rates of water erosion of soils. Soil degradation caused by water takes two main forms, sheet erosion and gully erosion.

Sheet erosion is the removal of the surface soil to an even depth over a wide area (figure 3.25). It often occurs on bare, cultivated ground. If run-off becomes sufficiently concentrated and turbulent, channels (gullies) are eroded into the soil.

3.25 *Sheet erosion near Konso, Ethiopia.*

Gully erosion is very obvious on cultivated land, and it occurs mainly after intense or prolonged rainfall (figure 3.26). Gullying can be a major problem in areas where people have cleared the natural vegetation, although it is important to remember that gullying is a natural process that can occur in areas where there has been no human impact. Nonetheless, human activities do often accelerate the rate of already existing erosion.

3.26 *Gully erosion near Arba Minch, Ethiopia.*

3.27 *Wind eroded farming land in the Manakah region of Yemen.*

Soil Erosion in Rural Areas

In rural areas, most soil erosion takes place on cultivated land. This is because land that has been left bare of vegetation for weeks or months at a time is more exposed to the actions of wind and water (figure 3.27). The loss of surface soil lowers crop yields because of reductions in:

- *chemical fertility* — the top layer, or horizon, of the soil usually contains more plant nutrients and organic matter than the lower horizons; and

- *physical constitution* — the lower horizons often contain more clay than the upper layers and are therefore less friable than the surface soil.

Even on cultivated land, the rates of erosion vary because of factors such as:
- local characteristics, such as the steepness of the slope;
- land management techniques such as the use of contour banks; and
- the soil's physical and chemical properties.

When cultivation occurs in arid areas with steep slopes, the soil is especially vulnerable to degradation. In such areas, soil degradation can be minimised by using techniques such as:
- constructing terraces or broad contour banks (figure 3.28);
- planting and harvesting crops on the contours;
- using grassed waterways to slow down and disperse runoff (figure 3.29);
- leaving crop residues rather than burning them;
- not overgrazing pasture areas (figure 3.30); and
- organising land uses in such a way that erosion is minimised.

3.28 *Terraces used for farming in the arid mountains of the Manakah region of Yemen.*

3.29 *Grassed waterways intersperse this farming land near Hossana in Ethiopia to slow down the flow of water, thus reducing erosion.*

The pressures of soil degradation are perhaps felt more keenly in Africa than any other continent because the productivity of crop cultivation is lower than many other regions of the world while population growth is more rapid. The Alliance for a Green Revolution in Africa (AGRA) estimates that 75% of Africa's farmlands suffer from soil degradation. Many of the soils in Africa were formed from granite rocks and are therefore quite low in nutrients that plants can use. Furthermore, granite-based soils tends to be quite coarse in texture, and therefore the minerals and nutrients are easily **leached** (dissolved by rainwater and removed from the soil). Given the long history of human farming in Africa and the traditional techniques used, such as hoes and ploughs, both wind and water erosion are significant problems (figure 3.31).

3.30 *Cattle grazing in the dry mountains of Nokhur, near the border of Turkmenistan and Iran.*

3.31 *Ploughing using traditional tools such as wooden ploughs and cattle near Sodo, Ethiopia.*

Like farmers using traditional methods elsewhere, farmers in many parts of Africa have have traditionally left their fields fallow, or unused, for a year every so often to allow the soil's natural fertility to return. Farmers who practised shifting cultivation would allow the field to return to its natural state of bushland, and then clear the field once again by burning the grass and bushes that had established themselves there. The ash produced in this process would replenish the soil and restore much of its productivity. However, population growth in recent decades has increased the pressure on farmland, and farmers have responded by shortening the fallow periods. As a consequence, soils in many parts of Africa have become increasingly degraded. Unfortunately, the traditional methods to restore fertility have not been replaced by new methods of soil management and cropping, partly because farmers cannot afford the necessary inputs and partly as they are unaware of the new techniques.

As soil nutrients are not replenished adequately, a vicious cycle begins in which yields decline, poverty increases, and farmers respond by placing still more pressure upon the soils, either by shortening the fallow period even more or by expanding farming into more marginal areas, starting the cycle once again.

One of the significant barriers to addressing the problem of soil degradation in Africa has been that most farmers are poorly educated and follow traditional methods handed on to them by their parents. In an effort to overcome this problem, an organisation called the Alliance for a Green Revolution in Africa (AGRA) was set up in 2006 with financial support from The Rockefeller Foundation and the Bill and Melinda Gates Foundation. In an effort to give the organisation international standing, it is chaired by the former Secretary-General of the United Nations, Kofi Annan, and has offices in Nairobi (Kenya) and Accra (Ghana).

AGRA has already begun working with African governments, NGOs, the private sector, other donors, and African farmers to improve the productivity and incomes of resource-poor farmers in Africa. AGRA is investing in four areas that are designed to address the problem of soil degradation:
- improving knowledge, application and adoption of integrated soil fertility management;
- improving economic access to fertilisers for poor farmers;
- increasing physical access to fertilisers for poor farmers; and
- developing policy and incentives for adoption of improved soil fertility management practices.

Soil Erosion in Urban Areas

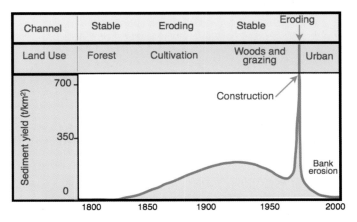

3.32 *Changing land use settlement yield in the Piedmont region of eastern USA.*
Source: After MG Wolman, 'A Cycle of Sedimentation and Erosion in Urban River Channels', Geografiska Annaler, vol. 49A, pp. 385-95.

Soil erosion often occurs when previously rural land is converted to urban uses. The removal of tree and shrub vegetation, which interferes with building construction and road preparation, accelerates erosion rates. Figure 3.32 shows the sharp increase in sediment loss that occurs when rural land is converted into an urban area.

When rural land is converted into urban land:
- soil is compacted by heavy earth-moving machinery used for site preparation;
- topsoil can be stripped in the levelling process, thus exposing the relatively impermeable subsoil to gully erosion;
- stockpiles of loose topsoil are reduced in storms by rills (small channels); and
- gullying and rilling are common on compacted roadways, especially if the road pattern has been designed to run mainly up-and-down the slope instead of along the contours.

These disturbances during the construction period for new urban areas can lead to severe soil erosion. Extra sediment can silt up local drainage lines and water storages. Once urban gardens are established and roadways have been paved, soil loss is markedly reduced (figure 3.32). Nonetheless, erosion in established urban areas can still be seen on steep or poorly vegetated roadside embankments, on unlined channel banks, and on the downstream side of some culverts and floodways.

QUESTION BLOCK 3E

1. What is soil erosion?

2. How can human activity increase 'normal erosion'?

3. What is the difference between the two types of water erosion?

4. Explain why soil degradation is of concern to farmers.

5. How does the removal of vegetation affect soil erosion?

6. How can soil degradation be minimised in farming areas?

7. Explain why soil degradation is particularly a problem in Africa.

8. Giving reasons, how successful do you expect AGRA to be in addressing the problems of soil degradation in Africa? Before answering this question, you should check for information updates at the AGRA website, which is at http://www.agra-alliance.org/.

9. How does construction in urban areas affect soil erosion? Explain why this is so.

Water and Change

Water Resource Management

Of the earth's surface, 70% is covered by water. Of this water, 97% is contained in oceans as salt water, and is therefore not usable for drinking or irrigation. Of the remaining 3 % that is freshwater, only 0.3 % is found in rivers and lakes, the rest being frozen. It is easy to understand why water is regarded as a scarce resource in many parts of the world.

The result is that water must be conserved and used efficiently. Therefore, the need to manage water arises is a response to matching the supply of water to people with their domestic and industrial needs – needs such such as household use, manufacturing, irrigation, recreation and navigation (figure 3.33)

3.33 *Water is a very scarce resource in arid areas. Irrigation, using underground supplies from oases, is often necessary to enable food cultivation necessary to feed human populations. This aqueduct supplies water to a small community in the Drâa Valley in Morocco, near Zagora at the western edge of the Sahara Desert. The transformation of the oases can be seen by comparing the arid surrounds in the background.*

Humans cannot survive for more than a few days without water. Therefore, it must be argued that water is one of the most precious resources in the world for humans. For many people, however, access to clean drinking water is a major problem – more people die each day from drinking water than drinking alcohol, and over one billion of the world's population do not have access to safe drinking water (figure 3.34).

Access to safe drinking water is a major concern, and it is addressed in one of the targets of the Millennium Development Goals (MDGs) discussed in chapter 2. Specifically, the MDG is to halve the proportion of people without sustainable access to safe drinking water and basic sanitation by 2015. In looking at the factors that affect access to safe drinking water, it is important to understand what is meant by the terminology:

- *Drinking water* is water that is used for domestic purposes, including drinking, cooking and personal hygiene;

- *Access* to drinking water means that the source of water is less than 1 kilometre away from the place where it will be used, and it is possible to obtain at least 20 litres per member of a household per day on a reliable basis;

- *Safe* drinking water is water with bacterial, chemical and physical characteristics that meet World Health Organisation (WHO) guidelines or national standards for drinking water quality.

3.34 *A majority of the world's population does not have access to clean drinking water. In this view, a boy collects water from a heavily sedimented pond in the village of Minnanthu in central Myanmar.*

3.35 *Drawing water from a well in Djenné, Mali.*

Putting these three definitions together, **access to safe drinking water** is measured as the proportion of people using improved drinking water sources, which includes household connections (such as piped water), public standpipes, bore hole, protected dug wells, protected springs or rainwater (figure 3.35).

The problem with using unclean water is that there is a high risk of disease. Among the common water-borne diseases are diarrhoea, cholera, schistosomiasis and intestinal problems such as hookworm and hepatitis. About 1.6 million die each year from diarrhoea and cholera that were caught from unclean water supplies, while 6 million are visually impaired from schistosomiasis and 133 million suffer from intestinal infections caught from unsafe water.

The need to manage water is becoming more pressing as demand increases. Figure 3.36 shows the amount of water used in various regions of the world in 1995 compared with projections for 2025. In 1995 the world used 3,906 cubic kilometres (km³) of water. By 2025, water use for most uses (domestic, industrial, and livestock raising) is projected to increase by at least 50%. This significant increase will severely limit the water available for use in irrigation, which will increase by just 4%, restricting increases in food production in some parts of the world.

Although the world has abundant supplies of water, these supplies are unevenly distributed, both within and among countries. In some areas of the world, water use is growing so rapidly that surface stores are being depleted and even underground reserves are shrinking more rapidly than they can be replenished. One-third of the world's population live in countries that are experiencing moderate to high stress on their water supplies, which means that their consumption levels exceed 20% of the available supply.

It is expected that this situation will become worse in the decades ahead as the demand for water increases. The United Nations estimates that by the year 2025, two-thirds of the world's population will live in countries that are experiencing moderate to high stress on their water supplies. Much of the additional demand for water is expected to come from manufacturing, and if present trends of growth in manufacturing continue, global industrial water use will double between 2000 and 2025. Globally, agriculture accounts for 70% of water use, and the use of water for this purpose is expected to increase between 50% and 100% over the same period.

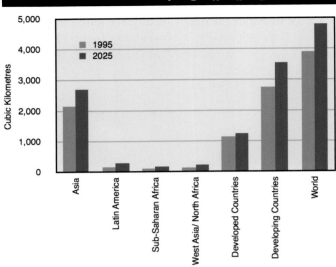

3.36 *Total water use by region, 1995 and 2025.*
Source: International Food Policy Research Institute

As shown in figure 3.36, much of the increase in demand for water will occur in the developing countries (LEDCs) as population growth and industrial growth is expected to be most rapid in those countries. This is important because it highlights the difference between physical water scarcity and economic water scarcity. **Physical water scarcity** occurs in places where the demand for water exceeds the supply. Physical water scarcity is most common in arid and semi-arid areas where rainfall is low and river flow fluctuates, perhaps even drying up at certain times of the year. **Economic water scarcity**, on the other hand, occurs when water is available but some people cannot afford to obtain it for reasons of poverty. Economic water scarcity is most common in LEDCs, especially among the urban poor living in shanty settlements in the cities.

3.37 *Water pollution aggravates local water shortages because it makes the water unusable for other purposes. In this view, a man defecates into an already heavily polluted open canal in Jakarta, Indonesia.*

When water is used, it often becomes polluted. Water pollution adds to the problem of scarcity of water because it removes additional volumes from the available supplies (figure 3.37). Many governments in LEDCs have become aware of the problem of water pollution in recent years,

and legislation has resulted in considerable improvements in many countries. However, in the rush to industrialise, water pollution is often placed as second in importance to manufacturing growth, and problems such as eutrophication, acidification, heavy metals and persistent organic pollutants (POPs) remain significant. A particular problem arises when pollutants seep downwards into groundwater, because dilution of pollutants is very slow and measures to purify the water are very expensive. This is a significant problem in many Asian countries, where more than 50% of domestic water supplies come from groundwater reserves.

As water supplies becomes scarcer, conflicts between rural and urban users may arise. Sometimes the competing demands are resolved by government legislation and quotas, as commonly occurs in the United States and Australia, while in other countries the scarcity simply results in higher prices for water. One strategy to manage the scarcity of water is to deliberately raise the price of water to force people to regard it is a valuable resource, and thus discourage waste and pollution. Understandably, this is not a popular strategy in LEDCs, where water for agriculture is a basic necessity for survival.

3.38 *Spray irrigation from pop up sprinklers is used to water decorative roadside date palms in one of the hottest, most arid parts of the world – at Jabal Hafit near the border of the United Arab Emirates and Oman. Most of this water will be lost to evaporation.*

Many geographers believe that better management of water resources could increase the availability of water. For example, it is estimated that in LEDCs, between 60% and 75% of irrigation water never reaches the crop because it is lost through leakage, evaporation or runoff (figure 3.38). Drip systems of irrigation use much less water than spray systems, but despite a 3000% increase in the use of drip irrigation globally between 1970 and 2005, it still makes up less than 1% of the world's irrigation systems.

Particular problems arise in LEDCs because low incomes make addressing water shortages very difficult. Many LEDCs are situated in arid areas of Asia and Africa, further exacerbating the problem. Lack of education sometimes leads to farmers using age-old methods of water management that cannot cope with the demands of a rapidly growing population, and erosion of the soil is one common consequence.

Another challenge for planners is that water is increasingly being used for non-essential uses, even in places that experience water scarcity. Urban planners often like to use water for ornamental purposes, even though this results in a loss through evaporation and diverts water from essential uses (figure 3.39).

3.39 *Ornamental water use in Uzbekistan's capital city, Tashkent, a city located in a hot, dry desert area.*

QUESTION BLOCK 3F

1. Discuss the proposition that 'water management arises from the need to match water supply to people's needs'.

Future Water Use

It appears very likely that the demand for water will continue to grow at a faster rate than the rate of population growth, placing even more pressure on scarce water resources. As shown in figure 3.36, it is expected that total water use in 2025 will have risen to 4,772 cubic kilometres (km³), a 22% increase on consumption in 1995. The increase is expected to be greater in LEDCs than MEDCs, the figures being 27% and 11% respectively.

The increase is expected to be mainly for domestic, industrial and livestock uses. The combined increase for these uses is expected to be 62% between 1995 and 2025, and the increase in domestic consumption is expected to be 71% of which over 90% will be in LEDCs.

Another significant area of increasing water use will be for manufacturing industries. The fastest growth will be in the LEDCs, and in 2025 the water used for industry in LEDCs is expected to be 121 cubic kilometres (km³) compared to 114 cubic kilometres (km³) for industries in MEDCs.

The increase in consumption of meat, especially in LEDCs, will also lead to a significant increase in the use of

water for livestock raising. Globally, the amount of water used for livestock raising is expected to rise by 71% from 1995 to 2025, the increase in MEDCs being 19% compared with the increase in LEDCs of 105%.

The largest use of water today is irrigating farmlands, which consumes about 35% of all the water used by humans globally. However, growth in the use of water for irrigation is expected to slow in the years ahead as the area of land used to cultivate food crops is expected to grow very slowly due to the effects of urbanisation, soil degradation and little investment in irrigation because a high proportion of arable land is already being farmed. It is also predicted that steady or declining prices for cereal crops will make it unprofitable for farmers to expand the area under cultivation. As a consequence, it is predicted that water used for irrigation will increase by 12% in LEDCs between 1995 and 2025, and it should decrease by 1.5% in MEDCs over the same period, resulting a global increase of just 4% in the total water used for irrigation.

However, the demand for water for irrigation is not distributed evenly across the world at the moment, and the uneven distribution is expected to continue in years to come. For example, the increase in demand for irrigation water is expected to increase by 27% in Sub-Saharan Africa between 1995 and 2025, and by 21% in Latin America. The large increases in these regions is partly because they have fairly small areas under irrigation at the moment, so the potential for growth is significant.

One of the consequences of physical water scarcity is that prices are likely to rise in the years ahead. This will aggravate economic water scarcity for many of the world's poor people. On the other hand, raising water prices should have the effect of encouraging all users to use water more efficiently, and it could also could generate funds to improve water facilities and build new infrastructure. However, because of the political opposition and concerns that higher prices could hurt poorer farmers and consumers, the price of water in most parts of the world has shown very little upward movement. Paradoxically, when water prices are subsidised, most of the benefits flow to richer urban dwellers who are connected to piped water systems, and poorer people remain underserviced because the investment funds are lacking to provide the access to safe drinking water that they need.

QUESTION BLOCK 3G

1. Explain why the future increase in demand for water for irrigation is expected to be less than for other purposes such as domestic, industrial and livestock use.

2. Explain why the policy of maintaining low prices for water makes it more difficult to meet the Millennium Development Goal to halve the proportion of people without sustainable access to safe drinking water and basic sanitation by 2015.

Case Study — Managing Water Scarcity in Turkmenistan

Turkmenistan emerged as an independent country in 1991 as a result of the break-up of the Soviet Union. Today, Turkmenistan serves as a region separating Iran and Afghanistan to the south, from Uzbekistan and Kazakhstan to the north. Although most of the country (90%) is covered by the vast sands of the Karakum (Black Sands) Desert, Turkmenistan has vast reserves of natural gas (figure 3.40). In 2007, Turkmenistan, Russia and Kazakhstan agreed to build new gas pipeline that will allow Turkmenistan to export gas to Russia.   Despite its huge energy resources, Turkmenistan does face a significant challenge in its economic development, which is the scarcity of water.

its HDI was 0.728, placing Turkmenistan 108th out of the 179 countries surveyed by the UNDP.

Although the USSR ceased to exist in 1991, many aspects of the the former Communist system continue to operate in Turkmenistan. The country continues to have a one-party system of government, controlled by the Democratic party of Turkmenistan, most of whose members were senior officials and politicians during the Soviet era. The leader of the Turkmen Soviet Socialist Republic, as Turkmenistan was known up until 1991, was Saparmurat Niyazov. After independence, he remained in power as Turkmenistan's leader, calling himself 'Turkmenbashi', or 'leader of the Turkmen people', and established a dictatorial rule with a highly developed personality cult (figure 3.41).

3.40 *The Karakum Desert in Turkmenistan.*

3.41 *There are many monuments in Turkmenistan celebrating the President's book, 'Ruhnama'.*

Some idea of Turkmenistan's extreme continental climate can be seen in the statistics shown in table 3.1. These statistics refer to the nation's capital city, Ashgabat, which lies in the relatively well watered foothills of Kopet Dag mountain range that separates Turkmenistan from Iran to the south. In the central parts of the country, tempera- tures frequently fall below freezing between December and February, while in summer, temperatures above 40°C are common and temperatures of over 50°C occur on several days every year.

The population of Turkmenistan is 5.2 million people, but because of the country's large area (488,100 km²), the average population density is just 10.7 people per square kilometre. In 2006, the GDP per capita was $US4,826 and

The strength of Niyazov's authoritarian rule increased and in 1999 he declared himself President for Life. He died suddenly on 21 December 2006, and his position was taken over by Gurbanguly Berdimuhammedow following the arrest of Niyazov's constitutionally appointed successor, Öwezgeldi Ataýew. Berdimuhammedow has continued the authoritarian policies of Niyazov, and this has been significant for all aspects of Turkmenistan's development, including its water management.

The management of water has always been important for human settlement in the region. The area now occupied by Turkmenistan has a long history of settlement dating right back to Mesolithic (Stone Age) times. It is known

Table 3.1
Climatic Statistics for Ashgabat, Turkmenistan (Latitude 38°N, Longitude 58°E, Altitude 208 metres)

	Jan	Feb	Mar	Apr	May	Jun	Jul	Aug	Sep	Oct	Nov	Dec
Average Maximum Temperature °C	7	10	16	24	30	36	38	37	32	23	17	10
Average Minimum Temperature °C	-1	0	5	11	16	21	23	21	15	9	5	1
Average Mean Temperature °C	2	4	10	17	23	29	31	29	23	15	10	5
Average Precipitation (mm)	22	27	39	44	28	4	3	1	4	14	20	21

that animals were being raised and both wheat and barley were being cultivated in Turkmenistan as long ago as 6000 BC. Shortly afterwards, several early urban settlements had been established near water sources such as oases. One particularly significant centre located on an oasis was Merv, located near the modern city of Mary. In its day, Merv was one of the largest and most cosmopolitan cities of the ancient world, rivalling Damascus , Baghdad and Cairo as a trading centre (figure 3.42). It held a key strategic position on the ancient Silk Road trading route between Europe and China, and during the 12th century it was the largest city in the world for a while with a population of 200,000 people. Being situated in the Karakum Desert, it is clear that very effective water management must have been practised in Merv to enable the population to grow to such a number (figure 3.43).

3.42 *The remains of the ancient city of Merv, Turkmenistan.*

3.43 *Ancient plumbing excavated in Merv.*

Today, one of the main reasons that Turkmenistan's scarce water must be managed carefully is because the nation's farming is so important, both for people's survival and for the economy. In 2006, agriculture contributed 20% of Turkmenistan's GDP and it employed 48% of the workforce, even though only 4.7% of the country's area was used for farmlands.

In its agricultural organisation, Turkmenistan still uses the Soviet system of state and collective farms, with production quotas set by the central government and fixed prices for the purchase of farm produce.

3.44 *Vegetables grown using irrigation water for sale in the large market in Ashgabat, capital city of Turkmenistan.*

Because of Turkmenistan's arid climate, irrigation is necessary for almost all the land that is cultivated land. A variety of fruits and vegetables are grown, most of which are sold in local markets as well as larger markets in the cities (figure 3.44). The most important food crop, however, is wheat. About 8,000 years ago, Turkmenistan became one of the first areas in the world where wheat was cultivated, as it is a native grass in the area.

3.45 *A display in Ashgabat celebrating Turkmenistan's wheat production.*

It is difficult to know exactly how much wheat is being grown in Turkmenistan, as the official government statistic of 2.6 million tonnes (2008) is not accepted by international agencies, who claim annual production is closer to 1 million tonnes. Either figure is insufficient to meet local demand (figure 3.45). Production is limited by the scarcity of water as well as the low level of technology available to farmers in Turkmenistan (figure 3.46). The country's wheat yields of about 1.5 tonnes per hectare are very low compared with neighbouring countries such as

Kazakhstan, where yields can reach 4.5 tons per hectare. Unlike Turkmenistan, Kazakhstan exports wheat, and uses it almost entirely for human consumption. The wheat produced in Turkmenistan tends to be of a lower quality and therefore 55% to 60% of production is used to feed animals. Whatever the production figure, the estimated area used for wheat cultivation is 880,000 hectares — 90% of which is under irrigation.

3.47 *A farmer shows a cotton plant in the irrigated cotton fields of eastern Turkmenistan.*

3.46 *Soil erosion generated by mechanised farming near Mary, Turkmenistan.*

By far the most important crop in Turkmenistan is cotton, which also requires large-scale irrigation (figure 3.47). Cotton growing began during the Soviet era, when huge areas of land were transformed from desert to farmland to grow cotton. Despite the high cost of irrigating the desert for cotton growing, the government is continuing to expand the land area for cotton, and in 2007 announced that an additional 100,000 hectares of virgin land (20,000 hectares in each province) would be brought under cultivation at an estimated cost of $US74 million. In order to achieve this goal, 3,200 kilometres of irrigation and drainage channels will be dug, placing additional demands on Turkmenistan's scarce water resources.

These new canals will continue the development of a pattern of water management that was initiated during Soviet times. Turkmenistan is home to the world's

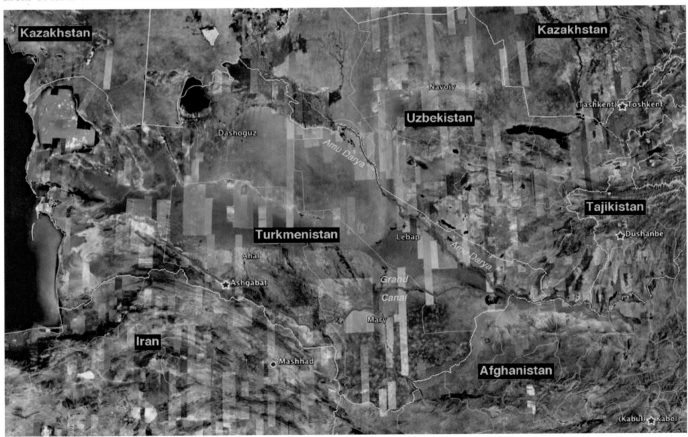

3.48 *Enhanced satellite image showing the Karakum Canal. (after Google Earth)*

longest irrigation and water supply canal, the 1,375 kilo-metre long Karakum Canal (also spelt as the Qaraqum Canal, Garagum Canal and the Kara Kum Canal). The canal was a major achievement of Soviet engineering, taking almost 13 cubic kilometres of water annually from the Amu Darya, a major river that flows through the far north of Turkmenistan. The canal begins in the far east of Turkmenistan and flows westwards across the Karakum Desert, past the capital city of Ashgabat to the town of Bereket in western Turkmenistan (figures 3.48 and 3.49).

3.49 *Water being pumped from the Karakum Canal to irrigate nearby cotton fields.*

3.50 *Irrigated cotton fields near Mary, Turkmenistan.*

Construction of the canal began in 1954. It reached Ashgabat in 1962 and Bereket in 1981. A future extension of the canal to Etrek in the far south-west of Turkmenistan is planned. Apart from a very small area in the far north of Turkmenistan that is irrigated directly from the Amu Darya, the Karakum Canal carries the water to supply all of Turkmenistan's irrigated farmlands (figure 3.50). Turkmenistan's cotton industry simply could not exist without the irrigation waters from the canal.

The flow of water is controlled by a series of large hydrau-lic structures near the Merv oasis, and water is diverted for irrigation into many branch canals (figure 3.51). However, silting of the canals is becoming a significant

problem as the Amu Darya brings large volumes of silt into the system. The efficiency of the canal has also been reduced because the poor quality of construction allows almost half the water to escape as it flows, creating lakes and ponds along the course of the canal.

Other environmental problems have emerged over the years. The main method of irrigation used is traditional surface irrigation, which means the water flows along a hierarchical network of canals through the fields. Efficient management of the water supply is very difficult using surface irrigation, and over-watering has been a widespread practice. This has led to a rise in the water table towards the surface, drawing salts to the surface and leading to salinisation of the soil in many areas (figure 3.52). In some areas, salinisation is so bad that fields have been abandoned as white salts take over the surface of the soil, making it useless for agriculture.

3.51 *Water being pumped into canals from the Karakum Canal.*

3.52 *White salt deposits on the surface indicate salinisation from inefficient irrigation practices.*

Further problems arise when the excess water drains back into the irrigation canals. However, the water flowing back into the canals has been percolating through the soils on the farms where large quantities of pesticides and chemical fertilisers are used. In the case of the cotton fields, it is normal practice in Turkmenistan to make extensive use of herbicides to defoliate the cotton plants to make harvesting easier for mechanical harvesting. For these reasons, the water flowing back into the canal tends to contain a variety of toxic substances. As more and more waste water flows back into the canal, the toxicity of the water rises as the water flows further downstream, and it is heavily polluted by the time it reaches western Turkmenistan.

Even before it starts to flow through the Karakum Canal, the water flowing into Turkmenistan from the Amu Darya is quite polluted. The headwaters of the Amu Darya are in the mountains of Tajikistan and Afghanistan. In spring each year, there are sudden rises in the levels of mercury, cadmium and lead in the waters entering Karakum Canal. The levels then fall again towards the end of summer. It is thought that mining operations in the mountains near the source of the Amu Darya are responsible for the heavy metals, and the annual spring melting of the snow washes the pollutants downstream into Turkmenistan.

Pollution of the waters in the Karakum Canal is a concern for the 700,000 residents of Ashgabat as 50% of the city's drinking water comes from the canal. The remaining 50% comes from surface runoff from the Kopet Dag mountain range south of the city, which is a cleaner source of water.

3.53 *New urban development and irrigated parklands in Ashgabat.*

Given its origins, it is not surprising that the quality of water in Ashgabat does not meet World Health Organisation (WHO) standards. In fact, no water supply in Turkmenistan meets the WHO standards. Although the water quality in Ashgabat is probably the best in the country, it fails 87% of the WHO indicators. Part of the problem is that the government lacks the funds to pay for upgrading Ashgabat's water treatment works, some of which date back to the 1960s. Nonetheless, the government has no plans to charge the public for water, as this would violate a presidential decree stating that electricity, gas, and water should all be free in Turkmenistan.

The shortage of funds has meant that it has not been possible to bring in experts to advise on the country's

water problems, and aid agencies have not so far seen Turkmenistan as a priority. As a consequence, wastage of water and poor quality drinking water continue to be problems. Moreover, Turkmenistan does not manufacture pipes, and so the government must pay hard currency if it hopes to replace, maintain, and expand water facilities.

3.54 *Fountains in Ashgabat, Turkmenistan's capital.*

Notwithstanding these problems with water, the Turkmenistan government is proceeding to rebuild Ashgabat as a city worthy of the 'Golden Age' of Turkmenistan as a personal political statement of the former leader, Saparmurat Niyazov. Vast new public buildings and apartment blocks are being built, all faced with white marble tiles and surrounded by green, irrigated lawns (figure 3.53). It is said that every week several hundred people are left homeless without compensation as a frantic demolition program works to clear the city's traditional single-storey courtyard-centred houses to make way for the reconstruction. Water is a feature of the redevelopment as elaborate fountains feature in many public areas and vast parks are built in honour of the country's leaders, sometimes including entire forests planted in the desert and irrigated with water from the Karakum Canal (figures 3.54 and 3.55).

3.55 *New irrigated parklands are being established in Ashgabat in an attempt to create a green, monumental capital city in the aridity of the Karakum Desert.*

In spite of the the problems encountered in managing its water in the past, the Turkmenistan Government is pressing ahead with some bold plans for the future. In 2004, the former President Niyazov announced "I am building the Turkmen Lake. I am building it for future generations. It will cost $8 billion... This lake is like a big sea. It will solve the water problem for the next generations. If we do not solve this problem, we will face water shortages."

The lake will be located in the far north of Turkmenistan. The water management plan states that the lake is to be filled with runoff water (i.e. recycled waste) from agricultural fields. If this works in practice, then the lake will not draw any additional water from the Amu Darya or any other source. However, critics of the plan have expressed doubts that the volume of runoff water will be enough to fill the lake, and they fear that yet more scarce water from the Amu Darya will have to used.

When completed in 2020, the planned surface area of Turkmen Lake will be almost 3,500 square kilometres. According to government planners, the new lake will enable the creation of 4,000 square kilometres of new farmland, which will represent a 20% increase in the country's arable land, enabling the annual production of 450,000 tonnes of cotton and 300,000 tonnes of grain.

Turkmenistan experiences chronic water shortages, and the extent of the water scarcity is increasing annually. Unfortunately, inadequate central controls of water management, shortages of capital and inadequate understanding of environmental consequences have hindered informed decision making.

QUESTION BLOCK 3H

1. *How has Turkmenistan's structure of government affected its water water management? Refer to both the Soviet and Post-Soviet periods.*

2. *To what extent is water scarcity in Turkmenistan a consequence of the country's climate?*

3. *Describe the importance of the Karakum Canal for Turkmenistan's water management.*

4. *Describe the problems and inadequacies of the Karakum Canal in addressing Turkmenistan's issues of water scarcity.*

5. *Explain why the waters of the Karakum Canal are so polluted.*

6. *Outline the consequences of polluted water for the residents of Ashgabat.*

7. *Critically evaluate the proposals to address Turkmenistan's water shortages in the future.*

Biodiversity and Change

Biomes, Ecosystems and Biodiversity

The **biosphere** is that part of the earth where all life exists. It is the shallow layer of soil, rock, air and water around the earth's surface that is only about 20 kilometres thick. If the earth were a soccer ball, the biosphere would be less than half a millimetre thick! Within this thin layer, there are both organic components (such as plants, animals, insects, micro-organisms and their dead remains and body wastes) plus inorganic components.

The biosphere represents a huge reserve of energy. There are three main sources of energy for the biosphere — gravity, solar radiation and internal earth forces. Of these, by far the most important is solar radiation. Plants use solar energy to make energy through the process of photosynthesis, and this energy is then available for use by animals and people. Without solar energy, there could be no life as we know it on earth.

3.56 *Large scale harvesting of rainforests is reducing the area of the world's tropical forests. In this area near the east coast of Malaysia, a large area of secondary forest has been logged in preparation for the planting of oil palms.*

An **ecosystem** is an interdependent community of plants and animals together with the habitat to which they have adapted. All the elements of an ecosystem are interrelated, being either directly or indirectly dependent on every other element of the ecosystem. A single ecosystem extends as far as the inter-relationships extend, and it follows from this that ecosystems can vary enormously in size. An ecosystem may simply comprise a small coastal estuary, or it may embrace an entire forest. It has been suggested that the world's largest ecosystem is the **rainforest** of Brazil that contains thousands of species with millions of interactions between them covering an area of almost 6 million square kilometres. The sum total of all the world's ecosystems is the biosphere.

An ecosystem such as a rainforest can be thought of as being similar to a large tapestry in which each thread builds up the total picture and where every thread is supported by every other thread. If one thread is removed, the effect is imperceptible. If several threads are removed, the picture becomes somewhat distorted but still hangs together. As more and more threads are removed, the picture loses its coherence until a point is reached where the tapestry collapses altogether. In the same way as the tapestry, the rainforest ecosystem can be remarkably resilient, but paradoxically they can also be very fragile (figure 3.56).

The factor linking the different parts of an ecosystem is the flow of nutrients and energy. Figure 3.57 shows the general movement of nutrients and energy with an ecosystem. Like the biosphere in general, ecosystems have organic components (such as plants and animals) and inorganic components (such as air, rock, water and soil). The main source of energy for any ecosystem is the sun. The sun supplies energy that is absorbed by plants through their green leaves by the process of photosynthesis. Some of this energy is lost to the atmosphere by respiration, but most of it is converted by plants into plant tissue and thus becomes an energy store. Plants also take in simple nutrients in solution from the soil in which they grow, and use these to produce plant tissue. Because plants are the first stage in the **food chain**, they are known as **primary producers**.

The energy and nutrients that are stored in the plants can be released, or made available to other organisms, in three ways. First, plant tissue falling to the ground (such as leaves, twigs, fruit, branches, or the entire plant when it dies) decomposes by bacterial action and forms **humus**, which is decayed organic material. This process of **decomposition** releases the minerals and nutrients into a storage pool for use by other plants.

The second process is **combustion**, which occurs when a plant is burned. Burning can occur due to natural forces or due to human activity. Either way, burning releases gases to the atmosphere and ash to the ground.

The third process is **consumption** of the plant material by plant-eating animals, or **herbivores**. Because herbivores eat the plant, which was the primary producer using the solar energy, the herbivore is known as the **secondary producer**. The herbivore in turn releases the nutrients by both **respiration** and the production of faeces. Some of the nutrients from the plant are used up as energy which is used to walk, run, breathe, and so on, while the remainder is converted into animal tissue in the herbivore. This energy may in turn be released if the herbivore is eaten by a meat-eating animal, or **carnivore**. Carnivores may be eaten by other carnivores, and thus a **food chain** is said to exist. Each carnivore in turn also releases nutrients through respiration and the process of defecating. Dead animal tissue that is not consumed by a carnivore is available for decomposition by micro-organisms, after which the nutrients are returned to the storage pool for use in the future by plants.

When a plant or animal is eaten by the next consumer in the food chain, most of the energy is lost. Of the incoming solar energy received by a green plant, only one to two percent is converted into plant tissue, meaning that 98% to 99% of the solar energy received is unavailable for use by the secondary producer. This means that each stage in the food chain requires a larger and larger number of organisms lower in the food chain to support it. This is

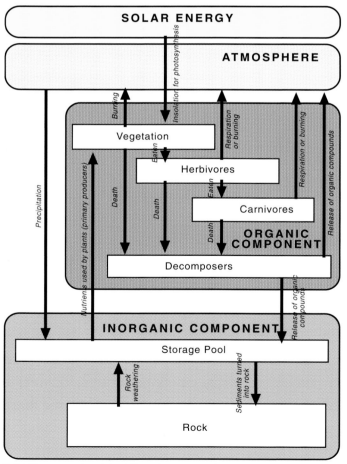

3.57 *Energy and nutrient flows in an ecosystem.*

known as the **pyramid of numbers** (figure 3.58). At the first energy level of the food chain, there is a large number of green plants. Green plants are also known as **autotrophs**, which means 'self-feeder', because they have the ability to produce their own food directly from the sun's energy by photosynthesis. All the later stages in the food chain comprise **heterotrophs** ('other-feeders'), which are also known as **consumers**. Each stage in the food chain represents a higher energy level, or **trophic level**. At the highest trophic level, the ecologically dominant species is found. In many ecosystems, this ecologically dominant species is human beings.

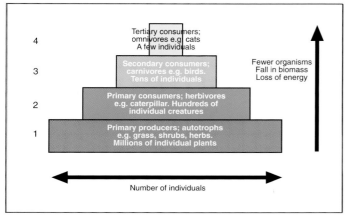

3.58 *The pyramid of numbers.*

Food chains are rarely longer than four trophic levels. This is because of the high loss of energy at each stage through respiration; the number of organisms required at the first trophic level to sustain a fifth trophic level in a given ecosystem would normally make that ecosystem unsustainable. To express this in another way, the shorter a food chain is, the greater will be the proportion of energy within the total food chain consumed by the ecological dominant species.

Although the concept of a food chain is a convenient way to understand the processes operating in an ecosystem such as a rainforest, it is really an over-simplification. In reality, most animals do not just consume a single species of plant or animal, but prefer to vary their diets somewhat. Most herbivores consume several species of plants, and most carnivores consume a variety of other animals. Moreover, **omnivores** such as human beings consume both autotrophs and heterotrophs. In some ecosystems, including rainforests, there are **detritivores** that consume organisms that are already dead and are decomposing. In reality, food chains are interconnected with other food chains, and the more realistic view of an ecosystem would be as a complex **food web**.

All ecosystems operate within certain tolerance levels. For example, if the precipitation becomes too high or too low, or if the temperatures become too hot or too cold, or if the purity of the water is disturbed, and so on, then the ecosystem may be placed under such stress that it collapses. Cold-blooded organisms such as fish and reptiles are especially dependent on stable environmental conditions, and if large numbers of these organisms were to die, then there would be a chain reaction throughout the food web.

All ecosystems have a particular **limiting factor** that controls their stability. For instance, a desert area may have sufficient solar radiation and soil nutrients to sustain abundant plant life, but water would be the limiting factor. A glacial area may have sufficient water and nutrients, but lack of incoming solar radiation limits plant growth, which in turn limits the numbers of all other organisms in the ecosystem. Limiting factors may not only be a minimum level — there may be an excess of water, or heat, or nutrients, and so on. For example, if a farmer releases an overflow of fertiliser nutrients into a stream, the excess of nutrients can kill many organisms and disrupt the ecosystem quite severely. Therefore, ecosystems have three critical levels for their limiting factors. First, there is the minimum level below which productivity ceases altogether. Second, there is the optimum level where productivity is greatest. Finally, there is the maximum level above which productivity ceases once again.

3.59 *Monsoon forests have a thick understorey of vegetation because, unlike equatorial rainforests, they have an open canopy. This area of monsoonal forest is near Darwin, Australia.*

Each species within an ecosystem fills an **ecological niche**. A niche is a particular function within the ecosystem, and it may be performed by one or several species. In different parts of the world, different animals can adapt to fill the same ecological niche. To take just one example, the kangaroo in Australia fills the same ecological niche (i.e. eating grass) as the zebra and antelope in Africa and the bison in North America.

When an ecosystem is disturbed, it can leave a particular ecological niche vacant. A species might be removed by hunting, a change in climate, pollution, and so on. Occasionally, another species can adapt and fill the vacant niche. More commonly, the removal of a species reduces the flow of energy through the entire ecosystem, causing stress and even the possible breakdown of the ecosystem.

The term **biome** refers to the world's total collection of a particular type of vegetation community, such as rainforests, deserts, grasslands and tundra, together with the fauna that are associated with it. The extent and nature of any particular biome depends on several environmental factors, the most important of which are climate, landforms, soils and biotic factors.

One measure of a biome's resilience is its **biodiversity**, which is simply how much variety there is in the life forms found there. At its most basic level, biodiversity can be measured or described by the number of different species in a given area. As a general rule, we find more species variation, and this greater biodiversity, in biomes which are found near the equator than those in colder climates (figure 3.59). We can therefore hypothesise that the biodiversity of rainforests even before we begin to examine them in detail.

QUESTION BLOCK 3I

1. *What is the difference between an ecosystem, a biome, and the biosphere?*

2. *Describe the linkages shown in figure 3.57.*

3. *How are nutrients made available to heterotrophs in an ecosystem?*

4. *Explain the cause of the pyramid of numbers shown in figure 3.58.*

5. *Why would greater biodiversity tend to make a biome more resilient?*

Tropical Rainforests

The hot, wet climates of equatorial areas create an environment that encourages year-round vigourous plant growth. In these areas, many species compete for light and nutrients in the somewhat poor, heavily leached soils. All trees are evergreen because any tree that remained dormant for part of the year could not compete with the constantly growing evergreens. This fierce struggle for light produces the distinctive vertical stratification, or layering, of rainforests (figure 3.60). The layers, or tiers, form because different plants have different levels of tolerance for light and shade. The tallest trees are the **emergents**, and these can be more than 60 metres high. In order to have support in the thin rainforest soils, emergents often have thick **buttress roots** spreading out above ground level to give stability (figure 3.61).

3.61 *Buttress roots give support to this tall tree in an Australian rainforest.*

Beneath the emergents is a layer of interlocking tree crowns called the **canopy** (figure 3.62). These trees require less light but more moisture than the emergents, and the canopy formed by their leaves is almost

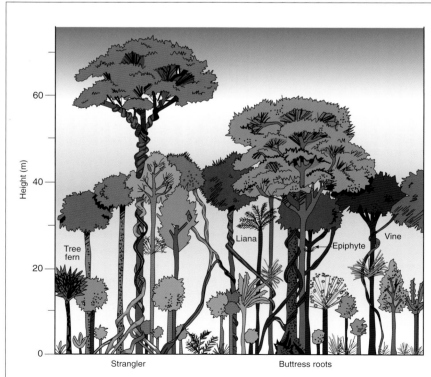

Emergents

Canopy (upper storey) with interlocking tree crowns

Lower storey (understorey) of smaller trees and tree ferns

Treelets

Forest floor (ground layer) - mostly too low to be seen here

Tree fern

Liana

Epiphyte

Vine

Strangler

Buttress roots

3.60 *The structure of the rainforest.*

continuous, making the floor of the rainforest quite a dark environment in spite of the intense sunlight overhead. Because the floor of the rainforest is so dark, there may be little vegetation at ground level except where patches of light can enter, such as beside a river or a road. Perhaps surprisingly, there is even very little leaf litter and humus on the floor of the rainforest because there are so many micro-organisms present to cause rapid decay.

One of the characteristics of a rainforest is that there are many plant species, and thus biodiversity is high.

3.62 *This view looking down on the rainforest from an elevated walk in the Kakum National Park in Ghana (West Africa) shows the thick canopy of trees (foreground), with a few emergents rising through it (background).*

3.63 *This fern in the Minnamurra Rainforest of Australia is a parasite, drawing its nutrients from the tree on which it is growing.*

Moreover, rainforests contain large numbers of woody climbing plants (lianas) and epiphytes, which are plants that rely on other trees for their physical support. Lianas may be several hundred metres in length and stretch from tree to tree, binding together the trees of the canopy into a tangled mess. In many rainforests it is common to find plants that depend on others to survive. One example of this is **parasitic plants** which grow on other trees, obtaining all their nutrient and water needs by sending their roots into the trunk of the host tree (figure 3.63). Stranglers are another type of parasitic plant found in rainforests. Stranglers, such as the strangler fig, begin as epiphytes, germinating in the branches of another tree. As they grow, however, they send their roots downwards towards the soil and become independent of the host tree. They then enclose the host tree, killing it (figure 3.64).

3.64 *This strangler fig beside the Zambezi River in Zimbabwe has almost succeeded in surrounding and killing its host tree.*

QUESTION BLOCK 3J

1. *Why is rainforest vegetation arranged in tiers, or layers?*

2. *Why are buttress roots such as those shown in figure 3.61 necessary in rainforests?*

3. *Comment on the biodiversity of natural rainforests.*

Human Impact on Tropical Rainforests

The tropical rainforest is a luxuriant vegetation biomass. In its natural state, there is great biodiversity of both plant and animals forms, although the animal biomass may be less than the plant biomass by a factor of a few thousand.

The ultimate source for the mineral nutrients that plants in rainforests require for survival is weathered rock. However, in a mature rainforest, the nutrient pool is contained largely in the living biomass and decaying organic matter of the forest floor (figure 3.65). Phosphorus and potassium are cycled almost entirely from biomass to litter and back again. Most of the roots lie at a depth of less than half a metre, and indeed many roots are found on the ground surface.

3.65 *Decaying vegetation covers the ground of rainforests.*

Some tropical rainforests have developed on rich, recent or alluvial material. However, in many rainforests the mechanisms for recycling nutrients are largely independent of the nutrient supply from the soil. Because of this, such forests are able to prosper even on poor soils.

However, the fragile mechanisms for recycling may stop functioning when a forest is disturbed, and the nutrients can be irretrievably lost.

Rainforests have adapted to the low nutrient levels of the soil under conditions of high rainfall and high temperatures. A dense root-mat forms over the soil in contact with the litter layer above it. Root tips grow upward and become attached to the fallen litter. The root mat also acts to absorb nutrients from sources such as rainfall. The leaves of many tropical rainforest trees have long, active lives and some transfer of nutrients back into the plant takes place before leaf shedding occurs. Some plants also have leathery leaves, or leaves which contain chemicals repellant to insects, to discourage herbivores eating the leaves while they are still active.

The multi-layered structure of the forest, together with its epiphytes and micro-organisms, acts to filter nutrients from rainwater. Nitrogen fixation occurs in the root-humus-soil zone and also on bark and leaf surfaces. Despite the intricate plant-animal relationships with exist in the rainforest, the nutrient flow through animal food chains is very small compared with other pathways.

How does such a system react to human interference and control? Clearly, activities which destroy the mechanisms of the natural rainforest that absorb and recycle scarce nutrients could result in disastrous nutrient losses.

3.66 *Shifting cultivators in northern Thailand near Chiang Rai clear the land for planting by burning.*

For centuries, humans have used the tropical rainforest lands to produce crops using the technique of **shifting cultivation**, or **swiddening**. Shifting cultivation is sometimes referred to as **slash-and-burn** agriculture, as it involves cutting down the vegetation and burning it to clear the plot for farming (figure 3.66). This type of land use allows human subsistence in vast areas of the tropics covered with forests growing on poor soils such as the Tierra Firme forests on lateritic gravels in southern Venezuela. These form part of the half million or so square kilometres of tropical rainforest in that part of

Venezuela which drains into the Amazon Basin. The area receives 3600 mm of rain per year; all months average more than than 100 mm. Average monthly temperature is 26.2°C, and there is only 1.3°C difference between the hottest and the coldest months.

Traditional shifting cultivation, with small (typically about one hectare) plots planted with various crops simultaneously, with the land being used for three or four years and then abandoned to fallow, has often been condemned as destructive. However, the practice involves a delicate balance with the environment and is now seen to be relatively harmless when practised by low density populations. The length of time a plot is cultivated, and the length of the fallow period before cultivation is repeated are critical (figure 3.67).

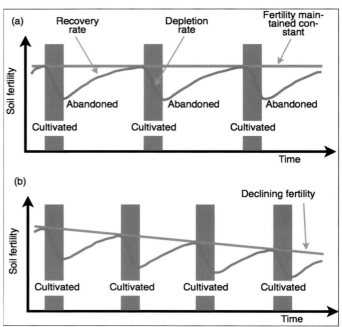

3.67 *Land Rotation Under Shifting Cultivation*

(a) Where population density is low, cycle-time is long, and the recovery of soil fertility is complete before a fresh cycle begins.

(b) Shorter cycle-time (more frequent cultivation) associated with increased population density results in long-term decline in soil fertility.

Note that the rates of depletion and recovery are the same (i.e. same slope on line), but the cycle-time is changed.

Source: After P Haggett, Geography: A Modern Synthesis, 1979.

The more successful forms of shifting cultivation establish a plant structure that is like a miniature of the former forest. The swidden plot has a **closed cover**, like the forest, because a few trees are usually left standing, and partly because some tree crops are planted, such as banana or paw-paw (figures 3.68 and 3.69). Within the swidden plot there is also great **diversity**, because many different types of crops are grown together, not in plots and rows, but distributed randomly, so that the result is a dense and complex plant mosaic. Moreover, like the rainforest, the swidden plants have a great deal of nutrients locked up in plant tissue. The effect of felling and firing the forest vegetation is not merely to clear the land but to transfer the rich store of nutrients to a plant complex whose usefulness to humans is a great deal larger than that of the original forest.

3.68 *A swidden on the steep slopes of Chimbu Gorge, Papua New Guinea. The slopes are so steep that ladders are needed to move across the gardens. People are killed from time to time by falling off their gardens into the gorge below.*

3.69 *Evidence of interculture (intercropping) can be seen by the different plant heights in this swidden in the Highlands of Papua New Guinea.*

Of greater significance than the activities of shifting cultivators is the conversion of tropical rainforests to **other forms of land use**. Globally, between 1% to 2% of the world's remaining area of rainforest is lost annually, with the most extensive deforestation occurring in Brazil and Indonesia (figure 3.70).

In certain areas, such as the Amazon Basin, clearing of rainforests is proceeding at a rate that alarms many observers. On appropriate soils, such as fertile alluvial soils or young volcanic soils, clearance of the rainforest for cultivation may result in stable and repeated cropping for generations. However, on poorer soils, conversion is often disastrous. The system of clear felling of trees for pulpwood results in the immediate export of nutrients

from the system, and the disturbance of the soil cover by logging equipment, together with its exposed state, frequently leads to spectacular soil erosion. Eroded lands may take many years to recover, if at all, but the problem is compounded because soil erosion also results in the destruction of roads and the siltation of reservoirs, reducing their life considerably. Indiscriminate use of fire can also result in a loss of nutrients from the system and lead to erosion.

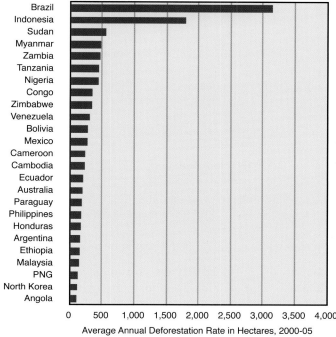

Average Annual Deforestation Rate in Hectares, 2000-05

3.70 *Average annual deforestation by country, 2000 to 2005.* Source: Derived from FAO data

When the rainforest is cut, plants cease taking up nutrients. This leads to larger quantities of drainage water passing through the system and to increased rates of decomposition resulting from higher soil temperature and soil moisture.

The large-scale clearing of tropical rainforests is thought by some to be a potential factor in causing **climate change**. However, the impact of tropical deforestation is bi-directional, which means it has impacts that lead to both global cooling and global warming at the same time.

The rate of reflection of solar energy (albedo) from tropical rainforests is only about 9%. By way of contrast, the albedo of desert can be as high as 37%. When rainforests are cleared, the albedo increases and therefore more incoming solar energy is reflected, meaning that less heat is absorbed at ground level. This leads to a series of effects, including global cooling, that are outlined in table 3.2.

On the other hand, when tropical deforestation occurs, burning of the trees releases large volumes of carbon dioxide into the atmosphere. It is estimated that tropical deforestation accounts for about one-third of all anthropogenic (human-induced) emissions of carbon dioxide. As shown earlier in this chapter, carbon dioxide is widely regarded as a key greenhouse gas, and there seems to be a positive correlation between the atmospheric concentration of carbon dioxide and rising global temperatures.

Table 3.2

Possible Climatic Effects of Tropical Deforestation

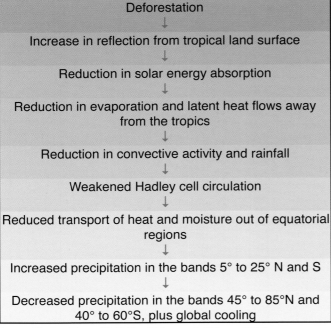

Source: Derived from GL Potter, *Nature*, vol. 258, pp. 697-8

Another important consideration when examining tropical deforestation is that **robust biodiversity** is not only necessary to maintain the natural food web, but loss of species deprives humans of beneficial products. Tropical rainforests have long been known as a rich source of natural products. Some rainforest trees such as the sandalwood have been collected for thousands of years because of its aromatic nature and natural oils. Some rainforest species have medicinal value, such as quinine. Still other species have had important economic value, some examples being rubber, palm oil, cocoa, teak and mahogany.

Many rainforest species have never been analysed to ascertain the benefits they might bring to people. Some rainforest plants have shown potential as medicines, such as one tropical periwinkle plant which is providing a chemical used to fight leukaemia. UNESCO estimates that fewer than 10% of the world's tropical flowering trees have been screened for even a single class of chemical compounds. It is reasonable to expect that when the rainforest species are analysed many will be found to have useful properties such as providing new sources of energy or industrial products such as resins, dyes, waxes, gums, oils and sweeteners. The disappearance of rainforest species before they have been examined represents a significant potential loss to humanity.

Fortunately, the world-wide rate of deforestation seems to be declining, and has been doing so since the 1980s at an accelerating rate. Based on current trends, it appears likely that the net movement will be an increase in the area of the world covered by forests within a decade or two, and it is predicted that global forest cover will increase by approximately 10% by 2050, this being the equivalent of an area about the size of India. Nonetheless, the rate of deforestation remains highest in tropical LEDCs where rainforest timber is seen as a valuable resource to earn hard currency through exports. The problem is that the short-term economic gains from clearing rainforests, either for agriculture or to exploit the timber resource, may be more than offset by a long-term loss of income as well as the long-term loss of biodiversity.

QUESTION BLOCK 3K

1. *On balance, do you think shifting cultivation is harmful to the rainforest environment?*

2. *How does deforestation change the natural nutrient flows of the rainforest environment?*

3. *Explain how tropical deforestation is leading to both global warming and global cooling simultaneously.*

4. *Discuss the causes and consequences of reduced biodiversity in rainforests.*

Sustainability and the Environment

Sustainability

In the previous chapter, the concept of sustainable development was discussed as a way to reduce global disparities. Another way of looking at sustainable development is as using resources in such a way that human needs are met while at the same time preserving the environment so that these needs can be met not only in the present, but into the indefinite future.

Although sustainability does not focus entirely on environmental issues, as we saw in figure 2.68 in the previous chapter, environmental considerations are very important. Indeed, as we noted in the previous chapter, environmental sustainability is one of the Millennium Development Goals (Goal 7). Several of the targets under this goal refer to three of the earlier sections in this chapter, namely greenhouse gas emissions, access to safe drinking water and reducing biodiversity.

At its most basic level, **sustainability** is maintaining something at a certain rate or level. It follows from this that **environmental sustainability** is achieved when any process that interacts with the environment replenishes at least what it uses so that the process is capable of continuing in perpetuity. If resources are used at a rate that is faster than they are replaced, then the use of those resources is **unsustainable**.

These concepts are developed in more detail in chapter 4 with respect to the use of resources and conservation.

QUESTION BLOCK 3L

1. *When we are looking at a process such as a farming operation or the work of a factory, what is the basis for deciding whether the process is environmentally sustainable or not?*

Case Study of a Management Strategy at the National Level to Achieve Environmental Sustainability — Iceland

In many ways, the Nordic countries (Norway, Sweden, Finland, Denmark and Iceland) are at the forefront of global efforts to achieve environmental sustainability. To some extent, this is the result of the strong emphasis they place on universal welfare, equality and environmental protection. Furthermore, the Nordic countries are very affluent and therefore have the financial means to implement effective management strategies that support their concern for environmental sustainability.

Following independence from Denmark in 1904, Iceland emerged from its position as one of Europe's poorest countries into an affluent nation with one of the highest standards of living in the world. Indeed, Iceland is ranked 1st place in the world according to its HDI, which in 2007 was 0.968. The foundation for this change was new technology that enabled Iceland to use its land resources and its surrounding fishing grounds. Fishing emerged as the backbone of the Icelandic economy during the 20th century, a position of importance that it still holds today.

Although Iceland's agricultural industries have declined, farming is still fundamental for the settlement of much of the country and makes Iceland largely self-sufficient in food production, though at quite a high price financially. The country's energy resources, especially geothermal power, provide heat and electricity as well as providing the basis for a growing export industry. Icelanders place importance on maintaining a pristine environment, not only for its own sake, but because Iceland's natural environment is the main attraction for foreign tourists (figure 3.71). Although Iceland's economy was — and probably still is — over-dependent on fishing, and despite a major financial crisis in 2008, sustained economic growth during the second half of the 20th century allowed sufficient resources to be accumulated for the government to develop a very comprehensive health care and welfare system for the nation's 305,000 people.

3.71 *Iceland's pristine natural environment.*

In 2002, Iceland announced a national strategy for sustainable development called 'Welfare for the Future'. The strategy, which is over 80 pages in length, has as its centrepiece the achievement of environmental sustainability. It is notable that this national policy was produced by the Ministry for the Environment.

In the preamble to the Policy, the Icelandic Minister for the Environment, Ms Siv Friðleifsdóttir, makes this statement:

> *"It can be said that Icelanders were well aware of the necessity of sustainable development long before the term became part of the Icelandic language. We have tried to reverse soil erosion and reclaim man-made deserts. We manage fisheries in a sustainable way so that not more is taken than the fish stocks' renewable strength can handle. These tasks remain important, but we must also pay attention to the tasks relating to the future development of Icelandic society, which call for the guidance of sustainable development. We have ample renewable energy resources that are very valuable, especially when we see the increased problems related to the burning of fossil fuels. Iceland's rugged but beautiful landscape is a magnet for tourists and a treasure for Icelanders. Long-range pollution is a current and future threat, and Iceland has been especially active in working on curbing the pollution of the oceans."*

The policy is designed to carry Iceland forward to 2020 following a philosophy of environmental sustainability. The program is seen as an evolution of earlier initiatives such as various laws to preserve and protect the environment, international environmental agreements and planning procedures that place great importance on protecting the quality of the environment. This is supported by a strong program of environmental education in Iceland's schools in an effort to make young Icelanders both aware of and sympathetic to environmental priorities.

One of the challenges for Iceland in implementing the national strategy is that very little work has been conducted in Iceland to define and develop indicators in the field of environmental sustainability, and this is a

Table 3.3
The Relationship between key sectors of the economy (column headings) with policy goals (row headings) in 'Welfare for the Future', Iceland's national strategy for sustainable development to 2020

	Agriculture	Fisheries	Industry	Energy	Mining	Transport	Tourism
1. Clean air		●	●	●		●	
2. Clean freshwater	●	●	●				
3. Safe food products	●	●	●				
4. Chemicals	●	●	●				
5. Outdoor activities	●					●	●
6. Natural disasters		●		●		●	
7. Iceland's animal and plant life	●	●	●	●		●	●
8. Geological formations				●	●	●	
9. Wilderness areas	●			●	●	●	●
10. Living marine resources		●					
11. Soil conservation	●			●			
12. Renewable energy		●	●	●		●	
13. Waste	●		●				●
14. Clean ocean		●	●				
15. Climate change	●	●	●	●		●	
16. Ozone layer		●	●				
17. Biological diversity	●	●		●			

Source: *Welfare for the Future*, Iceland's National Strategy for Sustainable Development, 2002–2020

barrier to effective goal setting. Although Iceland does collect statistics relating to environmental issues and resource use, which it publishes regularly, the information was not designed to be a measure of progress in achieving environmental sustainability. Part of the 'Welfare for the Future' strategy is to start the process of relating statistical information to goal setting with regard to sustainable development.

The core of the national strategy is a set of 17 goals, each of which relates to several key sectors of Iceland's economy and administration (table 3.3). The plan calls for national and local authorities to work with people and companies in each of the sectors to integrate the environmental sustainability goals into their own development objectives.

Goal 1: Clean air — In general, the air in Iceland is cleaner and less polluted than in most MEDCs. This is because of Iceland's low population density and its isolation from the major sources of air pollution in the northern hemisphere. Furthermore, clean sources of power such as geothermal energy and hydroelectricity

also contribute to the cleanliness of the air. Air pollution outside of Iceland's capital city, Reykjavik, is usually not regarded as a problem in Iceland, except in isolated places where there are polluting industries that produce foul odours such as fishmeal plants.

People in Iceland do regard air pollution in Reykjavik as a problem, even though the level of pollution is far less than in most similar cities in MEDCs (figure 3.72). The main cause of pollution is road traffic, and the national strategy calls for people to use more environmentally sound means of transport.

Outside Reykjavik, particulate air pollution (dust) can be a problem, especially in areas where soil erosion has occurred when winds blow strongly. Reducing soil erosion in rural areas can therefore reduce air pollution.

The national strategy has targets to achieve the goal of cleaner air:
• monitor air pollution ore closely and provide better information to the public;

- reduce particulate matter in the air by reducing the use of studded tyres (through increased taxes); and
- promote cleaner fuels (by adjusting the price structure of different types of fuel) and promote more use of public transport (by raising taxes on cars that are fuel-greedy).

3.72 *Reykjavik, capital city of Iceland.*

Goal 2: Clean freshwater — Iceland is fortunate in that its fresh water is generally the purest in Europe. Unlike people in many parts of the world, everyone in Iceland has access to safe drinking water and good sanitation.

Iceland's heavy average annual rainfall (2000 mm) and the low population density (the lowest in Europe) mean that there is more than enough water for everyone's needs. Over 95% of the water is untreated groundwater from springs, bore holes and wells (figure 3.73). Some parts of the country still depend on surface water, which is usually irradiated by ultraviolet light to eliminate any microbial contamination from animals and soil. A few populated areas still use untreated surface water that is well below the required standards.

3.73 *Fjarðrárgljúfur, one of Iceland's many natural rivers, near the town of Kirkjubæjarklaustur.*

The national strategy has targets to achieve the goal of cleaner water:

- introduce legislation to protect water and aquatic ecosystems;
- improve the monitoring of the quality of freshwater and drinking water; and
- ensure that all drinking water measures up to the required health standards.

Goal 3: Safe food products — Greater contact with the international community has changed the patterns of food consumption for Icelanders, reducing fish as a proportion of the diet and increasing the variety of almost every other kind of food. The more diverse diet has added nutrients to the diet, sometimes in excessive quantities, as well as artificial additives. Therefore, the national strategy is seeking to improve the dietary information provided so that people can take measures to prevent diseases that are caused by excessive intake of nutrients.

The national strategy has targets to achieve safer food products:

- conduct regular checks for pollutants, additives and pathogens in foods;
- limit the use of drugs and pesticides in food production;
- provide better nutritional information to consumers; and
- control environmental pollution near places where food is produced.

Goal 4: Chemicals — The national strategy sets a goal to make Iceland free from hazardous materials. Although laws and regulations require the monitoring of imported pesticides, toxic and ozone-depleting substances, and some other chemicals, the import and production control of toxic materials is said to be patchy and in need of reform, as is the control of other hazardous materials.

The national strategy has targets to achieve an environment free from hazardous materials:

- start compulsory registration of hazardous chemicals whether they are produced domestically or are imported;
- decrease the use of biocides and pesticides; and
- develop an action plan to limit the disposal of hazardous substances.

Goal 5: Outdoor activities — According to Iceland's Nature Conservation Act, the public may travel the country, but every traveller must treat it with respect and take care not to damage the environment. Both international and domestic tourism have grown rapidly in Iceland, and outdoor activities are a major focus of most travellers. Pressure from tourism can damage the natural environment, especially with off-road driving, horse riding and even hiking through sensitive vegetation such as that found in the highlands (figure 3.74). It is therefore important that outdoor activities are carried out in ways which are in harmony with nature.

3.74 *Tourists at Jökulsárlón, an iceberg filled lagoon in south-eastern Iceland.*

The national strategy has targets to encourage outdoor activities that are in harmony with nature:
- conduct research to determine the carrying capacity of tourist sites;
- improve the condition of tourist sites, such as by clearing paths, making parking spaces and improving access;
- provide better information for tourists;
- get tourists to cover the costs of monitoring and developing tourist sites; and
- include the value of outdoor activities in planning the potential of tourist sites.

Goal 6: Natural disasters — Being located on the Mid-Atlantic Ridge, which a plate tectonic boundary, Iceland experiences a wide range of natural hazards, including volcanic eruptions, lava flows, earthquakes, landslides and avalanches (figure 3.75). Furthermore, being located near the Arctic Circle in the Atlantic Ocean, Iceland experiences violent storms, floods and freezing winters. Structures such as houses, dams, harbours, bridges and electrical lines all have to withstand these hazards if possible.

3.75 *The lava flow from the 1973 eruption of Eldfell on Vestmannæyjar Island buried a large section of the town of Heimaey.*

The national strategy has targets to achieve protection against natural disasters:
- design structures to withstand pressures from storms, earthquakes and other natural threats;
- improve the monitoring system of natural hazards and improve people's preparedness to respond to danger;
- promote research into natural hazards; and
- conduct mapping and risk analysis so that land uses can be managed in response to natural hazards.

3.76 *Puffins on the exposed cliffs of Vestmannæyjar Island.*

Goal 7: Iceland's animal and plant life — Iceland's ecosystems have been shaped the country's isolation as well as its frequent volcanic eruptions and loose volcanic soils. The country's islands are important habitats and breeding centres for some 76 species of birds, 32 of which are endangered, including water birds and puffins (figure 3.76). About 270 species of fish have been identified in the waters surrounding Iceland. Of the 485 species of vascular plants in Iceland, 51 are endangered.

There has been considerable disturbance of Iceland's ecosystems since the beginning of human settlement in the year 874. Birch forests are thought to have covered about 25% of the country at the time of first settlement, but today this figure is only about 1%. Very little remains of the undisturbed wetlands on the lowlands, mainly because of drainage and the cultivation of marshes. Of all the wetlands in the southern part of Iceland, only 3% are undisturbed, while in western Iceland, only 18% of wetlands remain undisturbed.

The national strategy has targets to achieve the protection of Iceland's biota:
- map Iceland's biota and possible threats to use as a basis for regular monitoring;
- protect key habitats, such as the wetlands and birch woodlands;
- reclaim wetlands that have been damaged; and
- ensure that hunting and fishing in rivers and lakes is conducted on a sustainable basis.

Goal 8: Geological formations — Iceland has a unique set of geological formations because it is a volcanic island set on the Mid-Atlantic Ridge. The landforms have been dramatically shaped by the actions of ice and water, producing volcanic craters, lava flows, spectacular waterfalls and freshwater springs (figures 3.77 to 3.79).

However, various human activities threaten many of these geological formations. One example of this is mining for building materials, where the best and most accessible materials are often found in volcanic cones and lava fields.

The national strategy has targets to achieve the protection of Iceland's unique geological structures:
• systematically survey geological formations to produce a better geological map;
• preserve geological formations wherever possible; and
• reduce the number of mines and seal mines that are currently open.

Goal 9: Wilderness areas — Iceland is one of the few places in Western Europe where it is still possible to find large expanses of wilderness. These areas have value both as tourist attractions and as centres of biodiversity. The national strategy has targets to achieve the goal of conserving Iceland's wilderness areas:
• monitor industrial projects in wilderness areas on an annual basis;
• limit human structures and projects in wilderness areas;
• conserve continuous wilderness areas, including establishing a new national park (the Vatnajokull National Park, which will be Europe's largest conserved wilderness area and will include Europe's largest glacier as well as important volcanic and geothermal areas); and
• closing roads and banning traffic in some wilderness areas.

3.77 *The land is ripped apart at the Mid-Atlantic Ridge in Þingvellir, east of Reykjavik.*

3.78 *Gullfoss (Golden Falls), near Reykjavik.*

3.79 *The blue lake in the crater of Leirhnjúkur, near Krafla.*

3.80 *The fishing port of Húsavik on the north coast of Iceland.*

Goal 10: Living marine resources — The living marine resources in Iceland's fishing grounds are the backbone of the Icelandic economy. Marine exports account for about 45% of Iceland's exports. Management of the marine environment is clearly very important to Iceland (figure 3.80). The national strategy has targets to achieve the sustainable use of living marine resources:
• establish a legal framework to manage Iceland's fishing industry;
• adopt an ecosystem approach to the management of the marine environments; and
• take greater account of the environmental impact of fishing gear.

Goal 11: Soil conservation — Soil erosion and desertification have often been said to be Iceland's greatest environmental problem. The forested area of Iceland is smaller than any other European country and over half the country's vegetation has disappeared since human settlement began (figure 3.81). Studies have shown that clearing of woodlands and overgrazing have led to 52% of the country's soils (excluding the area covered by the highest mountains, glaciers and lakes) being seriously eroded. Grazing of animals continues to threaten the stability of soils in many parts of Iceland (figure 3.82).

3.81 *Wind erosion on the dry uplands of Iceland's Central Plateau.*

3.82 *Animals grazing near Lake Mývatn.*

The national strategy has targets to achieve sustainable use of vegetation and reclamation of land:
- achieve sustainable use of grazing lands, which means that the state of the vegetation should be stable or improving, and barren or eroded lands should not be used for grazing animals;
- government support for land improvement by farmers by providing data and suggestions for farm improvement;
- develop a long-term strategy for soil conservation; and
- increase afforestation projects.

Goal 12: Renewable energy — Iceland already uses renewable energy sources for 70% of its total energy use;

this is more than any other country in the world. For heating, 89% of Iceland's energy comes from geothermal energy, with a further 10% coming from hydroelectricity (figure 3.83). For Iceland's total electricity production, 17% comes from geothermal energy and 83% comes from hydropower. Fossil fuels are used for most transport, however.

3.83 *The geothermal power station at Krafla, central Iceland.*

The national strategy has targets to increase the utilisation of renewable energy:
- continue working to develop a master plan for the use of geothermal energy and hydroelectricity;
- conduct thorough research into new options to harness geothermal power and hydropower;
- test vehicles that are powered by clean and renewable energy;
- improve the efficiency of existing power sources; and
- create incentives to encourage more efficient use of energy, including educating the public about ways to save energy and setting the prices of energy in ways that encourage energy efficiency.

Goal 13: Waste — Each year, about 250,000 tonnes of waste are produced in Iceland. Of this amount, 60% is disposed of in landfills, 30% is recycled in ways other than for energy production, and 7% is incinerated. In total 67% of the waste was disposed of, 32% was recycled and 1% is unaccountable. The national strategy has targets for the reduction and improved handling of wastes:
- processing charges will be introduced on domestically produced goods and imports to cover the cost of recycling, supporting both the 'polluter pays' principle and creating an economic stimulus to decrease the quantity of waste and find better ways to recycle it;
- develop a national waste management plan;
- set annual recycling targets, including that no less than 50% to 65% of all packaging waste will be recycled;
- improve the handling of construction waste such as concrete and ground materials, 97% of which go into landfills today;

- introduce hazardous waste charges to support the safe disposal of hazardous wastes; and
- ensure that the best available technology is used for waste handling.

Goal 14: Clean ocean — The oceans around Iceland contain some of the cleanest waters known, and contaminants in Icelandic fish are virtually unknown. Some pollutants have been found at minimal but measurable concentrations in Icelandic waters, some being due to human activity in Iceland, but mostly due to sources in other countries. Nonetheless, because of the importance of the oceans to Iceland's survival, the national strategy has targets to ensure the concentration of pollutants should always fall below the strictest international standards:

- participation in international actions to combat the release of Persistent Organic Pollutants (POPs) and heavy metals into the oceans;
- develop an action plan to combat land-based marine pollution;
- improve the treatment of sewage;
- improve the monitoring of pollutants in line with international agreements;
- eliminate radioactive pollution in the North Atlantic by continuing to press for the closure of nuclear reprocessing plants in nearby countries (mainly the United Kingdom, but also France and Japan);
- improve the ability of ships to retain their waste and sewage (figure 3.84);
- include environmental liability into Icelandic law, which means there would be serious fines for ship-based as well as land-based polluters; and
- promote international action to undertake a global assessment of the state of the world's marine environments.

3.84 *Fishing vessels in the port of Höfn, south-east Iceland.*

Goal 15: Climate change — The possible impacts of climate change, and especially global warming, on Iceland are unclear. The Icelandic government has fulfilled its commitments to the Kyoto protocol, but nonetheless has set further targets in the national strategy to limit climate change:

- changes in the structure of fuel taxes will be used to encourage greater use of diesel-powered cars, import duties will be modified to encourage the importation of more more fuel-efficient cars, traffic lights will be synchronised to reduce fuel consumption, and taxes will be changed to make public transport more attractive;
- the aluminium industry will be required to minimise pollution emissions;
- energy use by the nation's fishing fleet will be reduced by introducing more efficient systems of refrigeration and by educating ship captains in more efficient ways to use energy;
- the disposal of gas-producing organic wastes in landfill tips will be reduced;
- carbon sinks will be created by afforestation and re-vegetation projects (figure 3.85); and
- Iceland will participate actively in international efforts to reduce global warming, such as through the Kyoto protocol and the United Nations Framework Convention on Climate Change.

3.85 *Grass planted to stabilise loose volcanic soils at Lakagígar.*

Goal 16: Ozone layer — The thinning of the ozone layer was first discovered in the late 1970s when a so-called hole in the ozone layer was detected above Antarctica. The thinning is caused by the emission of certain pollutants such as chlorofluorocarbons (CFCs) from refrigerants that react with the ozone in the stratosphere, destroying it under certain conditions. This is significant because the upper atmosphere ozone shields the earth from hazardous ultraviolet component of the sun's radiation. Reduced upper atmospheric ozone can lead to serious health problems for human such as skin cancer and genetic damage. Although the thinning of the ozone layer has been less serious over Iceland than in many places at similar latitudes, the national strategy has targets to protect the ozone layer:

- a complete ban on the import of ozone-depleting substances; and

- removal of ozone-depleting substances from older equipment, together with safe recycling of old air conditioners, fire extinguishers and broken refrigerators.

Goal 17: Biological diversity — Although biodiversity is a global issue that crosses international borders, the main threats to biodiversity in Iceland are the destruction of habitats due to cultivation and built structures, together with the deterioration of habitats due to land uses such as grazing and the use of fishing gear that can damage marine habitats. The use of imported species of plants and animals have also had some negative effects on biological diversity. It is uncertain what impact climate change will have on biodiversity in Iceland.

The national strategy has targets to achieve the protection of biodiversity:
- a comprehensive national strategy on conserving biodiversity will be developed and implemented;
- regulations will be introduced to restrict the importation of invasive animal species, as well as their breeding within Iceland; and

- Iceland will ratify the Cartagena Protocol on Biosafety (which is a supplement to the Convention on Biological Diversity) as well as limit the import and distribution of genetically modified organisms.

QUESTION BLOCK 3M

1. *Compare Iceland's national strategy on ecological sustainability with measures in your own country. Giving reasons and examples, say which strategy you think shows the better understanding of the concept of environmental sustainability.*

Patterns in resource consumption

4

Resource consumption, especially energy, and conservation strategies

Patterns of resource consumption
Page 145

Ecological footprint as a measure of the relationship between population size and resource consumption, looking at international variations in its size. Neo-Malthusian and anti-Malthusian views of the relationship between population size and resource consumption.

Changing patterns of energy consumption
Page 154

Global patterns and trends in the production and consumption of oil. The geopolitical and environmental impacts of these changes in patterns and trends. The changing importance of other energy sources.

Conservation strategies
Page 161

The reduction of resource consumption by conservation, waste reduction, recycling and substitution, including a strategy aimed at reducing resource consumption.

Patterns of Resource Consumption

ToK BoX — Page 150
The Ethics of Resource Use

The Nature of Resources

A **resource** is something that is useful to humans. Of course, something that is a resource to one person may not be a resource to someone else. A bicycle may be very useful to an 8 year-old boy, but it will be of very limited use to the 8 year-old's ageing grandparents. Therefore, the bicycle is a resource (or something useful) to the 8 year-old, but not to that child's grandparents.

It follows from this that whether something is a resource differs from culture to culture. Uranium is a resource in France because electricity is generated in nuclear power plants. However, uranium is not a resource to an isolated person living in the remote Highlands of New Guinea except in the sense that it, like some other kinds of rock, can be fashioned into a stone tool. Of course, if the High-

lander is not quite so isolated, and can sell the uranium, then it becomes a resource – as long as the Highlander has become part of the cash economy and money is therefore useful (or a resource) to that person. In a similar way, pigs are resources to the New Guinea High-landers because they are both a source of food and a symbol of wealth. However, a pig would not be a resource to a Muslim person living in Saudi Arabia because Islam regards the pig as an unclean animal that cannot be eaten.

Two small sticks from a bush are a resource to New Guinea Highlander. However, they are of little use to most urbanised people in the world for whom twigs are so common that they are worthless, and who would use a match or a cigarette lighter to start a fire (figures 4.1 and 4.2). What is a resource and what is not also changes over time. To take the example of uranium that was mentioned earlier, although it is a resource in France today it would not have been useful several centuries ago.

We can say, therefore, that the concept of a resource is dependent on technology as well as culture.

4.1 *The bicycle that is a resource to a resident of Hong Kong, where there are extensive networks of dedicated bicycle tracks, would be of almost no use to a person who lives in the mountains of Irian Jaya, where steep narrow trails with sharp rocks, crossing creeks and climbing steep mountains, make using a bicycle impossible.*

4.2 *For this man who lives in the mountains of Irian Jaya, the large stone axe used to butcher the pig that was just killed with a spear is an important resource. It would, however, be useless to a person in Hong Kong who rides a bicycle to the supermarket to buy refrigerated meat.*

Coal, oil and sand provide additional examples of the changing nature of resources. By the time Europeans first settled in Australia, coal had been used as a fuel in many parts of the world. However, the culture of Aboriginal people had developed over thousands of years without the use of this natural resource. The potential had always been there, especially where coal seams outcropped in coastal cliffs, and lumps of coal were scattered along

beaches, but coal only became a natural resource in those places where a use was found for it.

Oil, likewise, occurred naturally in places where it oozed to the surface and even formed shallow lakes in various parts of the world. It was a minor natural resource until drilling for it proved successful in 1859 and refining techniques were developed and spurred along with the development of the internal combustion engine.

Sand has been part of the building industry as an ingredient of mortar and concrete for thousands of years and glass, made from silicon via its dominant constituent, silica, has been used for about 2000 years. Only in the 1980s and 1990s have the techniques been developed to allow sand to become an important contributor to our computer-based and high energy-using society. The silicon chip is now part of our way of life even though computer chips are now being made from new compounds that allow even greater computing power. Silicon is also a key component of the solar panels that should contribute a growing proportion of the pollutant-free energy the world uses. Sand's changing role as a natural resource is another example of the way technological advances can radically alter natural resources.

If a resource is something useful to humans, then a **natural resource** can be thought of as anything in the biophysical environment that can be used by people. Thus, a natural resource can be defined as a naturally occurring material that a society perceives as being useful to its economic and/or social well-being, and which can be used or exploited.

There are several groups into which natural resources can be classified or categorised. One of the most common classifications is to separate resources into renewable and non-renewable resources. **Renewable resources** are those materials that can be regenerated in nature faster than they are being exploited by a society. Examples of renewable resources include solar radiation, water, wind, soil, plants (including forests) and animals. Sometimes, mismanagement of a renewable resource can lead to its depletion (or 'mining'), causing it to become exhausted. For example, if trees in a forest are cut down more quickly than they can re-grow, or if soils are cultivated in a way that allows erosion to occur, then the resource becomes effectively non-renewable.

A **non-renewable resource** is a material generated so slowly in nature that for all practical purposes it exists in a finite quantity. Examples of non-renewable resources include the fossil fuels (oil, natural gas and coal), minerals (both metallic and non-metallic) and nuclear fuels (such as uranium). Many non-renewable resources can be **recycled**, which means they can be used repeatedly. Examples of non-renewable recyclable resources include most metals (such as aluminium, zinc and lead), some non-metallic minerals such as diamonds, and materials manufactured from fossil fuels such as plastics.

There are other ways of classifying resources besides the simple division into renewable and non-renewable. For example, it is possible to divide resources into five broad categories:

- **energy resources**, such as fossil fuels, geothermal reserves, water (when used for hydro-electricity); nuclear materials, biomass, solar energy, tidal energy and the wind;
- **mineral resources**, both metallic and non-metallic;
- **organic resources**, such as soils, forests and animals;
- **water resources** and
- **landscape**.

These are not the only ways of classifying resources, and there is nothing to stop a group of students devising their own original system of classifying resources according to quite different criteria.

QUESTION BLOCK 4A

1. *What is a 'resource'?*

2. *Explain how the things that are considered to be resources change (a) over time and (b) between cultures.*

3. *Explain the difference between renewable and non-renewable resources.*

4. *Of the two ways of classifying resources mentioned in this section, which do you prefer? Explain why. Can you think of a third way of classifying resources that you might prefer?*

The Debate Between Neo-Malthusians and Anti-Malthusians

The distinction between renewable and non-renewable resources partly rests on the assumption that non-renewable resources are finite and therefore exhaustible. This view is shared by **neo-Malthusians** such as Paul Ehrlich who, like Thomas Malthus whose ideas were discussed in chapter 1, believe that there is a close relationship between population size and resource consumption. Neo-Malthusians believe that limited resources keep populations in check and reduce economic growth. Therefore, according to neo-Malthusians, population growth should be controlled, because if it is not controlled by choice, then pressure on scarce resources will force a catastrophe that will cause widespread deaths through famine, disease or war.

In 1968 Paul Ehrlich published an extremely popular book, *The Population Bomb*, which opens with the following declaration: "The battle to feed all of humanity is over. In the 1970s the world will undergo

4.3 *The Club of Rome's 'standard' world model plotted a predicted future for the world to the year 2100. It assumed no major change in the physical, economic or social relationships that historically governed world relationships. All variables plotted on the graph followed historical values from 1900 to 1970. Food, industrial output and population were predicted to grow exponentially until the rapidly diminishing resource base forces a slowdown in industrial growth. Because of natural delays in the system, both population and pollution continue to increase for some time after the peak of industrialisation. Population growth is finally halted by a rise in the death rate due to decreased food and medical services. N.B., B = birth rates, D = death rates, S = services per capita.*

famines – hundreds of millions of people are going to starve to death." Shortly afterwards in 1972, a group known as the Club of Rome headed by Dennis Meadows wrote *The Limits to Growth*, in which the authors argued that the combination of population growth and finite natural resources would create mass misery (figure 4.3). The group then ran several computer simulations on the future of humanity under various scenarios, all of which seemed to end in disaster. These views seemed like common sense in the context of the trends at the time. Their arguments paralleled those of Thomas Malthus two centuries earlier.

4.4 *Price is a measure of scarcity. Petrol prices rise if petrol becomes scarcer; prices fall if petrol becomes more abundant. Over time, prices have fallen, indicating greater abundance.*

However, **anti-Malthusians** such as Julian Simon disagree with this view, and quote statistics and historical examples to support their case. In his 1996 book *The Ultimate Resource 2* in 1996, Julian Simon argued that the true measure of scarcity is not the physical quantity of a resource, but price (figure 4.4). If something is becoming scarcer, its price will increase. Similarly, if something is becoming more abundant, its price will fall. Although it seems contrary to common sense, the evidence seems to be that over time, the price of almost every natural resource (adjusted for inflation) is decreasing, indicating that resources are becoming less scarce or more abundant.

In 1931 Harold Hotelling, one of the most respected resource economists at the time, predicted that the real price of oil and of other fixed resources would rise as the amount left on earth decreased. However, the evidence shows that apart from politically-motivated price increases such as occurred in the 1970s and early 1980s, and again in 2007 to 2008, the price of petrol has declined steadily in the long-term (figure 4.5). Furthermore, if the price of petrol is related to the 'real' cost of purchasing it, which is the number of hours needed by an average person to earn the money to buy a litre of petrol, then the decline in price is even more marked (figure 4.6). In 1920, the director of the U.S. Geological Survey announced that annual production of crude oil had almost peaked. How-

ever, by 1948 annual US production was at four times its 1920 level, and it has continued to increase since then.

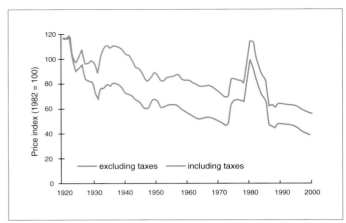

4.5 *Index of inflation-adjusted US prices for petrol, 1920-1999.*

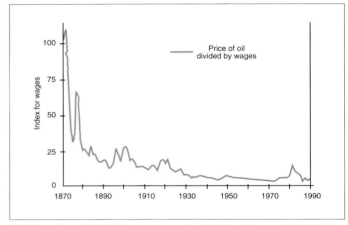

4.6 *The price of oil relative to wages in the United States, 1870-1990.*

The same analysis could be applied to almost every natural resource. In 1950, the world's reserves of iron were estimated at 19 billion tonnes. Over the next 30 years, 11 billion tonnes of iron were smelted from those reserves. That should have left a reserve of 8 billion tonnes, but in 1980 iron reserves had increased to 93 billion tonnes. A combination of new discoveries, recycling, new technology that allows less concentrated deposits to be used and previously inaccessible deposits to be mined has meant that as resources have been used, the estimates of known reserves for many natural resources have been revised upwards (figure 4.7). Long-term studies show that the prices of most natural resources have declined over time, indicating greater abundance rather than scarcity (figures 4.8 and 4.9).

In a famous incident, Julian Simon publicised his views with a bet. In 1980 he challenged Paul Ehrlich to a bet of several thousand US dollars that natural resources would become cheaper rather than more expensive over the next ten years. Simon's reasoning was that if natural resources were to become scarcer, their prices should rise. Paul Ehrlich confidently accepted the bet.

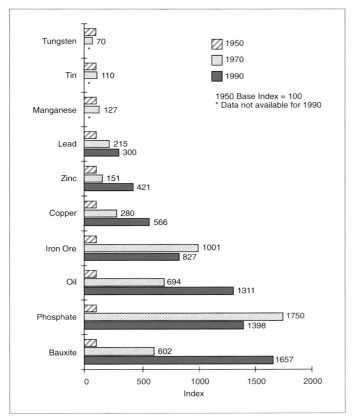

4.7 *Known world reserves of a range of natural resources, 1950, 1970, 1990.*

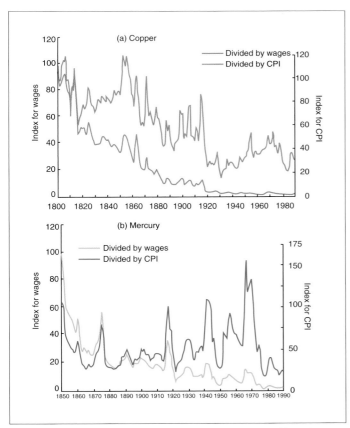

4.8 *The scarcity of selected natural resources as measured by price relative to wages and the consumer price index. Graphs show trends for copper 1800-1980 (top), mercury 1850-1990 (bottom).*

Paul Ehrlich was given the choice of natural resources and chose five metals – copper, chrome, nickel, tin, and tungsten – to follow over a period of a decade. Julian Simon won the bet. During the ten years 1980 to 1990, the prices of all five minerals fell: copper by 18%, chrome by 40%, nickel by 3%, tin by 72%, and tungsten by 57%. Although Paul Ehrlich paid the bet, his views about resource scarcity did not change, and he continues to insist that resources will become scarcer – and therefore more expensive.

Following this success, Julian Simon decided to expand both the bet and the set of potential bettors. In 1996, he told the *Washington Post* that he would bet "any prominent doomsayer" $100,000 that by any material measure, living standards would only improve. "I'll bet on anything pertaining to material human welfare – life expectancy, price of a natural resource, number of telephones per person in China," he told the *Washington Post*. No-one ever took up his offer, which Julian Simon's supporters claim means he won the debate.

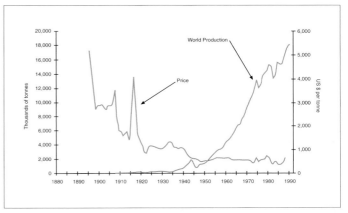

4.9 *Price and world production of aluminium, 1880-1990.*

It can be difficult to understand why Malthus' and Ehrlich's arguments that population growth will reduce resources seem to be incorrect. It is true that in the short run, population increases will drive up the demand for natural resources and therefore their prices. However, when this happens, the high prices prompt entrepreneurs and innovators to find new resources, or new ways of getting existing resources more cheaply.

Julian Simon quoted the example of billiard balls that used to be made from the ivory of elephants' tusks. As the demand for billiard balls increased, elephants became a scarce resource, because their breeding time was slower than the increase in demand for ivory. Consequently, researchers looked for substitutes, and this resulted in the development of celluloid, which was the prototype of plastic. As a result of the shortage of ivory, therefore, we now have plastics, which are a much cheaper alternative.

Simon argued that the net result of this is that resources are more plentiful and cheaper than they were before the

ToK BoX

The Ethics of Resource Use.

At its most elementary level, geography is concerned with three basic questions:

1. Where is it?

2. Why is it there?

3. And so what?

The third question could be re-phrased as "what are the implications of location?", and it raises many ethical issues of justice, equity and fairness.

This can be seen very clearly when we look at the global pattern of resource distribution, and the very different global pattern of resource consumption.

When we are confronted with ethical questions of fairness and equity, it can be easy to suspend rational judgement and appeal purely to the emotions. Fortunately, philosophers over the centuries have provided us with tools to analyse moral and ethical issues using more robust systems of analysis than a simple 'how do you feel about this?' approach.

It has been suggested that there are four standards of morality to which all moral decisions can be reduced:

1. The powerful decide what is right

2. Morals are determined by culture

3. Morals are determined by the individual

4. Morals are determined by a good God

It is probably fair to say that different individuals operate on different moral bases depending upon the issue in question, and even according to the time and circumstances. For example, a very experienced teacher in an international school once commented "Students are universalists when it comes to environmental issues, but relativists when it comes to moral questions." In other words, according to that teacher, students tend to insist that everyone without exception should adopt the same attitude on improving the environment, but they are willing to accept other people's rights to do whatever they like on moral and ethical issues.

If that teacher is correct, then students (and maybe other people as well) behave inconsistently on ethical issues, sometimes being ethical subjectivists and at other times ethical objectivists (see the table in the top right of this ToK Box).

Although *some* values are relative and people are *often* selfish, it does not follow that *all* values are relative or that people are *always* selfish. This suggests

Ethical Subjectivism	Ethical Objectivism
Whatever a person thinks or feels is morally right, is right, at least for that person	*A binding moral order exists independently of human opinion and/or approval*
The rightness or wrongness of actions depends on a person's thoughts, opinions, intentions, and desires. **Moral truth is relative to the individual**	Universal and valid ethical principles exist outside the minds and wills of human beings. **Moral truth stands apart from human convention**
Moral values are: • subjective • invented • widely accepted • relative • descriptive • consequential • particular for each individual	*Moral values are:* • objective • discovered • not necessarily conventional • absolute • prescriptive • non-consequential • universal

that there is such a thing as moral knowledge and people are capable of acting on this knowledge. There are several approaches to looking at this, known as theories of ethics.

One approach is Religious Ethics. The world's religions are sources of moral insight and guidance to millions of people. In the case of theistic religions, such as Judaism, Christianity and Islam, ethics flow from revealed truth that comes from a divine source. Many believe that the 'Golden Rule' — treat others as you want to be treated — is a common ethical factor in all the world's religions. As one who drew from religious ethics, the Russian novelist Fyodor Dostoevsky (1821-1881) said that "if God is dead, everything is permitted".

On the other hand, the Greek philosopher, Plato (428-348 BC) said we cannot derive ethics from religion. He explained it like this: is something good (1) because God says it is good, or (2) does God say it is good because it IS good? Plato said that if (1) is the case, then God could suddenly say evil was good, which would be absurd and unacceptable. If (2) is true, then values are independent of God and we do not need to appeal to the authority of God's word.

Most religious people would claim Plato had a very limited concept of God, but whether this is true or not, religion-based ethics will not satisfy atheists. This leads us to consider other theories of ethics.

A second group of ethical theories is called Duty Ethics. A leading advocate of this approach was Immanuel Kant (1724-1804), who said that the way to decide if something is right or wrong is *not* to use feelings, but to use *reason* to see whether or not you can consistently generalise it.

For example, if you are trying to decide whether or not it is okay to jump the lunch queue in the canteen, Kant would say you should answer this question by asking yourself — what would happen if everyone did that?.

The answer is that there would be chaos and anarchy, and there would be no queue left! If we regard chaos and anarchy as bad, therefore we have a duty *not* to jump the queue whenever we feel like it.

Kant used similar arguments to say we have a duty not to tell lies, not to steal, not to murder and not to commit suicide. Using Kant's logic, you could consider the morality of using resources at a rate that is faster than they can be replenished, or whether people should recycle their wastes.

The third approach to ethical issues is utilitarianism. This is the doctrine that an action is right insofar as it promotes happiness, and the greatest happiness of the greatest number should be the guiding principle of conduct.

From a practical point of view, utilitarianism breaks down, as many short-term pleasures bring long-term suffering (such as smoking, drinking, drugs) —

while short-term pain can bring long-term happiness (such as the dentist, exercise, learning the piano). Utilitarianism ignores the difference between long-term and short-term happiness. This can cause complications if, for example, a policy is being considered to relocate 10,000 people to build a dam that will bring electricity to one million people. Happiness is extremely difficult to measure; how could the unhappiness of relocating 10,000 people be measured against the happiness of bringing electricity to one million people?

In modern geopolitical terms, utilitarianism seems to fail in providing a practical basis of ethical decision making. For example, a group of six soldiers tortures a prisoner to get pleasure — utilitarianism says this must be morally ethical and right because six people have gained happiness at the expense of only one other person.

Whereas Kant emphasised the motives behind an action in judging whether or not it is ethically right, utilitarianism ignores motives. Therefore, duty ethics and utilitarianism (and religious ethics) would give quite different answers to the questions:

Is it right for Palestinians to kidnap one Israeli soldier to release 100 women and children?

Is it right to shoot down an airliner we suspect might be heading for the World Trade Tower?

Is it right to punish attempted murder less severely than actual murder?

The next ToK BoX is on page 178.

---

population grew. In *The Population Bomb*, Ehrlich generalised from animal behaviour to human behaviour – he was a biologist and had studied butterflies. On the other hand, Simon (an economist) argued that humans are fundamentally different from animals in their behaviour. He liked to quote the 19th-century American economist Henry George: "Both the jayhawk and the man eat chickens, but the more jayhawks, the fewer chickens, while the more men, the more chickens."

To quote Julian Simon:

"Our supplies of natural resources are not finite in any economic sense. Nor does past experience give reason to expect natural resources to become more scarce. Rather, if history is any guide, natural resources will progressively become less costly, hence less scarce, and will constitute a smaller proportion of our expenses in future years."

EXTRACT – A DIALOGUE ON 'FINITE'

The following imaginary dialogue between Peers Strawman (PS) and Happy Writer (HW), written by Julian Simon, highlights some of the tensions between the neo-Malthusian and anti-Malthusian viewpoints on resources.

PS: Every natural resource is finite in quantity, and therefore any resource must get more scarce as we use more of it.

HW: What does "finite" mean?

PS: "Finite" means "countable" or "limited."

HW: What is the limit for, say, copper? What is the amount that may be available in the future?

PS: I don't know

HW: Then how can you be sure it is limited in quantity?

PS: I know that at least it must be less than the total weight of the Earth.

HW: If it were only slightly less than the total weight of the Earth, or, say a hundredth of that total weight would there be reason for us to be concerned?

PS: You're getting off the track. We're only discussing whether it is theoretically limited in quantity, not whether the limit is of practical importance.

HW: Okay. Would you say that copper is limited in quantity if we could recycle it 100 percent?

PS: I see what you're saying. Even if it is limited in quantity, finiteness wouldn't matter to us if the material could be recycled 100 percent or close to it. That's true. But we're still talking about whether it is limited in quantity. Don't digress.

HW: Okay again. Would copper be limited in quantity if everything that copper does could be done by other materials that are available in limitless quantities?

PS: The quantity of copper wouldn't matter then. But you're digressing again.

HW: We're talking about scarcity for the future, aren't we? So what matters is not how much copper there is now (whatever the word 'is' means) but the amounts in future years. Will you agree to that?

PS: That I'll buy.

HW: Then, is copper limited for the future if we can create copper from other materials, or substitute other materials for copper?

PS: The size of the Earth would still constitute a limit.

HW: How about if we can use energy from outside the Earth-from the sun, say – to create additional copper the way we grow plants with solar energy?

PS: But is that realistic?

HW: Now it's you who are asking about realism. But as a matter of fact, yes, it is physically possible, and also likely to be feasible in the future. So will you now agree that at least in principle the quantities of copper are not limited even by the weight of the Earth?

PS: Don't make me answer that. Instead, let's talk realism. Isn't it realistic to expect resources such as copper to get more scarce?

HW: Can we agree to define scarcity as the cost of getting copper?

[Here an extended dialogue works out the arguments about scarcity and price given on pages 48 to 50 in this chapter. Finally PS says "okay" to defining scarcity as cost.]

HW: Future scarcity will depend, then, on the recycling rate, on the substitutes we develop, on the new methods we discover for extracting copper, and so on. In the past, copper became progressively less scarce, and there is no reason to expect that trend to change, no matter what you say about 'finiteness' and 'limits', as we just agreed. But there is more. Do you really care about copper, or only about what copper does for you?

PS: Obviously what matters is what copper can do for us, not copper itself.

HW: Good. Then can we agree that the outlook for the services that copper provides is even better than for copper itself?

PS: Sure, but all this can't be true. It's not natural. How can we use more of something and have it get less scarce?

HW: Well, this is one of those matters that defies common sense. That's because the common-sense view applies only when the resource is arbitrarily limited – for example, limited to the copper wire in your cellar. But that quantity is only fixed as long as you don't make another trip to the hardware store. Right?

And so we close

Source: Simon, J.L. (1996) *The Ultimate Resource 2*, Princeton: Princeton University Press. pp.68-69

Julian Simon died in February 1998. Paul Ehrlich continues to give lecture tours on the subject of our dwindling resources.

Shortly before he died, Julian Simon made this forecast:

> "This is my long-run forecast in brief:
>
> The material conditions of life will continue to get better for most people, in most countries, most of the time, indefinitely. Within a century or two, all nations and most of humanity will be at or above today's Western living standards.
>
> I also speculate that many people will continue to think and say that the conditions of life are getting **worse**."

These words are quoted at the beginning of a book by Bjørn Lomborg, published in 2001 called *The Sceptical Environmentalist*. Lomborg, who is also an anti-Malthusian, has developed Julian Simon's arguments in book of over 500 pages, quoting statistical evidence that he believes challenges widely held beliefs that the world's environmental situation and resource use are getting worse.

Lomborg is especially critical of the way many environmental organisations make what he calls selective and misleading use of scientific data to influence decisions about the allocation of limited resources. Lomborg argues that the cost of cleaning up many of the world's environmental problems (such as global warming) is so high, and the benefits so limited, that the money would be far more effectively spent directly to improve the quality of living of people in LEDCs.

Lomborg's views have generated a great deal of controversy. Eleven pages of the January 2002 issue of *Scientific American* were devoted to criticisms of Lomborg's ideas. Under the heading 'Science defends itself against the Sceptical Environmentalist', four scientists were invited to critique Lomborg's book in the areas of global warming, energy, population and biodiversity. They questioned Lomborg's incomplete use of some scientific and statistical data. While some agreed with Lomborg that conditions on earth are generally improving for human welfare, all felt that the book was a failure in overall terms. Another respected journal, *The Economist*, was more supportive of Lomborg, labelling the *Scientific American* attack 'strong on contempt and sneering but weak on substance'.

The May 2002 issue of *Scientific American* carried three pages of readers' letters, most of which were critical of Lomborg and supportive of *Scientific American*. The same issue also carried a short two page response by Lomborg. Lomborg said in part:

> "I take the best information of the state of the world that we have from the top international organisations and document that generally things are getting better. This does not mean that there are no problems and that this is the best of all possible worlds, but rather that we should not act on the myths of gloom and doom. Indeed, if we want to leave the best possible world for our children, we must make sure that we first handle the problems where we can do the most good."

Lomborg's views are controversial and they are debated widely in the media and on the internet. Amidst the many black-and-white opinions offered, the view of Stein Bie is worth considering. Bie is Director-General of the International Service for National Agricultural Research, and he wrote:

> "Lomborg's book questions the scientific basis why good news is suppressed and bad news amplified… In a world where 1.5 billion people live on less than one US dollar a day and 2.5 probably on less than two dollars a day, we should be seriously concerned about the human dimension of our interactions with the environment. In our efforts to rescue the environment, Lomborg suggests that exorbitant sums may be invested in environmental efforts that mean little to the poor, whilst only a handful of countries set aside as much as 0.7% of their GDP for development aid. If we are developing a setting, based on flawed data analysis, where rich people let butterflies count more heavily in their budgets than hungry and sick people, then we are morally on very thin ice."

QUESTION BLOCK 4B

1. *Explain the message presented by the Club of Rome. In your answer, refer to the data in figure 4.3.*

2. *Describe the relationship between 'scarcity' and 'price'.*

3. *Describe the long-term trend of commodity prices. What does this suggest about the scarcity of those commodities?*

4. *What is your opinion of Julian Simon's viewpoint that resources are not finite?*

The Ecological Footprint

One approach to examining the relationship between population size and resource consumption is the **ecological footprint**. First developed by Mathis Wackernagel and William Rees at the University of British Columbia (Canada) in the early 1990s, it compares the human demand for resource consumption with the Earth's ecological capacity to regenerate.

The approach taken in calculating the ecological footprint is to assess the biologically productive land and marine area required to produce the resources a population consumes and to absorb the corresponding waste using prevailing technology. It uses units of bio-productive area (global hectares) to assess the nature and scale of the environmental impact of a country, region, community, organisation, product or service.

Using the ecological footprint, it is estimated that the average biologically productive area per person world-wide is approximately 2.7 global hectares (gha). In other words, about 2.7 hectares of land are needed to provide the resources to support each person on the planet. This compares with a global average bio-capacity of 2.1 gha per person, leaving a deficit of 0.6 hectares per person. According to the Global Footprint Network, this means that humanity uses the equivalent of 1.3 planets to provide the resources we use and absorb our waste. In other words, it takes the Earth one year and four months to regenerate the resources that are used each year.

This figure varies widely for people in different countries, however. For example, the average ecological footprint for each person in the US is 9.4 gha, while that of the Netherlands is 4.4 gha per person and China is 2.1 gha per person.

When they first developed the ecological footprint measure, Wackernagel and Rees estimated that the available biological capacity for the planet's 6 billion people at the time was about 1.3 hectares per person. This figure is smaller than the current average figure of 2.1 gha because the original figure did not include marine resources such as fisheries.

Table 4.1 compares the ecological footprints of 30 selected countries with the total bio-capacity of those same countries. As each of these figures can be expressed using units of global hectares per capita, they can be readily compared to see whether there is an ecological reserve or deficit.

As shown in table 4.1, countries that have ecological reserves tend to be those with large areas compared to their

Table 4.1 Ecological Footprint for 30 Selected Countries

	Total Ecological Footprint *global hectares per capita*	Total Bio-capacity *global hectares per capita*	Ecological Deficit or Reserve
HIGH HUMAN DEVELOPMENT			
Norway	6.9	6.1	-0.8
Australia	7.8	15.4	+7.6
Sweden	5.1	10.0	+4.9
Japan	4.9	0.6	-4.3
USA	9.4	5.0	-4.4
United Kingdom	5.3	1.6	-3.7
South Korea	3.7	0.7	-3.0
UAE	9.5	1.1	-8.4
Mexico	3.4	1.7	-1.7
Malaysia	2.4	2.7	+0.3
MEDIUM HUMAN DEVELOPMENT			
China	2.1	0.9	-1.2
Iran	2.7	1.4	-1.3
Vietnam	1.3	0.8	-0.5
Indonesia	0.9	1.4	+0.5
Bolivia	2.1	15.7	+13.6
India	0.9	0.4	-0.5
Myanmar	1.1	1.5	+0.4
Nepal	0.8	0.4	-0.4
Papua New Guinea	1.7	4.4	+2.8
Kenya	1.1	1.2	+0.1
LOW HUMAN DEVELOPMENT			
Eritrea	1.1	2.1	+1.0
Nigeria	1.3	1.0	-0.3
Tanzania	1.1	1.2	+0.1
Rwanda	0.8	0.5	-0.3
Malawi	0.5	0.5	0.0
Zambia	0.8	2.9	+2.1
Ethiopia	1.4	1.0	-0.4
Mali	1.6	2.6	+1.0
Niger	1.6	1.8	+0.2
Sierra Leone	0.8	1.0	+0.2

Source: Global Footprint Network

population sizes, or those countries with lower levels of economic development that therefore consume fewer resources (figure 4.10). Conversely, countries with significant ecological deficits are those with higher resource consumption from higher levels of economic development and countries with large populations relative to the area of the country (figure 4.11). This shows that the ecological footprint is a neo-Malthusian measure of the relationship between population size and resource consumption.

4.10 *The Himba people of Namibia use very few resources but have the ability to survive in the aridity of the Namib Desert.*

4.11 *Dubai uses large quantities of energy and resources to maintain a comfortable lifestyle for its residents in a hot, dry, desert environment.*

It is estimated that about half the average ecological footprint is caused by the the use of hydrocarbon fuels. This has led to the development of another 'footprint' indicator, the **carbon footprint**, which can be defined as the total quantity of greenhouse gas emissions caused by an individual, organisation, event, product or nation. It is usually expressed in units of tonnes of carbon emitted.

As concerns about global warming grow around the world, more focus is being given to carbon footprints, both of individuals and of nations as a whole. It is recognised that it is not practical to eliminate carbon emissions entirely, and this has led to the development of **carbon offset schemes**. Although the details of such schemes vary, the general principle is that individuals or companies identify the carbon footprint of their actions

and then pay money to a fund or a company that does something to absorb an equivalent quantity of carbon. Carbon offsetting projects include afforestation and reforestation, industrial gas sequestration, projects that increase energy efficiency or fuel switching, methane capture from coal plants and livestock, and projects to establish renewable energy.

QUESTION BLOCK 4C

1. *What is meant by the term 'ecological footprint'?*

2. *Use the data in table 4.1 and the information in the text about the global ecological footprint to draw a column graph comparing the ecological footprints and the total biocapacity for (a) the USA, (b) Australia, (c) the United Arab Emirates, (d) China, (e) Bolivia, (f) Ethiopia, (g) Zambia and (h) the world.*

3. *What conclusions can you draw from the data you graphed in your answer to the previous question?*

4. *Ecological footprint calculations tend to present consistent conclusions about the relationship between population size and resource consumption. These conclusions would not be accepted by most anti-Malthusians. What arguments would an anti-Malthusian give to counter the types of conclusions suggested by ecological footprint calculations?*

5. *Conduct some research into carbon footprints and carbon offsetting. On balance, do you think carbon offsetting is a helpful response to the use of hydrocarbon fuels? Give reasons to support your answer.*

Changing Patterns of Energy Consumption

The Uneven Distribution of Natural Resources

In general people have settled this planet in places and in densities directly related to the available natural resources. Concentrations of people have occurred in places where resources have been abundant. Hunting and gathering societies moved within the forests, grasslands and coastal shores that gave them seasonal sustenance. Once agriculture began to replace such nomadic existence, fixed or sedentary settlement led to dense concentrations of people along the valleys of the great, reliable river systems and in areas where the soils were naturally fertile (figure 4.12) This was especially true in the mid-latitudes where temperatures were not extreme, where a wide range of plants could grow and people could easily tolerate the seasonal range.

The earliest civilisations needed a good water supply, reasonably fertile soils (which usually meant regular deposition of silt), material to build houses, a good range of

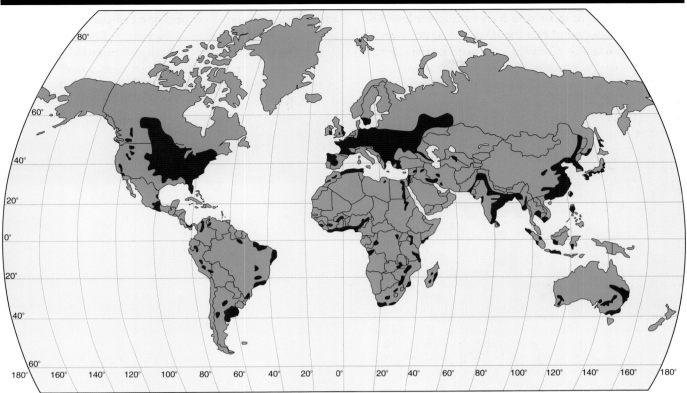

4.12 *Areas with naturally fertile soils (shown in brown) mostly correspond with areas of high population density as well as producing most of the world's grain.*

plant species and possibly animals that could be domesticated as beasts of burden. It is not surprising then that the valleys of the Yangtze (or Chang Jiang) in China, the Ganges in India, the Mekong in south-east Asia and the many rivers of Europe and the Mediterranean area provided sites for early settlement (figure 4.14).

As we saw in chapter 1, and as shown in figure 4.13, today's world population densities mirror the pattern of fertile soil resources in figure 4.12 very closely. However,

this is not entirely due to soil resources. The pattern of industrialisation has affected the distribution of population also. Towns and cities have grown where there are natural resources such as coal, oil and other minerals to fuel industrial employment, as well as in other areas such as along the coasts.

Australia, even though it has few people, is an excellent example of this tendency (figure 4.15). Cities such as Broken Hill and Mount Isa grew during the years when

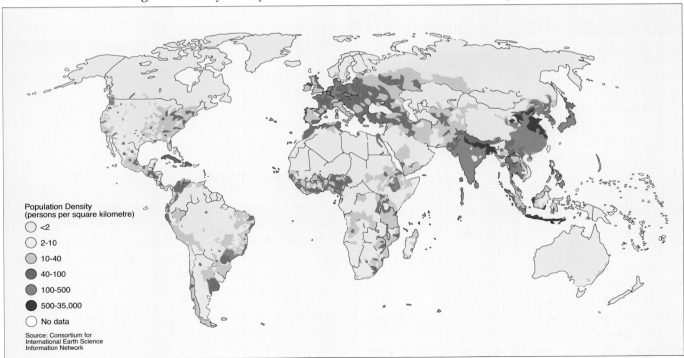

Population Density
(persons per square kilometre)

⬤ <2
⬤ 2-10
⬤ 10-40
⬤ 40-100
⬤ 100-500
⬤ 500-35,000
⬤ No data

Source: Consortium for
International Earth Science
Information Network

4.13 *World population density.*

workers rather than machines were needed to mine the resources discovered at those inland places. However, the rest of the population settled along the coastline. It is to those areas that workers who have become surplus to needs in the natural resource-based towns have drifted.

4.14 *When people wish to use resources that are not found locally, trade and transport become necessary. In this view, slabs of rock salt mined in the Sahara Desert have been brought by camel to the inland riverside port of Mopti where they await transport down the River Niger to large centres of population.*

4.15 *One of the larger settlements on the road that crosses Australia from north to south is Alice Springs. This view shows the transport links passing through a convenient gap in the ridge beside which the town has been built. The hostile, desert environment of the area can be seen clearly; for this town the most valuable resource is water.*

So we can see that the location of reliable water supplies and fertile soils has led to an uneven distribution of people throughout the world over many centuries. However, this is beginning to change as modern transport systems can move the products of one area to another, and trade is an integral part of the global economy. The potential exists for a more even distribution of people and wealth across the world in the future.

Table 4.2 shows the top 10 countries in the production and consumption of coal. It can be seen that among those top nations there is a more than twenty-fold difference from first to last. Of more significance in understanding the

uneven distribution is the fact that 70% of the world's nations produce no coal whatsoever.

Table 4.2
Production and Consumption of Coal
The Top 10 Countries, 2008

Production			Consumption		
Rank	Country	Million tonnes	Rank	Country	Million tonnes
1	China	2847.98	1	China	2829.52
2	USA	1171.48	2	USA	1121.71
3	India	568.32	3	India	637.52
4	Australia	438.51	4	Germany	269.89
5	Russia	356.19	5	Russia	269.68
6	Indonesia	313.23	6	Japan	203.98
7	South Africa	259.60	7	South Africa	193.65
8	Germany	214.35	8	Australia	160.52
9	Poland	157.88	9	Poland	149.33
10	Kazakhstan	119.81	10	South Korea	112.84

Source: US Energy Information website
http://www.eia.doe.gov/emeu/international/contents.html

It can be seen that there is quite a close similarity between the lists of the top coal producers and coal consumers. Nonetheless, many countries lack coal resources. In some cases they substitute other resources, such as water to generate hydro-electricity, or burn oil instead in the case of many Middle East oil producers. Other countries simply have to import coal from coal exporting countries which produce a surplus to their own needs (figure 4.16).

QUESTION BLOCK 4D

1. *Describe and account for the relationship between fertile soils (figure 4.12) and world population density (figure 4.13).*

The Production and Consumption of Oil

Figure 4.17 shows the trend in **world energy consumption** since 1970, together with the projected energy consumption to the year 2025. It can be seen that the main source of energy world-wide is oil (which includes petroleum), and that consumption is rising and is expected to continue rising. When we look at the projected energy use in 2025, we see that 87% of energy use is expected to be using hydrocarbon fuels — oil, coal and natural gas. For many people, the **environmental**

consequences are quite alarming as increasing quantities of greenhouse gases are produced with consequent effects on global warming.

4.16 *Trade is an important means to overcome the lack of coincidence in resource production and consumption. This view shows part of the huge port in Vladivostok, Russia.*

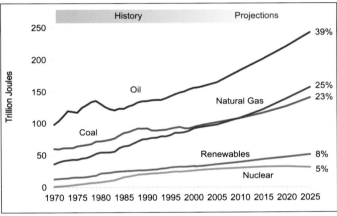

4.17 *World energy consumption, 1970 to 2025.*

The trend shown in figure 4.17 has led many researchers to speculate about the question of when oil production will peak and begin to decline. On the assumption that

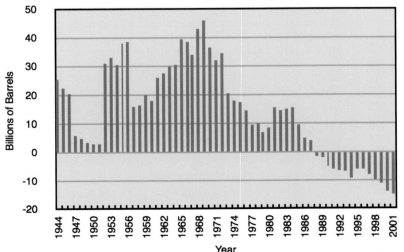

4.18 *Net difference between annual world oil reserves additions and annual oil consumption.*

oil reserves are finite, economists predict that the combination of rising demand and falling supply of oil will drive oil prices upwards, making alternative fuels relatively more attractive, thus reducing the need for oil as other sources of energy grow in importance. The term **peak oil** is used to define the point in time when the maximum rate of global petroleum extraction is reached, after which the rate of production enters terminal decline.

Predicting the timing of peak oil is extremely difficult because the number of variables is so great, and the variables are changing so rapidly. Some of the variables include price of oil, the known reserves, the locations of the reserves, the impact of oil substitutes, and so on. Researchers have been speculating about the date of peaking of world oil production ever since oil became an important fuel in the late 1800s. As little was known at the time about oil reserves, or even the types of geological areas where oil is found, the early predictions were simply guesses.

One of the first serious studies to look at a large number of variables affecting global resource use was the book *Limits to Growth*, written by Donella Meadows, Dennis Meadows and Jørgen Randers and published in 1972. In that book, the use of complex computer models predicted that the world's supply of oil would run out in 1992. Needles to say, the prediction was wrong, but it did cause widespread concern at the time.

The predictions about oil being used up by 1992 in *Limits to Growth* were wrong because the computer modellers underestimated the technological improvements that would find new ways of extracting oil from previously uneconomic sources. They also underestimated the number of new oil supplies that would be discovered. Nonetheless, the concept of peak oil continues to attract many followers as it seems obvious that oil supplies are indeed finite as the rate at which we are using oil is faster than the rate at which new oil is being formed — the arguments of anti-Malthusians such as Julian Simon notwithstanding.

More recent predictions of the timing of oil peak generally focus on the first quarter of the 21st century (table 4.3). These predictions are based on measurements which show that the net difference between annual world oil reserves additions and annual oil consumption is declining, as has been the case for several decades (figure 4.18).

Of course, the trends in oil production and oil consumption are **not uniform** in all parts of the world, and there is a marked difference in the locations where oil is produced compared with the places where it is consumed. This can be seen by looking at the data in table 4.4.

Table 4.3
Projections of the Peaking of World Oil Production

Projected Date	Source of Projection	Background	Date of projection
2006 - 2007	AMS Bakhitari	Oil executive, Iran	2004
2007 - 2009	MR Simmons	Investment banker, USA	2003
After 2007	C Skrebowski	Petroleum journal editor, UK	2004
Before 2009	KS Deffeyes	Oil company geologist, USA	2003
Before 2010	D Goodstein	Vice-Provost, Cal Tech, USA	2004
Around 2010	CJ Campbell	Oil geologist, Ireland	2003
After 2010	World Energy Council	Global NGO	2003
2012	Pang Xiongqi	Petroleum executive, China	2005
2010 - 2020	J Laherrere	Oil geologist, France	2003
2016	Energy Information Administration	Government authority, USA	2000
After 2020	CERA	Energy consultants, USA	2004
2025 or later	Shell	Large oil company, UK	2003
After 2020	MC Lynch	Author, *Oil and Gas Journal*, USA	2003

Source: RL Hirsch, 'The Inevitable Peaking of World Oil Production', *The Atlantic Quarterly*, vol. 16(3), p.9, and updates

Since coal and oil have helped to generate the greatest wealth during the last two centuries, this uneven distribution has contributed to today's wide gaps in affluence. Where countries have a surplus of natural resources such as coal and oil after their own needs have been fulfilled, wealth can be been generated by exports. Table 4.5 shows some of the most striking examples of the imbalance, using **crude petroleum** as the basis for comparison of production and consumption.

4.19 *Large scale urban development in Dubai, United Arab Emirates.*

Table 4.4
Production and Consumption of Oil
The Top 20 Countries and Regions, 2009

Production			Consumption		
Rank	Country	Barrels per day ('000)	Rank	Country	Barrels per day ('000)
1	Russia	9,931	1	USA	18,686
2	Saudi Arabia	9,764	2	China	8,200
3	USA	9,056	3	Japan	4,362
4	Iran	4,172	4	India	2,980
5	China	3,991	5	Russia	2,850
6	Canada	3,274	6	Brazil	2,460
7	Mexico	3,001	7	Germany	2,437
8	UAE	2,798	8	Saudi Arabia	2,430
9	Brazil	2,571	9	South Korea	2,216
10	Kuwait	2,494	10	Mexico	2,178
11	Venezuela	2,472	11	Canada	2,157
12	Iraq	2,399	12	France	1,875
13	Norway	2,350	13	Iran	1,809
14	Nigeria	2,210	14	UK	1,669
15	Algeria	2,133	15	Italy	1,552
16	Angola	1,948	16	Spain	1,482
17	Libya	1,789	17	Indonesia	1,115
18	Kazakhstan	1,539	18	Australia	946
19	UK	1,501	19	Netherlands	923
20	Qatar	1,213	20	Thailand	922

Source: US Energy Information website
http://www.eia.doe.gov/emeu/international/contents.html

Small countries, such as Brunei with only about 400,000 people and Kuwait with some 2.7 million, are able to use the wealth from their relatively huge surplus to meet the needs of their people. Although the distribution of wealth in these countries and other oil producing states is uneven, there is no reason for poverty (figure 4.19). Other nations such as Japan, France and Germany, which have to buy huge quantities of oil each year, are able to do this because of manufacturing wealth and expertise which they can sell. In the cases of France and Germany, access to coal during the early industrial revolution was the key to their current success, but they have not had similar luck with reserves of petroleum.

Table 4.5

Production and Consumption of Crude Oil, 2009
Selected Nations and Regions

Nation or Region	Production of Crude Oil (thousands of barrels per day)	Consumption of Crude Oil (thousands of barrels per day)
Australia	593	946
Brunei	142	16
Chile	10	277
France	71	1,875
Germany	158	2,437
Israel	4	231
Japan	131	4,362
Kuwait	2,494	320
Norway	2,350	204
Sweden	5	328
Taiwan	17	910
United Arab Emirates	2,798	435
United States	9,056	18,686
Venezuela	2,472	740

Source: US Energy Information website
http://www.eia.doe.gov/emeu/international/contents.html

New technology has brought other countries into oil production as techniques have been developed to allow deeper drilling under the oceans. Venezuela was one of the first countries to win large quantities of oil from under shallow, near-shore waters in protected bays and it is still producing from some offshore wells along with onshore drilling in the Orinoco Basin.

Norway on the other hand, like the United Kingdom, is winning oil from under the very turbulent waters of the North Sea. There have been some catastrophes as severe storms have toppled platforms, helicopters have crashed and supply vessels have sunk but the value of the resource is so great that the effort to extend human capacity to reach new reservoirs of oil goes on. It is not only the sources of natural resources that are distributed unevenly around the world, but the pattern of resource consumption is also uneven. For example, the pattern of energy use per capita is shown in figure 4.20. This global distribution mirrors the world pattern of development quite closely, as reflected by other indicators of development shown in figures 2.46 to 2.48 in chapter 2. The difference in distribution between the production and the consumption of oil results in large-scale movement of oil around the world, and the pattern of this is shown in figure 4.21.

The combination of energy supplies becoming more scarce with the uneven pattern of production and consumption could easily lead to **geopolitical tensions**. For example, the importance of oil as a natural resource is so great that most arguments about ownership of small rocky islands far from any coastline are really about who will own the oil or gas in the vicinity if any is found. The Spratly Islands of the South China Sea have been claimed

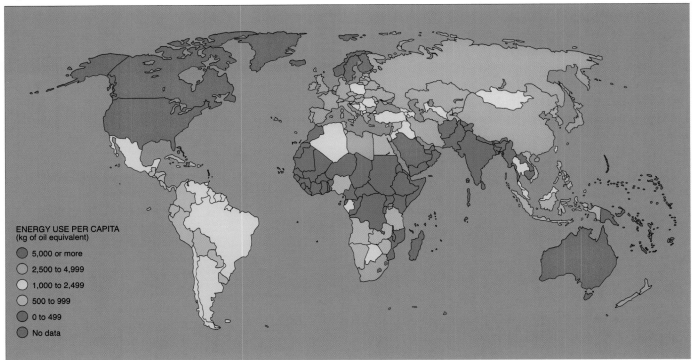

ENERGY USE PER CAPITA
(kg of oil equivalent)

- 5,000 or more
- 2,500 to 4,999
- 1,000 to 2,499
- 500 to 999
- 0 to 499
- No data

4.20 *Energy use per capita, 2008. This map shows the annual consumption of commercial energy divided by the population, expressed in kilograms of oil equivalent.*

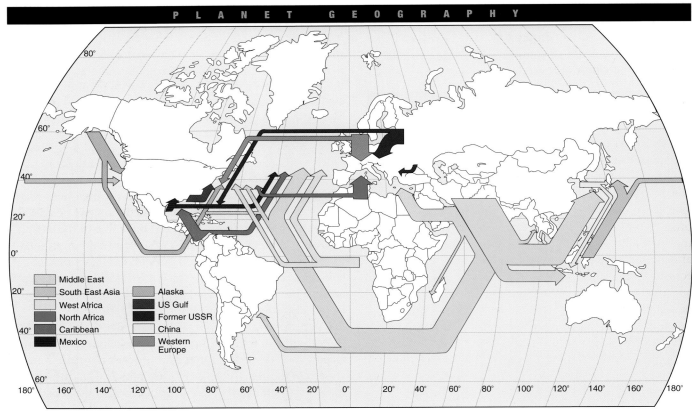

4.21 *The international flow of crude oil by sea.*

Legend:
- Middle East
- South East Asia
- West Africa
- North Africa
- Caribbean
- Mexico
- Alaska
- US Gulf
- Former USSR
- China
- Western Europe

by six different nations even though they are virtually uninhabitable as they contain no surface resources.

Since occupation may prove to be more important than legal claims in international courts, Brunei, China, Malaysia, the Philippines and Vietnam have made attempts to build shelters and keep small garrisons of defenders on whichever islands they think they stand a chance of holding. Vietnam currently has about 14 such islands, some just bare rock a few metres across, while China has about six. A sudden strong military push could change the situation very quickly. This was seen in April 1995 when China raised some buildings and its flag on Mischief Reef, a small rock previously regarded by the Philippines as theirs. China then stationed several warships nearby to make certain of the safety of any troops who were onshore and to supply them with provisions in that lonely area.

As long ago as 1981, President Jimmy Carter declared that the US had a right to treat any attempt to control the Persian Gulf (a major source of oil) as "an assault on the vital interests of the United States." Since that time, the United States has spent tens of billions of dollars each year maintaining a military presence in the Middle East, and many commentators claim that the major reason behind the US invasion of Iraq in 2002 was to protect supplies of affordable oil.

If oil becomes scarcer in the future as many predict, prices will rise and major exporters such as Russia and Iran are likely to become more influential in world politics (figures 4.22 and 4.23). On the other hand, if there is a sustained

4.22 *Heavy traffic congestion in Moscow, Russia.*

4.23 *Much of Iran's wealth comes from oil exports. This view shows the city of Esfahan in central Iran.*

fall in oil prices, perhaps triggered by a widespread switch to new sources of energy, then a long-term decline could begin for producers such as Saudi Arabia, Kuwait, Iran and Russia.

If the predictions about the world supply of oil are accurate, then by 2025 there will be a major transition from oil and other hydrocarbon fuels such as natural gas into new sources of energy. That could shift the balance of power in some parts of the world as some countries benefit and others are disadvantaged. For example, the level of oil production in many of the traditional energy producers (Yemen, Norway, Oman, Colombia, the UK, Indonesia, Argentina, Syria, Egypt, Peru, Tunisia) is already in decline. The production levels in other countries such as Mexico, Brunei, Malaysia, China, India, and Qatar, have flattened. Overall, it is expected that the number of countries capable of significantly expanding production will decline, leaving only six countries—Saudi Arabia, Iran, Kuwait, the UAE, Russia, and perhaps Iraq, to produce 39% of the world's total world oil production by 2025.

It is expected that most of the major producers will be located in the Middle East, which today contains about two-thirds of the world's known oil reserves. Oil production in the Persian Gulf countries is projected to grow by 43% to the year 2025, with Saudi Arabia alone contributing almost half of all oil production from the Gulf region. Just three countries — Russia, Iran, and Qatar — hold over 57% of the world's natural gas reserves, and when we consider oil and natural gas together, two countries — Russia and Iran — emerge as the key centres of energy production, and thus wealth and influence, in the future decades.

QUESTION BLOCK 4E

1. *Describe the overall pattern of oil production and consumption shown in table 4.4.*

2. *The pattern of movement shown in figure 4.21 is the result of the situation described in table 4.4. Explain why this pattern of movement exists.*

3. *With reference to table 4.5, what are the consequences for countries with (a) a deficiency of oil compared with needs, and (b) a surplus of oil above needs.*

4. *Describe the world pattern of energy consumption shown in figure 4.20.*

5. *Outline the relationship between the pattern of energy consumption shown in figure 4.20 and the global pattern of economic development described in chapter 2.*

6. *Explain the link between geopolitical tensions and the patterns and trends of oil production and consumption.*

Conservation Strategies

A wide range of resources is used to sustain life, provide shelter and support increasingly complex lifestyles. Therefore, it is not surprising that disputes will arise over obtaining adequate resources. These conflicts, as well as fears of dwindling reserves of certain resources, has led to greater interest in **strategies to conserve resources**.

Before examining specific conservation strategies, we will look at some of the issues that cause the pressures upon resources in the first place. These can be grouped into several broad areas – environmental issues, social issues, political issues, management issues and ecologically sustainable development.

Environmental Issues

4.24 *Water pollution causes serious risks to people's health, as seen here in Jakarta (Indonesia). However, as the pollution of Minamata Bay in Japan showed, it can be the pollutants that cannot be seen which cause most harm.*

Unfortunately, profits are easier to make if one does not have to clean up, restore or replant areas where natural resources have been obtained. Any mineral extraction causes some environmental impact, and the effluents from any industry may contain potentially harmful chemicals. In some cases, such as pollution from lead, mercury or other heavy metals, the cost of cleaning up the environment may be very great. The cost in damaged lives may be horrendous.

The importance of caring for the environment first captured public awareness as a result of a famous case of **water pollution** in Japan during the 1970s (figure 4.24). Minamata Bay on the east coast of Kyushu in Japan was polluted for years by mercury that poured into the water in the effluents from a chemical factory. By 1980, 305 people in the small fishing community had died, and thousands more had suffered from what became known as **Minamata disease**. The symptoms included numbness, loss of vision and hearing, clumsiness of movement, tremor, degeneration of nerve cells and there was mental retardation in the children. The victims were mainly fishing families. It was several years after birth defects began to be reported that steps were taken to identify the cause. The source of the problem turned out to be high mercury concentrations in the local fish caused by the Chisso Chemical Factory dumping untreated mercury wastes into the sea near Minamata Bay. Since fish was a staple food for many people, the damage that had already been done was extensive. The issue here seemed clear enough. Since the factory was responsible for death and grotesquely malformed children it should cease such operations and pay damages to those affected.

4.25 *The Ranger Uranium Mine in Kakadu National Park, east of Darwin, Australia.*

The company, fought for years to avoid paying any money to those affected, continuing meanwhile to discharge its wastes into the bay. By 1988, 1079 people had died and thousands more had suffered symptoms of Minamata disease. Finally, the company had to accept responsibility. It paid high compensation and helped with the setting up of special hospital facilities to deal with the terrible aftermath.

Of course, no amount of compensation could really help those children and their families whose lives had been changed forever by the heavy metal pollution. Fishing was banned from the area because there is no way that the mercury can be successfully removed from the sediments in the bay.

Most pollutants do not have such a severe impact. Indeed, some pollutants may seem fairly innocuous since they are a normal part of our environment. Water that has to be continually pumped from underground or open-cut mines contains salts which will raise the salinity of natural watercourses if they are released. This raises many issues such as the following:

• Should mines be allowed to add such pollutants to rivers or wetlands?

• Will retention of the salt water make the cost of mining unprofitable?

• Will it even be possible to hold the water in dams during periods of high rainfall?

• If a river is used for irrigation, will the salt ruin the farming land?

• If the salt water invades a freshwater wetland will it destroy that ecosystem?

4.26 *People fear that bird-nesting areas such as Yellow Waters in Kakadu National Park will be affected by pollution from the Ranger Uranium Mine if mine wastes are not managed wisely.*

Kakadu National Park and the Ranger Uranium Mine in northern Australia highlight some of the issues, along with the underlying debate about extracting uranium at all because of the possible environmental damage with its probable uses (figures 4.25 and 4.26). Aboriginal custodians of the surrounding wetlands fear that the release of mine water might damage the local environment. In response to these concerns, plans were devised to release the waste water from the mine only during the high flow of the wet seasons, hoping that this would dilute the mine wastes. Debate and further discussion of the consequences seem likely to continue for a long while yet. Resolution of the issue is clouded by examples from various parts of the world showing that the impact of mining effluents is often greater than engineers calculate early in a mine's planning stage.

Another ongoing issue is related to **competing uses** for a particular natural resource. The debate can become particularly contentious where the uses are mutually exclusive. Much of the land development on Australia's Gold Coast, south of Brisbane, and in the region around Miami (Florida, USA) has been in the form of **canal estates**, many of which are the result of in-filling the original **wetlands** (figure 4.27). Although the development resulted in the complete destruction of the tidal wetlands, few people were aware that an important natural resource was being lost. Part of the life cycles of many of the fish and prawns that both amateur and professional fishers enjoyed catching were being destroyed, and ultimately this resulted in the lowering of local catches. The economic value of the new canal estates is probably far greater than the resource it replaced, but very little debate took place on the effect of all the changes on the estuarine ecosystem.

4.27 *Some of the canal estates to the west of Miami (Florida, USA). Because waterfront housing sells at higher prices than normal housing, the developers aim to give as many homes as possible a water frontage. Extensive dredging and filling is needed to create the canal estates.*

A basic issue is whether the fishing industry should be the victim of other people's desire to live so close to the water that populations of fish, prawns and other sea foods are reduced. The income from tourism and the lifestyle benefits for hundreds of thousands of residents in areas such as the Gold Coast and in Florida (USA) are probably persuasive arguments in allowing development to occur. However, the issue is not so clear in a world where sea foods are an important resource, which are already depleted by more and more efficient marine harvesting. In countless places, wetlands are now being filled or drained for industry, airports, housing estates or farming.

The environmental issues of natural resource use in LEDCs often differ from those in MEDCs. This is particularly clear in the area of **energy use**. The pattern of global energy use has shifted greatly during the twentieth century, and vast differences still exist between LEDCs and MEDCs. Some idea of these differences can be seen in table 4.6.

In 1900, renewable energy sources made up almost half the energy used in the world. Today, almost 20% of world energy comes from renewable sources, and in LEDCs the proportion is much higher. In Africa and Asia where most renewable energy is used, the most important source is fuelwood. **Fuelwood** is timber used for burning to provide fuel. It is estimated that at least 2 billion of the world's 6 billion people depend on fuelwood as their main or only source of domestic energy (figures 4.28 and 4.29). In table 4.6, fuelwood is the main component of 'renewable combustibles' in the Medium and Low Human Development Countries.

4.28 *Fuelwood is the main source of energy in many LEDCs. This view shows the fuelwood market in the central Malian town of Djenné.*

4.29 *Fuelwood is sometimes transported long distances from its source to where it is to be used. In this view, two traders are transporting valuable scarce fuelwood by donkey across the Sahel Desert north of Douentza in Mali.*

Although trees are a renewable resource, the rate of fuelwood collection means that in many parts of the world not enough time is being allowed for re-growth. For example, loss of forest is one of Nepal's greatest environmental problems. Most of the timber is cut down for fuelwood, which supplies 75% of Nepal's energy needs (figure 4.30).

Table 4.6
Changes in the Pattern of Energy Use for Selected Countries, 1990 - 2005
(order of selected countries shown follows that in table 2.1)

	Total Energy Production (million tonnes of oil equivalent)		Total Energy Use (million tonnes of oil equivalent)		Energy Use per Capita (kg of oil equivalent)		Types of Energy Used (% of total energy in 2006)		
	1990	2006	1990	2006	1990	2006	Fossil Fuel	Renewable Combustibles	Clean Energy
HIGH HUMAN DEVELOPMENT									
Norway	119.1	222.9	21.4	26.1	5,050	5,598	54.9	5.1	39.6
Australia	157.5	267.8	87.7	122.5	5,138	5,917	94.7	4.1	1.3
Sweden	29.7	32.8	47.6	51.3	5,557	5,650	34.9	18.4	44.5
Japan	75.2	101.1	443.9	527.6	3,593	4,129	81.6	1.3	17.1
USA	1,649.4	1,654.2	1,926.3	2,320.7	7,717	7,768	85.7	3.4	10.8
United Kingdom	208.0	186.6	212.3	231.1	3,708	3,814	89.2	1.7	8.9
South Korea	22.6	43.7	93.4	216.5	2,178	4,483	80.8	1.1	18.1
United Arab Emirates	110.2	177.3	23.2	46.9	12,416	11,036	100.0	0.0	0.0
Mexico	193.4	256.0	123.0	177.4	1,478	1,702	89.1	4.6	6.4
Malaysia	50.3	97.9	23.3	68.3	1,288	2,617	95.3	4.1	0.9
MEDIUM HUMAN DEVELOPMENT									
China	886.3	1,749.3	863.2	1,878.7	760	1,433	85.1	12.0	3.0
Iran	179.8	309.3	68.8	170.9	1,265	2,438	98.6	0.5	0.9
Vietnam	24.7	71.9	24.3	52.3	367	621	49.8	46.4	3.9
Indonesia	170.0	307.7	102.8	179.1	577	803	67.1	29.2	3.7
Bolivia	4.9	14.3	2.8	5.8	416	625	83.1	13.8	3.2
India	291.1	435.6	319.9	565.8	377	510	69.0	28.3	2.7
Myanmar	10.7	22.1	10.7	14.3	266	295	25.9	72.1	2.0
Nepal	5.5	8.3	5.8	9.4	304	340	11.3	86.2	2.4
Kenya	9.0	14.3	11.2	17.9	479	491	20.6	73.6	5.9
LOW HUMAN DEVELOPMENT									
Nigeria	150.5	235.3	70.9	105.1	751	726	19.8	79.6	0.6
Tanzania	9.1	19.4	9.8	20.8	385	527	8.3	91.0	0.6
Zambia	4.9	6.7	5.5	7.3	673	625	11.1	78.2	11.0
Ethiopia	14.1	20.4	15.0	22.3	313	289	8.8	90.0	1.3

Source: Derived from data supplied by the World Bank

Some of the timber that is cut is sold in towns, although most of it is gathered by villagers for their own use (figure 4.31). Many of Nepal's factories also use fuelwood. In the Kathmandu Valley's 100 brick kilns, 3 million bricks are produced each year using 24,000 tonnes of coal plus 24,000 tonnes of fuelwood. If the cutting continues and Nepal loses its remaining humid tropical forest, the world would have lost ten species of valuable timber, six species of edible fruit tree, four species that supply traditional medicines and 50 species of little known trees and shrubs. The loss of the trees would also wipe out the habitats for 200 species of birds, 40 species of mammals and 20 species of reptiles and amphibians.

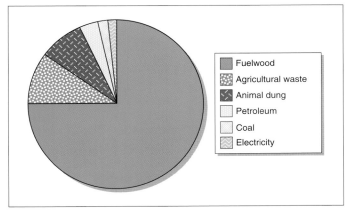

4.30 *Nepal's pattern of energy use.*

There are global consequences of forest loss. The world is losing over 20 million hectares of forest annually (figure 4.32). This releases about 2.8 billion tonnes of carbon, much of it as carbon dioxide. Many scientists claim that this change to the world's atmosphere could alter world temperatures, which in turn could change sea levels as polar ice caps melt or expand.

4.31 *A common scene in many LEDCs – a woman carries some scraps of fuelwood home after a long walk to find supplies. This scene is north of Tema in Ghana.*

The demand for fuelwood in LEDCs means that many of trees in these countries have been almost stripped bare. As the trees have died or have been cut down, soil erosion gets worse, as the trees' roots no longer bind the soil to-

gether. Entire hillsides have become eroded wastelands as a result of deforestation.

4.32 *Timber from a Malaysian forest at a sawmill where it is being processed for export.*

QUESTION BLOCK 4F

1. *Why was pollution in Minamata Bay so important in changing people's thinking about environmental issues?*

2. *Briefly describe two other examples of environmental issues in natural resource use.*

3. *What are the environmental issues concerning the use of fuelwood?*

4. *Using the data in table 4.6, list the countries shown which had (a) an energy surplus in 2006, and (b) an energy deficit in 2006.*

5. *Rank the countries shown in table 4.6 according to the percentage increase in their energy use from 1990 to 2006, with the countries showing the largest increases at the top of the list.*

6. *Comment on the pattern shown by your answer to the previous question.*

7. *Rank the countries shown in table 4.6 according to their energy use per capita. Describe the relationship between your ranking and the countries' level of development.*

8. *Discuss the relationship between types of energy used and economic development using the data in table 4.6.*

Socio-political Issues

There are social and political issues involved in any resource use. Where will workers live if a new resource is remote from settlement? What will be the impact of its transport on communities? What happens to communities when a resource on which their jobs depend is exhausted or replaced? What is the impact on groups with less political influence such as ethnic minorities, the poor and (in many countries) women and children?

Issues that arise from the exploitation of a resource in an area where the local people are displaced and have little say in the planning can have great consequences. Civil war may be an extreme case of the social unrest that can be caused, as happened during the 1990s in Papua New Guinea over the copper mine at Bougainville. In many cases of resource use, it is difficult to separate social issues from political ones as they become strongly mixed.

In the last few years arguments for a more managed, sustainable rate of logging have been called for along with programmes of ecotourism. **Ecotourism** occurs where local people are involved in the accommodating and guiding of people who respond to the growing world desire to see unspoiled areas such as equatorial rainforest. This is discussed in more detail in chapter 9.

4.34 *Political reality in Australia tries to find a balance between protecting native forests and managing exploitation of the resource. The balance often fails to satisfy either conservationists or industry workers.*

4.33 *Logging an old growth eucalypt forest on the escarpment between Bega and Cooma, New South Wales.*

Australia has about 5% of its total area under forest and only a small portion of that is **old growth forest** (i.e. unlogged forest with many mature trees which provide the variety of habitats in which many native birds and animals survive and which have developed stable ecosystems). Governments at all levels are aware of the need to protect our dwindling forests while still using timber as a renewable resource if managed well (figure 4.33).

Logging in Australia raises political issues that also have social and economic dimensions. To what extent should logging be regulated by government? If government intervention is necessary, which level of government should exercise the control? Should logs that are suitable for milling be chipped and exported for paper-making? If logging is stopped in traditional timber-getting areas, will displaced workers be compensated and, if so, by whom? Questions such as these apply to logging in many parts of the world, and indeed to resource use in many areas, and they are explored in greater depth in chapter 15 (figures 4.34 and 4.35).

4.35 *A mountain of woodchips awaits export to Japan from the Harris-Daishowa mill at Eden, on the New South Wales far south coast.*

Conservation Strategies

Management to conserve natural resources implies that there is a desire, or at least a recognised need to limit the use of particular resources. **Conservation** certainly indicates that there should be no waste of the resource.

In practice, the development of more efficient ways to use a resource is the most common conservation measure. However, this is usually because of the chance to increase the profits that can be made from the resource rather than a specific desire to reduce its rate of use.

In general, great efforts are put into finding new supplies and finding better ways to obtain, modify and market the resource to potential users. This is because owners of resources will make greater profits if they control larger amounts of a progressively improved product.

For this reason efforts to conserve a resource are often low on corporations' lists of priorities. As a result, more efficient resource use often springs from interventionist action by governments or special interest groups who see the resource in a different way, or who understand better some of the implications of the use of the resource. Earlier in this chapter, we saw that burning fossil fuels without adequate pollution controls can harm the environment, and that the lifestyles of indigenous people may be destroyed by the environmental change that resource use may cause. Even if governments see the need to act to conserve a resource, they may be constrained by the voting strength of those who would be affected and conservation may not take place or it may be less effective than it should be.

We can sum this up by saying that genuine conservation is usually forced on people, countries and the world. This will be illustrated with reference to some specific natural resources in the points that follow.

Conservation strategies for petroleum products

During the 1960s and 1970s many people were concerned about the long-term future of world oil supplies. The concern arose because of the rapid rate at which petroleum products were being used, and fears arose that oil would run out in a decade or two. Some experts at the time felt that by 2000 there would be such pressure on the remaining oil supplies that the price would climb steeply, and many oil-poor countries would have difficulty affording the product. Thoughts about how an industrial society would be able to operate without oil, lubricants and oil-fired power stations made alarming reading.

In the 1970s the world faced oil 'shocks'. The price jumped steeply and especially in Japan there was something close to panic as industry leaders considered a future in which their supplies could not be guaranteed. A movie studio heightened concern by producing a movie in which the Japanese islands gradually sank below the Pacific Ocean due to a geological subsidence of spectacular proportions. It was all fiction but many Japanese left the theatre comparing the physical disappearance of their country with an economic disappearance based on the loss of oil supplies. The data in table 4.5 earlier in this chapter gives some idea why Japan's fear was so real.

The oil-producing nations suddenly gained a political power out of all proportion to their size, or even their contribution to world history. Deals were made between countries that were large oil purchasers and the countries with large surplus supplies. Some dependent countries even failed to criticise or challenge the internationally unacceptable behaviour of terrorists from oil-rich nations in case it affected their future supplies.

Nations generally sought to ensure a supply of oil rather than take action to conserve supplies or reduce the use of oil, though OPEC (the Organisation of Petroleum Exporting Countries) did introduce limits on the amount of oil

they were producing as a way of lengthening the time oil would last.

However, there were some clear examples of attempts to reduce oil and petroleum use. New Zealand, for example, imposed a statutory 80 kilometres per hour road speed limit across the country – a reduction from 100 kilometres per hour – and policed it carefully until people accepted the change. Consumption of petrol fell by about 20% as a result. However, not all of that saving could be attributed to the reduced speed, since price increases were quite steep at the same time. In addition there was an emphasis in many countries on more compact cars as heavier taxes were imposed on cars with engines of six cylinder or more (figure 4.36).

4.36 *Petrol prices in Europe are about three times higher than in Australia and about five times higher than in the USA. That is why European cars tend to be smaller, lighter and more fuel efficient than cars in Australia or North America. These cars in Amsterdam are extremely small, not only to save fuel but to occupy less space in expensive parking areas.*

Across the world there were stories of countries trying to stockpile supplies and expand exploration rather than work to conserve the resource. On the other hand there was stimulation of research in a number of fields designed to reduce the use of oil. Car engines changed markedly with higher power to weight ratios. Engine components were reduced in weight, as were body panels and structural components as greater strength was built into light alloys. Fuel efficiency in engines improved with fuel injection and electronic/computer controlled ignition.

More aerodynamic body shapes for cars and trucks cut down fuel use. Emission control rules for motor vehicles were strengthened to protect the atmosphere and lead began to be removed from fuel to protect the health of people forced to live with motor vehicle exhaust gases. A spin-off from this was generally better maintenance and tuning of cars and this also reduced the amount of petrol consumed.

Orbital, rotary and other innovative engine designs have been stimulated by a market that began to demand

Patterns in resource consumption

engines that could deliver more power with less fuel. So far rotary engines have gained a small share of the car market and orbital engines are used in some smaller machines, but the promise of great reduction in petroleum use from this experimentation is yet to be achieved. The great saving has so far come from many improvements in conventional car engines.

Research has also looked at replacing our great reliance on the petrol-driven internal combustion engine altogether. Solar powered cars get interesting publicity every year, with competitions being held in countries that have a reasonable guarantee of many hours of sunshine each day. Electric cars have been produced by many large makers of motor vehicles, but both solar and electric cars have been unable, for various reasons, to match the performance of cars with petrol-driven internal combustion engines.

This is especially true since two things have helped to ensure the continued dominance of petrol-driven internal combustion engines. The petrol engine itself has been greatly improved as has been noted, and the great oil price rises of the 1970s have largely been forgotten as the world has been surprised by the large amount of crude oil produced since that time. Greater certainty of oil supplies has resulted from new techniques of locating and recovering oil, new locations for oil reservoirs where once it was considered there would be no chance of their existence, less waste at the point of extraction and refining techniques that produce a more combustible and therefore more efficient fuel. This means that the time when the world will again really worry about oil running out has been pushed into the future.

Conservation strategies for coal

Coal is used for many manufacturing purposes in industrialised countries. However, the most important use for coal in terms of the amount used is for generating electricity (figure 4.37). Because of the abundance of coal as a natural resource, its conservation (like oil) has been of the 'find a more efficient way to use it' variety rather than getting people to reduce their use of the resource.

Countries such as Australia and the United States have such abundant reserves of coal that even if the current rates of use continue, supplies will last for several thousands of years. In coal rich countries such as these there have been great savings in the amount of coal used to produce each megawatt of electric power. Research by those who control the generating stations has been based on the desire to be able to sell more of their product by reducing its price than by a need to save coal. The coal industry is funding university research by providing buildings, equipment and professorial salaries to make the industry more efficient at every stage – exploration, mining, transportation and use. In fact, a continuing

search for new markets overseas for coal has stimulated the mining of coal so that Australia is using its known reserves at an increasing rate, even though the use of each tonne of coal produces increasing pollutants. The extension of reserves by drilling to prove their existence has continually reassured Australia that this fuel will go on for as long as anyone is prepared to forecast.

4.37 *A coal burning power station near London, United Kingdom. The two tall structures to the left are cooling towers, where water that has been turned into steam is released.*

Conservation strategies for forests

Exploitation of other countries' forests by countries and companies that are able to afford this, while leaving their own forests intact, is one way that forests are conserved at the local scale. Economic arguments are used to justify actions of this type. If countries in Europe, North America and Australasia find it is cheaper to buy timber from South-East Asia than to grow and use plantation softwoods for internal mouldings or furniture, then local forests are conserved, but South-East Asia's are not. If Japan finds it cheaper to buy into forestry enterprises in Australia, chip the wood and ship it back to its own factories than to develop techniques of using lesser quality timber from its steep, difficult to access hillsides, Japan's resources are conserved but Australia's are not.

Such examples abound throughout the world and the decisions are made on the grounds of economic efficiency. In most cases there are arguments to say that the LEDC is being exploited. Indigenous people may not only fail to receive much financial return from the timber sales, but may have their way of life substantially changed by the activity.

Because of constant news about the rate of destruction of the world's forests, research and development of alternative products to timber for house building and furniture making does lead to conservation, as does recycling of paper. In some cases the plastics, fibreglass, cement, aluminium or steel that become the replacements are large users of fossil fuels in their manufacture and there is a transfer of resource pressure rather than genuine conservation (figure 4.38). Nevertheless, the regional saving of a particular resource may be achieved even if the world does not benefit as a whole.

4.38 *Timber being used as the framework for new houses in Auckland (New Zealand). Having extensive forests, New Zealand tends to use timber for more uses and in larger quantities than many other countries. If a steel framework replaced this timber, the forests would be conserved, but the total resource and energy use would be much greater.*

Conservation strategies for renewable energy sources

Renewable energy sources such as wind, the sun, tidal movements and wave action hold the promise of low pollution alternatives to fossil fuels. They are especially attractive to countries that want to reduce reliance on imported energy resources, and where pollution-free energy is desired. One of the great advantages of most renewable energy resources is that they have a wide distribution. Most places have enough sunlight, wind, rainfall or plant growth to provide some form of renewable energy. Furthermore, many types of renewable energy do not require expensive advanced technology.

4.39 *Patties of cow dung drying on a wall in Kathmandu (Nepal), to be used as fuel for cooking.*

Biomass in one form – fuelwood – was discussed earlier in this chapter. Other important forms of biomass include grain and sugar crops, oil-bearing plants (such as sun-flowers), garbage, and wastes from animals and plants (figure 4.39). Biomass is converted into fuel in a variety of ways, including burning, gasification and anaerobic digestion. In China, human sewage is collected in the cities and taken to farms, or collected directly on farms, for use as fertiliser as well as making fuel. The value of this 'black gold' as it is known in China is shown by the fact that the most productive farms in China encircle the cities that provide an abundant supply of sewage.

Hydro-electricity can be thought of as a form of solar energy, because the sun drives the water cycle that provides the precipitation. Globally, hydro-electricity is the most widely used form of renewable energy. Some countries with abundant rainfall and mountainous areas for water storage, such as New Zealand and Nepal, produce more than half their electricity using hydro-power. Hydro-electricity is generated when water falls downwards over turbines that it spins around. This means that the initial costs of obtaining hydro-electricity – building the dam, installing the turbines and constructing a network of power lines – are quite high (figure 4.40). Once the dam is finished, the ongoing costs of obtaining power are quite small.

4.40 *The huge Hoover Dam on the Colorado River of the United States is an example of a large hydro-electric power station. Large dams like this are controversial because of their environmental impact.*

Hydro-electricity is generally thought of as 'clean' power because it does not cause the pollution of coal, oil and nuclear power. However, the construction of large dams and reservoirs does cause some severe impacts on the environment, and for this reason it is becoming increasingly controversial. Among the environmental effects of large dams are the following:

- dams catch sediments flowing down the river, causing siltation upstream of the dam and erosion scouring downstream;

- dams drown river valleys, and the weight of the water can cause earthquakes and tremors;

- drowning of the valley destroys large areas of vegetation and many animal habitats;

- in inhabited areas, many people may have to move their homes or abandon productive farming land to make way for the dam's lake;

- lakes forming behind the dam are often acidic and anaerobic (oxygen-starved) where water floods valleys with vegetation; and

- the bottom of the lake is likely to be so cold and dark that it is lifeless.

Despite these problems, many countries are continuing to build large dams. Perhaps the most spectacular example of a large dam presently under construction is the controversial Three Gorges Dam on China's Yangtze River. By the time it is completed, it will dam a lake that is 600 kilometres long with 22.15 billion cubic metres of water. It will have flooded 657 mines and factories, flooded 23,800 hectares of farming land, and caused 1,130,000 to have to move. On the positive side, it will produce 84 billion kilowatt hours of hydro-electricity per year, which is the equivalent of burning 40 million tonnes of coal.

There are various ways of managing hydro-electric facilities to conserve the water resource. For example, it is possible to build several dams on the same river, multiplying the productivity of the water flowing through. Another technique to conserve resources is to develop **pump-storage dams**, which work well when hydro-electric dams are used to supplement coal power stations rather than replace them. Coal stations take several days to 'power-up', and so they are left running day and night. On the other hand, hydro-electric dams can respond well to sudden demands for power because they produce electricity with only a few minutes warning, simply by turning open a valve. At night, demand for electricity is much less than during the day, and so coal stations are generating electricity for which there is no need. A pump-storage dam uses some of this surplus power to pump water uphill from one lake to another during this time. This means the water is effectively recycled and available for re-use when the next peak in demand occurs.

Geothermal power is a valuable source of power in those countries that have active volcanic areas such as New Zealand, Iceland, Japan, and the Philippines. In volcanic areas, the hot rocks beneath the surface heat up water that has seeped downwards from the surface. While the water is trapped beneath the surface, it is under great pressure. A well is drilled into the underground reservoir, the pressure is released and steam rushes upwards (figure 4.41). Where turbines have been installed, the rushing steam drives the turbines and produces electricity. Although geothermal power does not produce large quantities of greenhouse gases like burning coal, there are environmental side-effects. The escaping steam often

contains other gases such as carbon dioxide and hydrogen sulphide (which is poisonous). To prolong the life of geothermal power stations, hot water is often pumped down into the underground reservoir once again, and over time this can make the water saline, leading to corrosion of the turbines and pipes. Because geothermal power is always generated in volcanic areas, earthquakes are an additional risk.

4.41 *Geothermal power generation at Krafla, Iceland.*

Wind power has been used for centuries to pump water and grind grain, but in recent years it has also been used to generate electricity. About 80% of the world's wind-generated electricity is produced in three areas of California (USA), where 1% of the state's electricity is wind-generated (figure 4.42). Although wind power is becoming more popular in western Europe, especially in the Netherlands, Denmark and the United Kingdom, it still represents a minute proportion of electricity generated there. Like hydro-power, wind turbines are expensive to construct, but cheap to run once completed.

4.42 *A large wind farm at San Gorgonio Pass near Palm Springs, California (USA).*

Although wind power is pollution free, it is not without its problems. Each turbine is between 30 metres and 50 metres high, with blades up to 35 metres in diameter (figure 4.43). They are built in windy places such as ridge tops or coastlines, and are criticised as ruining the scenic beauty of these areas. Furthermore, the swishing noise of the blades has been blamed for frightening wildlife and making life unpleasant for nearby residents, who also complain of reduced radio and mobile phone reception near turbines. In western Europe, some farmers are building wind farms to earn extra income, as the land between the turbines can still be farmed effectively.

4.43 *Wind turbines near Burnley, England. Critics claim the turbines ruin the scenic resource of rural areas.*

4.44 *The Usine Marémotrice de la Rance tidal power station at the mouth of the River Rance in France. The turbulent water in the foreground shows that water is passing through the turbines under the barrage that the cars are crossing.*

Tidal power is still fairly rare, but seems to be effective where it has been used. The world's first tidal power station was built near the mouth of the River Rance in France (figure 4.44). The only other operational tidal power station is on the Bay of Fundy in Canada. In each of these places, the difference between high and low tide can be as much as 10 metres, resulting in the movement of a huge volume of water into and out of the river estuary, twice daily. By building a barrage across the mouth of the estuary, the moving water turns turbines almost constantly, as the turbines turn both when the tide is rising and falling. Tidal barrages are among the most expensive types of

power stations to build, but once finished they are cheap and reliable. They produce no wastes or pollution, and the only environmental criticism is that they interfere with the migration of spawning fish into and out of the coastal estuary where the barrage is built.

The sun is certainly one source of energy that will not run out in a time span that need worry us. **Solar energy** is clean, safe and can be considered unlimited. However, the solar cells needed to produce electricity from the sun are expensive to produce and remain fairly inefficient. Although there is a small solar power station in southern France, solar power is usually used on a small scale, such as individual homes or factories. Solar energy also has the disadvantage that the times when power is most needed (at night and on cold, wet days) are the times when it is least available.

Recycling of natural resources

There is now such pressure on natural resources that there are regular calls for the responsible use of all resources. Even though continual improvements in technology mean that we are able to recover greater proportions of the available coal, oil, natural gas, gold, or timber from the source, this is more than matched by the greater use of each resource. Ways to conserve must be found and recycling is one of them.

Recycling has always been part of human existence but the 20th century brought ways of life that are very wasteful of resources. The packaging required to let people choose their own items in a supermarket accumulates in such mountains that our attention is drawn to the waste. Large cities generate as much as 20,000 tonnes of garbage per day and much of it is material that could have been used again (figure 4.45).

4.45 *A sign in Singapore that encourages recycling.*

In most rural economies there has always been an emphasis on recycling plant and animal wastes. Generally this takes the form of using the wastes to fertilise soils for future crops – part of soil renewal. It can also take the form of passing waste from one animal to another and another in a food chain that is controlled for the benefit of the human planners. In the first case, food scraps or inedible parts of the plants, along with animal droppings (particularly from those that are herbivores) are composted to speed up the bacterial breakdown of the material into soluble plant nutrients. This has been done on a huge scale in rural economies such as China for thousands of years (figure 4.46).

4.46 *A mixture of human and pig manure matures in a small well at this farm near Wuhan, China. From time to time, some is scooped out and used as fertiliser on the farm's crops of vegetables.*

Many urban dwellers throughout the world now compost kitchen refuse, lawn clippings, prunings and any other organic matter such as animal or poultry manure when it is available in order to produce better flowers, shrubs or vegetables in the home garden. Such growing of vegetables where the input of chemicals can be controlled or eliminated altogether is now becoming very popular. In many advanced societies it is a partial return to the way things were done several generations ago (figure 4.47).

4.47 *'Muck spreading' on a farm in Lancashire, England. Many English farms recycle organic wastes rather than using chemical fertilisers.*

Subsistence farmers often take this process some steps further. Food scraps and parts of plants not considered to be human food may be fed to pigs. Their droppings may be washed into ponds used for fish breeding where they contribute to increased growth rates. The fish become human food and the scraps return to the compost or become food again for the pigs.

As part of community recycling efforts, some Australian city councils are now looking at the experiences of overseas cities that have installed total waste treatment facilities incorporating recycling, composting and landfill (figure 4.48). Because the system can reduce the amount going to landfill by 80%, this lengthens the life of existing sites and reduces the need to lock up large areas of land for this environmentally unsound way of disposing of waste. The end products are recyclable by industry (glass, metals and some plastics) and as compost that will be sold to home gardeners and horticulturists.

4.48 *A comprehensive recycling depot in suburban Sydney.*

These are examples of organic matter being the main item recycled. In the industrialised world, there is a great need to recycle manufactured products and to reduce the huge quantities of natural resources, especially fossil fuels, used to make them. In some cases a pattern of recycling is well established (e.g. scrap steel, copper, aluminium) but in others (especially packaging materials) greater and greater quantities are being dumped each day.

Paper and its re-use

Timber has some scope for recycling or re-use, but its continued supply is influenced more strongly by forestry practices designed to make the forest a **sustainable resource**. In other words removal of trees must be equal to or less than the replacement rate, and removal must not change the forest in ways that will destroy the natural, sustainable system of re-growth.

To manage forests on a sustainable basis, **silviculture** (the breeding, propagation and nurture of trees) aims to achieve a greater rate of growth in the managed, replacement forest than was achieved in the original forest. This already occurs in many plantations such as those grown by New Zealand paper makers to supply their mills.

Pressures to increase recycling of paper have grown with the rising perception that forests are being depleted at an unsustainable level throughout the world. Since landfill often destroys valuable natural resources such as wetlands, the pressures to recycle increase still further. Germany has been a leader in encouraging manufacturers to develop techniques for the recycling of paper. Acceptance by many users that bleached, white, high quality paper is no more useful for their purposes than slightly grey or coloured paper has helped the cause, and has reduced the toxic effluents from paper factories that pose a danger to land and rivers.

Although convenient separation systems and collection points for metals, glass, paper and so on have been available for several decades in most MEDCs, recycling of paper has been slower to gain wide acceptance. A particular problem with paper recycling is that paper products are easily contaminated by putrescent and other waste materials – even moisture may be enough to make them unsuitable for recycling. Given present technology, any additional costs involved in the recycling can make the process uneconomic. Unfortunately, this can lead to paper that has been recycled by concerned citizens later being dumped at landfill sites.

In LEDCs, sorting through mountains of garbage for anything that might stand re-use in its discarded form (such as a cardboard box) or might fetch some money as a raw material (newspaper, cardboard pieces) is a source of work for many people. Where the need is great, the proportion of paper and other potentially recyclable items within garbage dumps is substantially reduced.

In general, the MEDCs generate more waste products and are currently doing proportionately less to re-cycle and re-use than the LEDCs. Having said that, perceptions of the need and the ways and means are growing. The paperless office was to be an affluent world way of saving paper but it has not happened. Some argue that the communication wizardry generated by the computer actually results in more paper being wasted. The saving may yet occur but it is some way off in the future.

Geosequestration

Many commentators believe that global warming has now reached crisis point. Fossil fuels, coal, oil and natural gas, currently supply around 85% of the world's energy needs. In spite of many international agreements, the International Energy Agency predicts that fossil fuels will continue to be heavily used for many years to come. The burning of fossil fuels is a major source of excess carbon dioxide, the gas that has contributed most to the increased

concentration of greenhouse gases in the atmosphere (figures 4.49 and 4.50). There seems to be an urgent need to reduce the atmospheric concentrations of greenhouse gases that are likely to produce rapid, human-induced climate change.

4.49 *Air pollution from factories with outdated technology are major sources of greenhouse gases. Such factories are still common in Eastern Europe, the countries of the former Soviet Union, China, India and some other economies. The example shown here is Pyongyang, capital city of North Korea.*

4.50 *Motor vehicles (cars and trucks) are among the most significant sources of human greenhouse gases. Older vehicles tend to produce more greenhouse gases than newer vehicles. This heavily polluting old truck is near Kaesong, North Korea.*

Greenhouse gas emissions can be lowered through increased energy efficiency, switching to lower carbon-intensive fuels, and by making greater use of renewable energy. Recently, a radical solution has been proposed, known as geosequestration.

Geosequestration is the storage of compressed near-liquid carbon dioxide in underground chambers. It involves capturing the carbon dioxide before it is pumped into the atmosphere, transporting it (usually by pipeline) and injecting it deep underground in rock reservoirs for thousands of years (figure 4.51).

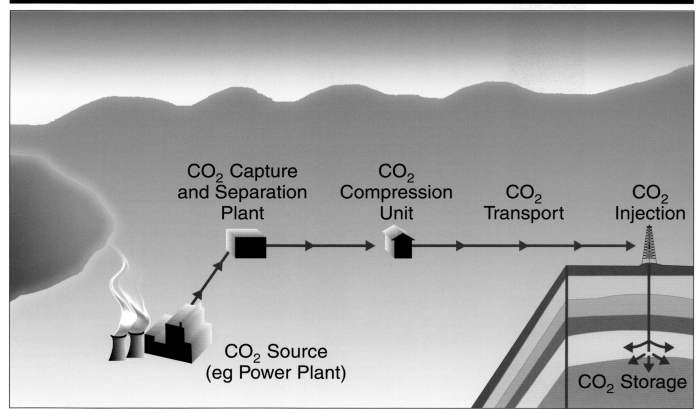

4.51 *The process of geosequestration.*

Some commentators see geosequestration as the solution to the earth's global warming problems, whereas others see it as a desperate last gasp from the coal industry as it wants to delay the move to alternative energy solutions.

In geosequestration, carbon dioxide is separated from burnt coal, oil or gas and then liquefied. The carbon dioxide can then be buried in geological sites with porous rocks, including old oil and gas wells, unmined coal seams, or in saltwater trapped underground. Advocates of geosequestration claim that the process could reduce carbon dioxide emissions from electricity production by up to 40% by 2030, assuming all new coal power stations sequestered 100% of their carbon dioxide emissions.

The process remains experimental, with only two test projects started by 2010, one in the North Sea off the west coast of Norway (rather than in porous rocks) and the other near Natchez (Mississippi, USA). The concept is also attracting considerable attention in Australia, where the government is investing heavily in geosequestration research.

However, the proposal is quite controversial, partly because one possible site, at Barrow Island off the north-west coast of Australia, is a nature reserve. It is also criticised as diverting funds and attention away from ways to reduce carbon dioxide emissions in the first place. Moreover, some people would question the morality of storing large volumes of carbon dioxide underground that may be released, either through seepage or by accident, with catastrophic consequences for future generations.

QUESTION BLOCK 4G

1. *Describe the management issues involved in any two of the following natural resources: petroleum, coal, forests.*

2. *Outline the advantages and disadvantages of each of the renewable energy sources described in this section.*

3. *Why is recycling important? Describe the pressures which promote and retard recycling of paper and water.*

4. *Investigate geosequestration on the internet. Outline the benefits and problems of the process as a way to reduce global warming.*

5

Freshwater issues and conflicts

Water on the land is a scarce resource which poses challenges for human management and use.

ToK BoX — Page 178
The Scientific Method

The Water System

The Hydrological Cycle

Water is constantly being moved through the environment in a never-ending process known as the water cycle, or **hydrological cycle** (figure 5.1). As water moves through the hydrological cycle, its state is changed between solid (ice and snow), liquid (water) and gas (water vapour). Water moves downwards by gravity, in forms such as rain and rivers, sideways in winds or ocean currents, or vertically in the atmosphere by convection.

Water in any state can be changed into any another state by heating or cooling. When water exists as a solid (as ice), rigid bonds that connect the atoms hold together the molecules of water. If enough heat energy is provided, some of these bonds can be broken and the molecules become free to slide past each other as a liquid. This process is called **melting**. Should yet more heat break the remaining bonds, the molecules may then escape from each other

and fly about freely as a gas; this is known as **evaporation**. It is also possible for ice to turn directly into a gas if enough heat energy is provided, and this process is known as **sublimation**.

The opposite processes occur when heat is removed from water. As water vapour becomes liquid water, **condensation** is said to occur – the opposite of evaporation. When water cools to become ice, **freezing** occurs. The direct change from water vapour into ice is known as **sublimation**, the same as the reverse process. The entire process of the hydrological cycle is driven by energy from the sun.

The hydrological cycle may be thought of as a **system**. A system is a network of related elements that work together towards some end. There are many types of systems, both natural and created by humans. For example, an education system brings together government administrators, teachers, students and others work together to develop a wiser, more knowledgeable and more skilful population. Other examples of systems include political systems, transport systems and sewerage systems. The

>> Some Useful Definitions

Drainage basin — the area drained by a river and its tributaries.

Drainage divide (also known as a **watershed**) — the line defining the boundary of a river or stream drainage basin and separating it from adjacent basin(s).

Maximum sustainable yield — the maximum level of extraction of water that can be maintained for a given area, indefinitely.

Wetlands — areas that are regularly saturated by surface water or groundwater, including freshwater marshes, swamps and bogs.

hydrological cycle is sometimes called a **closed system** because, with just a few minor exceptions, no water enters or leaves the system. Tiny quantities of 'new' water enter the system, mainly during volcanic eruptions, but these are so insignificant compared with the total volume of water on the planet that they can be largely ignored. These inputs, plus the input of solar energy into the system, mean that the hydrological cycle is not a completely closed system, although it is one of the most closed systems to exist naturally on earth.

Water on the land's surface moves through streams and glaciers. Water also flows below the surface of the land, percolating through the soil and rock into rivers, lakes and ocean basins. Precipitation, such as rain or snow, is often intercepted by something before it reaches the ground.

Precipitation that has been prevented by vegetation from falling directly to the ground surface is said to be **inter-**

cepted. Although animals may sometimes be the interceptor, the most common interceptor is vegetation. Vegetation affects the movement of water in six ways:
- by storing intercepted precipitation;
- by providing points for the re-formation of raindrops;
- by providing protection of the ground surface from the impact of raindrops;
- by providing leaf litter for debris dams;
- by removing water from the soil (that is later evaporated back into the atmosphere as a gas); and
- by disturbing the surface soil and construction of root channels.

The process of interception impacts on the hydrological cycle in several ways. First, interception reduces the amount of water reaching the ground, simply because it is stored on leaves and stems, and then some of it is evaporated. Moreover, interception re-forms raindrops, redirects the flow of water to the ground, and alters the chemistry of the rain.

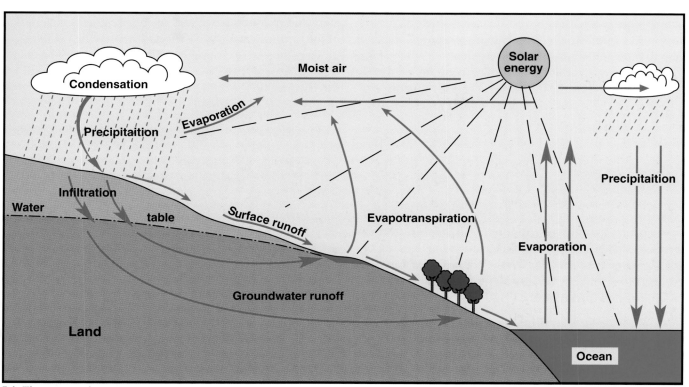

5.1 *The water cycle.*

Freshwater issues and conflicts

ToK BoX

The Scientific Method.

Although the IB classifies geography as a Group 3 subject (i.e. a humanities discipline), this is really a distortion of the nature of the subject. Geography developed as a bridge between the physical and human elements of the environment, and physical geography remains an important component of the subject, as this chapter of the book shows. Many universities around the world teach geography within the Faculty of Sciences as a reflection of the importance of physical geography and its use of the scientific method.

Although there are variations in the way the scientific method is applied by different researchers, the key elements are:

- observe some aspect of the universe (e.g. all swans are white);

- form a hypothesis that potentially explains what has been observed;

- make testable predictions on the basis of that hypothesis;

- make observations or experiments that can test those predictions;

- modify the hypothesis until it is in accord with all observations and predictions; which enables the development of ...

- laws, which can be can be tested conclusively (or least can be proved false), which are precise, make strong claims

about the real world, and which can be backed up by evidence.

Science uses inductive logic. This means that experiments and observations are undertaken to assemble a collection of individual results, which are then generalised into laws or theories. In starting from individual results to form general theories, scientific reasoning is the opposite of mathematical reasoning, which uses deductive logic (starting from a general situation and applying it to individual instances).

Scientific observations and experiments become more reliable as the number of observations and experiments increases. In the hypothesis mentioned above ('all swans are white'), European scientists found tens of thousands of swans that seemed to verify the hypothesis, and they therefore believed that the hypothesis was true. That changed, however, in the early 1800s when Europeans first visited Western Australia and found black swans. This is a good example to show that although the inductive logic used in the scientific method can provide high probability, it can never provide certainty.

There are other limitations to the scientific method that should also be acknowledged. For example, the traditional, perhaps naïve view of science is

that it generates truth from empirical evidence, and that it progresses by gradually improving on existing theories and data.

However, a simple historical survey shows that this is not always the case. Many earlier scientific theories are untenable today as they are completely inconsistent with contemporary data. Yet, in their day, these theories had what was believed to be conclusive empirical support and confirmed predictions. If the theories that earlier scientists believed have been proved false, why should we believe that the current theories will always remain true?

A philosopher of science, Karl Popper had an answer to this question, which has become known as falsificationism. Popper argued that for a theory to be scientifically valid, it must be falsifiable, or be capable of being proven false.

A strong conjecture is one that is easy to falsify. A weak conjecture is one that is difficult to falsify.

The French philosopher, Blaise Pascal (1623-1662) was not very confident that scientists actually follow the principle of falsificationism, commenting "People almost invariably arrive at their beliefs not on the basis of proof, but on the basis of what they find attractive".

The next ToK BoX is on page 241.

In any place where the ground surface is shielded by vegetation, interception of precipitation occurs. The degree of interception is influenced by the type of vegetation found in an area, and its density. For example, more water is intercepted by the dense forest canopy in a tropical area than by the sparse vegetation of arid and semi-arid areas. Similarly, broad-leafed trees are more effective interceptors than trees with needle leaves, such as pines.

If more rain falls than the vegetation is able to hold in interception storage, then the water rolls off the leaves, often re-forming into drops that are much larger than the ones that originally hit the vegetation. The increased drop size can lead to high rates of **rainsplash erosion** around the base of the tree or shrub, especially if the distance of fall is greater than 5 metres. Water that reaches the ground either directly or after being intercepted by vegetation is called **throughfall**.

Throughfall collects on the ground surface, first filling small depressions and hollows. Almost as soon as the water begins to accumulate, however, **infiltration** begins. As water enters the soil, it becomes part of the soil water

store and may, if it percolates deep enough, become part of the groundwater store. The ease with which water moves downwards through soil and rock material is called **permeability**. Where the water can move rapidly the permeability is high, but when the water moves slowly, the permeability is low.

Rainwater that has been intercepted by vegetation reacts chemically with the leaves and branches, and also with dust on the leaves. Minerals such as calcium, sodium, potassium and magnesium can be added to the throughfall water in this way, returning many chemicals from the trees back to the soil. This process can be important in recycling nutrients and in maintaining the fertility of forests.

Rainsplash erosion can be reduced by plant material that has fallen to the ground and accumulated. Accumulated leaf litter protects the surface, and can therefore reduce the quantities of soil that are moved downslope. Leaf litter can form small dams known as **debris dams**, and these provide small areas for water storage that increase the potential for infiltration.

Where plant roots have penetrated into the soil, and where lines of weakness in rocks open sub-surface cracks, water can move more easily from the surface into the sub-surface store. Having said this, it is usually when roots decay that the greatest access paths are provided for water to infiltrate downwards. Roots can also disturb surface material by pushing the soil surface upwards. When large roots are very close to the surface of the soil, surface depressions are formed, and these increase the depression storage (puddles) and the potential for both infiltration and evaporation loss. Furthermore, roots that trail across the ground surface impede overland flow and provide points for small pools of water to collect.

Except during rain, flooding or in swampy areas, soil is usually unsaturated at the surface. In this near-surface zone, water is held to the soil particles by electro-chemical bonds. This unsaturated zone is known as the **vadose zone**, and the water in the zone is known as vadose water. Below the vadose zone is the **phreatic zone**, which is where soil and rock voids are full of water. The water contained in this zone is known as phreatic water, or more commonly, as groundwater. Groundwater is an important source of water in many parts of the world, being the second largest store of liquid water in the water cycle. Stores of groundwater are referred to as **aquifers**.

In any area where is enough rainfall, large quantities of water will usually be stored on the surface in two main areas, the **hillslopes** and the **channels**. Most of the water that flows through lakes and rivers comes from the hillslopes, as they form the largest proportion of the area of any catchment. On any hillslope there are many irregularities in the surface. These depressions trap any water that might enter them, forming depression stores. When these are filled, water begins to flow over the land surface.

Large volumes of water may be held in these depression and surface storages. This can be seen by observing the large number of puddles on the ground following a rainstorm. Because of surface irregularities, the actual depth of water at particular sites may be greater (such as in swamps) or less (such as on bare rock).

Some of the water that reaches the ground surface moves rapidly over or through shallow soil into a stream, and this water is called **quickflow**. Quickflow contributes to the rapid rise in water level in streams during and following a storm. On the other hand, the slow seepage of water from hillslopes contributes to the base flow of streams, which is the low flow between floods.

QUESTION BLOCK 5A

1. Explain the difference between an open system and a closed system.

2. Discuss the role played by vegetation in intercepting water.

3. List the ways in which water can move under the influence of gravity.

4. List the (a) stores, and (b) flows, of water in the hydrological cycle.

Drainage Basins and Flooding

The Drainage Basin

Running water has shaped most of the earth's land surface. Even in coastal areas and desert landscapes, running water is the main agent of erosion and deposition that shapes the land's surface. Areas where running water is the main influence on the formation of landforms are known as **humid terrains**, because there is usually an abundance of water. Humid terrains include not only the streams and valleys, but also the slopes and ridges.

Water flows from high areas to low areas, usually taking the path where the least amount of energy is needed. The higher the altitude of water in a stream, the greater the amount of **potential energy** it possesses to erode the landscape. As water flows downhill, it uses up this energy **eroding** (or wearing away) the land surface. A stream cannot erode below a certain **base level**. For most rivers, base level is sea level, although certain streams may have a local base level, such as a lake.

Streams can be thought of as **systems**, with inputs and outputs. Each stretch of river receives **inputs** of water and sediment from upstream. These inputs combine with the water and sediment in the section of river, and a quantity of water and sediment will leave the stretch of river as **outputs**. If there is an imbalance between the inputs and the outputs, then changes will occur in the river. If more sediment enters the stream than leaves it, then **deposition** will occur. If less sediment enters the stream than leaves it, then **erosion** occurs. The input of water and sediment equals the output of water and sediment. Changes in the shape (or form) of the stream are unlikely, and the stream is said to be in **dynamic equilibrium**. This means that while individual particles of water and sediment are constantly moving (and are therefore 'dynamic'), the overall pattern is not changing (and is therefore in 'equilibrium').

The area that supplies water to a stream is known as its **drainage basin**, or catchment. The highest ridge between two valleys divides adjoining drainage basins, and these ridges are known as **watersheds**, or **interfluves**. Any ridge top therefore forms the border of a drainage basin.

Drainage basins can be described by the order of streams within them. Streams that have no **tributaries** (or streams flowing into it) are termed **first order streams**. When two first order streams join together, they become a **second order stream**. Two second order streams join to form a third order stream, two third order streams join to form a fourth order stream, and so on (figure 5.2). However, a stream may have a tributary with a lower order without becoming a higher order stream, and this is shown at several points labelled x in figure 5.2.

In the drainage basin shown in figure 5.2, the highest order stream is third order, and thus we can refer to the basin as a third order drainage basin. Within the third order basin, there are several second order and first order drainage basins. It is likely that the third order drainage basin shown is in turn part of a fourth order basin. We can therefore see that drainage basins occur in hierarchies.

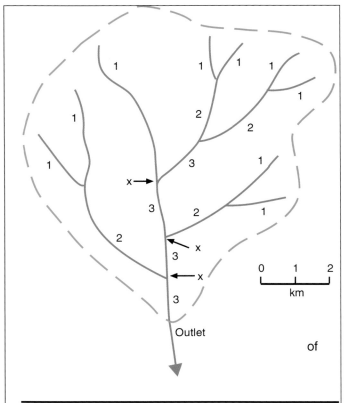

Order	Number of streams	Length of streams (km)
1	9	17.6
2	4	10.5
3	1	5.8
		TOTAL 33.9

Area = 53km²

Drainage density = $\frac{33.9}{53}$

= 0.64km / km²

5.2 Stream order. The inset shows calculation of drainage density.

The **drainage density** is the ratio of the total length of the streams in a basin, measured in kilometres, to the total area of the basin, measured in square kilometres. This measure indicates the length of channel needed to drain each square kilometre of the catchment.

The **bifurcation ratio** measures the number of streams of one order to the next highest order, such as the first order to second order, second order to third order, and so on. Typically, bifurcation ratios range between 3 and 5. In figure 5.2, there are four second order streams and one third order stream; this gives a bifurcation ratio of 4. If we had a sixth order drainage basin with a bifurcation ratio of three, then the number of streams would be as follows:

> 6th order streams = 1
> 5th order streams = 3 (1 x 3)
> 4th order streams = 9 (3 x 3)
> 3rd order streams = 27 (9 x 3)
> 2nd order streams = 81 (27 x 3)
> 1st order streams = 243 (81 x 3)

As one travels downstream from the source of a stream, several trends can be observed. Usually, the valley floor widens, the average angle of the slopes decreases, and the heights of the interfluves diminish. The **profile**, or side-view, of the longest stream in the drainage basin is usually concave, which means that the stream's **gradient**, or slope, declines further downstream (figure 5.3).

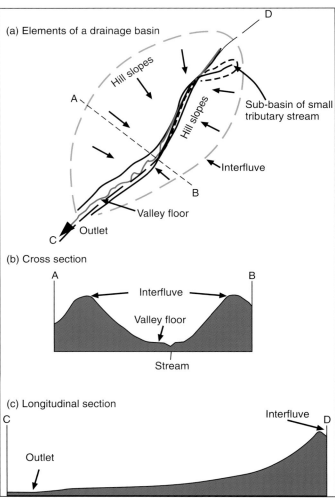

5.3 The parts of a drainage basin.

Drainage basins comprise several components – slopes, valley bottoms, stream channels and watersheds, and of these, slopes comprise the largest part in terms of area. Water and sediment are supplied to the channels and valley bottoms from the slopes. After it is eroded, the material from the slopes moves downhill by mass movement, wash and gully erosion (figures 5.4 to 5.6). When it reaches the valley floors, the eroded material may be removed further down the drainage basin through the running water of the stream. In this way, the valley floor can be thought of as a corridor for the removal of sediment and water.

5.4 *Mass movement is the movement of material downslope by gravity. The ribbed pattern on this slope at Whangaparaoa near Auckland in New Zealand is evidence of soil creep. The surface layer is breaking down into small steps called 'terracettes' that move downhill slowly.*

5.5 *A huge landslip in Arthur's Pass (New Zealand) presents a hazard for motorists who use this road linking the eastern and western coasts of New Zealand's South Island.*

Streams can therefore be thought of as the natural transport routes of a drainage basin. Water moves more rapidly than sediment through streams, and as they flow, they often trace out regular patterns when viewed from above.

5.6 *Gully erosion, caused by running water on a farm near Bega in south-eastern Australia.*

QUESTION BLOCK 5B

1. *What is a humid terrain?*

2. *Explain why the ocean is the 'ultimate' base level.*

3. *What would be the impact of an increase in the input of water in a stream?*

4. *What is a drainage basin?*

5. *Which part of a drainage basin do you think is most important for (a) landform development, and (b) human life – the stream, the slopes or the watershed? Give reasons.*

Discharge

The volume of water that passes through a stream's cross-section in a given period of time is known as its **discharge**. Discharge is measured in cubic metres per second (m^3/s), which can be shortened to 'cumecs'. Discharge can be calculated using the equation $Q = VA$, where Q is discharge, V is mean velocity and A is cross-sectional area of the stream.

Water flowing without any sediment is able to scour rock because of hydraulic action and turbulence. **Hydraulic action** is simply the erosive force of water beating on rocks – erosion by the impact of water. When water cascades down a waterfall and hits the rocks below, it exerts a hydraulic force that can scour holes into the rock, in much the same way that a hole is drilled into soil by a water jet from a hose. Weak rocks, and rocks with cracks and fractures, are easily broken down, although massive rocks (those with no jointing) resist breakdown by hydraulic action.

Although water by itself can produce landforms, most work is done by water that is carrying sediment. Materials carried by a river are referred to as the **load** of the stream. The rocks, sand, sediment and minerals that comprise the load can be carried by rolling along the river bottom (**bed load**), by being suspended in the water (**suspended load** or **wash load**), or by being dissolved in the water (**solution load** or **dissolved load**). Often, all four of these forms of transport take place at the one time.

Material that is dragged or rolled along the bed of the stream because it is too heavy to be lifted is called **bed load**. Typical bed load materials have diameters greater than 2 millimetres, such as gravel and cobbles (figure 5.7). Because of its large size, bed load usually moves slowly and is often broken down into smaller particles after being transported only short distances. Bed load particles are usually rounded because irregularities are removed rapidly during frequent collisions.

5.7 *Bed load of rounded boulders and an undercut outside edge of a meander – Haast River, New Zealand.*

Smaller particles with diameters between 0.02 and 2.0 millimetres are known as sand, and these are usually carried as **suspended load**. Suspended loads are carried by the water above the level of the bed of the stream. Larger particles are carried by **saltation** motion, which means a series of repeated jumps. On the other hand, fine sand may be suspended for long periods and even carried to the stream surface before falling back to the bed.

Wash load comprises very fine particles of silt and clay that are suspended permanently in the stream. These particles are so fine that they can be carried by flows with velocities less than 0.1 cm/s, and even minor turbulence may hold them in the water for long periods. Some rock materials are dissolved during the process of weathering, and when these materials are carried by a stream, they are known as **solution load** or **dissolved load**.

Water flows in a stream in two main ways, laminar flow and turbulent flow. **Laminar flow** occurs when water particles move in sheets parallel to the channel bed, flowing slowly in a smooth and shallow channel. However, laminar flow is fairly rare, and **turbulent flow** is much more common. When water moves in turbulent flow, the water particles move in erratic paths down-stream, criss-crossing and mixing with other particles (figure 5.8). Turbulent flow results in much more erosion of the stream channel than does laminar flow and it is capable of keeping particles suspended for longer periods of time.

5.8 *The irregular bed of this river in New Zealand causes the water to move in a turbulent flow.*

5.9 *This stream, the Merced River in Yosemite National Park in the USA, appears to flow quickly through its steep, rocky channel.*

5.10 *In contrast with the stream in the previous photo, the lower reaches of the Mekong River seem to flow slowly through the wide channels of its delta in southern Vietnam. In fact, this stream would flow much faster than the one on figure 5.9, because there is much less friction with the channel banks.*

When people compare the rushing water in the small channel of a stream near its source, with the apparent sluggishness of water downstream, they often conclude that water flows more quickly near the source (figures 5.9 and 5.10).

This was shown to be wrong as a result of the work done in 1891 by the Irish engineer, Robert Manning, who attempted to quantify the roughness of stream beds. Table 5.1 shows typical values of Manning's roughness coefficient depending on the material that makes up the bed of the stream.

Table 5.1
Typical Values of Manning's Roughness Coefficient

Bed profile	Vegetation (weeds, tree roots)	Manning's Coefficient Value		
		Sand and Gravel	Coarse Gravel	Boulders
Uniform	None	0.020	0.030	0.050
Undulating		0.030	0.040	0.055
Uniform	Some	0.040	0.050	0.060
Undulating		0.050	0.060	0.070
Highly Irregular	None	0.055	0.070	0.080
	Extensive	0.080	0.090	0.100

Source: Based on Goudie, A. (1984) p.286

Manning developed his roughness coefficient into an equation that described the velocity of flow. Manning's equation is:

$$V = \frac{(R^{2/3}S^{1/2})}{n}$$

where V is velocity (in metres per second), R is the hydraulic radius (in metres; in wide channels the mean depth is used instead), S is channel slope, or gradient (in metres per metre), and n is the roughness coefficient described above. This equation shows that if bed roughness increases, then velocity and discharge will decrease. Furthermore, if the hydraulic radius or the gradient increases, then the velocity and the discharge will increase.

Manning's roughness coefficient shows us that the water flows more quickly in the downstream stretch of a river than upstream. This is because a greater proportion of the volume of water is in contact with the channel sides and bottom upstream, causing more friction that in turn slows the flow of the water.

As the discharge and velocity of a river increase, the stream becomes capable of transporting greater volumes of sediment, and sediment of larger sizes. The largest particle of sediment that a stream can carry defines the stream's **competence**. The more 'competent' the stream, the larger the particles it can carry. Competence tends to increase exponentially with velocity. In other words, if velocity doubles, then the maximum size of the particle that can be carried increases six-fold. Naturally, neither wash load nor solution load concentrations are related to the velocity of flow.

The amount of sediment carried by a stream over a certain period is its **sediment discharge**. In general, sediment discharge triples when discharge doubles. This relationship is not precise, however, because it depends on factors such as how much sediment is available, the sediment size, velocity of the stream and the shape of the channel. The sediment yield of a catchment is the total quantity of sediment exported from a catchment in a year.

The main sources of sediment in a drainage basin are the stream bed and the banks (figure 5.11). Most of the material comprising the bed and bank material is sediment that has been weathered elsewhere in the catchment and deposited by the river. This is known as **alluvium**. Alluvium sometimes has a long history of transport, deposition and re-deposition, especially in streams with large catchments. The beds and banks of some streams are composed of bedrock, but even they may still provide some sediment as a result of the hydraulic action and **abrasion** of the stream by the particles that are being transported.

5.11 *The sediment comprising the bed of this stream near Âït-Benhaddou in Morocco is clearly seen. The sediment is being supplemented by weathered material from the outside bank that is being undercut by the river. In this view, a herd of goats is being brought to the river to drink.*

In the lower (or downstream) stretches of many rivers, **floodplains** develop over a long period of time. Floodplains are wide, flat areas of material beside rivers that are deposited during floods. Valley floors may consist of alluvium that has been deposited over many years. Because the sediments deposited by the river often contain useful plant nutrients, they make fertile soils that are often used by farmers for cultivation (figure 5.12). Much of the sediment is moved and rearranged whenever the river floods or changes course.

which cover periods of six months or more show several flood events separated by periods of low flow or base flow (figure 5.13). Hydrographs of small intermittent or ephemeral streams show floods separated by periods without flow, because there is no slow groundwater flow , the source of base flow.

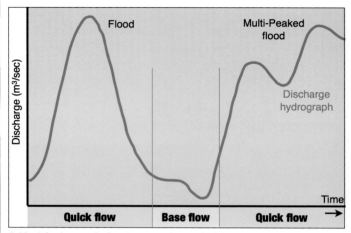

5.13 *A hydrograph showing a multi-peaked flood.*

Flood hydrographs usually have a short rising limb and a longer receding limb (figure 5.14). The rising limb goes from the start of run-off to the peak of the flood. The receding limb goes from the peak and continues until base flow is dominant. The total time shown in the rising and receding limbs is the period of the flood hydrograph, or the **flood period**. Not all flood hydrographs are as simple as the one shown in figure 5.14, as storms with different rainfall intensities can give rise to multi-peaked hydrographs.

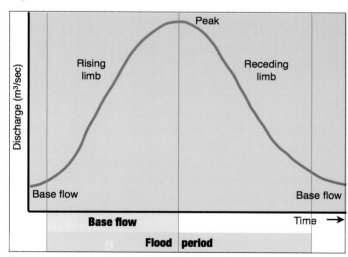

5.14 *Components of a typical flood hydrograph.*

People who live near a stream are not usually concerned about its velocity or discharge except when it either dries up completely or floods (figure 5.15). **Flood frequency** is the number of times that a flood of a given magnitude will occur, on average, in a specified period. A flood with a frequency of 0.1 per year would occur at an average of once every ten years. The opposite (or inverse) of flood frequency is the **recurrence interval**. A flood of frequency 0.2 per year has a recurrence interval of five years.

5.12 *Part of the extensive floodplain of the Chao Phraya River, north of Bangkok, Thailand. The fertile soils of the floodplain support a high population density and very productive agriculture.*

QUESTION BLOCK 5C

1. *How is it possible for water that is not carrying any sediment to erode a stream channel?*

2. *Describe the pattern shown in table 5.1, which outlines Manning's roughness coefficient.*

3. *What is the difference between hydraulic action and abrasion?*

4. *'Floodplains are created by both erosion and deposition, whereas potholes are created by erosion only'. Giving reasons, do you agree or disagree with this statement?*

Hydrographs and Flooding

For most land use planning and water resource engineering projects, there is a need to measure stream discharge over a period of years. The graph that relates discharge to time is known as a **hydrograph**.

Heavy rain for a short period of time produces runoff that is concentrated into a short time span. This concentrated runoff is called a **flood**. Most long-term hydrographs

Flood frequency and recurrence interval are only statistical estimates of the number of floods over a long period and they cannot, of course, be used to predict the exact period between floods. It is possible to find instances where the 5-year flood did not occur for fifty years, or where two 5-year floods occurred in one year.

5.15 *The Bega River (Australia) in flood, inundating farmlands.*

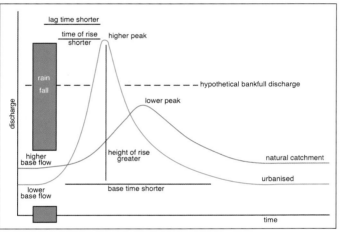

5.16 *Natural and urban hydrographs.*

Figure 5.16 shows the hydrographs for two streams, one that is natural (or unaltered by humans) and the other that is urbanised. Because an urbanised drainage basin has fewer trees, less grass and more paved areas than a natural catchment, there is less infiltration and more quickflow. Consequently, when there is a fall of rain, the stream in the urbanised catchment rises more quickly and is more likely to flood. Furthermore, because there is less ongoing seepage from groundwater in the urbanised catchment, the stream there is more likely to dry up between falls of rain.

Streams that flow all the time are known as **perennial streams**, and they have a seepage flow source. In other words, they are fed by water from a place where the water table rises to the surface (such as a spring) to create a source for the stream. The stream continues to flow as long as the water table on each bank is above the channel level. If the water table falls below the channel level, then the water in the stream will seep underground and there will be no surface flow. Streams that flow only after rain

do not have a permanent seepage source, and these are known as **intermittent** or **ephemeral streams**.

The rate at which water is delivered from the hillslopes to the channel determines the volume of water in a stream at any one time. If delivery times are long, **flood peaks** are low and the **flood periods** are also long. On the other hand, rapid delivery results in a short flood period and high flood peak, as shown in figure 5.16.

QUESTION BLOCK 5D

1. *How can hydrographs explain the magnitude, spatial extent and timing of floods?*

2. *Describe the differences between the urban and natural hydrographs shown in figure 5.16. Explain why the differences exist.*

Management Issues and Strategies

Water and its Re-Use

5.17 *This sign in Siem Reap (Cambodia) reminds people how important it is to keep the river water clean.*

Most of the world's people do not have access to an adequate supply of safe water. In fact many of the world's major health problems would be more quickly relieved by a safe water supply than by the provision of medicines, trained medical workers and well-supplied hospitals. Care in the use of such an essential resource is clearly needed (figure 5.17). Recycling water is not as easy as the recycling of paper, but in many ways it is more important.

The problem of water supply is the result of many interacting factors. Water is an example of a natural resource that is distributed very unevenly across the world. Rainfall and surface runoff are abundant and reliable in some places, while they are almost non-existent in others. In most places where large populations have grown, the water supply is adequate. This may be from local rainfall or runoff being carried by rivers from other wetter areas.

Egypt is an extreme example of the latter where true desert actually supports a large population because of the reliable flow in the Nile River.

5.18 *Retrieving water from a well that serves a few hundred families in a village near Kumasi in central Ghana. It is an effort to collect water, and the quality cannot be guaranteed.*

In almost every inhabited part of the world the retention and distribution of water consumes vast resources. This varies from the individual effort and time needed to dig wells and carry water to homes in semi-arid rural communities (figure 5.18), to the building of massive dams and canal/pipeline systems to ensure water is available to cities of millions and even tens of millions of people.

The daily task of collecting water consumes an enormous amount of time for hundreds of millions of people in LEDCs. An offer was made by international development agencies to Myanmar in the late 1990s to replace hundreds of village wells and reservoirs with piped water

(figure 5.19). However, the offer was turned down, and the reasoning provides an interesting insight into the place of women in many LEDCs. Collecting the water is traditionally women's work, although boys and very young men do also collect water from time to time. The offer of piped water was refused because the men wanted their wives kept busy collecting water. They argued that while the women were collecting water they could not get into mischief and have illicit relationships while they (the husbands) are away during the day working. In the view of the Myanmar decision-makers, it was worth the peace-of-mind it gave to forego the piped water.

5.19 *A boy collects water from a small reservoir in Minnanthu village, central Myanmar.*

Figure 5.20 shows the very uneven distribution of rainfall and consequent availability of water at the surface. Of course the terrain and the temperature regime influence the run-off. Runoff is also affected by the seasonal distribution of rainfall, although it is total rainfall that sets

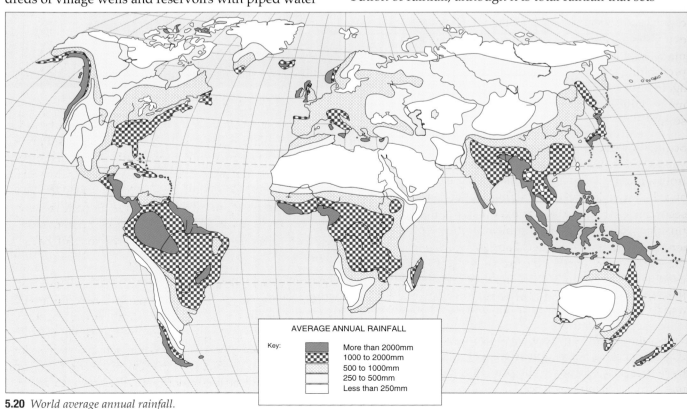

AVERAGE ANNUAL RAINFALL

Key:
- More than 2000mm
- 1000 to 2000mm
- 500 to 1000mm
- 250 to 500mm
- Less than 250mm

5.20 *World average annual rainfall.*

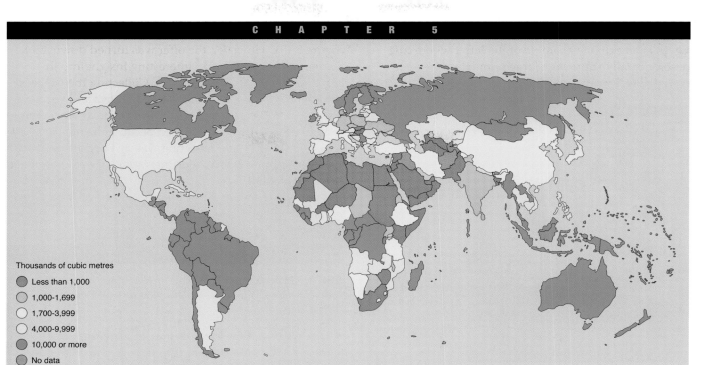

5.21 *Freshwater resources per capita. This map shows each country's renewable water resources, including river flows, divided by the population.*

basic limits to the availability of water. It is then up to human ingenuity to get water to where it is needed (figure 5.21).

Most of the massive worldwide efforts to control water have been focussed on first-time use and much more work must be done on how to re-use water (figure 5.22). Both industry and modern urban lifestyles waste a high proportion of water that is supplied through expensive reticulation schemes. In addition, most homes have the capacity to collect about 50% of the fresh water used every day if rainfall run-off were retained. However, many local government authorities still have regulations prohibiting tanks, even though there is growing encouragement for people to use such a source for garden watering to reduce the consumption of treated, reticulated supply.

So far, only dedicated environmentalists use the special valves which are available to re-direct grey water (water from a number of household uses such as baths, clothes and dish washing where contamination is not great) to a second use for garden watering, car washing and possibly flushing toilets. There are problems with the inconvenience of making regular decisions about when to activate the valve, where to store the grey water until it can be used, what organisms will be in the water and whether they will be a problem, and whether gravitational flow will be possible to the area of re-use.

The cost of water is generally too low to act as an incentive to recycle it, but people in the developed world may have to face steep rises in the price to force more efficient use of this precious resource.

5.22 *A sign encouraging tourists in Zimbabwe to conserve water.*

Industry has dual incentives to do a better job with water. Cost is one factor but restrictions on the effluents that can be returned to rivers or the sewer system can be enforced by heavy fines. Treatment on-site may be costly but it is essential that it be built into the feasibility study for any new manufacturing or mining venture. Extracting heavy metals, acids, dyes and bleaches allows companies to re-use water as a way to recoup some of the costs of treatment.

The technology exists to purify water that has been used for almost any purpose. The cost can prove prohibitive if fresh supplies are reasonably abundant. However, such abundance is becoming less common, and so people everywhere are going to have to become better at preventing water from being polluted in the first place and then more ready to pay for the treatment that will allow it to be re-used (figure 5.23).

5.23 *A sign at a village market in the Mekong Delta of Vietnam encouraging people not to pollute the water (in various ways).*

5.24 *Part of the reservoir of the huge Atatürk Dam, the largest reservoir in the GAP (South-eastern Atatolian) water management project in south-eastern Turkey.*

The political, environmental, economic and social implications of water use will be linked together and considered in the case study of the Aral Sea later in this chapter.

Dams and Reservoirs

For human use, water is usually stored on the earth's surface, although groundwater storage is being used more frequently as surface supplies become depleted. Artificial surface storage is usually achieved by building dams. Reservoirs thus formed range in size from the small farm dam that may store less than 100 m³ to the very large dams that supply urban and irrigation complexes. At the extreme end of large dams is the Three Gorges Dam, currently under construction on China's Yangtze River. When completed, the dam will create a reservoir that is about 660 kilometres long with an average width of 1.1 kilometres and a capacity of 22.1 billion cubic metres of water.

Surface water stores such as the dam shown in figure 5.24 have several effects on the water cycle:

• Reservoirs usually **increase evaporation losses** in the local area. Large surfaces of water that are exposed to the wind and sun lose more water than bare ground surfaces.

• Reservoirs **increase the groundwater stores**. No reservoir bed is entirely sealed from water seepage. The great depth of water in a large reservoir creates a head which forces water down into the underlying soil and rock. The groundwater may reappear downstream of the dam wall or may lead to the development of springs in areas that are quite distant from the dam. The actual losses and routes that the groundwater takes are dependent on the geology of the area in which the reservoir is located.

• Reservoirs **reduce the volumes of water** moving through the downstream channels. Reduced frequency of flooding and discharge are typical results. Some rivers have been dammed to the extent that they only flow during exceptionally wet years or because legal requirements demand that certain volumes of water be released downstream. A good example of this is the Colorado River, where US dams have markedly reduced the flow of water to Mexico. There is an agreement between Mexico and the USA that a minimum volume of water must be released through the Colorado River into Mexico each year. This situation is explored in more detail later in this chapter.

• Reservoirs can increase the frequency and severity of **earthquakes** if they are built in areas with unstable geology and many fault lines. Earthquakes can be triggered when the increased weight of water on the surface causes downward pressure on sensitive seismic faults in the underlying rocks.

• Reservoirs have **several effects on water quality, water flow and sediment transport**. First, there are the effects within the reservoir itself:
  • Increased water may encourage the **growth of weeds** and water-borne plants, some of which are noxious, such as water hyacinth and alligator weed.
  • Large bodies of water can **deteriorate chemically** as plant and animal debris decays within them. Extreme deterioration results in all the oxygen in the water being used up, a condition which produces stagnant pools that only support anaerobic life forms.
  • Water-borne **diseases** or diseases carried by organisms that favour water may be introduced. Mosquitoes that carry malaria and snails that carry schistosomiasis (bilharzia) have been introduced in to many tropical lakes as a result of dam construction, such as in Lake Kariba, Lake Nasser and Lake Volta.

- Second, there are the effects downstream of the reservoir:
  - Reduced flow may cause the death of riverbank and floodplain **vegetation**.
  - Lowered frequency of flooding **reduces the flushing effect** of floods and therefore water quality may deteriorate.
  - Sediment loads decline because sediment is trapped in the reservoir. **Erosion** of the bed and banks by **scouring** may result because the stream below the reservoir has a sediment load deficit, and therefore great capacity to erode.
  - **Lowered nutrient content** of the downstream water (because nutrients are trapped in the reservoir) may cause **deterioration of aquatic life**.
  - Groundwater tables may fall because less water is available for recharge.

Of course, dams and reservoirs also have beneficial effects. The water and power provided may encourage economic development through increased agricultural and other economic activity. Reservoirs are often used for recreation. Regulated flows may reduce flood risks and improve the quality and availability of water. Downstream scouring, or erosion, may even be beneficial in streams used for navigation. Wildlife attracted to reservoirs may improve the ecological balance as well as attractiveness of the area.

QUESTION BLOCK 5E

1. *Make three lists of the hydrological changes resulting from the construction of dams and reservoirs, the first list being beneficial changes, the second being harmful impacts, with the third being neutral effects.*

Case Study of the Aswan High Dam, Egypt

An example of what can go wrong when a reservoir is constructed can be seen by the water management of the Nile River in Egypt.

Throughout history, Egyptians have found the Nile River to be both the source of their wealth and the cause of their famines. This is because Egyptian agriculture has always depended on the size and timing of the river's floods. Although the floods could be very destructive, they also deposited large amounts of rich, fertile silt on the Nile floodplain. Farming in Egypt was and still is almost completely confined to this area of alluvial silt.

The Egyptian people have always wanted to control the Nile's flooding. Two thousand years ago they threw virgins into the Nile to appease the river gods in an effort to try and stop the floods. The results were not very successful. During the 19th century, two dams were built to store water on an annual basis for irrigation. These were the Gebel el Awlia Reservoir and the Aswan Dam. They

were also not very effective because the Nile's flood level can vary so much from year to year.

In 1952 it was proposed to build a new, much larger dam upstream from the Aswan. This project became known as the Aswan High Dam. The idea behind this dam was that it would be so large that several years' floodwaters could be stored and released as the need arose. With Soviet assistance, the dam was built in ten years using a labour force of 35,000 people (figure 5.25).

5.25 *The Aswan High Dam, Egypt.*

Besides regulating the flooding, there were two main aims in constructing the Aswan High Dam. First, additional irrigation water from the dam was to expand the area under agriculture in Egypt. Second, it was to be the basis of a new hydro-electric power scheme for the country. The project was therefore a **multi-purpose scheme**.

Since its completion in 1970, the dam has provided an extra 400,000 hectares of farming land which was not previously under cultivation. In southern Egypt, an additional 300,000 hectares of land which was previously flooded once a year and which was single-cropped, is now permanently irrigated and can produce two or three crops each year. The power station now produces 10 billion kWh (kilowatt hours) per year, the equivalent of saving two million tonnes of oil annually (figure 5.26).

Despite these successes, the dam has had several undesirable side-effects. While it was being planned, it was realised that the 500 kilometre long lake that the dam would form (Lake Nasser) would flood priceless 3000 year old temples and statues. This included the colossal temples of Abu Simbel and 22 other temples in the Nubia Valley that would be lost forever (figure 5.27).

Several solutions to this problem were proposed. One suggestion was to bury the temples in sand to protect them from the waters, but it was soon realised that the water would seep through and destroy the stone. Another proposal was to build a wall around the temples, but once again water seepage would have been a problem. Finally, it was decided to move the temples stone by stone and reassemble them on higher ground. The operation was co-ordinated by UNESCO and took eight years with a labour force of 900 to move 1,035 blocks of stone weighing over 20 tonnes each. The cost of this operation alone was US$24 million.

5.26 *The hydro-electric power station at the Aswan High Dam.*

5.27 *The Isis Temple Complex, Aswan.*

However, it was the environmental costs of the Aswan High Dam project that caused the greatest concern. These effects include:

• The Nile River floods were reduced by 90%, so the fertile silt from floodwaters is no longer available in effective quantities. As a consequence, the farmers in the lower Nile Valley now have to import fertilisers. To overcome the loss of silt, a new chemical fertiliser factory was built, but this factory needs so much electricity to produce the fertiliser that it is using the bulk of the hydro-electricity produced by the dam. Between the dam's completion in 1970 and 2009, chemical fertiliser use increased by 400% (although during the same period, Egypt's population doubled, while calorie intake and meat consumption per person rose by more than a third).

• Downstream erosion has caused the undermining of many bridges and small dams. The reason for this

downstream erosion is that like all dams, the Aswan prevents the passage of silt. Silt collects in the reservoir and only clear water is discharged. Therefore, the water downstream of the dam has a great capacity to collect additional sediment. The cost to repair the damaged structures was estimated at 25% of the construction cost of the Aswan High Dam.

• The Mediterranean shoreline of the Nile Delta is now eroding, with erosion rates of up to 2 metres per year being recorded.

• Nutrient loss resulted in a decline of the fishing industry in the Nile Delta and nearby Mediterranean waters. However, as the use of chemical fertilisers increased from the early 1990s, the outflow of chemical fertilisers began to boost nutrient levels, leading to a reversal of this effect. By 2009, fishing yields in the Nile Delta were three times higher than before the dam was built.

• Bilharzia, a disease spread by water-borne snails, has been introduced, not only in the dam but also in the many canals of the irrigated areas. Larvae pierce the skin and the disease produces fever , stomach pain, coughing, skin rash, diarrhoea and swelling of the liver. After some time, the disease can lead to cystitis and anaemia.

• Half the water that flows into the reservoir is lost to evaporation and groundwater seepage.

QUESTION BLOCK 5F

1. Use an atlas to locate the Aswan High Dam. Draw a sketch map to show its location within Egypt. Annotate (or label) the map to show where the dam's side-effects are apparent.

2. Compare the costs and the benefits of the Aswan High Dam as a multi-purpose scheme.

Floodplain Management

The main agent of change for landforms in a drainage basin is water. Water can both erode and deposit sediment, and it is the interplay between these two processes that determines the landforms found in any particular area. This is especially so on the floodplain of a river.

The interaction between erosion and deposition can be understood by examining the **Hjulström curve**, developed by the Swedish geomorphologist Filip Hjulström in 1935. We saw earlier in this chapter that more velocity, and thus energy, is needed to erode larger particles than smaller ones. Hjulström examined the stream velocity needed to erode and then transport particles of varying sizes, and compared these to the velocities at which streams lost competence to continue carrying them. He used his research to construct a curve showing these relationships (figure 5.28).

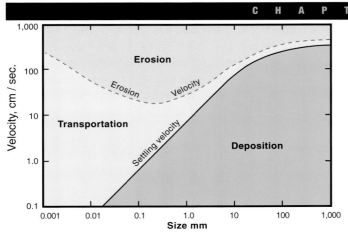

5.28 *The Hjulström curve shows the relationship between water velocity and the size of particles carried.*

The Hjulström curve shows that when the stream velocity is low, the water can only pick up very small particles such as clay and fine silt. As velocity increases, larger particles can be transported. The erosion velocity curve shows the velocity needed to erode and transport particles of various sizes. The settling velocity curve shows the velocity at which particles of varying sizes will be deposited because they are too heavy for the water to continue carrying. It is important to realise that the velocity needed to pick up a particle is greater than the velocity needed to keep it in motion.

5.29 *Two levels of terraces can be seen beside the Waimakariri River on New Zealand's South Island.*

The **valley floor** can be thought of as comprising three major parts – the channel, the floodplain and the terraces. **Terraces** are elevated remnants of abandoned floodplains (figure 5.29). They are known as **relict** features because they are the result of processes that have ceased long ago. Where terraces are found, **rejuvenation** has often occurred. This means that the base level has fallen relative to the land where the stream is found, increasing energy and causing a renewed phase of downward erosion. This change in base level can be caused either by a lowering of sea level, such as happens during an ice age, or a rise in the land, as happens with tectonic uplift.

The second component of the valley floor, the **channel**, is the major route for the movement of water and sediment

through the valley. There are two main channel patterns – braided and meandering. The differences between these two patterns arise mainly because of differences in the river's discharge and the amount of sediment carried.

Braided channels are made up by a large number of minor channels that are interconnected between bars of sediment (figure 5.30). They usually have one or more of the following characteristics:

- coarse sediment in the bed and banks, often material of gravel size and larger;
- steep gradients along the channel;
- discharges which vary greatly from one season to another, such as on the edges of glacial areas;
- a shallow depth relative to width (a high width:depth ratio);
- banks and a bed that are easily eroded because they are not cohesive; and
- a channel that does not meander very much.

5.30 *A large braided stream, the Rakaia River near Christchurch, New Zealand. This view looks downstream towards the southeast to the point where the river flows into the Pacific Ocean, shown in the background.*

It is thought that braided channels form when a river carries a large load of sediment relative to its discharge. As the sediment load of a river increases, a larger **bed load** (sediment on the stream bed) needs to be carried. By braiding, the river is able to maximise the energy spent on the stream bed. In this way, it seems that braiding is the most efficient way for a river to carry a large bed load. Braided channels also shift rapidly across the floodplain, and it is common for them to change their appearance completely after only one flood, with an entirely new set of channels and bars appearing.

In contrast with braided channels, **meandering channels** comprise a single stream channel that follows a sinuous course, resembling a sine curve (figure 5.31). The extent to which a stream meanders is measured by its **sinuosity**. This is measured as the distance between two points measured along the curving stream channel, divided by the straight line distance between the same two points. A stream with wide meanders would have a sinuosity index of 3 or more. In other words, the distance along the river channel is three times greater than the straight-line distance along the same valley. On the other hand, a low sinuosity would be less than 1.5, while a straight stream would have a sinuosity of 1.

5.31 *A stretch of meandering channel – the Brazos River, west of Dallas in Texas (USA).*

It is known that most streams meander rather than braid, although it is not fully understood why this is so. It used to be thought that a fallen log or rock would obstruct the stream, causing it to divert in one direction. Then, when it diverted back again, it would over-compensate, creating another meander, and so on. We now understand that an obstruction such as fallen tree is not necessary for meanders to develop. Indeed, if you were to take a perfectly smooth surface (such as a laminated desk top) and allow a trickle of water to flow down, the water would meander even though there were no obstructions.

Modern research suggests that meandering occurs due to the oscillation of the bipolar water molecule. Because the water molecule, which comprises two hydrogen atoms and one oxygen molecule, is bent rather than straight, each molecule has a positively charged end and a negatively charged end. In a moving stream of water, there is a complex set of attractions and repulsions as the molecules come into contact with each other at seemingly random angles. It is thought that these attractions and repulsions

initiate microscopic oscillations that take on a resonance as they work together. This causes small vibrations that send the water slightly off course. Once this happens, a pattern of meandering is initiated, and this pattern becomes established and grows as sediment is displaced.

One **meander** is defined as a complete loop or bend in a stream (figure 5.32). The point where one bend crosses to another is the **point of inflection**, and it is often the shallowest part of the meander. These shallow inflection points are called **riffles**. When water flows in a meandering stream, it tends to do so in a spiral pattern. As the water flows downstream, it is thrown outwards towards the outside bank by centrifugal force as it flows round the bend of each meander. This causes the water level at the outside banks to rise above the level at the inside bank, which in turn sets up bottom currents of water that flow inwards. This circular motion erodes the bed on the outside of the meander, scouring the bed and causing pools to form, and undercutting the outside bank (see figures 5.7 and 5.11 earlier in this chapter).

As a result of this effect, the line of fastest flow in a stream (known as the **thalweg**) is usually an exaggerated variation of the stream channel shape that crosses to the outside of each meander at the point of inflection (figure 5.32). Because erosion is greatest where stream flow is fastest, the thalweg is also the deepest channel in the stream.

Braided and meandering streams tend to construct floodplains in different ways. Braided channels migrate across their valley floor, usually in times of flood, leaving bars of

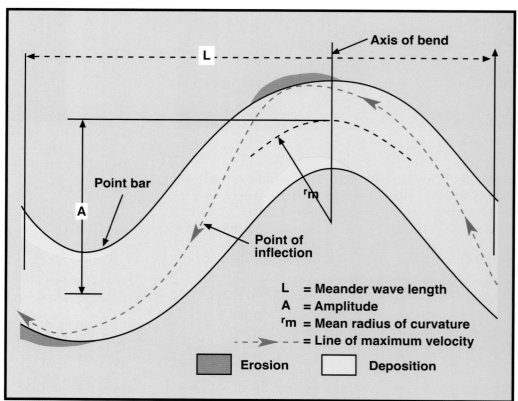

5.32 *The parts of a stream meander.*

sediment behind them. The direction of this movement depends on the looseness of the bank material, the rock through which the stream is cutting, and the shape of the valley. Small channels that have been abandoned become infilled with plant material and with fine sediment deposited by floods and wind action (figure 5.33).

5.33 *A floodplain formed by a braided stream flowing from New Zealand's Southern Alps, west of Christchurch.*

By contrast, most floodplains built by meandering streams are formed by the deposition of point bars. **Point bars** are deposits of sediment found on the inside banks of meanders (see figure 5.31). They form as part of the same process that causes meanders to widen as water erodes the outside banks of meanders. This process also means that the flow of water on the inside of each meander decreases, reducing the ability of the stream to transport sediment at the inside bank. Deposition of sediment therefore occurs, forming a point bar. The point bar continues to grow upwards and outwards as the stream migrates across the floodplain. This sideways movement of the meander is called **lateral migration**.

The process of lateral migration causes rivers to shift their courses constantly. If meanders did not migrate laterally, floodplains would be very narrow and valleys would only be widened by the processes occurring on the hillslopes (figure 5.34).

Streams migrate laterally in three ways – the process of concave bank scour, instability due to build up of the bed, and flood scour. All three of these processes may occur in the same valley and it is sometimes difficult to separate them.

Concave bank scour, or the wearing away of the outside banks of meanders, accounts for most of the lateral migration that takes place in rivers. As explained earlier, the concave (or outside) banks are the areas where most erosion occurs, and so meanders tend to migrate outwards. As time goes on, meanders begin to intersect with other meanders. This usually occurs in time of flood, when the river cuts through the narrow neck of the meander, leading to the abandonment of segments of channel (figure

5.35). Once they have been abandoned, these segments are called **oxbow lakes**, cutoffs or billabongs (figure 5.36). After some time, ox bow lakes fill in with sediment and become swamps called **backswamps**. Later still, they dry out and become colonised with vegetation, leaving only a depressed area of land called a **meander scar**.

5.34 *The wide floodplain and scars of old meanders indicate that the Brazos River, west of Dallas in Texas (USA), has a long history of lateral migration of meanders and concave bank scour.*

When valley walls are undercut by migrating meanders, the angle of the hillslope is increased, resulting in instability. This instability leads to an increase in local rates of mass movement, which in turn increases the width of the valley floor.

Much of the deposition that forms floodplains occurs during times of flood when the river level rises so high that the water overflows the river's banks (figure 5.37). Rivers that carry large sediment loads can therefore eventually build up their beds to levels above that of the valley floor. During a flood, the channel wall will be breached and the stream will take a completely different course when the floodwaters recede. The former elevated channel then forms a ridge (or series of ridges) that remains until destroyed by later floods or lateral migration.

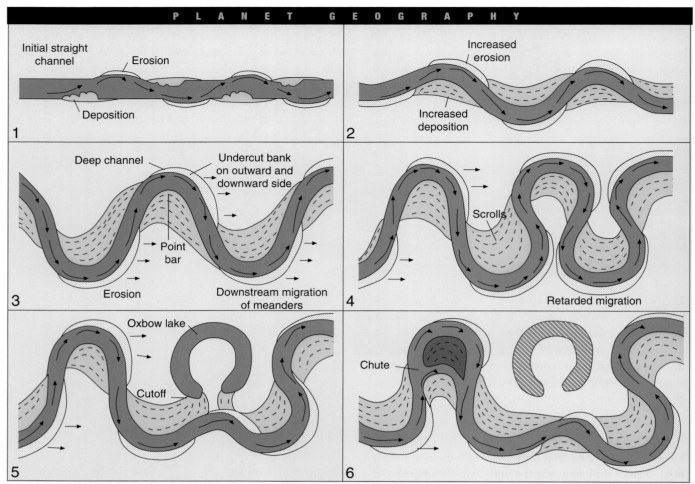

1. Initial straight channel — Erosion — Deposition

2. Increased erosion — Increased deposition

3. Deep channel — Undercut bank on outward and downward side — Point bar — Erosion — Downstream migration of meanders

4. Scrolls — Retarded migration

5. Oxbow lake — Cutoff

6. Chute

5.35 *Stages in the process of concave bank scour, which leads to the growth and downstream migration of meanders, and eventually the formation of oxbow lakes and chutes.*

5.36 *Ox bow lakes and meanders are highlighted by the sun's reflection of Australia's Murray River, near Adelaide.*

smaller tributary may flow parallel to the main channel for some distance before joining it. These smaller parallel streams are called **yazoo streams**, named after the Yazoo River, a tributary of the Mississippi.

Levees are ridges or embankments of sediment, parallel to the channel, that are built up by floods as they burst over the channel banks. As the water overflows the banks and flows onto the surrounding floodplain, it slows down, rapidly losing energy. The decreased competence means that the stream drops large quantities sediment near the bank. With the passage of time, these deposits (which usually consist of sand) build up into a ridge or levee. Levees are essential to the development of raised channels. Sometimes, levees prevent a tributary stream reaching the main channel. When this happens, the

5.37 *The Yangtze River (Chang Jiang) in flood at the city of Wuhan, China. The brown colour of the water indicates a large sediment load.*

5.38 *This tree beside the Irrawaddy River near Bagan (Myanmar) has been undercut by flood waters.*

5.39 *A spectacular example of rejuvenation – the huge volume of the Grand Canyon (USA) has all been eroded by the small Colorado River that flows through it.*

The third process of floodplain formation is **flood scour**. Considerable erosion can occur during flood times (figure 5.38). Where the sediments that make up the floodplain do not hold together well or are unprotected by vegetation, large floods can scour the valley floor. Usually, the scour channel has a steeper gradient than the meandering channel, because it is straight, and this may serve to speed up its capture of the meandering stream. Scour channels often develop across meander necks.

Floodplains may be abandoned for two major reasons. First, a river may **aggrade** (i.e. build up sediment) and bury its former floodplain. Second, the river may **incise** (cut deeply) and create a lower floodplain. The remnant of the former floodplain on the valley side is then known as a terrace. Aggradation and incision are triggered by a change in base level, which in turn may be caused by a number of processes such as a rise or fall in sea level, movements in the earth's crust, or climatic change. When base level is lowered (or the land is raised), **rejuvenation** is said to occur as the stream gains more energy to erode downwards (figure 5.39).

Another landform that may result from a change in base level is the nick point. **Nick points** are breaks in the smooth long profile of a stream. In the field, they appear either as rapids or a waterfall (figure 5.40 and 5.41).

Nick points can form in a variety of ways (figure 5.42). Sometimes a resistant layer of rock creates a temporary base level, and the stream has difficulty eroding below this level. This is common in areas of sedimentary rock where bands of rock may have different degrees of hardness, and thus resistance to weathering.

A second way that nick points can form is when sea level falls. When this occurs, rivers adjust to the lower base level by constructing a new long profile. Over time, headward erosion of the nick point thus formed gradually replaces the earlier long profile. There is a break in slope occurs at the junction of the two long profiles.

5.40 *The spectacular 27 metre high waterfall of Hafragilsfoss in north-east Iceland cuts through the resistant rock of the volcanic dyke that formed it.*

5.41 *Dettifoss, in Iceland, has the greatest volume of any waterfall in Europe, with a flow of up to 500 cubic metres of water per second. The water has a milky dishwater grey colour because of the huge amount of fine silt it carries.*

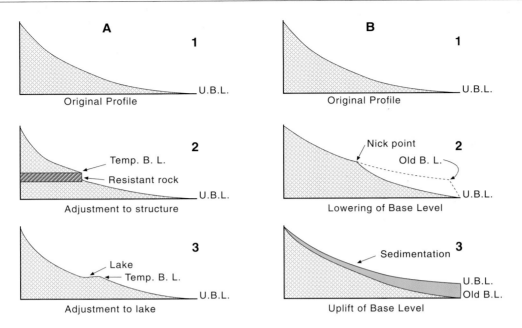

5.42 *Long profiles of streams showing nick points that have formed due to a variety of reasons. Note that U.B.L. is universal base level, or sea level.*

QUESTION BLOCK 5G

1. *Construct a table to compare the origins and characteristics of braided and meandering channels.*

2. *Explain why pools are usually found in the apex of a meander while riffles are usually found at the point of inflection.*

3. *Why does a stream erode on the outside of its meanders and deposit sediment on the inside? What happens to the course of the stream as a result of this?*

4. *Draw a series of diagrams to illustrate the formation of oxbow lakes.*

5. *Draw a table to classify the landforms described in this module as either (a) erosional or (b) depositional.*

6. *Choose any two erosional landforms and any two depositional landforms, and make a point form list to explain how they are formed.*

7. *Choose one photograph in the chapter to this point, and draw a photosketch of it, labelling the main features of the river shown. Identify and describe the main landform features of the area, paying particular attention to evidence of change in the river system.*

8. *Name and locate a floodplain you have studied in the field. Select three landforms studied, and explain their formation. Comment on how closely the landforms you studied resembled those described in textbooks.*

9. *Name and locate a floodplain you have studied in the field. Describe the human modifications to the floodplain and their effect on the size and probability of floods.*

Groundwater Management

Earlier in this chapter, the formation of groundwater was discussed. Groundwater is important in many drier countries for both farming and mining. If an aquifer is confined above and below by layers of rock with low permeability (aquicludes), then water may flow through the rock and emerge on the sides of cliffs or slopes (figure 5.43). Indeed, whenever an aquifer intersects with the surface of the ground, a **spring** arises. If the top surface of the water table has no confining bed of rock, then the surface of the unconfined saturated zone is generally referred to as the **water table**.

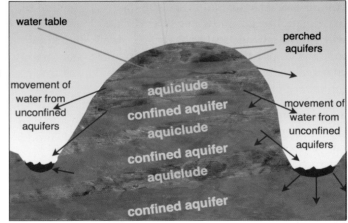

5.43 *The movement of water through aquifers.*

If the water in the confined aquifer has the potential to rise above ground level, as shown by the piezometric surface in figure 5.44), then the aquifer is **artesian**. A bore sunk into such a confined aquifer would result in water flowing to the surface without pumping.

In areas where there is a large artesian aquifer covering an expansive area, it is referred to an an **artesian basin**. One example of is the Great Artesian Basin, the largest artesian basin in Australia and one of the largest in the world. It occupies an area of 1.7 million square kilometres, or about 20% of Australia's land surface area. A total of 536 million cubic metres of water is withdrawn from the basin each year.

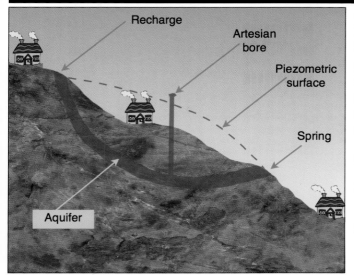

5.44 *The formation of artesian bores.*

Intensive use of groundwater in Australia for over a century has resulted in major sources such as the Great Artesian Basin being over-used (more water taken than replaced). The upper level has fallen 120 metres since it was first tapped. As a consequence, many of the bores are no longer artesian and the water has to be pumped to the ground surface.

Storage of water in groundwater is another way in which groundwater can be used by people. In some areas, it is economical to pump excess surface water into the ground to maintain the groundwater store. Sometimes waste water from sewage treatment works is pumped back, although this practice may create problems of water quality control.

There are two main ways in which water is inserted into a groundwater reservoir. First, water can be pumped down a bore hole, usually the same one from which water has previously been withdrawn. Second, it is possible to use **recharge basins**, which are large surface reservoirs with porous bottoms to allow water to seep into aquifers.

Basins are often built beside streams so that they can refill when floods occur. Recharge basins work best when the aquifer is near the surface and has no major aquiclude between it and the ground surface.

Groundwater stores can be over-pumped, or 'mined'. **Mining** takes place when more water is taken out of the aquifer than flows into it. In most rocks the rate of movement of water is slow, and the recharge rates are therefore slow. For example, water in the Great Artesian Basin in Australia is thought to take tens of thousands of years to move from the recharge areas to the deep stores.

Mining of groundwater has two effects. First, the 'head' (surface level) falls and it is harder to get water out of the bore or well. The further the level falls, the more expensive the cost of pumping becomes. Second, the rocks may compress as a result of the removal of water, and this consolidation may lead to subsidence of the surface. Mexico City, which is built on an old lake bed, has sunk by more than 8 metres as a result of the withdrawal of groundwater. There are old buildings that have subsided to the extent that one must now walk down a flight of steps to reach the original ground floor. London experienced subsidence of about 8 centimetres between 1865 and 1931 as a result of groundwater use.

QUESTION BLOCK 5H

1. Summarise the principles needed to use artesian water on a sustainable basis.

2. What are the effects of 'mining' groundwater? What can be done to overcome these problems?

Case Study of Groundwater Management in an Urban Environment — Bangkok

Bangkok has been the capital city of Thailand since 1783. In that year, an invading army from Myanmar forced the Thai king to abandon the old capital city, Ayutthaya, which was situated about 120 kilometres north of present-day Bangkok. Bangkok is located close to the mouth of Thailand's largest river, the Chao Phraya (*phraya* means 'river'), which drains the large Central Plain of Thailand to the north. Bangkok is built on soft deposits of river sediments that extend into a large delta-like deposit into the Gulf of Thailand to the south of the city.

Bangkok is only a few metres above sea level. Consequently, for much of Bangkok's history, people have used rivers and artificial canals (called *khlongs*) for transport (figure 5.45).

5.45 *A floating market at Damnern Saduak on the outskirts of Bangkok. This view shows the congestion which can occur on busy canals.*

Many of the *khlongs* are still used for transport, especially towards the edges of the city, although others have been filled in since the 1950s to create space for road construction. Traditionally, Thais have built their homes beside a waterway which provides them with a means of transport, a place to bathe, a source of food, and a waste disposal system (figure 5.46).

5.46 *A typical scene in Bangkok, with houses built beside the khlongs. Canals such as this criss-cross the entire urban area of Bangkok.*

Water pollution

Bangkok has a population of some 7 million people. This concentration of a large number of people in a fairly small area has caused quite serious water pollution. As long ago as 1970 an official report in the *Bangkok Post* stated:

"The condition of the Chao Phraya river is getting worse... The reasons for the increasing pollution of the river water are various; they can, however, be summed up in the statement that practically none of the waste water from industries and households goes through any form of treatment. A huge river like the Chao Phraya can definitely 'digest' a substantial amount of waste, but there are limitations. These limitations are especially serious during the dry season when the water discharge drops as low as 25-50 m^3 per second (compared to peak flow in the wet season of 700 m^3 per second)."

Today, about 30% of Bangkok's water pollution is caused by manufacturing industry, while the bulk (70%) is caused by private individuals. People have traditionally dumped their garbage in the *khlongs*, and in the absence of either garbage collection or sewerage systems, they will probably continue to do so in the future. The dumping of sewage into the *khlongs* is a direct cause of death from diseases such as cholera, diphtheria and diarrhoea. Millions of people in and around Bangkok wash their clothes in the *khlongs* every day, and detergent foam which cannot dissolve is spreading, killing other life forms in the canals and rivers into which they flow (figure 5.47). As Donner comments in *The Five Faces of Thailand*:

"The once romantic canals, which were part of the environment of the people who had built their houses alongside and which they used for kitchen and household purposes, are now filled with a black, stinking liquid or, during low tide, black mud covered with solid waste. A means of water supply and transport has been transformed into open sewers."

5.47 *A typical scene in front of a khlong home, where people wash and bathe in the water of the canal.*

5.48 *Water hyacinth in the Chao Praya River, Bangkok, Thailand.*

Some nutrients flow into the Chao Phraya from the agricultural areas to the north of Bangkok. The increased nutrient levels from fertiliser runoff has caused a significant growth of water weeds such as water hyacinth, a floating plant which causes problems for navigation in the rivers (figure 5.48). Another problem with nutrient enrichment of the water from farming areas is that algal blooms cover many of the *khlongs* where the flow of water is too slow to flush away the pollutants. This affects many areas where houses have been built over the *khlongs*, making it difficult for residents to catch fish as they are accustomed to doing (figure 5.49).

5.49 *A large algal bloom covers the water under these Bangkok houses. In this case, the algal bloom is caused by nutrient enrichment from the faeces of geese being raised, some of which can be seen through the trees.*

Thailand is one of the world's most rapidly growing economies at present – it is known as an Asian Tiger economy because of its rapid growth. Pollution control is a luxury that most Thai people seem to agree cannot be afforded because it might slow down this economic growth. Therefore, most Thai people seem to accept that water pollution is an inevitable result of industrial expansion. Officially there are 1800 factories on the Chao Phraya between Ayutthaya and the coast, although in reality there are many hundreds of additional unregistered factories. Every one of these factories has some impact on the river, with the worse pollution coming from distilleries, paper or rice mills, and factories producing noodles, paint, dyes or dairy foods (figure 5.50). Several distilleries have been threatened with closure for discharging wastes which have killed large populations of fish, prawns or shellfish.

In a country such as Thailand, which is trying hard to industrialise, little attention is often paid to water pollution until it interferes with industrial advancement. When the produc-

5.50 *Polluted water being dumped into a khlong in northern Bangkok from the Yakult yogurt factory. The waste water contains detergents and bacteria as can be seen by the foam forming in the khlong.*

tion of shellfish in some rivers near Bangkok declined by 20% due to effluent from sugar mills up-stream, the factories were forced to treat their wastes. It has been reported that in the Tha Chin River, near Nakhon Pathom on the north-west outskirts of Bangkok, the 400 industrial plants along the banks had so depleted the oxygen supply in the water that fish have been seen coming to the surface for oxygen.

An illustration of the decline in quality of water in the Chao Phraya near Bangkok is given in table 5.2. Three stretches of the Chao Phraya are shown, from north of Bangkok at the left of the table and passing through the city in the centre of the table.

Table 5.2
Water Quality of the Chao Phraya, Bangkok

Stretch of River	Nakhon Sawan to Ayutthaya	Ayutthaya to Nonthaburi	Nonthaburi to Samut Prakan	WHO Standard
BOD	4 mg/L	5 mg/L	7 mg/L	1.5 mg/L
DO	5 mg/L	3 mg/L	0.5 mg/L	6.0 mg/L
Coliform	5000 mpn	200,000 mpn	None (not drinkable)	5000 mpn

BOD = biochemical oxygen demand
DO = dissolved oxygen
mpn = most probable number per 1000 millilitres
WHO = World Health Organisation
Source: National Environment Board of Thailand

The biochemical oxygen demand (BOD) is a measure of the amount of oxygen needed to decompose organic matter in the water. The increase in BOD indicates that there is an increase in nutrients flowing into the river as it flows south towards Bangkok. This would probably be a combination of agricultural wastes and sewage.

The dissolved oxygen (DO) level is a measure of the amount of oxygen dissolved in the water. Although DO depends on water temperature, it can indicate whether water is fresh or infected. When the levels fall below 2 mg/L, it is a sign that there is not enough oxygen to enable most aquatic species to survive.

The coliform, or E Coli, reading is a measure of the disease-carrying bacteria in the water. Most coliform bacteria are introduced into water by human and animal excrement. It can be seen in table 5.1 that in the central section of the river these levels are 40 times higher than recommended by the World Health Organisation; this reading was taken at the point where the pumping station for Bangkok's water supply is located.

The National Environment Board of Thailand's limit for the BOD of effluent from factories into rivers is 20 mg/L. However, the normal emission from a noodle factory using current technology is about 1000 mg/L, while a normal distillery would discharge effluent with a BOD of

35 000 mg/L. In other words, the official standards which have been set down cannot realistically be enforced until the technology and the money are available to implement them. However, in recent years many *khlongs* in Bangkok have been equipped with small water wheels to churn up the water, enabling the oxygen level of the water to be raised (figure 5.51).

5.51 *The water in many Bangkok khlongs is now being re-oxygenated by churning with water wheels such as these ones outside a dairy products factory.*

Another aspect of water pollution is heavy metals in industrial waste water. Mercury is probably the most dangerous of these heavy metals, and fish have been found in some *khlongs* near a caustic soda factory in Phrapadaeng to have mercury levels well above the National Environment Board's standard. Indeed, half of the population tested in coastal areas of 21 provinces around Bangkok have been measured to have a blood mercury count 44.6% higher than the safety limit. Poisoning with mercury can cause serious damage of the mind and body, leading to paralysis and even death.

Subsidence of the city

Perhaps the most spectacular example of human impact on the Bangkok environment concerns the 'sinking' of the city. Bangkok is built on loose, waterlogged sediments near the mouth of the Chao Phraya. With its low elevation and network of canals, Bangkok became known as the 'Venice of the Orient' by travellers during the early part of the twentieth century. The foundations of the city have always been unstable, and they cannot even support an underground railway. Bangkok's railways are all above ground, causing traffic congestion at the city's many level crossings. For the same reason, there are few high rise buildings in the city.

In the decades after 1950 when it was no longer possible to treat polluted river water for drinking, people began to 'mine' the groundwater supplies under Bangkok to provide extra drinking water. Some 15,000 wells were dug into the aquifers beneath Bangkok during the 1960s, 1970s and 1980s. In the past decade or so, Thai officials have

realised that this 'mining' has taken away the hydraulic pressure within the sediments which support the city. Bangkok has been sinking at a rate of about 10 cm/year and already one part of the central city lies below sea level.

The Chao Phraya has always flooded annually in Bangkok during the monsoons when heavy rainfall of 60 to 120 millimetres per day may fall. However, with the lowering of the land these floods are now lasting longer each year and they are becoming more severe. Consequently, the Thai government is seriously considering abandoning Bangkok and moving the capital to a new site, perhaps back to Ayutthaya. The problem is made worse because groundwater movement is very slow, and so problems have been created by pumping water at a rate which is much faster than the rate at which nature can replenish the supplies. The unconsolidated sediments on which Bangkok is built have slumped in response to the lower pressure of the reduced reservoir of groundwater. The vibration of Bangkok's traffic shakes down the level of the ground even further, while the filling in of canals to make roads makes the flooding worse by filling in escape routes for the monsoon waters (figure 5.52). Other impacts of the city's subsidence have included the breaking up of footpaths and roads, and the need for adding additional lower steps to connect buildings with the falling level of the ground.

5.52 *Filling in khlongs to make roads makes urban flooding in Bangkok, caused by the city's subsidence, even worse. Note the small drain holes which have been left in this expressway to enable water to drain into the khlong beneath.*

In the 1980s, when the subsidence problem was recognised, city officials introduced strict controls on the pumping of groundwater and imposed new taxes and charges to discourage the practice. These measures have succeeded in reducing the rate of groundwater pumping and this has in turn led to a small rise in the groundwater level beneath Bangkok. However, even if the pumping of groundwater were to cease entirely, the slumping of sediments would continue for some time because of the lag effect.

QUESTION BLOCK 5I

1. *Describe the physical features of Bangkok that make it less than ideal as a site of a large metropolitan area.*

2. *What is the condition of Bangkok's khlongs today, and how did they get to be like this?*

3. *What impact has Thailand's rapid economic growth had on the cleanliness of water in Bangkok?*

4. *Describe the situation that is outlined in table 5.2.*

5. *Explain why Bangkok is sinking.*

6. *What can be done to stop or slow the rate of subsidence in Bangkok?*

Freshwater Wetland Management

As recently as half a century ago, wetlands were often referred to in derogatory words such as 'swamp'. Looking through the eyes of farmers or land developers, wetlands were seen as wastelands. Worse, they were often seen as breeding grounds for pests such as mosquitoes and therefore drained with the aim of improving people's health and livelihoods.

5.53 *An area of wetlands near Mombasa, Kenya.*

Today, wetlands are generally seen as a valuable biotic resource. Wetlands serve as valuable wildlife habitats, fish breeding grounds and centres of biodiversity (figure 5.53).

Wetlands also have increasing economic value as tourist attractions. Indeed, the Okavango Delta (or Okavango Swamp), which is the world's largest inland delta, is Botswana's major tourist attraction. Each year thousands of tourists visit the region to watch wildlife and enjoy the pristine environment (figure 5.54). Provided it is conducted responsibly, recreational use of wetlands is non-consumptive, although it may reduce the availability of water for other users at specific times and places.

5.54 *The natural environment of the Okavango Delta.*

Case Study of Freshwater Wetland Management — the Norfolk Broads

A **broad** is a term used in eastern England for a large, shallow sheet of fresh water (figure 5.55). Broads, which are a form of **wetlands**, are found in the eastern English counties of Norfolk and Suffolk, forming an area in East Anglia between the towns of Norwich and Great Yarmouth which is also known as **Broadland** (figure 5.56). More precisely, the Broads are located in an area centred at latitude 52°45'N, 1°30'E. The area is dominated by three larger rivers which converge and flow into the sea at Great Yarmouth. These rivers are the Bure, the Yare and the Waveney, which in turn have smaller tributaries called the Thurne, the Chet and the Ant.

5.55 *General view of the broads landscape; this view shows part of Horsey Mere.*

Each of the broads has quite a different character. They vary in size from the large Hickling Broad, which is about 140 hectares, down to small relict pools with areas of 0.25 hectares of less. Most of the broads are very shallow, and none has an average depth of more than four metres; most are much shallower than this. The rivers which join the broads are quite wide and flow slowly, and they are made salty by sea water in their lower reaches. For most of their length, the broads and the rivers are lined by marsh and swamp vegetation such as reeds and water plants.

5.56 *Location of the Norfolk Broads.*

The Broadland area is very well known in Britain and other parts of Europe for its natural beauty, as the lakes are joined by some 200 kilometres of rivers and canals which are well suited to recreational boating, fishing and other water activities. Thus, the Broads are a major area of tourism in Britain

The natural background to the Broads

The Broads environment is really a combination of individual inter-related natural systems. The main natural systems are the climate, the soils and geology, the relative levels of the land and water, and the vegetation.

Today's Broads have evolved over a period of 2000 years. During that time, the climate has changed several times, although there has always been a marked contrast between cold dry winters on one hand, and warm dry summers on the other. The average daily maximum temperature for the year is 14°C, ranging from 6°C in January to 22°C in July. The average daily minimum temperature for the year is 6°C , ranging from 1°C in January to 12°C in July. Overall, the average monthly temperature (average of maximum and minimum) for the year is 10°C.

The average annual rainfall is between 600 mm and 700 mm. As rain falls on about 50% of days, and the relatively cool climate means there is little evaporation, the area seems much more damp than one might expect where the average rainfall is so low. Rain is distributed quite evenly throughout the year.

The soils of the area have formed from a thick layer of chalk, the type of rock found beneath the whole of East Anglia. However, in most parts of Broadland, the chalk is quite deep beneath the surface, and it is covered by deep layers of shell-sands deposited in marshes between 300,000 and 2 million years ago. In places, the sands are quite deep, being up to 40 metres in places. These in turn are covered in many parts of Broadland by still more recent deposits of sand and gravel which were deposited by melting ice. These were deposited towards the end of the last ice age, which ended only 20,000 years ago. Most

of the surface soils have formed from these newest sands and gravels. These produce quite rich soils which are well suited to agriculture.

In the lower areas, where the marshes and swamps called **fens** were found, the soils were somewhat different. In those areas, the soils were quite young and were formed as a result of changes in the relative levels of the sea and land. At the end of the last ice age, sea levels were lower than today because much more of the world's water was trapped in glaciers and larger polar ice caps. In England, the bottoms of valley floors were up to 30 metres lower than today, and the rivers in the valleys flowed more quickly than they do today.

As temperatures increased after the ice age, the ice caps and the glaciers melted somewhat, causing a rise in sea levels. As this happened, the rivers flowed more sluggishly, allowing swamps (the fens) to form in the valley floors. Over time, this change in vegetation allowed deposits of peat to form as the decaying swamp vegetation built upwards, layer upon layer. However, sea levels continued to rise for a long time after the end of the ice age because of the 'lag' effect, causing siltation at the mouths of the rivers where they entered the sea. This had the effect of slowing the flow of the rivers even more than previously.

Most of Broadland is a very flat area which lies at or slightly below high tide level. The area is separated from the sea only by a long ridge of sand dunes lining the coast. As the sea rose relative to the land, there were occasions when the sea broke through the coastal dunes, flooding the lower areas of land and forming shallow lakes – the broads. Particularly serious floods have occurred in this way, with major floods in 1608, 1617, 1622, 1717, 1718, 1720, 1770 and 1791. In 1806, the coastal dunes were strengthened, preventing major floods until the land subsided still further. This had happened by the beginning of the 20th century, and severe floods occurred again in 1912, 1938 and, most recently, in 1953.

Human occupancy of the Broads

Human occupancy of Broadland has continued for many centuries, and over this time there has been a great variety of impacts on the Broads ecosystem. Traditional economic activities have included farming and sedge-cutting (cutting the reeds for roof thatching), and these continue today, but compete with newer activities such as recreational walking and boating. Over the years, these impacts have taken many forms, and have become more and more intense up to the present day.

The Broads in the English counties of Norfolk and Suffolk were formed by a combination of human and natural factors. During the Middle Ages, **peat** was dug for use as a household fuel. Peat is highly organic soil, largely consisting of decaying vegetation, and mining of it in eastern

England began in about 1100. In the late 1400s England's climate became wetter, and at about the same time the land sank relative to sea level. These effects combined to flood many of the old peat-mining sites, and they became the shallow broads. This is why we can say that the broads are both a natural and a human landform. There are 48 broads together with 200 kilometres of lock-free, navigable waterways.

In the centuries that followed, the broads became the basis of peasant life in eastern England. Channels were built to join broads together for transport, marsh hay was cut, eels and fish were trapped and birds were snared or shot for food. Over time, the pressures on the broads from various human uses have increased. From the late 1700s onwards, some of the broads and their adjoining swamps (the **fens** or **carrs**) were drained to expand agriculture for the growing population. Another intention of draining the fens was to try and remove breeding grounds for mosquitoes. During the twentieth century, there has also been pressure to use the broads for disposal of sewage and for tourism, especially recreational boating.

Changes in the chemistry of the water

The broads are fresh water lakes. The chemical composition of each broad depends on the water which flows into them. It is these chemical flows which determine the type and quality of the ecosystem. The presence of phosphorus is especially important because phosphorus is a scarce chemical which is nonetheless necessary for algae and other plant growth. **Algae** are simple water-borne plants, some of which are microscopically small. A typical clear mountain lake would contain about 5 μg (micrograms) of phosphorus per litre, while a natural lowland lake would contain about 10 to 30μg. Before 1800, the broads fitted this typical lowland pattern, with between 10 and 20 μg of phosphorus per litre. The water was clear, and there was little growth of algae, although there were low-growing water plants on the bottoms of the broads. These provided breeding grounds for fish and other animals such as crustacea. Reed swamps grew around the edges of the broads, and these were also essential for fish breeding and feeding.

An important new phase of human impact began around 1800 when draining of the broads by wind pumps began (figure 5.57). The aim was to lower the water table and so create 'dry land' suitable for arable crop production. Although the draining succeeded in its aim of providing extra farmland, it led to some environmental side effects. Peat forms only in swampy, saturated conditions. Therefore, the loss of flooded areas meant that the area of peat production shrank. Banks had to be built to prevent the new farmlands being flooded. These banks stopped the movement of fish and wildlife between the rivers and swamps, thus restricting the habitat of the fish. However, the most important impact of these changes was in the chemical balance of the broads, and especially in the quantities of phosphorus and nitrogen present.

When the new farmlands were created, much of the swamp vegetation at the edges of the broads was destroyed. The phosphorus and nitrogen stored in these plants was then released into the rivers. This led to an increase in phosphorus levels to about 80 μg / L over a very short period of time. The vast addition of extra nutrients such as these into a stream or body of water is called **eutrophication**. Problems occur when eutrophication leads to greatly increased growth of algae in the water.

5.57 *Horsey Windpump, one of many used since the late 1700s to drain swampy parts of the Broads. Drainage of the peaty soils caused the land surface to subside, and river embankments (dykes) became necessary to prevent flooding.*

In the broads, eutrophication led to strong growth of algae at the surface, which prevented light from reaching the lower parts of the water. Because of the shading of the deeper water by the algae, the low water plants on the bottom surface could no longer survive, and they were replaced by tall water weeds. The amount of weed increased greatly as this trend continued over time. By the 1940s weed growth had become so profuse that many thought that the broads would be choked by the weeds.

However, they provided a very good environment for fish breeding, and the area became a resort area for fishing.

Eutrophication only occurred to a fairly minor extent from changes in agriculture. Until the 1800s, sewage was disposed of in the district by septic tanks. Sewage contains up to 1000 times more phosphorus than any water draining from natural lands. When septic tanks were used, a little effluent percolated down to the groundwater, but the broads themselves were not affected. In the mid to late 1800s, sewerage systems were introduced. The effluent was treated and then dumped into the rivers of the broads. Sewage inputs have built up since that time, resulting in major additions of phosphorus to the broads. Today, some twenty sewage outlets discharge into the rivers of the broads.

5.59 *In contrast with the view in the previous photo, the brown turbid water of Ranworth Broad prevents light penetrating to the bottom of the water, causing the elimination of aquatic plants which require light.*

5.58 *Water lilies growing on the surface of the clear water of an isolated section of Cockshoot Broad. The bottom of the broad is clearly visible through the water.*

The typical levels of phosphorus today are between 150 to 300 μg / L, although levels of up to 2000 μg / L have been recorded. The levels are highest in those broads which are downstream from centres of population and connected to the rivers. On the other hand, isolated broads such as Upton Broad and Martham Broad have phosphorus levels which are only 5% of those in the 'connected' broads such as South Walsham Broad, Ranworth Broad and Barton Broad. Levels of this magnitude produce serious changes in the balance of the ecosystem. Very large crops of algae have grown, eliminating other water plants from many areas. A consequence of this growth of algae was the loss of breeding and feeding grounds for fish, and none of the broads now has its pre-1800 ecosystem. All the broads have new communities of both flora and fauna. The growth of algae has also resulted in visual pollution, in that natural clear water has been replaced by turbid green or brown water. There has been a consequent decline in recreational fishing (figures 5.58 to 5.60).

5.60 *Recreational fishing on the shores of Salhouse Broad.*

Effects of bank erosion

The effects of agriculture and sewage have been further aggravated by the increased use of the broads for boating. Recreational boating began in the broads in the late 1890s, first with sailing boats plus a few steam boats. By 1920 there were 165 hire boats, of which only four were motor cruisers. Since the Second World War, the number of boats has increased enormously, with greater use of motor boats, privately-owned launches and hire cruisers. By 1949 there were 547 hire boats, of which 301 were motor cruisers; by 1979, these figures had increased to 2257 hire boats, of which 2,150 were motor cruisers. The figures have declined a little since then, and currently there are 2,000 hire boats available in the Broads, plus another 6,000 private licensed boats and holiday facilities for almost 250,000 people (figures 5.61 and 5.62).

5.61 *Typical motor cruisers on the River Bure.*

5.62 *This large shallow bottomed paddle steamer is one of several boats taking tourists through the waterways of the Broads.*

The increase in boating has resulted in greatly increased erosion of river banks. The wash from pleasure boats (particularly power boats) undercuts the river banks, which in turn release sediment into the streams (figures 5.63 to 5.65). This problem has been aggravated by the loss of water weeds, which would have dampened the wave energy from the wash of the boats (figure 5.66).

5.63 *Wash from a motor boat approaching the reeds beside the River Bure. In the foreground a reinforced bank with pilings has been built as protection from the wash of boats.*

At times, eroded banks have had to be protected by pilings (figure 5.67). It has been estimated that maintenance

of these flood walls in the broads costs tens of thousands of pounds each year.

The boats also stir up the bottom sediments, particularly now that the bottom grasses have gone, leading to a steady movement of sediments downstream. Many of the broads are filling at a rate of over a centimetre per year, and with depths already less than a metre, will be full in less than a century. Sedimentation rates are now reported to be between 10 and 100 times the pre-1800 levels.

5.64 *Although wash from boats is the main cause of this bank erosion around the tree roots, trampling by recreational fishers has made the problem worse. Where the reeds are healthy they absorb the energy caused by the wash from boats.*

5.65 *Speed limits have been imposed on many waterways in the Broads to minimise erosion from the wash of boats.*

Persistent siltation and eutrophication of the broads has led to a loss of habitats for many species (figure 5.68). Large-scale destruction of broadleaf plants such as water lily, water soldier and hornwort has occurred. These plants provide the habitat for many small creatures such as snails and beetles and also provide the source of food for many larvae. Thus, the first steps in many food chains have been removed from parts of the broads, leading to reduced numbers of fauna higher in the chain.

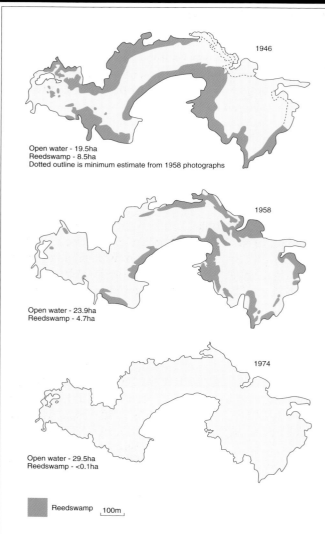

Open water - 19.5ha
Reedswamp - 8.5ha
Dotted outline is minimum estimate from 1958 photographs

1946

1958

Open water - 23.9ha
Reedswamp - 4.7ha

1974

Open water - 29.5ha
Reedswamp - <0.1ha

Reedswamp   100m

5.66 *Changes in the amount of reedswamp in Hoveton Great Broad between 1949 and 1974. (Source: George, M. [1992] p.181)*

5.68 *Refuges have been created in several parts of the Broads where loss of habitat has occurred, forming zones where water weeds can become established — protected from the wash of boats. Birds and fish are attracted to these refuges to breed.*

All the losses of reed-banks cannot be attributed to boating activities. The reeds seem to pass through cycles of growth and decline, and a naturally occurring decline might coincide in time with an expansion of boating activities. Another possible reason for the decline in reed-banks could be that birds which once fed on broad-leaf plants such as water lilies (which are now being replaced by weeds) have now switched their feeding to the reed shoots to survive. This may be causing greatly increased demands on the reed species.

Agriculture has accelerated these trends (figure 5.69). Trampling by cattle causes the sides of bank to collapse, increasing siltation and leading to the decline of plant species which provided the habitat for dragonflies and some species of butterflies, which are now endangered in the broads. Some species of birds (such as the heron and some breeds of ducks) whose feeding and breeding depend on the same habitats are also threatened (figure 5.70). Thus, the complex structure of the environment has meant that factors which first affected one or two natural systems have now spread throughout the natural systems of the area (figure 5.71).

5.67 *Protective defence has been built in an area where bank erosion has occurred.*

5.69 *Arable (wheat) farming beside Ranworth Broad. European Community policies have encouraged Broads farmers to replace cattle grazing with grain cultivation.*

Planning on the Broads

One of the obstacles to solving the environmental problems of the broads has been that control rests with many different organisations. For most of its history, overall land planning has been carried out by two county councils and six district councils.

At the same time, water management has been controlled by two authorities, one controlling boating (including registration and speed limits), and the other looking after water supply, water quality, sewage treatment, recreation, fisheries and land drainage.

To overcome the problem of uncoordinated control, it was recommended in 1947 that the Broads become a national park. The proposal was rejected on the basis that the area was already developed too intensively for this to be possible. In 1970 another study committee developed a management plan for the region, and this still provides the basis for decisions made by all authorities which have jurisdiction over the broads.

In the mid-1970s, there was a second attempt to have the Broads declared a national park. The controlling bodies could not agree to all that this involved, and the proposal again failed. Nonetheless, in 1978 the Broads Authority was formed to supervise overall control of the area. This was merely an advisory body, consisting of representatives of local councils, water commissions and some other government authorities Since its formation, it has set up committees to study the environmental problems of the region, particularly the effects of motor boats.

5.70 *A ducks' nesting area on Cockshoot Broad.*

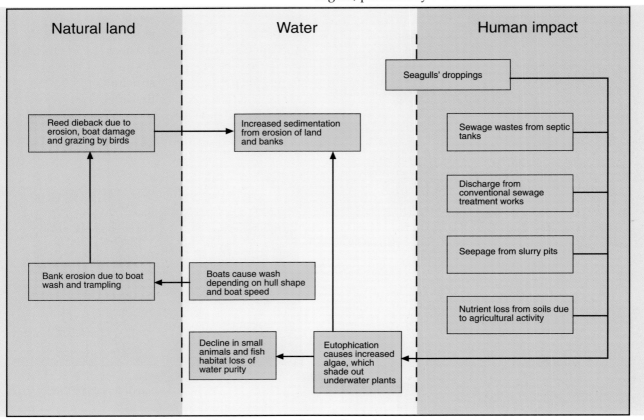

5.71 *The Broads ecosystem, showing the relationships between several types of impact.*

Finally, the Broads Authority was re-constituted in 1989 with much greater powers, including control over navigation of boating. In effect, an area of 287 square kilometres is now governed similarly to a national park by the Authority, which has three main tasks:

- conserving and enhancing the natural beauty of the broads;
- promoting the enjoyment of the broads by the public; and
- protecting the interests of navigation.

In its new, more powerful form, the Broads Authority has certainly played a valuable part in informing the wider community of the importance of the Broads fragile ecosystem as well as restoring the natural environment (figure 5.72).

QUESTION BLOCK 5J

1. What are the broads? Describe their location.

2. Describe the different natural systems which combine to form the Broads environment.

3. How did the broads form?

4. Draw a timeline to illustrate the changes in human impact on the broads over time.

5. Describe the human effects on the environment which are displayed in the photographs in this section.

6. Describe and account for the ways in which phosphorus concentrations have been affected in the Broads.

7. What is eutrophication? What are its (a) causes, and (b) effects in the Broads?

8. List the environmental effects of recreational boating. You may find the easiest way to do this is to draw a flow diagram, so that effects which cause other effects can be linked together.

9. What overall plan should be implemented for the Broads? Justify your opinion.

Irrigation and Agriculture

We are now heavily dependent on water management through irrigation to produce about one-third of the world's crops. These irrigated crops are grown on land that is, on average, about twice as productive as land that is watered only by rainfall. Irrigation is an important component of any program to increase the world's food supply. The spread of irrigation has been a key factor behind the 300% increase in world grain production since 1950 that is described in chapter 10.

This growth in irrigation has brought many benefits, such as more availability of food, lower food prices, higher employment and faster agricultural and economic development. These benefits sometimes blind people to the environmental consequences, however.

5.72 An explanatory sign about bank stabilisation erected by the Broads Authority.

At its most basic level, the most obvious effect of irrigation is that the downstream flow is reduced when water is removed from the river. For this reason, many countries impose government controls on the volumes of water that farmers can remove to ensure a fair share of water use.

The physical effect of using water for irrigation is that water is removed from the stream and added to fields where there was previously little or no water. The water then soaks downwards into the soil store, after which it can either percolate downwards and be added to the groundwater store or it can be lost to the atmosphere by evaporation.

One of the common consequences of irrigation is **salinisation**. As water passes over and through the soil, it dissolves various minerals and nutrients. Salts are very easily dissolved and therefore if there is salt in the soil it is likely to be absorbed into the irrigation water. This problem can be aggravated if too much irrigation water is added to the soil. This can lead to **waterlogging** (where the water table rises to the ground surface), which frees salts that have been washed downwards by rainwater infiltration over many years to rise once again by capillary action into the root zone of the crops, and perhaps even right up to the surface.

Many good farming areas are ancient sea beds, and so contain salts, although usually at levels that are too deep to affect plant growth. When the salts are liberated in saturated soils to rise to the surface they reduce crop productivity and, if the trend continues on a particular piece of land, it can poison the soil and make it useless for cultivation. In this way, irrigation can cause desertification.

Excess water from fields usually runs off back into the irrigation channels and eventually back to the river. As it does so, it carries dissolved salts from the rocks and soils where it has been flowing. On farms where pesticides and chemical fertilisers are used, the runoff also carries pollutants from these sources. When irrigation water is used and re-used in several fields, quite high concentrations of salt and **agro-chemical pollutants** can build up, severely reducing the quality of the water for downstream users.

According to estimates made by the United Nations Food and Agricultural Organisation (FAO), about one-third of the world's irrigated land is badly affected by salinity. Salinity that is caused by irrigation is equally likely to occur in large-scale and small-scale irrigation systems, and it has been the reason that many farmers have had to abandon their fields in some places such as the Sahel region of sub-Sahara Africa and the arid regions of northern Australia.

QUESTION BLOCK 5K

1. *Outline the benefits of irrigation.*

2. *Describe the process whereby irrigation causes salinisation.*

3. *Explain why water quality often deteriorates as one moves downstream in areas where irrigation is practised.*

Irrigation for Rice Farming in Bali

When practised properly, irrigation can be implemented on a long-term sustainable basis. A good example of this is the Indonesian island of Bali, where irrigation has been practised for more than a thousand years.

Bali is a small Indonesian island with an area of 5,620 square kilometres and a population of over 2.5 million people. It is situated to the east of Java (Indonesia's most populated island) and west of Lombok. As shown in figure 5.73, Bali's location is just 1,000 kilometres south of the equator, lying between latitudes 8°04'S and 8°52'S, and

5.73 *The location of Bali.*

between longitudes 114°26'E and 115°42'E. Shaped like a diamond, Bali measures about 140 kilometres east to west and about 80 kilometres north to south.

Rice is more central to the lives of the Balinese people than anything else. The cultivation of rice has radically transformed the landscape and the ecosystems of the island. Rice forms the centre of the Balinese diet, economy, culture and way of life.

The field where rice is grown is called a **padi** and it can be thought of as a manipulated ecosystem, an artificially created structure designed to copy the natural wetland ecosystem that was described in the previous section of this chapter. To create a padi, the natural biophysical environment must be totally transformed, and in many areas of rice cultivation, this manipulation of the natural ecosystem has been going on for many centuries. The key element in controlling the ecosystem is water management through irrigation.

Farmers have no control over the quantities of rain that fall on their fields. However, they can exert quite a deal of control over the water by irrigation and drainage techniques. At its simplest level, this involves building earth banks called **bunds** around the padi fields (figure 5.74). The bunds act as small dams preventing water from flowing to the next padi field down slope until the farmer chooses to release the water.

5.74 *Bunds separate padi fields near Tampaksiring in Bali, Indonesia. A complex system of water management allocates water to a succession of farmers, starting at the top of the hill and working down slope. Several flows of water downhill can be seen in this view.*

At a more sophisticated level, terraces can be constructed on the sides of hills to control the water. Terraces form a series of steps up the side of the hill, creating a succession of flat padi fields each one of which can be flooded with an even depth of water. Some terraces are engineering masterpieces, being centuries old and having been constructed by hand with almost no tools but a massive communal effort. Maintenance of the bunds and (especially) the terraces is a crucially important task for rice farming families. If the terraces were poorly maintained and allowed to slide downhill, the means of livelihood of

an entire community would be lost, together with the labours of many decades or even centuries.

Like rice cultivators in other parts of the world, farmers in Bali replace the natural pattern of drainage through creeks and rivers by a complex network of irrigation canals, bunds and terraces (figure 5.75). Irrigation reduces the farmers' dependence on rainfall and enables water to be used over and over again. For example, water used by a farmer at the top of a slope may be used by ten or even twenty other farmers further down the hill, as the water is released successively by each farmer. Furthermore, the water will carry nutrients down the hill, making highly efficient use of both the water and any fertilisers that are applied to the padi fields.

5.75 *Irrigation canals near Penestanan, Bali. A complex system of irrigation using canals and gravity-fed channels has been organised co-operatively in Bali for about 1,000 years.*

5.76 *Pura Ulu Danau is the water temple beside Lake Bratan which controls most of the irrigation water used by farmers in Bali.*

The key to successful rice farming in Bali is water management. The Hindu beliefs of the farmers have a strong influence. Almost all the water used by farmers in Bali comes from two mountain lakes that have formed in the craters of volcanoes. Beside each of these lakes is a water temple. The temple called Pura Bata Kau controls all the irrigation water for use in western Bali, while another called Pura Ulu Danau controls the irrigation for the rest of Bali (figure 5.76). Channels flow from the lakes near these temples to provide irrigation water for every farm in Bali. As the water flows across the soils of each farm, it dissolves nutrients and minerals that are carried on to other farms down slope. In this way the irrigation water provides fertiliser for the padi fields as well as moisture.

The complex system of irrigation channels has worked in Bali for more than 1,000 years, although it has been updated, expanded and maintained during that time. The organisation of water management and irrigation is done through a uniquely Balinese system of co-operative groups called *subaks*. The rice growers in each valley or area group themselves into a *subak*. The members of each *subak* elect a leader from their number, often the farmer who lives at the bottom of the slope because that farmer has the most to lose if the water is not allocated fairly.

Each *subak* has its own water temple where offerings are made twice each year. The aim of the *subak* system is to regulate the supply of water and distribute it fairly to all farmers. This means that farmers must discuss among themselves who will plant in which months of the year, as the demand for water would be very erratic if every farmer in a *subak* decided to plant at the same time. Fortunately, the temperatures in Bali are very even throughout the year, so planting is possible all year. This is why it is possible to see every stage of rice cultivation at any time of the year in Bali. Farmers within each *subak* agree to stagger their times for planting so that the demand for both water and labour will both be spread out. In this way, the *subak* becomes an agricultural planning unit. The *subak* is probably the most important unit in Balinese society – it is a religious community, a social unit, a legal entity and a definable area of land.

5.77 *The network of irrigation channels in Bali is complex and well established. In this view, water from a canal is diverted to two different farms in measured proportions according to the width of the channels.*

The other task of the *subak* is to maintain the complex network of irrigation channels (figure 5.77). This requires a large amount of co-operation among all the farmers in each *subak*. If irrigation canals become damaged, then all the farmers downstream will suffer as the quality and quantity of water deteriorate. As farm numbers change, new areas are opened and old areas close down, the

network of irrigation channels must change accordingly. Like all *subak* activities, this is done co-operatively and by general agreement among the members.

The planning of irrigation channels varies according to the type of topography under the control of the *subak*. In fairly flat areas, padi fields can be quite large (figure 5.78). However, even in flatter areas, there will be differences in the height of the land that must be taken into account in planning irrigation. Main canals are usually built along ridges, with smaller canals branching off, and smaller ones again forming a hierarchy of canals.

5.78 *Rice fields beside the Ayung River near Kedewatan. In the flatter valley floor, padi fields can be quite large.*

5.79 *The landforms have been transformed on this slope near Pujung, Bali. Balinese terraces are lush and peppered with trees, unlike the more stark terraces of the Philippines and Nepal.*

As slopes become steeper, the problems of drainage become more complex. Terraces need to be built on steeper slopes (figure 5.79). As Eiseman (1990, 284) comments:

> "The padi fields are also marvels of hydraulic engineering. Streams are dammed far uphill from the fields, and the water is directed by hand-built aqueducts to fields far away from the dams. Weirs and smaller dams divide and re-divide the streams, settling basins allow the silt to drop out, and finally the water reaches the highest terraces".

However, the water continues working as it flows step by step down the terraces of the hillside. The water is released in measured amounts, carrying nutrients down slope to the lower levels, being used over and over in successive rice terraces.

QUESTION BLOCK 5L

1. *Describe the evidence that supports the claim that Balinese padis are 'a manipulated ecosystem'.*

2. *What is the subak, and why it so important in the organisation of irrigation in Bali.*

3. *Suggest why irrigation in Bali has been sustainable for so long when irrigation has caused so many environmental problems elsewhere.*

Case Study of Water Management in Agriculture and Irrigation — the Aral Sea

In contrast to the sustainable irrigation practices in Bali, water management in the areas surrounding the Aral Sea in Uzbekistan and Kazakhstan has caused major environmental problems. The Aral Sea is a large inland sea, or more precisely, a huge inland lake that has no outlet. It is situated across the border of Kazakhstan and Uzbekistan, in central Asia. Until 1991, Kazakhstan and Uzbekistan were two of the republics within the Soviet Union (USSR). When the Soviet Union disintegrated in late 1991, Kazakhstan and Uzbekistan emerged as two separate independent nations (figure 5.80).

5.81 *A bridge crossing of the Amu Darya, north of Nukus, Uzbekistan.*

through Turkmenistan and Uzbekistan, entering the Aral Sea from the south (figure 5.81).

The two rivers are quite large, with a combined average annual flow of 111 cubic kilometres; this compares with the average annual flow of 90 cubic kilometres for the River Nile (in Egypt) and 225 cubic kilometres per annum for the Zambezi River (which flows through Zambia, Zimbabwe and Mozambique). Although much of the water is lost naturally to evaporation, transpiration and seepage as the rivers flow across the deserts, there is enough water in the rivers' natural state to maintain the Aral Sea's normal surface area of 68,000 square kilometres, an area which makes the Aral Sea the world's fourth largest lake. Unless there is human intervention, water entering the Aral Sea leaves only either by seepage downwards into the rocks below or upwards by evaporation.

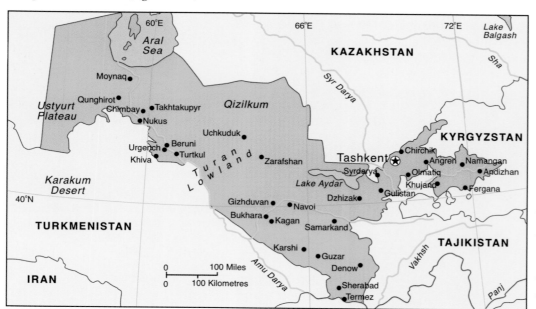

5.80 *Map of Uzbekistan and surrounding countries, showing the location of the Aral Sea.*

QUESTION BLOCK 5M

1. *Draw a sketch map of central Asia to show the location of the Aral Sea.*

The Aral Sea has only two tributaries, the Amu Darya and the Syr Darya. Both rivers rise in the Tian Shan mountains to the east, in the border areas of China, Tajikistan and Kyrgyzstan. From their sources, the two rivers take different courses before flowing into the Aral Sea. The Syr Darya flows west through Uzbekistan and Kazakhstan, entering the Aral Sea from the north-east edge. The Amu Darya flows towards the north-west

The biophysical environment

The area around the Aral Sea comprises dry, flat plains with few rivers. Being near the middle of the Asian land mass, Uzbekistan and Kazakhstan experience hot, dry climates which have made most of the land in the two countries into either desert or steppe grasslands. Average annual precipitation rarely exceeds 150 mm per year. The range in temperatures is very large, with minimum temperatures dropping to -20°C in winter and maximum temperatures rising to 47°C in summer.

The air around the Aral Sea is very dry. The relative humidity by day in summer is always less than 25% and around midday it can fall below 10%. Even in winter, relative humidity averages only 40 to 65% during the day. Many parts of Kazakhstan and Uzbekistan experience hot, dry winds called the *sukhoveya*, which can cause severe damage to crops.

5.82 *This area of irrigated farmland near Nukus shows the exposed sandy soils of western Uzbekistan.*

The soils of the area's deserts and semi-deserts are sandy (figure 5.82). This means that they do not retain even the little moisture that falls on them. Moreover, many of the soils are salty. The Aral Sea has affected the soils over a wide area; the sea was once much larger and salt infiltrated down into the soil at that time. Even today, salt is blown from the shrinking Aral Sea across Kazakhstan and Uzbekistan, continuing to make the soils salty. This process is called **salt deflation**, and it averages about 8,200 tonnes per square kilometre each year.

Scattered through the desert area are oases, areas where the underground moisture from groundwater comes close enough to the surface for people to drill and use it for irrigation. It is around these oases that most naturally occurring plants are found, and it is where the towns have been established.

QUESTION BLOCK 5N

1. *Describe the biophysical environment of the area around the Aral Sea, mentioning:*
   - *climate (temperatures and precipitation)*
   - *soils*
   - *landforms*
   - *water*

Water management in the desert

According to historical records, agriculture using irrigation water has been practised in Kazakhstan and Uzbekistan for up to 6,000 years, making this one of the world's oldest areas for practising irrigation. Indeed, farming would be practically impossible in the dry deserts of the two countries without taking water from the rivers and using it for irrigation. Nonetheless, agriculture is so difficult in the dry desert that the large plain between Tashkent and Samarkand became known as the Hungry Steppe (figure 5.83).

5.83 *Farming on the Hungry Steppe of Uzbekistan.*

A **steppe** is a large flat plain, and the name 'Hungry Steppe' referred to the starvation that the population often experienced. After the Russians conquered Uzbekistan in the late 1800s, irrigation expanded by a massive program of canal building. The area of irrigated land in Uzbekistan increased from 1.2 million hectares in 1928 to 2.2 million hectares in 1950, increasing further to a peak of 4.2 million hectares in 1990 before falling back to about 3.3 million hectares today. Unfortunately, figures for Kazakhstan have never been released, and with the break-up of the Soviet Union, the figures for Uzbekistan have been quite imprecise.

5.84 *Building a new irrigation canal, Uzbekistan.*

5.85 *Irrigated cotton fields west of Samarkand, Uzbekistan.*

By 1990, Uzbekistan had 20 large reservoirs and over 150,000 kilometres of irrigation ditches (figure 5.84). It is important to note that the main reason irrigation expanded under Soviet rule was not to grow more food, but to grow cotton. The dry climates of Kazakhstan and Uzbekistan were ideal for the cultivation of cotton, and vast areas to the east of the Aral Sea were made the Soviet Union's chief cotton producing areas (figure 5.85). In 1921, three years before it officially became part of the USSR, Uzbekistan produced 14,000 tonnes of raw cotton. By 1935, the cotton harvest reached one million tonnes, and it passed two million tonnes in 1950. By 1990, annual cotton production in Uzbekistan had reached six million tonnes and the combined total for the five countries using water diverted from the Aral Sea (Uzbekistan, Kazakhstan, Turkmenistan, Tajikistan and Kyrgyzstan) was over eight million tonnes. Under Soviet rule, cotton exported from these five republics was exchanged for food grown elsewhere.

5.86 *Mechanised harvesting of cotton on the Hungry Steppe near Tashkent (Uzbekistan).*

To transform cotton farming and make it easier to plan centrally, the Soviet authorities reorganised agriculture. Huge collective farms were formed. These huge farms were owned by the state, and the workers became like employees. Formation of these large collectives made it easier for traditional wooden ploughs to be replaced by

modern machinery such as combine harvesters (figure 5.86).

Cotton is not the only crop produced in the desert areas near the Aral Sea. The area also produces desert roses for commercial sale locally and for export. Large crops of melons are also produced, largely for export but also for local consumption (figure 5.87).

5.87 *Melons for sale in the markets of Khiva, Uzbekistan.*

QUESTION BLOCK 5O

1. Why is the area between Tashkent and Samarkand called the Hungry Steppe?

2. Why were the area's water resources developed on such a large scale?

3. Describe the changes in Uzbekistan's cotton production since the 1920s.

4. How was farming organised during the Soviet period?

Environmental consequences of water resource management

Irrigated cotton growing in Kazakhstan and Uzbekistan has had quite a number of environmental side-effects. As cotton production expanded, more and more water had to be diverted from the rivers flowing into the Aral Sea, with the result that less and less water has flowed into the Aral Sea. Although in the natural state these rivers brought an average of 111 cubic kilometres of water annually into the Aral Sea, this figure had been reduced to just 2 cubic kilometres per year by the early 1980s. At the same time as this was happening, more and more pesticides and fertilisers were draining into the rivers from the cotton fields, and industrial pollutants from factories beside the rivers were growing rapidly.

These agricultural and industrial pollutants all made their way to the Aral Sea. Evaporation and seepage are the only ways water leaves the Aral Sea, and so the concentration of pollutants became stronger and stronger with the passage of time.

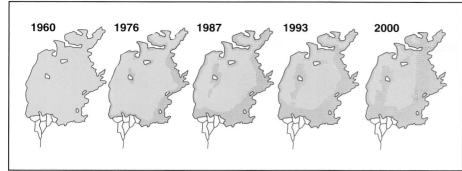

5.88 *The shrinkage of the Aral Sea, 1960 to 2000.*

As a result of the shrinkage of the Aral Sea, the remains of the pesticides and fertilisers have become exposed on the dry bed. These exposed deposits have then become free to blow over the farmlands and villages of Kazakhstan and Uzbekistan to the east, dumping poisons as well as salt across a huge area. The salt is toxic for plant growth, and is resulting in an expansion of the deserts near the Aral Sea. The soils of the area are naturally salty, and without adequate rainfall to flush away the newly deposited salt, more areas of land can be expected to become unusable for agriculture.

Because of the reduced flow of water into the Aral Sea, its surface area has shrunk by over 40% and its volume has fallen by 70% over the past few decades. Between 1960 and 2000, the area of the Aral Sea shrank from 68,320 square kilometres to about 24,000 square kilometres, and the level of the water fell by 20 metres. The volume of water in the Aral Sea fell from 1,090 cubic kilometres to 175 cubic kilometres. This has meant that salts, pesticides and fertilisers washed into the sea have become even more concentrated as the water has evaporated. Indeed, between 1960 and 1990, the concentration of salt in the Aral Sea increased from 10 grams per litre to up to 70 grams per litre. As the Aral Sea has shrunk, the shoreline has receded by up to 80 kilometres (figures 5.88 and 5.89).

The changes to the Aral Sea are summarised in table 5.3. To place the salinity figures in context, the average salinity of sea water is 33 grams per litre. The average level of the sea fell by 20 centimetres per year during the 1960s as water was diverted for irrigation. The rate of fall of the sea surface accelerated to 60 centimetres per year during the 1970s, and then to almost one metre per year during the 1980s.

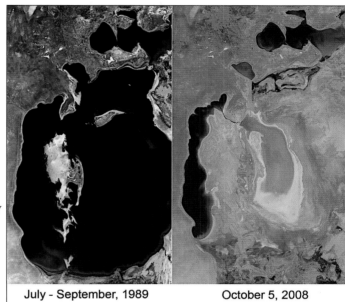

July - September, 1989   October 5, 2008

5.89 *Satellite images of the Aral Sea, 1989 and 2008. (Photo: NASA)*

Farmers have responded by putting even more water onto their crops, hoping that the excess water will wash away the salts. Unfortunately, the poor drainage of the area means that the excess water usually raises the water table, bringing upwards even more salts to the surface zone of plant growth. As long ago as 1985, Soviet soil scientists were claiming that 60% of the irrigated soils in Uzbekistan and almost 70% of the irrigated soils in Kazakhstan were experiencing moderate to strong problems of salinity.

The increased salinity of the soils is the main factor being blamed for declining yields of cotton in Kazakhstan and Uzbekistan. In the early 1990s, cotton yields declined by an average of 4% per annum. By 1994, cotton yields per hectare were only 70% of the average for the period 1976 to 1980.

The chemicals which are being blown from the exposed Aral Sea bed are causing severe damage to people's immune systems, and have resulted in hepatitis, throat cancer and respiratory diseases. Between 1970 and 1990 the death rate among Uzbekistan's population doubled as

Table 5.3
Changes in the Aral Sea, 1960 to 2007

Year	Level (metres)	Area (km²)	Volume (km³)	Salinity (grams/litre)
1960	53.41	66,900	1090	10
1976	48.28	55,700	763	14
1987	40.5	41,000	374	27
1993		33,642	300	
large sea	36.89	30,953	279	37
small sea	39.91	2,689	21	30
2000		24,154	175	
large sea	32.38	21,003	159	65 to 70
small sea	40.97	3,152	24	25
2004 (3 lakes)	n.a.	17,160	n.a.	n.a.
2007 (3 lakes)	n.a.	6,700	n.a.	100

Source: Saiko & Zonn (1994), p.14, Micklin, Nikolay & Aladin, *Scientific American* March 2008

people have had to drink increasingly poisoned water. Kazakhstan's death rate is expected to rise further from its 2000 level until at least 2020, although demographic changes in Uzbekistan will offset the health problems caused by the Aral Sea and its death rate should fall in the coming decades.

Nonetheless, over 80% of women of child-bearing age in the areas of Kazakhstan and Uzbekistan east of the Aral Sea are affected by anaemia. The rate of typhoid has risen by 3000% since 1970 and the rate of viral hepatitis has risen by 700% during the same period. The rate of cancer of the oesophagus in the area east of the Aral Sea is 50 times greater than the world average.

There are well-founded fears that health problems from the shrinking of the Aral Sea will become disastrous at some stage in the period leading up to 2015. This is because it is now known that during the 1980s, the Soviet Armed Forces conducted germ warfare experiments in the deserts near the Aral Sea. Deadly left over bacteria such as anthrax, plague, tularemia, brucellosis, typhus, Q fever, Venezuelan equine encephalitis and smallpox were subsequently buried on an island in the Aral Sea, near its western coastline.

As the Aral Sea shrinks, it is expected that the bacteria will become exposed, leading to the dangerous possibility that some will escape and spread over vast areas nearby. The bacteria were especially developed to be resistant to any conventional forms of treatment. Many cans of bacteria were buried on an island, known as Vozrozhdeniye Island, which became joined to the surrounding mainland as the sea shrank in 2001. This has enabled rodents such as gophers and marmots, which are natural carriers of plague and other diseases, to burrow into the bacteria stores, and spread disease over vast areas. It is suspected that two environmental disasters have already resulted from the shrinking Aral Sea exposing bacteria near Vozrozhdeniye. In 1976, a mass death of fish in the Aral Sea occurred which has never been explained, and in May 1988 some 500,000 Saiga antelope died in the steppes north-east of the Aral Sea in a single one hour period.

5.91 *A ship lies stranded in the sands of what used to be the Aral Sea at Moynaq, Uzbekistan.*

Life for people living around the Aral Sea has also changed for the worse. As the world's fourth biggest lake, the Aral Sea used to provide food for people living on its shores. It supported a large fishing industry, with catches averaging 50,000 tonnes of fish per year. As the concentration of salt in the water has increased from 10% to 23%, 20 of the Aral Sea's 24 species of fish have disappeared. The fishing industry has collapsed and the fishing boats lie where the edge of the Sea used to be, many kilometres from the shore (figures 5.90 and 5.91).

5.92 *Although Moynaq now lies about 100 km from the Aral Sea, the town badge recalls its former fishing industry when it was a port beside the sea.*

The town of Moynaq in Uzbekistan had a thriving harbour and fishing industry that employed approximately 60,000 people. Today, Moynaq lies about 100 kilometres from the shoreline (figure 5.92) and the only significant fishing company remaining in the area brings its fish all the way from the Baltic Sea, thousands of kilometres away. As a result of the decline in fishing, the town's economy is dying (figure 5.93).

The Aral Sea also provided a breeding ground for migratory birds. The breeding grounds were in swampy delta fringes of the Aral Sea. In the 1950s, 173 different species of animals and birds were recorded in the delta lakes of the Syr Darya and Amu Darya. By 1980, most of these

5.90 *A general view of what used to be the Aral Sea at Moynaq, Uzbekistan.*

5.93 *The town centre of Moynaq.*

lakes had dried up, the forests had dwindled to only 20% of their earlier size and only 38 animal species remained.

The Aral Sea is now divided into three parts, and the shrinkage is continuing. It is estimated that to maintain the Aral Sea at its present (reduced) size, average annual inflows from the two rivers needs to be increased to about 30 cubic kilometres. As the surface area of the Aral Sea declines, the loss of water by evaporation also declines. It is estimated that if present rates of inflow of water into the Aral Sea continue, the Sea will continue shrinking until it could disappear altogether in about 2015, by which time its salt concentration would have reached about 175 grams per litre. As table 5.3 showed, the sea's area was just 10% of its original size in 2007.

The shrinking of the Aral Sea has also led to a change in the climate of the surrounding area. Because less water is available for evaporation, average humidity has been reduced by 9%. The number of days without rain each year has increased from 30 in the 1950s to about 150 today. Summers are now hotter and drier, and winters are colder and longer – they now last four months rather than three as previously. As well as being disastrous for agriculture, these climatic changes make living in the area much less pleasant and comfortable for the inhabitants.

The Kazakh and Uzbek governments recognise the environmental problems of water mismanagement in the past. However, as economically less developed countries, little money is available for large-scale remedies. One plan involves trying to save the Aral Sea by enclosing the irrigation canals in concrete. It is hoped that this will slow the seepage of much needed water while allowing poisoned runoff to be diverted across Russia to the ocean. Although work has started, the project is too expensive to be completed without foreign assistance.

One problem is that each of the five countries using water diverted from the Aral Sea pursues its own individual water management policy. For example, as described in chapter 3, in 1995 Turkmenistan lengthened the Karakum Canal (which takes water from the Amu Darya) by 300 kilometres in order to irrigate additional areas in the country. This increased the amount of water diverted from the Amu Darya to 18 cubic kilometres per year, making the task of stopping the shrinkage of the Aral Sea even more difficult. Of the five countries, only Uzbekistan has reduced the amount of irrigated land used for cotton.

The continuing use of heavy machinery is leading to other environmental problems that are not directly related to water management. The soils of the area are very dry and loose in structure. Therefore, the use of heavy machinery has disturbed the soil much more than traditional implements used to do, leading to extensive soil erosion. Nowadays, it is very common to see huge clouds of soil being blown across the Hungry Steppe as machines disturb the soil structure (figure 5.94).

5.94 *Wind-blown soil erosion on the Hungry Steppe, caused by a tractor.*

Loss of the area's scarce water does not only occur due to farming activities, of course. Under Soviet rule, grand schemes of urban planning tried to transform Uzbekistan's and Kazakhstan's cities into socialist showpieces. Large, wide avenues were laid out, huge high-rise buildings were built and grand fountains were constructed in public places. These fountains make life in the dry, desert climate more bearable, but they also result in huge losses of water through evaporation (figure 5.95).

To some people, the environmental challenges in the region surrounding the Aral Sea seem out of control.

5.95 *One of Tashkent's many ornamental fountains.*

Nonetheless some experts have suggested measures that they believe might help the situation, including:

- improving the quality of irrigation canals to minimise water loss by seepage;
- installing desalination plants to improve the quality of water in the Aral Sea;
- charging farmers to use the water from the rivers as a way to regulate water use and minimise wasteful use;
- growing alternative species of cotton that require less water;
- using fewer chemicals on the cotton to improve the quality of water flowing into the sea; and
- installing dams to store and divert water into the Aral sea;
- diverting water from large rivers in Russia; and
- pumping diluted sea water from the Caspian Sea via pipeline into the Aral Sea.

The challenge in implementing any of these solutions is that the countries surrounding the Aral Sea do not have the resources needed to tackle the problems. Without an international program of co-ordinated co-operation it is difficult to see many solutions being implemented in the short-term future.

QUESTION BLOCK 5P

1. *The section above describes the effects on the environment of human actions. Make a point form list of these effects in descending order of your opinion of their importance.*

2. *Note 2 to 3 lines on each of these effects.*

3. *What practical measures can be implemented to remedy the environmental situation of the Aral Sea?*

Competing Demands for Water

Water Resource Management

In chapter 3, the general principles of water management were discussed, with special emphasis on the ways that humans respond to issues of scarcity. These principles will now be expanded by looking at two case studies of conflicts involving water, one at the local scale, and one at the international scale.

Case Study of Water Management at the Local Scale — The Florida Everglades, USA

The Everglades is a vast area of low lying wetland in south Florida, USA that forms the lower part of the Kissimmee River basin. It is so flat and low that no part of the Everglades is higher than 2.5 metres above sea level. The Everglades is also a complex **ecosystem**, a term that means a community of plants and animals which depend upon each other, together with the surrounding environment to which they have adapted. In an ecosystem, disturbing one type of living thing has a

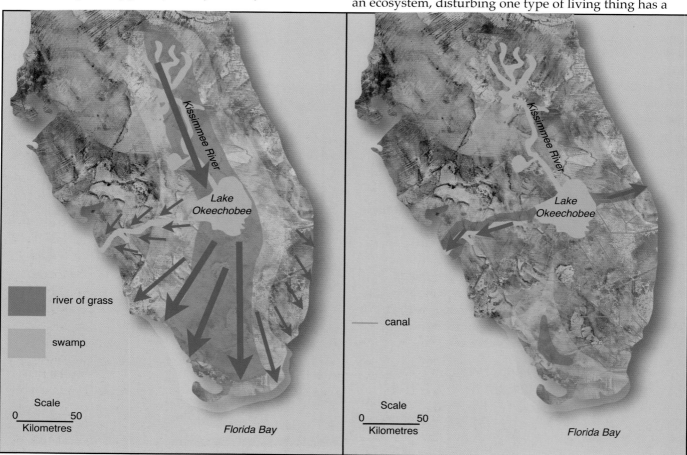

5.96 *The flow of water in southern Florida before human impact (left) and after human impact (right).*

chain reaction. This is because every living thing feeds upon another organism, and it in turn is the food for yet another organism. In the Everglades ecosystem, plants and animals were in harmony with each other and with their surroundings. However, this fragile, delicately balanced ecosystem which had developed over a period of 6,000 to 8,000 years has been disturbed as a result of the **competing demands for water** by humans.

In the 1940s, the pioneering conservationist Marjory Stoneman Douglas studied the Everglades and called the area a "River of Grass". Before the impact of humans, that was an accurate description of the Everglades. To understand the impact of people on the Everglades, it is necessary to look at the area as it was before humans arrived.

The 'natural' Everglades

The source of all life in the Everglades has always been water. South Florida receives quite heavy rainfall, between 1000 and 1500 mm each year on average. About 70% of this rain falls during the warmer months of May to October; winter is much drier. Before humans interfered with the Everglades, 80% of this rainfall was lost through evaporation, transpiration and runoff. The remaining 20% of the water flowed through the Kissimmee River into a large, shallow lake in central Florida called Lake Okeechobee, where the water was stored. This lake was less than 4 metres deep but covered an area of 1900 square kilometres.

5.97 *A water bird wades through the Everglades' "River of Grass".*

Each year, when the heavy rains came in summer, Lake Okeechobee would overflow and the water would flow slowly southwards across the Everglades in a wide shallow 'river'. This 'river' was about 80 kilometres wide and 160 kilometres long, but only one metre deep in the deepest channel and about 15 centimetres deep elsewhere (figure 5.96). This vast river flowed southwards very slowly about 30 metres each day towards the Gulf of Mexico. The speed of flow was very slow because the gradient was so flat — only three centimetres fall per kilometre. The water was not deep enough to cover the tall grass, which is why it was labelled the 'river of grass' (figure 5.97).

During the winter dry season, the 'river of grass' was reduced to a series of swampy water holes. The wildlife of the Everglades retreated to these water holes to await the next summer's overland flow. As the water flowed slowly southwards, large quantities of it soaked down into the porous rocks beneath. The rocks beneath the Everglades were a limestone aquifer and they acted like a sponge, soaking up the fresh water from the surface. The rocks remained saturated from the surface downwards, even during the dry seasons.

5.98 *Periphyton, a yellow-brown algae commonly found in the waters of the Everglades.*

All the plants and animals depended on each other, directly or indirectly, in the natural ecosystem. The main vegetation was the tough, long grass called '**saw grass**', named because of the small, sharp teeth along the edges of each blade of grass. Growing in the water around the saw grass was a yellow-brown ooze-like algae called **periphyton** (figure 5.98). The periphyton was the first step in the food chain and had several other uses as well. It provided refuge for fish when they were under attack, it sealed moisture in the ground during droughts, it provided a home for minute crustaceans and it actually decomposed to make the soil in which the saw grass grew.

Across the Everglades were some slightly higher mud islands called **hammocks**. The hammocks were only a few centimetres higher than the surrounding land. Nonetheless, a very different type of vegetation was found on these islands. On the hammocks, a complex tangle of ground ferns, air plants and tropical hardwoods such as cabbage palms and mahogany trees were found (figures 5.99 and 5.100).

The animals and birds of the Everglades were species that had adapted well to the swampy conditions. The Ever-glades region was infested with alligators, probably numbering about 2 million in 1950 (figure 5.101). The alligators were at the top of the food chain, and fed on other creatures such as turtles and fish which in turn fed on shrimps and small marine organisms. The Everglades had huge numbers of birds of many species, many of them wading species (figure 5.102). In the 1930s there were 265,000 wading birds, in contrast to today's figure of just 18,500. Species of birds included anhingas, ibises, herons and egrets. Other species of wildlife in the Everglades included otters, racoons and small deer.

5.99 *A hammock rises above the flat land of the Everglades.*

5.101 *An alligator in the Everglades.*

5.100 *Vegetation on the hammocks is quite different from the vegetation covering most of the Everglades.*

5.102 *A water bird in the Everglades.*

Fire was an important part of the natural Everglades environment. They were common during the dry months, being started by lightning strikes during storms. The fires were useful in clearing away old vegetation and making way for new growth. The burnt grass returned to the soil as nutrient, providing 'fertiliser' for new plants. The saw grass was protected from the fire because its roots and lower stems were covered in water. This meant that only the top part of the saw grass burned and the plant survived.

QUESTION BLOCK 5Q

1. The Everglades environment comprises many individual parts. Show the individual parts of the environment on a diagram to show how they link together.

2. We say that the parts of the Everglades environment are interdependent. What do we mean when we use this word?

3. Why could the Everglades ecosystem be labelled 'fragile'?

Human impact on the Everglades

In the early 1900s, more and more people began to move into southern Florida. Although some moved into the large cities like Miami, others came to start farms. The farmers wanted to grow vegetables in the warm climate to supply the colder northern states during winter (figure 5.103). The Everglades seemed like an ideal area. As well as having a warm climate, its soils were rich and fertile as they were made from the organic periphyton. Large areas of the Everglades were cleared for farming.

5.103 *Vegetable cultivation near the Everglades.*

The farmers faced one serious problem, and that was the annual flooding. In an effort to solve the problem, **drainage canals** were built to carry the water away to the ocean in the east (figure 5.96, right map). However, during the 1920s, there were several tropical cyclones which dumped huge amounts of rainfall on the Everglades. Even the drainage canals could not cope with the large amount of water, and widespread **flooding** occurred. A major flood in 1928 killed over 2,000 people. The farmers demanded that better flood control be put into place. In 1930, a long,

low dam called the Herbert **Hoover Dyke** was built around the southern edge of Lake Okeechobee. This stopped the flooding, but it also stopped the annual spill-over. The 'River of Grass' began to dry up.

Over the years, the water of south Florida has become more and more **regulated**. This occurred because of the competition for water, especially amount of water demanded by Florida's residents. Today, Florida's population is growing by 23.5% per annum. As well as its permanent population, more than 90 million people holiday in Florida each year, of whom about 30 million go during the dry winter months when water is most scarce. This population growth requires that water be provided. The trend in water use in Florida in recent years is shown in figure 5.104.

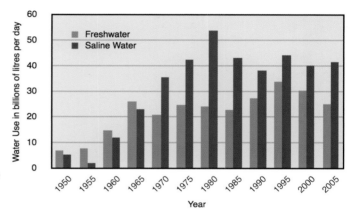

5.104 *Water use in Florida, 1950 to 2005.*
Source: Florida Department of Environmental Protection

QUESTION BLOCK 5R

1. How did the natural environment of the Everglades affect people in the early 1900s?

2. Describe the ways in which people's use of water has changed over the years in Florida.

The impact of human water use on the Everglades

To meet the needs of the population, wells have been sunk into the porous limestone rocks beneath the Everglades and groundwater has been pumped out from the aquifer. However, this has caused major problems.

As the fresh water has been pumped out, salt water from the nearby ocean has soaked in to replace it. The underground water is now becoming **saline** because of human actions. To make matters worse, all the new construction of roads and buildings seals off the surface so that water can no longer seep down and replenish the underground water. Drillers are having to go further and further down into the rocks to find fresh water, and when they do pump it out they make even more room for useless salt water. Humans cannot drink salt water, plants cannot grow with it and it destroys plumbing and appliances when used in manufacturing.

5.105 *A layer of dry crusty algae appears in many areas where the formerly moist soils have dried.*

There is now little water available to flow across the Everglades because so much is taken away in canals for use elsewhere. This has caused a chain reaction of disruptions to the environment. As a result of the loss of water, the ground has dried out in many areas (figure 5.105). Consequently, **fires** now cause much more damage than previously. Fires now burn the entire saw grass plant, the roots of which are no longer protected by water. Therefore, when a fire burns through the Everglades, large areas of saw grass are killed. In 1971, there were some particularly bad fires during the dry season. Almost 500 fires burned in the Everglades during that year, of which all but nine were lit by people. These fires burnt out over 200,000 hectares of the Everglades, killing large amounts of wildlife.

The drying out of the **soil** has had other effects. The soil of the Everglades is made up almost entirely of pure organic matter — periphyton and decaying saw grass. As the soil is exposed to the air, it oxidises and literally disappears — dissolves — into the atmosphere. This is happening at a rate of 2 to 3 centimetres per year in areas where the water cover has gone. This is lowering the level of the soil, exposing tree roots and some underground pipes and power cables.

Outcries by conservationists forced government officials to allow some water to flow across the Everglades once again. However, this has not solved all the environmental problems. Water is released when it is not needed elsewhere by farmers and others. The timing of the releases of water might be quite different from the natural cycle upon which the ecosystem is dependent. Alligators build their nests at the high water level when water levels are high. However, if more water is released later, the nests are flooded and the eggs destroyed.

QUESTION BLOCK 5S

1. *People's use of water has affected the Everglades environment in many ways. What have been the positive effects of people?*

2. *What have been the negative effects of people on the Everglades environment?*

3. *Make another copy of the diagram you did when answering question 1 in Block 5Q. Modify the diagram to show how the causes-and-effects of human impact on the Everglades environment.*

The impact of tourism

In an effort to restore the biophysical environment, the Everglades was declared a **national park** in 1947. However, much of what happens in the National Park is affected by actions outside it. Farmers 'upstream' release fertilisers and pesticides into the waters which will flow into the Everglades. When water is enriched with nutrients, it affects the growth of plants and the natural pattern of vegetation. High levels of mercury have been discovered at all levels of the Everglades food chain — fish in the marshes, racoons and alligators. The Florida panther is now so rare that there may be less than 30 in all Florida and less than ten in the Park. Indeed, a panther with mercury levels so high that they would be toxic to humans was found dead in Everglades National Park.

5.106 *An elevated boardwalk protects the Everglades ecosystem while still allowing visitor access.*

Declaring the Everglades a national park has had both good and bad effects. On the positive side, boardwalks and other facilities such as bird watching towers, information boards and wildlife viewing trams have been built. Such facilities enable visitors to see the Everglades while causing little damage to plant and animal life (figure 5.106). Another positive effect is that more people are encouraged to visit the Everglades and thus understand their biophysical environment.

5.107 *A group of tourists visiting the Everglades.*

Ironically, encouraging visitors is also a negative factor. Although tourists are only allowed to enter some parts of the park in organised groups, some environmental damage cannot be avoided (figure 5.107). The Everglades attracts hundreds of thousands of visitors each year. Some of these visitors camp in their mobile homes, while others are day trippers keen to view the wildlife by tram or air boat (figure 5.108).

5.108 *Tourist facilities at the Everglades.*

QUESTION BLOCK 5T

1. Explain what is meant by 'enriched with nutrients'.

2. Has making the Everglades a national park helped or hurt the quality of its environment? Give reasons for your answer.

Case Study of Water Conflict at the International Scale — The Colorado River in Mexico and the USA

The Colorado River drains much the south-western United States and a small part of Mexico. Its source is in the Rocky Mountains of north-east Colorado and it flows in a generally south-western direction for 2,334 kilometres to the Gulf of California (also known as the Sea of Cortez). The river flows through the US states of Colorado, Utah, and Arizona, and it marks the boundary between Arizona and Nevada and California. The final 120 kilometres of the river flows through Mexico into the Gulf of California (figure 5.110).

The area where the river flows is a region of very low rainfall. Indeed, much of the course of the river flows through desert, including the spectacular gorge of the Grand Canyon, which was carved by the Colorado River (figure 5.109).

5.109 *The Colorado River in the Grand Canyon.*

In the early 20th century, the warm climate made the area attractive to farmers wishing to grow crops using irrigation. This is not unique, of course, such as parts of Egypt which have almost no rainfall but very successful crop growing using the Nile River's water for irrigation. Australia and Israel have also converted large areas to farming using irrigation water brought from areas of surplus rainfall. However, the large demand for water in an area of scarcity led to significant international tensions between the US and Mexico over issues of water quantity and water quality.

As a result of the large-scale use of water for irrigation and urban use in the south-western USA, the Colorado River effectively **dries up** before it even reaches the sea. Furthermore, the water that does reach Mexico is of such **poor quality** that the Mexican Government has complained. For example, **salinity** at the headwaters of the Colorado is 50 parts per million (ppm). However, at the point where the Colorado River crosses the border into Mexico, salinity was about 400 ppm in the early 1900s (as one of the tributaries of the Colorado flowed across a

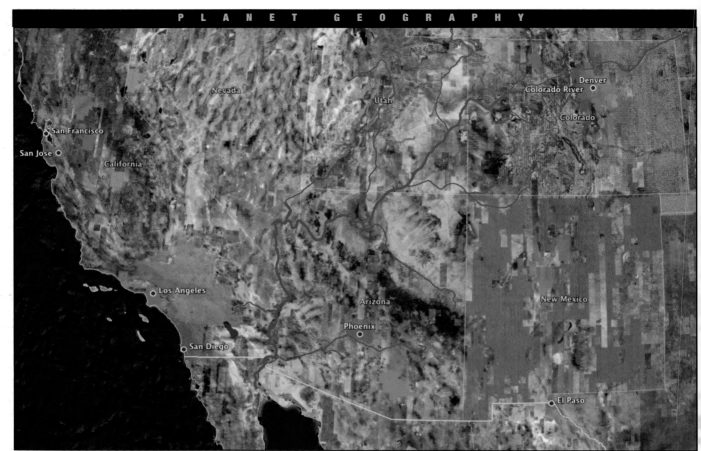

5.110 *Enhanced satellite image of the Colorado River (after Google Earth).*

layer of rock salt), but this figure rose to 1200 ppm in the 1960s as a result of increased irrigation runoff. Early agreements between the US and Mexico dealt with the quantity of water in the Colorado River that the US agreed to deliver. However, with the decrease in the quality of water, Mexico pursued new negotiations that would ensure a maximum level of salinity in water reaching Mexico from the US.

Background to the conflict

The conflict over water in the Colorado River arises because the **aridity** of the area makes water a scarce resource. The aridity is caused by the cool ocean currents that travel south along the Canadian and United States coastline from Alaska. Moisture blowing onshore from the Pacific Ocean bring high rainfall as they meet the coastal ranges in the north of California, but as they blow mainly from inland in southern California there is little moisture left. The descending winds near Los Angeles are very dry and, for many months each year, quite hot.

Ironically, it is this dry, warm, coastal climate that leads to a water shortage that has attracted people to the area in ever increasing numbers. At the end of World War II the state of California had approximately the same population as the whole of Australia — about seven million people. Now this one state has over 37 million people, with Los Angeles alone having over 15 million in its metropolitan area. In fact the dry southern one-third of California has more than 25 million people, or two-thirds of the total

state population. In nearby states such as Nevada new cities were being established in the desert, one of the largest being the tourism and gambling centre of Las Vegas (figure 5.111) .

5.111 *Las Vegas, a city in the Nevada Desert, survives on water piped in from the Colorado River.*

At the same time as the increasing urban population was demanding more water, the state's farmers were also needing more water to expand the area under cultivation (figure 15.112). Increasing affluence has added to the water shortages, and in the area around Palm Springs alone, which is a desert in its natural state, more than 70 golf courses stand out for their rich green colour, while surrounding urban areas are dotted with lakes while the surrounding homes of the wealthy are pictures of watery lushness.

5.112 *Farmland near Yuma, Arizona, that is irrigated with Colorado River water.*

The whole built environment stands beside desert sands from below which the water is pumped. This is common in California as a whole where close to half the water used for irrigation is from aquifers or underground supplies. The difference with Palm Springs is the great depth from which the water is pumped. This suggests it is geologically trapped water and will not be replaced. In the Central Valley, water being pumped to the surface is replaced by surface water soaking down to refill the aquifer.

How did the water shortage evolve?

To the casual observer, regulating the allocation of water of the Colorado River might seem a simple task. After all, if too much water is being used by upstream users, why not simply restrict access to water by upstream people to allow sufficient flow for downstream users, including those south of the international border with Mexico.

Perhaps surprisingly given the problems experienced by downstream users, this approach has been followed since the early days of using Colorado River waters. Attempts were made to measure the flow of the river as early as the 1890s, and several **measuring stations** were built at various points on the river from the 1890s to the 1920s.

On the basis of these measurements, the Colorado River basin was divided into two sections, the upper basin and the lower basin, with the boundary being placed somewhat arbitrarily at Lees Ferry, a point in the channel of the Colorado River in Nevada, about 50 kilometres south of the Utah-Arizona boundary, immediately downstream of the Glen Canyon Dam.

Each US state with the Colorado flowing through it entered into an agreement known as the 'Colorado River Compact' in November 1922. The allocation of water between the two parts of the basin were based on an estimated annual river flow of about 18.5 billion cubic metres (18,502,228,000 m³). It was known that the annual flow of the Colorado River fluctuates greatly, so this figure was obtained by taking the average of several years of meas-

urements at Lees Ferry in the years leading up to the signing. According to the Colorado River Compact, 9.25 billion cubic metres of water per year from the Colorado River was allocated to each of the upper and lower basins in perpetuity. The needs of Mexico were not considered.

5.113 *The Parker Dam, Colorado River, USA.*

Signing the Colorado River Compact cleared the way for a large number of **dams** to be built along the river to regulate the flow (figure 5.113). Some dams were built to provide hydroelectric power, while others were built for flood control, to provide water for irrigation, recreation, and municipal use. One of the dams, the 221 metre high Hoover Dam, is the largest producer of hydroelectric power and the main flood-control dam (figure 5.114). To carry the irrigation water from the dams to urban and farming areas, a network of long canals was also constructed. These include the Colorado River Aqueduct, which goes all the way to the southern California coast, the All American Canal, which carries water just north of the US-Mexican border to California's Imperial Valley, and the Gila Canal, in Arizona (figure 5.115).

The engineering behind the works is impressive, and includes tunnels through the Continental Divide to bring water from the Colorado River to cities and farmlands on the high plains of Arizona. Despite the impressive engineering, the problem of insufficient water persisted in the lower basin and especially in Mexico.

Recent studies in the Colorado River Basin using dendrochronology (analysis of tree rings), which measures the extent of wet and dry years over long periods by examining the thickness of the annual growth in tree trunks, have shown that the early 1920s was a period with unusually wet conditions in the mountains near the source of the river. Tree ring analyses for the past 300 years indicate that the correct long-term average flow of the Colorado River is about about 16.65 billion cubic metres. Furthermore, it seems that the river's discharge is highly erratic, ranging from 5.4 billion m³ to over 27 billion m³. Therefore, the assumed annual flow of 18.5 billion m³ seems to have been an over-estimate of the typical flow, which would explain the water deficiency in the lower sections of the river into Mexico.

5.114 *The Hoover Dam, USA.*

This promise was put into effect with the construction just over 20 years later of the Yuma Desalting Plant, which processes 270 million litres of water per day using a process known as reverse osmosis. Although completed in 1992, the high costs of operation forced its closure for every year except one during the period 1993 to 2008. The Mexicans, whose protests 47 years earlier in 1961 had led to the construction of the plant, are perhaps understandably disappointed by the continuing poor quality of the water they receive.

5.115 *A section of the All American Canal, channelling water westwards from the Colorado River just north of (and parallel to) the Mexican border.*

The water shortages in the lower Colorado River led to representations from the Mexican Government, and as a result, the United States and Mexico entered into a **treaty** on February 3, 1944 which guaranteed Mexico 1.85 billion cubic metres of Colorado River water annually, this figure being subject to increase or decrease under circumstances provided for in the treaty.

Nonetheless, over-allocation of water in the US means that the 1.85 billion cubic metres allocation does not arrive every year. Consequently, the Colorado River often soaks into its river bed and evaporates before reaching the sea. Many regard this as an **environmental tragedy** because this area, which is now often a dry salt flat, was a vast wetland, teeming with more than 400 species of plants and animals, before the waters of the Colorado were diverted.

The river's delta was also the traditional home of the Copacha Indians, who lived by fishing in the estuary. Today, many of the fishing boats are stranded and the Indians and Mexicans share widespread poverty as a result of the water shortages.

Unfortunately, much of the water that does reach Mexico contains runoff from alfalfa and cotton farms in Arizona and California. Many of the soils in these areas are salty, as they comprise an ancient sea bed. Therefore, the waters that reach Mexico are heavily saline and polluted.

When **salinity** levels of Colorado River water flowing into Mexico reached 1200 ppm in 1961, the Mexican Government complained to US officials that the poor water quality was reducing crop yields in the Mexicali Valley. As a result, the United States agreed to limit the salinity of water flowing into Mexico to a level less than 115 ppm.

The future

Climatic records across the Colorado River basin over the past century suggest that temperatures in the region are rising. If this trend continues, the higher temperatures are expected to result in less precipitation in the upper basin of the Colorado River. As much of the precipitation in this area falls and is stored as snow, the combination of reduced precipitation and increased losses due to evaporation could shift the timing of peak spring snow melt to earlier in the year. The overall effect of this could be to reduce discharge and water availability in the future, thus making Mexico's problems even more severe. Reduced discharge could also contribute to greater frequency of droughts, with such droughts becoming longer and more severe.

QUESTION BLOCK 5U

1. *Describe the physical features of the Colorado River basin.*

2. *Explain why the Colorado River often dries up before it reaches the sea.*

3. *What is the cause of the Colorado River's salinity?*

4. *Explain why the Colorado River Compact allocated more water to US states than was usually available in the river..*

5. *Describe the impact on Mexico of the management of the Colorado River in the US.*

Oceans and their coastal margins

6

The physical characteristics and processes of oceans with special reference to the atmosphere, and the management of coastal margins.

ToK BoX — Page 3
Linking Natural and Human Sciences

Introduction to Oceans

Distribution of Oceans

About 71% of the earth's surface is covered by water. Although some of this area comprises lakes and seas, most of the 71% consists of the five interconnected oceans, these being the Arctic, Atlantic, Indian, Pacific and Southern Oceans. The boundaries that separate the oceans from each other are somewhat arbitrary and blurred, but the general limits of each of the oceans is shown in figure 6.1.

The sizes of the oceans varies markedly, and when ranked from the largest to the smallest, the list is:

• Pacific (155,557,000 sq km)
• Atlantic (76,762,000 sq km)
• Indian (68,556,000 sq km)
• Southern (20,327,000 sq km)
• Arctic (14,056,000 sq km)

Sometimes, the five oceans are referred to collectively as the **world ocean**. This is because the divisions are imaginary rather than real and the water from each ocean mixes with water from the others at various points.

The world's oceans hold at vast quantity of water, a volume that has been estimated to be 1.185 billion cubic kilometres. This amounts to 97.3% of all the water on the planet.

The chemical composition of the water in each of the oceans is also very similar from place to place, and this composition varies very little from year to year. In fact, we can think of the oceans as being a single giant chemical mixing tank. There is an inflow of water and chemicals (in the form of dissolved minerals and materials) from the world's rivers, glaciers, rain and wind. There is also a smaller but very important input of chemicals from the **hydrothermal** (hot water) reactions between the sea water and hot basalt rocks that ooze to the surface along the mid-ocean ridges along the bottom of some of the world's oceans.

Balancing these inputs to a large extent, the oceans are continually losing water from their surfaces to the atmos-

>> Some Useful Definitions

Advancing coasts — depositional coasts that are accreting as a consequence of deposition of sediment and/or the infill of coastal marshes. Advancing coasts may also arise from a negative change in sea level (sea level fall or up-lift of land).

Exclusive economic zone (EEZ) — an area in which a coastal nation has sovereign rights over all the economic resources of the sea, seabed and subsoil, extending up to 200 nautical miles from the coast.

Littoral drift — the movement of sediments along a coast by wave action, also called longshore drift.

Oceanic conveyor belts — a global thermohaline circulation, driven by the formation and sinking of deep water and responsible for the large flow of upper ocean water.

Retreating coasts — coasts along which the dominant processes are erosional, resulting in the coastline moving inland. Retreating coasts may also arise from a positive change in sea level (sea level rise or fall in land level).

phere by evaporation, and this loss almost precisely matches the various inputs of water. The dissolved components of the sea water all contribute to various chemical and biological reactions that eventually cause them to precipitate out of the sea water onto the ocean floor. This is why the ocean's salinity remains constant over time. Overall, the precipitation of chemicals from the ocean waters to the ocean floors equals the total inputs of all dissolved materials from weathering on the continental land masses plus the hydrothermal activity at the ocean ridges.

The reason that the composition of all the oceans is similar is that there is a general pattern of circulation of water between the oceans. Water moves in a constant pattern of clockwise and anti-clockwise movements through **ocean currents** which flow like giant rivers through the oceans.

The general pattern of ocean currents is shown in figure 6.2, which is based on a United States Army map com-

piled in 1943; being a US-centric map means that the Pacific Ocean circulation can be seen clearly compared with the more common Euro-centric maps that split the Pacific Ocean (as seen in figure 6.1). The ocean currents can be seen to comprise five major ocean-wide **gyres** (a term that means a swirl, spiral or vortex). The two gyres in the northern hemisphere (one in the North Atlantic and one in the North Pacific) spiral in a clockwise direction, while the three gyres in the southern hemisphere (Southern Atlantic, Southern Pacific and Indian Ocean) spiral anti-clockwise. The reason for this difference in the **Coriolis Force**, which is a consequence of the earth's rotation that causes all moving objects in the northern hemisphere to be deflected to the right while moving objects in the southern hemisphere are always deflected to the left.

Ocean currents occur because there is very little friction between the ocean waters and the solid Earth. Therefore, as the earth rotates, the water moves differently to both

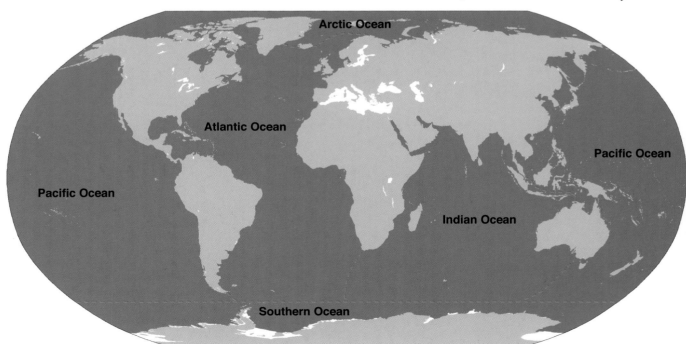

6.1 *The location and extent of the world's five oceans.*

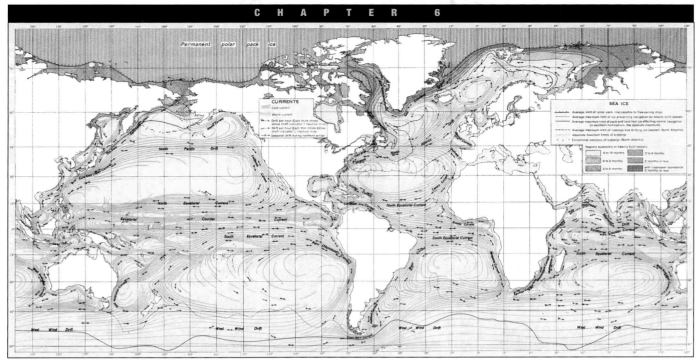

6.2 *The world's ocean currents, as shown on 1943 American military map.*

the solid crust beneath and the lighter atmosphere above. The speed of ocean currents varies according to depth, but in general, currents near the surface of the oceans may move at speeds of about 9 kilometres per hour. On the other hand, deep currents move much more slowly at speeds of about 1 kilometre per hour.

As currents move through equatorial areas, the water becomes warmer. In the same way, ocean currents cool as they flow in polar areas. Therefore , ocean currents flowing along a coast from equatorial areas will bring warm water, while flowing from polar areas will bring cooler water. This is shown in figure 6.2, where warm ocean currents are shown in orange while cool ocean currents are shown in green.

6.3 *The Namib Desert extends all the way to the western coastline of Namibia due to the influence of the cold ocean current in the area.*

Because of the clockwise and anticlockwise movements of the currents, continents in both hemispheres therefore tend to experience warm currents on their eastern sides and cool currents on their western edges. Warm ocean currents tend to bring more rain than cold currents, and

this helps to explain why many deserts are found on the western sides of continents, as seen in Australia, Namibia, Chile, California and Morocco (figure 6.3).

QUESTION BLOCK 6A

1. *Using the data in this section, calculate the percentage of ocean water found in each of the five oceans.*

2. *Explain why the chemical composition of the oceans remains fairly constant over time.*

3. *Describe and account for the pattern of the world's ocean currents. Relate this pattern to the ocean-wide gyres.*

4. *Outline the impact of ocean currents on the climatic differences between the eastern and western sides of the continents.*

Morphology of Oceans

As long ago as 1620, when the shapes of the continents were still being charted, geographers were commenting on the similarities between the shapes of the east coast of South America and the west coast of Africa. Some people suggested that the continents may have been joined at one time, later splitting and 'drifting' apart. At first, people who made this suggestion were not taken very seriously.

Geographers were determined to explain the shapes of these coastlines, because they seemed too similar to be a coincidence. Research was undertaken, and it was discovered that layers of rocks which crossed into the sea in West Africa seemed to continue on the east coast of South America, like a perfect match of two jigsaw pieces that had become separated. Other similarities were also observed, such as common types of plants and landforms,

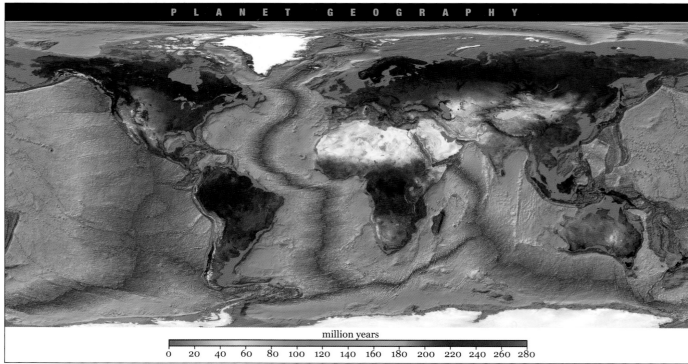

6.4 *The shape of the ocean floor, coloured to indicate the ages of the rocks (for details, see text).*

and eventually it was agreed that Africa and South America were once joined together. Like many discoveries, this 'answer' raised many more questions, such as 'how did the continents move apart?'.

The answer to the puzzle lay in the morphology (shape) of the ocean floor. The main features of the ocean floor may not be as well known as the mountain chains of the continents, but they tell us a great deal about the way the planet was formed. The shape of the ocean floors can be seen in figure 6.4. In this figure, the age of the ocean floor has been coloured to indicate the age of the rocks. Red indicates the youngest rocks, with yellow and green representing older rocks, through blue and purple to the oldest rocks. Ocean areas shown as grey are shallow continental shelves covered with recent sediments. Figure 6.4 shows clearly that the youngest rocks are found along lines along the ocean beds. This suggests that the ocean morphology arises from **tectonic processes**, which means they relate to the large-scale forces that build the earth's structure.

The process of **sea floor spreading** is explained in more detail at the beginning of chapter 8. In summary, the earth's crust consists of a number of large plates that move slowly, driven by currents in the liquid mantle beneath. New crustal material comes to the surface from the mantle beneath at the mid-ocean ridges, such as the Mid-Atlantic Ridge that can be seen clearly in figure 6.4.

The mid-ocean ridges, where new surface rocks are being formed, are known as **constructive plate margins**. In other parts of the world, plates collide and crustal material is destroyed, either by being forced downwards into the mantle (in which case it is known as a **subduction zone**), or by crumpling upwards to form mountain

ranges. Such plate margins are known as **destructive plate margins**.

Deep **ocean trenches** may form along the subduction zone where the two plates are forcing each other downwards into the mantle. Some of these trenches are extremely deep, and they typically extend three to four kilometres below the surface of the ocean. The deepest ocean trench and thus the lowest point on the planet is thought to be a point in the Mariana Trench off the east coast of the Philippines which is 10,920 metres below sea level.

QUESTION BLOCK 6B

1. *Explain the pattern of colour shown in figure 6.4.*

2. *Explain how ocean trenches are formed, and why they they are so deep.*

Oceanic Water

As anyone who has tried swimming in winter as well as summer will testify, the temperature of the ocean is not always constant. Ocean temperature not only varies through the seasons, but by latitude. Waters near the equator are warmer than ocean temperatures towards the poles. This can be seen in figure 6.5, which shows sea surface temperatures (SSTs) during a typical northern hemisphere summer (figure 6.5). Although we talk about sea *surface* temperatures, these are usually recorded remotely by satellites that are tuned to detect temperatures one metre below the surface.

The impact of the ocean currents discussed earlier in this chapter can be seen clearly in figure 6.5. On the western sides of the continents, the cooler waters from ocean

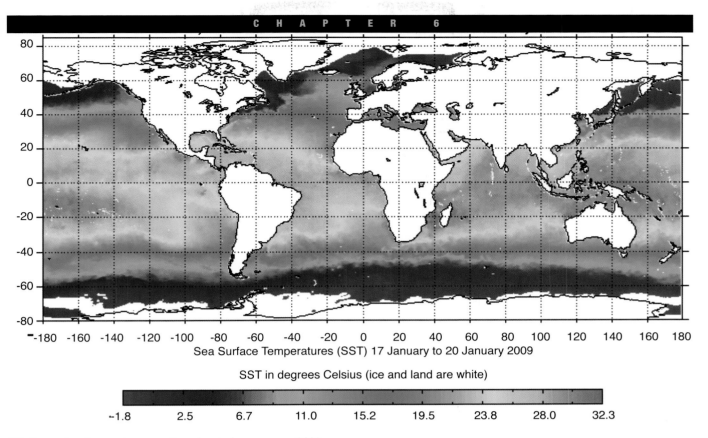

Sea Surface Temperatures (SST) 17 January to 20 January 2009

SST in degrees Celsius (ice and land are white)

-1.8   2.5   6.7   11.0   15.2   19.5   23.8   28.0   32.3

6.5 *Sea surface temperatures, northern hemisphere summer, 2009.*
Computerised digital image used courtesy of the National Geophysical Data Centre, National Oceanic and Atmospheric Administration, U.S. Department of Commerce, http://www.ngdc.noaa.gov/.

currents can be seen intruding towards the equator. Similarly (if not quite so clearly), the warmer waters of ocean currents flowing from the equatorial regions can be seen on the eastern sides of several continents.

As we would expect, ocean water also varies considerably with depth. Two of the significant variations with depth are temperature and salinity. Ocean waters vary in temperature between summer and winter down to a depth of between 500 and 1000 metres; below that level the rate of temperature decline is much slower. Figure 6.6 shows a fairly typical example of the relationship between water temperature and ocean depth where temperature decreases with increasing depth.

A boundary usually occurs at a depth of between 200 and 800 metres called the **thermocline**, below which the surface waters do not mix with the deeper layers. This boundary region is marked by a rapid decrease in temperatures as depth increases. About 90% of the total volume of ocean water is found below the thermocline, and in these deeper waters, the temperatures approach 0°C.

Other changes also occur as depth increases. For example, the density of ocean water increases constantly with decreasing temperature until the water freezes. Because ocean water is saline (salty), its normal freezing temperature is -1.94°C, a significant difference from the freezing point for pure water, which of course is 0°C. In the polar regions, it is quite common for water to reach -1.94°C and

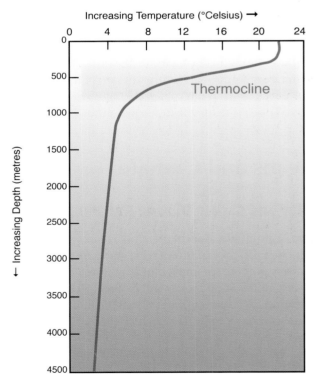

6.6 *The relationship between ocean temperature and water depth in the mid-latitudes.*

therefore turn to ice. As it does so, some of the dissolved salts in the water are usually rejected by the ice that is forming, and therefore sea ice is only about 1% salt whereas normal sea water is about 3.5% saline. For this reason, sea ice is usually okay for humans to consume even though sea water is not.

Salinity and density show the opposite trend to water as the depth of ocean water increases. Temperature declines with increasing depth, but salinity and water density both increase. In the same way that temperature shows a rapid fall at the thermocline, salinity shows a rapid increase at about the same depth, which is referred to as the **halocline**. Because temperature declines as salinity increases, the net effect is to increase water density as depth increases. Because the thermocline and the halocline occur at about the same depth, the water density also increases most rapidly in the same zone, which can also be referred to as the **pycnocline**, which is defined the layer in the ocean where the water density increases rapidly with depth.

These changes are seen more sharply in tropical areas than polar areas because the surface temperatures are warmer in equatorial areas than near the poles. At great depths, the temperature of ocean water shows very little difference between the equator and the poles. The relationships described are shown in a simplified graphical way in figure 6.7.

QUESTION BLOCK 6C

1. *Describe the pattern of sea surface temperatures shown in figure 6.5.*

2. *What is the relationship between the thermocline, the halocline and the pycnocline?*

3. *Describe and account for the information shown in figure 6.7.*

Oceans and Climate

Energy and Carbon Dioxide Transfers

At the beginning of the chapter, it was noted that the water from each ocean mixes with water from the others at various points. An important way in which this happens is a global-scale movement called the **thermohaline circulation** (THC), sometimes also referred to as the **oceanic conveyor belt**. The path of the THC is shown in figure 6.8.

The starting point for the thermohaline circulation is usually thought of as the warm, salty surface ocean water from the Gulf Stream. The Gulf Stream is a current of warm water that flows from the Caribbean across the Atlantic Ocean to the western coast of Europe. When it reaches the cold, polar conditions of the North Atlantic Ocean, the water becomes chilled and increases in density. The chilled surface water sinks in the North Atlantic and

then flows south near the bottom of the ocean towards Antarctica. When it reaches the Antarctic, the water is cooled even more and flows north at the bottom of the oceans into the Indian, and Pacific Ocean basins. As it approaches the equatorial areas of the Indian and Pacific Oceans, the water warms and becomes less dense, and therefore rises towards the surface, returning then as surface flow to the North Atlantic Ocean. It takes water almost 1,000 years to move through the entire cycle of the thermohaline circulation.

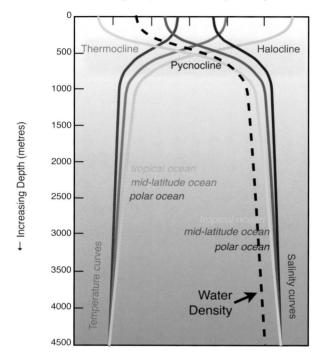

6.7 *Relationship between water temperature, salinity, water density and depth of the ocean in tropical, mid-latitude and polar regions of the world.*

The changes to the thermohaline circulation are shown in figure 6.8 by the different colours of the arrows. Cold water flowing a great depths is shown by the blue arrows, while warmer surface flows are indicated by red arrows. Waters that are dense due their cold temperatures and high saline concentrations are shown as blue and green belts. On the other hand, the yellow and orange belts indicate flows that are lighter in density because they are warmer and less saline.

The THC represents much more than a slow flow of density-driven water. As the thermohaline circulation flows at great depths near the bottom of the ocean, the water becomes enriched with important nutrients such as phosphates, nitrates, silicates and dissolved carbon dioxide. These minerals are then distributed through all the oceans by the THC, reducing the physical and chemical differences between them and making the world's oceans a single global system.

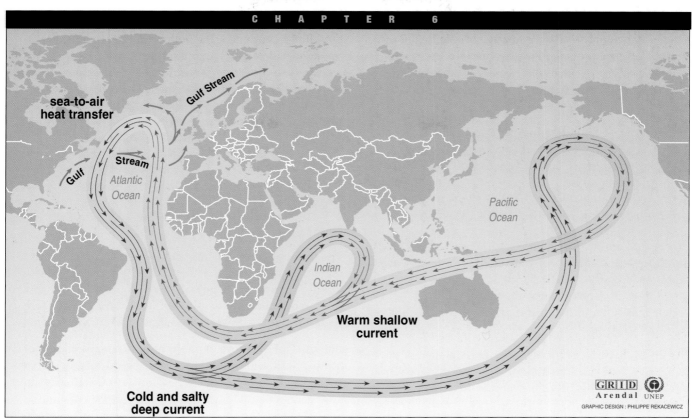

6.8 *World ocean thermohaline circulation.* (Courtesy: Grid Arendal and UNEP, graphic design by Philippe Rekacewicz)

In addition to redistributing minerals, the thermohaline circulation also moves **energy** (in the form of heat) around the globe. In brief, the thermohaline circulation moves heat from equatorial regions to the polar regions, and therefore plays an important role in controlling the quantity of sea ice near the poles. Some researchers claim that it is changes in the thermohaline circulation rather than climate change which are influencing the size of the polar ice caps. Other researchers suggest that **global warming** is itself an important factor affecting the density of the ocean's surface water, and as the flow of the THC is density-driven, this is the main factor in altering the circulation of the THC.

The rate of flow of the thermohaline circulation governs the rate at which deep waters are brought to the surface and exposed to the atmosphere. As the CO_2-rich THC is a source of adding carbon dioxide into the atmosphere, its rate of flow is an important factor in determining the concentration of carbon dioxide in the atmosphere. This in turn is important in analysing the rate of global warming as carbon dioxide is one of the more important greenhouse gases.

We can therefore say that the thermohaline circulation and global temperatures are interdependent, as each has the potential to influence the other.

QUESTION BLOCK 6D

1. *The Gulf Stream is powered by the wind and flows at an average speed of 6.5 kilometres per hour. Using this information, compare the speed of wind-generated ocean currents and the density-driven thermohaline circulation.*

2. *What is said that the thermohaline circulation is 'density-driven'?*

3. *In what ways does the thermohaline circulation transfer energy and minerals around the world?*

4. *Describe the role of the oceans as a store and source of carbon dioxide.*

5. *What evidence is there to support the claim that 'the thermohaline circulation and global temperatures are interdependent'?*

El Niño Southern Oscillation (ENSO)

The term **El Niño** translates from the Spanish meaning 'the boy child'. It is a term used for many years by Peruvians who fish for anchovy in the eastern Pacific Ocean. They referred to a warm ocean current that appeared off the coast of Peru, Ecuador and Chile each year at about Christmas time – hence the reference to the Christ child. The fishers noticed the warm current because it replaced the nutrient-rich cold current that usually flowed along the coast, thus reducing the food supply for the anchovy. When the current was especially strong, it ruined the anchovy harvest and caused economic ruin to the fishers.

The term El Niño has now been broadened from its original meaning where it referred to the annual weak warm ocean current that flows southwards along the coast of

Peru and Ecuador at about Christmas-time. The term now refers also to the large warmings that occur every few years in the Pacific Ocean which impact on global weather and climate patterns.

Normally, when El Niño is not operating, the waters off the west coast of South America (near Peru and Ecuador) comprise cold water that is rich is nutrients. This cold water is brought up from the ocean depths to replace surface water that has been driven west by prevailing winds. Because the waters near the South American coast are cooler than the waters further west in the Pacific Ocean, a giant convection cell forms in the atmosphere over the Pacific Ocean. Air descends over the cool oceans near South America, and rises over the warmer oceans near Australia, New Guinea and Indonesia (figure 6.9, top left). This situation usually exists during the southern hemisphere's summer and autumn period – from December to May each year.

During an El Niño event, the warm ocean current moves to the east, and the atmospheric convection cell follows it, altering the entire pattern of wet-and-dry weather in the Pacific (figure 6.9, bottom left). In a prolonged El Niño event that extends through to March, April and May, the warm water moves even further east, bringing rains to South America and drought to eastern Australia – the opposite of the 'normal' situation (figure 6.9, right).

During an El Niño event, the cool waters that are usually brought to the ocean surface near South America remain at a deeper level, allowing the surface waters to become warmer (figure 6.9, bottom). In other words, the permanent thermocline in the tropical waters of the Pacific Ocean lies at a deeper level than normal, during an El Niño event.

The thunderstorms release enormous amounts of heat energy that affect the circulation of the earth's atmosphere. Therefore, the global circulation of the atmosphere is altered whenever the thunderstorms are shifted from their normal position, such as during an El Niño event.

El Niño can therefore be thought of as a combination of atmospheric and ocean processes. The atmospheric component of El Niño is called the **Southern Oscillation**, and

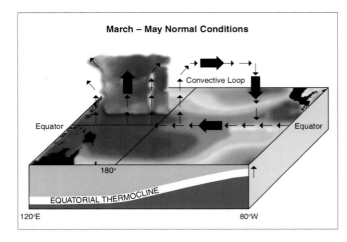

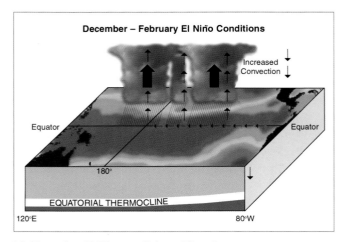

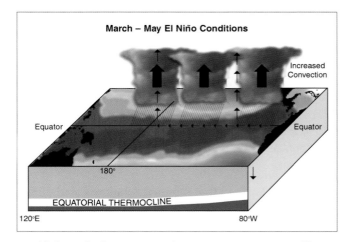

6.9 *Normal vs El Niño conditions. The colours represent ocean temperatures, with 'hotter' colours representing warmer temperatures. The two top diagrams show normal (not El Niño) conditions. A convection cell in the atmosphere is driven by heat at the ocean surface. Water from the surface evaporates and the warm, moist water rises in the western Pacific, pulling in cool, dry air from South America, creating a loop that transfers heat and moisture out of the hot zone. The cool water from the ocean depths near South America is drawn upwards to replace the surface water that has been moved to the west by the convection cell. The two bottom diagrams show an El Niño event. During this time, the hot spot in the ocean moves east, creating two convection cells and altering climates around the Pacific basin.*

when the atmosphere and ocean collaborate together, **ENSO** is said to occur, short for El Niño-Southern Oscillation.

An El Niño event, therefore, corresponds to the warm phase of ENSO. The opposite can also occur, in which the tropical waters of the Pacific Ocean become cooler, and a cold phase of ENSO begins. This is known as **La Niña**, from the Spanish word for 'the girl child'.

Table 6.1 lists some past El Niño and La Niña events. Both types of events are natural occurrences, and neither is predictable or regular. Figure 6.10 shows the world's ocean temperatures at the peak of the extreme El Niño event of 1997-98.

Table 6.1

A Selection of Past El Niño and La Niña Events

Cool ENSO Phase		Warm ENSO Phase
Extreme El Niño Events	Moderate El Niño Events	La Niña Events
1661	1567-68	1904
1694-95	1630-31	1908
1782-84	1641	1910
1790-93	1650	1916
1844-48	1715-16	1924
1876-78	1802-04	1928
1899-1900	1827-28	1938
1940-41	1832-33	1950
1982-83	1864	1955
1997-98	1867-69	1964
	1901-02	1970
	1913-15	1973
	1918-20	1975
	1965-66	1988
	1972-73	1995
	1986-88	1998-2001
	1990-95	2007-08
	2002-03	
	2004-05	
	2006-07	

tropical cyclone activity was suppressed, with the number and severity of cyclones being reduced significantly. On the other hand, tropical cyclone activity became more severe and plentiful in the Pacific Ocean. Flooding occurred in South America, whereas Australia, Indonesia and West Africa experienced severe drought conditions. Indeed, conditions were so dry in Indonesia that huge forest fires broke out that took several weeks to extinguish. In the United States, the north-western states facing the Pacific Ocean experienced a warmer-than-normal winter, with less snow but with more rain. The heavy seas on the west coast of the United States led to severe coastal erosion, with many homes in California being washed into the sea of undermined (figure 6.11). It has also been found that tornadoes are somewhat less numerous during El Niño events.

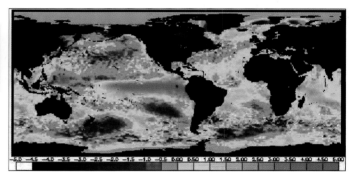

6.10 *World sea surface temperatures on 24th January, 1998. Yellow, orange and red colours show areas where the ocean temperatures are warmer than usual. The blue and purple colours show areas where the oceans are cooler than usual. The gradient below the map shows the deviation from normal temperatures in degrees Celsius. © NOAA (National Oceanic & Atmospheric Administration).*

6.11 *Severe erosion at Santa Cruz, on Monterey Bay (California, USA), caused by intense El Niño-related winter storms in early 1998. This view was taken six and a half years later in mid-2004, and shows that the beach had not recovered.*

The impacts of La Niña are the opposite of El Niño. In general, La Niña aggravates tropical cyclones over the Atlantic Ocean and Gulf of Mexico and suppresses cyclone activity in areas of the Eastern Pacific. La Niña leads to heavy rainfall in Indonesia, South Asia and Australia, often with severe flooding, and stronger monsoon

El Niño events can cause many drastic effects on world climate that affect tens of millions of people. Figure 6.12 shows the major impacts of the extreme El Niño event of 1997-98. In the Atlantic Ocean and the Gulf of Mexico,

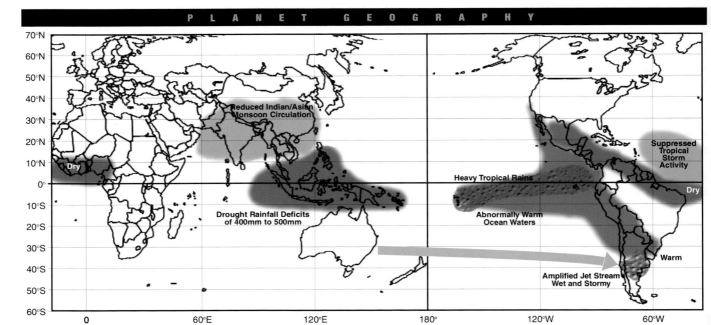

6.12 *Impacts of the El Niño event, June to September 1997.*

rains in south-east Asia. La Niña also enhances the number and strength of tornadoes in the mid-states of the USA.

Although researchers now understand the impact of ENSO events, they are still unsure what triggers the movement of the warm ocean currents. In the past, it had been suggested that volcanic eruptions may play a part, but this theory is no longer widely accepted because many El Niño events have not been preceded by eruptions. Other theories that have been suggested involve sea floor venting and sunspots, but no positive proof has yet been found to support these theories.

QUESTION BLOCK 6E

1. *Explain the meanings of the terms (a) El Niño, (b) La Niña, and (c) ENSO.*

2. *With reference to figure 6.9, explain how El Niño conditions vary from normal conditions.*

3. *Describe the pattern of sea surface temperature anomalies shown in figure 6.10. Explain why this pattern is typical of an El Niño event.*

4. *Describe the impact of El Niño events in different parts of the world.*

5. *Describe the impact of La Niña events in different parts of the world.*

The Value of Oceans

Resource Base

The world's oceans represent a valuable resource base for the planet. In addition to its role in regulating the earth's climate, the oceans provide many products that are useful for humans. Because accessing resources is more difficult in the deep oceans than in the shallow continental shelves, the margins of the oceans tend to have the greatest demands placed upon them to provide resources for humans. However, as technology develops and cost structures change, even the deepest and remote ocean areas are seen as being able to provide resources for human use.

6.13 *A fisherman in Dar-es-Salaam, Tanzania, repairing nets on the beach.*

Perhaps the most obvious **biotic resource** that the ocean provides for humans is **fish** — certainly fishing has a history of thousands of years. Today, fish supply 16% of the world's protein to humans, and this figure is higher in the LEDCs.

Fishing is conducted at a wide range of scales, from individual people casting nets to casting nets to large trawlers that operate like highly mechanised factories (figure 6.13). While most fish that are caught are used for human consumption, some fish are used to feed animals or to provide oils as raw materials for industrial processes. The management of fishing is discussed in more detail in the next section.

Another way in which oceans are used by humans is for **transport** (figure 6.14). Although people tend to travel only short distances by ship these days, long-distance shipping is widely used to transport cargo in various types of ships including bulk oil tankers and container ships. In a related use, the oceans are also used for communications as long-distance telephone, internet and data cables are laid across the ocean floor.

6.15 *Using the beach for recreation, Dubai, United Arab Emirates.*

6.14 *A ferry on Hong Kong harbour, China.*

Tourism is an increasingly important use for oceans as a resource. Although most tourism relating to oceans occurs on the margins, such as on beaches and the shallow waters of the continental shelves (figure 6.15), some larger cruise liners carry passengers across the oceans between continents.

The ocean floors are increasingly being used as a source for **minerals** and other **abiotic resources**. In general, it is much more difficult and therefore more expensive to mine the oceans than the land, but if the resource is sufficiently valuable then the profits may sufficient to justify the high costs. Unfortunately, mining in the oceans often causes so much devastation that the natural ecosystems are devastated. For example, when dredging occurs, the ocean floor is totally destroyed, wiping out all marine habitats including fish, invertebrates and breeding grounds.

Fishing

Traditional fishing methods were designed to obtain food for subsistence purposes (figure 6.16). Even today, fishing within most LEDCs takes only the quantities of fish needed for food in the local community. Under these circumstances, fish remain a renewable resource.

6.16 *Traditional fishing methods, Arba Minch, Ethiopia.*

This situation changes, however, with commercial fishing. In commercial fishing, there is an incentive to catch as many fish as possible to make as much money as possible. Under these circumstances, the fishing industry has great difficulty in conserving resources partly because fish can move across local and national boundaries. Within any country there can be the enforcement of rules about the size of fish that can be taken and about the bag limit for individual fishers. Such rules are made to ensure that each species has fish reaching breeding age. These actions can help to conserve fish stock in estuaries and coastal waters wherever there are sufficient inspectors to police regulations. Of course, as we have seen, the destruction of breeding habitat may be counteracting such conservation measures.

Where ocean stocks are being considered, there is the problem that fish may move great distances during their life cycle and this will mean crossing the boundaries of countries' controls. Territorial waters now extend some 320 kilometres from the shore and that means there is an overlap between many countries, or at least dispute as to where the line should be placed. Many maritime countries accidentally and deliberately enter other countries' territorial waters and remove fish and other marine sources of food. Adequate patrolling can go some way to seeing that any conservation measures are observed. However, with dwindling fish stock there is pressure to move into parts of the ocean where intruders could argue they were unaware they had strayed over the border. In any case if they are taking undersized fish near an ocean border they are depleting breeding stock on both sides.

6.17 *Selling fish from fishing boats, Zanzibar, Tanzania. Fishing on this scale does not usually threaten fishing stocks by over-exploitation.*

Much more efficient fishing techniques have been developed in recent years, including:

- air surveillance and various radar devices to locate fish schools;
- larger, faster, better equipped factory ships to process and preserve the catch (figures 6.17 and 6.18); and
- better netting techniques that often require the team work of a number of fishing boats.

6.18 *While medium-sized fishing vessels such as these boats in Greenland (top photo) usually do not over-exploit fishing stocks, the same cannot be said for ships such as the large Russian 'factory vessel' (lower photo), which uses radar to search for dense schools of fish.*

At the same time as these changes were occurring, the size of the world's fishing fleets grew enormously. As a result of all this, fish can now be caught in quantities that threaten the survival of species. The drift net is still being used by fishers from some countries, despite being banned in international agreements. This extensive and almost invisible net snares virtually everything that is unlucky enough to swim into it, including unwanted as well as protected marine species.

Where there are special markets for particular fish such as the tuna in Japan or the coral trout in Hong Kong the price that fishers can obtain encourages them to take greater risks of breaching territorial waters. In some cases a country such as New Zealand can benefit from gearing its methods of fishing, storage and preparation of fish such as tuna to reap the profits while they feel the fish is not endangered in their waters. On the other hand, a fish such as the coral trout has been taken from the protected marine park of the Great Barrier Reef to appear later in Hong Kong restaurants as the result of illegal fishing. The price that people are prepared to pay for fish ultimately influences whether conservation is likely to be successful or not.

6.19 *Typical Hong Kong coastline, near Sai Kung.*

Conservation measures are really having only a minor impact. The trend in marine fish catches has been downwards since about 1970 in spite of greater success in catching what fish are actually there. This indicates that the traditional fish sought by the industry are probably over-exploited. Thus, the total catch is being maintained by some non-traditional species such as the sprat and pollock, which are smaller than the more popular fish. Ways of marketing small fish, such as canning and making of fish-meal, will continue. In this way, the protein yield from fish may be maintained for some years but it is not going to be because of active conservation of the better types of fish.

Breaches of restrictions on whaling receive more publicity than the steep reductions in the stocks of some of the world's most popular fish, although it is one area where there have been successful conservation measures. Although Japan and Norway still do not recognise some international agreements, numbers of most whale species have shown a steady increase in the last two decades. In many places they contribute significantly to ecotourism. People are fascinated by the inshore passage of these huge sea creatures as they migrate for breeding and feeding.

QUESTION BLOCK 6F

1. *Describe the issues involved in the management of fish as a resource.*

Case Study – Management of Fishing in Hong Kong

Like many coastal areas in southern China, fishing has been an important function in Hong Kong for hundreds of years. An important part of the diet for people in southern China, fish provide both a source of protein and a major source of income.

Hong Kong is located beside a wide continental shelf on a rocky coastline with many small inlets and bays, a large number of islands and many small rocky reefs (figures 6.19 and 6.20). The waters are generally shallow, being between 10 and 20 metres deep. These circumstances combine to provide Hong Kong's waters with a rich variety of habitats in a relatively small area and thus a diverse and abundant supply of sea life.

6.20 *Tolo Harbour, Hong Kong.*

Hong Kong's fishing fleet expanded greatly in the years following World War II, and its boats ventured well beyond Hong Kong's local waters. In Hong Kong's spirit of imposing very few government regulations on business activities, there have been very few restrictions on fishing operations both inside Hong Kong and in its surrounding waters. Regulations have essentially been limited to bans on the uses of explosives, poisons and some other destructive methods, as well as fishing bans in certain shipping channels, especially Victoria Harbour in the central business district of Hong Kong.

It became obvious in the late 1980s that the number of fish in Hong Kong's waters was **declining sharply**. The decline in fishing stocks was due to four main factors:

1. Government authorities were focussed on increasing the overall catch and were paying little attention to either the health or sustainability of the industry.

2. Statistics collected at the time did not separate catches made solely within Hong Kong's waters and those made elsewhere, and this hid the declining trend of fishing within local waters.

3. The basis of collecting government statistics had been inconsistent from year to year, also making trends difficult to discern.

4. Hong Kong's waters had been impacted by a variety of factors that lowered the yields from fishing, including water pollution, large-scale reclamation, dredging and dumping operations, all of which disturbed or destroyed habitats in many areas.

The first step towards developing a conservation policy for fishing in Hong Kong occurred in 1995 when the government introduced the Marine Parks Ordinance. Under the Ordinance, four Marine Parks were declared in 1996, these being Hoi Ha Wan, Yan Chau Tong, Sha Chau and Lung Kwu Chau, together with one Marine Reserve, Cape d'Aguilar. Another Marine Park, Tung Ping Chau, was designated five years later in 2001 (figures 6.21 and 6.22).

Within the Marine Park areas, commercial fishing was permitted provided only small-scale equipment was used. The restrictions were a little tighter within Tung Ping Chau Marine Park where all fishing was banned. It is important to remember that these Marine Protected Areas were not intended as a way to restore the number of fish for catching; Marine Parks were intended for the conservation of marine life and habitats and to encourage recreation, while the Marine Reserves were intended to encourage scientific study in areas where there would be minimal human disturbance.

6.21 *Tung Ping Chau Marine Park, Hong Kong.*

6.22 *Lung Kok Shui Beach on Tung Ping Chau.*

At the time of writing, statistics suggested that the intro-duction of the Marine Parks and Marine Reserves were having very little effect on increasing numbers of fish. One possible reason for this is that the Marine Protected Areas are all quite small in size, the most extreme exam-ple being the Cape d'Aguilar Marine Reserve which cov-ers an area of only 18 hectares and which in several areas is less than 10 metres wide. Another factor could be that the regulations are not strongly enforced (figure 6.23).

6.23 *Rubbish on the beach, Tung Ping Chau.*

6.24 *A fishing boat using nets in the waters of Tolo Harbour, Hong Kong.*

The most intensive type of fishing conducted on the sand and mud sea-bed of the continental shelf, including

within Hong Kong's waters, is **bottom trawling**. Under this system, one or more heavily-weighted nets are dragged over the sea-bed by fishing boats to harvest shrimps, fishes, crabs and other edible species (figure 6.24). As the nets are dragged at quite high speed, and the mesh size of the net is small, bottom trawling is indis-criminate in what it catches. It is also extremely destruc-tive to sensitive and fragile sea-bed communities such as sponges, sea-fans, and soft corals.

The Hong Government has acknowledged the damage done by bottom trawling and has forbidden its practice in Hong Kong's Marine Parks. However, the shrimp trawl fishery industry continues to be financially viable as the market price for invertebrates is always high in Hong Kong (figure 6.25). This makes the practice very difficult to limit within the framework of Hong Kong's practice of imposing few controls over economic activities.

6.25 *Seafood is extremely popular in Hong Kong, leading to a constant and strong demand. These fish are for sale (for eating) in Sai Kung, a fishing village in eastern Hong Kong.*

Concern about dwindling fish stocks led the Hong Kong Government to commission several expert studies to investigate strategies for improving the situation. As a result of the investigations, **six recommendations** were made to the Government, these being:

i. establish a fishing license program;

6.26 *Fish traps, Lamma Island, Hong Kong.*

ii. limit new entrants to the fishing industry to reduce fishing pressure;

iii. establish nursery and spawning ground protection areas (Fisheries Protection Areas, Marine Parks and Reserves;

iv. enhance habitat;

v. restore habitat; and

vi. conduct fish re-stocking trials.

Of these recommendations, the Government accepted only two, which were to enhance habitat (by starting an Artificial Reef Program) and to conduct fish re-stocking trials.

The objectives of the **artificial reef program** were four-fold: (i) to enhance marine resources, (ii) to rehabilitate degraded habitats, (iii) to protect spawning and nursery grounds and (iv) to enhance habitat quality in open sea-bed areas. The government allocated a total of HK$100 million to build artificial reefs, and by 2003 a total of 529

ToK BoX

Linking Natural and Human Sciences.

When the academic journal 'The Australian Geographer' began publication in 1929, it described the scope of the subject on its front cover using the diagram shown to the right. Although views about the subject of geography have developed since 1929, the diagram still represents very well the interactive and integrating role that geography plays in linking the physical and human facts of our environment.

In the ToK Box in the previous chapter, the importance of the scientific method was outlined. It seems a fairly straightforward matter to apply the scientific method to physical geography, but how relevant is this approach to the human side of geography?

The IB regards geography as one of the human sciences. This means that the IB groups geography with other subjects such as archeology, anthropology, economics, ethnology, philosophy, psychology and sociology.

Some practitioners in the human sciences apply the same methods and standards to their work as the natural sciences. Others argue that we cannot apply the methodology of the natural sciences to the human sciences because people's behaviour is not predictable in the same way that the physical environment is predictable.

This raises the question of whether the human sciences are fundamentally different from the natural sciences? Are the human sciences actually "sciences"?

We can consider, for example, the role of models and theories, methods for

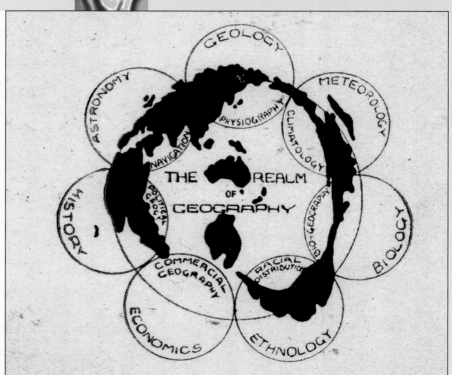

collecting data, the nature of facts, the role of observation and experimentation, the impact of the observer on things being observed, and so on. Researchers of the human sciences do employ many of these methods, but do they do so in the same ways as physical scientists, and are the results as reliable?

It may be that different approaches are required among those disciplines that are mainly historical (such as archeology) compared with those that are mainly behavioural (such as economics)

and with those that are mainly experimental (such as psychology)? If that is so, then how does geography (which seeks to tie together elements of all these human as well as natural sciences) fit in?

It seems that the great atomic physicist, Ernest Rutherford (1871-1937) was frustrated by the apparent inconsistencies of human behaviour, as he once claimed "The only possible conclusion that the human sciences can draw is — some do, some don't".

The next ToK BoX is on page 282.

had been built with a total volume of 158,300 cubic metres (figure 6.26).

There is some dispute about the effectiveness of the artificial reefs. Over 200 fish species have been identified and recorded on the reefs, but researchers disagree as to whether they have been attracted away from nearby natural reefs, or whether they exist solely as the result of the additional habitat provided by the artificial reefs. In Hong Kong, this is sometimes known as the 'aggregation vs enhancement' debate.

In 2004, a **fishing licence scheme** was introduced in which all ships involved in commercial fishing would require a fishing licence. This has been a successful measure to regulate the number of ships harvesting fish at any one time. However, the scheme does not include recreational fishing, and conservation organisations such as the WWF (World Wildlife Fund) have been pushing to have the licensing scheme widened to include this.

Since 1999, China has enforced an annual **'closed season'** policy towards fishing in the South China Sea. This has been intended to give fish time to reproduce without being disturbed by fishers in the hope that fishing stocks will increase in numbers as a consequence. The closed season takes place each June and July and covers the main reproductive season for marine life in the region. Although the 'closed season' restrictions do not apply in Hong Kong waters, it does apply to Hong Kong ships that fish outside local waters in the South China Sea. Reports suggest that the 'closed season' management strategy has been successful in increasing both the numbers of fish and the biodiversity in the region's oceans.

QUESTION BLOCK 6G

1. *Explain why the number of fish in Hong Kong's waters was declining in the 1980s.*

2. *Describe the elements of Hong Kong's fishing conservation policy and comment on the effectiveness of each element.*

3. *In what ways can (and should) Hong Kong's approach towards fish conservation be applied elsewhere?*

Waste

Pollution in oceans is a major problem in all parts of the world that has negative impacts on marine life and therefore indirectly, on humans. Oil spills, toxic wastes, dumping garbage and sewage, along with agricultural wastes, dirty water and other harmful substances are all significant sources of pollution in the oceans.

In 2008 the National Centre for Ecological Analysis and Synthesis produced the first detailed map showing the impact of humans on marine ecosystems in all the world's oceans (figure 6.27). In compiling the map, the researchers combined the impacts of six different types of fishing, inorganic pollution, invasive species, nutrient input, acidification, the impact of oil rigs, organic pollution, population pressure, the impact of commercial shipping and two aspects of climate change (sea surface temperatures and ultraviolet impacts). This information was combined with our current understandings of the vulnerability of different marine ecosystems to pollutants and other forms of human impact.

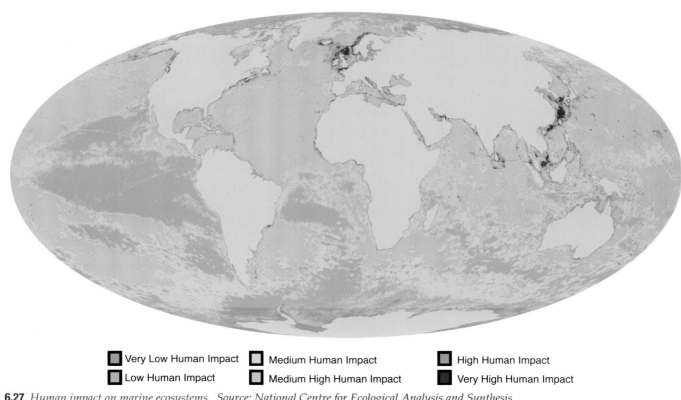

Very Low Human Impact   Medium Human Impact   High Human Impact
Low Human Impact   Medium High Human Impact   Very High Human Impact

6.27 *Human impact on marine ecosystems. Source: National Centre for Ecological Analysis and Synthesis*

The data in the map shows that the most heavily impacted ocean areas are the North Sea, the South and East China Seas, and the Bering Sea. Furthermore, many of the coastal areas of Europe, North America, the Caribbean, China and Southeast Asia are heavily affected by human impacts.

On the other hand, the areas that are least impacted by humans are mainly near the poles, but other less impacted zones are found along the northern coast of Australia, and in small, scattered places along the coasts of South America, Africa, Indonesia and in the tropical Pacific. Not surprisingly, oceans which are further away from areas of dense human settlement and away from major shipping lanes are likely to be the least impacted areas.

The information in figure 6.27 provides useful insights into the **sources of pollution** that make the most significant impact on the oceans. For example, there are some activities that have little impact on the oceans, while other more harmful activities perhaps need to cease or be relocated to less sensitive areas.

Poisonous materials that are dumped into the oceans are known as **toxic wastes**, and they are probably the most harmful form of pollution both for aquatic life and humans. When toxic waste harms an organism, the damage usually becomes magnified as it quickly passes through the food chain, sometimes finishing as seafood consumed by humans. In any food chain, smaller organisms are consumed by larger organisms, and as this process continues the concentration of any pollutants increases, hence the risk to humans from eating contaminated seafood. Toxic wastes enter the oceans from various sources such as discharges from ships, and leakage from landfills, dumps, mines, and farms. Toxic chemicals from farm wastes and heavy metals from factory wastes have especially serious impact on marine life.

Farm wastes are a serious form of ocean pollution. When pesticides and fertilisers are used, the excess quantities flow through rivers and into the oceans. Runoff containing fertilisers bring extra nutrients into the ocean, and these can cause **eutrophication**, which is an excessive richness of nutrients in a body of water which causes a dense growth of algae and other plant life, which in turn depletes the available oxygen supply , thus causing the suffocation of other marine life. Eutrophication has created enormous 'dead zones' in several parts of the world, including the Gulf of Mexico, parts of the Mediterranean Sea and the Baltic Sea.

Toxic wastes may have devastating impact on fishing industries. One particularly dangerous toxic chemical in oceans is lead as it can cause serious health problems such as damage to the brain, kidneys, and reproductive organs. Lead has been found to cause birth defects, both in marine organisms and in humans, as well as birth defects, nerve damage, lowering IQ scores, stunting growth, and causing hearing problems in children. The main sources of lead pollution are wastes from paint, lead batteries, fishing lures and water pipes.

Boats and **shipping** are very significant causes of pollution. The main types of pollution from boats are waste oil and other petrochemical fuels, but garbage is also often dumped from boats directly into the oceans, adding a variety of organic and inorganic wastes. Although oil spills can be catastrophic when they occur, and they receive a great deal of publicity, they are only responsible for about 12% of the oil entering the oceans each year. According to a study by the US National Research Council, and widely publicised by the WWF (World Wildlife Fund), 36% of the oil entering the oceans does so by flowing through drains and rivers as waste and runoff from cities and industry.

However, about 80% of all ocean pollution comes from land-based activities. **Human wastes** that are dumped in oceans directly from the shore include household garbage, factory wastes, sewage, waste water from bathing and plastics. Most types of garbage that are dumped into the oceans takes a long while to break down, and this is especially so for plastics and radioactive wastes.

Some types of rubbish cause special problems in marine habitats, such as **plastic bags**, which can be mistaken for food by many marine organisms. Fish are attracted to plastic bags and may become entangled in them, or the bags may block the breathing passages and stomachs of species such as whales, dolphins, seals and turtles, causing death by suffocation.

Particular problems arise in places where **sewage** pipes share tunnels with storm water drains. When heavy rainfall occurs, the contents of the sewage pipes may overflow and the sewage waste becomes mixed with household wastes and storm water runoff, which then flows into the ocean. In many parts of the world, sewage flows untreated (or inadequately treated) into the ocean, and as an example, it has been estimated that 80% of the human sewage discharged into the Mediterranean Sea is untreated. Like fertiliser wastes, sewage can lead to eutrophication as well as spreading infectious diseases.

QUESTION BLOCK 6H

1. *Describe the sources and distribution of pollution in the oceans.*

2. *What are the implications of the pollution of oceans by the disposal of toxic materials such as oil and chemical waste?*

3. *Which of the types of pollution discussed in this section worries you the most? Give reasons to explain your answer.*

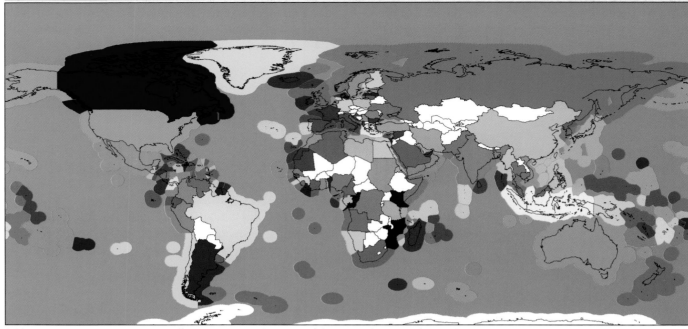

6.28 *National control over the world's oceans. Note that some of these boundaries are disputed.*

Geopolitics of Oceans

Sovereignty Rights

The territory of a country does not end at its shoreline. Countries which are connected to the sea or oceans have **sovereignty rights** over the section of water that is nearest to them. The extent of those sovereignty rights into the oceans is governed by the United Nations Convention on the Territorial Sea and the Contiguous Zone, which was approved in 1958. Among the key provisions of the Convention are the following points, which are quoted directly from the Convention (note that when the State is referred to, it means the nation-state, or the country):

• The sovereignty of a State extends, beyond its land territory and its internal waters, to a belt of sea adjacent to its coast, described as the territorial sea.

• The sovereignty of a coastal State extends to the air space over the territorial sea as well as to its bed and subsoil.

• The normal baseline for measuring the breadth of the territorial sea is the low-water line along the coast as marked on large-scale charts officially recognised by the coastal State.

• In localities where the coastline is deeply indented and cut into, or if there is a fringe of islands along the coast in its immediate vicinity, the method of straight baselines joining appropriate points may be employed in drawing the baseline from which the breadth of the territorial sea is measured.

• Where the coasts of two States are opposite or adjacent to each other, neither of the two States is entitled, failing agreement between them to the contrary, to extend its territorial sea beyond the median line every point of which is equidistant from the nearest points on the baselines from which the breadth of the territorial seas of each of the two States is measured.

• Subject to the provisions of these articles, ships of all States, whether coastal or not, shall enjoy the right of innocent passage through the territorial sea.

• The coastal State must not hamper innocent passage through the territorial sea.

• The contiguous zone may not extend beyond twelve miles (22 kilometres) from the baseline from which the breadth of the territorial sea is measured.

Most countries would argue that 20 kilometres of territorial water is not enough to guarantee security from smuggling and other illegal activities, or to ensure adequate space for controlling illegal entrants. Therefore, the United Nations agreed to create **exclusive economic zones (EEZs)** beyond the 12 nautical mile (22 kilometre) territorial waters. In general, each country's EEZ extends for 200 nautical miles (370 kilometres) from the shoreline, or 188 nautical miles (348 kilometres) beyond the limit of territorial waters.

An exception to this rule occurs when the EEZs for two countries would overlap, which would happen whenever their shorelines were less than 400 nautical miles (740 kilometres) apart. When such overlaps occur, the two countries are required to define their actual boundaries. In general, the boundary is drawn along the mid-point of the line separating the two countries.

Within its EEZ, a country has the right to explore, use, conserve and manage whatever natural resources are situated there. Countries may also use the EEZ to produce energy from the water, currents and winds. The pattern of control over the world's oceans arising from the combination of territorial limits and exclusive economic zones is shown in figure 6.28.

Conflict

Countries are not always able to agree on the boundaries of their EEZs. This is especially the case when significant natural resources, such as oil, may lie beneath the ocean waters. Some conflicts have arisen between countries over the boundaries of their EEZs, including the following:

- the Cod Wars in the North Sea between the United Kingdom and Iceland from 1958, 1972 and 1976.

- the ongoing dispute over Rockall, a tiny rock in the North Atlantic Ocean, claimed by Ireland, the UK, Denmark and Iceland.

- the ongoing dispute over various islands in the South China Sea (such as the Spratly Islands) that are claimed by China, Malaysia, Vietnam and the Philippines..

- the dispute between Peru and Chile about where their boundaries should be drawn in the Pacific Ocean; this dispute involves control of tens of thousands of square kilometres of rich fishing territory.

- the dispute between Italy and Slovenia on one side and Croatia on the other over Croatia's proposal to establish a Protected Ecological Fishery Zone (ZERP) in the Adriatic Sea.

QUESTION BLOCK 6I

1. *What rights and responsibilities does a country possess when it has sovereignty over an area of ocean?*

2. *Explain the difference between sovereignty rights of countries within their territorial limits and exclusive economic zones (EEZs).*

3. *Figure 6.28 shows the extent of control over the world's oceans by nation-states. Who do you think controls the other ocean areas (shown in light blue)?*

4. *Choose a current (ongoing) geopolitical conflict over an ocean resource that is not fishing. Research the conflict and then suggest a realistic solution to the conflict.*

Coastal margins

The Shoreline Environment

The coast is a narrow zone that is especially active in the shaping of landforms. In the coastal zone the sea, land and air all meet together and interact to shape the landforms, which are in turn heavily influenced by human activity. The **shoreline** is the actual boundary of the land and sea. However, when we study the **coastal margins**, we usually look a little more widely than the shoreline. **Coastal terrains** extend inland as far as the sea water, salt spray or wind-blown sand extends. They extend seawards to the depth of the **wave base**, which means the depth to which waves can move sediment on the sea bed.

It follows from this that the width of a coastal terrain in one area may be very different from its width somewhere else. The coastal terrain may be only a few tens of metres wide on steep, rocky coasts, but it could be tens or hundreds of kilometres wide where estuaries move sea water far inland or where there are wide shallow continental shelves. On the high energy coastlines of southern Australia, the wave base may be 20 metres below sea level, but on the low energy coastlines common in western Europe, the wave base may be only a few metres below sea level (figures 6.29 and 6.30)

6.29 *The cliffs, rocky outcrops and powerful waves indicate this coastline at Port Campbell in southern Australia is a high energy shoreline.*

6.30 *The wide expanse of sand and low waves indicate that this coastline at Bahia de los Piratas in Costa Rica is a low energy shoreline.*

With the exception of some glacial processes, all the processes that form landforms anywhere in the world operate on coastal terrains. In addition, there are many unique processes that operate in coastal terrains. The inputs and outputs used to describe fluvial landforms in the previous chapter could also be applied to the shoreline environment. The processes acting on coasts are mostly marine or atmospheric, although other important processes include the work of chemical and biological factors.

Marine Processes

Marine processes are the action of waves, tides and currents – these supply most of the energy that shapes landforms in the coastal zone. The original sources of energy that drive marine processes are solar radiation and the gravitational pull of the sun and moon.

The superficial undulations of the water surface produced by the wind blowing over the ocean are called **wind waves**. Small circular movements in the wind produce minor undulations in the water surface, and some of these are reinforced by subsequent gusts of wind. The stronger the wind, the larger the waves will be. Although wind waves are highly visible to someone standing on the shoreline, they are not the waves that perform most of the work of landform formation.

Larger waves are formed by a wind that blows for a long time or which has a long fetch (the distance over which the wind blows). When these larger wind waves leave the area where they were formed and begin to travel freely, they become more even and longer crested, and become known as **swell**. These waves have considerable potential to shape landforms on the shoreline.

It is possible to measure waves, and this helps us to distinguish between constructive or destructive waves. Many of the measurements focus on the **crests**, or tops of the waves, and the **troughs**, or dips between them. Some of the important measures commonly used are the following:

Wave height (H) is the vertical distance between a crest and its adjoining trough.

Wave length (L) is the horizontal distance between two successive crests.

Wave period (T) is the time taken for two successive crests to pass a fixed point.

Wave velocity (V) is the speed of the wave crests.

Wave steepness (H/L) is the ratio of wave height to wave length.

Wave steepness cannot exceed a ratio of 1:7, or 0.14, because at that point the wave breaks (figure 6.31). It is possible to calculate the wave length if the wave period is known. This can be done using the formula $L = 1.56T^2$.

The size of a wave determines how much energy it exerts. Larger waves posses more energy, and therefore have a greater potential to cause damage. Wave energy (E) is proportional to the square of the wave height (H), and directly proportional to the wave period (T), using the formula $E \propto LH^2$. In other words, a 4 metre high wave has 16 times more energy than a 1 metre wave, assuming the same wave length. Similarly, a wave with an 8 second period has 4 times more energy than one of the same height with a period of 2 seconds, assuming the same wave height. This shows us that long period, high waves can do as much work in a few days as it takes smaller waves several weeks or months to do.

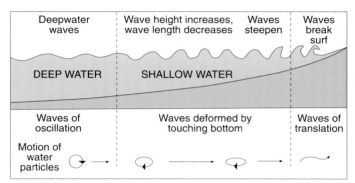

6.31 *Changes in the shape of a wave as it approaches the shoreline.*

6.32 *These very different coastlines are found close to each other near Auckland, New Zealand. The land mass of the North Island is very narrow in this area, and New Zealand's east and west coasts are separated by just a few kilometres. The high energy of Muriwai on the west coast, facing the Tasman Sea (top photo) contrasts strongly with the lower energy of Tawhranui (lower photo) on the east coast, facing the Pacific Ocean.*

Wind velocities, and therefore wave heights, are greatest in the mid-latitudes where strong winds blow for long periods across large stretches of ocean. Wave velocities and wave heights decrease towards both the equator and the poles. Because the prevailing winds over the oceans blow from the west, more moderate waves tend to be found along the east coasts of continents in the mid and low-latitudes, as these coasts are protected from the west coast swell (figure 6.32). In the tropics, where very gentle winds blow or calms prevail, low waves are most common.

Waves approaching a coastline do not distribute their energy evenly along the shoreline. We can regard each wave as a bundle of energy moving towards the shoreline. Each wave (or bundle of energy) can be divided into equal 'parcels' of energy, divided by lines drawn at right-angles to the wave crest, known as a **wave orthogonal** (figure 6.33). As each wave approaches the shoreline, it meets shallow water in front of the headlands while the water is still deep in front of the bays. The shallower sea bed slows the wave in front of the headlands, while still allowing the wave to travel more quickly into the bays. The effect of this is that waves **refract**, or bend, around the headlands and meet the shoreline approximately at right-angles.

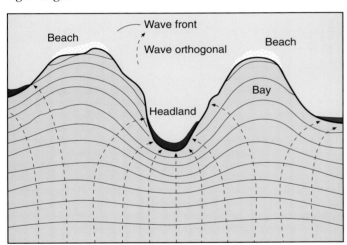

6.33 *The distribution of energy along a shoreline that comprises alternating headlands and bays. Each incoming wave is divided into equal segments of energy. The wave orthogonals show that the energy is concentrated onto the headlands and dispersed in the bays.*

The pattern of the wave orthogonals shows that energy is concentrated on to the headlands and is dispersed in the bays (figure 6.33). This uneven distribution of energy focuses erosion on most headlands, while deposition will occur in most bays. For this reason, cliffs are common on headlands while beaches will usually form inside bays (figure 6.34).

Wave refraction is also responsible for forming **tombolos**, or tied islands. When an island is located close to the coastline, waves refract round it as if it were a headland, and meet behind it. When the waves collide they lose competence to carry sediment. Deposition therefore

occurs behind the island, first in the form of a cuspate foreland that eventually grows to join the island to the mainland to form a tombolo (figure 6.35).

6.34 *Alternating cliffs and bayhead beaches, near Kiama, Australia.*

6.35 *A tombolo, or 'tied island'. The wave refraction around the island can be seen. This example is at Bournda in south-eastern New South Wales, Australia.*

Waves can be constructive or destructive. Waves are generally **constructive** during periods of low energy, when deposition occurs. On the other hand, waves are **destructive** during periods of high energy, when erosion is likely to occur. Beaches tend to go through cycles of erosion or

DEPOSITIONAL SEQUENCE

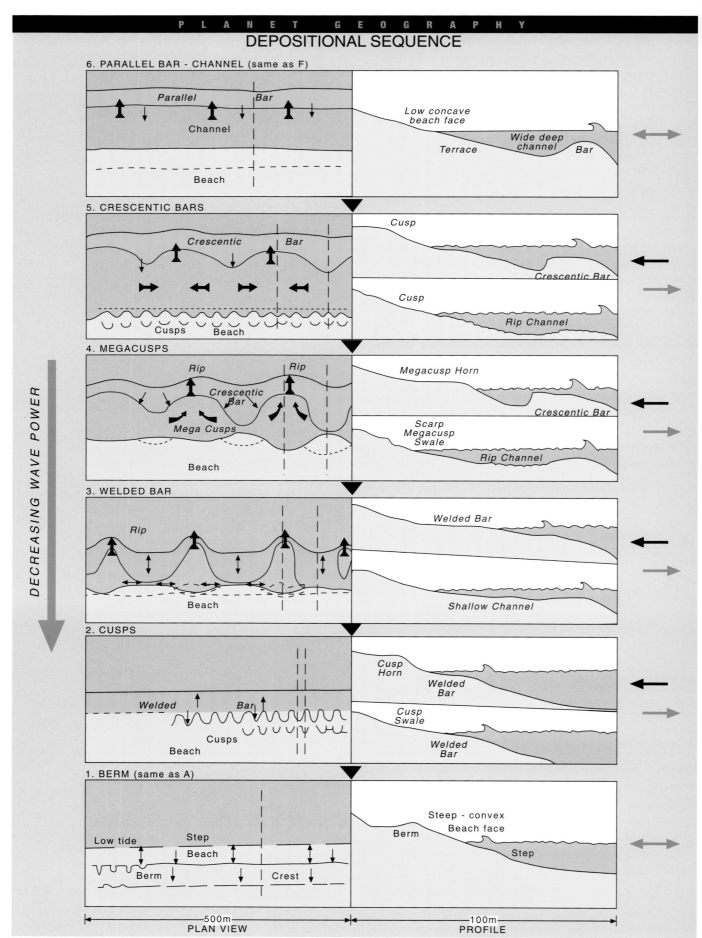

6.36 *A model of beach erosion and deposition. The depositional sequence is shown on the left (i.e. this page), with decreasing wave energy from stage 6 (at the top) through to stage 1 (at the bottom). The erosional sequence is shown on the right (i.e. page 249), with increasing wave energy from stage A (at the bottom) to stage F (at the top). A beach may change from the depositional sequence to the erosional sequence, and vice versa,*

EROSIONAL SEQUENCE

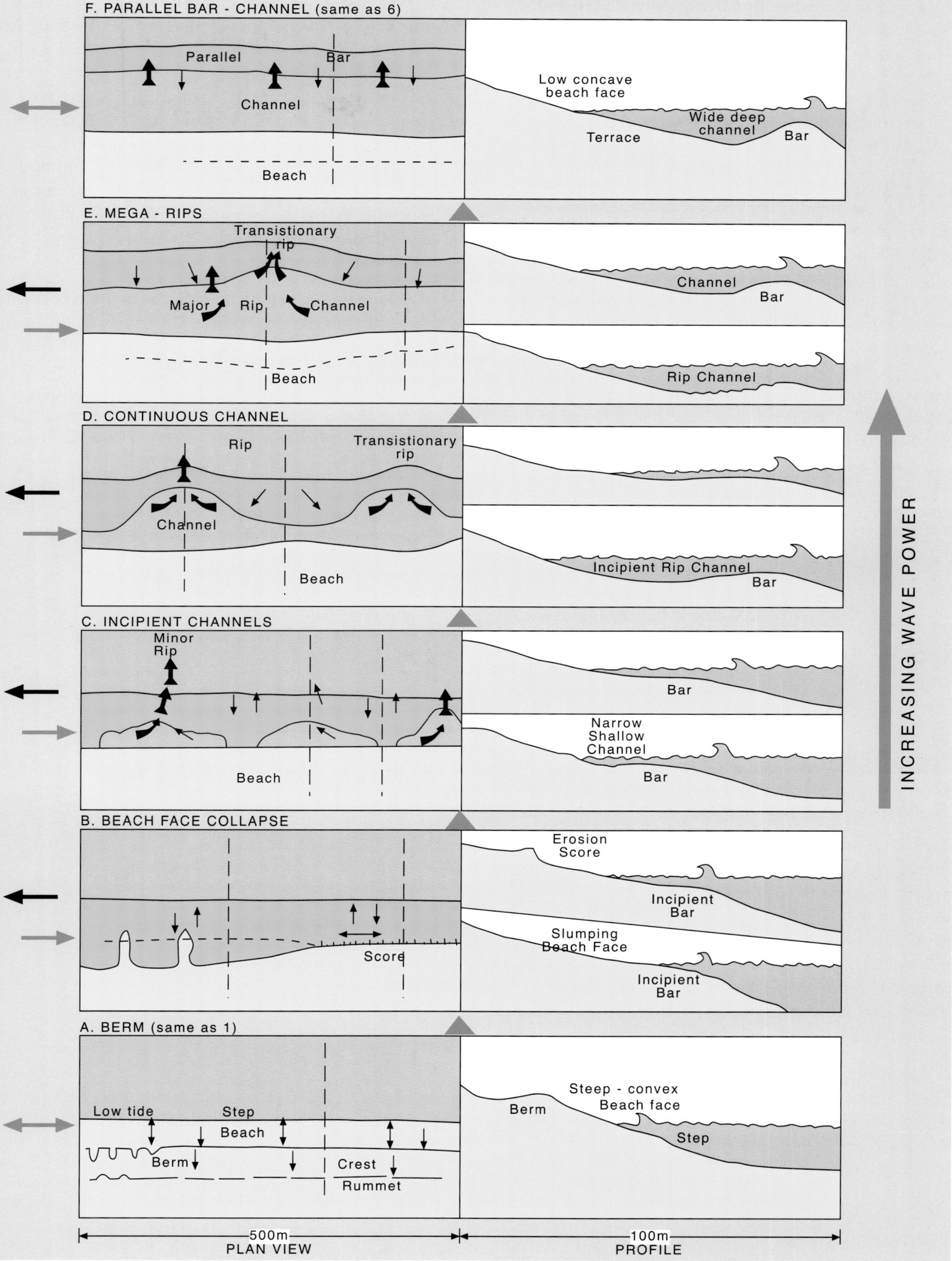

F. PARALLEL BAR - CHANNEL (same as 6)

Parallel Bar

Channel

Beach

Low concave
beach face

Terrace

Wide deep
channel

Bar

E. MEGA - RIPS

Transistionary
rip

Major Rip Channel

Beach

Channel

Bar

Rip Channel

D. CONTINUOUS CHANNEL

Rip Transistionary
rip

Channel

Beach

Incipient Rip Channel

Bar

C. INCIPIENT CHANNELS

Minor
Rip

Beach

Bar

Narrow
Shallow
Channel

Bar

B. BEACH FACE COLLAPSE

Score

Erosion
Score

Incipient
Bar

Slumping
Beach Face

Incipient
Bar

A. BERM (same as 1)

Low tide Step

Beach

Berm Crest

Rummet

Berm

Steep - convex
Beach face

Step

INCREASING WAVE POWER

500m
PLAN VIEW

100m
PROFILE

at any time, as shown by the arrows between pages 248 and 249. In each stage of the sequence, the left hand diagram shows the beach in plan view from above, while the right hand view shows the cross-section. On the plan views, yellow indicates sand above the water, orange indicates sand below the water, and the dashed lines show the locations of the cross-sections.

deposition depending on the wave energy available (figure 6.36). In the depositional sequence, decreasing wave energy changes the shape of the beach from stage 6 to stage 1, unless it is interrupted by an increase in wave energy. In the erosional sequence, increasing wave energy changes the shape of the beach from stage A (or wherever the starting point is) through to stage F, unless interrupted by lower energy conditions.

Landforms are changed when there is a change in the levels of water, sediment or energy. **Deposition** will occur if there is an extra input of sediment. The extra sediments available will be formed into depositional landforms such as deltas, beaches, dunes and so on. On the other hand, if there is a loss of sediment, **erosion** will occur. Whether a landform is erosional or depositional depends on the supply of sediment and energy available. By comparing the appearance of a beach with the model shown in figure 6.36, we can get good indication as to whether the beach is undergoing a depositional or an erosional sequence at the time (figure 6.37)

6.37 *The large welded bar at this beach at Gladstone (Queensland, Australia) suggests it is at stage 3 of the depositional sequence.*

Coastal sediment comes from two main sources. The first is the land, which supplies gravels, quartz sand, silts and muds. These sediments may be brought to the coast by rivers, or they may result directly from the erosion of cliffs. The second source of sediments is the sea. When marine organisms die, their shells and skeletons supply carbonate sediments to the coast. We can therefore say that coastal sediments are supplied by rivers, by marine erosion, or they can be produced on site.

A rare (though extreme) type of wave is the **tsunami**. These form as a result of disturbances in the earth's crust, such as an earthquake or volcanic explosion. These disturbances create long wavelengths at the ocean surface, radiating out from the earthquake centre at speeds of up to 900 kilometres per hour. The height of a tsunami in the open sea might be only a few centimetres, but like tides, their height increases in shallower coastal waters. The combination of their great speed and height can result in immense devastation and loss of life.

The twice-daily rises and falls in local sea level caused by the gravitational attraction of the sun and moon are known as **tides**. Although the moon is smaller than the sun, it is much closer to the earth and so it exerts a 2.16 times stronger gravitational force. Consequently, lunar tides are more significant than solar tides. Every two weeks, at the new and full moon, the moon is aligned with the sun, and this alignment produces the highest tides called **spring tides**. At the moon's first and last quarter, it is perpendicular to the sun, and lower **neap tides** result. When the spring tides coincide with periods of high winds or storm activity, a strong force capable of severe erosion may result.

The difference between high and low tide on a particular day is known as the **tidal range**. The tidal range can vary greatly from place to place around the world. In the deep oceans, the tides average only 18 centimetres in height. On the other hand, the height of the tides usually increases at shallow continental shelves and in coastal inlets. Depending on the shape of the sea bed and coastline, some coasts receive tides with a small range (less than 2 metres), while others receive tides over 10 metres in range. The coastline of South Wales that faces the Bristol Channel is one example of an area with a large tidal range.

QUESTION BLOCK 6J

1. *Explain why wave energy is unevenly distributed along a coastline. What are the effects of this?*

2. *Draw a diagram to show the relationship between wave height and wave length.*

3. *How are waves formed?*

4. *What determines whether a coastline will experience erosion or deposition?*

5. *Describe the changes seen on a beach as it progresses through (a) the depositional sequence, and (b) the erosional sequence.*

Other Coastal Processes

Subaerial processes

Not all the processes operating on coasts are marine processes. Subaerial processes are those processes that occur in the open air or on the surface rather than underwater. The atmosphere plays a very important part in these processes.

We have already seen that winds generate ocean waves, which provide most of the energy that leads to change in coastal environments. The role of the atmosphere in coastlines is much greater than this, however. The atmosphere produces precipitation, which in turn leads to weathering of nearby rocks. Together with the force of gravity, this force produces and delivers sediments that are then available to be rebuilt into beaches, deltas and continental shelves in the coastal zone.

Atmospheric processes shape the land's surface by reworking marine sediments and chemicals in areas well above the reach of the waves and tides. The wind provides energy to blow beach sand inland to form dunes. In tropical areas, temperature influences the growth of coral and algal organisms that produce the coral reefs on many tropical coasts. Temperature also affects plants (such as mangroves and salt marsh plants) and animals of the inter-tidal zone in the mid-latitudes. Atmospheric forces also play a role in the polar latitudes; when the sea temperature falls below −4°C the water freezes, forming sea ice that stops most activity on the coast.

Biological processes

The most important biological contribution to coastal landforms is the supply of calcium carbonate sediments from the skeletons and shells of marine organisms. This occurs especially in tropical and temperate regions of the world. In the tropics, reefs of coral and algae are important in influencing the development of the coast. In other areas, the plants and animals of the coastal dunes, rocky coasts and inter-tidal regions all contribute sediments. As a general rule, biological influences on the coast decrease towards the poles.

Chemical processes

Chemical processes tend to be related closely to weathering caused by atmospheric processes. Nonetheless, there are some additional and unique effects that are found in the coastal zone. Salt spray carried by the wind speeds up weathering and the breakdown of the coastal land surface. As the salt water evaporates, the dissolved salt forms crystals in small cracks and pores in the rock. As the crystals grow, they can cause the fracturing of the rock. Salt crystallisation often leads to a distinctive pattern of **honeycomb weathering** in coastal areas where evaporation rates are high (figure 6.38).

6.38 *Honeycomb weathering in the rocks at Barragoot Beach, Australia.*

In warm tropical waters in the inter-tidal zone of many beaches calcium carbonate is precipitated, cementing the sand grains together to form **beachrock**. In warm to hot semi-arid regions, calcium carbonate cements the grains of coastal sand dunes together to form **dune-rock** (see figure 6.39).

6.39 *This cliff at Robe (South Australia) is composed of dunerock made from limestone sand, with a resistant layer of capping rock. Undercutting by wave action has produced many boulders at the foot of the face of the cliff.*

Sea level changes

The earth's temperature has risen and fallen on many occasions over the past few million years. In general, these changes in temperature are just a few degrees Celsius. During the cooler periods, called **glacial periods**, much of the world's water is stored in glaciers and continental ice sheets, resulting in a lowering of world sea levels. During warmer periods, called **interglacials**, this trapped water is released once again into the world's oceans, causing a rise in sea levels.

6.40 *A section of the ice sheet off the south-western coast of Greenland.*

The changes in sea level resulting from these changes in temperature have been between 100 and 150 metres during the last two million years. At present the earth is relatively warm compared with past times, so the world's ice sheets are smaller than their average sizes, and sea level is also higher than average (figure 6.40). Indeed, at the end of the last great ice age only 18,000 years ago, the world sea level was about 125 metres below the present level. At that time, most of the world's shorelines lay near the edge of the continental shelves. The previous occasion when sea levels were as high as now was about 120,000 years ago.

The last ice age, called the **Pleistocene**, ended about 18,000 years ago. At that time the large ice sheets began to melt, causing oceans to rise to their present levels. This process took some time to complete, and the oceans continued rising until about 6,000 years ago. This post-glacial rise in sea level was called the **Holocene**, and because it was very recent in geologic time, almost all of today's coastal landforms are very young, being 6,000 years old or less. All the older coasts were submerged out on the continental shelf, except the old coastal features formed 120,000 years ago.

6.41 *Milford Sound, New Zealand — an example of a fjord.*

As the sea rose across the continental shelf between 6,000 and 18 000 years ago, it swept along with it many of the sand size sediments lying on the shelf, such as soils, river beds, old beaches and dunes. These sediments were reworked and moved inland with the rising waters, and eventually they were deposited along the present shoreline. As a result of the recent rise in sea level, the continental shelf has been a major source of coastal sediment. This is particularly so in areas with moderate to high waves, such as the southern half of Australia.

With the rise in sea level, many coastal valleys were drowned. This formed deep estuaries such as the **fjords** in the formerly glaciated valleys of Norway and New Zealand, and drowned river valleys (or **rias**) in temperate countries such as Australia (figures 6.41 and 6.42). Because the fjords and rias are very young in geological terms, the rivers which flow into them are still depositing their coarser materials (sand and gravel) in the upper reaches of the estuaries rather than at the coastline. At the same time as this is happening, waves and tides are pushing sediments up into the estuaries, and the sediments are lost to the coastal system. In this way, many coastal estuaries are acting as **sediment sinks**, trapping sediment that

would otherwise be available at the coast. This will continue until sediments fill the estuaries and the rivers can flow directly to the coast.

Not all sea level changes result from climatic change. Sometimes the land will rise or fall because of local tectonic pressures. Unless an area is compared with other areas, it is difficult to tell in the field whether it is the land or the sea that has changed height. If the land has risen relative to the sea, then **raised beaches** may result. These are relict features found at a level well above the zone where marine processes currently operate (figure 6.43). Changes in sea level are known as **eustatism**. Therefore, relative changes in the levels of the land and the sea caused by climatic change are often referred to as **glacioeustatic** changes.

6.42 *The shape of Port Hacking (foreground) and Sydney Harbour (background) show the typical shapes of rias, or drowned river valleys.*

6.43 *Although this raised beach at Rhossili (Wales) is now used for farmland, it provides evidence of a glacioeustatic rise in the land of this area.*

If natural cycles were to operate, we would expect the world's sea level to begin falling in the next few thousand years. However, changes in the atmosphere brought about by human activities such as pollution could upset this balance. If temperatures were to rise as a result of human impact on the atmosphere, and the Greenland

and Antarctic ice sheets both melted, sea level could rise by 70 metres, drowning all the world's ports and most coastal cities.

QUESTION BLOCK 6K

1. *How typical of the planet's history are the world's current sea levels?*

2. *Explain the causes of sea level change.*

3. *Describe the processes that form (a) honeycomb weathering, (b) raised beaches, (c) beachrock, and (d) rias.*

4. *What are the two main sources of coastal sediments? What role has sea level change played in creating them?*

Depositional Landforms

Depositional landforms cannot form unless three conditions are met. First, the inputs of sediment must exceed the losses. Second, the coastal processes must be operating to transport and deposit the sediment. Finally, the existing surface must be suitable to receive or mould the sediment. Of these three conditions, the coastal processes are probably the most important, and we will focus on these in this section. We will look first at beaches and dunes built by waves and wind, and then we will explore estuaries and deltas built by tides and rivers.

Beaches

A **beach** is the accumulated sediment deposited by waves on a coast. Where beaches occur at the head of a bay, they are known as **bayhead beaches**; if they occur on the side of a bay, they are known as **bayside beaches**. Beaches form when water moving onshore brings and deposits sediment. The water that moves up a beach after a wave has broken is known as **swash**, while **backwash** is the water returning to the sea from the beach.

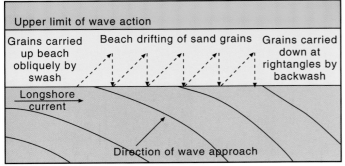

6.44 *The process of longshore drift.*

If the waves approach the beach at right angles to the shoreline (or **wave-sediment interface**), the backwash will return to the sea at the same place as the swash went up the beach. In this way, a grain of sand being moved by the water will be returned to its original position. On the other hand, if the waves hit the shoreline at an angle, then the swash will go up the beach at that same angle, but the

backwash will return along the steepest route, straight down the beach (figure 6.44). In this way, a grain of sand may be moved along the beach. This process, known as **longshore drift**, can go on for many years, during which time a significant amount of sediment can be moved along the beach in one direction. On some shorelines, longshore drift causes so much movement of sediments that barriers called **groynes** are erected to trap the moving sands (figure 6.45).

6.45 *Groynes, Botany Bay, Australia.*

Beaches usually consist of sand and/or gravel, although sometimes they are built of boulders, as in figure 6.46, in which case they are called **boulder beaches**. Boulder beaches are usually found in high-energy environments where all the sand-sized particles have been re-moved, leaving only the heavier boulders. They can also occur where the supply of sediment is restricted for some reason.

As we saw earlier when referring to figure 6.36, beaches form from sediment that lies just off the shoreline in an underwater reserve called an offshore bar. When beaches erode during storms, the sand is moved off the land and is stored in this offshore bar. When beaches build up during times of calm weather, sand from the offshore bar moves onto the beach.

6.46 *A boulder beach at Heimaey, Vestmannæyjar Island, Iceland.*

Most beaches are made up of two main sections. Beside the water is the **beach face**, which is the steeply sloping section against which the wave swash and backwash move up and down. The second part of the beach is the **berm**, which is nearly horizontal and consists of sediments deposited by the swash. As we shall see later in this section, some beaches have a third zone of dunes behind the berm.

Some other features are often found on beach faces and berms. One such feature is **cusps**. These are regularly spaced crescent-shaped 'horns' that are deposited on the beach face by wave action (figures 6.47 and 6.48). The spacing between the ridges, or **cusp horns**, is usually 15 to 30 metres, and each ridge is separated by a depression called a **cusp swale**. Sometimes, much larger cusps form with a spacing between 150 and 300 metres. These are a different type of feature, formed by deposition in the lee of crescentic bars, and they are called **megacusps** (see figure 6.36 earlier in the chapter).

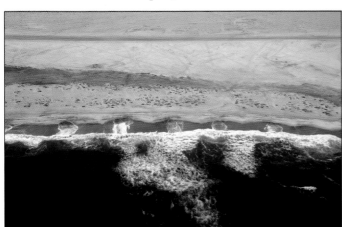

6.47 *Cusps forming on the beach face, Skeleton Coast, Namibia.*

Wave height is the main determinant of the shape of a beach. Low waves (one metre high) tend to form **low energy beaches**. This means that waves surge at the shoreline forming a small 'step', and then rush up the beach face and return as backwash. Often, the backwash is then reflected up onto the beach by incoming waves.

Low energy beaches are found in well protected bays and on open beaches after weeks of low waves (figure 6.49).

Where moderate waves occur (one to two and a half metres high), **medium energy beaches** form (figure 6.50). These have **rip currents** along them, which are formed by the return flow of water 'piled up' against the shore by incoming waves. Rips are seaward moving currents of water that transport sediments beyond the surf zone. In between rip currents, shallow bars extend into the sea. Rips are a constant danger to swimmers as they can drag people out to sea away from the safe and shallow area of the beach.

6.48 *Cusps along the steep beach face of Hahei Beach, on New Zealand's Coromandel Peninsula.*

6.49 *A low energy beach, Mombasa, Kenya.*

High energy beaches are produced by high waves (over two and a half metres). High energy beaches tend to have a steep beach face and a wide surf zone (figure 6.51). They have long channels and parallel offshore bars that form a reservoir of sand, which is available to move up onto the beach during a depositional sequence. This reserve of sediment begins to move onshore during calm conditions, although as shown in figure 6.36, the bar does not move forward in one continuous line – instead, 'fingers', or protrusions, of the offshore bar begin to move onshore. These fingers are more or less at right-angles to the shoreline, and they occur at intervals about 150 to 300 metres apart.

These fingers are termed **crescentic bars**, and they can be defined as ridges of sand more or less at right angles to the shoreline comprising the sediment moving from the offshore bar to the beach during a depositional sequence. As the crescentic bars attach to the shore, they become welded onto the beach. In this way, the beach moves from a high energy to medium energy state. The areas where the crescentic bars are moving onshore later become the megacusps, separated from each other by rip channels.

6.50 *A medium energy beach at Tathra, Australia.*

6.51 *A high energy beach made from the black sands of volcanic rocks, Reynisdrangur, near Vík, southern Iceland.*

When all the sediment in the offshore bar has moved up onto the beach, the beach will have become a low energy beach. Cusps may remain as a 'reminder' of where the bars moved onshore, and the beach face is very steep because of the large amount of sand stored there. Low energy beaches have either a very small offshore bar or none at all.

Coastal sand dunes

Coastal sand **dunes** are ridges of sand deposited by the wind, which lie on the inland (and leeward) side of beaches. Like offshore bars, they represent a store of sediment that is available to replenish the beach during erosional sequences. In reality, they are a capping on top of wave-built beaches.

6.52 *Spinifex grass stabilises these dunes at Wallagoot Beach, Australia.*

Three conditions are required for sand dunes to form. First, moderate to strong onshore winds are required. Second, there must be a supply of fine to medium beach sand, and third, vegetation is needed to trap and stabilise the sand (figure 6.52). In some cases dunes extend several kilometres inland and to heights of 100 metres or more.

The large dune nearest the sea is often called a **foredune**, while the dune furthest inland is often called the **hindune**. The **incipient foredune** is a small dune forming immediately behind the swash limit. Plants colonise the incipient foredune and stabilise the shifting sands. Because they are the first plants to grow on any particular dune, the first species to grow on a dune is called the primary stabilising species. These plants must be very hardy, being both salt tolerant (halophytic) and sand tolerant. Typical examples are marram grass (introduced in many countries) and spinifex (in Australia) (figure 6.52). Over time, more advanced species establish on the dunes, stabilising the dune and forming soil from the combination of decaying leaves and sand (figure 6.53).

6.53 *A stabilised dune with a range of vegetation species at Punta del Este, Uruguay.*

While ever the foredune remains stable, no beach sand will move further inland. However, on beaches which receive some high waves and strong onshore winds, waves occasionally erode and cut away the foredune. This leads to breaches in the sand dune, allowing sand from both the foredune and the beach to blow inland. These breaches are called **blowouts** (figure 6.54). If the onshore winds move the blowout inland beyond the hindune, it is called a **parabolic dune** because of its U shape. The curve of the U points in the direction of movement. On coastlines with strong winds and high waves, a series of parabolic dunes may join together into a sheet of unstable sand. Wind-blown sand will continue moving inland until stabilised, first by vegetation and later by soil-forming processes.

6.55 *Dee Why Lagoon (foreground) and the tombolo of Long Reef (background), in suburban Sydney, Australia.*

6.54 *A series of blowouts on a beach north of Coffin Bay (which is seen towards the background) on the western side of the Eyre Peninsula of South Australia.*

6.56 *The mid-bay barrier of Palm Beach joins the island of Barrenjoey to the mainland in Sydney's northern suburbs. In the background is the ria of Broken Bay.*

Coastal sand dunes form behind beaches that are stable or growing. If a beach continues to build out towards the sea, then a series of relict (abandoned) foredunes are left behind. These provide geographers with evidence of former shorelines. They occur in lines and are called **beach ridges**.

Barrier systems

Beaches, dunes and beach ridges are all parts of a large **barrier** system. Barriers are strips of sediments joining two headlands, or lining the head of a bay, or forming a strip across the mouth of a bay.

Depending on the surface of the coast, four types of barriers may occur. **Bayhead barriers** rest against the mainland, and are often called beaches. **Mid bay barriers** link two headlands and are backed by a lagoon (figure 6.55), or in some cases, the barrier joins an island to the mainland (figure 6.56). **Baymouth barriers** join the outer points of two headlands, and often form a lagoon as a consequence. Finally, **barrier islands** are long sandy islands that are parallel to the coast and lie seaward of it.

Depressions that are usually filled by a lagoon are found behind all types of barriers except bayhead barriers. Sometimes, these lagoons are difficult to see as they have become partly or wholly filled by sediments and marsh vegetation over time. Those lagoons that are not filled are often connected to the sea by an inlet (such as in figure 6.57). Lagoons exit into the ocean where the incoming waves offer the least resistance, such as at one end of a beach where it might be protected from the incoming waves by a headland or a rock platform.

6.57 *Lagoons, southern New South Wales near Nowra, Australia.*

When a barrier, or any strip of sediment, is only joined to land at one end, it is known as a **spit**. Spits may form as a result of longshore drift, or they can form behind offshore islands or reefs where wave refraction and lower wave energy cause the beach to build out seawards. If the spit advances to reach the island, a tombolo is formed.

Deltas

Deltas are deposits of alluvial material at the mouth of streams or rivers. They are made up of both land sediments and biological remains that are deposited where the river enters to sea, lake or lagoon. Several major world rivers have deltas at their mouths, and examples include the Nile, Mississippi, Irrawaddy and Mekong.

Deltas are named after the Greek letter delta (Δ), because the classic shape of a delta is triangular. However, deltas may form in many different shapes depending on how much sediment is available, the coastal processes and the shape of the coastal surface. As with beaches and barriers, it is the coastal processes that exert most influence.

Deltas with the classic shape most similar to the Greek letter delta are called **arcuate deltas**, and these have smooth shorelines and slightly protruding river mouths (figure 6.58). They occur where the waves have moderate energy and so can realign the river's sediments. The Nile and Niger Rivers in Africa have formed arcuate deltas.

6.58 This arcuate delta has formed on the south-west coastline of Greenland, near Narsarsuaq.

Birdsfoot deltas have quite a different shape, with highly extended channels and levees, often shaped like a bird's foot (figure 6.59). They form where the waves are of low energy, such as where a river flows into a calm lagoon or a bay. Large marshes and mud flats are usually found between the channels. The Mississippi delta in the United States is a classic example of a birdsfoot delta.

6.59 This small birdsfoot delta has formed in a coastal lagoon south of Nowra, on the south-east coast of Australia.

6.60 A cuspate delta in Narrabeen Lagoon, Sydney.

Streams flowing into coastal lagoons will sometimes form a similar feature called a **cuspate delta**, as in Narrabeen Lagoon in Sydney (figure 6.60). Cuspate deltas form when the waters of the stream enter the lagoon and the sediments carried by the stream are deposited. The velocity of the water is slowest near its edges, and so when the creek meets the still water of the lagoon, sediment is deposited at the edges first. Over time, the edges of the creek build out as spits of sediment into the lagoon.

QUESTION BLOCK 6L

1. What is meant by the terms 'swash' and 'backwash'?

2. With reference to figure 6.44, describe the process of longshore drift.

3. Explain why offshore bars are important in maintaining sand on beaches.

4. List in point form the main features you would look for in the field to recognise a high, medium or low energy beach.

5. How does sand move onshore? What do (a) rips and (b) cusps tell us about this movement?

6. Why are sand dunes important?

7. *Explain why the first plants to colonise incipient sand dunes are halophytic.*

8. *Draw sketch maps to show the four types of coastal barriers.*

9. *What causes a barrier to advance, recede or stay still?*

10. *What is a spit? How can a spit become a tombolo?*

11. *What is a delta? Sketch the three types mentioned.*

12. *Make a point form list of depositional coastal landforms.*

Erosional Landforms

Erosional landforms form when there is a net loss of sediment from a coastal system. Erosion may also result when the input of energy or water increases, such as during a period of storms. Sometimes the landforms eroded may be former depositional landforms, such as barriers and deltas, which are now losing sand. On other occasions, they may be formed by direct erosion of the coastal rock surface.

When depositional landforms begin to erode, there must have been a reversal in the inputs of sediment. Many forces could lead to this situation. A decline in the supply of sand from rivers could lead to erosion. Alternatively, less sand may be available from the continental shelf. Sand may have been lost to longshore drift, flood tide deltas in estuaries and coastal sand dunes. During very severe storms, sand may be removed out beyond the offshore bar and wave base. When this happens, it is 'lost' to the coastal system as it cannot be brought back by wave action.

A low energy beach, which has the sand from the offshore bar up on the beach, is easily eroded during heavy seas. As the wave height increases, small channels are eroded in the beach face which carry water and sediment offshore. In very heavy seas, the waves may erode a scarp in the beach face. As shown in figure 6.36 earlier in this chapter, erosion continues and the sand moves offshore in crescentic bars similar to those used when the sand moved onshore, except that they are much further apart (about 200 to 500 metres). Megacusps form, with rip channels between the horns marking where sand is being taken offshore. If the heavy seas continue long enough, a high energy beach will be formed with much of the beach sediment in the offshore bar.

Processes operating on rocky coasts

Rocky coasts usually contain steep sea **cliffs**. If a cliff has retreated landward, a **platform** extending seaward from its base will also be present (figure 6.61). The seaward edge of the platform marks the original seaward edge of the cliff. The level of the shore platform depends on the rock type and the exposure to wave attack, but it is usually somewhere between the low tide level and up to about 3 metres above sea level.

The processes that cause the cliffs to retreat are the most important processes on rocky coasts. These processes are both physical and chemical. Rocky coasts are exposed to all the normal weathering processes that occur in humid terrains, plus the effects of salt spray and wave attack. The marine forces acting on cliffs include the continual wetting and drying effects of spray, swash and tides, and the physical attack by waves and stones carried by waves.

6.61 *Cliff, Port Campbell, Australia.*

These processes reach maximum efficiency just above sea level when they act together. For this reason, the greatest degree of weathering occurs at a level immediately above the level of permanent saturation of the rock. Below this level, chemical weathering processes are restricted because of the lack of free oxygen. Above this level of saturation, however, chemical weathering is accelerated greatly by the continual wetting and drying and the action of salt spray.

So, a zone of rapid weathering occurs just above the level of saturation on many rocky coastlines. In this zone, the weakened rock fragments are then easily removed (eroded) by wave attack. As the cliff is eroded and undercut, rocks fall and slide downwards to the cliff base or platform, where it collects as **talus** or **scree**. Talus (also known as scree) is the build up of rock debris at the foot of a cliff. During storm times when wave energy is greatest, the talus may later be removed by wave action.

Wave quarrying is a specific process that acts on rocky coasts. This involves the physical removal of rocks from the cliff face or platform by direct hydraulic action, usually by waves quarrying out the rocks along joint or bedding lines. Rocks weighing several tonnes can be removed in this manner, and it is the main form of erosion of the seaward edge of the platform. It is particularly common in the jointed and layered rocks such as sandstones and shales.

Abrasion is the wearing away of the rock surface by rocks and sediments carried in waves. The rocks and sediments carried in the waves are called toolstones. They are rolled and dragged across the surface, physically abrading (wearing away) themselves and the surface. This leads to a rounding of the toolstones and smoothing and polishing the rock surface. A special form of abrasion can lead to the formation of **potholes**. Potholes are eroded by rocks that abrade downwards, and often outwards, to form steep-sided depressions in the surface of the rock platform. When abrasion combines with salt crystallisation, differential weathering can occur leading to strangely shaped formations, such as the **pedestal rocks** shown in figure 6.62.

6.62 *Pedestal rocks formed in sandstone at Yehliu on the northern coast of Taiwan. Wave quarrying has broken up the sandstone along joint lines, and salt crystallisation has caused honeycomb weathering. Abrasion has eroded the base of the resistant pillars of rocks, causing the pedestal formations.*

Organisms that inhabit the intertidal zone have a mixed impact on rocky coastlines. On one hand, their presence provides protection against abrasion and drying out. On the other hand, they may also erode the rock surface by their own actions. Boring organisms and those that graze on the rock surface can produce local but severe erosion. Sea urchins are very effective in eroding soft rock layers underwater.

Biological processes become increasingly important in the warmer waters that are found towards the equator. In cold climates, on the other hand, sub-zero temperatures cause water to freeze in the rock joints, producing frost wedging and eventual shattering of the rock surface.

Landforms of rocky coasts

Large-scale features on rocky coasts include the sea cliff and shore platform, as described in the previous section and shown. In certain rocks that are soft or which have lines of weakness, the cliff may be stranded seaward to form **sea stacks** (figure 6.63). An earlier stage in the formation of stacks is when they remain connected to the mainland or to each other, but are being undermined by sea caves linking together. This stage produces a landform called the **sea arch** (figure 6.64). If arches, stacks or cliffs are undermined, such as occurs by wave quarrying

along a joint of line of weakness in the rock, a **blowhole** may form (figure 6.65).

6.63 *The Twelve Apostles, a collection of stacks near Port Campbell, Australia.*

6.64 *Sea arch, Port Campbell, Australia.*

6.65 *A blowhole erupting at Muriwai, New Zealand.*

Cliffs often possess ledges, which are layers of rocks that are more resistant to weathering. Often the top of the cliff will consist of a resistant layer of rock that protects the cliff from erosion from above. Where this occurs, the vertical shape of the cliff is maintained by wave action undercutting the rocks above (seen earlier in this chapter in figure 6.39). If the base is eroding rapidly, a notch may be cut into the base, which may lead to further undercutting and undermining of the cliff. Many 'notches' coincide with weaker bands of rock, and are not at wave level.

Platforms sometimes rise towards their seawards edge where a **rampart** (a raised 'lip') is found. The rampart occurs because that part of the platform is more saturated than other parts of the platform due to the constant wave wetting. For this reason, the edge of the platform is not subject to the continual wetting and drying that accelerates weathering.

Several factors work together to encourage the development of **shore platforms**, including:
- warm to temperate climates which encourage wetting and drying;
- moderate to high wave energy to remove cliff debris;
- a small tidal range to concentrate the level of saturation and erosion;
- sedimentary and metamorphic rocks (or basalt), as these are porous and permit saturation and rapid chemical weathering; and
- horizontally bedded rocks with heavy jointing.

In general, platforms do not form on granites and other massive rocks, especially when they are in protected areas of low wave energy.

QUESTION BLOCK 6M

1. What factors lead to coastal erosion?

2. What could cause the supply of sediment on a coast to decline?

3. Referring to figure 6.36, describe the stages in the erosion of a beach due to high waves.

4. What does the presence of a shore platform tell you about the cliff next to it?

5. At what height is weathering concentrated on the coast? Explain why this is so.

6. What is the difference between the processes of wave quarrying and abrasion?

7. Describe the stages in the erosion of a cliff to form a sea stack.

8. Explain the reasons for the different shapes of the cliffs shown in figures 6.39 and 6.61.

9. List the factors that assist formation of shore platforms.

10. Make a point form list of erosional landforms.

11. Select one photograph from this chapter that shows several coastal landforms. Draw a full page photosketch of the photograph, labelling the significant coastal features of the

area shown. Choose two of these features and explain their formation.

12. 'All landforms are the result of erosion and deposition.' Discuss this statement with reference to coastal landforms.

13. Name and locate a coastal terrain you have studied in the field. With reference to three landforms, discuss the processes operating in the area.

Management Strategies

People are attracted to coasts, both to live and for recreation. Population densities in coastal areas are therefore often high, and this can place stress on coastal environments. Residential development, tourism, recreation, manufacturing and ports are among the functions that are attracted to coastal areas. Where these uses are incompatible in an area, **land-use conflict** is said to occur.

Coastal erosion has important implications for land use planning. In recent decades, people's preference to live near the sea has often meant that houses (and even high-rise home units) have been built on the foredune area of many beaches (figure 6.66). As discussed earlier in this chapter, dunes represent a reservoir of sand for the beach in times of wave attack. Houses and buildings built on dunes are therefore at risk during heavy seas. Every year, houses in various countries around the world are lost when heavy seas erode their dune foundations.

6.66 *Urban development along the beach front at Surfers Paradise on Australia's Gold Coast.*

In some areas, walls (revetments) are built at the back of the berm to protect structures behind the beach. In general, this does help to stabilise the buildings on the dune, but it means that storm waves passing over the beach do not have their energy absorbed by the dunes at the back of the beach as would happen on a 'natural' beach. Rather, the waves reflect off walls that are built too far seaward in the active beach, and therefore impose a double dose of wave energy across the beach. In this way, walls built at the backs of beaches may lead to even more erosion of the beach, sometimes to the extent that **beach**

nourishment is needed (figure 6.67). This involves supplying sand to beaches to compensate for natural erosion.

Usually the beaches that are nourished are those with high economic value, such as for tourism. Beach nourishment may also be used on beaches that are losing sand due to longshore drift if the cost of beach nourishment is less than the perceived loss of income from tourism. Longshore drift also poses problems in inhabited areas where the mouth of streams and coastal inlets can become blocked by the shifting sand. In such places, the construction of groynes and breakwaters is often used to avoid siltation (figure 6.68)

6.69 *Motor vehicles on the beach front, North Carolina, USA.*

6.67 *Beach nourishment, Miami Beach, Australia.*

6.68 *These breakwaters at Glenelg, a suburb of Adelaide (Australia) prevent siltation of the mouth of the stream where it enters the ocean.*

6.70 *Two examples of timber walkways with fences that have been built across the dune zone on this beach at Punta del Este (Uruguay) to protect the vegetation which is stabilising the dunes.*

Excessive use of beaches by people can cause erosion and a loss of sand. This can occur when people drive on beaches, as happens in some countries (figure 6.69). Erosion of sand dunes can be a significant problem when people walk across them. People's footsteps can destabilise the sand and destroy the vegetation that binds the sand together, leading to wind-blown erosion. This problem can be managed with the construction of fences to concentrate the human traffic, or the more expensive construction of elevated walkways over the top of the dune, provided people stay within the areas allotted (figure 6.70).

Because of the popularity of coastal areas as a place to live, waterfront views command premium prices on the property markets in many countries. One response to this by land developers has been to create **canal estates**, dredging networks of canals in low-lying swampy coastal areas to increase the proportion of properties with waterfront views (figure 6.71). The properties created are often very expensive, and represent a major re-working of the natural coastal environment. Because they are only just above sea level, such properties may be prone to flooding, especially if they are developed within reach of the tidal zone.

6.71 *A canal estate, near Surfers Paradise, Australia.*

QUESTION BLOCK 6N

1. *Outline the uses people make of the coastal margins. Explain how some of these uses conflict with each other.*

2. *Discuss how an understanding of coastal landforms can promote wise use of the coasts. Illustrate your answer with specific examples.*

Coastal Hazards

Coastal areas are especially vulnerable to various types of hazards. Many people are attracted to coasts as attractive and comfortable places to live. As a result of this, large numbers of people and their property are exposed to any hazard that arises.

The job of coastal resource managers is to assess the risk along the coast and make decisions about how people will cope during a possible future disastrous event. Sustainable development requires a dynamic balance of the human, social, economic and political systems within an area, allowing opportunities for growth while maintaining quality of life, water, and air, and at the same time protecting the natural and built environments. Although some coastal hazards cannot be prevented, hazard mitigation can improve the resilience of people and property.

Hazard mitigation is defined as sustained action that reduces or eliminates long-term risk to people and property from natural hazards and their effects. Hazard mitigation is important from an economic viewpoint to minimise property losses and large insurance claims. Of course, the cost in human lives can be even greater, and so it is important to protect the safety of the population and sustain the environment of coastal environments.

6.72 *The coastal change hazard scale.*

Coastal changes such as erosion of beaches, dunes and sea-cliffs, pose significant hazards to buildings and infrastructure that are built too close to vulnerable shorelines. The cost to society, in both money spent and lives lost, can be staggering.

Coastal planners must be able to predict where and how much coastal change will occur in order to locate new construction where it will be safe from coastal hazards. To be able to make accurate predictions, planners must take into account factors such as the climate of the area, the frequency of events such as tsunamis and tropical cyclones (known as typhoons in Asia and hurricanes in North America), the resilience of local landforms such as beaches, dunes and barriers, and the human land uses of the coastal zone.

The impact of a storm on a beach or barrier island depends not only on the strength of the wind and the size of the storm surge and waves, but also on the shape of the beach face. This is especially important when the beach is in the form of a barrier island, as these are especially vulnerable to wave attack during storms. By considering the size (both height and length) of the approaching waves, and the highest reach of the waves on the beach, it is possible to classify the storm hazard according to **four levels of impact**, as shown in figure 6.72.

At impact level 1, waves affect the beach face through the alternating movement of swash and backwash. Overall, there is no (or minimal) net change to the beach. When storms occur, presuming wave action is confined to the beach face, the beach will usually erode and the sand will be stored offshore (as shown earlier in figure 6.36). However, during a period of several weeks to a few months after the storm, the sand will return naturally to the beach, restoring the beach to its original condition.

More severe erosion begins to occur if wave action exceeds the elevation of the base of the dune. In this situation, the swash will collide with the dune causing erosion and dune retreat. Unlike the temporary changes of impact level 1, this change is considered a net, or semi-permanent (and maybe even permanent) change to the dune, and is shown as impact level 2 in figure 6.72.

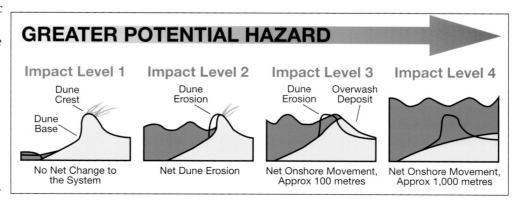

If wave action is even higher and exceeds the elevation of the dune, or in the absence of a dune, the beach system will be covered by the incoming waves, transporting sand landward on a large scale. This is shown as impact level 3 in figure 6.72, and leads to the migration of the barrier island landward, usually to a distance of about 100 metres.

If the storm surge is still higher and the elevation of the beach or barrier island is low, the barrier can become completely covered by the ocean water (see impact level 4 in figure 6.72). This is usually a major disaster, and sand is transported inland to distances of about one kilometre.

6.74 *Driving on the sand dunes, Bodie Island, North Carolina, USA.*

Case Study of Coastal Management Strategies — North Carolina

North Carolina is a state on the eastern coast of the USA. Situated south of Virginia and north of South Carolina, the length of the state's coastline is 484 kilometres. Because of the area's relatively warm climate and low costs, large numbers of families have been attracted to move into the coastal strip. Many of the in-migrants have built large houses, often right near the beach front (figure 6.73).

6.75 *Cars parked on the foredune of the beach, Bodie Island, North Carolina, USA.*

6.73 *Beach front residential development, Rodanthe, North Carolina, USA.*

6.76 *Boardwalks have been erected on some beaches in North Carolina to reduce the impact of trampling.*

The region's beaches also attract large numbers of tourists. This can place particular pressure on the stability of the beaches and dunes as many of visitors prefer to drive all the way to the water's edge rather than walk over the dunes (figures 6.74 and 6.75). Dunes are very vulnerable to disturbances such as car tyres, and this makes the dunes less resistant to wave action during times of storms. In an effort to protect the dunes, elevated wooden pathways have been built across the dunes in many parts of North Carolina, often connecting car parks in an effort to discourage driving onto the beaches (figure 6.76).

The shape of the coastline is such that it protrudes into the Atlantic Ocean, and this makes it especially vulnerable to frequent **hurricanes** (also known as tropical cyclones, or typhoons). Frequent storm damage has led to a long-term trend of **coastal erosion** along the North Carolina coast, and on average, the North Carolina coast recedes about one metre per year with an average annual loss of about 5 square kilometres of land.

Because this strip of coastline has been experiencing high levels of erosion for many years, and yet is located in a fairly affluent country where funds are available to invest in well researched coastal management strategies, it is a particularly good example of how different approaches can be used to manage a stretch of coast.

6.77 *Bodie Island, North Carolina, USA.*

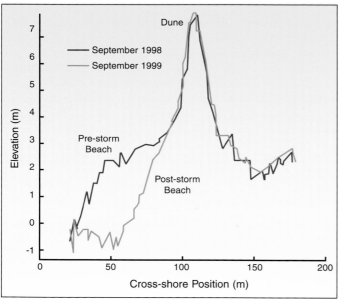

6.78 *The cross-section profile of the beach shown in figure 6.77, showing the impact of Hurricane Dennis in 1999. The seaward edge of the beach is at the left of the profile.*

Each hurricane affects different sections of the coastline in various ways. For example, in the area shown in figure 6.77 at Bodie Island, a sandy barrier on the North Carolina coastline, wave action from a recent hurricane was confined to the beach, even during the storm. As a consequence, the beach was eroded but the dune remained untouched. Most of the eroded sand returned to the beach over the following weeks and months, although when the photo in figure 6.77 was taken, evidence of beach erosion could still be seen. Figure 6.78 shows the 'before' and 'after' profile of the same beach as a result of one tropical cyclone, Hurricane Dennis in 1999. This diagram shows that the severe impact was confined to the beach, leaving

the dunes untouched. In this case, the effects of the storm were restricted to impact level 1 in figure 6.72.

More severe erosion from the same storm occurred a little further south on Bodie Island where the angle of the coastline made it more exposed to the waves generated by the hurricane. At Bodie Island, the swash reached the dune zone and removed most of the dune sand. This was an example of impact level 2 erosion, and can be seen in figure 6.79.

6.79 *Level 2 erosion at Bodie Island.*

Impact level 3 erosion occurred at Cape Hatteras, a very exposed sandy headland south of Bodie Island. At Cape Hatteras, the incoming waves were so high in energy that they completely destroyed the dune zone, flattening and moving the sand landward by about 100 metres (figure 6.80).

6.80 *Level 3 erosion at Cape Hatteras, North Carolina, USA.*

Hurricane Dennis, mentioned above, was not the strongest hurricane to affect North Carolina in recent years. Hurricanes are categorised according to their strength. One common system for measuring their strength is the Saffir-Simpson Hurricane Scale, the details of which are shown in table 6.2. On the Saffir-Simpson scale, Hurricane Dennis was a force 2 hurricane. As table 6.3 shows, it was certainly not an unusual event in the context of North Carolina.

Table 6.2
The Saffir-Simpson Scale of Hurricane Intensity

Category	Air Pressure	Wind Speed	Storm Surge	Damage Potential
1 (Weak)	980 millibars or more	120 to 150 km/hour	1.2 to 1.5 metres	Minimal damage to vegetation
2 (Moderate)	965 to 979 millibars	151 to 175 km/hour	1.5 to 2.4 metres	Moderate damage to houses
3 (Strong)	945 to 964 millibars	176 to 210 km/hour	2.4 to 3.7 metres	Extensive damage to small buildings
4 (Very Strong)	920 to 944 millibars	211 to 250 km/hour	3.7 to 5.5 metres	Extreme structural damage
5 (Devastating)	Less than 920 millibars	More than 250 km/hour	More than 5.5 metres	Catastrophic building failures possible

Table 6.3
Numbers of hurricanes that made landfall in North Carolina or severely affected the State, 1850 to 2009

	Force 1	Force 2	Force 3	Force 4	Force 5
1850 - 1859	1	3	4	-	-
1860 - 1869	5	3	-	-	-
1870 - 1879	7	2	5	-	-
1880 - 1889	7	9	8	2	-
1890 - 1899	2	3	4	1	-
1900 - 1909	9	2	-	-	-
1910 - 1919	3	3	-	2	-
1920 - 1929	4	2	-	3	1
1930 - 1939	2	1	3	2	1
1940 - 1949	4	1	2	4	-
1950 - 1959	2	4	5	4	-
1960 - 1969	4	2	2	2	2
1970 - 1979	6	1	2	1	2
1980 - 1989	6	-	1	2	1
1990 - 1999	4	3	5	1	1
2000 - 2009	7	2	2	2	2

Source: State Climate Office of North Carolina

6.81 *Many houses are built dangerously close to the surf zone at Rodanthe, North Carolina, USA.*

6.82 *The wooden pillars beside the house show the location of another building that was destroyed during storm erosion. The house that is visible was rebuilt in the same location after the storm that destroyed both houses.*

As a result of long-term coastal erosion in North Carolina, there has been large-scale loss of buildings along the coastline. Houses in the coastal areas are especially vulnerable to coastal erosion because loose building regulations have allowed many of them to be built very close to the ocean, in some cases on the dunes and even on the seaward side of the dunes (figure 6.81). There have been many examples of houses that were destroyed by waves and then re-built in the same locations (figure 6.82).

In response to the threat of erosion, coastal management strategies can help to protect people and property against more common coastal erosion. Most management strategies have attempted either to divert wind or wave energy away from the beach, or else to absorb the energy when it arrives at the beach. Devices used to achieve these goals may be placed on the beach itself, or in the water near the beach.

Two types of device that have been placed in the water near beaches are breakwaters and artificial seaweed. **Breakwaters** are structures that are built offshore parallel to the shoreline, either submerged or floating. They dissipate wave energy by forcing waves to break before they reach the shoreline, creating a 'wave shadow' causing a loss of wave energy and deposition of sand. However, problems have arisen when breakwaters have been constructed. Wave action may cause scouring (erosion) near the breakwater, they may cause downdrift erosion by removing sediment from incoming waves, they can reduce water quality by impeding natural patterns of circulation, and they may endanger swimmers or boaters.

Artificial seaweed consists of low-lying devices made from materials such as plastic, wire, concrete or old tyres, that are anchored to the sea floor. They are designed to slow down incoming waves and reduce energy, causing the waves to drop any sand that they are carrying. They are also designed to slow down the waves returning to the sea from the beach, causing sand that is being removed from the beach to be deposited close to the shoreline. Problems with these devices have been that they can be hazardous to swimmers and boaters when they are placed in shallow water. Furthermore, many examples lack the mass or design to remain anchored to the sea floor during storms and therefore they can create debris on beaches when washed up during storms,.

6.83 *A groyne at Cape Hatteras, North Carolina, USA.*

Perhaps because they are easier and usually cheaper to install, devices placed on the beach are more commonly used than devices that are placed in the water. One common device is the groyne, as mentioned earlier in this chapter. **Groynes** are walls or fences that are built at right-angles to the shoreline, extending from the beach into the water, and they are designed to trap sediment that is moving along the shoreline (longshore drift). Groynes have been installed at several points on the North Carolina coastline, including the exposed beaches near Cape Hatteras (figure 6.83). Although they are generally successful in slowing or stopping longshore drift, they can cause erosion of downdrift beaches as they become starved of sediment, they may create hazardous

rip currents, and they are a nuisance to recreational beach use.

An 'engineering' response to the problem of coastal erosion that has been used in North Carolina is **dewatering**. In the process of dewatering, a drain and pump system extracts water from the saturated zone beneath the sand, allowing more percolation of incoming waves. When water percolates through the sand, the sand being carried by the incoming wave is deposited on the surface, causing the beach to receive additional supplies of sand that would normally have simply returned to the sea with the backwash. The water that is pumped out from under the beach is either piped out to the ocean or, if it is fresh water, collected as a resource. Three main problems have been identified with dewatering. First, dewatering must be turned off during the nesting season of animals such as turtles because it affects the temperature of the sand (figure 6.84). Second, the system does not seem to withstand the additional pressure of waves during storm times. Finally, swimming must be banned in front of the extraction pipes because of the possible hazard.

6.84 *Efforts are made to protect breeding grounds on some beaches in North Carolina.*

One response to the erosion of natural dunes in North c Carolina has been to replace them with **artificial dunes**. This is a form of **beach nourishment** where sand is brought from elsewhere, usually a place where the beach has less economic value as an attraction to tourists, and dumped on the beach that has lost sand due to erosion. Often, the artificial dunes have an unnatural appearance, but they nonetheless provide protection for beach dwellings, until the next storm anyway (figures 6.85 and 6.86).

Dune stabilisation is a technique used in many parts of the world, and it has become important in North Carolina. This is achieved in various ways, such as placing low lying barriers on the beach to prevent erosion, planting grass to trap wind and thus stabilise the dune, or covering the dune with some protective layer such as cutdown tree branches, spray-gel, rock-filled mattresses, old tyres or polymer yarn (figure 6.87). Shortcomings of these devices are few, although it should be noted that walls and fences only protect the land on the leeward side of the structure and offer no protection to the area of the beach in front of it. Furthermore, dune stabilisation may lead to passive erosion in that sand is trapped by the device, and the beach is therefore unable to respond to a rising sea level be retreating.

6.85 *Artificial dunes, North Carolina, USA.*

6.86 *Artificial dunes have been built in an effort to protect houses on this heavily eroded beach in North Carolina, USA.*

6.87 *An elevated footbridge has been erected above this sand dune, which has been re-vegetated in an effort to stabilise it and protect it from erosion.*

Following the loss of several homes to storm damage in the late 1990s and early 2000s, the North Carolina Department of the Environment and Natural Resources es-

tablished stricter guidelines for the location of new buildings. The Department's Division of Coastal Management has produced maps showing the rate of coastal retreat for each local area. Based on this information, residents are now required to construct new buildings at certain distances back from the sea, the precise distance depending on local circumstances. The Division defines an **erosion setback line**, which is the closest distance that a house can be built to the shoreline. The erosion setback line is measured inland starting at the first line of stable, natural vegetation. The minimum erosion setback line is now set at 18 metres, and within that limit is calculated by multiplying the average annual erosion rate (in metres per year) by 30. Therefore, in areas which are experiencing the average rate of coastal retreat (one metre per year), then any new building would need to be at least 30 metres inland from the first line of stable, natural vegetation found on the dunes nearby.

QUESTION BLOCK 6O

1. *Describe the pressures placed upon North Carolina's beaches by tourists.*

2. *Why is North Carolina vulnerable to hurricanes?*

3. *List the management strategies that have been used on North Carolina's beaches in your opinion of their descending order of effectiveness. Then explain why you ranked the management strategies in the order that you did.*

Coral Reefs and Mangroves

Development of Coral Reefs

Although they are as hard as rock, corals are a type of living organism, built when organisms called **polyps** secrete calcium carbonate skeletons.

Although all **coral reefs** are found in the warm waters of the tropics, there are three different types with different shapes that reflect the different ways in which they were formed (figure 6.88).

Fringing reefs form in areas where free-floating coral larvae attach themselves to the shallow, rocky seabed surrounding a tropical island. As a living organism, coral needs an abundant amount of sunlight, which is why fringing reefs grow best in shallow, clear water. Fringing reefs are the most common type of reef in the Caribbean Sea and parts of Hawaii and Micronesia (figure 6.89).

Unlike fringing reefs, which may come right to the shoreline, **barrier reefs** form in a line roughly parallel to the shoreline but separated from it by a shallow lagoon. Barrier reefs often start as fringing reefs, but as the land sinks the coral grows upwards to maintain growth within the shallow water than sunlight can penetrate. The Great Barrier Reef on the north-east coast of Australia is an

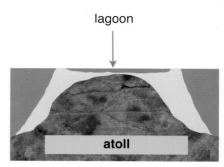

lagoons

lagoon

fringing reefs

barrier reefs

atoll

6.88 *Types of coral reefs.*

example of a very large barrier reef, being about 2000 kilometres in length (figure 6.90).

The third type of reef is the **atoll**. Atolls start as fringing reefs which become barrier reefs around an island as it begins sinking. The corals keep growing upwards on the outside of the island, and when all the land of the original island has disappeared below sea level, a circular ring of coral with some sediment in the middle is all that remains. This is the atoll, and it represents the final stage of a sinking island. Atolls are quite common in the South Pacific where old volcanic islands have sunk into the ocean (figure 6.91). The largest atoll in the world, Kwajalein in the Marshall Islands, encircles an oval lagoon that is about 100 kilometres long.

6.90 *Barrier reef, Heron Island, Australia. (Photo: Jaroslav Pozdisovce)*

6.89 *Fringing reef, Micronesia. (Photo: Jaroslav Pozdisovce)*

6.91 *An atoll in the Tokelau Islands. (Photo: Jerilyn Potasi)*

Most of the coral reefs found in the world today are of quite recent origin in geological terms, having formed since the end of the last ice age during the past 10,000 years. As the ice age ended and the glaciers and ice caps melted, the world's oceans rose. As the water level rose, the coral had to grow upwards also to survive.

The rate of growth of a coral reef depends on many variables, including temperature, solar radiation, calcium carbonate saturation of the water, turbidity, sedimentation, salinity, acidity, nutrients, level of pollution — and the species of coral in the area. To give some idea of the differences in growth rates, the growth rate of Australia's

Great Barrier Reef is said to vary between 0.8 millimetres per year to 80 millimetres per year.

Because of their beauty and their location in warm, tropical areas, coral reefs are significant tourist attractions. This gives reefs a high economic value, and the net worth of coral reefs is currently estimated at about US$30 billion each year. Expressed in another way, the United National Environment Program (UNEP) estimates the value of coral reefs to be somewhere between US$100,000 and US$600,000 per square kilometre per annum. Most of this value is generated from nature-based tourism such as scuba diving and snorkelling. On the other hand, the

UNEP estimates that the annual cost of protecting coral reefs (mainly management costs of marine protected areas) is just US$775 per square kilometre.

In addition to their value for tourism, coral reefs provide a variety of benefits, some of which are easier to measure than others. For example, reefs help reduce beach erosion by absorbing much of the energy of incoming waves. It has been estimated that each one square kilometre of coral reefs reduces coastal erosion erosion in Sri Lanka by 2,000 cubic metres each year. Furthermore, coral reefs help fishing by providing breeding grounds. According to the World Resources Institute (WRI), properly managed coral reefs can yield an average of 15 tonnes of fish and other seafood per square kilometre each year, and coral reef fisheries in South-east Asia are estimated to yield US$ 2.4 billion annually.

Development of Mangrove Swamps

Mangroves are a type of tree that grows in muddy, chiefly tropical coastal swamps that are exposed at low tide but flooded at high tide. Mangroves usually have a mass of tangled roots above ground and they form dense thickets. Because they need to survive in oxygen-starved (anaerobic) environments, they use aerial roots known as **pneumataphores** to survive (figure 6.92). Because they are difficult to penetrate and often have a foul smell (caused by the anaerobic conditions), mangrove swamps used to be considered as an undesirable waste of space and they were often cleared away. Today, we understand the value of the mangrove swamps more clearly.

Mangroves play an important part in stabilising tidal flats by slowing the movement of water around their roots. This causes the sediment in the water to be deposited, providing a foundation for **halophytic** (salt-tolerant) plants to establish themselves. In this way, mangroves serve as the pioneer vegetation community in many tropical estuaries, helping mud flats to form that can then support other types of vegetation, causing more deposition to occur, which leads to the expansion of the mud flats, and so the process continues.

Mangroves form best in calm, sheltered waters where there is little wave action. Because their extensive root systems are very efficient in **dissipating wave energy**, mangroves serve a useful role in protecting coastal areas from erosion, including extreme events such as surge storms and tsunamis. For this reason, mangroves are increasingly seen as an important element in conservation programs, especially where biodiversity is being encouraged.

On the other hand, it is important not to over-estimate the importance of mangrove swamps. Wave energy is usually low in areas where mangroves grow, so their effect on limiting erosion is really limited to extreme events such as tsunamis (tropical cyclones). In the aftermath of the large tsunami in the Indian Ocean in December 2004, it was found that coastlines protected by mangrove swamps were less damaged than areas without protective vegetation, and if the density of mangroves was at least 30 trees per 100 square metres then the maximum flow of the tsunami was reduced by about 90%.

6.92 *These mangroves are growing on an inter-tidal flat in Fannie Bay, Darwin (Australia). In this view, the flats are in the process of being covered by the waters of a rising tide. Because the mud flats are anaerobic (lack oxygen), the mangroves use the aerial roots (pneumataphores) to 'breathe'.*

For biologists, mangroves are seen to have special value because they support unique ecosystems, especially on a microscopic scale within their intricate root systems. Furthermore, the sheltered environment of the mangroves' root system provides **spawning grounds** and an attractive environment for many young marine organisms.

Mangroves provide other important biological functions such as the purification and **detoxification of wastes**. Some mangrove swamps have been found to reduce the concentration of nitrates in waste water by more than 80%.

Causes and Consequences of the Loss of Coral Reefs

Because of their slow rates of growth, coral reefs are vulnerable to damage and destruction. The World Resources Institute (WRI) estimates that 58% of the world's coral reefs are potentially threatened by human activity, and according to Seaweb (an online organisation that advocates better conservation of ocean environments), coral reefs are threatened in 93 of the 109 countries where they are found. According to Cesar Environmental Economics Consulting (a Dutch research organisation), the world has already lost 27% of its coral reefs, and if present rates of destruction continue, 60% of the world's coral reefs will be destroyed over the next 30 years.

One of the main threats to coral reefs comes from **coral bleaching,** which is the whitening of the coral polyp due to a reduction of photosynthetic pigment (figure 6.93). Bleaching occurs due to a change in the relationship between the coral polyp and microscopic algae known as **zooxanthellae**. Coral and zooxanthellae live in a **symbiotic relationship**, which means that each depends on the other for survival. The coral receives about 90% of its energy requirements from the zooxanthellae.

6.93 *Bleached coral. (Photo: NOAA)*

Bleaching occurs when the coral expels its zooxanthellae. As most of the colour of coral comes from the photosynthetic pigments of the zooxanthellae, the tissue of the coral animal becomes transparent when the zooxanthellae are expelled and the bright white skeleton of the coral is revealed, giving the reef a sickly white colour.

Bleaching is a sign of stress, and it can be caused by a variety of factors including changes in the ocean temperature, changes in the water chemistry (especially acidification), increasing sedimentation (especially from soil erosion), and dilution of the saline content by freshwater.

Acidification, the decrease in the pH of the Earth's oceans, is a consequence of **global climatic change**. Acidification occurs when the ocean surface absorbs carbon dioxide from the atmosphere. It has been estimated that from 1751 to 1994 the pH of the ocean's surface fell from approximately 8.179 to 8.104. However, current measures suggest that the current rate of pH decline is 100 times faster than the natural rate of decline.

When ice sheets in the Arctic and Antarctic collapse as a result of global warming, minerals and nutrients from eroded soil and bedrock are released into the sea that encourage the growth of photosynthetic plankton, which boost the absorption of carbon dioxide from the atmosphere. It is estimated that each year, Antarctic icebergs deposit 120,000 tonnes of iron into the Southern Ocean which promotes enough growth in plankton to sequester (absorb) 2.6 billion tonnes of carbon dioxide — the equivalent combined annual emissions of India and Japan. Although this has a positive effect in reducing the build-up of atmospheric carbon dioxide, it makes the problem of acidification of the oceans worse, and scientists warn that it may make most of the world's oceans inhospitable to coral reefs by 2050.

Once bleaching occurs, corals begin to starve. If conditions return to normal quickly, then the corals can regain their zooxanthellae, return to normal colour and survive. However, the stress of even short-term bleaching usually leads to decreased growth of coral and reduced reproduction as well as less resistance to disease. If the cause of the bleaching lasts more than ten weeks, it usually leads to the death of the coral.

Some of the causes of coral bleaching are natural. For example, strong winds, exposure at low tide and certain weather conditions can all cause bleaching. Annual bleaching of coral each summer is also a normal occurrence as increases in solar radiation affect the reef.

Another threat to coral reefs (that also causes bleaching) is **destructive fishing practices**, such the use of poisons. Some large-scale fishing operations deliberately try to reduce coral cover to make fishing easier or remove fish that are important elements in the food chain of the reef. In places where overfishing occurs, the food chain is disrupted and there is a decline in zooplankton, which in turn starves the coral.

Once bleaching begins, corals usually continue to bleach even if the stressor is removed. If the coral in a community survives the bleaching, it often takes weeks or months for the food web to re-establish itself, and it is fairly common for a bleaching to result in the colonisation of the reef by new species.

Many researchers argue that the greatest threat to coral reefs is global warming because corals are so vulnerable to small changes in ocean temperature. Temperature increases of only 1.5C° to 2C° for six to eight weeks are usually sufficient to trigger coral bleaching, and if those temperatures continue for more than eight weeks, the coral will almost certainly not survive. According to the IPCC

(Intergovernmental Panel on Climate Change) 2007 assessment, coral reefs will be highly vulnerable to increased and more frequent bleaching events as a result of global warming, and this negative impact will be magnified by the additional problem of acidification from increased carbon dioxide during the period leading to 2040.

According to some estimates, about half of the world's coral reefs will die within the next forty years from human causes unless significant measures are taken to save them from the impact of global warming. Mass bleaching has now been seen to affect every reef region in the world, and both the frequency and severity of bleaching events seem to be increasing. A very severe worldwide bleaching event that has not been fully explained occurred in 1998 in which about 16% of the world's coral reefs were destroyed. Australia's Great Barrier Reef was affected by this event as well as by other significant bleaching events in 2002 and 2006 (figure 6.94).

Causes and Consequences of the Loss of Mangrove Swamps

It is estimated that almost half of the world's mangroves have been destroyed by humans who, until recently, often regarded mangrove swamps as 'wastelands' or 'useless swamps'. Current estimates are that 15 million hectares of mangroves remain in the world, a significant loss from the original natural figure of 32 million hectares. According to the Food and Agricultural Organisation (FAO), about 150,000 hectares of mangroves are lost each year, representing an annual loss of 1%.

This destruction is not evenly distributed, however. Since 1960, Thailand has lost half of its mangroves, and the Philippines has lost almost 80% of its mangroves since the 1920s.

Mangroves are cleared for a variety of reasons, including commercial harvesting of their durable and water resistant wood, medicines, tea, livestock feed and charcoal production. All these uses destroy the mangroves. However, the United Nations Environment Program (UNEP) estimates that the biggest danger to mangrove swamps is clearance to make way for **shrimp aquaculture**. The UNEP estimates that about 25% of the destruction of mangrove forests comes from this cause alone.

However, this view is disputed by academic research in the 'Journal of Biogeography' which claims that the **expansion of agriculture** is the most significant cause of mangrove destruction. According to this research undertaken by the Chandragiri Science Application International Corporation (CSAIC), which analysed over 750 Landsat satellite images covering most tropical coastal parts of Asia, 81% of mangrove swamp destruction from 1975 to 2005 was the result of agricultural expansion. Shrimp aquaculture accounted for a further 12% while urban development accounted for another 2%.

Conservationists worry about the long-term consequences of this loss, especially with respect to the loss of habitat and breeding grounds that results.

6.94 *Undertaking monitoring of coral. (Photo: James Cook University ARC Centre of Excellence for Coral Reef Studies)*

QUESTION BLOCK 6P

1. *Explain how the formation of the three types of coral reefs is related.*

2. *What benefits do coral reefs bring to humans?*

3. *What benefits do mangroves bring to humans?*

4. *Explain the causes of coral bleaching and why it is a problem.*

5. *Compare the causes and consequences of of the loss of coral reefs and mangrove swamps.*

7

Extreme environments

Cold and high altitude environments (polar, glacial areas, periglacial areas, and high mountains), and hot arid environments (hot deserts and semi-arid areas).

Outline

Challenging environments
Page 272

The global distribution of extreme environments, and their relationship to population.

Physical characteristics of extreme environments
Page 282

Glacial, periglacial, and hot arid environments.

Opportunities and challenges for management Page 298
Agriculture, mineral extraction and tourism.

Sustainability
Page 318

The degree to which human activities in extreme environments are unsustainable, and the potential impact of global climatic change on indigenous people, settlements and economic activities.

ToK BoX — Page 282
Perception and Theories of Reality

Challenging Environments

Extreme Environments

In this chapter, two quite different extreme environments are examined. One type of extreme environment is **hot, arid environments**, which consist of the world's deserts and semi-deserts. The second type is **cold and high altitude environments**, which comprise a mix of polar, glacial and periglacial areas, together with the high mountains of non-tropical latitudes.

Although these two types of environments contrast with each other in many ways, they share the common characteristic of being inhospitable to human habitation as well as being relatively inaccessible. Nonetheless, people do live in these areas and they provide opportunities — as well as many challenges — for economic activity. For the geographer, the natural processes operating in these environments make an excellent study in contrasts.

Global Distribution of Cold and High Altitude Environments

A **mountain range** is a group or chain of mountains that are clustered together and thus form a continuous belt of elevated land. The world's longest mountain range is the Andes on the west coast of South America, which has a length of over 7000 kilometres. The highest mountain range in the world is the Himalayas, which contains the highest mountains in the world, including Mount Everest on the border of Nepal and China which has a summit altitude of 8,848 metres. The Himalayas have more than 30 peaks with summits higher than 7,600 metres.

The distribution of the world's mountain ranges is shown in figure 7.1. The pattern of the mountain ranges is closely related to the pattern of tectonic plates that is shown in figure 8.2 in chapter 8. As shown in figure 8.3 (also in the next chapter), mountains form where two converging plates of light sial material meet. The sial buckles upwards forming complex folded mountain

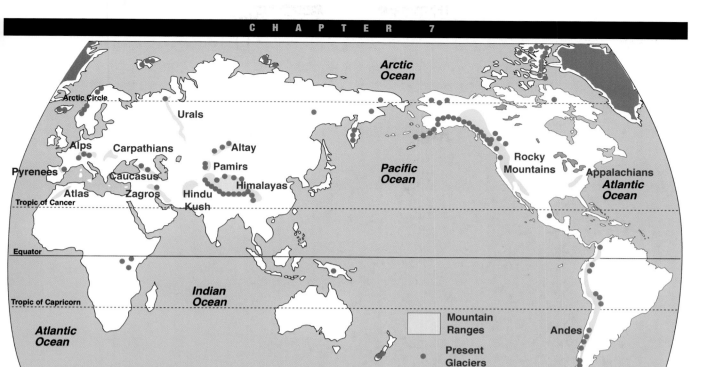

7.1 *The distribution of the world's mountain ranges and glaciers.*

chains that mark the approximate plate boundary. Older, lower mountain ranges may be remnants for former plate boundaries that are now inactive, or they may occur along lines of weakness called faults where the energy from moving plates is transferred.

Figure 7.1 also shows the locations of the world's **glacial areas**. A glacier is a slowly moving mass or river of ice formed by the accumulation and compaction of snow on mountains or near the poles. Although composed of solid ice, the glacier behaves like an extremely thick liquid, bending and flowing at a very slow rate under the influence of gravity. Areas that are shaped and influenced by glacial ice are known as glacial areas, and they tend to be found at high altitudes in non-tropical latitudes or at lower altitudes in high latitude (polar and sub-polar) regions. The areas adjacent to glaciers or ice sheets that experience repeated freezing and thawing are known as **periglacial areas**.

Why are Cold and High Altitude Environments Extreme?

In chapter 3, we saw that the amount of heat received at the earth's surface varies according to latitude. Figure 3.4 of chapter 3 shows that there is a net heat deficit from 38° north and south of the equator to the poles (90°).

To summarise the information detailed in chapter 3, there are three reasons that high latitudes (latitudes with high numbers) receive less heat from the sun than tropical areas. First, the sun's rays strike the earth's surface at a lower angle near the poles, meaning that an equivalent amount of solar energy is spread over a larger area in po-

lar areas than equatorial areas. Second, the sun's rays must penetrate a greater thickness of atmosphere near the poles than near the equator and therefore less heat reaches the surface. Third, a greater proportion of the heat that does reach the surface in polar areas is reflected back into space because the light shiny surfaces of the high latitudes, such as ice caps and snow, have a high **albedo** (reflectivity).

In mountain areas, the main factor causing differences in the landscape is **altitude**. The differences that are found globally from latitude 0° to 90° are mirrored by the differences we see rising from sea level to 9,000 metres elevation. In terms of geographical variations, the distance from the equator to the poles is the same as from sea level to the highest point in the world, even though the vertical distance is less than 10,000 metres.

This transition is particularly evident in Nepal, which is situated just north of the tropical zone, between latitudes of 26°N to 31°N. The southern part of Nepal, known as the Terai, is really part of the low flat plain of northern India, and with an altitude of only 60 to 300 metres, it experiences high temperatures and the seasonal wet-and-dry of a monsoonal climate. In contrast, the highest mountains in the world — the Himalayas — make up the northern fringe of Nepal. Because of their high altitude, many of the peaks of the Himalayas are permanently snow-capped, even though they lie close to the tropics.

Switzerland, on the other hand, is situated further from the equator, lying between the latitudes of 46°N and 48°N. Therefore, Switzerland has a cooler, more temperate climate than Nepal. This is shown in the comparative temperature figures given in table 7.1.

Extreme environments

Table 7.1

Average Temperatures in Selected Towns in Switzerland and Nepal

	SWITZERLAND						NEPAL					
Town	Geneva		Zürich		Saint Moritz		Biratnagar		Kathmandu		Jiri	
Altitude	375 metres		409 metres		1856 metres		72 metres		1336 metres		2003 metres	
	Min °C	Max °C	Min °C	Max °C	Min °C	Max °C	Min °C	Max °C	Min °C	Max °C	Min °C	Max °C
January	-2	4	-3	2	-16	-3	10	22	2	18	-3	13
February	-1	6	-2	5	-14	0	12	26	5	21	0	14
March	2	10	1	10	-10	4	14	26	10	25	3	20
April	5	15	4	15	-4	8	20	36	11	29	6	23
May	9	19	9	19	0	13	24	33	16	31	12	26
June	13	23	11	22	3	18	25	32	19	28	17	24
July	14	25	13	24	5	20	26	32	20	28	18	24
August	13	24	13	23	4	19	26	32	20	28	17	24
September	12	21	10	20	2	16	25	33	19	28	16	23
October	7	14	7	13	-2	10	21	31	14	26	10	22
November	3	8	2	7	-8	3	15	29	8	24	3	19
December	0	5	-1	3	-13	-3	10	26	3	21	-1	15

Both Nepal and Switzerland have a variety of altitude zones. In Nepal, there are three main landform regions:

a. The Terai region is the southern region, forming the border region with India. It comprises a long belt of alluvial plains, ranging in altitude from 60 to 300 metres. This belt is between 25 kilometres and 32 kilometres wide, and comprises 17% of Nepal's area.

b. The hilly region stretches across the middle of Nepal, and it ranges from 1,525 to 3,660 metres in altitude, making up 64% of the land area. This region contains some important rivers and valleys that support much of Nepal's population. Among the important valleys are Pokhara in the west, and Kathmandu, which contains Nepal's capital city.

c. Bordering China's province of Tibet in the north is the Himalayan region. This is the highest zone, and extends from 3,660 to 8,848 metres in altitude. There are 17 peaks higher than 8,000 metres, and over 240 snow peaks which are over 6,000 metres in altitude.

In Switzerland, the Alps comprise 60% of the country's area. The other 40% of Switzerland is also elevated, comprising another lower mountain range, the Jura Mountains, near the French border (10%) and the Central Plateau the remaining 30%. The Swiss Alps are not as high as the Himalayas, with the highest peak (Dufour Summit) being 4,634 metres. There are several peaks well over 3,000 metres in altitude, including the famous Matterhorn at 4,478 metres, Jungfrau (4,158 metres), Mönch (4,099 metres) and Eiger (3,970 metres).

QUESTION BLOCK 7A

1. *Explain the distribution of mountain ranges and glaciers shown in figure 7.1.*

2. *Plot the data shown in table 7.1 on a single sheet of graph paper. Then describe and explain the pattern shown.*

Altitude and the atmosphere

There is a direct relationship between altitude, air pressure and temperature. This is shown by the average figures in table 7.2. The tendency for the atmosphere to become cooler with increasing altitude is the reason that countries that are situated fairly close to the tropics may have many high mountains with summits that are permanently covered in snow. To a large extent, the fall in temperature with increasing altitude mirrors the fall in temperature with increasing latitude (figure 7.2).

QUESTION BLOCK 7B

1. *Plot the data in table 7.2 on two graphs, one showing the relationship between altitude and air pressure, and the other showing the relationship between altitude and temperature.*

2. *Is rainfall more likely in areas of high air pressure or low air pressure? Use this information to predict on which parts of mountains (the tops or the bottoms) rain is more likely to fall.*

Table 7.2
The Relationship between Altitude, Air Pressure and Temperature

Altitude (metres)	Air Pressure (kilopascals)	Temperature (°C)
-500	806.2	18.3
0	760.0	15.0
500	716.0	11.7
1000	674.1	8.5
1500	634.2	5.2
2000	596.2	2.0
2500	560.1	-1.2
3000	525.8	-4.5
3500	493.2	-7.8
4000	462.2	-11.0
4500	432.9	-14.2
5000	405.1	-17.5
5500	378.7	-20.8
6000	353.8	-24.0
6500	330.2	-27.3
7000	307.8	-30.5
7500	286.8	-33.7
8000	266.9	-37.0
8500	248.1	-40.3
9000	230.5	-43.5
9500	213.8	-46.7
10000	198.2	-50.3
10500	183.4	-53.3
11000	169.7	-55.0
11500	156.9	-55.0
12000	145.0	-55.0

Source: Panday (1995) p.375

Altitude affects more than just air pressure and temperature. As altitude increases, there are also decreases in air density, water vapour, carbon dioxide and impurities. With the fall in air pressure with altitude, the boiling point of water also decreases, and at the summit of Mount Everest (8,848 metres) water would boil at 72°C. On the other hand, increases in altitude bring increases in the intensity of ultra violet radiation, which is why sunburn is more likely at higher altitudes. Indeed, as a result of the reflected heat from the snow that can occur in the clear at high altitudes, temperatures of 80°C have been recorded in the Swiss Alps at 2,070 metres, the maximum ever recorded on the earth.

7.2 *Snow on the peaks of these mountains in the Eastern Himalayas shows the cooler temperatures at higher altitudes.*

7.3 *A typical house in Nepal, showing adaptation to the alpine climate. In Nepal, the houses are made from thick mud brick (adobe), which is an excellent insulator, and have small windows to contain heat loss. They are built on northern slopes to allow heating by the sun's rays.*

7.4 *In Switzerland, many houses are made from thick timber (a good insulator) and the roofs have spikes to reduce the risk of avalanches of snow from the roof.*

Extreme environments

At high altitudes, a greater proportion of sunlight reaches the earth's surface than is the case at lower altitudes because of the cleaner, clearer air at high altitudes. However, the heat that is then reflected from the ground cannot be retained very effectively in the thinner air, and therefore temperatures vary greatly in alpine areas according to whether the sun is shining or not at the time. This is the reason that houses in mountainous areas tend to be well insulated (figures 7.3 and 7.4).

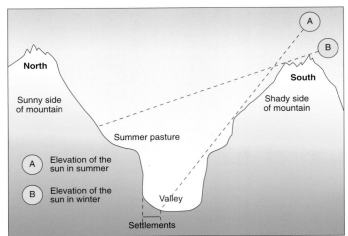

7.5 *The effect of aspect on a mountain valley in the northern hemisphere.*

7.6 *Hills on the edge of the Southern Alps of New Zealand, north of Invercargill, are covered with snow on the southern sides, whereas the snow on the northern aspect facing the sun has melted.*

Another factor that affects temperatures with altitude is slope aspect. In the northern hemisphere, where most of the world's high mountains are located, slopes which face towards the south (i.e. towards the equator) receive sunshine for longer intensive periods than slopes with a northern aspect (figures 7.5 and 7.6). A slope receiving direct sunlight will warm up very quickly, but will also cool quickly as soon as the sunlight disappears. Thus, slopes facing south receive more solar radiation and are exposed to the summer prevailing winds, rising air and

soil temperatures. As a result of this, there are significant differences in the vegetation and land uses found on the northern and southern slopes of alpine areas.

Because mountains change the circulation of air, mountain regions often have their own microclimates; for example windward slopes may receive heavy precipitation while leeward slopes remain almost desert-like.

Wind direction also changes with altitude, and isobars become almost parallel. Moreover, wind speed increases with altitude, sometimes creating gale force winds in one direction for hours or even days on end (figure 7.7). Exposed slope and summit winds are much stronger than those in the valleys, especially as there are much less friction between the air and the land surface at high altitudes. In general, winds blow up the slopes during the day as the sun warms the land creating areas of low pressure. At night, as the air cools, the winds reverse and blow down the slopes; this flowing downwards of cool air is known as katabatic wind.

7.7 *The strong winds blowing from left to right near the summit of this mountain in the Himalayas near Mount Everest are shown by the snow being blown from the tops of the arêtes.*

Altitude and the biosphere

Because altitude affects temperature, mountain areas show a vertical series of bands of vegetation. The precise height at which one type of vegetation ends and another begins varies from mountain to mountain, but the pattern on Mount Everest is shown in figure 7.8. This pattern arises because of a combination of two factors – altitude and aspect. The upper limit at which trees can grow is called the tree line. On the shaded (northern) side of Mount Everest, the tree line is lower than on the sunny side (about 4,000 metres). In Switzerland, the tree line is lower than this, often at about 1,500 to 1,800 metres because of the higher latitude and cooler temperatures. Similarly, the snow line (the lower altitude limit of permanent snow) is lower in Switzerland than in Nepal – 2,700 metres on the Matterhorn in Switzerland compared with 5,500 metres on the southern slope of Mount Everest in Nepal (and 3,600 metres on the northern slope).

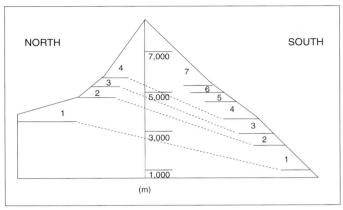

7.8 *Vertical zones of vegetation on Mount Everest. The zones are as follows:*

Northern Side	Zone	Southern Side
	7	Alpine névé (permanent snow) [above 5500 metres]
	6	Alpine frozen moraine lichens [5200 to 5500 metres]
	5	Alpine frozen meadow cushion plants [4700 to 5200 metres]
Alpine névé (permanent snow)	4	Sub-alpine cold bush meadow [3900 to 4700 metres]
Alpine frozen moraine lichens	3	Frigid-temperate mountain needle-leaf forest [3100 to 3900 metres]
Alpine frozen meadow	2	Warm temperate mountain needle-leaf and cushion vegetation broadleaf mixed forest [2500 to 3100 metres]
Alpine frigid semi-arid steppe	1	Sub-tropical mountain ever-green broadleaf forest [1600 to 2500 metres]

Because many alpine animals depend on vegetation for their food, the distribution of fauna is also arranged in altitude zones that parallel the vegetation zones. Animal species such as snow leopards, large cats, bears, eagles, wolves and bears are seldom seen in the lowlands where human habitation dominates the natural ecosystems. Furthermore, because of the hostility of highland climates, the number of species declines with increasing altitude. In Nepal, there are 600 different animal species recorded in the cloud forest zone of 2,000 to 2,800 metres altitude, but only 43 recorded species in the sub-alpine cold bush meadows above 4,200 metres. In the high altitudes, only birds of prey such as eagles, buzzards and falcons are found.

Cold-blooded reptiles cannot survive the cold temperatures of high altitudes. In the high altitude grasslands, some herbivorous animals with thick fur and coarse hair can be found, but they migrate down-slope during the winter months. In Nepal, for example, the highest dwelling mammals are yaks, which can adjust to altitudes as high as 6,100 metres.

7.9 *Mount Everest, looking towards Tibet to the north from the Nepalese side.*

QUESTION BLOCK 7C

1. *How would the diagram in figure 7.8 be different for a valley in the southern hemisphere?*

2. *Figure 7.9 shows the summit of Mount Everest from the southern (Nepalese) side. Using the information in figure 7.8, state the lowest altitude (in metres) that could be shown in the photograph.*

Altitude and the lithosphere, and its effect of population

Ranges such as the Himalayas, the Swiss Alps, the Rockies and the Andes have been formed by tectonic uplift, caused by the collision between two crustal plates. For example, the Himalayas are forming on the edge of the Indo-Australian plate that is moving north into the Asian land mass. This process is still occurring, and thus

Extreme environments

the Himalayas are still being pushed higher and higher. Because of the continuing instability, countries in the Himalayas such as Bhutan and Nepal suffer from periodic earthquakes (figure 7.10). Particularly severe earthquakes occurred in Nepal in 1833, 1934 and 1988. In the 1988 earthquake, which measured 6.7 on the Richter scale, 121 people were killed, 66 000 houses were destroyed and over $US100 million damage was caused.

7.10 *An earthquake damaged house in Patan, Nepal.*

The Swiss Alps are also situated on the boundary between two crustal plates. The mountains are forming as the land is pushed upwards as the African Plate forces its way into the Eurasian Plate to its north. This is the same plate boundary that causes earthquakes and volcanic activity in Italy, Greece and Croatia. Although Switzerland experiences earthquakes, they tend to be less severe than those in Nepal. Moreover, being a more economically developed country (MEDC), Switzerland can afford to construct its buildings to withstand earthquakes and to provide extensive rescue services in the event of a disaster. Indeed, the major effect of Switzerland's relatively minor earthquakes is to destabilise accumulated snow on steep slopes, leading to major avalanches that can kill people and damage property.

There are two altitude belts where snow avalanches occur. The first is above the snow line. In this zone, avalanches can occur all year round, although they are more common in the summer when some snows melt a little. These are not usually harmful to settlements because they stop in the cirque basins about the zone of habitation. The second zone of avalanches occurs below the snow line. Freezing during the night and melting during the day makes the underlying rock very weak, and only a minor disturbance may cause a great avalanche. These avalanches are very dangerous as they often come without warning and occur in areas of settlement or tourism. A summary of the different landform hazards that affect people at various altitudes is shown in figure 7.11.

The high mountains of the world are geologically young structures formed by folding. Therefore, they have steep gradients and weak rock structures. The processes that have created today's high mountains are therefore quite complex (figure 7.12). The loose structures, steep slopes and the action of water and ice combine to make many areas unstable and prone to weathering, erosion and mass movement due to gravity. The high diurnal range of temperatures in alpine areas helps to shatter rocks as they expand and contract, perhaps with the assistance of water freezing and expanding in the cracks of the rocks. This process is especially strong on the exposed mountain slopes (figure 7.13).

All these factors combine to limit the appeal of high mountains as areas of human settlement. The atmospheric and lithospheric hazards described above make the

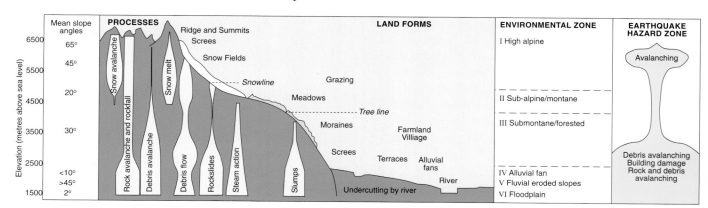

7.11 *The vertical zonation of landforms and landform hazards in Nepal.*

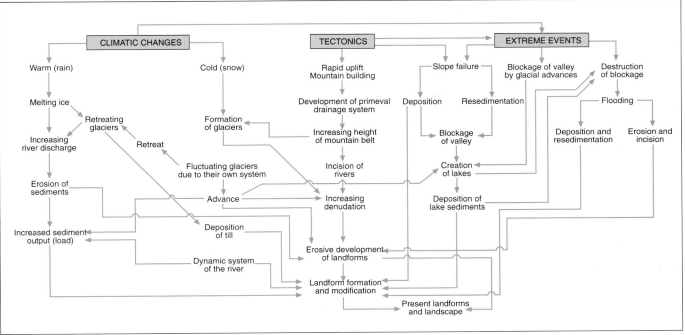

7.12 *The interaction between the different processes responsible for the evolution of the Swiss Alps and the Himalayas.*

high mountains uncomfortable places for human habitation. The steep terrain also limits accessibility, making the high mountains somewhat remote. On the other hand, the steep slopes and cold climate can create excellent ski fields which attract those with the financial means to overcome the obstacles to access.

QUESTION BLOCK 7D

1. Explain how the physical characteristics of high altitude environments affects the density of population.

7.13 *This slope in the Altay Mountains of western Mongolia shows the somewhat unstable shattered rock debris typical of alpine areas. The thin, patch vegetation cover is evidence of the slope's instability. This is a summer view of slopes that would be covered in snow during winter.*

Why are Arid Environments Extreme?

The word **desert** literally means a deserted land or wasteland. Although the common mental image of a desert is endless sand dunes, the word has come to be used in everyday speech for any arid land, whether it is occupied or not (figure 7.14). We can define an **arid environment**, or desert, as one where the potential evaporation exceeds the average precipitation. The land areas of the polar regions, and particularly the vast expanses of the Antarctic continent, are sometimes called 'cold deserts' because of the very low levels of precipitation that fall there. However, polar landscapes are not usually considered to be 'arid', and as the processes that operate on the landscape there are very different from the hot deserts, they are not discussed in this chapter. The term 'cold desert', or more correctly 'cold winter desert', is often applied to the arid regions of the mid-latitudes, such as those of Central Asia.

We need to understand arid environments, and particularly the landforms found there, if we are to understand one of the world's significant global environmental issues – desertification. **Desertification** is the process whereby deserts expand into semi-arid areas or become more intense. The expansion of deserts is a significant environmental issue in many

Extreme environments

countries today, and it threatens the livelihood of many people, especially in the Less Economically Developed Countries (LEDCs).

7.14 *Sand dunes in the Namib Desert, north-western Namibia.*

Traditionally, deserts have been described in terms of deficiencies – rain, soil nutrients, vegetation and population. We now understand that many desert areas have quite fertile soils, and can be very productive if managed wisely. Furthermore, most desert areas have quite an abundance of vegetation and wildlife, although the species found in deserts have made significant adaptations to cope with the aridity. It is important that aridity is not confused with infertility.

Deserts do not have clearly defined boundaries. They are bordered by semi-arid lands, and these in turn have sub-humid margins. Each of the climatic zones merges with the next. Nonetheless, about one-third of the world's surface can be classified as arid or semi-arid, and

as a result of desertification, this figure is probably growing.

Moisture deficit defines deserts

Regardless of the type of desert, it is the lack of rain that determines the characteristics of an arid environment. However, lack of precipitation is not the only influence. Some very dry areas have a significant vegetation cover, and they could at first sight be mistaken for a semi-arid or sub-humid land. On the other hand, some semi-arid areas have very sparse vegetation and look more like true deserts. The reason for these differences is often the soil characteristics, because good soils that can hold water helps the growth of vegetative, whereas poor soils, or thin immature soils such as skeletal soils or **lithosols**, which lead to run-off of rain, may have difficulty in supporting vegetation at all. Furthermore, human activities, especially grazing, can cause such deterioration of semi-arid and even sub-humid lands that they lose their natural vegetation, suffer badly from soil erosion, and come to resemble deserts. Such deterioration is a cause of desertification.

Global Distribution of Arid Environments

The distribution of the world's deserts – arid and semi-arid lands – is shown in figure 7.15. There are four important groups of deserts, although the differences between them are not always precise.

Cold winter mid-latitude deserts

The most important cause of the mid-latitude deserts of Central Asia is remoteness from sources of atmospheric

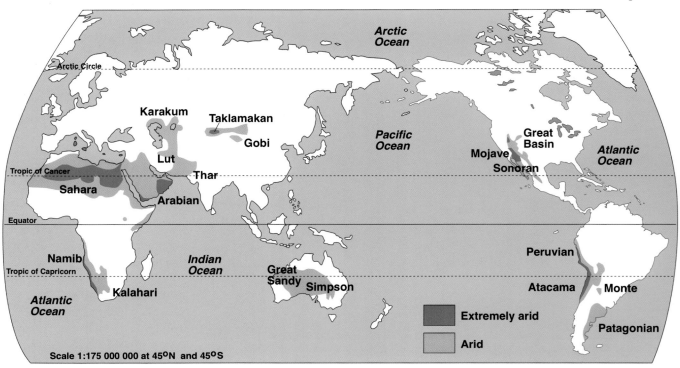

7.15 *The distribution of the world's deserts.*

moisture. In these areas, rain-bearing winds have to cross great expanses of land and high mountain ranges before reaching the interior of the continent. As the winds travel inland, they lose most of their moisture. Consequently, a group of 'cold winter deserts' extends from latitude 35°N to latitude 50°N, and beyond. The most important cold winter deserts are the Karakum Desert of Kazakhstan, Uzbekistan and Turkmenistan, and the Gobi Desert of north-western China and Mongolia (figure 7.16). These deserts have extremely cold winter temperatures.

Rainshadow deserts

When a moist air mass is forced to rise over a mountain barrier, it cools adiabatically, dropping precipitation on the windward side of the mountains that is known as **orographic rain**. By the time this air mass has passed across to the leeward side of the mountains, its moisture content has been greatly reduced. As a result, further precipitation is unlikely, especially if the air descends and experiences an adiabatic rise in temperature. The reduced rainfall area leeward of mountains is known as a **rainshadow** area.

There are several deserts of this type in the south-west of the United States The driest of these deserts is Death Valley, just east of the High Sierra Mountains, which obstruct the moisture-laden westerly winds blowing in from the Pacific Ocean. In the southern hemisphere, the best known rainshadow deserts are the Monte and Patagonian deserts east of the Andes in South America. The Patagonian desert extends right across to the east coast of Argentina where its aridity is partly due to the cold Falkland current.

Deserts of the subtropical highs

The equatorial zone receives more constant heating from the sun than anywhere else on earth. As the air is heated it expands, rises, and in the upper atmosphere spreads both north and south away from the equator. Eventually, the air descends in the subtropical zones about 30° north and south of the equator. As the air descends it becomes warmer through an adiabatic rise in temperature. The warmer the air becomes, the more moisture it can contain in the form of water vapour, and the less chance there is for precipitation to occur. This latitude zone therefore has clear skies and dry weather. It is known by different names, such as the zone of subtropical high pressure, the subtropical belt of anticyclones, and sometimes by the old term 'horse latitudes'.

The world's largest desert, the Sahara, is an example of a subtropical high pressure desert. Other examples found in the northern hemisphere are the deserts of Arabia, Iran, north-west India (the Thar) and the Sonora desert of North America. In the southern hemisphere, the Kalahari Desert of southern Africa, and most of the desert areas of Australia are of this type.

7.16 *Part of the Karakum Desert in central Turkmenistan.*

West coast deserts

Although coastal deserts are found in many parts of the world, the most distinctive group occurs in the tropics and subtropics on the west coasts of continents. In these areas, aridity is partly due to the subtropical high pressure systems that were described in the previous section. However, the main factor is the cool ocean currents that flow along the western coasts of most continents. The cold sea water cools the air above, and stabilises it. Although the cooling process often leads to fogs (a form of condensation), there is not usually enough atmospheric activity to cause rain.

There are only two west coast deserts in the northern hemisphere. These are the Baja California sector of the Sonoran desert in Mexico, and the extreme western sector of the Sahara. In the southern hemisphere, important west coast deserts include the Peruvian and Atacama deserts of South America, the Namib of southern Africa, and the coastal parts of the Great Sandy Desert in Western Australia.

The arid environments discussed in this chapter will focus on hot, arid areas (hot deserts and semi-arid areas).

QUESTION BLOCK 7E

1. *Explain what is meant by the term 'arid environment'.*

2. *What is desertification?*

3. *Draw up a table which lists the four types of deserts, summarises the cause of each, and gives two examples of each.*

ToK BoX

Perception, and the Theories of Reality.

An ancient Chinese proverb says "Two-thirds of what we see is behind our eyes."

Consider the illustration below:

When asked to describe it, various people will suggest different things, such as 'nothing', 'a white rectangle', 'a white cat in a snowstorm', or perhaps 'fibres of paper emitting light of uniform wavelengths'. As the French author Henri Thoreau (1817-1862) commented, "It's not what you look at that matters, it's what you see".

Similarly, when many people asked to describe what they see when they are looking at a desert, they reply 'nothing'.

The word 'perception' is often misused. When two people are having a disagreement, a common expression is "well, that's my perception", when they are really trying to say "well, that's my opinion". The title of this chapter is 'Extreme Environments', but should we argue that whether or not an environment is 'extreme' depends on each individual's perception? An Inuit person from the north of Canada, for example, may argue that the urban environment of Tokyo is 'extreme'.

It is important to remember, however, that perception is NOT the same as opinion, or understanding, or perspective. It would be a wrong use of the word to say something like "my perception is that Tokyo's environment is challenging".

Perception is the awareness of things through our five senses — sight, sound, touch, taste and smell. Some researchers refer to additional senses, such as intuition and sense of balance.

Unfortunately, our senses can be easily tricked into providing false information or incomplete information. Optical illusions are an obvious example of this. In geography, the important thing to remember is that even our own observations may not be as they first appear, and some cross-checking (such as through other people or using some of our additional senses) may be helpful.

In order to overcome the shortcomings of perception, philosophers have developed theories of reality, of which three are commonly discussed.

One theory of reality is known as common-sense realism. With this approach, the way we perceive the world mirrors the way the world is. Of course, as mentioned above, what we perceive is determined in part by our five senses, so maybe there are good reasons for rejecting the reliability of common-sense realism.

An alternative approach is scientific realism. With this approach, the world exists as an independent reality, but it is very different from the way we perceive it. The familiar, comfortable, sensuous world of our everyday experience is replaced by a colourless, soundless, odourless realm of atoms whizzing about in empty space. Consider Sir Arthur Eddington's description of a kitchen table as an example of scientific realism:

"It does not belong to our comparatively permanent and substantial world, that world which spontaneously appears to me when I open my eyes. My scientific table is mostly emptiness. Sparsely scattered in that emptiness are numerous electric charges rushing about with great

speed; but their combined bulk amounts to less than a billionth of the bulk of the table itself. Notwithstanding its strange construction, it turns out to be an entirely efficient table. It supports my writing paper as satisfactorily as an ordinary table, for when I lay the paper on it the little electric particles with their headlong speed keep on hitting the underside, so that the paper is maintained in shuttlecock fashion at a nearly steady level. If I lean upon this table I shall not go through; or, to be strictly accurate, the chance of my scientific elbow going through my scientific table is so excessively small that it can be negated in practical life".

The third theory of reality is known as phenomenalism. With this approach, matter is simply "the permanent possibility of sensation". Therefore, it makes no sense to say that the world exists independently of our experience of it. A phenomenalist would interpret "there are tables in the room at school" not as the physical presence of tables, but if you go into the room you are likely to have various table-experiences.

Phenomenalists make no claim that the world does not exist beyond our experience of it, because that too would be to make a claim that goes beyond the limits of our experience. Phenomenalists claim that beyond our experience of reality, there is simply nothing to be said, and that humans have no right to speculate about things we have not perceived or the nature of ultimate reality.

The three approaches can be summed very simply as follows:

Common-sense realism: "What you see is what is there".

Scientific realism: "Atoms in the void".

Phenomenalism: "To be is to be perceived".

The next ToK BoX is on page 345.

Physical Characteristics of Extreme Environments

Processes Operating in Glacial Environments

As discussed in chapter 3, the earth has experienced many changes in climate through its history. The planet is currently experiencing an unusually warm period – the average climatic conditions of the planet suggest that the 'normal' state of the world is more like an ice age than the conditions we experience today.

When the earth cools, the ice caps and glaciers expand, retreating again when the climate warms. Although we do not understand the reasons, the warming and cooling of the earth occurs in broad cycles, and we experience severe ice ages about every 200 to 250 million years. Ice ages are known as **glacial periods**, and the warmer periods between ice ages are known as **interglacials**.

During the last ice age, which ended about 12,000 years ago, ice covered about 30% of the earth's surface – about three times more than today. The ice caps spread further from the poles in both the northern and southern hemispheres, and ice and snow cover descended to lower altitudes than we find them today. Therefore, we find evidence of glaciation in parts of the world today that are located quite long distances from today's ice caps and glaciers, both in terms of latitude and altitude.

Mountain areas receive large volumes of orographic precipitation. Depending on the altitude, this can be in the form of rainfall (lower altitudes) or snow (higher altitudes). If the temperatures are cold enough, many streams flowing from higher altitudes take the form of **glaciers**, or 'rivers of ice' (figure 7.17). Glaciers form where snow that has fallen during winter does not completely melt away, even during summer time. Under the pressure of over-lying snow, the individual crystals of snow are changed into granular particles of snow (called **firn**), and after a few more years of pressure, this is transformed into blue glacial ice.

7.17 *Two views of the Potanini Glacier in the Altay Mountains of western Mongolia near the border with Russia, China and Kazakhstan. The lines of moraine in the upper view indicate the direction of flow through the U-shaped valley. The lower view shows a closer view of the rough surface of the glacial ice.*

If the ice is sufficiently thick, the initially rigid ice mass starts to flow like a plastic body, flowing slowly through the valley, scraping its course as it does so. Glaciers typically flow at a few centimetres per day. Of the world's

fresh water, 80% is stored in ice and snow, and thus glaciers are an important resource. Moreover, without the meltwater from glaciers, many rainshadow areas would be deserts or semi-arid grasslands.

7.18 *A U-shaped valley in the Altay Mountains of western Mongolia.*

One of the most noticeable features arising from this process is the **U-shaped valley**, or **glacial trough**, in which the valley floor may be quite flat and the sides extremely steep (figures 7.18 and 7.19). This is the shape left behind by a glacier after it has scraped and plucked rocks from the sides. In general, these valleys were formed originally by another process such as a river in warmer times or land shaped by lava flows. Quite often the abrasive action of the glacier on the valley sides will lead to major **landslides** onto the surface of the glacier, increasing the angle of the valley sides further and adding dramatically to the surface moraine on the glacier (figure 7.20). Furthermore, meltwater from the glacier can seep into cracks in the rock and as it refreezes and expands it loosens more rock to be carried away by the glacier.

High tributary valleys which fed the main glacier, but which were not big enough to carve valleys as deep as the main valley, are often left high above the main valley when the climate warms. These are called **hanging valleys** and the water from them has to drop down the steep slope to reach the present valley floor. The spectacular **waterfalls** that result are often strong attractions for tourists (figures 7.21 and 7.22).

In some cases the high tributary valleys will themselves leave distinctive features because of the special action of small glaciers near high alpine peaks. The best known are **cirques**, which are dish-shaped hollows eroded by these glaciers as the ice rotates under the force of gravity. When the ice retreats, the result is often a small lake called a **tarn** and maybe a waterfall (figures 7.23 and 7.24).

Where two or more cirques cut into both sides of a ridge, distinctive landscapes are formed that are unique to glacial areas. When cirques cut headward into a smoothly rounded flat or rounded ridge, then a **scalloped upland** results. If the divides between the cirques are eroded

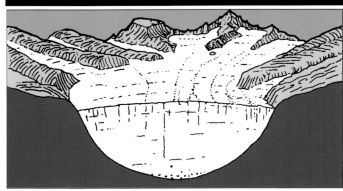

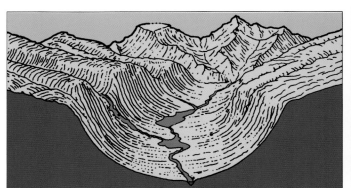

7.19 *The process of the formation of a U-shaped valley.*

backwards into themselves, a narrow, steep, rocky ridge called an **arête** forms. An example of an arête can be seen to the right of the U-shaped valley shown in figure 7.25. When an arête is reduced to a single rocky peak by ice erosion on all sides, the angular remnant is termed an **horn** (figure 7.26).

The surface of a glacier varies throughout its length. In its highest parts, a glacier is basically a snow field (the **névé**) with little evidence of erosion (figures 7.27 and 7.28). This

is because even the rock fragments that fall because of freeze and thaw action in any exposed mountain peaks are often buried by the next snow fall. In the middle and lower sections of the glacier, the surface is usually very convoluted with a mixture of dangerous **crevasses** and tall ice peaks (figure 7.29). These cracks initially form as the glacier twists around the curves of its valley. Once formed, the surface irregularities tend to deepen each summer as the surface layer of the glacier melts and the running water flows down and along the cracks and grooves, deepening them as it does so (figure 7.30).

7.20 *Surface moraine on a glacier near Grindelwald, Switzerland.*

7.21 *Waterfalls plummet from hanging valleys in a former glaciated area of Yosemite National Park, USA.*

Spectacular **fjords** are formed when glaciers carve valleys that reach or reached the sea, or where sea level rose after the last ice age to flood deep U-shaped valleys. The Atlantic Coast of Norway, the Alaskan Coast and New Zealand's Fjordland are the best known examples of coastlines dominated by fjords. Here the steep sides of the valleys extend into the water resulting in a great depth of water even right at the shoreline (figure 6.41 in chapter 6).

As glaciers flow down-slope, they erode and carry material from the sides of the valley. Evidence of the scraping action of glaciers can often be seen by **striations**, which are small scratches on the surface of the rocks on the sides of a glacier that were made as the ice moved slowly

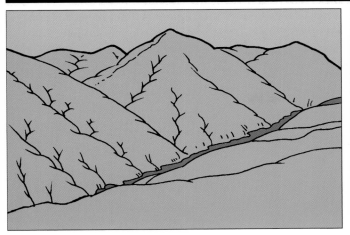

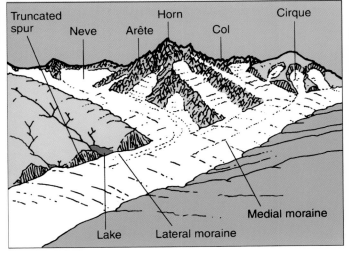

7.23 *A tarn, Snowdonia National Park, north Wales.*

7.24 *Tarns in cirques, fed by glaciers, Swiss Alps.*

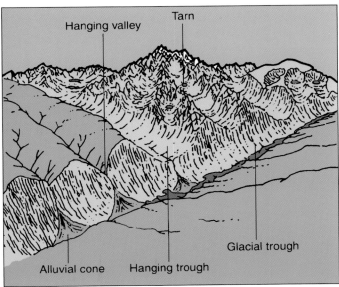

7.22 *The formation of hanging valleys and other typical glacial landforms.*

7.25 *Arêtes along the right hand edge of a small glacial valley in the Andes Mountains, east of Santiago (Chile).*

downhill, carrying smaller rocks as it did so (figure 7.31). Because the scratches were made by the ice as it moved, the scratches indicate the angle of movement of the ice. The scratches are usually parallel, but if the glacier retreated and then advanced at a later date from a different angle, the striations may show multiple sets of parallel scratches.

Rocks and sediment that is carried by a glacier is called **moraine**. Rocks that are carried on the sides of glaciers are known as **lateral moraine**. We can say, therefore, that striations are caused by lateral moraine being scraped against the rocks at the side of a glacier by the moving ice.

Extreme environments

7.26 *A horn near Zermatt, Switzerland.*

7.27 *A nevé (snow field) feeds a glacier in the Altay Mountains of western Mongolia.*

7.28 *This nevé feeds a glacier which in turn feeds a tarn in central Switzerland.*

A moving glacier also collect rocks and sediments that have fallen from the sides of the valley onto its surface, and this is known as **surface moraine** (figure 7.32). Where two glaciers join together, the lateral moraine that was at the sides of the two glaciers becomes a strip of moraine in the middle of the enlarged glacier, known as **medial moraine** (figures 7.33). All the moraine carried by the glacier is then deposited at the snout of the glacier where it melts, and this is known as **terminal moraine** (figure 7.34). One way to measure the rate of retreat of a glacier

is to examine the terminal moraine that has been left behind after the ice has melted.

The ice at the bottom of glaciers may be centuries old. When the ice forms it traps tiny bubbles of air, and studying these bubbles in centuries-old ice helps us to analyse long-term changes in the earth's atmosphere and air pollution. In spite of their huge size, most glaciers are receding and it is feared that several will disappear in the decades ahead (figure 7.35). Although many people claim this is due to global warming, the fact that glaciers in some places are advancing has called this explanation into question. Some scientists suggest that glacial retreat may be due mainly to fluctuations in local rainfall conditions, such as drier conditions, rather than global warming, and cite the example of Mount Kilimanjaro in Tanzania as an example of this.

7.29 *The surface of most glaciers is very rough, being marked by cracks and crevasses. This example in in southern Iceland.*

7.30 *This surface crevasse is being deepened by the flow of melting water during the summer melt period.*

7.31 *Striations on the rocks in this glacial valley in Mongolia were made when the moving ice scraped rocks along the edges of the valley. Two sets of scrape lines can be seen, indicating at least two periods of advancing ice. The animal carvings have been cut into the striations, proving they were made after the last ice age.*

7.32 *Surface moraine on the Potanini Glacier in western Mongolia.*

7.33 *The lateral moraine of two glaciers joins to form medial moraine in this glacier near Zermatt, Switzerland.*

Outwash plains form when the meltwater streams from glaciers deposit gravel, sand and moraine from glaciers each year during the summer retreat (figure 7.36). Where the outwash of many glaciers has combined, extensive outwash plains may develop. The Canterbury Plains of New Zealand are an example of a large area that has been built up by the terminal moraine from many glaciers that existed on the Southern Alps in past ice ages.

As ice sheets and glaciers expand, the scraping action of the ice has a drastic erosive impact on the surface beneath. When the ice erodes down to bedrock, it can form tear-drop shaped hills that have a streamlined appearance. These are called **roches moutonnées**, and they have smooth gently sloping ends and sides with a steeper lee-ward side that may be either smooth or plucked (figure 7.37). The size of roches moutonnées can vary greatly from miniature examples to large hills.

7.34 *The large area of deposited material in the foreground of this photo is the terminal moraine of the Athabasca Glacier, part of the Columbia icefield near Banff in the Canadian Rocky Mountains.*

7.35 *Another view of the Athabasca Glacier, giving some idea of the glacial retreat since 1992.*

7.36 *The extensive outwash plain of the Skaftafell Glacier, southern Iceland.*

Extreme environments

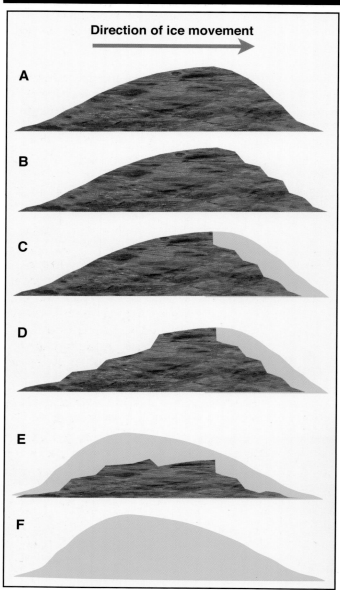

Direction of ice movement

A

B

C

D

E

F

7.37 *Some streamlined glacial landforms. In these cross-section diagrams, brown represents rock and yellow represents deposited sediment. The past ice movement is from left to right in all cases. A and B are roches moutonnées, C and D show crags and tails, E and F are drumlins.*

Drumlins can vary in size, and some have been observed which are up to 50 metres in height and more than 800 metres in length. They are often found in 'swarms' on flat plains called **drumlin fields** with other similarly shaped, sized and oriented hills.

The cause of drumlins is not known for certain, and debate about their origins continues among academic geographers. As the materials in drumlins are always the same as the surrounding ground moraine, deposited in layers, most geographers believe that the base of drumlins were formed at the same time as the ground moraine was deposited. In other words, the material in drumlins was deposited under the ice as the glacier or ice sheet advanced. When the ice melted, the drumlin remained as evidence of the former ice cover.

Erratics are rocks that are made of a different material from the type of rock native to the area where it rests (figure 7.38). The normal explanation is that the rocks were carried to their current location by a glacier or an advancing ice sheet, and then left there when the ice melted. Erratics can vary greatly in size, and some have been estimated to weigh over 5,000 tonnes — strong testimony to the energy of moving ice!

7.38 *Glacial erratics in a previously glaciated area of Yosemite National Park, USA.*

Sometimes, the steep lee side of a roche moutonnée might be covered with a streamlined tail of glacial debris, such as broken rocks and gravel. This is known as a **crag and tail** and they can vary considerably in shape and form (figure 7.37).

Roches moutonnées are erosional landforms because they result from the scouring of the bedrock by moving ice. A similar looking landform, called a **drumlin**, is formed by depositional processes. Drumlins are smooth oval-shaped hills of glacial debris (broken rocks and gravel). Unlike roches moutonnées, the steeper end of a drumlin is on the upstream side, while the leeward side is generally more gently sloping (figure 7.37). Although the shape can vary, drumlins are always smooth in shape, somewhat like an inverted spoon or an egg that has been split along its axis.

QUESTION BLOCK 7F

1. *Explain why glacial landforms can be seen in areas where there are no glaciers.*

2. *Look at the photos in this section and list as many landform features as you can see under the headings (a) erosional, and (b) depositional.*

3. *Choose four landforms you listed in your answer to the last question, of which two are erosional and two are depositional, and describe their formation.*

4. *Explain the difference between lateral, medial and terminal moraine.*

Processes Operating in Hot Arid Environments

Before we can explain the processes operating in hot arid environments, we must understand aridity. Aridity, or lack of moisture, is the key characteristic of deserts, but how can aridity be measured?

The degree of aridity is governed by the amount of moisture at ground level. This is heavily influenced by the degree of evaporation, which is in turn determined mainly by temperature. Therefore, the driest deserts are those that experience both low rainfall and high temperatures. It follows that tropical and subtropical deserts are drier than deserts with the same rainfall in mid-latitudes. This is because mid-latitude deserts are affected by seasonal changes, and they experience much lower temperatures in winter than in summer.

Several systems have been worked out for determining the degree of aridity for an area, and for drawing climatic boundaries. Most of these are based on climatic formulae, and some of them are quite complex. The most commonly used system was developed by a scientist called Meigs, and the map of the world's arid lands in figure 7.15 is based on his calculations. As a generalisation, we can assume that most subtropical deserts have a mean annual rainfall of less than 250 mm, while mid-latitude deserts (where evaporation is lower) have less than 200 mm. It is more difficult to suggest a simple definition for semi-arid environments, because more variables can affect them. In southern Australia, most areas with a rainfall less than 450 mm would be regarded as semi-arid.

There are no areas, even in extremely arid deserts, where it never rains. However, one weather station in the Atacama desert of Chile experienced 13 consecutive years without rain, while another station in the same desert has recorded 25 years with a mean annual rainfall of only 1.7 millimetres.

Rainfall variability, or the extent to which the rainfall for single years varies from the mean annual rainfall, is very high for arid regions. It is difficult to predict if or when rain is likely to occur in arid environments. It used to be thought that most desert rain comes from thunderstorms, and it is true that thunderstorm rain is characteristic of a few deserts, like the Sonora desert in the United States. However this is not generally the case, and it is certainly not the case in Australia except for the far north-west, which experiences summer monsoons and tropical cyclones.

Temperatures in arid regions are notable for their large **diurnal** (or daily) range; the exception to this is deserts on sea coasts. The heat during the day can be scorching as the sun rises high towards midday, but at night conditions cool off rapidly. Temperatures at a weather station in the Sahara Desert south of Tripoli (Libya) once varied from 37.2°C to -0.6°C within 24 hours, a difference of 37.8C°. It is claimed that this diurnal range is the greatest ever recorded. The highest temperature ever recorded was also at a weather station in Tripoli; 58°C.

Although the diurnal range is great, there is little **seasonal** change in temperatures in equatorial deserts. In subtropical deserts, however, the variation between summer and winter temperatures may be great, especially at high altitudes. In the mid-latitude deserts, seasonal variation is extreme. Summer temperatures in parts of the Turkestan desert may rise as high as 54°C, while winter lows may sink to -26°C, or even lower. This extreme seasonal range is more than 80C°.

Water is lost to the atmosphere by evaporation directly from the ground surface, and also by transpiration from vegetation. Together, these losses are known as **evapotranspiration**. The evaporation loss from a free water surface in an arid region is many times greater than the precipitation, a fact that causes concern to those storing water in lakes and reservoirs. Even on the rare occasions that rain falls, the dry air and high temperatures above the desert often cause the water to be evaporated even before it reaches the ground (figure 7.39).

7.39 *Rain from this evening shower above the Mojave Desert in the USA is evaporating even before it reaches the ground.*

Why then is there any water at all in the ground? When rain falls, some water evaporates immediately from the ground surface, some runs off to accumulate in local depressions, and the balance is absorbed by the soil. Moisture in the soil is to some extent protected from evaporating as it is not directly exposed to the atmosphere, and it is this moisture that enables desert plants to grow.

If soil water builds up to the extent that saturation point is reached, then a water table is established, and water from it may be tapped by wells and bores. Sometimes natural depressions are deep enough to cut into the water table, so that permanent or semi-permanent water is available at or near the surface. These areas, known as **oases** (singular **oasis**), can support vegetation and even cultivation because of the availability of water, and some of the oases in the Sahara are depressions of this type (figure 7.40). Not all water tables yield fresh water; often it is saline and may be unfit for use.

Artesian water is groundwater trapped in porous beds, known as **aquifers**, by relatively impervious beds above and below called **aquicludes**. The source of artesian water is usually far away from the desert, often in the mountains where orographic rain falls before reaching the rainshadow area of the desert. The rain infiltrates the aquifer and eventually seeps down to the area under the desert. The artesian water is under pressure since it has come from higher altitudes. Therefore, when an artesian aquifer is pierced by a bore, water rises to the surface, and sometimes above ground level. Artesian water was discussed in more detail in chapter 5.

7.40 *The oasis of Tinerhir on the western edge of the Sahara Desert in Morocco. Date palms cultivation is possible because of the availability of water in the low valley. The aridity of the surrounding areas can be seen clearly in the background.*

7.41 *Wind sweeping across this area of desert between Goulimime and Er Rachidia in Morocco, is causing a dust storm as it erodes the surface soil.*

Arid areas are notoriously windy, and this can lead to widespread erosion (figure 7.41). One reason for this is the sparse vegetation, because the frictional drag of trees and shrubs (where they are present) can be significant in reducing wind velocity near ground level. Moreover, most of the world's arid lands are comparatively flat or undulating, with little to obstruct the passage of the wind.

One significant cause of wind in the desert is convection. Each day, the sun rapidly heats the ground and the dry air above it, and as this air expands and rises, cooler air from elsewhere rushes in to replace it. Then, with falling temperatures towards sunset, the wind may gradually drop. Most desert nights are cool and still. There is more to wind behaviour in the desert than simple convectional replacement of air, however. Most of the subtropical deserts are subject to the influence of anticyclonic swirls. The influence of the seasons can also be very pronounced. Indeed, some desert winds are so regular in their seasonal patterns that they are known by specific names, such as the Sirocco that blows from North Africa across the Mediterranean Sea into Europe, and the Khamsin that blows towards the south-east from North Africa and Arabia.

QUESTION BLOCK 7G

1. *What is a typical rainfall in an arid environment? Is this figure the same for all parts of the world?*

2. *Describe the rainfall variability of arid environments.*

3. *Comment on the (a) diurnal and (b) seasonal fluctuations in the temperatures of arid environments.*

4. *How do oases form?*

5. *Why are arid environments so windy?*

Weathering in Hot Arid Environments

Weathering is the process of breaking down a rock. Weathering is usually classified into two broad categories, physical weathering and chemical weathering. **Physical weathering** is the disintegration of a rock by mechanical forces that do not change the rock's chemical composition. **Chemical weathering** is the decomposition of a rock by alteration of its chemical composition. Traditionally, geographers assumed that most of the weathering in arid environments was essentially physical weathering. It was argued that chemical action requires water, and arid environments are water deficient. However, no desert is completely dry, and even small amounts of moisture can bring about chemical change, given enough time. Since all weathering processes operate very slowly under dry conditions, chemical weathering is very significant in arid regions, and in fact it is generally more effective than physical weathering. In any case, most chemical and mechanical processes are not mutually exclusive, but operate together and supplement the work of the other.

Because arid environments experience large diurnal ranges of temperature, we might think that **insolation weathering**, which shatters the rock by alternate heating and subsequent rapid cooling (causing expansion and contraction) is an important weathering agent (figure 7.42). In deserts, the temperature of the ground surface may be 20C° hotter than the air temperature. Rock surface temperatures greater than 80°C have been recorded, but because it is such a poor conductor of heat, the temperature just a few millimetres below the surface would be much less. Because the temperature gradient is so steep, stress is placed on the surface of the rock as it expands relative to the rock beneath. Perhaps surprisingly, measurements have shown that the forces operating through insolation are enough to cause shattering in only a few types of rock. Even in these cases, insolation weathering occurs only when there are unusually sudden temperature changes, such as might result from cool rain falling on very hot rock. In this way, desert rainstorms probably aid the breakdown of rocks.

7.42 *Exfoliation, or onion skin weathering, causes sheets of a rock to fall away like layers of skin on an onion. It is thought to be caused by insolation weathering.*

Processes of chemical weathering can take place above the ground surface, but they are very much more effective underground where there is more moisture. In most cases, rocks on the surface today that show advanced chemical weathering were weathered long ago when they were underground.

Salt crystallisation can be an important agent of weathering in arid environments. This is the process of breaking down rocks by the growth of salt crystals in cracks. When rain falls in the desert, some of the salts in the soil and

rocks are dissolved, and they penetrate porous rocks such as sandstones. Later drying results in recrystallisation of the salts. This process exerts great pressure and tends to break down the rock.

Another process that was once thought to be important, particularly with respect to undercutting rock masses is **sand blasting**. This process was thought to produce **pedestal** or **mushroom rocks**, which are found in some arid regions. There is no doubt that sand blasting can weather soft materials at ground level. Wooden telegraph poles erected last century across inland Australia were undercut in this way, and blasting can also be responsible for polishing rock faces at or close to ground level. However, it is now known that most undercutting of hard rock is due to chemical weathering. Moisture tends to concentrate and remain for longer periods on the lower parts of rock masses, and these are the parts that weather most rapidly. Mushroom rocks in arid environments are therefore dominantly the result of chemical weathering.

It is important to remember that most of the world's deserts are old enough to have experienced episodes of wet climates over geological time. Many of the weathered features seen today in arid environments are not the result of current processes, but are relics from wet climates thousands, or in some cases millions, of years ago. Erosion, like weathering, is very slow under conditions of aridity, and once the climate has changed from humid to arid, the erosion of features produced by weathering in a former humid environment is a very slow process indeed.

QUESTION BLOCK 7H

1. *List the types of weathering which are important in arid environments. For each type, say whether it is physical or chemical, and comment on the landforms or other features that might result from its actions.*

2. *How could past climatic changes have affected arid environments?*

Weathering and Landform Development in Hot Arid Environments

It is very significant that all weathering processes are extremely slow in arid environments, because weathering is the initial process in the sequence of events that leads to the development of arid landforms. **Erosion**, or the removal of weathered rock fragments, can only take place when weathering processes have provided enough material to be transported. Therefore, the rate of landform development is ultimately dependent on the rate of weathering. It follows from this that landform development is much slower in arid than in humid environments.

Weathered products are removed from rocks exposed to the atmosphere almost as soon as they are produced. For this reason, mountains and hills in arid environments display many bare rock surfaces (figure 7.43). Furthermore, rock faces tend to be angular and sharp as opposed to the more rounded shapes found in humid environments. Soft rocks that erode easily may give rise to a complex of steep, narrow valleys and knife-edge ridges known as **badland topography** (figure 7.44).

7.43 *Bare rock surfaces dominate the desert environment in many desert areas, such as here at Wadi Dhar in Yemen.*

7.44 *This example of arid mountains with badland topography in the foreground is in Death Valley, California (USA).*

7.45 *The layered bands of rock in the geology of this area in northwestern Namibia have a strong influence on its appearance.*

The bare rock surfaces of and hills and mountains tend to accentuate the geological features of the underlying rocks. Features arising due to rock type, differential erosion,

sedimentary bedding, and folds or faults are not only conspicuous but they may actually determine the entire appearance of the landscape (figures 7.45 and 7.46). Furthermore, the slow rate of chemical weathering on the surface means that the natural colours of the rocks tend to be preserved. Sometimes, these colours are very bright, as in rocks stained by oxides of iron or manganese. The great scenic beauty of the arid environments of central Australia and the south-west of USA owes much to the colour of the rocks (figure 7.47).

7.46 *The geology has a strong influence on the appearance of the steeply-sided 300-metre deep Charyn Canyon Gorge in south-eastern Kazakhstan.*

7.47 *Uluru, or Ayers Rock as it is also known, is the world's largest monolith.*

QUESTION BLOCK 7I

1. What is the impact of the slow rate of weathering in arid environments on the development of landforms?

Water and Landform Development in Hot Arid Environments

Although water is scarce in arid environments, it plays a very important part in erosion, transport and deposition. In fact, apart from areas that are covered by sand plains and sand dunes, water is far more effective than wind in the processes of arid landform development. When it does rain, the rocky surfaces of the arid hills shed water freely into dry creeks, which then experience **flash flooding** – a short-lived, fast-flowing stream that results from the sudden heavy fall of rain. Further downslope, where soils cover the surface, some of the rain that falls does penetrate the ground surface.

Because of the sparse vegetation, runoff is much greater in arid environments than on similar slopes in humid regions. In some areas, a thin platy layer of fine sediment caps the soil and this resists penetration by water. Much bare soil is exposed in arid areas, and this favours runoff and aggravates soil erosion. The physical impact of individual raindrops on the soil causes **rainsplash**, which dislodges the soil particles and puddles them. When this happens on a sloping surface, soil particles are easily taken into suspension and carried into stream courses.

7.48 *The Colorado River, seen here flowing through the Grand Canyon, is an exotic stream that has its source is mountain areas with a high rainfall, well away from the desert. The deep canyon has been eroded by this river.*

Very few streams in arid regions flow to the sea. There are exceptions, such as the Nile, the Indus, and the Colorado, which have their catchment areas in heavy rainfall country outside the desert boundaries (figure 7.48). Such rivers are known as **exotic rivers**, because their source is outside the desert area. Most streams in arid environments follow patterns of **internal drainage**, where

streams are ephemeral, and either dissipate on the desert surface or terminate in local depressions where water collects briefly, then evaporates (figure 7.49). The ephemeral lakes formed in this way are often called **playas** or **playa lakes**. When they dry out, the lakes reveal beds of fine alluvial sediment together with **evaporites** like salt, calcrete and gypsum (figure 7.50). Dry lakes are common landforms in arid environments, and their beds are very conspicuous when white, salty surfaces are exposed.

7.49 *An ephemeral stream in western Oman, near Wadi Hatta.*

7.50 *Evaporites surround Lake Assal a large heavily saline lake in Djibouti.*

The ephemeral streams of arid regions, known as **wadis** in Arab countries, **arroyos** or **washes** in North America, and **dry creeks** in Australia, have many features in common with those in humid landscapes (figure 7.51 and 7.52). However, some characteristics, particularly those relating to channel patterns, are a distinctive part of an arid environment.

Alluvial fans are characteristic features that may develop in a variety of climatic regions. In order to form, alluvial fans require a flat or gently sloping plain near the foot of a hill or plateau, where a stream carrying sediment emerges abruptly from a mountain front and spreads out. As the stream reaches the flat plan, known as a **piedmont**, its velocity slows and it loses competence to carry the sediment load. The sediment is therefore deposited at the junction of the hill and the piedmont, and a fan-shaped deposit builds up (figure 7.53). Arid environments are very well suited to alluvial fan development because they are prone to flash flooding. Furthermore, they have hillslopes that erode easily and therefore provide alluvial material suitable for deposition.

7.51 *A wadi in Oman, near the UAE oasis of Wadi Hatta.*

7.52 *The vegetation in the bed of this dry stream in Namibia indicates the presence of underground water.*

7.53 *A number of alluvial fans have joined together to form a bajada where several ephemeral streams flow from the hills down to the valley near Ulgii (Mongolia).*

In many deserts, several nearby streams flow from the same mountain scarp to form alluvial fans. When this happens, the edges of adjacent fans usually coalesce to build up a continuous mantle of deposition known by the Spanish term **bajada**, usually anglicised to **bahada**. A bahada is thus virtually a piedmont plain composed of fan material (figure 7.54).

Alluvial fans in arid environments are found only next to escarpments, and they are associated with steep gradients. Where gradients are moderate, and the local sediments include a mixture of sand, silt and clay, desert streams have a flat, sandy bed with steep banks. This gives a rectangular cross-section known as a **box canyon** (figure 7.55).

7.54 *A large bahada in the Namib Desert of northern Namibia.*

When gradients are even less, a single stream channel may branch into one or more distributaries called **ana-branches**. These can flow parallel to the main channel for many kilometres before rejoining it. A well-known example is the Darling River anabranch in western New South Wales, Australia.

7.55 *A box canyon near Mount Isa, Australia. The stream has been dry for a long while, as shown by the many animal tracks in the bed of the canyon. Bank collapse caused by water undercutting the edge of the canyon can be seen to the right.*

On flat plains in arid environments where the gradient is extremely low and the stream flow infrequent, there are often many small channels that continuously divide and converge to form what is known as a **reticulate drainage** pattern. When occasional heavy floods come, these channels quickly overflow, resulting in wide expanses of shallow water. The Channel Country of south-west

Queensland (Australia) provides many examples of this type of drainage, incorporating the lower courses of the Georgina, Diamantina, and Cooper's Creek.

QUESTION BLOCK 7J

1. *Why is water more effective than wind in shaping landforms in arid environments? Give specific examples.*

2. *What is meant by the term 'internal drainage'? How common is this in arid environments?*

3. *How do alluvial fans form?*

4. *Make a list of landforms typical of arid environments whose formation is dominated by the action of water.*

Wind and Landform Development in Hot Arid Environments

As noted earlier in this chapter, arid environments tend to be windy. Although wind (or **aeolian** action) is not as effective as water in erosion, it plays an important part in the transport of fine sediments and sand. Wind is partly responsible for the transport and deposition of the sand in sandy deserts, and it is wholly responsible for the shaping of sand into dunes.

Dunefields, or **ergs** as they are called in the Sahara, are spectacular features, but they are not as widespread in deserts as many people perceive (figure 7.56). Sandy surfaces comprise only 2% of the North American deserts, 15% of the Sahara, and 30% of the Arabian desert. Although about 50% of the Australian desert is sandy, the sand is mainly in the form of vegetated sand plains and dunes that do not fit the popular image of sandy deserts as moving hills of sand.

7.56 *An oasis in the dunes of the Gobi Desert at Dunhuang, China.*

Deflation is the term used to describe the removal of any kind of material from the ground surface by wind. In some arid areas, large bodies of sediment may be removed, leaving behind **deflation hollows**, while elsewhere deflation may merely sort the sediments by taking away the finer particles.

There are several ways in which wind activates and transports dust and sand. At the surface of the ground there is a very thin layer of air which is virtually stationary, regardless of the wind velocity higher up. Because of this, a surface layer of very fine material with a particle size less than 0.06 mm (silt or clay) is very stable until disturbed by an unusual circumstance. This could be an unusual eddy of wind, or some mechanical factor such as moving sand, trampling animals, or the passage of a motor vehicle. Once in the air, the fine particles may be lifted as dust to considerable heights and carried great distances. During droughts, Australian dust has been carried as far as New Zealand and deposited on the snow of the Southern Alps. Sometimes, dust particles are picked up by the wind from the surface of a desert and carried outside the arid region, to be deposited as unstratified material known as loess. The famous loess deposits of China, some of which are more than 100 metres thick, comprise sediments blown from the great deserts of Central Asia.

Unlike clay and silt particles, particles of sand on the ground surface are large enough to extend up into the zone of moving air, and they can therefore be rolled along by the wind. Rolling grains of sand strike one another, and the impact throws some of them into the air, to be blown a short distance downwind before falling back and activating other grains. This kind of jumping action is known as **saltation**, and it is largely restricted to particles of fine sand. In general, coarse sand is too heavy to be lifted by this means, and it is usually rolled along the ground instead.

7.57 *The wind blows sand across this road near Liwa Oasis in the United Arab Emirates.*

A wind speed of more than 30 kilometres per hour is usually required to initiate the movement of sand on flat surfaces. On the slopes of dunes, however, a much lower wind speed of only 15 kilometres per hour may be sufficient (figure 7.57). Sand blown by the wind is mostly restricted to a zone below 0.6 metres above the ground. Even in quite strong winds, the maximum height to which sand can rise is about 2 metres.

Extreme environments

It is the quantity and particle size of the sand that largely determines which landforms will develop in sandy deserts. Other important influences are the velocity and direction of the winds, and sometimes, whether or not there is a hard rock base.

Sand sheets are areas of sand with more-or-less level surfaces. They form when there is enough coarse sand to restrict saltation, which therefore prevents the sand from forming dunes.

7.58 *A dunefield of migrating barchans (foreground), with a high hill of sand behind near Liwa Oasis, United Arab Emirates.*

Barchans are crescent-shaped (**crescentic**) sand dunes. The wings (or horns) point away from the wind. Sand is driven up the windward slope, which has a relatively gentle gradient, and rolls over the crest to form, on the leeward slope, the steep angle of repose for sand, which is constant at 33° to 34° (figure 7.58). Barchans form on hard, flat surfaces, where there is a limited sand supply, and where winds usually blow in one direction only. Barchans are quite common in many of the world's deserts, but they are very rare in Australia.

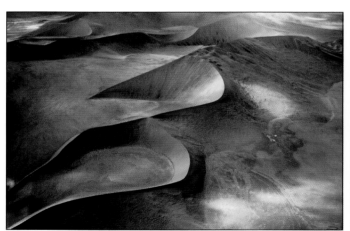

7.59 *The sand dunes at Sossusvlei in the Namib Desert rise to almost 400 metres above the surrounding plain.*

Parabolic dunes are U-shaped mounds of sand with elongated arms, and they are common in coastal deserts such as the Namib. Unlike barchans, the arms of parabolic dunes follow the movement of the wind rather than lead it, and thus the arms point towards the wind. The

arms are usually fixed by vegetation, whereas the bulk of the sand in the dune migrates away from the prevailing wind. Parabolic dunes can become very large, and the dunes at Sossusvlei in the Namib Desert rise to almost 400 metres above the surrounding plain (figure 7.59).

Unlike barchans and parabolic dunes, **longitudinal** or **seif dunes**, are formed by winds that blow from at least two directions. The general alignment of the dunes reflects the directions of these winds (figure 7.60). During the time that a dune is growing longer, sand movement is in the direction of the long axis. The prevailing winds increase the length of dunes, but cross-winds increase their height and width. Longitudinal dunes are parallel to each other, and they may extend for great distances. Indeed, individual longitudinal dunes may reach heights of 100 metres, and they can be as far as 1,000 metres apart. Longitudinal dunes occur in almost all of the world's deserts, but they are particularly extensive in Australia where they make up half of the total area of sandy desert.

Lunettes are crescent-shaped dunes that lie at the leeward, or downwind, edge of some ephemeral lakes. When the lakes are dry, salt crystals in the beds cause clay sediments to re-form into small pellets. These pellets are then blown by the wind and deposited on the downwind

7.60 *An oblique aerial photograph of longitudinal dunes in Central Australia.*

edges of the lake's shores. When the lakes are filled, wave action may form sandy beaches on the downwind shores, and some of this sand is then blown on to the dunes. For this reason, lunettes may include amounts of sand even though most of them are essentially made up from clay.

7.61 *Wind has eroded these rocks in the Gobi Desert at Yadan, north-west of Dunhuang (China). The prevailing wind direction is from the right hand side of the photo, and this has led to undercutting of the rock near ground level on the side of the rock facing the wind. The people standing in the shade of the rock give an indication of scale.*

QUESTION BLOCK 7K

1. What does the term 'aeolian landform' mean? List five aeolian landforms.

Desert Residuals and Stony Deserts

Many of the landforms found in arid environments today are relict features, being remnants from former landscapes. Changing climates over millions of years have transformed areas that were once well-watered into today's deserts. Therefore, much of the present desert landscape could be described as **residual**.

7.62 *The rounded shape of this inselberg is a result of the action of running water when the area was less arid. This is part of Kata Tjuta (the Olgas), in central Australia.*

When the term 'residual' is used to describe a land-form, the word refers to an elevated topographic feature such as an isolated mountain or segment of a plateau that is a remnant from a former, much more extensive, and usually higher land mass. For example, **inselbergs** are prominent steep-sided residuals rising in isolation above extensive and plains (figure 7.62). They usually have somewhat rounded outlines acquired long ago under humid conditions, often as a result of underground weathering. Sometimes, however, the roundness is due to the weathering characteristics of the rock type. Among the best-known inselbergs are Central Australia's Uluru (Ayers Rock) and Kata Tjuta (the Olgas) (figure 7.63).

7.63 *Kata Tjuta (also known as the Olgas) in central Australia is an example of an inselberg.*

7.64 *A mesa, near Er Rachidia, Morocco.*

The **mesa**, which is a table-topped mountain with steep and often vertical upper slopes, is the most common residual in arid environments (figure 7.64). Mesas can occur in humid as well as arid environments. When humid weathering processes influence mesas, however, they tend to have somewhat rounded profiles. In arid environments, it is the sharp break in slope between the flat top and the scarp on the one hand, and the scarp and the talus slope on the other, which makes mesas so distinctive. This profile shape is particularly obvious because of the absence of vegetation. The top of a mesa is the flat and roughly horizontal remnant of some former plateau surface, which is resistant to weathering compared with the rocks beneath it. This hard layer may be a basalt flow, a tough sedimentary bed, or a former erosion surface cemented and hardened by weathering products such as silica, or oxides of iron and aluminium.

Mesas erode by the backwearing of slopes, usually assisted by undercutting of the hard, caprock surfaces. As they erode, therefore, the angles of the slopes remain constant and their distinctive shape remains constant until all the capping rock disintegrates (figures 7.65 and 7.66). Mesas that have very little of their capping rock remaining are known as **buttes**.

7.65 *This former mesa in Arizona (USA) was eroded to form a butte.*

7.66 *Further erosion of this butte near Mount Isa in Australia can be expected to remove the last traces of the hard capping rock, leading to the rapid disintegration of the softer rock beneath it.*

As erosion removes material from the surface of an arid environment, rocks tend to be left behind because they are more resistant. When a stony layer is all that is left behind, the area is termed a **stony desert**. Several types of stony deserts can be identified depending on the nature of the rocks. Where the surface is covered with small rocks, the desert is known as a **gibber desert** in Australia, and **reg** or **serir** in the Sahara (figure 7.67). When the stones are packed so tightly together that no spaces remain between them, then the surface is termed **desert pavement** or **desert armour**, because the surface protects the underlying soil from erosion.

7.67 *This reg, or gibber desert, is situated between Goulimime and Er Rachidia in Morocco.*

QUESTION BLOCK 7L

1. *Give two examples of residual landforms, and describe their formation.*

Opportunities and Challenges for Management

Managing Agriculture in High Altitude Environments

7.68 *Zermatt is typical of many Swiss villages in that it is situated in a sheltered valley.*

In general, people in mountainous areas prefer to live at lower altitudes (figure 7.68). In Switzerland, only 5% of the population live at altitudes above 1000 metres, which is approximately half the country's total land area. In Nepal, the proportion of people living at higher altitudes is greater, as table 7.3 shows. Factors at high altitudes

Table 7.3
Population Distribution by Altitude, Nepal

	Below 300m	300 to 900 m	900 to 1500 m	1500 to 2100 m	2100 to 2700 m	2700 to 3300 m	Above 3300 m
% of population	38.6	11.5	27.4	14.8	5.4	1.7	0.6

Source: Panday (1995) p.196

which discourage settlement include the harsh climate, lack of communication facilities, difficulty of cultivation and the additional expense in bringing in materials to build warm, substantial housing.

In many mountainous areas, the vertical distribution of population is seasonal. Farming activities move to higher altitudes during summer and down to lower altitudes during winter – a process known as **transhumance**. In Nepal, transhumance applies mainly to cattle grazing activities. Animals such as sheep, goats and yak are well adapted to high altitudes, and they make good use of higher altitude grazing pastures up to 4,100 metres during the summer months. During the cooler winter months, the herds are brought to lower altitudes of between 2,000 and 3,000 metres. As lower altitude livestock such as cows, buffalo and pigs also use these altitudes, there is considerable pressure on feed supplies during the winter months.

7.69 *Vegetable farming on the lower slopes near Stalden, Switzerland.*

In the Swiss Alps, a typical farm comprises arable croplands in the valley floors, leading up to the forest zone and above that the natural pastures that are used only in summer (figure 7.69). The main type of animal raised is the cow, usually for the production of milk although increasingly also for meat. Traditionally, the cows in Switzerland were taken to higher alpine grazing pastures during summer and then brought back to the valley floors for the winter months where they were housed inside a barn attached to the farmer's house.

Upper altitude lands are tending to cease agricultural use in Switzerland because of the difficulty of making a living from farming in the harsh environment with its thin soils, rocky ground, steep slopes, heavy precipitation and pastures covered by snow for up to six months of each year. Swiss farms tend to be very small, with an average size of only five hectares, and many farmers are choosing to leave their farms in search of higher incomes in office jobs in the towns or in the tourist industry. The Swiss government is trying to stop the exodus of farmers by setting artificially high prices for farming products, and by providing generous grants for farm improvement. In spite of these measures, the number of Swiss farmers continues to decline. By contrast, there is no similar decline in Nepal, where most farmers are subsistence producers - over 80% of Nepal's work force are farmers.

QUESTION BLOCK 7M

1. *Contrast the willingness of people in Nepal and Switzerland to live at high altitudes.*

2. *Explain the concept of transhumance.*

3. *Why are farmer numbers in Switzerland declining?*

Managing Tourism in High Altitude Environments

Tourism is an important industry in many high altitude areas where the scenic beauty of the mountains attracts many people each year. Tourism as an industry began in Switzerland. In 1863, an English excursionist, Thomas Cook, conducted the first tour to the Jungfrau region of Switzerland from Britain, escorting a large group of 62 people in search of spectacular scenery. When Swiss tourism began, there were of course no trains or cable cars, and part of the adventure was the hardship (figure 7.70). The trip proved to be a great success, and numbers of tourists to Switzerland began to grow and have continued to grow ever since. Currently, about 120 million tourists visit Switzerland each year, providing 6% of the country's GNI. Over half the tourists come from Germany, France and the USA, with other important source countries being Britain, Austria and the Netherlands. The nature of Swiss tourism has changed over the years, as table 7.4 shows, although most tourists are still attracted by the spectacular scenery (figure 7.71).

Table 7.4
The Changing Nature of Tourism in Switzerland

Period	Type of Tourists	Means of Transport	Type of Accommodation	Main Areas Visited
1700s	Scientists interested in alpine plants and wildlife	Horse-drawn carriages	Local houses and inns	Alpine peaks
1800s	Climbers from Europe wanting to climb the main peaks	On foot, or horse-drawn carriages	Local houses and inns	Matterhorn, Eiger, and other alpine peaks
Late 1800s	Aristocrats taking advantage of clean air and water. People suffering from tuberculosis who were sent to health spas (sanatoria) to recover	Train	Large hotels	High altitude areas like St Moritz, famous for spa waters
1920s	Higher socio-economic groups for skiing	Train	Large hotels with access to a variety of skiing areas	New' alpine areas such as Wengen, Mürren and Gstaad
1950s onwards	Most socio-economic groups, for winter and summer holidays	Car, train and air	Smaller hotels and self-catering apartments	Location varies with the time of year. Newer skiing areas in winter and lakeside resorts or walking areas in summer

Source: Adapted from Davis and Flint (1986) p.230

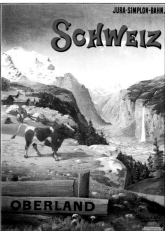

7.70 *Early posters promoting Switzerland as a tourist destination.*

7.71 *Tourists relaxing while admiring Switzerland's famous peak, the Matterhorn.*

Tourism brings both benefits and problems to Switzerland. It certainly generates a great deal of wealth for the country, which is used to develop roads, services, railways, schools and industry in remote areas (figure 7.72). It generates employment in hotels, transport and other service facilities. It is estimated that one job is created for every six to eight hotel beds, or for every 60 to 80 self-catering apartment beds. The disadvantages are that prices are raised for local people, traditional customs and dances may become commercialised for the tourists' pleasure, and employment opportunities are somewhat seasonal. Because Swiss people do not seem to enjoy working in hotels and restaurants, much of the seasonal labour is supplied by employing migrant workers from other European countries such as Italy and Spain.

Another problem that can be caused by tourism is damage to the fragile alpine environment. Highland areas are very slow to recover from damage caused by tramping or littering, and the Swiss have undertaken extensive education campaigns to alert tourists from other areas of these problems (figure 7.73).

In contrast to Switzerland's long history of tourism, Nepal was a closed country until 1952, with no outsiders being permitted to enter the country. Since then, the number of tourists has grown steadily – 4,017 tourists in 1960, 45,000 in 1970, 223,000 in 1986, 363,000 in 1995 and 550,000 in 2008 (despite political instability at the time). At present, tourism contributes significantly to Nepal's total foreign earnings. However, the earnings from tourism can fluctuate widely as a result of economic recessions, famine and political disturbances, both within Nepal as happened between 2001 and 2008, and elsewhere around the world.

When Nepal first opened for tourism, a large proportion of the tourists were hippies who came either in search of spiritual enlightenment from Hindu gurus (teachers) and sadhus (holy men), or en route from South-east Asia to Britain, driving overland on what was known as 'the hippie trail' through Thailand, India, Afghanistan, Iran and Turkey. During this period of the 1960s, Kathmandu became known as a centre of drug use, chiefly around the area known as Freak Street. However, the hippie days have long since passed in Nepal, and of the tourists who came to Nepal in 2008, just over 50% came for sightseeing, 23% for trekking and mountaineering, 6% for business, 5% on government business, 2% for religious pilgrimages, 2% for conventions and conferences, and just over 11% for other purposes.

through an agency (organised trek), by hiring their own guides and porters (tea shop trek) or by doing the trek themselves unaccompanied (budget trek). Trekking fees are imposed to control numbers, and treks to environmentally sensitive mountain areas such as Lomanthang and Mustang cost over $US500 per day, and permits are limited to 1,000 treks annually. The fee for climbing Mount Everest is $US7,000 per person with a minimum charge of $US35,000 per expedition.

7.73 *This small sign on a seat provided beside a walking track reminds tourists of the need to 'take nothing but photographs and leave nothing but footprints'.*

7.74 *Tourists are attracted to Nepal's mountain scenery, but ironically this means hotels and tourist facilities are often built in places that can spoil the natural beauty of the landscape. These hotels overlook the Himalayas from the hill town of Nagarkot.*

As is the case in Switzerland, tourism in Nepal brings both benefits and problems. The main benefit is economic – tourism contributes 3.5% of Nepal's GDP and 15% of its total foreign exchange earnings. On the other hand, tourism can generate environmental and social problems. The sudden influx of large numbers of tourists into Nepal's traditional society brought about big social changes in Nepal. Tourists bring new ideas, new modes of dress and new goods with them from elsewhere in the world. In an effort to earn money from tourists, local Nepalese people sometimes compromise their own culture to make tourists feel more at home. The effects of this can be seen in the streets of many towns in Nepal where tourists travel.

7.72 *An example of tourism leading to transport services being provided in remote areas is the rack railway to the 2132 metres high summit of Mount Pilatus near Lucerne in Switzerland. With a gradient of 48% in places, this is the steepest cog-wheel railway in the world.*

Nepal's attraction as a tourist destination lies in its spectacular mountain scenery (figure 7.74). Sightseeing and trekking are concentrated in eight designated national parks and two conservation areas spanning a wide variety of ecosystems. Trekking is controlled to protect the environment as much as possible. Tourists can organise a trek

The most significant problems caused by tourism affect Nepal's biophysical environment. In high mountains where the temperature is often cold, garbage left behind by trekkers does not break down for decades. About 90% of trekkers in Nepal use just three trekking areas, and this places great strains on the fragile local environment. By the end of the 2007 climbing season, there had been 3,679 ascents to the summit of Mount Everest since it was first climbed in 1953, and rubbish from these climbs still litters the routes to the top of the mountain. Even faeces left behind by climbers will still be intact after many decades in the alpine air if it is not buried. In recent years this problem has become even worse as trekkers have begun taking food in plastic as well as metal containers. It is estimated that there are some 600 tonnes of garbage lying on Mount Everest alone, and each expedition leaves an additional 400 to 500 kilograms of waste.

In an effort to keep the mountain environments clean, the Nepalese Government now imposes a $US4,000 expedition deposit from climbers, refundable upon return to Kathmandu on condition that all the group's rubbish and equipment has been removed from the mountain. A Nepalese initiative, the Sagarmantha Pollution Control Project (SPCP) has begun to educate tourists and local people about the importance of not leaving rubbish in alpine areas. However, proposals to install incinerators to destroy rubbish had to be abandoned as local people believe that the smell of burning rubbish is offensive to the mountain gods. Shortly before his death in 2008, Sir Edmund Hillary, who with the Nepalese climber Sherpa Tenzing, was the first person to climb Mount Everest, called for the mountain to be closed for at least five years so that some of the environmental damage can heal.

7.75 *A Nepalese woman carries scarce fuelwood past stalls with souvenirs for tourists. Tourists add to the pressure on scarce fuelwood, often being prepared to pay higher prices than local people can afford. Ironically, revenue from selling souvenirs to tourists helps local people to pay for fuelwood!*

Rubbish is not the only cause of environmental damage. Trekkers need fire for heating and cooking, and this is leading to the cutting down of scarce timber. Fuelwood is Nepal's main source of energy, and tourists are now competing with local people for the dwindling supply. The

lodges in one small village on the Annapurna trekking route consume one hectare of virgin rhododendron forest each year to serve the needs of the trekkers. Each trekker consumes six to seven kilograms of firewood per day. This forces the local people to go further and further away in search of fuelwood (figure 7.75).

These problems have led to calls for 'Green Trekking', where tourists are made more aware of the damage they can cause. Some suggestions made to tourists to reduce environmental impact have included:

- trek with a guide who uses kerosene instead of timber for fuel. This costs more but leave the forests intact.

- co-ordinate menu and eating times with other trekkers to reduce the use of fuel.

- dress warmly to reduce the need for heating at night.

- burn paper wastes and bury biodegradables (food wastes and excreta).

- urinate and defecate at least 30 metres away from any water source. If possible, burn toilet paper and carry out excreta in plastic bags.

- bathe away from drinking sources and use biodegradable soap.

- avoid buying hot water from a lodge that does not have a hydro-electric heating system.

- keep non-biodegradables to a minimum, especially batteries.

QUESTION BLOCK 7N

1. On balance, is tourism beneficial or detrimental for (a) Switzerland, and (b) Nepal? Explain your answer fully.

Case Study of Managing Agriculture, Mineral Extraction and Tourism in a High Altitude Environment - The Altiplano of Bolivia

Bolivia is the highest, poorest and most isolated nation in South America. It is a landlocked nation, one of only two in South America. This means it has no access to the ocean. Bolivia covers an area of 1,098,581 square kilometres and spans an area from the top of the Andes Mountains down to the floodplain of the Amazon River. Within this area live ten million people, 65% of whom are indigenous people from 'Indian' groups such as the Quechua and Aymará (figure 7.76). The remaining 35% are descended from Spanish immigrants who came to Bolivia in the 14th and 15th centuries in search of silver. The Spanish declared Bolivia a colony in 1531. Spanish culture continues to have quite an influence on Bolivia, even though independence was achieved in 1824.

7.76 *Indigenous groups celebrating Carnivale in Bolivia's capital La Paz.*

The Altiplano is the most densely populated part of Bolivia. The name 'Altiplano' means 'High Plain', although it is anything but flat. The Altiplano has basins at about 3,500 to 4,000 metres in altitude, but ranges up to snow-capped peaks exceeding 6,500 metres in altitude (figure 7.77). The region stretches down the western side of Bolivia, from the border with Peru down to the border with Argentina.

7.77 *La Paz is situated in a valley of the Andes Mountains.*

The Altiplano climate

As one would expect in such an elevated area, temperatures are quite cool throughout the year. The statistics for Bolivia's capital city, La Paz, which is just below 4000 metres in altitude, give some idea of the climate (table 7.5).

Most of the rain falls in summer when much of the Altiplano becomes wrapped in mists and cloud. During this time, lakes on the Altiplano grow in size and the cattle

stand knee deep in swamp. In the winter, almost no rain falls, and the area turns shades of brown and grey, becoming like a semi-desert. Because the air is so thin at high altitudes, the temperature drops dramatically every time the sun passes behind a cloud.

QUESTION BLOCK 7O

1. *Where is the Altiplano?*

2. *Why does the Altiplano house a multi-cultural society?*

3. *Why is the temperature in La Paz so even through the year?*

4. *La Paz is located quite close to the equator. Therefore, we might expect temperatures in La Paz to be quite hot. So, why are the temperatures in La Paz so cool?*

5. *Describe the rainfall in La Paz, mentioning when it falls through the year and its amount compared with your own city.*

Silver mining

The Spanish came to Bolivia in search of silver. One of the world's largest deposits of silver was found at Potosí in 1544, and a few years later it had a population of 160,000 people - the largest settlement in the Americas at the time. Other silver mines were found and a huge influx of Spanish people followed. Local Bolivian people were forced to work in the mines in work gangs under terrible conditions. Thousands died, either in accidents or through diseases such as pulmonary silicosis. Nonetheless, it was mining that led to the region's first large-scale inmigration of people from other areas.

The mining has also had adverse effects on the biophysical environment. Large areas were cleared of vegetation, and this resulted in massive soil erosion on the steep slopes of the mountainous areas (figure 7.78). Land became wasteland, especially where the soils were soft or comprised fine, clay particles. The eroded soil was washed down the hill side and into the streams below. Many of the Altiplano's rivers and streams have thus become choked with sediment from the mining erosion (figure 7.79).

QUESTION BLOCK 7P

1. *Describe the processes which combined to form the landscape shown in figures 7.77, 7.78 and 7.79.*

Table 7.5
Climatic Statistics for La Paz, Bolivia (Latitude 16°S, Longitude 65°W, Altitude 3759 metres)

	Jan	Feb	Mar	Apr	May	Jun	Jul	Aug	Sep	Oct	Nov	Dec
Average Temperature °C	18	18	18	19	17	17	17	17	18	19	19	19
Average Precipitation (mm)	138	87	80	32	2	2	2	3	25	50	51	88

Extreme environments

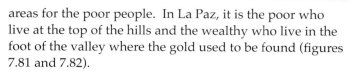

areas for the poor people. In La Paz, it is the poor who live at the top of the hills and the wealthy who live in the foot of the valley where the gold used to be found (figures 7.81 and 7.82).

7.78 Badly eroded hillsides in the Valley of the Moon, Bolivia.

7.80 An oblique aerial view of La Paz. The CBD can be seen in the centre foreground, marked by the large high rise buildings.

7.79 This stream near La Paz is filled with sediments from mining operations upstream.

7.81 A poorer residential area of La Paz, situated on the upper edges of the canyon.

Urban growth - the city of La Paz

With a population of over a million people, La Paz is Bolivia's largest city. Like many of Bolivia's towns and cities, it began as a **mining settlement**. It was founded in 1548 and was named *La Ciudad de Nuestra Señora de la Paz*, which means 'The City of Our Lady of Peace'. The river which flows through La Paz, the Río Choqueyapu, contained alluvial gold, and a settlement was established beside the river in the bottom of a steep canyon specifically as a mining settlement (figure 7.80). The site of the first settlement still marks the centre of La Paz, and it is where the city's modern, high-rise buildings are found. In this respect, La Paz is unusual. Most cities in developing nations have a zone where wealthy people live on the tops of the hills where there is a view, leaving the low

7.82 A wealthier suburb of La Paz, situated in the valley floor near the CBD.

Because La Paz is at a high altitude, its temperatures remain quite cool throughout the year. This enables open air markets to sell foods such as meat without the use of refrigeration (figure 7.83). A poor nation such as Bolivia has limited electricity, and so refrigeration is rare. Other services often lacking in La Paz are rubbish collection and sewage disposal. Like governments in many developing nations, Bolivia's government raises little taxation to provide services for its people. This means that many areas of La Paz become open garbage tips and open toilets. This poses a hazard for people's health as well as lowering environmental quality (figure 7.84). Diarrhoea is a major problem in La Paz, and many children die each year from the effects of intestinal upsets.

7.83 *Meat for sale in open air street markets, La Paz, Bolivia.*

7.84 *Rubbish and an open drain carrying sewage characterise this slope in a poor residential neighbourhood of La Paz.*

7.85 *Sub-standard housing in La Paz, Bolivia.*

These **environmental problems** have become worse in recent years due to **rural-urban migration**. Thousands of people move to La Paz each year from smaller towns and rural areas of the Altiplano. Many of these people do not have jobs or the money to buy housing. Great pressure is put upon the limited amount of housing in La Paz, and shanty settlements have sprung up to meet the demand for housing (figure 7.85). These shanty settlements appear on vacant land, often land which is too steep for 'normal' building, and put more pressures upon the limited services available in La Paz such as transport, waste disposal and electricity.

QUESTION BLOCK 7Q

1. *Describe the impact of mining and landforms on the development of La Paz.*

2. *In what way is the urban pattern of La Paz different from that in most other cities? Why did these differences arise?*

3. *Why are there shanty settlements in La Paz?*

4. *Describe the environmental problems faced by the residents of the shanties.*

Agriculture on the Altiplano

Figures 7.86 to 7.90, show aspects of farming and agriculture on the Altiplano. Life is difficult in the harsh, windswept climate and most of the people spend their lives producing their own food. The farmers must put up with the bitter cold, strong winds, droughts and the lack of oxygen at high altitudes with little electricity or modern conveniences.

7.86 *Animal herding on the Altiplano.*

Most farmers produce a mixture of crops and animals. Animal raising is very labour intensive. It is rare to see animals outside without someone in the fields to look after them to prevent them being stolen. Animals raised include pigs, cattle, sheep and llamas. The crops which are grown must have a short growing season to survive in the harsh, cold conditions. Special varieties of vegetables are produced, often on terraced hillsides where the land is steep.

The surplus food which is produced is usually sold in open markets in the towns and villages of the region. These villages are also centres of communication and exchange of information. In a society with few radios and almost no televisions, information is spread by word of mouth. Towns and villages tend to be small and are often centred on a Catholic church. Buildings tend to be constructed from mud bricks or fired bricks, made with local clay. These provide some protection against the cold winds when used in a building which has glass windows.

7.87 *A woman and her children look after some sheep.*

7.88 *The town of Copacabana and its surrounding farmlands.*

7.89 *Hills with very little vegetation are used for animal grazing.*

7.90 *Terraced hillsides near Lake Titicaca.*

QUESTION BLOCK 7R

1. *Are the farmers on the Altiplano affected by their biophysical environment? In your answer, consider how each of the following parts of the biophysical environment might affect farmers: climate, soils, landforms, vegetation.*

2. *Do the farmers in the Altiplano in turn affect their physical environment? Consider again the parts of the biophysical environment: climate, soils, landforms, vegetation.*

3. *What is meant by the term 'labour intensive'? What would be the opposite of this term?*

Tourism and change in the Altiplano

Although Bolivia is an isolated nation, **tourists** are starting to arrive, although the numbers are still very small. Tourists come in search of the exotic lifestyles and spectacular scenery of the Altiplano, although services for tourists remain poorly developed (figures 7.91 to 7.94). However, tourists bring new ideas with them and change the values of local people. In recent years, there have been increasing reports of robbery, theft and muggings of tourists by local people who envy the material wealth of tourists.

7.91 *Selling foetuses and various plants and animals for witchcraft in La Paz.*

7.92 *A typical village scene in the Altiplano.*

7.93 *Selling household goods in the street markets of La Paz.*

7.94 *Evidence of transnational corporate investment can be seen in the advertising in central La Paz.*

As more and more tourism develops, a demand arises for improved services, known as infrastructure. Often, though, the nation may be unable to afford these improvements. Transport services in the Altiplano provide one example of such services. Bus transport in many parts of the Altiplano are very basic and accidents are common (figure 7.95). Petrol is scarce and very expensive for local people. Petrol stations are few and far between. In recent years, new buses have been bought, some with air conditioning, but these are rarely used by local people.

Tourism has so far brought few benefits to local people on the Altiplano.

Perhaps more worrying is that some tourists might regard the local people merely as interesting curiosities. Tourists who travel on package tours rarely take the time to learn about the culture and history of the people in the places they are seeing. When this happens, there is a real danger that tourists from the richer nations will simply see the poverty of the people, not the richness of their culture and heritage. Moreover, when tourists are cut off from the local people in air conditioned buses the local people cannot afford, then local people could well feel resentment. They may see the tourists as intruders whom they did not invite into their area.

7.95 *Inter-urban public transport in the Altiplano often relies on old buses or trucks.*

In an LEDC such as Bolivia, where there is little money to provide services, tourists can make great demands upon the limited facilities available. This can lead to local people having to take second place to tourists in the demand for services, and it can lead to problems such as traffic congestion in the cities. If it is well managed and well informed, tourism can break down cultural barriers. However, at its worst, tourism can lead to resentment and environmental degradation.

QUESTION BLOCK 7S

1. *Is tourism a positive or negative factor in the Altiplano?*

2. *Outline the effects of tourists on the environment of the Altiplano.*

3. *Why would local people rarely use the air conditioned buses?*

Management Issues in Hot Arid Environments

Desertification, which is the process whereby deserts expand into semi-arid areas or become more intense, has been identified as a significant global issue (figure 7.96).

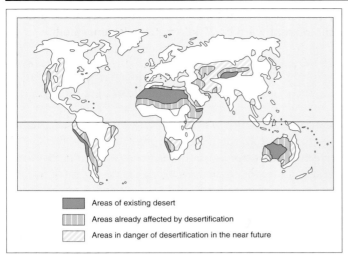

7.96 *The world distribution of areas threatened by desertification.*

Legend:
- Areas of existing desert
- Areas already affected by desertification
- Areas in danger of desertification in the near future

Less Economically Developed Countries (LEDCs) are especially vulnerable to desertification, partly because many of the world's semi-arid areas are on the edges of deserts in LEDCs, and partly because poverty pushes farmers in those countries to over-utilise the land in an effort to increase their meagre incomes. Where farmers cannot afford remedies that involve land and water management, or where they are not able to see the 'big picture' because of their own needs driven by poverty, then solutions become very difficult.

7.97 *Nomadic Tuareg people camping near their demountable shelter in the Sahara Desert, north-west of Timbuktu, Mali.*

More Economically Developed Countries (MEDCs) are also vulnerable to desertification, however. Serious soil erosion is occurring in Australia's arid areas, and most of this has been the result of mismanagement of pastoral grazing activities. As a consequence of the deteriorating environment, the economic productivity of Australia's arid terrains may even now be declining.

The Gascoyne Basin of Western Australia currently supports about 320 people, about 400,000 cattle and an unknown number of wild animals. It produces several million dollars of export income per year in a deteriorating physical environment. Before the arrival of Europeans, the area is thought to have supported 500 Indigenous people, engaged in hunting and gathering, with minimal

impact on their environment. Today, about 16,000 subsistence nomads and farmers occupy similar areas in northern Africa in an environment that is even more degraded (figures 7.97 to 7.100). It therefore comes as no surprise that desertification is a much more serious problem in Africa than in Australia.

7.98 *Nomadic animal herders use camels for transport as these animals have adapted to the hot dry conditions of the desert.*

7.99 *The nomadic animal herders have brought their animals into the town of Timbuktu in search of water. They have erected their huts in an area of vacant land and used mud bricks to build a temporary pen to hold their animals.*

7.100 *Although it is the largest town in northern Mali, Timbuktu has just one sealed road. Like Timbuktu itself, the road is becoming buried in sands that blow in from the surrounding Sahara Desert.*

Most researchers now argue that desertification is caused by a combination of human and natural forces. **Natural causes** of desertification include a long-term trend towards receiving less precipitation, either in the form of reduced amounts of rainfall or as less reliable rainfall. Other long-term climatic conditions such as dry winds, higher temperatures, reduced condensation and a higher rate of evaporation can exacerbate the effect of reduced precipitation.

The negative effects of these natural forces may be exaggerated by **human actions** such as deforestation, the over-exploitation of resources, the mismanagement of water, intensive agricultural or ranching practices. In China, for example, the cultivation of light textured soils in marginal, semi-arid areas for wheat has led to reduced plant productivity, a decline in soil quality and desertification. The problem is that as crop productivity declines, farmers often respond by farming the land even more intensively than previously to compensate for the reduced production, and this accelerates the process of desertification (figure 7.101).

7.101 *Placing too many cattle on marginal semi-arid farmlands may be a cause of desertification. This image shows animals grazing near Timbuktu, Mali.*

Desertification is not irreversible. Natural processes such as changes in precipitation and temperature seem to come in cycles. During the 1970s and 1980s, it was noticed that satellite images showed the Sahara Desert expanding southwards into the area known as the Sahel at a rate of about five kilometres per year. It was believed that this provided evidence for either global warming or over-grazing of the Sahel lands by the cattle of local herders. However, satellite images of the same area in the 1990s shows the southern boundary of the Sahara was retreating to the north once again. In fact, the trends were somewhat complex. From 1980 to 1984, the Sahara Desert expanded southwards, with the boundary shifting 240 kilometres. However, from 1984 to 1985, the trend reversed and the boundary moved north by 110 kilometres in a single year (1984), and then a further 30 kilometres north the following year. In 1987, the boundary moved southwards by 55 kilometres, and then northward

by 100 kilometres in 1988. In 1989 and 1990, the boundary shifted southward by 77 kilometres. Recent satellite measurements suggest that there is no long-term trend for the Sahara Desert to expand, although the pressures for farmers to put too many animals on small areas of marginal land does continue as a response to their poverty.

Desertification can be controlled if people can make more rational use of scarce water resources, collect and channel water more effectively, reduce or substitute activities that are damaging the environment, or manage the soil more sensitively. A particularly effective means of arresting desertification is to plant trees (reafforestation), as this binds the soil together and reduces erosion as well as increasing humidity, thus potentially increasing precipitation (figure 7.102).

7.102 *An area of reafforestation at Yadan (China) in the Gobi Desert, which is designed to stabilise the sands and soil of the region's wind-blown landscape.*

Access to water is a key factor in managing arid environments effectively. In some countries, irrigation is seen as the answer to these problems. **Irrigation** means bringing water from another area through canals or pipes in order to grow crops or vegetation. This can be a very expensive process requiring huge investments to establish and then maintain the infrastructure (figure 7.103).

7.103 *This Soviet-era irrigation canal near Lake Issuk-Kul in Kyrgyzstan has fallen into disrepair. Large sections of the concrete structure have been stolen by local people for use as building materials.*

In the south-west of the United States, a huge scheme has been built to divert water from the Colorado River across the deserts of southern California. Water is collected in a series of dams on the Colorado River. These dams serve other purposes in addition to water storage. Several are used to generate hydro-electricity, and the lakes of the dams are also used for tourism. From the dams, the water is pumped along several canals to irrigate fruit and vegetable cultivation in southern California (figure 7.104). This enables food to be grown that would otherwise have to be brought to the area from elsewhere (figure 7.105). Water management in the Colorado Basin was discussed in more detail in chapter 5, and this can be compared to water management in Turkmenistan that was discussed in chapter 3.

7.104 *An irrigation canal bringing water from the Colorado River to southern California. There is considerable loss of water due to seepage and evaporation.*

7.105 *Cultivation using irrigation in the Imperial Valley of southern California. The transformation of the landscape can be seen by comparing the irrigated farms in the foreground with the arid terrain of the background.*

Arid environments are being used more and more as sources of energy generation. Because they are rarely affected by cloud cover, deserts make excellent places to generate solar energy. Most of Australia's long distance telephone lines have now been replaced with solar powered optical fibre links. Many desert areas comprise wide, flat areas of plains. In such areas, wind power is an effective way to generate electricity because there are few barriers to block the movement of air. The United States is a leader in this type of power generation, and several large wind farms have been built in the deserts of the south-western USA.

7.106 *An isolated homestead near Alice Springs, central Australia.*

7.107 *Mudstone badlands scenery at Zabriskie Point, near Furnace Creek, Death Valley.*

Traditionally, deserts were areas of sparse population where travel was difficult and slow (figures 7.106 and 7.107). Greater ability to harness and divert water supplies has enabled arid environments to develop in ways that were previously thought to be impossible. However, conflicts can arise when competing land uses are incompatible. For example, it is very rare that tourism and mining can co-exist in the same area. Similarly, conflicts can arise when there is competition for scarce water resources among uses such as urban centres, hydroelectricity, irrigation and recreation.

QUESTION BLOCK 7T

1. *Is desertification caused by natural or human factors? Give reasons for your answer.*

2. *Why are LEDCs especially vulnerable to desertification?*

3. *Describe some of the new ways that deserts are being used, and outline the conflicts that may arise as a consequence.*

Case Study of Managing Agriculture, Mineral Extraction and Tourism in a Hot, Arid Environment - Death Valley

The name 'Death Valley' implies desolation and lifelessness. Sun-baked, barren **badlands** rise from the valley floor, and plants and animals seem totally absent (figures 7.44 and 7.107). Travellers to Death Valley in summer are handed leaflets entitled 'How to survive your summer trip through Death Valley'. The leaflet contains advice such as the following:

- Thirst, like pain, is a warning. Suppressing thirst by sucking a pebble or chewing gum will conceal your body's need, not satisfy it. Carry plenty of water and drink it freely. Stop to drink every hour or so - whether you feel thirsty or not.

- Salt is not a substitute for water. You should replace salt you lose in perspiration, but you cannot slow your perspiration rate with more.

- Clothing retains perspiration and keeps you cooler. Clothing also protects you from solar radiation. If you are not wearing a shirt, sunglasses, and a broad-brimmed hat, you are not prepared to walk anywhere in Death Valley.

- Avoid wind. It speeds up your evaporation rate and stirs up the low-level hot air layer created by radiation from the ground.

- Ground temperature in summer is seldom less than 65°C and may reach 93°C. Rest when you need to, but do it in the shade. Do not sit or lie in the sun.

- If storm clouds gather, be alert. Thunderstorms in the mountains can cause flash flooding in the washes that cross the highways several kilometres distant. If there are clouds over the mountains, watch for water running in the washes or road dips even though the sun may be shining.

This travel advice makes Death Valley seem like a very hostile environment for people. Even the names in Death Valley suggest hostility – Coffin Canyon, Deadman Pass, Funeral Mountains and Last Chance Range to name a few. However, it is known that Native Americans have lived in the area for at least 10,000 years before European settlement.

Death Valley is one of many desert basins between the Sierra Nevada mountains near the west coast of California in the United States and the Colorado Plateau to the east. The extreme aridity of Death Valley is the result of this situation – orographic rain falls over the mountains to each side of the valley, creating a rainshadow effect within the valley.

7.108 *The sign at the entrance to Death Valley gives a stylised cross-section of the valley.*

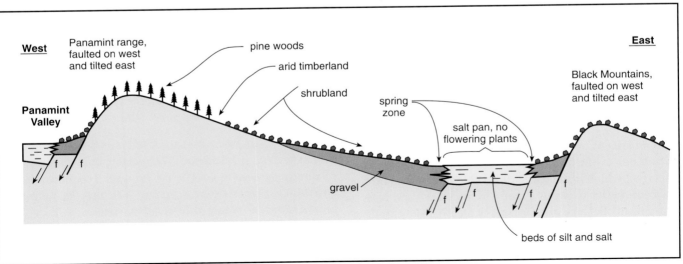

7.109 *Simplified cross-section through Death Valley. Fault lines are shown by the letter 'f'.*

Extreme environments

Death Valley is located on the border between the states of California and Nevada, approximately 300 kilometres in straight line distance from Los Angeles. Because of its unique topography (it includes the lowest point in North America) and climate (it is the hottest and driest part of the United States), the area was declared a national park in 1933 (figure 7.108).

Death Valley comprises three quite distinct environments (figure 7.109). Bordering Death Valley to the west are high, rocky mountain ranges, known as the Panamint Range, while to the east are another set of mountains known as the Black Mountains. As figure 7.110 shows, these two mountain ranges are both uplifted blocks which have been tilted towards the east, forming steep western slopes and gentle eastern slopes. Death Valley is thus a structural sag, separated from the two mountain ranges by fault lines in the rocks.

7.110 *After crossing the flat land in the foreground, this road climbs the gentle slope of the gravel fan before ascending up across the Panamint Range.*

Sloping into Death Valley from each of the mountain ranges are gravel fans of rock debris washed down from the mountain sides (figure 7.110). The gravel fans end at the edge of a broad salt-crusted mud flat which is the dry bed of a playa lake which last contained permanent water during the last ice age 10,000 years ago. Groundwater is close to the surface at the point where the gravel fans meet the playa lake, and a strip of springs sustains a few plants. The playa lake is too salty for flowering plants to survive, however. Desert shrubs grow up to about 2,000 metres on the mountain slopes, and above this pine trees grow.

Salt and water

With an area of over 500 square kilometres, the Death Valley salt pan is one of the world's largest playa lakes. The salt crust, which is mainly sodium chloride, varies from a few centimetres to about a metre in thickness, and rests on damp mud. Because the streams of Death Valley all flow into the playa, the concentration of salts becomes stronger and stronger over time, and the concentration of salt is considerably stronger than sea water.

Water in Death Valley comes largely from rain and snow in other places. The water seeps through the ground and enables fresh water to be available from three sources. In the mountain areas, small springs bring water to the surface, although it usually seeps away into the surface downslope. In the gravel fans bordering the salt pan, the groundwater is close enough to the surface to allow hand-dug wells to retrieve it, although much of this water is too salty to drink (figure 7.112). The third source of fresh water is the large warm springs which discharge water along some of the rock faults, and it is this source that supplies the small town of Furnace Springs. The springs supply enough water to irrigate a plantation of date palms and a golf course at Furnace Creek (figure 7.111).

The drainage basin of Death Valley covers about 23,000 square kilometres, with altitudes ranging from 85 metres below sea level on the valley floor near Badwater to 3,350 metres at Telescope Peak in the Panamint Range 21 kilometres west of Badwater (figure 7.113). Within the drainage basin there are several streams, of which Salt Creek brings the largest volume of water into Death Valley. All the streams in the drainage basin flow into Badwater Basin, the lowest point in Death Valley.

7.111 *This small creek carries water from a spring east of Furnace Creek into the centre of Death Valley.*

QUESTION BLOCK 7U

1. *Explain why Death Valley is so dry.*

2. *Referring to figure 7.109, describe the different environments of Death Valley.*

3. *Account for the general distribution of water springs in Death Valley, shown in figure 7.112.*

4. *Draw an east-west cross section of the area shown on the topographic map in figure 7.113 passing through Natural Bridge (labelled number 19 on the map). Label any features which appear on the cross section. Note that the contours are marked in metres at 50 metre intervals.*

5. *Interpret the symbols shown on the map in figure 7.113 to list the services provided in Furnace Creek village.*

7.112 *Map of Death Valley showing the principal springs (shown as solid circles) and seepage areas (shown as open circles) around the salt pan. Heights are shown in metres.*

Deposition - sand dunes and gravel fans

Although sand dunes are found in many desert areas, Death Valley has only one area with them, although this is a large area of several square kilometres (figure 7.114).

They have formed in the north of Death Valley along the course of Salt Creek and Mesquite Flat, where the winds have a long tract of open valley to collect the fine sediments into sand dunes.

The gravel fans of Death Valley are very extensive, especially on the western side of the valley beside the Panamint Range. In places, the gravel fans on this western side of the valley are 10 kilometres in length and rise 500 metres higher than the salt pan. On the eastern side, the fans are smaller, being usually about one kilometre in length and peaking about 50 metres above the salt pan. The difference reflects the angles of the two mountain ranges as they border Death Valley; being a gentler slope the Panamint Range has a larger catchment area for the gravel.

The gravel fans include areas that are the driest ground in Death Valley. The gravel fans receive less rainfall than the nearby mountains, and scarcely more than the valley floor. However, the gravel fans are highly permeable, and therefore they cannot retain moisture; the water that runs onto them quickly seeps into the ground. Thus, vegetation cannot become established in these areas.

Climate

In 1868, the author of the first United States mineral resource report, J. Ross Browne, wrote this of Death Valley's climate:

"The climate in winter is finer that that of Italy, though perhaps fastidious people might object to the temperature in summer... I have even heard complaint that the thermometer failed to show the true heat because the mercury dried up. Everything dries: wagons dry; men dry; chickens dry; there is no juice left in anything, living or dead, by the close of summer".

Death Valley is indeed the hottest and driest part of the United States south-western desert areas. Winter temperatures rarely fall below 0°C, but summer temperatures average over 40°C and have reached much more than this.

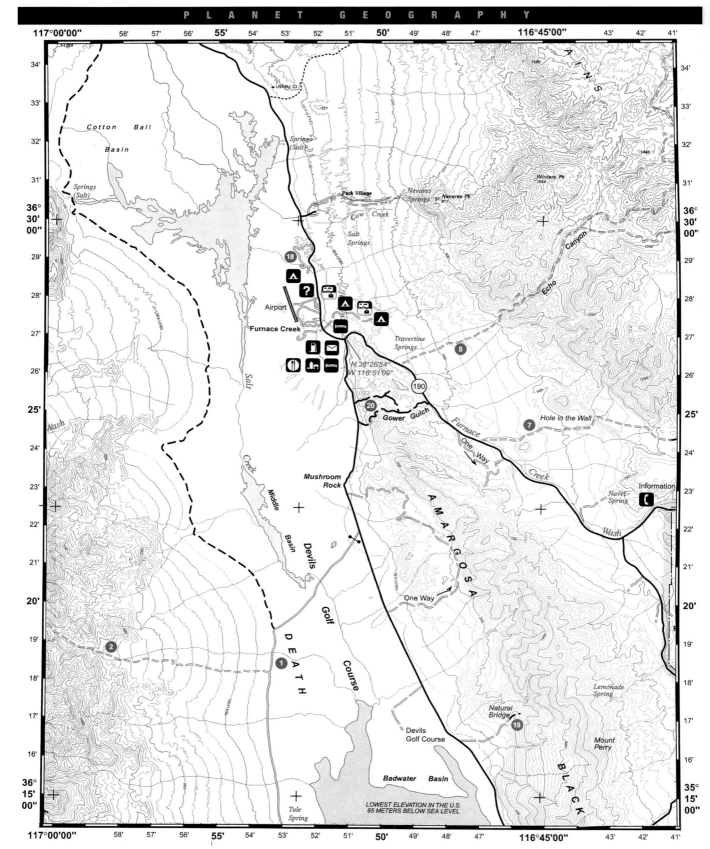

7.113 *Death Valley 1:160 000 topographic map extract. (Map provided courtesy of National Geographic Maps)*

The specific details of Death Valley's climate are given in table 7.6.

Annual precipitation averages less than 50 mm per annum. Weather records have been kept for less than a century, and twice during that period there have been entire years with no rainfall whatsoever. Only twice has the annual rainfall exceeded 100 mm since records began - in 1913 and 1940. Like all desert areas, rainfall fluctuations in Death Valley can be extreme, such as the change from 86 mm of rain in 1953 to zero in 1954. Over longer periods, the fluctuations have been much greater. In the

Legend

Paved Road	————————	Unpaved Road	═══════════
High Clearance Road	═ ═ ═ ═ ═ ═	4WD Road	─ ─ ─ ─ ─ ─ ─
Maintained Trail / Route	— — — — —	Unmaintained Trail / Route	- - - - - - - -
Cross Country Route	··················	National Park Boundary	▬▬▬▬▬▬
Campground, Ranger Station	▲ 🏠	Wilderness Area Boundary	▬▬▬▬▬▬
Picnic Area, Restrooms	🏕 🚻	Wooded Cover	⬭
Handicap Access, Information	♿ ❓	Drainages	⌒
Gas Station, Grocery Store	⛽ 🛒	Dry Washes	⬬
Telephone, Post Office	☎ ✉	GPS Way Point	⟋ N 36°20'23" W 117°28'05"
Lodging, Food Service	🛏 🍴	Interstate Highway	80
R.V. Camping, Dump Station	🚐 🚽	U.S. Highway	84
Showers, Gate	🚿 ⎯	State Road, County Road	30

period from 3000BC to 1AD, Death Valley contained a lake that was 10 metres deep, and during the last ice age (Pleistocene) the lake was almost 200 metres deep.

Although rainfall in Death Valley is unpredictable, there tends to be more rain in winter than in summer. At altitudes over 1,800 metres, rainfall is several times higher than on the floor of the valley. When rain does come, it tends to be sudden, causing flash flooding, gullying and landslides (figure 7.115).

The aridity of Death Valley is amplified by the high rate of evaporation. On the floor of the valley, the potential rate of evaporation is one hundred times greater than the precipitation. The temperature of the ground surface during the day is much higher than the air temperature, and a ground maximum of 95°C has been officially recorded. However, even where extremely high surface temperatures are recorded, the temperatures a few centimetres beneath the surface are much cooler, and this is what enables plants and animals to survive.

QUESTION BLOCK 7V

1. *How do the gravel fans in Death Valley form?*

2. *Draw a climatic graph for Death Valley, showing average maximum and minimum temperatures, and average precipitation.*

3. *Explain how and why Death Valley's climate becomes wetter with increasing altitude.*

4. *Explain why Death Valley has a high diurnal range in temperatures.*

Plants and animals

The wide range of temperature and moisture conditions in Death Valley means that there is quite a variety of plant and animal forms to be found. The length of the growing season for plants is determined by the temperatures, and for this reason there are altitude zones of different plant types found on the edges of the Valley (figure 7.118). In the centre of Death Valley, the extreme temperatures to which the land surface is subjected accounts for the total absence of vegetation in this area (figure 7.116).

7.114 *A large area of sand dunes near Stovepipe Wells in the north of Death Valley. This view looks east towards the Funeral Mountains.*

Near the edges of the Valley, different plant species use different techniques to gather and conserve water. Those plants which are found near the shallow groundwater where the gravel fans and the salt pan meet tend to be salt tolerant and have extensive shallow root systems. These plants, known as **phreatophytes**, send their roots to the water table and thus ensure a permanent water supply for themselves. The distribution of phreatophytes is governed both by the quantity of water available and its quality (i.e. saltiness). The main types of phreatophytes found in Death Valley are the willow (*Salix* spp.), reed grass

Table 7.6
Climatic Statistics for Death Valley, USA (Latitude 36°N, Longitude 117°W, Altitude 85 metres below sea level)

	Jan	Feb	Mar	Apr	May	Jun	Jul	Aug	Sep	Oct	Nov	Dec
Average Maximum Temperature °C	18	23	27	31	38	43	47	45	41	33	24	19
Average Minimum Temperature °C	4	8	12	16	22	28	31	30	25	17	9	5
Record High Temperature °C	31	36	39	44	49	53	57	53	49	45	36	31
Average Precipitation (mm)	6	8	6	3	2	1	3	3	3	2	5	5

Extreme environments

(*Phragmites communis*), salt grass (*Distichlis stricta*) and pickleweed (*Allenrolfea occidentalis*). The salinity of the groundwater varies from a few parts per million for the willow to 6% for the pickleweed, the most salt-tolerant of the phreatophytes.

Where water is less abundant or is deeper, xerophytic plants such as desert holly (*Atriplex hymenelytra*) are found. These plants have adapted to survive long periods of drought. They depend on ephemeral water in the ground above the water table. Moreover, they have made special adaptations to conserve water, such as by having very small leaves to minimise water loss and being able to tolerate salty water. The average density of desert holly plants is 10 to 500 shrubs per hectare. In areas which are a little less salty, creosote bushes (*Larrea tridentata*) are found. Creosote bushes, which are shown in figure 7.117, cover most of the lower halves of gravel fans, up to an altitude of about 180 metres. The density of creosote bushes varies from a few to 250 plants per hectare, with the average being about 80. Creosote bushes depend on ephemeral water, and therefore grow better near roads because of the slight additional runoff from the pavement.

7.115 *Although Death Valley is very dry, evidence of erosion by water is easily found. These two views show evidence of a washout (upper photo), and a box canyon (lower photo), both caused by the action of running water.*

7.117 *In the zone where the gravel fans meet the flat salt pan, springs allow the growth of a few scrub plants. In this view, the density is about 80 bushes per hectare.*

In summary, on the gravel fans where the water table is deep, xerophytes tend to be found, whereas phreatophytes are found at the foot of gravel fans where the groundwater ponds against the lower sediments.

The main types of fauna found in Death Valley are rabbits, rodents, lizards and insects. This wildlife is concentrated in the areas of shallow groundwater where the gravel fans and the salt pan meet. They are less numerous on the gravel fans themselves, and almost totally absent from the salt pan and the badland hills. Indeed, the only type of animal that has been observed to cross the salt pan is the coyote. Most of the pools of water in Death Valley evaporate too quickly or are too salty for fish to survive.

QUESTION BLOCK 7W

1. *With reference to figure 7.118, describe the distribution of vegetation in Death Valley.*

2. *Account for the distribution of vegetation shown in figure 7.118.*

3. *Describe the ways in which vegetation in Death Valley adapts to the dry conditions.*

7.116 *The extremely high surface temperatures at the centre of Death Valley prevent any vegetation at all from growing.*

4. *What is the difference between phreatophytes and xerophytes, and where are each found in Death Valley?*

5. *From what you have studied about the interaction of vegetation and rocks in forming soil, suggest what the soils in Death Valley would be like. Comment on how deep you think they would be, their texture and the amount of humus and water they would contain.*

People

The sections above describe the various natural systems which combine to form the Death Valley ecosystem. The natural ecosystem has survived for many centuries without threat of change other than from changes in the climate. However, the presence of humans has brought many changes.

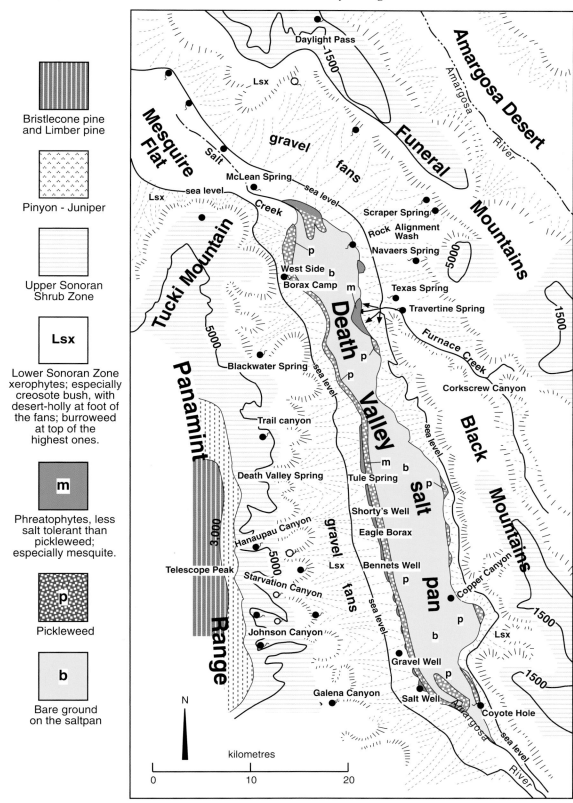

Bristlecone pine and Limber pine

Pinyon - Juniper

Upper Sonoran Shrub Zone

Lsx

Lower Sonoran Zone xerophytes; especially creosote bush, with desert-holly at foot of the fans; burroweed at top of the highest ones.

m

Phreatophytes, less salt tolerant than pickleweed; especially mesquite.

p

Pickleweed

b

Bare ground on the saltpan

7.118 *Vegetation map of Death Valley.*

Extreme environments

It is thought that the first humans lived in Death Valley about 10,000 years ago. These people were hunters, and from the evidence of their tools that have been found, they hunted large animals such as buffalo or bighorn sheep. This indicates that the climate must have been considerably wetter at that time than it is today.

There is also evidence that native Americans lived beside the lake (that has since dried up) about 2,000 years ago. They seem to have hunted smaller game such as rabbits and rodents, and gathered seeds.

The first Europeans visited Death Valley in 1849 on their way to the California gold rushes. However, European settlement did not begin until 1880 when borax was discovered. Borax is a compound of boron that looks like small white crystals and which has many diverse uses, such as making glass, porcelain, enamel, soap, detergents, fertilisers, ceramics, cosmetics, building materials, fire retardants, car anti-freeze solutions and as shields for nuclear reactors. The borax mined in Death Valley is used for fibreglass production.

The borax in Death Valley formed in hot mineral springs and was then deposited in the remains of old lake beds (figure 7.119). Later, partial alteration and solution of these deposits moves some of the borates to the floor of Death Valley, where evaporation left a mixed crust of salt, borates and alkalis.

7.119 *The ruins of an old house sits in an area of abandoned borax mining.*

When Death Valley was declared a national park in 1933, it was left open for mining and prospecting. Therefore, the borax mining continues to the present day. Today, most of the permanent residents of Death Valley are rangers of the Parks Service, people engaged in providing services to visitors, and some miners who continue to extract borax and talc. Although there is a post office in Death Valley, the nearest primary school is 80 kilometres away in Shoshone.

QUESTION BLOCK 7X

1. Suggest reasons that Death Valley seems to have had higher population densities in the past than it does today.

2. Do you think humans are a genuine threat to the Death Valley environment, or that the ecosystem is a greater threat to humans? Justify your answer.

3. It is said that "many environments have a limiting factor, such as solar energy, temperature, water or nutrient supply". What is the limiting factor in the Death Valley environment? Explain your answer.

Sustainability

Human Impact on High Altitude Environments

High altitude environments can be very fragile when exposed to the pressures of human activities. All the mountain environments explored earlier in this chapter — Switzerland, Bolivia and Nepal — have reputations as clean, pristine mountain environments, and yet as we saw when we looked at tourism on Mount Everest, the reality may be quite different. It is impossible for people to live in fragile mountain environments without making any environmental impact, and sometimes this impact can become too severe for nature to repair. Environmental impact can take many forms as the following sections indicate, developing the contrast between a high altitude environment in an LEDC (Nepal) with one in an MEDC (Switzerland).

Air pollution

7.120 *Oblique aerial view over Kathmandu showing the polluted air over the city.*

Although Nepal's air is clean compared with many parts of the world, it is heavily polluted in the towns. Furthermore, Nepal's **urban air pollution** is becoming rapidly worse as more and more second hand cars and trucks are imported from India. In 1989 there were 100,000 motor vehicles in Nepal; by 2008 this figure had risen to about

300,000. Air pollution comes from many sources, including dust from fires and burning, gases from motor vehicle exhausts, and both dust and gases from factories. On the other hand, although Switzerland has many more motor vehicles than Nepal (over 4 million), it imposes strict emission controls on exhaust gases, and therefore Switzerland has cleaner air than Nepal's urban areas (figures 7.120 and 7.121). Along with its neighbouring countries, Switzerland signed the Alpine Convention in 1991; this is an international agreement seeking to minimise the damage caused to the environment by motor traffic and tourism. This is an important need in Switzerland, which receives about 120 million tourists each year.

7.121 *Oblique aerial view over Grindelwald showing the clean air of Switzerland.*

Most of Nepal's factories are small-scale, but they are concentrated in certain areas. The Kathmandu Valley has the biggest concentration of factories (figure 7.122). Most of the motor traffic also occurs in this region. In contrast, Switzerland's manufacturing industries are dispersed across the country, and tend to be non-polluting activities.

7.122 *The Himal Cement Factory, south-west of Kathmandu, is seen here pumping large volumes of polluting gases into the air beside the Buddhist temple of Adinath Lokeshwar, built between 1400 and 1640.*

Deforestation

People in both Switzerland and Nepal use timber from their forests as an important resource (figure 7.123). The impact of forestry is much greater in Nepal than in Switzerland. Indeed, loss of forest is one of Nepal's greatest problems. Between 1965 and 1979, Nepal lost about 70,000 hectares of forest every year. Since then the rate of loss has been reduced to about 12,000 hectares per year, but this is still a major problem. Most of the timber is cut down for fuelwood, which supplies 75% of Nepal's energy needs.

7.123 *Fuelwood stored at the houses of a family in Patan, Nepal (top) and near Brienz, Switzerland (bottom).*

Although some of the cut timber is sold in towns, most of it is gathered by villagers who intend to use it themselves. Many of Nepal's factories also use **fuelwood** rather than other sources of energy. In the Kathmandu Valley's 100 brick kilns, 3 million bricks are produced each year using 24,000 tonnes of coal plus 24,000 tonnes of fuelwood. It is claimed that if the cutting continues and Nepal loses its remaining humid tropical forest, the world will lose ten species of valuable timber, six species of edible fruit tree, four species supplying traditional medicines and 50 species of little known trees and shrubs. The loss of the trees would also wipe out the habitats for 200 species of birds, 40 species of mammals and 20 species of reptiles and amphibians.

7.124 *A forestry ranger comparing a healthy branch from a forest tree (left) with one which has been stunted and defoliated as a result of acid rain (right).*

Soil erosion

Soil erosion is a major problem in Nepal, but much less so in Switzerland. Switzerland's population is growing much more slowly than Nepal's, and for this reason there is less pressure placed on the land to produce more.

Deforestation in Nepal leads to soil erosion, but other factors are also important. Nepal has thin, shallow, stony soils that are easily eroded. On average, Nepal loses the equivalent of between 20 and 50 tonnes of fertile topsoil per hectare per year due to soil erosion. In some areas, 200 tonnes of topsoil per hectare are lost annually and entire hillsides have been laid bare. Each year, about 240 million tonnes of Nepal's soil are washed away from Nepal down to the Bay of Bengal. So much soil erosion has occurred that a new island has risen from the sea off the coast of Bangladesh in the Bay of Bengal. Although this island, which is hundreds of square kilometres in size, comprises the eroded soil from Nepal, it is India and Bangladesh that are each claiming sovereignty (ownership) of it.

Some of Nepal's soil erosion occurs because of natural factors. These natural factors are the steepness of Nepal's hillsides, the coarse texture of the soils and the frequent earthquakes and tremors. However, the main causes of soil erosion are human activities such as grazing too many cattle on small parcels of land, expanding villages on steep land without planning permission, and over-farming (figure 7.125).

Switzerland's forestry industry is managed with tight government regulations controlling the quantities of timber that can be cut. However, Switzerland's forests are suffering from the effects of another factor over which the Swiss have little direct control – acid rain. **Acid rain** is caused by air pollution from cars and factories in areas upwind of Switzerland, which means principally in Britain, France and Spain. Sulphur dioxide caused by burning hydrocarbons mixes with the water in the atmosphere producing rain that is a diluted form of sulphuric acid ($SO_2 + H_2O \rightarrow H_2SO_4$). This is then blown by the prevailing winds over to Switzerland where the orographic uplift causes rain - rain which, because of its acidity, kills the trees on which it falls (figure 7.124).

Deforestation has become such a problem in Nepal that the government has conducted a two-decade long campaign to regenerate the country's forests. The government hopes to meet people's timber needs from plantation forests. Moreover, it hopes to reduce the overall demand for timber by encouraging people to use other fuels, such as kerosene and animal dung, instead. The government plans to connect more households to electricity, thus reducing the need for fuelwood. At present, only 3% of rural households have electricity. The cost of the 20-year program has been about $US2.5 billion, a huge sum for a poor nation like Nepal. Switzerland faces even greater problems in halting its deforestation because the acid rain affecting its forests is caused in areas over which it has no control. It is for this reason that the Swiss have been at the forefront of efforts to get international agreements limiting the production of air pollution gases.

7.125 *Severe gullying near Kathmandu is eroding farmlands. Some efforts to stabilise the erosion can be seen near the mouth of gully where tree planting has taken place.*

Landslides are a very extreme form of soil erosion in which both lives and property are lost. The higher a slope, the greater is the potential energy exerted by gravity. Like soil erosion, landslides can occur naturally but human actions often make them worse. It is estimated that of every 15 landslides in Nepal, 14 are the result of human actions while only one is entirely due to natural factors. Most landslides occur in the summer months of June to September when the monsoon winds bring heavy rainfall to Nepal. At this time, the topsoil gets soaked, making the soil waterlogged and much heavier, as well as better lubricated, and so more likely to slide downhill.

Landslides are also a major problem in the mountain areas of Switzerland. In Switzerland, however, the causes are usually natural. Many of the alpine areas of Switzerland have slip-off slopes – areas of unconsolidated rock sediments that have fallen from upslope and come to an angle of rest that is usually about 35° (figure 7.126). If something happens to destabilise the slope, such as a mild earth tremor, a period of heavy rain, or even a person walking on the slope, then the rock material can slide downhill, taking with it anything and anyone in its path.

7.126 *A large slip-off slope on the side of Mount Pilatus. The size of the slope can be seen by the size of the walkers at the foot of the slope. Such slopes are very unstable, which is why vegetation has not been able to establish itself.*

7.127 *Terraces are a major feature of water management in Nepal. Water is used by the top terrace first and then re-used by each successive terrace down the slope. These terraces are at Nagarkot.*

The Nepalese government is making a strong effort to remedy soil erosion because it is costing so much money in lost production. Among the soil conservation practices being encouraged are:

- improving terraces to improve the flow of water down hillsides (figure 7.127);
- re-routing walking trails so that they do not go straight up and down steep slopes;
- planting grass in gullies that have been eroded to stabilise them;
- stabilising the banks of rivers so that they do not get undercut and washed away;
- planting trees on hillsides.

Water quality

Water is necessary for everyone's survival. Sadly, maintaining clean water quality is often seen by developing nations to be a luxury they cannot afford. Although Switzerland has over 400,000 farmers, the country's waterways are remarkably free from agricultural wastes and contaminants. Indeed, Switzerland has generally embraced the green movement enthusiastically. On average, each Swiss person produces 450 kg of waste per year, half the figure for each American person.

Switzerland has an active policy of recycling under the slogan 'Reduction, Recovery and Recycling'. Most local government authorities have recycling facilities for paper, glass, plastic, aluminium and used oil. Most containers for food and drinks are recyclable, and the rate of recycling is very high. A law designed to reduce excess packaging entitles consumers to unwrap unnecessary packaging in the shop where the purchase was made and leave it for the shop to throw away — and many consumers do exercise this right.

Most Swiss cantons have introduced specially marked bags for rubbish that cannot be recycled. These are very expensive (up to $5 each including the incineration fee), and this high cost encourages as much as possible to be recycled. Sadly, the high cost also encourages residents to travel to other cantons that have not introduced the bag tariff and dump their rubbish there.

Water pollution in Switzerland is therefore quite rare. Dumping of chemicals into Swiss waterways is banned, but sometimes other forms of pollution are less easily avoided, such as sediment from river gravel mines (figure 7.128).

As an LEDC (less economically developed country), water pollution is a more significant problem in Nepal, especially near the urban areas. Hindus regard several of Nepal's rivers as holy, and the demands made upon the water of such rivers are very great indeed. For example, the Bagmati River which flows through Kathmandu is at the one time a source of irrigation water, a bathing channel for washing, a toilet, a garbage dump, a grazing area for cattle, a source of drinking water, a place for disposing cremated human remains, and an object of worship (figures 7.129 and 7.130).

7.128 *This gravel mine in the Bernese Oberland causes sediment pollution in the river downstream.*

7.130 *This view of the Bagmati River flowing through Kathmandu shows the garbage that has been dumped in the river-bed in preparation for the higher waters in the monsoon season to flush it away.*

Water quality is made even worse because of the ways the water is then used. Water is pumped from the river into wells distributed throughout the towns for communal clothes washing. Here, soap, dirt and animal droppings become mixed with the water before it is returned to the river (figure 7.131). The water is then taken further downstream for washing again, and the concentration of pollutants increases. The mixture of pollutants becomes even greater when combined with the remains of bodies cremated beside this holy river.

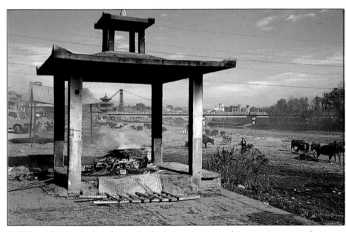

7.129 *A funeral ghat has a body being cremated in preparation for remains to be dumped into the Bagmati River in the background. Cattle are grazing on the stream bed between the ghat and the river channel.*

7.131 *Washing clothes in river water. The dirty water will be returned to the river, causing a problem for those downstream needing clean water.*

All these competing uses for the water have caused the quality of the water in Nepal's rivers to deteriorate. Water is taken from the Bagmati River and other streams for chlorination and drinking in Kathmandu. Even after chlorination, the water is heavily contaminated, especially with faecal bacteria.

There are many sources of water pollution in Nepal's rivers. Most of the Kathmandu Valley's factories are situated beside the rivers, and these factories dump waste chemicals such as chlorides, nitrates and sulphates into the rivers. Most of Kathmandu's sewage is dumped into the river, either through pipes from houses or directly into the river by people who have no toilets in their houses.

QUESTION BLOCK 7Y

1. *Draw up a table to compare the state of the environment in the high altitude areas of Switzerland and Nepal.*

2. *Why is Nepal's environment dirtier than Switzerland's?*

3. *What realistic policies could be introduced to improve Nepal's environment? Is the Swiss experience of environmental management applicable to Nepal?*

4. *Having examined human impacts on the environments of Nepal and Switzerland, to what extent do you think human activities in high altitude areas in general are unsustainable?*

The Impact of Global Climatic Change on Extreme Environments

There is a growing consensus among geographers that the world is experiencing global warming at a rate never previously experienced on the planet. As discussed in chapter 3, if this trend continues, there will be significant implications for all parts the world. When the physical conditions are 'extreme', as in the hot-arid and cold-high environments treated in this chapter, then the effects of climate change are likely to have serious impacts on the people, settlements and economic activities in those environments.

Some degree of speculation is needed to predict the future impacts of global warming. Many of the effects of global warming are thought to be non-linear in nature, which means the potential exists for certain changes to trigger further feedback effects. Some researchers claim that this means that the earth's climate could enter a critical state where even quite small changes could trigger runaway or catastrophic climate change. Other researchers dismiss such claims as alarmist.

Nonetheless, some trends do appear clear. For example, NOAA (National Oceanic and Atmospheric Administration) research suggests that the impacts of global warming are already irreversible. The reports of the IPCC (Intergovernmental Panel on Climate Change) claim that human actions are the major cause of global warming, although the IPCC reports do not attempt to quantify the proportions of global warming that arise from human and natural causes. Among the expected direct consequences of global warming, the IPCC lists rising sea levels, retreat of glaciers and polar ice caps and changing distribution of agriculture. Secondary and regional consequences predicted by the IPCC include greater frequency of extreme weather events, further spread of tropical diseases, altered seasonal patterns in various ecosystems, and severe impact on the economies of many nations.

One of the consequences of global warming is that rates of evaporation increase. Perhaps surprisingly, during the 20th century, the world's average evaporation rates decreased. Geographers speculate that the reason evaporation rates declined was **global dimming**, which is the gradual reduction in the amount of solar radiation received on the earth's surface. Although the measurements of solar radiation received in different different parts of the world vary, there was an average global decline of 4% during the 30 year period from 1960 to 1990.

Measurements since 1990 have been less clear. Some measurements in the mid-1990s showed an increase in solar radiation received at the earth's surface, possibly because 1990 was about the time that the world-wide use of aerosols began to decline, thus reducing the amount of particulates in the atmosphere.

If that trend continued, and the earth's climate continued to become warmer, evaporation rates would increase as the surface of the oceans become warmer bringing increased rainfall to arid and semi-arid areas.

An **increase of rainfall** in hot, arid environments would bring some benefits for people as more grass and bushes will grow in areas where there is presently too little rainfall to support such growth. On the other hand, it would also increase soil erosion as the desert soils are not capable of absorbing large increases in rainfall, and this would lead to **desertification**.

However, more recent measurements released by the UNEP (United Nations Environment Program) in 2009 seem to confirm that the world is becoming progressively dimmer, and the 1960 to 1990 trend has re-established itself. This is the result of pollution from human activities creating semi-permanent **atmospheric brown clouds** (ABCs). According to the UNEP, a three-kilometre thick layer of soot and other particles produced by burning fossil fuels and biomass stretches from the Arabian Peninsula to China and the western pacific Ocean, and other smaller ABCs are found over Europe, North America, southern Africa and the Amazon Basin. The UNEP found that dimming was especially severe over some cities such as Karachi, Delhi, Beijing, Shanghai and Guangzhou.

Global dimming represents a special danger because it may mask the full impact of global warming, making people complacent. The **masking** of the full impact of global warming occurs because atmospheric brown clouds reflect solar radiation back into space and absorb heat. In other words, the human causes of global warming may be having a more severe effect than the measurements at ground level indicate.

7.132 *A small oasis near Zakati, Yemen.*

If global dimming is increasing as the UNEP suggests, then **evaporation rates** would decrease from the surface of the oceans, reducing the rainfall to arid and semi-arid areas. This could lead to the **expansion of deserts** and the drying up of oases and other sources of water (figure 7.132). The drying up of limited water supplies also increases the concentration of pathogens in drinking and bathing waters used by indigenous community, increasing the risk of serious **water-borne diseases** and health problems (figure 7.133).

Lower rainfall in arid and semi-arid areas would mean that the daily task of gathering **fuelwood** may become even more onerous as scarce vegetation struggles to survive — especially population pressures continue to increase the demand for fuelwood more quickly than the trees and bushes can grow. If fuelwood becomes even less accessible to indigenous peoples, the impacts will be felt especially by women, as it is usually the women's role to carry the heavy bundles of wood in many of the world's arid and semi-arid areas (figure 7.134).

7.133 *This polluted water hole in Djibouti is used as a source of drinking water for the local population.*

7.134 *This woman from the Erebora tribe in southern Ethiopia is doing the daily chore of many women in LEDCs — carrying a heavy load of fuelwood.*

It has been suggested that climate change may already be causing problems for people in the arid regions of the Horn of Africa (Somalia, Eritrea, Djibouti an Sudan). Since 2003 there has been a **civil war** in the Darfur region of western Sudan which has led to a 'humanitarian crisis' (to quote the words of UN Security Council) in which as

many as 300,000 people have been killed and 2 million displaced from their homes. Although the direct causes of the conflict are tribal and ethnic differences, climatologists suggest that several decades of drought, combined with desertification and overpopulation, have fuelled the ill-will between the various groups. This claim is based on the fact that prolonged drought forced nomadic Arab Baggara animal-herders to take their livestock in search of water onto land that was mainly occupied by other ethnic groups.

Darfur is not the only place where people have been forced to migrate because of environmental change. In Eritrea, situated to the east of Sudan, desertification is also a serious problem. The country suffers from frequent droughts and it has still not recovered from a decades-long war for independence. Less than 3% of Eritrea's total land area is forested, and many marginal lands have been cultivated and overgrazed, leading to soil erosion and desertification (figure 7.135).

7.135 *Animals forage for scarce food in the arid lands near Massawa in northern Eritrea.*

This has led many outside observers to assume Eritrea's nomadic **pastoralists** (people who raise animals) are locked into a destructive cycle of increasing their numbers of livestock to survive at the times when drought should be forcing them to reduce livestock numbers. Although Eritrea's pastoralists may not be living in perfect harmony with nature, they are skilled and knowledgeable herders with a long tradition of making the best of a very tough and often hostile environment. Many of the pastoralists are able to adapt quickly to changing circumstances as they apply their traditional techniques.

Outside observers have accused Eritrea's pastoralists (as well as other pastoralists in Sub-Saharan Africa) of having little incentive to conserve communal grazing lands by reducing the sizes of their herds because they have no guarantee that others will do the same. In reality, however, land resources in Eritrea (and most other places) are not communally owned, but managed by particular groups. The local knowledge thus gained has enabled many of Eritrea's pastoral communities to remain viable in spite of continuing droughts and global warming.

Indeed, enabling local pastoralists to retain their traditional methods, which have served them well for many centuries, may provide much better protection against the threat of global warming than outside 'experts' imposing a system that may not be sustainable in Eritrea's extreme environment.

Similar pressures exist in even more arid environments. The Himba people of southern Angola and northern Namibia are nomadic pastoralists who survive by raising goats and sheep in the driest parts of the Namib Desert (figure 7.136). In the 1980s, a severe drought killed 90% of the Himba's livestock and many gave up their herds and became refugees. Many fear that of global warming continues, the pressures on the Himba could become impossible to bear and their traditional lifestyle will be lost forever. On the other hand, the Himba have shown a deep understanding of the climatic fluctuations of the desert as shown by their survival for many centuries. This has led some researchers to investigate traditional societies such as the Himba to learn more about ways of adapting to climate change in extreme environments.

7.136 *The nomadic Himba people of the Namib Desert have developed a lifestyle that enables them to survive by raising goats and cattle despite the area's extreme aridity.*

One of the factors that makes the Himba so resilient to the pressures of their extreme environment is their **tribal structure**. The Himba organise their society around a system called **bilateral descent**. Every person belongs to two clans, one through the father and another through the mother. The relatives in both clans are equally important for emotional ties and for the transfer of property or wealth. Sons live with their father's clan and when daughters marry they go to live with the clan of their husband. However, the inheritance of wealth does not follow the father's side of the family but is determined by the mother's clan. In this way, a son does not inherit his father's animals, but he inherits the animals of his mother's brother. The bilateral descent system seems to give groups such as the Himba that live in extreme environments a huge advantage in adapting to the pressures of climate change because individuals can rely on two sets of families living in different local conditions over a wide area.

Having said this, indigenous peoples leading traditional lifestyles may be vulnerable to climate change in other ways. The ways that indigenous people cope with their extreme environments are often based on traditional knowledge, and although this traditional knowledge has proven adaptable to many climatic fluctuations in the past, some researchers worry that more extreme global warming may stretch traditional adaptations beyond their breaking points. For example, if farmers plant crops at certain times of the year that are based on weather cycles, and those weather cycles are disrupted, the consequence could be widespread famine. In general, indigenous peoples receive the least 'western' education among the general population. Therefore, indigenous peoples are more likely to lack the wider scientific understandings of climate change that would be helpful to illuminate their traditional knowledge to cope with extreme environmental changes.

Despite the adaptability of indigenous peoples, environmental migration does occur in hot, arid environments. **Environmental migration** is the forced movement of people as a result of environmental degradation and resource depletion. It is often associated with poverty, food deficiency, conflicts and inequity. Indeed, historians explain the collapse of many of the world's great civilisations on environmental factors, including climate change (figure 7.137).

7.137 *Hecang, one of many abandoned settlements in the deserts of western China that provide evidence of thriving settlements based on well managed water resources in the less arid past.*

In the context of today's world, Dr Norman Myers of Oxford University has suggested that the combination of sea level rise and agricultural distribution caused by climate changes (global warming) could displace millions of people in LEDCs in the coming decades (figure 7.138). The term **environmental refugees** is often used to describe people who must flee (either temporarily or permanently) from their traditional habitat because of a marked environmental disruption that threatened their existence or seriously affected their quality of life. Myers estimates by 2050, 1.5% of the the world's population (150 million people out of 10 billion) will be environmental refugees due to the impact of global warming, compared to 0.2% of the world population who are environmental refugees today.

Scientists warn that prolonged drought conditions are another possible consequence of global warming in desert areas. This presents another possible adverse impact on local people, many of whom raise animals for their livelihood, as they will be forced to move their animals onto land that is more and more marginal in search of feed and water (figures 7.139, 7.140 and 7.141). When animals are forced to over-graze on marginal semi-arid land, there is a real risk that the land may turn into desert.

7.140 *These goats are resting in the shade of some trees in the marginal arid to semi-arid lands of the Erebora tribe in southern Ethiopia.*

7.138 *Global warming could make the arid conditions in countries such as Eritrea (shown here) even less hospitable in the future.*

7.141 *Himba herdsmen in the Namib Desert moving their goats, and stirring up soil erosion as they do so.*

7.139 *Goats grazing on marginal arid lands at Dimeka in southern Ethiopia.*

The large **shanty settlements** that exist on the outskirts of many towns and cities are another sign of environmental migration in hot, arid environments (figure 7.142). Nomadic peoples who are unable to survive the extreme aridity brought about by global warming are forced to migrate to settlements where water is available, even if employment is not. The Worldwatch Institute estimates that one billion of the world's three billion urban dwellers live in 'slums', which are defined as areas where people have no access to key necessities such as clean water, a nearby toilet, or durable housing. Although it is impossible to quantify the role of climate change in forcing rural-urban migration, there is concern that global warming will aggravate this problem in the years ahead.

7.142 *Shanty settlements made by rural-urban migrants from Eritrea on the outskirts of Djibouti City.*

Cities have a long history in extreme hot, arid environments. It is said that the world's first city was Sana'a, which today is the capital city of Yemen (figure 7.143). Tradition says that Sana'a was established by Noah's son, Shem, but whether that is true or not, Sana'a is a very old city with a long history of adaptation to changing environmental conditions. For example, the tall tower houses are built from mud and stone, which are natural insulators protecting the people inside from the scorching outside heat. The design of the tower houses uses the natural movement of air to create cooling convection currents without the use of any electricity or other energy.

On the western edge of the old city of city, an ephemeral stream called Wadi as Sa'ilah flows after heavy rainfall. City planners have converted the stream bed into a canal which is used as a main road for most of the time (figure 7.144). As well as providing a much-needed roadway through the narrow streets of the old city, this canal has also prevented the flooding that used to afflict residents. Another way in which the residents of Sana'a have adapted to their extreme climate is growing fruit and vegetables within the city wherever possible (figure 7.145). Because the city was established on a natural oasis, this provides protection against droughts and aridity in the surrounding countryside. In these ways, Sana'a has shown that traditional thinking can provide protection against the threats of global warming.

7.143 *Sana'a, Yemen's capital city, is claimed to be the world's first city.*

7.144 *The ephemeral stream known as Wadi as Sa'ilah, in Sana'a, has been converted into a canal which is used as a roadway when the stream is not flowing.*

Newer cities in hot, arid environments often follow the urban models of cities in Europe and North America, and thus lack the traditional wisdom and planning of settlements such as Sana'a. One example of a modern desert city is Dubai, the commercial centre and largest city in the United Arab Emirates (figure 7.146). In trying to create a modern city in a desert environment, Dubai uses large quantities of water for irrigation, creating not only green parklands but extensive golf courses and grassy median strips on the roads (figure 7.147). Dubai also uses large quantities of fuels such as oil to air condition the buildings, which unlike the traditional architecture used in Dubai, are seldom designed to catch the cool ocean breezes and circulate the air. Dubai's use of fossil fuels is among the highest in the world on a per capita basis, making the city both a significant contributor to greenhouse gases that are thought to cause global warming as well as increasing vulnerability as the economic pressures of global warming increase.

7.145 *Fruit and vegetable cultivation within the old city of Sana'a, Yemen.*

The impact of global warming may be even more marked in **cold and high altitude environments**. Glacial retreat and shrinking of the polar ice caps has been widely noted in recent decades, and global warming is the main cause suggested to explain these trends. In the Arctic, the shrinking of the ice caps is predicted to allow stronger waves to hit the coastlines, thus increasing coastal erosion. In mountain areas, melting glaciers are likely to increase stream discharge, thus increasing riverbank erosion.

7.146 *Dubai, the largest commercial centre in the United Arab Emirates, is an example of a modern desert city with a large energy footprint.*

Extreme environments

7.147 *Irrigation creates a verdant green median strips along many of Dubai's roads and expressways.*

In the periglacial expanses of the tundra, global warming is thawing permafrost. **Permafrost** is a thick layer of soil below the ground surface in polar regions that remains frozen throughout the year. In the early 2000s, some regions of northern Canada were reporting that during summer the permafrost was thawing, causing the earth to become spongy and the land to sink by as much as a metre, about 20 times more than the 'normal' rate. In parts of Canada and Russia, thawing permafrost is already causing damage to infrastructure such as roads, railway lines and buildings (figure 7.148). As permafrost melts, it releases large quantities of greenhouse gases such as methane that had been frozen into the atmosphere. In this way, melting permafrost and global warming are though to have a **positive feedback relationship**, with each reinforcing the other.

7.148 *These buildings in Dawson City (Yukon, Canada) show what can happen when heated buildings are placed on frozen permafrost ground. The permafrost melts, mixing soil with water forming a paste into which the footings settle at different rates.*

Another consequence of glacial retreat and thawing permafrost is that the frequency and size of **landslides** in cold and high environments are expected to increase. Water in liquid form on steep slopes acts as a lubricant, reducing cohesion and allowing gravity to take over and cause slope failure (figure 7.149). When permafrost melts and the ground slumps, the angle of a slope may become too steep to remain stable, thus triggering landslides.

Warmer temperatures in cold climates are likely to change the balance of animal species and their **habitat distribution**. Researchers predict that many areas, and the peoples within them, will have to adapt to the intrusion of new species and changing patterns of animal movement and migration routes. For indigenous peoples such as the Inuit of northern Canada and Greenland, changing distributions of fish could threaten the livelihood of large numbers of people who depend on fishing for their survival (figure 7.150).

7.149 *A landslip in the Rocky Mountains of Canada, near Jasper.*

Indigenous peoples in polar and sub-polar areas depend for their survival on **hunting** animals such as polar bears, seals and caribou. These activities have always been an important part of indigenous people's cultural identity, and as they have moved into the cash economy, this hunting has also come to be an important element of the local economies in places such as northern Canada, Greenland and northern Russia. With the threat of global warming, indigenous peoples such as the Inuit have expressed concern about the future of their traditional food sources.

7.150 *Indigenous people in Greenland depend on fishing for their survival and livelihood. The fishing may be threatened by global warming.*

Concerns have also been expressed by indigenous peoples about the increasing difficulties of **predicting the weather** in cold environments, a very important factor for people who depend so heavily on the weather and have very little capacity to modify their environment. Indigenous peoples in polar and sub-polar areas have been reporting an increase of rainfall each autumn and winter and more extreme heat each summer. Many have expressed concern about their future if global warming continues.

At a United Nations University (UNU) conference in Darwin in 2008, the plight of **indigenous peoples** in the face of climate change was the focus of discussions. In summing up the conference, the UNU Director, Dr A Zakri said "Indigenous peoples regard themselves as the mercury in the world's climate change barometer. They have not benefited, in any significant manner, from climate change-related funding, whether for adaptation and mitigation, nor from emissions trading schemes. Most indigenous peoples practice sustainable carbon neutral lives or even carbon negative life ways which has sustained them over thousands of years."

7.152 *A summer walker in the Swiss Alps, near Zermatt.*

7.151 *Another view of the Athabasca Glacier in Canada, shown earlier in figures 7.34 and 7.35. The marker locates the toe of the glacier in 1959. Today, the glacier has retreated out of sight behind the large hill of terminal moraine seen in the background.*

The retreat of glaciers is one of the most obvious effects of global warming. The retreat of many glaciers has been measured for over a century, and in some places it is possible to see markers where the earlier limits of the ice were found. For example, the marker in figure 7.151 shows the extent of the Athabasca Glacier in the Rocky Mountains of Canada; this is the same glacier that was shown in figure 7.35 earlier in this chapter. The current end of the glacier is still visible from the 1992 marker, but to walk from the 1959 marker past the 1992 marker to the current limit of the glacier, one must walk about 50 metres over the large hill of terminal moraine shown in the background of figure 7.151.

7.153 *Visitors stand on the outwash plain to study information about the Skaftafell Glacier in southern Iceland from a board, while viewing the glacier (background).*

The retreat of glaciers is expected to have a serious impact on the **economic activities** in cold and high altitude environments if global warming continues. Many of the economies of alpine areas depend on tourism which is based on skiing in winter and hiking in summer (figures 7.152 and 7.153). It is clear that if the main attractions in the mountain environments of places such as Switzerland, Canada and New Zealand — the glaciers and the snow fields — disappear, then the economies of those places will suffer greatly unless they can adapt and develop new ways of attracting tourists, perhaps replacing skiing and snowboarding with attractions such as cycling, horse riding and canoeing (figure 7.154).

Any collapse or contraction of the tourist industry in alpine areas would have a wider impact beyond the tourist industry itself, as many supporting industries and enterprises cluster in settlements based on tourism. Indeed,

Extreme environments

many of the settlements in high altitude environments would probably not exist if it were not for the tourist industry (figure 7.155).

7.154 *Preparing to go canoeing on Moraine Lake, Alberta, Canada.*

7.155 *Substantial infrastructure supports tourism in alpine areas these days. These accommodation chalets are in the Canadian town of Jasper.*

Despite the hot and dry conditions, many desert areas have small but growing tourism industries. In some areas this is based on the lure of exploring stark and beautiful environments, while in other areas the dry climate attracts tourists from cool, moist climates who are in search of sunny weather (figure 7.156).

7.156 *Tourists ride on the backs of camels to explore the large sand dunes of the Gobi Desert near Dunhuang, China. The area also provides facilities for paragliding and sand boarding.*

7.157 *Some places have very basic facilities to cater for tourists. This view shows Liwa Oasis in the United Arab Emirates.*

However, if global warming continues at the accelerating rate that many scientists predict, perhaps the future of tourism in more and more parts of the world will be something resembling the scene in figure 7.157!

QUESTION BLOCK 7Z

1. *Explain what is meant by global dimming. Describe the trend of global dimming and its relationship to global climate change.*

2. *There is disagreement among scholars whether global warming will increase or decrease rainfall in desert areas. However, most of the predictions seem negative either way. Giving examples, explain why this is so.*

3. *Although indigenous peoples in hot, arid environments are among the most vulnerable groups when global warming occurs, they may also be among the most resilient. Giving examples, explain why this is so.*

4. *Explain the terms 'environmental migration' and 'environmental refugee'. Why is global climate change likely to increase environmental migration in hot, arid environments?*

5. *What are the characteristics of settlements in hot, arid environments make them more resilient to global warming?*

6. *What are the consequences of thawing permafrost?*

7. *How might global warming affect indigenous peoples in cold and high altitude environments?*

8. *Overall, do you think there is more potential for global climatic change to affect hot, arid environments or cold and high altitude environments?*

Hazards and disasters —
risk assessment and response

8

Earthquakes and volcanoes, hurricanes (tropical cyclones, typhoons), droughts and human-induced hazards.

**ToK BoX — Page 345
Reasoning**

Characteristics of Hazards

hazard event that actually has an **impact** on people. An 'event' only becomes a 'hazard event' if it has a negative impact on people or their property.

Hazards

At its simplest level, a hazard is anything that poses a risk to humans. In our study of geography, we take a slightly more sophisticated view, which is to regard a **hazard** as any threat (whether natural or human) that has the potential to cause loss of life, injury, property damage, socio-economic disruption, or environmental degradation. Examples of natural hazards include earthquakes, volcanoes, hurricanes (also known as tropical cyclones or typhoons), droughts and tsunamis. Hazards can also be caused by humans, and examples of these include collapses of mines and industrial explosions.

It is important to distinguish between a hazard and a **hazard event**, which is the occurrence (or realisation) of a hazard, together with the changes in demographic, economic and/or environmental conditions which result. Hazards have the **potential** to affect people, but it is the

Earthquakes and Volcanoes

Earthquakes and volcanoes occur in the earth's **lithosphere**. This is the solid zone of rock on the earth, including the Earth's crust and the upper part of the mantle, that extends downwards from the earth's surface to a depth of about 70 kilometres. Figure 8.1 shows that the earth consists of several layers, like an onion. In the centre of the Earth is a very hot core. The temperature of most of the core is so high that its rock material has melted into a flowing liquid. Perhaps surprisingly, the inner core at the centre of the earth (where temperatures are highest) is solid. It is solid because of the enormous pressures pressing in on it. Surrounding the core is a mantle of semi-solid rocks. The closer we go to the earth's surface, the more solid the mantle becomes, although the rocks in the mantle are still able to flow like a thick honey.

>> Some Useful Definitions

Disaster — a major hazard event that causes widespread disruption to a community or region, with significant demographic, economic and/or environmental losses, and which the affected community is unable to deal with adequately unless it receives outside help.

Hazard — a threat (whether natural or human) that has the potential to cause loss of life, injury, property damage, socio-economic disruption, or environmental degradation.

Hazard event — the occurrence (realisation) of a hazard, and its effects which change demographic, economic and/or environmental conditions.

Risk — risk is the probability of a hazard event causing harmful consequences (expected losses in terms of deaths, injuries, property damage, economy and environment).

Vulnerability — the geographic conditions that increase the susceptibility of a community to a hazard or to the impacts of a hazard event.

A thin crust forms the surface of the earth. The crust varies in thickness from about 4 kilometres under the oceans to about 40 kilometres under the mountain ranges of the continents. The continents are made up of the lightest rocks, known together as **sial**. The term 'sial' is made up of the letters 'Si' and 'Al', short for silica and alumina. These are two of the most common minerals in granite, which is the most common rock in the continents. The heavier, denser layer of the crust is known as **sima**, made up of the letters Si and Ma (silica and magnesia). The world's ocean beds are made up of sima. If the earth were the size of a wet soccer ball, the crust would be as

thick as the layer of water on the outside of it. We can think of the crust as being like a hard shell, 'floating' on the liquid mantle beneath it.

As discussed earlier in chapter 6, the earth's crust is not one continuous shell. The crust is made up of several plates, some large and some small. There are only a few main plates, and these are shown in figure 8.2. The rates at which the plates move varies greatly, from about 1 to more than 18 centimetres per year. It seems as though the plates are being carried 'piggy back' by the currents moving slowly in the liquid mantle. The plates are all moving

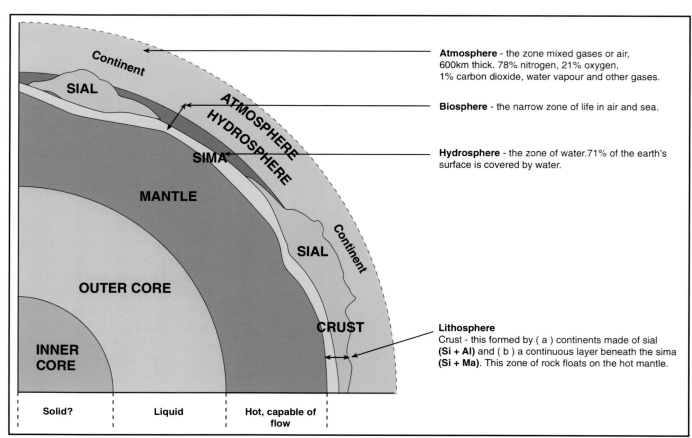

8.1 *The structure of the earth (not to scale).*

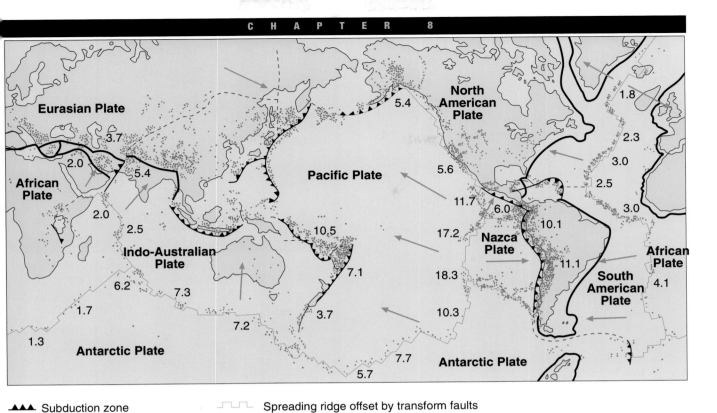

Subduction zone
Earthquake zone
- - - - Uncertain plate boundary

Spreading ridge offset by transform faults
Collision zone
Movement of plate

8.2 *The world's major crustal plates. The rates of sea floor spreading and plate convergence are shown in centimetres per year.*

in different directions. They are coming together in some parts of the world and moving apart elsewhere.

Because the earth's tectonic plates are less dense than the **mantle** under them, they 'float' on the mantle, moving across the earth's surface at the rates shown in figure 8.2. The forces driving the plates across the earth's surface are not fully understood, however. It seems that convection currents occur in the mantle in much the same way that they occur in the atmosphere.

There is, however, a significant difference — convection currents in the mantle occur from heat generated by **radioactive decay**. Where a convection current rises in the mantle, volcanic activity occurs and the plates are pushed apart as new crust is formed. This creates a number of **spreading ridges**, such as the Mid Atlantic Ridge, where new oceanic crust is added to the earth's crust (figures 8.3 to 8.8).

8.3 *The movement of the earth's crustal plates. Heavy plates sink into the mantle (a and c), pulling the rest of the plates behind them. This tears open the crust at the mid-oceanic ridges (b), creating ragged transform faults, where new material comes to the surface, helping to push apart the plates. Volcanic island arcs are created (a) where two sima plates collide. Where one plate is sial and one is sima (c), mountain ranges of the lighter sial buckle upwards, and volcanoes erupt. Where two sial plates collide (d) the mountains buckle upwards and are torn in different directions along a transcurrent fault.*

At the Mid-Atlantic Ridge, new material is forced to the surface, forcing apart the edges of the South American and African plates. This is the force that causes Africa and South America to 'drift' apart. The Red Sea and the East African Rift also represent areas of plate margins moving apart, but in the case of East Africa, it is land rather than the sea that is pushed apart. Because new material is created at the spreading ridges, they are called **constructive plate margins**.

Convergent plate margins occur where plates collide. Because crustal material is destroyed at these margins, they are known as **destructive plate margins**. The Indo-Australian plate moves northwards at a rate of between 5 and 7 centimetres per year as a result of the sea floor spreading between Australia and Antarctica.

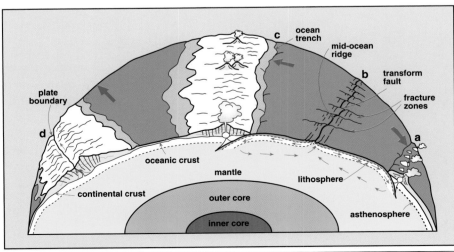

Hazards and disasters

8.4 *The Mid-Atlantic Ridge on the earth's surface in Iceland. This view shows Lakagígar crater row and lava flow from the 1783 eruptions.*

8.7 *A fumarole expelling sulphurous steam under high pressure at Hverarönd, near Reykjahlid, Iceland.*

8.5 *The Strokkur geyser at Geysir.*

8.8 *A fissure in the Krafla area in Iceland that marks the line of the Mid-Atlantic Ridge.*

To the north, the Pacific plate is moving north-westwards at about a similar rate, and therefore the two plates collide. Along the plate margins where the collision occurs, the edge of one plate is usually thrust under the other and a **subduction zone** is formed. As one plate (usually the heavier one) is forced under the other plate, it descends down-wards, and the friction causes **earthquakes**. As the plate is forced deeper into the hot mantle, it is heated up by the surrounding material. Eventually, the descending plate melts, and gives off gases as it does so. These gases rise to the earth's surface where they cause a **volcanic eruption** and sometimes even the formation of volcanic peaks as islands in the ocean (figure 8.9).

In an eruption, hot gases such as steam burst up from the surface, together with molten lava, solid blocks of rock, dust, cinders and ash. In places where this happens repeatedly, layers of ash and lava build up and a **cone volcano** may form (figure 8.10). An example of a volcano that formed in this way under the ocean but rose above the surface to become visible is White Island, situated off the northern coast of the North Island of New Zealand (figures 8.11 and 8.12).

Volcanic island arcs, such as the Aleutian chain south-west of Alaska, also form from volcanic activity resulting from subduction. Where the edge of one of the

8.6 *The explosion crater and lava flow at Krafla that is still hot following the 1984 eruption.*

colliding plates carries continental material (sial, which is relatively light), it is thrust upwards to form a mountain chain such as the Andes. Where two plates with continental material (sial) at their margins collide, high mountains such as the Himalayas are formed. For these reasons, areas where plates collide are not only the major areas of high mountains on the earth's surface, but are also the areas of most violent earthquakes and volcanic activity.

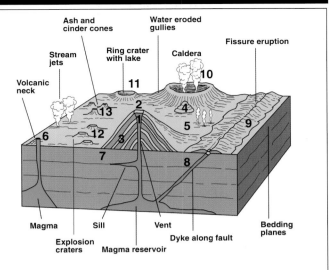

8.9 *Gases from a subduction zone are released in a volcanic eruption at White Island, New Zealand.*

1. Side vent *or* parasitic cone *or* subsidiary cone *or* subsidiary cone
2. Crater containing lake
3. Composite volcanic cone of layers of ash and lava
4. Lava flow
5. Steam and gas jets
6. Volcanic neck (the hard rock or plug remains, much of the rest has been eroded away).
7. Sill : an intrusion of lava along the bedding planes
8. Dyke: an intrusion of lava across bedding planes
9. Lava sheet which has welled up along a fault line.
10. Caldera (often with a lake)
11. Ring crater: the raised rim is formed of ash and cinder.
12. Explosion craters
13. Ash and cinder cones

8.10 *Features formed by volcanic activity.*

Volcanic activity is also found away from plate margins, however. The Hawaiian islands are situated in the mid-Pacific Ocean, well away from the margins of the Pacific Plate. However, Hawaii's volcanoes are very active. Hawaii is situated on a **hot spot**, where rising currents in the liquid mantle are concentrated near the earth's crust. The Hawaiian islands form a chain of volcanoes that are younger towards the south-east. The Pacific Plate, where Hawaii is situated, is moving towards the north-west. As the plate passes over the hot spot, new volcanoes are created that migrate towards the north–west (figure 8.13).

From time to time, lighter 'blobs' of magma are squeezed out of the slowly swirling magma in the hot spot beneath Hawaii, and they move towards the surface under pressure in a tadpole-shaped form known as a **diapir**. As the diapirs approach the surface, they encounter sial rocks that are made up of lighter material, so their rise is slowed down and the magma accumulates in large magma chambers beneath the surface.

As more magma rises from below, the pressure increases and the land surface bulges upwards, forming a **shield volcano**, named because its gentle slope resembles a shield resting on the ground. Eventually, the pressure from below forces the magma to the surface where it erupts, often producing a flow of liquid lava (molten rock) as it does so (figures 8.14).

8.11 *White Island is New Zealand's most active cone volcano. It has been erupting continuously since December 1996.*

8.12 *The plume of white ash from White Island. The ash is highly acidic and represents the main hazard from White Island.*

Hazards and disasters

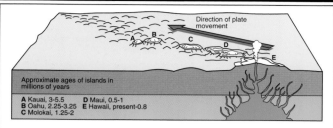

8.13 *Hawaii's volcanoes are older towards the north-west, reflecting the movement of the Pacific Plate over the hot spot.*

8.14 *The Eldfell volcano in Iceland erupted in 1973, creating the ash cone in the foreground and the extensive lava flow in the background.*

On Hawaii, two different types of lava form during eruptions, and they in turn form very different surfaces when they solidify. The first flows cool to form **a'a**, which has a very sharp, rough surface. Lava that takes longer to solidify forms **pahoehoe**, which has a smooth surface, sometimes with a rope-like surface (figure 8.15). The chemical compositions of the two types of lava flow are identical despite their very different appearances. Once cool, pahoehoe is very easy to walk on, but a'a can cut the soles of shoes and even car tyres in a matter of seconds.

8.15 *Two types of lava are shown in this view at Mauna Loa in Hawaii. The smooth lava in the foreground is pahoehoe, while the rough dark lava behind it is a'a.*

Eruptions have caused hundreds of millions of dollars in damage in recent years, as homes and other buildings have been destroyed, and as roads have been destroyed,

re-built, destroyed again, re-built again, and so on (figure 8.16). Lava flows have also realigned several sections of the coastline that will take many years of wave activity to establish a stable, recreational area once again. On the other hand, the ease of access to Hawaii's volcanoes brings curious tourists, and this generates considerable income that compensates to some extent for the economic damage that has been done. Less economically developed countries have much less financial capacity to cope with natural disasters.

8.16 *The Eldfell eruption produced a lava flow that buried several homes in the town of Heimaey, the largest settlement in the Vestmannæyjar islands off the south coast of Iceland.*

QUESTION BLOCK 8A

1. *Using figure 8.2, describe the relationship between the world distribution of earthquakes and the location of plate boundaries. Comment on the relationship.*

2. *Where is the earth's crust (a) created, and (b) destroyed?*

3. *Describe and explain the distribution of ages of volcanoes in Hawaii.*

4. *Describe the relationship between the spatial distribution of earthquakes and volcanoes.*

Hurricanes (tropical cyclones, typhoons)

The weight of the atmosphere is about 5 million billion tonnes. This weight exerts a downward pressure because of the effect of gravity, and this is known as the air pressure, or **atmospheric pressure**. Air pressure is usually expressed in kilopascals (kPa) or millibars (mb), the two measures being equivalent. The average atmospheric pressure at sea level is 1012 kPa. Lines joining points of equal air pressure are called **isobars**, and the isobars indicating a low pressure area on a weather map (or **synoptic chart**) look like a series of concentric circles with the numbers getting lower towards the centre. This can be seen on the synoptic chart of Australia shown in figure 8.17, which also includes a tropical cyclone named 'Katrina' centred at 13°S, 159°E.

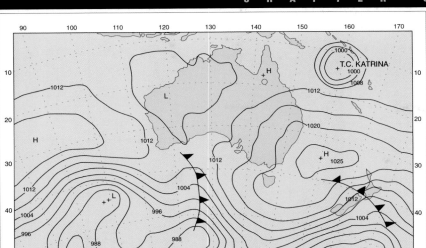

8.17 *Synoptic chart for Australia, 12th January 1998.*

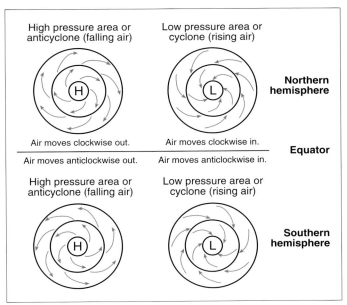

8.18 *The wind direction around high and low pressure cells is different in the two hemispheres.*

Another name for a low pressure area is an **cyclone**. Similarly, another name for any high pressure area is an **anticyclone**, and these appear on synoptic charts as a series of concentric isobars with numbers getting higher towards the centre.

Very intense low pressure areas in tropical areas which cause great damage are known as **tropical cyclones** in Australia, or **typhoons** in Asia, or **hurricanes** in North America. Hurricanes have isobars that are very close together, and this indicates very strong winds. As a general rule, closer isobars mean stronger winds, and both high and low pressure areas have essentially calm conditions in their centres.

Air moves from high pressure areas to low pressure areas, but it does not do so in a straight line. Air circulates around a pressure cell almost parallel to the isobars. Because of the rotation of the earth, an effect known as the **Coriolis force** comes into play. The Coriolis force affects any moving object, diverting it towards the right in the northern hemisphere and to the left in the southern hemisphere. Therefore, when air moves out of a high pressure area, it does so in a clockwise direction in the northern hemisphere but in an anticlockwise direction in the southern hemisphere. However, when air heads into a low pressure area, it does so in an anticlockwise direction in the northern hemisphere but in a clockwise direction in the southern hemisphere. The directions in which winds move around pressure cells are summarised in figure 8.18.

The satellite image in figure 8.19 shows Tropical Cyclone Katrina as an intense swirl of clouds over the Coral Sea to the north-east of Australia. On the false colour satellite image, the tropical cyclone appears as an intense white centre, surrounded by red, then orange, then yellow and then green zones as one moves away from the white centre. There are also clouds over the north-east coast, shown as red and yellow patches, where the moist easterly winds from the tropical cyclone are forced to rise over the mountains near the coastline. On the day this satellite image was taken, the area under the coastal clouds was experiencing floods as a result of the moist air being blown onshore from Tropical Cyclone Katrina. A report on the web on that day stated the following:

Record rainfall hitting Australia's north-eastern coast over the weekend left one person dead and caused millions of dollars in damage. Mop-up operations were under way and people were preparing to return to their homes Monday as the flood waters receded. Experts estimated that the damage bill would total at least $6.5 million. The port city of Townsville was declared a disaster area, freeing federal funds for clean-up and repairs. The government offered to pay up to 75% of the damage bill. The weather bureau said almost 700 millimetres of rain had been dumped, giving Townsville half its normal annual rainfall in a 24-hour period and its highest recorded downpour in history. Police recovered the body of a wheelchair-bound man whose car had been swept away. But another man was still missing and feared drowned after he disappeared in the churning floodwaters north of this city. More than a dozen other missing people were accounted for by Monday. The flooding caused landslides and rockfalls, disrupted road and rail links and left 20,000 people without electricity. Other services, including water and telecommunications, were also affected. More than 120 people were evacuated from their homes and about 60 tourists, many from Europe on a snorkelling vacation, were evacuated from the nearby Barrier Reef resort of Magnetic Island after a mudslide destroyed parts of the facilities.

Hazards and disasters

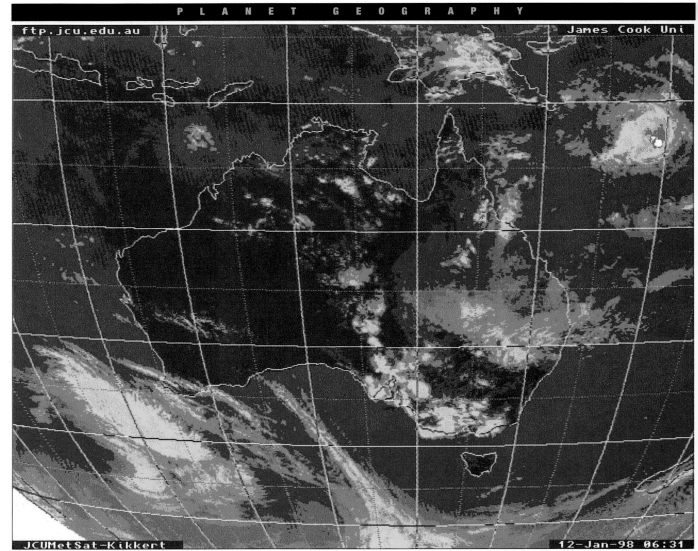

ftp.jcu.edu.au

James Cook Uni

JCUMetSat-Kikkert

12-Jan-98 06:31

8.19 *Satellite image of clouds over Australia on 12th January 1998. Black areas have no cloud cover. Clouds are shown as thin (turquoise), light (yellow), medium (orange), thick (red) and very thick (white). (Source: James Cook University, ftp.jcu.edu.au)*

The cloud pattern shown in the satellite image in figure 8.19 represented just a small part of the global picture. Figure 8.20 shows the pattern of clouds for the Pacific Ocean hemisphere on the same day as the Australian satellite image (figure 8.19) was compiled. This image shows that Tropical Cyclone Katrina was neither the only tropical cyclone nor the largest one at the time. The image shows quite intense storm activity to the east of the Philippines, to the south of India and in the eastern Pacific Ocean.

Because the winds from each hemisphere converge near the equator, a belt of low pressure forms around the equator, known as the **inter-tropical convergence zone**, which is sometimes abbreviated to **ITCZ**. The pattern of tropical cyclones and the cloud cover associated with the ITCZ show even more clearly in figure 8.21, which shows the global pattern of cloud cover on the same day. The belt of low pressure areas encircling the earth (the ITCZ) can be seen clearly as a line of cloud cover just south of the equator, the normal position for summer. To the north and south of the ITCZ, there are bands of cloudless skies representing the belts of high pressure.

QUESTION BLOCK 8B

1. What is 'air pressure'?

2. What is the difference between a cyclone and an anticyclone?

3. Look at the synoptic chart in figure 8.17 and the satellite image in figure 8.19. Describe the appearance of Tropical Cyclone Katrina in each.

4. Describe and account for the broad pattern of clouds shown in figure 8.21.

Droughts

The word **drought** means a long period (usually months or years) during which an area experiences a shortage of precipitation. Droughts occur when the amount of water vapour in the air is low, especially when stable air masses linger for extended periods of time.

Air masses can be either stable or unstable. A **stable air mass** is one where a parcel of air cannot rise, and therefore where clouds and rain are unlikely to form. On the

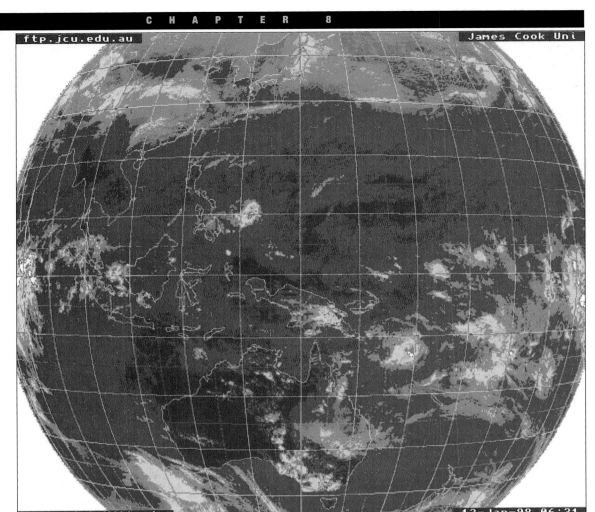

8.20 *Satellite image of clouds over east Asia, Australia and the Pacific Ocean on 12th January 1998. (Source: James Cook University, ftp.jcu.edu.au)*

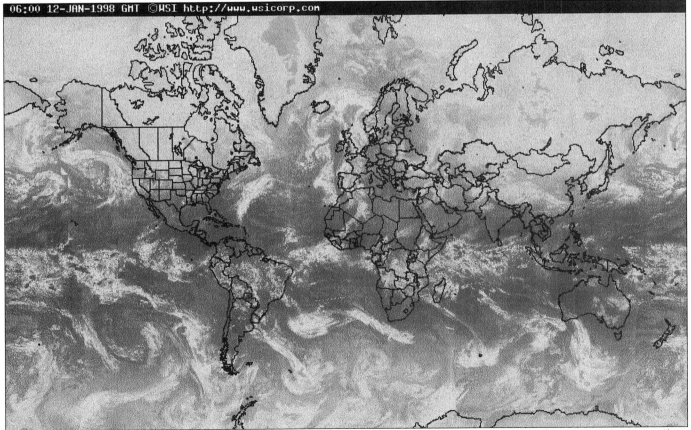

8.21 *Satellite image of global cover on 12th January 1998. Light clouds appear as white, medium clouds as yellow/green, thick clouds as red/brown, and very thick clouds as dark brown. (Source: WSI)*

Hazards and disasters

other hand, an **unstable air mass** is one in which a parcel of air can rise, and therefore where clouds and rainfall are likely.

To understand whether or not a parcel of air is likely to rise or not, we need to understand a little about **lapse rates**, which measure the relationship between temperature and altitude. If we plot the temperature of the air at different altitudes, we are likely to find that the air becomes cooler with increasing altitude. The rate at which the air becomes cooler is the **environmental lapse rate**. This can vary from place to place and from day to day, but an average value of about 6C° per 1,000 metres is common.

However, a body of rising air does not cool at the environmental lapse rate. Air rising from the earth's surface cools at a fixed rate of 10C° per 1,000 metres it rises, and this is known as the **dry adiabatic lapse rate**. Similarly, air which was descending would warm at 10C° per 1,000 metres. If a body of air rises far enough, it will cool down to the point where it becomes **saturated**. In other words, as the air cools, it condenses, and a point is reached at which the spaces between the molecules of air can no longer hold the water vapour that is in the air. The temperature at which this happens is called **dew point**. Once dew point has been reached, the air cools at a slower rate as it rises. This slower rate is known as the **wet adiabatic lapse rate**, and it is a fixed rate of 5.5C° per 1,000 metres. Clouds that appear to have flat bottoms appear that way because the air above the flat bottom is saturated, but the air beneath is not. The flat bottom of such clouds indicates dew point at that place on that day.

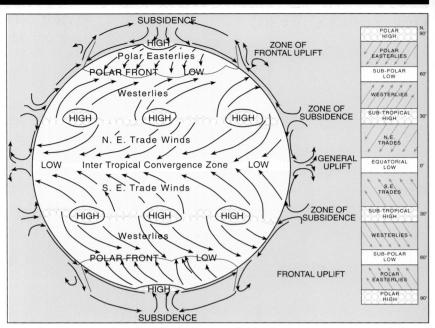

8.23 *The general pattern of the earth's atmospheric circulation.*

An air mass is stable if a body of air cannot rise. This occurs when the environmental lapse rate is less than the dry adiabatic lapse rate. An air mass is unstable if the environmental lapse rate is greater than the dry adiabatic lapse rate, as this allows a parcel of air to rise. This is shown in figure 8.22.

Stable air masses often occur when high pressure systems (**anticyclones**) are present. This is because high pressure areas tend to contain air that is descending from the upper atmosphere to the earth's surface. As the air descends, it warms up, making precipitation very unlikely.

High pressure areas, and therefore droughts, occur most often where **ocean currents** are cool. This is the opposite situation to when tropical cyclones form, where warm oceans cause the air to rise rapidly, forming clouds and precipitation. The locations of the world's cool ocean currents were shown by the green arrows in figure 6.2 in chapter 6; these areas coincide with arid areas and places where extensive droughts are common. Droughts are also common in the mid-latitude belts of high pressure that encircle the earth at latitudes of about 30° to 40° north and south of the equator (figure 8.23).

The route taken by ocean currents can fluctuate from time to time, and this was discussed in chapter 6 in the section on the **El Niño Southern Oscillation** (ENSO). During an ENSO event, drought can occur almost anywhere in the world, but research suggests that the strongest links between severe droughts and ENSO events occur in Australia, Brazil, India, Indonesia, the Philippines, eastern and southern Africa, Central America, and some parts of the US. In general, ENSO events are more likely to cause severe droughts in equatorial and tropical areas than in the mid-latitudes.

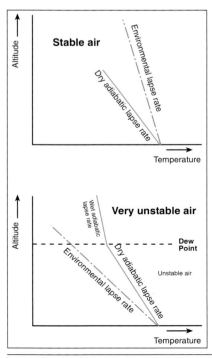

8.22 *Stable and unstable air.*

QUESTION BLOCK 8C

1. *Describe the difference between a stable and an unstable air mass.*

2. *What is the relationship between the spatial distribution of droughts, ocean currents and anticyclones?*

3. *Give reasons for the relationships you outlined in your answer to the previous question.*

A Human-Induced Hazard Event

One of the seemingly inevitable consequences of industrialisation and economic development is that the number of human-induced hazard events is increasing. Two of the best-known examples of explosions or escapes of hazardous materials are:

- the explosion in the Union Carbide chemical plant in **Bhopal**, India, in 1984. A faulty tank released poisonous methyl isocyanate that resulted in the almost immediate deaths of 2,259 people, with an additional 15,000 later dying from from related illnesses.

- the explosion and fire in the nuclear power plant in **Chernobyl**, Ukraine, in 1986. Following the explosion, a radioactive cloud spread across much of Europe, poisoning grazing lands and exposing tens of thousands of people to radioactive poisoning . The immediate death toll was 31 people, but the ultimate death toll can probably never be calculated.

In this section, we will examine a human-induced hazard event where hazardous material (natural gas) is still escaping and presenting a danger to people and animals almost forty years after it was first accidentally released. This hazard is seen at the **Darvaza gas craters** in central Turkmenistan.

Turkmenistan has one of the world's largest underground natural gas fields in the world, the proven reserves amounting to 2.86 trillion cubic metres. Before the disintegration of the USSR in 1991, Turkmenistan was part of the Soviet Union.

In 1971 and 1972, geologists working for the Soviet government began drilling for gas in Darvaza, a remote location in the Karakum Desert of central Turkmenistan, about 250 kilometres north of the country's capital city of Ashgabat. They found a large underground cavern filled with natural gas, but unfortunately the ground on which the drilling rig was placed collapsed. This triggered a succession of further collapses in the crumbly sedimentary rocks of the area, eventually creating several open craters, the largest of which has a diameter of about 60 metres and a depth of 20 metres (figure 8.24).

8.25 *Gas still burns in this crater at Darvaza almost 40 years after the land collapsed.*

8.26 *Another view of the largest gas crater at Darvaza.*

The leaking gas soon began to cause environmental problems as animals roaming in the area began to die from the gas that was escaping into the atmosphere. In order to protect the wildlife, a flaming tyre was rolled into the crater which set the gas alight and started a large fire which has been burning with intense heat in a spectacular fashion ever since (figures 8.25 and 8.26). Unfortunately,

8.24 *The main Darvaza Gas Crater in Turkmenistan.*

Hazards and disasters

animals find the fire mesmerising, and are still attracted to the crater, especially at night. From time to time, swarms of thousands of local spiders gather at the edge of the flaming crater and then run en masse into the crater to their deaths. The authorities in Turkmenistan today believe that the country has so much gas that it is easier simply to let the gas burn than to try and stop the gas escaping.

8.27 *Gas bubbles up through the water in the bottom of this gas crater in Darvaza.*

8.28 *Gas bubbles through mud in yet another of the Darvaza gas craters.*

It is now several decades since the fire in the large Darvaza crater began, and the flames are still burning very fiercely. At night, insects are attracted in huge numbers to the light and warmth of the crater. However, because of the intense heat and lack of trees, there is nowhere to rest and after flying above the warm, bright crater they collapse from exhaustion and plummet downwards into the flames. Birds are also attracted by the large numbers of insects to the flaming crater at night, but like the moths, many of them too become so exhausted that they collapse and fall into the crater's flames. Larger birds such as hawks come to prey on the smaller birds, but many of them also die each night, overcome either by the intense heat of the flames or by escaping gas fumes. It is small wonder that locals refer to the crater as the 'Gateway to Hell'.

Only one of the estimated 20 or so craters at Darvaza contains a fire. The other craters are still emitting gas into the atmosphere, albeit at a slower rate than the large, burning crater. Evidence of the escaping gas is the strong smell of sulphur near the craters, caused by pollutants in the natural gas (which itself is odourless), and bubbles formed by the escaping gas which can be seen in the bottoms of those craters that contain water (figures 8.27 and 8.28).

QUESTION BLOCK 8D

1. *Explain how and when the Darvaza gas craters formed.*

2. *In what ways are the gas craters a continuing hazard?*

3. *Consider the hazards described in the preceding sections — earthquakes, volcanoes, tropical cyclones, droughts and human-induced hazards. Compare these hazards in terms of (a) their speed of onset, (b) their frequency, (c) their predictability, (d) their spatial extent, (e) their magnitude, and (f) their duration.*

Vulnerability

Vulnerable Populations

Many people wonder why anyone would choose to live in an area where hazards might threaten their lives. Why would anyone choose to live near an active volcano, or on an active fault line, or in an area that frequently experiences disasters of any kind?

Of course, for many people, there is no choice. Most of the world's people have no option but to live in the place where they were born, perhaps because of extended family ties, perhaps they are in debt to a landlord or money lender, or perhaps because they lack the finances to move. Many farmers lack the skills required to gain employment if they were to move to an urban area.

Many people living in hazardous areas simply do not realise that there might be a hazard in that location. For example, earthquakes do not always strike in places where there have been earthquakes in the past. Even if hazards have affected an area, many people subscribe to the old (erroneous) superstition that "lightning never strikes the same place twice".

For other people, there is a conscious decision to live in an area where there is a hazard. In many parts of the world, such as the Highlands of Papua New Guinea and the islands of the Philippines, the most densely populated areas are on the sides of active volcanoes (figure 8.29). The reason for this is that when volcanoes erupt, they distribute ash that aids the fertility of the soil. In other words, the most fertile areas for cultivation are near active volcanoes, and as cultivation occurs annually but volcanoes erupt only infrequently, it seems to be a good rational decision to live there.

8.29 *Despite its hazardous location, these people have built their homes on the side of the Taal Volcano in the Philippines.*

8.30 *Heavily polluted water flows through this canal in a poor residential area of Manila, capital city of the Philippines.*

Vulnerability

Vulnerability to a hazard refers to the geographic conditions that increase the susceptibility of a community to a hazard or to the impacts of a hazard event.

Unfortunately, some groups of people are more vulnerable to hazards than others. In the same week of September 2004, tropical cyclones (hurricanes) swept through the south-east of the United States and the nearby island nation of Haiti. Although the hurricane in Haiti (Tropical Storm Jeanne) was much weaker than the one in the US (Hurricane Ivan), the death toll was 2,500 in Haiti compared with 25 deaths in the US.

Although several factors made the Haitians more vulnerable, including a lack of early warning systems and extensive deforestation, the main reason for the difference was the relative **poverty** of Haiti compared with the US. Even poorer people in the south-east of the US had more resources than most Haitians to cope with the hurricane, as well as having more substantial homes for protection from the strong winds. According to ISDR (the United Nations International Strategy for Disaster Reduction), 94% of people killed by natural hazards since 1975 were people with low incomes or lower middle incomes. Furthermore, about half of all disaster deaths since 2000 have occurred in LEDCs. The ISDR has expressed concern that the future impact of climate change may increase the vulnerability of people in LEDCs to an even greater extent.

Many of the world's poorer people live in **shanty settlements** (slums) in the rapidly expanding cities of LEDCs. People who live in shanty settlements are especially vulnerable to hazards because their housing usually lacks even the most basic facilities, such as clean water, drainage, fire services and telecommunications (figure 8.30). Furthermore, shanty settlements are often built in the most high-risk locations, such as on the steep sides of valleys, near flood-prone rivers, or on the fault lines of tectonic plates.

Poorer people in LEDCs cities are often **marginalised** culturally, socially, politically and geographically from the majority of residents in the city. Therefore, they are less likely to receive early warning of an approaching hazard event such as a typhoon (see figure 3.16 in chapter 3). because of their fear of dispossession, many are reluctant to leave their shanty settlement even if they do hear of an approaching hazard event.

It is therefore not surprising that according to the IFRC (International Federation of Red Cross and Red Crescent Societies), natural hazard events claim an average of 51 lives per disaster in MEDCs, but 589 deaths per disaster in LEDCs.

It is not only poorer people who have greater vulnerability to hazards. According to the ILO (International Labour Organisation), **women** are more vulnerable to hazards because they tend to have less access resources, and because they tend to be the main caregivers to children, the disabled and the elderly. Consequently, they are less likely to be able to respond to a disaster with the resources needed to make a large-scale difference. The ILO has also noted that women are specially vulnerable to sexual violence and exploitation — including human trafficking for prostitution or slave-labour — in the period following a hazard event.

Elderly people are another vulnerable group during a hazard event. Although the elderly often cannot move as quickly or with as much agility as younger people, they are often neglected in the aftermath of a disaster. In a major earthquake in Kobe (Japan) in 1995, about half the deaths were elderly people, even though only 14% of Kobe's population were elderly at the time.

At the other end of the age scale, **children** are another vulnerable group in hazard events. Children often experience long-term psychological problems when hazard events occur because they cannot fully understand what is happening (figure 8.31). Furthermore, like women, children are sometimes vulnerable to trafficking and abuse after a disaster, especially if they have been orphaned and are hungry. If the child has also experienced poverty, inadequate diet could make the child especially vulnerable to disease and even death if infections break out in the aftermath of a disaster.

In a major earthquake in China's Sichuan province in 2008, over 69,000 people were killed in spite of the valiant efforts of government officials and the army, and of this number, over 19,000 were schoolchildren. This was because many of the schools in the area had been built using inadequate construction materials, making the children more vulnerable to the earthquake than the general population. During the earthquake, at least 7,000 school buildings in Sichuan collapsed, more than any other type of building.

8.31 *Children in Manila (Philippines) in the immediate aftermath of a tropical cyclone in which their home was destroyed.*

8.32 *Buildings in Massawa, Eritrea, that were destroyed in the civil war have still not been repaired.*

Political conflict can make people more vulnerable to hazards. During 1984 to 1985, there was a major famine in Ethiopia and Eritrea, which government officials blamed on a drought at the time. Although this was a dry period when the rains failed, Ethiopian people had coped with similar droughts on many previous occasions without famine becoming a problem. The difference in the 1980s was that two civil wars were taking place in Ethiopia, one of which was Eritrea's war of independence, and these conflicts forced many people off their traditional lands while making the movement of food and

supplies extremely dangerous (figures 8.32 and 8.33). There have been many other examples of political turmoil making people more vulnerable to hazards, such as the drought in Afghanistan in 1999 and the tropical cyclone in southern Myanmar in 2008.

8.33 *War damaged buildings in Massawa, Eritrea.*

QUESTION BLOCK 8E

1. *What are the differences between direct and indirect effects of hazards?*

2. *With reference to one hazard event that has been in the news recently, assess whether direct or indirect effects were more significant.*

3. *To what extent is vulnerability to hazards a demographic and socio-political phenomenon? Give reasons and examples to support your answer.*

Risk and Risk Assessment

Analysis of Risk

Analysing the risk from potential hazards, and trying to predict their likelihood, are very specialised activities. Insurance companies try to analyse and predict hazards in a very detailed manner, but even when sophisticated computer models are used, errors occur much more frequently than anyone would wish.

One of the challenges in analysing risk is that there are many variables as well as different time scales to be considered. For example, if we were considering the risk of mortality (death) from a tropical cyclone in a particular area, we need to consider both **direct effects** (deaths caused during the cyclone, such as when a tree or a building falls on a person), as well as **indirect effects**, which are consequences that occur after the event. Indirect effects can be short-term or medium-term, periods that are difficult to define with very much precision. Short-term effects might include deaths resulting from respiratory, infectious or parasitic diseases that start to spread as a result of the tropical cyclone.

ToK BoX

Reasoning.

An important aspect of studying hazards is understanding and explaining the causes and effects of certain hazard events. Sometimes, the cause-and-effect links are unclear, and reasoning is required to explain the sequence of events.

Quite simply, reasoning is the use of the mind to think, understand and form judgements using a process of logic. There are two types of reasoning, inductive and deductive.

Deductive reasoning is chain of logic where one proposition leads to another, and thus the conclusion has 100% certainty, provided the assumptions are accurate. For example:

All men are mortal

I am a man

Therefore, I am mortal

On the other hand, in inductive reasoning, a number of observations provides evidence that leads to a conclusion. The greater the number of observations, the more reliable the conclusion. For example:

We see 30 swans

They are all white

We see 3000 swans

They are all white

Therefore, all swans are white

Inductive reasoning never gives certainty because it takes only one exception (which may not yet have been tested or discovered) to make a claim invalid. On the other hand, deductive reasoning, which is used widely in mathematics, is capable of giving certainty provided the assumptions are correct.

However, it is important to understand the logical patterns used in deductive reasoning. Consider the following argument, and ask yourself whether it is valid:

If human-induced global warming is really happening, then the polar ice caps will be melting.

The polar ice caps are melting.

Therefore, human-induced global warming is really happening.

In this case, the argument is not valid. It follows the form:

If p, then q

q

Therefore p

This is an example of a particular type of logical fallacy known as 'affirming the consequent'. It may be easier to see why it is a logical fallacy if we use a different argument that follows the same structure:

If it's Monday the banks will be open.

The banks are open.

Therefore, it's Monday

You can test how well you understand logical fallacies and reasoning by considering the seven 3-line arguments that appear below. For each argument, decide whether (a) the assumptions are true or false, (b) the conclusion is true or false, and (c) whether the argument is valid or invalid.

For each argument, the assumptions are found in the first two lines. The conclusion is found in the third (last) line. Whether the argument is valid or not is determined by whether or not the conclusion flows logically from the preceding assumptions (regardless of whether it is true or false).

When you have decided whether (a) the assumptions are true or false, (b) the conclusion is true or false, and (c) whether the argument is valid or invalid, write the number of the argument in the correct rectangle in the appropriate box below.

Argument 1:
China is in Africa
Moscow is in China
Therefore Moscow is in Africa

Argument 2:
China is in Africa
Moscow is in Africa
Therefore Moscow is in China

Argument 3:
China is in Asia
Shanghai is in Asia
Therefore Shanghai is in China

Argument 4:
China is in Asia
Shanghai is in China
Therefore Shanghai is in China

Argument 5:
China is in Africa
Cairo is in China
Therefore Cairo is in Africa

Argument 6:
China is in Africa
Shanghai is in Africa
Therefore Shanghai is in China

Argument 7:
China is in Asia
Shanghai is in Asia
Therefore Shanghai is in China

You should be able to write one number in each of seven rectangles, leaving one rectangle blank.

Check your answers in the next ToK BoX, which is on page 346.

VALID ARGUMENTS	True Conclusion	False Conclusion
True Assumptions		
False Assumptions		

INVALID ARGUMENTS	True Conclusion	False Conclusion
True Assumptions		
False Assumptions		

ToK BoX

If you analysed the logical arguments in the ToK Box on page 345 correctly, your tables should match those to the right of this column.

You will notice that one rectangle remains empty. Can you make up an argument that would fit into this rectangle?

Logically, the only way you can find an argument to fill the empty square would be if the argument contained a fallacy, such as a shifting meaning. One example could take the form:

A is located in B

B is located in C

Therefore, A is located in C (but in the process, B has shifted meaning).

To summarise this discussion on reasoning, if you provide a valid argument with true assumptions, you must inevitably get a true conclusion.

TRUTH IN → TRUTH OUT

In other words, validity preserves truth in any argument.

Inserting truth into an invalid argument can give a false *or* a true conclusion. That is why invalid arguments have no value.

Invalid arguments do not preserve truth. If the conclusion is true, it is for reasons that have nothing to do with the process of deductive reasoning.

For these reasons, a purely deductive argument will not reveal any truth that

VALID ARGUMENTS	True Conclusion	False Conclusion
True Assumptions	4	
False Assumptions	5	1

INVALID ARGUMENTS	True Conclusion	False Conclusion
True Assumptions	3	7
False Assumptions	6	2

was not already known. On the other hand, induction *does* provide new discoveries, but at the price of certainty.

In the words of Cornman, Lehrer & Pappas in their book 'Philosophical Problems and Arguments', "valid arguments preserve truth as good freezers preserve food. If the food you place in the freezer is spoiled to begin with, then even a good freezer cannot preserve it. Good freezers and valid arguments preserve fresh food and truth, respectively. But just as the former cannot preserve food when the food is spoiled, so the latter cannot preserve truth when the premises are false. Garbage in, garbage out."

The next ToK BoX is on page 383.

Medium-term effects might include deaths resulting from the deterioration of living conditions, a deterioration of basic services that affect health standards, or factors that increase people's vulnerability, such as poverty and malnutrition.

In analysing the risks presented by different hazards, it is important to take into account the factors that aggravate the vulnerability of individuals and groups of people. Figure 8.34 identifies some of the most important such factors.

One of the key reasons that risks are often misjudged is that planners and individuals **under-estimate the severity or the frequency of hazards**. This indicated by the second box from the left on the bottom line of figure 8.34. Underestimating hazards can occur for many reasons. In the case of some governments in LEDCs, the seriousness of hazards may be deliberately minimised in order that certain individuals or companies are spared the expense or effort of dealing with the remedies required. More

commonly, hazards are under-estimated because people do not have the necessary long-term data and information to access the risk accurately. In the case of many people living in hazard-prone areas, the risk may be known and understood, but it is psychologically suppressed so that the benefits of living in an area (such as access to employment or to good soils for cultivation) are not challenged. This is known as **psychological denial** of the risk.

Once the risk of a hazard has been assessed for a particular area, taking effective measures to prepare for a hazard event or to minimise its impact can be initiated. For example, the shanty settlement shown in figure 8.35 would be assessed as a high-risk area for several reasons. Located in Caracas, the capital city of Venezuela, this area shows a very steep, unstable slope, with poorly constructed buildings that house large numbers of people from very poor backgrounds in an area that experiences periodic hurricanes. For example, in 1993, Hurricane Brett passed very close to Caracas, causing 173 deaths.

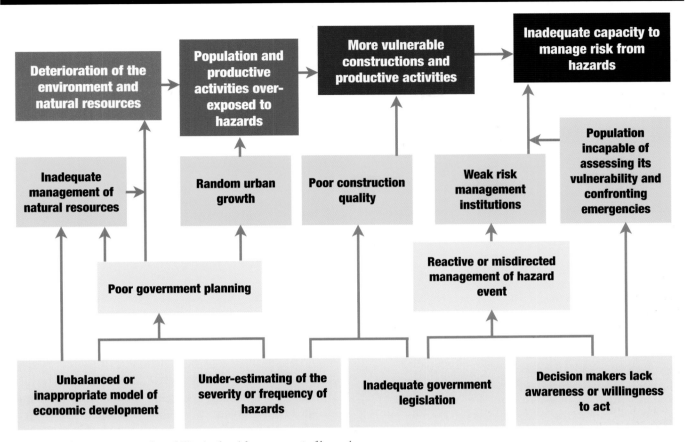

8.34 *Factors that aggravate vulnerability in the risk assessment of hazards.*

In 1988, Hurricane Joan caused 11 deaths in Caracas due to flash flooding, and in 2004, Hurricane Ivan caused 44 fatalities, led to the widespread evacuation of thousands of people and brought a 4 metre high storm surge to the nearby coastline that damaged 60 homes. The area also experiences moderate earthquakes quite frequently.

In a situation such as this, the hazard risk can be reduced through measures such as land use planning, relocating people to safer areas, ensuring that construction standards are met, and trying to reduce the level of poverty of the people in the area. Many researchers agree that the best way to protect people from the risk of hazards is to reduce poverty, as this is the most effective way of reducing vulnerability.

QUESTION BLOCK 8F

1. *Why do people live in hazardous areas?*

2. *Explain the reasons why some sectors of a population might be more vulnerable to hazards than others.*

3. *With reference to figure 8.34, explain why under-estimating the importance of hazards can cause major problems.*

4. *Why do individuals and communities often under-estimate the probability of hazard events occurring?*

5. *With reference to the earlier section on vulnerability, discuss the factors that influence a person's perception of the risk posed by hazards.*

8.35 *A vulnerable shanty settlement in Caracas, Venezuela.*

Hazard Event Prediction

As discussed in the previous section, estimating the risk of hazard events, or predicting their probability, is notoriously difficult to do with precision. The best hazard predictions are usually based on examining **historical records** of past events. This information is meshed with understandings of the **physical geography** of an area, such as its geological stability, whether it lies near a war tropical ocean that might trigger hurricanes, whether it is situated near a cold ocean current that might induce extended droughts, and so on.

There are many methods used to estimate the probability of hazards, some of which are extremely complex and use sophisticated computer algorithms. One of the simpler approaches is the **Disaster Reduction Index** (DRI), developed by the United Nations Development Program (UNDP). The DRI estimates the risk of loss of life that might occur from a hazard event, ignoring the possible damage to livelihoods and the economy. The advantage of this measure is that it highlights the hazard risk in a clear and simple way that avoids the problems of comparing different exchange rates when looking at different countries. Risk is calculated using the formula $R = H \times P \times V$, where R is the risk (expressed as the number of deaths), H is the hazard (measured by its frequency and expected strength), P is the population size of the exposed area, and V is the vulnerability of the population, a factor that depends on the socio-economic and political context of the location being assessed.

The DRI does suffer from shortcomings. Estimating the number of deaths from an event is rather imprecise, and it has been criticised for failing to include any measure of the capacity of the government to improve the state of development in a way that reduce the risk. It is seen as being particularly imprecise in urban environments because of their greater complexity and diversity compared with rural areas.

In an attempt to overcome these shortcomings, the IADB (Inter-American Development Bank) in Latin America worked with the United Nations Foundation (UNF) and IDEA (the International Debate Education Association) to develop four alternative indices of risk assessment and hazard prediction.

The first of the IADB measures is the **Disaster Deficit Index** ((DDI). This index models the consequences of a hazard event in macro-economic and financial terms, representing the maximum probably loss over a determined period of time and the capacity of the country to deal with it. The DDI is designed to allow planners to know in advance what the the gap will be between need for funds resulting from a hazard event and the capacity of the government in terms of its access to local or foreign money to restore the goods that have been lost or affected. The DDI is calculated by dividing the cost of the impact of the hazard event (as measured by its financial cost) by the economic resilience of the government (as measured by the funds the government can raise to deal with the event). If the DDI is greater than 1.0, then the government cannot raise sufficient funds to cope with extreme hazards. The greater the gap between the probable losses and the capacity to cope with them, the greater the country's indebtedness.

The second IADB measure is the **Local Disasters Index** (LDI), which measures the risk of social and environmental problems resulting from regular hazard events at the local scale, especially those which have the greatest impact on the poorest groups. To do this, the LDI adds the number of expected deaths, the number of people affected and the losses of the people affected for different local areas.

A third measure of hazard risk is the **Prevalent Vulnerability Index** (PVI), which is a composite indicator of vulnerability to the risk of hazards based on three other indicators — the Indicator of Exposure and Susceptibility (PVI_{es}), the Indicator of Socio-economic Fragility (PVI_{sf}), and the Indicator of (Lack of) Resilience (PVI_{lr}). This is a more complex measure requiring considerably more data — which is a problem when used in many LEDCs that may lack the resources to gather detailed data. Nonetheless, if the data is available, the PVI has the advantage of providing a comprehensive picture of vulnerability in terms of exposure in each area, socio-economic fragility and lack of social resilience.

The fourth measure used to assess the risk of hazards is the **Risk Management Index** (RMI). The RMI is another composite measure that estimates the effectiveness of risk management in terms of institutional organisation, capacity and development to reduce losses. It does this by combining four factors, each of which is also a complex composite indicator: risk identification, risk reduction, hazard reduction and effectiveness of governance.

Any system of predicting hazards must consider the probability that a certain type of hazard event will occur, as well as the potential impact of that event on lives and property. Obviously, the probabilities of different types of hazard vary from place to place and from environment to environment.

The United Nations International Strategy for Disaster Reduction (ISDR) maintains a database of hazard events and disasters dating from 1900 to the present day. ISDR categorises hazards into three groups:

- **Hydro-meteorological disasters**, which includes floods and wave surges, storms, droughts and related disasters (extreme temperatures and forest / scrub fires), landslides and avalanches;

- **Geophysical disasters**, which includes earthquakes, tsunamis and volcanic eruptions; and

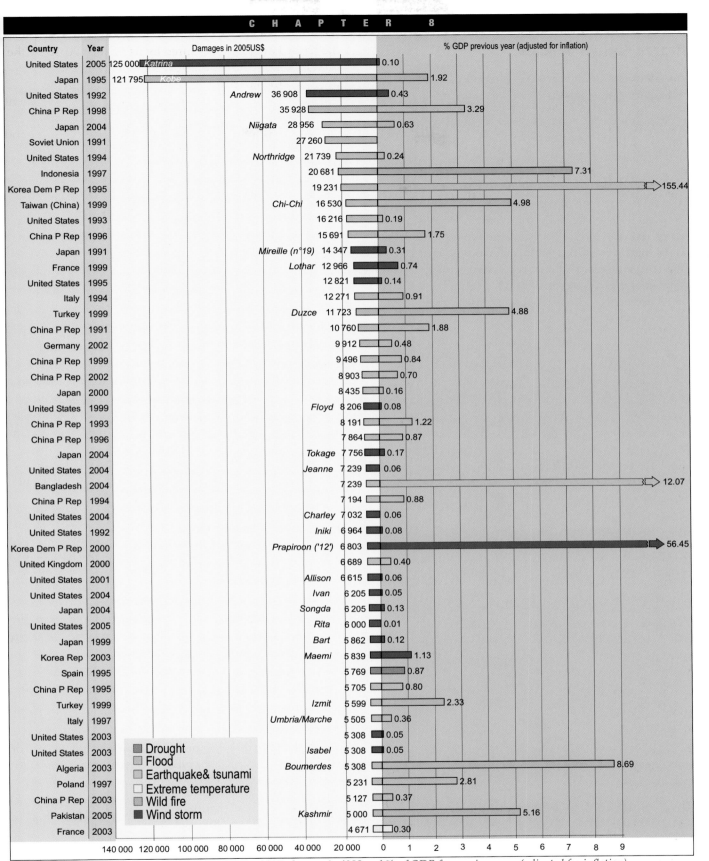

8.36 *Economic damage from hazard events, 1991 to 2005, damage in $US and % of GDP for previous year (adjusted for inflation).*

- **Biological disasters**, covering epidemics and insect infestations.

According to the ISDR, the number of disasters has been growing markedly since 1900, both in terms of the number of disasters and the value of the damage they cause.

The greatest growth has been in hydro-meteorological disasters, which have increased by a factor of about 40,000% since 1900. The increases in the numbers of geophysical and biological disasters have been considerably less, being a 6,000% increase in the number of biological disasters and an 800% increase in the number of geologi-

Hazards and disasters

cal disasters. It is quite possible that many of the earlier disasters were not reported and thus the actual increase in the number of disasters has been much less than these statistics might suggest.

When more recent hazard events are analysed, we find that the largest amount of economic damage was done in MEDCs (figure 8.36). This is probably to be expected as MEDCs have higher value assets and resources, and therefore when damage occurs it will cost more to repair, especially when the higher wages in MEDCs are considered. As we saw earlier in this chapter, measuring economic damage is very different from measuring loss of life or injuries resulting from hazards. As figure 8.36 also shows, even hazards that result in less economic damage (by value) may cause significantly greater hardship if they happen in an LEDC, because the damage is likely to

represent a greater proportion of an LEDC's total wealth (as measured by Gross Domestic Product).

The difference between the economic impact of hazards and the deaths they can cause is shown in figure 8.37. Both parts of the diagram show the world distribution of a wide range of hazards. As these maps are based on actual historical events over a long period of time, they can also be used as a broad basis for predicting future hazards on the assumption that future hazard events will be distributed in a similar way to those of the past.

Both maps indicate the top three deciles (i.e., the most likely 30%) of areas experiencing particular types of hazards, as shown in the key. Although there are some minor differences depending upon the hazard, on the basis of the information in figure 8.37, we can conclude that the economic loss from particular hazards tends to be greater

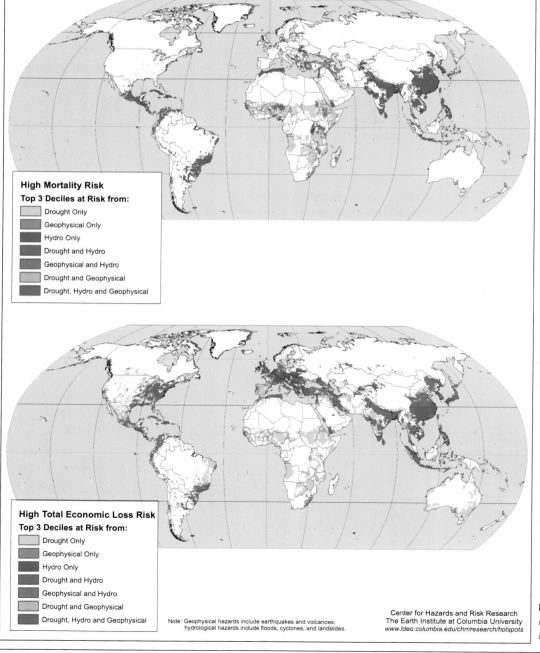

in MEDCs, but the loss of life from the same hazards tends to be greater in LEDCs. This supports the conclusions we reached earlier in this chapter.

When we examine particular hazards in greater detail, this conclusion is confirmed. Figure 8.38 shows the mortality and the economic losses that result from just one hazard — drought. In this map, the 8th to 10th deciles (red) represent the highest values, and the 1st to 4th decile (blue) represent the lowest values recorded. Although the broad pattern of areas affected by drought is similar on each map in figure 8.38, being the result of world climatic patterns, the economic impact is greater in MEDCs whereas the impact on mortality is greater in LEDCs.

High Mortality Risk
Top 3 Deciles at Risk from:
- Drought Only
- Geophysical Only
- Hydro Only
- Drought and Hydro
- Geophysical and Hydro
- Drought and Geophysical
- Drought, Hydro and Geophysical

High Total Economic Loss Risk
Top 3 Deciles at Risk from:
- Drought Only
- Geophysical Only
- Hydro Only
- Drought and Hydro
- Geophysical and Hydro
- Drought and Geophysical
- Drought, Hydro and Geophysical

Note: Geophysical hazards include earthquakes and volcanoes; hydrological hazards include floods, cyclones, and landslides.

Center for Hazards and Risk Research
The Earth Institute at Columbia University
www.ldeo.columbia.edu/chrr/research/hotspots

8.37 *Mortality (top) and economic loss (bottom) from a selection of hazards.*

QUESTION BLOCK 8G

1. *Five different measures of risk analysis are discussed in this section. What are the different emphases of each? Giving reasons, explain which approach you prefer.*

2. *List the five biggest disasters in figure 8.36 in descending order of their percentage of the country's GDP (Gross Domestic Product).*

3. *Suggest four significant conclusions you can draw from the data in figure 8.36.*

4. *Using the information in figure 8.37, describe (a) the world distribution of deaths from geophysical hazards (including areas where deaths also arise from other hazards), and (b) the world distribution of economic losses from geophysical hazards (including areas where losses also arise from other hazards). Then suggest reasons to explain these distributions (remembering to include factors from the physical environments of these areas as described in the early part of this chapter.*

5. *With reference to figure 8.38, predict the likely future distribution of droughts around the world, mentioning the likely impact on (a) lives, and (b) property.*

Disasters

Definition

At the beginning of this chapter, the term **hazard event** was defined as the occurrence (or realisation) of a hazard, together with the changes in demographic, economic and/or environmental conditions which result. This is not quite the same as a disaster, which we began discussing in the previous section. The difference is largely one of magnitude. A **disaster** is a *major* hazard event that causes widespread disruption to a community

or region, with significant demographic, economic and/or environmental losses where the affected community is unable to deal adequately with the situation unless it receives outside help.

Measuring the Intensity of Earthquakes

Earthquakes are a major hazard to people living on plate margins (see chapter 6). Measuring earthquakes presents a challenge to geographers. Two methods are used, one devised by Mercali and the other by Richter. Although the **Mercali scale** is not used as widely as the Richter scale, it is useful because its descriptions can be related to observations. The Mercali system is outlined in table 8.1. The more common way to measure the intensity of an earthquake is to use the **Richter Scale**, a scheme developed in 1935 by an American geographer, Charles Richter. On the Richter Scale, figure of 2 or less can hardly be felt. A figure of 3 is ten times stronger than a figure of 2. A figure of 4 is ten times stronger than a figure of 3, and one hundred times stronger than a figure of 2. An earthquake

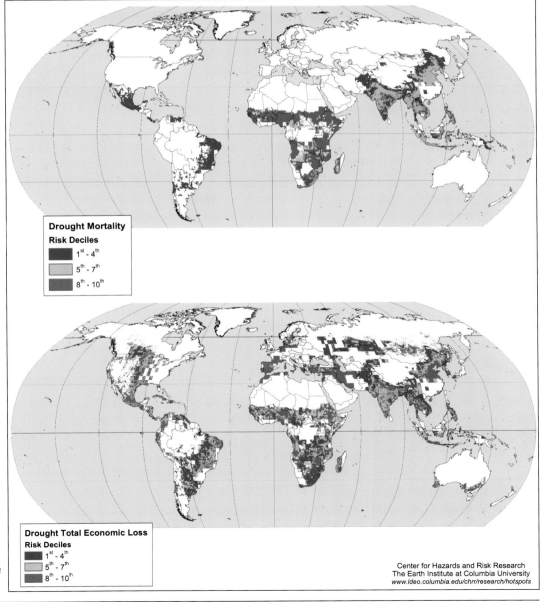

Drought Mortality Risk Deciles
- 1ˢᵗ - 4ᵗʰ
- 5ᵗʰ - 7ᵗʰ
- 8ᵗʰ - 10ᵗʰ

Drought Total Economic Loss Risk Deciles
- 1ˢᵗ - 4ᵗʰ
- 5ᵗʰ - 7ᵗʰ
- 8ᵗʰ - 10ᵗʰ

Center for Hazards and Risk Research
The Earth Institute at Columbia University
www.ldeo.columbia.edu/chrr/research/hotspots

8.38 *Mortality (top) and economic loss (bottom) from drought.*

Hazards and disasters

Table 8.1
The Mercali Scale of Earthquake Intensity

Scale	Description
I	Not felt except by a very few people under especially favourable circumstances.
II	Felt by only a few people at rest, especially on upper floors of buildings. Delicately suspended objects may swing.
III	Felt noticeably indoors, especially on upper floors, but many people do not recognise it as an earthquake. Standing cars may rock slightly. The vibration is like a passing truck.
IV	During the day, felt indoors by many, outdoors by a few. At night, some people are woken up. Dishes, windows and doors are disturbed. Walls make a creaking sound. Sensation is like a heavy truck striking a building. Cars rock noticeably.
V	Felt by nearly everyone. Many are awakened. Some dishes and windows are broken. Some plaster on walls may crack, unstable objects fall. Disturbances of trees, poles and other tall objects may be noticed. Pendulum clocks may stop.
VI	Felt by all, many are frightened and run outdoors. Some heavy furniture is moved, a few instances of fallen plaster or damaged chimneys. Damage slight.
VII	Everybody runs outdoors. Damage negligible in buildings of good design and construction; slight to moderate in well-built ordinary structures; considerable in poorly designed or badly built structures; some chimneys broken. Noticed by people driving cars.
VIII	Damage slight in specially built structures; considerable in ordinary substantial buildings, with partial collapse; large damage in poorly built structures. Panel walls thrown out of frame structures. Fall of chimneys, columns, factory stacks, monuments, walls. Heavy furniture overturned. Sand and mud ejected in small amounts. Changes in well water levels.
IX	Damage considerable in specially designed buildings, well-designed frame structures thrown out of plumb; great damage in substantial buildings with partial collapse. Buildings shifted off foundations. Ground cracked conspicuously. Underground pipes broken.
X	Some well-built wooden structures destroyed; ground badly cracked. Rails bent. Landslides considerable from river banks and steep slopes. Water splashed over banks.
XI	Few, if any, masonry buildings left standing. Bridges destroyed. Broad fissures in the ground. Underground pipelines completely out of service. Earth slumps and land slips in soft ground. Rails bent greatly.
XII	Damage total. Waves seen on ground surfaces. Lines of sight and level distorted. Objects thrown upwards into the air.

Table 8.2
The Richter Scale

Scale	Intensity	Description
1	*Instrumental*	Detected only by seismographs.
2	*Feeble*	Noticed only by sensitive people.
3	*Slight*	Like the vibrations due to a passing truck, felt by people at rest, especially on upper floors.
4	*Moderate*	Felt by people while walking, loose objects and stationary cars are shaken.
5	*Strong*	Trees sway and suspended objects swing; some damage from loose and falling objects.
6	*Destructive*	General alarm, walls crack, plaster falls, car drivers seriously disturbed, chimneys fall, poorly constructed buildings are damaged.
7	*Disastrous*	Ground cracks badly, many buildings destroyed and railways bent, landslides on steep slopes.
8	*Very disastrous*	Few buildings remain standing, bridges destroyed, all services (railways, pipes, cables) out of action, great landslides and floods.
9	*Catastrophic*	Total destruction, objects thrown into the air, ground rises and falls in waves.

measuring 5 or over may cause destruction. An earthquake of 7 or more will cause major damage if it is centred near a settled area. Table 8.2 gives details of the measures used in the Richter Scale. The San Francisco earthquake of 1906 had a force of 8.25 on the Richter Scale, while the Tokyo earthquake of 1923 had a force of 8.2. The strongest known earthquake ever measured was a shock in Chile in 1960 that measured 8.9.

QUESTION BLOCK 8H

1. *With reference to the Mercali Scale of earthquake intensity, suggest which of two earthquakes of equal intensity, one in an LEDC and one in an MEDC, would likely to cause more damage.*

The Tangshan Earthquake, July 1976

8.39 *A view of Tangshan, taken several hours after the earthquake on 26th July, 1976. (Photo: Xinhua)*

8.40 *The ruined library of the Tangshan Mining and Metallurgical Institute. The building was moved sideways 1.5 metres during the earthquake.*

8.41 *This line of trees ran at right-angles to the fault line that developed during the Tangshan earthquake. Before the earthquake, the trees in the foreground were in a straight line with those in the background; now they are offset by 1.5 metres.*

One of the most destructive earthquakes the past 100 years occurred in Tangshan, China, on 28th July, 1976, striking at 3:42 am (figure 8.39). This earthquake resulted in the deaths of 242,769 people and 186,851 injuries, a significant proportion of the city's population of 1,060,000 people at the time. The earthquake lasted just 23 seconds, but the force was equivalent to 400 atomic bombs of the kind that devastated Hiroshima. In that time, every building in the city was either destroyed or damaged so badly that it had to be demolished (figure 8.40). Local mines were flooded, water storage dams were damaged and all transport, communications, water and power supplies were cut. The Tangshan earthquake measured almost 8 on the Richter Scale, and its focus, or epicentre, was right below the city, only 12 kilometres beneath the surface.

When the earthquake struck, a fault line developed and the earth shifted one and a half metres on each side of the fault line (figure 8.41). It is still possible to see lines of trees, gutters and other features which are offset by an abrupt one and a half metres at the fault line. One survivor of the Tangshan earthquake was Zhang Yunxing (figure 8.42). She told the author of her experience of the earthquake:

"I was very lucky to survive the earthquake. I think I survived because I was living in a very small, old style house. They were built more strongly than the tall high rise flats.

When the earthquake struck. I woke up immediately. At first I thought that Tangshan had been attacked by the Russians with bombs. The government had been telling us for several years that the Russians might attack, and that we must be on guard. I thought that this was the beginning of a war.

My first thought was for the safety of my mother. She was an old lady who lived in a high rise flat on the other side of the town. I went outside, but I could not see very much as it was still dark. There was rubble everywhere. I had only walked a few metres from my home and I was completely lost, even though I have lived in Tangshan all my life! I could not find my way through the damaged streets and buildings.

I just sat down and cried. But then I heard calls for help and I forgot all about my own predicament. I joined in with some soldiers from the People's Liberation Army and some men of the People's Militia and tried to uncover injured people from the collapsed buildings. I started digging wherever I heard a voice. I thought only of Chairman Mao's love for the Chinese people and his command to us — "Serve the People!". I worked for two, or maybe three days, without sleeping — I can't remember exactly. Sadly, I never saw my mother again."

Hazards and disasters

8.42 *Earthquake survivor Zhang Yunxing points to the ruined foundations of a building that was lifted and moved sideways one and a half metres during the Tangshan earthquake.*

8.43 *People's Liberation Army soldiers help clear damaged buildings after the earthquake. (Photo: Xinhua)*

In 1976, China was an economically less developed country (LEDC). Like many LEDCs, China was poorly equipped to cope with a huge natural disaster, and the political turmoil of the Cultural Revolution made matters worse. It took a few days for the Chinese government even to announce that an earthquake had occurred. Once the enormity of the damage was realised, however, aid began to flow into Tangshan. More than 100,000 army officers and soldiers were sent to the area, together with 30,000 medical workers, 30,000 construction workers and 20,000 government office workers (figure 8.43). Wounded people and orphans were evacuated to be cared for elsewhere. Aid came from all parts of China. However, the Chinese government refused to accept aid from foreign countries as it wanted to prove that China was capable of managing the disaster relief itself.

Within a few weeks of the earthquake, it was decided that Tangshan's resources were so great that the city would have to be re-built. It would be unthinkable to abandon an area with such great coal reserves — 800 million tonnes of high grade coal reserves, enough to last for 400 years at the current rate of excavation. Even though the coal mines had been flooded during the earthquake, coal was being produced once again just ten days later.

The first priority in rebuilding Tangshan was to provide housing for the survivors. Thousands of temporary shelters were built with walls of mud bricks or fired bricks, and roofs of bitumen sheeting held down with stones and tree branches (figure 8.44). Most of these structures had no electricity or gas, and so both heating and cooking were done using open wooden fires. Lacking chimneys, the smoke from the fires seeped out through the gaps in the bricks.

The next problem arose with the removal of the rubble. In large factories, huge steel girders had been twisted into weird shapes and massive blocks of concrete had been tossed about. In some cases, the destroyed buildings were so damaged that the bodies of those trapped were simply left inside as memorials to the earthquake.

8.44 *Temporary housing like this provided accommodation for many of Tangshan's people for several years after the earthquake. Some examples were still found in Tangshan 12 years after the earthquake, although they have all gone now, replaced by high rise housing like that seen under construction.*

Tangshan has been completely re-built since the earthquake. Urban planners used the opportunity of the earthquake to redesign Tangshan completely. Today's Tangshan is the Chinese 'dream city' — the city that planners in China would build if they could start a new city afresh. Although Tangshan's reconstruction began when China was economically less developed, rapid economic growth in China during the 1980s and 1990s has enabled planners in Tangshan to develop a modern city that reflects China's greater prosperity (figure 8.45).

For residents of Tangshan, the biggest question is whether there is likely to be another earthquake or not. All new buildings in Tangshan are claimed to be earthquake-proof. China has had an Earthquake Prediction Centre for many years. Indeed, along with the Americans, the Chinese lead the world in the science of earthquake prediction. In February 1975, the Centre successfully predicted a force 7.2 earthquake at Haicheng in nearby Liaoning province. Although the earthquake destroyed 90% of the buildings in Haicheng, very few people were killed because they had advance warning. However, although there were some small warning tremors at Tangshan, the scientists disagreed about the size and date of the expected quake. For that reason, no warnings were issued.

8.45 *The rebuilt city of Tangshan, arranged in a grid layout that bears no relationship the pre-earthquake urban pattern.*

QUESTION BLOCK 8I

1. *Suggest how the outcome of the earthquake in Tangshan may have been different if it had struck (a) in a poorer country than China, and (b) in a more affluent country than China.*

The Indian Ocean Tsunami, December 2004

Often wrongly called tidal waves (they have nothing to do with tidal changes), **tsunamis** are very large sea surface waves that are caused by underwater earthquakes, underwater landslides, volcanic activity or even a meteorite strike. When they first form, they can only be detected by very sensitive measurements of changes in deep water pressure. However, when they reach the shallow waters of coastal regions, wave height may rise to several metres, leading to severe property damage and loss of life.

The word *tsunami* is Japanese and means 'harbour wave' because of the destructive impact these waves have had on low-lying Japanese coastal communities. Tsunamis usually travel at speeds averaging 700 (and up to 1,000) kilometres per hour in the open ocean. In the open ocean, a tsunami would not be felt by ships because the wavelength would be hundreds of kilometres long, with an amplitude of only one metre or so. For this reason, tsu-

namis also cannot be seen from the air when they are in the open ocean. However, as the waves approach the coast, their speed decreases and their amplitude increases as they are affected by the submarine topography approaching the shoreline. Unusual wave heights have been known to be over 30 metres high, but waves that are 3 to 6 metres high can be very destructive and cause many deaths or injuries (figure 8.46).

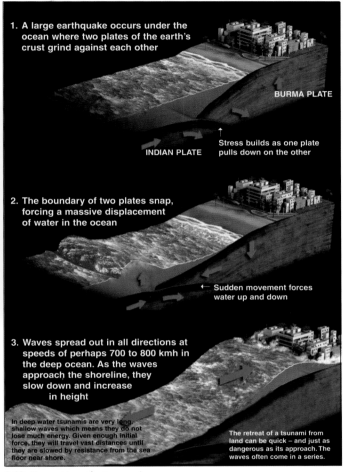

8.46 *Formation of a tsunami.*

The areas which face the greatest risk from tsunamis are those which are less than 8 metres above sea level and within one kilometre of the shoreline. Most deaths caused by a tsunami arise from drowning. Secondary risks include flooding, being hit by heavy debris carried by the moving water, contamination of drinking water, fires from ruptured tanks or gas lines, and loss of vital community infrastructure (police, fire, and medical facilities).

As soon as the shock first occurs, waves travel outward in all directions like the ripples caused by throwing a rock into a pond. As these waves approach coastal areas, the time between successive wave crests varies from 5 to 90 minutes. The first wave may be preceded by a few minutes of abnormally low water, and when it hits, it is usually not the largest in the series of waves, nor is it the most significant. Furthermore, one coastal community may experience no damaging waves while another, not that far away, may experience destructive deadly waves.

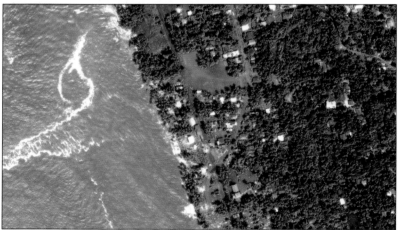

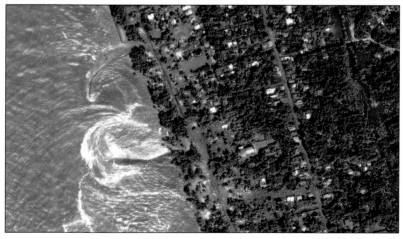

Because of its large size and extent of earthquake activity, the Pacific Ocean is especially vulnerable to tsunamis. Consequently, a network of tidal gauges has been established through the region, centred on Hawaii, providing 26 countries with warning messages.

One of the most severe tsunamis in recent times occurred on 26th December 2004 when an earthquake of magnitude 9.0 on the Richter Scale occurred at a depth of 30 kilometres under the ocean off the western coast of northern Sumatra (Indonesia). The earthquake was caused by a shift of about 15 metres along a 1,200 kilometre long boundary section between the Indian and Burmese crustal plates. The shift did not happen instantaneously, but in two phases over a period of several minutes. Aftershocks, some as large as 6.6 and 7.1, continued for several days after the initial earthquake. As a result, several tsunami waves were created during the period in which the plates were shifting.

Because the surface of the ocean shifted upwards by several metres over the long distance of movement (1,200 kilometres), the tsunamis that were created affected areas around the edge of the Indian Ocean, and there was even some impact as far away as New Zealand, Mexico and Chile. Six weeks after the earthquake, remnants of the wave could still be measured going back and forth across the Indian Ocean.

The tsunami that struck many areas around the Indian Ocean on 26th December caused an estimated death toll of about 300,000 people. The largest number of deaths occurred in Indonesia, near the epicentre of the earthquake, followed by the eastern coastlines of Sri Lanka and India which were openly exposed to the earthquake epicentre. Smaller numbers of deaths were reported in Thailand, Myanmar, Somalia, Maldives, Malaysia, Tanzania, Bangladesh, Kenya, South Africa and the Seychelles. About one-third of the deaths were children because they did not have the strength to resist the surging waters of the tsunami. In addition to the people killed, it was estimated that about 1.5 million people were displaced from their homes by the

8.47 *Four views of Kalutara Beach in Sri Lanka. In the top view, the beach is seen on 1st January 2004, almost one year before the tsunami. In the second view, the beach is seen on 26th December 2004 just before the tsunami hit, and the wide expanse of exposed sand is evident. In the third view, the waters of the tsunami flood the area behind the beach. In the bottom view, the waters recede back to the ocean. (Photos: courtesy DigitalGlobe)*

tsunami. Death rates were lower in areas where coral reefs or mangroves protected the shorelines, and where people had not built dwellings too close to the beach.

Despite a lag of several hours between the earthquake and the impact of the tsunami, most victims had no warning of the danger. The first warning sign of a possible tsunami is the earthquake itself, but as tsunamis can strike

8.48 *Two vertical views of Banda Aceh in Indonesia, the town that was closest to the epicentre of the earthquake and tsunami on 26th December 2004. In the upper view, the town is shown on 23rd June 2004, about six months before the earthquake. The lower view shows the same area on 28th December 2004, two days after the tsunami. Note that most of the buildings in the town were destroyed. The shoreline has either been heavily eroded or is missing entirely. Note also the complete devastation of the rice padis. (Photos: courtesy DigitalGlobe)*

Hazards and disasters

thousands of kilometres away, the earthquake may be felt weakly or not at all in the tsunami hazard zone. In the minutes preceding a tsunami, the ocean often recedes temporarily away from the coast (figure 8.47). Many people around the Pacific Ocean recognise this as a sign to head for higher ground because they are familiar with tsunamis. However, around the Indian Ocean on 26th December 2004, this rare sight apparently encouraged people, especially children, to visit the coast to investigate and collect stranded fish on as much as 2.5 kilometres of exposed beach, with fatal results.

One of the few coastal areas around the Indian Ocean to evacuate before the tsunami hit was the Indonesian island of Simeulue, very close to the epicentre of the earthquake. Island folklore told of an earthquake and tsunami in 1907, and the islanders fled to inland hills after the initial shaking, well before the tsunami struck, and no lives were lost. On Maikhao beach in northern Phuket, Thailand, a vacationing 10 year old British girl named Tilly Smith had studied tsunamis in geography class at school and recognised the warning sign of the receding ocean. She and her parents warned others on the beach, which was evacuated safely with no loss of life

With no recorded history of widespread tsunamis in the Indian Ocean, no tsunami warning system existed for Indian Ocean countries at the time of the earthquake. In the aftermath of the 2004 tsunami, a multi-national effort began to construct a tsunami warning system with seismometer gauges in the Indian Ocean to track and measure tsunami waves near the epicentre and at a distance from the epicentre. Furthermore, it was agreed to include a warning system with forecast tsunami models, and an emergency communications system to warn Indian Ocean countries when a potentially destructive tsunami forms so that people can be warned and evacuated if necessary.

Beyond the heavy toll on human lives, the Indian Ocean earthquake caused a huge impact on the environment that will affect the region for many years. There was severe damage to ecosystems such as coastal wetlands, mangroves, coral reefs, forests, vegetation, sand dunes and rock formations, animal and plant biodiversity and groundwater. Furthermore, the spread of solid and liquid waste and industrial chemicals, water pollution and the destruction of sewage collectors and treatment plants caused major impacts on the environment.

One significant environmental impact was the poisoning of fresh water supplies and the soil by salt water infiltration and the deposition of a salt layer over arable farming land (figure 8.48). In the Maldives, 16 to 17 coral reef atolls that were covered by sea waves were without fresh water and will be uninhabitable for decades. Huge numbers of water wells were invaded by the ocean and filled with salt water, sand and earth. Large areas of rice fields in India and Thailand, together with thousands of mango and banana plantations in Sri Lanka were destroyed almost entirely and will take years to recover.

At a global scale, the earthquake and tsunami shifted the location of the North Pole about 2.5 centimetres to the east, reduced the earth's oblateness (the tendency to flatten on the top and bulge at the middle) and changed the earth's rotation. It is estimated that the earthquake shortened the length of a day by 2.68 microseconds (or about one billionth of the length of a day).

More spectacularly, some of the smaller islands southwest of Sumatra, together with the northern tip of Sumatra and parts of the Malay Peninsula moved south-west by over 20 metres, while parts of overlying oceanic plate moved to the north-east. Several airports shifted by distances of over a metre and needed a correction to their GPS (global positioning systems) for aircraft to use their automatic landing systems.

QUESTION BLOCK 8J

1. *Explain how a tsunami forms.*

2. *Why did the tsunami in the Indian Ocean on 26th December 2004 cause so much damage?*

3. *Describe the impact of the tsunami shown in figures 8.47 and 8.48.*

The Eruption of Eyjafjallajökull, April 2010

Eyjafjallajökull is a small ice cap in southern Iceland that covers the caldera of a gently sloping shield volcano, also called Eyjafjallajökull, which has a summit elevation of 1,666 metres (figure 8.49). As it located right on the Mid-Atlantic Ridge, the volcano is very active, having erupted many times since the last Ice Age. The most recent major eruptions were in 920, 1612, 1782 and from 1821 to 1823.

8.49 *The location of Eyjafjallajökull in southern Iceland. Its precise location is latitude 63°38'N, longitude 19°36'W. The light blue areas on the map show the several ice caps that cover much of the surface area of Iceland.*

In late December 2009, many small earthquakes were recorded in the area around Eyjafjallajökull, suggesting that magma was accumulating in the magma chamber under the volcano. February 2010, GPS devices recorded a displacement in the local crust of 3 cm towards the south, of which movements of 1 cm occurred during a single four day period. These events were seen as further evidence that magma was flowing into the magma chamber beneath the volcano, increasing the pressure for an imminent eruption. The main eruption of Eyjafjallajökull began on 14th April, 2010 (figures 8.50 and 8.51).

8.50 *Eyjafjallajökull during a dormant phase in 2007.*

8.51 *A webcam image of Eyjafjallajökull erupting in April 2007. (Photo: Mila ehf., Reykjavík)*

The eruption of Eyjafjallajökull was marked by a huge cloud of ash, known as tephra, that rose up to about nine kilometres (9,000 metres) into the atmosphere. During the four weeks in which the eruption continued, it was estimated that about 250 million cubic metres of ash were sent into the atmosphere.

The cause of the huge ash cloud was the millions of tonnes of ice that had built up since the previous eruption in 1823. When the eruption began, this ice melted and collapsed into the volcano. As it did so, superheated steam began generating large-scale explosions that shot the ash up into the atmosphere.

Volcanic ash represents a major hazard to aircraft because ash clouds can travel thousands of kilometres and affect areas that are far away from the volcano. The ash plume from Eyjafjallajökull in April 2010 shut down most flights over Europe for the first six days of the eruption, causing major disruptions and economic losses.

Several factors combine to make volcanic eruptions with large ash plumes a danger to aircraft. First, the particles in volcanic ash are made up of hard and extremely sharp materials such as rock, glass and sand. When these particles are ejected into the upper atmosphere, they may be carried by the high winds over long distances that may disperse them over large areas. Another factor is that ash plumes are usually not dense enough to be seen easily by airline pilots, although they are dense enough to cause severe damage to the engines, which may cut out and fail. Failure happens when the fine dust particles block up the air vents or melt in the hot engines to form a solid mass of glass-like substance.

The nervousness about flying through an ash cloud can be partly explained by an incident that occurred in 1982. On 24th June of that year, a British Airways Boeing 747 airplane flew unexpectedly into the ash cloud of Mount Galunggung, an erupting volcano over Indonesia. The pilots were not aware of the ash plume because it was night time, and aircraft radar does not detect volcanic ash. As soon as the plane entered the ash cloud, all four engines failed and the plane lost power and the pilot famously announced to the passengers "Ladies and gentlemen, this is your captain speaking. We have a small problem. All four engines have stopped. We are doing our damnedest to get them under control. I trust you are not in too much distress".

The pilot was eventually able to glide the plane down to a lower altitude, where the force of the air blowing through the engines cleared the ash, enabling the engines to be restarted in flight one-by-one. Nonetheless, damage to the aircraft amounted to $80 million, including the replacement of all four engines.

Smoke and ash from eruptions causes other hazards for aviation by reducing visibility for visual navigation, and microscopic particles in the ash can sandblast aircraft windscreens.

The ash cloud from the eruption of Eyjafjallajökull spread quickly across Europe, forcing the cancellation of almost all flights within, to and from Europe (figures 8.52 and 8.54). Most airliners in Europe were kept on the ground, often with plastic wrapping around the engines to protect them from any stray ash that might blow into them (figure 8.53).

It was estimated that the closure of European airspace left five million travellers stranded around the world. Although most travellers were stranded in Europe, several

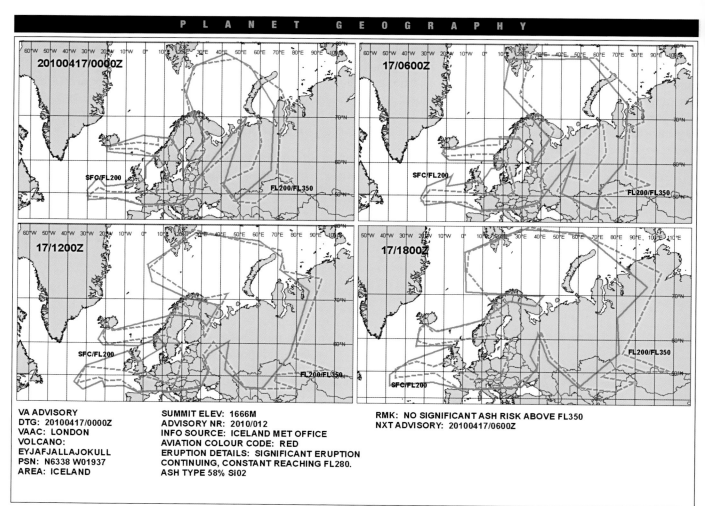

VA ADVISORY
DTG: 20100417/0000Z
VAAC: LONDON
VOLCANO:
EYJAFJALLAJOKULL
PSN: N6338 W01937
AREA: ICELAND

SUMMIT ELEV: 1666M
ADVISORY NR: 2010/012
INFO SOURCE: ICELAND MET OFFICE
AVIATION COLOUR CODE: RED
ERUPTION DETAILS: SIGNIFICANT ERUPTION
CONTINUING, CONSTANT REACHING FL280.
ASH TYPE 58% SiO2

RMK: NO SIGNIFICANT ASH RISK ABOVE FL350
NXT ADVISORY: 20100417/0600Z

8.52 *Aviation warning maps for Europe on 17th April 2010, the third day of the eruption of Eyjafjallajökull. The top left map shows the situation at midnight at the start of 17th April. The top right map shows the situation six hours later, at 6:00 am. The lower left map shows the situation after another six hours (at midday), while the map in the lower right shows the situation after a further six hours (at 6:00 pm). On all four maps, the green dotted lines show the extent of the ash cloud as a result of wind movements between 20,000 feet and 35,000 feet (6,100 metres to 10,700 metres). The red fixed line shows the flying exclusion zone that was being enforced at the time between sea level and 20,000 feet (0 to 6,100 metres) as a result of the hazard caused by the ash plume. (Map: Met Office)*

thousand passengers were also stranded in Asia, the United States and Australia. The disruption had a particularly significant effect on schools in the United

8.53 *During the period they were grounded by the eruption of Eyjafjallajökull, many airliners had their engines wrapped in plastic to protect them from possible damage by wind-blown volcanic ash. This Boeing 737 aircraft was grounded at Cologne, Germany. (Photo: Michael Frische)*

Kingdom because the eruption began at the end of the annual Easter Holidays and many students and teachers were thus stranded abroad. In some cases, travellers took very long and arduous journeys by bus, train and ferry to complete their journeys. Meanwhile, the International Air Transport Association (IATA) estimated that airlines were losing about $200 million per day during the period of the disruptions to flights.

Within the first few days of disrupted flights, shortages of imported flowers, fruit and electronic hardware were being reported across Europe. At the other end of the supply chain, Kenya's flower growers, who depend on the European markets for their livelihood, were unable to air freight their fresh flowers to the markets. On each day the flights were disrupted, 400 tonnes of fresh flowers were destroyed in Kenya, causing the loss of vast sums of money. Exports of hi-tech equipment from Europe were especially affected as companies were unable to transport their products to overseas buyers.

Pharmaceuticals companies in Europe also lost large sums of money because many of their products were time-sensitive, meaning that a delay of even a few days meant the medicines became unusable. Imports of medications into Europe were also affected for the reason, and organs for transplants could not be moved for surgery. Some shortages of fresh foods were also reported in many parts of Europe because of the disruptions to air freight. Perhaps most significantly for business, air freight of documents ceased, disrupting many business transactions.

Within Europe, many sporting, entertainment and other events were cancelled, delayed or disrupted as either individuals or teams found themselves unable to travel to their destinations.

The disruptions to air transport did not only affect people in Europe. As far away as Hong Kong, the press reported that air freighted fresh Norwegian salmon was in short supply, and some people began buying tickets on the Trans-Siberian Railway to get home to Hong Kong from London.

After about six days, Eyjafjallajokull's eruption stopped producing the large ash plume that had caused the widespread disruption to transport. This change in the volcano's behaviour came about because the supply of ice that had built up on top of the volcano following the previous eruption in 1823 was exhausted, and the explosive force created by tonnes of ice falling into the hot chamber of molten magma was thus removed.

Paradoxically, during the period of the eruption, prevailing winds kept Iceland's major international airport at Keflavík free from Eyjafjallajokull's ash cloud. Although air transport was shut down across most of Europe, Iceland's air links with non-European destinations continued without impact.

QUESTION BLOCK 8K

1. *Why is significant about Eyjafjallajökull's location that suggests it will be a very active volcano?*

2. *Why are airliners vulnerable to damage by volcanic ash?*

3. *Describe the pattern of spread of the ash cloud over Europe on 17th April 2010 as shown in figure 8.52.*

4. *Describe the economic and other consequences of the eruption of Eyjafjallajokull in 2010.*

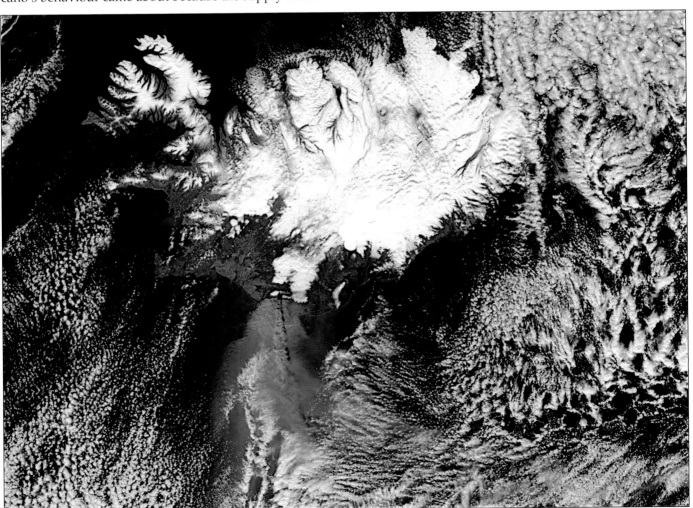

8.54 *The ash plume from the eruption of Eyjafjallajökull on 17th April 2010. In this view, north is at the top of the satellite image. A large cloud covers much of the area of Iceland. The ash in this image is at two different altitudes. A concentrated brownish plume from an explosive phase blows to the south, throwing a shadow on a wider plume that is also moving south, but at a lower altitude. At the time the photo was taken, the volcano had been emitting ash in puffs that reached between 5,000 and 7,500 metres. (Photo: NASA)*

5. *Explain why the size of the ash plume diminished after about a week even though the eruption of Eyjafjallajokull continued.*

Adjustments and Responses to Hazards and Disasters

Responses to the Risk of Hazard Events

People's responses to hazards fall into three phases. The **first phase** takes place before the hazard event, and involves preparation, prevention and education. This includes identifying the hazard, analysing the potential for the hazards that have been identified, providing warning of the developing threat and ascertaining the vulnerability of the community. Prevention and mitigation involves either preventing the threat eventuating or minimising the impact of the threat, such as by land-use zoning that attempts to separate people from known hazards. Preparation also includes alerting people to the threat, raising awareness of the need to prepare, allocating responsibilities and stockpiling essential food and equipment.

The **second phase** is the response during the hazard event and immediately after the hazard event has occurred. The response during the event usually ranges from panic, psychological paralysis, and through to the implementation of co-ordinated emergency measures by organisations such as the police, army, fire brigades, ambulances and emergency service teams.

The initial response immediately following the hazard event may be migration to other areas, outbreaks of disease and medical problems. The immediate response also involves combating the cause and effect of the hazard, assisting people affected and minimising the impact of repeated events.

The **third phase** is the medium and long-term actions taken to repair major damage and minimise the suffering from any repeats of the event if possible. Recovery includes cleaning up and repairing damage, ongoing medical treatment, counselling victims, financial and legal support, revision of the hazard analysis, and evaluation of prevention and mitigation measures.

In all three phases, people in MEDCs are better placed than those in LEDCs to cope (figure 8.55). Buildings in MEDCs tend to be more substantial, education is usually more wide-spread, government agencies are better funded and more adequately trained, lines of communication have more back-ups, and there is more money to pay for repairs. As we saw earlier in this chapter, when disasters strike LEDCs, the value of the property destroyed may be less, but the loss of lives is usually greater.

Responding to the Earthquake Hazard

Of all the hazards discussed in this chapter, earthquake remain the most difficult to predict. If there are small tremors before an earthquake, then adequate warning can be given. However, some earthquakes come almost without warning, such as the Tangshan earthquake described earlier in this chapter, and these are almost impossible to predict.

Residents in LEDCs have less ability to cope with natural disasters, such as earthquakes, than residents of more affluent countries. Tokyo, capital of one of the world's most affluent countries, Japan, experiences about 50 significant earthquakes each year. A major earthquake in Tokyo in 1923, that measured 8.2 on the Richter Scale, killed 143,000 people. Japan experiences a large number of earthquakes because it is situated above the subduction zone that marks the boundary between three plates, the Pacific Plate moving in from the south-east, the Eurasian Plate to the north-west, and the Philippine plate moving in from the south. Indeed, about 10% of the world's earthquakes each year occur in Japan.

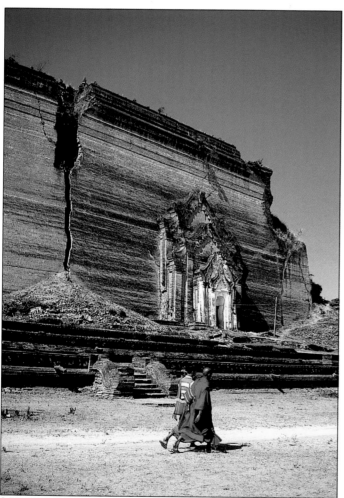

8.55 *The Mingun Pagoda near Mandalay, Myanmar, would have been the world's largest Buddhist structure had it not been destroyed by an earthquake before completion in 1838. It had still not been repaired when another earthquake in 1975 caused even more damage.*

8.56 *Overhead electrical wires in Tokyo, Japan.*

8.57 *The Tokyo suburb of Shinjuku .*

Because Tokyo is so prone to earthquakes, most of the city has very few high-rise buildings and services such as electricity and telephone lines are built above ground level (figure 8.56). In recent years, the high price of real estate in Tokyo has encouraged the construction of some 'skyscrapers' in order to earn more revenue from each square metre of ground space. Japanese engineers have used several techniques to make these tall buildings resistant to damage from earthquakes. In addition to using additional reinforced steel, some buildings are constructed with widened bases to encourage stability, while others have foundations of fluid, rubber or springs to enable movement during earthquakes without becoming brittle (figure 8.57). Another technique used in Japan is to employ electronically controlled counter-weights that offset the shocks from an earthquake. Measures such as these are quite expensive, and well beyond the capacity of most LEDCs.

QUESTION BLOCK 8L

1. *Apply the three phases of responses to hazards to one of the following examples of a hazard event that you have heard. about recently in the news: earthquake, volcanic eruption, tropical cyclone, drought, a human-induced hazard.*

2. *Summarise the measures that people take to minimise the impact of earthquakes.*

9 Leisure, sport and tourism

The geography of tourism, sport and recreation.

**ToK BoX — Page 383
Education and Indoctrination**

Defining Leisure

Tourism is now the world's largest industry. Indeed, if 'tourism' were a country whose wealth was being measured by its gross domestic product (GDP), then tourism would be the third richest country in the world.

In MEDCs, sport is becoming increasingly commercialised and profit-driven. When we consider tourism and sport together, perhaps under the broad label of 'leisure', we are looking at a significant and rapidly expanding global economic sector. However, like all economic activities, the wealth within the leisure industry is not evenly distributed.

In this chapter, we will look at many aspects of tourism and sport, including the distribution and diversity of leisure activities, their increasing popularity and their impact on environments, cultures and economies at a variety of scales.

The terms used in leisure studies are not always clear. Before proceeding too deeply into this topic, it is recommended that you become familiar with the definitions at the top of the next page.

Leisure at the International Scale — Tourism

Changes in the Demand and Supply of Tourism

Tourism can be thought of as the short-term circular migration of people to places outside their normal place of work or residence for the purpose of leisure. People have always travelled, and indeed much of the early interest in Geography arose from the fascination people have with other places that are different (figure 9.1). The growth that has seen tourism emerge as the world's biggest

>> Some Useful Definitions

Carrying capacity — the maximum number of visitors/participants that a site/event can satisfy at one time. It is customary to distinguish between **environmental carrying capacity** (the maximum number before the local environment becomes damaged) and **perceptual carrying capacity** (the maximum number before a specific group of visitors considers the level of impact, such as noise, to be excessive). For example, young mountain bikers may be more crowd-tolerant than elderly walkers.

Leisure — any freely chosen activity or experience that takes place in non-work time.

Primary tourist / recreational resources — the pre-existing attractions for tourism or recreation (that is, those not built specifically for the purpose), including climate, scenery, wildlife, indigenous people, cultural and heritage sites. These are distinguished from **secondary tourist / recreational resources**, which include accommodation, catering, entertainment and shopping.

Recreation — a leisure-time activity undertaken voluntarily and for enjoyment. It includes individual pursuits, organised outings and events, and non-paid (non-professional) sports.

Resort — a settlement where the primary function is tourism. This includes a hotel complex.

Sport — a physical activity involving events and competitions at the national and international scale with professional participants.

Tourism — travel away from home for at least one night for the purpose of leisure. Note that this definition excludes day-trippers. There are many possible subdivisions of tourism. Subgroups include **ecotourism** — tourism focusing on the natural environment and local communities; **heritage tourism** — tourism based on an historic legacy (landscape feature, historic building or event) as its major attraction; **sustainable tourism** — tourism that conserves primary tourist resources and supports the livelihoods and culture of local people.

9.1 *In the 1800s, tourism was enjoyed only by a privileged few. Maymyo (now Pyin Oo Lwin) in Myanmar was a 'hill station' where British soldiers and administrators took their holidays to escape the lowland tropical heat of what was then colonial Burma. Many buildings in Pyin Oo Lwin are relics of the privileges of the colonial era.*

tic tourists who travel within their own countries. Travel, once a luxury for the privileged few, now appeals to a mass market.

Despite factors such as international terrorism, economic stagnation in More Economically Developed Countries (MEDCs), and worsening of poverty in some Less Economically Developed Countries (LEDCs), international tourism is expected to grow strongly in the future. It is estimated by 2010, 1,018 million people will travel internationally.

industry has only occurred in the last half-century or so. Between 1950 and 1990, annual world tourist arrivals increased from about 25 million to 455 million (table 9.1). In 2000, international annual tourism arrivals reached 682 million, and despite temporary slow-downs following the 9/11 terrorist attacks in the US and the outbreak of SARS in 2003, the figure had reached almost 900 million by 2007, almost 15% of the world's population. In addition to these figures, there are even larger numbers of domes-

9.2 *The USA is one of the world's most popular tourist destinations, with over 40 million tourist arrivals each year. Although many visitors are attracted by spectacular scenery or family reunions, others are attracted by the country's many famous theme parks, such as Disneyland near Los Angeles which is shown here.*

Table 9.1

International Tourist Arrivals, 1950 - 2009

Year	Tourist Arrivals (millions)
1950	25
1960	69
1965	113
1970	166
1975	222
1980	288
1985	330
1990	455
1995	534
1996	570
1997	594
1998	611
1999	634
2000	682
2001	682
2002	702
2003	691
2004	761
2005	801
2006	846
2007	900
2008	919
2009	880

Source: World Tourism Organisation

Among the MEDCs, the top tourist destinations are France, Spain, the United States and Italy (figure 9.2). Other MEDCs with a significant share of the world tourism market are the United Kingdom, Canada, Poland, Austria, Germany and Russia. Some MEDCs are concerned about the loss of tourism income to LEDCs as their people travel overseas, and have actively promoted domestic tourism to their residents.

There are very few LEDCs that are not seeking to develop tourism because of the potential to earn foreign income that it brings. In general, LEDCs try to encourage wealthier tourists from MEDCs because of the extra money they spend. LEDCs with well-developed tourism industries include Brazil, China, Egypt, India, Indonesia, Malaysia, Mexico, Morocco, Thailand and Tunisia.

The rapid growth of tourism since 1950 has been caused by several factors. Important causes include the increased mobility and affluence of many people in MEDCs, stimulation of demand by advertising and greater media coverage of exotic tourist destinations, organisation of mass tourism by transnational companies, and improvements to facilities and infrastructure for tourists, especially in LEDCs. Another important factor has been the reduction in cost of travel due to technological developments in mass transport (figures 9.3 and 9.4).

9.3 *The development of wide-bodied airliners reduced the costs per seat of air transport to the point where it became affordable by large numbers of people.*

9.4 *Large cruise ships have increased the appeal of mass travel, but they have not reduced costs to the same extent as large aircraft because they take longer to complete each journey and thus passenger turnover is slower. This cruise ship is visiting the Icelandic port of Akureyri.*

Tourism can be classified according to the purpose of the travel and the way in which it is organised. **Group tours** tend to be cheaper than individual travel because a common set of arrangements is made for a number of people simultaneously (figure 9.5). Groups travel together, stay together and eat together. This works well if everyone in the group has common interests in the tour program. Some destinations, such as North Korea, require tourists to travel in a group at all times. A variation on group tours is the **packaged tour**. Packaged tours also tend to be cheaper than individual travel because travel agents make bulk purchases of airline seats and hotel rooms,

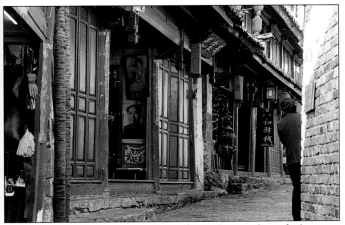

9.5 *Lijiang (China) attracts visitors who are interest in exploring China's cultural heritage..*

9.7 *Beaches are an important tourist attraction in warmer climates, such as here at Tamarindo in Costa Rica.*

9.6 *Recreational travel can take many forms, but it usually involves a change of scenery and lifestyle from normal. At its best, it also educates the traveller, such as here where tourists are learning about Europe's largest valley glacier, the Skeidarársandur, in south-east Iceland.*

9.8 *The hill at Medjugorje (in Bosnia-Herzegovina) where the Virgin Mary is said to have appeared on many occasions to give a message of peace and love. Medjugorje is the focus of pilgrimage for many Catholic Christians.*

gaining preferential rates because of the large volume of advance purchases made. Of course, tourists do not gain all the benefits of these savings because the travel agent takes a commission from the saving.

Individual travel is favoured by more experienced travellers, by those wanting a unique travel experience, and by the more adventurous. Individual travel can be very cheap when backpacking, and it can open the way to destinations that may not be able to handle the larger numbers of group and package travellers. Much individual tourism is for family reasons, such as visiting relatives and reunions. Other purposes for tourism include recreation, cultural enrichment, adventure, religious pilgrimages and sightseeing (figures 9.5 to 9.9).

Tourist destinations can be classified in many ways. In the United States, the Outdoor Recreation Resources Review Committee (ORRRC) classifies recreation resources into six broad categories:

1. **High density recreation areas**. These are areas where there is a variety of tourist attractions in a small area that use most of the local available resources. They are

9.9 *Sightseeing may focus on anything that interests the tourist. In this view, a group of trekkers enters Tiger Leaping Gorge in China by horseback.*

characterised by intensive development of resort hotels and facilities managed for maximum visitor usage, such as Disneyland, beaches on the Mediterranean coast of Spain or Greece, and Club Med resorts (figures 9.10 and 9.11).

2. **General outdoor recreational areas**. These are characterised by a wide variety of tourist attractions (though not as many as high density recreation areas), with substantial development. They tend to offer a wide choice of activities (figure 9.12). Resorts tend to be some distance from main population centres, and examples include ski resorts and sailing centres.

3. **Natural environment areas**. These are areas with multiple types of land use with a variety of activities available depending upon the nature of the area. National Parks are good examples of this type of recreation resource.

4. **Unique natural areas**. These are areas of outstanding natural beauty or scenic grandeur, where the main activity is sightseeing. Examples include the Grand Canyon in the United States, Victoria Falls on the border of Zambia and Zimbabwe, and Geysir in Iceland.

5. **Primitive areas**. These include undisturbed wilderness and areas with no roads where natural wild conditions can still be found. Tourist activities in these areas would include trekking in the Sahara Desert or exploring the Highlands of Irian Jaya or the jungles of the Amazon Basin.

6. **Historic and cultural sites**. These are places of significance at a local, regional, national or international scale. Examples may include places of pilgrimage, buildings, archaeological sites and places associated with important historical events. For example, the Pyramids in Egypt, the Taj Mahal in India and the Temple Mount in Jerusalem, among many others.

QUESTION BLOCK 9A

1. *Show the data in table 9.1 as a line graph, making sure that you show the time intervals between each statistic correctly.*

2. *Suggest reasons why each of the following MEDCs has a large share of the world's tourism market: France, Spain, the United States and Italy, the United Kingdom, Canada, Poland, Austria, Germany and Russia.*

3. *Suggest reasons why each of the following LEDCs has a large share of the world's tourism market: Brazil, China, Egypt, India, Indonesia, Malaysia, Mexico, Morocco, Thailand and Tunisia.*

4. *Explain why international tourism has grown so much since 1950.*

9.10 *An example of a well developed tourist area — Punta del Este on the coast of Uruguay.*

9.11 *At Vouliagmeni (Greece), the high density of tourism is an attraction to some, although others might be repelled by such tourism.*

9.12 *Outdoor recreational facilities at a hotel in Bangkok in Thailand, overlooking the brown waters of the Chao Phraya River.*

Stages of Tourism

Several geographers have attempted to describe the processes and the impacts of tourism by developing models. One of the best known is the **Butler Model**, which attempts to describe the cycle of evolution of a tourism area (figure 9.13).

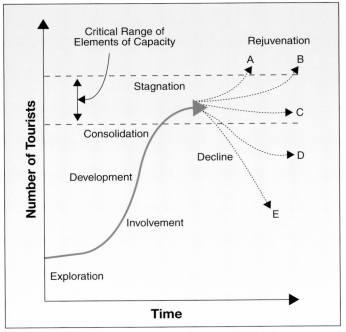

9.13 *Butler's model of the evolution of a tourist destination.*

The model identifies seven stages of tourism development over time:

Exploration: A small number of tourists independently explore a new location for reasons such as personal adventure or to experience new cultures. At this stage, the economic, social and environmental impacts are virtually zero (figure 9.14).

9.14 *Very basic tourist facilities characterise the 'exploration' stage of tourism, such as this accommodation facility at Turmi in southern Ethiopia.*

Involvement: As acceptance of tourists by the locals increases, the destination becomes better known and more popular. Travel and accommodation facilities are improved, and some local people become more

9.15 *A typical scene in an emerging area of tourism. Tiger Leaping Gorge in China's south-western province of Yunnan is a relatively remote and undeveloped tourist destination that appeals to limited numbers of adventurous trekkers. Accommodation in the Gorge is provided by local people of the Naxi ethnic group, typically in guest houses like this one, included as part of the family compound.*

involved in the emerging tourist industry (figure 9.15).

Development: Investment by outsiders begins to flow in to the area, and local people become more involved, attracting more visitors. The area begins to emerge as a well-known tourist destination, pitched towards a defined market. In LEDCs, control often passes from local people to organisations based in MEDCs. This leads to more package holidays, increasing tourist numbers and less local involvement (figure 9.16).

9.16 *In contrast to the scene shown in figure 9.15, this view shows the next stage of tourism when local people are employed by overseas companies in lower order jobs such as cleaning and waiting. This view shows part of a resort hotel in Tamarindo (Costa Rica) that is owned by a Spanish company.*

Consolidation: Tourism becomes established as an important economic and social activity. It begins to have a serious adverse impact traditional economies and lifestyles. Agricultural land is taken over for building resorts, usually without significant benefits for the local community in terms of increased wealth or employment. Resentment often occurs in the local population. Tourist numbers continue to rise, although rate of increase slows down.

Stagnation: Local opposition to tourism continues to grow, and there is a growing awareness of the environmental, social and economic problems brought by tourism. Negativity effectively stops further growth. There is a decrease in the number of tourist visits, suggesting that the original cultural and physical attractions have been lost.

Decline: The area decreases further in popularity, either severely or mildly (paths E and D in figure 9.13). Multinational tour operators move elsewhere and local involvement may increase to fill the vacuum. However, these local operators may be under-funded, leading to a further decline in the area's attractiveness to tourists.

Rejuvenation: A secondary growth spurt may occur, induced by some new factor such as new investment, falling prices or advertising (paths A, B or C in figure 9.13). The loss of original natural attractions may be compensated for by new constructed facilities. A new and different type of tourist may be attracted, perhaps with different socio-economic backgrounds or demographic profile.

Another tourism model attempts to explain the changes described in the Butler Model. The **Hawkins Model** examines the factors that affect the demand for tourism in a particular area, and the forces that may limit the carrying capacity of an area to develop a tourist industry (figure 9.17).

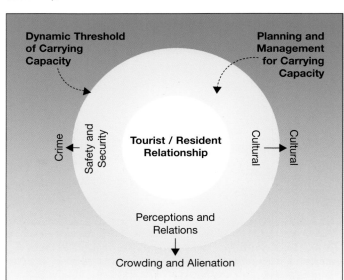

9.17 *Hawkins model of the carrying capacity of tourism in an area.*

Whereas Butler's Model describes the carrying capacity of tourism in an area when tourism is market-driven, the Hawkins Model attempts to take into account as broader set of factors. The Hawkins Model shows how the positive attitudes that may exist at first between tourists and local residents can change and become more negative as the threshold of the carrying capacity is reached.

At the centre of the model is the relationship between tourists and local residents. The outer edge of the coloured ring is the limit of tourist numbers that an area can support. The inner edge of the coloured ring is the minimum, or threshold, number of tourists in an area. The width of the coloured ring will oscillate in and out according to many variables, the most important of which are shown on the diagram – safety and security, perceptions and relations, and the nature of the contact between people of different cultures. In reality, there is a wide range of factors that can limit an area's tourism carrying capacity:

Ecological factors:
- climate
- vegetation
- animal life
- landscape
- water.

Political factors:
- legislation
- administrative capability
- individual priorities, goals and aspirations.

Physical factors:
- accommodation
- water supply
- sewage systems
- transportation and access
- visual attractiveness.

Economic factors:
- personal income
- living costs
- labour costs
- resort technology
- resort investment.

Local residents' experiences:
- invasion of privacy
- involvement in tourism
- benefits from tourism
- tourists' sensitivity and behaviour.

Visitor experiences:
- volume of people
- visitor behaviour
- levels of service
- local hospitality
- visitors' expectations.

QUESTION BLOCK 9B

1. *Do you think the names of each stage in Butler's Model are adequate labels? Can you suggest better names?*

2. *Describe what happens during the third phase of Butler's Model (Development).*

3. *Using examples that you know about, explain why some resorts have declined in popularity.*

4. *With reference to a tourist resort that you know about, describe its attractions and its problems.*

Leisure at the International Scale — Sport

International Participation and Success in an international sports event — The Olympic Games

The Olympic Games, which are held every four years in cities around the world, are an international multi-sport event established in 1896. The organisation that controls the Olympic Movement is the International Olympic Committee (IOC), based in Lausanne, Switzerland. The IOC oversees the planning of the Olympic Games, including the selection of the host city and the program of events for each Games. The Games are divided into summer and winter events. For cities that are selected to host the Games, there are often significant costs in building sports facilities, although these remain available for use many years after the event (figure 9.18).

Since 1896, the cities which have been selected to host the Summer Olympic Games have been:

- 1896 - Athens, Greece
- 1900 - Paris, France
- 1904 - St Louis, USA
- 1908 - London, UK
- 1912 - Stockholm, Sweden
- 1916 - Berlin, Germany (cancelled due to war)
- 1920 - Antwerp, Belgium
- 1924 - Paris, France
- 1928 - Amsterdam, Netherlands
- 1932 - Los Angeles, USA
- 1936 - Berlin, Germany
- 1940 - Tokyo, Japan (cancelled due to war)
- 1944 - London, UK (cancelled due to war)
- 1948 - London, UK
- 1952 - Helsinki, Finland
- 1956 - Melbourne, Australia
- 1960 - Rome, Italy
- 1964 - Tokyo, Japan
- 1968 - Mexico City, Mexico
- 1972 - Munich, Germany
- 1976 - Montreal, Canada
- 1980 - Moscow, USSR
- 1984 - Los Angeles, USA
- 1988 - Seoul, South Korea
- 1992 - Barcelona, Spain
- 1996 - Atlanta, USA
- 2000 - Sydney, Australia
- 2004 - Athens, Greece
- 2008 - Beijing, China
- 2012 - London, UK (scheduled)
- 2016 - Rio de Janeiro (scheduled)

The Winter Olympic Games began in 1924, and until 1992 were held in the same year as the Summer Olympics. From 1994, the Winter Olympics were held two years before the subsequent Summer Olympics. The cities that have hosted the Winter Olympic Games have been:

- 1924 - Chamonix, France
- 1928 - St Moritz, Switzerland
- 1932 - Lake Placid, USA
- 1936 - Garmisch-Partenkirchen, Germany
- 1940 - Sapporo, Japan (cancelled due to war)
- 1944 - Cortina d'Ampezzo, Italy (cancelled)
- 1948 - St Moritz, Switzerland
- 1952 - Oslo, Norway
- 1956 - Cortina d'Ampezzo, Italy
- 1960 - Squaw Valley, USA
- 1964 - Innsbruck, Austria
- 1968 - Grenoble, France
- 1972 - Sapporo, Japan
- 1976 - Innsbruck, Austria
- 1980 - Lake Placid, USA
- 1984 - Sarajevo, Yugoslavia
- 1988 - Calgary, Canada
- 1992 - Albertville, France
- 1994 - Lillehammer, Norway
- 1998 - Nagano, Japan
- 2002 - Salt Lake City, USA
- 2006 - Turin, Italy
- 2010 - Vancouver, Canada (scheduled)
- 2014 - Sochi, Russia (scheduled)

9.18 *The Olympic Stadium in Beijing, China.*

QUESTION BLOCK 9C

1. *For the Summer and the Winter Olympics (separately) classify each host city by its continent, and then tally the number of times the Olympics have been held in (a) Europe, (b) Asia, (c) Australia, (d) North America and (e) South America.*

2. *From your answer to the previous question, comment on the relationship between economic wealth and hosting the Olympic Games.*

The Olympic Games raise many interesting geographical questions, such as 'which countries and parts of the world are the most successful in winning medals at the Olympic Games?', 'do the MEDCs win more medals than LEDCs?', and 'do countries with larger populations win more medals?'.

Medal tallies at the Olympics

Although the IOC discourages the ranking of countries by medal tallies, newspapers and television stations around the world calculate and release daily counts of the numbers of medals won by each country, especially when the home country has been successful (figure 9.19).

9.19 *A medals presentation ceremony at the Beijing Olympic Games.* (Photo: Laptin Ho)

The competition between countries as a matter of national pride began in the 1950s as superpower rivalries between the capitalist USA and the communist USSR intensified. During this period, sporting prowess was seen as a way to promote political ideology, and vast resources were pumped into developing sports facilities and training

athletes. The rivalry between countries continues today, though more as a result of media hype than political ideology.

Comparing the medal tallies of countries can be misleading unless certain factors are taken into consideration. Table 9.2 shows the medal tallies of the top ten countries in the Summer Olympic Games since 1980. In raw figures, the most successful country in the 2008 Olympic Games in Beijing was China, which won 51 gold medals, followed by the United States with 36 and Russia with 23. It seems clear from these raw statistics that countries with **large populations** have a better chance of doing well as there is a greater chance that all things being equal, a larger population will produce a larger number of elite athletes.

There are, however, exceptions to this general trend. In the Beijing Olympics, Australia was ranked 6th, winning 14 gold medals from a population of 21.3 million people, whereas India with 1,149.3 million people ranked 50th, behind countries such as Azerbaijan and the Dominican Republic, winning just one gold and two bronze medals. This suggests that wealth and the **level of economic development** may also play a role in sporting success.

Related to wealth is the **availability of resources** to support athletes in a country. Until a few decades ago, all athletes competing in the Olympic Games had to be amateurs. Nowadays, professional sportsmen and sportswomen may compete in the Olympics, and this has led to a growth in the demand for high quality training and competition venues. Depending on the country, expensive sporting facilities usually have to be provided by governments or the corporate sector through sponsorships, donations or grants.

Table 9.2
Top 10 medal winning nations, Summer Olympic Games, 1980 to 2008

	Moscow 1980	Los Angeles 1984	Seoul 1988	Barcelona 1992	Atlanta 1996	Sydney 2000	Athens 2004	Beijing 2008
1st	USSR	United States	USSR	Russia	United States	United States	United States	China
2nd	East Germany	Romania	East Germany	United States	Germany	Russia	China	United States
3rd	Bulgaria	West Germany	United States	Germany	Russia	China	Russia	Russia
4th	Cuba	China	West Germany	China	China	Australia	Australia	Great Britain
5th	Italy	Italy	South Korea	Cuba	Australia	Germany	Japan	Germany
6th	Hungary	Canada	Bulgaria	Hungary	France	France	Germany	Australia
7th	Romania	Japan	Hungary	South Korea	Italy	Italy	France	South Korea
8th	France	New Zealand	Romania	Spain	South Korea	Netherlands	Italy	Japan
9th	Great Britain	Yugoslavia	China	France	Cuba	Cuba	South Korea	Italy
10th	Poland	South Korea	Great Britain	Australia	Ukraine	Great Britain	Great Britain	France

Table 9.3

Top 10 medal winning nations by Population and GDP per capita, Beijing Summer Olympic Games, 2008

	Country	Gold Medals	Population (millions)	Population per Gold Medal	Country	Gold Medals	GDP ($US mill.)	GDP per capita per Gold Medal
1st	Jamaica	6	2.714	452,333	North Korea	2	2,220	47
2nd	Bahrain	1	0.760	760,168	China	51	3,299,000	49
3rd	Mongolia	2	2.629	1,314,500	Ethiopia	4	16,900	53
4th	Estonia	1	1.340	1,340,600	Kenya	5	29,500	157
5th	New Zealand	3	4.274	1,424,800	Zimbabwe	1	3,418	263
6th	Georgia	3	4.395	1,465,000	Russia	23	1,286,000	394
7th	Australia	14	21.394	1,528,165	Ukraine	7	140,500	436
8th	Norway	3	4.778	1,592,667	Jamaica	6	8,905	547
9th	Slovakia	3	5.402	1,800,758	Georgia	3	9,553	725
10th	Slovenia	1	2.029	2,029,000	Mongolia	2	3,854	733

In some countries, sport is seen as an important factor in **national identity**. For example, Australian are often seen by outsiders as being obsessed with sports, and they like to present themselves to the rest of the world in this way. This can lead to a culture that values sport and competition, which in turn is likely to lead to more resources being diverted into sports and training.

Different sports tend to dominate in different countries, often for **cultural** or historical reasons. Thus, basketball and baseball are associated with the United States, table tennis with China, swimming with Australia, marathon running with Kenya and Ethiopia, and gymnastics with countries in Eastern Europe. Countries in East Asia tend to dominate in certain sports such as judo, table tennis and badminton for historical and cultural reasons.

Climate is also a factor in influencing success in sporting competitions such as the Olympics. Countries with cold climates tend to dominate the sports in the Winter Olympics, such as skiing, whereas these countries are seldom very successful in the Summer Olympics. The success of countries such as Australia and the United States in swimming can be partly explained by the warm climates of these countries.

Table 9.3 shows the relationship between gold medals won at the 2008 Olympic Games and two other factors, population size and wealth (as measured by GDP per capita). On a per capita basis, Jamaica was the most successful country, winning six gold medals from a population of 2.7 million people. When wealth is considered, North Korea was the most successful country, winning just two gold medals, but achieving this with a ratio of just $US47 per person per gold medal of GDP (figure 9.20).

9.20 *Pak Hyon Suk from North Korea won the gold medal for women's weightlifting at the Beijing Olympic Games in 2008.*

Because many sports require expensive facilities such as stadiums, velodromes and swimming pools, LEDCs that excel in sports tend to achieve in sports that do not require such facilities, such as long-distance running (which is dominated by Ethiopia and Kenya) or weight lifting (where the North Koreans do very well). On the other hand, sports that demand expensive resources such as cycling, rowing, canoeing and yachting tend to be dominated by richer countries in Western Europe.

However, there are exceptions to this general pattern. For example, at the Beijing Olympics in 2008, Luxembourg, which has one of the world's highest GDP per capita figures, failed to win a single medal of any type.

QUESTION BLOCK 9D

1. *Outline the factors that influence participation and success in international sporting events such as the Olympic Games.*

2. *Using the information in tables 9.2 and 9.3, which three nations do you think should be considered the most successful at the Olympic Games held in Beijing in 2008? Give reasons to explain your answer.*

Geographic costs and benefits of hosting the Olympic Games

From a financial viewpoint, holding the Olympic Games can be a mixed blessing for the host cities. The costs can be huge, but so can the benefits. For example, the cost of hosting the 2008 Olympic Games in Beijing was US$42 billion, spent over a period of about seven years. This figure included US$3 billion to upgrade Beijing Airport, and US$500 million to build the 'Bird's Nest' Stadium (figure 9.21). This figure of US$42 billion was a comparatively small price, however, considering the Games were estimated to have added US$4 trillion to China's Gross Domestic Product in 2008 alone.

9.21 *The 'Bird's Nest' Stadium, built for the 2008 Olympic Games in Beijing.*

In recent decades, larger numbers of cities have become more enthusiastic about bidding for the Games in the expectation of boosting income from tourism and raising the city's (and the nation's) profile internationally. On the other hand, some cities have reported huge losses as the income earned has fallen short of the expenditure required to host the event.

Before the Barcelona Olympics in 1992, the number of cities bidding to host the Olympic Games generally was quite small. From 1960 to 1984, the small number of bidding cities was due to a widespread feeling that the Olympics were becoming too large and too expensive, as well as presenting significant problems of political interference and terrorism. Terrorism at Olympic Games was highlighted by the attack on Israeli athletes at the 1972 Games in Munich, while superpower rivalries affected performance and participation at the Olympics in 1956 (Melbourne), Moscow (1980) and Los Angeles (1984).

However, the huge commercial success of the Los Angeles Olympic Games in 1984 made hosting the Games seem more attractive, as did the significant urban renewal that occurred in Barcelona as a result of the 1992 Games. As a result, the process of bidding for Olympic Games has taken on a much larger scale involving publicity teams, advertising and lobbying (figures 9.22 and 9.23).

9.22 *A large street sign in Beijing supporting the city's bid for the 2000 Olympic Games.*

9.23 *Another example of the public campaign in support of Beijing's 2000 Olympics bid.*

As we saw earlier in this section, the cities that have hosted the Olympic Games have been heavily concentrated in Europe, and to a lesser degree, in North America and Asia. The Olympics have never been held in either Africa or South America, nor in West/Central/South/South-east Asia. The distribution of Olympic host cities is a mirror of levels of economic development as well as the traditional origin of athletics within Europe.

The pattern of cities selected to host the Olympic Games generally reflects the pattern of offers received by the IOC. In recent decades, the largest numbers of bids have come from cities in Europe and North America (table 9.4).

Although bids have been received from a few cities in Africa and South America, they have never offered the large-scale input of resources and facilities promised by cities in MEDCs.

Table 9.4
Bidding Cities for the Summer Olympic Games
1992 - 2016

	Successful Bidding City	Runner-up Bidding Cities (in descending order of success; runner-up in bold)	Other Bidding Cities (in alphabetical order)
2016 Olympics	Rio de Janeiro	**Madrid** Tokyo Chicago	Baku Doha Prague
2012 Olympics	London	**Paris** Madrid New York Moscow	Havana Istanbul Leipzig Rio de Janeiro
2008 Olympics	Beijing	**Toronto** Paris Istanbul Osaka	Bangkok Cairo Havana Kuala Lumpur Seville
2004 Olympics	Athens	**Rome** Cape Town Stockholm Buenos Aires	Istanbul Lille Rio de Janeiro San Juan Seville St Petersburg
2000 Olympics	Sydney	**Beijing** Manchester Berlin Istanbul	Brasilia Milan Tashkent
1996 Olympics	Atlanta	**Athens** Toronto Melbourne Manchester Belgrade	
1992 Olympics	Barcelona	**Paris** Brisbane Belgrade Birmingham Amsterdam	

When cities wish to bid to host the Olympic Games, they submit their initial applications to the IOC nine years before the games are scheduled. Thus, cities wishing to bid for the 2016 Summer Olympics had to submit their initial applications by September 2007. From these initial bids, a short-list of four candidate cities was devised by June 2008, the finalist cities being Chicago, Madrid, Rio de Janeiro, and Tokyo. Three other cities, Prague, Doha and Baku, were eliminated. In October 2009, it was announced that Rio de Janeiro was the successful bidder.

This process was similar to that followed for many years to select the host city. The factors that influence the final decision of the host city are complex and not always transparent. For example, because the IOC makes a large profit from selling the television and media rights of the Games, it is understood that one important criterion for selecting a city is that the timing of events can be synchronised with peak viewing times in North America, where the highest media fees are paid. When the Games are scheduled outside North America, then individual events that are likely to feature North American finalists are often scheduled at unusual times of the day. It is thought that a considerable amount of lobbying precedes the final announcement of a host city.

The impact of the Summer Olympic Games on host cities needs to be seen in an historical context. There have been four phases of infrastructure impact on cities hosting the Olympic Games:

Phase 1, 1896 to 1904: The Games were small in scale, poorly organised and did not necessarily require the building of any new facilities.

Phase 2, 1908 to 1932: The Games were still small in scale, but were better organised and involved the construction of purpose-built sports facilities.

Phase 3, 1936 to 1956: The Games became large in scale, well organised, and involved the construction of purpose-built sports facilities that made an impact on the surrounding urban infrastructure.

Phase 4, 1960 to the present: The Games are very large in scale, well organised and involve the construction of purpose-built sports facilities with significant impact on the urban infrastructure of the host city (figure 9.24).

9.24 *The National Aquatic Centre, also known as the Water Cube, is an example of urban infrastructure from the 2008 Olympics in Beijing.*

During Phase 1, the Olympic Games were held in conjunction to World Exhibitions or Expos, and therefore they were really supplements (or side-shows) to the main event that lacked much genuine international interest or urban impact. Today (Phase 4), hosting the Olympic

Games usually brings significant new urban development and upgrading of urban infrastructure which receive a high priority in government funding.

The **infrastructure** built for the Olympics provide an ongoing resource for the host city, which generally leads to an improvement in the quality of life for the residents. The Olympic Games held in Sydney (2000) and Beijing (2008) were regarded as having the widespread approval and support of the local population, but this has not always been so in other cities. Some have argued that the money spent on sports facilities and urban infrastructure diverts finance away from the less visible needs of the local population, and such arguments were often heard in Atlanta, Barcelona and Athens. In some cities, organised anti-Olympic groups have been organised to oppose the bids by their home cities.

One response by Olympic host cities to criticism has been to raise the significance of **environmental sustainability** in the planning for the Games. This trend began with the Sydney Olympics in 2000, when ambitious promises were made that the city would host 'the Green Games', with a special emphasis on energy and water conservation, waste minimisation, recycling of water, use of public transport, the improvement of air, water and soil quality and the protection of significant cultural and physical environments. Part of the motive to highlight environmental sustainability arose because the site of the Sydney Olympics was an area of reclaimed swampland called Homebush Bay where toxic industrial wastes had been dumped in earlier decades (figure 9.25).

9.25 *An oblique aerial view of the site of the 2000 Olympic Games in Sydney, which was a reclaimed swamp where toxic industrial wastes had been dumped in earlier decades.*

Although the **economic benefits** of hosting the Olympic Games are often debated and are perhaps difficult to quantify precisely, some commonly accepted factors include:

• **tourism** is boosted, both by people coming to attend the Games, and because of the wider international media

publicity that the Olympics brings to the host city and the nation;

• the inflow of visitors raises **incomes**, and the impact of these higher incomes infuses many facets of the economy through the multiplier effect (which means the same money is spent several times as it passes through the economy);

• the construction of new sporting facilities and other **infrastructure** creates employment, and some types of development such as roads, buses, housing, airports and new hotels provide a basis for ongoing efficiency in the economy (figure 9.26); and

• the **demand for labour** increases in response to the extra services needed to support the Olympic Games, although if poorly managed, the employment created by the Games can evaporate as soon as the events have finished.

9.26 *The Athlete's Village, under construction for the London Olympic Games of 2012.*

9.27 *Banners such as this were erected in many cities throughout China (including Hong Kong, shown here) to express support for the Beijing Olympics during the torch relay.*

Other benefits of hosting the Olympics are even more difficult to measure, and these generally fit into the category of **social benefits**.

These include:

- **national pride** across the entire country invariably increases with the greater international focus on the host city, which usually tries to present itself in as positive a way as possible (figure 9.27);

- a related factor is the sense of goodwill generated by hosting the Olympics, which can serve a nation's **foreign policy goals** and make diplomacy easier and more effective;

- hosting the Olympics usually increases **awareness of sports** throughout the host country, leaving an ongoing legacy of improved fitness and involvement in sporting activities;

- since 2000, Olympic Games have relied heavily on voluntary labour, which has helped create a stronger **sense of community** among the population;

- much of the extra employment generated by hosting the Games is in the building and construction industries, and these jobs are typically taken by unskilled or semi-skilled unemployed workers, and this leads to the **empowerment of low income residents** of the host country; and

- hosting the games usually leads to large-scale **urban renewal** as Games venues tend to be built on disused or run down areas of land.

QUESTION BLOCK 9E

1. *What motivates a city to bid for the Olympic Games?*

2. *With reference to table 9.4, which types of cities tend to be most successful when bidding for the Olympic Games?*

3. *Outline the economic, social and environmental costs and benefits of hosting the Olympic Games.*

Leisure at the National/Regional Scale — Tourism

Case Study of a National Tourist Industry – North Korea

North Korea, or as it is officially known, the Democratic People's Republic of Korea, is one of the world's last examples of a centrally planned government tourism industry. Before the fall of communism in the USSR and Eastern Europe in the period 1989 to 1991, all tourism was controlled by single national government authorities such as Intourist (USSR), Cedok (Czechoslovakia) and Orbis (Poland). In a similar way, KITC (Korea International Travel Company) controls every aspect of tourism in North Korea today.

QUESTION BLOCK 9F

1. *Tourism in North Korea almost certainly provides a strong contrast with tourism in the country where you live. As you read this section, make a point form list of differences between the two..*

North Korea is perhaps the last hard-line communist country left in the world, and it has one of the world's smallest tourism industries. Although the government authorities do not release statistics, it is understood that fewer than 2,000 foreign tourists are allowed to enter North Korea each year.

This is much less than during the 1970s and 1980s when former communist countries (the USSR, East Germany, Poland, Czechoslovakia, Bulgaria, Romania, Hungary, Yugoslavia and Mongolia) sent about 10,000 tourists annually to North Korea. Of this number, about 70% came from the Soviet Union. During this period, the national airline (Air Koryo) had direct flights to such diverse destinations as Moscow (USSR), East Berlin (East Germany), Sofia (Bulgaria), Prague (Czechoslovakia) and Conakry (Guinea).

9.28 *North Korea's national airline, Air Koryo, still uses many Soviet-era aircraft such as this Ilyushin Il-62, seen at Pyongyang Airport.*

Today, Air Koryo operates just three regular international flights, these being twice-weekly to Beijing, once a week to Shenyang (China) and once a week to Vladivostok (Russia). Because the numbers of tourists today are so small, the infrastructure to support tourism is quite underdeveloped (figures 9.28 and 9.29).

Chinese visitors were first permitted to enter North Korea in 1989, and initially they were restricted to a zone that extended only 40 kilometres in from the Chinese border. Although this was relaxed in 1991 and Chinese were also permitted to visit Pyongyang (the capital), Kaesong (near the border with South Korea) and Mount Myohyang, the restriction was re-imposed in 2000.

The issuing of visas for all nationalities is strictly controlled, and this is achieved by requiring formal letters of invitation from an official organisation within North

Korea as well as routinely delaying the issue of necessary travel documentation until less than a week prior to the planned date of entry. Similarly, air tickets on the country's national carrier, Air Koryo, are usually issued only the day before departure. The authorities reserve the right not to issue either the visa or the air ticket right up to these dates.

9.29 *The waiting area at Pyongyang Airport, shortly before the departure of the one flight for the day.*

Other restrictions are enforced during a visitor's stay in North Korea. Mobile phones may not be taken into the country (they are left at the airport upon arrival and collected upon departure), binoculars are banned, and males are required to conform to the hair regulations, which limit hair length for men to between two and five centimetres, or up to seven centimetres for men over 50 to hide emerging baldness. This requirement apparently derives from a North Korean academic study that showed long hair reduces intelligence (for men only?) by sapping oxygen from the brain.

Furthermore, foreigners are forbidden from holding any local currency (the 'won'). All purchases by foreigners must be made using foreign currency, which in the order preferred is the Euro, the Chinese Renminbi, and the US dollar.

As is the case in all countries, visitors are required to conform to local laws and regulations. In North Korea, this includes not criticising the leadership. In the early 2000s, a German tourist was detailed for several months for asking her interpreter why Kim Jong Il was the only fat man in North Korea.

On the other hand, because the general law and order in North Korea is so effective, with almost zero crime rates, plus the fact that foreigners are under the care of their guides during almost every waking moment, North Korea is one of the safest destinations in the world for travellers. No foreigner has ever reported being attacked, robbed, threatened or mugged in North Korea.

The reasons that tourists travel to North Korea are quite different to the motives of tourists who visit most other destinations. North Korea does not appeal to tourists who are seeking beach resorts, theme parks, self-drive exploring or time to relax. All tourists in North Korea are required to travel as part of an all-inclusive group tour which is accompanied at all times by two guides (who act as interpreters) and a driver. Tourists may not leave their hotel compounds without permission, and then only if accompanied by a guide and usually without their camera.

Tourists are not normally permitted to speak with local people other than their guides, and they may only take photographs with the permission of their guides. Tourists are forbidden from photographing military or strategic objects, soldiers, poverty, or anything that might portray the country in a negative way. If any citizen sees a foreigner taking a photograph, they are obliged to report the incident to the police, although this seldom happens in practice.

These very tight regulations on photography may be explained in part by the country's turbulent history. From 1950 to 1953, the Korean peninsula was devastated by a brutal war that resulted in almost three million deaths. The fighting ended with an armistice signed on 27th July 1953, but a peace treaty has never been signed. Technically, North Korea is still at war with South Korea, which accommodates large numbers of US combat soldiers in its territory.

9.30 *This 20 metre high bronze statue of Kim Il Sung has pride of place on a hill overlooking the city of Pyongyang. Local people and visitors show their respect by bowing before the statue.*

Paradoxically, it is the distinctive characteristics of the country that emerged from that turbulent history that are the main attractions to tourists who visit North Korea. Tourists are taken to innumerable socialist monuments and memorials to the brilliance of the country's founder, the Great Leader Kim Il Sung, and his son, the Dear Leader Kim Jong Il (figures 9.30 and 9.31). Although he died in 1994, Kim Il Sung still serves as President (he is currently the world's longest serving Head of State), although this is now a ceremonial rather than decision-making role.

Most major tourist sights have a strong political and ideological flavour. For example, the museum in the country's capital city, Pyongyang, that is devoted to the Korean War (known as the Victorious Fatherland Liberation War Museum) features captured American tanks, guns and aircraft that were shot down (figure 9.32). The Museum also displays documents captured from the US Embassy in Seoul when the North Koreans took over the city that purportedly prove that the US and South Korean forces planned and initiated the Korean War (unlike the story that is generally accepted outside North Korea). Throughout the museum, and indeed throughout North Korea, the US is generally referred to as "US imperialist aggressors", while South Korea is generally referred to as the "South Korean puppet regime".

9.31 *A bronze statue of Kim Il Sung on a horse. In the background are large portraits of Kim Jong Il and his mother, Kim Jong Suk.*

9.32 *A display of captured American equipment in the Victorious Fatherland Liberation War Museum, Pyongyang.*

Although it is somewhat difficult to access from the southern side, visitors to North Korea are often taken inside the negotiating huts that straddle the border with South Korea at Panmunjom. Figure 9.33 is a view looking from North Korea looking into South Korea, with some tourists on the northern side leaving the negotiating huts.

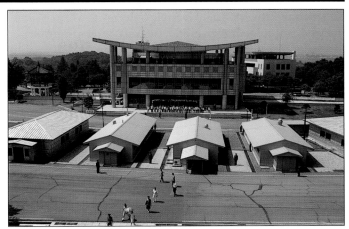

9.33 *The border between North and South Korea at Panmunjom, seen from the northern side. Some tourists are walking back from one of the blue negotiating huts that straddle the border. A group of tourists in South Korea watches from the other side.*

The border between the two Koreas is the thin concrete strip that passes through the middle of each blue building, with light coloured clay on the northern side and darker grey gravel on the southern side.

Other tourist sights may at first seem a little less political in character. For example, most tourists who visit Pyongyang are shown the Grand People's Study House, which overlooks Kim Il Sung Square in the city centre. The Grand People's Study House is a combination of a large central library and an adult education centre. Even here, however, there is a political dimension as visitors are invited to try a special type of desk with a swivelling desktop that was inspired when Kim Jong Il visited the library and gave some 'on-the-spot guidance' on how to make using the desks 'more convenient for the masses' (figure 9.34).

9.34 *Anyone using the Grand People's Study House in Pyongyang is welcome to visit the office of this 'philosophy expert' to have their question on any topic answered.*

Tourists are sometimes shown one of two restored Buddhist monasteries in North Korea, although neither is functioning as a place of worship for North Koreans (figure 9.35). While visiting these monasteries, visitors are told how the original buildings had been destroyed during bombing by 'US imperialist aggressive forces', but that the buildings had been rebuilt 'out of deep concern for the people under   the loving care and wise leadership of the Great Leader, Comrade Kim Il Sung'.

9.35 *The monk at this restored Buddhist temple on Mount Myohyang was trained in Buddhism at Pyongyang's Kim Il Sung University.*

In general, holders of US passports are not issued with visas to visit North Korea. However, exceptions are sometimes made (for short periods and at a high price) when performances of mass gymnastics are held in Pyongyang. Mass gymnastics (also called 'mass games') are synchronised gymnastics, dance, acrobatics and drama, often accompanied by music and a strong political message, featuring about 100,000 people in each 90 minute performance (figure 9.36). The mass gymnastics are held in one of several large stadiums in Pyongyang, and they include rapidly changing backdrops involving tens of thousands of school children, each of whom holds up a large book, changing the pages on cue to form a 'pixel' of the world's picture (figure 9.37).

9.36 *A scene from a mass gymnastics display in May Day Stadium, Pyongyang.*

Unlike sports competitions, where athletes compete for prizes or awards, the mass gymnastics are designed to represent a pure model of communism where each individual sacrifices his or her individuality for the greater common good of the excellence of the collective perform-

ance (figure 9.38). All the performers are volunteers, and in the case of the tens of thousands of school children who participate, practice takes several hours every day after school for about six months prior to the performance, often outside in sub-zero temperatures.

Not all tourism in North Korea is undertaken by foreigners. There is a domestic tourist industry, and although no statistics are available, it is also extremely small in scale. North Koreans require special permission to travel beyond the limits of their home town, and frequent road blocks check the papers and documents of all travellers. Access to some parts of the country are completely forbidden to domestic and foreign travellers alike.

9.37 *A close view of a section of the backdrop at a mass gymnastics display. The heads of the children holding the display books can just be seen, giving an idea of the large scale of the picture formed.*

9.38 *Mass gymnastics, Pyongyang.*

Domestic travel is usually organised by a person's work unit, and members of the same work unit usually travel together. Usual travel destinations for North Koreans are revolutionary sites such as Mount Paektu in the country's north or the birthplace of Kim Il Sung in Pyongyang (figures 9.39 and 9.40).

One of the most special destinations for local people, and for a few specially invited foreign visitors, is the Kumsusan Memorial Palace where the body of the President, Kim Il Sung, is preserved and displayed. This huge building was the residence of Kim Il Sung during his later life, and after his death in 1994, it was converted into a mausoleum (figure 9.41).

9.39 *Employees of a work unit, and their families, visit the house where Kim Il Sung was born on the outskirts of Pyongyang.*

9.40 *The plaque marks the spot where, as a boy, Kim Il Sung fought a Japanese bully, and won. It is now a significant tourist destination for North Koreans.*

9.41 *Immaculately dressed North Koreans leave Kumsusan, the mausoleum of Kim Il Sung, having paid their respects before his preserved body that is on display in a glass case.*

Admission to the mausoleum is carefully controlled and must be pre-arranged. Everyone must be dressed formally for the visit as they are meeting a Head of State, and visitors pass through security checks, have the soles

of their shoes disinfected, and pass through strong air blowers to remove any insects. Visitors file past the carefully preserved body of the President and pay their respects, and then visit several rooms where his personal belongings (including his private railway carriage and Mercedes-Benz) are displayed, and then other rooms to see his awards and medals, some of which were presented several years after his death. He was, for example, awarded an honorary doctorate in information technology by a university in Belarus in 2002.

Some North Korean tourist destinations focus on the beauty of the natural environment. For example, for several years, groups of South Korean tourists were permitted to visit Mount Kumgang, a resort developed by Hyundai (a South Korean company) in a scenic area in the far south of North Korea, remote from any areas of North Korean settlement. Although access was expensive and visitors saw no North Korean settlements, the trips were very popular as South Koreans could say they had been into 'the North'. However, these trips were suspended in 2008 after a North Korean soldier shot and killed a South Korean tourist who had wandered off the approved pathway.

Another popular area of natural beauty is Mount Myohyang, about 160 kilometres north of Pyongyang. This area features many trails for walking through a picturesque landscape of steep mountains, valleys and waterfalls (figure 9.42). Even here, however, the bare rock cliff faces are engraved with inspiring slogans and quotes from Kim Il Sung. The area also houses the International Friendship Exhibition, which is an underground building with 120 rooms displaying almost 250,000 gifts presented by world dignitaries and governments to Kim Il Sung to show their esteem and admiration for his innate genius and his work. The exhibits include bulletproof cars given by Josef Stalin, many portraits of the Great Leader in various national styles, and even a stuffed crocodile holding a tray of wine glasses that was given by the revolutionary Sandinista National Liberation Front in Nicaragua.

9.42 *This boulder at a rest stop on a scenic walk up the slopes of Mount Myohyang has been beautified with quotes from Kim Il Sung..*

When North Koreans have free time, they usually do not travel, which is why domestic tourism is poorly developed in North Korea. In general, North Koreans relax by doing activities that are often considered old-fashioned or quaint in most parts of the world today. For example, many families spend weekends and holidays as a family in a park, perhaps joining in communal singing of patriotic songs or dancing with other families (figure 9.43). Alternatively, some of the larger cities have amusement parks with rides and games for very low prices. Figure 9.44 shows one example of a Pyongyang amusement park where children can try their skill at throwing fake hand grenades at US soldiers.

9.43 *Communal singing and dancing, a popular weekend activity in Pyongyang's parks.*

9.44 *At the Pyongyang Fun Fair, children can try their skill at throwing fake hand grenades at US soldiers.*

All hotels in North Korea are state-owned and managed, and according to government statistics, there are about 6,000 rooms available (figure 9.45). This figure seems somewhat excessive when the number of tourists annually is only 2,000, and probably explains why visitors report staying in multi-storey hotels but finding that the floor where they are staying is the only one which is being used.

The excess of rooms also explains why construction of the world's largest hotel in Pyongyang, the Ryugyong Hotel, which began in 1987, was stopped in 1992. The hotel, which is already the world's 24th highest building, is 105 stories (330 metres) high, with seven revolving restaurants at its top and 3,000 rooms (figure 9.46). Construction resumed in 2008 under the control of an Egyptian building company, with a planned opening in 2012 to coincide with the 100th birthday of the President, Kim Il Sung.

9.45 *A large tourist hotel at Mount Myohyang. Most of the rooms are usually empty.*

9.46 *Construction of the Ryugyong Hotel began in 1987, and is due for completion in 2012 to mark the 100th birthday of Kim Il Sung.*

ToK BoX

Education and Indoctrination.

In this chapter, and in chapter 18, North Korea has been used to illustrate some important themes in Geography. Critics of the government in North Korea claim that the authorities use indoctrination to 'brain wash' its citizens, feeding lies and half-truths in a way that does not encourage questioning.

To some extent, what outsiders interpret as indoctrination and blind acceptance of authority is part of Korea's traditional educational ethic, based on Confucianism. Although originating in China, Confucius' thoughts have been very influential in Korea (and elsewhere in Asia), leading a a high level of respect for those in authority (and especially scholars) combined with a very positive attitude towards the importance of academic learning as a means of self-improvement. In Confucian societies, education is seen as being important not only for personal improvement, but to help the harmonious and progressive development of society as a whole.

In North Korea, this respect for authority figures has been elevated to new heights by the imposition of a personality cult around the country's founding President, the Great Leader Kim Il Sung,

and his son, the Dear Leader Kim Jong Il. It is this personality cult that leads critics of the regime to claim that widespread indoctrination occurs.

The IB aims to be a mind-broadening model of education that opens new possibilities for the students who complete it. By asking open-ended questions in subjects such as geography, the IB is probably the complete opposite of closed and rigid models of education, such as those operating during the Soviet era in the USSR or in Germany during the Nazi period.

It is interesting to consider the differences between 'education' (the process of receiving or giving systematic instruction) and 'indoctrination' (teaching a person or group to accept a set of beliefs uncritically).

Some possible differences between education and indoctrination might be:

- 'Education' has a positive connotation, 'indoctrination' is negatively loaded;

- 'Education' broadens the mind whereas 'indoctrination' narrows the mind;

- 'Education' is a dialogue, 'indoctrination' is a monologue;

- 'Education' transcends 'indoctrination';

- 'Education' lights fires whereas 'indoctrination' fills buckets

In mathematics classes, students are commonly taught "you must never divide by zero". When the author of this book studied mathematics in high school, he was taught that it was okay to divide by zero, and the answer would always be ∞. Is the statement "you must never divide by zero" an example of education or indoctrination?

Actually, it is an example of an axiom — a statement or proposition that is regarded as being established, accepted, or self-evidently true in order to provide the foundation of other understandings.

In general, 'education' minimises the number of axioms, whereas in 'indoctrination', everything becomes an axiom.

Giving reasons and examples, do you think your study of IB geography is 'education' or 'indoctrination'?

The next ToK BoX is on page 438.

One question that many outsiders ask is whether it is appropriate a country such as North Korea. Some argue that as everything in North Korea is government-owned, all profits made from tourism would be used to support a regime that has been accused of human rights abuses and disregarding international laws.

9.47 *Bison Waterfall, Mount Myohyang, North Korea.*

On the other hand, the United Nations World Tourism Organisation endorses visits by outsiders as the best way to break the government's monopoly on information to North Koreans. Defectors who have escaped from North

Korea say the regime's grip will loosen only when North Koreans learn more about the outside world.

Furthermore, the historical experience in Eastern Europe during the 1980s suggests that keeping North Koreans isolated only cements the government's monopoly of information and control over the people. It is illegal for North Koreans to listen to foreign radio broadcasts, and all televisions used by local people are permanently tuned into the government's channel. Indeed, one of the main reasons that the North Korean government restricts tourism in the first place is to control the flow of information to the local population.

SWOT analysis of tourism in North Korea

One way to analyse the impact of tourism is to conduct a **SWOT analysis**. SWOT analyses examine the Strengths, Weaknesses, Opportunities and Threats of a situation or a proposal. A SWOT analysis of tourism in North Korea undertaken by PATA (the Pacific Asia Travel Association) highlighted the following areas:

Strengths

- wide range of natural attractions, such as lush mountains and tranquil lakes (figure 9.47)

9.48 *Korean food, of the type served to foreign visitors.*

- acceptable 3-star hotels in Pyongyang and at key locations around the country
- good choice of local Korean cuisine (figure 9.48)
- ancient and well-preserved historical and cultural heritage
- warm people and hospitality
- impressive monuments and government buildings
- good network of highways (figure 9.49)
- clean and well-maintained tour coaches (figure 9.50)
- well-trained guides with excellent foreign language skills

9.49 *The Reunification Highway is a wide expressway that runs south from Pyongyang to the border with South Korea. It is intended to link Pyongyang with Seoul after the two Koreas are reunited.*

9.50 *A typical tourist coach operated by the government's KITC (Korea International Travel Company).*

- facilities capable of handling small conferences

Weaknesses

- limited air access
- stringent visa requirements
- public image of North Korea in international markets is driven by politics and hostile media presentations
- tourism infrastructure needs upgrading
- limited training for personnel dealing with foreigners
- does not enjoy 'Approved Destination Status' recognition from China
- limited choice on non-Korean food
- limited range of souvenirs, which when available are very expensive (figure 9.51)
- relatively expensive ground costs because of government monopoly pricing
- restrictions of foreign private investments
- harsh winter reduces the tourist season to nine months or less

9.51 *A foreign languages bookstore in Pyongyang. The range of authors is quite limited, with most books being either by Kim Il Sung or Kim Jong Il, or about the two leaders and their philosophies. In addition to books, the bookstore sells flags, posters, lapel badges, videotapes and stamps.*

Opportunities

- a trip to North Korea is perceived as a novelty and has 'bragging rights'
- perception as the last bastion of socialism/communism attracts the curious traveller
- focused marketing and destination brand development
- attract foreign airlines to open scheduled or charter air services
- foreign tourism investments (subject to relaxation of private investment regulations and new regulations to protect foreign and private investments)
- huge potential markets in neighbouring countries such as China, Japan and South Korea
- potential niche products such as winter sports, ecotourism, VFR (visit friends and relatives), and small-scale regional conferences
- accelerating co-operation with South Korea and potential for joint destination marketing

Threats

- government bureaucracy
- lack of tourism infrastructure funds
- lack of destination marketing funds
- negative impact on markets of ongoing political developments
- possible instability if and when the country's leadership changes
- fear of an invasion by US and South Korean forces

QUESTION BLOCK 9G

1. Why do such small numbers of tourists travel to North Korea?

2. For you personally, what factors (a) would attract you to visit North Korea, and (b) would stop you going?

3. Classify the points in the SWOT analysis into (a) economic, (b) socio-political and (c) environmental factors.

4. Using the framework in this section, undertake a SWOT analysis of tourism in your home country, or a country of your choice. Identify the factors that are the same or similar as those for tourism in North Korea.

Ecotourism

As a reaction to criticisms that tourism causes environmental degradation, there is a growing interest in **ecotourism**, which is based on environmentally sound principles and which seeks to encourage interaction between local people and tourists on an equal basis. Ecotourism encourages preservation of environmental quality and of traditional cultures, education of tourists and participation by local people (figure 9.52). Ecotourism operates under many labels, including adventure tourism, contact tourism, green tourism, low-impact tourism, sustainable tourism, and wilderness tourism.

The Talamanca Association for Ecotourism and Conservation in Costa Rica defines ecotourism in the following way:

> *"Ecotourism means more than bird books and binoculars… more than native art hanging on hotel walls or ethnic dishes on the restaurant menu. Ecotourism is not mass tourism behind a green mask. Ecotourism means a constant struggle to defend the earth and to protect and sustain traditional communities. Ecotourism is a co-operative relationship between the non-wealthy local community and those sincere, open-minded tourists who want to enjoy themselves in a Third World setting".*

9.53 *These two schoolgirls have volunteered to help build a medical clinic in China's Guizhou province.*

Where governments and tour operators wish to develop ecotourism, management of tourism is usually undertaken through tools such as visitor management techniques, carrying capacity calculations, and consultation and participation with local people. However, ecotourism remains a minor part of the total picture of world-wide tourism, and many tourism operators feel that ecotourism reduces profits and the speed with which money can be made. Consequently, most of the growth in tourism in LEDCs tends to be mass-tourism.

9.52 *Ecotourism seeks to make minimal impact on the environment and maximise understanding of one's surroundings. In China's spectacular Tiger Leaping Gorge (shown here) local people are directly involved in tourism as they own and run all the guest lodges for trekkers in the gorge.*

9.54 *One of the attractions of Africa for tourists is its wildlife. These zebras are in Nech Sar National Park, Ethiopia.*

Ecotourism tends to appeal to ecologically and socially conscious individuals. It can take many forms, such as communing with nature or learning to understand the environment more deeply, volunteering, personal growth and learning new ways to live on the planet (figure 9.53). It typically involves travel to destinations where the primary attractions are the distinctive flora, fauna and cultural heritage (figure 9.54).

Ecotourism usually minimises the negative impacts of tourism on the environment and it tries to preserve and dignify the culture and influence of local people. An example of how this works in practice is the **ecotourism camps of Hartmann's Valley**, situated in the arid Namib Desert in the far north-west of Namibia.

One example of such a campsite is Serra Cafema, which is located on the banks of the Kunene River that forms the border between Namibia and Angola. The canvas and thatched buildings are constructed from local materials where possible, and they are elevated above the flood-plain, both to avoid floodwaters intruding into the cabins and to minimise the impact on the local ecosystem (figure 9.55). By using designs inspired by local indigenous architecture, air circulates naturally and thus neither heating nor air conditioning is needed despite the camp's location in the heart of the Namib Desert.

9.55 *These cabins at Serra Cafema have been built on stilts above the banks of the Kunene River (on the border of Angola and Namibia) to protect the riverbank ecology and avoid problems from floodwaters.*

The camp is set among the Albida trees on the banks of the river, and it shares the area with the indigenous Himba people (see chapter 7). As the Himba are one of the last truly nomadic groups remaining in Africa, the opportunity to interact with the Himba and develop a deeper understanding of their culture is one of the attractions of Hartmann's Valley. The camp managers employ a young Himba woman and share the profits of the camp with the local people. In return, the Himba, who are normally extremely shy and reclusive, have agreed to welcome visitors on the basis that this will help the tourists understand their indigenous culture more fully. As a

9.56 *These Himba women are selling handicrafts to visitors in front of their home, representing their first tentative steps into the cash economy.*

side-effect, the Himba also sell some of their handicrafts, thus dabbling in the cash economy in a small way (figure 9.56).

The main focus of the Hartmann's Valley ecotourism camps, however, is gaining an understanding of the desert ecosystem. Unfortunately, ecotourism in remote locations is often a more expensive exercise than mass conventional tourism. The advertising for Serra Cafema describes the ecotourism experience of the camp in these words:

> *The variety of activities to explore the breathtaking landscape includes informative nature drives that tread lightly on the fragile habitats and boating on the Kunene River, where crocodiles and waterbirds seem out of place in this moonscape environment (figures 9.57 and 9.58). Walking in the remote mountain and river valleys are also a highlight, as is a visit to a Himba settlement, should the nomadic people be in the area. One of the highlights of Serra Cafema is the carefully guided quad bike excursions that tread lightly on the dunes, while allowing guests to experience a true desert (figure 9.59). The fairy circle phenomenon is best viewed in the Hartmann's Valley (figure 9.60).*

9.57 *The Kunene River marks the boundary between Namibia and Angola.*

9.58 *The natural ecology of the Kunene River.*

9.59 *Quad bikes allow visitors to the Hartmann's Valley to explore vast tracts of the desert environment with minimal environmental impact.*

9.60 *When animals are killed, the release of nutrients is too much for the hardy desert grasses to tolerate, as they have evolved to cope with a nutrient-poor environment.*

A key to sustainable ecotourism is operating in low-density environments and restricting the numbers of visitors. This ensures that human impact on fragile environments is minimised, that the integrity of the local area is not compromised, and that the act of tourism will lead to positive outcomes — environmentally, socially, culturally and financially.

Ecotourism is therefore based on the belief that local wildlife and indigenous communities who live in the areas being visited both have inalienable rights to their heritage. In the case of indigenous peoples, this implies that they are brought into the mainstream of conservation and tourism, thus providing a sustainable future both for their communities and the area's flora and fauna (figure 9.61).

In the case of Hartmann's Valley camps, this philosophy is expressed by monitoring wildlife in the area, maintaining the local infrastructure, and setting up a permanent research camp on lichens (an important part of the Namib Desert ecosystem).

9.61 *Fauna in the Hartmann's Valley.*

Ecotourism is often imperfect in its implementation for practical reasons, however. For example, while the Hartmann's Valley's isolation limits the number of visitors, it also means that motor vehicles are necessary to transport people to and from the camp, and to see wildlife (figure 9.62. While the drivers are extremely careful to stay on formed tracks, thus protecting the vegetation and the dunes, 4-wheel drive vehicles do produce exhaust fumes and create quite high noise levels.

9.62 *Four wheel drives are used in Hartmann's Valley to cover long distances.*

For this reason, perhaps a purer model of ecotourism is found in **Tiger Leaping Gorge**. The Gorge is situated in China's Yunnan province at the eastern end of the Himalaya Mountains, where the upper reaches of the Yangtze River have cut one of the world's deepest canyons. Tiger Leaping Gorge is 16 kilometres in length, and the height of the snow-capped mountains that line each side of the Gorge rise 3,900 metres from the waters of the river (see figure 7.2 in chapter 7).

Foreign as well as Chinese tourists come to Tiger Leaping Gorge to trek a narrow pathway that was originally developed as a track for horses to carry tea between Tibet and Yunnan (figure 9.63). The track gives spectacular

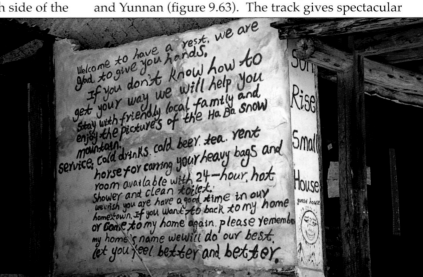

9.66 *Some of the services offered by guest houses are described in this painted sign on the wall of a guest house in Tiger Leaping Gorge.*

9.63
The upper path used by trekkers in Tiger Leaping

views of the area's pristine landscape, but because of its steep and narrow nature, it must be traversed either by walking, or by a combination of walking and horse or donkey riding (figure 9.64).

Tiger Leaping Gorge is inhabited by an ethnic minority called the Naxi people. The Naxi typically live in two-storey wooden homes arranged around a central courtyard. When trekking first began in the area, many Naxi people welcomed visitors as guests into their homes for overnight stops. This has now developed into a sideline business for many Naxi farmers who have extended their homes by adding guest flats, charging visitors about US$3 per night for accommodation, plus about US$2 for Naxi-style cooked meals (figures 9.65 and 9.66).

9.64 *Donkeys are used by some trekkers, although most enjoy the walking.*

9.65 *Many of the guest houses operated by Naxi nationality people in Tiger Leaping Gorge also offer snacks and drinks to trekkers.*

9.67 *Advertising beside the pathway in Tiger Leaping Gorge.*

Because tourism in Tiger Leaping Gorge causes minimal environmental impact and as its benefits accrue to local people through guest houses and horse rental, it is an excellent example of effective small scale ecotourism. This is not to say that there are no adverse impacts, however. Naxi people advertise their guesthouses by painting advertisements in red or yellow paint on the rocks beside the pathway, and many trekkers criticise this as a form of environmental vandalism (figure 9.67).

QUESTION BLOCK 9H

1. *What is ecotourism?*

2. *What characteristics of tourism in Hartmann's Valley characterise it as 'ecotourism'?*

3. *What characteristics of tourism in Tiger Leaping Gorge characterise it as 'ecotourism'?*

4. *Which example of ecotourism do you prefer — Hartmann's Valley or Tiger Leaping Gorge? Give reasons to explain your answer.*

5. *Outline the strategies that are used to manage and sustain ecotourism in Hartmann's Valley and Tiger Leaping Gorge.*

Tourism as a Development Strategy

During the period of mass tourism (1950 to the present), the MEDCs' share of world tourism has declined, while the share of the LEDCs has increased at an accelerating rate (table 9.5).

Large scale tourism of people from MEDCs to the LEDCs began in the 1970s. Before that time, travellers to LEDCs were small in number, and they tended to be specialist purpose travellers such as explorers, traders, colonisers, missionaries, scientists and administrators. In the 1970s, transport improvements and a desire by governments in LEDCs to raise income from tourism led to a substantial growth in numbers. By 2000, LEDCs such as China, Mexico and Thailand were all receiving more than 8

million international tourists per annum, and in China's case, the figure was almost 30 million.

In a similar way that some LEDCs look towards industrialisation as a pathway to economic development, others look towards tourism. Many people in LEDCs regard it as a 'smoke-less industry'. In other words, they see tourism as bringing substantial income in the same way as manufacturing, but without the environmental pollution which manufacturing industries produce. Many planners in LEDCs see tourism as a more reliable earner of income than minerals, cash crops and manufactured goods, all of which have experienced unstable prices from time to time. Furthermore, tourism was seen by the authorities in many LEDCs as an opportunity to define and raise money to preserve national culture, wildlife and unique natural features.

The size of tourism as a global industry doubles every 15 years, and it is the biggest growth industry, employer and source of revenue in the world. It is perhaps not surprising that LEDCs want to gain some of the revenue from this industry. Table 9.6 shows the importance of tourism for the 30 countries examined in several tables in chapters 1 and 2.

In general, countries with high numbers of international departures are the more affluent countries where residents can afford to travel. Countries with low numbers of departures but high numbers of arrivals tend to be LEDCs which have successfully developed a tourism industry. It should also be remembered that European countries tend to have higher tourism figures than elsewhere because of the short distances and ease of travel required to cross national borders within Europe.

The attraction of tourism for many LEDCs is that there is a constantly renewable supply of tourists available in the More Economically Developed Countries (MEDCs), and profitability can be high. It is often a quicker way to raise national income than exporting primary products or developing a manufacturing sector.

Table 9.5
Trends in International Tourist Arrivals by Region, 1950 - 2009

Region	1950 Share (%)	1995 Share (%)	2009 Share (%)	Difference 1950 to 2009	% Change 1950 to 2009
Americas	29.6	19.7	15.9	-13.7	-46.3
Europe	66.6	59.4	52.3	-14.3	-21.5
East Asia / Pacific	0.7	14.8	19.5	+18.8	+2685.7
Africa	2.1	3.3	5.2	+3.1	+147.6
Middle East	0.8	2.0	6.0	+5.2	+590.0
South Asia	0.2	0.8	1.1	+0.9	+450.0

Source: World Tourism Organisation

Leisure, sport and tourism

Table 9.6
International Tourism (for countries listed in table 2.1, where data is available)

	Thousands of Inbound Tourists, 1995	Thousands of Inbound Tourists, 2007	Thousands of Outbound Tourists, 1995	Thousands of Outbound Tourists, 2007	Inbound Tourism Expenditure US$ mill. 2007	Outbound Tourism Expenditure US$ mill. 2007	Inbound Tourism as a % of Exports 2007	Outbound Tourism as a % of Imports 2007
HIGH HUMAN DEVELOPMENT								
Norway	2,880	4,290	590	3,395	5,021	14,109	2.8	12.1
Australia	3,825	5,064	2,519	5,462	29,065	19,844	15.9	9.9
Sweden	2,310	3,434	10,127	12,681	13,706	15,696	5.9	7.8
Japan	3,345	8,347	15,298	17,295	12,422	37,261	1.5	5.1
USA	43,490	55,986	51,285	64,052	144,808	109,578	8.8	4.7
United Kingdom	21,719	30,870	41,345	69,450	47,109	88,478	6.5	10.7
South Korea	3,753	6,448	3,819	13,325	8,974	23,359	2.0	5.4
United Arab Emirates	2,315	7,126			4,972	8,827		
Mexico	20,241	21,424	8,450	15,089	14,072	9,843	4.9	3.2
Malaysia	7,469	20,973	20,642	30,761	16,798	6,245	8.2	3.7
MEDIUM HUMAN DEVELOPMENT								
China	20,034	54,720	4,520	40,954	41,126	33,264	3.1	3.2
Iran	489	2,735	1,000		1,834	6,526		
Vietnam	1,351	4,244			3,200		7.1	
Indonesia	4,324	5,506	1,782	4,341	5,833	6,120	4.5	5.6
Bolivia	284	556	249	476	294	325	5.9	8.0
India	2,124	5,082	3,056	9,780	10,729	9,296	4.5	4.0
Myanmar	117	248			59	40	1.2	1.4
Nepal	363	527	100	469	234	402	16.3	11.0
Papua New Guinea	42	104	51		4	56	0.1	2.1
Kenya	896	1,644			1,507	262	22.1	2.7
LOW HUMAN DEVELOPMENT								
Eritrea	315	78			60			
Nigeria	656	1,111			340	3,494	0.5	7.6
Tanzania	285	692	157		1,053	666	26.7	10.5
Rwanda					66	69	18.2	7.6
Malawi	192	714			48	84		
Zambia	163	897			138	98	2.8	2.2
Ethiopia	103	303	120		792	107	29.8	1.5
Mali	42	164			175	196	9.4	9.1
Niger	35	60	10		39	42	6.5	3.9
Sierra Leone	38	32	6	71	22	17	6.6	3.5

Source: Derived from data supplied by the UNDP and the World Bank

9.68 *Tourism spawns new occupations in LEDCs such as selling souvenirs or providing new experiences to tourists. In this view, enterprising local farmers have built rafts to transport tourists along the Yulong River near Yangshuo, China.*

9.69 *Viña del Mar in Chile can be thought of as a 'golden ghetto' of tourism. It has very comfortable purpose-built tourist facilities (top photo) within a few kilometres of the poor housing in the port city of Valparaíso (bottom photo).*

When tourism comes to LEDCs, many people who were involved in other industries, or were unemployed, establish themselves as part of the industry (figure 9.68). Although this is preferable to unemployment, it creates problems when they have diverted their attention away from food production and farming. Indeed, some scholars criticise tourism because it perpetuates the dependence of people in LEDCs on people from MEDCs, continuing a tradition of exploitation from colonial times. This may be especially so when the tourism infrastructure, such as hotels, airlines, bus companies and restaurants are owned by foreign interests which may siphon away the profits of the industry to other countries. Indeed, the World Bank estimates that 55% of the gross revenue from tourism in LEDCs leaks back to the MEDCs.

Another criticism of tourism in LEDCs is that it is an enclave industry that brings few benefits to local people. It is argued that tourism is largely confined to 'golden ghettos', or pockets of wealth near major tourist destinations, and the wealth does not become widely distributed. The situation can be aggravated if substantial investment is made in developing tourist facilities in these 'golden ghettos', diverting funds away from the needs of the general population (figure 9.69).

QUESTION BLOCK 9I

1. *Why is tourism attractive to many LEDCs?*

2. *Describe the pattern shown in table 9.5, and suggest reasons for it.*

3. *Using table 9.6, list the countries that have (a) an excess of arrivals over departures, and (b) an excess of departures over arrivals in the latest year available. What generalisations can you draw from these lists?*

4. *Referring to table 9.6, what types of countries are most dependant on tourism in terms of (a) absolute income, and (b) percentage of foreign funds earned?*

5. *How can LEDCs ensure that they gain effectively from tourism?*

Tourism is welcomed, or perhaps tolerated, in many countries because of the income in foreign exchange that it often brings into an economy (figure 9.70). Some countries with traditional cultures and developing economies rely on tourism as a major part of their economy as millions of tourists from wealthy nations visit each year. This is especially so for countries in the south Pacific such as Fiji and Tahiti, countries in the Caribbean such as Bermuda and Barbados, countries in Africa such as Kenya and Tunisia and countries in Asia such as Thailand and Malaysia.

There is widespread debate regarding the benefits and disadvantages of tourism. Tourism can generate substantial **economic benefits**, both in the destination country and in the tourists' home country. Indeed, one of the primary motivations for many LEDCs to promote tourism is the expected economic improvement. Tourism brings along both positive and negative consequences. According to the World Tourism Organisation, 924 million people travelled to another country in 2008, spending more US$ 993 billion.

9.71 *Bayan-Ulgii Airport in Mongolia brings tourists to visit the spectacular glacial scenery of the Altai Tavan Bogd National Park. It is unlikely that this airport would exist if it were not for the tourist industry. It should also be noted that very few local residents fly.*

9.70 *The importance of tourism to the economy of Yangshuo is illustrated by this sign, describing tourism in both English and Chinese.*

Positive economic benefits flow from tourism in several ways. First, tourism generates **income** for the local economy, and it can encourage investment in other economic sectors. Some countries try to accelerate this growth by requiring visitors to bring in a certain amount of foreign currency for each day of their stay, which they do not allow to be taken out of the country at the end of the trip. In 2008, tourism was one of the top five export earners for 83% of the world's countries, and was the main source of foreign exchange earnings for 38% of countries.

Government revenues also flow from tourism, both as direct contributions that come from departure taxes and taxes on the tourism industry, and indirect contributions, which are taxes and duties on goods and services supplied to tourists. Tourism also **generates employment** for local people in areas such as hotels, restaurants, night clubs, taxis, and souvenir sales. In 2008, it was estimated that tourism supported about 9% of the world's workers.

Tourism can enable governments to make improvements to **infrastructure**, such as better water and sewerage systems, roads, electricity, telephone and public transport networks (figure 9.71). These improvements usually benefit local residents as well as the tourist industry.

It can be difficult to quantify the economic benefits of tourism in LEDCs because not all tourist expenditures are counted in national statistics. Money is earned from tourism through informal employment such as street vendors, informal guides, rickshaw drivers, and so on, but this is almost never counted by the authorities in LEDCs. Money earned in the informal sector is returned very

effectively to the local economy, however, and this has a big multiplier effect as it is spent over and over again.

There are also **negative economic impacts** of tourism. Many of the potential benefits of tourism are lost through **leakage**. Leakage refers to the losses to the local economy from taxes, profits and wages that are paid to people and organisations outside the area. It is estimated that in most all-inclusive package tours, about 80% of travellers' expenditures go to the airlines, hotels and other international companies, most of whom have their headquarters in the travellers' home country.

9.72 *The American-owned Hilton Hotel dominates the skyline of Kuching and the scenery of the Sarawak River, adopting a fashion that owes nothing to the indigenous culture of East Malaysia where it is located.*

Leakage can occur in two main ways. First, **import leakage** occurs when tourists demand standards of facilities, equipment, food, and other products that the host country cannot supply. In many LEDCs, food and drinks are often imported to meet tourists' expectations. The average import-related leakage for most LEDCs is between 40% and 50% of gross tourism earnings for small economies. Second, **export leakage** occurs when transnational corporations and foreign businesses send profits back to their home countries. Foreign companies are often the only ones in LEDCs that have the necessary capital to invest in the construction of tourism infrastructure and facilities (figure 9.72).

Other economic losses arise from **infrastructure costs**. The development of tourism can consume a large proportion of the scarce revenues that governments in LEDCs possess. Expenditure on airports, roads and other infrastructure are sometimes at the expense of important development sectors such as education and health. Another economic problem is that tourism often **drives up the prices** for basic goods and services for the local population, whose incomes cannot sustain the rises that tourists can afford. Development for tourism can lead to rises in real estate demand, which increases building costs and land values for local residents. As well as making it more difficult for residents to meet their basic daily needs, rising land values can also disempower residents by giving wealthy outsiders effective control over land and property development.

9.73 *These women and men sell handicrafts to tourists in a floating market near Ywama on the Shan Plateau. Whenever they see a boat with foreigners approaching, they row across and surround the boat, eager to make sales.*

9.74 *At its best, tourism can build bridges of understanding between people of different cultures. Unfortunately, the scene shown here is more common where lack of language prevents meaningful exchanges and commercial transactions are reduced to a few angry words.*

Although income from tourism can be a benefit, this can become a problem when a country develops its tourism so much that it becomes **over-dependent on tourism**. Over-reliance on tourism brings significant risks to tourism-dependent economies. Economic recession in MEDCs, loss of confidence due to terrorism, and the impacts of natural disasters such as tropical cyclones can devastate an economy that is over-dependent on tourism. Over-dependence can also be a problem at a personal level, such as when local people develop a dependence on selling things to tourists and neglect education of children or the cultivation of food (figure 9.73).

As well as affecting the economy, tourism has an impact on the **culture** of LEDCs. As with economic effects, the impact of tourism on a country's culture has positive and negative aspects. On the **positive** side, tourism brings people from different cultures and backgrounds into contact with each other (figure 9.74). As such, it can **foster understanding** and provide authentic two-way cultural exchanges between hosts and guests. This can lead to greater tolerance, understanding and mutual respect.

Tourism often adds to the **vitality of communities**. Events and festivals are often rejuvenated and developed in response to tourist interest, helping to preserve local identity, and often leading to a renewal of indigenous cultures, cultural arts and crafts. The vitality of local communities can be strengthened further when the jobs created by tourism act as an incentive to reduce emigration away from rural areas to the cities.

9.75 *A young tourist joins in Uzbek dancing at the invitation of local people.*

Negative cultural impacts can occur when visiting tourists from wealthier nations create **hostility** among local people. Tourists may, out of ignorance or carelessness, fail to respect local customs and moral values. When they do, they can bring about irritation and stereotyping. Tourists may take a quick snapshot and then be gone, without realising that they have intruded into local peoples' lives in an insensitive way. On occasions, local people feel they must behave in a certain way, such as adapting local customs or wearing traditional dress to please tourists rather than for special occasions, and this displeases other members of that community (figure 9.75).

On other occasions, the free spending attitudes and loud behaviour of tourists from wealthier backgrounds cause resentment among local people. Furthermore, some local people resent being placed in a role of servitude that they find demeaning. This has led some writers to label tourism to developing countries as 'cultural bastardisation' and 'trinketisation' where people in developing countries are assimilated into the materialistic attitudes of the developed world.

9.76 *There can often be a stark contrast between the lifestyles of tourists and the population of the country where the tourists are visiting. The contrast can be seen in difference between this resort hotel in Penang, Malaysia (top photo) and the nearby houses of local residents (lower photo).*

Tourism can place further pressures on local cultures by highlighting the stark **contrast in lifestyles** between tourists and the local population (figure 9.76). It is common to see high-rise, well maintained glass and concrete hotels towering over modest timber or iron housing of local people. Moreover, by engaging in behaviour that is offensive to local people, such as wearing minimal clothing for swimming, tourists who do not understand local sensitivities can unwittingly cause further offence.

Where cultures meet through tourism, a process known as **transculturation** often occurs. In transculturation, people

in a traditional culture are exposed to new and alien ideas by outsiders (figure 9.77). They selectively choose those parts of the new culture they wish to accept, and reject those that they do not. This leads to **adaptation** of the traditional culture to accommodate the preferences of tourists. Adaptation can cause resentment in two ways. First, defenders of the traditional culture within that society resent the dilution of the culture by outside influences. Second, those entrepreneurs who bring tourists to see the 'exotic' culture resent the convergence with 'mainstream western' culture that results. Such entrepreneurs are said to **commodify** the local culture, preserving it to make it a commodity with an economic value. They are said to prefer the **zooification** of traditional cultures, which means preserving them as a curiosity for others to see and observe.

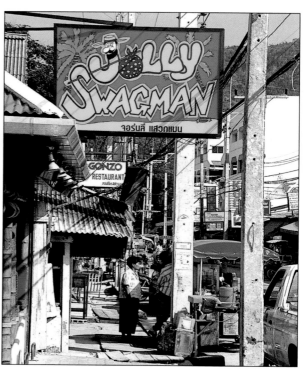

9.77 *Commercially-based transculturation – an Australian bar in the Thai beach resort of Phuket.*

Where people such as tourists insensitively impose their own ideas, traditions and culture on others who are in a less powerful position, it is known as **cultural imperialism**. However, it is important to see this concept from different perspectives. It is often people in wealthy developed countries who tend to decide what is good (untouched traditional cultures) and what is bad (tribal people gambling, drinking or watching television). However, it is not appropriate to dictate that certain people should be prevented from modernising if they wish to do so, simply to be preserved as items of curiosity for outsiders. In this sense, it is often useful to distinguish between 'tourists' who engage in self-oriented mass travel, and 'travellers' who make an effort to preserve the environment and understand other cultures.

9.78 *In order to protect the fragile environment of the mountains and glaciers of the north-western border areas of western Mongolia (top photo), the Altai Tavan Bogd National Park was established to regulate the number of visitors, and their behaviour. Special permits are required to enter the national park, and access in 4-wheel drive vehicles must be organised through registered agencies (lower photo).*

9.79 *An elevated pathway has been built to protect the fragile alpine ecosystem of Mount Kosciuszko (Australia) from damage by tourists.*

Finally, there are positive and negative **environmental consequences** of tourism. Negative impacts arise when the level of visitor use is greater than the environment's ability to cope with this use within the acceptable limits of change. Uncontrolled conventional tourism poses potential threats to many natural areas around the world (figure 9.78). Tourism can place great pressures on certain areas

and lead to impacts such as soil erosion, increased pollution, loss of wildlife habitats, pressure on endangered species and greater vulnerability to forest fires. Tourism may place pressure on water resources, and it can force local populations to compete for the use of critical resources. On the other hand, tourism can place **positive pressures** to improve the environment, as tourists are unlikely to want to travel to heavily polluted or degraded environments (figure 9.79).

Where tourism is successful, it tends to follow three essential principles that make it sustainable in the long-term. First, the local population should remain prosperous and retain its cultural identity. Second, the landscape of the place being visited should remain attractive to tourists. Third, any impact on the ecology of the tourist destination should be minimal.

QUESTION BLOCK 9J

1. *Draw up a table summarising the three main arguments (a) in favour and (b) against tourism to LEDCs.*

2. *Explain the terms 'transculturation', 'zooification' and 'cultural imperialism'.*

Leisure at the National / Regional Scale — Sport

National Sports Leagues

A **sports league** is an organisation that co-ordinates a group of individual clubs that play each other in a specific sport over a period of time for a championship. Some leagues may be as simple or as small as a group of amateur athletes who form teams among themselves and compete on weekends in their local area. At the other end of the spectrum are the international professional leagues that involve dozens of teams, thousands of players and millions of dollars.

A **league system** may form when a number of leagues are tied together in a hierarchical fashion. This might occur when the best teams playing in one league are promoted to a higher league, while the poorly performing teams in the higher league may drop to a lower league. League systems exist in a variety of major sports, and they are especially common in football (soccer) competitions in Europe and Latin America.

A **sports division** comprises a group of teams which compete against one another for a divisional title. Teams that get to the top of their division then compete for championships in the league. In this way, it can be seen that there is a **hierarchy** of teams.

The hierarchy of teams often mirrors the location of the teams in a competition. There tend to be more teams at the lower rungs of the league, and these represent smaller, more local areas than the major teams, which often represent larger centres of population or places with a greater drawing area (geographical spread).

Traditionally, sporting teams tended to represent particular areas, and players were drawn from their local area to represent that place. As some sports have become more professional, the traditional relationship between the team's home area and the area from which it draws its players has broken down. In the same way, the supporters of teams in major sporting leagues are less and less likely to live in the area represented by the team they are supporting.

QUESTION BLOCK 9K

1. *Explain what is meant by the 'hierarchy of a sports league'.*

2. *Examine one sporting league in the area where you live, and describe the relationship between the location of the teams and the residential areas of its main supporters.*

Leisure at the Local Scale — Tourism

Tourism Management in Urban Areas — the case of St Petersburg, Russia

When looking at tourism in urban areas, we can distinguish between primary and secondary tourism resources. **Primary tourism resources** are those factors or attractions which are the main reasons that tourists may want to visit a particular city. Primary tourism resources may be broadly categorised into groups such as scenic, cultural, historical, religious, ecological or climatic resources.

Secondary tourism resources are the facilities provided to support tourism in the city, such as accommodation, shopping, catering, entertainment, transport, and information services. These facilities are important for the success of urban tourism, but they are not the main attractors of visitors.

To understand the nature of these concepts, we will examine one of the world's great cities for tourism — St Petersburg, in north-west Russia. As a former capital city of the Russian empire, St Petersburg (Санкт-Петербург), which was known as Leningrad (Ленинград) between 1924 and 1991, attracts tourists who are interested in art, architecture, music, culture and history.

St Petersburg is located on a collection of flat delta islands and the surrounding banks of the mouth of the Neva River where it empties into the Gulf of Finland, which in turn empties into the Baltic Sea. The oldest part of the city was established in 1703 when the Czar (king) of the time, Peter the Great, established the Peter and Paul Fortress on a small island in the Neva River (figure 9.80). The city expanded on the nearby islands and river banks, and by 1725 the population had already grown to 40,000 people.

9.80 *The Peter and Paul Fortress in St Petersburg, Russia.*

The *Lonely Planet Guide to Russia* describes the appeal of St Petersburg to tourists in these words:

> *"If much of Russia recalls its Eastern rather than Western roots, St Petersburg is where you'll feel Russia's European influences and aspirations. The city was founded under gruelling conditions by Peter the Great as his 'window on the West' at the only point where traditional Russian territory meets a seaway to northern Europe. Built with 18th and 19th century European pomp and orderliness, mainly by European architects, the result is a city that remains one of Europe's most beautiful. Where Moscow intimidates, St Petersburg enchants".*

Because of its history, St Peterbsurg's most important **primary tourism resources** are architectural features in the old historical centre of the city. This concentration is highlighted in figure 9.86, which shows a sketch map of the city prepared for English-speaking tourists. The location of the Peter and Paul Fortress can be seen clearly on this map, and the concentration of other historical buildings around this area is also evident.

The defensive walls of the Peter and Paul Fortress are still the oldest buildings in St Petersburg, and the island is thus an important primary tourism resource for the city (figure 9.81). Within the walls of the fortress, the Cathedral of Saints Peter and Paul, with its distinctive needle-like spire (figure 9.80) is a major attraction. Furthermore, during the summer months, the sandy and grassy surrounds of the fortress serve as an important sun bathing and swimming area (figure 9.82). In winter, when the angle of the sun's rays is much lower, many people sun bake by leaning in a standing position against the sloping fortress walls facing the sun, even when the river beside them is frozen.

9.81 *A close view of the walls of the Peter and Paul Fortress.*

9.82 *Local residents sun-bake beside the walls of the Peter and Paul Fortress during summer.*

As with most popular primary tourism resources in almost every city in the world, the large number of tourists visiting the Peter and Paul Fortress cause management and environmental challenges. In many cities that have good international connections, large numbers of visitors are likely not to speak the local language, which encourages signage using symbols rather than words. In the case of the Peter and Paul Fortress, many signs such as the one shown in figure 9.83 have been erected in an effort to minimise damage and pollution in the area.

9.83 *This sign attempts to manage the impact of tourism in the Peter and Paul Fortress.*

Just across the Neva River from the Peter and Paul Fortress is perhaps St Petersburg's best-known primary tourism resource, the green, while and gold buildings of the Hermitage Museum (figure 9.84). Claimed by many to be the world's most famous art gallery, the Hermitage is located in five connected buildings that comprised the Czar's former Winter Palace. Many people visit the Hermitage as much for its architecture as its works of art (figures 9.85 and 9.87). It was the storming of the Winter Palace by the Bolsheviks in 1917 that started the Russian Revolution, bringing communism to Russia for the subsequent 74 years.

9.84 *The Hermitage Museum is in the former Winter palace that was used by the Czars (kings) of Russia before the 1917 Communist revolution.*

9.85 *The extravagant interior architecture of the Hermitage.*

The scale of the hermitage is vast, consisting of 1,057 rooms and 117 staircases. Even so, there is only enough space to display about 10% of the total collection at any one time. In order to control numbers, and perhaps also to maximise profits, foreigners pay an entry price that is 15 times greater than the fee paid by Russians.

Another important primary tourism resource in central St Petersburg is St Isaac's Cathedral (figure 9.88). The cathedral, which is built in an Italian rather than Russian style, dominates the skyline of central St Petersburg.

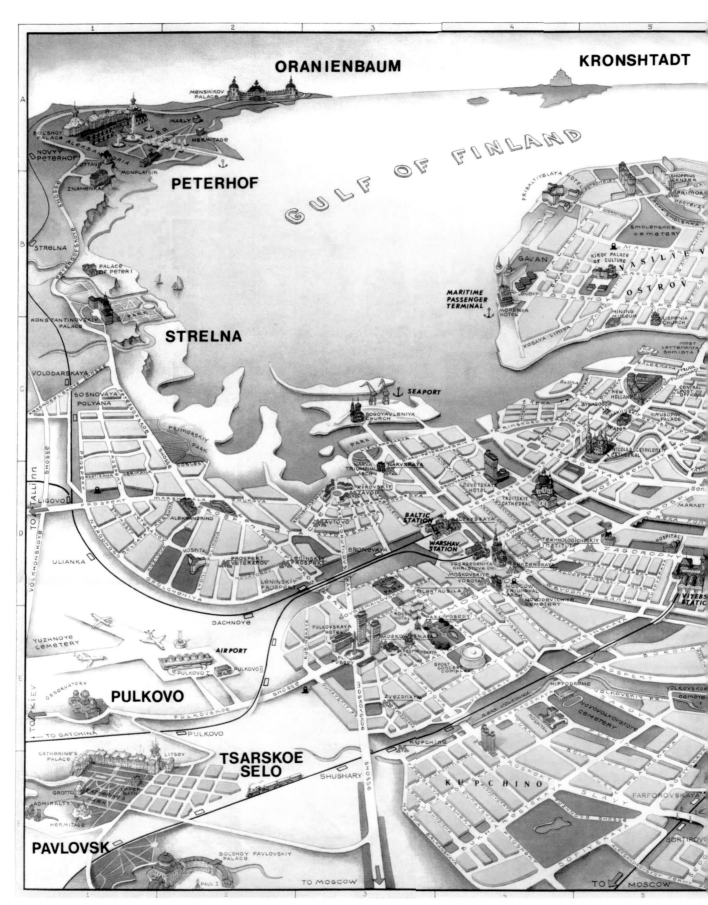

9.86 *Tourist map of St Petersburg. (courtesy: Aeroflot Russian International Airlines)*

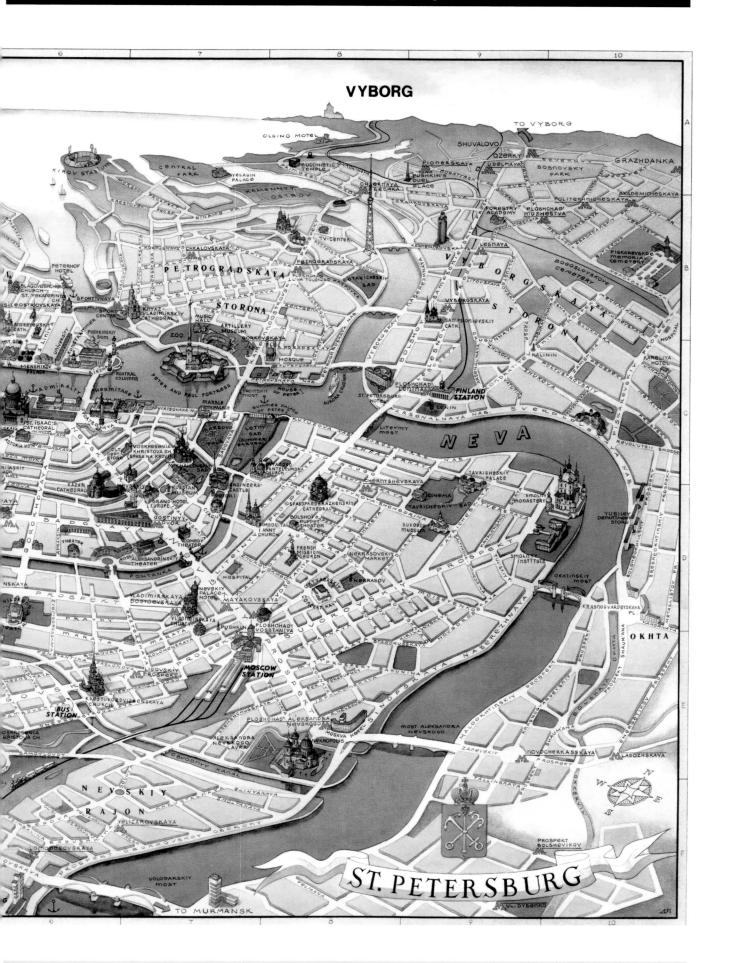

VYBORG

ST. PETERSBURG

Leisure, sport and tourism

9.87 *One of the many galleries within the Hermitage.*

9.88 *St Isaac's Cathedral, St Petersburg.*

9.89 *The interior of the dome in St Isaac's Cathedral.*

9.90 *A view across St Petersburg from the dome of St Isaac's.*

The attractions of the cathedral for visitors are both its elaborate architectural interior and the views from the external gallery that surrounds its golden dome, reached after a steep climb of over 250 stairs (figures 9.89 and 9.90). Between 1928 and 1990, St Isaac's Cathedral was simply a museum as the communist authorities banned religious services in the building. Today, the cathedral is once again a fully functioning centre of Christian worship.

Some of the attractions in central St Petersburg are of more recent historical interest. As seen in figure 9.86, St Petersburg's main street is the elegant Nevskiy (or Nevsky) Prospekt (*prospekt* — проспект — means 'grand avenue'). During World War II, St Petersburg was under siege from the German Army for 872 days from 9th September 1941 to 27th January 1944. During the 'Siege of Leningrad', as this event was known, the city was almost encircled by German forces, resulting in the deaths of almost 1.5 million local residents from starvation (in addition to about 350,000 deaths from military actions). The city survived only because the winters were usually severe and a large lake to the east of the city froze, enabling convoys of Soviet trucks to drive across the frozen lake and bring food through what became known as the 'Road of Life'.

While the siege was in force, Leningrad (St Petersburg) was under constant artillery fire from the German forces on the southern outskirts of the city, with the result that one side of Nevskiy Prospekt was sheltered while the other was exposed. The siege is remembered today with a simple memorial in Nevskiy Prospekt which consists of a renovated sign typical of many that lined Nevskiy Prospekt during the siege (figure 9.91). Still replenished every day with fresh flowers, the sign reads 'Citizens! At times of artillery bombardment, this side of the street is more dangerous'.

9.91 *A sign in Nevsky Prospekt dating from the siege of Leningrad warning residents to take shelter during artillery bombardment.*

Although most of St Petersburg's primary tourism resources are found in the old historic centre of the city, this is not always the case. One example of a major tourist site on the outskirts of St Petersburg is Peterhof (also known as Petrodvorets), which is located 30 kilometres west of central St Petersburg on the shoreline of the Gulf of Finland (figure 9.92).

Sometimes referred to as 'Russia's Versailles', Peterhof was Peter the Great's palace in the early 1700s and is set in extensive landscaped gardens with grand pavilions, artificial lakes and lavish fountains. The palace complex was almost destroyed during December 1941 and January 1942 when Stalin heard that Hitler was planning to hold a grand victory celebration there. The current buildings were reconstructed by Soviet authorities after World War II using photos, drawing and anecdotes.

9.92 *Peterhof, a palace on the outskirts of St Petersburg.*

9.93 *Mass graves at the Piskarevskoe Memorial Cemetery.*

Another example of a primary tourist resource that is found in the outer suburbs because of the large amount of land it occupies is the Piskarevskoe Memorial Cemetery (figure 9.93). This cemetery accommodates the mass unmarked graves of almost half a million of those people who died during the Siege of Leningrad. The graves cover many hectares, and are simply slightly raised mounds of earth, marked simply by the year of death. The entrance to the cemetery has an exhibition of historical photographs that need no translations.

For the same reason that Peterhof and the Piskarevskoe Memorial Cemetery lie in the outer suburbs of St Petersburg (i.e. they require large areas of land), some of the city's important **secondary tourism resources** are also found in the suburbs.

One example of this is St Petersburg's main airport, known as Pulkovo, which is situated 17 kilometres south of the city centre. There are two parts to the airport, Pulkovo-1 for domestic flights and Pulkovo-2 for international flights. Covering an area of 1,479 hectares, Pulkovo serves over six million passengers annually, making it Russia's fourth largest airport in terms of passenger capacity. By international standards, the airport is somewhat poorly equipped, lacking many of the facilities taken for granted in other countries, including air-bridges to connect the terminal with most aircraft (figure 9.94).

9.94 *The domestic terminal at St Petersburg's Pulkovo Airport.*

However, with the exception of some cheaper hotels that are situated on the city's outskirts to take advantage of cheaper land prices, most of St Petersburg's secondary tourism resources are found in the inner city areas where the primary tourism resources (and therefore most of the tourists) are situated. This applies especially to accommodation and transport services.

9.95 *The huge Moscow Hotel in St Petersburg was built during the Soviet era.*

Many of St Petersburg's hotels date from the Soviet era when large, institutional, characterless, concrete structures were the norm, usually featuring rude service and broken plumbing (figure 9.95). Being built during the

Soviet era, the location of these hotels bear no relationship to land values and are as likely to be located in central city locations and suburban areas.

Since the fall of communism, home stays and private flats have become available to tourists. Many of these flats are small in size but centrally located, making them very popular with travellers who want to avoid the expense and coldness of institutional hotels.

9.96 *A station in the Metro underground railway.*

St Petersburg has a cheap, clean and reliable underground railway network, known as the Metro, which is used by tourists as well as the local population (figure 9.96). Trains usually come every three minutes or so, and the network of routes serves the entire metropolitan area from the centre to the periphery. Being underground, the Metro is not affected by the city's climatic extremes such as heavy rain, sleet or snow. The Metro is supported by bus, trolley-bus and tram routes. Although the buses, trolley-buses and trams are older and more crowded than the Metro, they are also very cheap to use and the total public transport system means that few tourists are forced to rely on the more expensive taxis or less reliable private cars.

9.97 *A tourist boat on the Neva River in St Petersburg.*

One type of transport that is commonly used by tourists rather than local people in St Petersburg is canal and river

boats (figure 9.97 and 9.98). Because St Petersburg is situated on a delta, rivers and canals criss-cross many parts of the historic old centre of the city, which is also where many of the tourist attractions are located. Therefore, during the summer months from May to September, when tourist numbers are high and the rivers are not frozen, excursion boats provide river and canal tours as well as transport between key points, such as the Hermitage to Peterhof.

9.98 *A sightseeing boat on one of St Petersburg's canals.*

9.99 *Small privately owned stalls sell souvenirs near the entrance to the Peter and Paul Fortress.*

9.100 *This man has a small bear, and charges tourists to have their photo taken with it.*

Wherever tourists are found in significant numbers, retail outlets will spring up to cater for their needs and wants. During the communist era, retail outlets for tourists were restricted to shops in hotels and a few government-operated souvenir shops. Since the fall of communism, there has been rapid growth in small private enterprise stalls for tourists (figure 9.99). These stalls usually sell refreshments, souvenir handicrafts such as matryoshka dolls and (ironically) Soviet-era memorabilia, and T-shirts. In recent years, informal retailing has sprung up, where entrepreneurs establish a mobile presence in parks or gardens frequented by tourists to get donations in return for performing animal acts (figure 9.100).

An important group of secondary tourism resources is places to eat, such as cafés and restaurants. As one might expect in a large city with four and a half million people, St Petersburg has a vast range of dining options for tourists, from cheap stand up cafeterias to very expensive restaurants. The distribution of these dining places closely follows the broad pattern of tourist distribution in St Petersburg, which means there is a concentration of services in the old historic city centre. As Russia has opened up to outside countries, more and more overseas influence has become apparent in the city's dining options — evidence of globalisation — and Chinese, Japanese, Korean, Indian and American offerings are now widespread (figure 9.101).

9.101 *A McDonald's restaurant in St Petersburg, Russia.*

QUESTION BLOCK 9L

1. *Explain what is meant by the terms 'primary tourism resource' and 'secondary tourism resource'. Give five examples of each in St Petersburg.*

2. *Study figure 9.86. Note that Metro stations are marked by the red letter "M". Describe the distribution and location of (a) primary tourism resources, and (b) secondary tourism resources.*

3. *Using the information in this section, and any other information you can find about St Petersburg, suggest reasons for the pattern you described in question 2.*

4. *What strategies have been put into place in St Petersburg to manage tourist demands, minimise conflicts between local residents and visitors, and avoid environmental damage?*

Tourism Management in Rural Areas

The issues confronting tourism in rural areas are quite different to those concerning urban tourism, such as in St Petersburg. In many rural areas, concerns have been expressed about the impact of tourism and other land uses on the wildlife population. This led to the development of the concept of **carrying capacity**, which was defined by the United Nations World Tourism Organisation in 1992 as *"the maximum use of any site without causing negative effects on the resources, reducing visitor satisfaction, or exerting adverse impact upon the society, economy or culture of the area"*. It follows from this that **carrying capacity analysis** is the application of the concept of carrying capacity to a particular area.

Other definitions of carrying capacity have been a little more straightforward. In 1982, Mathieson and Wall defined carrying capacity as *"the maximum number of people who can use a site without an unacceptable alteration in the physical environment and without an unacceptable decline in the quality of the experience gained by visitors"*. In 1997, Middleton and Hawkins Chamberlain defined it as *"the level of human activity an area can accommodate without the area deteriorating, the resident community being adversely affected or the quality of visitors experience declining"*.

There are other definitions also, but the basic idea of the concept of carrying capacity is that there is a limit, or threshold, beyond which tourists cause damage or strain to the environment as well as to the quality of their own experience (figure 9.102). In other words, tourism (and most human activities) bring pressures upon the natural and cultural environment, and if a certain limit (the carrying capacity) is exceeded, these pressures threaten the conservation of the environment, quality of life and the sustainability of development.

9.102 *This group of tourists seem to overwhelm the temples at Angkor, Cambodia.*

To some extent, analysing the carrying capacity of an area requires an element of subjective judgement. If environmental or cultural damage is being analysed, a value judgement is needed to decide at which point the impact exceeds some acceptable standard. For example, in an area where hiking occurs, a certain number of walkers could lead to compaction of the soil. Although this represents a change to the natural environment, the decision on whether it also represents damage to the environment depends on the consequences of the soil compaction (if any), the fragility of the environment being analysed, the other land uses in the area, and in the end, value judgements by those undertaking the analysis.

Four types of carrying capacity have been identified that relate to tourism. **Economic carrying capacity** relates to how dependent the economy is upon tourism. **Psychological carrying capacity** refers to the level of satisfaction the tourist expresses for the destination. **Environmental carrying capacity** is concerned with how much impact tourism has on the physical environment. Finally, **social carrying capacity** focuses on the reaction of a local community to tourism. Each of these types of carrying capacity overlaps to some extent with the others, but it is still possible for one type of carrying capacity to be exceeded for a period of time before it starts to impact on the others.

In the 1960s and 1970s, researchers tried to use the concept of carrying capacity to calculate the number of tourists that certain areas could sustain without causing unacceptable social or environmental changes. Nowadays, most researchers realise that the issue is far too complex for such a simplistic quantitative approach. This is because it is now recognised that different types of tourists will display quite different types of behaviour — an individual backpacker does not have the same impact as a member of a football supporters' tour group, for example — and this makes it very difficult to legislate maximum numbers of people allowed into an area (figure 9.103).

Andrew Holden, who is Professor in Environment and Tourism at the University of Bedfordshire, suggests that there are ten factors which influence the carrying capacities of tourism destinations:

- fragility of the landscape to development and change;
- existing level of tourism development and supporting infrastructure (such as sewage treatment facilities);
- the number of visitors;
- the type of tourist and their behaviour;
- the degree of emphasis placed on the environmental education of tourists and local people;
- economic divergence and dependency upon tourism;
- levels of unemployment and poverty;
- attitudes of local people to the environment and their willingness to exploit it for short-term gain;
- the existing level of exposure of cultures and communities to outside influences and other lifestyles; and
- the level of organisation of destination management.

Case study of Etosha National Park, Namibia

Applying the concept of carrying capacity can be a useful tool when developing strategies to manage tourism in rural areas. This will be illustrated with reference to one particular case study, Etosha National Park in Namibia.

9.104 *The white salt surface of Lake Etosha.*

Etosha National Park is centred on a large salt pan in central Namibia — the word '*etosha*' means 'Great White Place' (figure 9.104). The park is located about 400 kilo-

9.103 *This sign at the entrance of Mago National Park in southern Ethiopia outlines the regulations for visitors.*

metres north of Namibia's capital city, Windhoek. The salt pan covers about 4,730 square kilometres, and at its widest point it is about 110 kilometres long by 60 kilometres wide. The pan is usually dry, although it does flood after heavy rains swell its two tributary rivers, the Ekuma and Oshigambo, which flow into Etosha from the north.

Until about two million years ago, the Etosha salt pan was a large inland sea. However, tectonic movements and climatic changes altered the course of the Kunene River that fed the sea, which began to flow westwards into the Atlantic Ocean. As a consequence, Etosha today is a depression made up of clay, silt and mineral salts that were left behind as the water evaporated.

9.105 *Zebras drink water at a waterhole in Etosha National Park.*

The park, which covers an area of 22,912 square kilometres, embraces the salt pan and its surrounding lands. When it was first established in 1907, it covered an area of about 80,000 square kilometres, but several reductions resulted in its present size. Because the salt pan represents a source of moisture, the park has an abundance of wildlife, with 114 mammal species, 340 bird species, 16 species of reptiles and amphibians and huge numbers of insects. The park contains many well developed water holes that enable visitors to see lions, zebras, giraffes, elephants, springboks, rhinoceros, warthogs, jackals, hyena, wildebeest and kudu, among many other types of animals, with relative ease (figures 9.105 and 9.106).

9.106 *Elephants at a water hole in Etosha National Park.*

Because of the area's dry climate, the way water is used is an important aspects of managing the park's carrying capacity. Some animals have adapted to the dry climate by developing the ability to obtain the moisture they need from their food. These animals are therefore mostly independent of surface water for their survival. However, most animals and birds in the park, and especially the larger species, must have access to drinking water every day. The feeding range of these species is limited to a distance within one day's walk of a water source.

The Etosha salt pan provides no drinkable water. It is only during a few months of the wettest years that the pan holds water, and even then, the water is twice as saline as sea water, and is thus not drinkable. Fortunately, there are perennial natural springs and water holes in the lands on the southern rim of the salt pan, and these explain the abundance of wildlife in the park (figure 9.107).

9.107 *An oryx at a waterhole in Etosha National Park.*

In order to minimise conflicts with the park's neighbours, who complained that lions were killing their livestock, fences were built to enclose Etosha National Park in 1973. This changed the feeding patterns of larger grazing animals such as elephants which had previously been free to migrate over huge distances, following the changing availability of water with the seasons. As a result, the animals in the park now depend exclusively on food and water available within the fenced perimeters. In order to maintain wildlife numbers, this forced the park management to build artificial watering points and to manage the water holes to prevent unnaturally large concentrations of animals which could cause overgrazing.

Etosha's wildlife is its major primary tourism resource, attracting over 850,000 visitors in 2006 (the most recent year for which statistics are available), an increase of 7% over the previous year. The revenue from tourism is very important to Namibia's development. Government statistics suggest that the income from tourism in the country's national parks exceeds US$150 million per annum, while the annual cost of maintaining and running the parks is only US$5 million.

9.108 *One of the entry gates into Etosha National Park.*

9.109 *Cabins at the Okaukuejo campsite in Etosha National Park.*

9.110 *This sign at Okondeka waterhole reminds visitors that they may not get out of their cars for reasons of safety.*

Visitor numbers are controlled in two major ways. First, an entry fee of $4 per person plus $3 per vehicle is charged at the entry gate to the park (figure 9.108). Second, and more significantly, the amount of accommodation (secondary tourism resource) within the park is controlled. There are three camps run by NWR (Namibia Wildlife Resorts), a government (Ministry of Environment and Tourism) agency that operates campsites throughout Namibia. The three campsites — Namutoni, Halali and Okaukuejo — are spaced at intervals of about 70 kilometres along the southern side of the salt pan to disperse the

concentration of tourists (figure 9.109). All visitors must stay in the designated camps, which are within fenced compounds to keep out dangerous animals after dark. Camping or staying outside the compounds is strictly forbidden for safety reasons. Each of the campsites has a floodlit water hole for nocturnal wildlife viewing.

In order to minimise the impact of tourists on the park environment, strict enforcement of rules and regulations is carried out. The most common tourist offences are speeding, off-road driving, littering and getting out of vehicles at non-designated areas (figure 9.110). Driving speeds within the park are limited to 50 kilometres per hour to protect the wildlife, and park officials are purchasing speed measuring equipment to enforce this limit more strictly (figure 9.111).

9.111 *A typical road in Etosha National Park.*

Other regulations are enforced in Etosha to control human impact on the environment. For example, access to the western part of the park is restricted to registered Namibian tour operators; individual visitors are not allowed to enter this section of the park. Weapons such as firearms, air guns and catapults are prohibited. Furthermore, there is a total prohibition on removing wildlife or plants from the National Park area. Making noise of any kind at any water hole is forbidden between the hours of 9:30 pm and 6:00 am.

QUESTION BLOCK 9M

1. *Having considered the various definitions of 'carrying capacity' express a definition in your own words.*

2. *How might each of Holden's ten factors relate to the carrying capacity of Etosha National Park?*

3. *Classify the strategies to manage carrying capacity in Etosha National Park according to the four categories: (a) economic, (b) psychological, (c) environmental, and (d) social.*

Leisure at the Local Scale — Sport and Recreation

The Leisure Hierarchy

A **hierarchy** is a system or organisation in which people or groups are ranked one above the other according to status or authority. Earlier in this chapter we looked at sports leagues, and noted that they usually operate as a hierarchy. Hierarchies exist at many levels in geography. Within cities, most people understand that there is a hierarchy of retail activities. In other words, we tend to find a small number of very large department stores (usually in the city centre), a larger number of medium sized stores (perhaps in the suburbs), and an even larger number of small shops selling convenience goods that are purchased at a high frequency.

Hierarchies also exist for urban settlements. Most countries (as well as states and regions within countries) have a large number of small settlements, and a smaller number of progressively larger settlements. In general, most people have to travel shorter distances to reach smaller shops and settlements than large ones because there are more small hops (and settlements) than large ones.

The same principle applies is the area of sports and recreation, where it is termed the **leisure hierarchy**. Figure 9.112 shows the leisure hierarchy as it might apply in one country, but the principle could be applied to most places.

At the top level of the hierarchy are international cities with a strong attraction to tourists, such as New York, Paris, London, Hong Kong, Sydney and Singapore. These cities tend to have large international airports that have the potential to draw visitors from all parts of the world with famous attractions, galleries and museums. Furthermore, they have well developed leisure facilities that appeal to people of many disparate tastes (figure 9.113).

9.113 *The signs in Hong Kong's Central district indicate a wide range of tourist-oriented services, including shops and restaurants.*

At the second level, towns and cities whose leisure facilities are significant at the national scale are found. Some of these cities have particular attractions that draw visitors, such as beaches in the case of Penang (Malaysia) and Coolangatta (Australia), or perhaps significant cultural attractions, such as those found in Angkor (Cambodia) and Lalibela (Ethiopia, figure 9.114).

9.114 *St George's church in Lalibela (Ethiopia) is a rock-hewn building, creating by excavation from the surrounding stone.*

The third level of the hierarchy includes towns that lack the attraction of second level towns, but which nonetheless attract visitors from their surrounding region. These cities may have weaker transport connections that limit visitor numbers (such as Akureyri in Iceland and Lijiang in China, figure 9.115), or simply fewer features to attract visitors from far afield despite their relatively large size (such as Birmingham in the UK or Novosibirsk in Russia).

International scale tourism cities
e.g. Sydney

Cities that provide leisure facilities to a national population
e.g. Coolangatta

Cities that provide leisure facilities to a regional hinterland
e.g. Cooma

Small cities and towns that provide leisure facilities to a local population
e.g. Bega

9.112 *The Leisure Hierarchy (using Australia as an example)*

9.115 *Shops in Lijiang, China.*

9.117 *Sports facilities at their most basic — a public ping-pong table in Konso Ethiopia.*

Intra-urban Spatial Patterns

As described above, leisure hierarchies exist between urban centres. The economic forces that operate to develop the leisure hierarchy also work within urban centres to develop distinctive spatial patterns of recreational and sports facilities.

9.116 *A cinema in Whitehorse, Canada.*

At the lowest level of the leisure hierarchy are towns that provide leisure facilities to the local population, but which attract few if any tourists from further afield. The types of leisure facilities in such towns will depend on cultural factors, but may include cinemas, parks and video games halls (figure 9.116). In LEDCs, the range of leisure facilities may be even more limited, and in many villages in developing countries, they may be limited to a foosball facility or a public ping-pong table (figure 9.117).

In general, land towards the centre of towns and cities in MEDCs have higher values than land on the periphery. Therefore, recreational facilities that need large areas of land are more likely to be found near the outskirts of such towns, while leisure activities that need less space and return higher profits are usually concentrated towards the town centre where accessibility is greatest. Examples of leisure facilities commonly found in town centres include cinemas, restaurants and theatres, while typical outer urban leisure facilities include swimming pools, tennis courts, ovals, sports grounds and football fields (figure 9.118). Of course, exceptions occur to this pattern, usually for specific historical or political reasons.

Another common intra-urban spatial pattern is that the quality of leisure facilities may decline with distance from the city centre. We can describe this as being an **inverse**

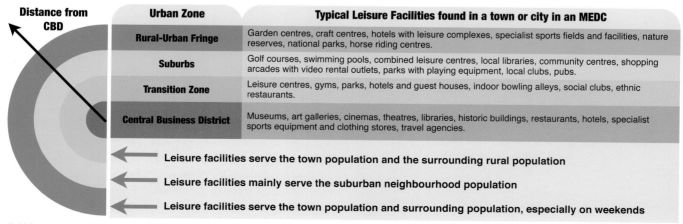

Distance from CBD	Urban Zone	Typical Leisure Facilities found in a town or city in an MEDC
	Rural-Urban Fringe	Garden centres, craft centres, hotels with leisure complexes, specialist sports fields and facilities, nature reserves, national parks, horse riding centres.
	Suburbs	Golf courses, swimming pools, combined leisure centres, local libraries, community centres, shopping arcades with video rental outlets, parks with playing equipment, local clubs, pubs.
	Transition Zone	Leisure centres, gyms, parks, hotels and guest houses, indoor bowling alleys, social clubs, ethnic restaurants.
	Central Business District	Museums, art galleries, cinemas, theatres, libraries, historic buildings, restaurants, hotels, specialist sports equipment and clothing stores, travel agencies.

← **Leisure facilities serve the town population and the surrounding rural population**

← **Leisure facilities mainly serve the suburban neighbourhood population**

← **Leisure facilities serve the town population and surrounding population, especially on weekends**

9.118 *Provision of leisure facilities in a typical town in a More Economically Developed Country.*

9.119 *Cricket facilities in central Mumbai (India).*

9.120 *Cricket facilities in inner Mumbai (India).*

9.121 *Cricket facilities in suburban Mumbai (India).*

9.122 *The area of bare earth in the right foreground shows a field used for playing cricket in a shanty area of outer suburban Mumbai.*

relationship between distance and quality, meaning that as one factor (distance) increases, the other factor (quality of the leisure facility) declines. This effect is known as **distance-decay**, and an example can be seen in the four photos of cricket facilities in Mumbai (India) in figures 9.119 to 9.122.

Urban Regeneration

In recent years, sport and tourism have been recognised as significant factors in regenerating rundown sections of urban areas. The role of sport in urban regeneration was first highlighted on a major scale when several cities such as Rome, Munich, Seoul and Barcelona hosted the Olympic Games and used the event as a catalyst to revitalise run-down parts of the city. This had led national and even local governments, especially in Europe, to recognise the potential of sport as a way to initiate urban regeneration.

The use of sport to boost urban regeneration has been especially strong in the United Kingdom. Many local government authorities in the UK offer funding for projects that will boost tourism (especially business tourism, conferences and heritage tourism), and when combined with other government grants that promote development projects in economically depressed areas, the result can be sports or leisure-driven urban regeneration.

One example of such a project was the Millennium Stadium in Cardiff (figure 9.123). The Stadium opened in June 1999 as the new home of the Wales national rugby union team and the Wales national football (soccer) team. With a seating capacity of 74,500 people, it is the largest stadium in the world with a fully retractable roof.

9.123 *The Millennium Stadium in Cardiff (Wales, UK).*

Despite its location on very valuable land near the centre of Cardiff, it was decided to build the Millennium Stadium on the same site as an older stadium, known as Cardiff Arms Park. Although Cardiff Arms Park was a relatively new structure, having been renovated most recently in 1982, its seating capacity of 53,000 was considered too small and its facilities were regarded as inadequate. The construction resulted in the demolition of several adjacent buildings, including a swimming pool, a telephone exchange and several office buildings. The result was a much more open space with access to the river and more accessibility to local residents.

When urban renewal occurs through sport and leisure activities, or indeed any economic trigger, there is a **multiplier effect** through the local economy. This means that as each dollar spent on urban renewal moves from person to person through the local economy, the actual benefits of the inflow of cash becomes multiplied several times. Thus, a leisure project that generates many new jobs (such as a new hotel) will have a greater multiplier effect than a more capital-intensive leisure development, such as a sports ground (once the initial construction phase has been completed). On the other hand, if the new developments are mainly in the hands of foreign operators, there will be a considerable leakage of profits to the home country, therefore reducing the beneficial effects of the multiplier effect in the location the new leisure facility.

Conflicts sometimes arise between different interest groups when new leisure-oriented urban developments are proposed. This is especially likely when demolition of people's homes is threatened. Residents are likely to claim that money would be better spent on improving housing quality or local people's welfare than on leisure facilities that are designed to attract outsiders and change the character of the area. Developers are likely to claim that land values will be enhanced by the new development and that it will boost the local economy by creating new jobs and supporting services. Of course, rising land values are unlikely to please many local residents who may be forced to move as they can no longer afford rents in the area. Furthermore, rising land values usually mean that the character of the urban area changes as more upwardly mobile professional people are attracted to the refurbished housing and new developments that become viable with rising land values.

For these reasons, tourist and leisure developments are often divisive and emotional as claims and counter-claims are argued, frequently through the media if any high-profile or well-known companies or individuals are involved. The response of some governments is to require that new leisure developments include provisions for enhancing the quality of life or job opportunities of local residents.

QUESTION BLOCK 9N

1. *Using the information in this section and figure 9.112, define the term 'leisure hierarchy' and give examples of each level from two countries, one of which is your home country.*

2. *In your own words, describe the pattern shown in figure 9.118.*

3. *Discuss the accuracy of the pattern shown in figure 9.118 with respect to the town or city where you live.*

4. *Using specific examples, including some from your own personal knowledge and research, discuss the role of sport and recreation in regeneration strategies of urban areas.*

Sustainable Tourism

Sustainable Management of Tourism

The former President of the Royal Geographical Society, Sir Crispin Tickell, made the following comment about sustainable tourism:

"Is sustainable tourism' a contradiction in terms?

Some people certainly think so. Sustainability carries the idea of self-regulating societies in which economic and social change are broadly accommodated. But tourism means intrusion, disruption and damage, no matter its scale.

Yet tourism can be good too. It is now the world's largest industry, generating wealth and employment, opening the minds of both visitors and visited to different ways of life, and promoting that adjustment to change known as globalisation. The right to travel has become an icon of personal liberty, but rights carry obligations, and if tourism isn't to be like the Indian god Kali, both creator and destroyer, we need a balance."

Tourism is **sustainable** if it can be conducted in its present form in perpetuity. For this to happen, what is used must be matched to what can be renewed or re-placed. Sustainability has four facets – environmental sustainability, social sustainability, cultural sustainability and economic sustainability. As tourism extends towards increasingly exotic locations, the concept of sustainability becomes all the more important (figures 9.124 and 9.125).

Tourism to **Antarctica** is a new industry, and it is still very small in scale. In 1983, about 2,000 tourists visited Antarctica. This figure had risen to 6,700 in 1993, and 14,700 by

9.124 *This sign in Lijiang (China) encourages tourists to behave in a sustainable way.*

9.125 *This bilingual sign at a hotel in Costa Rica lists the measures being taken to ensure tourism is sustainable.*

9.126 *Travellers who seek remote places in extreme climates often have a greater affinity with the environment than tourists who head to resorts and more commercially oriented destinations.*

2000. Tourists who venture to Antarctica are usually in search of a wilderness experience, hoping to go somewhere that is 'off the beaten track', and interested in an 'environmental' rather than a 'restful' experience (figure 9.126). There are health risks – hypothermia, sun-burn, dehydration, frostbite and snow blindness. Tourism is only possible in summer. In fact, tourism is prohibited in winter because pack ice extends for 1,000 kilometres around the continent, making access by ship impossible. In any case, Antarctica is dark for 24 hours per day during winter, and its temperatures can fall as low as –80°C to -90°C, so there is limited appeal to tourists anyway. The high cost of Antarctic tourism, about $US5,000 for 14 days, limits the numbers of tourists to the area also.

The main human activity carried out in Antarctica is scientific research, and tourism has to conform to the needs of the researchers. Antarctica's value for research will be lowered if it becomes polluted or significantly disturbed.

In a cold, fragile environment such as Antarctica, almost every human activity has some impact on the environment. The activities that take place in Antarctica tend to have a significant local impact, but of greater concern are the activities taking place outside Antarctica that have significant, widespread and long-lasting impacts. A well-

known example of this is the annual 'ozone hole' above Antarctica. This is caused by the release of human-manufactured chlorofluorocarbons (CFCs), mostly from the industrialised northern hemisphere.

The fragility of the Antarctic environment was recognised in 1991 when an international Protocol on Environmental Protection to the Antarctic Treaty was signed.

The protocol aims to protect the Antarctic environment, and it makes the following points:
- Antarctica is designated as a 'natural reserve devoted to peace and science';
- Mineral activities are prohibited for at least 50 years, except for scientific minerals research; and
- All activities are to be conducted in a manner that limits adverse environmental impacts.

Tourists who go to Antarctica are given strict instructions on how to preserve the fragile environment. Typical advice would include the following:
- Do not dispose of litter or garbage on land. Open burning is prohibited;
- Do not disturb or pollute lakes or streams. Any materials discarded at sea must be disposed of properly;
- Do not paint or engrave names or graffiti on rocks or buildings;
- Do not collect or take away biological or geological specimens or human artefacts as a souvenir, including rocks, bones, eggs, fossils, and parts of buildings;
- Do not deface or vandalise buildings, whether occupied or unoccupied, especially emergency refuges.

QUESTION BLOCK 9O

1. *Why do some people regard ecotourism as important?*

2. *What is meant by the term 'sustainable tourism'?*

3. *Explain how tourism to increasingly exotic locations, such as Antarctica, can cause conflicts. How can these conflicts be managed?*

10

The geography of food and health

The health of a population is the direct consequence of having enough food, a balanced diet and reduced susceptibility to disease.

Outline

ToK BoX — Page 438
Human Welfare

Health

Variations in Health

Most societies regard people as their most precious resource. Few things matter more to people than their good health. Good health affects the way people feel and ultimately the length of their lives. Even in economic terms, a healthy population is important. A population which is weakened with sickness and disease will not work well and will cost the society large sums of money in health care.

Like many features in the world, health is distributed unevenly. Many different indicators are used to measure the quality of health, but perhaps the most basic is **life expectancy**, which is defined as the average number of years that a person may expect to live at the time of their birth. There has been a long-term trend for average life expectancies to increase in most parts of the world, and this has been very evident in the period from 1950 to the present day (figure 10.1). Nonetheless, there are significant differences, as can be seen by looking at the present world pattern of life expectancy (figure 10.2).

Despite the overall improvements in health standards, even today Africans can expect to live an average of only 52 years, compared with Asians 66 years and South Americans 69 years. The average life expectancy in Sierra Leone (West Africa) is only 43 years, while half of all Zambians die before reaching 38. The average life expectancy in Swaziland is 40, although twenty years earlier in 1990 it was 58 years, the difference being due to the impact of AIDS. Indeed, figure 10.1 shows a general downward trend in life expectancies in southern Africa, and this is largely the results of AIDS. Further evidence of this pattern is provided in figure 10.3, which shows the twenty countries with the largest changes in average life expectancies since 1970. This figure shows an overall trend towards longer life expectancies (in green), the exceptions being several African countries (nine of the ten countries shown in red) where life expectancies have decreased markedly because of the impact of AIDS.

On the other hand, medical advances have improved the health of Europeans, who live to an average age of 73 years, as well as Americans (78 years), Canadians (81

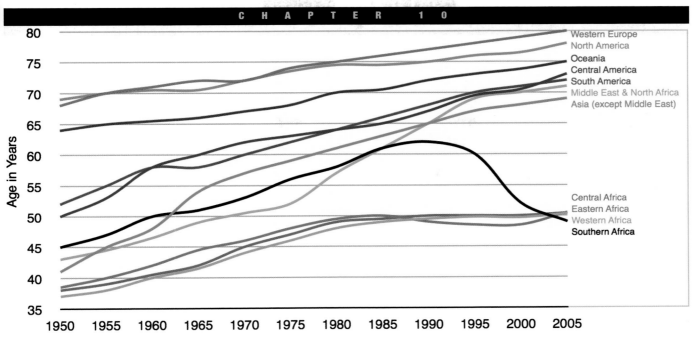

10.1 *Life expectancy at birth, selected regions, 1950 - 2005. Source: UNAIDS and the World Bank*

years) and Japanese, who have the world's longest average life expectancy — 83 years.

There are significant differences between the diseases which affect people in traditional societies compared with the diseases that affect people in industrialised nations. Some of the diseases and health conditions which are found in LEDCs, such as malnutrition, malaria, river blindness and cholera, are sometimes referred to as **diseases of poverty**. On the other hand, health problems that become more common as a country industrialises and becomes wealthier, such as heart disease, obesity, strokes and cancers, are sometimes called **diseases of affluence, or diseases of over-development**.

Question Block 10A

1. *Describe the pattern shown in figure 10.2.*

2. *Describe and account for the contrast in life expectancies between developed and developing countries.*

3. *Compare the patterns shown in figures 10.2 and 1.37 (in chapter 1), and suggest reasons for any similarities you can identify.*

4. *Describe the overall trend shown in figure 10.1, noting and explaining any exceptions.*

5. *Suggest reasons for each the 20 trends in life expectancy shown in figure 10.3.*

Measuring Health

Life expectancy, as discussed in the previous section, is a somewhat crude measure of health standards as it fails to consider the negative impact that poor health can have on quality of life. To overcome this shortcoming, in the early 1990s Canadian statisticians developed a more finely-tuned measure called the **HALE** (**health-adjusted life expectancy**). Whereas the conventional measure of life expectancy considered all years of life as being equal, the HALE weighted years of life according to health status, with healthy years being regarded as more valuable than

>> Some Useful Definitions

Disability-adjusted-life years (DALY) — a health measure based on years of "healthy" life lost by being in poor health or a state of disability.

Food miles — a measure of the distance that food travels from its source to the consumer. This can be given either in units of actual distance or of energy consumed during transport.

HALE — Health-adjusted life expectancy, based on life expectancy at birth, but also including an adjustment for time spent in poor health (due to disease and/or injury). It is the equivalent number of years in full health that a new-born baby can expect to live, based on current rates of ill-health and mortality.

Transnational corporation (TNC) — a firm that owns or controls productive operations in more than one country through foreign direct investment.

Food and health

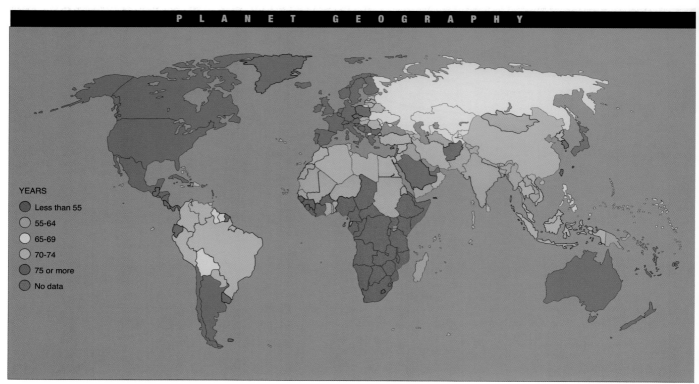

10.2 *Life expectancy at birth, 2008.*

years spent in poor health (due to disease or injury). In essence, the HALE is measured by calculating the number of years that a person can expect to live in full health, based on current rates of ill-health and mortality in that society. The gap between HALE and life expectancy represents society's **burden of ill health**.

The statisticians who developed HALE applied it to Canadian society at the time to ascertain the burden of ill health. The results of that initial study, which are shown in table 10.1, revealed that there is a greater gap between HALE and life expectancy for women than for men, and hence a greater burden of ill health. This suggests that although they live longer lives than men, women are more likely to be affected by the types of conditions that place a burden on the health care system than men.

As shown in table 10.1, the burden of ill health varied according to age group. At age 15, the difference between life expectancy and HALE in Canada was 14% for women

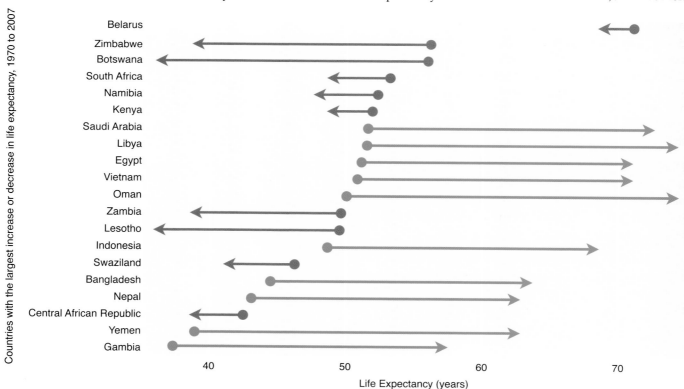

10.3 *Changes in life expectancy, selected countries, 1950 - 2007. Source: World Bank*

Table 10.1
Life Expectancy and HALE, Canada, 1990-92

BOTH SEXES	Life Expectancy	HALE	Difference		MEN	Life Expectancy	HALE	Difference		WOMEN	Life Expectancy	HALE	Difference	
At Age...	years	years	years	%	At Age...	years	years	years	%	At Age...	years	years	years	%
15	63.4	55.6	7.8	12	15	60.3	53.7	6.6	11	15	66.6	57.4	9.2	14
25	53.8	46.7	7.1	13	25	50.9	44.9	6.0	12	25	56.8	48.4	8.4	15
35	44.3	37.9	6.4	14	35	41.5	36.1	5.3	13	35	47.0	39.4	7.6	16
45	34.8	29.2	5.6	16	45	32.1	27.5	4.6	14	45	37.4	30.7	6.8	18
55	25.9	21.3	4.6	18	55	23.4	19.6	3.8	16	55	28.3	22.7	5.6	20
65	17.9	14.3	3.6	20	65	15.7	12.9	2.9	18	65	19.9	15.4	4.5	23
75	11.2	8.5	2.7	24	75	9.6	7.5	2.1	22	75	12.5	9.0	3.5	28
85	6.3	4.4	1.9	30	85	5.4	3.8	1.6	29	85	6.9	4.4	2.5	36

Source: Social and Economic Statistics Division, Statistics Canada.

and 11% for men, indicating a higher burden of ill health for women. One of the reasons for the gender difference is that on average, women live longer than men. As chronic health problems are more prevalent in old age, it follows that women tend to spend a longer period of life with chronic health problems than men. The Canadian research also showed that chronic health problems are less common among the wealthier members of society, who also tend to live longer than poorer people.

A more complex way of measuring the cost burden on a society imposed by poor health is the **disability-adjusted life year (DALY)**. DALY was developed by the World Health Organisation and the World Bank in the mid-1990s to provide a single figure that measures the impact on a society of premature death and disability.

A number of other indicators of health were discussed in detail in earlier chapters. For example, infant mortality rates were discussed in chapters 1 and 2, while calorie intake, access to safe drinking water and access to health services were discussed in chapter 2. All these measures are more useful in some areas than others, which is why it is helpful to consider a range of indicators when assessing the standards of health for a given population.

Disability-adjusted life years are calculated using the formula DALY = YLL + YLD, where YLL represents Years of Life Lost and YLD represents Years Lived with Disability. On this basis, one DALY represents one year of healthy life that is lost.

As a result of applying the DALY measure, the World Health Organisation announced that five of the ten main causes of disability in MEDCs were psychiatric conditions, and that psychiatric and neurological conditions accounted for 28% of all the years that are lived with disabilities.

The use of DALYs has been criticised by some researchers because of the value judgements said to be implicit in the measure. For example, because future years of life are discounted for disabilities, it has been calculated that 3,300 DALYs would equal 100 infant deaths or 5,500 people aged 50 living for one year with blindness. While such comparisons may be helpful for planners who are assessing priorities for health care, critics argue that the age-weighting and discounting are discriminatory, and may lead to a diversion of health care resources away from needy cases.

QUESTION BLOCK 10B

1. *Explain the difference between life expectancy and HAST.*

2. *Explain what is meant by the term 'burden of ill health'.*

3. *Study the information in table 10.1. Describe the main patterns evident and suggest reasons for these patterns.*

4. *Discuss the arguments for and against the use of DALYs as a useful indicator of health.*

Prevention Relative to Treatment

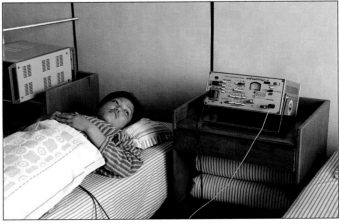

10.4 *The ward of a typical hospital emphasising curative health care.*

Most nations in the world emphasise **curative health care** facilities. In other words, governments spend money on hospitals and medical facilities which are designed to cure illnesses rather than prevent them (figure 10.4). Curative health care needs large numbers of hospitals, doctors, medicines and facilities. The results can be impressive where enough resources are allocated, with heart transplants, surgery and other techniques saving many lives. However, the sums of money involved are beyond the resources of many of the world's countries if curative health care is to be adequate.

10.5 *A lens grinding workshop using simple low-cost, low-tech equipment in Msalato, Tanzania.*

Primary health care is different to curative health care in that it combines prevention with cure. Many nations are coming to realise that it is better to prevent diseases where possible than to wait for people to get sick. Keeping people well enables them to work productively, feel better and not be a drain on government spending by being in hospital. Screening for diabetes, doing pap smears to detect cervical cancer in women, using sputum cytology to detect tuberculosis and mass inoculations for dis-

eases such as polio and Hepatitis B are cheap and could save millions of lives in LEDCs. It is estimated that providing all the primary health care needed in the world would cost an extra $50 billion per year for the next 20 years. This sounds like a large sum of money, but it is only a small percentage of what is spent on cigarettes around the world in a year, or $1/24$ what is spent annually on arms and the military.

In the 1960s, China introduced widespread primary health care. Thousands of paramedics, called barefoot doctors, were trained in the basics of medicine and sent to work in rural areas to care for farmers and their families. Similar systems have since been established in many countries, including Iran, Sudan, Jamaica, Botswana, Tanzania and Sri Lanka. Many LEDCs have realised that it is impossible, and inappropriate, to copy overseas health care systems without questioning their basic assumptions and financial demands. It is usually better to develop a system of health care which is affordable and suited to the specific needs of the country concerned (figure 10.5).

Reflecting (or perhaps contributing to) the differences in the quality of health standards around the world is the distribution of health care. There are vast differences between the ratio of doctors to people among the nations of the world. The countries with the most people per doctor are Ethiopia (60,000 people per doctor), Burkina Faso (57,220), Guinea (46,420) and Niger (39,730). The countries with the fewest people per doctor are Russia (180 people per doctor), Italy (230), the Czech Republic (270) and Bulgaria (280).

The broad world pattern of medical care provision, as measured by the number of doctors per 1,000 people, is

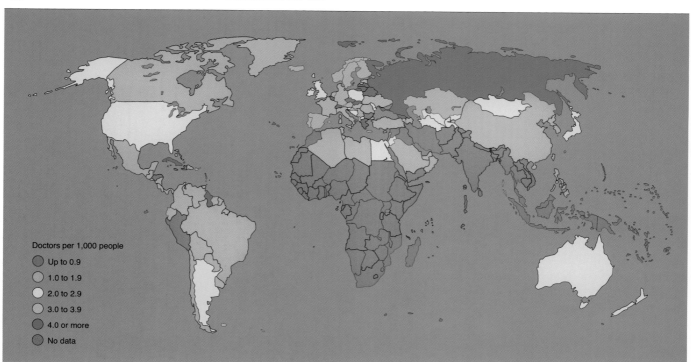

Doctors per 1,000 people
- Up to 0.9
- 1.0 to 1.9
- 2.0 to 2.9
- 3.0 to 3.9
- 4.0 or more
- No data

10.6 *World distribution of the quality of medical care, indicated by the number of doctors per 1,000 people.*

shown in figure 10.6. World scale maps such as this are useful to provide a broad general overview, but they can also be a little misleading, because even within countries, there can be vast differences in the standards of health care.

In most countries, one of the greatest differences occurs between urban and rural areas. Figure 10.7 shows a large hospital in the Chinese city of Harbin. Like most urban hospitals in China, it is well equipped, clean and efficient. However, people living in rural areas in most countries lack access to the equivalent standards of health care (figures 10.8 and 10.9).

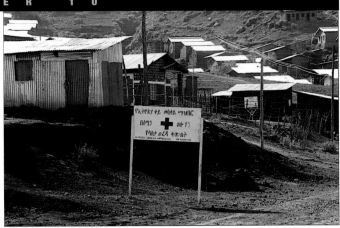

10.8 *A very simple hospital and medical clinic, Lalibela, Ethiopia.*

10.7 *A large hospital devoted to treating patients with traditional Chinese medicines in Harbin, China.*

10.9 *A small medical clinic in the village of Chengzhong (Guizhou, China) that serves a poor rural farming community in the surrounding area.*

Enlightened medical planners and policy-makers are increasingly emphasising **prevention**, as opposed to treatment, of disease. One example of a region where a focus on prevention is transforming the lives of poor, isolated farmers is **Majiang County** in China's Guizhou's province (figure 10.10).

Because of its isolation and difficult physical environment, Guizhou is one of China's poorest provinces. According to a local saying, Guizhou is the province of "The Three Noes" — there are no three days without rain, no three kilometres without a mountain, and no three coins in anyone's pocket (figure 10.11).

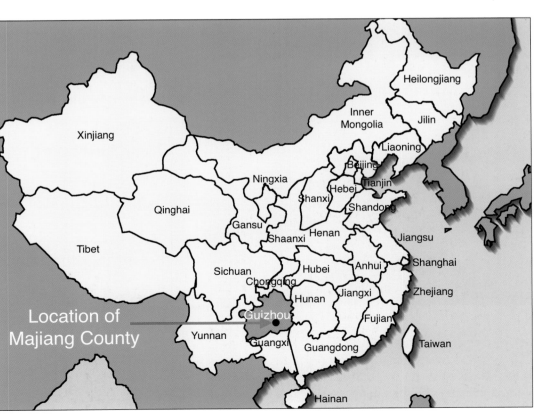

Location of Majiang County

10.10 *Location of Majiang.*

Food and health

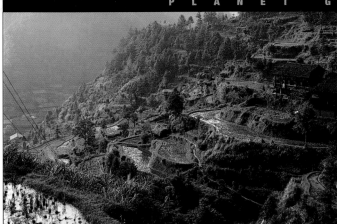

10.11 *Typical scenery in Majiang county, Guizhou province, China.*

Majiang is a rural county that has been designated by China's government as a 'poverty county' of national significance. It is situated near the centre of Guizhou province, about one and a half hour's drive east from the provincial capital of Guiyang. Situated beside the Qingshui (Clearwater) River, Majiang County has an area of 1,200 km² and a mild, wet, sub-tropical climate.

10.12 *Miao women in Majiang County.*

10.13 *Typical farmland in Majiang County, China.*

The area is populated by many minority ethnic groups, with the Miao group being the most populous (figure 10.12). Most of the county's 220,000 people live in small farming villages, although there are also nine designated townships in the county. The main farming products are rice, corn, and vegetables (figure 10.13). The town of Xiase in the east of Majiang county is famous for its dogs; its guard dogs are specially trained to maximise their aggression, which is perhaps easy to understand given the fact that they also are part of the local diet.

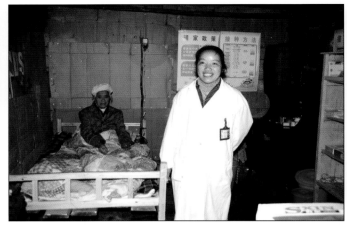

10.14 *A medical clinic in Chengzhong village, Majiang County.*

Majiang is an area with significant medical needs. Of the county's 129 villages, only six had clinics of an acceptable standard as at 2007. The clinic shown in figure 10.14 was fairly typical of the rural clinics available at the time, with leaking roofs, bare earth floors, open cabinets used for storing medical supplies, cardboard lining on the walls to keep out the wind, and damp, unhygienic conditions. Many of the clinics were so small that there was no room even for a bed to handle intravenous drips, which are the most common way of treating many conditions in the Chinese rural health care system. Consequently, the majority of rural doctors performed most of their work as house calls, carrying a heavy medical kit box long distances through the rice fields by foot (figure 10.15). It was (and is) quite common for doctors' house calls to require a walk of up to five kilometres, which can take about three hours in the difficult terrain of Majiang (figure 10.16).

10.15 *A doctor walks across a rice field to make a house call. On this visit, the doctor walked about ten kilometres each way from his village clinic.*

10.16 *A doctor makes an open-air house call near Gonghe village, Majiang County.*

Many of the doctors were poorly trained and were really paramedics rather than doctors, being equipped to handle only basic and routine medical issues. As an example, when asked by the author if he knew how AIDS is spread, one doctor in Majiang blushed heavily, and in a hesitating and embarrassed manner said "it depends on where you are sitting", noting that if you sit downwind of an AIDS-infected person you are more likely to become infected. The need for training of medical workers in Majiang ranked with the poor conditions of the clinics as a significant barrier to overcome if a preventative health care program was to be implemented.

The rural doctors keep very long hours, working on a 24/7 basis. It is quite common that if patients come to the clinics at meal times, they join the doctor's family for lunch or dinner, as most rural doctors live in their clinics, sleeping on the beds at night that are used for intravenous drips during the day. The most common problems dealt with are arthritis, high blood pressure, hepatitis B, tuberculosis and gynaecological issues.

The doctors' monthly salaries vary, but typical figures are 400 Renminbi Yuan per month (US$56), comprising 120 RMB (US$16.90) per month from the government, the balance coming from profits made on medicines sold. All consultations for basic medical issues are free for the patients. Even so, many people in the villages cannot afford treatment (because of the cost of the medicine), so most of the rural clinics operate on an IOU system. Over the course of a year, the IOUs can amount to about 5000 RMB (US$700), which is more than the doctor's annual income.

Another health-related issue facing medical policymakers in Majiang was that like many rural areas of China, Majiang was depopulating as young men left in search of work in the coastal cities of Guangzhou, Shenzhen and Xiamen. All the village's farming was (and still is) subsistence cultivation, and thus the only way for the county's poorly educated population to make money was

to send its young people to the coastal cities for work in construction and other labouring jobs. This has resulted in more and more women having to take on the farming work, but it also created fears that AIDS might spread when the men returned.

In 2004, concern with the low standards of health care and the desire to develop better preventative health care led the officials from the Majiang County Health Bureau to form a partnership with the Amity Foundation, an independent Christian voluntary NGO based in Nanjing, China.

10.17 *IB students provide voluntary labour to help build a new medical clinic in Chengzhong village, Majiang County.*

10.18 *The same clinic shown in figure 10.17 after completion.*

This led to the launch of a program by the Amity Foundation's Hong Kong bureau to raise the funds to build 100 new medical clinics in Majiang County. The aim was to provide well-built and well-equipped clinics built in highly accessible locations with sturdy concrete block construction and equipped with running water, electricity, a street-fronted medicine dispensary, several consultation rooms and a welcoming waiting area (figure 10.18). Being a partnership, the government agreed to match the funds raised, and by early 2009, 44 clinics had been built, 21 funded by the Amity Foundation and 23 by the Chinese government — some using voluntary labour to minimise costs and encourage deeper levels of understanding and commitment by outsiders (figure 10.17).

Significant geographical factors needed to be considered in locating the new clinics. According to Majiang County health officials, the priorities in deciding when and where to build clinics are determined by factors such as (1) whether or not the existing clinic building is actually collapsing, (2) how far the village is from the county hospital, and (3) the density of the local population.

As part of the partnership between Majiang County and the Amity Foundation, Amity has begun a program to upgrade the skills of village health workers, providing training and ongoing professional development. Having seen the early improvements in health care that this training has brought, the government has followed Amity's lead and has become involved in supporting the training of village doctors.

10.19 *Manure from pigs is combined with human excrement and stored in an underground tank to produce methane gas to power stoves and lights in Nabai village, Majiang County.*

10.20 *A resident of Nabai village turns on the biogas that will fuel her household stove and room lights.*

Another aspect of preventative health care in rural areas is improving hygiene. To this end, Amity began an innovative project in Majiang to promote the use of environmentally sustainable biogas energy. Centred on a Han nationality village called Nabai, Amity installed a total of 52 underground tanks in which a mixture of pig manure and human excrement is fermented to produce biogas, which is used to fuel small gas stoves and household lights (figures 10.19 and 10.20). Although the tanks need cleaning out every two years or so, the sludge is a very useful fertiliser for the fields. Local officials have noted how the biogas project seems to have resulted in a much cleaner and tidier town than many of the others in the county, and Nabai seems likely to become a model for other villages to emulate .

As a result of the improvement in Majiang's standards of preventative health care since the partnership between the county government and the Amity Foundation was established, Majiang now fulfils 95% of the government's health vaccination targets, which helps to explain why the county has experienced no serious epidemics since the partnership began. As a result of a vigorous public health education campaign, the percentage of pregnant woman delivering their babies in hospitals rose from just 2% in 2002 to over 80% in 2007.

10.21 *Anti-AIDS posters are prominently displayed in this medical clinic in Xuetou village, Majiang County.*

Within China, Guizhou appears in the middle of provincial rankings of AIDS, but within Guizhou, Majiang has the lowest incidence of HIV/AIDS among all counties — no cases whatsoever. To some extent, this can be explained by Majiang's high proportion of ethnic minorities, who tend to have more conservative attitudes towards sex than other groups. However, because of the fears of a possible epidemic when the county's migrant workers return, a large-scale preventative anti-AIDS campaign is underway throughout the county, even in the smallest and remote rural clinics (figure 10.21).

Majiang is an example of how careful planning and adequate funding of preventative health care can bring huge improvements in medical standards very quickly. Nonetheless, many challenges remain in Majiang. Because of the conservative attitudes of the county's population, women refuse to be treated by male doctors for gynaecological problems, and even for routine pregnancy checks. This means that most young doctors entering the rural clinics tend to be female, although there are also some husband-and-wife medical teams (figure 10.22).

10.22 *This husband and wife team share the role of doctor in this small medical clinic in Dachong village, Majiang County.*

At the time of publication of this book, many old clinics remained waiting to be replaced. Nonetheless, Majiang has emerged as a model county in terms of health care, and policy-makers visit Majiang from many other areas to learn from its example. This bodes well for the future development of preventative health care in rural areas of China.

QUESTION BLOCK 10C

1. *Look at the Tanzanian lens grinding workshop in figure 10.5. Explain why the level of technology in this workshop is most appropriate for an LEDC such as Tanzania.*

2. *Compare the types of countries that have low ratios of people to doctors with the countries that have high ratios of people to doctors, and relate this information to the pattern of life expectancy shown in figure 10.2.*

3. *State the location of Majiang County, and describe its geography.*

4. *List the ways in which Majiang County and the Amity Foundation have co-operated to promote preventative health care in Majiang County.*

5. *Describe the geographical factors that influence the location of new medical clinics in Majiang.*

6. *How successful do you think the promotion of preventative health care in Majiang has been?*

Food

Global Availability of Food

Why do farmers produce food? If your answer was 'to eat', you would only be half right. Food is grown by subsistence farmers to eat, but in the case of commercial farmers, food is grown to sell, usually for the highest price that can be found. Perhaps that is why we now have a situation in the world where we produce enough grain (mainly wheat and rice) to feed every man, woman and child in the world more than 3000 calories every day. This is **more than enough food** to feed everyone adequately, indeed more than adequately, even without allowing for any other food production such as vegetables, fruit, fish and meat (figure 10.23).

10.23 *A weight loss workshop does brisk business, surrounded by fast food outlets in New York, USA.*

10.24 *This American farm near Boulder, Colorado, has abandoned food cultivation and is now growing cut flowers as a result of U.S. government incentives to reduce the amount of land producing food crops.*

Indeed, the world has never before produced so much food per person than is happening now. In Europe and North America there are huge surplus stocks of wheat, butter, wine and other foods that simply cannot be sold for a price that would cover the cost of production. Farmers would often prefer to **dump** food into the ground or

Table 10.2
Average Annual Rate of Growth of Food Production and Per Capita Food Production, 1970 - 2005

All figures are percentages	Total Food Production				Per Capita Food Production			
World / Region	1970 - 1980	1980 - 1990	1990 - 2000	2000 - 2005	1970 - 1980	1980 - 1990	1990 - 2000	2000 - 2005
WORLD	**2.5**	**2.4**	**2.5**	**2.0**	**0.6**	**0.6**	**1.0**	**0.7**
MEDCs	**2.0**	**1.0**	**0.2**	**-0.3**	**1.2**	**0.3**	**-0.3**	**-0.6**
Industrialised countries	2.3	0.7	1.4	-0.8	1.4	0.0	0.7	-1.3
Transition economies	1.5	1.8	-3.6	1.8	0.6	1.0	-3.5	2.0
LEDCs	**3.0**	**3.6**	**4.0**	**3.2**	**0.7**	**1.5**	**2.3**	**1.6**
Latin America & Caribbean	3.6	2.5	3.4	3.7	1.1	0.4	1.7	2.2
Middle East & North Africa	3.1	3.5	2.9	3.4	0.3	0.7	0.7	1.3
Sub-Saharan Africa	1.1	2.9	3.1	1.9	-1.7	-0.1	0.4	-0.5
East and South-east Asia	3.3	4.4	5.2	4.0	1.4	2.7	3.9	3.0
South Asia	2.7	3.8	3.3	1.3	0.4	1.5	1.3	-0.4
Oceania LEDCs	2.2	1.7	1.9	1.2	-0.1	-0.6	-0.5	-0.9
North America LEDCs	-2.3	1.2	-0.9	0.5	-3.5	0.3	-1.3	-0.2
Continental groupings								
Africa	1.4	3.0	3.1	2.4	-1.4	0.1	0.6	0.1
Asia	n.a.	n.a.	4.3	3.1	n.a.	n.a.	2.6	1.8
Latin America	3.7	2.6	3.6	3.8	1.2	0.5	1.9	2.2
Caribbean	1.3	1.1	-1.1	1.1	-0.4	-0.5	-2.1	0.2
North America	2.8	0.6	2.2	-0.3	1.8	-0.4	1.1	-1.3
Oceania	2.2	1.4	3.8	0.0	0.6	-0.2	2.3	-1.3
Europe	n.a.	n.a.	1.4	-0.5	n.a.	n.a.	-1.7	-0.4

Source: Food and Agriculture Organisation *Summary Food and Agriculture Statistics.* Note: n.a. = not available

into the ocean than sell it for a price that is too low. In the United States, the government tries to reduce farming production by paying farmers *not* to produce a certain crop and take their land out of farming production (figure 10.24). This is because the government believes that a surplus of food on world markets will lower prices to farmers and reduce their incomes to an unacceptable level. In other words, the interests of the farmers in developed nations are being put before the interests of hungry people overseas.

The growth in world food production has not been consistent in all parts of the world, however. Table 10.2 shows the trends in world food production, both in terms of absolute production levels and food per capita. Although the quantity of food production has grown in most parts of the world, production per capita was declining regions,

with the largest declines occurring in Sub-Saharan Africa, the industrialised MEDCs and the LEDCs of Oceania. On the other hand, the largest increases in food production per capita have been occurring in East and South-east Asia and Latin America.

In spite of the overall glut of food on world markets, there has never been so many people suffering from **starvation** or **malnutrition** than now. To be malnourished, a person consumes fewer calories and less protein than they need to maintain health. **Chronic hunger** is long-term, whereas **periodic hunger** is short-term, caused by factors such as drought, famine, war, conflict or political upheavals. It has been estimated that about 850 million of the world's people suffer from chronic malnutrition, 220 million of them children. Of this number, between 18 and 20 million people die of starvation or starvation-related disease each year, a figure that translates to 50,000 people each day.

According to the World Health Organisation, one-third of the children in LEDCs are malnourished (figure 10.25). Over half the deaths of children under 5 years of age in LEDCs are related to malnutrition. Because of malnutrition among young mothers, many babies in LEDCs are born with very low birth weights, defined as below 2,500 grams. Children with low birth weights often have shortened life expectancies, greater risk of disease and sometimes retarded brain development.

Fortunately, the trend in world hunger is downwards, although like trends in food production per capita, the trend is not uniform in all parts of the world (table 10.3). Between 2000 and 2010, it is estimated that the rate of malnutrition in the world should fall by more than 10%,

10.25 *The small boy in the right foreground of this photo has a swollen belly that is a symptom of malnutrition. There is no evidence of malnutrition among the adults dancing at the sing-sing, or celebration, near Banz in the Highlands of Papua New Guinea; it is often the children who receive least food in some traditional societies.*

Table 10.3
Extent of Malnutrition, 1969 - 2002

World / Region	Percent of Population Malnourished				Number of Malnourished People (millions)			
	1969 - 1971	1979 - 1981	1990 - 1992	2000 - 2002	1969 - 1971	1979 - 1981	1990 - 1992	2000 - 2002
WORLD	n.a.	n.a.	n.a.	14	n.a.	n.a.	n.a.	852
MEDCs	n.a.	n.a.	n.a.	3	n.a.	n.a.	n.a.	38
Industrialised countries	n.a.	n.a.	n.a.	1	n.a.	n.a.	n.a.	9
Transition economies	n.a.	n.a.	n.a.	7	n.a.	n.a.	n.a.	28
LEDCs	37	29	20	17	961	925	824	815
Latin America & Caribbean	20	13	13	10	55	46	59	53
Middle East & North Africa	23	9	8	10	42	20	25	39
Sub-Saharan Africa	36	37	36	33	93	128	170	203
East and South-east Asia	43	28	16	12	504	401	277	217
South Asia	37	37	26	22	265	329	291	301
Oceania LEDCs	n.a.	n.a.	n.a.	n.a.	n.a.	n.a.	n.a.	n.a.
North America LEDCs	n.a.	n.a.	n.a.	n.a.	n.a.	n.a.	n.a.	n.a.
Continental groupings								
Africa	32	29	28	26	114	137	178	212
Asia	40	30	20	16	793	744	588	551
Latin America	19	12	12	9	50	41	52	46
Caribbean	26	20	27	21	5	5	8	7
North America	n.a.	n.a.	n.a.	n.a.	n.a.	n.a.	n.a.	n.a.
Oceania	n.a.	n.a.	n.a.	n.a.	n.a.	n.a.	n.a.	n.a.
Europe	n.a.	n.a.	n.a.	n.a.	n.a.	n.a.	n.a.	n.a.

Source: Food and Agriculture Organisation *Summary Food and Agriculture Statistics*. Note: n.a. = not available

Food and health

although that will still leave 680 million people malnourished. Africa is the main region where malnutrition is expected to increase, although some increase in South Asia is also expected.

At the same time, millions of people in more affluent societies are dying with diseases that are caused by over-consumption of food, or at least aggravated by over-eating the wrong types of food. Examples of such conditions include heart disease, strokes and some types of cancer. Over the past 50 years, United States aeroplane manufacturers have found that the average width of American bottoms has increased by almost 10 centimetres and that seats in aircraft must be widened accordingly. This is an enormous change in human evolutionary terms in a very short space of time, and it reflects the consequences of over-consumption of food combined with lack of exercise in that society.

Overall, the problem is certainly not that the world is producing insufficient food. Rather that there does seem to be some major problems with the **distribution** of the food that is produced. One problem is that commercial farmers (perhaps reasonably) will usually sell their produce to the person (or company) that will **pay the highest price**. Unfortunately, for many poor people in developing nations, they are usually the ones who cannot afford to pay the top prices (figure 10.26). As a result, the quantities of food available to humans (as measured by calorie intake) varies considerably from one part of the world to another (table 10.4).

Table 10.4
Food Availability Per Capita

All figures in kilocalories per day	Per Capita Food Availability			
World / Region	1969-71	1979-81	1989-91	2000-02
WORLD	**2,410**	**2,550**	**2,700**	**2,790**
MEDCs	**3,140**	**3,220**	**3,290**	**3,280**
Industrialised countries	3,050	3,130	3,290	3,450
Transition economies	3,320	3,390	3,280	2,920
LEDCs	**2,110**	**2,310**	**2,520**	**2,660**
Latin America & Caribbean	2,470	2,700	2,690	2,840
Middle East & North Africa	2,380	2,830	3,010	2,970
Sub-Saharan Africa	2,100	2,080	2,110	2,200
East and South-east Asia	2,010	2,320	2,630	2,870
South Asia	2,070	2,080	2,330	2,400
Oceania LEDCs	2,220	2,390	2,460	2,520
North America LEDCs	2,550	2,420	2,300	2,280
Continental groupings				
Africa	2,180	2,270	2,340	2,420
Asia	2,090	2,290	2,550	2,690
Latin America	2,480	2,710	2,710	2,860
Caribbean	2,340	2,530	2,430	2,520
North America	3,020	3,160	3,420	3,750
Oceania	3,010	2,930	3,040	2,960
Europe	3,210	3,320	3,390	3,290

Source: Food and Agriculture Organisation *Summary Food and Agriculture Statistics.*

10.26 *In the global food market, food tends to be sold to the highest bidder. In such a situation, children like these who are living in a poor village in southern Ethiopia will almost always miss out.*

Wheat is an important staple food for much of the world's population. However, wheat is also in demand by beef farmers in developed nations who feed it to their cattle to produce high quality, lean meat. A beef farmer in the United States will always be able to afford to pay a higher price for wheat than a hungry peasant in Mali, which means that the peasant in Mali will usually miss out. The problem is made worse when we realise that the food energy a person would get from a tonne of wheat is reduced by 90% if it is eaten in the form of wheat-fattened beef rather than as bread. Put another way, economic factors work to reduce the food energy available to people from wheat by 90% when the wheat is fed to cattle, and it is not even the people who most need the food energy that will be able to afford the lean beef.

Another problem concerns the role of **agribusiness**, or large corporations that are involved in farming. With the backing of organisations such as the World Bank, large profit-driven corporations have persuaded many subsistence farmers in LEDCs to abandon food production and switch to commercial production of non-food crops — a programme known as **crop substitution**. The argument put to farmers is that they could sell their cotton or rubber or coffee on the world market, and use the money earned to buy the food they used to grow, having a handsome surplus of money left over for other purposes. On the basis of such arguments, large numbers of farmers in LEDCs began producing cocoa, cotton, cut flowers, asparagus, strawberries, grapes and other crops for export (figure 10.27). This also helped farmers in Europe and

North America to sell some of their surplus production as new markets opened up in LEDCs.

Unfortunately, crop substitution has not worked well for many farmers in LEDCs. Prices for the export crops have often failed to meet expectations, so farmers have not even been able to buy the amounts of food they had previously grown for themselves. The farmers are trapped because of their contracts, obligations and commitments to the large corporations and the loans they have received from these corporations. Crop substitution schemes were very popular in African nations such as Sudan and Ethiopia – countries that used to be self-sufficient in food production but now experience widespread malnutrition.

10.27 *Crop substitution in Africa. Farmers in the Tanzanian village of Matumbulu have abandoned their subsistence food crops to grow grapes for the manufacture of wine for export.*

Addressing the Imbalances

Ironically, **food aid** from MEDCs can make the situation even worse. When farmers in LEDCs are trying to establish a commercial food growing industry in their country, there could be no greater blow than to have to compete with free or subsidised grain or other food from the United States or Europe. Food aid is important on humanitarian grounds when there is a natural disaster, but it really hurts farmers in LEDCs when it continues for a long period of time (figure 10.28).

How did this situation come about? In the late 1960s and early 1970s, there were many predictions of famine and starvation in the world. The opening words of one famous book at the time (1971), *The Population Bomb*, by Paul Ehrlich, stated boldly:

> *"The battle to feed all of humanity is over. In the 1970s and 1980s hundreds of millions of people will starve to death in spite of any crash programmes embarked upon now. At this late date nothing can prevent a substantial increase in the world death rate..."*

It was predicted that in the decades to come, the growth in world food production would fall behind the growth in world population. It was thought that most of the world's arable land was already being fully used, that crop yields in the developed nations were already high and had little potential for further increases, and that rises in yields in developing nations were unlikely because subsistence farmers could not afford the technology necessary.

The predictions were half right. World population did increase rapidly. During the period 1950 to 2007, world population rose from 2.5 billion to 6.6 billion, an annual average increase of less than 2% per year over the whole period. Entering the 1980s and 1990s, the rate of growth slowed somewhat. Between 1980 and 1985, the average annual rate of growth of world population fell to 1.75%. It fell further to 1.70% between 1985 and 1990, to 1.68% between 1990 and 1995 and to 1.42% between 1995 and 2000. During the period 2000 to 2007, the average annual rate of growth of world population was 1.20%.

The widespread famines that Ehrlich and others forecast did not occur The reason was that over the same period (1950 to 2007) **world food production** rose by an average of about 2.6% per year, a rate faster than world population growth. Indeed, in the ten-year period 1982 to 1992, world food production rose by 23%. Despite a slowing in the rate of increase in food production (as shown earlier in table 10.2), by 2007 the annual increase in food production (2% per year) was still almost double the annual increase in world

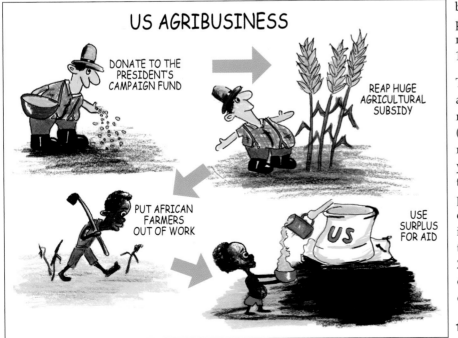

10.28 *US agribusiness — a cartoonist's view.*

population (1.2% per year). It is because food production has grown more rapidly than population that we find ourselves in the situation where there is (on average) more than enough food for every person in the world to be well nourished.

10.29 *One way that the area of land under cultivation can be expanded is by terracing hillslopes, thus creating steps of flat land. These terraces are near Xijiang in Guizhou province, China.*

10.30 *The productivity of farmland can be increased when the microclimate is made more suitable for crop cultivation. This extensive area of clear plastic 'glasshouses' is near Kunming, China.*

This trend has been made possible for two main reasons. First, the **amount of land used for cultivation** has increased slowly but steadily (figures 10.29 and 10.30). Between 1980 and 2002, the area of land used for growing crops increased by 33.5% (figure 10.31). This increase was not uniformly distributed around the world, however. In Africa the area under permanent cultivation increased by 30.3%, and in Asia by 73.3%. On the other hand, smaller increases in the area under crops were reported between 1980 and 2002 in Europe (16.7%), in Latin America (13.7%) and in North America (11.8%). Although the amount of land used world-wide for cultivation has increased, the amount of land per capita has decreased. In 1964, there were 0.44 hectares per capita used for growing crops in the world. By 1984 this figure had fallen to 0.25 hectares and by 2002 to 0.21 hectares. If less land per person is producing more food per person, it follows that the productivity of the land has increased. This is the second reason that the forecast widespread famines did not occur.

It is important to be able to explain why this increase in the **productivity** of the world's farmlands occurred. If we can find sustainable ways to make less land produce more food, then we may have found some important lessons for avoiding (or at least minimising) malnutrition in the future. There are six main reasons that land productivity increased since 1970:

First, many farmers adopted new **high yielding varieties** of crops, especially rice and wheat, which were genetically engineered to shorten the growing cycle, enabling double cropping and even triple cropping of farmland. Many of these high yielding varieties (HYVs) were also more resistant to diseases that affected traditional species of crops. Between 1955 and 2005, India more than quadrupled its food production and the main reason was said to be the adoption of HYVs. However, the benefits brought by the HYVs were offset by some problems, and these are explored elsewhere in this chapter.

Second, **irrigation systems** became more widespread in many areas of the world (figure 10.32). Between 1980 and 2002, the percentage of the world's croplands under irrigation increased from 15.7% to 19.7%, although in Asia the increase was considerably greater – from 31.3% to 37.9%. Some nations saw quite

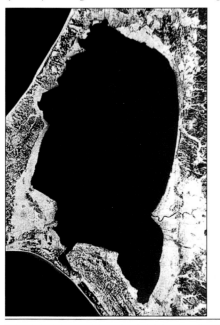

10.31 *In northern Japan, a huge coastal lake known as Lake Hachiro-gata was reclaimed to increase the land available for growing rice. These vertical aerial photographs show the area before (a) and after (b) reclamation. The reclaimed land has an area of about 22,000 hectares (220 square kilometres), measuring 12 kilometres from east-to-west and 27 kilometres north-to-south.*

spectacular increases in irrigated croplands, with examples including Bangladesh (17% to 37%), Nepal (22% to 35%) and North Korea (59% to 73%).

Third, there was a big increase in the use of **chemical pesticides and fertilisers** on farms. Although there can be undesirable side-effects on the biophysical environment from the widespread use of chemicals, there is no doubt that they can increase farm productivity, at least in the short-term. In 1964, an average of 29 kilograms of fertiliser were used on each hectare of the world's croplands. By 1981 this figure had increased to 87 kilograms, rising further to 99 kilograms by 1991 and 101 kilograms by 2003. In some countries, the amount of fertiliser being used by 2003 was vastly greater than the world average, with examples being Iceland (3433 kg/ha), Netherlands (592 kg/ha), South Korea (472 kg/ha), Egypt (361 kg/ha), China (309 kg/ha), United Kingdom (381 kg/ha) and New Zealand (212 kg/ha).

10.32 *Irrigated farmlands in south-eastern Turkey, fed from the Atatürk Dam as part of the GAP scheme.*

10.33 *Increased mechanisation has raised farming productivity around the world. In this view, combine harvesters are being used to harvest wheat near Gyula, Hungary.*

The fourth factor was **mechanical technology**, which has become much more widespread on the world's farms, enabling a small number of people to achieve tasks that used to require a huge work force. Between 1980 and 2002, there was a 16.6% increase in the number of tractors used on the world's farms and an 11.5% increase in the number of harvesters (figure 10.33). Some countries have seen spectacular increases in mechanisation. The percentage increase in the number of tractors between 1980 and 2002 in South Korea was 903%, in Indonesia 353%, in Burkina Faso 150% and in India 136%.

Fifth, the **changing nature of the agricultural work force** has also affected productivity. The number of people engaged in agriculture around the world is declining. This decline is found in every part of the world, and is expected to continue into the future as figure 10.34 shows. The decline in agricultural labour force was made possible by farm amalgamations, where neighbours or corporations have bought farms and enlarged them to make the use of machinery easier. This has enabled an increase in the productivity of farmers so that each farmer is now capable of producing more food than was the case previously.

Finally, food shortages have been alleviated by the growth of free trade and fair trade. **Fair trade** refers to the organised social movement that promotes a market-based approach to empowering farmers in LEDCs to sustain their viability as farmers. The key to 'fair trade' is paying farmers in LEDCs a fair price for their produce, rather than exploiting them as some would claim may be done by transnational corporations or corrupt government officials. Advocates of the 'fair trade' movement also emphasise the importance of requiring farmers in LEDCs to meet environmental and social standards in their farming practices. 'Fair trade' explicitly aims to help poor and marginalised farmers in LEDCs, and for this reason the products of 'fair trade' are often distributed by international development aid and religious organisations such as Oxfam, World Vision and Caritas International.

QUESTION BLOCK 10D

1. *Why do farmers in some MEDCs dump food rather than sell it when there are so many hungry people in the world?*

2. *'The problem with food today is not that we can't grow enough. The problem is that we grow too much but we can't seem to distribute properly'. Critically evaluate this statement.*

3. *Explain the term 'crop substitution', and say why it is significant in explaining food shortages in some countries.*

4. *Using table 10.2, describe and explain the trends in world food production in different parts of the world.*

5. *Describe the patterns and trends shown in table 10.3.*

6. *Show the information in table 10.4 as lines on a graph.*

7. *Describe and give reasons to explain the pattern of global food availability shown in table 10.4.*

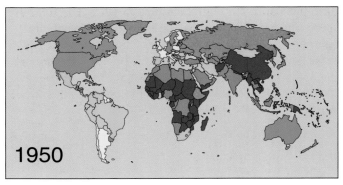

1950

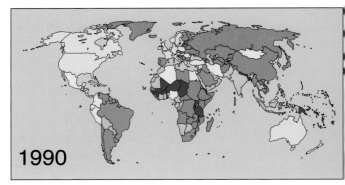

1990

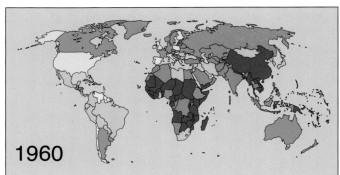

1960

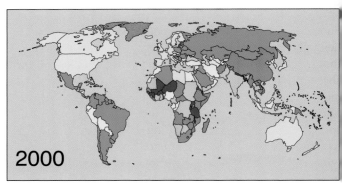

2000

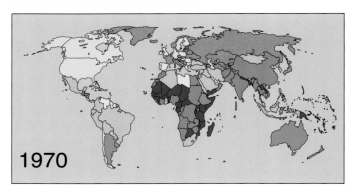

1970

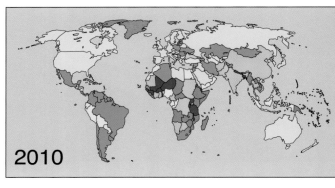

2010

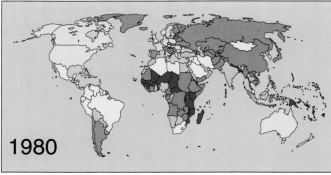

1980

- 80.41% and over
- 64.58% to 80.41%
- 44.15% to 64.58%
- 24.68% to 44.15%
- 9.5% to 44.15%
- less than 9.5%
- no data

10.34 *Proportion of population employed in agriculture, 1950 to 2010.*

8. *How can food aid actually make hunger worse? Who benefits most from food aid?*

9. *Why has food production risen more than expected in recent decades?*

10. *In 2007, the world population was about 6.612 billion people. Using this information, and the information contained in this section on the area per capita used for growing crops in the world, calculate the approximate area in the world used for crop production in 2007.*

11. *What is meant by the term 'productivity'?*

12. *Explain why land productivity has increased in recent decades.*

13. *Using the information in figure 10.34 (and an atlas if you need one), attempt a classification of the countries shown according to their agricultural labour force as a percentage of total labour force. It is suggested you use three categories; high, medium and low. Make a list of five countries in each category.*

14. Look at the information in figure 10.34. Select one country that appears to have experienced a large change in the agricultural work force engaged in agriculture as a percentage of total population between 1950 and 2000. Then select one country that appears to have experienced a very small change in the agricultural work force engaged in agriculture as a percentage of total population in the same period. Try to give reasons for the differences in the trends in these two countries.

Areas of Food Sufficiency and Deficiency

Figure 10.35 shows the global pattern of farming activities. Even though this map is a simplification of reality, the pattern shown is quite complicated. The pattern shown in figure 10.35 is the result of a complex set of biophysical, economic and socio-political factors. Many of these factors are shown in figure 10.36, which shows something of the decision making process which farmers (consciously or unconsciously) go through in deciding what to produce and what methods to use.

One of the most important factors affecting the pattern of farming is **climate**. All plants need sunlight, water and warmth to survive. Heat is necessary for plant seeds to germinate, and although the figure varies a little, a minimum temperature of about 6°C is necessary for plant growth. That is why few crops are found in areas close to the poles or in alpine areas; temperature falls by about 1°C for every 200 metres rise in altitude. Different crops need varying amounts of warmth to survive. Thus, wheat cannot be grown beyond the latitudes 60°N and S of the equator, whereas the limits of maize and cotton are 50°N and S and 35°N and S respectively. In general, farmers in economically less developed countries are more dependent on the climate than farmers in more advanced economies, who have greater capacity to change the climate (figure 10.37). Having said this, it is important to remember that farmers in traditional societies have made huge changes to their environment using irrigation, sometimes for thousands of years.

Similarly, plants require **water** to survive. Water can often be an important factor in deciding what crop will be grown, or even if it is possible to farm an area at all (figure 10.38). If the rainfall is inadequate, then either a different crop must be grown or water must be provided artificially by irrigation. This becomes especially important as plants need water in different amounts at different times of their growth cycles. Unless extra water is provided by irriga-

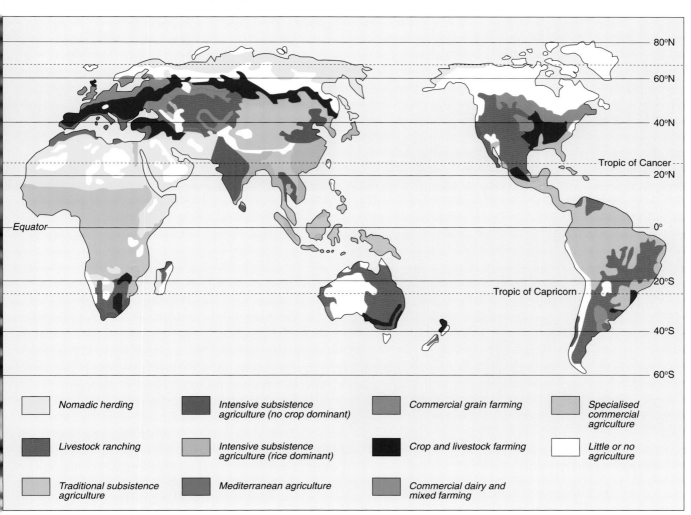

Nomadic herding	Intensive subsistence agriculture (no crop dominant)	Commercial grain farming	Specialised commercial agriculture
Livestock ranching	Intensive subsistence agriculture (rice dominant)	Crop and livestock farming	Little or no agriculture
Traditional subsistence agriculture	Mediterranean agriculture	Commercial dairy and mixed farming	

10.35 The global pattern of farming activity.

Food and health

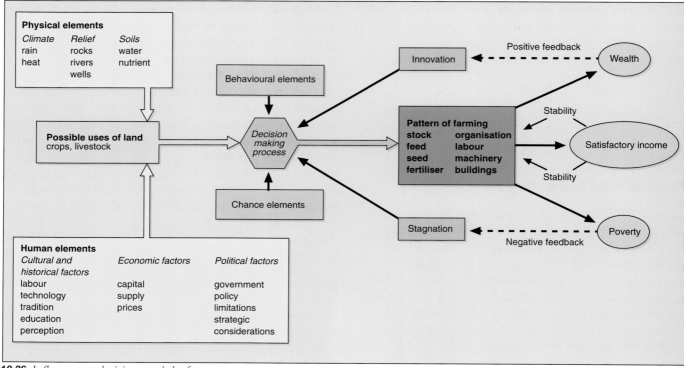

10.36 *Influences on decisions made by farmers.*

10.37 *Greenhouses made with clear plastic, Cengong, China.*

10.38 *An oasis in the Asif Imini Valley of Morocco. Water seeps from the bottom of the slope to the dry river bed, providing just enough water for crops to survive.*

10.39 *These cattle near Taungdwingyi in the dry central area of Myanmar are causing erosion of the soil, and possible contributing to desertification.*

tion, cotton must be grown where annual rainfall is at least 550 mm and not more than 1,150 mm. On the other hand, a crop like rubber needs at least 1700 mm of rain each year.

The **lithosphere** can impose additional biophysical limits. Areas with hard, igneous rocks such as granite are usually poor for farming because these rocks produce coarse soils with few nutrients that are easily eroded. In fact, soils that are too acidic, too alkaline (as in swamps) or too salty (as in coastal areas) result in reduced crop yields. Furthermore, in mountainous and cool areas, soil formation takes place more slowly than in warmer areas, and so soils tend to be quite thin, again reducing crop yields. That is why areas with poor soils and marginal climates often concentrate on livestock raising rather than crop growing (figure 10.39). On the other hand, the best soils for cropping are often the alluvial soils found near rivers, and volcanic soils that are found, not surprisingly, near active volcanoes. Alluvial and volcanic soils are normally only slightly acidic, with a friable texture and with a rich supply of minerals that make them very fertile.

Important though biophysical factors are in influencing the pattern of agriculture, **cultural** factors are also very important. Tradition can be particularly important; if farmers in an area have been producing a particular crop for generations, farmers will be most comfortable if they continue to grow that familiar crop, about which they will know a great deal (figure 10.40). Cultural traditions can also be important. For example, the pig is highly valued animal in places like New Guinea and China, and so pigs play a central role in farming activities. However, in Muslim societies such as most parts of Indonesia and Malaysia, the pig is regarded as an unclean animal and would almost never be found. As time goes on, education can reduce the influence of these and other traditional beliefs.

10.40 *Cultural influences on agriculture can be expressed in many ways. The Intha people live on Inle Lake (Myanmar), and have adapted so well to the water that they grow their crops on floating islands which they construct on the surface of the lake.*

10.41 *The woman who grew these beans is preparing them for consumption by her household in Konso, Ethiopia.*

The level of **economic development** of a particular society is another important influence on the type of agriculture practised. Countries that are largely pre-industrial tend to have large proportions of their populations involved in farming. For example, the proportion of the work force employed in agriculture in Malawi is 91%. The equivalent figures for other less industrialised countries include Nepal (92%), Papua New Guinea (84%), Tanzania (81%) and Thailand (80%). On the other hand, the figures for more industrialised countries include the United Kingdom (3%), the United States (4%), Australia (8%), Canada (8%) and Germany (9%).

10.42 *Using a wooden plough pulled by a bull — an example of traditional farming techniques near Sodo, Ethiopia.*

10.43 *Combine harvesters are being used to cut wheat near Gyula, Hungary.*

The reason for this difference can be explained by looking at the types of farming practised. A majority of farmers in pre-industrial countries are **subsistence** farmers, which means that the main intention in producing food is to feed the farmer and his or her immediate family (figure 10.41). This does not mean that nothing at all will be sold, only that the farmer's intention is to consume most of the crop produced. In strong contrast to this, most farmers in industrialised countries are **commercial** farmers, who produce food with the primary intention of selling most of it for profit. There is little reason for subsistence farmers to produce a large surplus. Once the family is fed

Food and health

and a small surplus has been kept as insurance against disasters and for trading, there is little sense in working hard to produce more while only a few linkages with a commercial market exist. On the other hand, commercial farmers can use some of their profits to invest in technologies which will increase productivity, enabling one farmer to produce enough food to feed tens or perhaps hundreds of families (figures 10.42 and 10.43).

10.44 *Shifting cultivators near Samyaek in northern Thailand.*

10.45 *An air-conditioned glasshouse near Boulder, Colorado, USA.*

It follows, then, that **economic influences**, such as the cost of wages, equipment, transport, and the prices received, will have a much stronger impact on commercial farmers than on subsistence farmers. Similarly, **political influences** such as government policies, trading treaties, subsidies and taxes will affect commercial farmers much more strongly than subsistence producers. Commercial farmers can use money to overcome the constraints of the biophysical environment much more easily than subsistence farmers. A commercial farmer may be able to afford

pesticides, fertilisers, machinery, irrigation systems and even climate modifying structures that would be an impossible dream for a subsistence farmer. Subsistence farmers must largely live within the confines of their biophysical environment, whereas many commercial farmers have the means to change their biophysical environment. In figure 10.44, shifting cultivators in northern Thailand have burnt grass to create a clearing, or 'swidden', to grow crops. The ash made by the burning is being dug into the soil. This will be the only fertiliser added to the poor soils used for cultivation. Providing a strong contrast in environmental manipulation, the air conditioned glasshouse in figure 10.45 has been built to create an artificial environment to grow vegetables in the United States. The farmer controls every aspect of the growing environment, including the water, humidity, light and soil fertility.

QUESTION BLOCK 10E

1. *Describe the main features of the distribution of world agriculture shown in figure 10.35.*

2. *Account for (i.e. explain) the main features of the distribution of world agriculture shown in figure 10.35.*

The Changing Nature of Food Production

Just as there are differences in the state of world food supply in different parts of the world, there are also differences in the trends and changes occurring in food production in different countries, and even within countries.

Increasing commercialisation: An increasing proportion of the food grown by farmers is being sold and traded in markets, and this is perhaps the most marked trend today in global food production. Sometimes, food is simply sold in markets in nearby towns (figure 10.46) although in other cases the food finds its way to large companies and international trade. One of the problems faced by farmers who sell food commercially is that the price is declining on a long-term basis.

10.46 *Food is sold to the public by the farmers who grew the food in this market in Key Afar, Ethiopia.*

Increasing commercialisation means that there is an increasing flow of money into farmers' households for the first time. This is resulting in improvements in the standards of living of farmers such as larger houses and even some consumer goods. One of the most extreme examples of rapid commercialisation of food production has occurred in China. In China, increasing commercialisation is being strongly encouraged by the government under a scheme known as the 'responsibility system'. Under the responsibility system, farmers take out a contract with their township government to supply an agreed quantity of a crop such as rice or vegetables to the township government in exchange for the right to cultivate a particular parcel of land. Once this agreed quantity is supplied, any excess produce from the land belongs to the farm household to use as it wishes. Households usually give the worst quality produce to the government, keeping the best produce for the next year's seed stock and to sell the remainder in the market for a premium price. The responsibility system was introduced into China over the period 1978 to 1984, and it has resulted in huge increases in both agricultural production and farmers' standards of living.

Increasing specialisation: As farmers become more involved with commercial production, they are able to earn money which can be used to buy types of food which they previously had to grow themselves. Once a farming family does not have to grow all the food it will eat, it can afford to specialise in growing the crop that will bring the greatest economic profit. With the extra income earned, they can afford to purchase a variety of other foods rather than having to grow these crops themselves.

10.47 *Farmers in central Myanmar use bullock carts to bring harvested rice to the market, in this case a government buying station. The store of purchased rice can be seen in the background.*

Increasing spatial integration: With the increasing trend towards commercialisation, two-way links between farmers and markets must develop. First, transport links must develop for farmers to transport their produce to town markets (figures 10.47 and 10.48). Second, other supportive service industries such as marketing, banking and

insurance develop. The links that arise are two-way in that farmers sell their produce in the market towns, but then use their new earnings to purchase items from other businesses in the town. In this way, the economies of the towns and the countryside become much more integrated and interdependent. Spatial integration extends beyond the nearest market town, of course. The prices received by farmers will be influenced by forces operating on a global scale – prices that reflect the demand for food in other countries and the availability of food from competing producers. As a result of all this, the factors that can affect a farmer become much more complex with spatial integration.

10.48 *As rice farming becomes more commercialised, more efficient transport links become necessary, such as motor lorry transport, seen here in central Myanmar.*

Spatial integration affects social and cultural aspects of farmers' lives also. As farmers begin to earn extra cash income, one of their frequent purchases is often a television set. The purchase of a radio or television transforms farmers' views of the world. Traditionally, farmers in isolated areas relied upon word of mouth – conversations with other people at the markets – to learn about events outside the local area. With a television in the house, farmers and their families are in instant contact with the rest of the world through satellite news broadcasts — as well as dramas and comedies from Hollywood!

After the Communist Party came to power in China in 1949, one of their earliest policies was to bring electricity to the countryside, even to peasants in the most remote areas (figure 10.49). This policy was considered important so that government propaganda could be instantly distributed to farmers (who made up 85% of the population) via the radio. Rural electrification throughout Asia and other developing parts of the world now puts even poor farmers in contact with global information, changing their world outlooks irreversibly.

Of course, new ideas can still spread without the aid of electricity. When a new idea or technique is introduced, nearby farmers will often wait and see how it works over time before rushing in and changing their familiar techniques. Subsistence farmers tend to be very conservative, preferring to continue with the proven techniques used by their parents and their parents before them. This is understandable as such farmers do not produce a large surplus and so they have little spare production with which to experiment. However, once farmers start commercialising their production, they are more likely to innovate and change in search of extra production and extra profits. Thus, change becomes more rapid in an area of commercial food production.

10.49 *The wires crossing this field, which is being cultivated by a woman of Miao nationality in China, provide evidence of rural electrification. Electrification allows even very isolated farmers to become integrated with the global information and communication network.*

The way in which new ideas spread is known as **diffusion**. A new idea that originates at a certain point will spread out from that point. If there is little or no communication by radio or television, the new idea will spread by word of mouth, either from one neighbour to the next or between family and friends at the markets in town. In general, ideas will spread fastest along lines of communication, while physical barriers such as rivers or mountains will slow the spread of ideas. As distance increases from the centre of the new idea, fewer and fewer farmers will have adopted the innovation.

10.50 *Small hand held tractors like this one in Bali (Indonesia) are used in several nations to perform the same tasks as water buffaloes used to do much more slowly.*

Increasing mechanisation: There is a very strong trend for farmers to replace people with machines as they become more involved with commercial production. The type of machinery used varies from place to place and is influenced by the profitability of the farmer. In many parts of Asia, small hand held tractors are replacing water buffaloes (figure 10.50). The tractors enable the farmer to perform tasks such as ploughing and puddling much more quickly than when they were done using water buffalo. Tractors are also less temperamental than water buffalo, although they cost much more to buy and to operate. In some areas, these hand-held tractors are owned by a few operators who use them to do the work for local farmers under contract for payment.

In China, a unique type of tractor is found throughout the country in rural areas (figure 10.51). These walking tractors have become a symbol of rural mechanisation in China. Originally introduced by Russian agricultural engineers in the 1950s as a small, hand-held plough, the Chinese adapted the design into a tractor, and then began producing them in small factories throughout the country. Today, millions of these slow-revving tractors are used to haul produce, transport farm equipment and even provide local bus services in isolated areas.

10.51 *A Chinese 'walking tractor' on a farm in Yunnan province, China.*

In MEDCs, farming is heavily mechanised. In Japan, small machines have been developed to perform most of the unpleasant menial tasks of rice cultivation such as ploughing, planting, harvesting and winnowing. These machines enable many Japanese rice farmers to have regular paid employment through the week and carry out their rice farming only on weekends. On the other hand, the machines require that standard, uniform practices are adopted. For example, the mechanised rice planter shown in figure 10.52 can only operate if the rice seedlings have been planted in standard sized boxes that are fed automatically through the planter as it crosses the **padi** field (a padi is the field where rice is grown). The machine can plant five rows of rice at the time with even 20 centimetre spacing.

10.52 *A mechanised rice planter (top) and a tractor used for ploughing (bottom), both in Hachiro-gata, Japan.*

10.54 *Steel tools such as these forked hoes in Bali are the simplest level of purchased inputs used by rice cultivators.*

On the other hand, the farms of most subsistence rice farmers in LEDCs remain largely non-mechanised, relying on human power and that of animals such as the water buffalo (figure 10.53). This is probably a very efficient use of the resources available to most rice cultivators, however. In most Asian nations, it is land that is a scarce commodity rather than labour, or as the author John King Fairbank (1992, 16) expresses it, "good muscles are more plentiful than good earth". It is very doubtful that replacing large numbers of people who can farm the land intensively with machinery on a large scale would increase the very high yields already being obtained. Using more machines would, however, create large-scale unemployment and social problems as (perhaps) millions of displaced farmers migrated to the cities in search of jobs for which they had no skills.

10.53 *A farmer near Selakarang on the Indonesian island of Bali uses cattle to plough and pound the mud in a padi field into a thick, structureless mud.*

It is likely that the increasing use of machinery is actually making food cultivation less and less efficient. We can measure efficiency by comparing the input of energy used to produce a crop with the output of energy contained in the food. This **efficiency** can be measured as a ratio of energy inputs to energy outputs. On this basis, intensive rice production is among the world's most efficient

sources of food energy with a ratio of about 1:3, although this falls to about 1:1.5 for extensive commercial rice production. In other words, we obtain three times more food energy from growing rice in the traditional way than we put into producing it. This compares with ratios of 1:2 for cattle grazing, 1:1 for dairying, 2:1 for intensive poultry raising, and 10:1 for feedlot beef and deep-sea fishing. As farming becomes more mechanised, the energy inputs can become so great that we are spending more energy than we are obtaining from the food produced — in the case of feedlot beef 10 times more energy!

The issue of energy efficiency is discussed in more detail in chapter 15 in the section headed 'the impact of agro-industrialisation on the physical environment'.

Increasing purchased inputs: As soon as a farmer purchases machinery, an ongoing commitment to purchase other inputs is made. Machinery requires inputs of petro-chemicals, and these can prove to be expensive for a farmer. Machinery is also expensive to repair when it breaks down, and repairs must usually be paid for in cash. As a farmer becomes more oriented towards commercial production, greater priority is placed on maximising yields, and so pesticides and chemical fertilisers are more likely to be used. Once again, these must be paid for in cash. Even at a more simple level, many farmers want to replace simple wooden tools they can make themselves with tools made of steel because they are harder and will last longer (figure 10.54). Such tools must be fabricated, either in a factory or by a craftsman in a nearby market town. Either way, such tools are usually a purchased input that must be paid for in cash, forcing the farmer to engage in more and more commercial farming activity.

Increasing farm sizes: As farms become more commercialised and more machinery is used in an attempt to boost production, farmers feel the pressure to increase the area of their farm. More area means more production and, hopefully, more profits. Larger farm areas also make it easier to justify the use of machinery, and if a larger area also means the fields can be more rectangular, then it becomes easier to use machinery on a large scale.

The trend towards increasing farm sizes has occurred in some nations to a greater extent than in others. Following World War II, American forces occupying Japan forced **land reform** on the rural countryside, amalgamating farms and creating larger land units. Even following the Japanese land reform, however, average farm size had only increased up to about one hectare.

A more effective land reform programme was imposed by the Chinese Communist Party after it came to power in 1949. Before the revolution in 1949, most of China's farmlands were owned by rich peasants or landlords who collected extremely high rents from the farmers who worked the land. There were instances in the late 1940s of rents as high as 120% of the annual crop being collected by landlords from their farmers. Between 1949 and 1952, land was confiscated from the landlords and redistributed to the peasants who had been farming the land. In 1958, as part of a political campaign known as the Great Leap Forward, China's farmland was collectivised (brought into public owner-ship) and amalgamated into large communes. The area of communes varied somewhat, but in general they were between 40 and 120 square kilometres each. Each commune was divided into a number of production brigades, each of which roughly equated to a village. Each brigade was divided in turn into a number of production teams, each of which roughly corresponded to a neighbourhood. Finally, each production team was divided into households (extended families).

The formation of communes made enlarging and squaring off fields much easier (figures 10.55 and 10.56). However, the commune system was abandoned in the early 1980s when the responsibility system was introduced. Nonetheless, many of the effects of the communes such as the large rectangular fields that were introduced under the system continue today.

10.56 *These large, square fields are typical of the post land reform layout of farms in China. This area is near Kunming.*

Increasing control over the biophysical environment: Environmental manipulation occurs to some extent on any farm. When wet-rice is grown, a completely new wetland ecosystem is generated which relies on water management to maintain rice as the ecologically dominant species. However, commercialisation of rice production gives farmers the power to control or manipulate their biophysical environment to an even greater extent. Farmers with cash incomes may be able to afford to buy mechanical pumps to boost the irrigation capacity of their farms. Many farmers can use purchased inputs such as chemical fertilisers to boost yields and pesticides to control insect pests.

Farmers with increased power to control the biophysical environment must use this ability wisely or else unforeseen damage can occur. In 1954, the Chinese government launched a campaign around Beijing in northern China in 1954 to eradicate birds. It was thought that birds were eating much of the grain from the wheat and rice fields, and spreading encephalitis, a very dangerous disease that causes swelling of the brain which can lead to death. The government decided to 'mobilise the masses', which meant involving the entire population in the campaign. Every person in every neighbourhood was placed on a 24-hour roster to stand outside and beat pots and pans together for a few days. The idea was that the birds would be so frightened that they would not come down to rest and they would die from heart failure while continuously flying. The campaign worked as planned, and after three days there were no birds left in Beijing.

Unfortunately, the absence of the birds meant that the biological control on insects and spiders was removed from the ecosystem. As a result, insect and spider numbers increased to plague proportions, and massive doses of chemical pesticides were needed. Indeed, a new pesticide factory had to be hurriedly built near Beijing simply to supply the chemicals needed to control the insect plague that resulted from eradication of the birds.

10.55 *The rice fields near Yangshuo (China) show the small fields of irregular shapes that were common before land reform.*

Changing social structures: All the changes listed above have changed the lives of farmers enormously. Traditional social structures have been broken down and there have been upheavals in many societies as some people benefit but others lose as a result of the changes.

10.57 *Evidence of social change near Kunming, China: the house on the top of the hill was occupied by a landlord before the Communists came to power in 1949. Following land reform and collectivisation, the land was redistributed to the peasants who lived in the mud brick houses next to the rice fields. Today, the house on the top of the hill is vacant — a silent monument to an old social order.*

In China, farmers have experienced many social changes that have been enforced by government policy. The establishment of the communes in 1958 and their abolition in the early 1980s caused huge changes for farmers as they tried to adjust to reverses in economic policies and government priorities which even affected how families were structured and organised (figure 10.57). The model of Chinese communes was adopted in other nations also, including Tanzania and Cambodia, and in each case it resulted in a savage decline in rice production as farmers lost the incentive to work hard.

Increasing commercialisation is the main cause of changing social structures. Most traditional rice growing communities organise their society and festivals around the annual cycle of rice growing. Farmers who are growing rice for profit rather than for lifestyle are less inclined to spend resources such as time, money and rice to celebrate traditional religious beliefs. Traditional subsistence farmers see rice as a gift from the gods and the very sustenance of life. Commercialisation breaks down this traditional culture bit by bit. Eventually, farmers embrace the same attitude as many farmers in industrialised nations who see producing food simply as a means to make money, devoid of any religious significance. They come to see a successful rice crop as being the result of spending money on fertilisers, pesticides, machinery or irrigation — manipulating and controlling the ecosystem rather than working within its confines.

BLOCK 10F

1. Suggest reasons why the trend towards commercialisation of food production is so strong in the world today.

2. What is the Responsibility System in China? How successful has it been?

3. What are the advantages and disadvantages of small tractors compared with water buffaloes for rice farmers when they are ploughing a padi field?

4. What are the social costs of replacing people and animals with machines?

5. When farmers exercise greater control over their biophysical environment, is this a good or a bad thing?

The Green Revolution

In the 1960s, 1970s and 1980s, many predictions of widespread hunger and starvation were made. These predictions did not come true, largely due to the increase in yields during the 1970s and 1980s. Some people have described the increase in yields as nothing short of a miracle. The terms '**Green Revolution**' and '**seed-fertiliser revolution**' have been used to label the package of measures introduced by farmers in the 1960s and afterwards to boost production. The measures included introducing new 'miracle' high yielding varieties (HYVs) of rice and wheat, expanding irrigation, and using larger amounts of fertiliser. The Green Revolution was so successful in boosting production that nations like India, Indonesia, Malaysia and the Philippines, which were rice importers, became rice exporters.

The key to the Green Revolution for rice cultivators has been the development of **hybrid** (or cross-pollinated) high yielding varieties of rice. Much of the work to develop new strains of rice was done at the International Rice Research Institute (IRRI) in the Philippines, which was established in 1960. The IRRI was established specifically to modernise Asian rice production by helping farmers to introduce Western (or temperate climate) technology. At first, only types of *japonica* rice were developed into HYVs, but later varieties of *indica* rice were also developed. The first of the 'miracle' HYVs was known as IR8 and it was released to farmers in 1962. In some places, the first crop of IR8 produced a yield 600% greater than the traditional varieties of rice grown the year before. IR8 was a low growing, short stemmed variety of rice, meaning that its growing season was shorter than traditional rice plants and it was less prone to damage by strong winds and heavy rains.

However, in the early 1970s, large areas of IR8 were destroyed by tungro virus which was spread by green leaf hoppers. This showed both the danger to farmers of

Food and health

depending on one type of rice only, and the vulnerability of the new HYVs to disease. To overcome these problems, other varieties of HYV rice were developed in the years to come by the IRRI and other agencies. Among the new varieties are the following:

- IR17 and IR19 — developed for the flood plains of central Thailand where annual flood waters may be more than one metre deep;

- IR36 — a quick maturing variety of rice allowing three crops of rice to be gathered from each padi field each year, and high yields of over 30 tonnes per hectare;

- IR42 — a high yielding variety developed for areas with poor soils;

- IR48 — a variety of rice for farmers who cannot afford expensive fertilisers and which is adaptable to a wide range of temperatures and rainfalls;

- IR52 — a quick maturing variety that is resistant to drought and blight.

The HYV strains of rice brought both advantages and disadvantages for rice farmers. The obvious **advantage** was the increased yields and the shorter growing season, enabling the cultivation of an extra crop each year from many padi fields. Furthermore, the low height of the HYVs made them more resistant to damage from monsoonal rains and high winds.

However, there were also **problems**. The new strains of rice were more difficult to grow than traditional types. Most of the HYVs required large amounts of fertiliser to produce their potential yields, and this proved very costly for all but the wealthiest farmers. The new strains of rice

also needed more precise allocation of water, meaning that a great deal of work was needed in some areas to improve irrigation systems. The HYV plants were also more susceptible to attack by disease and chemical sprays were often needed to ensure a successful crop. These sprays were expensive for smaller farmers and had some harmful effects on the biophysical environment. Moreover, the seeds were expensive to buy, and some of the genetically engineered types were copyrighted and sterile. This meant that the farmer had to buy new seed every year rather than just keeping some of the previous crop for the following year's planting.

Other problems were also encountered. For example, the increased yields of rice put a great deal of pressure on poorly developed transport networks and storage facilities. In the early years of HYV introduction, much of the crop was left to spoil because storage and transport could not cope with the huge volumes being produced. Because of the high cost of switching to HYVs, governments and banks established credit facilities for farmers to borrow money. Many farmers used these new facilities, only to find themselves heavily in debt and unable to repay their new debts. Finally, the new strains of rice are unpopular with many consumers because they do not like the taste of the rice produced. Many people find that the HYV rice lacks flavour and becomes sticky and mushy when cooked. For this reason, traditional varieties of rice often attract a higher price in the markets.

The **Green Revolution** is much more than the simple introduction of high yielding varieties of seed. It is a package of measures carried out in full or in part. A summary of the components of the Green Revolution is given in figure 10.58.

ToK BoX

Human welfare.

When geographers study issues of health, nutrition and disease, they are focussing on the broader issue of human welfare. In brief, human welfare refers to the happiness and fortunes of a person or a group of people.

According to utilitarianists (see the ToK Box in chapter 4), happiness is one of the most important things we can aim to achieve.

However, many psychologists (notably the American Dan Gilbert) claim that our beliefs about what will make us happy are often wrong, and that our brains systematically misjudge what will make us happy.

Gilbert is a researcher in 'happiness studies', an interdisciplinary field that has brought together psychologists,

economists and other researchers. His research suggests that logic-processing errors in our brains make people think that they do not want the things that would make them happy — and the things that most people seem to want (such as more money, a bigger house or a better car) will not make us happy.

Gilbert and other psychologists challenge the idea that we will be miserable if we don't get what we want. In fact, their research says that our happiness is maximised when our choices are restricted.

For example, the American psychologist Barry Schwartz has undertaken research that demolishes a central belief of western societies: that greater freedom of choice leads to personal happiness. In

what he calls the 'paradox of choice', Schwartz argues that too many choices undermine happiness.

This seems counter-intuitive, and many people work very hard to find arguments against these clear research findings. This is an example of cognitive dissonance,which is a psychological state that describes the uncomfortable feeling caused by holding two contradictory ideas simultaneously..

We should be aware of our own preconceptions when we study issues of health, food and disease. It is quite possible that our assumptions about what is best for ourselves and others is not supported by the research!

The next ToK BoX is on page 476.

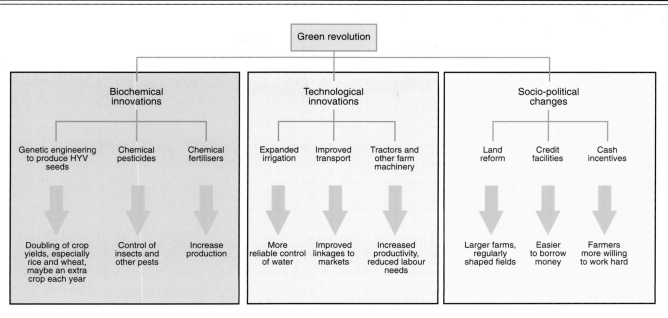

10.58 *The Green Revolution 'package'.*

There is no doubt that the Green Revolution has brought many benefits and many problems. Figure 10.59 attempts to weigh up and balance some of the main points for and against the Green Revolution. Of course, the situation is not as simplistic as this diagram might suggest, as many of the problems faced by rice cultivators are consequences of side-effects of the Green Revolution. This particularly applies in the area of the **biophysical environment**. For example, the high yielding varieties of rice have proved to be more vulnerable to attack by pests and diseases than traditional varieties. Farmers have been forced to use large quantities of toxic chemicals and pesticides to control these pests. These chemicals have been expensive, but even more importantly they have destroyed wildlife and cheap food resources such as fish and snails that were part of the padi field ecosystem.

Another effect of pesticide use has been the development of more resistant pests. The insect pests have become more and more resistant to the chemicals used against them through a process of selective breeding. Some insects always have greater immunity to the toxic effects of chemicals than others. These more resistant insects survive the pesticides and become the breeding stock of the next generation of insects. In this way, insects become more and more resistant to the pesticides over time, and so even more toxic chemicals must be used. Furthermore, as some insect species are reduced through toxic chemicals, other species (which may also be pests) will increase in number. This is because the insects destroyed will have been the natural predators of other species. By largely removing one link from the food web, then other species can multiply without the normal biological controls. In this way, pests which were once a very minor problem can increase in numbers to plague proportions.

The Green Revolution
Success or failure?

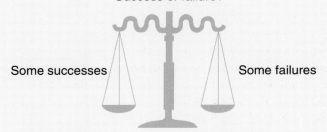

Some successes   Some failures

* Yields of some crops such as rice and wheat have increased greatly
* Shorter growing season means an extra crop may be grown each year
* HYV plants are often shorter, and so can withstand stong winds and monsoon without severe damage
* Farmers who can afford new seeds and mechanisation have become richer
* Mechanisation improves quality of life of farmers by reducing back-breaking tasks
* Land holdings have been enlarged and 'squared off', making them easier to farm
* Commercialisation of farming puts peasants in touch with the outside world through trading contracts and access to the media
* Transport linkages improve to cope with increased commercial production
* Millions of people fewer than before suffer from starvation

* HYV seeds are expensive, so only richer farmers can afford them
* HYV seeds often need expensive irrigation and fertilisers to thrive
* Farmers and consumers do not like the taste of the new HYV seeds as much as traditional types
* Some HYV seeds are sterile, so farmers must buy new seeds every year
* HYV seeds are copyrighted by the laboratory that developed them
* Some HYV seeds cannot tolerate difficult environmental conditions such as drought or floods
* Smaller peasant farmers who cannot afford the HYV seeds, fertiliser or machinery have become poorer
* Unemployed rural labourers who have been replaced by machines migrate to the cities in search of work, creating social problems
* Some farmers cannot repay the money borrowed to buy seeds or machinery
* We may lose the genetic stock of the traditional types of rice as they are replaced by HYV's

Conclusion: An economic success for richer farmers. Has increased yields and reduced hunger.

Conclusion: Has increased the gap between rich and poor farmers. Has caused social dislocation.

10.59 *Some benefits and problems of the Green Revolution.*

Food and health

And yet, it seems beyond dispute that the Green Revolution has produced more food. But this food has not always gone to the people who have needed it most. Much of the extra production went to the wealthier people who live in the towns, to other countries to earn export income, to fatten cattle and as ingredients to make luxury food products. As we said at the beginning of this chapter, commercial farmers do not grow food to eat but to sell, and it will be sold to the highest bidder, and this person will almost always not be the hungriest person!

The development of HYV strains of rice was a conscious choice. In making this choice, some other choices were not made. For example, it was decided not to improve traditional seeds that were already well adapted to local conditions. It was decided not to improve long-established traditional methods of farming, but to replace them with an adaptation of high cost, high technology 'Western' techniques. And it was decided not to develop a labour intensive technology that would create employment rather than replace people with machines.

The geographer Philip Woodhouse summed up the recent past and immediate future for rice cultivation in these words:

"The Green Revolution in Asian farming has exposed sharply both the strengths and weaknesses of twentieth-century science as an instrument for improving livelihoods in poorer, agriculturally based societies. It has demonstrated a capacity to produce enough food for a population believed to have grown perilously beyond the 'carrying capacity' of the fixed amount of land available. It has simultaneously demonstrated that this, though necessary, is not by itself sufficient to improve rural food security or living standards."

In the end, it may depend on your own perspective whether you think the Green Revolution has been a good or a bad thing. If you were a poor peasant, displaced from your farm because a wealthy farmer had bought your farm and replaced you with expensive machinery, forcing you to migrate to the city in search of work, you would probably be disappointed by the Green Revolution. On the other hand, if you were a fairly rich farmer whose wealth has been boosted by higher yields, you would appreciate the Green Revolution. Perhaps the most powerful argument in favour of the Green Revolution is that millions of people are alive today in developing nations who are adequately fed – people who may well have been malnourished if it had not been for the Green Revolution. Unfortunately, these may not be the poorest people who most needed it.

QUESTION BLOCK 10G

1. Why is the Green Revolution sometimes also called the 'seed-fertiliser revolution'?

2. What do the letters HYV stand for?

3. Why was IR8 known as the 'miracle rice'?

4. What have been the problems in growing the high yielding varieties of rice?

5. What measures have farmers had to implement to support the introduction of HYVs? Have these other measures created any problems?

6. Discuss the impact of the Green Revolution on the biophysical environment.

7. What social problems have resulted from the Green Revolution?

8. On balance, do you think the Green Revolution has brought more benefits or problems? Explain your answer fully.

9. Speaking of the Green Revolution, Philip Woodhouse wrote "It has demonstrated a capacity to produce enough food for a population believed to have grown perilously beyond the 'carrying capacity' of the fixed amount of land available. It has simultaneously demonstrated that this, though necessary, is not by itself sufficient to improve rural food security or living standards." What do you think he means by this statement? Do you agree or disagree with it?

Sustainable Agriculture and the Future of Farming

Few doubt that even with the successes of the Green Revolution in increasing yields, there is further potential to increase food production in the decades ahead. Yields can increase when labour intensive rice production becomes more mechanised, although this is at the cost of a considerable loss in energy efficiency. The Green Revolution has already increased rice production to the level that some areas such as Taiwan are facing problems of overproduction and rising surpluses. It is likely that future increases in production will come from subsistence farmers when they become more commercialised, and this is happening at quite a rapid rate.

The trend for farmers to move away from subsistence to commercial farming suggests that agriculture may become less efficient in terms of **energy efficiency ratios**. This ratio measures the input of energy into the farming system compared with the outputs of energy in the food that is produced. Typical energy efficiency ratios, in declining order of energy efficiency and sustainability, are:
1:20 - Shifting cultivation (figure 1.72 in chapter 1)
1:10 - Hunting and gathering
1:5 - Intensive rice cultivation
1:2 - Cattle grazing
1:1 - Dairy farming
1:1 - Coastal fishing
2:1 - Intensive poultry farming
10:1 - Feedlot beef raising
10:1 - Deep sea fishing

Some commentators question whether commercialisation and the rising standards of living in developing nations might lead to unsustainable practices in world food production. The President of the US-based Worldwatch Institute, Lester Brown, has written several articles that have been published around the world on this subject. In these articles, he expressed concern about a possible scenario. He noted that rapid increases in food production in China had resulted in big rises in income for Chinese people, about 70% of whom are farmers. As China becomes more affluent, he argued, its population will follow the trend which every other nation becoming richer has shown – it will increase its consumption of meat (figure 10.60). He argued that as this happens, the demand for grain to feed the cattle will skyrocket, and China will not only absorb its increased grain production but will have to import grain from overseas. Because China contains more than 20% of the world's population, this could create global food shortages and drive up the price of food around the world, leaving millions of poorer people hungry.

Brown believes that little capacity is left in China to increase grain production itself. Most of China's fertile land is already under cultivation, and vacant land is generally

very unproductive. Moreover, rapid urbanisation and industrialisation in China is reducing farmland by about 1% per year, or about 350,000 hectares per annum. There is little capacity to increase irrigation because large volumes of water are being diverted to non-farm uses that make more money.

There is also little capacity to increase yields. In China, rice yields have stabilised at about 4 tonnes per hectare per year. Increased fertiliser use will do little as it has reached the point of diminishing returns. In other words, if more fertiliser were applied in many areas, it would actually reduce the crop yield. Fertiliser use in China has already increased from 7 million tonnes in 1977 to 30 million tonnes in 1995. Environmental problems such as soil erosion, air pollution, global warming, waterlogging of the soil and siltation of irrigation systems will also work against increasing Chinese farm yields. Brown estimates that by the year 2030, China will need to import 216 million tonnes of grain, more than the world's entire grain exports of 200 million tonnes just three decades earlier.

Another factor affecting sustainability of agriculture is the increasing distances that food is transported. One way of measuring this is to use **food miles**, which measures the distance food is transported from the point of its production until it reaches the consumer. This measure was first developed in the United Kingdom (which may explain the use of 'miles' rather than 'kilometres'), but the measure can be expressed either in units of distance or as the amount of energy consumed during transport.

In 2007 it was estimated that the average distance travelled by food from farms to consumers in MEDCs had increased by 25% since 1980, leading to significant increases in greenhouse gases that cause global warming. This has led to more frequent calls to buy locally produced to reduce the distance that food is transported.

The concept of food miles serves as a useful reminder of the need to control the amount of energy used to move food from one location to another. However, the concept is somewhat simplistic and difficult to apply in a practical sense. For example, distance travelled is not necessarily the main determinant of the amount of energy used. This can seen by comparing two hypothetical farms. One is small in scale and produces just 10 tonnes of beans. The farmer has a small truck that can carry only one tonne at the time. If the farm is situated 100 miles (160 kilometres) from the market, each bean would travel 100 food miles, although the farmer would need to make ten return trips (2,000 miles) to deliver all his beans to the market.

The second hypothetical farm produces the same quantity of beans, but is located at a distance of 1,000 (1,600 kilometres) from the market. However, if that farmer has a larger truck that can carry 10 tonnes, the produce would travel 1,000 food miles, although the total distance trav-

10.60 *This food was prepared for a Chinese family's 'get together' to which the author was invited. As Chinese families become richer, they will eat more meat. This trend has already begun. What are the implications for the global food situation?*

elled would be the same. In fact, the amount of greenhouse gas produced may be slightly more because larger vehicles consume more fuel, but the difference is certainly not ten-fold as the measure of 'food miles' might suggest. The differences become greater when different forms of transport are considered. Trucks produce a different level of pollution when compared with an aircraft, a donkey cart or a train, but the measure of 'food miles' ignores such differences.

Recent research suggests that in many parts of the world, eating locally grown food may lead to an increase rather than a decrease in energy use and the carbon footprint. This is because certain areas are better suited physically for producing particular types of food than others, and thus eating locally produced food may increase energy use because of the need to grow crops or raise animals in sub-optimal conditions.

A widely publicised article in the *International Herald Tribune* and *New York Times* in 2007 claimed that raising lamb on New Zealand's natural grassland pastures and transporting it 18,000 kilometres by ship to the United Kingdom would produce 626 kilograms of carbon dioxide emissions per tonne. This figure compared with lamb produced in the United Kingdom, which would produce 2,580 kilograms of carbon dioxide per tonne between the point of production and delivery to the consumer. A large part of this difference was that the poorer British pastures and colder climate forced farmers to use feed in order to sustain their animals through the colder winter months (figures 10.61 and 10.62). Contrary to the implications of the 'food miles' concept, it was therefore four times more energy-efficient for a person in London to buy lamb imported from the other side of the world than to buy it from a local farmer.

10.62 *Sheep in Lancashire (UK) depend on hand feeding during the cold winter months.*

10.61 *Sheep grazing on grass fields near the Southern Alps of New Zealand's South Island.*

A 2008 study at Carnegie Mellon University, supported by a 2009 study in the Netherlands, showed that globally, only about 4% of the greenhouse gases produced by the food industry are the result of transporting produce from farmers to retail outlets. The same studies concluded that

a far more effective way to reduce greenhouse gas emissions than minimising food miles would be to adopt a **vegetarian diet**, even if the vegetarian food was transported over very long distances. The United Nations estimated in 2009 that the world's trillions of farm animals generate 18% of the world's greenhouse emissions, which is more than the greenhouse gases produced by the world's cars, buses and aircraft. This figure is expected to increase as the consumption of meat increases in LEDCs as they grow in affluence. The projected trend is shown in figure 10.63.

It is always difficult to predict the future. Certainly gloomy forecasts such as those of Lester Brown have been made many times in the past. In the 1960s and 1970s, before the Green Revolution, pessimistic predictions were commonplace. Perhaps the world can increase food production more than Brown has predicted. Indeed, each year the United States diverts more than 20 million hectares of good land away from food production because of grain surpluses. That area could immediately produce an extra 100 million tonnes of grain if it were needed. Similarly, another 100 million tonnes of grain could be produced in Argentina on former cropland that is being used as pasture for 30 million head of cattle because grain prices are so low.

Meanwhile, the International Rice Research Institute (IRRI) in the Philippines continues to work at increasing the quality of its hybrid strains of rice. It has developed a genetically engineered variety of rice that is resistant to tungro virus, and it expects to increase world rice yields by 50% to 75% by the year 2030. It hopes to do this by developing strains of rice that divert about 10% more of the solar energy the plants receive away from growing stalks and into growing rice seeds. The IRRI hopes to develop varieties of rice that will be resistant to pests such as stem borers and plant hoppers.

IRRI is currently working on a **genetically modified** pro-vitamin A-enriched 'golden rice' that is designed to increase vitamin intake among rice consumers. IRRI's

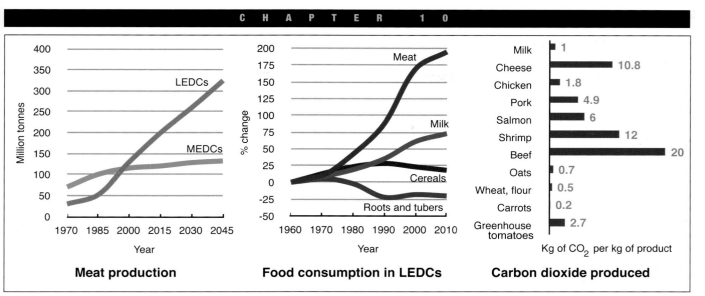

10.63 *Meat consumption and carbon dioxide emissions (past trends and future projections).*
Source: Food and Agriculture Organisation, *Livestock's Long Shadow*, Lantmannen (2006), New York Times (2009)

biotechnologists hope they will be able to create rice plants that deliver not only vitamin A, but also iron, zinc and increased levels of protein to those who eat the rice. IRRI hopes that with the development of genetically modified strains of rice, dietary benefits might be delivered free of charge to the poorest of the world's poor. The genetically modified 'golden rice' contains beta-carotene, which is the precursor of vitamin A. The strain was developed with the sole intention of combating vitamin A deficiency, which is responsible for about half a million cases of irreversible blindness and up to one million deaths per year among the poorest people in the world. However, like all genetically modified foods, the development of 'golden rice' is quite controversial.

Lester Brown's comments have been criticised from within Asia itself. As long ago as late 1994, an article by Dennis Avery appeared in the Far Eastern Economic Review arguing that Lester Brown did not really understand the Asian rice farming situation. Speaking of Lester Brown, the article commented:

"He stands as a vivid warning to a newly affluent Asia of the dangers that lie in wait when people get too far removed from fundamental realities. Brown has helped make high-yield farming politically incorrect in America and Europe, which itself has created a funding crisis for the international agricultural research centres that created and maintain the Green Revolution. Thanks to Brown and his followers, virtually all donor countries except Japan are shifting their aid money from agricultural research to population control.

The implications for Asia are clear. Lester Brown was wrong in 1974 when he said we were running out of agricultural research; we've doubled world crop yields since. Brown was wrong again in 1980 when he predicted a world soil erosion crisis; the prediction came just as we began to use conservation tillage, the soil-safest farming system in history. And he is wrong again, today, when he says the

world cannot feed an affluent China. Had his advice been followed before, Asia would not be eating as well as it is today."

Is Lester Brown or Dennis Avery correct? The only sure answer lies in the future.

QUESTION BLOCK 10H

1. *Describe the differences in energy efficiency and sustainability between different types of farming.*

2. *Describe the concept of 'food miles'.*

3. *Outline the shortcomings of 'food miles' as a measure of sustainability.*

4. *It has been claimed that the best way to promote sustainable agriculture is for the world's population to become vegetarian. What is the evidence for and against this claim?*

5. *Who do you think is correct – Lester Brown or Dennis Avery? In about 2 pages, briefly summarise the arguments of each and say which you agree with, justifying your opinions with facts.*

Disease

Global patterns of disease

There is a sharp difference in the types of diseases found in different parts of the world. As a broad generalisation, the main medical problems found in LEDCs are diseases of poverty, whereas the main medical issues found in MEDCs are increasingly diseases of affluence.

Diseases of poverty are medical conditions that are more commonly found among poorer people and in less economically developed countries (LEDCs). Poverty is often an important contributor to the cause of diseases in LEDCs, either directly or indirectly.

Food and health

There are five distinctive causes of poor health in LEDCs. These causes are poor diet, poor hygiene, water-borne parasites and bacteria, other pests, and poor public health facilities combined with lack of information or education. Each of these causes can lead to diseases of poverty, and some examples are shown in the pink sector of figure 10.64. In general diseases of poverty are communicable, which means they are contagious and can be passed from one person to another.

In contrast to the common medical problems in LEDCs, many of the significant diseases in MEDCs are **diseases of affluence**, which can be defined as medical conditions that are the consequence of increasing wealth in a country. There are three main causes of diseases of affluence (as shown in the blue sector of figure 10.64), these being increased longevity, environmental quality, and the combined impact of over-consumption and lifestyle. In contrast with diseases of poverty, diseases of affluence are usually non-communicable.

The global distribution of the diseases shown in figure 10.64 closely follows the broad world pattern of economic development described in chapter 2 using a variety of indicators. It is important to remember, however, that there are significant variations in wealth within most countries as well as internationally, and domestic disparities in wealth also affect the **patterns of health within countries**.

An example of fairly extreme internal variations in health standards occurs in Australia. Although Australians in general enjoy high standards of health, Indigenous Australians have notably poorer health. For example, Aboriginal and Torres Strait Islander peoples have average life expectancies that are 20 years lower than the Australian average, the figures for Indigenous Australians being 56.3 years for men and 62.8 years for women. Compared with Australians in general, Indigenous Australians are four times more likely to die from chronic kidney disease, three times more likely to die from circulatory diseases, eight times more likely to die from diabetes, and they have one of the highest rates of rheumatic heart disease in the world as well as double the average Australian rates of infant death and low birth weight (an indicator of poor health in later life).

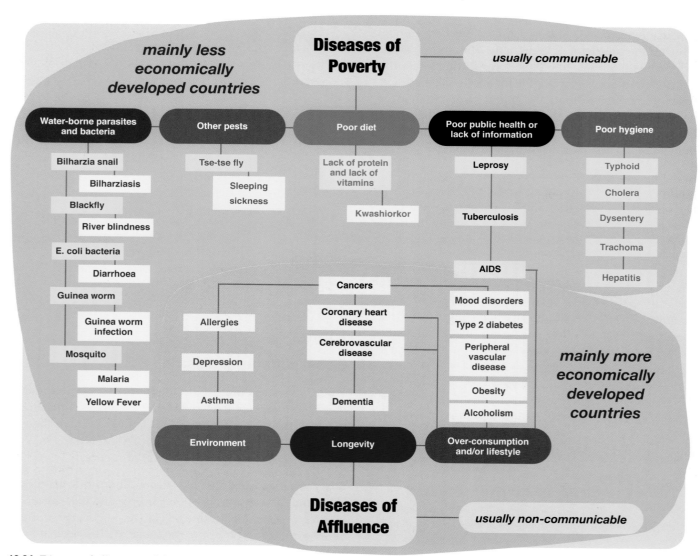

10.64 *Diseases of affluence and diseases of poverty.*

10.65 *This sign at the front of the Central Australian Aboriginal Congress in Alice Springs lists many of the services provided by the organisation to Indigenous Australians.*

Like many groups of indigenous peoples, Indigenous Australians have a different view of health compared with the concepts that are usually used for international comparisons. Indigenous notions of health tend to be holistic in nature, and in the words of Australia's National Aboriginal Health Strategy, "health (for Indigenous Australians) encompasses the social, emotional, spiritual and cultural well-being of the whole community."

For this reason, many indigenous communities around the world claim that a prerequisite for good health is maintaining close connections with the land, or home territory, of the group. Where successful programs to promote the health of indigenous peoples have been introduced in Canada, New Zealand, Australia and Alaska, a key element has been emphasising the connection between traditional cultural values and good health, and involving indigenous peoples in the decision making and implementation of the programs (figure 10.65).

Regardless of whether people live in LEDCs and MEDCs, there are some common overlapping factors that help to explain the state of people's health. These are sometimes known as **the causes of the causes of people's health**. The causes, which are explained in figure 10.66, include several facets of an individual's social context, which combine to affect the particular structures within their society, which in turn affect the environment in which a person lives, this in turn having an impact on their biological processes which finally determine the quality of their health. All these causes are in turn affected by wider external factors, including the country's health system and even the impact of globalisation as people become more internationally mobile and as transnational corporations become more and more involved in supplying medicines internationally.

QUESTION BLOCK 10I

1. *Define 'diseases of affluence' and 'diseases of poverty', and give five examples of each.*

2. *Describe the global distribution of diseases of affluence.*

3. *Suggest reasons that explain the distribution of diseases of affluence.*

4. *Describe the global distribution of diseases of poverty.*

5. *Suggest reasons that explain the distribution of diseases of poverty.*

6. *Explain how differences in the distribution of wealth within countries can affect the standards of health within those countries.*

7. *Conduct some research into the quality of health in two countries, one an LEDC and one an MEDC. Use the framework provided in figure 10.66 to explain the differences in standards of health in the two countries.*

The spread of disease

In 2009, a proposed speaker at the 2010 TED conference commented that "the greatest threat to our species is not global warming, warfare, poverty, or environmental degradation – the greatest threat is drug-resistant bacteria. Should a flesh-eating streptococcal infection someday exchange the right genes with drug-resistant Staphylococcal infection, the resulting super-bug could conceivably melt the human race like a wax museum on fire".

As in all evolution, and all natural cycles, diseases do mutate. This does pose significant potential threats to humanity. If this were to happen, some people will survive and it will have little to do with power, money or influence. Indeed, many medical experts warn that people in MEDCs are likely to be at a significant disadvantage compared with people in LEDCs, as many people in MECs have compromised immune systems because of the over-use of certain antibiotics both in the community and the food chain.

Although the 'causes of the causes' of health quality shown in figure 10.66 can be identified using the same general headings for both LEDCs and MEDCs, the way they operate in poorer societies is very different from their operation in more affluent areas.

In LEDCs, any factors combine to allow and even encourage the spread of diseases of poverty. Environmental factors include crowded working and living conditions, inadequate sanitation, and unclean water supplies. Social conditions include inadequate nutrition, low wages that make people reluctant to seek medical help, long working hours, inaccessible health care, and exposure to health risks and injury in unsafe working conditions.

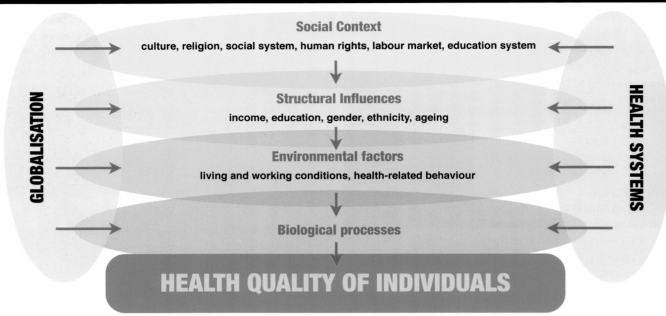

10.66 *Influences on the quality of health.*

Many diseases in LEDCs are spread through the process of geographic **diffusion**. Earlier in this chapter the

concept of diffusion was introduced (in the section headed 'the changing nature of food production'). In that section, it was noted that diffusion refers to the way in which new ideas are spread. The concept of diffusion also applies to the spread of most things across geographical space,   including the spread of communicable diseases.

There are two broad types of diffusion, expansion diffusion and relocation diffusion (figure 10.67). In **expansion diffusion**,   an innovation, an idea — or a disease — develops in a source area and spreads out from there while also remaining strong in its source area. This can happen in two ways. With **contagious diffusion**, the disease spreads out in several directions from the source, affecting most individuals who come into contact with it (even if they do not show the symptoms).

Not all diseases spread through contagious diffusion. Some diseases, such as AIDS, spread through **hierarchical diffusion**. In hierarchical diffusion, there are channels of diffusion among people or groups that are more susceptible to the disease, and the disease by-passes individuals or groups that do not share this vulnerability.

Expansion diffusion takes place in populations whose locations are stable and fixed. It is the disease that moves, not the people. Relocation diffusion, on the other hand, involves the movement of individual people who carry the disease to new locations (figure 10.67). When expansion diffusion occurs, the disease remains at the source area, often becoming more intense. When relocation diffusion occurs, the disease evacuates the source area along with the person who is the carrier.

The diffusion of disease can be thought of very simply as one person passing an infection to someone else, who in turn passes it on to others, and so on. However, this

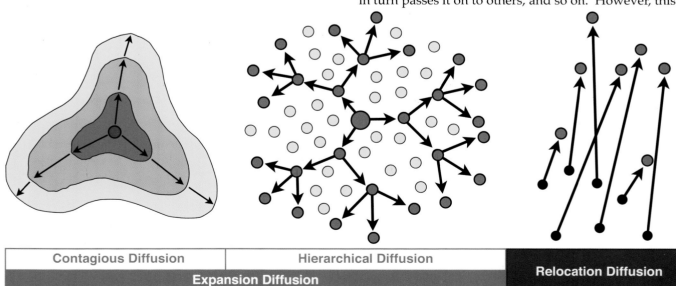

10.67 *Types of diffusion.*

simple process applies only to **directly transmitted diseases**, which are diseases that are transferred from one human to another. The processes involved with water-borne diseases and vector-borne diseases are slightly different, and will be considered later in this section.

One example of a directly transmitted disease of poverty is **leprosy**. Leprosy has a long history, first being identified in about 600BC. It affects the nerves and skin of affected people, leading to permanent damage to the limbs, skin and eyes (figures 10.68 and 10.69). Leprosy is not highly infectious, and 90% of the world's population have a natural immunity to it. It is spread via airborne droplets from the nose and mouth during close and frequent contacts with untreated cases. However, the bacteria multiply very slowly, and the incubation period is about five years; indeed, symptoms may not appear for 20 after infection.

10.68 *Two elderly leprosy sufferers in a remote area of Yunnan, China.*

10.69 *This woman in Ma Chan (China) had one leg amputated when she was young due to the impact of leprosy.*

Leprosy is easily treated, and if treatment begins in the early stages of the disease, then long-term disabilities are unlikely (figure 10.70). The fact that people still suffer from the disease highlights leprosy as a disease of pov-

erty, caused largely by lack of information or poor public health facilities, as often occurs in isolated regions of LEDCs.

10.70 *This young mother had leprosy, but it was cured before severe symptoms set in. The only visible damage from the leprosy is the sparse hair of her eyebrows.*

The World Health Organisation is trying to eliminate leprosy. Since 1995, WHO has supplied free Multi Drug Treatment (MDT) to leprosy patients anywhere in the world where leprosy remains a problem. The MDT comprises a combination of medications, including rifampicin, clofazimine and dapsone (which has been readily available for treating leprosy since 1930). In this way, WHO hopes to erect what geographers call a **barrier to diffusion** for leprosy.

10.71 *These two men suffer discrimination because of the facial disfigurement caused by leprosy when they were younger.*

One of the challenges in stopping the spread of leprosy is that the disease carries a strong social stigma because of the deformities that can arise in advanced cases (figure 10.71). The discrimination shown to leprosy sufferers is a major obstacle to self-reporting and early treatment as well as a major obstacle to former leprosy sufferers who have been cured returning to a normal life in wider society. As an example, none of the residents of a village populated with former leprosy sufferers where the author performed voluntary work over several years felt they would ever be able to return to their families because of the discrimination and ostracism they would face. As a result, they expected to spend the rest of their lives in the village where they were sent when first diagnosed with leprosy, in some cases three or four decades previously.

One of the main ways in which diseases spread in LEDCs is through dirty water (expansion diffusion), causing a variety of **water-borne diseases**. As recently as the early 1990s, 19% of people in urban areas and 42% of people in rural areas around the world did not have access to a safe supply of drinking water. As these figures were world averages, the figures for many LEDCs were much worse. Current statistics for 30 countries can be seen in table 2.1 in chapter 2.

A problem in LEDCs is that water is often used for many different purposes, and sometimes these uses are not compatible. For example, it is common to see people washing their clothes in the river even though the river bed might also be used to graze cattle and the water might be used as a toilet and garbage dump (figure 10.72).

10.72 *People bathe in the Hooghly River in central Kolkata (formerly Calcutta), India.*

One of the main pollutants of water in LEDCs is **human sewage**. Poorer people in such countries often have difficulty in affording hygienic disposal of human wastes. In some countries, a toilet is simply a hole in the ground or a river bank set aside for toileting. In such places, diseases can spread easily as flies and other vermin carry germs from the exposed excrement to people's food. It is hard for people to maintain personal hygiene under such conditions, and diseases such as diarrhoea can spread easily.

A more hygienic but more expensive way of disposing of human wastes is to dump them in a river. Usually, this involves building toilets over the water of a river or, occasionally, piping the wastes to the river from elsewhere (figure 10.73). When sewage is dumped in a river, bacteria known as E. coli feed on it. If large amounts of sewage are dumped in a river, the E. coli bacteria multiply greatly and can use up most of the oxygen in the water. When this happens, other forms of life may become starved of oxygen and die. When the oxygen in a body of water is

10.73 *These metal sheds above the river in a shanty area of Dhaka (Bangladesh) are toilets. The toilets have no storage facilities, causing water pollution as the wastes drop straight into the river.*

used up, the process of eutrophication is said to occur. Health problems occur when people use water with sewage dumped in it for other purposes such as washing and drinking.

Other water borne diseases are caused by parasites or organisms that live in the water. **Bilharzia** snails cause about 20 million deaths each year, and this is another example of disease that spreads by expansion diffusion. The snails live in warm, still waters of tropical areas. When people walk bare footed in the water, the snails enter the body through the soles of the feet or through a body orifice. Once in the human body, the snails reproduce in the kidney or the bladder. The person becomes weak and suffers from anaemia and failure of the bladder or kidney. When infected people urinate or defecate in a lake or river, the eggs of the bilharzia snail are released, starting the life cycle over once again.

Other water-borne diseases include guinea worm disease and river blindness. **Guinea worm disease** is caught by drinking water which contains water fleas which in turn contain guinea worm larvae. These larvae are found in West Africa and on the west coast of India. The disease causes an open sore, through which a worm up to 30 cm in length protrudes. **River blindness** is caused when the blackfly bites a human and deposits parasitic worms in the blood. One worm produces about a million offspring in a year inside the human body, causing swelling and intense itching. If the worms get under the eyelid, then blindness results. Most river blindness is found in West Africa.

Other diseases in LEDCs are caused by insects, many of which live and breed in water, such as mosquitoes. Diseases that are spread by insects are known as **vector-borne diseases**. **Malaria** kills thousands of people each year in tropical areas of the world. Malaria is a parasite which carried by one particular type of mosquito, the anopheles. The mosquitoes breed in stagnant water where the summer temperature is over 21°C (figure 10.74).

10.74 *Heavily polluted water in a poor residential district of Manila (Philippines).*

10.75 *A poster advocating immunisations in Mumbai, India.*

If an anopheles mosquito bites a person, the malaria parasite may be injected into the person's blood stream. Once in the blood, the parasite multiplies and can cause the person to suffer from the disease of malaria.

Malaria causes fever and fits of shivering. It can either kill a person directly, or else it can weaken a person so that they are unable to work properly. Sometimes, it weakens the immune system so that other diseases can infect and perhaps kill the sufferer. Malaria is largely found in tropical areas of developing nations. In previous centuries it was found in other areas also, including parts of Europe.

The spread of contagious diseases can be arrested or slowed by erecting **barriers to diffusion**. In cooler parts of the world, malaria was eradicated by draining swamps and marshes, and this represented a barrier to further expansion of the disease. However, in the tropics this task is so great as to be impossible. One effective barrier to the spread of malaria is to kill the mosquitoes by using pesticides such as DDT. However, pesticides have long lasting harmful effects on the environment. DDT builds up in living organisms, causing experts to fear that people may be poisoned by eating animals with DDT in their systems.

Another barrier to the diffusion of diseases is medication. People suffering from malaria are treated with medications such as chloroquine. However, these medications have significant side-effects — they can destroy the functioning of the liver and can cause blindness if used for long periods of time. Moreover, the ongoing use of anti-malarial treatments over many decades has caused the disease to develop a resistance to chloroquine and to other more potent medications. Thus, malaria is spreading in tropical areas today. About one in four children in Africa are infected with malaria every year. India now has over 10 million patients with malaria, causing great strains on the economy and the health system.

The spread of other diseases of poverty, such as polio, tuberculosis, whooping cough and diphtheria can be controlled by **vaccinations** and **immunisations** (figure 10.75). For many diseases, vaccinations provide the cheapest and most effective barriers to diffusion, although many people in LEDCs are unable to afford this preventative treatment.

There are also natural barriers to diffusion. Apart from climate that was mentioned previously, time and distance are both factors that works against diffusion (whether it is disease, ideas or innovations that are spreading). The further a disease (or an idea) moves from its source, the less likely it is to remain viable. Similarly, the passage of time reduces the effectiveness with which many diseases (and ideas) can spread. We refer to these natural barriers **time-distance decay**.

It may be possible to erect barriers to diffusion by eliminating the causes of these diseases, which are the blackflies, guinea worms and mosquitoes. However, it is difficult to drain all the stagnant water in tropical areas — after all, the staple food of much of the world (rice) is grown in flooded padi fields. Therefore, eliminating the parasites would probably involve the use of pesticides. The sprays involved are expensive for poor nations and they can cause significant damage to the environment. Perhaps the most effective barrier to diffusion in reducing the impact of these diseases would be to educate the local population in ways they can minimise the risks of catching the diseases.

QUESTION BLOCK 10J

1. *What is the difference between relocation diffusion and expansion diffusion?*

2. *What is the difference between the two types of expansion diffusion (contagious diffusion and hierarchical diffusion)? Name a disease that spreads by each of these types of diffusion.*

3. *What is time-distance decay?*

4. *Give examples of effective barriers to diffusion of diseases.*

5. *What problems might arise from the way the river is being used in figure 10.73?*

6. *Describe the effects of three water-borne diseases common in LEDCs. Why are these diseases so hard to eliminate?*

10.76 *A food market selling local produce in the streets of Axum, Ethiopia. The range of food available (tomatoes and potatoes) is insufficient for a balanced diet.*

Another common cause of diseases of poverty is **inadequate diet**. It is estimated that an average adult person weighing 70 kilograms needs about 2,500 calories each day to maintain body weight. However , there are many parts of the world where people are not receiving an average of 2500 calories per day. The areas where diets are deficient are mostly in Africa, western South America, south Asia and parts of south-east Asia. On the other hand, there are other parts of the world where the average person is eating much more than the amount of food needed to maintain body weight. These areas are mainly the developed nations of Europe, North America, Russia and Australasia.

It is estimated that over 20% of the world's population are chronically hungry. The problem is not simply the small amount of food that many people receive but that the diet may be unbalanced (figure 10.76). If people eat mainly carbohydrates and have insufficient protein , then their bodies cannot metabolise the carbohydrates. They can suffer from malnutrition even though their stomachs are full.

The most serious diseases of malnutrition are kwashiorkor and marasmus. Both these diseases are caused by not eating enough protein, found in meat, fish and beans (figure 10.77). **Marasmus** mainly affects children in their first year of life whereas kwashiorkor affects children from the age of two upwards. Children with marasmus are very underweight and are so thin that the shape of their bones protrudes through their skin. Muscles are thin, there is no fat and the face looks like that of an old person. On the other hand, children with **kwashiorkor** have a swollen belly, are listless with blotches on the skin and hair that has changed to a ginger colour. If young children have either of these diseases it may impede the development of the brain at a crucial stage of a child's life, causing mental retardation in adulthood — if the child survives to adulthood.

Other diseases of malnutrition are caused by insufficient vitamins. Insufficient vitamin B causes **beri-beri**. People with beri-beri waste away, become paralysed and may have disorders of the nervous system. Another vitamin deficiency disease is **rickets**, which is caused by having insufficient vitamin D. Rickets causes deformities in bones, especially the spine and the legs.

10.78 *Large flies cling to this meat on sale in the open air in a market in Chinsapo, Malawi.*

Diseases can be caused by food-related problems other than the amount consumed. In many parts of the world, **storage of food** is difficult because of lack of refrigeration (or even lack of electricity). Where meat is stored in the open without refrigeration, flies can contaminate the food and spread disease (figure 10.78). Furthermore, bacteria multiply in warm temperatures and diseases such as food poisoning and salmonella can result. That is why the markets in many places without refrigeration sell live animals; as seen earlier in figure 10.77, it is the cheapest and most effective way of keeping the food fresh.

As nations develop economically, **food preferences** change. These changes in diet affect people's health.

10.77 *Protein is available in this market in Lijiang (China) in the form of chicken, dog and pig meat.*

In general, people in wealthier societies tend to eat more red meat, more protein, more dairy foods, more sugar and less fibre than people in more traditional societies. People in wealthier societies are more likely to eat processed 'fast' foods. On the other hand, people in traditional societies are more likely to eat with the family at home. Some fast foods have been criticised as offering an unbalanced diet if eaten too frequently. Furthermore, low fibre and high fat foods have been linked to bowel cancer, strokes and heart disease — diseases of affluence.

In recent years, fast food has become very popular in many LEDCs where economic growth is occurring (figure 10.79). This is another example of expansion diffusion, this time a spread of new ideas and cultural values that in turn leads to a spread of **diseases of affluence into LEDCs**. Since 1960, Japanese people have more than tripled their per capita consumption of beef. Many doctors believe that this is the cause of a large increase in rates of breast cancer among Japanese women during the same period of time.

10.79 *A large KFC outlet in Hanoi, Vietnam.*

Another example of the diffusion of Western ideas and cultural values is the widespread advertising of cow's milk and baby formula foods (figure 10.80). Thus, women may be persuaded by large companies to **stop breastfeeding** their babies and bottle feed instead. This has caused significant health problems, especially in LEDCs where mothers have stopped breastfeeding. The best balanced and most appropriate food for any baby is the milk from the baby's own mother. Milk formula may cause problems for babies because it is often (of necessity) made in a non-sterilised bottle with impure water. Further problems can occur because uneducated mothers without literacy cannot read the instructions and may quite possibly mix the formula with the wrong concentration, leading either to malnutrition (if it is too weak) or dehydration (if it is too strong). Bottled baby's milk is made from cow's milk (to which many young babies are allergic). Moreover, milk formula costs money whereas breastfeeding is free (figure 10.81).

10.80 *A huge sign promoting infant cereals as a substitute for breast milk at a bus station in Harare, Zimbabwe.*

Severe illness and even death can result from babies being fed unhygienic milk formula instead of breastmilk. Most mothers in LEDCs do not have access either to pure water or to the means of purifying contaminated water. This can also be a problem in MEDCs.

In response to this problem, the World Health Organisation has called on all countries adopt a voluntary common code of conduct. Countries signing the code of conduct

10.81 *Milk powder for sale at the entrance to a maternity hospital in Tangshan, China.*

have agreed to halt to all advertising of powdered milk for babies and feeding bottles, to stop giving free samples of milk for babies, to ban milk company employees from acting as health educators and to require labels on baby milk which state the hazards of bottle feeding and the benefits of breastfeeding. Adopting the common code of conduct would be an example of a **regulatory barrier to the diffusion of diseases** related to unhygienic milk formula for babies. Several countries now have policies which support breastfeeding. In Papua New Guinea, for example, a baby's feeding bottle may only be obtained with a doctor's prescription certifying that the mother is unable to breastfeed.

QUESTION BLOCK 10K

1. *Give examples of some diseases of poverty that are diet-related.*

2. *With reference to types of diffusion, explain how these diseases spread.*

3. *Give examples of some effective barriers to diffusion of diet-related diseases of poverty.*

Some years ago, the-then Director of the World Health Organisation (WHO) stated:

"Global standards of health and well-being are declining. Life expectancy, after reaching a peak, is now decreasing. Cancer rates are rising; heart diseases are rampant; drugs, alcohol, cigarettes and traffic accidents nowadays kill more people than did all the epidemics together in earlier centuries."

He was referring mainly to **diseases of affluence** in that statement. Diffusion of diseases of affluence generally follows a different pattern from the spread of diseases of poverty. Increases in the rates of diseases of affluence are caused, perhaps ironically, those things that many people would regard as improving their quality of life, such as more labour-saving devices, less need for physical exertion, over-consumption of food, tobacco and alcohol, more use of mechanised transport, easy access to cheap fast-food, less exposure to infections throughout life (which means immunity is likely to be less fully developed), and the consequences of longer life expectancies.

Examples of diseases of affluence were listed in figure 10.64. Many people regard **obesity** as a classic disease of affluence because it thought to be caused by a combination of factors such as over-consumption of highly processed foods, insufficient exercise and stress. Obesity can be defined as having such an excess of body fat that a person's health is adversely affected. Obesity is measured in terms of a person's BMI (body mass index), which relates a person's weight to height. According to the WHO (World Health Organisation), a normal BMI is defined as being within the range of 18.5 to 25 kg/m². An overweight person has a BMI of 25 kg/m² or more, while obesity is indicated by a BMI of 30 kg/m² or more. By comparison, an underweight person has a BMI of less than 18.5 kg/m², while a BMI of under 16.5 kg/m² indicates severe underweight.

The world distribution of obesity is shown in figure 10.82. Although the general pattern is broadly related to affluence and economic development, there are many significant exceptions to this pattern. The six countries with the

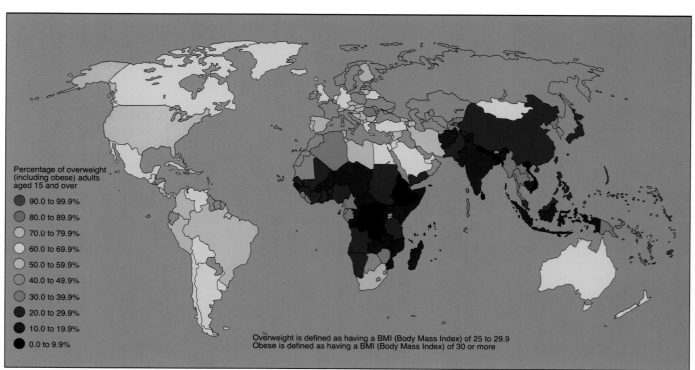

Percentage of overweight (including obese) adults aged 15 and over

- 90.0 to 99.9%
- 80.0 to 89.9%
- 70.0 to 79.9%
- 60.0 to 69.9%
- 50.0 to 59.9%
- 40.0 to 49.9%
- 30.0 to 39.9%
- 20.0 to 29.9%
- 10.0 to 19.9%
- 0.0 to 9.9%

Overweight is defined as having a BMI (Body Mass Index) of 25 to 29.9
Obese is defined as having a BMI (Body Mass Index) of 30 or more

10.82 *Percentage of overweight (including obese) adults aged 15 and over.*

highest percentages of obese adults are Nauru, Micronesia, Cook Islands and Tonga (with more than 90% of their adult populations being overweight), plus Niue and Samoa (with over 80% of adults overweight). All these countries are relatively economically less developed Pacific Island nations, suggesting that diet or culture is an important factor in influencing obesity. In fact, obesity is regarded in these societies as a positive attribute as it is thought to signify wealth and prestige.

Several affluent nations also have high rates of obesity, such as the United States, with 74% of its adult population being overweight, Kuwait (74%), New Zealand (68%), Australia (67%), United Kingdom (68%) and Canada (61%) (figure 10.83). On the other hand, several other affluent nations have much lower rates of obesity, such as Denmark (46%), Italy (45%), France (40%) and Japan (23%). At the other end of the scale, countries with low levels of obesity, such as Vietnam (6%), Bangladesh (6%), Ethiopia (5%) and Eritrea (4%) are LEDCs (figure 10.84). Overall, the pattern shown in figure 10.82 suggests that while obesity is a disease of affluence, it does not affect all countries and all cultures to the same extent.

10.83 *A family at Kitty Hawk, USA. The US has one of the world's highest rates of obesity.*

10.84 *Most of the people gathering water at this communal well in Eritrea are underweight. Eritrea has one of the world's lowest rates of obesity.*

Of course, obesity is just one example of a disease of affluence. It has been said that in the coming decades, rising affluence will bring a global 'plague' of **neurological diseases**. The reason that affluence is increasing life expectancies and ageing brings neurological disorders. Figure 10.85 shows the distribution of countries where 20% or more of the national populations are aged over 65 years today, and the projected pattern in 2050. This is because improved medical care has lengthened average life expectancies around the world, and at present, worldwide average life expectancies are increasing by about five hours per day.

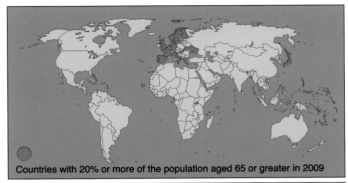

Countries with 20% or more of the population aged 65 or greater in 2009

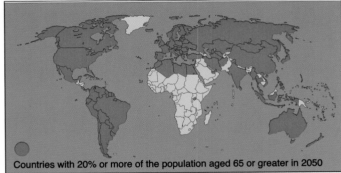

Countries with 20% or more of the population aged 65 or greater in 2050

10.85 *Percentage of the population aged 65 and over in 2009 (top) and predicted in 2050 (bottom).*

As a consequence of increasing longevity, age-related diseases such as Alzheimer's disease (a type of dementia) and Parkinson's disease will almost certainly increase. As people age beyond 65 years, the chances of getting either (or both) of these diseases increases exponentially. It is expected by by 2050, the United States alone will have about 32 million people over the age of 80, and unless there are significant medical breakthroughs before that time, about half of them can be expected to be affected by Alzheimer's disease while an additional 10% will have Parkinson's disease. On the brighter side, for reasons that are not yet understood, there is a significant negative correlation between the incidence of neurological diseases and most forms of cancers, meaning that those who get cancer are less likely to be also affected by dementia.

It can be seen from this discussion that the concept of diffusion relates somewhat differently to diseases of affluence than to diseases of poverty. Most diseases of affluence are to some extent 'lifestyle diseases', and thus they are generally non-communicable. Therefore, the spread of most diseases of affluence is the consequence of the spread of affluence, not a direct process of disease diffusion as occurs with infectious diseases. For that reason, the influence of globalisation (as shown in figure 10.66) is even more significant for understanding the spread of diseases of affluence than it is for diseases of poverty.

Because diffusion of diseases of affluence is a secondary process, barriers to diffusion become more difficult to develop. Although some might argue that MEDCs ought to reduce their standards of wealth, this is usually argued on the grounds of environmental sustainability of global justice rather than as a strategy to reduce the incidence of diseases of affluence. Suggestions to reduce the rates of diseases caused by longevity by shortening people's lives are also unlikely to attract widespread support. This, the barriers to diffusion are more difficult to identify and define for diseases of affluence than they are for diseases of poverty.

QUESTION BLOCK 10L

1. *Why are neurological diseases regarded as diseases of affluence?*

2. *Referring to data in figure 10.82, explain why obesity is (or is not) a disease of affluence.*

3. *Explain how the concept of diffusion relates to diseases of affluence.*

4. *It is claimed that "the barriers to diffusion are more difficult to identify and define for diseases of affluence than they are for diseases of poverty". Identify and describe (a) the factors that have led to reductions in the incidence of diseases of affluence, and (b) the factors that have the potential to reduce rates of diseases of affluence in the future.*

Geographic Factors and Impacts of the Spread of AIDS

One way of classifying diseases is according to the way they are spread. **Water-borne diseases** are spread when a person consumes or has contact with water that is contaminated by the disease. Examples include bilharziasis, guinea worm infection, cholera, dysentery and river blindness. **Vector-borne diseases** are transmitted to humans by an insect (such as a mosquito or tick) or an other type of arthropod such as a spider. **Directly transmitted diseases** are transferred from one human to another. This can occur in several ways, such as droplet contact (coughing or sneezing on another person), direct physical contact (touching an infected person, including sexual contact), indirect contact (such as by touching or eating something that an infected person has touched).

An example of the spread of a **vector-borne disease** (malaria) was provided in the previous section. However, the geographical factors influencing the spread of directly transmitted diseases are quite different, and this will be shown here with reference to AIDS.

The impact of AIDS in raising death rates in some parts of the world, and especially in Africa, was discussed earlier in this chapter. AIDS, or Acquired Immune Deficiency Syndrome, is a **sexually transmitted disease** that was first identified in 1981. It is caused by a virus known as HIV, or Human Immunodeficiency Virus. Between 1981 and 1994, about 15 million people became infected with HIV, and at that time (1994), the World Health Organisation estimated that between 30 million and 40 million people would have been infected by HIV by the year 2000. The forecast was only slightly pessimistic, and by the end of 2007, the figure had reached 33.2 million (table 10.5). As this table and figure 10.86 show, more than 90% of AIDS cases are in Less Economically Developed Countries (LEDCs). Because AIDS has become a large-scale global health problem in a short time, it is referred to as a pandemic.

As shown in figure 10.64 earlier in this chapter, AIDS affects both LEDCs and MEDCs. However, the causes and the effects of the disease are quite different in each case. Among the More Economically Developed Countries (MEDCs), AIDS is becoming a more significant cause of death, although it is still far behind cancer, heart disease and strokes. As long ago as 1986, AIDS was the main killer of young adult males in San Francisco. AIDS can be spread in several ways, including through intra-venous drug use, using infected needles, during sexual activity, from a blood transfusion using poorly screened blood and from an infected mother to her unborn baby. In MEDCs, AIDS is primarily (although certainly not only) a lifestyle-related disease.

The pattern in LEDCs is quite different, and in those countries AIDS is primarily a disease of poverty caused by lack of information and inadequate health care systems. In Sub-Saharan Africa, AIDS is the leading cause of death. Some countries with very high rates of HIV infection include Swaziland (33% of the population), Botswana (24%), Lesotho (23%), Zimbabwe (20%) and South Africa (19%).

Unlike most diseases in the world, and being a new disease, AIDS has been studied and recorded since its very beginnings. This enables us to study the spread of the disease, which we call **spatial diffusion**, and to learn something about the spread of diseases in general. In this way, geography makes a contribution to helping the welfare of humanity (see the ToK Box on page 438).

There have been two main types of HIV. These are known as HIV-1 and HIV-2. Most of the recorded cases have

Table 10.5

The World Distribution of HIV/AIDS, 2001 to 2007

Region	Year	Adults and Children Living with HIV	Adults and Children Newly Infected with HIV	Adult Prevalence (%)	Adult and Child Deaths due to AIDS
Sub-Saharan Africa	2007	22,500,000	1,700,000	5.0	1,600,000
	2004	21,400,000	2,000,000	5.7	1,500,000
	2001	20,900,000	2,200,000	5.8	1,400,000
Middle East and North Africa	2007	380,000	35,000	0.3	25,000
	2004	340,000	39,000	0.3	23,000
	2001	300,000	41,000	0.3	22,000
South and South-East Asia	2007	4,000,000	340,000	0.3	270,000
	2004	3,750,000	400,000	0.3	230,000
	2001	3,500,000	450,000	0.3	170,000
East Asia	2007	800,000	92,000	0.1	32,000
	2004	650,000	84,000	0.1	22,000
	2001	420,000	77,000	<0.1	12,000
Australia and the Pacific	2007	75,000	14,000	0.4	1,200
	2004	52,000	9,000	0.3	900
	2001	26,000	3,800	0.2	<500
Latin America	2007	1,600,000	100,000	0.5	58,000
	2004	1,450,000	120,000	0.4	55,000
	2001	1,300,000	130,000	0.4	51,000
Caribbean	2007	230,000	17,000	1.0	11,000
	2004	215,000	18,500	1.0	12,500
	2001	190,000	20,000	1.0	14,000
Eastern Europe and Central Asia	2007	1,600,000	150,000	0.9	55,000
	2004	1,000,000	190,000	0.7	32,000
	2001	630,000	230,000	0.4	8,000
Western and Central Europe	2007	760,000	31,000	0.3	12,000
	2004	610,000	30,000	0.2	9,500
	2001	620,000	32,000	0.2	10,000
North America	2007	1,300,000	46,000	0.6	21,000
	2004	1,200,000	45,000	0.6	21,000
	2001	1,100,000	44,000	0.6	21,000
WORLD	2007	33,200,000	2,500,000	0.8	2,100,000
	2004	30,667,000	2,935,500	0.8	1,905,500
	2001	29,000,000	3,200,000	0.8	1,700,000

Source: UNAIDS / WHO

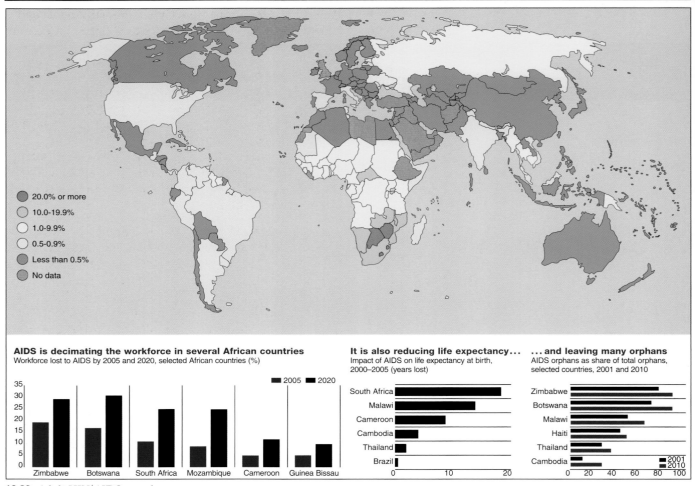

10.86 *Adult HIV/AIDS prevalence.*

been HIV-1. Most virologists (people who study viruses) believe that HIV-1 began with the transfer of a similar virus from chimpanzees to humans in central Africa, possibly in Congo, which then mutated. Although it is conceivable that the virus transferred from chimpanzees to humans through a sexual act, the commonly accepted theory is that the virus was caught as a result as a result of chimpanzees being killed and eaten, or perhaps when their blood entered a hunter's body through skin cuts or wounds. Although cross-species infection is fairly rare, chimpanzees and humans share a close genetic relationship, and it is certainly possible that a virus could have been caught by a human, after which the virus mutated to become HIV-1.

It is thought that HIV-1 was taken from central Africa to Haiti by vacationers returning home. From Haiti, HIV-1 was taken to the United States by American tourists, and from the United States it spread to Europe (figure 10.87).

HIV-2 was not identified until 1986. The spread of HIV-2 was quite different from the spread of HIV-1. HIV-2 seems to have begun in West Africa, probably in the small nation of Guinea-Bissau. Guinea-Bissau is a former Portuguese colony, and the disease spread from there to Portugal (in Europe) and to two other former Portuguese

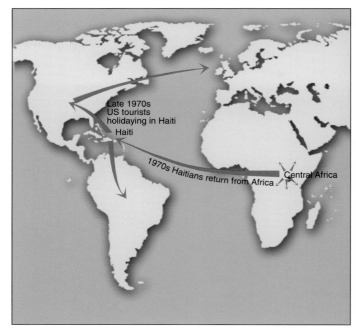

10.87 *The spread of HIV-1.*

colonies in Africa, Mozambique and Angola (figure 10.88). From these four nations, HIV-2 then spread elsewhere in Africa. The disease spread to North America from Guinea-Bissau, to South America from Guinea-Bissau and

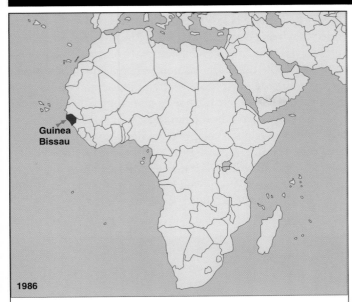

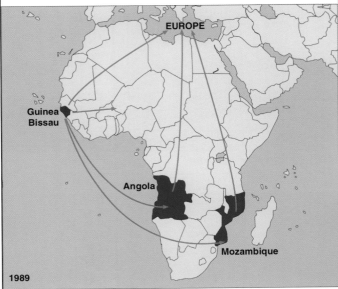

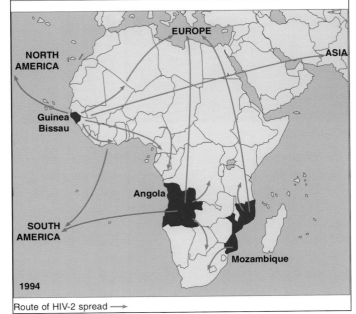

Route of HIV-2 spread ⟶

10.88 *The spread of HIV-2.*

Angola, and to Europe from Guinea-Bissau, Angola and Mozambique. By 1994, Portugal was still the main centre of dispersion of HIV-2 through Europe.

AIDS has now become a major cost to the world's health services. There are the **direct costs** of diagnosing and treating the disease as well as the **indirect costs** of the loss of earnings due to premature deaths. AIDS is a prolonged illness, and sufferers sometimes draw upon health services for many years as a result of the disease. Because AIDS usually affects young adults who would usually be the most productive sector of society, the indirect costs of AIDS are very significant.

The impact of HIV / AIDS in Sub-Saharan Africa is major. In the nation of Kenya, there are only 700 doctors, and they are overwhelmed by the AIDS pandemic. The expression which is often used in Kenya is "if you're not infected, you're still affected". In countries such as Kenya, AIDS has reduced the supply of teachers in schools, and many children are forced to stay home from school to look after family members who are sick. In these ways, AIDS will cause ongoing problems for national development in the coming decades. These problems are amplified when many children are forced to leave school to earn income, replacing the income earned by parents who have died from AIDS. It is understandable that many LEDCs are worried about AIDS and are trying to educate their populations about the dangers of it (figures 10.89 and 10.90).

10.89 *An AIDS awareness sign in a small village in southern Ethiopia.*

One of the problems faced in the fight against AIDS is the prejudice shown towards AIDS sufferers by a large part of the general population in many countries. In the early years of the pandemic, AIDS was sometimes referred to as the 'gay plague', causing many people to feel there was something sinister or immoral about the disease. Some even labelled the disease "God's revenge".

Although unprotected homosexual sex between men continues to account for most new cases of AIDS in many countries, such as Canada, New Zealand, Australia, the

Food and health

United Kingdom and many nations in Latin America, other causes account for the majority of new cases in other parts of the world. In Western Europe, for example, the largest proportion of new HIV infections comes from unprotected heterosexual sex, often between migrants from countries where the rate of HIV infection is high. In Western Europe, less than one-third of newly diagnosed HIV infections are due to unsafe sex between men, and only about one case in twenty to injecting drug use.

10.90 *An AIDS awareness poster in Lilongwe, Malawi.*

In Russia and other former Soviet republics such as Ukraine and Belarus, the main source of new HIV infection is injecting drug use. The causes in some LEDCs are also lifestyle-related, although in different ways to MEDCs. In Thailand, for example, almost half new cases are women who have caught it from their husbands or partners who had been infected either during unsafe paid sex or through injecting drug use. In Indonesia, the main cause is using contaminated injecting equipment, but other important causes are unprotected paid sex and, to a much lesser extent, unprotected sex between men. In other Asian countries such as Pakistan and Vietnam, the main cause of new HIV infections is injecting drug use (figure 10.91).

10.91 *A poster in Ethiopia educating people not to accept syringes because of the risk of catching AIDS.*

In Africa, lifestyle is less of a factor compared with other causes such as poor public health or lack of information. In most parts of Africa and some parts of Asia, the majority of new HIV cases are women (whereas most new cases are men outside of Africa). Many of these women have caught HIV from their husbands after they (the husbands) had been away from home having paid sex. The women's HIV infection is often diagnosed when they arrive at pregnancy clinics, meaning that their babies will be born with an HIV-infection. For many of these babies, they will grow up as HIV-infected orphans as their parents will have died from AIDS when they were still very young (figures 10.92 and 10.93).

10.92 *Children with AIDS sitting in front of their orphanage in Phnom Penh, Cambodia.*

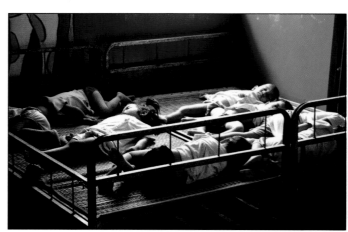

10.93 *Young AIDS sufferers in an orphanage in Phnom Penh.*

One of the problems faced by planners trying to combat the spread of AIDS is the high cost of treatment. For example, southern China's Guangzhou province, with a population of almost 90 million people, has only one dedicated AIDS treatment ward with 24 beds in a hospital, where one month's treatment (including medicines) costs almost $US5,000. Such a cost is typical of many countries, but in LEDCs it is clearly beyond the scope of many AIDS sufferers, who simply must leave the condition untreated. AIDS is an example of a medical condition where prevention is much cheaper and more effective than trying to cure the disease (figure 10.94).

10.95 *A long distance truck stop in Africa. The early spread of AIDS occurred along the trucking routes.*

QUESTION BLOCK 10M

1. *What do the letters (a) AIDS and (b) HIV stand for?*

2. *How serious is the AIDS pandemic? Use specific statistics from table 10.5 to support your answer.*

3. *Describe the world distribution of AIDS.*

4. *Using figure 10.87, describe the spread of HIV-1.*

5. *Using figure 10.88, describe the spread of HIV-2.*

6. *What are the (a) direct costs and (b) the indirect costs of AIDS?*

7. *What management strategies can be applied to reduce the impact of AIDS?*

8. *Contrast the geographic factors responsible for the incidence and spread of malaria and AIDS.*

10.94 *Condoms have been shown to reduce the risk of catching AIDS.*

In examining the geographical factors responsible for the incidence and spread of AIDS, it is clear that travel (relocation diffusion) played an important role in the early spread of HIV. In Africa, where the virus originated, AIDS almost certainly spread along long-distance truck routes (figure 10.95). International travel by young men who were enjoying the gay sexual revolution of the late 1970s and early 1980s then played a significant role in spreading the virus unknowingly on a global scale. It is also thought that several of the early outbreaks in African nations were not started by Africans infected with the early forms of virus, but by foreigners visiting from overseas where the epidemic had also been expanding — an example of **reverse diffusion**.

11 Urban Environments

Cities are places of intense social interaction and focal points of production, wealth generation and consumption. Their patterns of wealth and deprivation can result in conflict.

Outline

Urban populations Page 460
Urbanisation, inward and outward movement of people, natural change and the global megacity.

Urban land use Page 491
Land use patterns, especially in residential areas and other areas of economic activity.

Urban stress Page 505
Urban microclimates and air pollution, as well as other types of environmental and social stress.

The sustainable city Page 535
The city as a system, including case studies of sustainable strategies.

ToK BoX — Page 476
Collecting data

Urban Populations

Urbanisation

The world has never experienced urbanisation on the scale that it is occurring today. Writing in the mid-1990s, Philip Hirsch described urbanisation as 'one of the most dramatic demographic, economic and social changes occurring in the ... world'. It is fair to claim that urbanisation is one of the major changes of global significance in the world today. Its impact will continue for many decades at least, and so it is important for people today to understand something about this issue and its causes and consequences.

Geographers distinguish two main types of settlement — urban and rural. A **rural settlement** is a dwelling or group of dwellings that simply provides housing for farm workers. In other words, no services are provided other than the **dormitory** function of providing accommodation for the residents. On the other hand, an **urban settlement** is an area of habitation that provides services to the surrounding countryside. In other words, as soon as a rural settlement begins to have services such as shops or manufacturing, then it has become an urban settlement (figure 11.1).

In most nations it is usually statisticians (rather than geographers) who use the concept of 'urban settlement' to classify places. Statisticians prefer clear and precise defi-

11.1 *This fishing village on the coast of Ghana has only dormitory accommodation, and so is a rural settlement. When the village gets its first shop, it will become an urban settlement.*

Table 11.1

The minimum numbers of people needed to classify a settlement officially as 'urban' in selected countries

COUNTRY	MINIMUM POPULATION OF A SETTLEMENT TO BE CONSIDERED 'URBAN'	OTHER CONDITIONS
Sweden	200	and less than 200 metres between houses
Albania	400	
South Africa	500	or 100 people if the population is white
Papua New Guinea	500	
Peru	600	must have 100 or more occupied buildings
Australia	1,000	must have at least 250 dwellings of which 100 are occupied
Czech Republic	2,000	and having more than 75 people per hectare, three or more rooms in at least 10% of the houses, piped water and sewerage in at least part of the town, at least two doctors and one pharmacy and less than 15% of people engaged in agriculture
France	2,000	and with less than 200 metres between houses
Israel	2,000	and a non-agricultural community
United States	2,500	
Austria	5,000	
Bangladesh	5,000	and has streets, tap water, sewerage and electric lights
Ghana	5,000	
India	5,000	and population density must be at least 390 people per square kilometre and at least 75% of adult males are employed in non-agricultural pursuits
Switzerland	10,000	
Malaysia	10,000	
Senegal	15,000	
Japan	30,000	and with 60% or more people (including dependants) engaged in manufacturing, trade or other urban types of business
Serbia	15,000 5,000 3,000 2,000	unconditional urban classification if at least 30% of people are not farmers if at least 70% of people are not farmers if at least 80% of people are not farmers
Bulgaria	-	a town can be classified as urban regardless of size

Source: United Nations Demographic Yearbook

nitions that are easy to work with, even if they are not completely accurate. Therefore, each nation in the world has developed its own definition of 'urban' based on the population size of the settlement. For example, in Australia the statisticians say that services will begin to appear in settlements when they have about 1,000 people. Therefore, they generalise and say that settlements with more than 1,000 people are 'urban' while those with fewer than 1,000 people are 'rural'. In India, the statisticians found that services do not usually appear until there are at least 5,000 people living in a settlement, so in India 'urban'

settlements are defined as having 5,000 people or more. Table 11.1 shows the range of definitions of 'urban settlements' in some nations of the world.

The different definitions used for 'urban' around the world make international comparisons very difficult. For example, table 11.2 gives the proportion of people classified as 'urban' in a number of different nations around the world. However, when using the table it is important to remember that the definitions used in each nation are different. Moreover, the accuracy of data collection in many nations may be very poor, especially in nations that

Urban environments

lack the money to spend on data collection or where the culture of the people does not esteem accurate figures as Western societies tend to do. With this in mind, the data in table 11.2 should be viewed as approximations only.

There is an important difference between 'urban growth' and 'urbanisation', and unfortunately these two terms are often used in different ways in different books. **Urban growth** can be used correctly in two ways. First, it can mean the increase in size of a particular urban place. For example, if Sydney's population increases from 3.5 million to 3.6 million, we can say that urban growth has

occurred. The second way that the term 'urban growth' can be used is to mean an increase in the number of people living in urban centres. For example, we could say that the urban population of Australia increased from 7 million to 8 million people, and that therefore 'urban growth' had occurred.

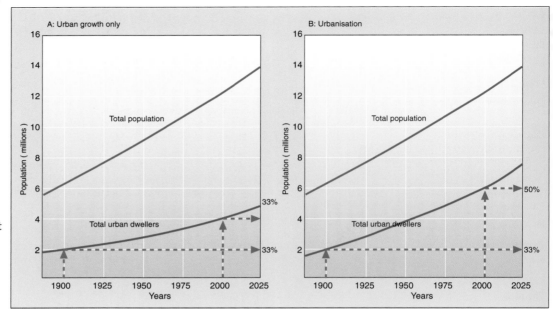

11.2 *Urban growth and urbanisation.*

>> Some Useful Definitions

Brownfield site — this refers to abandoned, derelict, or under-used industrial buildings and land, which may be contaminated but has potential for redevelopment.

Counterurbanisation — a process involving the movement of population away from inner urban areas to a new town, a new estate, a commuter town or a village on the edge or just beyond the city limits / rural-urban fringe.

Ecological footprint — The theoretical measurement of the amount of land and water a population requires to produce the resources it consumes and to absorb its waste under prevailing technology.

Megacity — a city with a population of at least 10 million people.

Reurbanisation — the development of activities to increase residential population densities within the existing built-up area of a city. This may include the re-development of vacant land and the refurbishment of housing and the development new business enterprises.

Suburb — a residential area within or just outside the boundaries of a city.

Suburbanisation — the outward growth of towns and cities to engulf surrounding villages and rural areas. This may result from the out-migration of population from the inner urban area to the suburbs or from inward rural-urban movement.

Sustainable urban management strategy — an approach to urban management that seeks to maintain and improve the quality of life for current and future urban dwellers. Aspects of management may be social (housing quality, crime) economic (jobs, income) and environmental (air, water, land and resources).

Urbanisation — the process by which an increasing percentage of a country's population comes to live in towns and cities. It may involve both rural-urban migration and natural increase.

Urban sprawl — the unplanned and uncontrolled physical expansion of an urban area into the surrounding countryside. It is closely linked to the process of suburbanisation.

Table 11.2
Urban Population Statistics for Selected Countries and Regions

	Urban population as a percentage of total				Average annual population change 2000 to 2005 (%)		Percentage of total population in cities with at least 750,000 people		
	1960	1980	2000	2020	Urban	Rural	1965	1995	2015
Africa	**21**	**27**	**38**	**49**	**4.0**	**1.6**	**7**	**11**	**n.a.**
Algeria	38	43	59	70	3.2	0.5	9	13	15
Burundi	2	4	9	17	5.9	2.1	0	0	0
Kenya	9	16	33	48	5.0	1.2	4	7	10
Libya	27	69	88	91	3.5	0.8	24	46	80
South Africa	47	48	50	59	2.7	1.5	23	30	34
Tanzania	5	15	28	42	5.2	1.7	2	9	14
Zambia	23	40	45	55	3.3	1.8	4	16	22
Asia	**22**	**27**	**38**	**50**	**2.8**	**0.3**	**10**	**13**	**n.a.**
China	18	20	34	49	2.9	-0.6	10	12	17
India	19	23	28	39	2.9	0.9	7	11	14
Indonesia	16	22	40	55	3.4	-0.3	7	9	12
Japan	67	76	79	83	0.4	-0.8	26	39	41
Myanmar	21	24	28	40	3.4	0.9	5	9	11
Nepal	3	7	12	21	5.2	2.0	0	0	0
Singapore	100	100	100	100	1.0	0.0	100	100	100
Thailand	13	17	22	33	2.5	0.2	8	11	15
North and Central America	**67**	**74**	**77**	**82**	**1.0**	**-0.3**	**36**	**39**	**n.a.**
Canada	73	76	77	81	0.9	0.2	29	41	42
Cuba	58	68	78	84	0.8	-1.4	20	20	21
Haiti	18	24	35	48	3.6	0.8	8	21	29
Mexico	55	66	74	79	1.7	0.6	25	33	32
United States	72	74	77	82	1.0	-0.4	39	42	42
South America	**56**	**68**	**80**	**85**	**1.8**	**-0.7**	**26**	**37**	**n.a.**
Argentina	76	83	89	92	1.4	-0.9	40	43	42
Bolivia	40	45	65	75	3.2	0.0	11	28	35
Brazil	50	66	81	87	1.7	-1.4	25	34	35
Peru	52	65	73	79	2.1	0.2	19	28	29
Uruguay	81	85	91	94	0.7	-1.4	43	42	41
Europe	**64**	**69**	**75**	**80**	**0.3**	**-1.2**	**23**	**24**	**n.a.**
Albania	31	34	39	51	1.9	-0.1	0	0	0
Belgium	93	95	97	98	0.2	-2.1	11	11	11
Estonia	62	70	74	80	-0.3	-1.8	0	0	0
France	67	73	76	81	0.5	-0.8	22	22	22
Germany	78	83	88	91	0.2	-1.5	42	44	45
Romania	38	49	58	68	0.6	-1.4	8	9	10
Russia	63	70	78	83	0.1	-1.8	20	21	22
Spain	61	73	78	83	0.3	-1.1	16	19	20
United Kingdom	87	89	89	91	0.2	-0.6	28	27	26
Oceania	**69**	**71**	**70**	**72**	**1.3**	**1.3**	**39**	**41**	**n.a.**
Australia	83	86	85	87	1.1	0.8	56	58	55
Fiji	33	38	42	54	2.6	0.8	0	0	0
New Zealand	79	83	87	90	1.3	-0.4	20	26	27
Papua New Guinea	5	13	17	27	4.0	1.7	0	0	0
Solomon Islands	9	11	20	32	5.8	2.3	0	0	0
WORLD	**36**	**39**	**47**	**57**	**2.2**	**0.4**	**15**	**17**	**n.a.**

Source: United Nations Population Division. *Figures after 2000 are projections*

Urban environments

The term **urbanisation** is quite different. Whereas urban growth refers to increase in the *number* of people living in urban areas, urbanisation refers to an increase in the *proportion* of people living in urban areas. The diagrams in figure 11.2 help to explain the difference. In part A of the figure, the national population in a hypothetical nation increases from 6 million people in 1900 to 12 million people in 2000. During the same period, urban population increases from 2 million people to 4 million people. In 1900, the urban population was 33% of the total population, and in 2000 the urban population was still 33% of the total. Urban growth had occurred but urbanisation had not occurred, as the *proportion* of people living in urban centres had not increased.

In part B of the figure on the other hand, the national population in our hypothetical nation still increases from 6 million people in 1900 to 12 million people in 2000. However, this time urban population increases from 2 million people to 6 million people during the same period. In 1900, the urban population was 33% of the total population, but by 2000 this had increased to 50% of the total. Urban growth has occurred once again and this time urbanisation has also occurred, as the *proportion* of people living in urban centres has increased.

The term 'urbanisation' can also be used in a slightly different, but related, way. We have just described the *process* of urbanisation, but we can also refer to the *level* of urbanisation. The level of urbanisation is the proportion of the population living in urban areas at a given time. In table 11.2, data is given headed 'Urban Population as a percentage of total population'. This column could have also been headed 'Level of Urbanisation'.

QUESTION BLOCK 11A

1. What is the difference between the following pairs of terms?
   a. rural settlement and urban settlement
   b. urban growth and urbanisation

2. Explain why it is very difficult to make international comparisons of urbanisation.

3. Using the information in table 11.2:
   a. List the continents/regions shown in descending order of urban population as a percentage of total population in 2000.
   b. Devise a classification of 'high', 'medium' and 'low' urbanisation and allocate the nations listed into the three categories you have defined.
   c. Describe the pattern of places where the most rapid urbanisation occurred between 1960 and 2000.
   d. Describe the expected changes in world urbanisation to the year 2020.

Early Experiences of Urbanisation

The process of urbanisation has been going on for many centuries, although not at the same rapid pace as is happening today. Indeed, urbanisation has been occurring since the first cities appeared about 6,000 years ago in the Middle East. The capital city of Yemen, Sana'a, claims the honour of being the world's oldest city, having been established (it is claimed) by Shem, one of Noah's sons (figure 11.3). Cities were 'invented' separately in various parts of the world to meet the needs of rural people. Among the places where ancient cities sprang up were south-western Nigeria and Egypt in Africa, the North China Plain, the Indus Valley and Mesopotamia in Asia, the central Andes Mountains in South America and Mexico.

11.3 *Sana'a, the capital city of Yemen, is said to be the world's first city.*

For cities to form several prerequisites were needed. First, the farmers in the area had to be able to produce an agricultural surplus to feed the townsfolk. In several areas where cities first developed, this was achieved by using elaborate large-scale irrigation works. Related to this first factor was the need to have a favourable biophysical environment with fertile soils, reliable and sufficient rainfall and warm temperatures. Other factors that encouraged the growth of the first cities were population growth, the need for communal defence against aggression from outside groups, the development of trade and the rise of organised religion. These last factors were significant because they allowed power to become concentrated in the hands of groups with an interest in developing towns, such as traders, priests and politicians. There are a few isolated parts of the world today where these forces can still be seen leading to the development of villages for purposes of defence and social organisation (figure 11.4).

Some of the ancient cities were quite large. The ancient capital of Egypt, Thebes, probably had a population of about 225,000 people in 1600 BC. There are a few places in the world left today where it is possible to see what these ancient Middle Eastern cities were like, giving us some idea of living conditions and the layout of the cities (figure 11.5).

The growth of ancient cities was limited by the productivity of farmers. People living in cities could not grow food, so they relied on farmers' surpluses. However, farmers produced only small surpluses until the Industrial Revolution of the late 1700s and early 1800s. No other European city reached Rome's first century population of one million again until the 1800s when London's population reached that same figure.

11.6 *Handicraft manufacture in Nepal. Apart from the clothes being worn by the people, this scene could have been taken from the early days of the world's first urban centres.*

11.4 *This village compound of the Dani people in the highlands of Irian Jaya gives some idea of the appearance of the world's first villages. Surrounded by a wall and trench for protection, the people who farm the surrounding lands gather together to talk politics, celebrate community events and defend each other. These Dani men are building a fire to cook a village community dinner.*

11.7 *Goods produced by artisans, such as these carpets in the main market in Ashgabat (Turkmenistan), have been exchanged for food with farmers since very early times.*

11.5 *Adobe (mud brick) houses line a street in Timbuktu, an ancient city in Mali. This scene gives us some idea what old cities in the Middle East and northern Africa were like centuries ago. Note the overhead pipes which empty waste water and sewage directly onto the earth street.*

When towns first developed urban functions, it was often the manufacturing of handicrafts and useful tools and utensils that first appeared (figure 11.6). Farmers and their families needed objects that they lacked the skills to make themselves. Artisans in the town developed their skills and began to produce these handicrafts, exchanging them with farmers who were willing to exchange food for the goods they needed (figure 11.7).

11.8 *The large market in Djenné, Mali, is still found in the open area surrounding the grand mosque, the world's largest mud brick building.*

As urban centres in Europe and the Middle East developed, the population became organised into guilds (or professional associations) of merchants, artisans and craftsfolk. These groups tended to live in separate parts of the cities, and each part of the city developed to meet their specific needs. Over time, the markets became larger and more organised, and those towns with the largest markets attracted farmers from nearby towns and villages, further aiding the growth of the urban centre — and the overall process of urbanisation. The markets were usually set up in the centre of the city, often in an open area around a church, town hall or some other building that bound the community together. The markets of many cities today are still found in these historic locations (figure 11.8).

11.9 *An example of a walled city, designed for defence — Dubrovnik, on the Adriatic coast of Croatia.*

11.10 *Narrow stepped streets in Dubrovnik (Croatia) make access by motor vehicles impossible.*

As cities developed in Europe and the Middle East, their wealth increased and they became targets for attacks by outsiders. Many old cities were surrounded by thick, high defensive walls, and often dominated by a castle (figure 11.9). Within the walls of the castle or the city walls, narrow winding streets and houses would offer protection to farmers who lived outside the walls if an enemy attacked. The central areas of many European cities still have these narrow winding streets, making motorised traffic difficult or even impossible (figure 11.10).

Once cities had become safe places with good defences, their functions were able to diversify, and this encouraged more **inward movement** of people. Providing education became an important role played by cities during the

middle ages, both in Europe and in the older cities of the Middle East (figure 11.11). Some important trading cities, such as Bukhara and Samarkand in Uzbekistan, became centres of learning producing scholars who went far afield to spread their teachings and their Muslim religion. Other cities, such as Oxford and Cambridge in England, became 'university cities' where higher education dominated the city to such a degree that all other activities were subordinate to it.

11.11 *The Mir-i-Arab Madrassa in Bukhara (Uzbekistan) was used for many centuries as an important Koranic university.*

European cities were transformed in the late 18th and early 19th centuries when the industrial revolution swept across the continent. Resources from the new colonies were used to start factories using machinery and mass production techniques for the first time, meaning that generalist handicraft makers were replaced by teams of specialist workers in factories. The first impact of the Industrial Revolution was to create entire new towns and cities where none had existed before. These new settlements were usually near the coal fields or important transport routes (figure 11.12). These new urban centres attracted more inward movement of people, further boosting the process of urbanisation.

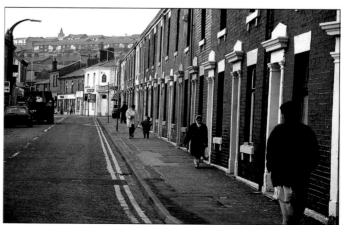

11.12 *A typical industrial revolution town: Blackburn, which is situated in Lancashire, England.*

Large factories were created for the first time to mass produce goods on production lines, with textiles manufacture typically being the first industry to become established. This led to a need for new raw materials such as cotton and rubber that had to be obtained from places with warmer climates than Europe. Colonies were established by many European nations, including Britain, France, Germany, the Netherlands, Spain and Portugal to guarantee their supplies of raw materials. This had a significant impact of the development of cities in areas away from Europe such as Africa, Asia, Australasia and South America.

QUESTION BLOCK 11B

1. What are the prerequisites for cities to develop?

2. Why did towns and cities first develop?

3. How did the Industrial Revolution affect the development of urban centres?

At the same time that urbanisation was occurring in Europe and the Middle East, a parallel process of urbanisation was happening in other parts of the world. For example, several large cities began to develop in Asia about 2,000 years ago. Examples of these ancient Asian cities include Angkor in Cambodia, Bagan in Myanmar, Varanasi in India, Kyoto in Japan, Ayuthaya in Thailand and Beijing and Xian in China (figure 11.13).

11.13 *Angkor Wat was the centre of religious life in Angkor (Cambodia) during the days of the great Khmer empire.*

However, rapid urbanisation only began when the European powers began colonising the other continents. The European powers were keen to send agricultural produce from their tropical colonies back to Europe by ship. Therefore, they established ports on the coast, where there was good shelter. Many of these ports were near the mouths of large rivers that functioned as 'highways', bringing goods to the coast from inland areas. Examples in Asia include Mumbai (Bombay) and Kolkata (Calcutta) in India, Dhaka in Bangladesh, Yangon (Rangoon) in Myanmar, Melaka (Malacca) in Malaysia, Shanghai, Hong Kong and Macau in China, Jakarta in Indonesia, and Singapore (figure 11.14). In Africa, examples included Mombasa (Kenya), Dar-es-Salaam (Tanzania), Banjul (Gambia), Kinshasa (Congo) and Accra

(Ghana). Many of these colonial port cities have now grown and become political capitals of independent nations, although several nations have preferred to establish capitals at inland locations where political control is more effective, some examples being Delhi (India), Naypyidaw (Myanmar), Nairobi (Kenya) and Dodoma (Tanzania). However, because the colonial cities had a different function (trading) to the ancient Asian cities (political control) when they were first established, they were situated on the coast rather than at inland locations.

11.14 *Dhaka, the capital city of Bangladesh, is located on the banks of the Buriganga River, which provides access to many inland areas.*

Like Asia, Africa has a long tradition of urbanisation, although this usually took the form of villages and small towns rather than cities. Very few large ancient cities grew up in Africa, one exception being the ancient city of Axum in Ethiopia, which controlled a vast empire in North-east Africa and the Middle East about 2,000 years ago (figure 11.15). A network of towns developed around the lakes of the Rift Valley in East Africa and one of these small villages, Kampala, has now grown to become the capital city of Uganda. Many of the villages and small towns later became large cities after trading contacts with foreigners had developed.

11.15 *The city of Axum, in northern Ethiopia, controlled a vast empire in north-east Africa and the Middle East about 2,000 years ago.*

Coastal parts of Africa have had a long history of trading contacts dating back to the Phoenicians, Egyptians, Greeks and Arabs. Small coastal trading towns such as

11.16 *The main street of Mombasa. This significant port on the east coast of Kenya has a long history of trade, especially with Arab countries to the north.*

Mogadishu, Lamu, Pemba and Zanzibar became established. Some, such as Lamu have declined to just a few thousand people while others such as Mombasa have grown to become major cities, with Mombasa having

about half a million people today (figure 11.16). Arab traders also established inland towns in arid areas on trading routes from the Mediterranean Sea across the Sahara Desert, and examples include Timbuktu (Mali) and N'Djamena (Chad).

Since the impact of European trading and colonisation, urbanisation has progressed at a very rapid rate in Africa. Indeed, as table 11.2 showed, Africa's urbanisation is happening at a rate that is even faster than that in Asia. Africa today is the least urbanised continent, but its urbanisation is the most rapid. The situation in Kenya has been fairly typical of the African experience and table 11.3 gives some statistics to illustrate the trend of urbanisation in that nation.

QUESTION BLOCK 11C

1. Why were the ancient cities of Asia usually situated inland and away from the sea?

Table 11.3
Urbanisation in Kenya, 1970 to 2010

	1970	1980	1990	2000	2010
Total Population	10,943,000	15,327,000	24,872,000	30,210,900	40,900,000
Urban Population	1,080,000	2,310,000	4,327,700	5,971,200	9,243,500
Urban Population as a % of Total Population	9.9	15.1	17.4	19.7	22.6
Population of Nairobi	450,000	835,000	1,389,000	2,150,000	3,500,000

Source: Government of Kenya, *Economic Survey*

Table 11.4
Population of the World's Ten Largest Urban Areas, 1950 to 2010
(cities in developing nations are shown in pink rectangles)

City	1950 (millions)	City	1980 (millions)	City	2010 (millions)
New York	12.3	Tokyo	16.9	Tokyo	34.0
London	8.7	New York	15.6	Guangzhou	24.2
Tokyo	6.7	Mexico City	14.5	Seoul	24.2
Paris	5.4	São Paulo	12.1	Mexico City	23.4
Shanghai	5.3	Shanghai	11.7	Delhi	23.2
Buenos Aires	5.0	Buenos Aires	9.9	Mumbai	22.8
Chicago	4.9	Los Angeles	9.5	New York	22.2
Moscow	4.8	Kolkata	9.0	São Paulo	20.9
Kolkata	4.4	Beijing	9.0	Manila	19.6
Los Angeles	4.0	Rio de Janeiro	8.8	Shanghai	18.4

Source: United Nations data

2. Why did European colonialism in Asia and Africa lead to rapid urbanisation?

3. In what ways did the location of colonial cities in Asia and Africa differ from the ancient cities in those places?

4. Using the information in table 11.3, draw one graph with two lines to show (a) the growth in Kenya's total population since 1970 and (b) the growth of Kenya's urban population over the same period. On the same graph, superimpose four bar graphs to show the urban population as a percentage of total population for each year shown.

5. Using the information in tables 11.2 and 11.3, say how typical Kenya's trend of urbanisation is compared with (a) the rest of Africa and (b) the rest of the world.

Processes of Urbanisation in Less Economically Developed Countries

As cities in Less Economically Developed Countries (LEDCs) have expanded in recent years, they have tended to **sprawl**. In other words, they have expanded horizontally over great distances. To take just one example, each year, Bangkok spreads out to cover an additional 32 square kilometres of former farmland. In 1900, only 10% of the world's population lived in cities — today the figure is approximately 50%. The recent growth in the largest cities is described in table 11.4. It shows clearly that most of the current growth is occurring in the large cities of LEDCs.

11.17 *A shanty settlement in Dhaka (Bangladesh), populated by rural-urban migrants.*

Much of the recent urbanisation in LEDCs has happened because of rural-urban migration. **Rural-urban migration** is the movement of people from rural areas into urban areas. In the cities of some LEDCs, well over half the population may not have been born in the city, but they moved there from rural areas. For example, in Port Moresby, the capital city of Papua New Guinea, 61% of the population were not born there. In Dhaka, the capital city of Bangladesh, 80% of the city's growth has come from rural-urban migration, with only 20% coming from natural increase (figure 11.17). In the Tanzanian

towns of Dar-es-salaam, Dodoma, Arusha and Zanzibar, the proportion of migrants (i.e. people born elsewhere) is 68%, 73%, 70% and 85% respectively.

Moving from a rural village to a big city is a major decision that is not made lightly. The decision whether or not to move is usually made after long consideration and many factors are considered. The factors that encourage a person to move can be divided into push factors and pull factors. **Push factors** are forces that send a person away from an area. **Pull factors** are the forces that attract a person into a certain area. As well as the push and pull factors that encourage a person to move, there are also **restraining factors**. These are forces that encourage people to remain in the rural areas where they are living. Some push, pull and restraining factors were shown in table 1.10 in chapter 1.

11.18 *Rural-urban migrants in southern Ethiopia on their way to the country's capital, Addis Ababa, in search of employment.*

Migration from a village to a large city is seldom undertaken in one jump. Most rural-urban migration is done in a step-wise manner, called **chain migration**. The rural-urban migrant will usually move from a village to a nearby small town at first, then to a larger town and only then to a city. The typical rural-urban migrant is a young, single, somewhat adventurous male who comes to the city in search of wealth before returning to his home town or village (figure 11.18). Some rural-urban migrants wind up staying in the city, especially if they find a marriage partner there. Others return to their rural area, either permanently or seasonally. Migrants who repeatedly return to their home areas and back to the city are said to engage in **circular migration**. Those rural-urban migrants who stay in the city but have family left behind will usually send money back to their family on a regular basis.

Most rural-urban migrants who come to the city do so with very few skills that would be useful in an urban environment. Many are peasant farmers who have been forced off their land due to mechanisation or changes to patterns of land ownership. These people may be highly skilled at growing rice or raising animals, but they lack even such basic skills as literacy. Arriving with very little money, they often have difficulty in finding even basic housing and so must sleep on the footpaths or construct temporary accommodation (figure 11.19).

11.19 *Pavement dwellers in Delhi, India.*

QUESTION BLOCK 11D

1. What is (a) urban sprawl, and (b) rural-urban migration?

2. Quoting some specific statistics, explain how important rural-urban migration is in LEDCs today.

3. What is the difference between 'pull factors', 'push factors' and 'restraining factors'? Give two examples of each.

4. What is the difference between 'chain migration' and 'circular migration'? Why does each occur?

5. Why do many rural-urban migrants have trouble finding employment in the city?

Consequences of Urbanisation in Less Economically Developed Countries

Shanty housing

One of the features of most cities in LEDCs is that they have large areas of **shanty housing**. This comprises self-help housing made from scrounged materials such as corrugated iron, packing cases, cloth and disused plastic sheeting (figures 11.20 and 11.21).

11.20 *A large shanty settlement in Addis Ababa, Ethiopia.*

11.21 *A shanty settlement on the outskirts of Pune, India.*

Shanty settlements are known by various names in different countries, including *bustees* in India, *bidonvilles* in West Africa, *ishish* in the Middle East and *favelas* in Latin America. The Worldwatch Institute estimates that between 70% and 95% of all new housing in developing nations consists of shanty settlements (figure 11.22). About 60% of the urban population in Africa live in shanty settlements, and the equivalent figures for Asia and South America are between 20% and 30%.

11.22 *A large shanty settlement covers the steep slopes of this hill in Caracas, Venezuela.*

Often, shanty settlements are occupied by **squatters**, a term for people who neither own nor have legal title to the land on which they are living. Squatters will build on land that has been left vacant, such as the strips along the sides of railway lines, or the edges of parklands or steeply sloping land that is unsuitable for building. In many cities in LEDCs, this can lead to the paradoxical sight of shanty settlements being situated almost next door to expensive real estate such as luxury housing or prestigious administrative or corporate office blocks (figure 11.23). Shanties can be found in all parts of developing world cities, but they are most commonly located on the outskirts of the cities where the most 'free' land is available. Many governments are embarrassed to have shanty settlements and use the police or the army to demolish them from time to time.

11.23 *Shanty settlements near prestigious high rise office blocks in Manila, Philippines.*

Other governments are a little more enlightened and realise that shanty housing is a self-help way of addressing the housing shortage, and that a housing shortage cannot be solved using a bulldozer! Some administrations even connect shanty housing to basic services such as electricity. Where this happens, the highly dangerous temptation is removed to steal electricity by connecting wires to the power lines with bulldog clips. Some governments that have enough resources have been highly successful in building public housing to rehouse the shanty dwellers. For example, the last shanty housing was removed from Singapore in 1989 when the new towns of Yishun and Boon Lay were opened, comprising hundreds of high-rise housing blocks (figure 11.24). However, the shanties in Singapore were not removed until there was sufficient public housing available for the residents who lived there.

The replacement of shanty housing is a major issue in many LEDCs. Not all countries have the resources available that Singapore was able to find to build large housing estates. Other possibilities include providing materials for people to build better quality self-help housing, providing people with loans or grants to improve their shanties or having the government pay to improve the

quality of shanty areas. However, problems can arise from these strategies. All these measures cost money, which is always in short supply in economically poor nations. People are often reluctant to move away from locations near the city centre, even if it does mean an improvement in the quality of their housing. Moving people can often destroy the spirit of community that binds people together, and job training may still be needed to make people employable. Finally, when shanty areas are improved they may be seen as being so attractive that even more people come to settle there, leading to problems of overcrowding and congestion.

11.24 *High rise housing in Jurong West, Singapore, which was used to re-house shanty dwellers. High rise housing in Singapore is among the best in the world.*

Population structures

Rural-urban migration distorts the population structures of many cities in LEDCs. Because the typical rural-urban migrant is a young single male, cities with high rates of rural-urban migration have a skewed population pyramid. Figure 11.25 shows the age-sex structure for a typical city in India that is influenced by a high rate of rural-urban migration. The population structures of the smaller towns and villages from which the rural-urban

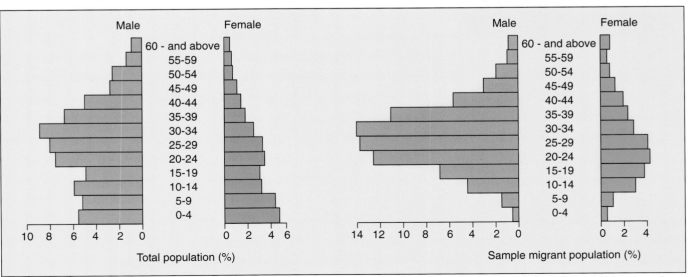

11.25 *Age-sex pyramids for the city of Kolkata (formerly Calcutta). The left hand graph shows the city as a whole, and the right hand graph shows a sample of rural-urban migrants.*

Urban environments

migrants have come will also be affected, but in the opposite direction. Whereas the large cities have an excess of males in the 20-45 year age range, small towns and villages will be deficient in such people, leaving an excess of females, children and the elderly. Fortunately, women do most of the farming work in many developing nations so food production is not affected by this imbalance. However, the excess of non-productive people (children and the elderly) can cause problems in many areas.

However, this trend has changed a little in recent years. It is still true that few women migrate to the cities independently of men because of the traditional roles they are expected to play in the villages and because of the limited job opportunities available to them in the cities. However, it is now becoming more common for men who have moved to cities to be followed by their wives after a few years. In Dar-es-Salaam, for example, the number of females per 1,000 men increased from 815 in 1967 to 865 in 1978 and 901 in 1988. By 1995, the number was estimated to have reached 921 females per 1,000 males — still an imbalance but of a smaller magnitude than previously.

11.26 *A girl holds her baby brother as she begs for money in a small village in Myanmar.*

The unskilled people who migrate to the cities often have difficulty surviving. Most developing nations do not have social security systems or pensions, and migrants who do not have family in the city must fend for themselves. Employment is usually difficult to find for people who possess only farming skills. In some nations, the women (and some men) resort to prostitution to make enough money, but this is really a last resort for the desperate. A number of people turn to crimes such as theft and mugging to obtain the money they need to survive. Others resort to begging, often using children to do the begging on behalf of the adults, or a person with some disability such as blindness, missing limbs or injuries

(figure 11.26). In most cities in the developing world, begging is organised with bands of beggars each having their own territory that is protected for them by their leader. Some rural-urban migrants create their own work by doing things such as washing drivers' windscreens when they are stopped at traffic lights, performing with trained animals and shining people's shoes (figure 11.27). These people are said to work in the informal sector.

11.27 *A man walks with his performing money on a crowded beach in Mumbai hoping to earn money with his animal act.*

Primate cities

Many of the large cities in LEDCs are **primate cities**. This means that they completely dominate the urban networks of which they form a part. Primate cities are usually the political, economic, social and cultural focus of their country. In general, a primate city has at least five times the population of the second largest city in the nation. Table 11.5 shows some cities which are primate.

Primate cities tend to emerge under certain circumstances. In LEDCs, foreign investors tend to place their money in the largest city because that is where the best infrastructure, supporting services and government assistance are normally found. Educational and research facilities are also usually found in the largest city, meaning that there is more likely to be a pool of skilled labour there. Transport routes, which are often poorly developed in developing nations, often focus on the primate city, encouraging growth in that city at the expense of smaller centres.

QUESTION BLOCK 11E

1. *Explain why shanty settlements are a common feature of most cities in Africa, Asia and South America.*

2. *Some governments tolerate shanty settlements while others oppose them? Which policy is better in your opinion? Give reasons for your answer.*

3. *For nations that do not have the resources to re-house shanty dwellers as Singapore did, what can be done about improving the quality of life for shanty dwellers?*

4. How does rural-urban migration affect the population structure in (a) cities in LEDCs, and (b) rural areas of LEDCs?

5. How do unemployed rural-urban migrants survive in the city?

6. What does the term 'primate city' mean? Give one example from each of Asia, Africa and South America.

7. Why do primate cities develop?

Table 11.5
Some Examples of Primate Cities, 2000

Country	Largest (primate) city	Population ('000)	2nd largest city	Population ('000)
Argentina	Buenos Aires	12,024	Cordoba	1,368
Chile	Santiago	5,467	Valparaiso	360
Congo	Kinshasa	5,054	Lubumbashi	965
Indonesia	Jakarta	11,018	Bandung	3,409
Iran	Tehran	6,979	Mashhad	1,990
Iraq	Baghdad	4,865	Mosul	1,131
Mexico	Mexico City	18,066	Guadalajara	3,697
Myanmar	Yangon	4,393	Mandalay	770
Nepal	Kathmandu	359	Bhaktapur	65
North Korea	Pyongyang	3,124	Nampo	1,022
Paraguay	Asuncion	1,262	Concepcion	40
Peru	Lima	7,443	Arequipa	784
Tanzania	Dar-es-Salaam	1,434	Mwanza	201
Thailand	Bangkok	7,372	Chiang Mai	302
Uganda	Kampala	1,213	Jinja and Njeru	112
Uzbekistan	Tashkent	2,148	Samarkand	640

Source: Geohive

Processes of Urbanisation in More Economically Developed Countries

Cities in More Economically Developed Countries (MEDCs) are experiencing much slower growth than cities in developing countries, and in some cases they are experiencing a decline in population. Therefore, the urban dynamics of developed world cities are quite different from cities in developing world cities. Perhaps the greatest impact that older cities have had to cope with is the introduction of the motor vehicle. The streets of most European cities were planned when the main means of

transport were walking and horses (figure 11.28). The narrow streets and twisting patterns of these streets cause problems of congestion and parking for the large numbers of motor vehicles now found in developed world cities (figure 11.29). The large numbers of motor vehicles cause other problems also. One of the worst of these is air pollution, which in turn causes respiratory problems for residents and can hasten the weathering of old stone buildings. Unlike many developing countries, most developed world governments have imposed strict emission controls on motor vehicles in an effort to address these problems.

11.28 Narrow cobble-stoned streets in the city centre of Maastricht (Netherlands) are not really suitable for motor vehicles, which are therefore restricted from parts of the historic city centre. This in turn encourages movement by walking and by bicycle.

11.29 Cars have taken over much of the area of the historic centres of European cities, such as Budapest (Hungary), which is shown here.

Because the population growth rates of developed world cities have slowed or declined, the inner city areas are often decaying. This **urban decay** is a reflection of the lack of demand for inner city land, and it shows as vacant blocks of land, derelict buildings or graffiti in public places (figure 11.30). When inner city land is left vacant for long periods of time, it becomes an unproductive resource that is not supplying employment, income or tax revenue.

11.30 *Graffiti is often a sign of urban decay. This example is in Milan, Italy.*

According to the bid-rent theory that was explained earlier in this chapter, inner city land should be in high demand and command high prices. Urban decay represents a lack of demand for inner city land, perhaps because inner city traffic congestion has made the area unattractive for industry or commerce, perhaps because the buildings require expensive upgrading, or perhaps because outer areas with more space, cheaper land and good communications has become more attractive.

The processes affecting urban environments in MEDCs can be categorised into three groups. The first group of processes involves the **inward (or centripetal) movement** of people to the urban area, and these processes include rural-urban migration, gentrification, and reurbanisation (with urban renewal). The second group of processes is **outward (or centrifugal) movements** of people, and these include suburbanisation, counterurbanisation and urban sprawl. The third group of processes do not involve movements of people, but comprises the **natural changes** to patterns of population density within urban areas.

Inward (or centripetal) movements

11.31 *These streets have been converted into covered pedestrian plazas containing expensive shops in Milan, Italy.*

Governments and citizens' groups in developed world cities often embark on projects to rejuvenate inner city areas which are experiencing urban decay. One common low-cost strategy is to convert streets that are lined with shops into pedestrian plazas (figure 11.31). This strategy is often opposed at first by shop keepers who are worried that their business will decline. However, business turnover invariably increases as people find that shopping in a car-free environment is much more enjoyable.

Urban renewal can take several forms. **Gentrification** occurs when middle class people move into run down inner city areas with the intention of renovating the old buildings. As a result of gentrification, old buildings are usually restored in keeping with their original character, raising their value considerably and repaying the people who carried out the renovations (figure 11.32).

11.32 *Gentrification, shown by restored historic buildings and resurfaced pathways in Prague, Czech Republic.*

Another approach is for governments to carry out a programme of **urban renewal** in run-down inner city areas. One of the most spectacular examples of urban renewal has been the London Docklands. In Sydney, Australia, a large area occupied by a largely disused railway goods handling yard at Darling Harbour was completely redeveloped by the New South Wales state government. Although the redevelopment has failed to attract as much private sector investment as the London Docklands, and although its transport system, a monorail, fails to link up with other public transport like the Docklands Light Railway, the project has been successful in attracting tourists and business folk to the convention centre, exhibition halls, shops and other attractions (figure 11.33).

Other examples of large-scale urban renewal include the Cardiff Bay redevelopment in Cardiff (Wales) and La Défense in Paris (France). La Défense was a run-down area west of the main CBD of Paris. It was redeveloped in the 1980s and 1990s into a major office and administrative centre with futuristic architecture on a grand scale.

Cardiff Bay redevelopment covers an area of 1,100 hectares, which is 20% of the area of the City of Cardiff, and involves large-scale construction of factories, housing and offices in an area of urban decay near the old Cardiff docks (figures 11.34 and 11.35). A one kilometre coastal barrage was built to control the tides of Cardiff Bay so that it is always covered by water to make the area more attractive – the natural range between high and low tides at Cardiff Bay is 12 metres. Construction of the barrage also created an additional 13 kilometres of waterfront land suitable for development. The total cost of the Cardiff Bay urban renewal scheme was about £2.4 billion.

11.35 *This former mill, which had fallen into disuse, has been converted into housing in the Cardiff Bay redevelopment area.*

11.33 *Darling Harbour in Sydney (Australia) used to be an area of derelict factories and warehouses before it was redeveloped to create exhibition centres, restaurants, shops and public areas.*

11.36 *An expensive housing estate in Washington D.C. built overlooking the Potomac River. The artist and the man standing are actually sculptures.*

11.34 *This former dock area of Cardiff Bay has been transformed into an area of expensive flats.*

In Washington DC (USA), Christian churches and other charitable organisations have seen the availability of cheap derelict land as an opportunity to be grasped. They have bought large areas of cheap land, demolished the old buildings, and used the land to build low cost housing for poor residents of the city, especially people from minority ethnic groups. Not only cheap housing is built on derelict inner city land, however. Figure 11.36 shows a housing estate which was also built in Washington DC. This high security block, known as Washington Harbour, comprises extremely expensive housing that overlooks the Potomac River.

11.37 *Demolition of old buildings to make way for new developments in Shanghai, China.*

Some of the largest scale urban renewal projects are taking place in economically developing countries. In China, large areas of major cities are being demolished to make way for new high-rise development. In Shanghai, the pace of redevelopment is so rapid that residents are known to have become lost looking for their own house

Urban environments

ToK BoX

In the mid-1980s, there was a popular satirical comedy on British television called 'Yes, Prime Minister'. The series followed the career of Prime Minister Jim Hacker as he battled with the Civil Service, headed by the Permanent Secretary, Sir Humphrey Appleby, and his Principal Private Secretary Bernard Woolley.

In one episode, Bernard Woolley gives Jim Hacker the results of the latest opinion poll showing that 73% of the population are against conscription. The Prime Minister is concerned about this result, so Bernard Woolley discusses the problem with Sir Humphrey Appleby. Sir Humphrey suggests that another opinion poll should be done to show that 73% of voters are in favour of conscription. Woolley can't understand how voters could be both for and against conscription at the same time. Sir Humphrey explained the dilemma as follows:

Sir Humphrey: "You know what happens: a nice young lady comes up to you. Obviously you want to create a good impression, you don't want to look a fool, do you? So she starts asking you some questions: Mr. Woolley, are you worried about the number of young people without jobs?"

Bernard Woolley: "Yes"

Sir Humphrey: "Are you worried about the rise in crime among teenagers?"

Bernard Woolley: "Yes"

Sir Humphrey: "Do you think there is a lack of discipline in our comprehensive schools?"

Bernard Woolley: "Yes"

Sir Humphrey: "Do you think young people welcome some authority and leadership in their lives?"

Bernard Woolley: "Yes"

Sir Humphrey: "Do you think they respond to a challenge?"

Bernard Woolley: "Yes"

Sir Humphrey: "Would you be in favour of reintroducing National Service?"

Bernard Woolley: "Oh...well, I suppose I might be."

Sir Humphrey: "Yes or no?"

Bernard Woolley: "Yes"

Sir Humphrey: "Of course you would, Bernard. After all you told me, you can't say no to that. So they don't mention the first five questions and they publish the last one."

Bernard Woolley: "Is that really what they do?"

Sir Humphrey: "Well, not the reputable ones, no. But there aren't many of those. So alternatively the young lady can get the opposite result."

Bernard Woolley: "How?"

Sir Humphrey: "Mr. Woolley, are you worried about the danger of war?"

Bernard Woolley: "Yes"

Sir Humphrey: "Are you worried about the growth of armaments?"

Bernard Woolley: "Yes"

Sir Humphrey: "Do you think there is a danger in giving young people guns and teaching them how to kill?"

Bernard Woolley: "Yes"

Sir Humphrey: "Do you think it is wrong to force people to take up arms against their will?"

Bernard Woolley: "Yes"

Sir Humphrey: "Would you oppose the reintroduction of National Service?"

Bernard Woolley: "Yes"

Sir Humphrey: "There you are, you see Bernard. The perfect balanced sample."

Of course, this dialogue is entirely fictitious. However, it does show how survey results can be manipulated, especially when only one or a few of the answers in the survey are reported. This is a form of 'selection bias'.

Whenever statistical material is presented, the first question you should always ask is: "What is the source?". If the source is not quoted, then the statistics may not be reliable as they are more difficult to verify. Even if the source is quoted, it is important to note whether the source is neutral or not. For example, statistics showing people's attitudes towards a proposed urban redevelopment are less likely to be reliable if they have been collected by a vested interest, such as either the land developer or a residents' resistance group!

It is also important to understand the methodology that was used in collecting the data. Was the sample random or was it structured in some way? Telephone surveys, for example, are known to be unreliable for many reasons, not least because they exclude people without access to a telephone. In many societies, this will eliminate one sector of society, specifically those with lower incomes.

The next ToK BoX is on page 559.

if they have been away for a few months! Urban renewal is particularly widespread in old cities in China, where traditional buildings are now regarded as being inadequately serviced and inefficient because they are not high enough (figure 11.37). Large areas of ancient cities such as Beijing, Xian, Kunming, Chengdu and Guangzhou now look like very modern cities with little sense of their historical past because of the large-scale urban renewal that has taken place.

Urban renewal can be smaller in scale than this and still transform an area of urban decay. In Amsterdam, the largest city in the Netherlands, the inner city area was experiencing urban decay in the 1960s. The area experienced urban renewal through the development of an entirely new industry – sex shops and brothels – during the 1960s and afterwards (figure 11.38). Today, central Amsterdam is an economically vibrant area with a buoyant tourism industry. A similar pattern of urban renewal

11.38 *The development of sex shops and brothels in central Amsterdam from the 1960s onwards led to urban renewal, enabling many old buildings to be preserved and restored for their new use. The area now attracts tourists from many parts of Europe and elsewhere.*

occurred on the south bank of the Yarra River in Melbourne during the 1990s, although this was based on gambling rather than sex. The entire riverbank area was cleared to make way for a casino, with associated hotels, restaurants and shopping centres (figure 11.39).

11.39 *The long building in the foreground of this photo is the Crown Casino complex, an example of urban renewal on the south bank of Melbourne's Yarra River.*

Outward (or centrifugal) movements

Suburbanisation refers to the overall movement and resettlement of people from inner city locations to vast new areas of housing further from the CBD. To some extent, suburbanisation (where residents move outwards) is a balancing process to gentrification (where residents move inwards), although it has occurred at a much larger scale. In the period between the end of World War I (1918) and the start of World War II (1939), manufacturing industries developed rapidly in most cities in North America and Europe. This led to technological, physical and institutional changes in the way cities functioned.

However, it was after the end of World II in 1945 that suburbanisation began to happen on a large scale. For the first time, ordinary families could afford their own motor vehicles, and these gave people a new freedom to live away from their place of work. Up until that time, workers had been dependent on public transport to get to and from work, and so they had to live close to bus routes or railway stations. Private motor vehicles meant people could live much further away from their work, shops and schools. Consequently, vast new areas around the cities were opened up for the first time for suburban development (figure 11.40).

In the United States, this led to **urban sprawl** on a large scale. The government made low interest loans available to families to build their own homes, and special grants were given to soldiers returning from the war. There was a large backlog of demand for housing because of the

effects of the Great Depression between 1929 and 1941. Between 1950 and 1970, the main trends in American cities were the urbanisation of the population, and within cities, the suburbanisation of the residents. The early suburbs tended to be medium density areas, often built on a grid pattern of streets (figure 11.41). However, during the 1970s, 1980s and 1990s, there has been a trend towards larger houses on bigger blocks of land in the suburbs. Modern principles of town planning such as curving the streets, building a hierarchical network of streets to minimise traffic flow and planting lots of trees in residential areas are now commonly practised.

11.40 *An area of new housing on the outskirts of Dallas (Texas, USA). The curved streets and hierarchical street pattern are sound principles of modern town planning.*

11.41 *This suburban area of Los Angeles (California, USA) was built during the 1950s, and shows the small blocks of land and grid layout of streets that were typical of the period.*

Accompanying the movement of people to the suburbs, manufacturing industries also moved away from crowded inner city locations to the edges of the cities where larger amounts of cheap land were available. These industries were followed by retail outlets, eager to maintain easy accessibility to a sprawling population. In American and Australian cities, the vast majority of shopping activity now takes places away from the CBD. The construction of expressways has accelerated the trend towards suburbanisation. Increasingly, major shopping areas being located at expressway intersections and along

Urban environments

Table 11.6
Population Change in Selected US metropolitan Areas, 1980 to 1986

NORTH AND EAST	Percentage Change in Population 1980 to 1986		SOUTH AND WEST	Percentage Change in Population 1980 to 1986	
Metropolitan Area	Central City	Suburbs	Metropolitan Area	Central City	Suburbs
New York	+2.7	+2.3	Los Angeles	+9.8	+7.2
Chicago	+0.2	+3.5	San Francisco	+10.3	+9.4
Philadelphia	-2.7	+2.9	Dallas	+11.0	+30.8
Detroit	-9.7	-1.0	Houston	+8.4	+26.6
Boston	+2.0	+2.1	Miami	+7.8	+10.5
Washington DC	-1.9	+12.4	Atlanta	-0.7	+24.9
Cleveland	-6.6	-1.3	Seattle	-0.2	+12.5
St Louis	-6.0	+4.6	San Diego	+16.0	+20.2
Pittsburgh	-8.7	-3.5	Tampa	+2.2	+21.9
Minneapolis	-3.8	+9.7	Denver	+2.6	+19.2

Source: Getis, Getis and Fellmann (1991) p.397

the approach roads to expressways, with large car parks being provided for shoppers to park their cars.

Where manufacturing industries and people relocate away from an urban centre, **counterurbanisation** is said to occur. In Australia, the government policies that encouraged residential and manufacturing growth in towns away from the major state capitals were known as **decentralisation policies**. Therefore, as industries and people relocated outwards from state capitals to centres such as Albury-Wodonga, Bathurst-Orange and Gosford-Wyong, decentralisation was said to be occurring. In fact, decentralisation can also occur within an urban area. For example, if an industry wishes to escape the pollution, congestion and high land prices of an inner urban area, and relocates to the suburbs or beyond, then decentralisation is said to occur. Therefore, suburbanisation is one type of decentralisation.

Table 11.6 provides some statistics which indicate the extent of suburbanisation in the United States during the early 1980s when the trend was at its peak.

Suburbanisation has only been possible because of the widespread use of private motor vehicles. During earlier times when people depended on walking for transport, the growth of urban areas was severely limited. However, the huge growth in the number of cars in most economically more developed countries from 1950s onwards removed the constraint on urban sprawl. In the United States, extensive networks of expressways developed (figure 11.42). Although these expressways were designed to speed up people's movement, they attracted such increased numbers of vehicles that movement on many routes actually became slower.

11.42 *Like many other US cities, large areas of Dallas (Texas) are devoted to cars, including expressways and large car parks.*

11.43 *In most cities of the world, cars use vast areas of land for roads and parking. This parking station is in Vancouver, Canada.*

The increased use of private motor vehicles also occurred in Europe, though to a lesser degree than in the United

States. Although many European cities had well-developed systems of public transport, use of private motor vehicles increased substantially from the 1960s onwards. The increased use of cars had a significant impact on the land use in many cities, as areas have had to be devoted to providing parking spaces for the cars (figure 11.43). This led many cities in MEDCs to restrict the amount of parking space available in the hope that making parking difficult would encourage more people to use public transport, and also to restrict the movement of cars into the city centre (figure 11.44). Most European cities also charge for parking space, either in parking stations or using parking meters. This has encouraged the development of cars that are so small that two of them can share the one parking space (figure 11.45).

11.44 *Electronic road pricing (ERP) is used in many cities (including Singapore, shown here), to regulate the number of cars in the CBD. The toll charged varies according to the type of vehicle and the time of day.*

11.45 *Perhaps the trend for the future – two small cars share one parking space in Amsterdam, where parking space is scarce and expensive.*

Another trend that has emerged towards the end of the 20th century was **counterurbanisation**, which is also sometimes called **deurbanisation** or **reurbanisation**. This does not mean, as the term might imply, that the proportion of people in urban areas is declining, but means that smaller and medium sized towns are growing at a faster rate than the large cities. Counterurbanisation is said to occur when there is a marked decline in the number

of people living in large metropolitan areas, or a slowing in the growth of large metropolitan areas. This is accompanied by the growth of smaller urban centres at the expense of the larger ones.

Counterurbanisation is a strong trend in certain nations of Western Europe. For example, in Britain from the late 1930s to the late 1990s, London's size was shrinking as people moved into smaller towns that were considered more desirable. To some extent, counterurbanisation is the opposite of rural-urban migration as it is a movement of people away from the largest cities.

In general, suburbanisation and counterurbanisation have affected different income groups in different ways. In the United States, for example, younger, wealthier and better-educated upwardly mobile residents who can afford cars have tended to move away from inner city areas into newer areas. An extension of this is the process of **exurbanisation**, which occurs when usually affluent people move from the city to rural areas. However, when they do so, they continue to maintain an urban way of life, either through long distance commuting or technology.

11.46 *Two elderly people lock up their house in an inner part of the Dutch city of Leiden as they leave it for a while. Like many buildings in inner Leiden, their home has been defaced by graffiti.*

11.47 *An inner area of Washington DC which has become an area of urban blight.*

On the other hand, poorer, older and less advantaged people, especially from minority ethnic groups, can not afford to move and they get left behind (figure 11.46). As table 11.7 shows, U.S. cities have become increasingly segregated by income and ethnicity as a result. This creates problems because entire neighbourhoods are coming to consist of poor people from minority groups who have little ability to pay taxes for government services such as education, health, police and fire protection which are needed. Many people in these inner city areas are forced to sleep on park benches, in doorways of public buildings, in underground railway stations or near the warm street level exhaust vents from the underground trains.

11.48 *Hong Kong's high rise residential blocks are a spectacular example of intensification. These housing blocks are at Ngau Chi Wan in Hong Kong's New Territories.*

As a result of suburbanisation and counterurbanisation, the inner city areas of many North American and some European cities have become very run down. This is a particular problem in the eastern United States, as people have moved to cities in the west, and in northern England, as people have migrated to cities in the south. The tax base of the cities declines, and so local government authorities have less money to maintain the city and provide services. This encourages more people to move away. Buildings have been abandoned, graffiti and vandalism have become endemic and the areas become afflicted with **urban blight** (figure 11.47). Once this happens, land prices plummet and the area becomes ready for redevelopment.

Natural change

In recent years, cities have been expanding so far that they have started coalescing in some areas. For example, in the north-east of the United States, a continuous corridor of urbanisation extends from Boston to Washington DC which also includes New York, Providence, Philadelphia and Baltimore. In New South Wales, Australia, Sydney has expanded so that it has incorporated towns such as Penrith, Campbelltown, Blacktown and Liverpool that were once separate country towns. This process whereby urban areas expand into each other to create huge metropolitan areas is called **conurbation**.

One way to reduce urban sprawl is to encourage **urban consolidation**. Urban consolidation is the process of

Table 11.7
Ethnic Groups and Incomes for Selected US Cities

NORTH AND EAST City	Ethnic Composition (%) White	Black	Hispanic	Median Annual Family Income ($)	SOUTH AND WEST City	Ethnic Composition (%) White	Black	Hispanic	Median Annual Family Income ($)
New York	60.7	25.2	19.9	26,740	Los Angeles	61.2	17.0	27.5	30,390
Suburbs	89.0	7.6	0.4	45,818	Suburbs	71.9	9.6	28.9	37,461
Chicago	49.6	39.8	14.0	29,530	Houston	61.3	27.6	17.6	35,665
Suburbs	90.8	5.6	3.9	47,885	Suburbs	86.3	6.7	10.9	47,955
Philadelphia	58.2	37.8	3.7	25,416	Dallas	61.4	29.4	12.3	31,318
Suburbs	89.8	8.1	1.7	40,344	Suburbs	92.2	3.9	5.3	41,111
Detroit	34.3	63.0	0.2	26,983	San Diego	75.4	8.9	14.8	31,669
Suburbs	94.1	4.2	0.1	46,393	Suburbs	85.9	2.6	14.6	34,369
Baltimore	43.9	54.8	1.0	24,725	San Antonio	78.6	7.3	53.6	26,586
Suburbs	89.2	9.0	1.0	42,985	Suburbs	88.1	5.2	23.4	37,542
Indianapolis	77.1	21.8	0.9	33,348	Phoenix	84.0	4.9	15.1	33,619
Suburbs	98.3	1.0	0.5	51,828	Suburbs	89.4	1.4	11.2	34,904
Washington DC	26.8	70.3	2.7	31,287	San Francisco	58.3	12.7	12.2	30,623
Suburbs	78.5	16.7	3.1	49,655	Suburbs	81.1	6.5	10.6	43,184
Boston	69.9	22.4	6.4	24,125	New Orleans	46.2	55.3	0.0	22,840
Suburbs	96.6	1.6	1.5	39,505	Suburbs	85.4	12.6	0.0	37,978

Source: Getis, Getis and Fellmann (1991) p.400

increasing the density of residential buildings in an urban area. This can be achieved in several ways. For example, urban consolidation can be achieved by infilling gaps in an urban area, by bringing disued buildings (usually in the inner city) back into productive use, or by replacing low density dwellings with medium or high density buildings which can accommodate more people on the same land area. This last option is also known as **intensification** (figure 11.48).

11.49 *Evidence of the Chinese presence in Penang, Malaysia — the long established Chinese Chamber of Commerce Building in Georgetown.*

Urban consolidation represents an alternative to urban sprawl as a way of accommodating a growing population. Urban consolidation has the advantage that services such as utilities and transport are more economic to provide in areas with higher population densities. On the other hand, people in countries such as Australia, Canada and the United States have traditionally valued abundant space, and there has been some resistance to urban consolidation.

11.50 *The entrance to a guarded residential compound at Shunde in southern China.*

Another process of natural change is the emergence of the urban village. An **urban village** is a residential district within a city that houses a community of people sharing a common cultural background. These areas have an identity that separates them from surrounding areas.

They usually have a strong community spirit, intense feelings of kinship, high levels of social and cultural contact, a well-developed sense of neighbourliness, and a desire to remain identified as separate community.

Most large cities in Asia and Africa have identifiable ethnic quarters, and these are good examples of urban villages. For example, Singapore has very clear areas of ethnic difference, with Chinatown, Little India and the Arab Quarter having quite different identities. Penang in Malaysia has a large Chinatown area (figure 11.49). Similarly, Sydney has several urban villages that can be defined on ethnic criteria, such as Chinatown (Chinese), Cabramatta (Vietnamese) and Auburn (Turks).

Urban villages can be defined on grounds other than ethnicity. Many urban villages are defined on economic grounds or where a minority group feels threatened by another group. Examples of urban villages that are defined by non-ethnic criteria include Montmartre in Paris, Greenwich Village in New York, Nowa Huta in Kraków and Notting Hill in London.

11.51 *A private residential compound in London, United Kingdom.*

The distribution of urban villages within a city evolves on the basis of many factors such as price of housing, the location of markets or an historic focal point. At times, urban villages can lead to **spatial exclusion**, a process where wealthy residents become so concerned about their security and defending their luxury lifestyles that spatial access and freedom of movement becomes restricted for other residents. Evidence of this process includes security systems on houses, walled estates and access-restricted industrial estates (figures 11.50 and 11.51).

QUESTION BLOCK 11F

1. *What has caused the parking congestion seen in figure 11.29? Suggest some realistic strategies that might relieve this problem.*

2. *Why do many cities in the developed world have inner city decay?*

3. Describe some successful programmes which have relieved the problem of inner city decay.

4. Explain the economic forces which cause 'urban decay' to lead into 'gentrification'.

5. Urban renewal occurs in many cities. Quoting specific examples, explain why such projects might be controversial.

6. What is 'suburbanisation'? How important has this process been?

7. Why has urban sprawl affected many cities in the United States between 1945 and the present time?

8. What is decentralisation? Give some examples of decentralisation.

9. Describe the pattern shown in table 11.6.

10. What is 'conurbation'? Why does it occur and where is it most strongly seen?

11. What have been the effects of motor vehicles on urban dynamics?

12. Explain the terms (a) urban consolidation, and (b) intensification.

13. What is 'counterurbanisation'? Where is this trend seen most strongly?

14. What is exurbanisation?

15. Write one page to describe and account for the pattern shown in table 11.7.

16. In a city with which you are familiar, make a list of some urban villages, and for each urban village, write a few words to describe its main characteristics.

Case Study of the Processes of Urbanisation in a City in an LEDC — Yangon

The processes described in the previous section also operate in cities in LEDCs, although not always in the same ways. This can be seen with reference to the largest city in Myanmar, Yangon.

Yangon, which used to be known as Rangoon, is one of the many cities in Asia with a population exceeding one million people. Located about 30 kilometres from the ocean on the fertile delta of the Irrawaddy River, Yangon was the capital city of Myanmar (which used to be called Burma) until 2005, when it was replaced by a new inland city called Naypyidaw. Yangon is also Myanmar's largest city, with an official population size of 4.4 million people. Myanmar's second largest city, Mandalay, has a population of about 1.1 million people, making Yangon the primate city of Myanmar.

From the early 1960s to the late 1980s, Myanmar was controlled by a military government that adopted a policy known as the 'Burmese Way to Socialism', which was a mix of nationalism, isolationism, Buddhism and socialism. As a result, Myanmar's economy stagnated and the standard of living of the population declined steadily. This policy was relaxed somewhat in the early 1990s when the military government undertook to improve people's quality of living by freeing the economy from many of its restrictions. It allowed foreign investment to occur, and this led to an inflow of funds from overseas, especially Singapore, Thailand and Japan. As a result of the changes, significant changes began happening in the urban processes within Yangon.

11.52 A typical colonial-era building in central Yangon, Myanmar.

11.53 A crumbling colonial-era commercial building in Yangon's CBD.

For most of the period following independence in 1948 until the late 1980s, Yangon saw almost new construction. During that period, the two main urban dynamics operating in Yangon were urban decay and urban sprawl. **Urban decay** was especially evident in the city centre, where the old British colonial buildings fell into disrepair because money was unavailable for necessary maintenance (figure 11.52). Some of the buildings were used by government authorities, while others were taken over by squatters or poor people as residences. Although extensive new construction is now occurring in Yangon's city centre, urban decay is still very widespread because of the huge backlog of neglect and the continuing shortage of funds for renovation. It is estimated that about 80% of the buildings in Yangon's Central Business District require urgent maintenance (figure 11.53).

During the four decades of economic stagnation, many people moved to Yangon from the countryside in search of work or new opportunities that were unavailable to them in rural areas. Although Yangon lacks many services and facilities that are found in other capital cities in Asia, it nonetheless offers much more than the rural areas and towns of Myanmar, and so **rural-urban migration** has been strong. Some of the rural-urban migrants moved into old dilapidated buildings in the city centre, while others settled in new suburbs on the outskirts of Yangon to the north of the city centre.

Urban sprawl has accelerated since Myanmar's economic reforms were introduced. Rural-urban migration has accelerated markedly as Yangon's development has made the city even more attractive for potential migrants. Although the official population size is 2.5 million people, government planners acknowledge that the 'real' population of Yangon is more like 5 million people, and some government officials quote a figure of 7 million people when unregistered rural-urban migrants are included. The wide discrepancy in estimates of population size highlights the problems of gathering accurate statistics in a developing economy such as Myanmar.

11.54 *Suburban houses in Yangon, typical of those found in areas such as Dagon, Dala and Okkalapa.*

Most of the migrants coming to Yangon since the 1990s have settled in the outer suburbs, building simple new houses that resemble the houses found in rural villages and small towns throughout Myanmar. Indeed, the urban sprawl in Yangon has led many residents to describe Yangon as an overgrown village (figure 11.54). The typical houses are separate dwellings built from timber and thatch, and many lack basic services such as running water or reliable electricity. Like most cities in nations with developing economies, Yangon also has considerable areas of self-help shanty housing, although the scale of

Yangon's shanties are quite small compared with cities in nearby surrounding countries such as India, Bangladesh and Thailand (figure 11.55). Nonetheless, shanty housing is a normal expectation in countries with developing economies and high rates of rural-urban migration.

11.55 *Shanty housing in the New Town of Dagon, on the eastern outskirts of Yangon.*

The area under the control of Yangon's city planners has been expanded to acknowledge the new suburbs that sprang into existence during the 1990s — a form of **suburbanisation**. The new suburbs have been designated 'New Towns' by Yangon's planners, and several areas have been classified in this way. Several of the New Towns are new extensions of Yangon's earlier urban sprawl, and these include Shwe Pauk Kan to the north-east and Shwe Pyi Thar to the north-west. Other New Towns represent a new expansion of Yangon across the streams that had contained the city's urban sprawl until the early 1990s. These New Towns include Dala, across the Yangon River to the south, Hlaing Tharyar, across the Yangon River to the north-west, and Dagon to the east (across Pazun Daung and Nga Moe Yeik Creeks).

11.56 *The roads in Yangon's New Towns have been laid out in long straight lines. However, shortages of finance mean they are often poorly maintained, as is the case with this road in Dala.*

Like the areas developed during the earlier pre-1988 urban sprawl, the New Towns largely consist of simple village style houses, although they tend to be constructed along long straight roads rather than the narrow winding tracks found in outlying villages (figure 11.56). In the late 1990s, the first condominiums and high-rise blocks of flats were built in Dagon, one of the New Towns. The condominiums appealed to Yangon's emerging middle class, and if the economic reforms continue to expand the numbers of middle class workers it can be expected that more condominiums will be constructed.

11.57 *A passenger train on Yangon's circular railway route.*

11.58 *Public bus, Yangon, Myanmar.*

11.59 *A truck being used to provide a bus service, Yangon, Myanmar.*

Until the late 1980s, Yangon's metropolitan area was about 10 kilometres east-to-west and 32 kilometres north-to-south. By 2009, Yangon's size had increased to about

25 kilometres east-to-west and 45 kilometres north-to-south. Yangon's increasing size has posed transport problems for the residents, although perhaps fortunately very few people living in the outer suburbs work in the Central Business District. Compared with cities in countries with more developed economies, there is very little separation of home and workplace in Yangon. Yangon has a circular suburban railway line that was built by the British before independence, and a programme of road widening and new construction was undertaken during the 1990s (figure 11.57). Nonetheless, public transport is heavily overcrowded, with far too many passengers using far too few antiquated buses and trucks (figures 11.58 and 11.59). Very few residents of Yangon own private motor vehicles, and so they rely on the public transport. Fares cost just a few cents per journey, and while this makes the transport affordable for almost everyone, it does little to limit the demand for transport services or provide funds to upgrade and maintain the vehicles.

11.60 *A mirror-fronted bank stands out in stark contrast to the somewhat run-down colonial-era buildings that line Strand Road in downtown Yangon.*

Urban decay and urban sprawl are two urban dynamics that have been seen in Yangon for many years, but their pace has become much more rapid since the economic reforms for 1988. However, the renewed development of Yangon in the 1990s also led to several new urban dynamics that had not been seen previously. Many of the people squatting in downtown colonial buildings were rehoused in the new suburbs, enabling many of the old buildings to be renovated as offices or more expensive apartments. In this way, the processes of **urban renewal** and **gentrification** began. In some cases, dilapidated buildings that had been used as government offices were sold to private developers who have renovated them for commercial purposes (figure 11.60). In other cases, more commercially viable businesses such as insurance companies or hotels have replaced former uses that were viable only in the non-competitive, government-controlled business environment which prevailed before 1988 (figure 11.61).

Urban renewal is not restricted to the Central Business District. In the suburban areas, many of the old colonial mansions built by the British have become seen as desirable buildings to renovate. Among the 'higher value' uses to which the old mansions are now being put are residences for foreign embassies, houses for wealthy businessmen or government and military officials, and, in some cases, company offices.

11.61 *The Grand Hotel and a number of street level small shops now operate in this former office building constructed during the British colonial era.*

Government policy is trying to support the new commercial pressures that encourage urban renewal. The government wishes to modernise Yangon, to transform its colonial appearance and make it appear more worthy of a modern business centre. The government is aware that Yangon contrasts strongly with most other large cities in Asia – whereas most Asian cities today are vibrant, hectic and dynamic, reflecting the strong economic growth in Asia's economies, Yangon is described as sleepy and relaxed, where until recently the tallest buildings have been pagodas (figure 11.62).

The city administration has decided to demolish most of the colonial buildings in the years ahead and replace them with higher, more modern 'international-style' buildings. In the mid-1990s, construction began of the first high rise buildings in downtown Yangon, and today a handful of high rise buildings dot the Yangon urban landscape (figure 11.63). These tall buildings are usually either hotels or office blocks built with foreign funds. As more and more of these buildings are constructed, the skyline and thus the character of Yangon will be transformed forever.

Accompanying the process of urban renewal have been the processes of **urban consolidation** and **intensification**. With new commercial pressures beginning to affect owners of buildings on Yangon's Central Business District, owners are striving to maximise the value of each square metre of land. This is the main reason that high-rise development has begun to be seen in Yangon. In other parts of the Central Business District, previously vacant blocks of land are being developed for buildings, and additional floors are being added to the tops of some older buildings. Urban consolidation has increased the

pressures on Yangon's old public transport system, as well as increasing congestion in inner city areas (figure 11.64). This has led to the purchase of newer second-hand buses from South Korea, Israel and Japan.

11.62 *The Sule Pagoda dominates the centre of Yangon's CBD.*

11.63 *Yangon's Central Business District.*

11.64 *Transport congestion in Central Yangon.*

Traditionally, Yangon has been a highly centralised city, with few services found in the suburbs. This has also changed with Myanmar's economic reforms, and suburbanisation is now taking many services to the suburbs. Some offices are being established in suburban areas, hotels are appearing away from the city centre, and some suburban shopping centres began to appear in the late

1990s (figure 11.65). Often, these services in the suburbs have appeared in new buildings with modern appearances constructed during the 1990s, often as part of high-rise developments. In this way, the appearance as well as the functions of Yangon's suburbs is changing rapidly.

Like many cities in Asia, Yangon has always had a number of **urban villages**, and this has not changed with the economic reforms in the city. Yangon's Chinatown is situated in the west of the CBD, focussed on the Kheng Hock Keong Chinese temple on Strand Road. Similarly, Yangon's Indian quarter is centred on the Sri Kali Temple in Anawratha Road (figure 11.66). In the area around these temples, many of Yangon's ethnic minority peoples live, and there are markets, restaurants and medicine stores in the same areas to support those communities. Yangon's substantial Christian minority tend to live near the city's several churches.

11.65 *Several suburban office buildings like this one have been built at key intersections in Yangon.*

11.66 *The Hindu Sri Kali Temple represents a focus for Yangon's ethnically Indian population.*

In Yangon, there are also several suburban areas with strong concentrations of ethnic minorities from within Myanmar's borders. One of the strongest minority concentrations is found in the northern suburb of Insein, which is largely an urban village of Karen people from the south-east border area of Myanmar with Thailand. The Karen presence is so strong that the large Buddhist

pagoda in Insein is markedly different architecturally from the usual local style of solid bell-shaped towers. It is expected that with the development of the New Towns, the sense of identity in Yangon's urban villages will increase in the future.

Spatial exclusion is less developed in Yangon than in many other cities. However, with increasing affluence, security devices are becoming more common. So far, this has usually taken the form of high lockable gates, barbed wire or broken glass topped fences, and guardhouses at the entrances to properties. In a few cases, electronic surveillance measures have been installed, but these remain rare in Yangon. Some houses have security measures augmented with barred windows and security doors.

11.67 *A secure executive housing estate in Yangon's CBD.*

In the late 1990s, Yangon's first walled housing estate for wealthy residents opened under foreign management at the northern end of the central business district's grid layout streets. This estate maintained privacy and security for its residents by requiring visitors to pass through a gate staffed by a security officer (figure 11.67). Since then, several similar estates have opened in the New Town of Dagon, and many more are planned to cater for the emerging elite as Myanmar develops economically.

11.68 *The gap between the rich and the poor in Yangon grew during the 1990s. This view shows some of Yangon's homeless people living amongst the garbage between Strand Road and the Yangon River.*

While Myanmar's economic reforms have brought many positive effects to the lives of Yangon's people and to the pattern of urban land uses of a city that had stagnated for decades, there have also been some negative aspects. Average incomes have risen substantially, although the benefits have not flowed evenly through the population. The gap between the wealthy and the poor grew during the 1990s and early 2000s. For this reason, the number of people who scavenge through garbage to make a living has increased, as have the numbers of beggars and people who are homeless (figure 11.68).

QUESTION BLOCK 11G

1. *How have Myanmar's economic reforms affected the appearance and urban land uses of Yangon?*

2. *What changes would you expect to see in Yangon's urban land uses during the next decade?*

3. *Which of the following urban dynamics would you expect to be important in Yangon today: suburbanisation, exurbanisation, counterurbanisation, decentralisation, consolidation, urban decay, urban renewal, urban villages, spatial exclusion. Give reasons for your choices.*

The Global Megacity

Speaking of the megacities of the developing world, the Indian author A.K. Jain wrote in 1996:

"A large section of human population is ravaged by chronic poverty, malnutrition, homelessness, inadequate shelter,

and hazardous living conditions. They often suffer from a high population growth rate, low standard of living, high mortality, low expectation of life and unsanitary environment".

Since the year 2006, over half the world's population has been living in urban areas. By 2015, more than 560 cities will have populations of over one million, compared with 83 in 1950 and 280 in 2000. Most of this rapid urban transformation is taking place in developing countries, which are in many ways least able to cope with the pressures of urbanisation.

The location of the world's great cities has changed enormously over the centuries. Table 11.8 shows the changing distribution of the world's ten largest metropolitan areas.

Table 11.8 shows that western industrial cities were dominant in the world for only a small part of human history, centred on the year 1900. In 1800, only three of the ten largest cities were in Europe. By 1900, nine were in Europe or North America, but by 2000 this figure had fallen to just two, neither of which was in Europe. In 1000 and 1800, at least half of the world's ten largest cities were in Asia, and in 2000 this was once again the case. Table 11.9 shows that the fastest urban growth is now occurring in the economically less developed nations.

Cities with more than 10 million people are commonly referred to as **megacities** because of their large size. Thus, there are 21 megacities shown in table 11.9 in 2008. All of these are in LEDCs except for six – Tokyo, New York, Los Angeles, Osaka, Seoul and Paris. These six cities also tend

Table 11.8
The World's Ten Largest Cities, 1000 to 2010
(figures show populations in millions)

1000		1800		1900		2010	
City and Country	Pop'n	City and Country	Pop'n	City and Country	Pop'n	City and Country	Pop'n
Cordova, Spain	0.45	Beijing, China	1.10	London, UK	6.5	Tokyo, Japan	34.0
Kaifeng, China	0.40	London, UK	0.86	New York, USA	4.2	Guangzhou, China	24.2
Istanbul, Turkey	0.30	Guangzhou, China	0.80	Paris, France	3.3	Seoul, South Korea	24.2
Angkor, Cambodia	0.20	Tokyo, Japan	0.69	Berlin, Germany	2.7	Mexico City, Mexico	23.4
Kyoto, Japan	0.18	Istanbul, Turkey	0.57	Chicago, USA	1.7	Delhi, India	23.2
Cairo, Egypt	0.14	Paris, France	0.55	Vienna, Austria	1.7	Mumbai, India	22.8
Baghdad, Iraq	0.13	Naples, Italy	0.43	Tokyo, Japan	1.5	New York, USA	22.2
Neyshabur, Iran	0.13	Hangzhou, China	0.39	St Petersburg, Russia	1.4	São Paulo, Brazil	20.9
Al-Hasa, Saudi Arabia	0.11	Osaka, Japan	0.38	Manchester, UK	1.4	Manila, Philippines	19.6
Fez, Morocco	0.10	Kyoto, Japan	0.38	Philadelphia, USA	1.4	Shanghai, China	18.4

Source: Data for 1000 to 1900 based on O'Meara (1999) p.135. Data for 2008 from United Nations
Note, place names and countries are those of the present day

Table 11.9

The World's 25 Largest Cities in 2008, showing the growth of those cities since 1950
(note that cities over 10 million are usually regarded as megacities)

City and Country	Population 1950	Population 1975	Population 2008	Growth rate (% p.a.)
Tokyo, Japan	6,920,000	19,771,000	34,400,000	0.15
Jakarta, Indonesia	1,452,000	4,814,000	21,800,000	2.38
New York, USA	12,339,000	15,880,000	20,090,000	0.24
Seoul, South Korea	1,021,000	6,808,000	20,010,000	0.43
Manila, Philippines	1,544,000	5,000,000	19,550,000	2.31
Mumbai. India	2,981,000	7,347,000	19,530,000	2.00
São Paulo, Brazil	2,528,000	10,333,000	19,140,000	0.78
Mexico City, Mexico	2,883,000	10,691,000	18,430,000	0.60
Delhi, India	1,391,000	4,426,000	18,000,000	2.40
Osaka, Japan	4,147,000	9,844,000	17,270,000	0.04
Cairo, Egypt	2,410,000	6,079,000	16,750,000	1.53
Kolkata, India	4,446,000	7,888,000	15,010,000	1.83
Los Angeles, USA	4,046,000	8,926,000	14,730,000	0.79
Shanghai, China	5,333,000	11,443,000	14,460,000	1.54
Beijing, China	3,913,000	8,545,000	12,770,000	1.60
Buenos Aires, Argentina	5,042,000	9,144,000	12,390,000	0.46
Guangzhou, China	1,498,000	2,650,000	11,810,000	1.48
Shenzhen, China	4,000	26,000	11,710,000	14.80
Istanbul, Turkey	1,077,000	3,601,000	11,220,000	1.11
Rio de Janeiro, Brazil	2,965,000	7,963,000	11,160,000	0.79
Paris, France	5,441,000	8,885,000	10,430,000	0.09
Karachi, Pakistan	1,028,000	3,990,000	9,380,000	2.54
Chicago, USA	4,945,000	6,749,000	9,030,000	0.54
Lagos, Nigeria	288,000	1,890,000	8,860,000	2.99
London, UK	8,733,000	8,169,000	8,320,000	0.07

Source: United Nations and government census documents

to have the slowest rates of growth of the megacities. This is to be expected, as the countries where these cities are found (Japan, USA, France and South Korea) are already highly urbanised. The changing distribution of large cities in the world has occurred fairly recently and rapidly, as the data in table 11.10 show.

Today, 70% of people in economically more developed countries live in cities. Because overall population growth in these countries has slowed, even the largest cities in developed countries (Tokyo, New York, Los Angeles, Moscow, Paris, and so on) are growing at rates of only 1% to 2% per annum, and some such as London have declined in size at times.

On the other hand, some cities in economically developing nations are growing at 4% to 5% per annum. By 2015, 27 of the world's 33 largest cities will be in Asia. In 2015, it is expected that Shanghai and Mumbai will each have 20 million people, while Jakarta and its surrounding cities are likely to have almost 37 million. As a result of this rapid growth, cities in developing nations today often seem more modern, sophisticated and dynamic than longer established cities in developed nations (figure 11.69).

Table 11.10
Population in cities with more than one million residents, 1950 to 2015

Region	Total population of all cities with more than one million residents (population in millions)			
	1950	1970	1990	2015
Africa	3	16	59	225
Latin America	17	57	118	225
Asia	58	168	359	903
Europe	73	116	141	156
North America	40	78	105	148

Source: Far Eastern Economic Review

11.69 *These two views show centrally located districts of two major world cities — London (top) and Jakarta (bottom).*

Only a small part of the growth of the megacities in developing countries comes from natural increase. Most of the growth comes from the process of **rural-urban migration**, in which people (mostly young, single, adventurous males or dispossessed farmers) move to the cities in search of work. The cities attract migrants because job prospects are perceived to be good, services are seen to be much better than in the countryside and fanciful tales often circulate in rural areas about the wealth to be made in the cities. For most rural-urban migrants, the reality turns out to be quite different from the perception. Few rural-urban migrants find that their experience in farming or village life qualifies them for obtaining a job in the city, and many become shanty-dwellers or live on the pavements (figures 11.70 and 11.71). The presence of shanty settlements is one of the characteristics of most megacities in the developing world. The problems of housing in the megacities of the developing world are discussed in detail later in this chapter.

11.70 *Shanty dwellers, Dhaka, Bangladesh.*

11.71 *A homeless street dweller, Kolkata, India.*

With the rapid economic growth of many LEDCs, the cities of these countries are becoming dichotomous — in other words, developing a dual character. An example of this is seen in figure 11.72. These three photographs show three views in two different cities. At first sight, one would think that views (a) and (b) show the same city, as the appearance of the two cities is somewhat similar, and certainly quite different from the character of the area shown in (c). In fact, photos (a) and (c) of figure 11.72 both show Jakarta, capital city of Indonesia, while view (b) shows Taipei, the largest city in Taiwan, China.

11.72 *Which two views show the same city? The answer is given in the body of the text.*

Many megacities in the developing nations of Asia, Africa and South America were established during the period of European colonial rule. Examples include cities that were established by the British (Mumbai, Kolkata), the Dutch (Jakarta), the French (Hanoi, Ho Chi Minh City) and the Spanish (São Paulo, Manila). Although only a few centuries old, these cities have grown rapidly and today they all have populations in the millions. The colonial powers

established these centres to facilitate their trade. For this reason, all the colonial cities are situated on the coast, often at the mouths of large rivers that gave trading access to inland areas. The centres of the colonial cities were laid out by town planners in Europe, and as shown earlier in figures 11.62 and 11.63 in the case of Yangon, they were usually marked by geometric layouts of streets as a consequence, often in a grid pattern (figures 11.73 and 11.74).

11.73 *Spanish architecture dominates the design of the Central Post Office and other colonial era buildings in the centre of Santiago, Chile. Chile was a Spanish colony from 1541 to 1826.*

11.74 *British architecture dominates the Victoria Railway Terminus in Mumbai, India.*

However, not all megacities in developing countries began as colonial cities. In countries with a long history of urbanisation before the arrival of the Europeans, such as India, China and Japan, indigenous inland cities were established with a view to controlling as much territory as possible. Examples of such cities include Delhi in India, Beijing in China, and Tokyo in Japan. One indigenous megacity in South-east Asia is situated on the coast. Thailand was never colonised by the European powers but its capital city, Bangkok, was established on the coast in 1782. Bangkok was established to replace an inland city, Ayuthaya, which had been destroyed by the Burmese, and it was situated on the coast to place Thailand in a strong position to trade with the European powers on an even basis, with the intention of avoiding being colonised. Not coincidentally, Bangkok is one of the very few large cities in South-east Asia that does not have a regular geometric layout for its streets in the city centre.

QUESTION BLOCK 11H

1. *Describe the trends shown in table 11.8, highlighting especially (a) the changing distribution of the world's largest cities, and (b) the changing size needed to qualify as one of the world's largest cities.*

2. *Using an atlas and a blank map of the world, plot the locations of the megacities listed in table 11.9.*

3. *Using the data in table 11.9, draw line graphs to show the changing populations of the cities that are megacities today. Use a separate line for each city shown.*

4. *Rank the megacities (in 2008) shown in table 11.9 from the fastest growing to the slowest. Then comment on the geographical distribution of the fastest growing cities.*

5. *What is rural-urban migration?*

6. *Draw up a table to list the common geographical features of Jakarta and Taipei as shown in figures 11.72a and 11.72b.*

7. *Draw up a table to list the contrasting geographical features within Jakarta as shown in figures 11.72a and 11.72c.*

8. *What are the differences between indigenous cities and colonial cities in Asia? Give three examples of each.*

Urban Land Use

Processes Influencing Urban Land Use in MEDCs

Earlier in this chapter, the process of urbanisation in LEDCs was discussed. The processes of urbanisation in economically more economically developed areas such as North America, Europe and Australasia have been quite different to those operating in the developing nations. These different processes have resulted in cities with quite different patterns of urban land uses to those seen in developing nations.

The term **urban morphology** refers to the shape and appearance of urban centres. The urban morphology of a city is the result of the **urban dynamics**, or processes, operating there.

Compared with cities in developing nations (LEDCs), the pattern of land uses in the cities of industrialised nations (MEDCs) depends very much more on land values. In developed world cities, land values will vary enormously from one part of the city to another. The parts of the city with the highest land values will be those near the centre as these have the greatest **accessibility** for the people who live in the city. Therefore, businesses that are located there can expect to attract extra business because of the highly accessible location. The point with the highest land values is called the **Peak Land Value Intersection**, or PLVI (figure 11.75). It is always located in the Central Business District (CBD). The land values at the PLVI can be very high in large cities, and in American cities the values can exceed $3 million per hectare.

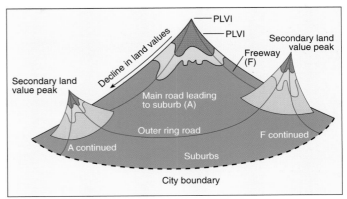

11.75 *Land values in a city in an economically more developed country.*

Land prices usually fall away quite sharply from the PLVI. This is the principle of **distance-decay**. As distance from the PLVI increases, land prices decrease, and reflecting this, building heights also decrease (figure 11.76). Only a few types of very profitable businesses that would benefit by being at the PLVI can afford to pay the high land prices demanded there. Typically, large retail shops have the most to gain from a highly central location, and these tend to be the highest bidders for the scarce land right at the PLVI. As accessibility declines as one moves away from the PLVI, so does the price that businesses are willing to pay for land also declines. Commercial enterprises such as financial companies, solicitors and corporate offices require high accessibility, but they cannot usually afford to pay the high prices that large retail shops can pay. Therefore, these types of businesses are situated further away from the PLVI, towards the edge of the CBD.

11.76 *Building heights decrease from the PLVI reflecting the decrease in land values. A graph showing the building heights in this part of Dallas (Texas, USA) would very closely mirror the land values.*

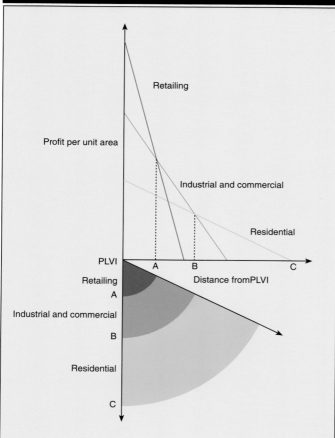

11.77 *The bid-rent theory.*

Figure 11.77 illustrates the pattern that emerges, and is called the **bid-rent theory**. Retailers can afford the highest rents, but they are not prepared to pay high prices if they are not in a highly accessible location. Therefore, the slope of the rent curve for retail shops is very steep. The rent curve for industrial and commercial enterprises does rise as high as that for retail shops, but it falls away a little more gently because accessibility is not quite as crucial for them. Similar forces operate for other land uses such as multiple family dwellings (flats and home units), single family dwellings (free standing houses) and, finally, agriculture. Agriculture is the least competitive land use, and so it is found beyond the urban limits.

It is assumed that land developers will try to maximise their profits. Therefore, the land use whose curve is highest in figure 11.77 will be the land use found in that area. Thus, retailing will be found closest to the PLVI. As we move away from the PLVI in this example, we will come in turn to an industrial and commercial area, an area of flats and home units, a zone of single family dwellings and finally to the farming areas which surround the city.

If we assume that the land on which the city is built is fairly uniform, then this pattern will be found in every direction as we move away from the PLVI. In the 1920s, an American geographer called Burgess carried out field-work in Chicago and concluded that this does in fact happen in reality. He developed a model of urban areas

which concluded that land uses are arranged around the CBD in concentric circles, with the most profitable land uses being found closest to the city centre (figure 11.78a).

Although Burgess' concentric zone model highlighted some important urban dynamics, it had several shortcomings. It was clearly an over-simplification, as it took no account of landforms (land prices are higher where there is a view), transport routes (which attract industry) or changes that can occur over time. The model suggested that there were sharp boundaries between land use zones, whereas in reality these fade and merge into one another. Furthermore, it was only applicable to cities in industrialised nations, as land uses in developing nations were not influenced as strongly by economic forces. That is why Burgess concluded that poorer people tend to live in inner city areas whereas developing world cities tend to have poorer people living on the outskirts, usually in shanty settlements.

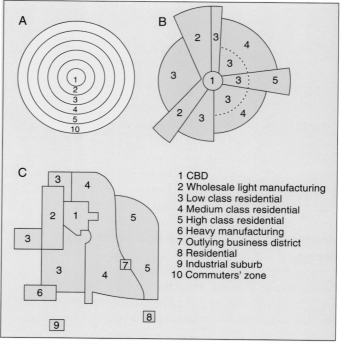

11.78 *Three simplified models showing urban land uses in cities of economically more developed countries:*
A the concentric model (after Burgess);
B the sector model (after Hoyt);
C the multiple nuclei model (after Harris and Ullman).

To overcome some of these difficulties, another American geographer called Hoyt suggested that land uses in cities are arranged in sectors rather than in concentric circles (figure 11.78b). Hoyt could not accept that all the land upon which a city is built is uniform, and his model took landforms and transport routes into account. He suggested that wealthier people tend to live on higher land while manufacturing industry will be aligned along transport routes such as roads, railways and rivers. In this way, he argued, land uses will be arranged in sectors that radiate out from the CBD.

However, two other American geographers, Harris and Ullman, argued that even this was too simplistic. They said that land uses are not arranged around just one CBD, but that large cities have several business centres (which they called nuclei) such as shopping centres and areas of office development (figure 11.79). These centres emerge as the city grows because the one central CBD is no longer accessible to residents who live towards the edge, or periphery, of the city.

11.79 *The taller buildings in this aerial view of Sydney show the suburb of Parramatta, an important nucleus serving Sydney's western suburbs.*

Therefore, Harris and Ullman argued that land uses tend to be arranged in cells or patches throughout the city depending on the availability and the quality of the land (figure 11.78c). Some activities, such as shops and factories, will cluster together for their mutual advantage. Other land uses that are incompatible, such as high-class residential land and heavy industry, will not locate near each other. Certain types of land use that need large areas of land, such as manufacturing industry, will locate towards the edge of the city where cheap land is available. Other land uses which need high levels of accessibility, such as offices, tend to be located close to the CBD. Higher-class residential areas will tend to be located on elevated land where land prices are higher.

In reality, most cities in industrialised countries show a land use pattern that is a combination of all three models. Getis, Getis and Fellmann suggest a model of a U.S. city that is probably applicable also to cities in Australia and elsewhere that combines the three earlier theoretical models (figure 11.80).

The bidding process for land in the CBD has the effect of causing a **population density hollow** in the middle of the city (figure 11.81). Apart from a few very costly apartment houses, the residential land use is usually out-bid by retailing and office space in the CBD. Where residential areas are located close to the CBD, they tend to be high-density flats and home units, as only these types of housing will provide the land owners with the necessary profit on the highly priced land in these areas. Thus, residential

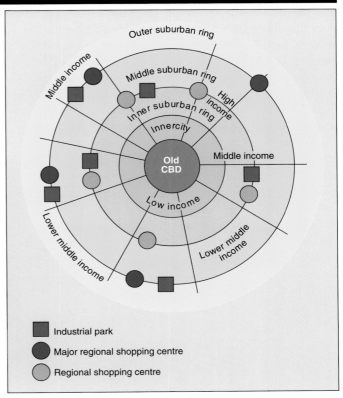

11.80 *The integrated model of a large US city (after Getis, Getis and Fellmann).*

density (and building heights) decline with increasing distance from the outskirts of the CBD, two more examples of distance-decay.

There is no country in the world whose rate of urbanisation (urban population as a percentage of total population) has fallen in the period following 1965. Even Cambodia, which had a forced programme of abandoning the cities and moving people to rural areas under the Khmer Rouge government between 1975 and 1979 had an increase in urban population from 11% in 1965 to 23% in 2000. However, the rate of urbanisation in the MEDCs of the world has been much less than that in the world's developing nations. This was shown in table 11.9 earlier in this chapter.

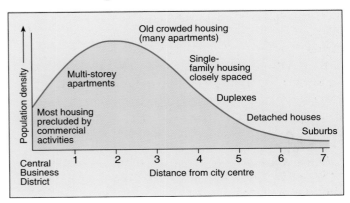

11.81 *The general population density curve for a large city in an economically more developed country.*

The processes of urbanisation operating in Europe, North America and Australasia today are quite different from those in the LEDCs. Rural-urban migration does not occur on a significant scale as happens in most of Asia, Africa and South America. Rather than rural-urban migration, the important dynamics operating in cities of industrialised nations are suburbanisation, gentrification and counter-urbanisation. These will be dealt with in more detail later in this chapter. Having said this, it is important to realise that as the economies of these countries develop, the economic force of the bid-rent mechanism grows in importance. It is becoming increasingly common to see evidence of this in large cities in Asia, Africa and South America as vertical expansion of the CBD and distinctive land-use zones develop (figure 11.82).

11.82 *The Central Business District of Santiago, capital city of Chile.*

QUESTION BLOCK 11I

1. *In what ways do the patterns of urban land use of cities in MEDCs contrast with the land uses of cities in LEDCs?*

2. *What are the processes that lead to the differences you described in your answer to the last question?*

3. *What is the PLVI? Suggest where the PLVI is in the urban centre where you live.*

4. *What is meant by the term 'distance-decay'? Give two examples of how distance-decay can be seen in a city.*

5. *Explain how the bid-rent theory predicts that the land use zones in a city will be arranged in concentric circles around the city centre.*

6. *Make a point form list of the main features of the urban models produced by (a) Burgess, (b) Hoyt, and (c) Harris and Ullman.*

7. *Why is there a population density hollow towards the centre of most cities in economically more developed countries?*

Cities in LEDCs

Cities in less economically developed countries usually develop bit by bit, growing outwards by adding shanty settlements on the outskirts of the city (figure 11.83). As time passes, these shanty settlements evolve into permanent buildings and a new 'ring' of shanties develops further out, causing the city to expand horizontally. In this way, cities in LEDCs tend to develop with the wealthy élite living close to the city centre, with people becoming progressively poorer towards the outskirts (figure 11.84). Bands of manufacturing industry are generally situated along major lines of communication such as roads and railways.

11.83 *Shanty settlements near the outskirts of Dhaka, Bangladesh.*

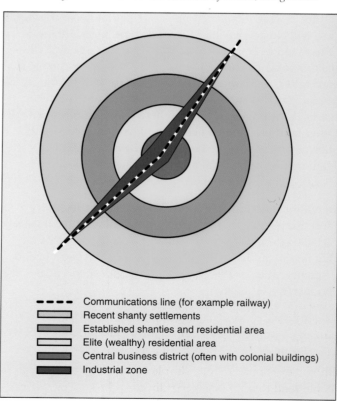

- - - - Communications line (for example railway)
☐ Recent shanty settlements
▭ Established shanties and residential area
☐ Elite (wealthy) residential area
▭ Central business district (often with colonial buildings)
▬ Industrial zone

11.84 *Simplified land use pattern in cities in the LEDCs of Asia, Africa and South America.*

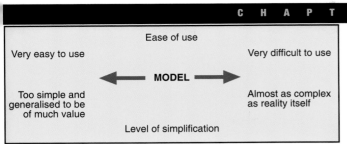

11.85 *The use of models in Geography.*

Any model such as figure 11.84 is a vast simplification of reality. As figure 11.85 suggests, the simplest models are the easiest to use but they are not very useful for predicting reality. The simplest models are most useful for highlighting broad patterns and processes. On the other hand, as we make models more realistic, they become more complex and more difficult to use. To be effective and useful, therefore, a good model will fall between the two extremes shown in figure 11.85.

With this in mind, we can make the model of the developing world city shown in figure 11.84 somewhat more realistic without making it too complex. One such more complex model of a developing world city is shown in figure 11.86.

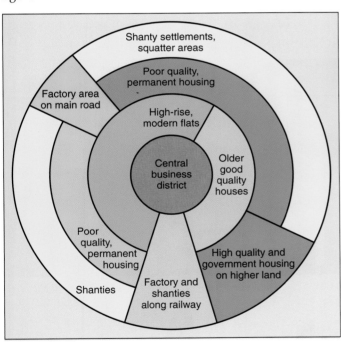

11.86 *A less simplified land use model of a city in a developing nation of Asia, Africa or South America.*

In the real world, of course, cities are much more complex even than the pattern shown in figure 11.84. Models are only simplifications of reality, designed to highlight the processes that are operating. Developing world cities almost never have a clear, simple pattern of land uses. People tend to segregate according to ethnic group as well as wealth. A city in South-east Asia may have separate areas for Chinese, Indian, Malay and European residents. Furthermore, land uses in developing world cities are seldom arranged horizontally, but they are more common

arranged vertically in buildings known as three-tier developments (figure 11.87). The buildings typically have a shop on the ground floor, with a warehouse or factory making goods in the middle level and the residence of the family operating the business on the top floor.

11.87 *An example of three-tier development in Bangkok, Thailand.*

11.88 *An advertisement for designer clothes dominates this area of shanties in Manila, capital of the Philippines, highlighting the gap between rich and poor in the city.*

One of the features of cities in Asia, Africa and South America is that there are often huge gaps in wealth within the population (figure 11.88). Many of the wealthiest – and the poorest – people in the world live in the developing nations (LEDCs). Social unrest based on differences in wealth is rare, however, and people tend to accept the differences in wealth, at least outwardly. In countries with a strong Confucianist, Hindu or Buddhist tradition, people traditionally accept their position in society as 'fate', the consequence of deeds or misdeeds in past lives. By accepting their position in society and working within it, Hindus and Buddhists who accept reincarnation believe that they can earn merit that will improve their positions in the next life. In contrast, societies which have embraced the Christian religion, the Muslim faith or a Communist ideology are less likely to accept wealth and position in society as 'fate'. More social unrest tends to occur in such societies as people work more actively to change their society.

Urban environments

11.89 *These two housing areas of Soweto, a suburb of Johannesburg (South Africa), are situated just a few kilometres from each other.*

The differences in wealth are reflected in the urban morphology of cities in Africa, Asia and South America. It is very common to find cities in developing nations having a Central Business District (CBD) that has modern high-rise buildings of the type that might be found in almost any large city in the industrialised world. However, nearby there will often be poor quality, overcrowded housing. Similarly, it is common to find housing for wealthy residents situated very close to residential areas for the poor (figure 11.89). Such differences occur over very short distances, and this is a feature of many large cities in LEDCs.

11.90 *This man operates a business on the pavement typing letters for illiterate residents of Kolkata (India) who need to correspond with official government bodies.*

Another consequence of the increasing wealth in many developing world cities is that new industries are created for which there was never previously a large demand (figure 11.90). These new industries create wealth for a new emerging group of entrepreneurs that become the 'middle class' of these countries. The emerging middle class tends to have high disposable incomes that are spent on things like fast food, cars and electronic consumer goods.

The one characteristic that is common to most cities in LEDCs is that they are changing rapidly. Often, there is a deliberate policy of encouraging growth in urban areas. For example, China has set aside several cities and made them targets for government and foreign investment funds. These cities include Shenzhen, Zhuhai, Xiamen and the Pudong and Hongqiao districts of Shanghai (figure 11.91). These areas have special tax concessions, streamlined regulations and labour laws that are designed to attract foreign investment funds. Other nations have introduced similar zones. However, with or without these special investment zones, the economies of most of the developing nations are expanding, and the first benefits of this expansion tend to be seen in the cities rather than the countryside. Consequently, the central business districts of many cities in LEDCs are at least as modern as any city in North America, Europe or Australia.

11.91 *Shenzhen, located beside the Hong Kong Special Administrative Region (SAR), was China's first Special Economic Zone (SEZ).*

QUESTION BLOCK 11J

1. *Which is the more useful model of a developing world city in your opinion, the one shown in figure 11.84 or the one shown in figure 11.86? Give reasons for your answer.*

2. *What is three-tier development?*

3. *Explain why there seem to be huge gaps between the rich and the poor in the cities of LEDCs.*

4. *It is suggested in the text that 'the one characteristic that is common to most cities in LEDCs is that they are changing rapidly'. Using specific examples, explain why you agree or disagree with this statement.*

Case Study of Urban Land Use — Yangon

Urban land uses are usually examined in the more developed countries where economic forces are dominant. This is because economic forces often give way to social and cultural factors as the main influences on the geography of cities in the economically less developed countries.

Nonetheless, rapid change is a characteristic of many cities in the developing world. In the 1990s, after decades of stagnation, Myanmar began a period of rapid economic change. This led to significant changes in the country's largest city and former capital, Yangon.

Yangon began as a small fishing village called Dagon. However, Dagon was quite different from other villages because it had a Buddhist pagoda (stupa) that has great religious significance. Construction of the pagoda, known as the Shwe Dagon Pagoda, began in about 500 BC, although it has been extended since that time (figure 11.92). It is said that the Shwe Dagon Pagoda is built on eight hairs from Buddha's head, and it has become a symbol of both Yangon and Myanmar. Today, the Shwe Dagon Pagoda comprises a 98 metre high solid central spire coated in a one centimetre thick layer of solid gold, topped with 5,451 diamonds and 1,383 other precious stones. The central spire is surrounded by about 70 pavilions, temples and halls.

11.92 *The main spire of the Shwe Dagon Pagoda, Yangon.*

QUESTION BLOCK 11K

1. *Using an atlas, draw a sketch map to show the location of Yangon. Include the latitude and longitude of Yangon.*

From the mid-1800s, the British occupied Burma (as it was known at the time) and made Rangoon the capital city. As the city had been destroyed during the fighting over political control, the British used the opportunity to re-plan the layout of those parts of the city near the river where they lived and worked. They decided to remodel the city according to a European-style grid layout with streets running at right angles, north-south and east-west.

A grid was surveyed centred on the Sule Pagoda, and this point still marks the administrative and commercial centre of Yangon today (figure 11.93).

11.93 *The Sule Pagoda marks the centre of the grid pattern of streets surveyed by the British for Yangon during colonial times.*

A port and industrial zone was established nearby along the northern bank of the Yangon River. Although some roads were built to other towns in Myanmar, the main means of transport was by boat. Even today, Yangon's river frontage is largely taken up with wharves, warehouses and trading houses. Because the area to the southeast of the Sule Pagoda comprised low-lying, reclaimed land, it was designated as parkland, and remains so today.

11.94 *The High Court Building in central Yangon, seen from the green expanses of Maha Bandoola Park.*

Meanwhile, at the northern edge of the city, the British military saw the hill where the Shwe Dagon Pagoda was built as having strategic value. Therefore, they made the

Urban environments

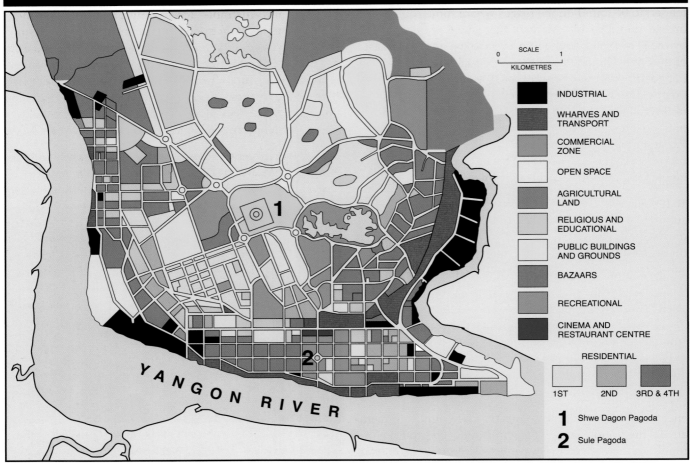

11.95 *Urban morphology of Yangon in the late 1930s. Because there has been so little new construction since that time, the map is still essentially accurate today.*

Shwe Dagon Pagoda their military headquarters. This caused great offence to most Buddhists, as it is the custom to show respect by removing one's shoes before entering the precincts of a pagoda; the British soldiers were certainly not willing to walk around their own base barefooted!

Notwithstanding all this, a substantial and elegant city arose as construction continued (figure 11.94). Population grew rapidly, reaching 92,000 by 1872, 141,000 by 1881, 177,000 by 1891, 221,000 by 1901 293,000 by 1911, 342,000 by 1921 and 400,000 by 1931. By 1930, half of Yangon's population was Indian, mainly labourers brought in by the British.

The pattern of urban land uses in Yangon in the late 1930s is shown in figure 11.95. The commercial core was found in a compact area around the Sule Pagoda, while banks and trading companies were found along Strand Road, the main street that ran along the northern side of the Yangon River. A large area of movie theatres was found to the north of the Sule Pagoda near the railway station.

West of the central core area was the main retailing area. The large Scott Market, a huge complex of covered alleyways and stalls was found there, together with the Chinese markets, street stalls, bazaars and small shops

(figure 11.96). Further to the west, approaching the Yangon River, an area of manufacturing industry was found, comprising food factories, saw mills, metal workers and rice mills. In general, the most elegant buildings, such as the High Court and the City Hall, were found near the Sule Pagoda.

11.96 *The Bogyoke Aung San Market (formerly Scott's Market, and still widely known by that name) in Yangon's CBD.*

Residential areas at the time fell into three types, as shown in figure 11.95. These three types of residential area were often separated from each other by open spaces. Type 1 residential areas, which were of the highest quality, tended to be found on the ridges where some cooling breezes could be felt. Many of these areas were occupied by the British, although large areas to the north and east of the Shwe Dagon Pagoda were occupied by higher ranking government workers and business families. At the other extreme, type 3 residential areas, which can also be termed 'slums', tended to be found on the low lying areas of flood-prone land on the eastern side of the city near Pazundaung Creek. The poorest areas were inhabited by Indian workers, and it had the highest death rates and highest infant mortality rates in Yangon.

To the north of the Shwe Dagon Pagoda, the outer suburbs resembled over-sized traditional villages in that they were sprawling areas with dirt roads and small timber houses with thatched roofs. Beyond these outer suburbs lay the countryside of rice fields and smaller, more isolated villages.

QUESTION BLOCK 11L

1. *In about two pages, describe and account for Yangon's urban morphology in the late 1930s, as shown in figure 11.95.*

On 4th January 1948 Myanmar was granted its independence from British rule. The country faced almost immediate disintegration as various ethnic minority groups fought to separate from Myanmar. By early 1949, most of the country was under the control of one rebel group or another, and there was even fighting in the suburbs of Yangon. The unrest continued until 1962 when a military coup gave control of the country to the army. The military government adopted a policy called the 'Burmese Way to Socialism', which cut Myanmar off from contact with most other nations.

11.97 *British colonial-era buildings near the port facilities in the Yangon River.*

This isolation meant that very little foreign aid and almost no foreign investment flowed into Myanmar. The isolation also cut off Myanmar from the world's air routes. Until the 1950s, Yangon had been a major refuelling stopover for airlines flying between Europe and South-

east Asia and Australia. Today, only a handful of airlines, most of them of only minor importance, fly into Yangon. Due to the policy of isolation, the economy stagnated and Myanmar drifted into poverty. Because of the civil unrest and then the policy of isolation, very little new construction, or even repairs, took place in Yangon. Yangon took on the appearance of a decaying, poorly maintained, 'living museum' of British colonial architecture (figure 11.97).

The Yangon River was the reason for the selection of Yangon's site, and it continues to influence the city. Yangon has grown to the north away from the site of first settlement near the river. Expansion to the west, south and east has been restricted by the river and its tributaries. Thus, there is a clear transition as one travels towards the north away from the river of rising elevation, less well planned street layouts and more recent development.

11.98 *The Yangon City Hall, across the road from the Sule Pagoda, once marked the centre of Yangon. Recent growth has since moved the geographical centre of the urban area many kilometres northwards.*

Because of the lack of new building activity since independence in 1948, the urban land use map in figure 11.95 is still generally accurate today for the area shown. The administrative and commercial core of Yangon is still where it was in the 1930s, although the growth of Yangon towards the north has meant that this core is no longer in the geographical centre of the urban area (figure 11.98). Lining the river is a zone of port facilities, warehouses

11.99 *British architecture in central Yangon, Myanmar.*

and manufacturing. These two zones owe their locations to the colonial origins of Yangon.

The intention of the British to build a European city in an Asian environment is seen very clearly in the centre of Yangon (figure 11.99). Although centred on the indigenous Sule Pagoda, the architecture of this area is almost entirely British. Other reflections of the colonial origins include the grid layout of the streets, the English street names such as Merchant Street, Strand Road and Mission Road, and the large open recreational areas in the city centre (figure 11.100). Among the buildings found in this city core are Yangon City Hall and National Library, several embassies (especially in Strand Road), the Office of Ministers, Office of the Workers' Council, General Post Office, Yangon General Hospital, the National Museum, the Central Railway Station and the High Court Building (figure 11.101).

11.100 *A street sign in central Yangon, recalling the days of British colonial rule.*

11.101 *Yangon Central Railway Station.*

Like most cities in developing countries that had colonial origins, Yangon's core is heavily influenced by port activities. Currently, Yangon handles most of Myanmar's legal foreign trade. Therefore, the city's river frontage is lined with some 6.5 kilometres of wharves with accompanying commercial activities such as warehouses and factories. Most of Yangon's manufacturing involves light processing of the raw materials brought in from the surrounding

countryside. Consequently, the main industries include textiles, jute, medicines, timber milling, rice milling and building materials manufacture. Many minor industries have been established in an effort to make Yangon largely self-sufficient in as many goods as possible to control the outflow of foreign currency.

11.102 *An example of one of Yangon's many decaying colonial-era mansions, originally built for upper class British settlers but now used by residents of Yangon.*

11.103 *Houses in one of Yangon's inner suburbs. Note the condition of the pavement in front of the house.*

The residential areas of most Asian cities are divided into ethnic groups, and Yangon is no exception. Yangon has a small Chinese quarter towards the western end of the commercial core, and an area of Indian housing in shanties along Pazundaung Creek to the east of the core. Otherwise, the city is almost uniformly indigenous in character. The former European areas are now occupied by wealthier locals, such as government and military officials. These areas have large houses that are on hill-sides facing the river to benefit from any breezes in Yangon's hot, tropical climate. Like many of the buildings in the commercial core of the city, little maintenance has been done on the old colonial-era houses since independence, and they present a somewhat crumbling, decaying appearance (figures 11.102 and 11.103). In Yangon, these wealthier housing areas are dispersed in pockets throughout the city wherever there is some higher land, although they are concentrated towards the city core.

11.104 *Housing in central Yangon.*

11.105 *Shops in outer suburban Yangon.*

11.106 *Dala, a new suburb of Yangon.*

In general, the quality of the residential areas deteriorates as one moves further away from the commercial core of Yangon. Much of the residential accommodation in central Yangon comprises converted colonial buildings (figure 11.104). Away from the city centre, accommodation is mostly in small houses with shops at the front

(figure 11.105) or more recently built traditional 'village' houses (figure 11.106). Dwellings are often single roomed with a minimum of furniture and lighting. Settlement becomes sparser towards the northern edge of Yangon because there is less pressure of the land. The buildings on the outskirts are typically two or three roomed of somewhat flimsy construction.

11.107 *Shanty housing on the eastern outskirts of Yangon.*

On the outskirts of Yangon some shanty settlements are found (figure 11.107). These are areas of temporary housing built on pockets of vacant land by squatters who have migrated to Yangon from rural areas. Rural-urban migration does not appear to have been as significant a force in the growth of Yangon as it has been in the growth of other Asian cities such as Jakarta, Dhaka, Kolkata or Bangkok. Push factors encouraging migration into Yangon include the lack of amenities in rural villages, natural disasters such as droughts and floods, civil wars in the hill areas near Myanmar's borders, and slow but increasing farm mechanisation. Pull factors that encourage people to leave their rural areas and migrate to Yangon include the higher standards of living in the city and the prospect of employment.

In most Asian cities, it is very difficult to construct maps of urban morphology showing the urban land use zones. There are several reasons for this. First, the economic forces that operate through the land-rent mechanism are often absent or weaker in Asian cities than in western cities. In Asian cities, tradition, ethnic groupings and politics are usually more influential than simple commercial forces. Second, many economic activities occur in the streets rather than in buildings. For example, many of Yangon's markets are on the footpaths, and they relocate to different positions at various times of the day (figures 11.109 and 11.110).

Third, a distinctive type of architecture has become increasingly common in Asian cities during the past few decades. Much of the recent construction has been building three-tiered buildings with retail activities at the street level, residential facilities on the upper level and light manufacturing on the middle floor. Where such buildings

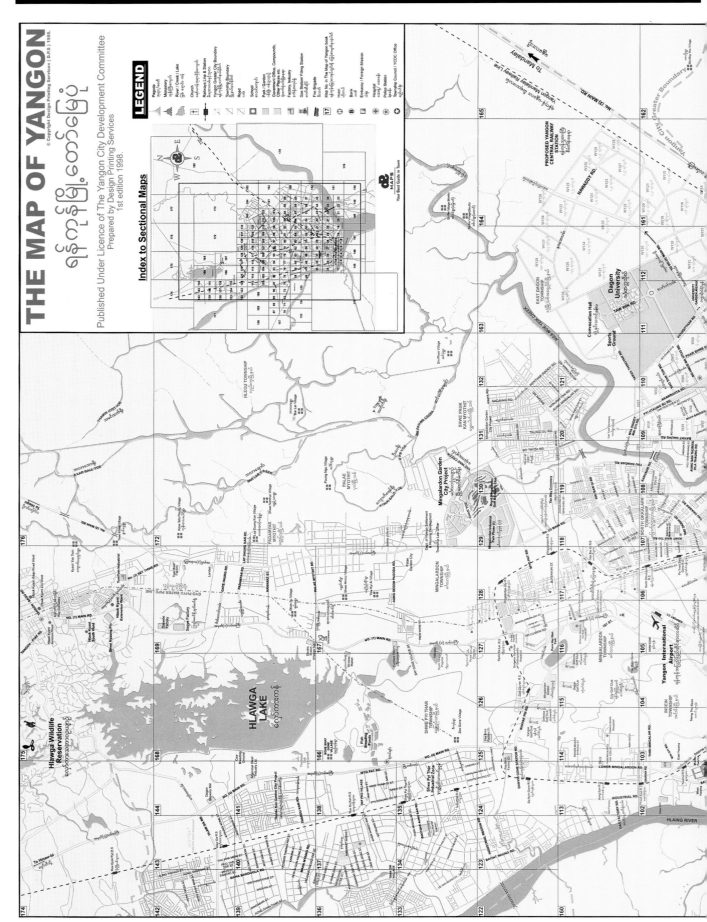

11.108 *Street map of Yangon, reduced to a scale of 1:100,000.* (Source: Design Printing Services, Yangon, Myanmar. www.dps.com.mm)

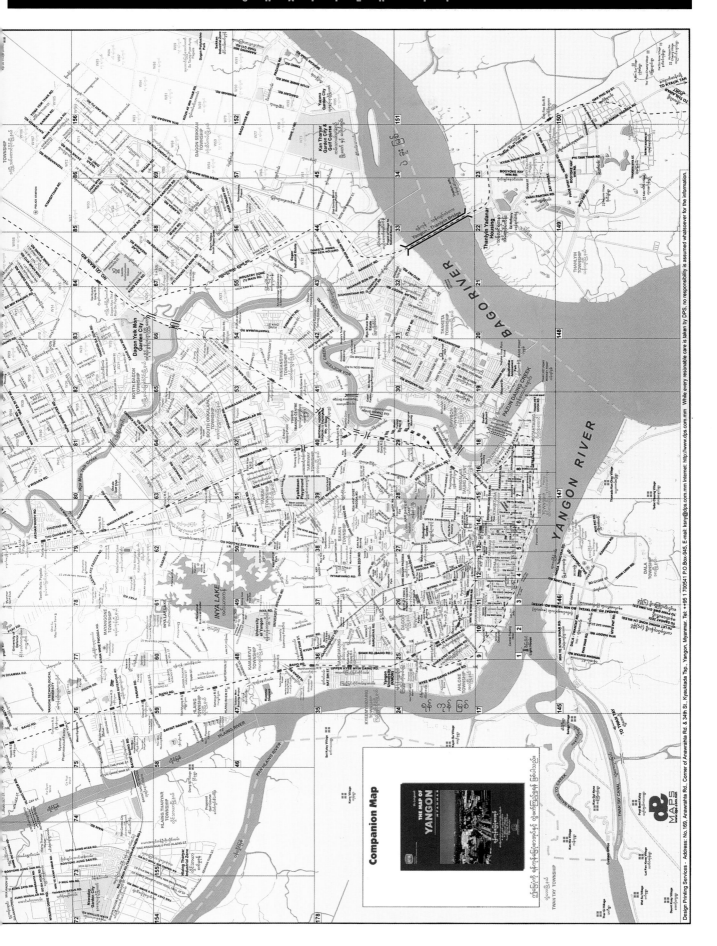

Urban environments

11.109 *Fruit and vegetables for sale in a street market in central Yangon.*

11.110 *A book seller sells books on the pavement in Yangon.*

11.111 *Three-tiered land use in an old colonial building in Yangon.*

occur, land use zones should probably be plotted vertically rather than horizontally as on a land use map.

Because there has been so little construction in Yangon since 1948, this three-tiered pattern of architecture has hardly emerged in Yangon. Many of the old colonial buildings in the city centre have been modified inside to accommodate more and more families, and in so doing a three-tiered pattern has often emerged with the buildings (figure 11.111). Nonetheless, with so little new construction of three-tiered buildings, Yangon has an unusually clear pattern of land use zones for an Asian city, and the

pattern is a clear reflection of the pattern that existed during colonial times.

In addition to the commercial, administrative, industrial, port and residential areas described above, Yangon has a number of zones set aside for special purposes. One such zone is the area set aside for the huge Shwe Dagon Pagoda complex that was described earlier. Other examples are the large areas of recreational land and parks surrounding Yangon's two lakes, Inya Lake in the north and the smaller Royal Lake to the south (figure 11.112). These are both artificial lakes that were expanded in the 1800s to provide a water supply for Yangon. Open space is also found around the University of Yangon to the north-west of the city, at Yangon racecourse to the north-east and in many other smaller areas within Yangon. Indeed, much of suburban Yangon has a park-like atmosphere with many tall trees hiding the buildings.

11.112 *Karaweik Hall, shaped by a mythical bird, dominates the shore-line of Royal Lake.*

Yangon's street pattern shows three major phases of development (figure 11.108). First, the grid pattern in the Central Business District beside the river at the southern end of the city reflects the city's colonial origins. British influence was concentrated in the port and administrative areas, and so these zones were surveyed according to the practices then current in Europe – a grid layout aligned with the cardinal points of the compass. To the north of this 'grid' area, extending up the southern side of Inya Lake, is a zone where the growth was largely unplanned and uncoordinated. In this area, a deranged street pattern emerged with roads following the traditional pathways and ridges. Finally, recent expansion to the west, north and east of Inya Lake shows increased evidence of town planning by government authorities, who have tried to plan urban development using a loose system of a very large scale grid layout.

QUESTION BLOCK 11M

1. Explain why there was so little new construction in Yangon between the 1950s and the mid-1990s.

2. *Compare the pattern of Yangon's urban land uses today with its pattern in the late 1930s. Give reasons for the changes (and lack of changes).*

3. *Compare the importance of rural-urban migration in Yangon with other Asian cities. What have been the reasons for and consequences of Yangon's different pattern?*

4. *Use the map in figure 11.108 to construct a sketch map showing Yangon's pattern of main roads and water areas today. Label the areas of the three main types of street pattern which reflect Yangon's growth.*

Urban Stress

Environmental Quality and Health Issues in Cities in LEDCs

As countries seek to develop economically, manufacturing industry expands and motor vehicle traffic increases rapidly. This has an enormous environmental impact on the world's cities, as it is in cities that industry, people and traffic are concentrated in high density. The problem of pollution can be particularly severe when governments and industry decision makers regard environmental quality as a luxury they cannot afford.

One major type of pollution in the developing world's cities is **air pollution**. Consider the following statement:

"A blood-red sun glows through the toxic haze. Commuters clog the arterial roads and their lines of cars resemble long sheets of steel, belching a miasma of pollutants. Stuck in the inevitable traffic jam, the drivers gaze out of their windows at the stark, inner urban landscape from whose broken buildings stagger impoverished drunks. On the street, young punks wearing tattoos like badges stare back so malevolently, the commuters quickly look away."

This description was written to describe Melbourne (Australia) on an autumn day, but it could also apply to any other major world city with a large volume of motor transport (figure 11.113). The gases produced by motor vehicles include nitrous oxides, carbon monoxide and sulphur dioxide. In warm climates, such as those found in Bangkok, Lagos, São Paulo, Dhaka, Delhi and Jakarta, the gases emitted through car exhausts 'cook' in the sun and ozone, or photochemical smog, is produced. This is very harmful for the residents living in the cities concerned. Pilots flying into many cities report that they can always locate the city from a great distance away because it is covered by a characteristic brown dome of photochemical smog (figure 11.114).

An indication of the extent of air pollution in some of the world's largest cities is given in table 11.11. Recent research shows that the most dangerous component of air pollution is not the poisonous gases, but the suspended particulate matter (SPM). SPM includes much more than dust, and a particularly dangerous component is microscopic particles of benzene. Less than 2.5 microns in size, these particles are inhaled into the deepest parts of the lungs where they remain, leading to cancer. Particles of benzene are almost never produced by a source other than motor vehicles.

11.113 *Traffic congestion in Dhaka, Bangladesh.*

A large part of the blame for urban air pollution is placed upon the construction of expressways. Many cities in the developing world, such as Bangkok, Jakarta and Shanghai now have extensive networks of expressways that span the entire metropolis. In such cities, public transport is poorly developed and even footpaths for pedestrians do not exist in many parts of the city.

11.114 *Air pollution over Santiago, Chile.*

On the other hand, not building expressways also brings problems of wasted fuel and air pollution as vehicles clog roads that are inadequate for the volume of traffic. In Bangkok, Thailand, expressways were not built for many years as the government felt that providing better roads would only encourage more people to use private cars rather than public transport. As a result, Bangkok has some of the worst traffic jams in the world as well as severe air pollution that causes many people's nostrils to sting when they inhale. Indeed, 20% of the Bangkok

Table 11.11
Air Pollution in Selected Large Cities

City	SO₂	SPM	Pb	CO	NO₂	O₃
Bangkok	✔	☠	✘	✔	✔	✔
Beijing	☠	☠	✔		✔	✘
Buenos Aires		✘	✔	☠		
Cairo		☠	☠	✘		
Delhi	✔	☠	✔	✔	✔	
Jakarta	✔	☠	✘	✘	✔	✘
Karachi	✔	☠	☠			
Kolkata	✔	☠	✔		✔	
London	✔	✔	✔	✘	✔	✔
Los Angeles	✔	✘	✔	✘	✘	☠
Manila	✔	☠	✘			
Mexico City	☠	☠	✘	☠	✘	☠
Moscow		✘	✔	✘	✘	
Mumbai	✔	☠	✔	✔	✔	
New York	✔	✔	✔	✘	✔	✘
Rio de Janeiro	✘	✘	✔	✔		
São Paulo		✘	✔	✘	✘	☠
Seoul	☠	☠	✔	✔	✔	✔
Shanghai	✘	☠				
Tokyo	✔	✔		✔	✔	☠

✔	*Low pollution. WHO guidelines are normally met*
✘	*Moderate to heavy pollution. WHO guidelines exceeded by a factor of two.*
☠	*Serious problem. WHO guidelines exceeded by a factor of more than two.*
	A blank rectangle indicates no date available or insufficient data for assessment.

SO₂	*Sulphur dioxide*
SPM	*Suspended particulate matter*
Pb	*Lead*
CO	*Carbon monoxide*
NO₂	*Nitrogen dioxide*
O₃	*Ozone*

police force suffer from heart and lung disease induced by the air pollution. Meanwhile, the average car in Bangkok spends the equivalent of 44 days every year with its engine idling in a traffic jam.

Beijing's residents have expressed concerns about environmental quality for generations. Beijing's air is heavily polluted with sulphur dioxide, solid particulate materials and ozone. These pollutants are worst in the city centre near Tian An Men Square, where traffic density is highest, and in the western suburbs where heavy manufacturing industries are concentrated (figure 11.115).

11.115 *Air pollution in Beijing, China.*

11.116 *A 'shelter belt' of trees in central Beijing.*

One of Beijing's major air pollutants, dust, has always been a problem in the city. When winds blow from the north-west into Beijing, huge clouds of dust are often blown in from the plains of Mongolia and the loess highlands north and north-west of the city. In recent years, the urban planners have tried to combat this problem by planting concentric rings of trees along the routes of Beijing's expressways and orbital ring roads and by planting trees along many of the streets of central Beijing (figure 11.116). Six circuits of trees are being planted, coinciding with the six ring roads around the city. As well as breaking up the winds and settling the dust, the tree planting along the roads provides shade for cyclists and gives the city a softer aesthetic appearance. In an effort to support the tree planting along roadways, the city's regulations now stipulate that any new building project must also include provisions for tree planting.

While the problem of solid particulate matter is being addressed in Beijing, air pollution from gases such as sulphur dioxide and ozone is increasing. A major factor in inducing this change has been the change in Beijing's traffic patterns. The two views in figure 11.117 show typical street scenes in Beijing about twenty five years apart. Since the early 1980s, there has been a very strong trend for bicycles to be replaced by small motor vehicles. Very few cars were visible in Beijing before the mid-1980s. By 2001 there were one million cars registered to individuals in Beijing; the 2010 the figure had reached more than three and a half million (figure 11.118).

11.117 *Typical Beijing street scenes in 1982 (top) and today (bottom).*

Until 1999, small yellow vans made up the bulk of Beijing's taxi fleet. The vans provided Beijing residents with cheap reliable transport in all types of weather, and they were available in plentiful supply. However, the authorities in Beijing ordered that all the vans be sent to the scrap yards for destruction in early 1999 because their small engines were creating too much air pollution. Although this provoked anger from many of Beijing's poorer residents who were unable to afford larger taxis, it has improved the quality of Beijing's atmosphere. It was decreed that the taxis must be destroyed in order to pre-

vent owners selling them in other cities, and thus raising levels of air pollution in other Chinese cities. In the years leading up to the 2008 Olympics in Beijing, the authorities emphasised the need to clean up the city's air, and new fleets of buses were introduced as an important step to meeting the ambitious targets set (figure 11.119).

Beijing's environmental stresses are developed in more detail in a case study later in this chapter.

11.118 *A view of Beijing's orbital ring road, showing the traffic congestion now found even on Beijing's widest roads during morning rush hour.*

11.119 *Beijing has made great efforts to clean up its air pollution by introducing eco-friendly buses.*

In Indian cities, where much of the freight transport is done by human power, the air pollution creates a severe hazard for the carriers who spend all say doing heavy labour, inhaling the heavily polluted air deeply (figure 11.120). Trucks are replacing humans, and as Indian trucks are often old and poorly maintained, this is leading to a large increase in the emission of polluting gases. Each day, 2,000 tonnes of air pollutants are released into the air in India's capital city, Delhi, comprising 323 tonnes of nitrogen dioxide, 320 tonnes of hydrocarbons, 179 tonnes of sulphur dioxide and 1,063 tonnes of carbon monoxide. The World Health Organisation recommends that 9 parts per million of carbon monoxide should be the limit for safety, but in Delhi, carbon monoxide concentrations reach peaks as high as 35 parts per million.

A concentration of 25 parts per million is enough to cause poisoning in humans. According to *The Times of India* newspaper, the average Delhi resident visits the doctor 15 times each year for pollution-related health problems.

11.120 *Air pollution is a serious hazard for human freight carriers who spend all day in the streets of Indian megacities such as Delhi, shown here.*

Motor vehicles and factories are not the only sources of air pollution in the cities of the developing world. The burning of biomass, wood and coal for cooking and heating purposes is also an important contributor to air pollution. In Delhi, street sweepers burn 8,000 tonnes of rubbish from the street dwellers each day, while the poor people living in shanty settlements burn plastic to keep warm, producing poisonous hydrochloric acid fumes while so doing. From these figures alone it can be seen that poor living conditions result in environmental pollution.

11.121 *With no other way of disposing of household rubbish, residents of this shanty settlement in Jakarta have simply dumped their garbage in the stream which runs past their houses.*

Water pollution is also a significant problem in most of the developing world's cities. Many houses are not connected to a sewerage system, and so dispose of sewage and other household waste directly into streams, canals and other waterways (figure 11.121). For example, houses built over the *khlongs*, or canals, in many parts of Bangkok (Thailand) discharge their wastes directly into the water under the house, polluting the water that flows between the other houses. When organic wastes are added to water in public areas like this, there is a severe risk of water borne diseases such as cholera, acute gastro-enteritis, diarrhoea, dysentery, typhoid, viral hepatitis A and E, and polio. Of these diseases, the major killers are cholera and acute diarrhoea.

One example of water pollution is the River Yamuna, which flows for a distance of 48 kilometres through the urban area of Delhi. Although the portion of the Yamuna flowing through Delhi is only 2% of the total length of the river, this stretch contributes 71% of the river's total pollution load. Every day, 17 open drains discharge 1.7 billion litres of human wastes and toxic effluents into the Yamuna as it flows through Delhi, and the river has been described as an open sewer as a result. Water-borne diseases such as cholera, jaundice, gastro-enteritis and typhoid are endemic in the areas near the river, especially during the rainy season when the river spills over its banks and floods many nearby homes.

The average child below the age of five in Indian cities experiences an average of 3.3 attacks of severe diarrhoea each year. This compares with an average of 1.2 attacks of diarrhoea per child per year in large Chinese cities, a reflection of Chinese residents' greater access to clean water supplies.

It is important to remember that urban residents have much greater access to clean water supplies than rural residents or people in small towns in economically less developed countries. Although the water quality in cities such as Kolkata, Lagos and Dhaka falls well below the standards of cleanliness and purity that people in industrialised nations take for granted, it is still much better than the water quality in villages and farming areas in the same countries.

QUESTION BLOCK 11N

1. *Why is air pollution becoming a more serious concern in large cities?*

2. *Describe in words the information shown in table 11.11.*

3. *Suggest reasons for the pattern shown in table 11.11.*

4. *Outline the arguments for and against building expressways in cities.*

5. *Explain the causes of Delhi's severe air pollution.*

6. *Why does poor quality of life in Indian cities cause environmental pollution?*

7. *Explain the impact of polluted water on people's health.*

Urban Microclimates and Air Pollution

It is well known that air quality in the world's cities is poorer than the air quality in rural areas. Dust and sulphur dioxide are produced from chimneys, and motor vehicles produce carbon monoxide and hydrocarbons. Nitrogen oxides are produced from both motor vehicles

The amount of air pollution in an urban area depends on two main factors. First, it depends on the quantity of pollution produced. As figure 11.122 shows, more air pollution tends to be created in cities in low income countries (LEDCs) than in high income countries (MEDCs). The second factor is the amount of wind that blows through the city. Winds can dilute and disperse urban air pollution, although whether winds blow through an urban area depends mainly on the surrounding topography and especially whether sea breezes are available. Tall buildings have an effect on winds, as the narrow canyon-like streets created between skyscrapers can funnel winds, causing dust and litter to irritate passers-by in the street. On the other hand, buildings of one and two storeys create friction with wind and therefore act to calm moving air.

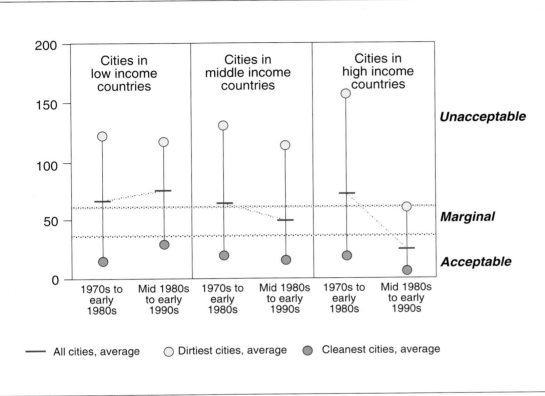

11.122 *Changes in urban air pollution (as measured by concentration of sulphur dioxide) in countries with different income levels.*

and chimneys. These pollutants produce cloud nuclei that increase both cloud cover and precipitation by about 10% in large urban areas compared with the pre-urban conditions in the same area.

A combination of processes increases temperatures in urban areas compared with their rural surrounds (figure 11.123). Sealed surfaces such as roads and paths together with dark roofs absorb large amounts of heat during the day – perhaps 85% of the solar energy that reaches them. The heat absorbed by these hard surfaces is retained

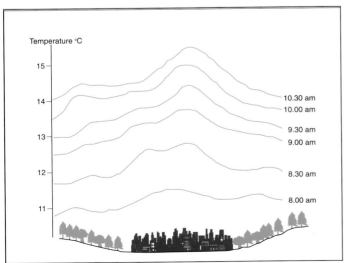

11.123 *The increase in temperatures over a small town at half hourly intervals between 8:00 am and 10:30 am shows the urban heat island.*

11.124 *The urban heat island can be seen by the reduced amount of mist in the CBD of Chicago (USA), marked by the tall buildings in this view.*

Urban environments

during the day and released slowly at night, warming the air of the city. Furthermore, heat is generated in urban areas by industrial processes, domestic heating, cars and people working. All these processes combine to make urban areas warmer than their surrounds, creating an effect known as the **urban heat island**.

During the day, the urban heat island is only warmer by a degree or two (figure 11.124). At night the difference is much greater, with urban areas being perhaps 3C° or 4C° warmer than their rural surrounds. The urban heat island effect explains why flowers in urban areas tend to bloom earlier each year than flowers in rural areas and why cities have fewer frosts each year than rural areas.

QUESTION BLOCK 11O

1. *With reference to figure 11.122, compare the trends in urban air pollution in low-income countries, middle-income countries and high-income countries.*

2. *Suggest reasons for the different trends in the three groups of countries shown in figure 11.122.*

3. *Describe some hazards posed to people's health in the three groups of countries by urban air pollution and suggest realistic strategies which could be implemented to improve people's quality of life as a consequence.*

4. *What causes the urban heat island effect?*

5. *With reference to figure 11.123, describe the changes which took place between 8:00 am and 10:30 am.*

6. *Explain why temperatures in figure 11.123 appear to have been higher over the town than over the surrounding rural area.*

7. *Choose two additional ways in which urban centres have an impact on the environment that are not shown in figure 11.123, and discuss the effects of these impacts.*

Case Study — Air Pollution in Beijing

A number of cities in China are becoming well known for the poor quality and high pollution of their air. Recently, a Chinese newspaper called the *Economic Daily* published an article about one city in the north-east of China called Benxi which has 'air like soot'. The article commented that: "Benxi has a population of 800,000 people, but they might as well be 800,000 vacuum cleaners". A recent book on China described the author's experience when she went to the city of Chongqing, an inland city of about three million people. She had gone to Chongqing to investigate air pollution and found that the smog was so bad she was unable to take any photographs – the air was so grey that they looked as though they had been taken underwater. The air pollution made the rain acidic with a pH of 3.0, about the same acidity as vinegar.

11.125 *Air pollution in Beijing varies according to wind direction and atmospheric pressure. This view was taken when a high pressure area trapped pollutants close to the surface.*

11.126 *This view of Beijing was taken the day after the previous photo after a cold front had moved through, bringing low pressure conditions allowing the pollutants to rise.*

Like all Chinese cities, Beijing has problems with air pollution. However, as China's capital city, more effort has been made to reduce the problem in Beijing than in most parts of China. The main source of air pollution in Beijing, as in most Chinese cities, is the burning of coal. Coal is the main fuel used for heating, cooking and for industry. China has huge reserves of coal, but most of it is of poor quality. The coal contains large quantities of sulphur and Chinese cities have large amounts of coal dust, especially in winter when coal is used for heating, and even more so when a high pressure area over Beijing traps pollutants close to the surface (figures 11.125 and 11.126). It is estimated that each year, China produces 11 trillion cubic metres of waste gases and 16 million tonnes of coal soot; each three years the production of soot equals the weight of all Chinese people!

Levels of air pollution in China's northern cities exceed the standards of the World Health Organisation by five or six times. In their book *China Wakes*, Kristof and WuDunn report that:

"Respiratory disease, often a result of lungs clogged with soot, is the leading cause of death in China, accounting for

26 per cent of all deaths. This mortality rate is 5.5 times the level in the United States. One careful study found that particles in the Chinese air cause 915,000 premature deaths each year, including those of 300,000 children who die from lung infections. Another 600,000 adults die early of respiratory blockage, and 15,000 fall victim to lung cancer caused by bad air".

The authors lived in Beijing for several years, and commented:

"After an hour or two outside in winter, we would come home and find our nostrils blackened from the soot. The coal dust would creep into our apartment through every cranny, and when I went on one of my six-mile jogs through Beijing, I would come back with a blackened tongue. Finally, I decided that running might be doing my health more harm than good. I stopped jogging in the winter".

Just over 60% of Beijing's total energy consumption is coal, representing a little over 30 million tonnes per annum. Of this quantity, manufacturing industry consumes about 70%, domestic households about 20% with the other 10% being used by other activities such as transport and shops. The use of coal is highly seasonal, however. In Beijing, heating is strictly regulated, and all heaters are turned on at the beginning of winter on the same date, and all are turned off simultaneously with the onset of spring. During the 'heating season', average daily consumption of coal rises 30% above the annual average. Beijing has over one million small coal pellet stoves and almost 8,000 heating furnaces that add pollutants into the atmosphere every winter.

However, the burning of coal adds more than just soot to air. One of the by-products of burning coal is sulphur dioxide (SO_2). During the 'heating season', small stoves and central heating devices account for 48% of Beijing's lower atmosphere sulphur dioxide. There is a dramatic increase in sulphur dioxide in Beijing during the 'heating season' (figure 11.127). At this time, the average sulphur dioxide content of the air is 0.23 milligrams per cubic metre compared with an average of 0.05 milligrams per cubic metre during the rest of the year. The main concentration is in the inner suburbs due to the high density of population in that area. By contrast, the main concentration in the 'non-heating season' is in Beijing's western suburbs where there is a high concentration of heavy manufacturing industries.

Government officials in Beijing are aware of the air pollution problems faced by the city. They propose that in the decades ahead the quality of coal available for residents is to be improved, meaning that fewer pollutants will be produced when it is burnt. In the long-run, they hope to encourage people to replace their coal stoves with gas appliances. Although about 85% of homes in Beijing now have gas stoves, only 15% of homes have replaced coal with gas for heating.

11.128 *When the wind blows from the north-west, Beijing's air becomes thick with fine dust, making life unpleasant for pedestrians and cyclists.*

There are two additional sources of air pollution in Beijing which, while less important than the burning of coal, are still important. One is fine dust from soil erosion which blows into Beijing from inland areas (figure 11.128). In many inland areas of China, the soil is composed of very fine clay particles called **loess** that are easily eroded by the wind. Overgrazing and deforestation has destabilised large areas of loess, and the prevailing north-westerly winds blow large quantities of dust into Beijing.

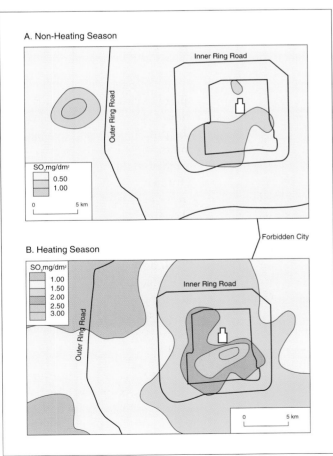

11.127 *Sulphur dioxide in the air over Beijing in the 'non-heating season' (top) and in the 'heating season' (bottom).*

Many Beijing women wear scarves, not so much as an item of fashion as much as to protect their hair from the dust. In recent years, trees have been planted on the outskirts of Beijing. They are designed to act as wind-breaks, causing the dust to settle before reaching the main residential areas of the city. Known as the 'Great Green Wall of China', this programme has reduced the problem, although it has certainly not eliminated it.

The other main source of air pollution in Beijing is exhaust fumes from motor vehicles. As recently as the early 1980s, Beijing had very few motor vehicles. Today, Beijing experiences the same traffic congestion as most major world cities despite massive programmes of road and expressway construction.

Exhaust fumes from motor vehicles produce nitrogen oxides (NO_x) and carbon monoxide (CO). Nitrogen oxides have risen markedly with the increase in numbers of motor vehicles in Beijing. In general, concentrations of nitrogen dioxides are highest at traffic intersections and along major road arteries (figure 11.129).

11.129 *Air pollution on Chang'an Avenue (Avenue of Eternal Peace) in Beijing.*

11.130 *A researcher measuring air pollution at a major intersection in central Beijing.*

There has also been a significant increase in concentration of carbon monoxide in Beijing. Carbon monoxide is produced by cars, especially those that are moving slowly, and by incomplete burning of coal in small coal stoves. Therefore, carbon monoxide concentrations are highest in the 'heating season' and where traffic congestion occurs. Like nitrogen oxides and sulphur dioxide, carbon monoxide is a poisonous gas that leads to breathing problems and some cancers such as leukaemia. Greater awareness of air pollution has led to the construction of several air pollution monitoring stations with public displays in Beijing over the past few decades (figure 11.130).

One of the most worrying aspects of Beijing's air pollution is the high concentration of BaP, or Benzo[a]-pyrene, a chemical which induces lung cancer and which is produced by heavy industry without adequate pollution controls. The death rate from lung cancer in Beijing in 1958 was 7.9 people per 100,000; by 1979 this had reached 15.5 people per 100,000 and by the early 1990s was estimated to be over 20 people per 100,000. There are three concentrations of BaP in Beijing – the highly populated centre of the city, the Capital Iron and Steel Works in the western suburbs and near a coking plant in Beijing's eastern suburbs. The problem is worst during the 'heating season' when an area of 500 square kilometres of Beijing exceeds the accepted standard of 1 milligram per 100 cubic metres of BaP; during the non-heating season only a few small areas exceed the standard. However, around the iron and steel works and the coking plant, the concentrations remain above 4 milligrams per 100 cubic metres for most of the year (figure 11.131). The solution to this serious problem seems to be to require stricter standards of pollution emission, especially from heavy industry in Beijing.

11.131 *Although taken on quite a clear day, this oblique aerial view of heavy manufacturing industries on the outskirts of Beijing shows dark clouds of sulphurous and BaP air pollutants.*

Air pollution in Beijing has given rise to some surprising new developments. One such development is the establishment of oxygen bars by new entrepreneurs. These bars typically charge about $6, or nearly half a Beijing worker's weekly wage, for 30 minutes of fresh air, with medicated and scented air costing more. One entrepreneur sold 60 U.S.-made oxygen machines during 1995, each costing $3,600, to hotels, discotheques and private buyers. The owner of one oxygen bar has even offered free 10-minute doses to traffic police who spend all day breathing carbon monoxide fumes.

Humans have affected the atmosphere above Beijing in other ways besides pollution, notably by the creation of an urban heat island. An urban heat island exists when there is a difference in average temperatures between a city's inner areas and its suburbs. In general, when the difference exceeds 0.5C°, a heat island is said to exist.

Beijing's heat island is among the strongest of the world's major cities. A study of 20 of the world's major cities showed an average temperature difference between city centres and outskirts of 0.7C°. In Beijing, the average annual difference is 1.7C°, while during the heating season the difference averages 2.5C°. Figure 11.132 shows the isotherms on one clear winter's day when there was very little wind.

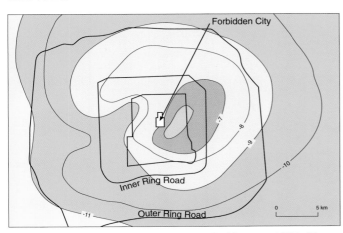

11.132 *Isotherms in Beijing at 8:00 pm on 2nd January 1987. The figures show the temperatures in °C.*

The difference in temperatures evident in heat islands causes movements of air through the formation of convection currents. The inner urban areas, having relatively warmer air, tend to have lower air pressures than outlying areas with cooler, descending air. Thus, air rises in the city centre, bringing in pollutants from outer industrial suburbs as air flows in from the cooler surrounds.

Beijing's authorities have committed themselves to cleaning up the atmosphere over Beijing. In late September 1999, factories in Beijing were closed for over a week to allow the air to clear for the celebrations on 1st October of the 50th anniversary of the Communist revolution (figure 11.133). During the period of the Beijing Olympic Games in 2008, air pollution was once again controlled by closing many factories and restricting cars by using an 'odds-and-evens' system (only cars with licence plates ending in an odd number were permitted on the roads on odd-numbered days of the calendar, etc). Of course, closing all the city's factories is not a viable long-term solution to the

problem of air pollution, but Beijing has nonetheless made significant strides towards improving the quality of its air.

11.133 *A vision of Beijing's future – new buildings and clean air. The clean air was possible because the authorities closed the city's factories for several days before a major national celebration.*

QUESTION BLOCK 11P

1. *What evidence is there that Chinese cities in general suffer from air pollution?*

2. *Identify the main source of air pollution in Beijing.*

3. *Explain the difference in levels of air pollution in the two views in figures 11.125 and 11.126.*

4. *What is the 'heating season' in Beijing, and why is it significant? In your answer, refer to the information in figure 11.127.*

5. *What can be done realistically in Beijing to reduce air pollution arising from (a) burning coal, (b) dust, and (c) car exhausts?*

6. *What is BaP, and why is it a problem in Beijing?*

7. *Use figure 11.132 to draw a cross-section graph of Beijing's temperatures on the date shown. Use the information you have plotted to describe Beijing's heat island on that day.*

Case Study — Air Pollution in Los Angeles

In contrast to Beijing where air pollution has only improved in recent years, air pollution in Los Angeles has shown a marked improvement since the 1980s. This can be illustrated with reference to the most dangerous type of air pollution in Los Angeles, photochemical smog or ozone (O_3). Ozone forms when the gases from car exhausts heat under strong sunlight, and it appears as a brown haze on the horizon, especially during calm conditions or when there is a high pressure area overhead (figure 11.134). Between 1955 and 1992, the peak level of ozone in Los Angeles decreased from 680 parts per billion (ppb) to 300 ppb, and by 2009 the figure had dropped further to 104 ppb. This was significant because ozone concentrations have a direct relationship to the number of deaths from respiratory causes.

Nonetheless, air pollution in Los Angeles remains the worst in the United States. According to the World Resources Institute:

"Pollution reaches unhealthy levels on roughly half the days each year — as opposed to 279 days in 1976 — causing irritation for many and illness for some. A recent study found that those living in areas where particulate pollution exceeded government standards for 42 days per year or more had a 33 per cent greater risk of contracting asthma".

11.134 *Brown haze, or ozone, over Los Angeles.*

There are several reasons that air pollution in Los Angeles is worse than any other US city. Los Angeles relies very heavily on private motor vehicles rather than public transport. Despite an attempt in the 1980s to reintroduce bus services in Los Angeles, three and even four-car households are the norm (figure 11.135). A common expression in Los Angeles is that *"You need a car in Los Angeles like you need your liver!"*. Los Angeles is a large, spread out, sprawling city. The built up area of the metropolitan area is 3,000 square kilometres, making it

11.135 *Express-ways divide communities in Los Angeles, as this view on an unusually clear day shows.*

second only to New York in size of US cities. The city's location is in a westward (seaward) facing basin, and this helps to trap the pollutants produced in the city. Furthermore, the area's climate, which is hot and semi-arid with low average wind speeds, provides ideal conditions for photochemical smog (ozone) to develop.

Air pollution in Los Angeles has been an important community issue for several decades. Back in the 1940s and 1950s, people were demanding action to reduce air pollution and there were many newspaper articles and editorials at the time demanding action. By the mid-1970s, local government authorities throughout Los Angeles had pollution control programmes, but it was clear that a less fragmented, more coherent approach was needed. In 1976, a new body known as the South Coast Air Quality Management District was established to have authority over air quality throughout metropolitan Los Angeles. Soon after establishment, the South Coast Air Quality Management District issued regulations on car exhausts and factory emissions that were the toughest in the United States, with emphasis on gases which are 'ingredients' of photochemical smog (figure 11.136).

11.136 *This oblique aerial view of Los Angeles (looking north) shows the suburb of Long Beach clearly in the foreground. However, the more inland suburbs are hidden by the air pollution trapped against the hills which back the city to the north-east.*

In 1987, the South Coast Air Quality Management District introduced a programme to encourage people to car-pool. This programme has been quite successful, although the scheme proved to be expensive for businesses due to lost hours with workers having to leave early or arrive late due to car-pooling – this cost was estimated to be about $125 per employee or almost $20,000 per tonne of pollution that had been reduced.

An even more ambitious plan to reduce air pollution was announced in 1990 when the State Government of California ruled that by 1998 2% of all passenger vehicles must be completely pollution free, a figure that rose to 5% by 2001 and 10% by 2003. At first, this regulation increased the interest in electric cars in California that had not been taken seriously before due to their high cost, limited performance (a range of only about 100 kilometres) and long battery recharge time (about 8 hours). However, the goal was never reached, and in 2008 the authorities re-defined the targets in two parts. First, car manufacturers will have to produce at least 7,500 zero-emission vehicles, such as hydrogen fuel cell or electric automobiles, although no date has been set. Under the old regulations, the car industry would have been required to manufacture 25,000 zero-emission vehicles for sale in California from 2012 to 2014. Second, car makers will have to produce 58,000 low-emission vehicles for sale in California between 2012 and 2014. This was a new requirement which will include cars such as plug-in hybrids that use both electric and petrol engines.

QUESTION BLOCK 11Q

1. *Identify the main type of air pollution in Los Angeles, and describe the way that it forms.*

2. *Explain why air pollution in Los Angeles is worse than in any other U.S. city.*

3. *How important has political opinion been in reducing air pollution in Los Angeles? How is this different from the situation in Beijing?*

4. *Having studied air pollution in Beijing and Los Angeles, what can you conclude about the relationship between air pollution and a nation's level of economic development?*

Other Types of Social and Environmental Stress in Urban Areas

As we have seen in this chapter, urbanisation is changing the face of our earth at an unprecedented rate. This growth poses significant challenges for the residents of large cities. These challenges directly impact on the quality of life of residents, affecting their housing, movement, services, and environmental quality.

Excessive size and movement

Cities in both MEDCs and LEDCs have experienced urban sprawl on a huge scale to accommodate their populations (figure 11.137). Moreover, as table 11.9 showed, the growth rates of cities in LEDCs continue to be very rapid. Indeed, the speed with which cities in developing countries are growing today is even more rapid than the growth of cities in the industrialised world a century ago (table 11.12).

Table 11.12
Rate and Scale of Growth of Selected Large Cities

City	Average annual population growth (%)	Population added (millions)
Cities in MEDCs, 1875 - 1900		
Chicago	6.0	1.3
New York	3.3	2.3
Tokyo	2.6	0.7
London	1.7	2.2
Paris	1.6	1.1
Cities in LEDCs, 1975 - 2000		
Lagos	5.8	10.2
Mumbai	4.0	11.2
São Paulo	2.3	7.7
Mexico City	1.9	6.9
Shanghai	0.9	2.7

Source: O'Meara (1999) p.136

11.137 *With a population of about 18 million people, it is not surprising that São Paulo in Brazil has experienced massive urban sprawl. This view shows just a small part of the metropolitan area.*

11.138 *New urban areas expanding on the fringes of Bangkok, Thailand.*

This rapid population growth means that **urban sprawl** is also continuing to expand the land area occupied by cities (figure 11.138). For example, the area of Bangkok expanded from 67 square kilometres in 1953 to 426 square kilometres in 1990 and to almost 800 square kilometres in 2009. In 1959, it was possible to walk across the entire city of Bangkok from north to south in three hours; today it is not possible to drive across Bangkok in three hours at most times of the day.

11.139 *Urban sprawl — new development on the outskirts of Bangkok, Thailand takes over land formerly used for farming.*

11.140 *Despite the construction of a broad expressway with additional overhead lanes, traffic congestion like this is a daily occurrence in megacities such as Bangkok.*

Continuing urban sprawl causes several problems that impact on the lives of the residents. First, expanding cities takes over land that was previously occupied by farms (figure 11.139). It is estimated, for example, that each year urban expansion takes up 200,000 hectares of arable land in China alone. This urban expansion in turn has three important impacts. First, many farmers become dispossessed of their land, and must either move outwards to new farming areas which are often less productive (which is why they were not already being farmed) or

move to the city in search of non-farming work for which they have experience or qualifications. Second, it means that food must be transported over longer distances from the countryside to feed the rapidly growing population in the city, raising the costs of food to urban dwellers. Finally, the additional burning of fuel adds to greenhouse gases that could in turn lead to global warming and climatic change. Between 15% and 20% of the six billion tonnes of carbon dioxide produced by human activities annually comes from transport. This is significant as carbon dioxide is one of the major greenhouse gases.

Urban sprawl has an even more direct impact on urban dwellers in the form of movement and **transport difficulties**. An expanding city means that more people will have their homes and places of work separated by long distances. This in turn means that people must commute long distances on roads that are often highly congested (figure 11.140). At a superficial level, traffic congestion is a nuisance for commuters, but in reality the problems are much worse than this. Traffic congestion represents a waste of scarce petrol resources as cars' engines run without moving as well as a waste of time that could otherwise be used productively in work or recreationally.

11.141 *An overcrowded bus in Ulaan Bataar, Mongolia.*

In most cities in LEDCs, private car ownership is rare compared with cities in more industrialised economies. This means that people are more dependent on public transport such as buses, trams and trains. These services are often inadequate for the numbers of people needing to use them (figures 11.141 to 11.143). Prices are low to make the transport affordable, but this means few funds are available to maintain and upgrade the vehicles. The low prices also attract more people to use the transport, leading to overcrowding and discomfort while travelling.

Increasing distances to travel within cities is a particular problem in the poorer countries where transport is often human-powered. In many cities, freight is transported on barrows or wagons that are pulled and pushed by humans, and transport of passengers in human-powered trishaws is also common (figure 11.144). Increasing distances caused by urban sprawl makes such transport

during the 1990s and early 2000s as more cars came on to Beijing's roads, bicycles still provide the main source of personal transport. There are still about 10 million bicycles in Beijing, and they are popular not only because they are cheap, but because they are seen to promote mass fitness. Fortunately, Beijing's very flat topography makes riding bicycles relatively easy, even for elderly folk. Other cities, including those in MEDCs such as Canberra, Ottawa, The Hague and Hong Kong, are now building extensive cycleways to promote the use of bicycles as a cheap, clean form of individual transportation (see figure 11.48 earlier in this chapter).

11.142 *A tram (streetcar) in Kolkata, India.*

11.143 *Suburban train in Mumbai, India.*

11.144 *Rickshaws provide taxi services in Dhaka, Bangladesh.*

increasingly difficult in two ways. First, the huge physical distances needing to be covered make the task of pushing or pulling carts increasingly unpleasant, especially in the hot and humid conditions of many cities (figure 11.145). Second, because human powered transport becomes inefficient over long distances, many labourers are replaced by trucks and cars, forcing unemployment on to the unskilled labourers.

In cities that have experienced rapid economic growth, such as Beijing, other transport problems have emerged. Although growth in the number of bicycles slowed

11.145 *Manual haulage of freight in Kolkata, India.*

Overcrowding and housing

Although urban sprawl has occurred in many cities in developing countries, average population densities are still higher than in most cities in Europe, Australia and North America. Rapid population growth has led to **overcrowding**, which can be defined as too many people occupying too little space and competing for too few services or jobs (figure 11.146).

One of the main consequences of overcrowding is a **shortage of housing**, a characteristic of every city in every LEDC. Although some cities have pavement dwellers, the

11.146 *A clothes and laundry washing service, located in a crowded shanty settlement beside the railway line in Mumbai, India.*

Urban environments

more common evidence of the housing shortage is **shanty settlements**. Shanties are makeshift dwellings erected without official permission, usually of makeshift materials such as cardboard, corrugated iron, plastic, straw mats, sacks, canvas and scrap timber (figure 11.147).

The shanties have no building standards and no standards for sanitation, and they often lack basic services such as water and sewerage. As a result, health problems are often a concern in the shanties, and diseases can spread quite easily in the cramped and inadequate housing conditions (figure 11.148).

11.147 *Shanty housing made with scrounged materials, near Pune, India.*

11.148 *Unhygienic conditions, including dirt and stagnant pools of water, aid the spread of disease in shanty settlements.*

The people who live in the shanty areas seldom own their home – they are **squatters** who live on land they do not own or for which no rent is paid. They commonly have very poor living conditions — open sewers, piles of fermenting garbage, electricity 'stolen' from overhead wires by connecting illegal lines with crocodile clips, and noxious fumes from cooking and burning rubbish. The numbers of people who live in shanty settlements in developing world cities is huge — more than half of the 10 million people in Dhaka, the capital of Bangladesh, live in shanty settlements for example.

11.149 *Shanties become a permanent feature of the landscape in many urban areas in LEDCs, such as in Gonder (Ethiopia) shown here.*

As mentioned earlier in the chapter (on page 470), most governments are embarrassed by the shanties, but recognise that they are filling a need, and so simply ignore them. This reaction means that shanties become a permanent feature of the urban landscape in many cities (figure 11.149). However, some administrations adopt a harsher policy and demolish the slums. This seldom removes the shanties for very long, however, as the residents re-build them, sometimes as quickly as within a few days. A few governments recognise the shanties as a form of self-help housing that places very little burden upon government funds. Such governments sometimes encourage shanty development by providing water, electricity and garbage collection services.

Cities in developing countries also commonly have **slum housing**, which is of a higher standard than the shanties. Slums are areas of authorised housing which are dilapidated, run-down or decaying. Slums may be old buildings that are no longer serviced by electricity or water, or they may be newer areas of sub-standard housing that are nonetheless better than the shanties (figures 11.150 and 11.151). In general, the older decaying slums are found near the city centres, while the newer housing is found towards the edges of the urban area.

11.150 *Housing in poor condition in a slum district of Massawa, Eritrea.*

11.151 *Much of the housing in Bosnia-Herzegovina is still in poor condition following the civil war of the early 1990s. This housing block is in Srebrenica, the site of large-scale genocide during the conflict.*

Provision of urban services

With large, rapidly growing populations, government administrations of cities in developing countries face great difficulties in providing the services that residents might like or expect (figure 11.152). Much of the problem arises because tax revenues collected by governments are insufficient to provide services such as street maintenance and garbage collection, and this in turn leads to problems such as poor roads and infrastructure, and a build up of rubbish in the streets.

11.152 *Under-investment in public infrastructure can cause problems, such as the rough and broken pavement seen here in Yangon, Myanmar.*

In many cities in LEDCs where rubbish collection services are provided, large communities of people live at or on the garbage tips and make a living from recycling the rubbish that is dumped there. For example, Dump Hill (also known as Stung Meanchey) is Phnom Penh's largest garbage tip. Thousands of poor people live at the tip and make their living from it, including many children who remain uneducated because they never attend schools (figures 11.153 and 11.154). Many of the residents of Dump Hill are chronically sick because of the unhealthy conditions of living and working in garbage, and many suffer poisoning from the toxic fumes of burning plastic.

11.153 *Poor residents of Phnom Penh sift through garbage at the city's major tip (Dump Hill) as a way to make money by recycling waste.*

11.154 *Some of Phnom Penh's poorest residents live at Dump Hill, making it both their place of work and place of residence.*

Table 11.13 gives a summary of some of the living conditions that affect the quality of life of residents in some of the world's cities. Some cities in economically more developed countries are included so that a comparison can be made with the developing countries. This table shows that large areas of many cities have houses without running water or adequate sanitation. People who live in such houses often have no alternative but to use nearby rivers for washing clothes and for personal washing as well as for garbage and sewage disposal. It is understandable that people who do not have access to clean running water in their homes experience problems of diseases such as gastrointestinal upsets and diarrhoea.

As cities expand, more and more surface area becomes sealed with concrete or bitumen. This prevents rainwater infiltrating into the soil, meaning that more water must be channelled through pipes and gutters. However, many cities in economically less developed countries have a poorly developed drainage system, because this type of infrastructure can be quite expensive to provide. As a result, urban flooding is becoming more and more of a problem (figure 11.155). Furthermore, as groundwater is not being recharged by infiltration as occurs in a more

Table 11.13
Living Conditions in Selected Large Cities

	Area	Population Size ('000)			Living Conditions					
	sq km	1980	1990	2008	% h'hold income spent on food	People per room	% houses with tap water	% houses with electricity	Phones per 1000 people	Cars ('000)
Argentina										
Buenos Aires	2,590	9,918	10,648	12,390	40	1.3	80	91	14	1000
Bangladesh										
Dhaka	311	3,290	6,578	7,310	63	2.4	60	85	2	n.a.
Brazil										
Rio de Janeiro	1,580	8,789	10,948	11,160	26	0.8	86	98	8	n.a.
São Paulo	2,590	12,101	18,119	19,140	50	0.8	100	100	16	4000
China										
Beijing	2,616	9,029	10,867	12,770	52	1.2	88	90	2	308
Shanghai	2,396	11,739	13,447	14,460	55	2.0	95	95	4	148
Egypt										
Cairo	1,269	6,852	8,633	16,750	47	1.5	91	98	4	939
India										
Delhi	1,425	5,559	8,171	18,000	40	3.1	50	81	5	1660
Mumbai	777	8,067	12,223	19,530	57	4.2	92	78	5	588
Kolkata	984	9,030	10,741	15,010	60	3.0	51	63	2	500
Indonesia										
Jakarta	2,720	5,985	9,206	21,800	45	3.4	75	94	3	1380
Japan										
Osaka	2,720	9,990	10,482	17,270	18	0.6	96	100	42	n.a.
Tokyo	7,835	21,854	25,013	34,400	18	0.9	100	100	44	4400
Mexico										
Mexico City	2,137	13,888	15,085	18,430	41	1.9	92	97	6	2500
Nigeria										
Lagos	971	4,385	7,742	8,860	58	5.8	47	53	1	n.a.
Pakistan										
Karachi	881	5,023	7,943	9,380	43	3.3	66	84	2	650
Philippines										
Manila	1,425	5,966	8,882	19,550	38	3.0	89	93	9	510
South Korea										
Seoul	1,943	8,283	8,979	20,010	34	2.0	100	100	11	2660
United States										
Los Angeles	5,812	9,523	11,456	14,730	12	0.5	91	98	35	8000
New York	11,264	15,601	16,056	20,090	16	0.5	99	100	56	1780

Source: United Nations, *World Resources*

natural environment, the hydraulic pressure under some cities is reduced, resulting in subsidence of the land, breaking water pipes and buckling railway lines. In coastal cities such as Bangkok, subsidence is aggravating the flooding even more as the land is lowered relative to the nearby sea. In Mexico City, the groundwater has been used to provide water for the growing city, and this has led to even more severe subsidence. In some parts of Mexico City, subsidence of more than 9 metres has occurred, giving the strange sight today of water pipes which are 7 metres higher than ground level.

Cities in LEDCs experience frequent power blackouts because electricity generation has often failed to keep up with the rising demand. The power shortages are aggravated by shanty dwellers who often steal electricity by connecting illegal or unauthorised lines to the official power lines. Because of the shortage of power, neon lights and flood lighting are less common in cities in the developing world than in industrialised nations, and air conditioning and refrigeration are also scarcer (figure 11.156).

As the cities of the developing world become more integrated with the global economy, people's expectations of services and needs expand. Communications technology such as telephones, faxes, computers and internet access become more closely integrated into everyday life (figure 11.157).

Unemployment and underemployment

The population structure of cities in developing countries differs from cities in industrialised nations. The developing world cities tend to have a high proportion of the population aged between 15 and 30 years of age. Many of these young people have migrated into the city from rural areas in search of work, and they lack skills that would equip them for many urban jobs. This creates enormous pressure on the job markets of cities in developing countries, and unemployment rates of up to 30% and 40% are common in many cities.

The response of people to this challenge varies. Many young people create their own work, by setting up small street stalls and selling goods that do not cost very much to buy wholesale (figure 11.158). Sometimes the goods sold are food obtained cheaply from farmers, while at other times small goods bought in shops are sold at a marked up price.

11.155 *Urban flooding in downtown Shanghai occurs several times each year on average.*

11.156 *Live poultry on sale in a market in Yemen.*

11.157 *An internet café in Asmara, the capital city of Eritrea, which is one of the world's poorest countries.*

11.158 *These two young men live half a world away from each other, but they have found identical solutions to their problem of unemployment. Both are selling food from mobile counters to passers-by, in Rio de Janeiro (top photo) and Delhi (bottom photo).*

Other job seekers manage to obtain jobs that are below their capabilities, which means they are **underemployed**. Another variation on underemployment occurs where more people are hired to do a job than is really efficient or necessary (figure 11.159). This occurs quite commonly when job applicants know the employer who would not have otherwise given them a job. This practice is common in economically less developed countries where labour is relatively cheap compared with machinery, which is scarce and expensive. This contrasts with the cost structure of economically more developed economies where labour is relatively expensive, making it economically more rational to justify replacing people with machines.

11.159 *Underemployment (overstaffing) on a building site in Dhaka, Bangladesh.*

11.160 *The entrance to the Jama Masjid Mosque in Delhi is a gathering point for many of the city's Moslem population. The man in the left foreground is begging with his crippled son who is lying on the trolley.*

The cities in developing countries also have many people working in the **informal sector** of the economy. The informal sector, which is also known as the 'black economy', includes those activities that are outside the legal and tax structures of a country. It includes begging and prostitution, which is a major industry in all cities outside China (where these industries are smaller), and it is especially significant in Bangkok and Manila.

Racial and ethnic issues

Many cities in developing countries have a number of ethnic groups. Often, these groups live in separate zones within the city, making it easier to preserve their ethnic, linguistic, religious and social identity. In general, these ethnic groups live in harmony, respecting one another's differences. For example, although India is a predominantly Hindu nation, there are large Muslim and Sikh minorities in its large cities (figure 11.160).

Where large numbers of migrants have come to a city from elsewhere, tensions sometimes arise between ethnic groups. This happened in the mid-1960s and again to a lesser extent in the late-1990s in Jakarta, when tensions arose between the Chinese community and the dominant Indonesians.

Westernisation vs modernisation

One of the challenges faced by many cities in developing countries is the tension between westernisation and modernisation. Governments in developing economies are keen to raise the living standards of their populations, and this implies **modernisation**. However, there is often a deep suspicion of **westernisation**, which means abandoning traditional cultural beliefs, values and way of life in favour of European or American lifestyles.

11.161 *Copacabana Beach in Rio de Janeiro is an example of a well developed tourist facility which attracts tourists in large numbers to a developing world megacity.*

This tension shows itself particularly in certain industries, such as tourism. Governments are often keen to promote tourism as a means of modernising the economy, seeing it as a large revenue raiser (figure 11.161). However, local people are much less comfortable with the 'western' values that are often seen to accompany tourism – values such as materialism and hedonism which local people equate with the developed West (figure 11.162).

Another aspect of westernisation that many people in developing world cities resent is the loss of identity in the appearance of their city. The architecture seen in the two cities in figures 11.163 and 11.164 could be anywhere in

11.162 *The side of tourism that local people in Rio de Janeiro are less comfortable with is shown here, as tourists look at souvenirs which include erotic videos and books which do not deepen understanding of local culture.*

11.163 *Nairobi, Kenya*

11.164 *Caracas, Venezuela.*

the world, as the appearance is an anonymous 'international' style. Other aspects of the westernisation of developing world cities include the construction of expressways, advertising, the use of information and communications technology, and the introduction of western 'fast food'.

New ideas have also been introduced through foreign investment from overseas. For example, fast food outlets are changing the diets of many people in the cities of the

developing world, even though the meals there may cost as much as a week's wages for many residents (figure 11.165). The reason that local people are prepared to pay such relatively high prices for food at foreign food outlets is that they see prestige in eating foreign food on very special occasions. Nonetheless, the opening of these restaurants is evidence of a rising standard of living in some cities. Sadly, the fact that many people in the same cities cannot afford to eat there is also evidence that the gap in incomes between rich and poor in many cities is growing as the economic reforms increase inequalities.

11.165 *A McDonald's outlet in Bangkok, Thailand.*

The tension between modernisation and westernisation is a topic of debate in most developing world cities. On one hand, some feel that westernisation is inevitable if modernisation occurs, because western culture and economics are the dominant forces that seem to drive modernisation globally. On the other hand, others argue that despite the outward appearance of westernisation, traditional values still permeate the lifestyles and attitudes of most of the population.

QUESTION BLOCK 11R

1. *What conclusions can you draw from the data in table 11.12?*

2. *What problems does urban sprawl cause for residents of cities in the LEDCs?*

3. *What transport difficulties do residents of cities in LEDCs face that are not normally faced by residents of MEDCs?*

4. *Why is there usually a shortage of housing in the cities of LEDCs?*

5. *What are shanty settlements, and why do they arise?*

6. *Describe the challenges facing residents of shanty settlements.*

7. *Why are the urban services in LEDC cities often inadequate?*

Urban environments

8. Using the information in table 11.13,

a. List the cities in descending order of their population sizes in 2008.

b. Using table 11.9, list the cities that are also shown in table 11.13 in descending order of population growth rate.

c. What can you notice about the list you completed in the last question?

d. Compare the living conditions in two cities with contrasting statistics.

e. Suggest reasons for the differences you noted in your last question.

9. Conduct a survey among the students in your class to collect data on the five sets of statistics listed under the heading 'Living Conditions' in table 11.13. Compare the results of your class with the statistics for the major world cities.

10. Explain why unemployment is a problem in many cities.

11. Define 'underemployment', and give some examples of underemployment.

12. Explain the tension between 'modernisation' and 'westernisation' for the residents of many cities in LEDCs.

Responses to Urban Stresses

Of course, it would be wrong to think that every aspect of living in the great cities is bleak. Half the world's population lives in urban centres, and most of these people do so by choice. There are many good things about living in cities, and there are measures being taken to improve urban dwellers' quality of life. Increasingly, governments are becoming concerned about the quality of urban living and they are framing regulations to control and improve the urban environment. In many parts of the world, public transport is being encouraged as a means to reduce **traffic congestion** and **air pollution**. In the cities of Brazil, drivers are encouraged to convert the engines of their cars to run on alcohol as a biofuel instead of petrol (figure 11.166).

The challenge of air pollution is one of the most significant barriers to the quality of life in many of cities. Among the realistic solutions to the problem that have been proposed, the following are generally well accepted as being necessary:

- While it is not practical to slow down modernisation and industrial growth, it is necessary to ensure factories control their pollutants much more than at present.
- As it is not practical to ban cars or return to the days before their use was widespread, it is essential to clear the obstructions and bottlenecks that cause traffic congestion and stagnation.
- Residential population densities should be reduced in areas where manufacturing industries are concentrated.
- As young children below the age of five who live in slums and shanties suffer most from indoor air pollution, cleaner cooking fuels such as gas should replace traditional inferior fuels such as cow dung, wood, plastic and household waste.
- Vehicles with old technology should be banned from large cities.
- Small two and three-wheeler vehicles which are found in many cities in the developing world use heavily polluting two-stroke engines, and these should be upgraded to four-stroke engines or replaced with four-wheeled vehicles (figure 11.167).
- Heavy-duty vehicles could be barred from inner city streets between (say) the hours of 8 am to midday, and between 4 pm to 8 pm to reduce traffic congestion at peak times of day.
- To encourage the use of more modern, less polluting technology in vehicles, the price difference between petrol and diesel could be adjusted, as diesel is a greater source of pollutants.
- Extensive tree planting should occur to purify the polluted air and provide wind-breaks to settle dust and particulate matter (figure 11.168).
- Cars with pollution-reducing technology such as electronic fuel injection should be encouraged.

11.166 This fuel station in Brazil sells alcohol biofuel (labelled Álcool) as well as petrol and diesel. The alcohol biofuel, which is cheaper than petrol and diesel, is made in Brazil from fermented sugar cane.

11.167 Indian manufactured two-stroke mini-taxis in Mombasa, Kenya.

- Catalytic converters could be made compulsory for all petrol driven vehicles, and particle traps could be required for all diesel-engine vehicles.
- Street hawkers could be regulated or banned, as they slow traffic at intersections in many cities, building up levels of exhaust gases in the atmosphere and exposing themselves to respiratory problems such as bronchitis.

11.168 *Tree planting beside some main roads in Jakarta provides shade, purifies the air and calms wind-blown dust and particles.*

11.169 *High rise housing blocks are replacing sub-standard housing in Beijing, China.*

In the cities of more prosperous countries, the **housing shortage** is being solved in quite a dramatic but expensive way — the construction of huge numbers of high rise housing blocks (figure 11.169). In cities such as Shanghai and Beijing, high-rise flats are divided into neighbourhoods, each within walking distance of a neighbourhood centre with shops, restaurants and markets. However, the governments in many poorer countries such as Nigeria, India, Bangladesh and Pakistan claim they do not have enough taxation revenue to be able to afford to build low-cost housing for the urban poor. On the other hand, the Brazilian Government does not become involved in building high-rise flats, but allows private companies to do so. In the Brazilian cities of Rio de Janeiro and São Paulo, there has been large-scale construction of high-rise flats, but they are generally too expensive for the poor people who continue to live in shanties (figure 11.170).

11.170 *These high rise blocks of flats in Rio de Janeiro (Brazil) have been built by private developers, but they are too expensive for the poor people who live in the city's shanties.*

Perhaps the most effective solution to the challenges of living in the cities of the developing world is **self-help. Self-help projects overcome the problem of being de**pendent on the continuing support of outsiders. Self-help schemes can be individual, but they are more effective if they are organised on a community basis. Examples of self-help include the construction of shanty housing, operating within the informal economy and self-job creation, each of which was mentioned earlier in the chapter, together with co-operative housing or employment projects (figure 11.171).

11.171 *This co-operative centre in Jakarta accepts homeless unemployed youth from the streets. It feeds and houses them, and creates employment opportunities. In this view, young people are making frozen ice confection for sale in the markets.*

A spectacular example of community self-help occurred in the 1980s and 1990s in La Boca, a suburb of Buenos Aires. La Boca was a run down, poverty-stricken area populated by poor Italian immigrants. Writing about a century ago, a British diplomat in Argentina, James Bryce, described La Boca as:

"a waste of scattered shanties… dirty and squalid, with corrugated iron roofs, their wooden boards gaping like rents in tattered clothes. These are inhabited by the newest and poorest of immigrants from southern Italy and southern

Spain, a large and not very desirable element among whom anarchism is rife".

Because the residents were so poor, they could not afford paint for their buildings, and used whatever was available from other left over sources regardless of the colour. As a result, buildings in La Boca were painted in a patchwork of uncoordinated colours. The residents have used this characteristic to advantage to make the area into an artists' colony and a tourist attraction, bringing in substantial revenue to revitalise the neighbourhood (figure 11.172).

11.172 Most parts of La Boca, a suburb of Buenos Aires, are run-down and poverty-stricken (top). However, the local residents have co-operated to convert parts of the suburb into a tourist attraction, building on the area's colourful traditions, bringing in revenue and raising the quality of life for the residents.

In some cases, residents of cities become so frustrated at the lack of progress in addressing their problems that they turn to more radical solutions. Cities are often the centres of political dissent and protect. For example, although India's national government is strongly anti-communist, the city government of Kolkata has been communist for most of the period since 1950. Cities in developing countries have seen urban protests and riots from time to time, such as in Jakarta in 1965 and 1999, and at a more local scale in many of the other cities (figure 11.173).

11.173 The graffiti on the walls of these buildings in La Boca (Buenos Aires, Argentina) are expressions of frustration by local residents and signs of their involvement in radical political processes as a means to improve their quality of life.

11.174 Today's Beijing; this view of Wangfujing Avenue is quickly becoming the typical scene in Beijing.

In rapidly modernising cities such as Beijing, very few remnants remain of a less affluent past (figure 11.174). Large projects in the late 1990s and early 2000s have tried to change the city's image from a developing world city into a modern, technologically advanced metropolis. Examples of these projects included widening Wangfujing (a major shopping street) and converting it to a pedestrian plaza, several expressways, a huge new terminal at Beijing Airport and construction of a large new park in the Xidan shopping district(figure 11.175). City planners in Beijing are trying to form a modern, showpiece city by replacing the old traditional buildings with high rise housing blocks, replacing the heavily polluting factories and heating systems with clean substitutes, and even replacing bicycles with new double deck buses.

11.175 The new park opened in Xidan to celebrate the 50th anniversary of Communist government in China. Beijing's planners are trying to clean the air by opening new areas of grass, trees and flowers.

In the late 1990s, efforts were made to construct buildings with individual appearances featuring a variety of building materials, different angles and architectural features. The Oriental Plaza office and retail complex, which occupies an entire block of land near the city centre was completed as a millennium project for the beginning of 2000, and is regarded by the Beijing authorities as a symbol of the future direction of Beijing's development – modern, high-rise, privately developed, grand in scale, and with

11.176 *Oriental Plaza, a huge office and retail complex which takes up an entire block of land on Chang'an Avenue. Like the park at Xidan shown in the previous photo, this project incorporates open space with grass and flowers.*

extensive green landscaping and open space (figure 11.176).

As the national economies of many LEDCs have advanced and their population growth has slowed, greater attention has been paid to environmental quality and the quality of life of the people." In the case of China, population planning policies have resulted in an ageing population, whose needs must be addressed by urban planners. In Beijing, recreation areas are now being designed especially for elderly people to gather and socialise, and to exercise on a regular basis (figures 11.177 and 11.178).

11.177 *A social gathering area for old people in an area of traditional housing in central Beijing, China.*

In the early 2000s, it became clear that the process of urbanisation had become intertwined with the process of globalisation (see chapters 12 to 18). **Globalisation** has brought many benefits for cities in LEDCs, but it has also brought some significant challenges. Among the benefits are improved diffusion of knowledge and information, greater awareness of environmental issues and human rights, improved communication between planners around the world, and an easier spread of shared technology that hastens infrastructure development (figure 11.179).

11.178 *This open-air park in Beijing provides exercise equipment designed to meet the needs of an ageing population.*

11.179 *Evidence of political activity — wall graffiti in support of Venezuela's leader, Hugo Chavez, in a slum district of Caracas.*

On the other hand, globalisation has brought a greater emphasis on economic rationalism, in which economic forces often take priority over social and environmental considerations. This is sometimes referred to as a shift from managerialism to entrepreneurialism.

Entrepreneurialism in urban planning tends to view the city as a product to be marketed and promoted with the aim of increasing investment income from elsewhere in the global marketplace. When such investment occurs, it typically benefits land developers and government officials rather than the poorer mass of the population.

Problems of self-interest can become very acute in nations where corruption is prevalent, and in such cases, most of the population may become poorer as an elite group profits from globalisation. The challenge of the coming years will be to ensure that the benefits of globalisation are channelled in ways that improve the lives of the millions of people who now live in the cities of the LEDCs.

QUESTION BLOCK 11S

1. *How do you think the housing shortage and problems of housing quality should be addressed in the cities of poorer economies, remembering the shortage of funds available?*

Case Study of Social Stresses — London

With a population of about seven million people, London is the third largest city in Europe (after Paris and Moscow). London is the capital city of the United Kingdom and a major centre of banking and international finance. It is a centre of political power, world trade and communications, world communications, entertainment, sporting spectacles, and a centre of tourism.

In many ways, London is a curious mix of **social extremes** (figures 11.180 and 11.181). On one hand, London is the wealthiest region of Britain and one of the four wealthiest regions of Europe. On the other hand, there are large areas of poverty and unemployment, with three-quarters of a million people living below the poverty line of £125 per week. In inner London, almost half the children live in households with no earner of regular income.

11.180 *The affluent side of London — an expensive car drives through the gate leading to the avenue that approaches Buckingham Palace.*

11.181 *The poorer side of London — a scene in London's East End.*

London's **social structure** is similar to the rest of Britain except that it has proportionally more in both the richest and the poorest groups. The **gap between the rich and the poor** in London began to widen throughout the 1980s and 1990s, and the trend is continuing. Part of the reason for the widening gap is government policy, which under Prime Ministers Margaret Thatcher and later John Major emphasised private sector investment and personal self-reliance.

London's **social structure** today reflects past patterns to a large extent. In the 1800s, while traders were making large profits and Britain's overseas empire was bringing in great wealth, many Londoners suffered from disease, overcrowding and poverty. Moreover, thousands of people were dying each year from cholera, smallpox and typhoid. These problems were most severe among the poor in the East End, but they were also felt to some degree throughout London.

11.182 *Closed shops and businesses for sale in London's East End.*

Today, the reasons for London's **social problems** are different. However, the problems still tend to be worst in London's inner areas, as it is these parts of the city which have seen the most factory, shop and office closures (figure 11.182). Unemployment in the inner areas of London is very high, and so crime, vandalism and violence have also become common. In these inner areas, rents and land prices are often high, and many residents have had to move elsewhere. The term **urban blight** is used to describe many of London's inner areas, where the factories, people and jobs that have disappeared from the area have been replaced with vacant land or deserted and derelict buildings.

Traditionally, people in London have placed great faith in the education system to narrow the gap between rich and poor. In London, many would argue today that the education system has widened the gap (figure 11.183). British education authorities publish annual tables of statistics comparing the performance of schools in external examinations. The tables highlight the polarisation of opportunity for London school students. In one year, it was reported that three London schools were among the top ten schools in England, while in the same year six London schools were among the bottom eight in the country (figure 11.184).

The gap in London's schools is reflected in London's workforce. On one hand, London has a very well educated workforce, with 20% of the population having

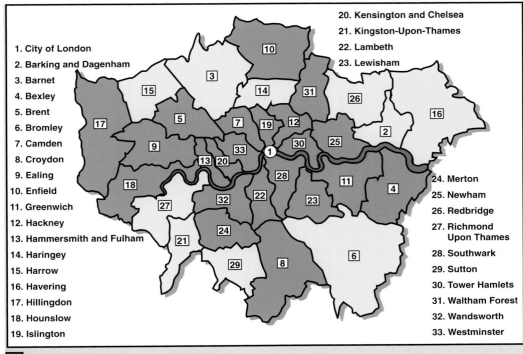

1. City of London
2. Barking and Dagenham
3. Barnet
4. Bexley
5. Brent
6. Bromley
7. Camden
8. Croydon
9. Ealing
10. Enfield
11. Greenwich
12. Hackney
13. Hammersmith and Fulham
14. Haringey
15. Harrow
16. Havering
17. Hillingdon
18. Hounslow
19. Islington
20. Kensington and Chelsea
21. Kingston-Upon-Thames
22. Lambeth
23. Lewisham
24. Merton
25. Newham
26. Redbridge
27. Richmond Upon Thames
28. Southwark
29. Sutton
30. Tower Hamlets
31. Waltham Forest
32. Wandsworth
33. Westminster

■ Majority non-white, below average exam results
□ Majority white, above average exam results
■ Other areas

11.183 *Schools in inner London often receive very little funding and operate in difficult conditions, as shown by the limited playground space in this primary school in London's East End.*

university degrees compared with the British national average of 13%. On the other hand, London has a larger percentage of its population without qualifications or skills than the national average. Over 50% of young people in London have no employment qualification whatsoever. In the early 2000s, one million people in London were receiving welfare payments from the government.

Like many features in London, unemployment is unevenly distributed. It is worst in the inner areas, and becomes less severe towards the edges. In part this is because many people with jobs have chosen to relocate their homes beyond the outer boundaries of London and commute to work each day. Today, about 750,000 people commute into and out of London on a daily basis for work. For London as a whole, 1 in 5 jobs is held by someone commuting, and for the financial centre, the proportion is 1 in 3.

The **distribution of wealth and poverty** in London is mirrored in the access people have to housing of different standards. In general, London's poorer suburbs are in inner areas, while wealthier people live on the outer fringes, and figures 11.185 and 11.186 illustrate this difference. There are exceptions to this pattern, however. For example figure 11.187 shows an area of very expensive terrace housing which is near Bedford Square, less than a kilometre from the area shown in figure 11.188. Some of London's most expensive housing is found near Regents Park in central London, only a couple of kilometres from Bedford Square and Russell Square (figure 11.189).

London's poorest housing tends to be in the East End district (figure 11.190). Typical of average, middle level London suburbs is Chiswick, about half way between the centre and the western edge of London. The average cost of houses such as those shown in figure 11.191 is about £200,000.

11.184 *The relationship between social structure and school performance in London. Schools with majority non-white populations are in London's poorest areas.*

11.185 *Outer suburban housing in London.*

11.186 *Inner city housing in London.*

11.187 *Terrace housing near Bedford Square in central London.*

11.188 *Housing near Russell Square, London.*

The ownership of **housing** in London reflects the social structure. There is a shortfall of some 600,000 dwellings in London. As a result, London over 30,000 squatters living in vacant houses they do not own or rent. On the other hand, many wealthy householders own two or more

homes. The distribution of ownership shows that the proportion of the population owning their own home increases with distance from the centre of London (figure 11.192). This measure of the distribution of wealth mirrors other measures such as average incomes, housing prices and average savings.

Many older London homes have **inadequate facilities**, and it is estimated that about 150,000 homes in London do not have their own bath or indoor toilet. The most poorly serviced homes, with no bath or toilet, poor heating and no insulation, are found in the poorer inner areas such as the East End.

11.189 *Chester Terrace, a street with very expensive housing near Regents Park.*

11.190 *Robin Hood housing estate in London's East End.*

Overall, there are about 250,000 applications from families waiting for low-cost council housing in London. The waiting lists vary from area to area, however, reflecting the distribution of wealth. In the inner suburbs, there is an average of more than 100 applications per 1,000 resident families, whereas in London's wealthier middle and outer suburbs the figure is fewer than 35 applications per 1000 resident families.

Many of those who are successful in obtaining low-cost council housing find themselves in high-rise housing estates. It has been found that people in high-rise housing

them with low-rise dispersed housing, but the high cost of such a dramatic policy means the campaign has little likelihood of success.

The estates have gained a savage reputation as centres of **crime** and **violence**, and as a result many of them have been declared 'no-go' areas by many milk vendors, doctors and rubbish collectors. This further disadvantages the residents of the housing blocks because they therefore may not have access to these services. It is quite common for upper-floor residents to throw their rubbish over their balconies or through their windows into the gardens

11.191 *Middle class housing in suburban London.*

estates are very disadvantaged compared with the general population. Residents in high-rise blocks have a higher likelihood of suicide, they are more likely than average to be bashed or murdered, and they suffer from frequent thefts.

Large numbers of people have no choice but to continue to live in **high-rise estates** in London, However, many of them resent having to do so, and they demonstrate this in various ways. Several tenants' groups have been organised to campaign for improvements in the quality of living in the estates. Many of these tenants' groups have suggested blowing up the high-rise estates and replacing

11.193 *The blackened area on the wall of Gloucester Grove Estate in south London is evidence of a fire lit by the resident of the flat, perhaps to dispose of their garbage or perhaps in frustration at the lifestyle.*

below because they are so frustrated that no-one will come and collect it. Fires are also common in the estates because residents attempt to burn their rubbish in the corridors to dispose of it, or to set fire to their flat in the hope that they can move out into different housing (figure 11.193).

There are other signs of **frustration** and **discontent** among the residents of the high-rise housing blocks. For example, large quantities of litter are found in corridors and in the grounds, there is widespread vandalism such as broken windows and smashed equipment, while piles of human excrement are often left on the floors of corridors or smeared on the walls. Graffiti, usually a sign of frustration, is almost always found on the walls of the housing estates (figure 11.194).

Some larger housing estates were designed to have shopping centres included on one floor of the high-rise blocks to supply everyday needs to the residents. However, because of the

Percentages, arranged in four quartiles, median = 38%

60% - 62%	22% - 37%
38% - 59%	4% - 21%

11.192 *Proportion of the population aged 65 and over who own their own home outright.*

combination of deliberate vandalism and the poverty of the often-unemployed residents, most of these shops have fallen into disuse and disrepair. As a result, many housing estates have an entire floor with boarded up shop fronts which provide little more than a derelict place for young people to meet (figure 11.195). Sadly, the only commercial activity on these floors now is drug selling and vice.

11.194 *A young boy caught in the act of defacing a wall with graffiti in the Aylesbury Estate, south London.*

11.195 *Now that the shops have closed in this housing estate, the entire level has become a waste-land with graffiti, vandalism, assaults and organic litter being common-place.*

Not surprisingly, most of the residents feel trapped in the environment of the high rise housing estates because they cannot afford to move elsewhere. Although there is a major shortage of housing in London, many high-rise estates have vacancy rates as high as 35%. This high vacancy rate shows how unpopular the high rise estates are, even for low income earners without any other form of housing. It is not uncommon for squatters to move into vacant flats, and this cause resentment among the tenants who are paying rents for their flats.

In spite of its problems, London continues to attract large numbers of **migrants** from other parts of Britain. The migrants are attracted by the job prospects, wealth, entertainment and education opportunities available in London (figure 11.196). The typical migrant into London is a young, single, ambitious, well-educated person, whereas the typical migrant out of London is a successful husband and wife team in their mid-forties or older (plus their children) in search of more open space in which to enjoy a more comfortable lifestyle.

11.196 *Evidence of multiculturalism in London — a sign in Hindi on a Christian church in Tower Hamlets, a district in London's East End.*

The **movement of people** into and out of London has created some further **inequalities** and unequal access to services, however. For example, urban planners have zoned areas for housing which are separated from areas of employment. This has been done to preserve the high quality of residential environments. However, the planning was done based on the transport costs for male heads of households. The planners are now criticised because they did not take into account the fact that over 40% of London's work force is now female. The separation of home and workplace is especially inconvenient for working women as most of them continue to do the household shopping and child raising in addition to their paid employment.

In addition to migrants from other parts of England, London also attracts migrants from other regions and countries. The influx of migrants gives London a distinctive multi-cultural character, but the diverse ethnic mix also mirrors patterns of advantage and disadvantage. These will be discussed in the next section.

As a port city, London has a long history of **immigration**. As long ago as the Middle Ages, groups of foreigners lived in separate neighbourhoods, notably Jewish traders

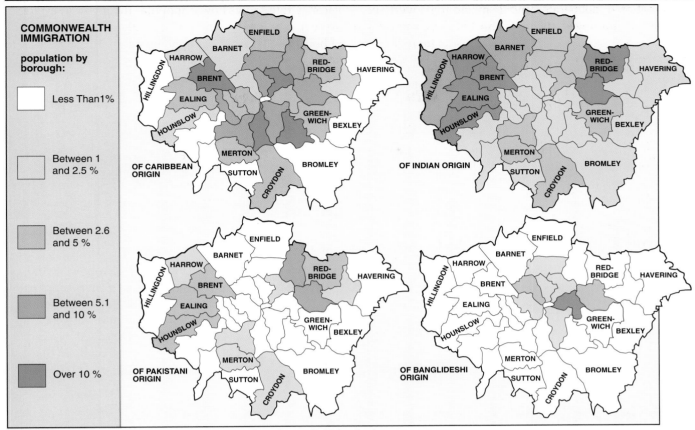

COMMONWEALTH IMMIGRATION

population by borough:

Less Than 1%

Between 1 and 2.5 %

Between 2.6 and 5 %

Between 5.1 and 10 %

Over 10 %

11.197 *The distribution of some immigrant groups from former British colonies.*

and German merchants. With the expansion of Britain's Empire, immigrants from the colonies began to enter London and settle, while many immigrants came to London during the two world wars of the twentieth century to escape the troubles in Europe.

Since the late 1960s, increasing numbers of immigrants have settled in London. The largest groups have come from former colonies in Asia (such as Pakistan, Bangladesh and Sri Lanka), East Africa (such as Uganda and Kenya) and the Caribbean (especially Jamaica and Trinidad). In the 1980s and 1990s, large numbers of refugees have been accepted from many of the world's trouble spots – Nigeria, Afghanistan, former Yugoslavia, Iraq, Somalia, and so on. London absorbs 90% of Britain's refugees.

When immigrants from former colonies or trouble spots first arrive in London, they tend to be quite poor and therefore they are unable to afford good housing. As a result, many new immigrants tend to cluster together in groups, generally in London's poorer suburbs (figure 11.197). The specific place where immigrants settle depends on where cheap housing is available at the time and where previous patterns of migration have seen people of the same nationality settle. As a general rule, new arrivals follow the settlement patterns of earlier settlers from the same country, and over time community facilities for that ethnic group develop in those areas.

As well as settling near other people from the same country, immigrants also tend to take up similar work to previous arrivals in the same ethnic group. For example, many Spanish immigrants work in the hotel and hospitality industry, Latin Americans often clean offices and West Africans manage car parks. Sometimes, the division of work can become quite specific, such as where many Nigerians are employed stacking shelves at '7-11' stores, whereas many Tamil Indians stack shelves in 'Europa' stores. At any one time, there are about 55,000 young Australians, New Zealanders and Canadians working in London – these are short term immigrants who typically work for a few months to earn enough money to go touring through Europe. Like other immigrant groups, the young Australians tend to live in the same area (Earl's Court) and work in the same industries (hotels, restaurants, child care and insurance offices).

Because they cluster together in **urban villages** for reasons of comfort, support and economy, immigrant groups have been able to retain many aspects of their own cultures in London, including continuing to practice their own religion, establishing their own food stores, speaking in their original languages and arranging their own marriages (figures 11.198 and 11.199). On the other hand, there have been instances of **hostility** towards immigrant groups in London, such as racist graffiti in buildings and trains and hostile personal behaviour. This is justified by some people in London simply on the grounds that immigrants look quite different or behave differently.

Although British government policy strictly forbids racism and discrimination on the grounds of **ethnicity**, many immigrants complain about racial **discrimination** shown to them by London's housing authorities. It is claimed that poorer quality housing tends to be allocated to immigrants than to white people. It is also alleged that immigrants with coloured skin are more likely than whites to be allocated the very unpopular high-rise housing, rather than more desirable semi-detached or terrace housing.

11.200 *This view of the main street of Brixton shows a representative sample of the diverse ethnic mix of the suburb.*

11.198 *Reflecting the multicultural character of London, this Jewish synagogue and Islamic mosque are found next door to each other in Whitechapel.*

However, most Londoners now seem to appreciate the positive contribution which immigrant groups make to the city's economic and social life, and such arguments are now seldom heard openly. One London citizen summed up London's ethnic mix as she saw it by describing the main street of her local shopping centre in the suburb of Finsbury Park:

> "Here in a hundred (metre) stretch can be seen an Irish pub, Indian newsagents, food shop and restaurant, a Greek-Cypriot delicatessen, a halal butcher, a variety of West Indian businesses, a West African restaurant with a taxi service above, a Chinese take-away, a Lebanese flower shop, a Jewish-run ironmongers, an Italian restaurant and a Spanish-run off-licence (take-away liquor store). It is this rich mix of cultures rubbing alongside one another that characterises contemporary London and adds so much to its vitality."

11.199 *This view of Whitechapel (inner London) has more similarities with a shopping street in Dar-es-Salaam, Mumbai or Nairobi than 'traditional' London, even though this scene is just one kilometre north of the Tower Bridge. Today, however, it is an authentic reflection of London's ethnic mix.*

Racial **riots** have broken out from time to time against Asian immigrants in parts of London. The best known race riots in London occurred in the suburb of Brixton. About 25% of the population of Brixton comprises immigrants of different racial background, which is why the suburb became the target of racist rioting (figure 11.200). Although it is less common today, some extreme political groups have arguing that coloured immigrants should be sent back to their original countries.

11.201 *Old Bond Street in Mayfair is an example of a famous London shopping street now owned almost entirely by Arab business interests.*

Not all the immigrants into London are economically disadvantaged. London is also attracting increasing numbers of **millionaire immigrants** from various countries, but especially the Middle East and the former Soviet Union. Like other immigrant groups they tend to cluster together, but in these cases it is in areas of London's top real estate – Mayfair, Knightsbridge, Kensington and Belgravia. Housing in these areas has always been expensive, but the arrival of foreign millionaires has raised prices of real estate in these areas beyond the reach of even wealthy British people. The shopping streets north of Hyde Park and parts of Mayfair (east of Hyde park) and Knightsbridge (south of Hyde Park) are now almost entirely owned by Arab immigrants from the Gulf (figure 11.201).

QUESTION BLOCK 11T

1. *Outline the evidence to support the claim that "London is a curious mix of social extremes".*

2. *Why is London's social structure so polarised?*

3. *Describe the spatial distribution of wealth and poverty in London.*

4. *Account for the pattern you have described in the previous question.*

5. *Why is the East End of London a particularly disadvantaged area?*

6. *Describe the pattern shown in figure 11.183.*

7. *List the disadvantages faced by residents of high-rise housing estates.*

8. *What realistic solutions would you propose to relieve the problems of people living in London's high rise housing estates?*

9. *What attracts migrants to London?*

10. *List the reasons that immigrant groups tend to settle near other people from the same ethnic group.*

11. *What is the relationship between the patterns shown in figures 11.183, 11.192 and 11.197?*

12. *Do you think London's wide ethnic mix is a positive or negative factor in influencing the city's culture of place? Give factual reasons and evidence to support your view.*

The Sustainable City

The City as a Sustainable System

The concept of **systems** should be familiar to most people as the word 'system' is commonly used in everyday speech. We often speak of transport systems, or the education system, or a hot water system, or the fuel system in a car. Geographers use the word 'system' in a similar way to the way the word is used in everyday speech.

Each of the systems mentioned above has certain common characteristics. For example:
- each system is made up of a number of objects;
- these objects are linked in a functional relationship to achieve a purpose';
- the objects and the links between them have a boundary, or a limit (even though it may sometimes be difficult to determine precisely where that limit lies);
- the system does not exist in isolation, but it functions within a wider environment;
- the systems described above are **open systems**, which means they receive inputs from the surrounding environment and they provide outputs to the environment; and
- the system shows a behaviour that is a consequence of all those things that relate to the system — the inputs, the links between the objects, and the surrounding environment. If any one of these elements changes, then the behaviour of the system is likely to change.

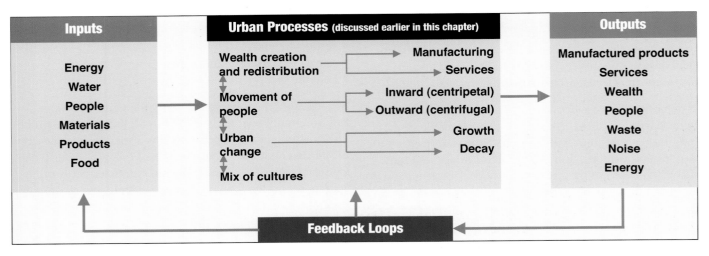

11.202 *The city as a system.*

Question Block 11U

1. *Consider a domestic hot water system and the education system where you study. List the details of each of these open systems under the headings: purpose, environment, linkages, inputs, outputs.*

The water cycle that was described in chapter 5 is an example of a system in the physical environment. Because the water in the system is constantly being recycled in different forms, with no water being removed or added to the system (apart from minute quantities during volcanic eruptions), the water cycle is often referred to as a **closed system**.

Systems are commonly found in human environments. Businesses such as farms, factories, banks and shops, are open systems with certain inputs (such as land, labour and capital) being organised through internal linkages and processes to produce certain outputs (such as products, profits, and perhaps environmental pollution). Churches, clubs, political parties and examination systems are all examples of human organisation systems.

Similarly, the city can be thought of as a system with certain inputs which are processed to produce certain outputs. Figure 11.202 shows a simple diagram of the city as a system. Inputs enter the city from both the physical and human environments. For example, energy inputs arrive in the form of sunshine and warmth from the physical environment, and these are supplemented by energy from the human environment in forms such as electricity and piped gas. Inputs of water also come from both the natural environment (rainfall and stream flow) and the human environment (piped water).

Once the inputs have entered the city system, they are processed in various ways. The processes that operate in the city to process the various inputs can be quite complex, varying from city to city, and they have been described in detail earlier in this chapter.

As a result of the processes, the city produces various outputs as shown in figure 11.202. Some of the outputs (such as wealth, services and manufacturing goods) are deliberate, while others (such as solid, liquid and atmospheric wastes) are usually unintended.

If this linear process operated as simply as summarised here, it would almost certainly be unsustainable in the long term. **Sustainable development** was defined by the Brundtland Commission in 1987 as 'development that meets the needs of the present, without compromising the ability of future generations to meet their own needs'. Computer modelling has shown that in the long-term, uncontrolled use of inputs and outputs results in an unsustainable situation as resources become exhausted and environmental pollution rises to alarming levels. On

11.203 *A collection bin for plastics recycling in Sydney, Australia.*

the other hand, if outputs can be recycled, the demand for new input resources is reduced and environmental pollution (such as dumping rubbish in ever-expanding landfill tips) is also controlled (figure 11.203).

Sustainable city management therefore refers to the process of managing the city's inputs and outputs in such as way that the quality of life for current and future urban dwellers can be maintained and enhanced. Sustainable management of cities is a **holistic** concept that includes all facets of the urban environment, including the social (such as housing quality and crime), the economic (such as income and employment) and the environmental aspects (air, water, land and resources).

In its implementation, sustainable city management is very similar to the concept of **ecocities** that was developed by Richard Register in the early 2000s. The policy principles underpinning ecocities are:
- restore degraded land
- fit the bioregion
- balance development
- halt urban sprawl
- optimise energy performance (figure 11.204)
- contribute to the economy
- provide health and security
- encourage community
- promote social equity
- respect history
- enrich the cultural landscape
- heal the biosphere.

In 2002, a workshop sponsored by the United Nations Environment Program was held in Melbourne (Australia). The outcome of this workshop was a set of guidelines for urban sustainability. Known as the *Melbourne Principles for Sustainable Cities*, the document contained ten simple statements on the ways in which a sustainable city must function, each of which was followed by an elaborate description providing additional information on its meaning and application. The *Melbourne Principles* were adopted at the Earth Summit 2002 in Johannesburg (South

11.204 *Some people question the wisdom of using energy to floodlight city buildings at night. This example is in Warsaw, Poland.*

11.205 *The ecological footprint is reduced when shared hired bicycles such as these Villos replace private motor vehicles. People with a Villo account can pick up a bicycle at any one of 180 Villo stations in Brussels (Belgium), and simply leave it at any other station when the journey is finished. The Villo stations are situated just 450 metres apart from each other throughout Brussels.*

11.206 *One way to reduce energy use for air conditioning and heating in buildings is to use 'green roofs' and 'green walls'. This building in Singapore uses vines on the exterior of the building to provide shade and insulation.*

Africa), and they have since become the standard by which the sustainability of cities is measured.

The *Melbourne Principles* aimed to create environmentally healthy, vibrant and sustainable cities where people

respect one another and nature, to the benefit of all. They are intended to provide a starting point for decision-makers as they work towards sustainability, providing holistic guidelines that can help promote sustainability in cities. The ten principles of city sustainability in the Melbourne Guidelines were as follows:

1. Provide a long-term vision for cities based on: sustainability; intergenerational, social, economic and political equity; and their individuality.

2. Achieve long-term economic and social security.

3. Recognise the intrinsic value of biodiversity and natural ecosystems, and protect and restore them.

4. Enable communities to minimise their ecological footprint (figure 11.205).

5. Build on the characteristics of ecosystems in the development and nurturing of healthy and sustainable cities (figure 11.206).

6. Recognise and build on the distinctive characteristics of cities, including their human and cultural values, history and natural systems.

7. Empower people and foster participation.

8. Expand and enable co-operative networks to work towards a common, sustainable future.

9. Promote sustainable production and consumption, through appropriate use of environmentally sound technologies and effective demand management.

10. Enable continual improvement, based on accountability, transparency and good governance.

QUESTION BLOCK 11V

1. *With reference to figure 11.202, give an example of each feature in the diagram that relates to the city where you live.*

2. *Write your own definition of 'sustainable city management' in a way that embraces the Brundtland Commission's view of sustainability.*

3. *What is your opinion of the Melbourne Principles as a framework for managing cities in a sustainable manner? Give reasons to support your opinion.*

Case Study — Sustainable City Management in London

A major influence on London's future will be the way it manages its environmental quality. As a city with a population of about 7 million people, London's ecological **sustainability** could well be the factor that determines how efficiently and effectively it continues to function.

Some measures suggest that inefficient and wasteful use of resources in London is making the city **unsustainable**. For example, London uses 45,000 tonnes of fuel to power its homes, factories, transport, offices and communica-

Urban environments

tions systems every day. This energy is the equivalent to a supertanker of oil every two days. Using this fuel produces about 160,000 tonnes of carbon dioxide into the atmosphere every day.

Another sign of extravagant energy use is transport. In spite of London's almost constant traffic congestion, almost 70% of all journeys within London are made by car. Government projections predict that the use of private motor vehicles will increase until at least 2020. Between 1974 and 2001, the proportion of seven and eight year olds going to school on their own fell from 90% to 8%, with most now being driven to school. The increase in car use means that the average speed of car journeys in London is now only 15 kilometres per hour. Furthermore, most of the 6,800 tonnes of food consumed in London each day is brought by road transport. However, large quantities of fruit and vegetables are now flown in to London from tropical areas. For example, it is now common to fly beans from Kenya, vegetables from California and mangoes from West Africa. It has been estimated that the energy required to fly each mango from Gambia to London is 600 times greater than the food value (kilojoules) in the mango!

One way of analysing this situation is to refer to the **urban ecological footprint**, which is theoretical measurement of the amount of land and water a population requires to produce the resources it consumes and to absorb its waste under prevailing technology. This was discussed in detail in chapter 4.

In many ways, cities make very efficient use of resources such as energy, water and land because the population is concentrated in higher densities than rural areas. London contains 12% of the UK population and it produces 20% of the nation's GDP, and yet London emits just 8% of the

country's carbon dioxide. Compared with the UK population in general, London's population consumed less electricity per capita, produced less waste per capita, consumed less water per capita, produced less carbon dioxide per capita and used less gas per capita.

Nonetheless, the United Kingdom ranks 8th among nations on the list of world-wide carbon dioxide emissions, so London's contribution of 8% to that total is significant globally. Of London's overall carbon dioxide emissions, 22% comes from ground-based transport, 38% from domestic (or household) uses, while 40% comes from industrial and commercial uses. Figure 11.207 shows the breakdown of each of these sources of carbon dioxide emissions.

In 2006, London produced 44 million tonnes of carbon dioxide, excluding the amount produced by civil aviation. It was estimated at the time that if action was taken to reduce this amount, London's annual CO_2 emissions would reach 51 million tonnes by 2025. London's planners have set a target to reduce the CO_2 emissions in 2025 to 70% of this amount (i.e. a 30% reduction). Planners believe that about 30% this reduction can come through public action in response to public education. However, it is expected that the remaining reduction will need government intervention, such as imposing carbon taxes, investing in research, funding low-carbon initiatives and removing regulations that make decentralising energy production difficult.

In an effort to reduce both inner city congestion and carbon emissions, London introduced a congestion charge in 2003. The congestion charge was applied to motorists who drove into an inner city area designated as the Congestion Charge Zone (CCZ). The aims of the charge were to reduce congestion, reduce CO_2 emissions, and

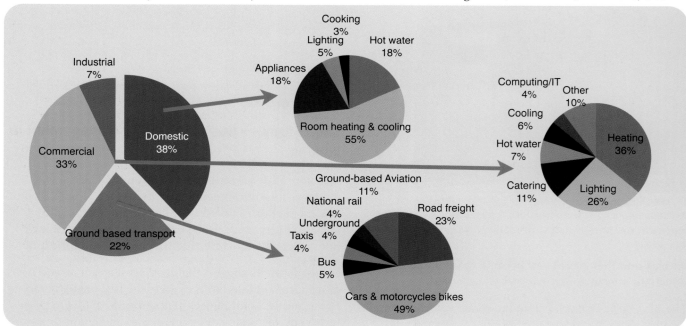

11.207 *London's carbon dioxide emissions.*

raise money to invest in London's public transport (figure 11.208). Despite disagreement over the effectiveness of the scheme, the CCZ was extended into parts of West London in 2007.

Perhaps the ultimate test of ecological sustainability in London will be how well the city manages its **waste outputs**. At present, resource use in London is **linear**, which means resources are taken from one place and the wastes are dumped somewhere else. In London, there are three key waste products which must be managed – air pollution, water pollution and solid wastes.

11.208 *In this view of Oxford Street in central London, almost every vehicle is a bus or a taxi.*

Because London has a long history of urban settlement, some of its **environmental problems** have been particularly severe for a long period. For example, as far back as the year 1257, **air pollution** was recorded as being a problem in London, especially smoke from burning coal. By the early 1600s, people were complaining that the outside walls of St Paul's cathedral were being stained by air pollution. In the mid-1600s, it was generally agreed that London's death rate was being raised because of air pollution. By the mid-1800s, London's air pollution was so severe that the city had become known as "the Smoke". Indeed, air pollution caused by smoke from factories and from coal burnt for household heating was so bad that it was altering London's climate. The smoke filtered out sunlight, reduced daylight hours and affected people's health.

Until the 1960s, London's atmosphere was almost always hazy. Fogs were common, especially in winter, when water droplets formed around the smoke particles that were always in the atmosphere. It was estimated that an average of 75 tonnes of carbon, ash and dust rained on each square kilometre London annually, and in some areas of the East End the figure was 175 tonnes per annum. Diseases of the lungs increased every winter, and peaked during times of heavy air pollution. By the early 1950s, London's air pollution was mainly smog, a mixture of smoke and fog. They were so thick that they became known as 'pea soupers'. As well as causing sickness, the smog stunted the growth of trees and made London's buildings look a uniform dreary grey colour.

In 1952 a particularly severe smog killed about 4,000 Londoners and reduced visibility so much that there were major traffic problems for many days. This incident led the government to introduce very strict air pollution control laws in London in 1956, laws which were tightened further in 1968. Most of London's smoke – 84% – was caused by burning coal in domestic houses for heating, so new forms of heating were introduced. The laws were very effective in reducing air pollution, and today the air in London is cleaner than in many other large cities in Europe. London's last major smog occurred in 1962, and in contrast with the 1952 incident, 340 people died.

London's air pollution in the 1950s and 1960s influenced decision making in less direct ways than air pollution regulations. As a result of the smog, planners increased the amount of parkland in London, encouraging tree and flower planting along railway embankments and other areas of open space (figure 11.209). Furthermore, planners surrounded London's urban area with a 'green belt' that had to be protected as open space, and began constructing tall buildings with white or off-white facades to replace the old, dark, soot-stained buildings.

11.209 *One of the parks that provide green space in central London.*

On the other hand, some new types of air pollution are beginning to cause problems. Examples of these new pollutants include carbon monoxide (from cars) and nitrogen oxides (from power stations, cars, and gas stoves in household kitchens). As well as producing pollution, cars make demands on the scarce space within London and detract from the beauty of the city (figure 11.210).

One of the problems caused by air pollution is weathering of buildings, This occurs when pollutants such as sulphur dioxide, carbon dioxide and nitrogen dioxide attack the stone used in many old buildings. It can be expensive to repair pollution damaged buildings, and many people argue that it would be cheaper (as well as healthier) to clean up the pollution rather than repair damaged old buildings and treat sick people.

11.210 *Scarce parking space in London.*

The amount of water used in London could also be a barrier to future ecological sustainability. Each day, London uses almost 3 million tonnes of water, which represents about 430 litres of water per person per day. This water must be disposed of after use, leading to another long-standing environmental problem in London – **water pollution**. During the 1800s, many Londoners took their water directly from the River Thames. This was not a healthy practice as the river also served as the city's sewer. Even today, some seven million tonnes of sewage sludge are pumped into the Thames each year. This sludge could be used as organic fertiliser on farms, saving large quantities of chemical fertilisers. However, although other areas in Britain are converting human sewage into pellets for farm fertilisers, this has not occurred in London.

Although many of London's factories have closed down or relocated to outer areas, quite a number of older factories are still located beside the Thames, and they continue to use the river as a dumping ground for wastes. Meanwhile, the Thames supplies 70% of London's water, although this water is taken from further upstream than the industrial areas. However, like London's air pollution, water management in the Thames Basin has improved dramatically in recent decades. Today, fish such as salmon are commonly found in the Thames, although in the 1960s, the river was so heavily polluted that no fish or marine life whatsoever could be found in it.

For many years, flooding was a serious problem in low lying parts of London. The flooding was caused by a combination of natural and human factors. The level of the sea near London is rising by about 85 centimetres per century. This rise in sea level has three causes. First, for the past 10,000 years, the British Isles have been tilting, with London and south-east England sinking and north-west Scotland rising. The tilting has resulted from the release of pressure at the end of the last ice age when thick ice caps over Scotland melted. The release of weight over Scotland is still causing the rise in northern Britain because of the lag effect.

A second reason for the rise in sea levels has been the melting of the polar ice caps at the end of the last ice age. This has put more water into the world's oceans in general, raising their levels. Indeed, the world today is going through an unusually warm period, and so sea levels are abnormally high as a result. Third, dredging of the Thames River has led to a rise in the level of high tide in London due to changes in the shape of the river channel.

11.211 *The embankment along the Thames River was built to prevent flooding. The green moss indicates the common level of the river.*

The flooding has also been affected by human actions. Like all major cities in developed economies, London has large areas of ground surface sealed with concrete or bitumen. This covering prevents rainwater infiltrating the soil. As a result, the rainwater remains on the surface, either in drainage channels or in ponds. Measurements have shown that new housing construction and industrial estates in north London have caused flood peaks three times higher than they were before building in the area. In order to overcome the threat of flooding in London, the embankment beside the Thames River has been raised (figure 11.211) and a costly flood control barrier with opening and closing gates has been built.

11.212 *Garbage awaiting collection in a central London street. The separation of paper rubbish into cardboard boxes is an example of recycling.*

The third key waste product that must be managed in London is **solid wastes**. Average daily waste disposal in London is 6,700 tonnes per household. In addition to household waste, building demolition and road works add 22,400 tonnes of waste per day and each commercial and industrial enterprise adds a daily average of 8,500 tonnes of waste. Although recycling is becoming more common, less than 5% of London's rubbish is currently recycled, although the government has set a target of 25% (figure 11.212). Meanwhile, large amounts of rubbish are simply dumped on vacant land or left in the streets, giving London the reputation of a somewhat dirty, litter-strewn city (figure 11.213).

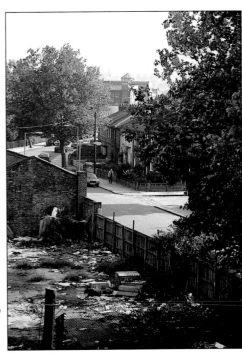

11.213 *Although this street looks clean, fences hide the garbage dumped on the vacant block of land.*

11.214 *The large complex across the middle of this aerial view of south-west London is a sewage treatment works. The residents who live nearby and experience the odours would no doubt welcome a more productive way of recycling sewage.*

Many people are now recognising that if London's ecology is to be sustainable, it must change from a linear (waste-producing) use of resources to a circular (recy-

cling) pattern. Six ways in which this could occur in London are:

- sewage works could become fertiliser factories to enriching farmland (figure 11.214). Toxic liquid wastes could then be kept separate from valuable household garbage
- washing powders, toilet cleaners and bleaches could be fully biodegradable
- companies could routinely invest in recycling technology and non-toxic production processes.
- liquid chemical wastes from factories could be recycled within factories and not discharged into sewerage systems.
- household and factory rubbish could be utilised as a resource rather than discarded as a nuisance
- forests would not be replanted only for timber but also for protecting watersheds and absorbing carbon dioxide.

In the end, ecological sustainability is important because of what it means for the quality of people's lives. As Girardet commented in a 1994 article published in *Geographical*, "A dejected, insecure and restless urban population will not be interested in the ecological viability of their city. Their concern is day-to-day survival rather than the existence of their city from century to century... Unemployment, alienation, boredom, homelessness and crime are all elements in the unsustainability of urban areas". As we saw earlier in this chapter, these social issues are real concerns in London, and therefore they must addressed if the issue of ecological sustainability is to be addressed.

If we assume present trends will continue, then it is likely that London's future development will follow two paths at the one time – **renewal** and **expansion**. The effects of de-industrialisation and the growth of service industries, such as finance and tourism, will have major impacts on London's future.

As industry and population have moved from inner to outer areas of London, space has been made available for inner urban renewal. One spectacular example is the former **Docklands** area. When London's inner city docks on the River Thames were replaced by new facilities nearer the sea, the abandoned area in the East End became a zone of high rise redevelopment. Sometimes known as Manhattan-on-Thames because its high-rise character was said to resemble New York more than London, the London Docklands was an example of inner city renewal on a massive scale (figure 11.215).

Perhaps the most famous new building in Docklands is Canary Wharf Tower, Europe's largest office block and Britain's tallest building. This building, together with a surrounding complex of ten buildings, provides 30 hectares of office space. Like many of the new buildings in Docklands, the appearance of Canary Wharf Tower was quite alien to the rest of London. The Docklands scheme did not include any philosophy for the design of buildings or their arrangement across the area. As one British architect described Docklands, "examples of young, exhilarating architecture (are) mixed in with the mediocre and the crass" (figure 11.216).

11.215 *High rise development in the London Docklands.*

11.216 *The light railway station at Canary Wharf Tower, London Docklands.*

Despite its financial successes, the pattern of development was criticised by long-term local residents for its alien architecture and intimidating landscape. Furthermore, the claims of economic success have also been questioned. Many offices remain unoccupied, and this adds ammunition to long-term East End residents who claim that the direction of development is flawed. Indeed, in contrast with the high rents being charged in the City of London, office space is available in Docklands for as little as £45 per square metre. For many executives, Docklands still carries the stigma of being in London's East End, which was traditionally a poor, working class area populated by wharf labourers.

About two-thirds of the investment in Docklands has been from foreign companies, especially corporations based in the Middle East, the Netherlands, Japan, Sweden, France, the United States and Denmark. This has also brought criticism, although to be fair, several large projects were underway by British firms in the

1980s but these firms went bankrupt before completion. Commenting on its characteristics, the British geographer Michael Hebbert wrote:

> *"The mainstream of the property sector continued to see the Docklands as a low-density business area similar in style to the emerging industrial landscapes of the urban fringe: trees, water, ample car-parking, crinkly tin sheds, offices and workshops for the business service and media sectors, some warehousing, and the occasional larger plant such as the relocated printing presses of the Fleet Street newspaper industry. In a word, as a convenient backyard to the real London west of the Tower (Bridge)."*

11.217 *The Docklands Light Railway.*

11.218 *Billboards outside the construction site for the Athletes Village for the London 2012 Olympics emphasise sustainability.*

It is likely that the type of development which is taking place in the Docklands area will increasingly be found in other parts of the city, despite the criticisms of the Docklands scheme (figure 11.218). However, London must overcome problems of outdated public transport, congested roads and old infrastructure such as water and sewerage systems if redevelopment is to be successful (figure 11.219).

Having said that, major **improvements in public transport** are planned for the coming decades. Extensions and major upgrades are planned for several of London's Underground railway lines, and the rail linkage with

Europe via the Channel Tunnel is to be expanded and upgraded. The fifth air terminal at Heathrow, opened in 2008, together with improvements to London's other airports, have helped London to maintain its role as a major tourist and financial centre. New buses are being purchased to upgrade the standard of London's public transport in an effort to entice commuters away from their private cars (figure 11.220).

11.219 *Russell Square station in the London Underground.*

The needs of the financial sector for 'instant' information means that many buildings constructed only 20 years ago have already become outdated. Many existing buildings cannot accommodate the computer cables or air-conditioning ducts which are expected in today's office environments. On the other hand, more companies are now prepared to move away from the congested inner area of London, as **information technology** frees them from older forms of communication which made the clustering of offices necessary. Indeed, some companies in London already let some of their employees work from home, and have found it has almost doubled productivity.

11.220 *An example of a relatively new double-decker bus in London.*

Although London's **population growth** remains quite slow, it seems certain that the urban area of London will continue to expand as people demand more space around their homes. In the same way that new types of transport last century allowed London to spread out, new technol-

ogy will continue the process in the years ahead. It is expected that the London of the mid twenty-first century will stretch across a diameter of about 200 kilometres filling much of the south-east corner of England. For most Londoners, this should mean a significant improvement in the quality of their environment as population densities decrease.

Whatever direction the future development of London takes, it is certain that the questions of ecological sustainability, patterns of advantage and disadvantage, social structures and economic change will be central to the city's future viability.

QUESTION BLOCK 11W

1. *Give three examples which suggest that London may not be ecologically sustainable unless significant changes are made.*

2. *Why are urban ecological footprints often lower for individuals who live in cities than for people in rural areas?*

3. *Describe the pattern of London's carbon dioxide emissions.*

4. *What steps are being taken to reduce London's urban ecological footprint?*

5. *Outline the measures that have been taken to improve the quality of (a) air and (b) water in London.*

6. *Why is flooding an increasing threat in London?*

7. *Suggest realistic ways of making London a more ecologically sustainable city in the future.*

8. *Is the type of urban development seen in the London Docklands helpful in promoting sustainability? Explain your answer.*

9. *If you were in charge of planning London over the next twenty years, what three things would you set as your key priorities? Give reasons for your choices.*

Case Study — Sustainable City Management in Curitiba, Brazil

Curitiba is a city in southern Brazil with a population of almost two million people. Capital of the state of Paraná, it has emerged as an example of outstanding city planning and sustainable development as a response to the challenges of urban growth.

Following the appointment of Jaime Lerner as Mayor in 1971, city planners in Curitiba have focussed on four main areas of sustainable city management — transport, recycling, parks and affordable housing.

Transportation

One of the first decisions made by Curitiba's planners in the early 1970s was that the city should be developed for people, not cars. They began by closing Curitiba's busiest street, Rua XV de Novembro, and converting it into Brazil's first pedestrian plaza (figure 11.221). Because there was considerable opposition from business owners to the plan, the conversion was completed in 72 hours over one weekend. However, subsequent experience showed that the change improved business for local firms because pedestrians were more relaxed and thus more willing to spend time shopping.

11.221 *Rua XV de Novembro, the first pedestrian plaza in Curitiba, Brazil.*

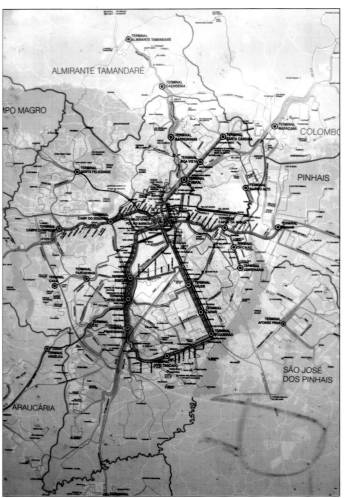

11.222 *This map of Curitiba's bus network prominently displayed at a bus stop highlights the five main radiating bus routes in red.*

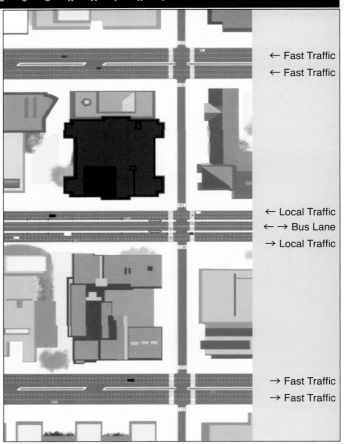

← Fast Traffic
← Fast Traffic

← Local Traffic
← → Bus Lane
→ Local Traffic

→ Fast Traffic
→ Fast Traffic

11.223 *Curitiba's trinary road system.*

11.224 *A six-lane, one-way street.*

In contrast to many cities around the world, where the growing number of cars is managed by building wider streets and more expressways, Curitiba's planners decided to emphasise public transport and make it attractive and affordable for commuters. Restrictions were introduced to prevent more tall buildings being constructed in the congested downtown area, and permits were only granted for new buildings in areas where mass public transportation could be provided. Five routes were identified radiating out from the downtown area, allowing urban expansion to occur in a regulated way (shown as red lines in figure 11.222). Thus, new schools and businesses were located along routes where buses could replace cars as the main means of transportation, replacing a concentrated city centre with multiple linear centres.

The five axes were converted into a distinctive trinary (three-part) structure. The axes used three parallel streets that were designed to work together to ease traffic flow (figure 11.223). The central street is divided into three sections. The central section of the central road is a two-way road that is reserved for Curitiba's large bi-articulated buses, with bus stops every 500 metres. Having separate bus lanes enables people to travel quickly regardless of traffic conditions on surrounding roads. The bus lanes are also used by emergency vehicles such as police and ambulances when needed.

On either side of the bus lanes are lanes for cars that need access to local businesses and buildings. One block away from the central road, in each direction, are the other roads that complete the trinary road system. Known as *hoppidas*, these are three to six-lane one-way avenues that provide high-speed cross-city roadways for cars (figure 11.224). This trinary road system covers about 70 kilometres of Curitiba's main roadways. One-way roads have been shown to reduce congestion because the waiting times at traffic lights are reduced and cars never have to wait for oncoming cars before turning into cross streets.

11.225 *Passengers disembark from a red bi-articulated bus into the tube station.*

11.226 *A red bus tube station.*

For the bus stops, a special tube station design was adopted to improve efficiency. Passengers can enter and leave buses without the inconvenience of steps, and they pay fares at the tube station, thus eliminating the collection of fares within the bus (figures 11.225 and 11.226).

The buses are colour-coded to indicated their function within the transport system. Red buses are either articulated or bi-articulated, and they travel exclusively along the dedicated bus lanes in the centre of the middle road of trinary road system, connecting outer areas of Curitiba with the downtown. Each bi-articulated bus can carry up to 270 passengers, and during peak hours, the average frequency of buses is just 50 seconds.

Grey buses travel along the fast lanes of streets, but stop only every two to three kilometres, using the special tube stations when they do so (figure 11.227). The grey buses are thus the fastest way of travelling over longer distances in Curitiba.

11.227 *A grey bus at a tube station.*

Yellow, orange and green buses connect local towns to transport hubs where passengers can transfer to other buses without paying additional fares (figure 11.228). This enables passengers to use connecting bus stations to reach their destinations, thus avoiding downtown areas and reducing the central city congestion that plagues many world cities. Thus, over 60% of Curitiba's residents use buses to get to work each day, even though Curitiba has the second highest rate of car ownership in Brazil (one car per three inhabitants). Evidence of Curitiba's emphasis on public transport planning is that no person in the city has to walk more than 400 metres to reach a bus stop.

Curitiba's public transport system represents a relatively low-cost solution to transport needs. The total cost of the infrastructure and vehicles is about US$1 million per kilometre, compared with the cost of building a subway system, which would be about US$100 million per kilometre. In practice, however, Curitiba's bus system functions like a subway system because it is separated from the rest of the road network and uses its own dedicated routes.

11.228 *Yellow buses provide access to local areas over short distances in Curitiba.*

It has been estimated that Curitiba's transport system has resulted in a reduction of about 40 million car trips per year, saving about 40 million litres of fuel annually. Compared to eight other Brazilian cities of similar size, Curitiba uses about 30% less fuel per person, resulting in one of the lowest rates of air pollution in Brazil. Today, about 1,100 buses make 12,500 trips every day, serving more than 1.3 million passengers, which is 50 times greater than the number 20 years previously. Perhaps most significantly, people in Curitiba spend only about 10% of their income on travel, a figure that is well below Brazil's national average.

Recycling

The incentive to introduce large-scale recycling in Curitiba arose from the city's rapid growth. In the late 1940s, Curitiba's population was just 150,000 people, but this had risen to over one million by the late 1980s. This rapid growth resulted in *favelas*, or shanty settlements on steep hills and undeveloped land. Because the *favelas* were built on such steep slopes, often in an extremely crowded way, normal methods of garbage collection and rubbish disposal were impractical, and rubbish was often dumped on open fields or into rivers.

11.229 *Already holding a plastic bag full of empty drink cans, this favela resident is asking people to give him their empty cans as they get off the bus.*

The response of city planners was to establish collection points near the *favelas* where residents could sell their rubbish, including organic wastes, to the government in return for bus tokens that could be used at off-peak times. This brought benefits for the environment and the local people without any significant cost to the government or the bus operators, who are paid per kilometre travelled rather than by passenger numbers.

As a result of this scheme, the environmental quality of the *favelas* improved almost instantly, and many street children even began collecting rubbish from the rivers and open fields to exchange for bus tokens (figure 11.229).

11.230 *The residents of this house have left their rubbish for recycling ready for collection on an elevated metal platform outside the front of their home. Most residences in Curitiba have these elevated platforms for recyclable waste.*

11.231 *These colourful arrays of five bins are found throughout Curitiba to encourage recycling. From left to right, the bins are for paper, plastic, metal, glass and organic wastes.*

The second phase of the recycling program was encouraging all Curitiba residents to separate recyclable rubbish in their homes before collection, a measure that adds about 25% to the life span of land-fill dumps (figure 11.230). Brazilians did not have a tradition of environmental awareness or recycling, so the city planners engaged school children in an awareness campaign called 'trash is not trash' in the hope that the children would in turn influence their parents to start recycling. For example, in the period before Christmas, children were asked to bring plastic to school to recycling. A few weeks later, the children received new plastic toys, a lesson that rubbish can be recycled into new goods. Just three months after the 'trash is not trash' campaign began, 70% of Curitiba's families were separating their garbage. This has since been expanded to encourage recycling everywhere in the city (figure 11.231).

In the 1990s, a recycling station was built to separate the wastes collected. The profits from the sales of recycled goods more than paid for the running costs of the station, and also funded a number of social welfare programs for Curitiba's underprivileged population. Many of the people working in the recycling station are either re-formed drug users undergoing rehabilitation or illiterate people who would otherwise probably be begging on the streets.

Affordable housing

In the mid-1960s, Curitiba introduced a program to provide affordable housing of standard designs to low-income earners (figure 11.232). In summary, the program allowed residents to pay rent that contributed to their eventual purchase of the flat. Unfortunately, these projects were usually located on the city's outskirts at long distances from jobs and other services.

11.232 *Older, low cost houses in Curitiba.*

In 1980, the program was rejuvenated by starting a project to provide more diverse designs in housing. There was concern that previous low income housing was remote and lacked appeal, and planners wanted to give low income housing the same feeling as regular housing in order to raise the dignity of the residents.

Low income residents were therefore provided with options for the way they wished to furnish and decorate their homes. In one area on Curitiba's outskirts known as Linhão do Emprego where low cost housing had been established by in-migrants on land owned by electricity company, government-sponsored facilities such as health clinics, schools and day care centres were provided to improve the quality of life of the residents, and these in turn encouraged small businesses to establish in the area. A nearby area called Linhão do Ofício was developed with the simple idea of building low cost housing with the owner's business (such as a small shop) on the ground floor and the residence above to eliminate the costs of travelling from home to work each day.

In several areas of low-cost housing, the government has built large warehouses where local people can be trained in basic work skills and then establish their business within the warehouse. Since the project began, over 6,000 business have been established, creating more than 50,000 jobs.

Parks

Despite its high altitude (about 900 metres above sea level), Curitiba used to suffer from frequent flooding. As rural-urban migration increased in the 1960s and 1970s, this became a major problem as migrants established their settlements along the floodplains. Every year, flood waters would invade their homes, destroying their property and spreading diseases.

Whereas many cities try to solve problems of flooding by building canals and levees, Curitiba's planners decided instead to relocate the migrants and transform the floodplains into public parks. However, there were no funds available to maintain the rapidly expanding areas of green parkland. As the parks were seen as an ecological resource, it was decided to use an ecological solution to find a cheap way to maintain the parks, so sheep are used to trim the grass.

11.233 *An elevated view showing the extent of the lake and its green surrounds in Parque Barigüi in Curitiba.*

The lake in central Curitiba's largest park, Parque Barigüi, replaced over 800 houses that experienced flooding every year (figure 11.233). Every resident was paid fair compensation to leave the area and relocate to a safer part of the city. Once the people have been evacuated from the floodplain, a water management system was introduced to create an artificial lake with landscaped surrounds. It was estimated that those cost of creating the park, including the cost of relocating the people, was only 20% of the cost of building a concrete canal, as well as providing a valuable recreational resource for Curitiba's residents and tourists. Furthermore, the development of the park attracted higher class residential development in the surrounding areas, increasing the value of properties and therefore the land and property taxes collected by the government to such a level that the cost of creating the park has been repaid many times over (figure 11.234).

11.234 *The creation of Parque Barigüi raised land values in the surrounding area, attracting affluent residents to relocate in the park surrounds.*

There are more than 30 parks in Curitiba today that were created to control flooding by converting land from old flood-prone residential and industrial areas or disused quarries (figure 11.235). The total area of parklands is over 80 million square metres. In the 1960s, Curitiba had about 0.5 square metres of green space per inhabitant; by 2000, this figure had increased to 55 square metres per inhabitant. This compares with the WHO prescribed amount of green space, which is 16 square metres per inhabitant.

11.235 *In an interesting example of recycling, the "Wire Opera House" was built in a beautifully landscaped former quarry.*

QUESTION BLOCK 11X

1. Explain the key points of each of the four aspects of Curitiba's sustainable city management.

2. A former mayor of Curitiba claimed that if every city in the world adopted Curitiba's sustainable city management, the world would not be facing the challenges of global climate change today. Do you agree?

3. It has been said that Curitiba shows what a city would look like if urban planners rather than politicians designed cities. What is your opinion on Curitiba's urban planning?

Sustainable Strategies to Manage Housing in Newington (Sydney, Australia)

Newington is a unique suburb in Sydney (Australia) that was originally developed to provide housing for the participants in the 2000 Olympic Games. An important component of Sydney's successful bid to host the Olympic Games was environmental sensitivity, and Newington was a key component of the plan.

Newington contains about 2,000 houses accommodating 5,000 people in an area of 90 hectares that was a **brownfield** site (which means the new development totally replaced the previous factories and poor quality housing on the site). A key aspect of the design philosophy was to use new technologies to minimise the urban ecological footprint. For example, all buildings include solar panels that are estimate to prevent the production of about 1,300 tonnes of carbon dioxide per year, which is the equivalent of removing 261 cars from Sydney's roads.

11.236 *The suburb of Newington is seen to the right of the lakes, overlooking the site of the Sydney 2000 Olympics across the water.*

Other strategies undertaken in Newington to promote sustainable development include the planting of native species of vegetation which are drought-resistant and thus use less moisture than exotic species (figure 11.236). Furthermore, the native species are well adapted to the local soils and produce very few allergens. The extensive use of plant cover ensures that on average, 40% of the runoff infiltrates into the groundwater supply, reducing the risk of flooding.

The water cycle of the area is managed in such a way that stormwater (water collected in drains from rooftops and roadways) is diverted and used to create natural wildlife habitats. Stormwater is cleaned by passing it through pollutant traps from which it is channelled into the water quality ponds that also attract wildlife. Newington also has a dual water water system that separates drinkable water (for use in kitchens) from non-drinkable water (for use in flushing toilets).

The layout of Newington was planned as three park-centred precincts, ensuring that no home is more than five minutes walk from parklands. A shortcoming of this ideal is that the clusters of houses are somewhat separated from each other, making the development of a strong sense of community more difficult. Nonetheless, a dense network of bicycle tracks and pedestrian pathways links the residential areas with the parklands.

11.237 *Every house in Newington has a solar panel incorporated into its design.*

11.238 *The window awnings in Newington are designed to provide shade in summer but allow sunlight into the house during winter when the angle of the sun is lower.*

When the construction of Newington began in 1997, it was the largest solar village in the world. Solar panels have been incorporated into the design of every home, with 780 homes having 1,000-watt peak power solar arrays, and 339 homes having 500-watt peak solar arrays (figure 11.237). Furthermore, every house has gas-boosted solar hot water. The houses are designed so that window awnings and glazing draw heat inward during winter and

provide shade in summer (figure 11.238). About 90% of the homes are oriented within 30° east of north and 20° west of north to maximise the use of natural sunlight. The use of wool insulation , slab construction and cross-ventilation also reduce the need for artificial heating and cooling of the homes. As a result of these measures, homes in Newington use an average of 50% less energy and drinking water than conventional homes in Sydney.

11.239 *Buses provide public transport in Newington.*

Transport in Newington has also been designed with sustainable development in mind. Bus services run throughout the suburb and connect to rail and ferry services (figure 11.239). Unfortunately, the residents have not really become used to utilising the public transport provided, and like most Sydney residents, prefer to use private motor vehicles. Perhaps this is because the private company that planned Newington allotted an average of two parking places for many of the houses.

11.240 *This automated garbage truck is collecting waste for recycling, which is placed in large bins with colour coded lids to indicate the type of recyclable waste.*

Waste disposal in Newington also shows evidence of sustainability. Residents sort waste into recyclable and non-recyclable rubbish, which is collected from separately coloured large bins using highly automated trucks that compress the rubbish as it is collected (figure 11.240). Waste that is designated for landfill is compressed by 90% for hard waste and by 60% for soft waste.

Urban environments

One criticism of Newington's planning is that no provisions were made to provide low cost housing for needy people. Although the variety of housing designs and sizes does ensure a mix of incomes, few low income earners can afford to live there, despite the strong appeal of its sustainable features.

Sustainable Strategies to Manage Pollution in Graz, Austria — an example of Ecoprofit

Western Europe has a strong tradition of concern for the quality of the environment, as shown by the strong support received by environmental groups and green political movements. It is perhaps therefore not surprising that some of the most impressive examples of sustainable strategies to manage environmental pollution are found in European cities.

One example is the Ecoprofit program in the Austrian city of Graz. Also known by its German language name of Ökoprofit, Ecoprofit is the 'ECOlogical PROject For Integrated environmental Technology', a program for sustainable economic development developed by the Environment Department of the City of Graz , Austria, in 1991.

The program is intended to educate local businesses and help them identify ways in which they can improve their production processes to reduce waste and resource consumption, and thus increase profitability. It is run jointly by the city's Environment Department and and the Graz University of Technology. As an incentive to participate in the program, companies that complete the program are awarded the Ecoprofit logo, which can then be used for promotional purposes for marketing as an 'ecological market leader' (figure 11.241).

11.241 *The logo for Ökoprofit that is awarded to companies that meet the requirements of the Environment Department of the City of Graz , Austria.*

The city of Graz has a long history as an industrial centre, and therefore long-term problems with environmental pollution, especially during winter months when atmospheric temperature inversions occur. The Ecoprofit program was seen as a way to improve environmental quality beyond the reductions in pollution required by government legislation.

The program involves several stages for participating companies and organisations. First, workshops are conducted to educate managers in closed loop production techniques that maximise recycling and minimise waste. Following the workshops, each company is required to appoint a multi-disciplinary task force to co-ordinate ways of increasing efficiency and minimising waste.

The Ecoprofit logo may only used by companies that have demonstrated a significant reduction in pollution and waste. These reductions are quantified, and include a 30% reduction in solid wastes and a 50% reduction in hazardous wastes and air emissions. The logo is awarded for only one year at the time, and to retain the use of the logo, further improvements must be made annually.

The ways in which urban firms reduce pollution varies according to the type of business. For example, a crash repair workshop developed new paint spray technology that reduced overspray, while a printing company switched to water-based inks. A Ford assembly factory in Graz adopted a number of changes in the production process, including a new technique that allowed the recapture and re-use of spray paint.

Because companies participate in the Ecoprofit program on a voluntary basis, the incentives offered are very important. The main incentive is the use of the logo for marketing purposes, but participating companies also gain access to research and support from the city's university. The participating companies claim significant advantages, both as a result of the marketing benefits of the logo and from reductions in their processing costs.

The success of the Ecoprofit program has led several other European cities to adopt similar strategies. In the city of Kolding, for example, over 200 businesses have formed the Green Network, which represents a commitment to setting goals to reduce environmental pollution and improve resource efficiency. Other cities that have adopted sustainable strategies to manage pollution include Albertslund, Ealing (a suburb of London), Leicester, and Den Haag (The Hague).

QUESTION BLOCK 11Y

1. *List the features of Newington that show evidence of sustainable urban strategies.*

2. *Do you think Newington is an effective example of sustainable urban planning? Give reasons for your answer.*

3. *Explain how the Ecoprofit program in Graz works.*

4. *To what extent could the Ecoprofit program be adopted effectively in the city where you live?*

Sustainable Strategies to Control Rapid City Growth in Sydney (Australia)

By world standards, Sydney is a young city, having been established by British settlers in 1788. Since that time, the city has grown rapidly, both in terms of population size and area. Today, metropolitan Sydney has a population of about four million people and an area of approximately 4,000 square kilometres. Much of the growth has occurred since the end of World War II, during which period urban sprawl has occurred as new suburbs were built based upon transport by private motor vehicles (figure 11.242).

11.242 *Since World War II, much of Sydney's growth has been dependent on private motor vehicles.*

In December 2005, the New South Wales state government released a strategic plan to co-ordinate the future growth of Sydney called *City of Cities: A Plan for Sydney's Future*. The plan covers the period to the year 2031, during which time an growth of 1.1 million people is anticipated. The plan has five stated aims:

1. Enhance Sydney's **liveability**, by ensuring a diverse choice of housing for an ageing and changing population, close to services, while protecting the character of the suburbs and communities.

2. Strengthen Sydney's long–term economic prosperity by increasing the city's **competitiveness** in globalised markets, and sharing the benefits across all parts of the city.

3. Ensuring **fairness** by provide fair access to jobs, services and lifestyle opportunities by aligning services close to where people live, and by providing access to high quality transport.

4. Protect Sydney's **environment** and reduce the city's use of natural resources and production of waste.

5. Improve the quality of **planning** and decision making, giving the community greater confidence in governing institutions.

The underlying assumption of Sydney's plan is that population growth will continue to 2031 and beyond. In 2031, the projected population size will be 5.3 million people. According to the plan, this growth will require the development of 640,000 new homes, planning for the creation of 500,000 more jobs, 7,500 hectares of additional industrial land, 6.8 million square metres of additional commercial floor space, and 3.7 million square metres of additional space for retail activities.

11.243 *Sydney's Central Business District. The Sydney Harbour Bridge (lower right foreground) joins the CBD to North Sydney.*

11.244 *A view of North Sydney from the Sydney CBD.*

The plan articulates a vision of Sydney in 2031 which contains eight elements:

1. **Stronger Cities within the Metropolitan Area**
   As the name of the plan (*City of Cities*) implies, a key element of the plan is shifting the emphasis of future growth away from Sydney's CBD to a number of nuclei within the metropolitan area. Sydney's CBD and North Sydney (which is today really an extension of the CDB at the other end of the Harbour Bridge) will continue to be the heart of Global Sydney (figures 11.243 and 11.244). According to the plan, the CBD and North Sydney will form the focus for international business, tourism, cultural, health, education and entertainment activities. This will be supplemented by several suburban cities that are located to the west of Sydney's CBD — Parramatta, Liverpool and Penrith —

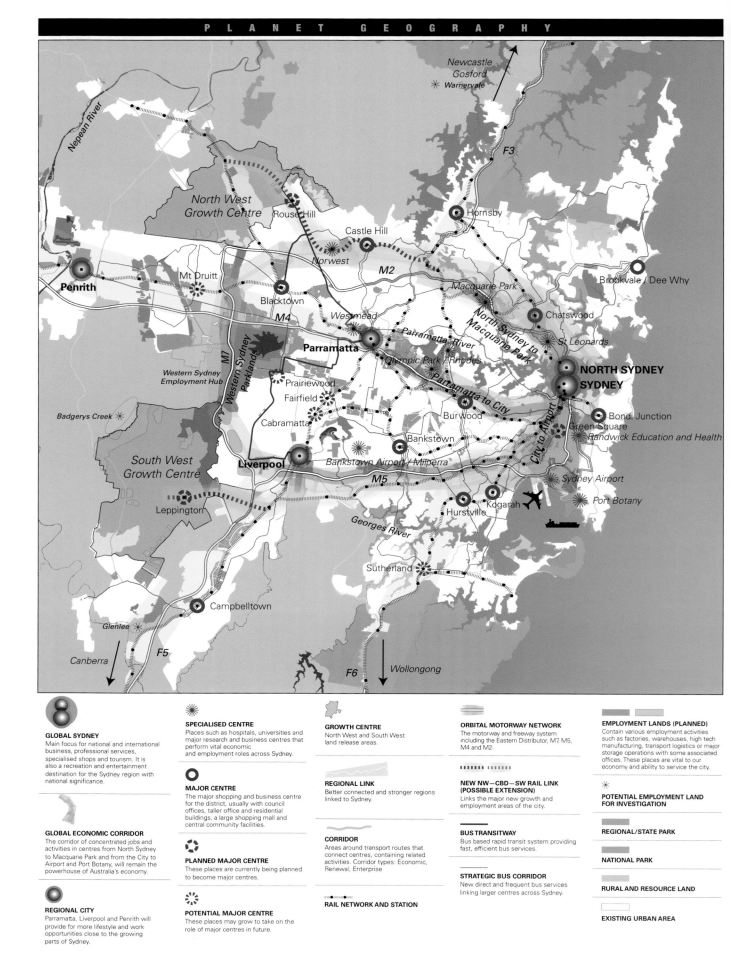

11.245 *A map showing the main elements of the Sydney Strategic Plan.*

Source: adapted from 'Cities of Cities - A Plan for Sydney's Future', © Copyright 2005, New South Wales Department of Planning.

GLOBAL SYDNEY
Main focus for national and international business, professional services, specialised shops and tourism. It is also a recreation and entertainment destination for the Sydney region with national significance.

GLOBAL ECONOMIC CORRIDOR
The corridor of concentrated jobs and activities in centres from North Sydney to Macquarie Park and from the City to Airport and Port Botany, will remain the powerhouse of Australia's economy.

REGIONAL CITY
Parramatta, Liverpool and Penrith will provide for more lifestyle and work opportunities close to the growing parts of Sydney.

SPECIALISED CENTRE
Places such as hospitals, universities and major research and business centres that perform vital economic and employment roles across Sydney.

MAJOR CENTRE
The major shopping and business centre for the district, usually with council offices, taller office and residential buildings, a large shopping mall and central community facilities.

PLANNED MAJOR CENTRE
These places are currently being planned to become major centres.

POTENTIAL MAJOR CENTRE
These places may grow to take on the role of major centres in future.

GROWTH CENTRE
North West and South West land release areas.

REGIONAL LINK
Better connected and stronger regions linked to Sydney.

CORRIDOR
Areas around transport routes that connect centres, containing related activities. Corridor types: Economic, Renewal, Enterprise

RAIL NETWORK AND STATION

ORBITAL MOTORWAY NETWORK
The motorway and freeway system including the Eastern Distributor, M7, M5, M4 and M2.

NEW NW—CBD—SW RAIL LINK (POSSIBLE EXTENSION)
Links the major new growth and employment areas of the city.

BUS TRANSITWAY
Bus based rapid transit system providing fast, efficient bus services.

STRATEGIC BUS CORRIDOR
New direct and frequent bus services linking larger centres across Sydney.

EMPLOYMENT LANDS (PLANNED)
Contain various employment activities such as factories, warehouses, high tech manufacturing, transport logistics or major storage operations with some associated offices. These places are vital to our economy and ability to service the city.

POTENTIAL EMPLOYMENT LAND FOR INVESTIGATION

REGIONAL/STATE PARK

NATIONAL PARK

RURAL AND RESOURCE LAND

EXISTING URBAN AREA

which will provide business opportunities, employment and lifestyle opportunities close to the rapidly expanding areas of Sydney's western suburbs).

2. Strong Global Economic Corridor

In an attempt to decentralise the focus of economic activity away from the CBD, two corridors of employment and economic activity have been identified which will radiate out of the CDB and into the middle suburbs (figure 11.245). One such corridor will extend from North Sydney to Macquarie Park (figure 11.246), while another extends from the CBD to Sydney Airport and nearby Port Botany (figure 11.247). As well as providing land for industrial and commercial development, these corridors were identified as priority areas for high quality transport access.

11.246 *New hi-tech factories and offices in the suburb of Macquarie Park tap into research undertaken at the nearby Macquarie University.*

11.247 *The container wharves at Port Botany, on Botany Bay in Sydney's southern suburbs.*

3. More Employment in Western Sydney

Most of the Sydney's growth in coming decades is expected in Sydney's western suburbs, where the land is flatter than elsewhere (making building costs cheaper) and land prices are lower. The Plan calls for a specific emphasis on job creation in Western Sydney, including support for emerging clusters of high value

health and education activities. Western Sydney's low population density makes the provision of profitable high-frequency public transport very difficult, so it is planned to link Western Sydney with other areas via a network of orbital motorways.

4. Contain Sydney's Expanding Area (Urban Footprint)

Sydney has already experienced urban sprawl which has developed a high dependency on private motor vehicles. Under the Plan, valuable remaining rural and resource lands will be recognised and protected. Furthermore, new land will not be released for urban development unless it meets the Government's sustainability criteria.

11.248 *The high rise buildings indicate the suburb of Chatswood, which has emerged as a significant business centre in its own right.*

5. Major Centres will emerge for Employment, Services and Residential Land-Use

Major suburban centres such as Bankstown, Blacktown, Bondi Junction, Brookvale/Dee Why, Burwood, Campbelltown, Castle Hill, Chatswood, Hornsby, Hurstville and Kogarah will become focal areas for shopping, health and tertiary education (figure 11.248). To support these functions, the density of housing around these centres will be increased to include medium and high density housing.

6. Fair Access to Jobs, Housing, Services and Open Space

As well as looking at the locations of future development, *City of Cities* looks at the quality of life to be enjoyed by Sydney's future residents. Planning for suburban centres and neighbourhoods will be intended to provide healthier environments and access to high quality and suitable housing, jobs, transport choices and open space (figure 11.249). The Plan calls for a mix of housing types interspersed with parks and public places throughout the metropolitan area.

7. Connected Centres

City of Cities calls for an expansion and improvement of the transport network to provide better access to jobs and services in the global economic corridor (fig-

11.249 *Cronulla, a residential area in Sydney's southern suburbs.*

11.250 *The future development of Sydney will rely increasingly on the suburban railway network, which uses double deck carriages to maximise capacity while also providing seats for most passengers.*

ure 11.250). Significant investment in the rail network is planned, and planned strategic bus corridors will provide faster and direct public transport linking suburban centres and areas where jobs will be concentrated.

8. **Better Connected and Stronger Regions**
City of Cities focuses on Sydney's links with surrounding regions, emphasising the importance of improving transport and communication links with the Central Coast and Hunter Valley regions to the north, and to the Illawarra region to the south. It is expected that

the Central Coast (focussed on the town of Gosford) will expand its current role as an outer commuter zone for Sydney and develop jobs within the region to provide more local employment options. The Hunter Valley (centred on Newcastle) has a long history of manufacturing and mining, but future development is likely to see these areas decline as the regional economy diversifies. The Illawarra region also has a long history of mining and manufacturing, and like the Hunter Valley, will probably diversify its economy in coming decades.

The release of *City of Cities* was welcomed by a majority of Sydney residents and commentators, many of whom were concerned about the growing unsustainability of Sydney's rapid growth. It is hoped that the plan may provide a realistic example for other cities in MEDCs that are experiencing rapid growth and urban sprawl.

QUESTION BLOCK 11Z

1. *What evidence is there that Sydney has been experiencing rapid growth, and how has this affected its environmental sustainability?.*

2. *Do you think the five aims of* City of Cities *are necessary? Do you think they are sufficient? Explain why or why not.*

3. *Rank the eight elements of* City of Cities *in what you think is their descending order of importance. Justify your rank order.*

4. *To what extent do you think the strategies in* City of Cities *to promote sustainable development could be used in other cities in MEDCs?*

12

Measuring global interactions

Geographers study global interactions with a broader perspective than more conventional studies of globalisation that emphasise a linear process involving the domination and imposition of western culture upon the world.

Global Participation

What is Globalisation?

Protests against globalisation are becoming common in countries across the world. Newspapers and television news broadcasts carry images of masked protesters trashing multinational brand shops, shouting and carrying placards. To the demonstrators, the word 'globalisation' seems to embrace all that anyone can find wrong with the state of the world.

Protesters claim that globalisation is to blame for such diverse problems as unemployment, child labour, and environmental decay, and the agents of globalisation are multinational companies, the World Trade Organisation, and even American fast food and pop music. They blame globalisation for sharp fluctuations in global finance, such as the Global Financial Crisis that occurred in 2008 and 2009.

And yet, others claim that globalisation is not inevitable and beneficial. Supporters of globalisation claim that it has created millions of jobs from Malaysia to Mexico, and

ToK BoX — Page 559
Bias

has brought a huge range of affordable goods to consumers in the More Economically Developed Countries (MEDCs) and elsewhere. Globalisation is also claimed to have brought telephone services to some 300 million households in Less Economically Developed Countries (LEDCs) and a transfer of nearly $US2 trillion from LEDCs to MEDCs through equity, bond investments, and commercial loans. It is claimed that globalisation has helped topple dictators by making information available in once closed societies. Furthermore, it is claimed that the internet is about to narrow the gap that separates MEDCs from LEDCs.

For supporters of globalisation, it is little wonder that the rage that is shown against globalisation is so puzzling.

In order to understand the debate, it is necessary to understand the term **globalisation**. Dictionaries differ in their definition of 'globalisation', but they tend to say something like 'to make world-wide in scope or application'. This is a very broad definition, and in this form, globalisation has been occurring since the beginning of human history, although at a slower pace than today. The sequencing of the human genome suggests strongly that

>> Some Useful Definitions for Chapters 12 to 18

Cultural imperialism — the practice of promoting the culture or language of one nation in another. It is usually the case that the former is a large, economically or militarily powerful nation and the latter is a smaller, less affluent one.

Globalisation — according to the International Monetary Fund (IMF): "the growing interdependence of countries worldwide through the increasing volume and variety of cross-border transactions in goods and services and of international capital flows, and through the more rapid and widespread diffusion of technology".

Globalisation Index — the A.T. Kearney index is one of several measures of globalisation. It tracks changes in four key components of global integration: trade and investment flows; movement of people across borders; volumes of international telephone traffic and Internet usage; participation in international organisations. (source: A.T. Kearney; *Foreign Policy*).

Glocalisation — a term that was invented in order to emphasise that the globalisation of a product is more likely to succeed when the product or service is adapted specifically to each locality or culture it is marketed in. The increasing presence of McDonald's restaurants worldwide is an example of globalisation, while the changes in the menus of the restaurant chain that are designed to appeal to local tastes are an example of glocalisation.

Out-sourcing — the concept of taking internal company functions and paying an outside firm to handle them. Outsourcing is done to save money, improve quality, or free company resources for other activities.

Time-space convergence — the reduction in the time taken to travel between two places due to improvements in transportation or communication technology.

---

the ancestors of all humans alive today came from Africa. It could be said that globalisation began when the first human beings began moving in search of better food and safety, and that movement has never stopped.

During the 1990s, the term 'globalisation' came to mean something much narrower – the rise of market capitalism around the world. The International Monetary Fund defines globalisation as 'the growing economic interdependence of countries world-wide through the increasing volume and variety of cross-border transactions in goods and services and of international capital flows, and also through the more rapid and widespread diffusion of technology'. The OECD, through the author Tatyana Soubbotina, defines 'globalisation' a little more simply as 'the growing interdependence of countries resulting from the increasing integration of trade, finance, people and ideas in one global marketplace'. The geographer Peter Haggett defines it as 'the process by which events, activities and decisions in one part of the world can have significant consequences for communities in distant parts of the globe'.

Most people are aware that ideas from one country move more quickly to other countries now than at any time in world history. The term 'globalisation' is often applied to the spread of economic, social and cultural ideas across the world, and the growing uniformity between different places that results from this spread. The result of globalisation is a dilution of economic, social and cultural differences between places.

Writing in the Hong Kong-based journal, *Far Eastern Economic Review*, the Indian economist Nayan Chanda offered the following comment on the debate over globalisation:

"Acknowledging globalisation as a secular trend of human history does not mean accepting the unfairness, injustice and inequality that have come in its wake. The leisurely pace of the past is over. Goods, ideas and culture are rushing across national borders with unthinkable speed and unprecedented volume – overwhelming many, and affecting their lives in ways that are beyond their control. Today's protesters are right to draw attention to these negative aspects. Certainly the pernicious aspects of globalisation need to be addressed and prudently remedied. However, protesters are wrong to think that the restless movement of people and ideas across the globe can be arrested, and by so doing solve its marginal ill-effects. To be sure, fix globalisation. But to demand a stop to globalisation is to demand that life as we know it should cease".

Globalisation is a significant geographical issue in today's world, and chapters 12 to 18 will attempt to explain it.

QUESTION BLOCK 12A

1. *Which of the definitions of 'globalisation' do you think is most useful? Explain why.*

2. *Having read the short piece on globalisation by Nayan Chanda, state whether you think his view of globalisation is overly-positive, overly-negative, or realistic. Give reasons to support your answer.*

Theories of Globalisation and Global Interactions

Globalisation is a complex and controversial concept. Some people regard globalisation as an economic process, some as political, while others see the concept more broadly, embracing a range of social, political, cultural and economic forces. Studying globalisation is complicated by the fact that it no longer a 'neutral' word, and many commentators use the word as a judgement – both positively and negatively. When used as an adjective, the word 'global' is useful to describe a scale that encompasses the entire planet – it has no connotation politically of 'good' or 'bad'. However, when used as a noun, the word 'globalisation' is very different. It was described by geographer Phil O'Neill as 'one of the most powerful words in human history, rivalling words such as religion, capitalism, war and poverty in terms of description of world events, concern for the human condition, and impact on ways of thinking'.

The various ways that people view globalisation can be grouped conveniently into four theories of globalisation, each of which overlaps to some extent with the others.

The World-Economy Theory (or Hyperglobalisation-ism)

Hyperglobalists would define globalisation as the process by which the capitalist world-system spreads across the entire globe (figure 12.1). They would argue that the global market place has become (or is becoming) so advanced and integrated that the nation-state is becoming obsolete; this argument is developed further in chapter 17. Some hyperglobalists argue that this is a good thing because the market is more rational than govern-ments could ever be. On the other hand, other hyper-globalists argue it is a bad thing because corporate power is usually less compassionate than governments, most of which are, after all, accountable to the population through elections (unlike companies and corporations).

12.1 *A symbol of hyperglobalisation, or world-economy theory — a McDonald's outlet in Shanghai, China.*

Many hyperglobalists would argue that this process nearly reached its geographical limit during the 1990s as the capitalist market system seemed to be operating, at least to some extent, in every country in the world. They would argue that it is simply the completion of a process begun in the late 1400s and early 1500s when European countries began exploring the globe for raw materials, often establishing colonies to guarantee the supply of the materials needed.

Hyperglobalists argue that the world-economy now comprises a single world market and a single, mobile labour force (that happens to be located in many nation-states which may have different cultural priorities and

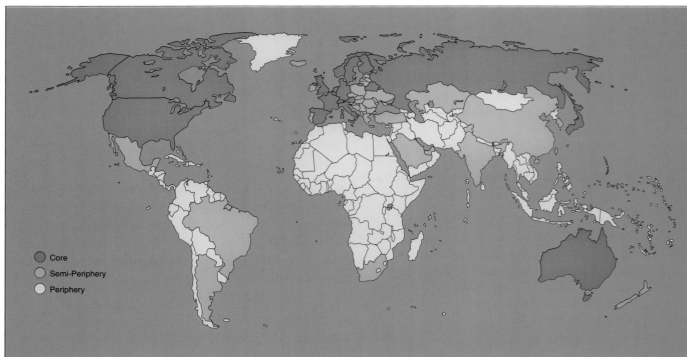

12.2 *Core and periphery in an era of globalisation.*

ToK BoX

Bias.

Globalisation is a controversial issue. Many writings on the subject are accused of being biased.

The term bias refers to prejudice in favour of or against one thing, person, or group compared with another, usually in a way considered to be unfair. It is a negatively loaded word.

There are three types of bias found in geographical writings:

• Hindsight bias — the account is different from what it would otherwise have been because with the wisdom of hindsight; this is especially so with historical writings;

• National bias — the written account reflects the perspective of one particular nation or culture, usually that of the writer;

• Confirmation (or selection) bias — the writer is tempted to use only evidence that supports a prior viewpoint.

In geographical writings on globalisation, the most common type of bias writers are accused of is selection bias.

It would be impossible for any author to include every fact or every point of view in a piece of writing on globalisation, or any other topic for that matter, just as it

would be impossible for any person to record every single detail of even one day of their life on paper. It is necessary to omit certain details that are less relevant in order not to drown the essential message in a deluge of irrelevant data.

Whenever a choice is made about what to include or what to leave out, the potential for bias arises. Bias may be deliberate or it may be accidental, but some bias is probably inevitable as soon as decisions are made about what points should be included and what points should be omitted.

When writings are criticised for being biased, it usually means that the reader disagrees with the viewpoint being expressed. Somehow, it sounds like a more sophisticated criticism to assert that writing is biased than for the reader simply to say that he or she disagrees with it.

However, any accusation of bias in writing should be supported with specific evidence of ways in which the writing lacks balance. It is not sufficient to claim that certain points have been omitted, because this is inevitable in any piece of writing, just as it is inevitable that many details must be omitted from any map.

More significant evidence of bias would be that the points chosen to have been omitted were in some way significant, or even pivotal, in preventing the reader gaining a complete understanding of the issue being discussed.

Even then, the bias arising may be intentional or unintentional. If the author's bias was intended to mislead the reader into adopting a certain point of view, then it could be regarded as a form of indoctrination.

Often, bias is in the mind of the reader. Two people may read the same piece of writing, with one concluding it is a biased piece of writing designed to manipulate the reader, while the other defends it as a fine and cogent statement of a particular argument or viewpoint.

Accusations of bias frequently reveal much more about the person making the accusation than the piece of writing being examined.

Now, after you have read Section 3 of this book, which deals with globalisation, ask yourself whether the things you read were biased, and if so, justify your opinion.

The next ToK BoX is on page 575.

---

aspirations). Countries in the core of this world-economy concentrate on higher-skill, capital-intensive production. These countries have strong armed forces, and they consume much of the profits of the whole world-economy. In contrast to the core countries, peripheral areas focus on low-skill, labour-intensive production and the extraction of raw materials; they generally have weaker armed forces and weaker economies. Between the two extremes of the core countries and the peripheral areas, there are semi-peripheral areas that are less dependent on the core than the peripheral areas are – these semi-peripheral areas have more diversified economies and stronger military forces than the peripheral countries (figure 12.2). Today, the core is made up of the wealthy industrialised countries, such as the USA, Britain, France, Germany and Japan. The semi-periphery includes many states with rapidly growing or emerging economies, such as China, India, Saudi Arabia, Brazil and Poland. Poorer, recently independent colonies are the main countries comprising the periphery.

The Regional Bloc Theory (or Global Scepticism)

Global sceptics disagree strongly with hyperglobalists. They would dispute that a single world market exists, and they would argue that the growing internationalisa-

tion of trade and investment is really the growth of regional economic blocs, such as the European Union.

The growth of regional trading blocs has benefited some countries (mainly those within the blocs) and disadvantaged others, marginalising them from the benefits of economic growth and development. Global sceptics view globalisation not as a reality, but as a strategy to expand capitalism, which is why sometimes violent protects against globalisation erupt from time to time.

According to the regional bloc theory, there is no single government or institution guiding the process (or, rather, strategy) of globalisation, although there is a general acceptance among economic decision-makers that capitalism is a worthwhile framework of reference. Many global sceptics see this unquestioning acceptance of capitalism as being the root of the problem of globalisation, as capitalism in its pure form emphasises competition and financial efficiency over compassion and care for oppressed and disempowered people. As former IB Director-General George Walker commented, "Globalisation looks very different when it is seen, not from the capitals of the West, but from the cities and villages of the South, where most of humanity lives".

The Third Way Theory (or Transformationalism)

A third view of globalisation seeks to find a relationship between economic processes occurring at the global and local scales. This theory is sometimes known as the **transformational** view because it looks for ways of transforming the powers of the nation-state to cope with the pressures of globalisation, rather than simply focussing on the global forces that reduce the powers of the nation-state. Transformationalists therefore seek to challenge existing institutions to reform or restructure, or encourage greater local autonomy. The transformational view is often linked to a political agenda, especially in Europe, where it is popularly known as 'the third way'. The Third Way theory is summed up by the commonly used exhortation: 'Think Globally, Act Locally'.

For transformationalists, the challenge of globalisation is to maintain diversity in the face of economic forces that encourage uniformity. This desire to preserve and celebrate difference against cultural homogenisation is shared with many people who see globalisation in terms of the fourth theory – the world-culture theory.

The World-Culture Theory (or Homogenism)

The three theories mentioned above all view globalisation primarily as an economic process, or economic force. The world-culture theory, in contract, sees globalisation more broadly, being the increasing uniformity (or homogenisation) of cultures across the world. Whereas the three previous theories view the growth of a single world culture as a possible consequence of globalisation, the world-culture theory views this as an integral part of globalisation.

This will be explored more fully in chapters 16 and 18.

QUESTION BLOCK 12B

1. What is meant by the term globalisation?

2. Explain the differences between the four theories of globalisation.

Globalisation Indices

Measuring globalisation is more difficult than describing it. Two attempts that have been made to quantify globalisation are the AT Kearney Index and the KOF Index.

AT Kearney is a global management consulting firm that advises large corporations on international competitiveness. Founded in 1926, the company's headquarters is in Chicago (USA) and it has 51 offices in 34 countries in five continents. In conjunction with *Foreign Policy* magazine, AT Kearney publishes an annual Globalisation Index. The AT Kearney Globalisation Index assesses the extent to which the world's most populated countries are becoming more or less globally connected.

The AT Kearney Index analyses the 72 countries that account for 97% of the world's GDP and contain 88% of the world's population. Twelve variables are examined, divided into four aspects of globalisation:

- **political engagement**, including participation in treaties, organisations, and peacekeeping

- **technological connectivity**, including the number of internet users, hosts, and secure servers

- **personal contact**, including telephone, travel and remittances

- **economic integration**, including international trade and foreign direct investment

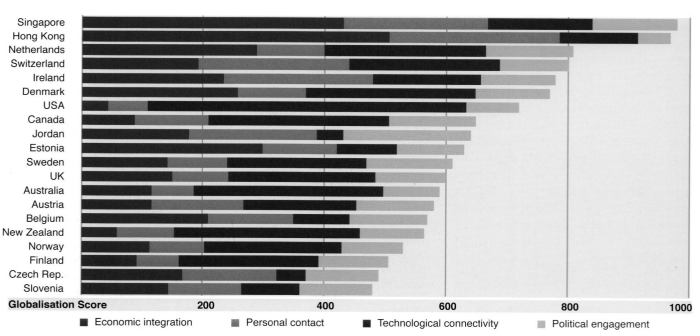

12.3 *The 20 most globalised nations according to the AT Kearney Index (2007).*

The result of the 2007 analysis is shown in figure 12.3, which shows the 20 most globalised countries at the time according to the index. Figure 12.3 also provides some insight into the factors contributing to globalisation in different countries. For example, Singapore (the world's most globalised nation according to the index) scores strongly on all four factors, and especially on economic integration. The United States ranked seventh overall, but this was largely due to its high level of technological connectivity. In contrast, Jordan had a low level of technological connectivity but higher levels of economic integration, personal contact and political engagement than the US.

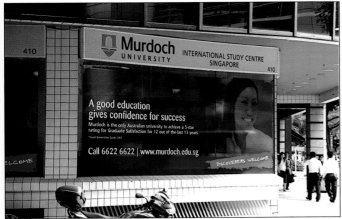

12.4 *Advertising for international education in Singapore, the world's most globalised nation according to the AT Kearney Index of Globalisation.*

Ghana (not shown in figure 12.3 because it ranked 33rd overall) came second in the world's rankings for political globalisation because of its high level of participation in treaties, peacekeeping, and international organisations, but lagged severely in technological connectivity.

At the lower end of the scale, the lowest five countries in the AT Kearney survey in 2007 were (from last to fifth last) Iran, India, Algeria, Indonesia, and Venezuela (figures 12.4 and 12.5). This does not mean these countries were the least globalised in the world, simply that they

12.4 *Advertising to promote national identity in Tehran, Iran, the least globalised nation on the AT Kearney Index of Globalisation.*

Table 12.1

Weightings of the components of the KOF Index of Globalisation

Indices and Variables	Weights
A. ECONOMIC GLOBALISATION	**38%**
i. Actual Flows	**50%**
Trade (% of GDP)	19%
Foreign direct investment, flows (% of GDP)	20%
Foreign direct investment, stocks (% of GDP)	23%
Portfolio investment ((% of GDP)	17%
Income payments for foreign nationals (% of GDP)	21%
ii. Restrictions	**50%**
Hidden import barriers	21%
Mean tariff rate	29%
Taxes on international trade (% of current revenue)	25%
Capital account restrictions	25%
B. SOCIAL GLOBALISATION	**39%**
i. Data on personal contact	**50%**
Telephone traffic	26%
Transfers (% of GDP)	3%
International tourism	26%
Foreign population (% of total population)	20%
International letters (per capita)	26%
ii. Data on information flows	**34%**
Internet users (per 1,000 people)	36%
Televisions (per 1,000 people)	36%
Trade in newspapers (% of GDP)	28%
iii. Data on cultural proximity	**32%**
Number of McDonald's restaurants (per capita)	37%
Number of Ikea stores (per capita)	39%
Trade in books (% of GDP)	24%
C. POLITICAL GLOBALISATION	**23%**
Embassies in the country	25%
Membership in international organisations	28%
Participation in UN Security Council missions	22%
International treaties	25%

Source: Dreher, A, Gaston, N & Martens, P (2008) *Measuring Globalisation - Gauging its Consequence*, New York: Springer.

were the least globalised among the 72 countries that were included in the survey.

Another attempt to measure globalisation is the KOF Index, which was introduced in 2002 and refined in 2008. KOF is the Swiss Institute for Business Cycle Research (Konjunkturforschungsstelle), a branch of ETH (Eidgenössische Technische Hochschule, or the Swiss Federal Institute of Technology) in Zurich, Switzerland.

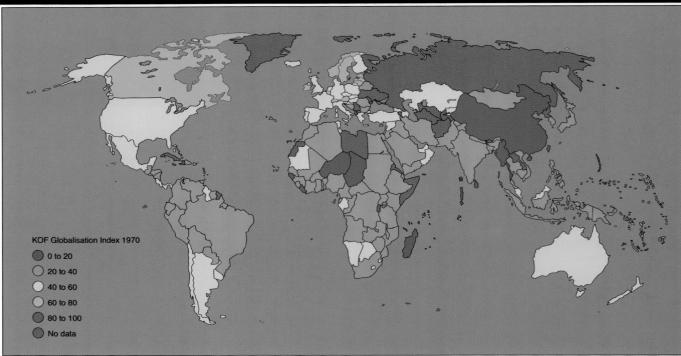

12.6 *World pattern of globalisation in 1970 according to the KOF Index of Globalisation.*

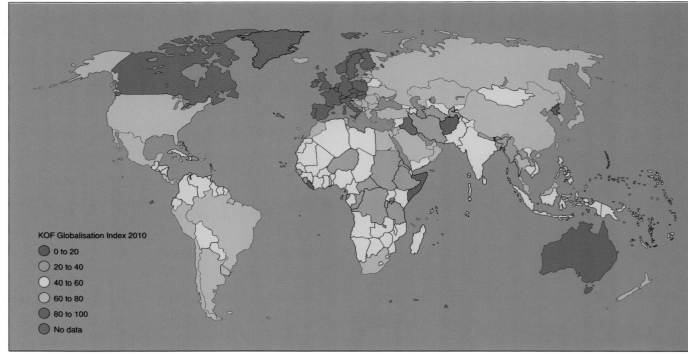

12.7 *World pattern of globalisation in 2010 according to the KOF Index of Globalisation.*

KOF defines globalisation as "the process of creating networks of connections among actors at multi-continental distances, mediated through a variety of flows including people, information and ideas, capital and goods". KOF then amplifies this by stating "Globalisation is conceptualised as a process that erodes national boundaries, integrates national economies, cultures, technologies and governance and produces complex relations of mutual interdependence."

Using this foundation, KOF examines 181 countries and territories with respect to three facets of globalisation:

economic globalisation, political globalisation and social globalisation. The components of each of these three facets of globalisation, together with the weightings that KOF gives to each, are shown in table 12.1.

To construct its Index of Globalisation, KOF transforms each of the variables in table 12.1 into an index using a scale of 1 to 100, where 100 is the maximum value for a specific variable during the period since 1970, and 1 is the minimum value for the same period. Higher values indicate a greater degree of globalisation in that country.

KOF's analysis shows that globalisation has been a growing pattern since 1970 (figures 12.6 and 12.7). According to the KOF Index of Globalisation, the world's most globalised country is Belgium, with a score of 92.95, followed by Austria (92.51), the Netherlands (91.90) and Switzerland (90.55). The least globalised countries according to the KOF Index are Myanmar (20.69), Kiribati (25.45), the Solomon Islands (26.35), Equatorial Guinea (26.85) and Laos (28.12). However, it should be remembered that KOF does not calculate precise figures for other countries that would certainly have extremely low rates of globalisation, such as Afghanistan, Somalia, North Korea and Liberia.

QUESTION BLOCK 12C

1. *Compare the factors that are measured in the AT Kearney and KOF Indices of Globalisation.*

2. *Describe the changing pattern of globalisation shown in figures 12.6 and 12.7.*

3. *Which of the two indices — AT Kearney and KOF — do you consider is more useful? Give reasons to support your answer.*

Global Core and Periphery

Global Core and Periphery

In chapter 2 the **core-periphery** model was discussed with reference to development. As explained in chapter 2, the core-periphery model attempts to explain the distribution of human activity in terms of the unequal distribution of power in politics, societies and economies. The model looks at the world as a single unit and suggests that **growth poles** have developed where economic and political power is concentrated. These areas, known as the **core**, tend to be in the MEDCs of Europe and North America, and they dominate world economic activity. On the other hand, there is a **periphery** (which means 'edge') — mainly the LEDCs — where there is a lack of power in the processes of economic and political decision-making. between these two extremes are the nations of the **semi-periphery** which have more power and influence than the periphery but not as much as the core.

Since the industrial revolution in the early 1800s, the nations of the core have tended to be where manufacturing has occurred, using raw materials obtained from the nations of the periphery (figure 12.8). The relationship shown in figure 12.8 allowed the world's major manufacturing regions to develop, often based on the location of coal fields (as coal was the major source of industrial energy), but also on the pattern of world trade that developed in the 1800s and early 1900s when European powers

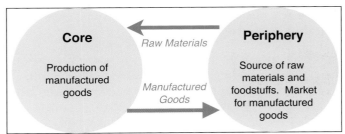

12.8 *Core and periphery in the global economy.*

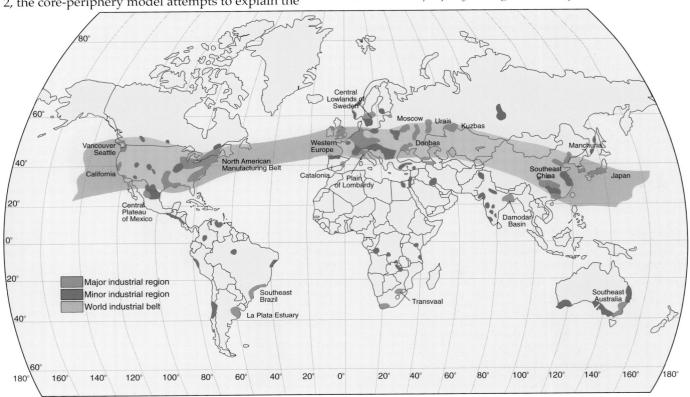

12.9 *The world distribution of heavy manufacturing.*

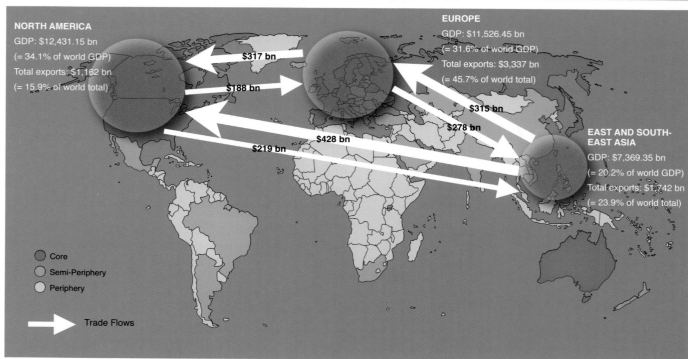

NORTH AMERICA
GDP: $12,431.15 bn
(= 34.1% of world GDP)
Total exports: $1,162 bn
(= 15.9% of world total)

EUROPE
GDP: $11,526.45 bn
(= 31.6% of world GDP)
Total exports: $3,337 bn
(= 45.7% of world total)

$317 bn

$188 bn

$315 bn

$278 bn

$428 bn

$219 bn

EAST AND SOUTH-EAST ASIA
GDP: $7,369.35 bn
(= 20.2% of world GDP)
Total exports: $1,742 bn
(= 23.9% of world total)

Core
Semi-Periphery
Periphery

Trade Flows

12.10 *Global core and periphery, showing world GDP and exports.*

brought raw materials from their colonies that were spread across the world (figure 12.9).

As the colonies of the European powers gained independence, trading relationships around the world became less predictable though not necessarily more just or fair (figures 12.12 and 12.13). Since the early 1970s, global economic growth has become more volatile, with periods of rapid growth interspersed with periods of recession or stagnation. As the world's economies have become more **interconnected** and integrated, fluctuations

in economic growth in certain major economies such as Japan and the US have had global consequences.

In 1985, the Japanese management author Kenichi Ohmae introduced the term **global triad** to describe the structure of the world economy, with a tripolar core in North America, Europe and East Asia. Today, these three macro-regions contain 86% of both world GDP and world merchandise exports, and they are the focus of most of the world's foreign direct investments (figure 12.10).

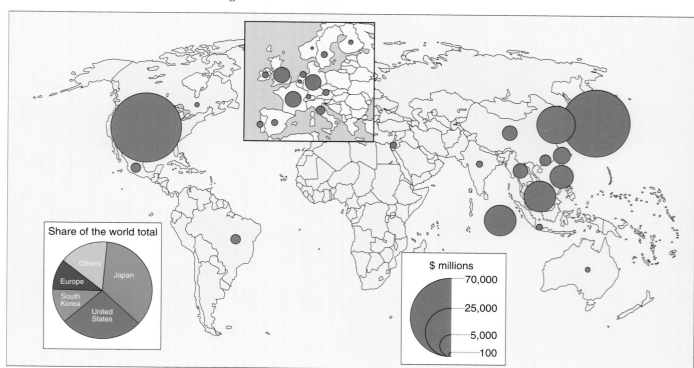

Share of the world total

Others
Japan
Europe
South Korea
United States

$ millions
70,000
25,000
5,000
100

12.11 *World production of active electronic components.*

12.12 *The flow of global capital now has an impact even in the world's most remote countries. In this photo, a large advertisement for the Capital Bank stretches right across the street in Ulaan Bataar, Mongolia. From 1921 to 1990 Mongolia was a communist country where capitalist activities such as investing in capital were strictly forbidden.*

As globalisation grows in importance as an agent of global integration, the gap between the core and periphery seems to be widening. Many manufacturers in MEDCs are shifting production to LEDCs where labour costs are lower, but the profits are tending to remain with the parent companies in the MEDCs. As shown in figure 12.11, which shows the state of the world's electronics industry, industrial relocation tends to be occurring to semi-periphery countries rather than those nations of the periphery. In this way, the gap between the core and the periphery is widening in the opinion of many commentators.

12.13 *Evidence of increasing global economic integration - the US-based KFC and the UK-based Tesco supermarket outlets are prominent features of the northern Chinese city of Dandong.*

QUESTION BLOCK 12D

1. Explain how the core-periphery model helps us to understand the distribution of economic and political power in the world today.

2. With reference to figures 12.10 and 12.11, describe the evidence that the world economy today is structured as a core and periphery.

13

Changing space: the shrinking world

Improved information and communications technology and transport are fundamental to all forms of global interaction.

Outline

Time-space convergence and the reduction in the friction of distance   Page 566

A reduction in the friction of distance results in time-space convergence. The relative changes in the speed and capacity of types of transport responsible for flows of goods, materials and people.

Extension and density of networks   Page 568

Changes in a network in terms of the extension of links and nodes, and the intensity of use at a national and global scale. The role of information and communications technology (ICT) in the transmission and flow of images, ideas, information and finance. Contrasting rates, levels and patterns of adoption of ICT.

ToK BoX — Page 575
Maps and reality

Time-Space Convergence

The Role of Global Transport

Changes in transportation are a powerful agent in globalisation. In recent decades, technological changes in air, sea and land transport have reduced travel times and lowered costs dramatically. A

journey by sailing ship across the Atlantic Ocean from Europe to North America that took 55 days in the mid-1600s was reduced to three weeks in the early 1800s with the introduction of steam-ships. By 1900, technical developments in steamships had reduced this travelling time to just one week. When aircraft were introduced in the 1920s, journey times fell to a day. Today, a trans-Atlantic flight

13.1 *While developments in transport such as jet airliners have resulted in time-space compression, many people in the world spend their lives in local space using transport that is no faster than this bullock cart.*

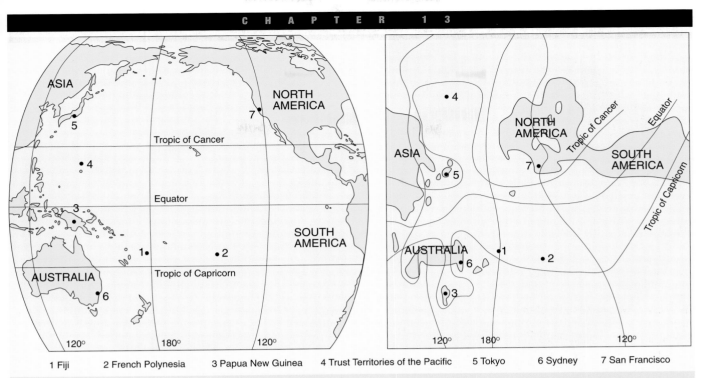

| 1 Fiji | 2 French Polynesia | 3 Papua New Guinea | 4 Trust Territories of the Pacific | 5 Tokyo | 6 Sydney | 7 San Francisco |

(a) 'Conventional' projection of the Pacific Basin.

(b) Time-space map of the Pacific Basin, based on relative time accessibility by scheduled airline.

13.2 *Mapping time-space convergence, where places appear to move together or apart.*

between London and New York takes about seven hours in a jet airliner (figure 13.1).

We often hear the expression 'the world is shrinking'. The expression is not meant literally, and fifty kilometres today is still the same fifty kilometres it was a century and a millennium ago. However, the expression conveys the idea that longer distances are becoming easier to cover in a shorter and shorter period of time. Developments in transportation, especially in rail and air transport, have resulted in shrinking the relationship between time and space.

The expression **time-space convergence** was devised by the geographer Donald Janelle in 1969 to define this process of shrinking time/space. Janelle said that improvements in transport technology have the effect of 'moving' places towards one another, reducing the significance of time as a measure of distance between the two places. He argued that the velocity at which places are moving towards each other can be measured as a 'time-space convergence rate'. For example, Sydney and Brisbane are approximately 1,000 kilometres apart. In 1909, it took three days to travel between Sydney and Brisbane by coastal steamer boat, but in 2009 it today just one hour and 25 minutes by aeroplane. Therefore, we can say that time-space convergence rate between Sydney and Brisbane was about 42 minutes per year over a 100 year period. In 1909 it took 4,320 minutes, and in 2009 just 85 minutes; the difference is 4,235 minutes, divided by 100.

On the other hand, if we were to make the journey between Sydney and Brisbane by ship, the reduction in time over the past century would be much less. Time-space convergence is greater with air transport than it has been by road or rail, which in turn have shown greater time-space convergence than ocean transport.

The result of time-space convergence is shown in figure 13.2. Figure 13.2a is a conventional map of the Pacific Basin. Figure 13.2b shows the same area distorted to reflect time-space relationships. In other words, distances in figure 13.2b are measured not by absolute distance, but by the time taken to travel between two points. When travelling time is taken into account, points with good connections such as Tokyo, Sydney and San Francisco appear to move towards each other, while others such as Papua New Guinea appear to move further away.

However, even places that were once remote in distance or distant culturally are now much more accessible than they used to be. This is evident in figure 13.3, which shows the travel time to major cities from all points in the world, together with major shipping routes. Better connectivity is shown by lighter colours and greater isolation is indicated by darker colours.

It is important to remember that time-space convergence has not occurred evenly for people in all parts of the world. There are many people in the world today who still spend their lives in 'local space', which means they remain in the area where they know everyone by sight even if they don't know all their names.

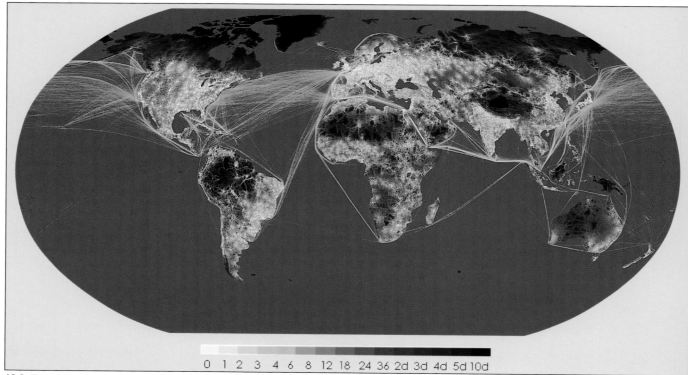

13.3 *Travel time to the nearest city of 50,000 or more people (in hours and days) and shipping lane density.* (Map copyright © European Communities, 2008)

QUESTION BLOCK 13A

1. *Explain why time-space convergence occurs at different rates in various parts of the world.*

2. *Write about 10 lines to describe the pattern shown in figure 13.3.*

Extension and Density of Networks

The Changing Nature of Air Transport in China

Transport is a key element in the development of any nation as soon as trading and communications links begin to develop. For some countries such as the United States and the United Kingdom, railways provided important transport links at key times of national development. For other more recently settled and more sparsely populated countries such as Canada and Australia, air transport have served an important role in opening up new areas for settlement.

Although China has a long history of human settlement, its period of rapid economic development is relatively recent. Therefore, more than many other countries, the growth of China's civil aviation transport network has both mirrored the nation's economic development and has been a vital factor in facilitating it.

Although aviation came to China in the early 1900s, the development of an effective civil aviation network was slowed by the country's low level of economic develop-

ment as well as civil unrest in the period leading up to World War II. The onset of the Second World War, which for China lasted from 1937 to 1945 meant that almost all aviation transportation was handled by the military. Soon after the defeat of the Japanese in 1945, China was again divided by a civil war. It was only following the Communist victory in 1949, known in China as Liberation, and the establishment of the People's Republic Of China, that matters stabilised and safe networks of transport could be established.

China's first civil aviation administration was established by the Political Bureau of the CPC (Communist Party of China) Central Committee as division of the People's Military Commission. This occurred on 2nd November, 1949, just one month after the People's Republic of China had been established.

China's first post-Liberation airline, the Sino-Soviet Civil Aviation Company (SKOGA), was founded on 1st July, 1950, a joint partnership between the governments of China and the USSR. SKOGA launched the country's first three international routes from Beijing to Chitta, Irkutsk and Almaty (then Alma-Ata), all cities in the former Soviet Union, soon afterwards. On 1st August, 1950, China formally launched its first two domestic air routes, one from Tianjin to Chongqing and the other from Tianjin to Guangzhou.

The joint airline agreement was annulled on 1st January, 1951, when the Soviet partner turned over its shares to China. This led to the formation of CAAC, the Civil Aviation Administration of China, which still controls

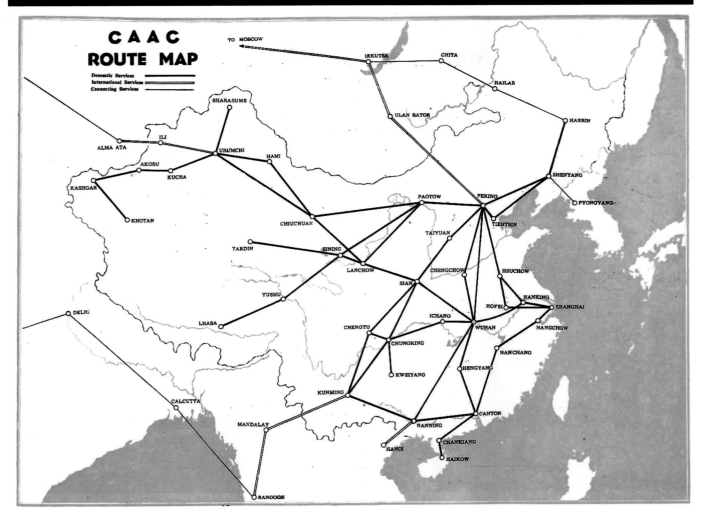

13.4 *The CAAC route map, showing all China's domestic and international air routes, 1957.*

China's civil aviation administration, and until 1988 was China's only airline.

In 1950, China had only 12 domestic and international air routes, with total traffic turnover and passenger transport volume standing at 1.57 million tonne-kilometres and 10,000 people respectively. By 1957, China had had 27 domestic and international air routes, with the total traffic turnover reaching 15.34 million tonne-kilometres and the passenger transport volume hitting 68,500 people.

Figure 13.4 shows China's domestic air network in 1957, as portrayed in a CAAC timetable at the time. The map shows clearly how few flights there were within China. For example, Shanghai, which was China's largest city, had just ten flights a week. At the time, there were no daily flights between Beijing (then Peking) and Shanghai, which was the route between China's two largest cities. Of the five flights a week between Shanghai and Beijing (Peking), three were routed via Nanjing (then Nanking) and Jinan (then Tsinan), and two were routed via Hefei (then Hofei) and Jinan (then Tsinan). These flights, which covered a distance of 1,075 kilometres if flown directly, took between seven to seven and a half hours and were flown with the standard equipment of the day, the Soviet-

13.5 *A Soviet-manufactured Ilyushin Il-14, the backbone of the CAAC fleet for many years.*

manufactured Ilyushin Il-14 (figure 13.5), seating 26 passengers.

It should be noted that figure 13.4 labels many Chinese cities using old names. Among cities on the map which are named differently nowadays are Peking (Beijing), Urumchi (Urumqi), Sining (Xining), Langchow (Lanzhou), Sian (Xian), Chengtu (Chengdu), Chungking (Chongqing), Kweiyang (Guiyang), Haikow (Haikou),

Tientsin (Tianjin), Canton (Guangzhou), Hangchow (Hangzhou) and Chengchow (Zhengzhou).

The expansion of China's civil aviation network progressed quite slowly through the 1960s and 1970s because of the turmoil of various mass campaigns such as the Great Leap Forward and the Cultural Revolution. However, as the period of economic reforms began under Deng Xiaoping in the late 1970s, aviation was identified as a key link in national development, and orders were placed for airliners in Western countries such as the United Kingdom and the United States (figure 13.6).

13.6 *A view of the main apron at Shanghai's Hongqiao Airport in 1982. One British-made Trident jet can be seen to the right, and the other three aircraft are Soviet-made turboprops, such as the Ilyushin Il-18 in the left foreground. This was probably China's second busiest airport (after Beijing) at the time the photo was taken.*

13.7 *Beijing's Capital Airport, 2010.*

In 1988, civil aviation had expanded to such an extent that the decision was made to break up CAAC into several smaller airlines. Initially CAAC was broken into six regionally-based airlines, but later mergers resulted in three large government-owned companies: Air China (based in Beijing), China Eastern (based in Shanghai) and China Southern (based in Guangzhou), which is now China's largest airline. The regulations were also relaxed to allow the development of privately owned airlines, and two of the largest private airlines to emerge were Shenzhen Airlines (based in Shenzhen) and Sichuan Airlines (based in Chengdu).

The break up of CAAC into regionally based airlines allowed further expansion of China's air network. Figure 13.9 shows the route networks of China's five largest airlines in 2008. The different regional hubs of the five airlines is very evident. It should be noted that in figure 13.9, the hub cities are labelled by their standard three-letter codes, so Beijing is shown as PEK, Shanghai as SHA (with Shanghai's second airport at Pudong shown as PVG), Guangzhou is CAN, Shenzhen is SZX and Chengdu is CTU. Other significant cities are URC (Urumqi), LXA (Lhasa), HKG (Hong Kong), HRB (Harbin), XIY (Xian) and CKG (Chongqing). The codes for many other cities shown on the map can be found in table 13.1, as well as on many websites such as http://www.mapping.com/cgi-bin/NEWairport.cgi and http://gc.kls2.com.

The expansion of China's domestic civil aviation network between 1957 (figure 13.4) and 2008 (figure 13.9) is very marked. By 2008, China's civil aviation industry included 1,336 routes covering a total distance of 2.11 million kilometres. Of these routes, 1,068 were domestic routes (including 43 routes to Hong Kong and Macau), connecting to 140 cities within China, with the total distance being 1.15 million kilometres. The remaining 268 routes were international connections to 91 cities in 42 countries, covering a total distance of 966,200 kilometres.

The expansion of China's air network has required large investment in infrastructure such as runways and terminal buildings. Table 13.1 shows the thirty busiest airports in China according to passenger numbers and aircraft movements. In contrast to the scenes shown in figure 13.6, China's airports today meet or exceed international standards in most cases (figure 13.7). Figure 13.8 shows part of the terminal buildings at Shenzhen Airport in south-east China. Shenzhen is now China's fifth busiest airport, a remarkable achievement as the airport only opened in 1991 and the city of Shenzhen itself was just a small fishing village until 1980 (figure 13.10).

Today, Shenzhen is a megacity with a population of 11.7 million (as shown earlier in table 11.9). As a Special

13.8 *The entrance to Terminal A building at Bao'an Airport, Shenzhen, China. Terminal B can be seen in the left background.*

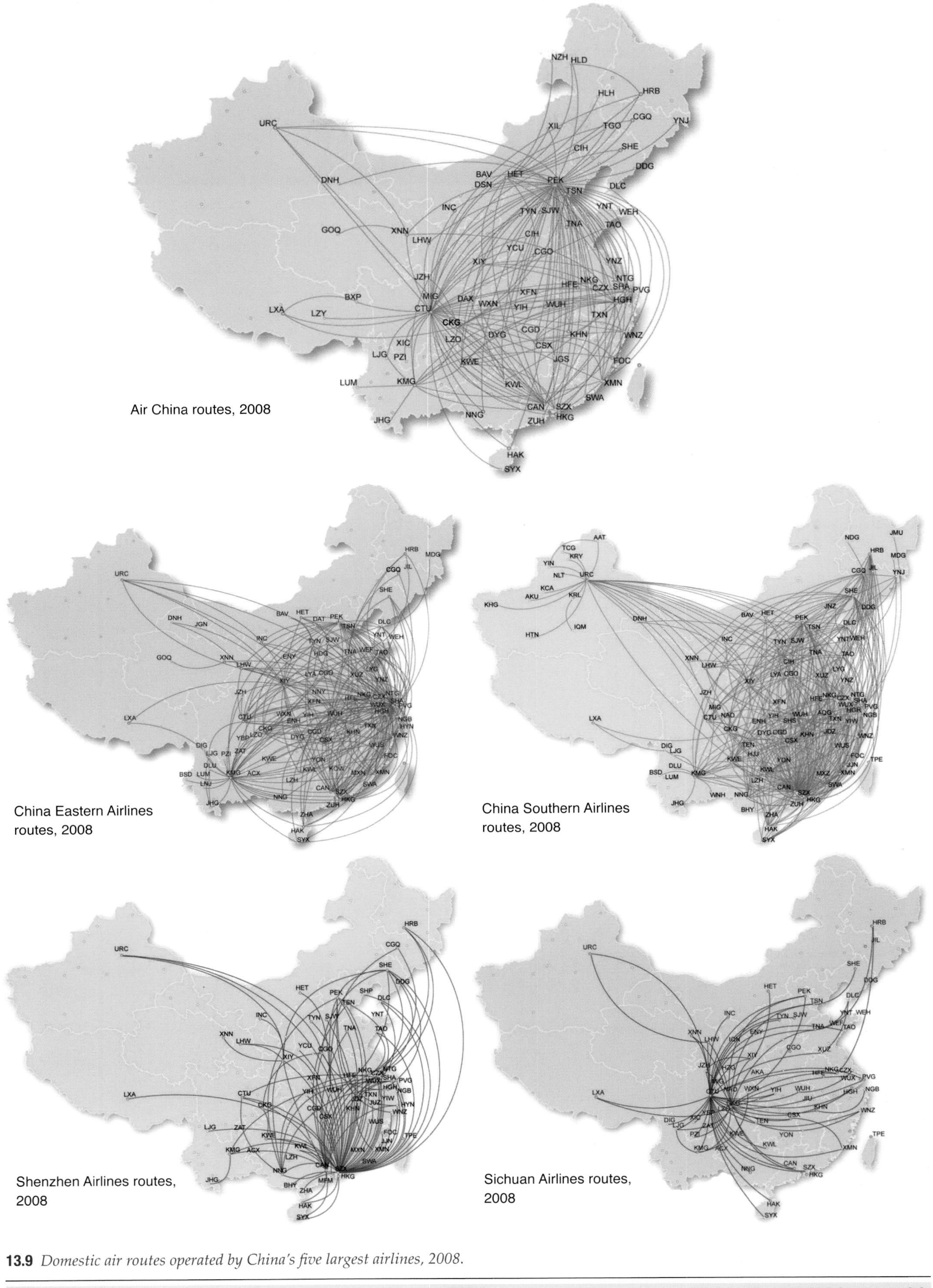

Air China routes, 2008

China Eastern Airlines routes, 2008

China Southern Airlines routes, 2008

Shenzhen Airlines routes, 2008

Sichuan Airlines routes, 2008

13.9 *Domestic air routes operated by China's five largest airlines, 2008.*

Changing space: the shrinking world

Table 13.1

China's Busiest Airports, 2007-08, by passenger traffic and aircraft movements.
(airports are arranged by descending number of passengers in 2008)

Airport	Location	Code	Total Aircraft Movements		Total Number of Passengers	
			2007	2008	2007	2008
Beijing Capital	Chaoyang District, Beijing	PEK	399,209	429,646	53,611,747	55,938,136
Guangzhou Baiyun	Guangzhou, Guangdong	CAN	260,828	280,392	30,958,467	33,435,472
Shanghai Pudong	Pudong District, Shanghai	PVG	253,532	265,735	28,920,432	28,235,691
Shanghai Hongqiao	Changning, Shanghai	SHA	187,045	185,304	22,632,962	22,877,404
Shenzhen Bao'an	Shenzhen, Guangdong	SZX	181,450	187,942	20,619,164	21,400,509
Chengdu Shangliu	Chengdu, Sichuan	CTU	166,312	158,615	18,574,284	17,246,806
Kunming Wijiaba	Kunming, Yunnan	KMG	148,128	150,353	15,725,791	15,877,814
Hangzhou Xiaoshan	Hangzhou, Zhejiang	HGH	114,672	118,560	11,729,983	12,673,198
Xi'an Xianyang	Xi'an, Shaanxi	XIY	119,341	121,992	11,372,630	11,921,919
Chongqing Jiangbei	Jiangbei, Chongqing	CKG	105,092	112,565	10,355,730	11,138,432
Xiamen Gaoqi	Xiamen, Fujian	XMN	85,251	92,785	8,684,662	9,385,436
Wuhan Tianhe	Wuhan, Hubei	WUH	93,498	98,372	8,356,340	9,202,629
Nanjing Lukou	Nanjing, Jiangsu	NKG	82,392	91,242	8,037,189	8,881,261
Changsha Huanghua	Changsha, Hunan	CSX	82,041	85,339	8,069,989	8,454,808
Haikou Meilan	Haikou, Hainan	HAK	60,579	66,411	7,265,349	8,221,997
Dalian Zhoushuizi	Dalian, Liaoning	DLC	63,416	73,082	7,281,084	8,205,454
Qingdao Liuting	Qingdao, Shandong	TAO	82,367	87,828	7,867,982	8,200,367
Shenyang Taoxian	Shenyang, Liaoning	SHE	56,879	62,531	6,190,448	6,807,235
Sanya Phoenix	Sanya, Hainan	SYX	42,292	47,373	5,311,622	6,006,300
Zhengzhou Xinzheng	Zhengzhou, Henan	CGO	54,470	62,288	5,002,102	5,887,598
Urumqi Diwopu	Urumqi, Xinjiang	URC	59,284	59,462	6,189,981	5,817,274
Harbin Taiping	Harbin, Heilongjiang	HRB	40,194	46,364	4,432,645	4,985,212
Jinan Yaoqiang	Jinan, Shandong	TNA	46,357	52,557	4,363,483	4,828,746
Tianjin Binhai	Dongli District, Tianjin	TSN	65,664	70,279	3,860,752	4,637,299
Fuzhou Changle	Changle, Fujian	FOC	43,928	45,336	4,247,236	4,533,889
Guiyang Longdongbao	Guiyang, Guizhou	KWE	47,685	46,259	4,248,005	4,324,085
Taiyuan Wusu	Taiyuan, Shanxi	TYN	43,061	47,909	3,613,308	4,312,910
Guilin Liangjiang	Guilin, Guangxi	KWL	43,733	42,919	4,665,021	4,259,410
Wenzhou Yongqiang	Wenzhou, Zhejiang	WNZ	34,762	38,697	3,587,940	3,976,546
Ningbo Lishe	Ningbo, Zhejiang	NGB	n.a.	n.a.	3,300,626	3,574,352

Source: Civil Aviation Administration of China

Economic Zone, Shenzhen is a city of in-migrants from all parts of China, and being integrated into the national air transport network with its own airline company has been an important factor in helping the city's development (figure 13.11).

13.10 *A view of central Shenzhen, China, in 1982.*

13.11 *A view of central Shenzhen, China, in 2008.*

QUESTION BLOCK 13B

1. *With reference to figures 13.4 and 13.9, describe and account for the expansion of China's domestic civil aviation network.*

2. *Using an atlas, plot the locations of China's busiest airports on a map. What do you notice about the distribution of the busiest airports? What does this suggest about the distribution of economic growth and development in China?*

The Changing Role of Telecommunications and ICT

In the 1960s, the Canadian thinker and theorist Marshall McLuhan forecast that the world would become a 'global village' in the coming decades. Few people at the time understood the full implications of this claim. McLuhan was trying to explain that global communications would improve so much that exchanging information with other people anywhere in the world would become as easy as communicating to another person in the same village. In this way, the world would effectively 'shrink' to the scale of a village. Although some parts of the world still lag in telecommunications, McLuhan's forecast is close to having come true today.

At the time McLuhan made his forecast, international telephone calls travelled by undersea cable that could each carry about 100 simultaneous calls. Communications satellites first began to be used in the late 1960s, increasing the number of calls that could be communicated simultaneously. By 2001, there were over 200 communications satellites in orbit, each capable of handling tens of thousands of phone calls plus several television transmissions at the same time. The growth in satellite numbers is shown in table 13.2.

Table 13.2
Actual and Projected Numbers of Satellites Launched
1957 to 2009

Period	Average number of commercial geostationary satellites launched each year
1957	1*
1962 - 1969	15
1970 - 1979	34
1980 - 1989	69
1990 - 1999	216
2000 - 2009	320

* This was the first satellite, Sputnik 1, and was not for commercial use
Source: *National Geographic*

The growth in telecommunications has allowed the internet to grow very rapidly in recent years also. The internet came into existence in the late 1970s as an outgrowth of a project known as the ARPANET initiated by the US Department of Defence. By the end of 1998, there were 147,800,000 internet users worldwide, of whom 52% were living in the United States. By late 2001, the number of internet users had increased to about 326 million, 67% of whom used English as their first language. This figure had grown still further to 801 million by September 2004, of whom only 35% used English as their first language. By 2009, the number of internet users had grown spectacularly to 1.464 billion, of whom 17% (253 million) were in China and 15% (220 million) were in the United States (table 13.3).

This change suggests spectacular internet expansion into new parts of the world. Today, virtually every country in the world has some internet access; as recently as 1993, only 60 countries had any connection to the internet.

Table 13.3

The Top 20 Countries with the Highest Number
of Internet Users, 2010

Rank	Country or Region	Number of internet users, 2010	Penetration (% of population)	% of world users	User growth 2000 to 2009
1	China	360,000,000	26.9%	20.8%	1500.0%
2	USA	227,719,000	74.1%	13.1%	138.8%
3	Japan	95,979,000	75.5%	5.5%	103.9%
4	India	81,000,000	7.0%	4.7%	1520.0%
5	Brazil	67,510,400	34.0%	3.9%	1250.2%
6	Germany	54,229,325	65.9%	3.1%	126.0%
7	UK	46,683,900	76.4%	2.7%	203.1%
8	Russia	45,250,000	32.3%	2.6%	1359.7%
9	France	43,100,134	69.3%	2.5%	407.1%
10	South Korea	37,475,800	77.3%	2.2%	96.8%
11	Iran	32,200,000	48.5%	1.9%	12780.0%
12	Italy	30,026,400	51.7%	1.7%	127.5%
13	Indonesia	30,000,000	12.5%	1.7%	1400.0%
14	Spain	29,093,984	71.8%	1.7%	440.0%
15	Mexico	27,600,000	24.8%	1.6%	917.5%
16	Turkey	26,500,000	34.5%	1.5%	1225.0%
17	Canada	25,086,000	74.9%	1.4%	97.5%
18	Philippines	24,000,000	24.5%	1.4%	1100.0%
19	Vietnam	21,963,117	24.8%	1.3%	10881.6%
20	Poland	20,020,362	52.0%	1.2%	615.0%
TOP 20 COUNTRIES		**1,325,437,422**	**30.3%**	**76.4%**	**359.9%**
Rest of the world		408,556,319	17.1%	23.6%	461.5%
TOTAL WORLD USERS		**1,733,993,741**	**25.6%**	**100.0%**	**380.3%**

Source: Internet World Stats: Usage and Population Statistics.
http://www.internetworldstats.com/top20.htm

13.12 *An advertisement for ADSL broadband internet in Mbabane, capital city of Swaziland.*

As the internet spreads to more and more countries, it has the capacity to influence local cultures and ways of thinking (figure 13.12). This is because the internet has great potential to introduce powerful new ideas very quickly, together with the opportunity to communicate rapidly and cheaply with other people through chat sessions, ICQ, Skype, and so on. In recent years, social networking sites such as Facebook and micro-blogging sites such as Twitter have had a major impact on the ways in which the internet is used as well as the profiles of those using the internet.

The internet is a particularly powerful agent of cultural change because it has the potential to reach so many users. An internet host might be an individual computer, a local area network (LAN) or a gateway to a wide area network. Therefore, a message sent through the internet may reach anywhere from one to several million users. The interconnectivity of the internet is one of its main advantages, and many users make use of this capacity to disseminate information very widely, cheaply and quickly.

As communications technology has improved global communications, several media networks have taken advantage of the technological improvements and established global networks. In the television field, notable examples are CNN of the United States, Sky and the BBC in the United Kingdom and Al Jazeera in Qatar. Major newspapers such as the New York Times and the International Herald Tribune have established a strong web presence, and several commentators have predicted that hard copy newspapers will start to cease production in the next few years in favour of subscription-based web distribution.

13.13 *A bus carrying advertising for Google in Beijing, China. In 2010, Google withdrew from China for various reasons including concerns about censorship of search results by the government.*

The attraction of such global media networks to the internet is that information and entertainment can reach most parts of the world almost instantly. The danger is that the culture of the media network's home nation may come to suppress the culture of the society into which the programs are being broadcast (figure 13.13). It is estimated, for example, that about half of the world's 6000 languages will disappear between 2000 and 2100 in the face of the more dominant languages spread by electronic media.

ToK BoX

Maps and Reality.

the world according to two different projections in which each red 'circle' covers an equal size of area with varying degrees of distortion.

Because each map has a theme, maps can be used to portray particular opinions or viewpoints. This introduces another element of selection bias. For example, the map below labelled 'The world according to the United States of America' was very popular on the internet a few years ago. What is the message that you think the map maker is presenting?

There is a convention in drawing maps that north will always be at the top. There is no rational reason for this choice to be made, as the earth is a sphere. The placement of north at the top seems to reflect the continuation of an historical tradi-

In the previous ToK Box, the issue of bias was discussed. In that discussion, it was noted that some amount of selection bias is inevitable in any writing or drawing because it is impossible to record every single detail. Indeed, if the aim of writing or drawing (say, a map) is to convey information, then including *every* piece of detail would actually obscure the clear communication of information because so much irrelevant data would be included. Data is not necessarily information.

Selection bias is an important issue when maps are drawn. Every map is distorted to some extent because maps are representations of curved surfaces on flat surfaces. The larger the area covered, the greater will be the distortion. This can be seen in the two maps above, which show

The world according to the United States of America

tion of the early European map-makers, who usually chose to place their home country of Spain or Portugal in the centre of the world. Is there any reason today (apart from convention) that the world could not be drawn with south at the top, as shown on the Hobo-Dyer equal Area Projection to the left?

The next ToK BoX is on page 579

Changing space: the shrinking world

13.14 *Movies such as Superman that showed American lifestyles in LEDCs had a huge impact on changing local people's expectations and aspirations.*

13.15 *Local residents access the national intranet in the Grand People's Study House in Pyongyang, North Korea.*

Movies also play a very important part in changing cultural attitudes and perceptions. Many movies are made in the United States, and to a lesser extent in other developed countries. These usually show the lifestyles and attitudes of the people who live in that country. When the movie Superman appeared in Shanghai in 1986, the wealth of the people and the modern nature of the high rise cities shown astounded the local population (figure 13.14). Many people believe that foreign movies appearing in China in the 1980s caused large numbers of locals to support economic development that would enable China to catch up with the rest of the world. Shanghai's skyline today resembles that in the Superman movie much more closely than it resembles the Shanghai skyline of 1986! The spread of movies and television shows via bit torrent sharing on the internet has accelerated this spread of new ideas and culture across national borders.

Although some countries (especially those in the Middle East) censor certain sites on the internet that are regarded as being incompatible with local moral and ethical values, for most places in the world the internet provides equal access to information for everyone who has an internet connection. In this way, the internet acts as a significant agent of globalisation.

There are very few exceptions today of countries that limit internet access. One example is **North Korea**, probably the most isolated and least globalised nation in the world. It does not provide any access whatsoever to the internet for its citizens. Instead, a national intranet that was entirely developed within the country by government officials is provided in a small number of major public libraries, such as the Grand People's Study House in Pyongy-

ang (figure 13.15). Access to outside information in North Korea is restricted in others ways also, as mobile phones are banned, modems (and computers containing modems) are banned, all landline telephone calls are monitored by government operators, short-wave radios are illegal, television sets can receive just one channel, and the import of printed materials from overseas is prohibited. As shown in chapter 18, the isolation imposed by such policies significantly limits the impact of globalisation in North Korea, which is of course the intention of such policies.

At the opposite end of the spectrum of internet availability is the **One Laptop Per Child** (OLPC) program. Originally known as the '$100 laptop program', OLPC aims to provide inexpensive sub-notebook computers on a no-profit basis to children in LEDCs so they can access knowledge and have opportunities to "explore, experiment and express themselves".

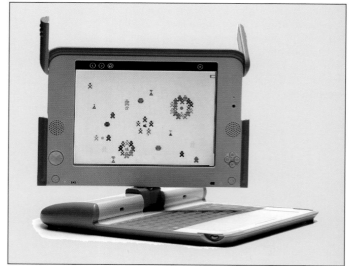

13.16 *The XO-1 laptop used by the One Laptop Per Child program (photo: OLPC)*

The vision of Nicholas Negroponte, a Greek-American architect and computer scientist who was the founder and Chairman Emeritus of Massachusetts Institute of Technology's Media Lab, OLPC is a non-profit organisation.

It was established specifically to manufacture and distribute the XO-1 computer, a distinctive, rugged, low-power laptop that uses flash memory rather than a hard drive, a Linux operating system, wireless internet access, sunlight display, a hand crank to recharge the batteries, and a choice of 18 different keyboards for different alphabets (figure 13.16).

13.17 *A boy in Cambodia uses an XO-1 computer from the One Laptop Per Child program.*

The first order for XO-1 computers came from Uruguay in 2007, when the government ordered 100,000 laptops. Since then, almost one million more XO-1s have been ordered for schools in LEDCs, and at the time of writing, they were being used by children in Uruguay, the USA, Peru, Mexico, Colombia, Ghana, Ethiopia, Rwanda, Haiti, Kiribati, Nauru, New Caledonia, Niue, Papua New Guinea, Solomon Islands, Tuvalu, Vanuatu, Afghanistan, Mongolia and Cambodia (figure 13.17). Additional pilot projects were underway in the Middle East (Iraq, Lebanon, Yemen), Africa (Mali, Mozambique, Nigeria, South Africa, Tanzania), Latin America (Brazil, Nicaragua, Paraguay, Suriname, Virgin islands) and Asia (India, Nepal, Pakistan, Philippines, Thailand).

QUESTION BLOCK 13C

1. *To what extent has Marshall McLuhan's forecast that the world would become a 'global village' come true? Provide evidence to support your answer.*

2. *Search the internet to find the latest statistics listing the top 20 countries in rank order of the number of internet users. Describe the pattern that you find.*

3. *Explain how global communications networks can affect traditional cultures.*

14

Economic interactions and flows

Global flows of finance, labour and information

Outline

Financial flows   **Page 578**
The importance of loans development aid, remittances, foreign direct investment, repatriation of profits in the transfer of capital between the developed core areas and the peripheries.

Labour flows   **Page 584**
The causes and effects of one major flow of labour between two countries

Information flows   **Page 585**
The role of ICT in the growth of outsourcing.

ToK BoX — Page 579
The use of language

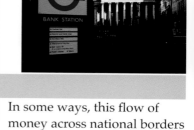

Financial Flows

Globalisation and Economic Activity

Professor Ron Martin is professor of economic geography at the University of Cambridge's Geography Department. In one of his many books on the subject, he wrote:

"The geographical circuits of money and finance are the 'wiring' of the socio-economy … along which the 'currents' of wealth creation, consumption and economic power are transmitted … money allows for the deferment of payment over time-space that is the essence of credit. Equally, money allows propinquity without the need for proximity in conducting transactions over space. These complex time-space webs of monetary flows and obligations underpin our daily social existence".

Whether people praise or detest the consequences of globalisation, there can be no doubt that world economic activity is becoming increasingly integrated. This is happening because of growing levels of international trade, the growth of transnational corporations (TNCs), international economic agreements, trading blocs and global movements of capital.

In some ways, this flow of money across national borders represents a return to the situation before World War I. Until 1914, an increasing share of the world's economy operated under the **gold standard**, which was the system where the value of a currency was defined in terms of pre-set, fixed quantities of gold, for which the currency could be exchanged. Under the gold standard, the world economy operated through a global financial market based in London.

Between the outbreak of war in 1914 until the end of the Second World War in 1945, the gold standard was abandoned as national currencies were used as agents of government policy throughout the world. In that context, international financial flows almost stopped and foreign investment was viewed with great suspicion.

Towards the end of World II, in July 1944, a conference was held among the 44 Allied countries at Bretton Woods (New Hampshire, USA). The aim of the conference was to plan the structure of the post-war international economic system. The underlying principle of the discussions was that international trade and global markets should be as open as possible. As a result of the confer-

ToK BoX

The Use of Language.

When you read articles on controversial subjects, such as some of the issues covered in this chapter, you should be aware of the way in which language is being used. Saying the same thing in different ways can alter the tone of the message being conveyed.

Some words not only have a descriptive meaning, but also carry emotional baggage. For example, words such as 'hero', 'peace', 'tolerance' and 'democracy' have positive connotations, while others such as 'thief', 'discrimination', 'pervert' or 'elite' have negative overtones. Emotional loading in words is part of the reason that everyone claims to be in favour of peace, but fewer people like to be labelled as a pacifist.

The way words are used within particular communities can affect their emotional overtones, so that being a 'socialist' is more acceptable in (say) Scandinavia than it is in the US, while the term 'capitalist' has very different implications in the US, Russia, Denmark, Iran and Venezuela.

In a similar way, a person who is labelled as a terrorist in one place may be called a freedom fighter in another. What some people refer to as genetically modified food is referred to by others as frankenstein food, and what some people call 'free speech' is branded 'hate speech' by others.

Euphemisms are a special type of emotionally-loaded language, where a mild or neutral sounding word is used in preference to a negatively sounding word. Thus, some people refer to 'land-scape management' instead of 'clear felling' of a forest, 'passing away' instead of 'dying' and 'pleasantly plump' or 'shapely' instead of 'fat'.

A more extreme form of euphemism is politically correct language, which tries to influence people's thought patterns by using words that convey a desired values position. Politically correct language is usually described as inclusive, left-wing or liberal, and is intended to avoid using words that might be exclusive, patriarchal, hierarchical or conservative.

The choice of words is a powerful way to influence the thinking of others, as George Orwell noted in his novel '1984'. If someone is capable of redefining words in such a way that alternative ways of thinking are eliminated, then that person has gained effective control over our thinking. That is why it is so important to use language precisely and not allow the meaning of words to drift into ambiguity.

Another way in which the meaning of language can be shifted subtly is by the use of weasel words, which are words like 'many', 'should' and 'probably'. Weasel words can be slipped into sentences to give the speaker (or writer) an escape route. For example, an international loan agency might say "This type of loan should work for you if you follow our instructions carefully". If a government agency in a poor country accepts the loan but it doesn't have the impact that was anticipated, the lender can claim that the agency didn't follow the instructions carefully enough.

Grammar is another way in which the meaning of language can be shifted to affect the way people see things. For example, the active and the passive voice can give quite different impressions, as can be seen in the difference between 'Many villages were bombed' as opposed to 'We bombed many villages'.

The distorted use of language during war has become so sophisticated that it is sometimes referred to as 'warspeak'. In order to get 'our boys' to be prepared kill foreign troops, 'the enemy' needs to be dehumanised. During the Vietnam War, Vietnamese soldiers were labelled by US troops as 'Gooks', while during the first Gulf War in the early 1990s, firing on Iraqi soldiers was known by US servicemen as a 'turkey shoot'. Psychologically, it is easier to kill 'gooks' or 'turkeys' than other human beings who might have wives and young children. Some other examples of 'warspeak' include the following:

collateral damage (bombed cities)
ethnic cleansing (genocide)
friendly fire (accidentally firing on your own troops)
liberate (invade)
neutralise (kill)
no longer a factor (dead)
pacification (bombing)
pre-emptive strike (unprovoked attack)
reporting guidelines (censorship)
service a target (drop bombs on a target)
strategic redeployment (retreat)
take out (destroy) .

The next ToK BoX is on page 600.

14.1 *The Airbus A380 airliner is the world's largest passenger jet, and is designed to carry passengers at relatively low costs per seat per kilometre. It is manufactured by a company with ownership in five countries that draws on components from over 1,500 companies in 27 countries. (Photo: Konstantin von Wedelstaedt)*

ence, agreements were signed to set up the International Bank for Reconstruction and Development (IBRD — later part of the World Bank), the General Agreement on Tariffs and Trade (GATT — later to become the World Trade Organisation), and the International Monetary Fund (IMF). Furthermore, an exchange rate management system was set up that remained in place until the early 1970s when fully floating exchange rates became the norm.

The widespread introduction of flexible floating exchange rates in the 1970s began a trend towards removing barriers to the movement of money across national borders. The world's financial markets responded accordingly, and by 2000, the mobility of capital (money) had reached the 1914 level once again.

The world's economies thus became more and more integrated during the period following World War II, and this process has continued to accelerate since the mid-1980s. In addition to the structural changes already mentioned, the trend towards increased financial mobility has arisen mainly due to two sets of forces. First, advances in technology have reduced the costs of transport, communication and information transfer so that firms can now locate different offices and parts of production lines in different countries economically. For example, the airliner shown in figure 14.1 is operated by an airline based in Dubai, but was manufactured by the European company Airbus Industrie. This company is owned jointly by aerospace companies in France, Germany, United Kingdom, Spain and Belgium, each of which manufactures parts of the aircraft. These companies in turn sub-contract the manufacture of some parts of the aircraft, so that altogether Airbus Industrie has more than 1,500 suppliers in 27 countries.

The second factor is that trade and the international movement of money was increasingly liberalised and deregulated during the 1980s and 1990s. Using policies and mechanisms to promote political stability, accommodate rapid flows of capital and promote foreign investment , governments have increasingly replaced protectionist trading policies with free trade policies. Free trade encourages importing and exporting with as few barriers as possible. Therefore, tariffs, quotas and import duties are actively discouraged. Several of the international institutions that were established at Bretton Woods or shortly thereafter have encouraged this trend, examples being the World Bank, International Monetary Fund (IMF) and World Trade Organisation (WTO). These organisations will be examined in greater detail a little later in this chapter.

It seems that globalisation has boosted economic growth in some parts of the world such as China, South Korea, and Singapore. However, many other economies are less integrated into the global economy and have missed out on this growth. Examples of economies that seem to have been hurt by globalisation include most of the countries in Africa and many of the countries of the former Soviet Union, as their shares of world trade have been declining steadily. It should be remembered that whether a country's economy benefits overall from globalisation or not, its impact will vary within the country. In many cases, the trend is that a small wealthy elite will become even richer as a result of globalisation, while a larger poorer section of the population could become even poorer.

As we saw in chapter 12, in spite of the problems, most countries have been trying to globalise their economies in recent decades. As long ago as 1986, the British academic, Susan Strange, devised the term **casino capitalism** to describe the global financial system, saying:

"every day games are played in this casino that involve sums of money so large that they cannot be imagined. At night the games go on at the other side of the world ... (the

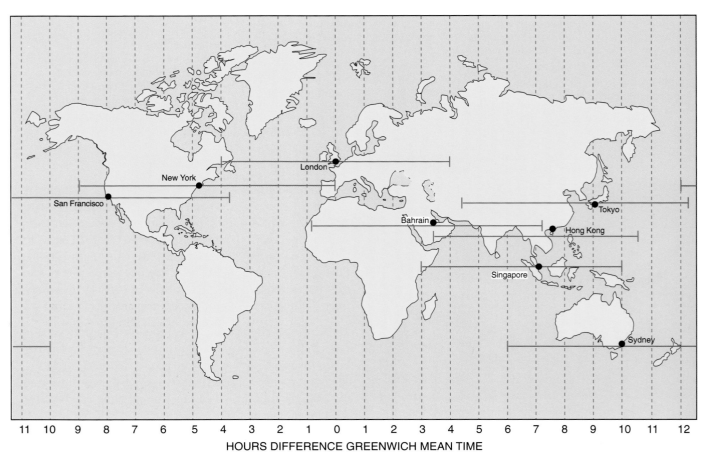

14.2 *Trading hours of the major financial centres.*

players) are just like the gamblers in casinos watching the clicking spin of a silver ball on a roulette wheel and putting their chips on red or black, odd numbers or even ones."

The same writer later used the term 'mad money' to describe the volatility of the financial system and the uncertainty it brings to people in most parts of the world. This is understandable, as the value of the flow of finance, including foreign currency transactions, speculative exchange rate movements and financial investments, now far exceeds the total value of international trade in manufactured products and services combined. These international financial flows are said to be the engine that drives the process of globalisation.

Technological developments in ICT (information and communications technologies) have been necessary for the large-scale financial flows that occur today. Indeed, as Professor Peter Dicken, an economic geographer from the University of Manchester, comments *"information is both the process and the product of financial services."* He describes the raw materials of the financial services industry as information — about markets, risks, exchange rates, returns on investments, and credit ratings. The products of the financial services industry are also information, mainly the value-added to the inputs of information. He quotes a financial services executive, who said *"we don't have warehouses full of cash, we have* information *about cash — that is our product."*

14.3 *The New York Stock Exchange symbolises New York's position as a Level 1 global financial centre.*

The **global financial system** is known as an industry which never stops, as financial trading is a 24-hours-per-day industry. When one financial centre closes, activity simply switches to another in a different time zone that is still operating (figure 14.2). This ability to switch trading from one city to another makes it very difficult for new cities to enter the world financial trade. The cities that control the world financial markets are more than centres of control and information processing – they are also centres of information interpretation. Although data can be transferred electronically, interpretation of data requires knowledge, expertise, and contact with other

people. These requirements further reinforce the dominant position of a few world cities that have established the corporate culture and expertise that supports information interpretation (figure 14.3). The cities which dominate the flow of global finance are:

Level 1:
    London (United Kingdom)
    New York (United States)
    Tokyo (Japan)

Level 2:
    Amsterdam (Netherlands)
    Frankfurt (Germany)
    Hong Kong (China)
    Paris (France)
    Zürich (Switzerland)

Level 3:
    Bangkok (Thailand)
    Basel (Switzerland)
    Beijing (China)
    Brussels (Belgium)
    Chicago (United States)
    Dubai (United Arab Emirates)
    Düsseldorf (Germany)
    Hamburg (Germany)
    Istanbul (Turkey)
    Jakarta (Indonesia)
    Los Angeles (United States)
    Madrid (Spain)
    Melbourne (Australia)
    Mexico City (Mexico)
    Milan (Italy)
    Moscow (Russia)
    Mumbai (India)
    Rio de Janeiro (Brazil)
    Rome (Italy)
    San Francisco (United States)
    São Paulo (Brazil)
    Seoul (South Korea)
    Shanghai (China)
    Singapore (Singapore)
    Sydney (Australia)
    Taipei (China)
    Toronto (Canada)
    Vienna (Austria)
    Warsaw (Poland)

This list is based on a variety of indicators, including the volume of international currency dealings, the size of the currency market, the volume of foreign financial assets, the number of headquarters of large international banks, and the degree of connectivity between the city and other financial centres. The list is, of course, not fixed, and the importance of various cities will change from time to time. For example, although New York and London have been two major financial centres for many decades, the place of Tokyo as a level 1 centre has fluctuated. Cities such as Dubai and Moscow would not have been on the list a decade ago, whereas Seoul and Shanghai would not have been on the list a couple of decades ago.

The pattern has become a little more complex in recent decades with the establishment of the so-called **offshore financial centres (OFCs)**. These are small places such as islands and micro-states that have set themselves up as financial centres that attract money by offering lower taxes and freer regulatory frameworks than the established financial centres (figure 14.4). Many of the financial institutions in the offshore financial centres are virtual entities — for example, in the Cayman Islands, there are more than 500 banking companies operating with hundreds of billions of dollars in their accounts, but only about 70 of the banks have a physical presence in the Cayman Islands. There are clusters of OFCs:

The Caribbean:
    Bahamas
    Bermuda
    Cayman islands
    Panama
Europe:
    Gibraltar
    Guernsey
    Isle of Man
    Jersey
    Liechtenstein
    Luxembourg

Middle East:
    Bahrain
    Kuwait
    Qatar
The Pacific:
    Cook Islands
    Nauru
    Tonga
    Vanuatu
    Western Samoa
Africa:
    Liberia
    Mauritius

Offshore financial centres provide banks, financial institutions, investors and transnational corporations with the flexibility to move money freely, declaring profits in whichever place charges the lowest (or zero) taxes. In recent years, there have been moves to force OFCs to tighten their regulations and decrease their secrecy, especially following the terrorist attacks on the US in September 2001, but as the viability of many OFCs relies on preferential treatment for foreign companies and tight secrecy, they have resisted these pressures.

14.4 *The tall buildings in this view of Doha, the capital city of Qatar, have appeared in recent years as Qatar has emerged as an offshore financial centre (OFC).*

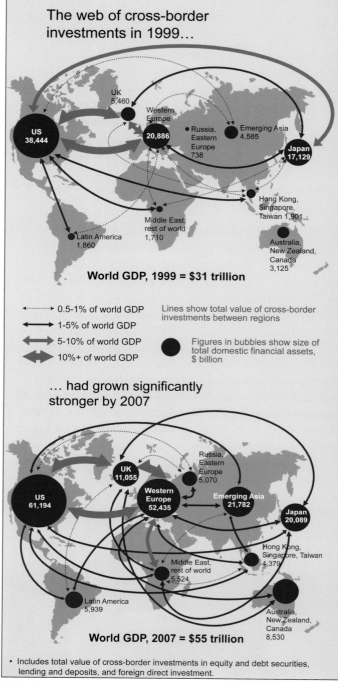

14.5 *The global web of cross-border investments, 1999 to 2007.*
Source: McKinsey Global Institute analysis.

In recent decades, and especially since the fall of communism in most parts of Eastern Europe in 1989 and the collapse of the Soviet Union in 1991, the flow of finance around the world has been increasing rapidly. This is shown by many indicators, such as the growth in world trade, the figures for foreign investments, the volume of aid money, loans (and the resulting repayments), the movement of speculative currency, and the transfer of profits between offices of transnational corporations.

Figure 14.5 gives a simplified visual representation of the growing volume and complexity of global financial movements. The maps in figure 14.5 show the growth in cross-border investments during the period 1999 to 2007. In these maps, cross-border investments include investments in equity and debt securities, lending and deposits and direct foreign investment.

QUESTION BLOCK 14A

1. *Using a blank world map, plot the locations of the cities that cities which dominate the flow of global finance, using separate colours for the level 1, 2 and 3 cities. Comment on the distribution of the cities on the map.*

2. *What is the significance of OFCs in global flows of finance?*

3. *Using the information in figure 14.5, describe the overall pattern of cross-border investments (a) in 1999, and (b) in 2007.*

4. *Using the figures that are in (or beside) the blue bubbles in figure 14.5, calculate the percentage change from 1999 to 2007 in the total domestic financial assets for each of the regions shown. What can you conclude about the changes in global financial flows from this information (focussing especially on which parts of the world have contributed most to the changes)?*

Not all movement of capital is done by private companies and speculators, of course, and financial flows can take many forms. Some of these, such as development aid, loans and debt relief, were discussed in chapter 2 where it was noted, among other points, that the need to repay debt on borrowings and the profits on investments means that the net flow of money in the world is now from LEDCs to MEDCs.

To some extent, the pattern shown in figure 14.5 can be explained by the policies of different governments in various parts of the world. Some governments have policies that encourage free trade, such as removing tariffs and import duties, where as others are more protectionist.

Three organisations have been particularly influential in influencing the size and direction of financial flows around the world, and because of this influence, have received criticism from anti-globalisation groups. These organisations are the World Trade Organisation, the International Monetary Fund, and the World Bank.

The **World Bank** was established by the victorious governments after the Second World War in 1947 to provide financial and technical assistance to LEDCs. It operates through two subsidiary organisations, the IBRD (International Bank for Reconstruction and Development) and the IDA (International Development Association). The IBRD works with middle income and credit-worthy poor countries, whereas the IDA focuses on the poorest countries in the world. The World Bank describes its roles as "providing low-interest loans, interest-free credits and grants to developing countries for a wide array of

purposes that include investments in education, health, public administration, infrastructure, financial and private sector development, agriculture, and environmental and natural resource management."

Also established by the victorious governments in the aftermath of World War II was the **IMF (International Monetary Fund)**. The role of the IMF is (in its own words) "to oversee the international monetary system to ensure exchange rate stability and to encourage members to eliminate exchange restrictions that hinder trade." Today, the IMF has 185 member countries and works in three main areas. First, the IMF monitors global economic and financial developments, and on the basis of this 'surveillance', provides policy advice which is designed to help countries avoid financial crises. Second, the IMF provides loans to countries that are having problems with their balance of payments, to countries that need temporary financing, and to low income countries to reduce poverty. The third area of IMF work is providing technical assistance and training in fields where it believes it has expertise. In recent years, the IMF has also played an active role in working to counter money laundering and financial flows that are thought to be supporting terrorist activities.

The **WTO (World Trade Organisation)** had more recent origins, having been founded in 1995. However, it succeeded another organisation, called GATT (General Agreement on Tariffs and Trade) that was established in 1947 under similar circumstances to the World Bank and the IMF. The WTO has over 150 countries as members, and its main role is to establish and regulate a set of rules to govern international trade. Its philosophy is to work towards the liberalisation of trade, and when problems arise, make effort to settle disputes.

14.6 *The banner at this protest in Jakarta (Indonesia) reads "Expel the World Bank from Indonesia! Get rid of SBY and JK and the parties of the political elite, the causes of the fuel price increase! National Liberation Front!." (Photo: Politik Rakyat Miskin)*

Critics of globalisation attack these three organisations because they are said to favour the rich and powerful at the expense of the poor and dispossessed (figure 14.6).

This is because free trade is said to increase the gap between rich and poor rather than decrease it. For example, it is claimed that free trade favours transnational corporations rather than small producers, because the latter need greater protection from competition as they tend to be less efficient. In this way, it is claimed that the three organisations have a bias against poorer countries and they discriminate against poorer people. These criticisms are explored in more detail in chapter 18.

QUESTION BLOCK 14B

1. *Describe the role of each of the following: (a) the World Bank; (b) the WTO; and (c) the IMF.*

2. *Why are these institutions criticised when their role seems to be specifically to help poor countries?*

Labour Flows

Causes and Effects of International Labour Flows

Like the global financial flows described above, the international movement of labour (migrants in search of work) peaked just before World War I, declined from 1914 until 1945 (especially during the Great Depression of the 1930s), and then began to increase once again as the forces of globalisation became stronger.

14.7 *The export of labour is encouraged by Bangladesh's government as an important source of foreign currency earnings.*

Migration, and the factors that influence a decision whether to migrate or remain in the same place, were discussed in chapter 1. In the case of international migration for work, the general pattern is for workers to migrate from economically less developed areas to places where the there is a heavy demand for labour because of rapid economic growth. Thus, during the 1950s, there was large-scale migration from southern Europe to Australia, the US and Canada; the 1970s saw a flow of labour from Africa and the Middle East to Europe; in the

1980s from LEDCs in south-east Asia to 'Tiger Economies' such as South Korea, Malaysia and Thailand; and since the 1990s from countries such as Bangladesh and India to the emerging Middle East economies such as Dubai, Qatar and Bahrain. Today, a significant proportion of Bangladesh's foreign currency earnings are the remittances sent by Bangladeshis working overseas, and the export of labour is actively encouraged as an export earner by Bangladesh's government (figure 14.7).

International migration is growing in importance as a result of globalisation of the labour market. Although it attracts a great deal of media attention and public comment, it is important to remember that international migration is much smaller in scale than than internal flows of migrants within the same country. Although there are significant barriers to the free migration of people for the purpose of working (including the often difficult process of obtaining a work visa), growing numbers of people are migrating internationally specifically to find work. This is largely explained by improvements in transport technology and infrastructure as well as better flows of information about the work possibilities in other countries.

14.8 *Rural villages like this one near Luang Prabang in Laos represent important sources of migrant workers to Thailand.*

14.9 *It is not only rural dwellers who migrate to Thailand in search of a better life. Many of the people in Cambodia's towns and cities also experience extreme poverty, such as the residents who live on Phnom Penh's largest garbage tip (Dump Hill).*

14.10 *Thailand's capital city (Bangkok) attracts many migrants from poor areas in Myanmar, Laos or Cambodia with the promise of a better life.*

14.11 *A young prostitute (wearing blue shorts) seeks work outside a hotel frequented by foreign tourists in the Thai beach resort of Phuket.*

One example of a cross-border labour flow is the movement of people into Thailand from surrounding countries such as Myanmar, Laos, Cambodia and Vietnam. Although all the countries in this region have been experiencing sustained rapid economic growth for many years, Thailand has been the most attractive destination for migrant workers because of its higher wages, more rapid rate of economic growth, and until 2008, its more stable political situation. By comparison, many of the rural areas and smaller cities of Myanmar, Laos, Cambodia and Vietnam were quite poor (figures 14.8 to 14.10).

For Thailand, the migrant workers have provided cheap labour that is willing to perform unpleasant tasks that many Thais prefer not to do. It is estimated that there are almost two million migrant workers in Thailand today, and that they add about 0.5% to Thailand's GDP each year.

However, there are problems with this labour flow. Although most of the migrant workers enter Thailand with valid working visas, it is estimated that more than half over-stay the expiry of their visas, thus becoming illegal workers. Most of the migrant workers are young, single, adventurous, males, which means that their homes areas are deprived of some of their most valuable workers. Although migrant workers from Myanmar tend to be poorly educated and sometimes illiterate, workers from Cambodia tend to have above average levels of education.

A less well publicised aspect of migration to Thailand is human trafficking. This occurs when girls (and a significant though smaller number of boys) are sold into prostitution by their poor, rural families in Laos, Myanmar and Cambodia. The human trafficking, which is a modern form of slavery, can involve girls as young as 9 or 10, and is also associated with drug dealing and money laundering. Often uneducated or illiterate, the girls are made to work in Thai tourist areas, such as the Patpong district of Bangkok or beach resorts such as Pattaya and Phuket (figure 14.11). Others are forced to work in brothels along Thailand's border. Some of the girls are later moved on from Thailand to work in other places such as southern Malaysia, Bahrain, the USA and western Europe.

With the exception of Thailand's estimated 35,000 sex slaves, the flow of migrant labour into Thailand leads to a flow of money in the opposite direction. Estimates vary of the amount of foreign remittances sent home from Thailand because many of the payments are made through unofficial (i.e. non-banking) channels, and are thus never recorded. However, the general estimates are in the order of US$200 million to US$300 million per year.

Another specific case study of international migration (from Mexico to the United States) is discussed in chapter 17.

QUESTION BLOCK 14C

1. *Explain why migrants might want to move to Thailand from neighbouring countries to work.*

2. *Discuss the effects of the flow of labour to Thailand from neighbouring countries.*

Information Flows

International Outsourcing

Outsourcing occurs when some aspect of a business operation is contracted out to an external company. **International outsourcing** refers to contracting services to an offshore, rather than a domestic, company. Outsourcing has become more popular as a management tool in recent decades as it is seen as a way for a company to identify those things which are best done by its own employees, and then contract out those services which can be handled more cheaply or more efficiently by a specialist contractor. However, for companies engaging in international outsourcing, there can be significant cultural, legal, political, financial, technological and managerial challenges to overcome.

Information and communication technologies (ICT) have played a leading role in the growth of international outsourcing during the past decade or two. ICT companies, especially in the area of software development, have been outsourcing ICT work to offshore destinations, as communications technologies have developed to the point where software can be developed independently of location provided the connections are adequate.

Although some ICT has been outsourced to China, South Korea and Mexico, India has been the favoured destination for many US and European software developers. India has proved attractive as a destination for offshore outsourcing because the cost of labour is relatively cheap, English is widely spoken, and there is an emerging middle class of well educated young Indian people with an interest in ICT. For India, the attractions have been that ICT is a rapidly growing industry with high profitability, it brings advanced skills to the country, and it is an environmentally friendly industry in that it does not damage the environment.

As a result of this outsourcing, the value of India's software outputs grew from just US$150 million in 1991-92 to US$5.7 billion by 1999-2000, of which over US$4 billion was software exports. This represented an average annual growth rate of more than 50% per annum. Since that time, the value of software produced in India has continued to grow by about 35% every year, and in 2008, India's software exports earned about US$50 billion (gross figure). Although precise and accurate up-to-date statistics are difficult to obtain from India, it is estimated that ICT exports now make up more than 20% of India's total exports (by value), and about 2.2 million people are said to be employed in India's ICT industry.

The development of India's ICT industry has been confined to several 'software development hotspots', such as Bengaluru (formerly Bangalore), Pune (formerly Poona), Mumbai (formerly Bombay), Chennai (formerly Madras), Kolkata (formerly Calcutta) and Hyderabad, and to a lesser extent, the Delhi-Noida-Gurgaon belt, Vadodara (formerly Baroda), Bhubaneswar, Ahmedabad (formerly Ahmadabad), Goa, Chandigarh, and Trivandrum (also known as Thiruvananthapuram). Unlike most parts of India, these cities boast state-of-the-art software facilities and the presence of many overseas companies.

Much of India's success in developing a software and ICT industry can be explained by the active policies adopted by the State of Karnataka (formerly Mysore) in which Bengaluru is situated. The Karnataka government helped to provide the telecommunications infrastructure that was necessary for software developers to communicate quickly with parent companies in other parts of the world, and this was supported by a set of policies that was designed specifically to encourage investment in software development. Bengaluru has become known as

'India's Silicon Valley', and it has become the city where most large software companies have established.

Although Bengaluru was the first major centre in India for outsourced ICT development in India, others centres are now developing rapidly. Perhaps the most notable of these is Pune (pronounced Poon-ah), situated about 160 kilometres east-south-east from Mumbai, to which is connected by one of India's very few freeways. For several decades, Pune has been one of the largest industrial cities in Maharashtra state, as was known as 'India's Detroit' because several large car companies had their headquarters in the city.

14.12 *A billboard near Pune advertising facilities in a new IT (information technology) park.*

Since 2005, Pune has been attracting investments in hi-tech software and computer hardware. Among the companies that have invested in Pune are Infosys, Satyam, IBM, and Wipro. In the coming years Pune intends to position itself as "India's other Silicon Valley", a twin city for Bengaluru. Rapid development in the area surrounding Pune has totally transformed the landscape, especially in the Kharadi-Kalyani-Nagar belt (figure 14.12). This has led to a real estate boom as Pune's land developers are convinced that there is a high demand for top-end residential units, and projects are under construction with global partners to provide the best technology and amenities to cater to the demands of the prospective purchasers.

Nonetheless, the benefits of Pune's ICT boom have not yet been shared widely through the community, nor even among many of the software developers (figures 14.13 and 14.14). There is an uncomfortable coexistence between modern new high-rise housing for IT technicians and the shanty huts for other parts of the population (figure 14.15). Although the ICT infrastructure has been developed to modern international standards, the same cannot always be said for services to meet the needs of the local population, including many of the software developers (figure 14.16).

can jobs to low-cost locations such as Mexico and South Korea during the 1970s and 1980s — such relocation to least cost (maximum efficiency) countries may be inevitable in an era of globalisation that encourages free trade.

Of course, there is another side to this argument. Although there may have been a loss of ICT jobs in the US, it has created high value employment among many needy people in India while also increasing economic efficiency. International outsourcing does not destroy jobs; it redistributes jobs to places where the efficiency gains are greatest. This in turn puts downward pressure on the prices of ICT products, which benefits consumers in MEDCs — provided they still have a job.

In the case of ICT outsourcing to India, it has also brought significant social benefits. Economic activity in India has traditionally been influenced by the caste system, which places very strict barriers on the progression of a person from one social status (including jobs) to another. However, the social barriers of the caste system have begun to break down as wealth has increased and many more parents have been able to educate their children. Despite the long-term benefits that this change brings, it does lead to short-term family disruptions as the uneducated parents of educated children see their children move away from to the cities (especially the 'software development hotspots') where jobs and new opportunities are available.

14.13 *Typical semi-rural housing on the outskirts of Pune, India.*

14.14 *New luxury apartments under construction for ICT workers near Pune, India.*

14.16 *Software developers stand in the open air as they travel to work near Pune on a local minibus.*

14.15 *Shanty huts (foreground) are situated within clear view of a new housing block for IT workers near Pune, India.*

International outsourcing is a controversial topic. In the United States, there is an increasing number of unemployed ICT workers, dismayed as they see their jobs exported to India. Although the loss of some jobs in the US can be explained by factors such as an economic recession and the collapse of many dot-com start-ups, the deliberate policy of several state governments in India to capture a share of the US ICT industry permanently has also been a factor. Some commentators draw a parallel with the US car making industry, which also saw an export of Ameri-

QUESTION BLOCK 14D

1. Explain the term 'international outsourcing'.

2. Why has international outsourcing become more popular in recent years?

3. Why has India attracted a large share of international outsourcing in the ICT industry?

4. Discuss the benefits and problems of international outsourcing (a) for India, and (b) for MEDCs.

15 Environmental change

Environmental degradation through raw material production, the effects of industrialisation, transboundary pollution and the homogenisation of landscapes.

Outline

Degradation through raw material production Page 588
The effects of agro-industrialisation and changes in international production and consumption on the physical environment. The environmental consequences of growing demand for raw materials.

The effects of transnational manufacturing and services Page 604
Reasons for the relocation of polluting industries to countries with weaker environmental controls and safety regulations.

Transboundary pollution Page 606
International pollution events, the growth of environmental awareness and the role of an NGO in fostering improved environmental management.

Homogenisation of landscapes Page 613
The evolution of uniform urban landscapes; the use of common commercial activity, structures, styles of construction and infrastructure.

**ToK BoX — Page 600
Certainty**

Degradation through Raw Material Production

The Impact of Agro-industrialisation on the Physical Environment

The term **agro-industrialisation** can be defined as the development of agriculture by incorporating corporate and industrial techniques. In a landmark analysis of agro-industrialisation in 2000 by US agricultural economists Thomas Reardon and Christopher Barrett, this definition was expanded and made somewhat more complex to mean (a) the growth of agro-processing, distribution, and farm input provisions off-farm; (b) institutional and organisational change in the relation between farms on the one hand and food processing and distribution companies on the other (such as a marked increase in vertical integration); and (c) simultaneous and consequent changes on farms, such as changes in product composi-

tion, technology, and market structures.

Agriculture is changing at least as quickly as other sectors in the global economy. Whereas the traditional picture of farming was once a family-owned and operated farm producing food for largely local markets, farming in MEDCs (and increasingly in some LEDCs) is becoming a very complex business activity run by large corporations with global marketing links. Increasingly, successful farms are seen as being large, mechanised, corporate-owned and having international networks for obtaining cheap inputs and selling the outputs. Sometimes the outputs are transported on trucks or in ships operated by subsidiaries of the same company, often after initial processing in a factory that is also operated by the same company.

However, it is important to remember that agro-industrialisation is not a uniform trend around the world. In many places, agro-industrialisation is widening the gap between rich and poor farmers, especially in places where significant subsistence agriculture is still found.

One of the consequences of the growth of agro-industrialisation is that the techniques adopted often cause significant damage to the natural environment. For example, many large-scale agro-industrialised farms plant hundreds of hectares with one single crop, a technique known as **monoculture** (figure 15.1). Monoculture is an environmentally unsustainable technique because any single crop draws the same narrow band of nutrients from the soil without the compensation of replenishment by other plant species. Where multiple crops are crown (**interculture**), the nutrients required by one crop species tend to be replaced by one of the other crop species, thus replicating a natural ecosystem and restoring a balanced set of nutrients to the soil.

15.1 *An example of a monoculture — a large rice field on the Chonsamri Co-operative farm near Pyongyang, North Korea. Only the potatoes in the foreground and the corn on the right of the photo add biodiversity to this scene.*

For this reason, a monoculture can only be sustained by adding fertilisers to replace the continual removal of the same nutrients. Many chemical fertilisers are derived from by-products of oil, and they can cause side-effects, such as changing the texture of the soil (often reducing the capacity of the soil to absorb moisture) and adding certain extra minerals that are not required by the particular crop. When this happens, the concentration of those minerals may accumulate over time to levels that can become toxic.

During the second half of the 20th century, large agro-industrial farms were regarded as being more efficient than small-scale farms. From a purely financial perspective, using traditional accounting methods, large capital intensive farms are often more efficient in MEDCs where labour costs are high and capital costs are relatively low. Of course, in LEDCs, where labour is relatively cheap but machines are expensive, the opposite is true.

Regardless of the financial efficiency, however, large-scale agro-industrial farms are very inefficient from an environmental perspective. The most common way to

measure efficiency is to examine the outputs produced compared with the inputs required. When examining environmental efficiency, we can examine the inputs of energy in relation to the energy contained in the foods that are being produced. As explained in chapter 10 (in the discussion on 'increasing mechanisation' in the section on 'the changing nature of food production'), as farming becomes more mechanised, the energy inputs can become so great that we often spend more energy than we are obtaining from the food produced.

Given that solar energy is free, the figures given in chapter 10 showed the ratio of additional energy input to food energy output. For example, a ratio of 1:20 for shifting agriculture shows that 1 kilojoule of muscular effort yields 20 kilojoules of food energy for the shifting cultivators. Hunting and gathering is somewhat less **energy efficient**, partly because energy is spent in the search and chasing activities. Wet rice or intensive rice cultivation is still energy efficient enough to support a farmer and dependants without outside energy input.

However, when we move along the spectrum to the types of activities normally associated with sophisticated commercial agriculture, we see that the energy spent to produce the food is greater than the energy the food actually contains. Dairying or coastal (continental shelf) fishing achieves an approximate balance between energy input and output, but the production of table chickens requires more input of fuel energy than its output in food energy. At the extreme are activities such as feedlot beef production, where the input of energy is about 10 times greater than the output. Ocean fishing also requires high energy input , largely because it is carried out in waters that are distant from the point of fish consumption. The energy subsidy required for ocean fishing also illustrates the fact that harvesting the oceans is not a simple solution to the world's food supply problems.

One of the ironies of agro-industrial farming is that the energy used in producing grain is compounded by the conversion of grain into animal protein. With the shift in tastes in many MEDCs from bread and cereals to beef,

15.2 *Extensive, irrigated energy-intensive agro-industrial farms in the mid-West of the United States.*

Environmental change

pork and chicken, most US grain production is now for animal consumption rather than human consumption (figure 15.2). In the US, about 90% of the corn crop is fed to livestock, and soybeans is the largest single source of protein food for animals. It is, however, extremely inefficient to convert plant material to animal tissue, and this inevitably means that only a tiny fraction of the energy present in the grain will become available to human users.

Of course, there are enormous benefits to humans in this system of energy-subsidised agro-industrial production. With this form of farming, the growth of large cities would be almost impossible, and farm workers would not be freed for culturally more desirable forms of employment. However, these benefits have only been possible with the support of increasingly heavy subsidies of energy. A challenge facing humanity in the years to come is maintaining the enormous benefits in the quality of life (cultural output, education, scientific advances, and so on) while at the same time moving into a declining or steady-state of sustainable energy use.

Another environmental cost of agro-industrial farms arises from the large amounts of pesticides, herbicides, insecticides, and chemical fertilisers that are required to support large-scale capital intensive monoculture farming. It is estimated that in the United States, about 430 million kilograms of pesticides are used each year. However, only about 10% of these chemicals actually reach the insects that they are targeting as excess poisons are released into the air and onto the ground, where they accumulate in streams and the groundwater.

15.3 *The algal bloom on this small water reservoir in Yemen indicates an artificially nutrient-rich environment.*

Wherever chemical fertilisers are used, there is always some runoff of excess nutrients into nearby creeks and rivers. The build up of nutrients in natural waterways can create artificially nutrient-rich environments that lead

to algal blooms (figure 15.3). When algal growth gets out of control, the algae consume all the available oxygen in the water, creating an anaerobic (oxygen-starved) environment which kills the natural plants and water life. Algal blooms and and foul odours are features of many types of agro-industrial farms, such as CAFOs (confined animal feeding operations) for poultry and livestock.

CAFOs present another environmental hazard, as they are places where disease outbreaks can easily and quickly spread due to the high density and close confinement of large numbers of the same species of livestock. In 2009, a world-wide outbreak of deadly swine flu (also known as H1N1, or influenza-A) was traced back to its point of origin, which was said to be a large pig farm in La Gloria, Perote Municipality, Veracruz State, Mexico (figures 15.4 and 15.5). The farm was an agro-industrial farm where 15,000 pigs were raised in 18 large warehouses, run by the subsidiary of a large US-owned transnational food conglomerate.

15.4 *Pigs being raised intensively in an agro-industrial complex in the United States. (Photo: Freeman-Wicklund)*

15.5 *Dead pigs on the farm in Veracruz, Mexico, where swine flu was said to originate. (Photo: Public Citizen Organisation)*

Water pollution from agro-industrial farming can affect areas a long way from the source of the pollution. Because many fertilisers are nitrogen-based, nitrogen compounds are a common type of water pollution downstream of farms where fertilisers are used. In the United

States, nitrogen pollutants from farms in the mid-western states flows down the Mississippi River and poisons coastal waters, leading to the degradation of the fishing industry in the Gulf of Mexico.

Through the financial impact of environmental degradation, we can now measure the economic costs of agro-industrial farming to put into perspective the so-called monetary efficiency of large-scale farming. On one hand, it is claimed that agro-industrial farming brings benefits for consumers through lower prices for food. It is also claimed that agro-industrial farming helps the national economy because the large profits generated by the giant agribusiness corporations boost the national economy, although how widely these benefits are spread throughout the economy is debatable. On the other hand, a full accounting system would offset these possible benefits with the social and environmental costs, including the opportunity cost of jobs lost (because of the small number of people who typically work on such farms), the cost of health problems caused by environmental poisoning, the real costs of extra farming inputs such as fertilisers, pesticides, heavy machinery and fuel costs, and the losses experienced by other industries as a result of environmental degradation.

According to the Union of Concerned Scientists in the United States, a major problem with assessing the environmental impact of agro-industrialisation is that we do not yet have an adequate understanding of the ways some agricultural chemicals impact on living creatures, including humans. One example of this is the potential for endocrine disruption that it seems many pesticides may have. Endocrine disrupters are molecules that have the ability mimic the actions of human and animal hormones, thus disturbing biological functions such as reproduction which are hormone-dependent. At this time, the full extent of the impact of endocrine disrupters is unknown, and many people are calling for a moratorium on their use until more research has been conducted.

QUESTION BLOCK 15A

1. *What is meant by the term 'agro-industrialisation'? In which parts of the world is it most commonly found? Why is this?*

2. *Comment on the energy efficiency of agro-industrialised farms.*

3. *Why are the inefficiencies in agro-industrialisation tolerated?*

4. *Is it fair to blame the global outbreak of swine flu in 2009 on agro-industrialisation?*

5. *Identify the effects of agro-industrialisation on the physical environment.*

Environmental Consequences of the Increasing Demand for Raw Materials

It was shown in chapter 4 that there is a long-term global trend for humans to use more and more resources. To some extent this is a consequence of population growth, but perhaps more importantly it is a result of increasing affluence and changing technology. Increased use of resources inevitably has an impact — usually negative — on the quality of the natural environment. This can be illustrated by the increasing international demand for one raw material resource — timber.

As the demand for raw materials increases, we can either carry on and continue to increase production and the use of resources, or we can plan alternative strategies that substitute one raw material for another, or perhaps find ways to lower expectations so that the demand for resources is reduced. From an environmental perspective, it is preferable not simply to continue using resources according to past patterns of consumption.

15.6 *The effects of over-harvesting timber for fuelwood; this example is near Gonder in northern Ethiopia.*

One example of a raw material that is used in large quantities is timber. In the United States, the amount of timber used annually (by weight) is roughly equivalent to the quantity of metals, plastics, and cement combined (also by weight). When we examine the global picture, the amount of timber used in relation to other materials is even greater (figures 15.6 and 15.7).

15.7 *Selling timber for fuelwood in a small market in Dimeka southern Ethiopia.*

Although finding substitutes for timber would ease the pressures on forestry management, the environmental effects of mining ores for metals, using petrochemicals to produce plastics or mining the raw materials to make cement are usually significantly greater (figure 15.8). Properly managed, timber is a renewable and a recyclable resource, whereas metal ores may be recyclable but they are not renewable.

15.8 *Open cut mining in Kalgoorlie, Western Australia.*

In the following section, a specific case study will be used to illustrate the environmental consequences of the increasing global demand for timber as a raw material for making paper.

Case Study — Forest Management on the Far South Coast of New South Wales, Australia

The forests of the New South Wales far south coast in Australia form a substantial resource base of timber. In an area from Narooma south to the state border between New South Wales and Victoria, trees are cut to provide woodchips, the raw material for making paper. The area extends approximately 160 kilometres from north to south and 60 kilometres west to east, and comprises the dark green areas in figure 15.9. The woodchips are exported to Japan where they are converted into paper, mainly low-grade paper for computing. At times, the forestry operations have led to significant conflicts within the local community. On one hand, conservationists object to the destruction of the forests, while on the other, many people support the forestry operations because of the employment and the facilities which they bring.

Environmental systems of the region

In order to understand the environmental impact of forestry in this region, it is necessary to understand the nature of the natural environment before human impact in order that the significance of the changes can be understood. The environmental systems of any area interact in a delicate balance. When people enter an area these environmental systems are modified. Sometimes this leads to a deterioration in the environment, although this is not always the case.

The **landforms** of the far south coast of New South Wales fall into two main groups. Near the coast is the first landform area, an undulating lowland which is well drained by creeks and rivers. However, about 40 kilometres inland this coastal lowland gives way to the second landform area, the steep escarpment of the Great Divide. In this area, slopes are much steeper, in some cases exceeding 30°, but frequently about 15°.

These landforms affect the **climate** of the area. The coastal plain receives about 850 mm of rain each year. However, the rainfall is considerably higher on the escarpment (about 1,000 mm) due to orographic uplift of moist air blowing in from the Tasman Sea. Precipitation is distributed evenly through the year. Nonetheless, the rainfall of the far south coast is extremely unreliable. Long droughts are frequent, while most of the rain comes in storms of a few days' duration when a stationary low pressure area is located over the Tasman Sea. The rainfall throughout the area is regarded as well above the minimum to sustain forests.

Geology varies greatly through the area. Near the coast is a thin strip of sedimentary rocks such as shale, although many of these rocks have been metamorphosed (heated and placed under pressure) into slate. Inland, most of the rocks are granite.

Soils formed from the granites are acidic, shallow, coarse in texture and fairly infertile. They are usually classified as red and yellow podzolics. These soils are easily eroded because of their loose structure, particularly when they are found on steep slopes. Where streams flow through steep, granitic soils, a great amount of natural erosion

15.9 *A map of the far south coast of New South Wales, with forests shown in dark green.* (Source: after Google Earth)

occurs, and this has resulted in the silting up of many of the district streams. On the other hand, soils on the coastal strip are much more stable, having more clay-sized particles.

Fires have always occurred naturally on the far south coast. Before human occupation, they were started by lightning strikes. After Indigenous occupation of the area, the number of fires increased somewhat due to spread from cooking, hunting and ceremonial fires.

However, since European occupation the number of fires has increased enormously.

There is abundant natural **fauna** in the area, such as wallabies, echidnas, bandicoots, wombats, possums and insects. There are also some introduced species which have become very common since the mid-nineteenth century. Examples of these include rabbits, European hares and rats. These animals have adapted to the forest ecosystem, each finding a specific **ecological niche** (see the section in chapter 3 headed 'biomes, ecosystems and biodiversity'). Few of the faunal communities yet studied are regarded as being rare, although some species present, such as the long-footed potoroo, the yellow-bellied glider and the eastern pygmy possum, are endangered.

From a raw materials perspective, the environmental system of most interest to humans in this area is the **vegetation**. Except for a thin coastal strip along the sand dunes, the vegetation communities on the far south coast are forest communities. The main vegetation types are coastal species of eucalyptus, such as *Eucalyptus sieberi* (silvertop ash) on the coastal plains and *Eucalyptus fastigata* (brown barrel) on the higher altitudes of the escarpment. In common with many areas of Australia, native flora has evolved under the influence of fire, and has thus adapted to it and, in many cases, become dependent on it for re-production to occur.

Background to forestry on the far south coast

The original inhabitants and traditional owners of the far south coast were the Yuin people, who first settled in the area about 20,000 years ago. Apart from some minor impact from fires, the Yuin people lived in harmony with the environment, taking only the resources which were needed by each family at the time. The impact of Indigenous Australians was mostly near the coast, and there are still remains of old camp sites in some areas. One of the tall mountains in the district, Mumbulla Mountain, is regarded as a sacred site by local Aboriginal people, who fought to prevent an expansion of logging into the area in the early 1980s. This resulted in the area being gazetted as the Biamanga Aboriginal Place in 1983 under the guidance of the National Parks and Wildlife Service.

European settlers began arriving in the district in the 1820s. These settlers saw the district differently from Indigenous Australians. The Europeans viewed it as being very rich in seemingly limitless resources that were simply waiting to be exploited. There was no competition for resources because there were plenty for the small numbers of people at the time. Consequently, resources such as water and timber were very cheap.

A timber cutting industry was established round Tathra and Bermagui, to the north of Eden, during the 1800s. Timber was cut for saw-milling and for railway sleepers, and was removed from the forest by bullock teams. The timber was either milled near Bega or transported to Sydney where it was sold as logs. This early logging involved **selective felling**; only a few trees were cut, leaving the forest ecosystem virtually intact. A more intensive form of selective felling ('sawlog plus salvage pulp log') is still practised in some areas, particularly around Bega and Narooma. However, since 1969 the focus of timber cutting has been felling for **woodchips**, which are small chips of wood shredded from low quality eucalyptus timber (figure 15.10). They are exported from the woodchip mill at Eden to Japan, where they are pulped for paper manufacture (figure 15.11).

15.10 *Woodchips at the Harris-Daishowa mill near Eden, Australia.*

15.11 *An oblique aerial view of the woodchip mill near Eden.*

Forestry operations

About 300 people are employed in harvesting the forests for woodchipping around Eden. Logging for woodchips is a **clear felling** operation. This means that every suitable tree in the working area is cut down, leaving only a scattering of unsuitable trees (crooked, fire damaged, or unwanted species). Even these trees are often cut down and simply left on the ground. Good quality logs are sent to a sawmill, while poorer quality timber is sent for woodchipping. Individual trees may be marked by foresters for retention as future sawlogs. These trees will be cut at a later time — probably after about 40 years. Clear felling means that the forestry operation is more profitable, with larger volumes of timber being obtained within each time period. Furthermore, the forests around Eden are regarded as old and derelict, with virtually no commercially useful growth and with the growth of new trees being balanced by the decay and death of others. Thus, the area is regarded by foresters as suitable for clear felling.

15.12 *Heavy machinery disturbs the soil on this logging operation in the hills to the west of Bega, Australia.*

Any forestry operation disturbs the soil, exposing it to soil erosion (figure 15.12). In order to minimise the effects of erosion, drains are built *across* the slopes to stop any long, fast runs of water developing. Furthermore, drains are built to empty into undisturbed areas where the water can be absorbed in the ground litter and soil. To stop sediments reaching streams and causing siltation, unlogged strips of forest 20 metres wide are left on both sides of all permanent streams (figure 15.13). Research shows that most eroded sediment does not move more than 5 or 6 metres through such an undisturbed area as long as the terrain is not too steep. On occasions, these 'filter strips' may be logged as long as the trees to be cut down are marked by a forester and the trees are felled away from the stream.

15.13 *Although Tantawanglo Creek is in a logging area, the sides of the creek are protected by a 20 metre strip on each side of the stream where trees may not be cut.*

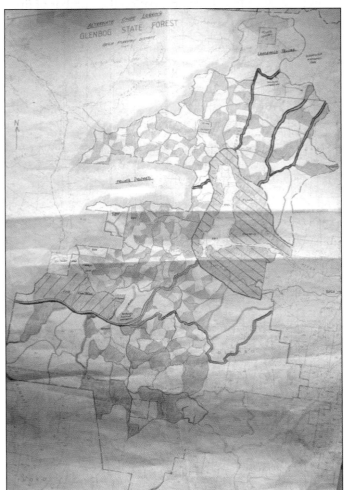

15.14 *This forester's map of part of Glenbog State Forest shows the 'chess board' pattern of logged (in white) and protected (in green) areas. The protected areas along streams and beside main roads can also be seen.*

Another way in which erosion is controlled is to conduct logging operations in small areas of a few square kilometres each, called 'compartments'. When seen from above, the compartments appear in a pattern that resembles the black and white squares of a chess board. Only 50% of a particular compartment may actually be logged, and this 50% must be in small patches of under 100 hectares each (figure 15.14). Other sections of the compartment may be logged after about 20 years, meaning that the entire area will have been cleared after about 40 years. Forests NSW (the government authority that regulates forestry in New South Wales) requires that at least five mature trees per 15 hectares, preferably grouped, must be left uncut to preserve wildlife habitats.

After clear felling, **regeneration** of the forest becomes necessary. This is not only to prevent erosion, but to provide timber for future harvesting. Re-growth comes partly from seedlings already growing before logging, but mostly from seeds which are shed during logging or from dead trees left lying in the forest. In most areas, natural regeneration has been considered adequate (figure 15.15).

Environmental change

However, in cases where the ground was compacted by heavy machinery during the logging operations, regeneration is slow. In such areas, Forests NSW workers rip the compacted soil and plant eucalypts. It is claimed that after regeneration, excellent conditions are provided for native herbivores such as wallabies, and the populations of many of these animals increase as a result of the logging.

15.15 *This area of regenerated forest was a logging road just one year before this photograph was taken.*

Pressures on the logging industry

During recent decades, the population of the far south coast district has grown very quickly. This has been the result of a growth in the district's tourist industry and prosperity from dairying as well as timber cutting. However, the greater numbers of people have increased pressures on the resources of the district. To meet these demands, exploitation of resources (including forests) has increased. In contrast with the situation during early settlement in the mid-1800s, the forestry resources are now seen as being finite.

According to conservationists, clear felling of natural forests has now reached the point where logging will soon have to rely solely on regenerated forests with trees about thirty years old within a decade or so. However, thirty years re-growth may not produce trees large enough for further harvesting. Many authorities consider that eucalypt forests in the district will require about fifty years' re-growth before a sustainable harvesting cycle can be established.

Conservationists argue that the quantities of timber cut for woodchipping amount to 'mining' the forest resource rather than 'managing' it so that the timber will last for all time. Foresters argue that one answer to this problem will probably be to expand the areas subject to clear felling, so that additional areas of state forests are used in this way. They argue that this would allow more time for forest regeneration and would reduce the concentration of damaging environmental effects in the area.

Effects of clear-fell logging on the ecosystem

Foresters and conservationists differ about the impacts of clear-fell logging on the ecosystem. Both points of view are presented here. It is up to you to consider the viewpoints expressed, and then make up your own mind about the issue and *justify* your opinion.

'Pro-logging' viewpoint

Foresters argue that clear felling is very suitable for the far south coast because the area regenerates immediately after cutting (taking from 1 to 5 years). The *density* of the re-growth is also very high, ensuring that the new trees grow very straight. The regenerated forest consists of the same species as the original forest, and the new growth is said to be comparable with the growth which occurs naturally after a severe fire. Foresters argue that the only difference is that the produce of the forest is now being used to benefit people rather than simply being converted to charred wood and smoke. Conservationists, on the other hand, argue that there are great differences between fire and logging. During a fire the nutrient loss is very small, whereas about 60% of phosphorus available from the tree leave the site in a debarked tree log.

Dieback disease appeared in district forests in the early 1980s. This caused death in trees, starting at the tips of the shoots and working downwards. Its cause is still unknown, although some have suggested that an imbalance of species within the ecosystem could cause it. This theory rests on the assumption that there are many insect species within the forest ecosystem which alone could cause the death of trees on a widespread scale. Generally they do not do so because they are held in balance by predator species. Suddenly, this control mechanism seemed to be absent from many areas of eucalypt forests of New South Wales from the mid-1970s onwards, leading to dieback. Others claim that the dieback is transmitted in the soil on logging machinery. It must be emphasised, however, that these are just two of several theories proposed, and the true cause is still unknown. However, some argue that as a result of dieback disease, the natural forests should be harvested while they may still have an economic use.

Eucalypts have a relatively high demand for light, so they rely on occasional severe site disturbance for their survival. In fact, it is claimed that without fire or some other major disturbance (such as logging), several major species of eucalypt such as blackbutt and stringy bark would become endangered species over a number of generations. If it were not for major site disturbances, they would be replaced by more shade-tolerant species.

Fires are seen as being part of the natural forest ecology, but they create several problems. Apart from destroying the timber, they destroy both food and habitats for wildlife, some soil nutrients (such as nitrogen) are lost to the atmosphere from the vegetation community, erosion is increased substantially, and the surface litter (a source of nutrients) is destroyed along with many of the decomposer organisms (figure 15.16). In order to preserve the forests for cutting, fire trails have been established and control burning is carried out in safe periods to reduce the litter on the ground. Although fire trails allow a greater potential for people to get into the forests to start fires, they also allow a much better chance of stopping fires of both natural and human origin once they have started.

15.16 *A forest fire send a dense plume of smoke over the nearby settled areas of the Bega Valley, Australia.*

New forestry roads and fire trails are also used by tourists, who would otherwise have found the remote sections of the forests inaccessible. Indeed, a number of forest drives and picnic areas have been provided in state forests of the area, along with some camping sites.

A further positive influence of logging concerns the habitats for wildlife. Existence of natural bushland does not necessarily mean that there is a large range of flora and fauna. Some old natural forests which are in a declining state may not have many habitats for wildlife. Because the forests which regenerate are thicker and healthier than the original, the habitats for many wildlife species are said to be improved after logging. However, because the re-growth has an even age throughout, the diverse range of habitats in a natural, multi-storeyed forest may be narrowed down to a smaller range of habitats. Some native animals increase in population after logging because of the greater supplies of food available in a thick, regenerated forest. Furthermore, specific habitats of some animals are not logged. It has been found that the favoured habitat of many tree-dwelling animals is the monkey gum trees next to creeks. Must of these are found in the strip of forest not logged because of the need for a **sediment trap** beside creeks and steams.

Diseases which could kill productive trees are more closely controlled in state forest areas than in natural forests because of the economic value of the timber.

Thus, positive effects on the environment are said to stem from woodchipping.

About 20% of the forests on the far south coast are preserved as national parks and state recreation areas. According to surveys, this is regarded by most people in the district as an adequate and substantial sample of the unlogged native forest, but most of these reserves are near the coast where tourists are most likely to visit. They do not provide a representative sample of environments; they over-represent coastal communities.

Although siltation into rivers increases after logging, the rates of siltation return to their previous levels after regeneration of the forests. Moreover, officers from the NSW State Fisheries Department claim that there has been no decline in the quality of fish life in local streams and estuaries since logging began.

'Anti-logging' viewpoint

Conservationists argue that forestry is the main environmental problem of the district. This is not so much because of any problems with regeneration — indeed, the quality of the regenerated forest is acknowledged by foresters and conservationists alike as being much thicker than the derelict natural forests.

Conservationists are chiefly concerned about the effects of fire in regenerated forests, particularly on the escarpment. Regenerated forest in these areas consists of *Eucalyptus fastigata*, a species common in areas of high rainfall. It grows very thickly, with some areas of regenerated forest having densities of nine plants per square metre (figure 15.17). This very dense growth means that fuel levels (material available for burning) are very high. Combustible material extends from the ground litter layer right up the branches to the tree tops.

15.17 *An area of extremely dense regenerated Eucalyptus fastigata forest.*

In November 1980 a forest fire began at Timbillica, south of Eden. This fire focussed the attention of conservationists on the environmental problems of forestry for the first time. The fire became the most destructive in the district's history, burning over 44,000 hectares (440 km²). Much of this fire was in *Eucalyptus sieberi* regenerated forest, and the result was a fuel resembling an explosive mixture of gas and air. The fire was too strong to be fought, and fire fighters simply had to wait for a change in wind direction. Because of the intensity of the flames, only the largest trees remained, and even they were killed by the fire. The landscape was reported to have resembled a desert after the fire. All plants and animals had been killed, and few remaining seeds were capable of regenerating.

Conservationists are concerned that the entire area being clear felled for woodchipping will be liable to the same type of damage. Certainly, they are concerned about those areas of regenerated forest on the escarpment consisting of dense *Eucalyptus fastigata* , even thicker than the *Eucalyptus sieberi* which burned at Timbillica. There is less concern about regenerated forests of *Eucalyptus sieberi* on the coastal plain. Nonetheless, all forests are liable to more severe fire damage than natural forests because all the growth is of the same age, concentrating fuel levels at one particular height, and because there is very abundant litter production in the dense regenerated forests.

The main problems with fire in young re-growth are:
- young forests have more leaves per hectare than a mature forest, and therefore more fuel for fires;
- leaves are closer to the ground, increasing the chance of a crown fire; and
- young trees may be sexually immature; if killed they may not be replaced as they will not have produced any seeds.

Another area of concern to conservationists is the **deterioration of water supplies** that follows logging. Many of the state forests being logged are in parts of catchments for district water supply. This applies particularly to forests on the steep escarpment to the west of the area. Areas in a natural state (before logging) retain soil moisture for long periods due to the undisturbed soil structure, the deep litter and the shade provided by the tree cover. Heavy falls of orographic rain from onshore winds sometimes occur on the escarpment, an example being one fall of 914 mm over three days in 1973 near Tantawanglo Creek. Uncut forests can absorb such heavy falls easily as the rainfall infiltrates the thick fern litter on the surface, with very little excess for overland flow.

On the other hand, after clear felling, the surface of the soil is disturbed and the leftover timber is burned on the site. This means that there is less infiltration, and the overland flow which results is about 40% higher than for a natural forest. This erodes large quantities of soil, and the fine sediment can be seen after rains as a muddy colour in the stream water. As shown in figure 5.16 in chapter 5, surface run-off after rainfall in human-affected catchments is of shorter duration, but much greater intensity, than run-off from natural catchments.

Apart from the actual logging operations, soil erosion can also arise from the roads and tracks associated with logging. Most forestry roads follow the ridge tops. However, the minor tracks leading to these extend down the sides of the hills, creating paths for running water to erode (figure 15.18). These tracks are usually only used for a few days or weeks, after which they are ploughed and drained, and sometimes sown with grass seed.

15.18 *Forestry roads tend to follow the ridge tops to minimise soil erosion during periods of rain.*

Fire can aggravate erosion. Two years after the fire at Timbillica, bare earth was still widespread and susceptible to erosion, although fortunately, very little rain fell during this period. After an intense wildfire, overland flow increases greatly. This is because the reduction in litter, the destruction of humus in the top few centimetres of soil and the destruction of ground level vegetation remove obstacles to overland flow. A further factor concerns the soil structure. Large cracks in the soil, called **macropores**, through which water usually infiltrates, become sealed at the surface during the fire, increasing overland flow which in turn increases erosion from the newly exposed soil.

Thus, flooding after rains becomes more likely after logging, and there is also greater chance of streams drying up during droughts. The eroded soil washes into nearby streams, causing silt burdens and degrading quality and reliability of the water for other uses (figure 15.19). Among these other uses which are affected are the district's main income earners, which are dairying (which needs clear, reliable water for irrigation) and tourism, which requires abundant water during the dry summer months to supply the influx of tourists. Each litre of milk produced requires 1,000 litres of water to produce it, while tourists may be reluctant to stay at places where a supply of water cannot be guaranteed.

15.19 *The bed of Wolumla Creek is heavily silted as a result of logging operations upstream.*

Another concern of conservationists is the destruction of the ecosystem by the removal of certain species which are key elements of the food web. As explained in chapter 3, the plants and animals in any ecosystem are mutually dependent in a complex web of inter-relationships. If one species is removed, it can wipe out all the other species that feed on it or are dependent on it. This can lead to a chain reaction, destroying the forest ecosystem.

Conservationists argue that forestry practices have already initiated this effect in the area's forests. For example, one of the many types of insects in far south coast forests is the psyllid (pronounced 'sigh-lid'), which is a jumping louse that lives on eucalypts by sucking sap.

Many kinds of birds eat psyllids, and this stops the numbers of psyllids exploding. One kind of bird, the bellbird, feeds on psyllids, but unlike other species of birds, it only eats the waxy coating on the psyllids' backs. Bellbirds do not kill psyllids.

Bellbirds inhabit the fringes, or edges, of the forest. They are aggressive towards other birds, and drive them away from their territory. After forestry operations have expanded in a chess board pattern, clearing alternate squares but leaving the alternating squares uncut, the entire forest becomes peppered with cleared zones. In other words, the entire forest becomes a fringe environment that is attractive to bellbirds. This has enabled the bellbirds to expand their territory through the entire forest. As the bellbirds' area has expanded, psyllid numbers have also increased because the birds that used to eat them have been driven away by the aggressive bellbirds.

As psyllid numbers have increased, the health of the eucalypts has declined because more of their sap is being sucked. This has led to the death of the trees in some areas, and some researchers speculate it may be one of the causes of dieback disease. Because the number of psyllids in the forest depends upon on the number of bellbirds, we say that bellbirds and psyllids are in an ecological association, usually labelled the **bellbird-psyllid association**.

QUESTION BLOCK 15B

1. Describe the environmental systems of the New South Wales far south coast before human impact.

2. Describe the environmental impact of the Yuin people.

3. What view of the district's environment was held by the district's early European settlers? Why has this view changed in recent years?

4. What is the difference between selective and clear felling of trees?

5. What are woodchips? Where are woodchips from Eden used, and for what purpose? Do you expect that the international demand for woodchips is increasing or decreasing?

6. How is soil erosion from clear felling minimised?

7. What is forest regeneration? Is it a good thing or a problem in the far south cost of New South Wales?

8. What pressures has population growth on the far south coast of New South Wales placed on forestry operations?

9. Using the following headings, write two to four lines on each of the suggested environmental advantages and disadvantages of woodchipping:
   Environmental advantages:
   a   quality of regenerated forests
   b   response to dieback disease
   c   response of eucalypt trees to fire
   d   fire control
   e   wildlife habitats.
   Environmental disadvantages:
   a   increased fuel levels
   b   much more severe fires
   c   increased soil erosion
   d   siltation of streams
   e   ecological disruptions, such as the bellbird-psyllid association.

10. Prepare a class debate on the topic "Woodchipping on the far south coast of New South Wales is not, on balance, harmful for the environment". There should be three speakers on each side — affirmative and negative. Each side should prepare a case, thoroughly researching the topic by reading and conducting research. During the debate, the class should note the arguments presented by both sides, being careful that all arguments have been supported by evidence, facts and reasoning (see the ToK Box in chapter 8 for more background on 'reasoning'). Selected members of the class can then adjudicate the debate and present their decisions. Remember that in both debating and adjudicating, it is essential to present the reasons for any statement that is made, but that no matter how sound the facts appear to be, achieving 'certainty' will not be possible (as demonstrated in the ToK Box on the next page).

ToK BoX

When we look at the issue of environmental change, one of the questions that arises is "how can we be *certain* that these things are really happening?". To generalise the question and express it more broadly, how can be *certain* of anything?

The French philosopher René Descartes (1596-1650) lived during a time when the prevailing philosophy was scepticism. Scepticism is the view that doubts whether any of our views can be supported by adequate or sufficient information. In other words, sceptics doubt everything.

Descartes refused to surrender to scepticism. He had an intense desire for certainty — to be so certain that no discovery could ever shake his beliefs again.

Descartes decided there is no need to test every opinion, which would be an 'endless undertaking', because opinions can be grouped together and categorised, enabling us to consider general types of belief.

Using this as a basis, Descartes claimed "If there is any reason for doubt, then the entire category ought to be treated as doubtful and unreliable."

His starting point was to say that that ALL ordinary information — including all scientific and mathematical information — is open to challenge because it is the product of human construction.

In his own words, "I did not imitate the sceptics, who doubt only for the sake of doubting, and pretend they are always uncertain. On the contrary, my purpose was only to obtain good grounds for assurance for myself — to reject quicksand and mud so that I might find the rock or clay".

He then proceeded to set aside anything that might contain the smallest element of doubt as though it was completely false until he was left only with what was absolutely certain.

His requirements for certainty were so strict that when he did this, he found that there was almost nothing about which he could be absolutely certain. As he said: "I became convinced that there was nothing in the entire world — that there was no heaven, no earth, that there were no minds, nor any bodies. Was I not then also convinced that I did not exist? Not in the least! I was certain that I myself existed since I convinced myself of something (or just because I thought of something)".

But then he thought: "Maybe there is some kind of a deceiver, who is very powerful and very cunning, who always uses his ingenuity to deceive me. Then, for certain I exist also if he is deceiving me, and let him deceive me as much as he wishes, because he can never make me nothing as long as I think I am something."

"So, after having considered this well, we have to arrive at the definite conclusion that the proposition 'I THINK, THEREFORE I EXIST' has to be true every time I utter it, or that I mentally think about it."

This certainty is more commonly expressed as "I think, therefore I am". As Descartes said, "As soon as you try to conceive any condition under which this might possibly be false, you engage in a thought that confirms and assures you that you must exist in order to think!". Descartes was convinced he had discovered a truth that "was so certain and so assured that all the arguments from the sceptics could not shake it".

From the truth "I think, therefore I am", Descartes claimed that we can discover a criterion for ALL truths. He said: "The only feature of this statement that convinces me it is true is that I clearly and distinctly see, or understand, what is being said". Therefore, he claimed, "Clarity and distinctness must be the marks of truth — the distinguishing characteristics by which you can tell the true from the false".

From this conclusion, Descartes formulated the rule: "Whatever is clearly and distinctly conceived, is true".

But how can we know if something is clear and distinct?

Descartes claimed that "An experience or thought is clear if it is so forceful that we cannot avoid being aware of it". He said there were two types of such thoughts and experiences. The first was 'vivid sense experiences' — something that was so powerful that it could not be ignored, such as a toothache. The second was 'certain types of ideas', such as mathematical ideas, thinking or wishing.

However, there was a problem with this categorisation. To be distinct, an idea had to be unrelated or able to be separated from all other ideas. To be clear, its source had to be identifiable. However, ideas can be clear without being distinct, and sense experiences could be distinct without being clear. For

example, a toothache might be distinct, but is the source of pain in the tooth, the nerves or the brain? The idea of a mermaid might be clear, but how can it be separated from other ideas such as women, fish and the oceans?

Descartes struggled with these thoughts and came to the point of saying "If we had the ability to distinguish an experience from everything else in the world, then the experience could not possibly be confused with anything else, in which case it would be distinct as well as clear."

After further struggles, he concluded "When I examine my ideas to see which of them are clear and distinct, I discover that most of them are either unclear or indistinct. They either come from my experiences or from ideas I have had."

But then he found another type of idea called innate ideas which do not come from experiences and which are not constructed or invented by the imagination. These are ideas which seem to be 'hard-wired' into our being.

Descartes said that there were two categories of innate ideas. The first was mathematical objects, such as the idea of a circle. No circle we see is perfectly round, but the one we can think about is, and therefore it is an idea that originates outside our experience. The second category was the idea of a perfect being (God). In Descartes' view, we are not perfect enough to invent the sort of perfection that exists in some of our ideas, especially that of God. "Therefore", claimed Descartes, "there must be a God who has created me and who has implanted in me the idea of a perfect being."

From this, Descartes concluded there are two truths:

1. I think, therefore I am.
2. God exists.

Many philosophers following Descartes have struggled to find either certainty or truth.

For example, the empiricists assumed that all knowledge comes from sense experiences. But as the senses are unreliable, we therefore can't be certain of anything.

Relativists claim that there are no such things as truth and certainty. They seem quite certain that this is a truth, and as we will see in chapter 17, that undermines their claim to a large degree.

The next ToK BoX is on page 634.

Environmental Impact of Air Freight

The concept of 'food miles' was discussed in chapter 10 (in the section headed 'sustainable agriculture and the future of farming'). In that discussion, it was stated that the concept of food miles can serve as a useful reminder of the need to control the amount of energy used to move food from one location to another, but the concept also has some serious limitations when applied in a practical sense.

In recent decades, the cost of air freight relative to other forms of transport has decreased. This has enabled air freight to become a financially competitive way to transport fresh food and produce over vast distances when compared with other forms of transport, especially when the costs of preserving food on ships over several weeks is considered.

Every modern airliner has an under-floor cargo area that enables large volumes of freight to be transported in the space not occupied by passengers' baggage (which is why many airliners are keen to limit the quantity of luggage passengers can take with them). Indeed, many airlines can fly profitably with an airliner carrying almost no passengers because of the high profitability of air freight. In addition to the freight carried on commercial passenger services, there has been a rapid growth in dedicated cargo aircraft over the past few decades (figure 15.20).

15.20 *The world's largest aircraft, the Ukrainian Antonov An-225, is used for transporting large cargo. (Photo: Glenn Beasley)*

However, air transport has been heavily criticised by environmentalists as a significant cause of global warming (as discussed in chapters 3 and 6). According to the Intergovernmental Panel on Climate Change (IPCC), fuel emissions from aircraft accounted for just under 3% of human contributions to climate change.

Air travel has been criticised on environmental grounds for three main reasons:

First, if the atmospheric conditions are 'right' (which is about 15% of the time if the upper atmosphere air is still and clear, the relative humidity is 100%, and the tempera-ture is below -38°C), aircraft may emit **contrails**. Contrails are long, thin clouds that condense from the water vapour emitted from the exhaust of jet engines at high altitudes (figure 15.21). When contrails form, the narrow bands of ice crystals emitted from the engines gradually expand into a cirrus type high altitude cloud, provided the atmospheric conditions are suitable. Contrails are inherently unstable, and most of the time, they fade away within a few minutes and they pose no threat. However, under certain conditions when the clear air is cold and extremely still, a contrail may remain for a longer period, especially in polar regions (figure 15.22). It is claimed that like clouds, contrails can trap heat in the atmosphere, especially at night, and are thus a source of global warming.

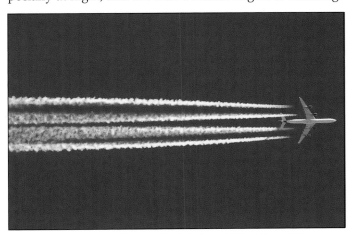

15.21 *Contrails from a four-engined Airbus A340 airliner. (Photo: Randall Johnson)*

Evidence that contrails affect the weather is often quoted by referring to the period in the United States from 11th to 14th September, 2001. During these three days, all flights over the United States ceased after a series of terrorist attacks in New York and Washington DC. For this three day period, no contrails were produced because there were no flights, and the average diurnal range in temperatures in the United States was reported to be the highest diurnal range over a three day period for over 30 years.

However, these results have been disputed on the bases that:

- if contrails are such a a significant cause of global warming, reversing their impact after 40 years of jet airliners should take longer than just three days;
- such a rapid shift in weather conditions is far more likely to be caused by a change in the air masses moving across the continent than suddenly removing contrails; and
- the evidence quoted is based on measurements taken at just five weather stations, and a few isolated readings during a three-day period is too small a sample to draw conclusions about a general, long-term global climate trend.

According to atmospheric scientists who have analysed US weather during the period in question, early September usually marks the time when a significant seasonal shift in weather occurs due to the arrival of frontal weather systems. The first of these frontal systems for 2001 moved across the United States immediately before the September 11th terrorist attacks. At the time, the atmosphere was relatively dry across the country and the skies were absolutely clear because of a strong high pressure system that did not move for several days. This, combined with the relatively high mid-September angle of the sun, caused daytime temperatures to climb rapidly. Because there were no winds, cold air sank quickly to the surface at night, causing the significant fall in night temperatures.

15.22 *The mass of contrails indicates very still and cold conditions over Frankfurt (Germany) on the day this photograph was taken. (Photo: Martin Boschhuizen)*

Although this type of weather pattern is an annual event in the United States in early September, environmentalists focussed greater attention on it than usual because the cancellation of all flights was thought to provide an 'experimental control' situation to measure the effect of removing contrails. However, the upper atmospheric conditions for most of the three days in question would not have allowed many contrails to form in any case. US government meteorologists have reported that the diurnal temperature range was precisely what would have been expected given the the surface dew points, atmospheric conditions, and air masses during the time period studied — with or without contrails.

The warming impact of contrails is said to be greater at night than during the day. This is because the earth's surface loses heat at night time, and clouds (or contrails) trap the heat and prevent it from escaping. By this same reasoning, if contrails have any effect, the impact during the daytime should be to cool the earth's surface in the same way as clouds, by reflecting a greater proportion of incoming solar radiation back into space.

According to the American Geophysical Union, contrails make up 1% of all the sources of human induced global warming. Even this small quantity is disputed, however, and there remains an absence of substantial evidence to

support the hypothesis that contrails cause global warming. As an aside, it is not only aircraft that produce contrails — geese exhaling warm, moist air into -38°C air have also been reported to produce small contrails.

The second area of environmental criticism directed towards air travel is that aircraft flying at high altitudes release chemicals that **disturb the composition** of the upper atmosphere. One example of these chemicals is **nitrogen oxide**, which reacts with the atmosphere to increase ozone concentrations. **Ozone** (O_3) in the atmosphere protects the earth's surface from harmful ultraviolet radiation by absorbing it; ultraviolet radiation causes skin cancer, cataracts and immune suppression in both animals and humans. During the 1980s and 1990s, the refrigerants and propellants used in many cooling and air conditioning systems (such as CFCs, or chlorofluorocarbons) reacted with atmospheric ozone to destroy it, leading to a thinning of ozone (especially over the poles). This increased the amount of heat and ultraviolet radiation reaching the earth's surface, causing widespread concern. Since that time, the use of CFCs has been heavily restricted, relieving the problem significantly.

Ozone near the earth's surface is the main component of photochemical smog, and it is dangerous for humans. On the other hand, ozone in the upper atmosphere can be seen as desirable, especially during a period of global warming, as it filters the ultraviolet radiation. In the 1960s, the introduction of supersonic transport aircraft (SSTs) such as the Concorde was criticised by environmentalists on the grounds that the airliners would produce upper atmospheric ozone that could trigger a new ice age — as discussed in the ToK Box in chapter 3, the main concern about climate change in the 1960s and 1970s was global cooling, not global warming. These days, by contrast, environmentalists' criticism is that the production of upper atmospheric ozone by aircraft is **masking** the full impact of global warming, and that by offsetting the rise in atmospheric temperatures it is causing people to be too complacent and thus not taking global warming seriously enough.

The third area of environmental criticism directed towards air travel is the high level of **carbon dioxide emissions** and their impact as a cause of global warming. It has been estimated that air travel (people and freight combined) contributes 3% to 5% to the world's carbon dioxide emissions. As explained in chapters 3 and 6, carbon dioxide (CO_2) is a 'greenhouse gas', which means there is a broad positive correlation between the atmospheric concentration of CO_2 and average temperatures world-wide. On the other hand, as the ToK Box in chapter 3 explained, there is a debate over the direction of the causal relationship — does CO_2 cause temperatures to increase or is a build up of CO_2 the consequence of increased temperatures?

The environmental impact of air travel has become a contentious subject over the past decade. One environmental lobby group's website claims "It (aviation) is one of the principal contributors to global environmental problems such as climate change, ozone depletion, and the wasteful use of scarce raw materials". The Advisory Council for Aeronautical Research in Europe (ACARE), a consulting group to the EU, has called for a 50% reduction in carbon emissions for all new aircraft designed and built from 2020 onwards. This should not be a difficult target to achieve when we realise that modern aircraft engines produce about 85% fewer emissions for every kilogram of fuel burned than engines built in the 1970s, and jet engines today burn about half the fuel per kilometre travelled compared with equivalent engines 30 years ago. Compared with the jet engines of 50 years ago, today's engines use 70% less fuel per kilometre.

Because of concerns with the environmental impact of flying, there is an increasing trend for **carbon offsetting**. People are urged to 'offset' the environmental impact of their flights (as well as their car driving and even their home air conditioning) by sending money to purchase an equivalent carbon saving. The money goes to one of many organisations that promises to neutralise an individual's carbon emissions, some by planting trees which they claim will absorb an equivalent amount of CO_2, others by providing cleaner energy to poor countries. Unfortunately, publicity about scam organisations that have stolen people's carbon offsetting money has meant that such schemes have lost credibility in the eyes of some people who now doubt whether the forest or the wind turbine actually exist, and question the regulations that govern the operation of such funds.

Typical carbon offsetting websites calculate the amount of CO_2 a person will be responsible for through flying. Some websites calculate what at first appear to be excessively **large amounts of carbon dioxide**. Using the example of a one-way flight between Hong Kong and Sydney (Australia), a distance of 7,372 kilometres, one widely used website (Atmosfair — http://www.atmosfair.de) claimed that the weight of CO_2 gas generated would be 856,000 kg (in a Boeing 747, economy class, carrying 400 passengers — figure 15.23). At first this figure seems absurdly large, as the empty weight of a Boeing 747 is about 162,000 kg, and the maximum take-off weight of the plane, fully loaded with all passengers, fuel and cargo is about 350,000 kg.

How could 856,000 kg of gas (even a 'heavy' gas like carbon dioxide) be generated by a fully loaded metal aircraft that weighed much less than half of the weight of the gas apparently produced? Part of the answer lies in the chemical reaction between the burnt aviation fuel and the atmosphere. One litre of aviation fuel weighs about 0.75 kg, and it is claimed that when burnt it produces 2.4 kg of

carbon dioxide (CO_2). This is explained by the fact that most of the weight of the CO_2 does not come from the fuel (which is a hydrocarbon), but the oxygen in the air. When fuel burns, the carbon and hydrogen separate. The hydrogen combines with oxygen to form water (H_2O), and carbon combines with oxygen to form carbon dioxide (CO_2). A carbon atom has a weight of 12, and each oxygen atom has a weight of 16, giving each single molecule of CO_2 an atomic weight of 44 (12 from the carbon and 32 from the oxygen). Therefore, to calculate the amount of CO_2 produced from a litre of aviation fuel, the weight of the carbon in the fuel is multiplied by $^{44}/_{12}$, or 3.7. Since aviation fuel is about 87% carbon and 13% hydrogen by weight, the carbon in a litre of fuel weighs 0.65 kg (0.75 kg x 0.87). The weight of the carbon (0.65 kg) can then be multiplied by 3.7, which equals 2.4 kg of CO_2.

15.23 *A Boeing 747 airliner of the type that typically flies between Hong Kong and Sydney. (Photo: Hans Schultze)*

A fully laden Boeing 747 from Hong Kong to Australia will carry about 91,000 kg of fuel. If the chemistry of the preceding paragraph is accepted, then about 289,000 kg of CO_2 should be produced (or about 720 kg per person), even assuming every drop of fuel was burnt and there was zero fuel reserve. This is well short of the 856,000 kg claimed by the website.

The figure of 720 kg per person represents about 0.01 kg (or 10 grams) of CO_2 per person per kilometre. This compares with a figure of 98 grams per kilometre for a typical modern small car (such as a Ford Fiesta Econetic or a Seat Ibizia Ecomotive), 166 grams per kilometre for a typical modern medium car (such as a Mazda 6), or 240 grams per kilometre for an SUV (such as a Toyota Land Cruiser or a Dodge Nitro). Each of these figures would need to be divided by the number of passengers in the car to obtain the figure for the CO_2 per person per kilometre.

As explained in chapter 3, the effect of carbon dioxide in the atmosphere is to reduce the escape of long-wave infrared radiation (heat) from the earth into space. Therefore, when we increase the concentration of carbon dioxide, we effectively increase the energy input to the earth.

However, the effect of surface level CO_2 is somewhat different to CO_2 which is in the upper atmosphere (where it is deposited by aircraft). Carbon dioxide is a gas with a high **albedo**, which means it is shiny and thus has a high rate of reflectivity. It is this high level of reflectivity that enables CO_2 to trap heat, because the radiation is reflected and re-reflected within the body of gas. In this way, CO_2 near the earth's surface traps surface heat and acts as an obstacle to delay its release back into space. On the other hand, CO_2 in the upper atmosphere acts as an agent of global shading. In a similar way that volcanic eruptions cause cooling as the clouds of ash they emit reflect incoming solar radiation back into space, the high albedo of CO_2 in the upper atmosphere also reflects incoming solar radiation.

In 1991, the ash cloud emitted by the eruption of Mount Pinatubo in the Philippines caused global temperatures to drop in the northern hemisphere by an average of 0.5C° to 0.6C° during 1992 and 1993, and globally by 0.4C° to 0.5C° during the same period. Although the physical properties of a volcanic dust cloud and carbon dioxide vary, they both have a high albedo and reflect incoming solar radiation from the upper atmosphere back into space, leading to cooler temperatures. Because of this, carbon dioxide emissions from aircraft are likely to become a reason for growing accusations in the future that aviation is masking the effects of global warming. Similarly, , if a trend towards global cooling recommences (as a growing number of scientists claim has been the case since 2002), then aviation can expect to receive part of the blame for this phenomenon.

15.24 *The 'biofuel' sticker on the outside engine of this Air New Zealand Boeing 747 shows it is one of the biofuel testing aircraft. (Photo: Jonathan Rankin)*

Because of public pressure and environmental criticism, aircraft manufacturers and airlines are experimenting with alternate fuels that will reduce carbon emissions from flights (figure 15.24). Some biofuel alternatives, such as jatropha, corn and algae, are said to have greater energy content than existing petrochemical aviation fuels, and they are said to generate less carbon dioxide. Of

these alternative fuels, the most promising is perhaps algae-based biofuels as they can be grown in laboratories with minimal sunlight, the algae can be grown in nearly every environment, and they do not compete with any human food crops for farming land. Furthermore, biofuels do not add any carbon to the biosphere that was not already there, whereas traditional petrochemical-based aviation fuels extract carbon from the the earth, burn it in aircraft and add carbon dioxide into the atmosphere.

QUESTION BLOCK 15C

1. *Why has the volume of air freight increased in recent years?*

2. *How do contrails form, and how common are they?*

3. *What are environmental effects of contrails?*

4. *Describe the impact of aviation on the amount and distribution of ozone in the atmosphere.*

5. *Compare the amounts of carbon dioxide produced by airliners and by cars.*

6. *What is your impression of the effectiveness of carbon offsetting?*

7. *Aviation has been accused of masking the impact of global warming. Are such accusations justified?*

8. *To what extent is the aviation industry responding to criticisms of its environmental impact?*

Effects of Transnational Manufacturing and Services

The Relocation of Polluting Industries

During recent decades, transnational corporations (TNCs) have been accused by environmentalists of relocating polluting industries and waste disposal from MEDCs to LEDCs where there are weaker environmental controls and safety regulations.

The incentives for LEDCs to attract manufacturing industries as a way of stimulating economic development are considerable. Manufacturing industries are seen in LEDCs as the key to transforming a rural-based agricultural economy into an urban-based industrial economy. As a result, foreign investment is welcomed by offering TNCs cheap land and facilities, attractive tax arrangements, and perhaps government-sourced infrastructure such as roads and railway links. For industries that generate large amounts of environmental pollution, slack regulations may also be seen by TNCs to be an attractive reason to relocate in an LEDC.

There is some debate among geographers as to whether there is a conscious strategy on the part of TNCs on one hand, and LEDC governments on the other, to relocate polluting industries into what are termed '**pollution havens**' (figure 15.25). The hypothesis that TNCs deliberately export polluting industries was first studied in the 1970s by the US Environmental Consultant, Barry Castleman, who compiled a long list of US factories that had been relocated to Mexico to produce asbestos, benzidine dyes, pesticides, arsenic and zinc.

15.25 *Some Western European companies have been accused of relocating polluting industries to Eastern Europe, where economic costs are lower and pollution regulations less stringent. This example shows the industrial zone of Kiev, capital city of Ukraine.*

However, several studies in the 1980s found (in the words of one study by H. Jeffrey Leonard, President of the Global Environment Fund) that "the costs and logistics of complying with environmental regulations are not a decisive factor in most industrial decisions about desirable plant locations or in the international competitive picture of most major industries". The 1980s studies concluded that while environmental factors may be included in a relocation feasibility study, they were never strong enough to outweigh all the traditional **forces that determine investment and location decisions**, which are:

Raw materials:
- Are raw materials bulky, awkward and costly to transport?
- Will these raw materials deteriorate quickly?
- Are the quantities sufficient for long-run production?
- If the raw materials at the original location are exhausted, should a move be made to a new site, should raw materials be transported to the original site, or should the factory be re-sited with regard to another factor such as transport or market?
- What is the relative importance of the different raw material inputs?

Energy
- Are large supplies of power needed in production?
- Which source of power is most suitable?
- What cost advantages exist between coal, gas, hydro-electric, wind, tidal, solar and nuclear energy?
- What pollution controls are needed?

Labour
- Are large amounts of labour required?
- In which proportions should it be: skilled, semi-skilled or unskilled?
- Would it be valuable to be near research institutions?
- In which towns are there relatively untapped supplies of labour?
- Which other firms will be competing for similar labour?
- How stable is the labour force?
- Is the environment attractive for the workforce?
- How common are industrial disputes?

Market
- What proportion of production can be sold locally?
- How affluent is the local population?
- Are there large cities nearby?
- Where are competitors located?
- Where are the suppliers located?
- How bulky is the finished product?

Transport and communications
- What types of transport are available?
- What types of transport are most suitable for the raw materials and the finished product?
- What linkages exist with a sea port, other markets and raw materials locations?
- Are there any problems of congestion?
- Are communication services such as telephone and the internet adequate?
- Do freight concessions exist?

Political considerations
- Is the area politically stable?
- Does the government encourage or discourage new firms?
- Is the area being redeveloped?
- To what extent is local planning legislation an advantage or a hindrance?
- Are there tax incentives?
- Is there a threat of terrorism?
- What are the personal preferences of management?

Climate
- Are there problems of frequent flooding or drought?
- Does the industry require certain temperatures?
- Is expensive climate-modifying equipment necessary?

Later studies during the 1990s presented a mixed picture. Some studies have confirmed the view of the 1980s analyses that environmental factors are not sufficient to outweigh all the other factors of location (and relocation) because any potential gains in pollution havens would only last for a short time. This based on the belief that environmental protests are no longer confined to MEDCs, but have spread to LEDCs through the efforts of environmental NGOs and civil societies (as discussed in chapter 18).

On the other hand, a theoretical study by the economists Baumol and Oates suggested that as free trade expanded in a globalised environment, competition between countries to attract foreign investment should lead to the creation of 'pollution havens'. Several empirical studies (i.e. based on evidence) at the same time, however, failed to find examples of such pollution havens. One study of Brazil's chemical industry, for example, concluded that the expansion of free trade through globalisation would actually remove any advantages offered by so-called pollution havens as financial factors grew in importance. Indeed, the same study showed that export-oriented chemical firms in Brazil chose to adopt global environmental standards because of fear of litigation, negative public relations and concern about the loss of export markets, and this occurred even in remote areas that were seldom visited or inspected by Brazil's increasingly powerful environmental movement.

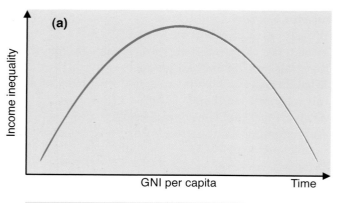

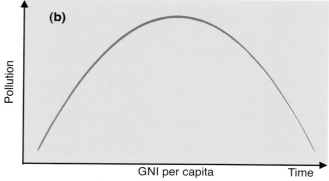

15.26 (a) *The Kuznets Curve.*
(b) *The Environmental Kuznets Curve.*

This has led some geographers and economists to hypothesise that there is an environmental Kuznets curve — which is the opposite of the 'pollution haven' hypothesis. The traditional Kuznets curve suggests that incomes become less equal for a period of time when a country begins a period of rapid economic development, but the gap in inequality decreases after a certain average income level has been reached (figure 15.26, top). The Environmental Kuznets curve suggests that in a similar way, a country's level of pollution will become worse during the early phase of rapid economic development, but will improve as development proceeds (figure 15.26, lower).

The 'pollution haven' hypothesis suggests that the movement of investment and manufacturing plants from MEDCs to LEDCs is harmful to the environment. The Environmental Kuznets curve, on the other hand, suggests that while the movement of investment and manufacturing plants from MEDCs to LEDCs may be initially harmful to the environment, in the longer term the results will be beneficial. Although the Environmental Kuznets curve has been substantiated by a large number of empirical studies, it has not found favour with environmental groups, perhaps in part because it has been advocated by the World Bank, which is viewed disapprovingly by many environmental groups (as discussed and explained in chapter 18). As a study by Lyuba Zarsky (Associate Professor in the International Environmental Policy Program of the Monterey Institute of International Studies, USA) concluded as long ago as 1999:

> "While 'pollution havens' cannot be proven, a pattern of agglomeration of pollution is discernible, one based not on differences in national environmental standards, but on differences in income and/or education of local communities. They may not be 'havens', but there are clearly 'pollution zones' of poorer people, both within and across countries, where firms perform worse and where regulation is less effective".

QUESTION BLOCK 15D

1. *Why might the government of an LEDC want to attract a highly polluting factory to relocate within its territory from an MEDC?*

2. *Think of a factory with which you are familiar. Rank the importance of the factors of location (or relocation) as they apply to the establishment of that factory.*

3. *Describe the message conveyed by the environmental Kuznets curve.*

4. *Which hypothesis do you find more convincing — the 'pollution havens' hypothesis or the environmental Kuznets curve? Give reasons to support your answer.*

Transboundary Pollution

Acid Rain

Transboundary pollution is defined by the OECD as 'pollution that originates in one country but, by crossing the border through pathways of water or air, is able to cause damage to the environment in another country.' Implicit in this definition is the concept that there are two main types of transboundary pollution, these being water pollution and air pollution.

In chapter 7, the formation and impact of acid rain was discussed as one example of atmospheric transboundary pollution. As noted in chapter 7, **acid rain** forms when sulphur dioxide caused by burning hydrocarbons mixes with the water in the atmosphere and produces rain that is a diluted form of sulphuric acid ($SO_2 + H_2O \rightarrow H_2SO_4$). The sulphur dioxide originates from cars and factories burning hydrocarbon fuels. Because the gases in the atmosphere are unaffected by national borders, acid rain thus becomes a transboundary issue in Europe where the territory of each nation-state is quite small compared the global average. Therefore, in the example discussed in chapter 7, acid rain produced in Britain, France and Spain may be blown by the prevailing winds over Switzerland, where the orographic uplift causes rain. Because of its high acid content, this rain may kill the trees on which it falls, and an example is shown in figure 7.124 (chapter 7).

In Europe, the prevailing wind direction is from the west or south-west. Therefore, air pollution in the United Kingdom commonly affects the Nordic countries of Norway, Sweden, Denmark and Finland. Similarly, pollution produced in France and Spain blows eastwards to Italy, Switzerland and Germany, pollution produced in Germany often affects Poland and pollution produced in Italy frequently affects Greece, Bosnia-Herzegovina and Croatia.

15.27 *The border zone between Bosnia-Herzegovina (left side of the photo) and Croatia (right side of the photo), near the coastline of the Adriatic Sea south of Dubrovnik.*

Figure 15.27 illustrates the point that air pollution cannot be stopped at national boundaries. The photo shows the Adriatic coastline of Croatia south of Dubrovnik, looking towards the south. Pollution blows onto this coastline from Italy (off to the right of the photo). However, there is another national boundary running through the middle of this photograph, approximately at the bottom of the escarpment — the dark green plains are mainly in Croatia and the drier hillslopes are mainly in Bosnia-Herzegovina. Obviously, onshore winds carrying pollutants from Italy will affect Bosnia as well as Croatia, and not stop at the national border! Because of the prevailing

winds, countries in central Europe tend to receive more acid rain than their 'fair share' in term of the air pollution produced in those countries.

As discussed in chapter 7, forests are especially vulnerable to the effects of acid rain (figure 15.28). This is partly because the deciduous and coniferous trees that make up most forest areas in Europe tend to be intolerant of environmental conditions that lie outside their niche, especially increasing soil acidity. It is also because Europe's remaining forests tend to be in high altitude mountain ares that experience clouds and fog, thus exposing the trees to even greater amounts of acidic water vapour and water droplets than mere rainfall. Needless to say, the impact of acid rain is greatest in areas that receive high rainfall.

15.28 *Trees on the side of Mount Kasprowy Wierch, near Zakopane, Poland, have been killed by acid rain.*

Acid rain is not only a problem for forests, but it also accelerates the rate of weathering of rocks. In Europe, many historic buildings and monuments are made from finely carved stone, and acid rain is therefore accelerating the destruction of these structures, some of which have survived many centuries before being challenged by the erosive power of acid rain (figures 15.29 to 15.31).

Although some supranational institutions such as the United Nations and the European Union attempt to

15.29 *The Parthenon in Athens (Greece) has survived for many centuries, but is now threatened by acid rain weathering.*

impose controls on the production of pollutants, there are few realistic options to prevent their movement across national borders once they have been released into the atmosphere or waterways. For that reason, transboundary pollution cannot be addressed using the same regulatory strategies as domestic pollution issues.

15.30 *These stone sculptures in Buda Castle (in Budapest, Hungary) were made in 1265. Acid rain in the past few decades has weathered the exposed statue (left) more than those which are more protected.*

The most effective way of reducing acid rain is to reduce the production of the polluting gases that cause it to form. In order to achieve this, fossil fuels that contain less sulphur would need to be used, and even better, fossil fuels would be replaced entirely by alternative energy sources that do not produce acid rain generating gases. These strategies could be achieved by regulation within individual countries. However, some governments have been reluctant at times to impose increased costs on their own industries when the benefits will mainly accrue to citizens in other countries.

15.31 *These ruins of the ancient city of Rome are now threatened by accelerated weathering and erosion caused by acid rain.*

As long ago as 1979, several governments in western Europe began to respond to the problem of acid rain by signing the Geneva Convention on Long-Range Transboundary Air Pollution (LRTAP). Since that time, the number of parties to the Convention has grown to 51 and the Convention itself has been expanded by eight

protocols that identify specific measures to be taken by parties to cut their emissions of air pollutants. The Convention is now governed by UNECE (the United Nations Economic Commission for Europe).

QUESTION BLOCK 15E

1. *What is meant by the term 'transboundary pollution'?*

2. *In what ways is acid rain a problem in Europe?*

3. *Outline the measures that are being taken to address the problem of acid rain in Europe.*

The Growth of Environmental Awareness

Expressions of concern about the quality of the natural environment were virtually unknown before World War II. However, the growth of post war industrial landscapes made people aware of the dangers of pollution for the first time. This emerging concern was reflected by the establishment in 1948 of the **IUCN** (International Union for Conservation of Nature, originally known as the International Union for the Protection of Nature) in Fontainebleau, near Paris, France. The IUCN remains the world's largest and oldest civil society organisation devoted to fostering environmental awareness and improving environmental management, and has over 1,000 government and NGO member organisations, with almost 11,000 volunteer scientists working in more than 160 countries.

The IUCN states its mission as being to 'help the world find pragmatic solutions to our most pressing environment and development challenges', and it achieves this by supporting scientific research, managing field projects in all parts of the world and bringing governments, NGOs, UN agencies, companies and local communities together to develop and implement policy, laws and best practice.

In the early years following the establishment of the IUCN, environmental awareness remained a concern of fringe groups. The prevailing view in capitalist and communist countries alike was that 'progress' was good (or, as it was often expressed at the time, 'you can't stop progress'), with 'progress' being understood as economic development through industrialisation. For many people, pollution was a necessary by-product of progress, and perhaps even a positive sign that progress was occurring.

This view began to change in 1956, however. In that year, as described earlier in chapter 4, the first person died from Minamata disease, the consequence of mercury poisoning from pollutants that had been dumped by a chemical factory into Minamata Bay. More than a thousand other people subsequently died from Minamata disease, and awareness began to grow that environmental pollution could pose genuine health hazards for humans. Concern about water pollution resulted in the first United Nations Conference on the Law of the Sea (UNCLOS) in Geneva (Switzerland) in 1958, which approved several conventions on environmental protection of the world's oceans.

As a sign of growing environmental concern, the WWF (first known as the World Wildlife Fund, and later the World Wide Fund for Nature) was formed in Morges (Switzerland). Originally an organisation to promote the protection of endangered animal species, the WWF has since expanded its conservation interests to include the wider issue of biodiversity, working towards the conservation of special places and habitats as well as species. Today, the WWF is one of the world's leading civil society organisations involved in conservation in many countries.

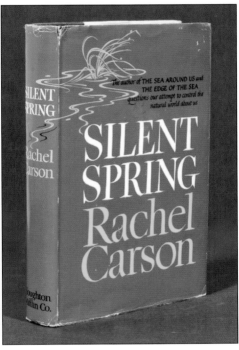

15.32 *The first edition of the book 'Silent Spring' by Rachel Carson, published in 1962.*

A significant step in raising the public's awareness of environmental issues occurred in 1962 when the book *Silent Spring* by Rachel Carson was published (figure 15.32). When this book was published, it generated a storm of controversy about the effects of chemicals such as DDT on human and animal health. *Silent Spring* provided documented evidence of the harmful effects of pesticides on the environment, such as the impact of DDT as a cause of thinner egg shells, problems with reproduction and even death. The book also accused the chemical industry of lying and spreading disinformation, and it accused civil servants of accepting the claims of large corporations with insufficient critical analysis. Today, almost half a century after its publication, many people claim that the book's publication marked the launch of the environmental movement on a mass scale.

Just four years later, another significant event occurred that changed — probably irreversibly — the perception humans had of earth, making millions of people aware

15.33 *The Earth as seen from the Lunar Orbiter I spacecraft, 23rd August, 1966. (Photo: NASA)*

for the first time of the tininess of their planet compared with the vastness of space. The event was the capture of the first photograph of earth taken from an orbiting spacecraft, and this occurred on 23rd August, 1966 (figure 15.33). The photograph, a rough black-and-white image showing the surface of the moon in the foreground, was taken from the US Lunar Orbiter I spacecraft, and was transmitted back to earth by radio. This photograph made a huge impact as it showed the planet from the perspective of an outsider looking in for the first time.

15.34 *The Earth as seen from Apollo 8, with the moon in the foreground, 24th December 1968. (Photo: NASA)*

Two years later, on 24th December 1968, the first colour photograph was taken of the earth from space by astronauts in Apollo 8, which was the first manned spacecraft on a mission to the moon (figure 15.34). During a live radio broadcast to earth on the day the photograph was captured, command module pilot Jim Lovell commented "The vast loneliness is awe-inspiring and it makes you realise just what you have back there on Earth." The astronauts ended the broadcast with the crew taking turns reading from the book of Genesis. The delicate fragility of planet Earth suddenly became apparent to many people, and for the first time many people began to visualise the planet as a finite entity, not the limitless expanse that many had previously unthinkingly assumed it to be.

The late 1960s and early 1970s saw a steady increase in environmental awareness among the general population, sometimes sparked by spectacular environmental disasters. In March 1967, a supertanker called the Torrey Canyon was shipwrecked off the south coast of the United Kingdom. The ship had been carrying a vast load of crude oil, and the accident resulted in the world's first oil spill, causing about 120,000 tonnes of crude oil to form an oil slick of 700 square kilometres that killed about 15,000 birds and huge numbers of marine organisms, as well as destroying hundreds of kilometres of coastal habitats on the British and French coastlines.

At about the same time, the effects of defoliants used by US troops in the Vietnam War started to become known. In order to expose communist soldiers hiding in the jungles of Vietnam and Cambodia, US forces spread defoliants such as Agent Orange over vast areas of rainforest, killing the trees and poisoning the soil (figure 15.35). The side-effects of exposure to the defoliants included severe birth defects in babies born in the exposed areas, large-scale miscarriages among pregnant women, skin diseases, cancers, leukaemia, and sterility among males. People in Vietnam are still living with the impact of Agent Orange more than three decades after the spraying occurred.

15.35 *A US helicopter sprays Agent Orange defoliant over the Mekong Delta region of Vietnam during the Vietnam War, 1968. (Photo: Brian K Grigsby)*

Another event at the time that raised public awareness of the extent of the environmental impact of humans on the planet occurred in 1971 when a Norwegian adventurer, Thor Heyerdahl, built a papyrus raft called Ra II, based on ancient Egyptian drawings, and sailed it across the Atlantic Ocean from Morocco to Barbados. During the voyage, Heyerdahl reported that most of the Atlantic Ocean was covered with human waste, including lumps of floating asphalt that were the result of oil pollution from tankers. This news was widely publicised, and almost coincided with other news reports that scientists had found evidence of DDT pesticides in the Antarctic. These two news stories made many people realise just how far reaching human destruction of the environment had extended.

As a result of the alarming stories about environmental destruction, the first Earth day was held in the United States on 22nd April 1970. On that day, 20 million people across the country participated in peaceful demonstrations and teach-ins. Many people remember this as the beginning of the modern environmental movement in the USA. Since that time, Earth Day has become an annual event around the world. By 1990, 200 million people in 141 countries participated in Earth day events, and by 2007 an estimated one billion people participated.

In 1972, a groundbreaking report on the environmental implications of resource use was published. The book, *Limits to Growth*, was prepared by The Club of Rome , which was a group of thinkers and leaders from 40 countries. Edited by Donella and Dennis Meadows, it was the first attempt to analyse the environment using computer modelling, producing a series of printouts such as the one shown in figure 4.3 in chapter 4. The book argued that if the then-current trends in population, food, pollution, and resource use continued, then the limits to growth on the planet would be reached within the next 100 years. The book was very controversial, with critics arguing that the assumptions built in to any simple computer simulation could be designed to produce any desired output — 'garbage in, garbage out' was a common criticism. Nonetheless, *Limits to Growth* led to a resurgence of Malthusian perspectives towards resource use for a time, and it highlighted the link between economic growth and environmental degradation in the public minds.

The early 1970s was a period of intense environmental concern across the world, and this was reflected in the creation of the United Nations Environment Programme (UNEP) in 1972 as an outcome of the United Nations Conference on the Human Environment in Stockholm, Sweden. The UNEP continues to be an important agent to bring together researchers and governments from all parts of the world. Today, the UNEP focuses on six priority areas; climate change, disasters and conflicts, ecosystem management, environmental governance, harmful substances and resource efficiency.

The establishment of the UNEP was followed by many other significant awareness-raising conferences and the establishment of more environmental groups, including the Bucharest Population Conference (1974), the Cocoyoc Declaration on the distribution of resources (1974), the Rome Food Conference (1974), the Dag Hammarskjöld Report (1975), the first United Nations Conference on Human Settlements (Habitat) in Vancouver (1976), and the United Nations Conference on Desertification in Nairobi, Kenya (1977).

Then, in 1979, a World Climate Conference in Geneva (Switzerland) concluded that 'the "greenhouse effect" from increased build-up of carbon dioxide in the atmosphere demands urgent international action'. This shocked many observers, as the primary concern for the previous two decades had been the possibility of a new ice age. Global warming had not been seriously considered as the prevailing trend in world temperatures from 1940 to 1980 had been downwards. With only a few exceptions, government leaders and the media did not take this conclusion seriously for at least a decade after the conference.

The following year (1980) saw the release of the Brandt Commission Report. More formally known as *The Independent Commission on International Development Issues*, the report focussed on inequalities in income levels and wealth around the world, introducing the terms 'North' for MEDCs and the 'South' for LEDCs for the first time. The report recommended a huge increase in aid to LEDCs as well as environmental impact assessments of development proposals before they are implemented. In the same year, the *World Conservation Strategy* was jointly released by IUCN, UNEP, and WWF. This report called for "global co-ordinated efforts" to achieve "sustainable development", the first time that this term was used officially in an international document. Also in 1980, a report was published in the United States entitled *The Global 2000 Report to the President*. This report, commissioned by US President Jimmy Carter projected what the world could be like if present trends of resource use and environmental degradation continued. The report was on the top selling book list for several months, and it played an important role in informing the general public about the consequences of unrestrained resource use.

During the mid to late 1980s, several ecological disasters occurred that further raised public awareness of the environment as a significant issue. The first of these occurred in December 1984 when a leak of deadly methyl isocyanate from the Union Carbide pesticide factory in Bhopal, India, exposed about 500,000 people to toxic gases. Estimates of the death toll range from 2,250 to 16,000, and it remains the world's most deadly industrial accident.

In the following year, 1985, the 'ozone hole' was discovered by a team of British scientists. Also known as seasonal stratospheric ozone depletion, the ozone hole referred to the area over the poles where the concentration of atmospheric ozone was lower than other parts of the world (figure 15.36). The research found that the size of the ozone hole was increasing as a result of ozone-destroying chlorofluorocarbons. As a result of this finding, widespread bans were imposed on chlorofluorocarbons, and the general public became even more acutely aware that the combination of individual actions (such as using air conditioners and spray cans) could have consequences that were significant on a global scale.

The next disaster occurred in April 1986 when an accident at a nuclear power station in Chernobyl, Ukraine (then part of the USSR) spread radioactive material across

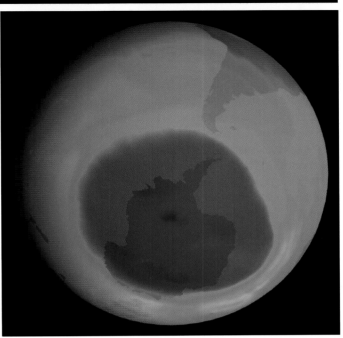

15.36 *The amount of ozone in the atmosphere is indicated by the colour, with lighter colours representing more ozone and blue representing the lowest percentage of atmospheric ozone. (Photo: NASA)*

central and western Europe. Over 300,000 people had to be evacuated and resettled, and large areas of farmland remained contaminated for several years after the explosion. It was estimated that radioactive fallout from the Chernobyl explosion was about 400 times greater than the fallout from the atomic bombing of Hiroshima in 1945.

Then, in March 1989, one of the world's worst oil spills (in terms of impact on fragile ecosystems) occurred when an oil tanker, the Exxon Valdez, hit a reef near Prince William Sound in Alaska. Although the oil spill was not great in terms of volume, the remote location made cleaning up difficult and the environmental impact was devastating as the area was a habitat for wildlife such as salmon, sea otters, seals and seabirds (figure 15.37).

At around the same time, another landmark study was published that further raised public awareness of envi-

15.37 *Dead sea birds are lined up on a beach in Prince William Sound Alaska after the Exxon Valdez oil spill. (Photo courtesy of the Exxon Valdez Oil Spill Trustee Council)*

Environmental change

ronmental issues. Commonly known as the Brundtland Report, but officially titled *Our Common Future*, the report was prepared by the World Commission on Environment and Development under the chairmanship of Norwegian Prime Minister, Gro Harlem Brundtland. Advocating the wider adoption of sustainable development strategies, the report expressed concern about the accelerating deterioration of the environment and use of natural resources, as well as the consequences of environmental deterioration for economic and social development. The report called for "a new era of economic growth, one that must be based on policies that sustain and expand the environmental resource base".

The 1970s and 1980s had seen a rapid growth in public awareness of the environment. The 1990s saw a slowing in the rate of awareness raising, partly reflecting a more growth-oriented attitude towards economic development. The slowing also occurred in part and because the degree of environmental awareness and sensitivity to ecological issues were already fairly high among the general population, at least in the the MEDCs of North America and Western Europe.

In June 1992, the United Nations Conference on Environment and Development (UNCED) was held in Rio de Janeiro, Brazil. The conference was the largest gathering to that time of heads of state, and became known as the 'Earth Summit'. Several significant statements and commitments emerged from the Rio Earth Summit, including international conventions on global climate change, biodiversity, principles of sustainable forest management, a fundamental 'umbrella' statement called the Rio Declaration, and a detailed plan of action called Agenda 21. Later that year, the United Nations General Assembly set up the Commission on Sustainable Development (CSD) specifically to oversee the effective implementation of Agenda 21 and ensure it would be integrated into the programs and processes of the UN system.

The next major event that brought environmental issues to wide public attention occurred in December 1997 when the third meeting of the Conference of Parties to the UN Climate Change met in Kyoto, Japan. At the end of this meeting, a landmark agreement to reduce global emissions of greenhouse gases was adopted which has since become known as the 'Kyoto Protocol'. This international treaty was designed to achieve (in the words of the Protocol) "stabilisation of greenhouse gas concentrations in the atmosphere at a level that would prevent dangerous anthropogenic interference with the climate system." The Protocol committed the countries signing it to reduce four greenhouse gases — carbon dioxide, methane, nitrous oxide, sulphur hexafluoride — plus two groups of gases, hydrofluorocarbons and perfluorocar-

bons. By 2009, a total of 183 nations and regions had ratified the Protocol.

Another significant event occurred three years later, in 2000, to bring environmental issues to the attention of the wider public. This event was publication of the Millennium Development Goals. As discussed in detail in chapter 2, the Millennium Development Goals represented eight international development and environmental goals that the 192 United Nations member states committed themselves to achieving by 2015.

Then, in 2006, the release of Al Gore's movie *An Inconvenient Truth* represented what many regard as the most important and influential act in increasing environmental awareness among the general public — ever. Although aspects of the film are controversial and some of its facts are disputed (as discussed in the ToK Box in chapter 3), Al Gore and the Intergovernmental Panel on Climate Change (IPCC) were jointly awarded the Nobel Peace Prize in 2007 for "their efforts to build up and disseminate greater knowledge about man-made climate change, and to lay the foundations for the measures that are needed to counteract such change." Al Gore was a former US Vice-President, and to have such a high profile person advocating environmental awareness made a deep impression on the world's population.

In the six decades or so since the establishment of the IUCN, environmental awareness has grown from an interest shared only by a fringe minority group to a general and widespread concern that environmental issues have the potential to threaten not only human health but human survival. In some parts of the world, this increased environmental awareness is now expressed through politics, as 'green parties' committed to environmental action have gained support. Green politics originated in Germany in the late 1970s and early 1980s, and spread through western Europe in the following decade. Today, green parties are found in several MEDCs, helping to raise environmental awareness by focussing on specific issues of concern to voters and advocating policies to address these issues.

With the growth in environmental awareness, it is easy for people in MEDCs to overlook an important limitation, however. Much of the increase in awareness since 1948 has depended on the flow of information through books, newspapers, television, and the internet. These information flows are still concentrated in the MEDCs, which helps explain why environmental awareness is significantly less in many LEDCs. Perhaps the great challenge for the coming decade is to disseminate these understandings to people in LEDCs so that environmental awareness can be truly shared at a global level.

QUESTION BLOCK 15F

1. *Examine the role of the IUCN in fostering improved environmental management.*

2. *Identify the three events that you feel were most important in raising awareness of environmental issues between 1948 and the present day. Explain why you chose these three events.*

Homogenisation of Landscapes

The Growing Uniformity of Urban Landscapes

As recently as a few decades ago, cities in different parts of the world had distinctive characters that reflected their national identity and their location (figures 15.38 and 15.39). As a result of globalisation, however, many large cities are losing the distinctive cultural characteristics that they once had. The pressures facing cities in different parts of the world are becoming more similar as more uniform economic systems are adopted. Increasingly, the transnational companies that make decisions in one city are making decisions in many parts of the world, so it is to expected that **homogenisation** of urban landscapes will occur. This was discussed in some detail in chapter 11 under the heading 'The Global Megacity', and the similarities were illustrated in a number of photos such as figure 11.72.

15.38 *With its distinctive canals, Venice in Italy is characteristic of older cities that possessed a distinctive local or national character.*

A major reason for the homogenisation of urban landscapes is the emergence of the **world city**. Over the past half century, a network of so-called world cities has evolved, these being cities that have significant global links. As discussed in chapter 11, the emergence of world cities has intensified the pressures towards uniformity among cities in different continents.

The task of identifying which large cities are world cities and which are not is not as easy as we might first think. **World cities** can be defined as those cities that have

outstripped their national urban networks and become part of the global economic system. World cities tend to perform similar urban functions, including being centres of political power, world trade and communications, leaders in banking and finance, and places where major entertainment and sporting spectacles are staged. They typically house headquarters or offices of NGOs and are centres that attract large numbers of tourists (figure 15.40). Their influence extends beyond the national boundaries of their own countries.

15.39 *Another view of Venice, Italy, showing its distinctive un-homogenised urban landscape.*

15.40 *Although Dar-es-Salaam in Tanzania has a large United Nations office, it lacks many of the other characteristics of a major world city.*

Peter Hall, the geographer who reintroduced the term 'world cities' in 1966, described them in this way:

"By what characteristics do we distinguish world cities from other great centres of population and wealth? In the first place, they are usually the major centres of political power. They are the seats of the most powerful national governments and sometimes of international authorities too; of government agencies of all kinds. Round these gather a host of institutions, whose main business is with government; the big professional organisations, the trades unions, the employers' federations, the headquarters of major international concerns.

15.41 *London — a major world city.*

15.42 *Kolkata, with a population size larger than London's lacks the international links that would qualify it as a world city.*

These cities are the national centres not merely of government but also of trade. Characteristically they are great ports, which distribute goods to all parts of their countries, and in return receive goods for export to the other nations of the world. Within each country, roads and railways focus on the metropolitan city. The world cities are the sites of the great international airports… Traditionally, the world cities are the leading banking and finance centres of the countries in which they stand. Here are housed the central banks, the headquarters of the trading banks, the offices of the big insurance organisations and a whole series of specialised financial and insurance agencies.

Government and trade were invariable the original raisons d'être of the world cities. But these places early became the centres where professional talents of all kinds congregated. Each of the world cities has its great hospitals, its distinct medical quarter, its legal profession gathered around the national courts of justice. Students and teachers are drawn to the world cities; they commonly contain great universities, as well as a host of specialised institutions for teaching and research in the sciences, the technologies and the arts. The great national libraries and museums are here. Inevitably, world cities have become the places where information is gathered and disseminated; the book publishers are found here; so are the publishers of newspapers and periodicals,

and with them their journalists and regular contributors. In this century also the world cities have become headquarters of the great national radio and television networks".

It is important to note that world cities are defined by their functions and links with other places, not their population size. Therefore, a city such as London with a population of just over 7 million would qualify as a world city, but Kolkata (Calcutta) with a population of almost 12 million would not (figures 15.41 and 15.42).

QUESTION BLOCK 15G

1. *List the key characteristics of a world city as outlined by Peter Hall. Then highlight those characteristics that are most central to defining a city as a 'world city'.*

2. *London has been identified as a 'world city'. Suggest three other cities which would be 'world cities' according to Peter Hall's characteristics, and explain your selection.*

Table 15.1 lists the major world cities in descending rank order, as calculated by AT Kearney Management Consultants in 2008. The ranking takes five factors of globalisation into account: business activity, human capital, information exchange, cultural experience and political engagement.

QUESTION BLOCK 15H

1. *For each of the five lists of functions in table 15.1, rank the top ten cities.*

2. *In each of the five lists you made in the previous question, give 10 points to the top ranked city, 9 points to the second ranked city, and so on down to 1 point for the tenth ranked city. Then, for each city that appears on a list, add its points.*

3. *What conclusions can you draw about the number of world cities?*

From the information in table 15.1, it can probably be concluded that there are only four genuinely 'world cities', these being New York, London, Paris and Tokyo (figure 15.43). Other cities have a range of world city functions, but in much smaller numbers than these four cities. Examples of these 'lesser world cities' would include Hong Kong, Los Angeles, Singapore, Chicago, Seoul and Toronto. Many of these cities are stronger in some areas of globalisation than others, such as Hong Kong which ranks 5 for business activity but only 40 for political engagement. Brussels is significant in international affairs, but much less so in business, human capital and cultural experience. Some cities that are often perceived as being world cities have insufficient headquarters to appear high on the list. Although most recent rapid urban growth has occurred in cities in LEDCs, table 15.1 shows that the most influential world cities are still located in MEDCs.

Table 15.1
The Top 40 Global Cities, 2008
arranged in descending rank order, with top 10 shaded red

Rank	City	Business activity	Human capital	Information exchange	Cultural experience	Political engagement
1	New York	1	1	4	3	2
2	London	4	2	3	1	5
3	Paris	3	11	1	2	4
4	Tokyo	2	6	7	7	6
5	Hong Kong	5	5	6	25	40
6	Los Angeles	15	4	11	5	17
7	Singapore	6	7	15	37	16
8	Chicago	12	3	24	20	20
9	Seoul	7	35	5	10	19
10	Toronto	26	10	18	4	24
11	Washington	35	17	10	14	1
12	Beijing	9	22	28	19	7
13	Brussels	19	34	2	32	3
14	Madrid	14	18	9	24	33
15	San Francisco	27	12	22	23	29
16	Sydney	17	8	27	36	43
17	Berlin	28	29	12	8	14
18	Vienna	13	31	29	11	9
19	Moscow	23	15	33	6	39
20	Shanghai	8	25	42	35	18
21	Frankfurt	11	43	19	13	34
22	Bangkok	18	14	23	41	13
23	Amsterdam	10	38	25	12	56
24	Stockholm	25	33	13	16	27
25	Mexico City	34	23	32	9	11
26	Zurich	30	20	8	31	54
27	Dubai	21	19	14	44	44
28	Istanbul	32	13	34	43	8
29	Boston	37	9	35	33	50
30	Rome	31	30	30	15	22
31	São Paulo	16	36	31	27	23
32	Miami	33	21	26	39	21
33	Buenos Aires	40	16	43	25	12
34	Taipei	20	49	21	40	15
35	Munich	29	27	49	18	36
36	Copenhagen	36	41	16	42	28
37	Atlanta	38	24	39	21	32
38	Cairo	48	28	17	45	10
39	Milan	24	42	41	28	37
40	Kuala Lumpur	22	46	40	49	38

Source: AT Kearney Management Consultants, 2008

15.43 *The high rise 'skyscrapers' of New York's Manhattan reflect the city's role as a world city of the first order.*

Although geographers may argue about whether some specific cities should be included as major 'world cities' or not, most geographers recognise a hierarchy of world cities. On the top level of the hierarchy are the world cities that have major global influence – London, New York and Tokyo. The second level of the hierarchy includes cities that have international importance within their region, such as Frankfurt, Los Angeles and Singapore. The third level of the hierarchy includes lesser international cities such as Madrid, Seoul and Sydney. A fourth level in the hierarchy would include cities with a smaller number or a less balanced range of international functions, such as Houston, Milan, Munich and Osaka. A variation of this hierarchy was produced by another geographer, John Friedmann, and this is shown in figure 15.44.

Regardless of the level of their specific 'world city' status, however, all these cities face similar economic forces which result in increasing homogenisation of their landscapes. An example can be seen in the urban redevelopment of Beijing, China's capital city. As China has opened to the outside world, it has been exposed to similar kinds of financial and commercial pressures that impact all cities with international links. The response to these

Environmental change

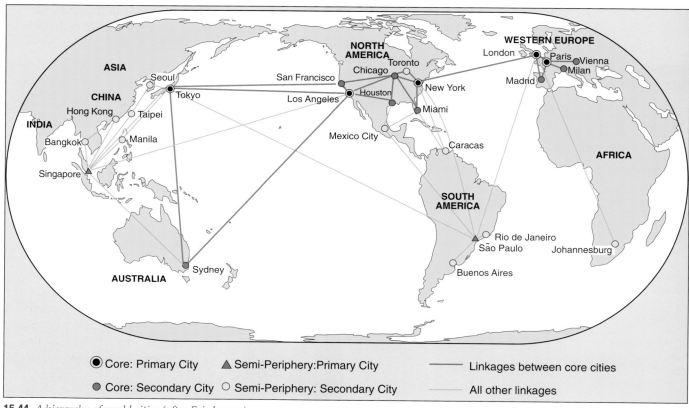

15.44 *A hierarchy of world cities (after Friedmann).*

pressures in Beijing, as elsewhere, has been to replace a distinctive urban landscape with a much more modern though homogenised landscape, featuring infrastructure, facilities and appearances that could be found in almost any modern large city (figures 15.45 and 15.46).

QUESTION BLOCK 15I

1. *Describe the pattern shown in figure 15.44.*

2. *Ignoring the specific locational differences such as the slope of the land, describe the changes in urban landscape that are typified in figures 15.45 and 15.46.*

15.46 *The modern landscape of Beijing shows the homogenised urban landscape typical of most large cities with strong international links.*

Because of their function and roles, world cities play a key role in the control of the global economy, and they tend to take on a similar appearance as well as common functions, structures and infrastructure (figure 15.47). The decisions made in the political and financial spheres of world cities have an impact on people in other urban and rural areas around the globe.

This is particularly so where a world city houses a large number of influential transnational corporations. Vast sums of money now pass around the world at the touch of a keyboard, and this can place many people in a state of dependence on decisions made in world cities. In the 1800s, it was decisions made in the manufacturing sector that often determined the economic well-being of the

15.45 *The traditional urban landscape of Beijing comprised small courtyard-fronted homes, linked by narrow laneways called 'hutongs'. Very few of these traditional areas remain; this example is in the outer suburb of Chuandixia.*

Table 15.2

Headquarters of the Largest 500 Manufacturing Firms

City	Country	Number of Headquarters
New York	USA	59
London	UK	37
Tokyo	Japan	34
Paris	France	26
Chicago	USA	18
Essen	Germany	18
Osaka	Japan	15
Los Angeles	USA	14
Houston	USA	11
Pittsburgh	USA	10
Hamburg	Germany	10
Dallas	USA	9
St Louis	USA	8
Detroit	USA	7
Toronto	Canada	7
Frankfurt	Germany	7
Minneapolis	USA	7
San Francisco	USA	6
Rome	Italy	6
Stockholm	Sweden	6

Source: Based on Clark, D (1996) p.148, and updated

population; today it is decisions made in the financial sectors of a small number of world cities. Indeed, decision making that takes place in the financial sectors of a few world cities is regarded by many economists as a new form of global control.

Much of the power of corporate decision makers in world cities comes from their small number and their concentration in just a few cities. Ten cities house the headquarters of almost half of the world's largest 500 transnational manufacturing corporations (table 15.2). Indeed, the top four cities alone house 156 of the top 500 companies. The remaining 344 headquarters offices are distributed across 47 other cities.

It is possible that this dominance of a small number of cities may begin to break down. Information and communications technology is bringing places closer together in terms of the time it takes to move information and money. As discussed in chapter 13, this is known as **time-space convergence**. However, as time-space convergence occurs, clusters of decision makers in a few world cities become unnecessary. In the future, it may be as easy to base decision making in Sydney as in London, or even in a remote centre such as Timbuktu in Mali — provided the internet and communications connections are sufficient.

15.48 *Emerging cities such as Dubai in the United Arab Emirates are investing heavily in infrastructure such as roads, airports, communications and buildings to attract a greater share of world business. The urban landscape being created here reflects the now-common international style that is found in many countries.*

So far, this possibility has not occurred, largely because some places in the world have better connected information services than others. Decision making requires large amounts of up-to-date information, and information technology connections are best developed in existing world cities. This reinforces the dominant position of existing world cities. It is probable that existing world cities will retain their dominant position, and perhaps strengthen it further, unless other centres can out-perform the world cities in cost, speed and convenience of information and communications technology — as is starting

15.47 *Fast food outlets are becoming a feature of homogenised urban landscapes across the world. These examples are in Bangkok, Thailand.*

Environmental change

to happen with certain key cities such as Dubai (figure 15.48). It has been reported that the New York suburb of Manhattan has twice the telephone capacity of the average nation, more computers than Brazil, and more word processors than all of Europe combined (figure 15.49).

15.49 *The high demand for space in the limited area of central New York has led to extreme vertical expansion of the city.*

The economic success of world cities has attracted migrants to those cities. Many of these migrants come from other countries, increasing the pressures for homogenisation of the urban landscape. This is not a new phenomenon, as much of London's population growth between 1800 and 1900 (when the population grew from 1 million to 6.5 million) was the result of migration rather than natural increase. Major US and Australian cities experienced large-scale immigration during the 1900s, and similar immigration is occurring today into large cities in economically developing nations. Much of the present rapid growth of cities such as Bangkok, Mexico City, São

Paulo, Rio de Janeiro and Cairo is coming from the migration of workers hoping to make their fortune in the big cities (figure 15.50). In some cases, migration to large cities is depriving smaller cities and towns of their bright, young, energetic labour force. This is leading to the decline of many medium and smaller urban centres in the source regions of migrant flows.

In spite of all that has been said in this section, some geographers question the concept of the 'world city'. Although few people would seriously deny the concentration of financial functions in a few cities, some would question whether it is really possible for a handful of cities to perform a role that covers the entire world. Nonetheless, it does seem clear that as the forces of globalisation impose pressures on urban areas to adopt a common set of functions and commercial activities, the homogenisation of urban landscapes seems inevitable as a common set of structures, styles and infrastructure emerges.

15.50 *São Paulo (in Brazil) is a huge, sprawling metropolis, with much of the growth coming from migration of people into the city in search of work.*

QUESTION BLOCK 15J

1. It is said that world cities exist because they are the chosen locations for the agencies of global capitalism. They are the places in which global financial and political control is concentrated. Giving reasons, say whether you believe this view is justified.

2. Explain why uniform urban landscapes have emerged, including the effects of common commercial activities, structures, styles of construction and infrastructure.

Socio-cultural exchanges

16

Globalisation is neither static nor inevitable.

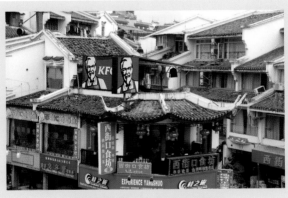

Cultural Diffusion

ToK BoX — Page 634
Plato's Cave and Enlightenment

What is Culture?

We take it for granted that people in different countries have different cultures. As Wood and McManus describe it:

"In India holy men go naked and stand in one position for years, bury themselves in sand or adopt painful postures, permanently distorting their bodies. In Japan, the simple act of pouring a cup of tea has become a ceremony which involves meditating for long periods and gently stirring the tea with a bamboo whisk. In England, wealthy people ride horses at high speed, following a pack of hounds and chasing a small fox, while one of the riders blows a horn."

We accept that these behaviours are part of the culture of the people in these countries.

Many aspects of people's behaviour, attitudes, beliefs and appearance make up culture. We can define **culture** as the

framework of shared meanings which people who belong to the same community (or group or nation) use to help them interpret and make sense of the world. In other words, a culture is the expression of people's world view.

16.1 *Maori people performing a powhiri, or traditional welcome. The dress, language, customs and beliefs of Maori people are important cultural traits of their total culture.*

Culture defines the lifestyle of people, and also their values and beliefs.

Culture shows itself in many ways. Culture is expressed through language, customs, beliefs, traditions, thinking, behaviour, faith, music, clothing, art, technology, images, food, architecture, dance, and in many other ways. Each of these individual features of a culture is known as a cultural trait. Therefore, for the Maori people of New Zealand, cultural traits include their traditional dress, their language, the architecture of their *marae* (or meeting place), and their spiritual beliefs and myths of origin (figure 16.1). It is the combination of these cultural traits, along with many other factors also, that defines Maori culture.

QUESTION BLOCK 16A

1. *What is meant by the terms (a) cultural trait, and (b) culture?*

The Diffusion of Mass Consumer Culture

The following item appeared on the internet:

"A group of American tourists arrived in Italy. 'Amazing!' said one to their tour guide. 'You have pizza here too'. A group of Japanese boy scouts landed in Chicago. 'Amazing!' they told their troop leader. 'They have McDonald's here too'."

This anecdote tells us a great deal about the globalisation of culture. A food that was invented by the Italians – pizza – is now accepted by people in the US and many other countries. Similarly, an American food chain – McDonald's – is now found in so many countries that children who have grown up with it consider it to be 'local' to their own country. And the fact that this anecdote was found on the internet, making it available instantly to anyone with an internet connection anywhere in the world, demonstrates how quickly ideas now move around the world.

16.2 *Ronald McDonald welcomes customers in Wuhan, China.*

Globalisation works against the preservation of traditional cultures. Traditions and ways of life that have survived for centuries in various parts of the world are finding it increasingly difficult to withstand the pressures of foreign influences. As the cultural theorist, Stuart Hall commented, "global consumerism … spreads the same thin cultural film over everything – Big Macs, Coca Cola and Nike trainers everywhere – inviting everyone to take on western consumer identities and obscuring profound differences of history and tradition between cultures" (figures 16.2 and 16.3).

16.3 *Donkeys carry Coca-Cola into the traditional markets of Fez, Morocco.*

The speed with which cultural influences move from place to place has never been more rapid than it is today. However, globalisation is not a new or recent process. For example, before 1000, the nations and tribes of Europe each had its own distinctive culture, with various languages, dress, architecture and beliefs. Around the year 800, the Serbian general Charlemagne conquered vast areas of Europe, including France, Germany, and parts of Spain and Italy. This led to the concept of 'Europe' emerging for the first time as a common culture based on Christianity and the Latin language spread through the empire.

16.4 *A sign reflecting the spread of both the Christian religion and the English language to Africa – the name of this business is typical of many in Ghana. Other examples may appear humorous to outsiders, such as the Rock of Ages Cement Works and the Only Jesus Can Do It Beauty Salon.*

European culture developed further as something distinctive with its own identity in the 1100s and 1200s when Christian Europe and the Islamic Middle East and North Africa came into conflict. This was perhaps the first clash between two cultures that were larger in scale than individual tribes or nations. Both Christian and Islamic cultural influences spread further over the following centuries and traders and conquerors travelled around the world (figure 16.4). Other cultures similarly spread their influence during the 1400s to 1800s, including especially the Chinese through South-East Asia (figure 16.5).

16.5 *Although this temple is Chinese in its architecture and religious practices, it is located in Penang (Malaysia), and is surrounded by colonial buildings built by the British.*

In past centuries, cultural diffusion has occurred through a series of processes:

- exploration by traders of areas around the world that were unknown to those people at the time;
- establishment of trading links in areas that produced goods different from the home areas;
- investment in new areas by traders, and a return of profits to the investors;
- expansion of production of raw materials, commodities and food in the new areas where investment has occurred;
- conquest and colonisation by the trading power, imposing new systems of government and culture on local cultures; and
- migration of colonists to new colonies, bringing further cultural impact to colonial areas.

In general, these processes were undertaken by people from European countries who established colonies overseas, usually in Africa, Asia, South America and Oceania. Occasionally, similar processes were followed by other cultural groups, notably Chinese and Arab traders, although these groups did not conquer and colonise to the same extent as the Europeans.

Traders and colonists exported the culture of their home societies into the areas where they travelled. This influence still shows today in the buildings found in many parts of the world (figure 16.6). However, the cultural influences also show in less visible ways such as the religion, language, legal systems and education found in many former colonies and trading areas. The result was often to suppress, or at least have an impact on, local cultures. In this way, the colonies and trading areas became **contact zones** that marked the 'frontier' of the expansion of one culture into a new area.

The process of **cultural diffusion** continues today at an accelerating rate. Today, colonisation is relatively less important than trade in promoting cultural diffusion. Colonisation does continue to play an important role in cultural diffusion, and notable examples include Indonesian influence in Irian Jaya, Chinese influence in Tibet, and until 1989, Russian influence in Eastern Europe.

Although tourism and migrant workers are often sources of cultural diffusion, as discussed elsewhere in this book, trade is probably the main agent of cultural diffusion. However, it is important to understand that the nature of today's trade is quite different from trade in the 1800s. Today, trade includes foreign investment, advertising and commercial media broadcasts which transfer cultural influences with great speed and strength. Cultural diffusion has now occurred to such a great extent that many people claim that 'places are all becoming the same' (or homogenised). We will investigate this claim later in the chapter.

16.6 *This building in Hanoi, Vietnam, shows two periods of cultural diffusion. The building is in European style, having been built by the French during colonial times. The posters show a more recent cultural infusion — socialism — which originated in Europe and spread to Vietnam through Russia (then the Soviet Union).*

It is important to understand that cultural diffusion can occur in two ways. First, in **expansion diffusion**, an idea develops or exists in a source area and then spreads into other areas while remaining strong at the source. For example, Islam developed in the Arabian Peninsula of the Middle East, and spread from there through North Africa, the rest of the Middle East, East Africa and parts of South-East Asia. However, it remained strong in its source area, the Arabian Peninsula, so this is an example of expansion diffusion. Expansion diffusion usually occurs where populations are stable or fixed; it is the idea that moves.

On the other hand, the second type of cultural diffusion is **relocation diffusion**. In this case, people who have adopted a new idea or belief carry it to a new destination. The spread of Christianity from Israel to Europe and then on to Africa, Asia and South America by traders and missionaries would be an example of relocation diffusion. It is possible that an idea transferred by relocation diffusion may lose its original strength in its source area, although this does not always happen. The longer an idea takes and the further it has to travel, the less likely it is to be adopted in new areas; this is known as **time-distance decay**. It explains why cultural diffusion by 'instantaneous' satellite television broadcasts are so powerful, why American speech and slang appear very quickly across the globe, and why 'foreign' products gain rapid acceptance in many other countries (figure 16.7).

The two types of diffusion were illustrated diagrammatically in figure 10.67 in chapter 10.

16.7 *An advertisement for Coca-Cola in Sana'a, Yemen. The global spread of this soft drink has been so strong that a slang term for the homogenisation of cultures is 'coca-colanisation'.*

QUESTION BLOCK 16B

1. What is meant by the term 'cultural diffusion'?

2. Explain the process of cultural diffusion which occurred in past centuries.

3. Describe the difference between 'expansion diffusion' and 'relocation diffusion', and give an example of each.

4. What is 'distance-time decay'? How does it help understand the process of cultural diffusion?

Adoption vs Adaption of Mass Consumer Culture

When confronted with the impact of a new culture, the choice facing people is whether they should reject the new influence, adopt it or adapt it. Where people **adopt** a new cultural trait, they take it on board in its entirety, perhaps abandoning some older tradition or belief to do so. Where a cultural trait is **adapted**, it is modified in

some way, usually so it can be accommodated within the framework of an existing culture or world view.

When Buddhism spread from India into Myanmar, the local people adapted it into their traditional belief system. Before Buddhism came to Myanmar, the people believed that spirits called *nats* inhabited every tree, rock, stream, house and other feature of the landscape. The people adopted Buddhism by making Buddha a supreme *nat*, enabling them to adopt Buddhism as well as retain their belief in the spirits. Even today, Buddhist temples and pagodas in Myanmar include important places to pay homage to the *nats* (figure 16.8).

16.8 *Worshippers at the Shwe Dagon Pagoda in Yangon look on as a devotee pours water over a small image of Buddha to earn merit. Behind the Buddha image is an image of a guardian nat, an example of cultural adaptation by the Myanmar people.*

One of the most obvious examples of the global spread of mass consumer culture today is McDonald's fast food (figure 16.9). It is claimed that a new McDonald's opens somewhere in the world every six hours. Because the foreign, or American, image of McDonald's is attractive to people in many countries, local businesses sometimes copy as much of the name and image as they believe they can get away with; an example of this is shown in figure 16.10. This is a contemporary example of cultural adaptation.

16.9 *Although American in origin, McDonald's 31,000 fast food restaurants are now found in 119 countries. This example is one of many McDonald's outlets in Moscow, Russia.*

16.10 *Perhaps imitation is a sincere form of flattery; this is a fast-food outlet in Yangon, Myanmar.*

16.11 *A McTurco meal in a McDonald's restaurant in Istanbul, Turkey.*

16.12 *The menu of a McDonald's restaurant in Mumbai, India. Note the vegetarian options near the top of the menu.*

Furthermore, McDonald's itself is a good example of **reverse adaptation**, where mass consumer culture has changed to become more easily accepted by local people. It is possible to buy teriyaki burgers at McDonald's outlets in Japan, McLaks (a grilled salmon sandwich) in Norway, and ayran (a chilled yogurt drink) and McTurcos in Turkey (figure 16.11). In India, the burgers are made from mutton and are called Maharaja Macs, as Hindus will not eat beef and Muslims will not eat pork. In addition, as many Hindus in India are vegetarian, McDonald's offer a spicy vegetarian patty made of potatoes and peas called a McAloo Tikki (figure 16.12).

Because of the adaptability of cultures, globalisation has not resulted in all places becoming the same, although there is certainly greater mixing (or **hybridisation**) of cultures. Cultural diffusion is not a new process, and although the pace of cultural change is accelerating, the impact is uneven across the world – some places are more accepting of global cultural changes while others are more resistant.

QUESTION BLOCK 16C

1. *Explain the difference between cultural adoption and cultural adaptation.*

2. *Define 'reverse adaptation', and give an example of it.*

3. *What does the term 'hybridisation' of cultures mean?*

Consumerism and Culture

Transnational Corporations (TNCs)

A **transnational corporation** (TNC) is a company that operates in several (or even many) different countries. According to the Instituto del Tercer Mundo, there are about 37,000 major transnational corporations with some 170,000 subsidiaries (local representative companies) in the world. Of these corporations, about 200 of them control the bulk of world trade. The growing influence of these top 200 TNCs is shown by their increasing share of world Gross Domestic Product, which has increased from 17% in the mid-1960s to 24% in 1982 and 33% in 1995. Although new figures have not been reliably estimated since that time, it is reasonable to assume that the percentage has continued to increase. In 1995, when they controlled 33% of world GDP, the same 200 corporations also controlled 76% of world trade.

All 200 of the largest TNCs have headquarters in just nine countries, all located within the tripolar core zone that was discussed in chapter 12. Japan hosts the headquarters of 62 of them, while others are found in the United States (53), Germany (23), France (19), United Kingdom (11), Switzerland (8), South Korea (6), Italy (5) and the Netherlands (4).

Manufacturing and petroleum companies hold many of the top positions in UNCTAD´s annual ranking of the world's 25 largest non-financial TNCs, even though TNCs in service industries have become increasingly important since 2000. In general, the larger TNCs from LEDCs tend to operate in a broader range of industries than TNCs from MEDCs, the most important industries being electronics and computers, petroleum and telecommunications.

Transnational corporations often have a wide-ranging impact in many countries, taking their production methods into a variety of economies and cultures. For example, one author describes the activities of Nike in the following words:

"Nike, the athletic footwear marketer, used to own manufacturing plants in the United States and United Kingdom, but presently subcontracts 100% of its production capacity to suppliers in South and East Asia. The geography of Nike's production partnerships has evolved over time, a change powered in part by changing labour costs in Asia. Initially, production of Nike shoes took place in Japan. Soon, subcontracting agreements diffused factories in South Korea and Taiwan. Presently, those partnerships are diminishing in importance as labour costs rise and new networks of subcontractors become established in Indonesia, Malaysia and China where workers involved in shoe production are paid about one-thirtieth of the wage their counterparts make, working for other companies, in the United States".

For many TNCs involved in manufacturing, the attraction of operating in economically less developed countries is low labour costs. Ironically, the attraction of TNCs involved in retailing to the same countries is the increasing wealth and spending power of the population as the economy grows and develops. Because of the widening gap between rich and poor in many developing countries, it is seldom the same people who would, for example, eat in an American fast food outlet in China as would work in an American shoe factory in China.

Fast-food TNCs have been especially vigorous in establishing themselves in many countries. Usually, these fast-food corporations are US-based, and they have established operations in many countries with quite different cultural backgrounds (figure 16.13). When these companies establish in developing countries, they usually charge prices that are similar to those charged in the United States, which means prices are much higher than local food restaurants. However, they often establish a very fashionable image of exotic 'foreign' American food that encourages local residents to spend a significant proportion of a weekly salary on a single meal. Compared with many local food outlets, the fast-food TNCs are clean and safe, and this encourages local people to change their dietary habits and eat there. As the fast-food TNCs tend to sell food that has a much higher fat content than local food, this is beginning to lead to problems of obesity and lack of fitness among people who dine at the outlets frequently.

16.13 *A not-entirely-official KFC restaurant in Moscow, Russia.*

It should also be recognised that fast-food TNCs have adapted to local conditions in many countries where they operate while retaining their American image. The adaptations to McDonald's menus was discussed in the previous section. The operations of the TNCs also adapt to local conditions where appropriate. For example, figure 16.14 shows the home delivery vehicles for Pizza Hut in Shenzhen, China. In a country where private motor vehicles are uncommon and bicycles are used more often, the pizzas are delivered in insulated boxes on the backs of bicycles.

16.14 *Part of the fleet of bicycles used for home delivery of pizzas in Shenzhen, China.*

1. Using relevant figures, describe the importance of transnational corporations in the world today.

2. Explain why transnational corporations may have a significant impact on cultures in many parts of the world.

Socio-cultural Integration

Homogenisation and Dilution of Culture

It is a common claim that 'places everywhere are becoming the same'. The claim arises from seeing people in many diverse places wearing similar blue jeans, brand-name trainers and drinking cola from a metal can. The claim also arises from the perception that cities around the world are losing their individuality and character, and taking on a uniform anonymous 'international' appearance. The trend towards uniformity in the character of different places is known as **homogenisation** of landscapes.

In general, homogenisation of landscapes also means 'westernisation' of place, or taking on the features of a European or North American landscape. This process does not refer only to buildings, but also to the shops and services found in cities around the world. Thus, fast food outlets and brand-name clothing outlets can now be found in many countries around the world, either in their authentic form or in an adapted or 'pirated' form. The inspiration for such shops is more likely to be a western cartoon, television show or corporation than the traditional culture of the country (figure 16.15).

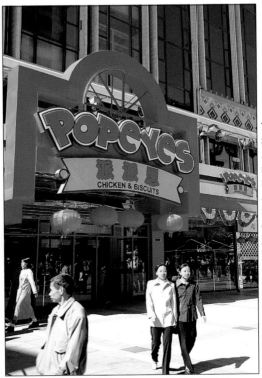

16.15 *This restaurant in Beijing (China) markets itself in an overtly American way to increase its appeal to young people, for whom 'American' equals 'cool' or 'modern'. There is no evidence here whatsoever of China's long history of food traditions.*

The study of geography first began because people were fascinated by the differences between places and the desire to explain those differences. The homogenisation of landscapes dilutes these differences, although it does not eliminate them. Because of the interaction between cultures, there is no longer a clear and simple correlation between culture and place. In today's world, there are very few 'pure', untainted cultures remaining, and it seems likely that this process will continue into the foreseeable future. Rather than remaining resistant to change, most cultures in the world today are open to change (willingly or otherwise), leading to hybridisation and homogenisation.

When **culture contacts** occur, they are often caused by the actions of powerful international corporations or media interests. In both cases, a common outcome is that the economies of developing countries become more dependent on the developed world.

16.16 *A Buddhist monk walks past a shop advertising Disney home videos in Yangon, Myanmar. Foreign media programmes were banned until recently in Myanmar because of the negative effects they might have on local people.*

When television programs made in one country are beamed into other countries with different cultural priorities, the values portrayed often have a great impact on the population (figure 16.16). Values that are taken for granted by children in the United States may be culturally challenging to a child in China, India, Tanzania, or even in Australia or Canada. However, because American culture is perceived in many countries as the road to wealth and affluence, these values can sometimes be accepted somewhat uncritically.

The imposition of other cultures is often sustained through **advertising** which supports foreign investment and economic activity (figures 16.17 and 16.18). Such advertising usually has one of two aims. One possibility is to portray a foreign product as part of the local culture in the hope that this will speed up acceptance of it. Such advertising aims to achieve the objective where children in Japan and Dubai perceive McDonald's as being Japanese or Arab.

The second possibility is to achieve the opposite of portraying a product as part of the local culture. Sometimes, it is the exotic foreign nature of a product that is highlighted in the hope that people will embrace this as an improvement over what they have traditionally used. An example of this is the advertising by transnational corporations promoting the use of infant feeding formulas or packaged foods in LEDCs (figure 16.19). The desire by young mothers to be 'modern' has led many to abandon breastfeeding, leading to poorer nutrition of infants and sometimes fatal disease such as diarrhoea.

16.17 *Advertising for Coca-Cola, which is an American product, in Ulaan Bataar, the capital city of Mongolia.*

16.18 *Another example of Coca-Cola advertising in an environment that is very different from its origins — in rural Djibouti.*

Where either of the two aims of advertising are followed, however, local people's perception of their own culture is challenged, diminished or modified in a way that encourages another foreign culture to emerge in a more dominant position.

When one culture is imposed upon another, a process known as **cultural imperialism** is said to occur. Cultural imperialism can be a deliberate, active, formal policy, or it may be nothing more tangible than a general active or

passive attitude. For example, when Australian Aboriginal people send each other Christmas cards with scenes that feature snow, or when maps of the world are drawn with Europe in the centre top, these are commonly regarded as examples of cultural imperialism.

The term 'cultural imperialism' is usually viewed negatively because it implies an unbalanced power relationship in which the culture of a stronger or more powerful nation or society suppresses the culture of a smaller or weaker society. Thus, powerful Western governments are capable of cultural imperialism that negatively affects people in many LEDCs, but almost all the people of LEDCs do not have the power required to exercise cultural imperialism in the opposite direction. Similarly, some observers claim that in today's globalised world, agencies such as the World Bank, the IMF (International Monetary Fund) and the WTO (World Trade Organisation) are also agents of cultural imperialism.

16.19 *The message of this sign to African mothers in Djibouti is in French, and says 'Blédina helps your baby to grow well — and makes your life easier!".*

Because the term 'cultural imperialism' has negative overtones, it is difficult to provide examples of it that people of all persuasions will accept. For example, many Palestinians assert that Israel's policies towards the Palestinian homelands reflect cultural imperialism, but few Israelis would agree. Similarly, many West Papuans accuse Indonesia of cultural imperialism in Irian Jaya, but few Indonesians from Java or Sumatra would agree.

With the dominance of English language around the world today and the decline of many minority languages, some commentators accuse native speakers of English of cultural imperialism if they refuse to learn and use other languages. English may also be an agent of cultural imperialism if it disempowers non-native speakers in important areas of business and commerce (figure 16.20).

It is not only landscapes and economies that are becoming more similar, but cultures and attitudes also. In many countries, **hybridisation of cultures** is occurring as traditional cultures take on values and aspects of other cultures with which they have come into contact. In

16.20 *Advertising in Ulaan Bataar (Mongolia) to encourage people to learn English. As English has become the international language of business, some argue that language is a form of cultural imperialism.*

16.21 *A man in Yangon (Myanmar) walks beneath a huge advertisement for music that is anything but traditional. The appeal of western culture is obvious.*

some countries, traditional cultures are sustained mainly through the economic value of tourism.

One aspect of culture that is becoming more uniform as a result of globalisation is **music** (figure 16.21). Modern western music is associated with progress and anti-establishmentism in the minds of many young people, and at times rebellion. This has led to the wide acceptance of modern music around the world. Furthermore, it has led many bands and musicians to try and copy the style, abandoning their own cultural traditions. In some cases, musicians have tried to combine their indigenous sounds with western music, and this results in a modification of traditional culture rather than its abandonment.

In the same way that colonialism during the 1800s threatened the sovereignty of nations that were forced to

become politically dependent, national sovereignty can be threatened by economic forces today. Where powerful **transnational corporations** operate in a country, a nation may find itself dealing with a company that is financially larger than the country itself. In such cases, countries are vulnerable to the wishes of companies who can threaten to sack local workers or even withdraw operations from a country completely if they do not get what they want.

A geographer, David Harvey, attempted to give **reasons** for the cultural homogenisation that is occurring in the world today. Harvey argued that because business interests are competitive by nature, investors are constantly searching for new places where a profit can be made more rapidly than elsewhere. Harvey called this waiting time for a profit the **turnover time of capital**.

Harvey argued that the search for shorter and shorter turnover times of capital is the real cause of the shrinkage of time-space. He said this shrinkage is quite different from the time-space convergence that was described in chapter 13. **Time-space convergence** involves physical travel between two points, but the shortening of the turnover time for capital does not. Therefore, Harvey devised the term **time-space compression** to describe the reduced turnover time for capital. The process of time-space compression can be measured by the declining cost of travel and communications, as shown in table 16.1.

Table 16.1
Declining Cost of Transport and Communications
1920 to 2010 (all figures in 1990 $US)

Year	Sea Freight (average ocean freight and port charges per tonne)	Air Transport (average revenue per passenger kilometre)	Telephone Call (3 minutes, New York to London)	Computers (index 1990 = 100)
1920	95	-	-	-
1930	60	0.42	245	-
1940	63	0.29	189	-
1950	34	0.19	53	-
1960	27	0.15	46	12,500
1970	27	0.10	32	1,947
1980	24	0.06	5	362
1990	29	0.07	3	100
2000	22	0.05	0.20	42
2010	19	0.04	0.05	26

Source: United Nations Development Program, updated.

Marshall McLuhan defined changes in cultures as **detraditionalisation**. Followers of David Harvey would argue that detraditionalisation is the result of local social practices being overwhelmed by foreign business and economic interests. The electronic media and developments in telecommunications have served to strengthen the power of business interests to impose their ideas and values on traditional cultures.

However, not all geographers agree with Harvey's analysis of corporate power. Some geographers argue that culture contact is not all one-sided, and that people from the dominant western culture are being influenced by concepts from other cultures. Examples of this include acceptance of Japanese management practices in many western companies, and the adoption of aspects of eastern religions by youth in developed countries searching for new meaning.

QUESTION BLOCK 16E

1. *What is meant by the term 'homogenisation' of landscapes?*

2. *Explain why homogenisation of landscapes usually results in the westernisation of local cultures.*

3. *Give some examples from your own knowledge of ways in which music (a) builds bridges between cultures, and (b) erodes individual cultures.*

4. *Explain how the concept 'time-space compression' differs from 'time-space convergence'.*

5. *The contact between cultures is often portrayed as a destructive process. How can contact between cultures be constructive instead?*

The Role of Diasporas in Preserving Culture

A **diaspora** is the scattering or dispersal of a community of people or a cultural group from its homeland to other parts of the world. The term was first used to describe the dispersal of Jewish people, but has since been used to describe the spread of many cultural groups such as the Irish, the Italians, Africans, Indians and various Pacific Islander groups. In general, the people of a diaspora share a common cultural and/or geographic origin, and although spread across many new areas, retain a strong sense of identity and common background.

The Jewish diaspora is found across the world, with concentrations in the US, Russia and South Africa that reflect historic migrations. The Indian diaspora is found in places such as southern and eastern Africa, Fiji, Singapore, Myanmar, Brazil and the United Kingdom. The Irish diaspora has particular concentrations in the United States, Australia, Canada and the United Kingdom. An Indo-Chinese diaspora from Vietnam and Cambodia has concentrations in Australia and the west coast of the USA.

During the 16th to 19th centuries a forced diaspora occurred in the form of the slave trade in which an estimated 12 million Africans were transported to North America, South America and the Caribbean to work as forced labourers for British, Dutch, Portuguese and other European land owners on plantations growing crops such as sugar and cotton (figures 16.22 and 16.23). The slave trade not only created an African diaspora in the Americas and the Caribbean but led directly to the development and spread of the concepts of racial differences and racial inferiority, not only among the slave-owning élites but among the Africans and Arabs who sold the enslaved people to the Europeans.

16.22 *One of the many fortresses on the coast of Ghana (West Africa) from which European traders sent thousands of captured men and women to the Caribbean and the Americas as slave labour.*

16.23 *A memorial to the suffering imposed by slavery at the site of the former slave market in Zanzibar, Tanzania.*

The slave trade created a connection between people on both sides of the Atlantic ocean and was thus an important agent of globalisation and cultural diffusion. One of the after-effects of slavery has been the rise of the Rastafari movement and the creation of yet another diaspora, that of Jamaicans returning to Africa.

The Rastafari Movement (also known as Rastafarianism, or Rasta) began in the slums of Jamaica in the 1930s when a Jamaican born black nationalist, Marcus Garvey, began calling on the descendants of slaves to take pride in their

African heritage. Garvey began to speak in religious terms, telling prophesies about a black king who would be crowned in Africa, and who would be a redeemer and liberator of the dispossessed black race. When the Ethiopian ruler Haile Selassie was crowned emperor in November 1930, many people believed that Garvey's prophesy had come true. Haile Selassie was also known as Ras Tafari Makonnen, from which the name 'Rastafari' derives. Haile Selassie took on a vast array of titles including 'Conquering lion of the tribe of Judah, Elect of God and King of the kings of Ethiopia', and the descendants of slaves in Jamaica started to see Ethiopia as their promised land.

Following the crowning of Haile Selassie in Ethiopia, the Rastafari movement in Jamaica began to develop as a religion. Black people were called upon to follow a path towards truth and reject the power of modern, oppressive white society (which they called 'Babylon') which was seen as rebelling against God, who was identified by the name Jah.

During the 1930s, six principles of the Rastafari movement emerged which still hold today:
- hatred for the white race;
- the complete superiority of the black race;
- getting revenge for the wickedness of white peoples;
- opposition to and humiliation of the government and all legal bodies of Jamaica;
- return to Africa (especially Ethiopia, which is 'the Promised Land'); and
- acknowledging the former Ethiopian Emperor Haile Selassie as the supreme being (living god) and only ruler of black people.

During the 1950s and 1960s, several additional Rastafari principles emerged:
- smoking cannabis (ganja) was seen as a spiritual act that brings a person closer to Jah;
- alcohol was to be avoided, as it is seen as a tool of white oppression;
- dietary guidelines were adopted that avoided pork, milk and coffee;
- wearing hair in dreadlocks was seen as a symbol of the mane of the lion of Judah (the Emperor Haile Selassie);
- the use of certain distinctive words was adopted, such as 'upfulness' (which means being helpful), 'overstanding' (as a higher form of 'understanding') 'irie' (to describe positive feelings, acceptance, or anything that is good), 'inity' (which means unity), and 'downpression' (which means oppression, but emphasises the downwards pressure applied by a powerful person to suppress a victim);
- women were forbidden from wearing trousers; and
- the use of reggae music, especially the music of Bob Marley, who is revered in Rastafari circles, was used to express mood and power (figure 16.24).

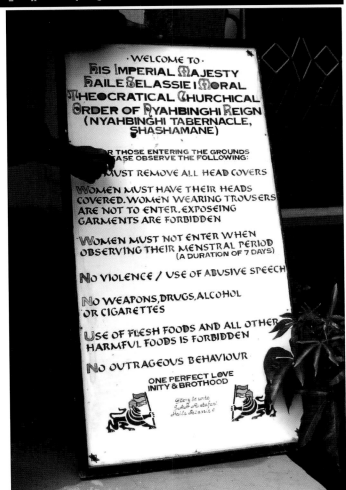

16.24 *The rules for entry to a Rastafari tabernacle in Shashemene, Ethiopia.*

16.25 *Many symbols of the Rastafari Movement are on display in this tabernacle in Shashemene, Ethiopia, including portraits of Emperor Haile Selassie, the colours of the Movement, a shrine to cannabis, and pictures of the Lion of Judah.*

During the mid-20th century, a large migration of Rastafari Jamaicans occurred to several overseas destinations, notably the United Kingdom, the United States, and South Africa. However, the largest migration of the Rastafari diaspora was from Jamaica to Ethiopia, and this took place due to a combination of three factors. First, racial relations were quite tense in Jamaica between the

British colonial rulers and the black descendants of former slaves. This was due to a range of British colonial government policies that local people believed were racist. Second, more people became aware of Marcus Garvey's teachings, especially his ideas that Blacks of the Diaspora could never prosper in countries governed by whites, and that therefore they must migrate to Africa to contribute to the creation of a strong Black-governed nation. Third, the crowning of Emperor Haile Selassie in Ethiopia seemed to fulfil Garvey's prophesy: "Look to Africa, to the crowning of a Black King that will be the Redemptor" (figure 16.25).

In adoration of Haile Selassie as a living god, the Rastafari in Jamaica declared themselves to be free citizens of Ethiopia, pledging loyalty to the Emperor and the Ethiopian flag, even adopting its colours of red, yellow and green as the colours of the Rastafari Movement.

16.26 *The main street in Shashemene, Ethiopia.*

16.27 *Two Rastas, a priest and his wife, in Shashemene, Ethiopia.*

During the 1950s and the subsequent decades, large numbers of Rastas migrated from Jamaica to Ethiopia, establishing a community in the town of Shashemene (about 250 kilometres south of the country's capital, Addis Ababa), where Haile Selassie gave the Rastafari a grant of 500 hectares of land in 1948 (figure 16.26). The situation deteriorated for the Rastafari in Ethiopia, however, when Haile Selassie was overthrown in a military coup in 1974. Army officers murdered Haile Selassie the

following year, although many Rastafari believed he was immortal and thus never died. Nonetheless, because the Rastafari were so closely associated with the former emperor, almost 98% of the land grant was confiscated by the new hard-line socialist government that came to power, and they were left with a mere 12 hectares in Shashemene. During the 1980s, persecution of the Rasta community caused its numbers in Shashemene to shrink to just 50 people (figure 16.27).

16.28 *The Nyahbinghi Rastafari Tabernacle in Shashemene, Ethiopia.*

Since then, numbers have grown once again, and today about 300 Rasta families live in Shashemene, but they experience widespread discrimination. The Rastafari diaspora is a highly visible group in Shashemene with their brightly coloured clothes, loud reggae music, dread-locked hair, and widespread marijuana smoking (figure 16.28). Although a few have opened shops, hotels and businesses in Shashemene, most of the Rastafari stay segregated from the general community, living in walled compounds where they can play reggae music and smoke marijuana without outside interference (figure 16.29).

16.29 *The wall and gate of the compound of the Twelve Tribes of Israel Rastafari community in Shashemene, Ethiopia.*

Ethiopian citizenship was taken away from the Jamaican settlers during the socialist period of the 1970s, and the loss of citizenship and loss of land continues to upset the Rastafari diaspora in Ethiopia. Although the Government is examining the possibility of granting citizenship to

Socio-cultural exchanges   630

Rastafari who have lived in Ethiopia for four years or more, restoring land that had been confiscated is almost impossible, as it was reallocated to local Ethiopians who have been using it for several decades for farming.

Nonetheless, the presence of the Rastafari community has had some impact on the local population. For example, the Rastafari demand for marijuana has created an expanding market for the crop with rising prices, and some local farmers have replaced their cultivation of potatoes with marijuana growing to supply the Rastafari. The Rasta presence also provokes debate among local people about the nature of the former Emperor Haile Selassie. Many Ethiopians see the former ruler as an autocratic and somewhat cruel absolute ruler, and certainly not the divine being that the Rastafari claim.

Overall however, the impact of the Rastafari diaspora on the host society in Shashemene has been minimal because the gap between Rasta culture and the culture of the host society is so great — in spite of their original common African origins. Most of the Ethiopians in the Shashemene area are conservative Orthodox Christians or Muslims. As such, they do not condone the marijuana smoking by the Rastafari or the reggae music they play. Furthermore, both the Christian and the Muslim commu-

nities object strongly to the Rasta claims that the former Emperor Haile Selassie was a divine figure who is worthy of worship. On the other hand, most people in the Christian and Muslim communities do acknowledge that the Rastafari are peaceful people who seldom cause any disturbances or problems. They also acknowledge the good work done by people such as Rita Marley, widow of the musician Bob Marley, who joined with local Rastafari aid workers to fund a school and a clinic in Shashemene.

QUESTION BLOCK 16F

1. *What is meant by the term 'diaspora'?*

2. *Identify some major diasporas in the world today.*

3. *What caused the African diaspora that is seen today in North and South America, and the Caribbean?*

4. *What are the main features of the Rastafari Movement?*

5. *How did the rise of the Rastafari Movement lead to a Jamaican diaspora in Ethiopia?*

6. *Describe the role of the Rastafari diaspora in Ethiopia in preserving culture.*

7. *To what extent has the host society in Ethiopia adopted traits of the Rastafari minority culture?*

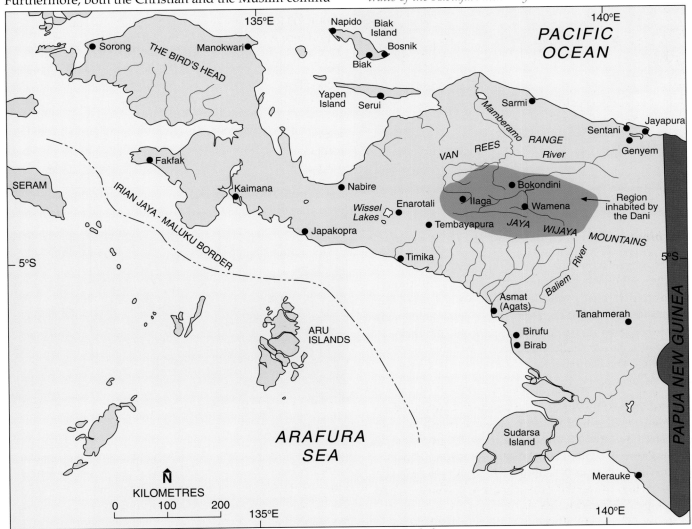

16.30 *Map of Irian Jaya, showing the location of the area inhabited by Dani people in darker green.*

Socio-cultural exchanges

Case Study of Socio-Cultural Integration — the Dani People of Irian Jaya

The western half of the island of New Guinea is part of Indonesia. Known as Irian Jaya, it is the eastern-most province of Indonesia, and it is home to the Dani people who live in the Highlands of the province (figure 16.30). They are found in the valleys of the rivers which cut deep valleys through the forest-covered mountains. Altogether there are about 194,000 Dani people, 100,000 living along the Baliem River which flows to the south and the rest along tributaries of the Mamberamo River which flows to the north.

The Dani were one of the last large groups of people to be 'discovered' by the outside world. Their existence was unknown by outsiders until a group of American adventurers , led by Richard Archbold, flew over the Baliem Valley in 1938. The fliers were astonished to find compact villages, neat gardens and well developed irrigation systems (figure 16.31). Since the 1950s, contacts with outside cultures have increased, although the Dani remain quite isolated because of the rugged terrain of the Highlands.

16.31 *An oblique aerial view of the Baliem Valley. This is similar to the view that amazed Richard Archbold in 1938.*

The biophysical environment of the Dani people

The biophysical environment of the Irian Jaya Highlands is a difficult one — harsh and unforgiving. Although there are rich, fertile soils in the wide floodplain of the Baliem River, most of the region has steeply sided valleys where is almost no flat land to grow food. On the hillsides, soils are shallow and stony, and they have few nutrients. The Dani people are farmers, so the poor soils are a major problem for them.

Rainfall in the Highlands is very heavy. Like mountain ranges anywhere in the world, orographic rain falls as the moving air is forced to rise and cool down. Average annual rainfall varies from 2,000 to 2,500 mm. This heavy rainfall causes leaching of the soils, washing away minerals and nutrients. It also leads to soil erosion and gullying on steep hillsides.

Temperatures do not change very much through the year because the region is so close to the equator. During the day, temperatures average about 20°C, although they often drop below freezing point at night because the air is so thin. Snowfalls are common, and several peaks are capped in snow throughout the year.

QUESTION BLOCK 16G

1. *Describe in words the location and type of country where the Dani people live.*

2. *In what ways is the biophysical environment of the Dani harsh?*

Pre-contact Dani life

Before contact with the outside world, the Dani people lived a very traditional lifestyle that was heavily dependent on their biophysical environment. Unlike people in industrialised nations, the Dani did not have (and still do not have) the resources to change their surroundings on a large scale. Therefore, the Dani live within the confines of their environment rather than live by changing their environment.

When outsiders made first contact with the Dani people, one of the first things they noticed was the traditional Dani style of **clothing**. The Dani wear surprisingly little clothing given the cold nights experienced in the Highlands. Women wear little more than a grass skirt, sometimes with a string carry bag over their backs. The string bag is used as protection against the sun, for warmth and for carrying food and small children. Men wear little more than a penis sheath made from the dried fruit of the gourd vine. Ornaments such as arm bands or 'neckties' made from shells are sometimes worn, especially on festival occasions (figure 16.32). All the materials for clothing worn by both men and women were traditionally grown in the village or gathered from the nearby forests.

16.32 *A group of men in Miagaima village, dressed for a pig kill ceremony, wearing traditional penis sheaths together with decorations such as armbands and head dresses. The black colouring worn by some comprises charcoal mixed with pig fat.*

The lifestyle of traditional Dani people centred on the growing of food. Unlike most traditional groups in New Guinea, which practised shifting cultivation, the Dani practised **sedentary agriculture**. This means that the same land was cultivated year after year, rather than being abandoned for a new plot. Sedentary agriculture meant that land could be individually owned, intensively farmed and neatly laid out, using a complex system of irrigation channels (figure 16.33). Farming plots were surrounded by fences with sharp spikes on top to keep wandering pigs out of the gardens.

16.35 *During this pig kill ceremony, the men have pierced the pig's heart with an arrow, and are now pumping the heart with their feet to hasten death.*

16.33 *A sweet potato garden under cultivation beside the Baliem River, with the irrigation channels clearly visible.*

16.36 *A group of men butcher the pig using bamboo and bone knives, and stone axes. The pieces of pig meat are wrapped in banana leaves for cooking.*

16.34 *Most farming is done by Dani women. This woman is using a digging stick to cultivate sweet potatoes.*

The main crop grown was the sweet potato and after the initial clearing of the land, work in the fields was usually done by the **women** (figure 16.34). Sweet potatoes are high in starch and need to be supplemented with protein to make a balanced diet. Although some protein came from hunting small birds and marsupials, most protein came from the raising of pigs. Pigs were a measure of a person's wealth, and so they were rarely killed except at large ceremonies. As a result, women and children often suffered from malnutrition, as they usually received much less pig meat at the feasts than the men. Pig kill ceremonies were held to mark births, deaths, marriages, and to make pre-battle magic, to cure illnesses and to make peace after war.

The **pig-kill ceremony** was the centre of traditional Dani life. Traditionally they were held only once every three to six years and long preparations were required. On the day of the pig kill, the men of the host village would

16.37 *Young men and women dance during the pig kill celebrations.*

Socio-cultural exchanges

ToK BoX

Plato's Cave and Enlightenment.

If the purpose of education is enlightenment and the development of wisdom, then by the time you finish your IB studies in Geography you will hopefully be well on the road towards acquiring both.

The ancient Greek philosopher, Plato, tried to explain how education leads to enlightenment. He said that knowledge is "justified true belief", which he explained in his tripartite (or three-part) theory of knowledge, as follows:

.... a person 'S' knows proposition 'P' if and only if:

1. P is true

2. S believes P

3. S is justified in believing P.

Plato said that all three points are necessary and sufficient conditions for knowledge. Almost everyone (except a hardened relativist) would accept the first two points. However, many people debate the precise form and degree of justification required for the third point.

Plato tried to explain what it means to be truly educated and enlightened in his most famous book, *The Republic*. In that book, Plato used the image of a cave, as follows:

Imagine a group of prisoners who are chained together in an underground cave. They have lived all their lives in that position, chained to face the wall of the cave in front of them.

Behind them is a blazing fire that provides light, and between the fire and the prisoners, there is a bridge with a safety wall. As people pass across the bridge, they will cast shadows on the wall in front of the prisoners, somewhat like shadow puppets. Some of them walk across the bridge talking, while others walk in silence.

The prisoners will see the shadows of the passing people, and they will hear their voices echoing from the wall. Because this is all they have ever experienced, they will assume that the shadows and the echoes are truth and reality.

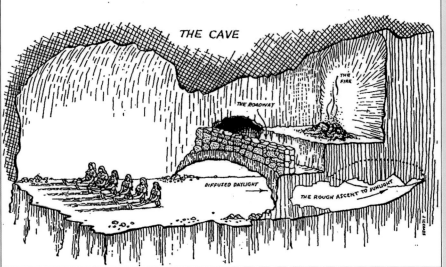

THE CAVE

If one of the prisoners was released, we can imagine he would stand up and turn around. When he saw the fire for the first time, he would probably be in great pain because of the strong glare, and he would take some time to process the realities that he was now seeing compared with the realities he had known all his life. Eventually, however, he would understand that the things he thought were realities were, in fact, illusions.

If the prisoner was then dragged up a steep and rugged tunnel to the earth's surface, he would suffer another round of pain when confronted by the glare of the sun. However, when his eyes had adjusted, he would start to see a new reality, first in the shadows, then actual objects, and eventually in the whole cosmos of the moon, the sky and the stars. Last of all, he would be able to see the sun, and begin to understand the importance of the sun in causing many of the other things he was seeing.

Eventually, he would be able to take in a deeper reality than anything he had ever known in the cave, either while he was chained or after he had been released. He would come to understand that the sun was the cause of day and night, the seasons and the life that he

was witnessing, and he would start to form hypotheses, explanations and reasons to explain what he was experiencing.

Moreover, if the former prisoner was subsequently led back into the cave, he would almost certainly take pity on his fellow prisoners, because he would understand that even if he tried to explain what he had seen, they could never fully understand. Having experienced enlightenment, the former prisoner would probably rather suffer anything than return to the false notion of truth he was living under previously and return to live in this miserable manner.

And yet, when he returned to the gloom of the cave, the other prisoners would notice that the man who had been to the surface would not be able to see clearly because his eyes had now adjusted to the light of the world above. The other prisoners would claim that he had returned without his vision, and that it would be better not even to think of ascending from the familiarity of the cave.

The message of Plato's allegory of the cave is that one must make the uncomfortable ascent from the gloom of ignorance if one is to become enlightened.

The next ToK BoX is on page 649.

dress in their finest outfits and would take turns to shoot arrows into the heart of a pig (figure 16.35). While the pig was dying, a fire would be started and the cooking rocks heated. Then the pig would be butchered using stone axes and bamboo knives, with the pieces wrapped in banana palm leaves (figure 16.36). When the stones were hot, they would be removed from the fire using wooden tongs and placed into an underground pit, together with

the pieces of pig and vegetables such as sweet potato. During the four to six hours that the food was cooking, dancing, singing and games would take place (figure 16.37). Eventually, after night had fallen, the pig would be eaten, first by the men, then by the women and children who would eat the remains (figure 16.38). Because the women received only the 'left-over' pig meat, they were poorly nourished compared with the men in

16.38 *After the pig meat has been cooked underground using hot rocks, the meat is distributed, first to the men, followed by the women and children as shown here.*

16.39 *Typical Dani huts have conical roofs and are surrounded by the gardens so that people do not waste time or effort walking long distances to the fields. The irrigation ditch can be seen clearly in the right foreground.*

16.40 *Smoke from the fire in the men's hut collects in the upper part of the hut where the men sleep at night. The black carbon deposits on the walls indicate the unhealthy interior environment of Dani huts.*

the fields. Men lived in **separate houses** from the women and children and the houses for both genders were always two storey. The lower level had an earth floor, covered with grass, and was used as a living and cooking area. There was a fire in the centre which filled the hut with smoke for warmth. The upper level, which had a bamboo floor, was for sleeping and (in the case of men's huts) for storing valuable or sacred objects. Dani huts had no chimney, so the smoke built up in the huts, eventually seeping out through open doors or through the thatched roofs. Dani people therefore spent most nights inhaling smoke from the fires, and this caused serious **health problems** (figure 16.40). The average life expectancy of Dani people (even today) is only 38 years as many die from pneumoconiosis. This is similar to the disease suffered by coal miners called 'black lung disease' when the alveoli of the lungs become clogged with carbon soot.

16.41 *Traditional vine and timber suspension bridges such as this one over the Baliem River at Wamena are still found throughout the Dani territory.*

traditional times. Through the pig-kill ceremony, the Dani's culture, ceremonies, wealth and nutrition were linked together.

Traditionally, the Dani people lived in round timber **houses with round grass roofs** (figure 16.39). Huts were almost always situated immediately beside the food gardens so that no time was wasted going to and from

Before outside contact, walking was the only means of land **transport** used by the Dani. A dense network of walking tracks criss-crossed the Dani territory. Small bridges of timber or vines spanned rivers and streams, while small bridges of logs crossed irrigation canals (figure 16.41). In order to cross a large river such as the Baliem, logs were strapped together into a raft, with the passengers standing up as the raft was paddled across the river.

An important part of traditional Dani life was **ritual warfare**. Watchtowers were built in each Dani village (figure 16.42). While the women gardened, the men would keep watch in case a surprise attack should come. Fighting used spears, bows and arrows. However, the purpose of the fighting was not to take territory or to kill the opposition. The fighting was done for the sheer enjoyment and excitement. Normally, a battle would not last more than a single day, and would normally end when first person had been killed — this would determine the winner of the battle. In some cases, people from the winning village would eat the body of the person killed to draw upon his spirit and strength. However, this often spread diseases, especially when the brain of the dead person was eaten. This was because any disease suffered by one human can be caught by another, unlike diseases carried by animals to which humans tend to be immune.

16.42 *A defensive watchtower at Miagaima village. Only a few decades ago, thousands of such watchtowers covered areas of Dani settlement. Now that ritual warfare has ended, most of the watchtowers have been cut down and destroyed. Only two now remain in the Grand Valley, these having been re-built as tourist objects. Note the smoke seeping through the thatched roof of the hut with no chimney in the background.*

The Dani people had a strong and rich culture. The **traditional religion** of the Dani saw the world as being filled with spirits and ghosts. The Dani made charms to protect themselves from the spirits. A special type of charm was the mummified bodies of special people. Many Dani villages have the mummified remains of great chiefs from the past hidden away on the top floors of the men's houses. In some cases, these remains may be over 300 years old, and are preserved by the smoke which fills the hut each evening. These mummified bodies are brought out only on special occasions (figure 16.43).

QUESTION BLOCK 16H

1. Why are traditional Dani houses unhealthy?

16.43 *A 350 year old smoked mummy in Pummo village.*

2. How appropriate is traditional Dani clothing? In your answer, consider (a) the climate, and (b) the difficulties of washing clothes.

3. In what ways was traditional Dani farming quite advanced?

4. What were the main traditional Dani foods? How adequate was the traditional Dani diet?

5. What advantages were there in using tools made from locally available raw materials such as stones, bones and timber?

6. How did the great pig kill feasts serve to bind together traditional Dani society?

7. What were the important traditional Dani measures of wealth?

8. Why did the traditional Dani people engage in ritual warfare?

First contact with the outside world — explorers and missionaries

For many centuries, the Dani existed in isolation. Some brief, isolated contacts were made in the early 1900s by mountain climbers, but these contacts were in the high mountains well away from Dani settlements. Following **Richard Archbold's 'discovery'** of the Dani in 1938, several visits were made to Dani villages over the next year. Archbold wrote of his travels in the *National Geographic* in 1941, and this was the first time most people were aware of the existence of the Dani people. Archbold described Dani society as a 'paradise on earth'.

World War II, which was fought in South-east Asia from 1941 to 1945, prevented contact with the Dani people for several years. However, several **Christian missionary groups** became interested in the Dani following the *National Geographic* article, and some groups made contact in 1950 and 1952. In April 1954, the first missionaries landed in the Baliem Valley to establish a mission station. Six years later in 1960, virtually all Dani people were in contact with one or another missionary group. The missionaries opened schools throughout the Dani area and began medical services, church services and literacy programs. Unlike government officers, the missionaries always learned the local language and lived as much as possible like the local people, and so they were able to communicate very clearly.

The missionaries came to convert the Dani people to Christianity. They felt that the traditional Dani people were 'lost souls', and that becoming Christian was the only way they could have eternal life. By the early 1990s, almost every village in the Dani area had one or more mission station attached to it (figure 16.44). It is estimated that over 80% of Dani people had been converted to Christianity. In fact, the efforts of the Christian missions has meant that Irian Jaya has become Indonesia's only province where Christianity is the dominant faith. Most of Indonesia is strongly Muslim.

16.44 *The 'Dr Bob Pierce Memorial Chapel' is attached to a Protestant mission conducted by The Mustard Seed Incorporated, Wamena.*

Culture contact with the Christian missionaries had great impact on the Dani people. When they were first converted to Christianity in the 1950s, many Dani people thought they would change colour and became white. By the early 1960s, Dani had come to terms with being black Christians. As a result, many Dani people have adopted Christian names such as Moses, Isaac, and even Epaphroditus.

Unlike missionaries in some parts of Papua New Guinea, the missionaries in Irian Jaya never insisted that Dani people who had become Christians should wear **clothing**. The missionaries were concerned that clothing would create skin problems for the Dani because it was so hard to wash clothes properly. Therefore, although some Dani people have chosen to adopt Western clothing, many Dani people today continue to wear traditional clothing.

Although the missionaries **eliminated ritual warfare and cannibalism**, ceremonies such as the **pig-kill** have continued. However, pig-kill ceremonies now take place

much more often, being used to celebrate Christmas, Easter, baptisms, marriages, the Indonesian Day of Independence or even the arrival of an important guest. More frequent pig-kill ceremonies mean that people's **nutrition** has improved, especially in the cases of women and children. The more frequent ceremonies have also strengthened the bonds between neighbouring villages, reducing tensions and the likelihood of **conflicts**.

16.45 *Women sometimes travel for several days to sell their produce at the markets in Wamena. Travel to the markets has opened up new channels of communication for Dani people. These days, a mix of traditional and Western dress is found.*

Before contact with outsiders, Dani people seldom travelled more than a few kilometres from their village. To have ventured further would have taken them into territory controlled by another village. The arrival of the missionaries has broadened the view of Dani people, as they were made aware for the first time that other people existed in the world. With the end of ritual warfare, Dani people now **travel** long distances without fear of attack. Women will often travel for several days to sell their produce in the markets in faraway towns and villages (figure 16.45). Such travel to markets has opened up entire new networks of **communication** and ex-changes of ideas which never previously existed. The missionaries also operate a transport system using light aircraft. Although mainly intended to take missionaries in and out of remote areas, the aircraft are also used to transport ill Dani people out of remote villages in cases of emergency. Such flights can reduce a three day walk over snow-capped mountains to a short half-hour flight. This can often mean the difference between life and death.

The missionaries have brought great changes to the traditional pattern of **farming**. They brought new tools — shovels, hammers and nails — which could make the traditional lifestyle more efficient. They also brought household implements such as saucepans and plastic dishes which made life in the villages easier (figure 16.46). However, manufactured goods such as these cost money, and for the first time Dani people came to see the need to earn some money. Over time, **money** has come to replace pigs as the measure of a person's wealth.

Traditionally, the Dani people were **subsistence cultivators**. In other words, they grew only enough food for themselves and their immediate families. When the missionaries arrived, they bought food from the Dani people, and this led to small **markets** being established. The main crop grown by the Dani was the sweet potato. The missionaries wanted a more diverse diet, so they handed out seeds to grow vegetables such as cabbages, tomatoes, carrots, corn and beans. The Dani people then began eating these vegetables also, and their diet became more balanced and malnutrition further decreased.

16.46 *Although living in a traditional hut in a compound near the mission station at Sinatma, this Dani boy dresses in western clothes and stands beside his plastic plates and metal can that are drying in the sun.*

Perhaps the biggest impact of the missionaries has been to change the **world view** of the Dani people. The main aim of the missionaries was to lead the Dani into a mature Christian faith. This meant that the Dani had to learn how to learn how to read and write, because otherwise they would not be able to read the Bible or other Christian literature. Each of the mission stations built a school, and both children and adults were encouraged to attend classes to learn basic **literacy** and numeracy. Over half the Christian missionaries in Irian Jaya were involved in translation and literacy programs with local people. Through education, the Dani have come to learn that the world is much bigger than they had thought possible. The Dani still believe the world is full of ghosts and spirits, but they now see these spirits as being subject to the higher authority of God.

QUESTION BLOCK 16I

1. *Why did it take until the 1930s for outsiders to learn of the Dani people?*

2. *Why were Christian missionaries attracted to the Dani people?*

3. *How successful were the missionaries in evangelising the Dani people?*

4. *What was the missionaries' attitude to traditional Dani dress?*

5. *How has missionary activity affected the traditional great pig kill feasts?*

6. *Why did the Dani abandon ritual warfare?*

7. *How did missionary work 'broaden the perspectives of Dani people'?*

8. *How did the missionaries affect the diet and health of the Dani people?*

9. *Why were the missionaries so keen to make the Dani people literate?*

Indonesian government impact

The Indonesians took control of Irian Jaya from the Dutch in 1962. The Indonesians were as different from the Dani people of Irian Jaya as were the Dutch. Almost the entire population of Irian Jaya in 1962 were Melanesians, closely related to the people of Papua New Guinea and other nations such as the Solomons and Fiji. The only historic link between Irian Jaya and the rest of Indonesia is that both were Dutch colonies. Some people argue that Indonesian control of Irian Jaya is an example of **colonialism**.

There was some resistance to the Indonesian take-over by Dani people. In 1977, fighting broke out in the Dani region. The Dani attacked the Indonesians with bows and arrows and the Indonesians responded with rockets, attack aircraft and helicopters to strafe Dani villages. About 500 Dani people were killed.

In general, the Indonesian officials in Irian Jaya seem to look down upon the Dani people, seeing them as savages who are little better than animals. For many years they tried to **ignore** the Dani people as much as possible, and this has helped to preserve their traditional culture. Travel to and from the Highlands by Dani people is heavily restricted by the government, and alcohol is banned from the Dani region by the government leaders, most of whom are Muslim.

One exception to this ignoring of the Dani concerned the wearing of **clothes**. The Indonesians were offended by the near-nakedness of the Dani, and a campaign was launched in the early 1970s to get them to wear clothes. The campaign was called 'Operation Koteka', *koteka* being the Indonesian word for 'tail', an insulting term for the penis sheath worn by Dani men. The Dani were usually too proud of their traditions to abandon their traditional clothing, and as they despised the Indonesians, the campaign failed. They resented the insulting comments about their traditional clothing and if anything, Operation Koteka encouraged Dani people to continue wearing traditional dress as a sign of defiance against what they saw as cultural imperialism.

Nonetheless, by the mid-1980s, the Indonesian government felt the need to try once again to improve the life of the Dani people. The authorities were concerned about the short life expectancy of the Dani, many of whom were dying in their late 30s from pneumoconiosis. The government began building Western-style square **houses** for nuclear families (figure 16.47). Most Dani people rejected these houses and have often built traditional houses beside them. Then they use the square houses for storing books or clothes or as animal shelter. They do not like the square houses because they are too cold- the metal roofs let out the heat at night and the smoke escapes through the doors and windows.

The Indonesians have had some influence on the Dani **diet**. In an effort to make the Dani people more Indonesian, new crops such as rice and new animals such as water buffalo were introduced. Most Dani people have not adopted these new foods because they cannot attach any wealth or prestige to them. Dani people see chickens and goats as something to sell rather than eat. They do not refuse to eat the new foods, but most cannot see a good reason to do so.

16.47 *Housing provided by the Indonesian government in Wamena.*

A **cultural conflict** arose between the Dani and the Indonesians over the value of pigs. The Dani people have traditionally seen pigs as the main source of wealth and prestige. However, to the Indonesians who are Muslim, the pig is an unclean animal. The Indonesians tried to convince the Dani people to stop eating pigs, but they were not successful. Then the Indonesians offered to improve the quality of Dani pigs by importing some new stock from Bali for breeding purposes. Bali is an Indonesian island, but being Hindu, had some pigs.

Unfortunately, the pigs from Bali carried a disease called **encephalitis**. This caused death by inflammation of the brain among people who ate the pig meat. The disease is still widespread among Dani pigs, and many Dani people believe that the Indonesians sent diseased pigs to Irian Jaya deliberately.

The Indonesian government is still trying to make the Dani people more 'Indonesian'. In the late 1980s, the government took over most of the mission schools so that Dani children would learn about Indonesian things — language, culture, religion — rather than Christian things.

School classrooms now carry portraits of the Indonesian president as the government wants the children to see themselves as Indonesians rather than Dani. However, most Dani children have difficulty with Indonesian education. Unlike the mission schools, which taught lessons in the Dani language using traditional systems of thinking and logic, schools now teach in the Indonesian language and use different ways of thinking. Even today, fewer than 1% of Dani children proceed to high school.

QUESTION BLOCK 16J

1. *Describe the differences between the Dani and most other Indonesians.*

2. *How do most Indonesians regard the Dani people?*

3. *What evidence is there that relations between the Dani and the Indonesian government lack harmony?*

4. *What were the aims of Operation Koteka? Why was the campaign unsuccessful?*

5. *Why does the government want the Dani people to abandon their traditional housing? Why have the Dani been reluctant to agree to this?*

6. *How have Muslim attitudes among Indonesians towards eating pork affected relations with the Dani people?*

7. *Why does the Indonesian government place so much importance on educating Dani children in schools? What problems does this cause?*

Tourism

Because of its isolation, few tourists come to the Dani region. However, since the mid-1980s, small numbers of adventurous trekkers have begun coming to the Irian Jaya Highlands (figure 16.48). **Tourism** has already had quite a significant impact on the Dani people.

16.48 *A trekking group, accompanied by Dani porters, on a walking track near Uwosilimo.*

Many of the tourists hire local people as guides and **porters**. This gives local people the chance to earn money, learn English and explore new areas. On the other hand, it also means Dani people may be diverted away from growing food or other village responsibilities. Tourists bring new styles of clothing, new ideas and new habits which many Dani people have tried to copy to be 'fashionable'. When tourists give novelties or gifts to local people, especially children, a 'cargo cult' can develop where Dani people come to expect gifts or charity whenever outsiders arrive. This is quite different from their traditional way of life which emphasised giving rather than receiving.

16.49 *This Dani man has dressed himself in an exaggerated form of traditional dress in the hope that tourists will pay him to be photographed.*

In an attempt to earn income from tourists, basic hotels for trekkers were built in the early 1990s, mainly by Indonesian entrepreneurs from Java and Sumatra. To support this, some Dani villages encourage trekkers to pitch tents in their compounds and local people produce souvenirs for sale to tourists. While this can help preserve traditional crafts, it can also corrupt the traditional culture (figure 16.49). There is a real danger that if tourism expands too much or too quickly, the Dani culture could be wiped out in a way that neither the missionaries nor the Indonesians were capable of achieving.

Of course, tourism can bring benefits also. Culture contact is a **two-way process**, and if tourists take the time and trouble to study the culture of the people they are visiting, important learning can take place. There is some evidence that the Indonesian authorities see tourism as a reason to preserve aspects of traditional Dani culture. For example, the airport terminal at Wamena, the biggest town in the Dani region, is modelled on traditional Dani huts (figure 16.50). Tourists visiting villages usually buy some Dani artefacts such as spears and arrows. If these are displayed back in their homes, then Dani culture may become better known and more appreciated around the world.

16.50 *Wamena Airport Terminal, modelled on the architecture of a traditional Dani compound.*

QUESTION BLOCK 16K

1. *Why would tourists wish to travel to a remote area such as the Grand Valley of the Baliem?*

2. *Draw up a table which lists the advantages of tourism for the Dani on one side, and lists the disadvantages on the other.*

3. *What conclusions about the costs vs benefits of tourism to the Dani people can you draw from the table you constructed in the last question?*

4. *Draw a time line from 1900 to the present. Mark in the important events in the history of Dani culture contact. Include the early explorers, Richard Archbold, the first missions, government actions, tourism, and all other noteworthy events.*

5. *What evidence is there that culture contact with the Dani has been a two-way process?*

6. *Do you think the Dani people should be protected from future culture contact? Explain your answer fully.*

7. *To what extent has cultural diffusion led to the globalisation of Dani culture?*

Political outcomes

17

The political aspects of globalisation — and the question of whether tolerance will be sufficient to build a better world in the future.

ToK BoX — Pages 649 and 659
Political ideologies
Tolerance and relativism

Loss of Sovereignty

What is a Nation-State?

The 1990s was a decade of enormous change for atlas makers. In the early 1990s, the Soviet Union disintegrated and 15 new countries were created as a result. At about the same time, Yugoslavia began a process of disintegration and turmoil that was still continuing a decade later. This turmoil resulted in the creation of yet more countries. This process was not new – new countries are created while others disintegrate, and the map of the world has always been changing to reflect political changes. Indeed, an atlas published a century ago is of almost no use today to study national boundaries except in an historical sense.

Each of these countries in the world should correctly be called a **nation-state**. A nation-state is a defined area of territory that is under the control of a single government that controls the economy, political organisation and external security. Although this may seem a simple definition at first sight, it often results in complex situations and conflicts that are difficult to resolve.

The world has not always been divided into nation-states. Through most of human history, groups of people organised themselves in tribes. Each tribe shared a common language, culture, religion and history. In Europe, alliances, conflicts and revolutions resulted in some tribes and communities being conquered or amalgamated with others, forming larger and larger political territories. In 1648, a peace treaty known as the Treaty of Westphalia acknowledged the existence of independent sovereign states for the first time, and the concept of the nation-state is often seen to date from that time. When Europeans began to colonise other parts of the world, the nation-state concept came to be applied in all continents as boundaries and territories were defined.

Some communities have only embraced the concept of the nation-state quite recently, if at all. Even today there are groups within countries such as Papua New Guinea, Congo and Ethiopia who see their 'nation' as their tribe, and their territory as the valley or area they have traditionally controlled. For such people, the tribe in the neighbouring valley is seen as a different nation with a different language whom they have traditionally fought against in war (figure 17.1). This creates quite a challenge for the governments of countries such as Ethiopia, Congo and Papua New Guinea government in Port Moresby as they try to build a strong loyalty to a single nation-state that includes traditional enemies.

The nation-state is different from the concept of nation, which is closer to the traditional smaller grouping just described in Papua New Guinea. A **nation** is a community of people bound together by a common culture and history, who have a collective sense of being different from others. Although nations and nation-states sometimes coincide, they usually do not. Thus, the Basque people who have their own language and live in the Pyrenee mountains of Europe are a nation which happens to inhabit some territory in the nation-states of France and Spain. In a similar way, Indigenous Australians are members of one nation within the nation-state of Australia. The Kurds are a nation of about 20 million people who mainly live in five nation-states – Iraq, Iran, Turkey, Syria and Armenia.

17.1 *Members of the Mursi tribe in southern Ethiopia. The Mursi have a strong loyalty to their tribe rather than to the national territory of Ethiopia, with which they do not identify. A distinctive feature of the Mursi is that the adult women identify themselves with large round lip plates that are up to 15 centimetres in diameter, inserted into a slit separating their lower lip and jaw.*

Having defined the 'nation-state', the common question many people ask is "how many nation-states are there in the world today?". This is a surprisingly difficult question to answer, because it is not always clear whether a place is a nation-state or not. For example, Scotland is part of the United Kingdom, but it has its own sports teams, its own flag, its own National Assembly and issues some denominations (but not all) of its own currency. Therefore, is Scotland a nation-state, or is it part of the United Kingdom?

Most authorities recognise very small micro-states as nation-states, examples being Andorra, Monaco and the Vatican. Some countries recognise the Republic of Kosovo as a separate nation-state, but other countries regard it as still part of Serbia (figure 17.2). No countries

recognise the Republic of Transdnestr (or Pridnestrovie as it is sometimes known), which is a breakaway region on the border between Moldova and Ukraine, and yet the area has functioned effectively as a separate nation-state since it declared its independence from Moldova in 1992.

17.2 *A general view of Priština, the capital of Kosovo.*

17.3 *The Governor's Residence in Macau during the time when Macau was a Portuguese colony, flying the Portuguese flag. Macau was returned to China in December 1999, and is now a Special Administrative Region (SAR) of China. It has the distinction of being the first European colony in Asia, and also the last.*

There are other examples of places that could be defined as a nation-state, but which are unclear. Figure 17.3 shows the Governor's Palace in Macau when it was still a Portuguese colony. Colonies are not nation-states. Although they have a defined territory, permanent inhabitants and sometimes a separate structure of administration, they lack full control over their internal affairs. In December 1999, Macau was handed over to China and it became a Special Administrative Region, like Hong Kong. Is Macau now a nation-state? It is issuing its own stamps and currency and has its own flag and administration, although is controlled ultimately from Beijing as being part of China. The case of Greenland is also difficult. It has its own flag, issues its own postage stamps and is entirely self-governing for internal affairs, but relies on Denmark for defence and foreign policy, uses Danish currency and is represented by several seats in the Danish parliament (figure 17.4).

17.4 *The Greenlandic flag, flying on a fishing vessel.*

One criterion often applied to whether a place is a nation-state or not is whether it is a member of the United Nations. However, this would have excluded Switzerland as a nation-state as it had chosen not to be a member until 2002. Furthermore, Yugoslavia was excluded from UN membership for a period of time, but obviously this did not mean it ceased to be a nation-state. Israel is a member of the UN, but about 20 Arab nation-states insist that Israel does not exist as a nation-state.

Another possible criterion is whether a country competes in the Olympic Games. This would allow both China and Taiwan (which competes as Chinese Taipei) to be seen as separate nation-states, even though the United Nations excludes Taiwan from membership because it considers the People's Republic of China to be "the only lawful representatives of China" at the UN and does not question China's claim that Taiwan is part of China. If participation in the Olympics became a criterion for status as a nation-state, Scotland would be excluded, although at another level, Scotland has its own soccer and rugby teams that compete in international competitions.

There is even disagreement over which is the smallest nation-state in the world. The smallest territory to make a claim is the Sovereign Military Order of Malta, which occupies 1.2 hectares in a building in Rome. It issues its own coins and has diplomatic relations with over 100 nation-states. However, it is not recognised by the majority of nation-states, is not a member of the UN, does not have sporting teams which compete in the Olympic Games, and is not viable without Italian support.

So there is probably no 'right' answer to the question of how many nation-states exist in the world. There are 192 members of the UN, although the UN also has several non-member observers, including the Vatican, Palestine and the Sovereign Military Order of Malta. There were 204 members of the Olympic movement registered to compete in the Beijing 2008 Olympic Games. The Guinness Book of Records used to list 191 sovereign states plus 65 non-sovereign territories (making a total of 256), but complaints from various groups opposing the status

of certain areas as nation-states led Guinness to stop publishing their list in 2004. The Instituto del Tercer Mundo in Uruguay which produces the biannual book the World Guide lists 217 countries, and the Travellers' Century Club, a US-based organisation for people who have visited over 100 countries, lists 319 (of which Alaska is a separate entity and each emirate of the United Arab Emirates is also separated).

Even these numbers are certain to change constantly. Currently, the world's newest country is Kosovo, which declared independence from Serbia in February 2008. Prior to that, the newest country was Montenegro, which became a country in June 2006 after separating from Serbia. Since 1990, 28 new nation-states have come into being, and unless history changes dramatically from past trends, other nation-states will separate, amalgamate and be invaded in the years ahead.

QUESTION BLOCK 17A

1. What is the difference between a 'nation' and a 'nation-state'?

2. Name some examples of nations which are not nation-states.

3. How many nation-states are there in the world today?

The Changing Role of the Nation-State

Since the mid-1600s when nation-states emerged as the dominant form of organising the territories of the world, they have performed two main roles. First, nation-states have exercised political and administrative control over areas of land and the people living within those areas. Second, they have dominated relations between people in different areas, sometimes through trade but at other times by conflict and war.

Nation-states exist in a world of differing **power relationships** in which some nation-states are stronger than others. As globalisation has occurred in recent decades, the role of nation-states changed somewhat as the rise of other powerful bodies – **transnational corporations** and **international organisations** – became more significant. Before the 1960s, nation-states had only to deal with each other; today they must also deal with these other powerful organisations, not only TNCs but organisations such as the United Nations, World Bank, International Monetary Fund and the World Trade Organisation.

Challenges to National Sovereignty

The growing importance of international organisations and transnational corporations has led some people to question the power of the nation-state today. As long ago as 1969, the historical economist and author Charles Kindleberger wrote "the nation-state is just about through as an economic unit", although another writer (Michael

Political outcomes

Porter) wrote much more recently that "while globalisation of competition might appear to make the (nation-state) less important, instead it seems to make it more so".

On balance, it seems that Porter's view is more realistic. Governments of nation-states continue to play a major role in global politics and international trade. All governments in the world influence the markets and economies in their own nation-states, and international agreements are always subject to government approval and control. Therefore, the nation-state is still extremely powerful in shaping the global economy.

To some extent, nation-states **compete** against each other globally in a similar way that companies compete within a national economy. Nation-states compete to attract **foreign investment**, to sell exports and to gain a competitive advantage over other nation-states. Some historians argue that the reason Japan declared war in 1941 was because it thought it could get access to resources more cheaply by invading the countries of East and South-east Asia than by trading with them. Many commentators also assert that the United States invasion of Iraq in 2003 was economically motivated, the main purpose being to secure reliable and affordable supplies of oil in the face of opposition from the-then Iraqi President, Saddam Hussein.

Of course, competition between nation-states is more complex than competition between companies. Corporations are usually solely (or primarily) driven by profits, and if they make a loss they go out of business. On the other hand, nation-states do not go out of business, however much they suffer when economic performance is poor. Furthermore, nation-states are not direct rivals in the same sense that Coca-Cola and Pepsi are rivals. When Pepsi's market share increases, it is almost always solely at the expense of Coca-Cola, and vice versa. However, if the economy of a nation-state performs well, it is not necessarily at the expense of another nation-state's economy.

17.5 *The powerful influence of TNCs such as Nestlé and Pepsi is demonstrated by their strong visible presence on these tall buildings in Caracas, Venezuela.*

The role and importance of transnational corporations was described in chapter 16. **Transnational corporations** (TNCs) are seen as posing an increasing threat to nation-states. Transnational corporations today are estimated to control more than a quarter of the world's economic activity. This gives TNCs enormous bargaining power when negotiating with national governments as they can easily threaten to relocate to another country if they do not easily get what they want in negotiations (figure 17.5). Governments are accountable for their actions to the voters (depending upon the system of government operating in the country), whereas TNCs are subject to the control of much smaller and more elite groups of people, notably the company's shareholders. Therefore, some commentators feel that TNCs are less likely than governments to make decisions that reflect the interests of the broad mass of the population.

With more nation-states recognising the advantages of co-operation rather than competition, several **regional economic blocs** grew during the period from 1950 to the present. There are four types of economic bloc with varying degrees of integration:

- **Free-trade areas** are groups of nation-states which have agreed to remove trade restrictions between themselves, but retain independent trade policies towards non-members.

- **Customs unions** extend the free-trade area arrangements by establishing common policies and tariffs against non-members.

- **Common markets** extend the customs union arrangements still further by permitting free movement of workers and goods between members.

- **Economic unions** integrate the economies of the members even more than in the common market by ensuring that each member's economic policies are in harmony and by agreeing to national control by international agencies established by the economic union. An economic union is the strongest form of regional economic integration short of political union.

The differences between these four types of regional economic blocs are summarised in figure 17.6. Over 100 regional economic blocs now exist, with notable examples including NAFTA (the 'North American Free Trade Agreement' between Canada, the United States and Mexico), MERCOSUR ('Southern Zone Common Market', a customs union between Argentina, Brazil, Paraguay and Uruguay) and AFTA ('ASEAN Free Trade Agreement' between the Association of South-east Asian Nations [ASEAN] of Brunei, Cambodia, Indonesia, Laos, Malaysia, Myanmar, Philippines, Singapore, Thailand and Vietnam). A free-trade agreement also exists between

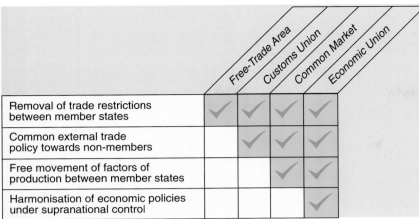

	Free-Trade Area	Customs Union	Common Market	Economic Union
Removal of trade restrictions between member states	✓	✓	✓	✓
Common external trade policy towards non-members		✓	✓	✓
Free movement of factors of production between member states			✓	✓
Harmonisation of economic policies under supranational control				✓

17.6 *Types of regional economic integration.*

17.7 *Expansion of the European Union.*

'euro', (€), and readjust national economic policies to conform to EU standards. Some nation-states have been reluctant to embrace all these reforms, Britain being the most notable example. Membership was further expanded during the 1990s with the addition of Austria, Finland and Sweden, and since 2000 with the addition of Bulgaria, Cyprus, Czech Republic, Estonia, Hungary, Latvia, Lithuania, Malta, Poland, Romania, Slovakia and Slovenia (figure 17.7). Membership is likely to expand in the future as other applications from Croatia, Macedonia and Turkey are being considered. Current membership of the EU is 27 nation-states.

The ultimate goal of the European Union is to be 'an ever closer union among the peoples of Europe, in which decisions are taken as closely as possible to the citizen'. The EU states its objective is to promote economic and social progress that is balanced and sustainable, assert the European identity on the international scene and introduce a European citizen-ship for the nationals of the Member States. The European Union has its own flag, its own anthem and celebrates Europe Day on 9th May. With many of the sym-bols of a nation-state, some people in Europe (and especially in Britain) fear that membership of the EU will mean a loss of sovereignty and a political union will be-come inevitable (figure 17.8).

Membership of the EU seems to have had a very positive impact on the economic development of member states. On the other hand, the formation of the EU has damaged the economic development of some other countries.

Australia and New Zealand, effectively creating a common market between the two countries.

Of the regional economic blocs, the largest and most successful has been the **European Union** (EU). The EU had its origins in the 1950s when six nation-states – France, Germany, Italy, Belgium, Netherlands and Luxembourg – formed the European Economic Commu-nity (EEC). In 1958, customs duties between the six members were abolished, and in 1968 they introduced a common external tariff. Membership of the EEC in-creased during the 1970s with the addition of Denmark, Ireland and the United Kingdom, and during the 1980s with the addition of Greece, Portugal and Spain.

A desire to further strengthen economic ties led to the signing in 1991 of the Treaty of Maastricht. This created the European Union, agreeing to abolish passport checks between members, introduce a single currency the

17.8 *The Headquarters of the European Commission, which is the executive body of the European Union, in Brussels (Belgium). The EU has become an additional layer of government for member states in Europe.*

Political outcomes

For example, before the United Kingdom (UK) entered the EU, Commonwealth countries such as New Zealand and Australia enjoyed preferential import taxes when they exported goods to the UK. When the UK joined the EU, the UK was obliged to treat Australia and New Zealand like any other non-EU member, and this caused a sharp fall in exports from those countries to the UK, forcing them to find new markets in other parts of the world.

QUESTION BLOCK 17B

1. *If the nation-state is becoming weaker in today's world, what other bodies are taking over the power?*

2. *Outline the differences between the four types of regional economic blocs.*

3. *Give three examples of regional economic blocs, and for each one, say what kind of regional economic bloc it is.*

4. *Do you think the European Union is strengthening or weakening the power of the nation-states that are members? Explain your reasons.*

Political Tensions and Conflicts

Political tensions and conflicts can arise in a nation-state for many reasons. However, many of the conflicts over the years can be traced to disagreements over resources, and the ownership of territory in which resources are found. We therefore need to examine the nature of **national boundaries**.

Although boundaries appear as simple lines on maps, complex sets of laws revolve around them. A boundary is actually like a vertical sheet that cuts through the rocks beneath the surface and the air above it (figure 17.9). The legal control of governments extends to the limits of these boundaries, including the air above the surface and the

17.10 *The white red-topped concrete posts mark the precise boundary between Poland and Slovakia on Mount Kasprowy Wierch. In general, the boundary follows the ridge line separating two watersheds.*

rocks (and mineral deposits) beneath. Where boundaries follow a natural feature, such as a mountain range or a river, the boundary usually follows the middle of the feature unless special circumstances apply (figure 17.10).

Boundaries above and below the surface can cause conflict. Nation-states insist that they control the airspace above their territory, and thus have the right to refuse entry to aircraft if they wish. It was for this reason that the Soviet Union insisted it was right in shooting down a Korean airliner that flew off course over Sakhalin Island in September 1983, causing the death of 269 passengers.

A war between Iraq and Kuwait in 1991 was caused by a similar way of thinking. When the boundary was drawn between Iraq and Kuwait, no-one knew that a large oil field called the Rumaylah reserve was situated beneath the surface. In 1990, the Iraqis claimed that Kuwait was drilling too many oil wells on its side of the border, depleting the underground oil deposits. Furthermore, the Iraqis claimed that the Kuwaitis were drilling oblique oil wells from the surface in Kuwaiti territory into Iraqi underground territory. The dispute led to war in early 1991 into which the United States, Britain and other major powers were drawn.

Boundaries are a common source of conflict, because they frequently do not coincide with ethnic or cultural differences (figure 17.11). Several types of national boundaries exist. **Geometric boundaries** are straight lines that bear no relationship to the physical environment or cultural groups living in an area. Several of the boundaries imposed by the colonial powers upon Africa are geometric boundaries, such as between Algeria and Mali, Egypt and Libya, and Namibia and Botswana. The long boundary between the United States and Canada is another example of a geometric boundary for most of its length, and most Australian state borders are also geometric.

17.9 *A political boundary affects the rocks beneath the surface as well as the air above it.*

17.11 *Ethnic territories and national boundaries in Africa. Tribal boundaries were largely ignored by the European colonial powers which drew the boundaries. This has resulted in great ethnic diversity in many nation-states, often leading to conflict.*

Amur River. This last example has caused conflict, as the course of the river has changed over the years. International law states that a boundary between two nation-states in a navigable river shall follow the central line of the main channel. However, shifts in the main channel meant that islands which were once in one country shifted to the other side of the channel. China and Russia, or the Soviet Union as it then was, fought a short and bitter border war in March 1969 over Chenpao Island, a desolate island in the middle of the Amur River which became disputed territory.

A third type of boundary is the **arbitrary boundary**. These boundaries usually arise following an armed conflict, and represent a compromise between two hostile groups. A well-known example of an arbitrary boundary was the division through Berlin between the occupying forces of the Soviet Union to the east, and the armies of France, Britain and the United States to the west (figure 17.12). In 1961, this boundary became a symbol of the divide between the capitalist west and the communist east when the Berlin Wall was built (figure 17.13). The Berlin Wall remained a symbol of division until 1989 when it was destroyed by a popular uprising, symbolising the re-unification of Germany.

Physical-political boundaries follow natural features, such as a river or the summit of a mountain range. The border between the Australian states of New South Wales and Victoria is a physical-political boundary for most of its length, as it follows the course of the Murray River. Other examples include the border between China and Nepal, which follows the Himalaya Mountains, and between Russia and north-east China which follows the

The fourth type of boundary is the **cultural-political boundary**. These boundaries attempt to follow the borders between ethnic or cultural groups, or linguistic

17.12 *This boundary marker has been preserved in Berlin, Germany, to mark the former international boundary between East and West Germany. Deutsche Demokratische Republik means 'German Democratic Republic', which was the official name of the communist nation-state of East Germany.*

17.13 *One of the few remnants of the Berlin Wall that is preserved. This view shows a section of the wall, looking from the former Communist, or eastern, side of the Wall.*

Political outcomes

groups. A problem with these boundaries is that boundaries between ethnic groups are seldom 'clean', and quite a degree of mixing occurs in a transition zone. Furthermore, the areas inhabited by particular groups are likely to change over time, and this can lead to conflict if the boundaries are not adjusted – and even if attempts are made to adjust them! The boundaries around former Soviet republics such as Armenia, Uzbekistan, Azerbaijan and Kazakhstan are attempts at drawing cultural-political boundaries.

During the 1990s, the former nation-state of Yugoslavia disintegrated into several smaller countries. A major factor in the conflict was that many ethnic groups with long histories of dispute had been grouped together in the one nation-state, but the traditional rivalries remained (figure 17.14). Attempts were made to re-draw cultural-political boundaries so that the ethnic differences could be accommodated, but the task proved too difficult because of the complex mixing of groups that had evolved over the centuries.

17.14 *Mine fields that were laid during the break up of Yugoslavia in the 1990s present a continuing danger in parts of Bosnia-Herzegovina.*

Tourist brochures used to claim that Yugoslavia had seven borders, six republics, five ethnic groups, four religions, three languages and two alphabets. In fact, the diversity was even greater than this because in addition to the five main ethnic groups (Serbian, Croatian, Macedonian, Montenegrin and Slovenian), there were 13 others in substantial numbers. In addition to the three major languages (Serbo-Croat, Macedonian and Slovenian), there were several others, and radio broadcasts were made in seven languages while newspapers were printed in eleven.

Ethnic diversity does not necessarily mean a nation-state is not viable. In addition to the ethnic differences within many African countries (shown earlier in figure 17.11), other countries have significant differences. For example, Belgium is divided almost evenly between speakers of Dutch in the north and speakers of French in the south without any conflict. In Yugoslavia, the conflict arose because of a combination of the ethnic diversity, a long

history of changing alliances and warfare, and the economic differences that had been allowed to grow between the ethnic groups.

Government investment had been concentrated in the major cities, especially in Serbia and Bosnia, while outlying areas inhabited by ethnic minorities such as the ethnic Albanians in Kosovo and the Muslims in Bosnia had been allowed to remain impoverished. The horror of ethnic conflict reached a climax in July 1995 when Serbian forces initiated a program of 'ethnic cleansing', or genocide, against ethnic Bosniaks (Bosnian Muslims) living in the small mountain town of Srebrenica (figures 17.15 and 17.16, as well as figure 11.151 in chapter 11). This resulted in the deaths of 8,000 men and boys within a three day period, the largest mass killing in Europe since World War II (figure 17.17).

17.15 *The town of Srebrenica in the mountainous north-east of Bosnia-Herzegovina.*

17.16 *Many of the buildings in Srebrenica still bear the scars of intense fighting in the 1990s.*

Ethnic differences have been responsible for many conflicts. One example of almost constant unrest, conflict and civil war caused by ethnic conflict is Myanmar during the period since independence in 1948. Myanmar, which used to be known as Burma, has eight main ethnic groups – Burmans (or Myanma), Karens, Chin, Shan, Rakhine, Kachin, Mon-Khmer and Kayah (figure 17.18).

ToK BoX

Political Ideologies.

Equality	The Political Spectrum	Order

| Communist | Socialist | Liberal | Moderate | Conservative | Fascist | Totalitarian |

In studying political ideologies, it is important to look deeper than the day-to-day ways in which politics are expressed. Some of the deeper questions that political philosophers ask include:

- What is the ultimate justification for the existence of any form of government?

- What ought to be the proper limits of government power over members of society?

- Should elected representatives be allowed to vote as they see fit, or should they merely reflect the majority opinion of their voters (or their party leaders)?

Political ideology means "a comprehensive set of beliefs about the political world". People who follow a particular political ideology usually do so because they believe that society can be improved by following certain doctrines.

Political ideologies are commonly labelled as 'left wing' and 'right wing'. Left wing political ideologies emphasise equality and collective ownership of resources, while right wing ideologies emphasise individual rights and private ownership of resources.

One of the earliest political philosophers was Heraclitus, who lived in Greece from 535 BC to 475 BC. Heraclitus argued strongly that democracy was an inferior form of government because when it comes to the search for wisdom and truth, the opinion of the greatest number may well be a poor guide, especially if they are poorly educated and uninformed.

Plato (429 BC to 347 BC) may well have been influenced by Heraclitus when he said that the best government would be that carried out by philosophers who were not self-interested and had been trained in the search for wisdom. Plato believed that ruling is a skill. Just as people's ability in all skills varies from person to person, Plato believed that people differ innately in their skills of leadership. Therefore, those with the greatest capacity for ruling should be trained into the skill, and then made

rulers. Furthermore, because they had the greatest skills to rule, they ought to be given absolute authority so their laws could be put into effect without frustrating and inefficient delays from ill-informed objectors.

Plato's viewpoint on leadership was possibly the most powerful argument ever directed against democratic government. There are, however, some commonly expressed objections to Plato's view of leadership:

1. Some people deny that ruling is a skill.

2. Even if ruling is a skill, and even if people differ in their skills to rule, perhaps rulers should still be accountable. The question then arises — to whom should a ruler be accountable if everyone else is less skilled in leadership than the ruler?.

3. Some feel that a society run by the few altruistic philosopher-kings will stop most people developing moral autonomy, and that this is a problem.

The next great leap in thinking about political ideology came almost 2000 years later from the English philosopher, Thomas Hobbes (1588-1679). Perhaps reflecting the view of the much earlier Chinese philosopher, Confucius, Hobbes claimed a chaotic society was to be feared more than anything else, noting also that chaos arises because people are innately selfish and egoistic.

According to Hobbes, the way to avoid chaos is compromise — securing an agreement among people to abide by certain rules or conventions, called laws. However, Hobbes realised that to be effective, laws must be enforced. Hobbes felt that enforcement requires absolute power to be effective, and he suggested that one person — a king — should be the ruler to avoid conflicts between those on a committee or a panel of rulers.

There are two commonly expressed objections to Hobbes' philosophy of leadership:

1. It is an expression of defeatism, a 'peace at any price' philosophy, and is

therefore unacceptable to non-submissive people.

2. It surrenders liberty in return for security — but which would most people regard as being more important?

Modern political thinking has seen ideologies fragment into a multitude of different perspectives. This book is not the appropriate medium to analyse the full range of political ideologies — there are whole books, websites and university courses to do that — but among the notable political ideologies in the world today, we can note the following:

Liberalism is the political ideology that places the highest value on individual freedom and claims that the role of the government should be quite limited. It is probably the dominant political ideology in the world today. In classical liberalism, it is assumed there are certain areas of conduct which are immune from the government's interference; these are called "rights". All people are seen as being equal as they have rights that are neither given by society nor taken away by society. The source of authority is the people ('the masses') who appoint the government, thus making democracy the most popular form of government for most liberals. Modern liberalism opposes the use of state power to enforce standards of behaviour, and it has thus evolved into an ideology that advocates minimum government and maximum individual liberty.

A more extreme form of liberalism is libertarianism. Libertarianism follows the teachings of John Stuart Mill (1806-1873), who wrote "it is wrong to suppress an opinion that the majority does not approve of because the suppressed opinion may be true", and "interference in personal matters will in the long run prove harmful to a democratic society". Libertarians therefore advocate minimal government as a way to maximise individual liberty, and they usually favour legalisation of drugs and prostitution, prohibition of censorship and the freedom for women to have abortions.

Political outcomes

Capitalism is an economic expression of the philosophy of liberalism, and in various forms, it is the dominant economic system in the world today. First defined by the economic philosopher, Adam Smith (1723-1790), capitalism is an ideology that advocates private ownership of property and minimal government intervention. In capitalism, almost no central planning of an economy is done by the government as the economy is guided by what Adam Smith called 'the invisible hand' — which in reality was the price mechanism which adjusts demand and supply to regulate prices.

The political ideology of conservatism combines elements of liberalism and capitalism. Conservatism promotes the importance of the individual as a means of preserving traditional moral and ethical values within society. Conservatism views inequality as natural and inevitable, although it also claims that privileged people should act with generosity towards those who are less privileged. This is the principle of *noblesse oblige*, a French term that literally means 'the nobility is obliged', but which is generally taken to mean that with wealth, power and prestige come responsibilities. Since the 1980s, a movement known as neo-conservatism has developed this ideology into a set of policy positions, which typically includes low taxes, small size of government, traditional moral values and an expansive foreign policy.

In contrast with liberalism and conservatism, which emphasise the rights of the individual, socialism emphasises the collective good and the welfare of the group as a whole. Socialism makes the claim that the most important goal of government is to provide high-quality, relatively equal conditions of life for everyone, and that a strong, interventionist government is necessary to overcome the selfishness of powerful individuals and to protect the weak and vulnerable in order to achieve this goal.

There are two main types of socialism. In democratic socialism, humans are seen as being intrinsically social and caring in nature, and thus they see the good of society as being more important than the good of the individual — and they will elect governments that reflect that view. The policy priorities of democratic socialist governments therefore tend to include public (government) ownership of resources and property, extensive government regulation, generous welfare systems (such as free education and free health care), often financed by relatively high taxes on in-

comes that redistribute incomes from the rich to the poor, and a large government bureaucracy to manage planning and delivery of services.

In contrast to Democratic Socialism, Marxism (named after the German economic philosopher, Karl Marx, 1818-1883) focuses on the struggle between different classes in society. During a period in the mid-1800s when Marx was living in Britain, he wrote "The history of all hitherto existing society is the history of class struggles… All class relationships are independent of people's wills, and in fact are really determined by the prevailing economic system."

Marx saw capitalism as the means whereby the rich exploit the poor, making profits from the labour of the working class. Based upon this observation, he developed a scheme to show the evolution of societies from primitive communism (as might be found in an isolated tribal society) through various

Name of Historical Period	Features of Historical Period	
	Class Situation	**Ownership of production**
6. Communism	*No class conflict*	*No private property*
The state withers away		
5. Socialism		
Progressive Revolution		*private*
4. Capitalism	*class*	*property*
Progressive Revolution	*conflict*	*exists*
3. Feudalism		
Progressive Revolution		
2. Slavery		
Fall of 'Communist Man'	*Introduction of private property leading to class divisions*	
1. Primitive communism	*No class conflict*	*No private property*

phases of exploitation to socialism, and eventually when the government has withered away, to communism. Marx saw this evolution as historically inevitable (see the table above).

The Russian revolutionary, Vladimir Lenin (1870-1924) disagreed that a peaceful transition to socialism was inevitable. Lenin translated Marxism into a form of political action to speed up the transformation of society. Developing an ideology that has become known as Leninism, Lenin claimed that violence is necessary to overthrow powerful power,

that the transformation from a capitalist society to a socialist one would be difficult, that a strong dictatorship group is needed to enforce change, and this enforcement could be through repression if it was necessary for the greater common good.

Although it has fallen into disfavour, fascism (which includes Nazism), combined the strong government of Leninism with the private ownership of resources of capitalism. Fascists argue that citizens can prosper only when the nation prospers (hence 'national socialism'). Following the principles of Darwinism ('the survival of the fittest'), fascism thus glorifies strength, rejects equality (as this is seen as artificially propping up the weak), advocates nationalism and rejects pacifism.

In recent years, the simple traditional left-right spectrum of political ideologies has become more confused. Some commentators label the times since 2000 as the post-ideological period. One important political ideology that grew in strength from the 1960s onwards was feminism. This ideology advocates psychological, political, social and economic equality for women with men. It rejects patriarchy and sexism, and promotes pacifism. There are many sub-types of feminism, each with particular emphases, including liberal feminism, radical feminism, black feminism, post-colonial feminism, multiracial feminism, socialist feminism, Marxist feminism, libertarian feminism, postmodern feminism, eco-feminism and lesbian feminism.

Environmentalism has emerged as an important new political ideology. Also known as ecologism, environmentalism differs from both liberalism and socialism in that it does not focus on people, either as individuals or collectively. Environmentalism advocates that the environment is endangered and must be preserved through regulation and lifestyle changes. It thus focuses on ecosystem health rather than human beings, and thus rejects anthropocentric (human-centred) beliefs. Arising from the ground-breaking writings of the American writer Rachel Carson, whose 1963 book 'Silent Spring' first drew the world's attention to environmental issues, environmentalism advocates ecological stewardship and sustainable development. In several parts of the world, most notably in Western Europe, environmentalism is expressed through what has become known as Green politics.

Fundamentalism of various types has always been a factor in political thinking. In recent decades, the rise of Islamic Fundamentalism has focussed more attention in Western countries on the role of religion in politics. Islamic fundamentalism, as expressed through groups such as the Taliban in Afghanistan, al-Qaeda in several countries and Lashkar-e-Taiba (LeT) in Pakistan, calls for a return to the centrality of religion in every day life and a literal (perhaps militant) interpretation of the Qu'ran. Islamic fundamentalism calls on its followers to live according to strict Islamic codes, it rejects Westernisation and the secularisation of Islamic societies, and some groups support the use of violence, sometimes in extreme forms such as beheadings or what is termed in the West as 'acts of terrorism'.

There are, of course, many other political ideologies in addition to the ones summarised here. Moreover, each of the ideologies mentioned here has various sub-groups and sometimes factions as well.

The next ToK BoX is on page 659.

17.17 *A small section of the Srebrenica-Potočari Memorial and Cemetery to Genocide Victims, where many of the victims of the genocide are buried.*

These groups are divided into many smaller tribal groups, however, and altogether there are almost 70 different ethnic groups and tribes in Myanmar. Each of these groups has its own style of dress, language or dialect.

It is estimated that the ethnic breakdown of Myanmar is 65% Burman, 10% Shan, 7% Karen, 4% Rakhine and 2.3% each of Chin, Kachin and Mon-Khmer. Other recently migrated ethnic minority groups, such as Chinese, Indians and Assamese make up about 1% each of the population. These ethnic groups migrated to Myanmar from different areas over the centuries. The Burmans migrated from Tibet, the Mon-Khmer from Cambodia, the Shan from Thailand, and so on.

This history of migration has led to a long history of conflict, especially between the Burmans and the Mon-Khmers, each of which managed to control the other at different times in history. The Burmans were in control in the late 1800s, when the British arrived and colonised all the feuding ethnic groups. However, the British never managed to control the ethnic minorities completely, and

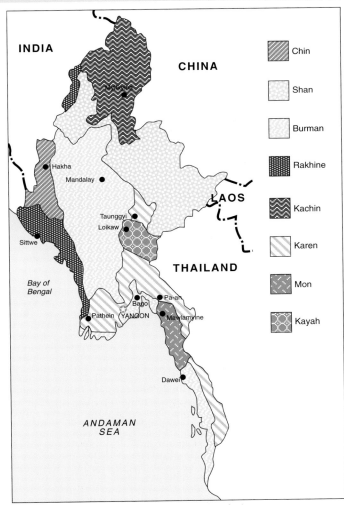

17.18 *The distribution of Myanmar's main ethnic groups.*

these groups were given some autonomy and self-government.

When Myanmar became independent in 1948, the ethnic groups were promised a degree of independence, but for various reasons this was never implemented. This led to armed conflict as several ethnic groups formed their own armies to fight to secede (separate) from Myanmar. By

Political outcomes

the early 1990s, there were 35 separate insurgent factions fighting the central government of Myanmar, mainly in the mountainous border areas. The numbers in these armies varied from as few as 50 (in the Tai National Army, Kayah New Land Revolution Council and Palaung State Liberation Organisation) to tens of thousands (Mon-Tai Army and Shan United Army). As well as fighting the government, these groups are often in conflict with each other, and conflict also exists between different factions within ethnic groups, such as the Karen People's Liberation Front and the Karen Liberation Army. Sometimes, the conflicts become confusing, such as the constantly changing alliances and conflicts between the Shan State Army, Shan United Revolutionary Army and the Shan United Army.

Several of these armies operate in the area known as the 'Golden Triangle', and so are financed by growing and selling opium, or by charging taxes on goods smuggled through their areas of control. The instability caused by the conflicts has led to major propaganda campaigns within Myanmar to develop loyalty to the central government (figure 17.19).

17.19 *A large sign designed to encourage loyalty to the central government in Myanmar.*

With the turn of the century in 2000, the situation began to calm for the first time in many decades. One large army that had been supported by Chinese Communist groups, the Wa National Army, negotiated a truce with the government of Myanmar. This enabled Chinese foreign aid to flow in Myanmar, and opened the border areas between Myanmar and China. Some 14 other truces were negotiated with ethnic groups, including some large and well-armed armies such as the Kachin Independence Organisation, the Mon National Liberation Front. However, ethnic conflict continues on a significant scale in many border regions of Myanmar and seems unlikely to abate.

QUESTION BLOCK 17C

1. Explain how national boundaries are three-dimensional.

2. Give two examples of national boundaries that have caused conflicts.

3. What are the differences between (a) geometric boundaries, (b) physical-political boundaries, and (c) cultural-political boundaries. Give an example of each.

4. Explain briefly why Yugoslavia experienced so much conflict during the 1990s.

5. Why has Myanmar experienced so much ethnic conflict since independence in 1948?

6. Suggest a realistic solution to the ethnic conflicts in Myanmar.

Can These Issues be Resolved?

Humans always seem to have been in conflict. However, during the twentieth century (1901 to 2000), the scale of conflict and warfare has been much greater than ever before (table 17.1).

Table 17.1
War-Related Deaths, 1 to 2000

Period	Total War Deaths (millions)	Deaths per 1000 people
1 to 1499	3.7	n.a.
1500 to 1599	1.6	3.2
1600 to 1699	6.1	11.2
1700 to 1799	7.0	9.7
1800 to 1899	19.4	16.2
1900 to 1999	115.8	44.5

Source: Based on Eckhart, W (1991) and Sivard, RL (1996), cited in Renner, M (1999) p.153

The wars of the twentieth century had a huge impact on countless millions of families, and even on the overall demographic structures of many countries. In World War I, France lost almost 20% of its military age males, and Germany lost 13%. Russia still has an imbalance of males and females because of the number of males killed during World War II. Moreover, the proportion of civilians killed during armed conflicts during the twentieth century was generally greater than earlier wars (table 17.2).

The causes of these conflicts can be grouped in two broad categories. First, conflicts arose in and between nation-states, either for control over resources or because of conflicting political ideology. Second, conflicts arose either within or between nation-states due to ethnic rivalry. Even where conflicts arose in the first category, ethnic conflicts were often part of the conflict. For example, of the 53,547,000 deaths in World War II, it is estimated that there were about 3,053,000 deaths from the attempted genocide of Jews, Poles and Gypsies by the Germans, 1,471,595 of which occurred in the Auschwitz death camp

Table 17.2
Death Tolls in Selected Conflicts, 1500 to the Present

Conflict	Period	Number Killed	Civilian Victims (%)
SELECTED WARS, 1500 TO 1945			
Peasants War (Germany)	1524 - 1525	175,000	57
Dutch Independence War (against Spain)	1585 - 1604	177,000	32
Manchu Conquest of the Ming Dynasty (China)	1616 - 1662	25,000,000	n.a.
30 Year War (Europe)	1618 - 1648	4,000,000	50
Spanish Succession War (Europe)	1701 - 1714	1,251,000	n.a.
7 Year War (Europe, North America, India)	1755 - 1763	1,358,000	27
French Revolutionary and Napoleonic Wars	1792 - 1815	4,899,000	41
Taiping Rebellion (China)	1851 - 1864	25,000,000	n.a.
Crimean War (Russia, France, Britain)	1854 - 1856	772,000	66
US Civil War	1861 - 1865	820,000	24
Paraguay vs Brazil vs Argentina	1864 - 1870	1,100,000	73
Franco-Prussian war	1870 - 1871	250,000	25
Spanish-American War	1898	200,000	95
World War I	1914 - 1918	26,000,000	50
World War II	1939 - 1945	53,547,000	60
CONFLICTS SINCE 1945 WITH MORE THAN ONE MILLION DEATHS			
Chinese Civil War	1946 - 1949	1,000,000	50
Korean War	1950 - 1953	3,000,000	50
Vietnam (US intervention)	1960 - 1975	2,358,000	58
Biafra (Nigerian Civil War)	1967 - 1970	2,000,000	50
Cambodian Civil War	1970 - 1989	1,221,000	69
Bangladesh Separation from Pakistan	1971	1,000,000	50
Afghanistan (Soviet intervention)	1978 - 1992	1,500,000	67
Mozambique Civil War	1981 - 1994	1,050,000	95
Sudanese Civil War	1984 - present	1,900,000 +	97
US Invasion of Iraq	2003 - present	1,308,000 +	97

alone (figure 17.20). It was largely as a response to the horrors of the **holocaust**, as the attempted extermination of Jewish people is known, that a separate Jewish nation-state, Israel, was established after World War II.

Many peace and disarmament treaties have been signed in an effort to reduce the risk of armed conflict between nation-states. Indeed, it is estimated that about 50,000 bilateral and multilateral treaties have been negotiated and signed.

Perhaps the most important initiative has been the establishment of the United Nations (UN). Most nation-states of the world are now members of the UN, whose objective is to get nation-states talking about their disagreements rather than fighting over them. Although the UN

Political outcomes

is sometimes criticised as being expensive, bureaucratic and ineffective, it does seem to have been effective when it has intervened and sent multi-national peace keeping forces into conflict situations.

17.20 *Part of the Nazi death camp at Auschwitz in Poland, where an estimated 1,471,595 Jews, Poles and Gypsies were killed, either in the gas chambers or by starvation, bashing, shooting or hanging.*

17.21 *The Hiroshima Peace Memorial Park is a memorial to those who suffered in the world's first nuclear attack, when the US dropped an atomic bomb here on 6th August, 1945, killing 140,000 people. In the background is the A-Bomb Dome, the skeletal ruins of the former Industrial Promotion Hall, which was the building closest to the hypocentre (ground zero) of the nuclear bomb that remained at least partially standing.*

Nonetheless, military expenditures remain high in many parts of the world. In 1988, towards the end of the Cold War that had existed between the United States and the Soviet Union since the end of World War II, the armed forces of the world comprised 28.7 million soldiers. With the easing of tensions since the end of the Cold War, military expenditures has fallen and the number of soldiers has also been reduced. Nuclear stockpiles have been reduced from about 70,000 warheads in 1988 to fewer than 26,000 today. However, it has been estimated that just 50 of today's nuclear weapons could kill 200 million people, and the numbers that still exist are far more than enough to destroy the planet (figure 17.21).

Although several nation-states have abandoned nuclear weapons during the 1990s (Ukraine, Kazakhstan, Belarus and South Africa), the use of nuclear weapons by remain-

17.22 *Each year, about 10 million origami paper cranes are added to the Hiroshima Peace Memorial Park as a symbol of people's aspirations for peace.*

17.23 *This memorial in the former Jewish ghetto in Warsaw (Poland) remembers the millions of men, women and children who were murdered in the gas chambers simply because of their ethnicity.*

ing nuclear countries or by fringe terrorist groups is still a real threat. The countries that are known to have nuclear weapons today are the United States, Russia, United Kingdom, France, China, India, Pakistan, Israel and North Korea.

People often feel powerless in the face of the huge military might of modern nation-states. One response is to form or join peace groups. With the increasing threat of war, the number of peace groups has grown markedly from their small beginnings in the US and UK in 1815 (figure 17.22). The cause of peace is also being advocated by many NGOs (non-government organisations) that advocate issues such as environmental quality, justice and equity, human rights and government accountability in addition to peace (figure 17.23).

It may be no coincidence that in the twentieth century, nation-states reached their most powerful position in world history, and we experienced the most horrific wars and conflicts ever (figure 17.24). With the decreasing power of nation-states as international organisations and regional economic groups gain more influence, many people hope that global conflicts are an accident of past history. On the other hand, globalisation and changes in the balance of development between peoples are creating new inequities, and these have potential to generate new conflicts. Furthermore, ethnic tensions remain in many parts of the world, many of which have long histories of reprisal and revenge.

17.24 *Scars showing the ferocity of armed conflict in 1956 can still be seen on this wall in Budapest, capital city of Hungary.*

In the end, conflicts will only be solved by the changed attitudes of human beings. As the UNESCO charter states, 'since wars begin in the minds of men, it is in the minds of men that defences of peace must be constructed'. This is a strong argument for educating young people in the importance of loving and harmonious relationships, because in the final analysis, it is people who choose to be in conflict.

QUESTION BLOCK 17D

1. *Draw a column graph to show the 'deaths per 1,000 people' data in table 17.1.*

2. *Do you think these treaties are a sign of desperation or a real source of hope?*

3. *Explain why the size of the world's armed forces may still be a threat to peace in spite of cutbacks during the 1990s.*

4. *Is there a solution to war and conflict? Write as much as you wish to explain your views.*

Responses to the Loss of Sovereignty

Nationalism

Nationalism is the ideology or belief that emphasises patriotism, loyalty to and the advancement of a particular nation. In general, nationalism refers to an existing nation-state, but it can be also refer to the yearning for the creation of a new state or independence for a colony or an occupied territory. Nationalism may also refer to a nation (as opposed to a nation-state), such as the Basques, the Kurds, the Indigenous Australian and the Inuit people.

The Professor Emeritus of Nationalism and Ethnicity at the London School of Economics, Anthony D. Smith, said there are certain criteria required to give a nation its identity:
- a fixed homeland (current or historical)
- high autonomy
- hostile surroundings
- memories of battles
- sacred centres
- languages and scripts
- special customs
- historical records and thinking.

When nationalism becomes extreme, such as when patriotism is expressed aggressively towards others, then it is known as **jingoism**.

There has been a resurgence of nationalism in many parts of the world in recent decades. One reason for this is that with the break up of the Soviet Union and the disintegration of Yugoslavia, many people have perceived a growing trend for ethnic groups to achieve autonomy and control their own destinies. This has encouraged groups such as the Palestinians, the Kurds, the Chechens and the Tuaregs to campaign for their own nation-states.

A second explanation for the resurgence is that nationalism is seen by many as a force to counter the cultural homogenisation that globalisation brings. In this way, nationalism can provide a sense of identity and stability in a rapidly changing world.

A third reason for the resurgence of nationalism is less idealistic, and this is the use of nationalism as a weapon of reaction against immigration. In several countries of western Europe, conservative people have become alarmed by what they see as large-scale immigration of migrant workers from Muslim countries such as Turkey, and nationalism has been invoked as a response.

One example of a country where the resurgence of nationalism is an important factor today is **Turkey**, a largely Muslim country that is situated in western Asia

Political outcomes

(occupying the Atatolian Peninsula), with a small piece of territory also at the far south-east corner of Europe.

Modern Turkey was founded as a democratic, secular republic by Mustafa Kemal Atatürk in 1923 following the collapse of the Ottoman Empire after World War I (figure 17.25). Since that time, Turkey has become tightly integrated with the West through its membership in organisations such as NATO, the OECD, the Council of Europe and the G-20 major economies. Turkey has applied for membership of the European Union.

17.25 *Like most government workers, this civil servant works under a portrait of modern Turkey's founder, Mustafa Kemal Atatürk.*

One of Atatürk's important foundations of Turkey was its secular government. A **secular** administration is one that has no religious or spiritual basis. In a nation-state where 98% of the population are Muslim, this was a decision that sent Turkey along quite a different path of development to many other countries in the Middle Eastern region.

17.26 *A large Turkish flag flies above the entrance to Istanbul University. Despite its official status as a secular state, Turkey's flag displays the crescent moon and star that symbolise Islam.*

Turkey's focus on secular nationalism rather than Islam has had consequences throughout the country's modern history. More than many other Muslim countries, Turkey has emphasised its secular nationalism by requiring that women not wear headscarves in schools, universities or government offices, and with prominent displays of the

national flag (figure 17.26). The ban on headscarves in government buildings is seen by many people as discriminatory as many Muslim women wish to express their religious faith and devotion to Islam by wearing their headscarves (figure 17.27).

There have been incidents in recent history when Turkey's nationalism has been expressed through violence. For example, in September 1955, about 100,000 took part in a government-sponsored program of attacking foreigners' homes, schools and churches in Istanbul, the country's largest city. Huge piles of materials taken from foreigners' shops were placed in the streets and either taken by Turks or destroyed. As a result of these attacks, almost everyone who could not claim to be Turkish left Istanbul, a remarkable change for a city that had for centuries been marked by tolerance and acceptance of people from many lands.

17.27 *When given the choice, many Turkish women choose to wear headscarves.*

Turkey's nationalism is also expressed at times by government suppression of 'alternative nationalisms', such as claims for autonomy by minority groups such as the Kurds and the Armenians.

In 2004, the Turkish government labelled university researchers who wanted to discuss the Kurdish and Armenians claims 'traitors'. In 2007, a famous Turkish writer, Hrant Dink, was murdered by Turkish nationalists after he wrote about the expulsion and killing of hundreds of thousands of Armenians in eastern Turkey in 1915. As an ethnic Armenian, Hrant Dink had labelled the action as genocide, but he was convicted of insulting the Turkish nation as a consequence. Turkish nationalists then surrounded his office with shouts of "Love Turkey or leave it!", and he received hundreds of death threats before being murdered shortly afterwards. Since that time, about 50 other writers have been put on trial, charged either with 'attempting to influence the outcome of judicial proceedings through their writings' or for 'insulting Turkishness'.

Turkey's application to join the European Union is having an impact on the resurgence of nationalism in Turkey. For

Turkish nationalists, joining the EU would mean a loss of Turkish identity, and the EU application has therefore led them to increase their efforts to oppose EU membership by emphasising Turkish nationalism and identity. On the other hand, supporters of EU membership realise that violent nationalism in Turkey will work against the success of their application. Therefore, they are making efforts to reduce nationalist tensions by showing greater tolerance for dissenting viewpoints, which is what the EU demands.

17.28 *These university students in Istanbul are protesting against the government policy that denies women the choice of wearing a head-scarf in government offices, schools and universities if they choose to do so.*

17.29 *The Hagia Sophia Mosque in Istanbul, one of the many great mosques found in the city that demonstrate Turkey's long association with Islam.*

Despite this, the government is resisting demands for freedom to wear headscarves in educational institutions and government buildings on the grounds that it does not want to be seen to be encouraging fundamentalist Islam (figure 17.28). Although Islam is seen as an important part of Turkish identity, Atatürk's secular foundation of the modern Turkish state is also seen as important (figure 17.29). Many Turkish people are demanding an Islamic state. For secular Turks, this is sometimes interpreted as a threat to nationalism and the distinctive identity of Turkey as a nation-state. An attempted Islamic revolution in Turkey failed in 1997 when it was suppressed by the

army. For many Turkish people, Islam is an important part of their identity with a long history, and they are demanding the freedom to express their faith in their day-to-day lives.

QUESTION BLOCK 17E

1. *What is meant by the term 'nationalism', and how is it different from 'jingoism'?*

2. *Why is there a resurgence of nationalism in many countries today?*

3. *To what extent is the resurgence of nationalism in Turkey a consequence of attempts to regain control of its culture and its resources?*

Controlling Immigration

The resurgence of nationalism is one response to the perceived loss of sovereignty brought by globalisation. Another response in several parts of the world is the introduction of tighter controls on immigration.

In this context, **immigration** can be defined as the international movement of people into a country for the purpose of permanent settlement. Traditionally, voluntary international migration usually occurred primarily for family reunification (the main cause to countries such as Australia and Canada) or for employment (the main cause to countries such as the United Arab Emirates and Germany). In recent years, however, these causes have diversified with other reasons becoming more significant, such as international education, arranged brides, adopted children and retired people. These changes have resulted in a significant shift in the gender balance of migrants and an increase in the rate of female international migration. Today, about 200 million people were born in a different country to the one where they are currently living; this represents about 3% of the world's population.

17.30 *In an effort to stop illegal migration from North Korea into China, the Chinese authorities are constructing concrete and barbed wire fences along many stretches of the border between the two countries.*

17.31 *Tijuana, Mexico's border city with the United States.*

17.32 *In contrast to towns in Mexico (see figure 17.31), even small towns in the US (such as Las Vegas, New Mexico, seen here) offer far greater resources, wealth, potential and opportunities.*

In an increasingly globalised world where people have better information about job opportunities and the differences in wealth from place to place, the rate of international migration is likely to increase among people in search of employment. This has led to very high rates of immigration in some countries and regions, such as the United Arab Emirates (+23 migrants per 1,000 population), Kuwait (+16 migrants per 1,000 population), and Macau (+15 migrants per 1,000 population). Similarly, some countries and regions that are sources of labour are experiencing significant emigration (loss of people) for the same reasons, some examples being Bangladesh, India, Morocco, Pakistan, Turkey and the Philippines.

The United States accepts more legal immigrants as permanent residents than any other country in the world, and the number of immigrants in the US today is about 38 million people (of a total population of 305 million). The most important source countries for immigrants to the US are (in descending order of importance) Mexico, China, Philippines, India and Vietnam. Almost 24% of US immigrants have come from Mexico (9.6 million people), much higher than the figure for the second largest source, China (5% of migrants).

Because they share a common land border, and there is a significant gap in wealth between them, there is large-scale movement of migrant labour from Mexico into the

United States (figures 17.31 and 17.32). The United States has a net migration rate of +4.31 migrants per 1,000 population (2009), whereas Mexico has an rate of -3.61 migrants per 1,000 population (2009) (figure 17.33).

The figures in the preceding paragraphs state the official statistics. However, a large number of the immigrants from Mexico to the US make the move illegally. It is estimated that there are about 11 to 12 million illegal immigrants in the US, of whom over half are from Mexico and a quarter are from other parts of Latin America. About 25% of the illegal immigrants live in California, which is the largest US state adjoining Mexico.

Many of the illegal immigrants from Mexico to the USA cross the land border between the two countries, usually at night. The border is fenced, heavily patrolled and the natural environment is hostile, being hot, arid desert (figure 17.34). Because of the difficulties of making a successful border crossing, many of those wishing to migrate illegally hire professionals who know the local terrain and situation, and agree to smuggle them across the border in return for a payment. In an effort to reduce illegal border crossings, US officials have agreed to build a separation barrier along the border and to increase the number of armed patrols that police the border zone.

17.33 *The road crossing between Mexico and the United States at Tijuana. The cars on the left are entering the US from Mexico, while those on the right are heading towards Mexico.*

17.34 *The harsh landscape immediately north of the US-Mexican border.*

ToK BoX

Tolerance and Relativism.

When people are confronted with political views they do not agree with, they often respond in one of two ways. One response may be open hostility, which in its most extreme form might be termed fundamentalism. An alternative response might be tolerance, respecting the other person's right to hold different views and perhaps agreeing to disagree. A more extreme form of tolerance may be relativism — which is the opposite of fundamentalism.

Fundamentalism is the uncritical, literal acceptance of what are supposed to be the founding doctrines or documents of a tradition. It demands a closed mind and the suspension of rational faculties. It could be summed up in the simple mantra '"We" are right, "they" are wrong!'.

Fundamentalism is attractive to people in search for security against the challenge of a universe where everything seems to be up for challenge. This security comes at a cost, however. For example, fundamentalism can promote irrational intolerance among some political or religious groups, it tends to close the mind to any authentic search for truth, or new insights or corrections, and its claims to truth are not subjected to the scrutiny of being measured against any external tests.

The alternative pathway — tolerance — seems like a more hopeful way to ensure peace and harmony. In the world of half a century ago, tolerance was not widely valued as a virtue. However, since the 1960s, tolerance has taught us to understand and listen to perspectives that differ from our own and even to learn from these alternative perspectives. Tolerance has challenged us to be less racist, less biased against alternative sexual orientations, more committed to gender equality, more committed to equality of opportunity for those with disabilities or those who are older, a greater unwillingness to discriminate against indigenous people or those with a different skin colour and it has opened us to be willing to listen to the views of other religious groupings.

Unfortunately, many people are confused by the differences between tolerance and relativism. Tolerance accepts that there may be a single truth but encourages understanding of alternative perspectives which may partially share this truth, and even acceptance of those people who sincerely operate within a completely different framework. On the other hand, relativism holds that every truth is deserving of equal respect and can be held to be equally valid — even if it conflicts with other truth. Tolerance acknowledges that there is such a thing as truth, whereas relativism denies that truth is anything more than an opinion or a view that has been shaped by culture or some other factor.

Relativism thus reduces truth to personal preferences, opinions, persuasion and power. In this way, relativism tends to empower those who are most articulate and persuasive, and disempower those who are weaker in society.

Moreover, relativism is an incoherent philosophy. For instance, relativists claim that 'there is no such thing as absolute truth'. If you agree with the statement, you are accepting an absolute truth and therefore negating the statement. If you disagree, you are saying that there IS such a thing as absolute truth. Either way, the statement actually argues that absolute truth DOES exist. Relativism is self-refuting like "I can't speak a word of English".

Even committed relativists do not live their lives as though there was no such thing as absolute truth. If a relativist disputes the balance of his or her bank account, then it is most unlikely that he or she will be happy with the answer "well, that's your truth, and I have my truth, and our truths have equal worth, so we will just have to agree to disagree".

Even on questions of morality, many people would argue that there are absolute truths. For example, many people would be prepared to argue:

• Gang rape of a 13 year old in war is always and everywhere wrong.

• Pedophilia is, always and everywhere, wrong.

• Beating up old people for amusement because they belong to a different racial group is, always and everywhere, wrong.

• Committing genocide is wrong, always and everywhere.

Each of these is an absolute statement about a moral position because of the 'wrong, always and everywhere' inclusion.

A committed relativist will reject these claims and will maintain that they are simply society's assumptions and that by stating a position on them, I am guilty of an imperialist mentality which seeks to subvert the values of other cultures.

However, most people are not relativists and would claim that these actions are always and everywhere wrong.

But on what basis could people argue against a relativist? What might make these and similar actions wrong in an absolute sense?

One response is to claim that "Those actions are wrong because they violate a divine command". However, there is a major problem with this argument because it raises the question of which divine commands from which religious tradition should be accepted as absolute. A Christian may say that cutting off a person's hand for theft is barbaric or stoning a woman caught committing adultery cannot be the command of God, and yet many Muslims would want to affirm these practices and ground them in Sharia (Islamic) law.

The ancient Greek philosopher, Aristotle (384 - 322 BC), attempted to provide a more universally satisfying response. His answer was to claim that "actions such as these are wrong because they go against what it is to be human."

Aristotle said that every creature has its own nature. All human beings share a common human nature — we are human; we are not cats, pine trees, earthworms or grasshoppers. Even though we may differ in many ways due to hair and skin colour, personality, intelligence, gender, sexual orientation and many other factors, nevertheless we all share certain attributes that define us as human beings.

Aristotle considered that each species of plant and animal had an individual nature depending on what the thing in question was — grasshoppers share a grasshopper nature and human beings share a human nature. This approach has had a huge influence on the development of western civilisation and international law. Genocide and rape are condemned in warfare because these are held to be crimes that go against our common humanity. They are held to be wrong because they are actions that go against the fundamental nature of what it is to be human.

If Aristotle is right, we can overcome relativism and discern what is true and right by exploring what it is to be fully human. This will be done in the next ToK Box.

The next ToK BoX is on page 672.

Political outcomes

Another route for illegal immigrants to the USA is to remain after a legitimate visa has expired. The illegal immigrants are known as 'visa overstays', and they tend to be better educated and more professional people than those who attempt the dangerous border crossings. About half the illegal immigrants in the USA are 'visa overstays', and to control this situation, US officials have tightened the data gathered for all foreign visitors, including the collection of biographic, travel, and biometric information such as photographs and fingerprints, and increasing insistence that all foreigners to the USA use electronically readable passports.

A third form of illegal immigration to the USA involves various types of visa fraud, which means obtaining a visa on false grounds. The most common type of visa fraud is the 'green card marriage' in which a foreigner marries an American specifically to settle in the USA, even though they have no intention to live together as a couple. Other examples of visa fraud include mail order brides, human trafficking (where the immigrant becomes a slave of the sponsoring person), or payment to an American citizen in return for writing a personal letter of recommendation. Other than running effective security checks, visa fraud is very difficult to control until it is exposed after the migrant has already arrived in the USA.

Paradoxically for a country that was built on migration, immigration is becoming an increasingly controversial issue in the United States. Public opinion polls are almost evenly split between those who believe illegal immigrants take jobs away from Americans and those who believe that illegal immigrants perform the jobs that Americans are unwilling to perform. To some extent public opinion in the USA has a discriminatory undertone as the majority view expressed is that the migration of Poles, Italians, and Jews was very positive for the US, whereas migration of people from Mexico, the Philippines and the Caribbean is overwhelmingly viewed negatively.

QUESTION BLOCK 17F

1. *Explain why globalisation has led to an increase in immigration in many parts of the world.*

2. *Why is the rate of migration from Mexico to the United States so large?*

3. *Describe the attempts of US officials to control migration from Mexico.*

Anti-globalisation Movements

During the 1990s and early 2000s, the world's increasingly globalised economy was hit with a series of financial peaks and troughs. In 2008, a severe global recession led many people in MEDCs to question whether globalisation was really the good thing that they had been led to believe. A poll was conducted by London's *Finan-*

cial Times in June 2007 in which 1,000 people were interviewed in six MEDCs. The results showed that people in the United Kingdom, France, the United States and Spain were about three times more likely to claim that globalisation was having a negative rather than a positive effect on their countries. Similar views were expressed in Italy and Germany, although the majorities there were smaller.

The pro-globalist view that opening economies to freer trade brings benefits to poor and rich countries alike is increasingly being questioned by people in MEDCs, regardless of whether they are conservative or liberal in their outlooks.

Growing cynicism towards globalisation has encouraged the growth of **anti-globalisation movements**. These groups are opposed to the unregulated expansion and globalisation of capitalism, and they are especially critical of the large profits they believe many corporations are making. Anti-globalisation groups tend to express themselves in the language of socialism, criticising 'ruling élites', 'corporate greed', 'capitalist colonisation', and 'dispossession' or 'oppression' of the masses. Since the first anti-globalisation groups began, they have tended to form coalitions with like-minded groups by adopting a broad spectrum ideological position that opposes:
- environmental destruction
- child labour
- third world debt
- exploitation of working people
- gender oppression
- oppression of minority groups
- discrimination
- capitalism
- transnational corporations
- militarisation
- genetically modified crops

and promotes:
- animal rights;
- the rights of indigenous peoples; and
- anarchism

17.35 *This café in Bethlehem is modelled on the well-known international chain, Starbucks.*

In an article in *New Formulation* in 2003, the American author, Chuck Morse, described anti-globalisation as a movement that "directly attacks global capital's economic and political infrastructure with radically democratic politics and a strategy of confrontation", adding that it is "bold, anti-authoritarian, and truly global — and also quite effective."

Morse also added the following analysis:

> *"The emergence of the anti-globalisation movement has produced a feeling of near euphoria among anarchists. Not only are our commitments to direct action and decentralisation shared broadly in the movement as a whole, but we are also enjoying a political legitimacy that has eluded us for decades. We can now articulate our anti-statist, utopian message to activists around the world and we are no longer dismissed as terrorists or cranks. In many respects it seems like we should just mobilise, mobilise, and mobilise.*

In addition to their opposition to large, highly visible, global corporations such as McDonald's and Starbucks (figures 17.35 and 17.36), anti-globalisation groups focus attacks on three organisations that are seen to promote globalisation — the WTO (World Trade Organisation, which argues for reduced tariff barriers and freer world trade), the World Bank (which gives advice and long-term development loans to LEDCs), and the IMF (International Monetary Fund, which gives countries crisis loans). Gatherings of world political and business leaders are seen by anti-globalisation groups as opportunities to demonstrate and attack those in positions of power, and anti-globalisation protecters have effectively closed and disrupted meetings of trade ministers and high ranking officials.

Perhaps one of the most surprising features of anti-globalisation movements is that although they are becoming more and more effective in mobilising support in MEDCs, they have found much less widespread support in LEDCs, even though they claim to exist to support the rights of the poor. This has led to complaints that people in LEDCs seem to be relatively accepting and supportive of globalisation, whereas the strongest opposition to globalisation comes from affluent activists in wealthy countries.

17.37 *This taxi driver in Bangladesh may never gain directly from the forces of globalisation, but he has portrayed his admiration for modernisation and internationalisation nonetheless. Globalisation tends to be rated more positively in LEDCs than in MEDCs.*

There is evidence that many people in LEDCs see the anti-globalisation movement as a threat to their jobs and livelihoods, and an intrusion by well-meaning but misguided outsiders into their affairs (figure 17.37). There is a genuine fear in many LEDCs that if the trend towards greater globalisation were to reverse, many people would be left in poverty with little prospect to achieve the riches to which they aspire.

Which of the various competing perspectives are realistic or persuasive probably depends on one's individual perspective and world view. Perhaps time will help the question become clearer as to whether globalisation is a constructive or destructive force — and for whom.

QUESTION BLOCK 17G

1. Suggest reasons why globalisation seems to be losing support in MEDCs, but is still seen as a positive force in LEDCs.

2. Why do anti-globalisation movements focus on many issues that seem to be unrelated to globalisation, such as gender oppression and animal rights?

3. Evaluate the effectiveness of anti-globalisation movements in the world today.

17.36 *The logo of this Shanghai coffee shop is reminiscent of Starbucks — a common target of attacks by anti-globalisation groups.*

Political outcomes

18 Global interactions at the local level

Global interactions may encounter local obstacles and resistance, which modify them and result in hybridised outcomes.

Outline

Defining glocalisation

Page 662

The difference between glocalisation and globalisation.

Adoption of glocalisation and local responses to globalisation   Page 664

The extent to which commercial activities at a local scale, and the reasons why the levels and rates of adoption vary from place to place.

Alternatives

Page 665

The role of local groups in raising awareness of local and global environmental, social and cultural issues. The role of local groups in supporting local economic activity and strengthening local cultural values. Anti-globalisation groups.

Defining Glocalisation

Glocalisation as a factor in cultural homogenisation

ToK BoX — Page 672
The Fulfilled Human Life

traditional communal priorities in many cultures (figure 18.1).

As the pressures for **cultural homogenisation** have intensified in recent years, there has been a consequent effect known as **glocalisation**.

The concept of a **world culture** has deep roots in the European tradition. Cultural homogenisation could be viewed as the continuation of a process that began several hundred years ago as Europeans began travelling around the world for exploration, trading, and evangelism. As the Europeans explored, they often established political control, bringing new models of central government as they did so. Central systems of political control were not uniquely European (the Chinese had developed complex bureaucracies over 1,000 years ago), but as European political influence spread into colonies around the world, the structures of government, politics, science, religion, philosophy and trade became the 'world norm'. Following independence, ideas of citizenship and individuality spread across traditional cultural boundaries, replacing

The word 'glocalisation' combines globalisation and localisation, and it can be defined as the modifying impact of local conditions on global forces. Glocalisation may be thought of as the balance that is achieved between forces which lead to homogenisation with forces that preserve diversity or difference. In other words, glocalisation recognises that the homogenising ideas imposed by globalisation are interpreted and absorbed differently according to local viewpoints and traditions. Taking the example that was mentioned in chapter 16, the spread of McDonald's restaurants across the world can be seen an example of cultural homogenisation (and globalisation), whereas the different menu items available in various countries represents glocalisation.

18.1 *Is it inevitable that 'foreign' pressures towards individualism will one day challenge the traditional communal priorities that are the foundation of many of the world's cultures? In this view, the women and children of the Erebora tribe in Ethiopia express their sense of 'community' by spending time together.*

Glocalisation operates through three processes: relativisation, emulation and interpenetration.

Relativisation: As globalisation occurs, there are pressures to align culturally with other parts of the world to aid communication and understanding. Each place in the world evolves in a way that is relative to the places in the world that interact with it. In this way, traditional cultural values tend to become diluted and replaced with what are seen as universal standards and values that flow from a common understanding (or perception) of what it means to be human (figure 18.2). Relativisation raises

18.2 *New York's Christopher Street, in Greenwich Village, is where the gay and lesbian movement began in 1969. The cultural values of the gay rights movement have since spread out to many countries, challenging long-standing intolerance of homosexuality.*

concerns in many parts of the world about a loss of traditional values and national identity, because basic foundation beliefs can no longer be assumed. In its most extreme form, **relativism**, there is no such thing as absolute truth, and no moral truth that holds for all people. Rather, it is left up to individual judgement to decide

what is right and wrong, good and bad. More detail on relativism is provided in the ToK Box in chapter 17.

Emulation: The improved flow of information between countries in recent decades has enabled people to compare their values, attitudes and ideas more easily with others than was previously possible. Information flows through the media and the entertainment industry are strong forces in encouraging emulation of other people and cultures (figure 18.3). This emulation is often labelled as 'the latest craze' when it is adopted widely by younger people.

18.3 *This teenage girl from the Himba tribe in Namibia dresses in the traditional way, including braiding her hair with a mixture of red ochre, sap and butter, and yet she chooses to demonstrate 'cultural emulation' and be 'modern' by drinking her water from a plastic bottle.*

Interpenetration: Culture contact is a two-way process, although the movements in each direction may not be of equal strength (figure 18.4). Therefore, cultural homogenisation and cultural diversity are not really opposites, but end-points on the continuum of glocalisation. The extent of glocalisation that occurs will reflect the balance of strength, or persuasiveness, of the ideas that are competing in the conflict of cultures.

18.4 *An example of cultural interpenetration – Yangon's Central Railway Station was built by the British during Myanmar's colonial era. Although essentially a British design, it incorporated Burmese 'temple-top' decoration, reflecting the local culture.*

Working against the process of cultural homogenisation is the process of deglobalisation. **Deglobalisation** is the process of deliberately replacing 'world culture' in a country or area with distinctive local cultural traditions. Deglobalisation is sometimes a reaction or organised resistance to the process of globalisation. A contemporary example is the growth of Islamic fundamentalism in recent years. Some Islamic nations have objected to a model of globalisation that sees all cultural traditions as having equal value, and have advocated a distinctively Islamic world view instead.

QUESTION BLOCK 18A

1. *Do the four processes of cultural homogenisation (relativisation, emulation, glocalisation, interpenetration) work in the same direction or against each other?*

2. *Explain what is meant by the term glocalisation.*

Adoption of Globalisation and Local Responses to Globalisation

The Globalisation of Commercial Activities at the Local Scale

The extent to which globalisation is adopted varies from place to place. In chapter 12, various indices were used to describe the extent to which the forces of globalisation had taken root in different countries, and the broad pattern of globalisation was related to the core-periphery model.

In general, those places with frequent and effective transport links to other countries tend to be more receptive to the impact of globalisation. For example, Hong Kong is a city in southern China with a long history of trade and business links with other countries. Therefore, it is perhaps not surprising that Hong Kong today has an

18.6 *Hong Kong International Airport is situated less than five flying hours from half of the world's population. It handles about 800 aircraft movements every day with 85 different airlines. It is the world's fifth busiest airport.*

18.7 *As a somewhat isolated nation, Laos is less affected by globalisation than most other countries. This view shows the main street of the city of Luang Prabang.*

18.8 *Traditional culture in Luang Prabang — in the pre-dawn morning, a line of Buddhist monks walks through the streets to receive alms (gifts) of rice and other food.*

ethnically diverse population, strong international business links, advanced communications technologies and a dense network of transport links with other places (figures 18.5 and 18.6).

On the other hand, places with fewer international links may be more resistant to the impact of globalisation.

18.5 *Chungking Mansions in Hong Kong contains a vast array of shops and businesses run by people from many nations.*

Although Laos is in the same region of the world as Hong Kong, it is a much more isolated place whose international links are poorly developed. It is therefore not surprising that its traditional culture remains largely intact, but on the other hand, its level of economic development is quite low, its internet and communications links are poorly developed and its trade with other countries is limited in scale (figures 18.7 and 18.8).

Adoption, Adaptation or Rejection of Globalised Goods

A growing number of people in highly globalised societies claim to be against globalisation, and they express this opinion in ways such as buying only locally produced goods, refusing to buy goods from certain overseas locations, and refusing to do business with certain transnational corporations that are believed to follow unethical practices such as paying workers in LEDCs unfair wages or engaging in environmental destruction.

On the other hand, the commercial success of globalisation suggests that large numbers of people willingly buy the cheapest items in the supermarket regardless of their country of origin. They also enjoy the benefits of broadband internet, and are prepared to work for companies with transnational connections. If this were not so, then globalisation could not have taken root at the local level to the significant extent that it has in many places.

Globalisation is seldom accepted unthinkingly by individuals at a local scale. In order to make foreign goods and services attractive to local people, adaptations are often implemented, as discussed earlier in this chapter in the section on glocalisation. The McTurco shown in figure 16.11 is an example of a transnational corporation adapting product to suit local preferences. Adaptation occurs in the opposite direction also, as local businesses may adapt in order to identify with the allure and glamour of globalisation, and an example of this is the coffee shop shown in figures 17.34 and 17.35.

Surveys show that those who want globalisation the most tend to live in LEDCs — paradoxically those who complain most about globalisation are those who perhaps benefit most from it and live in the MEDCs. However, as we will read in the next section, many people in LEDCs who acknowledge the benefits of globalisation also want radical changes to the power imbalance implicit in the way that globalisation is presently being implemented.

QUESTION BLOCK 18B

1. Survey the shops and businesses in your local area. To what extent have the commercial activities in your local area become globalised?

2. Why does the rate of adoption of globalisation vary from place to place?

3. Outline the ways people respond to the challenges of globalisation at the local scale.

4. Show how adaptation to globalisation can be a two-way process.

5. Conduct an investigation in your local area to evaluate the relative costs and benefits of local commercial production to (a) the producer, (b) the consumer, and (c) the local economy, when compared with the costs and benefits of globalised production.

Alternatives to Globalisation

The Alternatives Proposed by Anti-globalisation Groups

Several decades ago in 1980, the-then President of Tanzania, Julius Nyerere, made the following far-sighted claim on behalf of people in LEDCs about the emerging trend of globalisation:

"There is a world economy, and there are international institutions, even if there is no world government. Our national economies are linked; the poverty or prosperity of one country affects the economy of all others. When potential customers are too poor to buy, the manufacturer suffers — internationally as well as nationally. And under the present world economic order, the rich and the industrialised areas — regardless of whether they are capitalist or socialist — automatically, as well as by the exercise of naked power, extract from the poor and rural areas even that little which they have.

It is done through the pricing mechanisms of primary products relative to manufactured goods, by a virtual monopoly of international transportation facilities, by the control of world currency and credit which is exercised by the rich nations and by a hundred or so other so-called market forces. Among these should not be forgotten the industrial and financial activities of the great transnational corporations, and their manipulations to increase the wealth of of the already rich at the expense of the desperately poor.

Yet on a world scale, we are still being told that the solution to the present economic ills is for greater investment and greater wealth accretion in the already developed areas. We are told that the real problem comes from the oil producers among the developing countries, who have found a way of preventing their wealth being extracted in the interests of cheap transport and cheap power in the industrial economies. The fundamental imbalance between the world's rural and urban nations — between the industrial and the primary producer areas — is not yet universally recognised as the root cause of world economic problems and world poverty." (figures 18.9 and 18.10).

18.9 *This typical market in Julius Nyerere's nation-state of Tanzania shows the obvious importance of the local (rather than global) economy. This market is near the city centre of Zanzibar.*

18.10 *These fisher folk in Dar-es-Salaam, Tanzania, are less affected by globalisation than most other people, at least in the direct sense. Nonetheless, the forces of globalisation are rapidly approaching, symbolised by the large bulk oil tanker on the horizon.*

Frustration and antipathy towards the forces of globalisation among diverse groups of people has led to the growth of many anti-globalisation civil societies. **Civil societies** can be defined as organisations and movements that work to build bridges of understanding and facilitate negotiations between individual people, private companies and governments on matters of public concern.

The Centre for Civil Society at the London School of Economics explains the nature of civil societies in these words:

"Civil society refers to the arena of uncoerced collective action around shared interests, purposes and values. In theory, its institutional forms are distinct from those of the state, family and market, though in practice, the boundaries between state, civil society, family and market are often complex, blurred and negotiated. Civil society commonly embraces a diversity of spaces, actors and institutional forms, varying in their degree of formality, autonomy and power. Civil societies are often populated by organisations such as registered charities, development non-governmental

organisations, community groups, women's organisations, faith-based organisations, professional associations, trades unions, self-help groups, social movements, business associations, coalitions and advocacy group."

The term 'civil society' is increasingly used by activists and opponents of globalisation to describe their anti-globalisation groups, as the term emphasises principles such as democracy, liberalism and peace. Examples of such organisations include NGOs (non-government organisations) such as Oxfam, Globalise Resistance, Greenpeace, Médecins Sans Frontières, the Fair Trade Network, Christian Action, World Wildlife Fund, Amnesty International, the Stop the War Coalition, CAFOD, World Vision, and The Yes Men (figure 18.11).

18.11 *The most effective way to help people in need in LEDCs is often through small-scale projects handled through voluntary efforts. In this view, students from the Global Concerns Action Team of Li Po Chun United World College in Hong Kong work to build the first toilets for a village of leprosy sufferers in an isolated area of Yunnan province, China.*

However, as the ToK Box in chapter 17 showed, restricting use of the term 'civil societies' to anti-globalisation groups is contestable, as most pro-globalisation groups would claim that capitalism is a pure form of liberalism, which is a key element in the definition of a civil society. Furthermore, pro-globalisation groups often claim that they act more peacefully than the sometimes anarchic actions of anti-globalisation groups and protesters. The label 'civil society' becomes even more blurred when it is understood that many civil societies are funded and directed by businesses and institutions, especially by individual donors and companies.

As noted in chapters 14 and 17, and as shown in figure 14.6, anti-globalisation groups are especially critical of the role played by three organisations that are seen to promote globalisation — the WTO (World Trade Organisation, which argues for reduced tariff barriers and freer world trade), the World Bank (which gives advice and long-term development loans to LEDCs), and the IMF (International Monetary Fund, which gives countries crisis loans).

Some people are surprised that anti-globalisation groups target organisations that have been established specifically to promote the development of poorer countries. For example, the World Bank's stated mission is to "advance the vision of an inclusive and sustainable globalisation … by focussing on middle income and creditworthy poor countries as well as the poorest countries in the world." The World Bank claims to "provide low-interest loans, interest-free credits and grants to developing countries for a wide array of purposes that include investments in education, health, public administration, infrastructure, financial and private sector development, agriculture, and environmental and natural resource management."

Similarly, the IMF defines itself as "an organisation of 185 countries, working to foster global monetary co-operation, secure financial stability, facilitate international trade, promote high employment and sustainable economic growth, and reduce poverty around the world." It does this by monitoring global economic and financial developments, providing policy advice, lending money countries with balance of payments difficulties, providing loans to LEDCs that are targeted to reducing long-term poverty. The IMF also provides countries with technical assistance and training as well as research and statistics.

18.12 *The promise of globalisation for residents in LEDCs is symbolised by this sign advertising new housing above shanty dwellings near Pune, India.*

The main reason that anti-globalisation groups attack such organisations is because they see the policies of the World Bank and the IMF as being driven by a capitalist free-market ideology (see the ToK Box in chapter 17). Critics in civil societies and NGOs see such policies as divisive (because they take too long to assist the poorer groups in society) and often harmful to economic development. This is especially true if the policies are implemented too quickly, in the wrong sequence, or in very weak economies that are incapable of competing effectively in a global market. Furthermore, critics of the IMF and the World Bank argue that if money is needed by LEDCs it should be given, not extended as a loan because

borrowed funds will need repayment in the future, usually with interest (figures 18.12 and 18.13).

Many civil societies have expanded their roles to embrace anti-globalisation in recent decades. For example, when it was established in 1961, the WWF was known as the World Wildlife Fund, but in 1986 re-branded itself as the World Wide Fund for Nature to reflect a broader scope of interest. Originally focussing on protecting endangered species, the WWF now also campaigns on issues such as biodiversity, climate change, pollution and globalisation. Other NGOs which began as single-issue groups have similarly expanded their scope as a broad anti-globalisation coalition of civil societies has emerged.

18.13 *Pune (India) is expanding rapidly as a hub for information technology and computer companies, fuelled by the global economy. This sign advertises one of the new developments that is intended to appeal to India's emerging middle class.*

Through the actions and campaigns of these and other civil societies, the general public in MEDCs has become more aware of global environmental, financial and political issues. Consequently, an increasing number of people choose to purchase only 'fair trade' or 'organic' foods, while others make a point of not buying GM (genetically modified) foods. Others avoid dealing with companies that violate ethical principles or who are known to pollute the environment. Individually, such decisions might make little difference, but when large numbers of people choose to take such actions, then the price mechanism begins to drive globalisation in new and different directions.

QUESTION BLOCK 18C

1. *The quote by Julius Nyerere in the section above is several decades old. How accurately do you think it summarises the reality of globalisation in the world today?*

2. *Explain what is meant by the term 'civil societies'.*

3. *Give some examples of civil societies that you think are highly effective, and explain why you think they are effective.*

4. *Do you think the criticism of organisations such as the World Bank, the IMF and the WTO by anti-globalisation groups is fair? Give reasons for your answer..*

5. *What evidence is there that civil societies are raising awareness of significant environmental, social and cultural issues?*

6. *Explain how accurately each of the following quotes describes globalisation and the possible alternatives:*

   a. *"The third world is the cow, the second world is the dairyman, and the first world is the butcher."* — Oxfam Community Aid Abroad, an Australian community-based aid and development organisation

   b. *"If you're not part of the solution, you're part of the problem."* — Eldridge Cleaver, US author

   c. *"I sit on a man's back, choking him and making him carry me, and yet assure myself and others that I am sorry for him and wish to lighten his load by all possible means — except by getting off his back."* — Leo Tolstoy, Russian novelist

   d. *Terms are devised as though it is some kind of disgrace to be poor. The disgrace is inequality of incomes in an underdeveloped country. The disgrace isn't the suppression of basic human rights, of religious persecution, oppression on the grounds of race or tribe, suppression of political opposition, direct control of the news media and similar practices."* — Sir Robert Muldoon, former prime Minister of New Zealand

Case Study of a Non-globalised Society — North Korea

Probably the only country in the world today that totally rejects globalisation is North Korea, or as it is officially known, the Democratic People's Republic of Korea (DPRK). North Korea became a separate country in 1948 when the Korean peninsula was divided into two separate countries in the aftermath of World War II (figure 18.14).

18.14 *The raised concrete strip running across the ground and though the middle of the blue negotiating huts at Panmunjom marks the boundary between North and South Korea.*

North Korea (the DPRK) was a Communist country under the leadership of Kim Il Sung, whereas South Korea (also known as the Republic of Korea, or ROK) followed a capitalist approach under guidance from the United States. North Korea today has emerged as the world's most isolated country as it actively discourages visits by foreigners and forbids foreign investment. It is sometimes known as the 'Hermit Kingdom' because of its extreme isolation.

Kim Il Sung remained in control of North Korea until the time of his death in 1994. His son, Kim Jong Il was named leader of the country following the death of Kim Il Sung, and he continues in that role today, perpetuating the isolationist philosophies and policies of his father. Following his death, Kim Il Sung was named President for Eternity, and thus remains the country's President – in fact, he is currently the world's longest serving head of state! Kim Il Sung is thus still referred to as the Great Leader, whereas his son, Kim Jong Il, is known as the Dear Leader (figure 18.15).

18.15 *Every home and office in North Korea displays portraits of the Great Leader, Kim Il Sung (left) and the Dear Leader, Kim Jong Il (right).*

Under the leadership of Kim Il Sung and Kim Jong Il, North Korea has developed a unique philosophy known as *juche* (pronounced joo-cher) that is the foundation of its independent policies of anti-globalisation and isolation. *Juche* is a Korean word based on two syllables, *ju* meaning 'master' and *che* meaning 'oneself'. Therefore, the word *juche* literally means 'humanity as the master of its own destiny', although it is often translated more simply as 'self-reliance'. Sometimes, *juche* is referred to as Kimilsungism.

As *juche* emphasises self-reliance, it is the antithesis of globalisation

The origin of the *juche* concept was Karl Marx's concept of *homo faber* – humans as makers — 'I make, therefore I am'. Marx was adamant that there is no god, and that humans are the masters of their own destiny. Kim Il Sung extended this idea by saying that humans differ from animals in their self-consciousness and creativity, and that the source of all good human ideas – the Leader – replaces any god as the supreme deity for the masses. As the historian, Bruce Cumings commented in 2004, 'DPRK ideologues would embarrass even Stalin in their presumptions that the *juche* idea contains the solution to all problems, winning ever-greater victories, all the time – and for all time'.

Juche has been the guiding philosophy of the DPRK since its foundation, and it is stipulated in the country's constitution. It is celebrated in slogans across the country, and in a grand monument known as the Tower of Juche Idea in the country's capital city, Pyongyang (figure 18.16). Large slogans celebrating juche are found on hillsides and on buildings throughout North Korea, such as 'Everyone must have juche firm in mind and spirit', 'Only when juche is firmly implanted can we be happy', and 'Juche must not only be firmly established in mind but perfectly realised in practice'.

18.16 *The Tower of Juche Idea in Pyongyang, North Korea.*

North Koreans acknowledge that juche may not be appropriate for other countries, but they claim it provides a moral and philosophical basis that is highly appropriate for Korean society, given the history and culture of that country. North Korea claims that it does not seek to impose juche on any other country, but it also wishes to be left alone to implement its model of self-reliance in the DPRK without outside or foreign influence.

The basis of juche is that humanity is the master of everything, and everything should be decided in terms of what is best for people's moral welfare (as opposed to both capitalism and Marxism, which say that decisions should be based on people's material wealth). According to the juche idea, humans are unique because they possess the three attributes of creativity, consciousness and *chajusong*. *Chajusong* means 'independence', though in a very deep and broad sense that embraces the human will to live, to develop independently and to shape the future. Chajusong also involves humans subordinating the will of nature, adapting the environment to suit human needs, which are the most important bases for decision-making.

18.17 *The 'Three Revolutions' are symbolised by these three red granite flags at the Three Revolutions Exhibition in Pyongyang.*

Juche is seen as the means whereby humans can achieve chajusong. This is done, according to Kim Jong Il, through the three revolutions – cultural revolution, ideological revolution and technological revolution (figure 18.17). The cultural revolution is designed to bring every North Korean up to the high standard of literacy of an intellectual. The ideological revolution is designed to replace traditional ideas and outdated thinking with 'correct' progressive thinking that emphasises collectivism. The technological revolution is designed to introduce innovations that improve the welfare and living standards of people. It is said that a person's thinking determines his or her worth and quality. Thinking is therefore different from knowledge, because some knowledge encourages bad (i.e. individualistic materialistic) ideology, whereas correct thinking encourages good (i.e. collectivist moral) ideology that drives society in a positive direction.

According to the juche idea, a nation's chajusong can only be achieved through economic self-sufficiency. This is because any reliance on others shifts power into their hands. Therefore, globalisation is incompatible with the juche philosophy.

North Koreans call subordination to others 'flunkeyism', and like globalisation, it is the opposite of the juche idea. According to Kim Jong Il:

> *"Life contrary to the independent life is the flunkeyist, subordinate and slavish life. The life one leads at the expense of others, or becoming a slave to them, is not the life inherent to humanity. The life of those who consider it satisfactory to be well fed and to be better off even if they become slaves of others, and their country is reduced to the colony of another country, is not the life worthy of true human, but is an animal life such as a dog's or a pig's. The life of the flunkeyists and traitors to the nation who fawn upon foreign forces and sell the country to them, is an inhuman and mean life. The flunkeyist and submissive life of those who live off foreign forces and only seek an easy and comfortable life for themselves, kowtowing to foreign forces,*

cannot be said to be a life worthy of humanity. Genuine life is not the life lived for physical life, but is the life devoted to the society and collective, the country and nation, and having socio-political integrity as a social being".

From a materialist perspective, statistics suggest that the juche philosophy has not served DPRK well. South Korea is one of the world's fastest growing and most vibrant industrialised economies, whereas North Korea experiences severe shortages of power, manufactured goods and even food. The daily total energy consumption of North Korea is less than that of a medium-sized South Korean town (figure 18.18). Whereas South Korea's main exports are hi-tech electronics and manufactured goods, North Korea's main exports are weapons, drugs and counterfeit currency.

18.18 *Even North Korea's capital, Pyongyang, has a very dark, unlit appearance at night. There is an absence of street lights, interior lights are very dull, and the only floodlighting is on monuments to the Leaders and buildings with their portraits, such as the newspaper office in central Pyongyang, shown here.*

North Koreans would argue that it unfair to measure their philosophy against Western capitalist standards that are unrelated to the priorities of juche. On the other hand, most North Koreans are unaware of conditions elsewhere in the world, as the flow of information to North Koreans is extremely limited. The government controls all print and electronic media, mobile telephones

18.19 *A large mosaic of Kim Il Sung with the adoring masses, situated beside the road near a housing estate in Pyongyang, North Korea.*

are banned, landline telephone conversations are monitored, and the internet is unavailable. North Koreans have not yet been informed that humans have landed on the moon (this happened in July 1969) because that knowledge runs the risk of making people admire the United States. DPRK media focuses on government information, political statements, news of the Dear Leader providing 'on-the-spot guidance' around the country, and anti-capitalist stories. North Koreans defend their media, claiming that Western media organisations are controlled by a handful of wealthy entrepreneurs who portray a pro-US and pro-capitalist viewpoint that is 'brain washing'.

The juche philosophy is supported in North Korea through the government-controlled media, by large slogans displayed around the country, and by politically inspired art and posters (figures 18.19 and 18.20).

18.20 *Revolutionary 'advertising' beside the road, Pyongyang.*

Criticism of the DPRK leadership is illegal in North Korea. This adulation of the leadership, shown through large statues of Kim Il Sung at which people bow before and lay flowers, the twin photos of Kim Il Sung and Kim Jong Il that decorate every home and every office in the country, and the loyalty badges worn by all North Koreans that show a portrait of Kim Il Sung or Kim Jong Il, constitute a personality cult (worship of the leader) (see figure 18.21 and figure 9.30 in chapter 9). In addition to his title of Dear Leader, Kim Jong Il is also known as the Party Centre, Unique Leader, Wise Leader, Respected Leader, Supreme Commander, Father of the people, Great Leader, Morning Star of Mount Paekdu, Outstanding Military Strategist, Leader of Steel, Father of the Nation, Leader of the People, Our Father, Dear General, Great General, Our General, Leader of the Twenty-First century, Sun of the Twenty-First Century, Glorious Sun of the Twenty-First Century, Son of Mount Paektu, Sun of Mankind, Everlasting Sky, and more. Special strains of flower called the Kimilsungia and the Kimjongilia have been developed to honour the leaders, and large annual flower festivals featuring only these flowers are held in North Korea attracting extensive media attention within the DPRK (figure 18.22).

18.21 *Thousands of athletes dressed in yellow emulate an abundant field of wheat in a performance of mass gymnastics in Pyongyang to glorify the Great Leader Kim Il Sung.*

18.22 *This large roadside sign in Pyongyang shows the Kimjongilia flower.*

And yet, people who have become close friends with North Koreans say that the affection most people feel for the leadership and the juche philosophy is genuine. People admire Kim Il Sung's defeat of the Japanese during World War II followed by his perceived defeat of the US forces in the Korean War of 1950 to 1953, describing these achievements as 'defeating the two great imperialisms in a single generation'.

North Koreans are proud of their country's independent stand against foreign aggression, in contrast to the South Koreans who they see as puppets of US imperialism and aggression. They believe Kim Jong Il is a genius who solves major problems through his 'on-the-spot guidance' (they also believe that Kim Jong Il scored 11 holes-in-one the first time he played an 18-hole game of golf).

North Koreans see their country as one which shows compassionate care for children in general and war orphans in particular, has radically improved the status of women, provides genuinely free housing, provides free health care, and has improved life expectancy and literacy rates to levels comparable with the world's most advanced countries. North Koreans are proud of their unique juche philosophy which, although deriving from Marxist Communism, has been combined with Confucianism by Kim Il Sung to develop a uniquely Korean framework (figure 18.23 on the next page).

Juche is the opposite of globalisation. It relies on isolationism that is sustained by media control, propaganda and ignorance of the rest of the world to achieve self-sufficiency. This ignorance has resulted in a deep fear of the outside world in which all foreigners are seen as potential spies and where there is a genuine fear of US attack. School children learn Maths by adding and subtracting numbers of dead US soldiers, and learn foreign languages by translating sentences such as 'Yankees are wolves in human shape'. A North Korean phrase book for travellers gives the following sentence in the section on useful tips on the way to the hotel: 'Let's mutilate US imperialism!'. The author has often been greeted by North Koreans who introduce themselves with the standard sentence "I am a citizen of the Democratic People's Republic of Korea, and therefore I envy nothing in the whole world".

Outside North Korea, opponents of globalisation at protests and events such as the World Social Forum advocate principles such as justice, equity, sustainability, environmental responsibility and plurality. According to its charter of principles, the World Social Forum 'is opposed to all totalitarian and reductionist views of economy, development and history, and to the use of violence as a means of social control by the State. It upholds respect for Human Rights, the practices of real democracy, participatory democracy, peaceful relations, in equality and solidarity, among people, ethnicities, genders and peoples, and condemns all forms of domination and all subjection of one person by another.' It is unlikely, therefore, that most supporters of the World Social Forum would advocate North Korea as the ideal model of anti-globalisation. Nonetheless, the fact remains that North Korea's juche philosophy is the purest (and perhaps the only) example of anti-globalisation in action in the world today on a national scale.

18.23 *A large street-side poster in Pyongyang exhorts the masses of all classes (workers, soldiers, famers, intellectuals) to work harder to advance national development and self-reliance according to the anti-globalist juche philosophy.*

QUESTION BLOCK 18D

1. *What are the historical reasons that North Korea rejects globalisation today?*

2. *Summarise the concept of juche.*

3. *Explain why juche is incompatible with globalisation.*

4. *Quoting evidence, how successful is juche in North Korea today?*

5. *North Korea is the clearest example of an anti-globalist country in the world today. What other countries resist globalisation to some extent? In what ways are these countries distinctive because of their anti-globalist leanings?*

6. *Is there a realistic alternative to globalisation in today's world? Is globalisation inevitable?*

ToK BoX

The Fulfilled Human Life.

In the previous ToK Box, we raised the possibility that understanding what it means to live a fulfilled human life might help us understand both truth and morality. As one important goal of education — and especially of geography, even more than other subjects — is to help people lead fulfilled lives, it is appropriate that we conclude our ToK Boxes by looking at the question of what it means to live a fulfilled human life.

What is it to flourish as a human being, and what is it to live a fulfilled human life?

When a survey asked teenagers in one affluent Western society "what does it mean to live a fulfilled human life", the most common response was "being happy".

However, when pressed, most of the respondents had little idea what 'being happy' meant. At a material level, most young people in most countries have everything that should bring happiness, and yet research is clear that young people tend to be less happy in countries where affluence is greater. The same research suggests that amongst many young people, there is a deep sense of discontent and life too often seems to have little meaning and purpose.

All the great religious traditions would reject the idea of 'happiness' as an aim in life. The great Jewish prophets would

have despised the idea, Jesus never referred to it, the Qu'ran does not see it as an aim in life and nor does the Buddha.

The great religious traditions would have talked of something much more profound which would be linked with words like wisdom, peace, joy and truth.

Søren Kierkegaard, a Danish philosopher (1813-1855), claimed there were three stages in finding fulfilment as a human being:

THE AESTHETIC STAGE: This is the person who lives for self and for whom self-interest is the habitual centre of their life. Self-interest underpins all the person's choices and priorities.

THE ETHICAL STAGE: This is the person who has a genuine commitment to live a good, ethical life, putting the needs of others before their own. They will identify with the values of their community and seek to live a life of duty.

THE RELIGIOUS STAGE: This last stage represents the person for whom everything in their life is subsumed beneath an ultimate commitment to a higher service that transcends family, friends and society. It is a life of service that may be costly and demanding.

According to Aristotle, as well as many of the the great religious and philosophical teachings, certain behaviours

and understandings can fulfil us as human beings, while other forms of behaviour diminish us as human beings.

The search for wisdom is largely the search for those understandings and behaviours that fulfil us human beings — in other words, those insights that enable us to live a fulfilled human life.

However, it is important to remember that there is no formula for fulfilment, and it is something that each person must undertake an authentic search to find. Being an expert in philosophy most certainly does not guarantee a fulfilled human life.

In the words of Peter Vardy, in his book *What is Truth?*:

"Truth is something that will not be arrived at easily, but only by struggle, by searching and by a willingness to open up to alternatives. It will only be found by those who try to live the Truth and reject the easy option of living a lie. These individuals will stake their lives on the search and, with passion and commitment, seek to pierce through the veils of illusions, the masks of falsehood, the constructs of society and the self. Truth lies outside the comfort zone and the security blanket, and it may only be accessible by those who are troubled about existence and who are prepared to stake their lives on the search."